I0836994

A

# HISTORY OF GERMANY;

FROM THE

## EARLIEST PERIOD TO THE PRESENT TIME.

BY FREDERICK KOHLRAUSCH,

CHIEF COUNSELLOR OF THE BOARD OF EDUCATION OF THE KINGDOM OF HANOVER,
AND LATE PROFESSOR OF HISTORY IN THE POLYTECHNIC SCHOOL.

TRANSLATED FROM THE LAST GERMAN EDITION,

BY JAMES D. HAAS.

WITH A COMPLETE INDEX,

PREPARED EXPRESSLY FOR THE AMERICAN EDITION.

NEW-YORK:
D. APPLETON AND COMPANY,
346 & 348 BROADWAY.
M.DCCC.LIX.

# TRANSLATOR'S PREFACE.

---

The high merits and distinguished character of the original German work by Professor Kohlrausch, of which this is a translation, have long been acknowledged. A work which during a period of thirty years has enjoyed so much popularity as to have gone through several editions, embracing a circulation of many thousands of copies; a production which has extended and established its good repute, even in its original form, far beyond its native clime, to England, France, Belgium, Italy, America, &c., (in several of which countries it has been reprinted in German,) and has thus become a standard book of reference in almost all the universities and principal public, as well as private educational institutions—such a publication possesses ample testimony proving it able to create a lasting interest, and confirming its claims to consideration and esteem.

The aim of the distinguished author in this valuable history is thus simply but distinctly expressed by himself: "My sole object," he says, "has been to produce a succinct and connected development of the vivid and eventful course of our country's history, written in a style calculated to excite the interest and sympathy of my readers, and of such especially who, not seeking to enter upon a very profound study of the sources and more elaborate works connected with the annals of our empire, are nevertheless anxious to have presented to them the means of acquiring an accurate knowledge of the records of our Fatherland, in such a form as to leave upon the mind and heart an enduring, indelible impression."

That our industrious historian has attained his object, the intelligent reader will find in the interest excited, the clear views imparted, and the deep impression effected by his animated portrayals of both events and individuals. This has been the original and acknowledged characteristic of Herr Kohlrausch's work throughout its entire existence; but in the new edition from which this translation has been rendered, he has endeavored to make it as perfect as possible, both in matter and style, and besides this has enriched it with many valuable notes not contained in the former editions; thus making it in reality a concise, yet, in every respect, a complete history of Germany.

It is important to remark, that Professor Kohlrausch is a Protestant, and one distinguished not less for his freedom from prejudice and partiality, than for the comprehensiveness of his views and the high tone of his philosophy. The general adoption of the work—alike by Protestant and Romanist—is proof sufficiently convincing of the impartiality of his statements, and of the justice of his reflections and sentiments.

JAMES D. HAAS.

*London*, 1844.

# TABLE OF CONTENTS.

## INTRODUCTION.

ANCIENT GERMANY AND ITS INHABITANTS.



## THE MORE ANCIENT GERMAN HISTORY.

## FIRST PERIOD.

FROM THE MOST ANCIENT TIMES TO THE CONQUESTS OF THE FRANKS UNDER CLOVIS, 486 A. D.

### CHAPTER I.

B. C. 113—6 A. D.



### CHAPTER II.

7—374.



### CHAPTER III.

375—476.



## SECOND PERIOD.

FROM THE CONQUESTS OF CLOVIS TO CHARLEMAGNE, 486—768.

### CHAPTER IV.



## THIRD PERIOD.

THE CARLOVINGIANS FROM CHARLEMAGNE TO HENRY I., 768—919.

### CHAPTER V.

768—814.



### CHAPTER VI.

814—918.

## FOURTH PERIOD.

FROM HENRY I. TO RUDOLPHUS OF HAPSBURG, 919–1273.

### CHAPTER VII.

919—1024.



### CHAPTER VIII.

THE SALIC OR FRANCONIAN HOUSE, 1024–1125, TO LOTHAIRE THE SAXON, 1137.



### CHAPTER IX.

THE SWABIAN OR HOHENSTAUFEN HOUSE, 1138–1254.

1138—1190.



### CHAPTER X.

FROM 1190 TO THE INTERREGNUM, 1273.



### CHAPTER XI.

THE MIDDLE AGES.



## FIFTH PERIOD.

FROM RUDOLPHUS I., OF HAPSBURG, TO CHARLES V., 1273–1520.—EMPERORS OF DIFFERENT HOUSES

### CHAPTER XII.

1273—1347.



### CHAPTER XIII.

EMPERORS OF DIFFERENT HOUSES.

1347—1437.

## CHAPTER XIX.



## CHAPTER XX.



## CHAPTER XXI.

## CHAPTER XXII.



## CHAPTER XXIII.







## CHAPTER XXIV.



## CHAPTER XXV.

## CHAPTER XXVI.



# SEVENTH PERIOD.

FROM THE PEACE OF WESTPHALIA IN 1648, TO THE PRESENT TIME.

## CHAPTER XXVII.



## CHAPTER XXVIII.



## CHAPTER XXIX.

CHAPTER XXX.



CHAPTER XXXI.



CHAPTER XXXII.

## CHAPTER XXXVII.



## CHAPTER XXXVIII.



## CHAPTER XXXIX.



## CHAPTER XL.

# INTRODUCTION.

## ANCIENT GERMANY AND ITS INHABITANTS.

The Sources of the most ancient German History—The Nature of the Country—The Natives—The Germanic Races—Manners and Customs—Civil Institutions—War—Regulations and Arms—Religion—Arts and Manufactures—The Germanic Tribes.

### I. SOURCES OF OUR EARLIEST HISTORY.

THE history of the origin, and of the earliest state of the German nation, is involved in impenetrable obscurity. No records tell us when, and under what circumstances, our ancestors migrated out of Asia, the cradle of the human race, into our fatherland; what causes urged them to seek the regions of the north, or what allied branches they left behind them in the countries they quitted. A few scattered and obscure historical traces, as well as a resemblance in various customs and regulations, but more distinctly the affinities of language, indicate a relationship with the Indians, Servians, and the Greeks.*

This obscurity of our earliest history must not surprise us; for every nation, as long as it lives in a half savage state, without a written language, neglects every record of its history beyond mere traditions and songs, which pass down from generation to generation. But as these, even in their very origin, blend fiction with truth, they naturally become, in the course of centuries, so much disfigured, that scarcely the least thread of historical fact is to be found in them. Not a syllable or sound of even those traditions and songs, wherein, according to the testimony of the Romans, our ancestors also delighted to celebrate the deeds and fate of their people, has, however, descended to posterity.

Our authentic history, consequently, commences at the period when our ancestors, possibly after they had dwelt for centuries, or even a thousand years, in our native country, first came into contact with a nation that already knew and practised the art of historical writing. This happened through the incursion of the Cimbrians and Teutonians into the country of the Romans, in the year 113 before the birth of Christ. But this intercourse was too transitory, and the strangers were too unknown, and too foreign to the Romans, for them, who were sufficiently occupied with themselves, and besides which, looked haughtily upon all that was alien, to inquire very particularly into their origin and history.

And even the relation of this contest against the German tribes, howsoever important it was to the Romans, we are obliged to seek laboriously from many authors; for the source whence we should draw most copiously, is precisely here dried up,—the books of the Roman author, Livy, which treated of this war in detail, having been lost, together with many others; and we only possess—which we may even consider as very fortunate—their mere table of contents, by means whereof, viz., those of the 63–68 books, we can at least trace the course of the chief events of the war. Beyond this, we derive some solitary facts from Roman historians of the second and third class, who give but a short and partially mutilated account, and collectively lived too long after this period to be considered as authentic sources. To those belong—1, the "Epit. Rer. Rom." of Florus, (according to some, a book of the Augustan age, but according to others, the work of L. Annæus Florus, who lived

* According to more recent researches, it is concluded that the ancient Sanscrit and Zend languages may have formed likewise the basis of the German tongue, or at least have approximated more closely with the common primitive dialect.

at the commencement of the second century under Adrian;) 2, the "History of the World" of Velleius Paterculus, in a brief outline, down to the period of Tiberius, who lived about the time of the birth of Christ; 3, the "De Stratagematibus" of Frontinus (about 150 years after Christ) contains some good notices of the Cimbrian war; 4, the "Dicta et Facta Memorabilia" of Valerius Maximus, (about 20 years after Christ;) 5, the "History of the World" of Justin, (about the year 150;) and 6, the "Sketch of the Roman History" of Eutropius (about the year 375) present us with much; and again, much is supplied us, incidentally, by the Roman writers who did not directly write history.

Among those who wrote in Greek, must stand: 1, Plutarch, (about 100 years B. C.,) in his biography of "Marius," besides whom, good details may be gleaned from: 2, Diodorus Siculus, (about the period of the birth of Christ,) in his "Historical Library;" 3, Appian, (about the year 160,) in his ethnographically-arranged "History of the Romans," (particularly in the cap. "De Reb. Celt." and "De Reb. Illyr.;") 4. Dio Cassius, (about the year 222,) in the fragments which are preserved of his "Roman History;" and among those who treat of geography, Strabo (about the period of the birth of Christ) especially.

After the Cimbrian era, another half century passes before the Romans again mention the Germans. It was towards the middle of the last century before the birth of Christ, when Julius Cæsar advanced to the frontiers of what may be truly considered Germany. He himself mentions having fought with Ariovistus in Gaul, and afterwards with some German tribes on the left bank of the Rhine, and that he twice united the banks of this river by means of a bridge, and set foot upon the opposite side; besides which, he gives us all the information he could obtain from the Gauls, travelling merchants, or German captives, relative to the nature and condition of Germany and its people. His information is invaluable to us, although it is but scanty, fragmentary, and, to a certain extent, not to be depended upon. For this great commander, who strove for absolute rule—who used mankind (he cannot be freed from the charge) as the means to his end—who, from the depth of an already corrupted state of civilization, could not possibly estimate the simple, natural dignity of such a nation—and who, lastly, in order to be considered worthy of belief in every thing he relates, too well understood the art of representing events to his own advantage—such a writer, we say, cannot truly be regarded by us without some degree of mistrust.

After him there occurs another interval of about fifty years, during which the obscurity of our history is scarcely illuminated by a single ray of foreign observation, until about the period of the birth of Christ, and when, immediately after, the Romans again set foot upon, and, for a longer period, traversed the German soil. They then became tolerably well acquainted with the southwest and northwest of Germany; or, rather, they *might* have become well acquainted therewith, had their prejudiced and selfish minds, which were barred against all foreign peculiarities, been properly competent to it, and had not the difficult extremities to which they were reduced in Germany too much occupied them, and rendered them unjust in their judgment of the country and its inhabitants. In order to expose themselves to less shame for being several times severely cut up by the very force of arms borne by those they called barbarians, by whom they were frequently surpassed in prudence and warlike subtlety, they necessarily, notwithstanding the decisive victories of which they boasted, when driven from the German soil, extenuated their own misfortunes, and exaggerated those of their opponents, whom they accused occasionally of deceit, when probably, on the contrary, the most open conduct prevailed, and generally, in fact, they heaped upon the Germans and their country the most opprobrious charges. No impartial man among them, who was an eye-witness of their incursions, describes to us faithfully the events themselves, and the German nation generally. The only historian of the period who might have done so, Velleius Paterculus, the servant of the Emperor Tiberius, and the friend of his favorite, Sejanus, who, in the years immediately preceding and succeeding the birth of Christ, was himself in Germany—that is to say, on the banks of the Elbe, with the army of the emperor—shows himself, in the very scanty notices he gives, only as a flatterer of his despotic lord, whose deeds he elevates to the skies in inflated and extravagant language.

A second Roman writer, who also had seen Germany, Pliny the elder, (and who died in the year 79 A. D.,) had been upon the northern coast of Germany, among the *Chauci*, but certainly did not travel far into the land. In his "Hist. Nat.," which is an Encyclopædia of general knowledge, he gives us several valuable notices of the natural condition of our country, and of its tribes and nations. His information and judgment, however, must be used with precaution, as his critical sagacity is often questionable. But we have suffered an irreparable loss in his twenty books, which treated of all the wars of the Romans with the Germans, not the least fragment of which has come down to us. He lived so near the period, that he might have collected the information as correctly as it was to be obtained. We may, however, in some degree console ourselves that Tacitus, (about 100 years A. D.,) who cites his precursors as testimonies, availed himself of the work of Pliny; but Tacitus only relates the German wars in part, and does not treat them as the principal subject, while, also, much from him that was important is lost to us. His "Annals," which relate the Roman history from the death of Augustus to the death of Nero, commence after the great German battle of liberty with Varus; but of these annals all from the seventh to the tenth book is also wanting, and the fifth and sixteenth books have come down to us only in an imperfect state. We, nevertheless, acknowledge him to be by far the chief and most important author as regards our earlier German history, and revere his elevated feeling for moral dignity, for truth and justice, in what he also relates of the contests between the Romans and Germans, although, faultlessly on his part, he does not always draw his information from a pure source. But we value him for the treasure he has left us in his description of Germany and its people, ("De Situ ac Moribus Germ.") His deep feeling for simplicity of manners, and healthy energy of nature, had made him a warm friend towards the German natives; and it appeared to him that a faithful description of the German nation would be a work worthy of his pen, so that, when placed before his corrupted countrymen, it should present to their view a picture which might bring many of those whose minds were as yet not quite unsusceptible, to acknowledge their own unnatural condition. For this purpose he collected all that he could obtain from the earlier authors, from the oral information of the Romans who had been in Germany, and from the Germans who were in the Roman service. Thus arose this invaluable book, which may be called a temple of honor to the German nation, and which illuminates, like a bright star, the commencement of their otherwise obscure path. Some things, indeed, through too great a predilection, may be placed by him in too favorable a light; but, even if much be deducted, still sufficient that is praiseworthy remains, and that the material portion is true, we may be assured of by the incorruptible love of truth of the noble Roman, which speaks so triumphantly in all his works.

Among the remainder of the less important historians who contributed to our earliest history, and are already mentioned in the notice of the Cimbrian war, Dio Cassius may be included as important; for the later wars may be named, Suetonius, (110 years A. D., esteemed by Trajan and Adrian,) in his biography of the twelve first Cæsars; the "Scriptores Hist. Augustæ," towards the end of the third century; Ælius Spartianus, Julius Capitolinus, and Flavius Vopiscus; Aurelius Victor, (330,) in his biography of the Cæsars, from Augustus to Constantine; and Paulus Orosius, (417,) in his history. Among the geographical writers, besides Strabo and Pomponius Mela, (48,) we may name in particular Claudius Ptolomæus, (140,) who constructed a system of geography upon a lost work of Tyrian Marinos, and was particularly careful in the determination of longitude and latitude.

But even when we have brought together all of the best that ancient authors supply us with upon Germany, and console ourselves over the great chasms they leave, with the idea that still something has descended to us both great and important, we must nevertheless consider it but as the testimony of strangers,—of the people of the South, differing essentially from the Germans in nature and character, ignorant of their language, and, with the exception of one instance, indifferent, or rather inimically minded, towards them. Not a single German word, correcting the judgment of the Romans, or elucidating the thread of events which the Romans could neither see nor understand, resounds to us from yonder period. How much richer, and certainly more honorable, would the picture develop itself before us, did we also possess German records!

But it was not until many centuries later, after multifarious convulsions had taken place, and most of the constituent parts of ancient times had disappeared from their seat, that isolated and scanty sources of history commenced flowing from original German testimony, by writers who, driven with their countrymen to foreign lands, there endeavored to relate their career and fate. Their names will be mentioned at the commencement of the second period.

After what is stated above, we must rest contented with giving as true a picture as possible of ancient German history, derived as it is from the Roman and Greek writers, and by conclusions drawn from later testimony upon earlier times, admitting that much must necessarily appear obscure, fragmentary, and contradictory, and that upon many points opinions will forever remain divided. The period to which the following description belongs, is about the time of the birth of Christ, and the few immediately succeeding centuries.

## II. THE NATURE AND CONDITION OF THE COUNTRY.

According to the description of the Romans, Germany was, at the time they first became acquainted with it, a rude and inhospitable land, full of immense forests, marshes, and desert tracts. The great Hercynian forest, by Cæsar's account, extended from the Alps over a space, that in its length occupied sixty, and in its width nine days' journey; consequently, all the chief mountain chains and forests of the present Germany, must be the remnants of that one stupendous wooded range. But Cæsar, from the indefinite information he received, owing to his ignorance of the German language, applied the general German word, *Hart*, or *Harz*, for mountain, to the collective mountain forests of the land, which, however, the natives certainly already distinguished by different appellations. Later authors, viz., Pliny and Tacitus, circumscribe the Hercynian forests to those chains of mountains which, to the south of the Thuringian forest, enclose Bohemia, and in the east extend to Moravia and Hungary. They also, as well as Ptolemy, subsequently, mention many individual mountains by peculiar names; for example, *Mons Abnoba*, the Black Forest, (Ptolemy seems to imply by this, the mountains between the Maine, the Rhine, and the Weser;) the *Melibokos* mountains, the present Harz; the *Semana* forest, to the south of the Harz, towards the Thuringian forest; the *Sudeta* forest, a portion of the Thuringian forest; the *Gabreta* forest, the Bohemian forest; the *Askiburgish* mountains, according to some the *Erz*, or rather the *Riesen*-Gebirg; the *Taunus*, the heights between Wiesbaden and Homburg; the *Teutsburger* forest, the mountain and forest tracts which extend from the Weser through Paderborn, as far as Osnaburg. Cæsar mentions besides, the *Bacenis* forest, probably the western portion of the Thuringian forest, which extends into Fulda, and in the middle ages was called Bocauna, or Buchonia; and Tacitus names the *Silvia Cæsia*, between the Ems and the Issel, the remains of which may be the Haser forest, and the Baumberge, near Coesfeld; and that town itself may probably have preserved the name. Many other less important or uncertain names we pass over.

The large German forests consisted probably, as now, principally of oaks, beeches, and pines. The Romans admired, above all, the immense oaks, which seemed to them coeval with the earth itself. Pliny, who had been personally in the north of Westphalia, in the country of the Chauci, expresses himself thus upon them: "Created with the earth itself, untouched by centuries, the monstrous trunks surpass, by their powerful vitality, all other wonders of nature."

The Romans were also acquainted with the majority of German rivers: *Danubius*, the Danube; *Rhenus*, the Rhine; *Moenus*, the Maine; *Albis*, the Elbe; *Visurgis*, the Weser; *Viadrus*, the Oder; the *Vistula; Nicer*, the Necker; *Luppia*, the Lippe; *Amisia*, the Ems; *Adrana*, the Eder; *Salas*, (in Strabo alone,) the Saale; and some others. It is remarkable that the Romans do not mention the Lahn and the Ruhr, although they must surely have become acquainted with them in their campaigns in the north of Germany. The German rivers were not at that period made passable by means of bridges, which the native did not require, as he easily swam across the former, and for wider transits he had his boats.

The soil of the land was not cultivated as now, although the Romans call portions of it extremely fertile, and agriculture and pasturage were the chief occupations of the Germans. Rye, barley, oats, and, according to the opinions of some, wheat also, were cultivated; flax was everywhere distributed; various sorts of carrots and turnips it certainly produced; the Romans admired radishes of the size of a child's head, and mention asparagus, which they, indeed, did not praise, and a species of parsley, which pleased them much. The superior fruits of southern climates which have been subsequently transplanted among them, might probably not then thrive, although Pliny mentions a species of cherry found near the Rhine, and Tacitus names among the food of the Germans wild-tree fruits, (*agrestia poma,*) which must certainly have been better than our crab-apples.

The pastures were rich and beautiful, and the horned cattle as well as the horses, although small and inconsiderable, yet of a good and durable kind.

The most important of all condiments, salt, the Germans found upon their native soil, nor did it refuse them that most useful of all metals, iron, and they understood the art of procuring and manufacturing it; they do not, however, appear to have dug for silver.

Of the many strengthening mineral springs which the country numbers, the Romans already mention Spa and Wiesbaden.

The climate, in consequence of the immense forests, whose density was impervious to the rays of the sun, and owing to the undrained fens and marshes, was colder, more foggy and inclement than at present, but was nevertheless not quite so bad perhaps as represented by the Romans, spoiled as they were by the luxurious climate of Italy. According to them the trees were without leaves for eight months in the year, and the large rivers were regularly so deeply and firmly frozen that they could bear upon them the heavy field-equipages of the army. "The Germans," says Pliny, "know only three seasons, winter, spring, and summer; of autumn they know neither the name nor its fruits." The Romans found the country in general so ungenial, that they considered it quite impossible that any one should quit Italy to dwell in Germany.

But the ancient Germans loved this country beyond all, because, as free men, they were born in it, and the nature of the climate helped them to defend this freedom. The forests and marshes appalled the enemy; the severity of the air as well as the chase of wild animals strengthened the bodies of the men, and, nourished by a simple diet, they grew to so stately a size that other nations admired them with astonishment.

### III. THE NATIVES.

The Romans justly considered the German nation as an aboriginal, pure, and unmixed race of people. They resembled themselves alone; and like the specifically similar plants of the field, which springing from a pure seed, not raised in the hotbed of a garden, but germinating in the healthy, free, unsheltered soil, do not differ from each other by varieties, so also, among the thousands of the simple German race, there was but one determined and equal form of body. Their chest was wide and strong; their hair yellow, and with young children it was of a dazzling white. Their skin was also white, their eyes blue, and their glance bold and piercing. Their powerful, gigantic bodies, which the Romans and Gauls could not behold without fear, displayed the strength that nature had given to this people, for according to the testimony of some of the ancient writers their usual height was seven feet.

From their earliest youth upward they hardened their bodies by all devisable means. New-born infants were dipped in cold water, and the cold bath was continued during their whole lives as the strengthening renovator by both boys and girls, men and women. Their dress was a broad short mantle fastened by a girdle, or the skins of wild animals, the trophies of the successful chase; in both sexes a great portion of the body was left uncovered, and the winter did not induce them to clothe themselves warmer. The children ran about almost naked, and effeminate nations, who with difficulty reared their children during the earliest infancy, wondered how those of the Germans, without cradles or swaddling bands, should grow up to the very fullest bloom of health.

The Romans called our nation, from its warlike and valiant mode of thinking, GERMANS;* a name which the *Tungi*,—a body of German warriors, who, at an earlier period, crossed the Rhine, and colonized, with arms in hand, among the Gauls,—first bore, and subsequently applied to all their race, to express thereby their warlike manners, and thus to impress their enemies with terror. This name was willingly adopted, as a name of honor, by all Germans, and thus it remained.

The aboriginal name of the people is, however, without doubt the same which they bear to the present day. It springs from the word *Diot*, (in the Gothic, *Thiudu*,) which signifies *Nation*. A Teutscher or Deutscher, according to the harder or softer pronunciation, was, therefore, one belonging to the *nation*, which styled itself so prerogatively.

According to history, it was some centuries after the decline of the Roman dominion, that the name of the nation of Germans was again heard of, and it is found in but few records prior to Otto I., the earliest of which bears the date of the year 813.

It must not appear remarkable to us, that the original collective name of the people was little used in the earlier periods, and was probably unknown to the Romans. In the intercourse with a nation composed of so many septs, the names of only those septs transpired with whom that communication took place, because each held itself to be a nation, (Diot;) and so also later, when various tribes associated together in bodies, merely the name of the union appeared: as, the Suevi, the Marcomanni, the Allemanni, the Goths, the Franks, and the Saxons. It is, however, remarkable enough, that we meet with the original national name in that of the Teutonians, which is already used by Pytheas, 300 years before the birth of Christ, and which again recurs in the Cimbrian war.

### IV. THE GERMANIC RACES.

Ancient authors mention several German tribes, as well as their dwelling-places, with greater or less precision. Several of them also speak of the *chief tribes* among which the single septs united themselves. But their statements are not sufficiently unanimous or precise, to give us that clear view which we would, however, so willingly obtain. For how desirable would it not be for us to be able, even in the very cradle of our history, to point out the original distinctions of the races as yet discovered, and which display themselves in the different dialects of the German language, as well as in many essential differences in the manners of the people, particularly in those of the less sophisticated peasantry! But we are here upon too insecure a foundation, although it still yields us some few features always important.

The most obscure account presented to us is the five-fold division of tribes given by Pliny. Beginning at the extreme north coast, towards the estuary of the Vistula, he first mentions the *Vinilians* or *Windiler;* farther westward, towards the East Sea coast, and beyond the Cimbrian peninsula, towards the North Sea, as far as the mouth of the Ems, the *Ingavonians;* in the neighborhood of the Rhine, as far as the Maine, and higher up on the left bank of the Rhine, the *Istavonians;* and in the middle of Germany, particularly in the highlands along the Upper Weser, the Werra, Fulda, and towards the south, as far as the Hercynian forest, the *Hermionian* tribes. He gives no general name to the fifth tribe, but includes therein the *Peucinians* and *Bastarnians* in the districts of the Lower Danube, as far as Dacia.

Tacitus also mentions three of these names, but he derives them from the mythical origin of the people. Man, the son of Tuisko, had three sons, Ingavon, Istavon, and Hermion, whose descendants formed the three principal tribes of the Ingavonians, the Istavonians, and the Hermionians.

We would willingly, as before mentioned, bring the fourth or fifth-fold division of the tribes of Pliny, in conjunction with the subsequent times, and, on this head, we are not altogether without some histori-

* Most probably from the word *ger*, spear or lance, and the word *man*—the man, the lord or chief. Therefore, in any case, a warlike title of honor, which distinguished the manliness and valor of the nation. It is worthy of remark, that the name *Germanen*, which, before Cæsar, no Roman author mentions, appears on a marble slab discovered in the year 1547, and which is connected with the celebrated *Fastis Capitolinis*, in the year, before the birth of Christ, 223. The consul Marcellus gained in that year a victory over the Gallic chief Viridomar, who is inscribed upon that captured slab a leader of the Gauls and *Germanen*.

cal indications,—as, viz., when the Vandals, of their own accord, return later and join in the great Gothic union; when the Suevi, the flower of the Allemannic alliance, as the inhabitants of the internal and southwestern parts of Germany, thus bring to mind the Hermionians, the Ingavonians and Istavonians therefore remaining for the north and northwestern portions; so that as, even in the earlier times of the Romans, an essential difference, nay, a decided contrast, in comparison with the inhabitants of the North Sea, the Tresians and Chaucians, evidently occurs between the inhabitants of the Middle and Lower Rhine, extending itself onward towards the mountain districts of the Weser and the Harz, and which, in the subsequent league of the Franks and Saxons, becomes confirmed, we have thence furnished to us already the third and fourth principal tribes of Pliny.

The fifth he refers to as before mentioned. Proceeding further onward we may find again in Bavaria the remnant of the Gothic tribe, which, after the period of the migration of the people, remained stationary in Germany, so that between the later four principal nations in Germany, the Franks, the Saxons, the Swabians, and Bavarians, a connection is formed and established even to the original tribes of Pliny. Such links of connection convey assuredly a great charm; but we, nevertheless, wander upon ground too uncertain to enable us to succeed in acquiring authentic historical data.

Much more importance attaches, on the contrary, to what the ancients, but more distinctly Cæsar and Tacitus, relate of the peculiarities of one German chief tribe, which included many individual septs, namely the *Suevi.* From the combination of the picture sketched by them, in conjunction with other descriptions of German manners and institutions, we can define, with tolerable safety, the peculiarities of a second tribe, although the Romans give it no general name. We will first portray the *Suevi*, as Cæsar and Tacitus described them:

1. The nations forming the *Suevic* race dwelt in the large semi-circle traced by the Upper and Middle Rhine and the Danube, through the middle of Germany, and farther towards the north to the East Sea, so that they occupied the country of the Necker, the Maine, the Saale, and then the right Elbe bank of the Havel, Spree, and Oder. Nay, Tacitus even places Suevic tribes beyond the Vistula, as well in the interior as on the coasts of the Baltic, and beyond it in Sweden. Grounds of probability admit, indeed, of our placing a third—the Gothic-Vandal tribe, between the Oder and the Vistula, and along the latter stream; but as distinct information is wanting, we can but allude to it, of which more below. The Suevi, as Cæsar informs us, had early formed themselves into one large union, whose principles were distinctly warlike. The love of arms was assiduously cherished in all, that they might be always ready for any undertaking. Thence it was that individuals had no fixed landed possessions; but the princes and leaders yearly divided the land among the families just as it pleased them; and none were allowed even to select the same pastures for two consecutive years, but were forced to exchange with each other, that neither of them might accustom himself to the ground, and, acquiring a love for his dwelling-place, be thus induced to exchange the love of war for agriculture. They were afraid that, if an individual were permitted to acquire an extensive tract, the powerful might chase away the poor, build large and imposing dwellings, and that the lust of wealth might give rise to factions and divisions. Besides which, they were obliged, from each of their hundred districts, to supply the wars with a thousand men yearly, and those who remained at home cultivated the land for all. The following year, on the other hand, the latter marched under arms, and the former remained at home, so that agriculture as well as the art of war was in constant exercise.

They considered it a proof of glory when the whole tract beyond their frontiers lay waste, as a sign that the neighboring nations were not able to resist their force. They might also have considered it perhaps as a greater security against sudden invasion.

In these, although rude principles of the Suevic union, a great idea manifests itself, and proves that the ancient Germans, about the period of the birth of Christ, were by no means to be reckoned among the *savage tribes*. What Lycurgus wished to effect by means of his legislation among the Spartans, and for the same reason that he allowed his citizens no fixed and exclusive possession, seems to have been a principle and combining power of the Suevic nation, viz. a public spirit, so general and operative, that the individual should submit himself to the common good, and for which and in which he should only live; and not by selfishness, faction, or by idleness, desire to separate himself from the rest, or consider his own weal as more important than that of the collective body.

2. The Romans mention many individual tribes in the northwest of Germany, between the Lower Elbe and the Lower Rhine, consequently about the Aller, the Seine, the Harz, the Weser, the Lippe, the Ruhr, and the Ems, as high up as the coasts of the Baltic, (later also on the opposite side of the Rhine, in the vicinity of the Meuse and Scheldt,) without distinguishing them by a collective name. Subsequently, in the second century after the birth of Christ, the name of *Saxon* occurs in these districts, and in still later times it becomes the *dominant* title in the above-mentioned tracts of land; for in the third century, the tribe of Saxons spread forth from Holstein over Lower Germany, and gave its own name to all those tribes which it conquered or united by alliance. It has been customary to apply the name of Saxons, for even the earlier periods, as the collective appellation of all the tribes of Lower Germany, and thereby to express the very opposite character they presented in their whole mode of living to the Suevi. For as these unwillingly confined themselves to a fixed spot, and by their greater exercise and activity, kept themselves constantly ready for every warlike undertaking, so, on the other hand, the nations of Lower Germany had early accustomed themselves to settled dwellings, and had made agriculture their principal occupation. They dwelt upon scattered farms; each farm had its boundaries around it, and was enclosed by a hedge and bank of earth. The owner was lord and priest within his farm, and by voluntary union with a number of other proprietors was attached to a community; and several communities again were bound to a *Gau* or district. The name of *Saxon*, which is derived from *sitzen*, to sit, and has the same signification as to occupy, or hold, appeared effectively to characterize the peculiarity of *this* people; while on the other hand, the name of *Suevi* would indicate the roaming life led by the others. But these derivations are more ingeniously than historically founded. The name of Saxon is, according to all probability, to be derived from the short swords, called Saxens,(Sahs,) of this people; but that of the Suevi in its derivation is not as yet thoroughly explained. Meantime, however, the contrast between the Suevi and the non-Suevi is not to be mistaken. In the latter we find the greatest freedom and independence of the *individual;* in the former we perceive the combined power and unity of the *whole,* wherein the individual self is merged; in the latter again, *domestic life* in its entire privacy, and in the former, *public life* in the—although as yet rude—accomplishment of an acutely formed idea.

Saxon institutions were not the most favorable for the exercise of the strength of a nation against the enemy. But it gives a strong and self-dependent mind to the individual man, to find himself sole lord and master upon his own property, and knowing that it is his own power that must protect wife and child. In villages or even in towns where man dwells amidst a mass, he depends upon the protection of others, and thereby easily becomes indolent or cowardly. But the isolated inhabitant, in his, frequently, defiance-bidding retreat, is nevertheless humane and hospitably minded, and offers to his neighbor and his friend, and even to the stranger, an ever welcome seat by his hearth. For he feels more intensely the pleasure derived from the friendly glances of man, and the refreshment of social intercourse; while, on the contrary, the townsman, who meets a multitude at every step, accustoms himself to view the human countenance with indifference. When the Saxon, with his hunting-spear in his hand, had traversed, through snow and storm, the wilderness and forest, the huts of his friends smiled hospitably towards him, like the happy islands of a desert sea.

We shall enumerate subsequently the individual tribes of both branches, as well as the others mentioned by the authors of antiquity. It appeared necessary to notice thus early the chief distinction between the German nations, for many of the descriptions given by the ancients of their manners and customs, accord only with the one or the other branch, and their apparent contradictions are to be explained only by the confused mixture of the information. Cæsar, for example, notices chiefly the Suevi; and Tacitus, the Saxon tribes. Yet in the detail which we now enter upon, it will be perceived that the essential fundamental character of both was the same.

### V. MANNERS AND CUSTOMS.

The Germans loved the open country above every thing. They did not build towns, they likened them to prisons. The few places which occur in the Roman writers called towns—the later Ptolemy names the most—were probably nothing more than the dwellings of the chiefs, somewhat larger, and more artificially built, than those of the common freemen, and in the vicinity of which the servitors fixed their huts; the whole might possibly have been surrounded by a wall and ditch to secure them from the incursions of the enemy.

The Saxon tribes did not even willingly build connecting villages, so great was their love for unlimited freedom. The huts lay, as is already mentioned, in the midst of the enclosure that belonged to them, and which was surrounded by a hedge. The construction of these huts was most inartificial. Logs shaped by the axe were raised and joined together, the sides filled with platted withy, and made into a firm wall by the addition of straw and lime. A thatched roof covered the whole, which (as is still found in Westphalia) contained the cattle also; and by way of ornament they decorated the walls with brilliant colors.

Tacitus says, they selected their dwelling wherever a grove or spring attracted them. Advantage and comfort were consequently frequently sacrificed to their love of open and beautiful scenery, and it is probable that they so ardently loved their country from its presenting them with so great a variety of hill and dale, wood and plains, and rivers in every part.

This strong love of nature, which may be traced from the very first in our forefathers, is a grand feature of the German character. As long as we retain it, it will preserve us from sensual enervation and the corruption of manners, wherein the most cultivated nations of antiquity, by excess of civilization and luxury, and compression into large cities, gradually sunk.

Next to war, the most favorite occupation of the Germans was the chase; and that itself was a kind of warlike exercise. For the forests concealed, besides the usual deer, also wolves, bears, urocks, bisons, elks, wild boars, and many species of the larger birds of prey. The youth was, therefore, practised in the use of arms from childhood, and to him the greatest festival of his life was when his father first took him forth to hunt wild animals.

"Agriculture, the herdsman's business, and domestic occupations," says Tacitus, "they leave to the women and slaves; for it is easier to prevail upon the Germans to attack their enemies than to cultivate the earth and await the harvest; nay, it even appears cowardly to them to earn by the sweat of the brow, what the sanguinary conflict would procure." But this description of our forefathers, as is so often the case with the narratives of the Roman authors, represents the individual feature as the general characteristic. The small proprietor, no doubt, like our peasant, necessarily applied his own hand to the cultivation of his land, while the great land-owner reserved time for hunting, for festivities, and for all the pleasures of social intercourse.

And with respect to the description of their dominant warlike propensities, which preferred earning the necessaries of life by blood rather than by the sweat of the brow, this must be understood to refer more particularly to the conquering warlike trains of bold leaders, such as an Ariovistus, or to the frontier safeguards of the Germans against the Romans, as, for instance, the Marcomanni. For when once among a nation agriculture and pasturage have become prominent occupations, and without which life could not be supported, they can no longer belong to those employments despised by the free man, and which as such he leaves solely to the care and attention of women and slaves.

It is, however, no doubt true, that among the Germans of the more ancient period, warlike desires, and powerful natural inclinations for bold undertakings, and in particular for the display of an untamed strength with its violent concomitants, were a ruling passion. But the ennobling features of higher virtues are seen through these defects. History records no people who, in conjunction with the faults of an unrestricted natural power, possessed nobler capabilities and qualifications, rule and order, a sublime patriotism, fidelity, and chastity, in a greater proportion than the Germans. "*There*," says the noble Roman, who had preserved a mind capable of appreciating the dignity of uncorrupted nature ; "there no one smiles at vice, and to seduce or be seduced, is not called *fashionable ; for among the Germans, good morals effect more than elsewhere good laws.*"

This moral worth of the Germans, which beams through all their rudeness, has its true source and basis *in the sanctity of marriage*, and the consequent concentration of domestic happiness ; for it is these two features chiefly which most decidedly determine the morality of a nation. The young man, at a period when his form had taken its perfect growth, in the full energy of youth, like the sturdy oaks of his native forests, and preserved by chastity and temperance from enervating desires, at the time that his physical and moral nature had attained their equilibrium, selected then the maiden for his wife, little differing in age from himself. The exceptions were few, says Tacitus, and that only perchance —as in the case of a prince, who might wish to increase his own importance by an alliance with another powerful house—that a second wife was taken.

It was not the woman who brought the portion to the man, but the latter to the former, and who indicated the value he attached to his alliance with her by the quality of the present he made, according to the extent of his means ; and even this custom displays the consideration the German nation had for the gentler sex. The bridal gift comprised, besides a team of oxen, a war-horse, a shield, and arms ; a gift not useless among people with whom, particularly in long excursions, the wife, generally, accompanied her husband to the field. She was thus reminded not to consider valor, war, and arms, as wholly strange to her, but these sacred symbols of the opening marriage told her to consider herself as the companion of the labors and dangers of her husband, in war as well as in peace, and as such to live and die. She received what she was bound to transfer uncontaminated to her children, and what her daughter-in-law was to inherit in turn, in order to transmit to her grand-children. And this gift, as Tacitus says, was, as it were, the mystic holy consecration and guardian deity of marriage.

Such an alliance founded upon love and virtue, and calculated to continue for better for worse, in firm union unto death, must indeed be holy and inviolable ; and, in fact, the infringement of the marriage vow was, according to the testimony of Tacitus, almost unheard of. The deepest and most universal contempt followed a crime so very rare.

The children of such a marriage were to their parents the dearest pledges of love. From their very birth they were treated as free human beings. No trace was to be found in Germany of the tyrannical power of the Roman father over his children. The mother reared her infants at her own breast ; they were not left to the care of nurses and servants. The Germans, therefore, highly venerated virtuous women ; they even superstitiously believed there was something holy and prophetic in them, and they occasionally followed their advice in important and decisive moments.

This veneration for the female sex in its human dignity, combined with their strongly impressed love of arms, of war, and manhood, this noble feature in the German nature, which elevates him so high above the—in other senses, so gifted —Greeks and Romans, shows most clearly that nature had resolved her German son to be the entire man, who, by the universal cultivation of the human powers, should at some future period produce an age, which, as now, in its liberal and many-sided or multifarious views, should far surpass that of the Greeks and Romans.

The ancient German dress and food were simple, and agreeable to nature. Female decoration consisted in their long yellow hair, in the fresh color of their pure skin, and in their linen robes, spun and woven by their own hands, ornamented with a purple band as a girdle : the man knew no other ornament than his warlike weapons ; the shield and his helmet, when he wore one, he adorned as well as he could. Among the Suevi the hair was worn tied in a bundle on the top of the head, for the sake of its warlike effect. Among the Saxons it was parted, and hung down the shoulders, cut at a moderate length.

Their simple fare consisted chiefly of meat and milk. They prepared their favorite drink, beer from barley and oats.

They made mead also from honey and water. Their honey was collected by the wild bees in great quantity, and good quality. Upon the Rhine they did not despise or neglect the cultivation of the vine introduced there by the Romans.

No nation respected the laws of hospitality more than the Germans. To refuse a stranger, whoever he might be, admission to the house, would have been disgraceful. His table was free and open to all, according to his means. If his own provisions were exhausted, he who was but recently the host, would become the guide and conductor of his guest, and together they would enter, uninvited, the first best house. There also they were hospitably received. When the stranger took his leave, he received as a parting present whatever he desired, and the giver asked as candidly on his side for what he wished. This good-natured people rejoiced in presents. But they neither estimated the gift they made too highly, nor held themselves much bound by that which they had received in return.

At these banquets the Germans not unfrequently took counsel upon their most important affairs, upon the conciliation of enemies, upon alliances and friendships, upon the election of princes, even upon war and peace; for the joyousness of the feast and society opened the secrets of the breast. But on the following day they reconsidered what had been discussed, so that they might view it coolly and dispassionately; they took counsel when they could not deceive, and fixed their resolution when fitted for quiet consideration.

During these banquets they had also a peculiar kind of festival. Naked youths danced between drawn swords and raised spears; not for reward and gain; but the compensation for this almost rash feat consisted in the pleasure produced in the spectator, and the honor reaped by the display of such a dangerous art.

They gambled with dice, as Tacitus with astonishment informs us, in a sober state, and as a serious occupation, and with so much eagerness for gain, that when they had lost their all, they hazarded their freedom, and even their very persons upon the last cast. The loser freely delivered himself up to slavery, although even younger and stronger than his adversary, and patiently allowed himself to be bound and sold as a slave; thus steadfastly did they keep their word, even in a bad case: "They call this *good faith*," says the Roman writer.

### VI. CIVIL INSTITUTIONS.

The entire people consisted of freemen and slaves. Among the latter there seems even to have been an essential difference. The one class, which may be compared to the vassals pertaining to the land of the lord of the manor, and among whom the freedmen of Tacitus may be also reckoned, received from the land-proprietor house and home, and yielded him in return a certain acknowledgment in corn or cattle, or in the woven cloth which was made under every roof. The second class, on the contrary, the true slaves, who were bought and sold, and were mostly prisoners of war, were employed in the more menial services of the house, and the labors of agriculture. But their lot even was endurable, for their children grew up with those of their master, with scarcely any distinction, and thus in the simplicity of their living, there was formed a relation of mutual adherence. But the slave was held incapable of bearing arms; these were alone the privilege and prerogative of the *Free-men.*

They were divided into the nobles, *nobiles,* as Tacitus calls them, and the common Free-men, *ingenui.* In later periods the German language distinguishes *Adelinge* and *Frilinge.* The former word is probably derived from *Od,* Estate, and therefore denoted the large proprietor, who reckoned in his estate bondsmen and vassals, and who possessed already in his domains the means of exercising a more extensive influence. The Friling was, on the contrary, the common free man, who cultivated his small possessions with his own hands, or by the assistance of but a few slaves. If Tacitus, as is probable, indicates this distinction by his term *nobiles* and *ingenui,* we may therein trace the origin of the German nobility, founded as it is in the nature of all social relations. From the importance given by possessions and merit, individual as well as ancestral, those privileges may be adduced, which are held over the poorer, unnoticed families, and which in the course of time, and as it were by the antiquity of possession, pass into rights. But the information given by Tacitus does not, however, speak absolutely of *rights*,—implying, for instance, the offices of director and president in communities and districts,—but merely of the *custom* of filling them from the superior families.

A number of farms of great and small landowners, specially united by close ties, constituted a community, (*Gemeinde;*) several communities a league of the hundred, (*Markgenossenschaft,*) which exercised within a larger circuit the common right of herd and pasture; and, lastly, a number of these formed the larger confederacy of a district, (*Gau,*) formally united for protection against every enemy, and for internal security both of life and property.

As chief of the district, a judge was elected from among the oldest and most experienced, who probably may have borne in ancient times the name *Graf.** Cents or hundreds were subdivisions of the district, probably consisting originally of a hundred farms, whose chiefs were the centners or *Centgrafen.* These gave judgment in trifling affairs; and in matters of more importance they were the assistants of the Gaugrafen. The occupation of these functionaries was not limited to their judicial employments, but they had the guidance also of other affairs in the community; and together, they formed the *Principes* of the district, the foremost and first among their equals, whence is derived the German word *Fürst,* (prince.) The recompense for their trouble did not consist in a regular stipend, but in presents received from the chiefs of families.

But the *National assembly* was at the head of all, and counselled and decided upon the most important affairs. Every freeman, high as well as low, was a member of the national assembly, and took his part in the welfare of the whole.

In earlier times, perhaps, there never existed in many circuits, and during peaceful relations, a more extensive and firm confederacy than that of the *Gau.* But danger from without, and the relationship of the septs, chiefly produced, without doubt, the establishment of *Unions of whole tribes,* which may possibly have given to their collective body a form variously fashioned. A multifariousness of social regulations was welcome to the hereditary love of freedom of the Germans. The majority of these tribes appear to have had a very simple constitution of confederacy in the time of peace, inasmuch as all transactions in common were determined and regulated by the national community. In the individual districts all continued according to the customary mode of administration, and it consequently did not require the permanent appointment of a superior executive government. In war, on the contrary, an election was made, of the common *Herzog,* or duke, according to valor and manly virtue, whose office closed with the war. (Duces ex virtute sumunt.—*Tac.*)

Among other tribes peace had also its chiefs or directors, selected originally by the community from the most meritorious of the people, which election, in the course of time, when a natural feeling placed the son in the situation of the father, became invested with an almost hereditary right. (Reges ex nobilitate sumunt.—*Tac.*) We cannot ascertain whether these chiefs bore everywhere, or merely among some tribes, the title of *King;* the Romans called them *Reges,* because they found this name most applicable, and in contradistinction to the transitory ducal dignity, which terminated with the war. The king could also naturally be the leader in war, in which case the duke was superfluous. But in smaller expeditions, which were not to be considered in the light of a national war, or when the king, by reason of age or natural infirmity, was unable to act, a duke may have been appointed as his substitute.

Among some tribes we see a change of constitution. Among the Cherusci, when they fought against the Romans, there appears to have been no king; Arminius was the leader appointed by the people. Later, however, in the year 47 after the birth of Christ, the Cherusci appointed *Italicus,* the son of the brother of *Flavius,* who was brought up among the Romans, to be their king, in order to adjust the internal factions.

The peculiarity of the Saxon people consisted altogether in their free form of government, a constitution most conformable to their origin, springing as they did from the union of the heads of free families, each of whom ruled his domain according to the ancient patriarchal form.

* The derivation of the word Graf or Grav is uncertain. That from *grau,* gray, as well as from *alt,* old, is not tenable.

A common general was required only during war, which, in general, was defensive, and consequently national. Among the Suevi, on the contrary, whose constitution was one warlike throughout, wherein the individual was early accustomed to consider himself but a portion of the whole, a monarchical government became the natural form of the constitution, and we consequently find among them an Ariovistus, a Marbodius, and a Vannius, as kings of a warlike state.

These differences may assist in explaining the various characteristics and forms of the public institutions which the Romans mention, and which it is not always easy to distinguish, from their having confounded and mixed the individual details.

In the larger confederations there also occurred general assemblies, although more seldom than in the individual districts, and much that the Romans relate refers to these said larger assemblies, while on the contrary the leading subjects were common to both large and small assemblies.

These were generally held at a return of the full moon and new moon; as they considered those the most happy moments for any transaction. They came armed—arms being the symbol of freedom, and they preferred exposing themselves to the possibility of their misuse, rather than come without them. The right enjoyed by the youth of bearing them as an ornament when he had attained a fitting age, and was adjudged worthy, even in times of peace, was imparted by the national assembly itself; he was there solemnly invested by one of the princes, his father or a relative, with shield and spear. This was deemed among them the clothing of manhood, the ornament of youth; previous to this the youth was considered only as a member of the domestic hearth, but henceforth he was received as the representative of the common fatherland.

Priests ruled the communities; God only was the universally feared lord, whom it was no breach of freedom to obey; and in his name the priests kept the multitude in order. They commanded silence; the kings, dukes, counts, who derived experience from years—the nobles, who learned from their ancestors how the district was to be governed—the most valiant, who, by their deeds in war, stood in general respect, spoke in turn simply, briefly, and impressively, and not in a commanding tone, but by the force of reason. If the proposition displeased them, it was rejected by the multitude with hisses and murmurs; but if approved, they signified their satisfaction by the clashing of their arms, their most honorable mode of testifying applause.

In important affairs, the king and princes first counselled together, prior to the matter being brought before the people; a custom consistent with good government, for the multitude can form conclusions only upon a transaction being simply and clearly explained.

These few traits of aboriginal German institutions display the sterling sense of our forefathers, who therein sought to establish the principle, that the foundations of every community should be based on individual good feeling, obedience to the laws, and respect for religion. Thus an internal durability was given to the whole structure, which no external means could replace, howsoever artificially applied.

We have yet a word to say upon the larger unions of several tribes. In a common danger, they formed themselves into a *Confederation*, at the head of which stood one of the more powerful tribes. Thus it was with the Cherusci alliance against the Romans; thus the Suevi, at whose head, in earlier times, stood the Semnoni; and later, the confederations of the Goths, Franks, and Allemanni. In all that concerned the universal league, the laws were very severe. The slightest breach of faith, and treachery as well as cowardice, were punished by death.

Their principle was, "One for all and all for one, for life or death!" May this through every century be the motto of all Germans!

### VII. WAR-REGULATIONS, AND ARMS.

When the nation was threatened by impending danger, or the country of the enemy was to be invaded by a large force, all the freemen were summoned to arms by what was called the *Heerbann*.* The army thus proceeded under the banner of the national god, borne by the priests in ad-

* In the language of the earlier times *Heerbann*, (*Heribannus*,) the *penalty*, which was inflicted upon those who, at the general summons to the war, neglected their duty. This word, however, for its object, is at once so usual and significant, while it is so difficult to replace with another, that it may be here retained in its original form.

vance. The princes and judges of each Gau or district were also its leaders in war; the confederates of one mark or hundred, and of one race or sept, fought united; and when the invasion became a regular migration, or when the invading foe chased all from their hearths, the women and children followed them. Thus was all combined that could excite their valor; each warrior stood side by side to his nearest relations, companions, and friends, and in the rear of the order of battle were placed their wives and children, whose appeals could not fail to reach their ear. When wounded, they retired to the matrons and females, who fearlessly investigated and numbered their wounds. We read, indeed, of the women having occasionally restored a faltering battle by their incessant supplications, from the dread of slavery, and even by forcing, with arms in hand, the fugitives back to the contest.

Besides the general summons of the Heerbann, there was *a Companionship in arms*, founded upon a voluntary union, which was called the *Gefolge*, the reserve phalanx or sacred battalion. Warlike youths collected themselves around their most tried and esteemed leader, and swore in union with him to live and die. There was much contention among this Gefolge who should take the first place next to the leader, for this corps had its grades. It was high fame for a leader, not merely among his own tribes, but among all the adjacent ones, when he was distinguished by the number and valor of his Gefolge. He was appealed to for assistance; embassies were sent to him, he was honored by presents, and the mere celebrity of his name would frequently check a war. In battle it was considered a disgrace to the chief to be outvied in valor, and to the Gefolge not to equal that of their leader; but to return alive from battle, after the death of his chieftain, was a stigma that attached for life to the individual, and their fidelity was so great, that scarcely an instance of this occurs. It was considered the most sacred duty to protect and defend their brave brother in arms, and to attribute their own valorous deeds to his fame. The leaders contended for victory, and the Gefolge for the leaders. When the tribe to which they belonged continued in a state of long and monotonous peace, the majority of these bold youths, led by their captain, voluntarily joined those tribes which were at war. Repose was hateful to them; and, amidst danger, the valiant acquired fame and booty. The Gefolge received from the leader their war-horse, and their conquering and deadly spear; a large Gefolge, consequently, supported itself most easily by war and booty. It is thus that Tacitus describes the military institutions of the Germans. He wrote, however, at a period when long wars and their attendant chances may possibly have altered much Originally, perhaps, the alliance between the Gefolge and their chieftain was binding only during single excursions, and ceased at their termination. For it is not probable that a people so jealous of its liberty would have allowed individual princes to have surrounded themselves with such a troop, as with a body-guard. But when the dangers of war continued for a longer period, it became desirable, and even necessary, to be prepared for every casualty. The Gefolge remained long united, and they formed the experienced and élite portion of the army for attack, defence, or pursuit. In the migratory period, kingdoms were founded by these Gefolges, and from the essence of their internal organization, the laws sprung which regulated these new states, (feudal system.)

The chief arms of the ancient Germans were the shield and the spear, called by them *Framen*, (*Framea*,*) with a narrow and short blade, but so sharp and well adapted for use, that they could employ the same weapon, according to necessity, both far and near. Long heavy lances are also spoken of in the description of many battles. For close combat, the stone battle-axe, which is still frequently dug up, and the common club, were certainly used. From the scarcity of iron, few wore body-armor, and but here and there a helmet; even swords were scarce, and the shield was formed of wood, or of the platted twigs of the withy. Nevertheless, it was with these simple weapons that they achieved so much that was grand, inasmuch as natural courage and strength of limb effect more than artificial weapons.

Their horses were neither distinguished by beauty nor speed, but they were very durable, and the Germans knew so well to manage them that they frequently over-

* From *framen*, to throw.

threw the fully-armed and mounted Roman and Gallic cavalry. They held the latter in contempt because they used saddles, which appeared to them unmanly and effeminate; they themselves sat upon the naked back of the horse. But the chief strength of their army lay in their infantry, and they placed the boldest and strongest of their youth, mixed with their cavalry, in the van, in order to give an additional solidity to the ranks. The cavalry themselves selected their companions from among the infantry, and thus, even in the rude pursuit of war, esteem and affection exerted their influence. They thus held together in the tumult of the fight, and came to each other's assistance when the contest was desperate. If a horseman fell heavily wounded from his steed, the foot-soldiers immediately surrounded and shielded him. When sudden and rapid movements either in advancing or retreating were necessary, the quickness of those on foot, by means of incessant practice, was so great, that holding by the mane of the horse, they equalled the swiftest in their course.

Their order of battle was generally wedge-shaped, that they might the more speedily break the ranks of the enemy. Before battle they sang the war-song relating the deeds of their ancestors and the celebrity of their fatherland. Warlike instruments also, horns of brass or of the wild bull, and large drums, formed of hides expanded over hampers, beat the measure to their joined shields; and as they proceeded they became more and more excited. In the march against the enemy the song became ruder and wilder, a courageous and stimulating cry, which was called *Barrit;* at first deep-sounding, then stronger and fuller, and growing to a roar at the moment of meeting the foe. The chieftain felt excited with hope or fear, according to the louder or weaker tone of the *Barrit*. Frequently, to make the sound more strikingly fearful, they held their hollow shields before their mouths. This terrific war-song, combined with the sight of their gigantic figures, and the fearful threatening eyes of the Germans themselves, was so terrible in its effects upon the Romans and the Gauls, that it was long before they could accustom themselves to it.

To leave their shield behind them was to the Germans an inexpiable disgrace; he who had so debased himself durst not attend religious worship nor appear in the national assembly, and many who had thus effected their escape from the field of battle could not endure so miserable a life, but ended it by a voluntary death.

### VIII. RELIGION.

The religious worship of the Germans attached itself to, and was associated with nature. It was a veneration of her great powers and phenomena; but withal it was more simple and sublime than the worship of other ancient nations, and bore the impress of its immediate and profound feeling for nature. Although but rudely so, they yet had the presentiment of an infinite and eternal divine power in their breasts; for they considered it at variance with the dignity of the divinity to enclose him within walls, or to conceive and represent him in a human shape. They built no temples, but they consecrated to holy purposes groves and woods, of which nature had formed the pillars, and whose canopy was the infinite heaven itself; and they named after their divinity the mystery which their faith alone allowed them to contemplate. Even their aboriginal poetical descriptions of their divinities display the nobler sentiments of the Germans, who did not, like the Greeks and Romans, attribute to their deities all the infirmities of human nature, but represented in them the portraiture of strength, valor, magnanimity, and sublimity. And they still more strongly distinguish themselves from all other ancient nations by their firm and cheerful belief in the immortality of the soul, which entirely dissipated every fear of death; and in the confidence of a future state they committed suicide, when life itself could be purchased only by slavery.

This sublime natural feeling, and this purity of their religious ideas, made them, in after times, better adapted for the reception of Christianity. They were the vessel which God had selected for the pure preservation of his doctrines. For Jews, Greeks, and Romans were already enervated by sensuality and vice; they could neither comprehend nor retain the new doctrines, just as, according to the scriptural image, the old drunkard could not retain the new wine. The ancient Germans revered, like the Persians, the sun and fire; but worshipped as their superior God, *Wodan*, (*Guodan*, the *Goden*, *Guten*, *Gott*.) They called him also by a beautiful name, the Universal Father. They kept, in their sacred groves, white horses for the sun, which were harnessed to the consecrated chariot and driven by the priest or prince, who paid particular attention to their neighing, which they considered, as did the Persians, prophetic of the future, and indicative of the will of their divinity.

They venerated the mother earth as their most beneficent deity; they called her *Nerthus*, (the nourishing,*) and we have the following relation of her worship: "In the midst of an island in the sea† there was a sacred grove, in which was a consecrated chariot, covered with tapestry. Sometimes (as noticed by the priests) the goddess descended from the sacred dwellings above, and drove the chariot, drawn by consecrated cows, accompanied by the priests in the deepest reverence. The days were then cheerful, and the places which she honored with her presence, solemn and holy; they then entered into no war, seized no arms, and the iron spear reposed in concealment; peace and tranquillity then reigned in every bosom, until the priests reconducted the goddess, satiated with her intercourse with mortals, back into the temple. The chariot and carpet were immersed, and the goddess too, if we may believe it, bathed in a secret lake; slaves performed the offices of service, whom the same lake immediately swallowed up. Thence arose a mysterious fear and holy ignorance of what that might be which only those beheld who were to die."

The Germans placed great faith in prophecies and indications of the future, as shown already in the neighing of the sacred horses of the sun. When they were at war they often selected a prisoner taken from their enemy, and caused him to fight with one of their countrymen, each armed with his national weapons; the victory of the one or the other was received as prophetic, or as a divine judgment. They considered the raven and the owl as harbingers of evil; the cuckoo announced length of life. They prophesied of the future also with small staves cut from a fruit-tree, having peculiar or runic signs carved upon each staff, and these were then strewed upon a white raiment. And then, on public occasions, the priest, but in private the father of the family, prayed to the divinity, and, with upraised eyes, took up each individual rod thrice, the characters upon which indicated the event.

The holy prophetesses were highly esteemed, and history names some to whom the credulity of the tribes attached great influence in the determination of public affairs. Tacitus names *Aurinia*, (perhaps *Alruna*, conversant with the mystic runic characters;) again, the celebrated *Veleda*, who, from a tower on the banks of the Lippe, directed the movements of the tribes of the Lower Rhine; and, lastly, a certain *Gauna*, in the time of Domitian. In the incursions of the Cimbri, and in the army of Ariovistus, notice is taken of prophesying females.

There was no ceremony at their funerals; only the bodies of the most distinguished were burned with costly wood, and with each, at the same time, was offered up his arms or war-horse. The tomb which covered the ashes and the bones of the deceased was a mound of turf. Splendid monuments they despised as oppressive to their dead. Laments and tears they speedily gave over, but grief they indulged in much longer. *Lamentations* they considered as appropriate to females, but to men *remembrance* alone was deemed suitable.

### IX. ARTS AND MANUFACTURES.

Should we, after all that has preceded, inquire concerning the progress made by the ancient Germans in the arts of life, we shall find upon that subject the information of the Roman writers unfortunately very scanty. Looking down from the point of their very superior culture, they did not consider it worth their trouble to attend to the origin of the arts, trades, and knowledge, found among those nations which they considered as barbarians. This silence has misled to the supposition, that the Germans, about the period of the birth of Christ, were to be considered as half savages, resembling the North American Hurons. But history may, where she finds no express testimony, draw conclusions from uncontested facts. Therefore we can, with certainty, infer that about the time, and shortly after the birth of Christ, the Germans—who in arms and warlike skill could contest with an enemy who had acquired in a war of five

* Tacitus, Germ. xl

† Much here indicates the island to be Rügen; but there are important grounds for contradiction.

hundred years, with all the nations of the earth, the highest grade in the art of war, and consequent subjugation; these Germans, who had already far advanced in their civil institutions; to whom marriage and the domestic hearth, and the honor of their nation, and their ancestors, were sacred; who in their religious symbols displayed a deep feeling for the most profound ideas of the human mind; and who, lastly, by a dignified natural capacity, and exquisite moral traits, in spite of the undeniable ferocity of unbridled passions, were enabled to inspire that noble Roman, in whom dwelt a deep sense of all that was great and elevated in human nature—these Germans, we say, could not have been the rude barbarians described as resembling North American savages. Their cultivation, as far as their wild life and dispersed mode of dwelling admitted, advanced to a degree worthy of mention.

Agriculture and pasturage united, consequently a regulated and settled rural economy, presupposes the use of the necessary implements, howsoever simple they might be. The German made them himself. The iron necessary for that purpose, as well as for his weapons, he must have known how to work, and the manipulation of hard-melting iron is not easy; presuming they were only able to use that which lay upon the surface without understanding or practising the art of mining. Yet Tacitus names iron mines among the Goths, in the present Silesia. That the preparation of iron utensils must indicate already a higher degree of skill in art, in the earliest ages of nations, is shown by the very frequent use of copper in such instruments for which iron is much better adapted. Copper is much easier to manufacture.

In the irruptions and battles of the Germans, namely, among the Cimbri and Teutoni, chariots and cars are named, which conveyed the women and children, and which were placed around to defend the camp. The Germans appear also upon their rivers, and upon the coasts of their seas in ships, and contest also with the Romans in naval battles. Tribes which could build structures of this description, need no longer be considered savage.

The art of spinning and weaving is also not possible without complicated machinery, and this formed the daily occupation of the females.

Although the art of building houses was not carried to any extent, yet the towers or burgs of the superior classes, some of which are mentioned in the records of history, must have been essentially different from the huts of the community; and that walls of stone were used in their construction, we may infer from the subterranean excavations in which provisions were preserved, and wherein the women generally wove their linen, and which must therefore have been walled in.

Trade and commerce were not foreign to the ancient Germans; they were even acquainted with that pivot of all commerce, a general medium of barter—money. Tacitus remarks that they knew well how to distinguish the old good coins of the Romans, and took silver in preference to gold in their retail transactions. The great multitude of Roman coins, which by degrees have been dug out of the German earth, proves that their commercial intercourse was not trifling, although much may have fallen into the hands of the Germans as booty upon the defeat of the Romans. Arminius, before the battle of Idistavisus, offered to every Roman deserter daily 200 sesterces.

Their music was no doubt limited to their war-song, and the rude warlike instruments previously named, and to the heroic song at festivals. German antiquity had without doubt its inspired singers, equally as the Greeks had their Homerides; the testimony of Tacitus tells us so, and the inclination of the people for all that was great, and worthy of fame, as it evinces itself in their deeds, would even, without that testimony, have convinced us.

It has been disputed whether the Germans, about the time of the birth of Christ, had a written character. Tacitus expressly says, that neither men nor women understood writing, (literarum secreta viri pariter ac feminæ ignorant.—*Germ.* 19.) And although this passage might be interpreted in a more restricted sense, were there express witnesses to the contrary extant; still, for the want of them, it is sufficiently conclusive of the ignorance of writing among the ancient Germans. There are, indeed, letters mentioned of Marbodius and Adgandaster, a prince of the Chatti, to Rome; but these were certainly written in Latin, and only prove, if they were written by the princes themselves, that the upper classes, who had intercourse with the Romans, and perhaps lived a long time in Rome itself, learned there the Roman art of writing. The people generally, however, were, without doubt, ignorant of the art.

### X. THE GERMANIC TRIBES.

The seats of the Saxon tribes are already generally stated in the fourth division; the following are the names and situations of the individual septs:

1. The *Sigambri*, a considerable tribe in the neighborhood of the *Sieg*, whence they probably derived their name; and farther inward towards the mountainous districts of Westphalia, which was called, later, the Süderland, or Sauerland. Cæsar found them here about the year 56, and Drusus in the year 12, before the birth of Christ, at which time their domain extended as far as the Lippe. Weakened by the attacks of the Romans, to whom they were most exposed, a portion of them were driven by Tiberius to the left bank of the Rhine, as far as its mouths, as well as that of the Issel; another portion remained in their ancient dwelling-places, and fought with the Cherusci against Germanicus. In the subsequent centuries, the name was retained only by that portion which dwelt at the mouths of the Rhine, and which constituted the Salic Franks, and formed a leading tribe in the confederation of the Franks.*

2. The *Usipetri* and *Tenchteri*, almost always neighbors, and sharing the same casualties. Driven by the Suevi, about the year 56 before the birth of Christ, from their original seat, probably in the *Wetterau,* (the district between the Maine, the Rhine, and the Lahn,) farther towards the north, they were, upon their crossing the Rhine, beaten back again by Cæsar, and partly destroyed. The remainder were received by the Sigambrians; and in the time of Drusus, the Usipetrians dwelt north of the Lippe, on the Rhine. But the Tenchterians had already, about the year 36 before the birth of Christ, when the Ubierians were driven to the left bank of the Rhine, occupied their domain upon its right bank, so that both the tribes became again neighbors, and dwelt in the duchy of Berg and in a portion of Cleves. Finally, the Tenchterians appear to have formed a portion of the Franks.*

3. The *Brukteri*, a powerful tribe in the country north of the Lippe, as far as the more central Ems, and from the vicinity of the Rhine near the Weser, consequently more properly in the present Münster land, and some of the approximate districts. According to the most recent investigations, the country in the south of the Lippe, as far as the mountains of Sauerland, therefore, the so-called Hellweg, is considered a portion of the country of the Brukterians. They were divided into larger and lesser bodies, took an active part as the confederates of the Cherusci, in the war of freedom against the Romans, and they received as their booty, after the battle with Varus, one of the three conquered eagles. About the year 98 after the birth of Christ, in an internal war with their neighbors, they were almost annihilated, so that Tacitus divides their domain between the Chamavrians and the Angrivarians. But this account is certainly exaggerated, as their name occurs in Ptolemy much later in the same district; and even afterwards they appear as a portion of the Frankish confederation. After the alliance of the Saxons had more and more widely extended itself towards Westphalia, the country and tribe of the Brukterians became equally included therein; but whether by force of arms, or by alliance, is not to be decided. The Brukterians may possibly have derived their name from the marshes (brüchen) in their country.

4. The *Marsi*, neighbors of the Brukterians, also present themselves as active enemies of the Romans, about the time of the birth of Christ. In the battle with Varus they seized an eagle, which Germanicus afterwards reconquered; and this same leader commenced his campaign against Lower Germany, in the year 14 after the birth of Christ, by an incursion from *Vetera Castra* (near Xanten) through the Cæsian forest, into the land of the Marsi, in which he destroyed the celebrated sanctuary of *Tanfani*. These events show us the Marsi as a Westphalian tribe, dwelling not far from the Rhine. Beyond this, we cannot determine with certainty their

* Claud. Claudianus (about 400 years after the birth of Christ) de IV. Cons. Honor. 449; Gregory of Tours, ii. 31; and others. Clovis, on being baptized, was addressed by the Bishop Remigius: *mitis Sicamber.*

* Gregory of Tours, ii. 9.

dwelling-place, and antiquarians consequently entertain different opinions with respect to it. Some place them on the Lippe, others eastward of the Ems, towards Tecklenburg and Osnaburg, which latter is the most probable. The sanctuary of Tanfana, which has been sought for in different places, and among the rest near Münster, would, therefore, henceforth be considered to lie in the land of Tecklenburg.

5. The *Tubanti*, likewise neighbors of the Brukterians, are placed by some in the country between Paderborn, Hamur, and the Arnsberg forest, (the *Soester Börde ;*) by others, and with greater probability, on the opposite side of the country of the Brukterians, northwest of the Rhine, and the Vechte, the Twente of the present day.

6. Southward of the Tubanti, on the Rhine, dwelt the *Chamavi*, and bordered farther southward on the Usipetrians, to whom they had yielded a portion of the pasturage on the Rhine and the Issel, even before the time of Drusus. About the year 98 after the birth of Christ, they deprived the Brukterians of a portion of their country, and they appear later as forming a part of the confederation of the Franks. In the middle ages, their domain was called the Hamaland. Ptolemy mentions the Chamavi, as well as the Cherusci, at the foot of the Harz mountains, but which former were probably a very different tribe.

7. The *Ansibari* or *Amsivarians*, northward from the Brukterians on the Ems, (thence called Emsgauer or Emsbauer.) In the year 59 after the birth of Christ, a portion of them were driven away by the powerful Chauci; they long sought, in vain, another dwelling among the neighboring tribes, and they at last vanish among the Cherusci. A portion, however, must have remained in their ancient dwelling-place, as they appear later, forming part of the Frankish confederation.

8. The *Chasuari* and *Chattuari* were, according to some, two tribes, the first of which dwelt upon the Haase, northward of the Marsi, and were thence called Hasegauer, but the latter at the mouth of the Ruhr, where the Gau or district *Hatterun* gave testimony of them in the middle ages; but, according to others, they were but one tribe, which had their dwelling northward of the Chatti, on the Diemel.

9. The *Dulgibini* are placed, with probability, in the neighborhood of the Weser, perhaps precisely in the district of the Lippe, where the legions of Varus were destroyed, and where the name still exists on the heath of Dolger. In a stricter sense they belonged to the confederation of the Cherusci. Ptolemy places them on the right bank of the Weser; therefore, they very probably occupied both its banks. In this neighborhood Ptolemy also names *Tulisurgium*, perhaps wrongly copied for *Teutiburgium*, in the vicinity of Detmold, and *Tropæa Drusi*, the monument of the victory of Drusus on the Weser, perhaps in the neighborhood of Höxter.

The following are some other places, mentioned by Ptolemy, in Westphalia, unfortunately without indicating the domain wherein they were, and which are, consequently, very variously referred to by antiquaries :

a. *Bogadium*—Münster, according to some, but according to others, Bochold, or also Beckum ; according to Ledebur, Beckum on the Lippe, upon the great Roman road between Vetera and Aliso.

b. *Mediolanium*—Also supposed to be Münster, but now, probably, *Metelu* on the Vechte.

c. *Munitium*—is either Osnaburg, the Castle Ravensberg, or Stromberg in the neighborhood of Münster.

d. *Stereontium*—Warendorf, Stromberg, Steinfort or Steveren, all in the land of Münster.

e. *Amasia*—probably the same place as the *Amisia* of Tacitus, the hold on the left bank of the Ems, not far from its estuary, which was built by Drusus.

f. *Ascalingium*, near Minden on the Weser.

g. With respect to *Aliso*, the castle built by Drusus, in the second year before the birth of Christ, at the confluence of the Aliso and the Lippe, according to the information of Dio Cassius, opinions are so far unanimous that it was situated upon the Upper Lippe, not very far from the entrance of the Teutoburgian forest. The majority again have decided for *Elsen*, near Paderborn, not far from the confluence of the Alme and the Lippe ; the most recent, very careful investigation of Ledebur, however, has raised it to the highest probability that Aliso lay in the present parish or district of *Liesborn*, in the space which is formed between the junction of the *Liese* and the *Glenne*, and that of the Glenne and the Lippe, near the religious foundation of Cappeln.

h. *Arbalo*—where Drusus was pressed hard by the Germans, upon the frontiers of the country of the Cherusci, Sigambri, and Chatti, was, very probably, between Nühden and Gesecke, where the Haar mountains gradually dwindle into the plains of the Hellweg, and where in the middle ages a *Gau* or district, Arpesfeld, was situated. The syllable ending with *lo* in the name, implies a *forest; Feld*, in contradistinction to *Wald*, indicates old forest land made arable.

Close to the left bank of the Weser, beyond the Dulgibini, dwelt also the remaining smaller tribes of the confederation of the Cherusci; and on the opposite side of this river:

10. The *Cherusci* themselves, the most celebrated Germanic tribe of ancient times, when in their most flourishing state. About the period of the birth of Christ they possessed an extensive domain, but of which it cannot be exactly stated how much was properly their own hereditary land, and how much of the land belonged to their more closely attached confederates, who are often called by the Romans, off-handedly, Cherusci. This domain extended from the Harz, its centre, eastward as far as the Saale and the Elbe, northward nearly as far as the Aller, westward as far as the Weser, and southward as far as the Werra and the Thuringian forest. From the time of Drusus to the generalship of Varus, in the twenty years during which the Romans were almost settled in Lower Germany, and already spoke of a Roman province, the Cherusci were on friendly terms with them; the sons of their princes entered the Roman armies, Augustus had a German body-guard, and all seemed peaceable. But under Varus the Cherusci placed themselves at the head of almost all the tribes between the Rhine and the Weser; the smaller tribes, particularly on the left bank of the Weser, united themselves with them, whom the Romans often called clients of the Cherusci, naming them often absolutely Cherusci, whence has arisen the error that the Cherusci dwelt on both sides of the Weser. Later, when Arminius went forth against Marbodius, the Longobardi and Semnoni, their powerful neighbors in the East, united themselves with them. But after the death of Arminius the superiority of the Cherusci diminished. They became enervated in a protracted state of inactivity, and were by degrees so weakened by the Longobardi, Chauci, and Chatti tribes, that the shadow alone of their former greatness remained. Once again only does their name appear as a constituent portion of the confederation of the Franks. Ptolemy mentions in their domain *Lupia* or *Lupta*, now Eimbeck, *Callagri*, Halle on the Saale, *Brieurdium*, Erfurt.

With the Cherusci sank also their confederates, viz:

11. The *Fosi* on the Fuse, or Brunswick of the present day.

12. The *Angrivari*, on both sides of the Weser, below Minden, the neighbors and faithful confederates of the Chauci, with whom they appear again later as a constituent portion of the Saxon confederation under the name of *Engern*. The Saxon district on the Weser was called *Angaria*.

13. The *Chauci* dwelt on the Baltic, from the estuary of the Ems to the Elbe, surrounding the Weser, by which they were divided into the greater and the lesser classes.* Pliny, who had personally visited their country, sketches a melancholy picture of the inhabitants on the coast: "The ocean, twice a day," he says, "overflows an extensive district, and produces a constant contest in nature, so that we must continue doubtful whether to call this part land or sea. The miserable natives dwell upon the hills of the coast, or rather heaps of earth, thrown up by the hand upon the margin of the highest side. They dwell there at flood-tide like mariners, and at its ebb like shipwrecked beings. The fish driven hither by the sea they catch with nets of reeds and sea-grass. They have no cattle, and do not, like their neighbors, feed upon milk. They are not allowed even to hunt for game, for not a shrub grows near them. The turf, secured by hand, they dry more in the air than in the sun, wherewith to cook their food, and thereby to warm their bowels frozen by the north wind. They have no other drink than rain-water, preserved in holes; and yet, had these tribes been conquered by the

* Their name appears to have been derived from the nature of their country; *kauken*, *quaken*, means, in the vulgar language, to quake; and the marshy ground of the country quakes under the feet. *Quakenbrück* still retains the original denomination.

Romans, they would have called themselves slaves!" Tacitus, on the contrary, who had more in view the extensive tribe of the Chauci in the interior of the country, celebrates them as the most considerable tribe of the Germans, peaceably minded and yet warlike and valiant. They were long the faithful allies of the Romans, who frequently traversed their country, against the tribes on the more central Weser, probably emanating in an original feud with the Cherusci. Indeed, in the reign of Nero they pressed hard upon the Wehrmanni of the Cheruscian alliance—the Ansibarians, and spread themselves so far towards the south, that Tacitus makes them even extend as far as the Chatti. In the third century they devastated Gaul in the reign of the Emperor Didius Julianus, and at last they disappear under the confederate name of Saxons.

Ptolemy mentions some of the towns of the Chauci: *Tuderium*, probably Meppene; *Thuliphardum*, Verden; *Phabiranum*, Bremen or Bremenvörder; *Leuphana*, Lüneburg, and others.

14. The *Frisi*, on the Baltic, from the mouths of the Rhine, to the Ems, allies of the Romans in the German wars. In the fourth and fifth centuries they again appear in the Saxon alliance, and even embark with these for Britain.* The Romans call the island Borkum, *Burchana*, and Ameland, *Austeravia*, on their coast, and in their country: *Fleum* or *Flevum*, on the Dollart.

15. The *Saxons*, afterwards so important, are first mentioned by Ptolemy in the middle of the second century, as inhabitants of the present Holstein. They were skilful sailors, and in the fourth and fifth centuries became dreaded from their piracies. Tacitus and Pliny do not name them, probably because they comprise them under the name of Cimbri. We shall speak further on of the confederation they founded and called by their name.

16. The *Cimbri* remained for many centuries after their great irruption, with which our history begins, still in their old dwelling-place, called the Cimbrian peninsula, styled the present Jutland; Strabo expressly says, "they still dwelt in their old seat."†

Between the Saxon and Suevic septs is found one of the most remarkable of the German tribes, which appears to belong to neither side; viz.,

The *Chatti* or *Katti*, in high probability the Hessians of the present day, (Chatten, Chässen, Hessen.) They frequently came in contact with the Romans, upon whom they bordered, and are often named by them. Cæsar himself even knew them, for the Suevi, against whom he defended the Uberians, and whom he threatened by his passage across the Rhine, must, according to the locality of the dwelling-place, have been the Chatti. They even then, probably, belonged to the great Suevic confederation. Tacitus, on the contrary, expressly separates them from the Suevi, and we may, therefore, most rightly consider them as a self-dependent tribe, forming a separation between the two great tribes, the Suevi and Saxons. At the time of these great wars under Augustus, their country was often visited by the Romans; but in the age of Tacitus, after the entire reduction of the Cherusci, their domain seems to have acquired its greatest extent, for they spread themselves from the neighborhood of Hanau, and where they bordered upon the Roman tithe-land beyond the Spessart and the mountains of the Rhine as far as the Thuringian forest, and towards the southwest as far as the Franconian Saale, then towards the north, somewhat beyond the country where the Werra and Fulda join, and northwest as far as the heights of the Wester forest.

Tacitus celebrates the Chatti especially for their valor and prudent management of war. Their infantry was the best of all the Germans. They were more accustomed than all the rest to discipline and order, and knew how to form defensive camps; besides, they were large-formed, powerful, and fearless, and their warlike glance was intimidating. "They can all fight," says Tacitus, "but the Chatti alone know how to conduct a war; and what is very rare in savage nations, they depend more upon their leader than upon the army. *Good fortune they reckon among the casual, valor among the certain things.*" Their youths allowed their hair and beard to grow long, and they wore an iron ring upon their arm, the sign of minority, until a slain enemy proved their manliness; over whose body, and captured arms, they freed their face from the abundance of

* Procop. Goth. iv. 20

† Geogr. vii. 2, i.

hair, and only then first boasted of having paid the reward for their tenure of life, and of being worthy of their fatherland and ancestors.

At a later period the Chatti joined the extensive confederation of the Franks.

The ancient metropolis of the Chatti was *Mattium*, which many consider to be Marburg; but it is probably the present village *Maden*, near Gudensberg, on the river Eder.

The *Mattiaci*, a branch of the Chatti, which, in the expeditions of Drusus and Germanicus, appear only under this latter name, but by Tacitus are called by their individual name, dwelt between the Lahn and the Maine, as far as the Rhine, therefore in the present Nassau. The Romans located themselves very early in their country, constructed defences upon the Taurus mountains, and treated the Mattiaci as a conquered tribe. In the revolt of Civilis they took a part, and invested Mentz. Subsequently, their name disappears, and the Allemanni occupy their land. Pliny mentions warm springs here, which he calls *Fontes Matiaci*, doubtless Wiesbaden, where many remains of Roman buildings, baths, &c., have been found; and *Arctaunum*, the Roman fort upon the heights near Homburg, of which traces are yet extant. Ptolemy names also *Mattiacum*, probably the present Marburg.

SUEVIC TRIBES.

1. The *Semnoni* are called by Tacitus the most ancient and considerable among the Suevi; and Ptolemy fixes their seat between the Elbe and the Oder, in the southern part of Brandenburg, and in the Lausitz as far as the Bohemian frontiers. It is said that in their country the sanctuary of the confederation was a holy grove, wherein the confederate sacrifices were solemnized. They, consequently, appear to have stood, in more ancient times, in peculiar regard among all the Suevic tribes. After the second century of the Christian era, however, their name does not again occur in the annals of history; of the causes for this disappearance, we are ignorant.

2. The *Longobardi*, few in number, but the most warlike of all the Suevi. They dwelt, when history first becomes acquainted with them, about the period of the birth of Christ, westward from the Middle Elbe, opposite the Semnoni in the Alt-Mark and Lüneburg districts, where the name of the city, Bardewik, the villages of Barleben and Bartensleben, and the Bardengau, still preserve their recollection. They thence spread to the eastern banks of the Elbe, as far as the Havel. Under Arminius, they fought against Marbodius, but subsequently they assisted towards the reduction of the Cherusci, who appear to have been, for a period, in a certain degree of dependency on them. Ptolemy gives them, in the second century, a very extensive domain, from the Elbe over the country of the Cherusci, the Tubanti, and Marsi, as far as the Rhine. They may possibly, if Ptolemy's relation be true, have made successful, but short invasive expeditions. History then becomes silent concerning them, until towards the end of the fifth century, when they appear upon the Danube, in Hungary; and in the sixth, they establish their kingdom in Italy. They derived their name, according to their ancient legend, (as handed down of king Rothari,) from their long beards, but according to others, from their *Helle barden* or Halberts; more probably, however, from their dwelling-place, on the borders of the Elbe, where a tract of land is still called the *long Börde*, or fruitful plain. Ptolemy names *Mesuium* among them, perhaps the present Magdeburg.

3. Northward from the Longobardi and Semnoni, in the present Lauenburg, Mecklenburg, and Pommerania, dwelt, according to Tacitus, the Suevic tribes of the *Varini*, *Angeli*, *Reudingi*, *Avioni*, *Eudosi*, *Suardoni*, and *Nuithoni*; but little known or remarkable. We have already referred to their common worship of the goddess Nerthus.

The name of the Varini reminds us of the river Varne, in Mecklenburg; and, indeed, Ptolemy mentions, in their domain, a series of towns, which, according to his geographical determination, are comprised in the district on the north of the Elbe, from Hamburg as far as the estuary of the Varne. Hamburg itself appears under the name of *Marionis*; Lübeck under that of *Marionis Altera*. *Laciburgium* may be Wismar, and *Alistus*, Schwerin.

The *Angeli*, neighbors of the Varini, appear later in union with the Saxons, with whom they seemed to have joined themselves, in the vicinity of Silesia and upon the neighboring islands; then in England, which has preserved their name nobly down to the present day.

On the coasts of the Baltic, extending farther towards the east, Tacitus names a series of tribes, which he refers to the Suevic race. Perhaps we may recognise in them a third, namely, the Gothic, and we therefore quit, for the present, that direction, to turn ourselves towards the undisputed Suevic tribes in the interior of Germany. Here first we meet:

4. The *Hermunduri.* The information of the dwelling-places of this tribe, which, besides, is named by almost all the writers who mention the Germans, from Vell. Paterculus to Dio Cassius, (with the exception of Ptolemy,) is very contradictory, but which may, perhaps, be owing to their frequent change of locality. Tacitus is acquainted with them as the friends and neighbors of the Romans on the northern shore of the Danube, whence they stood with the Romans in a peaceful commercial intercourse, namely, in the capital of Rhœtia, *Augusta Vindelicorum,* Augsburg, and he makes them contend with the Chatti, on the Franconian Saale, for the possession of the salt springs, so that their domain, consequently, stretched between the Danube and the Maine, across the present Franconia. They had arrived here about the time of the Christian era, when the Marcomanni, under Marbodius, were moving towards Bohemia. They were received by the Roman general, Domitius Ænobarbus. Thence arose their friendship with the Romans. They probably dwelt, previously, farther northeastward, in the Franconian and Bohemian mountains, as far as the Elbe. The Hermunduri, from the middle of the second century, appear only under the collective name of Suevi; and it is they, probably, who, carrying it farther to the southwest, have preserved and brought it down to the present day under the name of Swabians.

Ptolemy mentions, in the present land of Franconia, *Segodunum,* perhaps Würzburg; *Bergium,* Bamberg; *Menosgada,* Baireuth, &c.

5. The *Nariski,* in the Upper Palatinate, between the Hermunduri and the Marcomanni.

6. The *Marcomanni,* the most important of the southern Suevic tribes, or perhaps, more properly, the advanced *Wehrmannei* of the Suevic confederation against the Gauls, and later, against the Romans—thence called mark or frontier-men—guarded the boundaries of Germany between the Rhine, the Maine, and the Danube. Upon the increasing weakness of the Gauls, they endeavored to make conquests in the country of their enemies. Ariovistus was, according to all probability, a Marcoman. History will inform us how about the commencement of the Christian era, they, under Marbodius, advanced, in front of the Romans, towards Bohemia; and how, subsequently, they became the terrific enemies of the latter. Their name disappears in the migration, probably merging in that of the Suevi, under which collective name they may have wandered, with other Suevic tribes, to Spain.

7. The *Quadi,* the most southeastern Suevic tribe, seated upon the Danube, in Austria and Moravia, as far as the river Grau, in Hungary, where they joined the Sarmatian tribe of the Jazygi. They lived in peace with the Romans until the great Marcomannic war, under Mark Aurelius, in which they took a share. From this time they always remained the enemies of the Romans. In the fifth century, their name likewise disappears, and merges in that of the Suevi, among whom they are again mentioned in Spain. Ptolemy names many towns in their country, as a great commercial road led from *Carnuntum,* Pressburg, through the land of the Quadi, and by this means conveyed life and spirit into it. We name only *Phurgisatis, Coridorgis,* and *Philecia,* probably Znaim, Brünn, and Olmütz.

8. Behind these, towards the east, ancient writers mention the names of many other tribes, without, however, giving more particular information about them, or even being able to state precisely that they were of German origin. Thus it is with the Gothini and Osi, in the mountains which border upon Moravia and Bohemia, running towards Upper Silesia, of whom Tacitus himself says, that the former spoke the Gallic, and the latter the Pannonian, accordingly, the Sarmatian tongue.

The *Marsingi* are mentioned by Tacitus alone; according to whom, their dwelling-place seems to have occupied a portion of Lower Silesia, eastward from the Riesengebirge. It is, however, doubtful whether the Marsingi of Tacitus were not a branch of the Vandals. In the district of the above-mentioned tribes, belong many of the names of towns which occur in Ptolemy; viz., *Strevinta*, in the vicinity of Neisse; *Casurgis*, in that of Glatz.

9. The *Lygi*, a powerful union of tribes in the eastern portion of Silesia, and in that part of Poland which is enclosed by the elbow of the Vistula, from its source as far as Bromberg. Tacitus considers them, perhaps rightly, as Suevi, although their manners and mode of life partake much of that of their savage Sarmatian neighbors, on which account several modern historians class them with the Sclavonic tribes. They belonged, when we first hear of them, to Marbodius' confederation of tribes, and their alliance with the Marcomanni and Hermunduri seems to have continued even much later. In the third century, they appear with the Burgundians on the Rhine, and are defeated by the Emperor Probus.* The chief stem, however, which remained behind, probably attached itself, at the time of the great migration, to the Goths, the name being no longer mentioned.

Among the Lygian tribes, Tacitus names the Ari, the Helveconi, Manimi, Elysi, and Naharvali; his *Buri* also, which he does not join to the Lygian union, belonged probably to it; they dwelt at the sources of the Oder and the Vistula. Tacitus describes the Ari as the most powerful, but also the most savage of the Lygians. They painted their shields black, colored their bodies, selected dark nights for their battles, and excited terror in their enemies by the fearful and almost infernal appearance of their ghastly, death-like ranks.

In the country of the *Naharvali*, there was a sacred grove, wherein a youthful pair of twins, similar to Castor and Pollux, were worshipped under the name of Alcis, and were attended by a priest in female raiment.†

The whole domain of the *Elysi*, who dwelt probably in Silesia, and perhaps gave its name to the principality of Oels, was certainly traversed by a Roman commercial road, which is proved by the many Roman coins that have been, and still continue to be found buried there in the earth.

In the great Lygian domain, Ptolemy mentions many names of towns; among others, *Budorgis*, probably Ratibor; *Lygidunum*, Liegnitz; *Calisia*, Kalisch, &c.

10. The *Goths*. Tacitus, who only knew the Suevi and non-Suevi among the German tribes, considers this tribe also, which he calls Goths, as Suevi. Pliny, on the contrary, who makes a five-fold division of the tribes, regards them as belonging to the stem of the Windili, namely, to that of the Vandals. That the tribes of this stem dwelt, collectively, in the extreme east of ancient Germany, these two, as well as the rest of the ancient authors who mention their names, are in opinion unanimous. Later history finds many of these tribes likewise in combination, or, at least, acting under the same impulses and towards the same purpose; and it was by them that the first grand blow was struck against the Roman colossus. If, therefore, nothing decided can be said upon these obscure relations, to the elucidation of which the light of history is wholly wanting, it will not be objectionable, but rather contribute to the easier survey of this manifold mixture, if we here collect these tribes together, as belonging, probably, to a third chief stem, allied to the Suevi, which, with Pliny, we may call the *Vandalian*, or, according to the title of the later principal tribe, the *Gothic* branch.

a. The true *Goths*, or *Gothones*, were known to Pytheas, about the year 300 before the birth of Christ, on the Amber-coast, near the estuary of the Vistula. Tacitus places them beyond the Lygi, therefore still on the Vistula, but no longer extending to the sea; for on the coast he names the Rugi and the Lemovi. Ptolemy, nearly fifty years later, places them likewise on the Vistula, in the interior of the country, and mentions, by name, the Venedi, or Wendi upon the coast. We may thence conclude that, even at this period, the great movement of the Wendian and Sclavonian nations, from the northeast towards the southwest, had already commenced, whereby the Germans were impelled forward in the same direction. At the beginning of the third century, we already find the Goths again further southward, namely, in Dacia, where they fixed themselves. At this time, also, they appear divided into two great branches, the Ostro-Goths and Westro-Goths, or East and West Goths. Their progress and fate,

* Fosimus i., 67.

† Tacitus calls it the Sanctuary or deity Alcis, probably the Gothic Alhs.

at the time of the great migration, will be further related in the history itself.

As single tribes, the Gepidi, Mosogothi, Therwingi, and Greuthungi, are named as branches of the Gothic stem, upon whose affinity and position towards each other a variety of opinions are still maintained.

b. The *Burgundians* are placed by Pliny at the head of the Vandal stem, but they are not named by Tacitus. Ptolemy points out as their dwelling-place the country between the Oder and Vistula, where the Netze and the Warthe flow. Driven by the Gepidi from this district, a portion of them turned towards the north and located themselves upon the island Bornholm, (Burganda-holm,) between Sweden and Denmark; but the greater portion drew off to the southwest, attacked Gaul, were beaten back by the emperor Probus, dwelt for a space of time in the vicinity of the Maine, then upon the Upper Rhine, and received from the Roman governor, Aetius, at the beginning of the fifth century, a dwelling-place in the southeast of Gaul, where their name still continues. In their ancient domain Ptolemy names the city Ascaucalis, where Bromberg now exists.

c. The *Rugi* are placed by Tacitus on the Baltic; he attaches close to them the Lemovi, who are mentioned by no one else, and who do not even again appear in the great migration. The name of the Rugi survives in the island of Rügen and some neighboring places. Tacitus does not enumerate them among the tribes who took part in the Nerthus worship on the isle of Rügen; but it was, perhaps, after the age of Tacitus that they spread themselves so wide towards the west, and gave its name to the island Rügen, with which he was unacquainted. At the time of the great migration they appear in the army of Attila, when he advanced against the Gauls; after his death they settled themselves upon the northern banks of the Danube in Austria and Hungary, which country was called Rugiland; and, shortly afterwards, Odoacer, king of the Heruli, Rugi, Sciri, and Turcilingi, (he being sometimes called by one and sometimes by the other of these titles, although by birth a Scirian,) came forth and destroyed, in the year 476, the west Roman empire. The said four named tribes were, according to all probability, closely allied, originating from the vicinity of the Baltic, between the Vistula and the Oder; and who, after several separations and a variety of adventures, of which isolated notices occur in history, are again found united under Odoacer. The *Herulians* are, next to the Rugi, the most remarkable. They appear as a portion of the great kingdom of the Ostro-Gothic king, Hemanrich, and form, after Attila's death, a powerful empire on the banks of the Danube, at last vanishing on different sides, after encountering the most adventurous fortunes.* A portion seems to have united itself into a nation with the Bojoarians or Bavarians.

d. The *Vandals* appear as an individual tribe in Dio Cassius only, who calls the Riesengebirge the Vandalian mountains, whence the Elbe has its source, and we indeed find upon its northeast side the original dwelling-place of the Vandalian tribes. We have already noticed that the Wendili race of Pliny is the Vandalian, and that Tacitus speaks really of the Vandalian as received by some others; later writers expressly say, that the Vandals were of the same stem as the Goths, had a similar appearance, the same laws and institutions. We shall further relate their history at the period of the migration.

Tacitus does not allow his country of the Suevi to end with the coasts of the Baltic only, as far as the estuary of the Vistula, but conveys his readers to the Æstyi, on the Amber coasts. They, according to their manners and dress, were Suevi, but approached nearer to the Britons by their language. They zealously cultivated grain, and collected amber, which they called hesum, (glass,) and received with astonishment the high price Roman luxury offered for it. Tacitus describes amber very distinctly and rightly.

11. Also, on the other side of the Baltic, in the present Sweden, according to him, are found Suevi, viz. the Suioni. "Equally strong," says Tacitus, "by their fleets as by their men and arms, kings rule over them with unlimited power. Beyond the Suioni there is another sea, calm and almost motionless. It is believed that this sea limits the earth, from the circumstance that the last dying splendor of the setting sun continues until its rise, and so brightly, that it obscures the stars." Thus it is evident that they had intelligence of the

* Procop. de Bell. Goth. ii., 11 and 12.

Polar circle. Tacitus also seems to hint at the great northern lights, by citing the tradition that particular rays are seen in the skies, and tones heard at the same time. To the Suioni are attached the races of the *Sitoni*, over whom a woman reigns. "Thus far," says Tacitus, "they are not only degenerated from freedom, but fallen into slavery. Here is the end of the Suevi."

That the Swedes are of German origin, may be considered as decided, and that they were closely related to the Goths is extremely probable. The name of the island Gotland, and many other names in Sweden, corroborate this. The Gothic historian, Jordanis, describes the Goths as having migrated and shipped themselves direct from Scandia, (Scandinavia, the general name given by the ancients to the northern countries,) and settled on the banks of the Vistula. But what he states assumes more the form of heroic tradition than a history of his people; and it may be received as equally correct, that the Goths passed over to Sweden from our coasts.

### TRANS-RHENISH TRIBES

In the west, the Rhine was not properly the boundary of the German tribes, but many of them had passed over it already, before the period of the birth of Christ, and had located themselves on its left bank. To these belonged:

1. The *Vangioni*, the *Nemeti*, and the *Triboci*, in the district on the left bank of the Rhine from Bingen, below Mentz, as far as Breisach. In their domain are many towns, which owe either their origin or enlargement to the Romans; viz., *Monguntiacum*, Mentz, an ancient Gallic city in the country of the Vangioni; under the Romans an important citadel. Already, in the year 70 after the birth of Christ, the 22d legion, which, on returning from the conquest of Jerusalem, was quartered in this place, brought with them probably, and introduced Christianity there. *Bonconica*, Oppenheim; *Borbetomagus*, Worms; *Noviomagus*, chief seat of the Nemeti, Spires; *Taberna*, Rheinzabern; *Argentoratum*, Strasburg, in the country of the Triboci, containing the chief arsenal throughout Gaul.

2. The *Ubi* dwelt earlier on the right bank of the Rhine, but were so hard pressed by the Suevi, that they applied to Julius Cæsar for help, and after he had procured them peace for a short time, they allowed themselves, in the year 36 before the birth of Christ, to be transplanted to the left bank by the Roman general *Vispanius Agrippa*. They were always the faithful allies of the Romans. Their country commenced at the confluence of the Nahe with the Rhine, and here was founded *Bingiune*, Bingen, the first seat of their domain; further, *Bontobrice*, Boppart; *Confluentes*, Coblentz; *Antunnacum*, Andernach; Bonna, Bonn; on the opposite side, as a bridge head or sconce, built by Drusus, was established *Gesonia*, the present village Geusen; *Colonia Agrippina*, Cologne, a chief city of the Romans on the Rhine, named after the daughter of Germanicus, and consort of the emperor Claudius, Agrippina, who was born in this city of the Ubi, and in the year 50, after the birth of Christ, sent hither a colony of veterans in order to distinguish her birth-place. Constantine also caused a bridge to be built here over the river, the remains of which are still to be seen at low water; on the right side was *Divitia*, the present Deutz, the bridge head. *Novesium*, Neuss; *Gelduba*, (often named by the Romans,) the present village Gelb, near the little town of Uerdingen.

3. The *Gugerni*, northward from the Ubi, commencing not far from *Gelduba*, down the Rhine to where the Waal divides itself from it. Places: *Asciburgium*, Asburg, near Meurs; *Vetera* (*castra*,) Xanten or Büderich, opposite Wesel.

4. The *Batavi* and *Canninefati*, both of the Chattic race, were, according to Tacitus, driven from their country by a revolt, and settled themselves near the mouth of the Rhine, in that part of the land surrounded by water, which was called the island of the Batavians. They were allies of the Romans until they revolted under Civilis in the year 70, after the birth of Christ. In their domain lay *Lugdunum*, Leyden; *Ultrajectum*, Utrecht; *Noviomagus*, Nimwegen.

Besides these tribes, there were several others in the Trans-Rhenish countries who had formerly wandered thither, and were still proud of their German origin, as if the celebrity of their race separated them from a connection with, and a resemblance to the weak and cowardly Gauls. The chief among them were the *Treviri*, with the capital *Augusta Trevirorum*, the present

Treves, the most important city of the Roman empire in our northern countries; and the *Nervi*, between the Meuse and the Scheldt.

The south of the Danube was no longer inhabited by the pure German tribes, but such as had become mixed with Gallic and other emigrants. The Danube may be considered as the boundary of Germany at that period, and the Roman provinces on its southern side from Switzerland to beyond Carinthia, and Carniola, were called: Helvetia, Rhetia, Vindelicia, Noricum, and Pannonia.

### ROMAN TITHELAND.

But more important for the ancient geography of our country is the consideration of the southern part of Germany, from the Rhine downward beyond the Maine, according to others still further morthward, and which was called the *Roman titheland*, (*agri decumates.*) From these districts the Germans, pressed hard by the superiority of the Romans, who threatened them from the Rhine and the Danube, had retired more and more into the interior—among the rest the Marcomanni especially—and the Romans considering the land now as a portion of their own provinces, allowed Gallic and other colonists to cultivate it, upon the payment of a tithe. Thence the country which was now considered as a frontier or foreland against the barbarians, received its Roman name; and as such it was already known to Tacitus. To secure it from the predatory irruptions of the Germans, a long line of fortresses, walls, ditches, walls with towers, and other defences, were by degrees constructed, the traces whereof by unwearied research have been discovered in the whole of the south and middle of Germany, so that we are enabled to follow these Roman frontier-defences almost uninterruptedly.

Their commencement is found in considerable remains of defensive works, three miles beyond Ratisbon, near the influx of the Altmühl into the Danube. The intrenchment, well known to the natives under the name of the Devil's Wall and the moat of piles, runs from here, for twelve miles uninterruptedly, towards the northwest, sometimes raised three or four feet above the ground, then again southwest and west into Wurtemberg, in the vicinity of the Necker, and at the distance of some miles from this river constantly northward, as far as the Oden forest. This wall was built of a stone found in the earth near the spot, and at every half league was almost regularly provided with towers. If here and there perhaps the traces of the line have become indistinct, we soon again meet with them more perfect. In the Oden forest we only discover the ruins of solitary towers more distinctly marked; and it is highly probable that here, where there was such an abundance of wood, they were connected by a fence of piles, or a row of palisades, all traces of which have naturally disappeared. But if we follow the remains of these isolated fortifications, we find at last that near Obernburg and eastward from Aschaffenburg, the line joins on the Maine, after it has completed from the Danube onward a distance of nearly two hundred miles.

Northward from the Maine, the traces of the line are very slight, yet it traverses Hanau and Darmstadt, to the north of the Nidda, where the moat of piles begins to be again visible, and runs past Butzbach towards Homburg. Here lies the Salburg, probably the fort or citadel of Arctaunum, erected by Drusus on the Taunus mountains. In this part the frontier wall is twenty feet high, and closed in by trees as old as the forest itself. It runs over the whole of the Taunus mountains, then through the latter on the right bank of the Rhine, as far as the Ems, and thence again over mountain and through forest to the neighborhood of Neuwied. Its traces are lost behind the Seven mountains. This Roman boundary line extended no doubt as far as the Sieg, near Siegburg, perhaps also still further northward. Tiberius, at least, according to Tacitus, built a border wall, *limes,* also in the Cæsarean forest; but no trace of any connection between this and the southern defences has been discovered. It is clear that even under the later emperors, the defensive works were constantly being extended, until the repeated irruptions of the Allemannic hordes destroyed them. At the commencement of the fourth century the Allemanni were in possession of the former Titheland.

As Roman colonies within the boundary line of defences, besides those in the north already mentioned, the following are further cited:

1. *Castellum Valentiniani*, in the neighborhood of Manheim.

2. *Civitas Aurelia Aquensis*, called also merely *Aquæ*, the present Baden; it is not cited, it is true, in Roman authors, but from inscriptions that have been found, it is at least clear that a Roman garrison and baths were here already at the end of the second century.

3. *Tarodunum*, near Friburg, in Breisgau, where the Mark or boundary, Zarten, is still found.

4. *Ara Flavia*, Rotweil, together with several others. The whole titheland is full of the remains of Roman buildings, forts, citadels, and temples, bridges, streets, towers, pillars, and baths.

# THE MORE ANCIENT GERMAN HISTORY

## FIRST PERIOD.

FROM THE MOST ANCIENT TIMES TO THE CONQUESTS OF THE FRANKS UNDER CLOVIS, 486, A. D.

### CHAPTER I.

B. C. 113–6, A. D.

The Cimbri and Teutoni, 113-101 B. C.—Cæsar and Ariovistus, 58 B. C.—Julius Cæsar on the Rhine—Commencement of the great German Wars—Drusus in Germany—Marbodius, King of the Marcomanni.

THE Roman and Greek writers who give information upon this period of our history, have already been mentioned at the commencement of the Introduction. In addition to those, we may include here the subsequent chronicles of Prosper and his continuators, Marius especially, Idacius and Marcellinus, which are collected together by Roncallius, in his "Vetustiora Latinorum Chronica," 2 vols. Further, is to be named Beda Venerabilis, a very learned English monk, who died in the year 735, and who has left behind him a chronicle, "De Sex Ætatibus Mundi," to 726, and a "Hist. Eccles. Gentis Anglicanæ." Finally, we have likewise collected largely, for this earlier epoch, from Jordanis, who will be referred to in the second period.

Efforts have been made to trace back the signs of migrations and contests of German tribes on Roman and Greek ground to very early times, and especially to the invasion of the Gauls under Brennus into Italy in the year 389 B. C., and the incursion of the Gauls again, under a second Brennus, through Thracia and Macedonia, as far as Delphi, in the year 278, as referring to German tribes from the vicinity of the Alps. But these indications are much too obscure and fragmentary, and to pursue the inquiry would produce no essential contribution towards a knowledge of our national records. We shall therefore commence the running thread of our history, after, as before, with the incursion of the Cimbri and Teutoni.

It was in the year 113 B. C., that a wild and unknown tribe crossed the Danube, and appeared upon the Alps, where the Romans guarded the passes into Italy. In this same year they defeated the Roman consul Papirius Carbo, who commanded the army here, near Noreja, in the mountains of the present Styria. Carbo had proved treacherous to them, for upon their request to remain on friendly terms with him, he had provided them with false guides, who led them astray among the mountains, while he advanced by a shorter road and fell unexpectedly upon them. For this breach of faith they punished him severely, and he and all his troops would have been utterly destroyed had not a heavy storm intervened and assisted his flight.

No one knew whence these fearful hordes originally came; they called themselves, according to the account of the Romans, *Cimbri* and *Teutoni*. Upon collecting together the isolated narratives of writers, it appears that the Cimbri had already, for a length of time, been wandering about, and had fought with many nations, especially with the *Boi*, and now, quitting the Danube, appeared upon the Roman frontiers. Whether they are to be considered as collective tribes intent upon migrating, or only as troops of warriors seeking adventures, (as was subsequently the practice of the Suevic warriors under Ariovistus,) or, forming themselves by degrees into one entire mass by the junction of women and children, they required a country wherein to settle, we cannot, owing to the deficiency of precise information, positively decide. If the Cimbri, as is the general opinion, proceeded from the Cimbrian peninsula, so called by the Romans, but which now is the present Jutland, it is very certain that only a portion of the tribe could have left it, as it was still occupied by that tribe at a much later period. But if the name *Kimber*, as others have surmised, implied merely *Kämpfer*, fighters, (Kamper, *Strenuus*,) they may then have belonged to other German tribes, probably to the Suevi. Opinions likewise differ upon the name of the Teutoni. Some believe it was not the name of an individual tribe, but that the Romans, hearing that these Cimbri were Teuten or Teutones, imagined that they had a second tribe to contend with, which they called Teutoni. According to the opinion of others, the Teutoni were wanderers of several tribes between the Vistula and the Elbe, who, urged forward by the eruption of the Cimbri from their northern peninsula, formed themselves into an individual horde, and called themselves Teuten, or Teutones, the collective name of all the German races. Others fix the home of the Teutoni in the northern Scandinavia, in favor of which their iron armor appears to say much already. But we shall follow the accounts of the ancient writers, who always name the Teutoni as an individual tribe, and remind us that Pytheas had already, more than three hundred years B. C., heard the name of the Teutoni on our northern coasts.

After the Cimbri had fought near Noreja, they advanced through the fruitful district that lies between the Danube and the Alps, towards southern Gaul, which appears originally to have been the aim of their exertions, and many tribes from Germany, Gaul, and Switzerland, strengthened their numbers, particularly the Ambroni from the Emmegau, and the *Tigurini*, (Zurichers,) a valiant tribe at the foot of the Alps. They demanded a country from the Romans, for which they promised military assistance for every war. The Romans, however, refused their request, when they determined to obtain by valor and the sword what they could not acquire by treaty. Four Roman armies, one after the other, were defeated and almost annihilated by them and their confederates—the first under the consul Junius Silanus, the second under the consul Cassius Longinus, who fell in the battle, the third under the legate Aurelius Scaurus, who was taken prisoner. When he was brought before the council of the Germans, in order to give them intelligence respecting the passage over the Alps, he advised them to forego their intention, calling the Romans unconquerable. Angered at this, a young German prince, Bojorix, stood forth and struck Scaurus to the ground with his sword.

The Romans, who already thought of conquering the whole earth, but saw themselves now defeated by a horde whose name they scarcely knew, collected together another large army, under the consul Marcus Manlius, and sent it to the assistance of the consul Scipio, whose legate, Scaurus, had just been vanquished. But envy and dissension existed between the generals, and the Germans taking advantage of this, gave such battle to this large army, that 80,000 of the Romans and their allies were left dead upon the field, with 40,000 of their slaves. Manlius fell with his two sons, but Scipio escaped, with, it is said, but ten men. This day was, henceforth, considered by the Romans as one of the most unlucky in their calendar, and the city of Rome, as well as the whole country, were seized with such a panic, that in Rome for a very long time after, any uncommon alarm was called a "*Cimbrian panic.*" The enemy, however, did not take advantage of this opportunity, the reason for which neglect is not known; but, instead of advancing upon Italy, they turned aside towards the south of France and Spain, and gave the Romans time to recover themselves.

The Romans possessed but one man who still sustained their hopes; this was Caius Marius, a rude, proud man, but a valiant warrior. He was of low origin, and had raised himself by his talents alone; he was, therefore, hated by the patricians, but they were obliged, in opposition to all hitherto followed rules and against the laws, to make him consul several years in succession, in order that he might free them from their terrific German foes.

Marius collected his army and conducted it over the Alps towards Gaul, as far as the river Rhodanus, (the Rhone,) and formed there a defensive camp. He re-established the ancient discipline and order in his army, which had been long neglected, and to which was to be attributed the mischances that had befallen them. He, therefore, kept himself for a long time quiet in his camp, that he might accustom his warriors to the view of the large gigantic forms of these strangers, and to the tone of their fearful voices. And whenever he observed that a small troop of his enemies were alone, he quickly took advantage of the favorable opportunity, and made a sortie upon them with great strength and superiority, that his troops might learn to conquer them by degrees. This delay was irksome to the war-hunting Germans, and they often came to the very walls of the camp, mocked at the Roman army, and called them out to battle, but Marius was not to be diverted from his plan.

The Germans had now divided themselves into two bodies. The Cimbri had passed up the Rhodanus through Switzerland and the Tyrol towards Italy, but the Teutoni remained opposed to Marius. When these latter perceived that their challenge was not accepted by their opponents, they also broke up, marched past his camp on the road to Italy, and called out jeeringly to the Roman soldiers, asking them "if they had any commissions to send to their wives?" The multitude was so great that they were six days passing the camp in uninterrupted ranks.

Marius followed at their side, continuing always upon the heights, that they might not unexpectedly attack him; he then re-encamped himself opposite to them near Aquæ Sextiæ, or which is the present town of Aix, in the South of France. In the spot he had selected there was but little water, and when his warriors complained of thirst, he pointed with his hand to a river that ran close by the enemy's camp, and said, "Behold, yonder is drink offered you—but only to be purchased with blood." They replied, "Why do you not then lead us at once against them while our blood still flows?" He however returned, in a steady voice, "The camp must first be secured." And the warriors, although unwillingly, obeyed his orders; to such an extent had this strict leader been able to re-establish military discipline. Of the baggage men, however, many hastened in a multitude to the river to procure water for themselves and the beasts of burden, when, meeting with a few of the enemy who were indulging in bathing, they speedily came to blows with them, and as the cries of the combatants drew to their aid more from both sides, there arose a sharp skirmish with the *Ambroni*, whose camp lay on the Roman side of the river. The Ambroni were driven back into their camp of wagons, and then a severe battle took place with the women, who burst forth with swords and axes, attacking as well their own countrymen who retreated, as the pursuing Romans. Night separated the combatants. But this night was in many ways terrific and dreadful. There arose from the camp of the Germans a strange mixture of voices, not like lamentation and sorrow—although it might have meant a mourning-cry for the dead—but resembling a deadened roar, as of wild beasts, which was re-echoed by the mountains around, and by the shores of the stream. Terror seized the Romans; they feared the enemy might make a night attack, which would easily have thrown all into confusion; for their camp, owing to the battle, was still without walls and ditches. But the enemy stirred not; they remained quiet, and continued so up to daybreak. Marius now laid down his plans for battle. He placed the infantry before the camp, but the cavalry he sent down into the plain, and he dispatched his lieutenant-general, Claudius Marcellus, with 3000 heavy armed soldiers forward to occupy the wooded heights behind the enemy, with the command to advance from his ambush at the commencement of the fray.

When the Teutoni observed the Romans place themselves in order of battle, they were seized with such a desire for the fight that they did not await them in the plain, but clambered the heights against them. But as they arrived, breathless and panting, the Romans received them courageously and with closed ranks, and drove them back again into the plain. Marcellus did not waste this decisive moment, but broke forth in full gallop, and shouting from the woods with his three thousand horsemen, fell upon the rear of the enemy, who, pressed on both sides, soon got into disorder, and took to flight. The Romans pursued them, and either killed or took prisoners more than one hundred thousand. Shortly afterwards, the prince of the Teutoni, *Teutobod*, was also taken prisoner in his flight across the mountains, and was subsequently forced to form in Rome the chief ornament in the triumphant train of Marius; and according to the account of the Romans, he was so tall and lofty that his figure rose above all the trophies, and so active, that he could leap over from four to six horses. But Marius burnt the arms and entire booty as a great and splendid sacrifice to the gods, excepting only what he selected and preserved of the most costly and rare. This battle, near Aquæ Sextiæ, took place in the year 102 B. C., and eleven years after the battle of Noreja.

The exultation of Marius and his troops was speedily damped by the intelligence that the consul Catulus had been repulsed by the Cimbri in Upper Italy. These latter had, although late in the year, crossed the Alps, and drove before them the enemy, who guarded the mountain passes. The latter looked with astonishment upon these powerful strangers, who, in their delight at their native snow and ice, as well as in the consciousness of their hardy powers of endurance, revelled naked in the snow, ascended over ice and deep snow to the summits of the mountains, and then, sitting upon their broad shields, slid down from the peaks of the most precipitous declivities. The consul was obliged to retreat behind the river Athesis, (the Etsch,) but erected defences on each side of the bridge he had built. When the Cimbri, advancing closer, had surveyed the river, they commenced, giant-like, to break rocks from the surrounding summits, and cast them, with stones and earth, into the stream, in order to check its course; they loosened the piles of the Roman bridge with great weights, which were driven crashing against them by the floods, so that the Romans, in their terror, deserted their defences and their camp, and took to flight; and not until they had crossed the river Po did they again take up a position.

The Cimbri now spread themselves over the rich and beautiful plains of Upper Italy, and delayed going at once and direct, as they should have done, upon Rome; the charms of the country completely enchanting them. Instead of their rude camp beneath the open sky, they now accustomed themselves to the shelter of a roof and its comforts; instead of their cold baths, they now took warm; instead of plain meat, they indulged in choice dishes; but, above all, they sank into intemperance by wine drinking. Catulus, in the mean time, waited beyond the Po until Marius returned from Gaul with his victorious army and joined him; when they both advanced forward over the river. As soon as the Cimbri were apprized of this, they collected their troops, and, in expectation of the Teutoni, whose misfortune they were either ignorant of or did not believe, they sent to Marius once more to demand of the Romans a country for themselves and their brethren. When they named their brethren, the Teutoni, Marius ridiculed them, and said, "Think no more of your brethren; they have their land already, and you likewise shall receive quite sufficient from us." The ambassadors censured him for his ridicule, and said he would speedily receive his punishment from the Cimbri on that very spot, as also from the Teutoni the moment they arrived. "They are here already," said Marius; "and it would not be right to allow you to retire without having greeted your brethren." And with that he ordered the captive princes of the Teutoni to be brought forward in their fetters.

Struck with amazement, the ambassadors returned to their camp, and the Cimbri immediately broke up; Bojorix, their prince, rode to the Roman camp, and challenged Marius, with the Romans, to battle, at any place which he might appoint. Marius replied, "It was not usual for the Romans to make their enemies acquainted beforehand with the day of battle, yet even in that he would show himself agreeable to the Cimbri;" and he accordingly appointed the *Raudian* plain, between Vercellæ and Verona, as the place of battle, and fixed the time for the third day following.

After the lapse of this interval, the Cimbri quitted their camp in good order; they placed their infantry in a square, but the cavalry, 15,000 men strong, turned to the right, and endeavored, by this manœuvre, to bring the Romans between themselves and the infantry. Their cavalry, for the greater portion, was equipped in the most sumptuous manner possible; they wore helmets which were made to resemble the throats of terrific animals, or other frightful objects, with a full waving crest, which increased the size of their gigantic figures, and their iron armor and shining shields glittered afar. Every rider had a double javelin, and for close combat a large heavy sword. They had obtained these choice arms very probably in victorious battles during their long incursions. The infantry, however, poured itself forth upon the plain like an immeasurable and moving sea. Marius, at this moment, washed his hands, raised them to the gods, and vowed to them a great sacrifice, should he conquer; Catulus also, with raised hands, made a vow for the success of this day. And when the entrails of the slaughtered animal were shown to Marius by the priests, he exclaimed with a loud voice, so that the multitude might hear him, "*Mine is the victory!*"

A severe and bloody battle now began. The heat, and the sun which shone in the eyes of the Germans, aided the Romans. For the former, brought up in cold and shady parts, could endure the cold, but not the heat; profuse perspiration enervated their bodies, and they held up their shields to shelter their eyes from the sun. It was precisely in the month of July, when the summer's heat is most intense, that the battle was fought. The dust also was opposed to them, for it completely enveloped them, and concealed from the Romans both their numbers and their terrific aspect, so that the latter, not being previously alarmed by their appearance, fell at once upon the ranks of their enemies. The most dreadful close conflict ensued, wherein the Romans derived a vast advantage over their enemies from their short broad-swords. They had also so accustomed their bodies to the labors and discipline of war, that not a single Roman was observed to perspire or to lose his breath, even in the most suffocating heat. Besides, Marius had invented a new weapon, a kind of long barbed spear, which the Romans hurled against the shields of their enemies, and with which they forced these down, so that the individual remained exposed.

Thus it happened that the largest and most warlike portion of the Cimbri were killed. The foremost rank had bound themselves together with long chains or cords, fixed to their girdles, that they might not be forcibly separated; and they now lay on the field as it were strung together. When the Romans, pursuing those who fled, arrived at their wagon-camp, their eyes beheld a sad and mournful scene. The wives of the Germans stood, dressed in black, upon their wagons, and themselves destroyed the fugitives as they arrived, nay, even their own little children they cast beneath the wheels of the wagons, and under the feet of the beasts of burden, that they might not fall into the hands of the Romans; and they then killed themselves. Many of the men also slew themselves, for they feared slavery more than death. Sixty thousand were, however, taken prisoners, and as many more upon this fatal day were exterminated.

Thus was concluded this severe and bitter war, which the Romans considered equally as critical as the earlier one, nearly three hundred years before, when the Gauls under Brennus burnt Rome; and thence they called Marius the third founder of the city. But the boys and youths of the Cimbri and Teutoni, who were made prisoners in these battles, and conveyed away as slaves, amply revenged hereafter the blood of their fathers and their brothers in that of thousands of Romans, whom they slew in the servile war under their leader, Spartacus.

Not quite fifty years had passed after this first essay at arms of the Germans with the Romans, when the former again advanced towards the Roman frontiers, in smaller numbers, certainly, than at the first time, and perhaps not with the clearly defined purpose of invading Italy; but conquest and the prospect of booty probably would speedily have increased their forces, and the fruitful pastures, as well as the full granaries, of the natives, would have allured them from province to province, until the fame of the smiling country beyond the Alps might have suggested to them the path over these towering frontier walls, had they not found an opponent who knew at least the art of war as well as Marius.

*Ariovistus*, a king of the Marcomannic Suevi, between the Danube and the Necker, was appealed to for assistance by a Gallic tribe, the *Sequani*, against another tribe, the *Ædui;* in the year 72 B. C., he passed over the Rhine at the head of an army, and obtained a victory for the Sequani; but the beautiful plains of the present Burgundy pleased him so much, that he would not again quit them. At enmity equally with the conquerors and conquered, he seized a space of land, and when the Gauls had united against him he put them to flight near Magetobria, (now Mumpelgard.) He, perhaps, originally went forth upon this adventure as a duke with his warlike train, but more and more Germans flocked to him, attracted by the celebrity of this beautiful country, so that he speedily had under him an army of 120,000 men. The whole of Gaul trembled before him; the tribes believed themselves already vanquished or driven from their ancient seats. The Romans, however, who possessed aleady in Southern Gaul a subjected province, acknowledged Ariovistus as king in his conquered territory, and called him friend.

But speedily afterwards Julius Cæsar, one of the greatest and boldest of Roman leaders, appeared in Gaul. Burning ambition excited him to great warlike undertakings, and he had arrived in these districts with no other view than to subject the whole of Gaul to the Romans. The Ædui and other Gallic tribes, now turned to him and demanded aid of him against the Germans. Cæsar gladly profited by this opportunity of advancing further into Gaul, promised them help, and demanded an interview with Ariovistus.

Ariovistus answered proudly and boldly, that, "If he himself desired aught of Cæsar he should come to him, and if Cæsar desired aught of him he must do the same. Besides, he could not understand what Cæsar or the Roman people in general had to do in *his Gaul*, which he had conquered by the force of arms."

Cæsar replied to him: "As he had refused his invitation to an interview, he at once would briefly state what he desired of him, viz., in the first place, that he should not bring any more Germans across the Rhine; and, secondly, that he should return to the Gallic tribes their hostages, and treat them no longer as enemies. If he fulfilled these conditions, the Roman people would hold constant peace and friendship with him; if not, Cæsar would not behold the injuries of the Ædui with indifference."

Ariovistus, in his reply to this, referred boldly and candidly to the right of arms, according to which the conqueror might treat the conquered as he pleased. It was thus the Romans themselves were likewise accustomed to act, who well knew too how to make use of their rights; he only required therefore to be left to do the same. And, with regard to Cæsar's announcement, that he would not let the injuries of the Ædui remain unrevenged, Ariovistus replied: "No one had hitherto contended with him but to their ruin. If Cæsar wished, he might begin the contest; he would then learn to know what unconquered Germans, perfectly practised in the use of arms, and whom no roof had sheltered for fourteen years, could perform." Truly, the language of a hero of the great tribes-migration; to whom his sword stood in lieu of hereditary right and title-deeds, and who, with his brethren in arms, was determined to repose under no roof until he had conquered the sought-for country of his new home!

With any other opponent this bold declaration might have produced its influence, and been effective; but Cæsar, who even in Rome itself could not endure to be the second, felt thereby the more excited to measure himself with such an enemy. He advanced against him and occupied *Vesontio*, (Besançon,) the chief city of the Sequani, which was very strong and richly provided with all the munitions of war. While he remained here a few days, a very dangerous despondency suddenly overpowered his army. The statements of the Gauls who had been so often beaten by the Germans, the descriptions given by the traders who had travelled through their country, the close proximity of the terrific enemy himself, tended, combined altogether, to present before the soul of the Romans so fearful a picture of the strength, the valor, and ferocity of the Germans, within whose annihilating glance it was impossible to stand, that many who had thus far voluntarily followed Cæsar, did not hesitate inventing any excuse to enable them to return home. Others whom shame retained, could however so little govern themselves, that they frequently broke forth in tears, and in their tents sorrowfully mourned their ill-fortune. Throughout the whole camp all were engaged making their wills publicly; and, at last, even those became tainted by the panic, to whom the dangers of war were by no means strange. And, in fact, there was a general murmur against their rash leader, for thus unnecessarily seeking so perilous a battle.

Cæsar, in order to subdue this impression in his army, summoned forth the whole force of his eloquence. He collected together the leaders of his host, and represented to them that a war with Ariovistus was as yet by no means certain; he much more expected that the latter would listen to the voice of justice and of peace. But should he, from a mad love of battle, absolutely desire it, they had only to remember the defeat of the Cimbri and Teutoni, and the servile war just ended, wherein the Germans also were conquered as well as the Helvetians, not being able to resist the Roman arms. But if, notwithstanding, all these reasons could not serve to tranquillize them, and none would follow him, he would at once advance against the foe with the tenth legion alone, for on *their* fidelity he could depend.

This address made a deep impression upon their minds. The tenth legion thanked him immediately for his confidence, and all the rest emulated each other in displaying their readiness. Cæsar broke up forthwith, and advanced nearer to the German army. An interview which he held with Ariovistus at his desire, was as fruitless as the previous negotiations, and Cæsar now wished for nothing but a battle. But Ariovistus took up a position in which he cut off from the Romans all the supplies, and caused his cavalry, which, by its mixture with the light infantry, was superior to that of the Romans, to make skirmishes. But the battle, although daily offered by Cæsar, he did not accept.

Cæsar then learned from some prisoners the cause of this delay, which otherwise was not in accordance with German custom. The *prophetic women*, according to whose oracles the army acted, had announced misfortune should they fight before the new moon. Cæsar now sought a battle more zealously than ever, and advanced close up to the German camp. They then at last drew forth their troops, and each tribe took up its position—the Harudi, Marcomanni, Tribocki, Vangioni, Nemeti, Sedusi, and Suevi; they surrounded their battle array with wagons and chariots, whereon sat the women with wild and loosely flowing hair, supplicating all the ranks as they passed by, not to allow them to fall into the bondage of the Romans. The battle commenced, and they were soon furiously engaged on all sides. The Germans rushed forward with so much speed, that the Romans had not time to cast their javelins, and their left wing was driven to flight; but their right wing conquered on its side, and now were displayed the advantage and superiority of perfect warlike order and discipline. The broken wing of the Romans was re-formed, when the third division advanced to its aid; the ranks of the Germans, however, remained in confusion, for their army, although extremely valiant, was deficient in strict discipline and order. They were therefore at last driven to flight on all sides, and hastened towards the Rhine. But the Roman cavalry overtook the greater part, and but few, among whom was Ariovistus, saved themselves by swimming or by traversing the river in small boats. His two wives were killed in the flight, and of his two daughters one was likewise slain, and the other taken prisoner. Of Ariovistus himself history says nothing further.

When Cæsar had driven Ariovistus across the Rhine he began the subjection of the Gallic tribes, who were not equal to the Germans in valor. He conquered one after the other, and kept constantly advancing to the Lower Rhine. Intelligence then came to him that two German tribes of the Lower Rhine, the *Usipeti* and *Tenchteri*, pressed by the Suevi, had passed over the Rhine to seek a new settlement in Gaul. They had with them their wives and children, their slaves and herds, as well as the rest of their property, and were upwards of 430,000 strong. As Cæsar now, however, considered Gaul to belong to him, he desired them to retrace their steps. They, however, replied, "That they had been forced by the Suevi to wander from their homes; they desired nothing but a land to dwell in; he ought therefore to leave them the fields they had conquered with their arms, or give them others instead. Besides, it was not German fashion to avert a battle by entreaties, but to make a stand against those who desired the contest; he was therefore free to choose their friendship or war. They yielded to none but the

Suevi, to whom in battle even the immortal gods themselves were not equal; but excepting those there dwelt none on earth whom they could not conquer."

They nevertheless were conquered by Cæsar, but only by Italian cunning, for as their princes and chieftains came to an arranged interview with him, he suddenly seized them as prisoners, fell immediately upon their camps, and beat and scattered the whole tribe, which was now without a leader. Some of them fled back across the Rhine to the Sigambri. Cæsar required them to be delivered up. The Sigambri answered: "The Rhine at least was the limits of the Roman empire; if he did not wish the Germans to cross the Rhine against his will, why did he presume to give orders on their side of the river?"

Such language vexed the proud Roman. He likewise still bore fresh in mind, that the Suevi under Ariovistus had already fallen upon Gaul; therefore, he determined to build a bridge over the Rhine, and make the German tribes feel in their own country the power of the Romans. In ten days he constructed with much ingenuity, in the country of the *Ubi*, below the place where the Moselle falls into the Rhine, (according to some near Bonn, according to others near Andernach,) a large wooden bridge, and passed with his army over Germany's noble stream. This was in the year 55 B. C. He wished to attack the powerful confederation of the Suevi; these, however, removed their whole property and their wives and children far back into the interior of the forests, and collected all their warlike forces in the middle of their domain, there to await their enemy. It appears they had selected their ground with great prudence, for Cæsar did not consider it even advisable to follow them thus far. He halted only eighteen days on the right bank of the Rhine, devastated with fire and sword the vicinity of the Sieg, where the Sigambri then dwelt, and then returned across the river. To the Ubi, who upon this occasion had been his faithful adherents, he gave the name of Roman allies.

But the Suevi had so little fear of the Romans, that they shortly afterwards sent assistance to the Treviri against them. Cæsar then determined to cross the Rhine a second time. He built a second bridge a little above the former place, (according to the opinion of some near Neuwied,) but scarcely placed a foot in Germany, for the Suevi had made their arrangements this time as prudently as before.

According to the connection of events, and of the locality where Cæsar crossed the Rhine, those whom he called Suevi must have been the Chatti, and these either then have belonged to the Suevic confederation, or Cæsar, in his ignorance of the German relations, has included them as such.

After this period Cæsar did not again pass into Germany, but he had become so well acquainted with the Germans, as being such strong and valiant men, that he endeavored to raise troops from among them to serve in his legions. This was easy to him among such a brave people, where there were always bold men ready to go forth for pay, booty, and the love of war. Cæsar was likewise a hero who well understood how to win the hearts of his warriors; he led them always to victory. German subsidies helped him henceforth to win his battles, and at *Pharsalus*, where he fought the last battle against Pompey, and where it was decided which of the two should rule the world, they afforded him important aid. After the battle had been hard fought, Pompey dispatched his cavalry against the enemy, that they might give decision to the battle; but these horsemen were chiefly proud Roman youths, of the superior classes, who idly thought they could not be defeated. Cæsar then gave command to his German infantry to drive back the cavalry, and called out to them: "Comrades, strike only at the face!" He well knew that the vain youths of the metropolis preferred their smooth faces to scars. And the Germans, who were sufficiently tall and strong, rushed against the cavaliers as if they were themselves mounted, and not on foot, and frightened them so much that they speedily took to flight. Thus the day was by them won for Cæsar. Henceforward, there were constantly German soldiers in the Roman service, and the succeeding emperors even formed of them their body-guard.

Julius Cæsar was murdered as he was about to make himself sole master of Rome; but the Romans were no longer worthy of being a free people; they therefore speedily fell into the hands of masters who were worse than Cæsar. The first among them was the emperor Augustus, whose reign lasted from the year 30 B. C. to the year 14 A. D.

During this time the Romans had subjected a greater portion of the then known earth. Of Europe, besides Italy, Greece and Macedonia, Hispania, and Gaul were also subject to them; with that they were not however satisfied, but coveted other countries which lay beyond the Alps and the Rhine; for the ambition and avarice of the Romans knew no limits, and no doubt it appeared very desirable to them to gain dominion over the powerful men of the German race, according to their own will, and to form the *flower* of their armies from their ranks, and by their aid to hold the rest of the world in obedience. They at first attacked those tribes which dwelt upon the sides of the Alps towards Germany, in the mountains of Graubünden, the Tyrol, Saltzburg, and Austria: wild tribes, partly of Gallic and partly of unknown origin, who could not resist the superiority of the Romans, and who were not only conquered, but exterminated or sold as slaves. This contest was concluded in the year 15 B. C. Henceforward the river Danube was on this side the boundary between the Romans and the Germans. From the other side, however, the river Rhine was no longer to remain so, and Augustus, therefore, sent his step-son, Claudius Drusus, to Gaul, to attack the Germans in their own country, and he was certainly a hero competent to accomplish what was great.

Drusus undertook four campaigns in Germany, in the years 12–9 B. C. He warred with the Suevi, Chatti, Sigambri, Usipeti, Tenchteri, Brukteri, and Cherusci. He passed on from the Lower Rhine to the rivers Lippe and Ems, as far as the Weser, and in his fourth incursion advanced even to the Elbe. But his irruptions were no conquests. The Germans well understood how to conduct war against such an enemy. They retreated from their isolated dwellings into the forests on both sides of the road he took, destroyed the supplies they could not take with them, placed their families in safety, and stayed there until the autumn. The Romans were then obliged once again to return, as they could not winter in the desert country, from the deficiency of provisions; and that was the moment the Germans had awaited with impatience. They now annoyed the enemy at every step he took; attacked solitary troops, rushing upon them suddenly from the forests, in the most dangerous places, destroyed the wearied stragglers, seized upon their baggage, and allowed them no rest either by night or day; and thus the Romans never returned to the Rhine without considerable loss.

The rapid and extensive incursions of Drusus into Germany gave him, therefore, great fame among the Romans, but did little harm to the Germans. In the autumn, winter, and spring, they dwelt quietly in the places which the enemy had again quitted. But Drusus would certainly have found at last the means of establishing his dominion in Lower Germany had he lived longer. He had made one commencement towards it already. He built strong forts at the mouths of the rivers which flowed into the Rhine and the North Sea, that he might retain in his power all their navigation; thus being enabled to convey into the country a portion of his army with greater security upon a fleet of small vessels, and to transport their provisions conveniently after. For this purpose he also commenced a canal, which was called after him the Drusus ditch, (and is still called the Drusus Vaart,) and united the Rhine between Doesberg and Isselort with the Issel. By means of this canal the Rhine was brought into connection with the Zuider Zee, the *Flevum ostium* of the ancients, and the Romans henceforth, by means of this outlet, were enabled to have communication with the North Sea from all their holds upon the Rhine. Drusus himself took this mode of uniting himself with the Friesi, and of reaching the mouth of the Ems by sea, and where he likewise built a fort, probably opposite to the present Emden. On the Rhine he built as many as fifty of these forts, strongly fortified, especially Bonn and Mentz, the last upon the border-limits against the Suevi, and provided them with bridges and flotillas for their defence; and upon the Taunus mountains, on the heights near the present Homburg, he built the fort *Arctaunum*, intended against the Chatti. Had he, therefore, from year to year advanced more and more with such fortresses into Germany, and so at last prevented his being obliged to quit the land again in autumn, the dominion of the Romans, together with the adoption of their language and manners might, perhaps, have maintained a firm ground in Germany. But his course was already stopped in the fourth year of his impellent irruptions.

We will here give a brief sketch of these incursions. The first he made was after his legate had revenged himself upon the Sigambri for the defeat of Lollius, with his fleet down the Rhine, through his canal and the Zuider Zee into the Northern Sea, entering the mouth of the Ems. The Friesi were allies; however, the Brukteri had collected a fleet in the Ems and opposed him, but they were beaten. Here Drusus built his fort at the mouth of the river, and then continued his course along the Oldenburg coast, as far as the afflux of the Yade, where his ships got stranded, but by the aid of the Friesi and the flood were set afloat again. The winter, however, obliged him to return.

In the second campaign Drusus gained the shore across the Lippe, as far as the Weser, in the vicinity of Höxter; but a revolt of the tribes in his rear forced him to make a retreat, when he found himself suddenly surrounded near Arbalo by the Germans. Their too great confidence in gaining a victory, which misled them to make an irregular attack, as well as their thirst for booty, were the means of his rescue. He built here, at the junction of the Aliso and Lippe, the fort or castle *Aliso*,* in order to have a *point d'appui* for his incursions against the tribes on the Weser.

The third campaign he made was against the Chatti, who, previously peaceable, had now united with the Sigambri against him, because he had built opposite to them the fort upon the Taunus mountains; they were beaten but not subdued.

In the fourth campaign Drusus advanced from the fort on the Taunus mountains into the land of the Chatti, beat them, as well as the Marcomanni under Marbodius, and forced the latter to retreat further eastward. These attacked the Bojians and forced them to yield. Thus did Drusus himself assist in causing the Germans to completely drive before them the Gallic tribes, and to extend their own settlements. Upon this Drusus turned again to the left against the Cherusci, marched on across the mountains to the Saale, and along this river downward as far as the Elbe, (perhaps in the vicinity of Barby.) It was while one day he was here standing alone on the banks of the Elbe, which in his mind was not yet to be the limits of his progress, that, as it is related, a supernatural figure in the form of a female appeared before him, and with a lofty, threatening air, addressed him thus: "How much further wilt thou advance, insatiable Drusus? It is not appointed for thee to behold all these countries. Depart hence! the term of thy deeds and of thy life is at hand!"

Whether this was the creation of his imagination, or was devised by the craft of one of the prophetic women among the Germans, inwardly bemoaning the fate of her country, is uncertain;—suffice it, that Drusus, on his return, fell from his horse, and died a few weeks afterwards in consequence.

After him his brother Tiberius commanded the legions which were opposed to the Germans. He was of an artful and deceptive disposition; and besides arms, he employed other and worse means against them. By craft he caused disputes among the tribes, and by want of faith he led them into ruin. The Sigambri, who were one of the strongest and most valiant tribes upon the Rhine, he could not conquer with arms. He, therefore, demanded an embassy from them to him for the sake of peace, as he said; and as the princes and leaders came in great numbers, he caused them to be taken prisoners and dispersed among the Gallic cities, transplanting also of the tribe, which was thus robbed of its chieftains, 40,000 towards the estuaries of the Rhine and the Issel.* The princes, however, to whom life among a strange people was an insupportable burden, and who would not that on their account their people should be withheld from a retributive war against the Romans, killed themselves.

By such means, indeed, it was not difficult to hold in trammels those districts which bordered on the Rhine, or on the rivers which flowed into it; and by the aid of the strong forts placed there, and of the frontier walls or land defences, (*limites*,) which enclosed the occupied country, the northwestern portion of Germany, as far

* Respecting the locality of Arbalo and Aliso, see the Introduction

* This transplantation of the Sigambri, by which Tiberius thought to exterminate the tribe, only produced their salvation; for from these new settlements arose afterwards the Issel-Franks, who laid the foundation for the greatness of the kingdom of the Franks.

nearly as the Weser, appeared even already subdued, and, as it were, a Roman province. *Domitius Ænobarbus*, the grandfather of the subsequent emperor Nero, who held the command in the years immediately preceding the birth of Christ, pressed forward, even across the Elbe. No one hitherto had been so far. He also built a road between the Rhine and the Ems, called *pontes longi*, namely dikes and morass bridges, which led from *vetera castra*, near Wesel, onward to the vicinity of the Ems, over moors and marshes.

When Tiberius came a second time to Germany, about the year 3 A. D., he completely subdued a recent rebellion among the Lower German tribes, embarked upon the ocean, and sailing as far as the mouth of the Elbe, fought with the Longobardi, and took up his winter-quarters among the quieted tribes near the sources of the Lippe, probably near the fort *Aliso*. Henceforth this place was the point whence the Romans directed all their undertakings against the middle of Germany, upon the frontiers of which they had now arrived; and with the nearest tribe therein, the *Cherusci*, they had just formed an alliance under the name of friendship and confederation; which kind of union had, more safely than the force of arms, led to the subjection of the tribes. The internal organization of this province appeared to be a task possible now to be put into operation. But under this great oppression of their country, the courage of the Germans did not sleep; for, the same as in all times, although it was possible to bend their proud spirit, still it had never yet been broken. The sources of their aid sprung from among themselves.

A multitude of noble German youths had by a variety of events arrived at Rome; some in the Roman service, others as deputies, or as hostages; some again perhaps from ambition. But in the metropolis of the world they beheld neither greatness nor freedom, on the contrary, only slavery, which carries with it these sins:—meanness by the side of arrogance, flattery, dissipation, enervation, and idleness. To be ruled by such masters as the Romans then were, seemed to them the most disgraceful of all things. At the same time, however, they became acquainted with Roman military affairs, their art of government, and their craft; and what the former had applied to the oppression of their country, they determined to employ for its redemption.

Marbodius, a noble Suevian of the frontier tribe of the Marcomanni, was a youth of this stamp. The Romans describe him as tall and stately, self-willed in disposition, and more by birth than intellect a barbarian, which name they in their pride gave to all who were not Romans or Greeks. He had been sent young to Rome, and at the court of the Emperor Augustus he, was particularly honored. When, however, he had seen sufficient of Rome, he returned to his own country, and as he saw that they could not, in their present settlements upon the Necker and the Rhine, well maintain themselves against the great powei of the Romans, which threatened them after the conquest of the Alps from the side of the Danube, and, since the almost completed subjection of the north of Germany, menaced them also from the Maine, he persuaded his people to quit their districts, and to withdraw to other settlements towards the east. The Marcomanni, who, by their warlike constitution, were speedily ready and resolved for any movement, broke up, and Marbodius led them to Bohemia, a country well defended on all sides by mountains; they drove hence the Gallic tribe of the Boji, which had for generations past wandered thither, subjected many tribes around, and founded a great, well-regulated Marcomannic kingdom. His capital was Bubienum, called also Marobudum, according to some the present Prague, according to others Budweis. The Hermunduri, Longobardi, and Senoni, the flower of the Suevi, became dependent, and thus his power extended from the Danube across the centre of Germany to the Elbe. Henceforward he addressed the Roman emperors not humbly, as one subordinate and weak, but as their equal.

He had thus far conducted his affairs laudably, and he might now have become, as it were, a frontier defence for the freedom of the whole of Germany; but it almost appears as if he had learned too much in Rome. He had acquired the love of dominion also from the Roman emperors, and had at the same time perceived the art whereby the exercise of power over men otherwise free born, may be confirmed. He maintained a body-guard, introduced all other Roman regulations, and hitherto no single individual had ever practised so much authority among the German tribes. His army consisted of 70,000 infantry and 4000 cavalry, and he kept it in constant practice by his continual wars with his neighbors, so that it could be well seen that he was preparing it for still greater purposes. This, however, constituted the condemnable and distinctive feature in his character, whence, in truth, he cannot be called a great man; inasmuch as all this was accomplished, not for the freedom and happiness of his people, but solely for himself, and in order that *he* might alone be called great and powerful, and become honored and feared.

He had already appeared so dangerous to the Romans, that Tiberius, the son of the emperor, in the year 7 A. D., advanced against him with a large army. He intended to attack him from two sides with twenty-two legions, and he was already in full march, when intelligence reached him that a great rebellion had broken out in Hungary, Dalmatia, and Illyria, and that all the tribes from the Adriatic to the Black Sea, who dwelt upon the Danube and among the mountains, had conspired against the Romans, and had collected an army of 200,000 infantry and 9000 cavalry, with which they were determined to invade Italy. Fright and terror seized upon all in Rome, and the Emperor Augustus exclaimed in the senate, "Ten days hence the enemy may be within sight of Rome!"

Tiberius immediately concluded a peace with Marbodius, which was favorable to the latter, and hastened with his whole army against the Pannonian tribes; and, after three years of the most obdurate war, he succeeded in diverting the great danger, and brought these tribes again under the dominion of his father. The latter rejoiced, however, but little in this good fortune; for, on another side of his empire, the Germans had caused him the greatest loss, and had involved him in calamities the most serious he had ever experienced during his whole life.

## CHAPTER II.

### 7—374.

**Arminius, or Hermann—Arminius and Varus—Arminius and Germanicus—The death of Arminius, 21 A. D.—Further Wars between the Germans and Romans—War with the Marcomanni, 167-180—The Germanic Confederations—The Alemanni—The Franks—The Saxon Confederation—The Goths—The Decline of the Roman Empire**

The campaigns and forts of Drusus, and the crafty, cunningly-devised arts of Tiberius, had effected so much in Lower Germany, as we have above seen, that as far as the Weser, no armed tribe any longer openly opposed the Romans. All was bowed down, the unions of the tribes were sundered, and the minds of many of the leading men had been poisoned by the seductions of the Romans. They already began to appear a different race of men; habit and intercourse with the strangers commenced already to obliterate their national manners. Markets sprang up and were established around the Roman camps, and enticed the Germans to purchase and barter. Even the earth and heavens, says a Roman writer, appeared to be more gentle and mild, for the forests had become penetrated and passable, and bridges and dikes were built across the morasses. Three complete legions, the best of the Roman army, kept guard in the numerous forts and camps, and in the midst of our lofty forests of oak, a Roman Prætorship was established, together with Roman laws, legal institutions, and appointed functionaries. The Roman governor, *Sentius Saturninus,* who was in Germany in the year 5 or 6 A. D., contributed much to these changes; he was a man who united old Roman honesty with affability. He took pleasure in feats and enjoyments, and imparted to the Germans a greater love for the refined mode of life among the Romans. *Quintilius Varus* succeeded him in the autumn of the year 6; a man of a weak mind, who was more adapted for the occupations of peace than of war, and besides which, was addicted to avarice. For it was said of him, that he entered the rich province of Syria, where he had just been governor, a poor man; but when he quitted it, he himself had become rich and left the province itself poor. The Germans, to this weak-minded man, appeared thoroughly subjected, because they were tranquil, and he endeavored to fix slavery among them by those gentle but effective means, which are more pernicious and destructive than the power of the sword, because they assume an innocent garb. He sat in judgment upon the Germans, as among

Romans; decided upon the freedom and property of Germans, and the Roman lawyers, instead of the straightforward and simple German custom, sought to introduce the subtle and perplexing arts of Roman jurisprudence. If it be desired to fix within the heart of a nation, a secretly devouring and destructive worm, which shall gradually reduce it to that state of degradation that it becomes careless to all magnanimous ideas, the love of country and compatriots—substituting instead, the more debasing, petty, selfish considerations—it is only necessary to imbue it with a love of law and disputation, that all may become embittered against each other, and that every one shall know nothing greater than his own advantage. And as all judicial proceedings were conducted in the Roman language, it was likewise intended thus to introduce and establish that tongue among the Germans. For, in order to thoroughly annihilate the idiocracy, freedom, and independent feelings of a people, and to mould it into an entirely new form, it is only necessary to deprive it likewise of its peculiar hereditary possession—its *mother tongue*.

Varus, however, had much miscalculated when he supposed the rude Germans were insensible to these cunning arts. The understanding of uncultivated nations is keenly alive to those who wish to enclose them within nets, and the Germans were supplied by nature with a healthy mind and good discernment. They quickly perceived the source and central point of ruin, and they were beyond all things filled with inward rage at the view of the lictors' rods or fasces of the Roman governor, which were the attributes of his power of awarding corporeal punishment, or even death itself. Nothing was more degrading to the free German than corporeal punishment, the disgrace of the most abject slavery; and the power of punishing with death, they did not even allow to their own princes, but conceded it to the divinity alone, who proclaimed the sentence through the voice of his priests.

Their wrath, however, durst not give itself utterance, but it remained long concealed in the breasts of individuals, for there was no one near, who with a bold mind could collect and fan the glimmering sparks into a broad flame. But it was Rome itself that was chosen to nurture and bring up to maturity the saviour of German freedom. This was *Arminius*, (whom we are accustomed to call *Hermann*,) the son of *Segimer*, prince of the Cherusci; a youth of valiant heart and arm, of a clear, quick mind, whose eyes proclaimed the fire of his soul. By distinguished military service he had acquired the right and dignity of a Roman citizen and knight, and had returned to his country well instructed and practised in all the arts of war and peace. He here perceived the disgrace and ruin which was being prepared for his native country; and his mind pondered upon the great means of remedy. He speedily discovered a similar feeling to reign among the noblest of the Cherusci and the neighboring tribes; his inflaming word inspired their courage; they prepared the grand blow of deliverance, and in order to destroy the Romans the more securely, they enticed Varus by a planned rebellion to the frontiers—as it is related by the Roman writers—still farther away from the Rhine, into the depths of the Teutoburger forest, which flanked the districts towards the Weser.

Varus, however, might still have escaped his fate, through treachery: the traitor being found among the Germans themselves, in the person of Segestes, a prince of the Cherusci, who was an enemy to Segimer; while he was envious also of Arminius's great reputation, and jealous because this much younger man, by the powers of his mind and his heroic virtues, attracted the eyes of all the tribes upon him. Even the day before the breaking out of the conspiracy, when Varus had collected the princes at a banquet, Segestes entreated him most earnestly to take Arminius prisoner on the spot; but a blind confidence in his own power, concealed from the governor the abyss that yawned beneath his feet. He advanced still deeper into the forest which covered the country of the Weser, and the princes quitted him with the promise of immediately joining him with their auxiliary troops. They came—their plan being well and happily laid—and in the midst of the Teutoburger forest, (in the present principality of Lippe-Detmol,) where there are on all sides mountains and narrow valleys, they met him. Nowhere around was a beaten path visible, nothing but a thickly grown and impenetrable wood. Trees were obliged to be hewn, pits and morasses filled up, and bridges built. It was in the stormy autumn season—the month of September; heavy rains had made the ground slippery and every step unsafe, while the tempest roared at the summits of the oaks, whence the tutelary deities of the country seemed wrathfully to threaten. Warriors, beasts of burden, loaded with baggage and munition, all passed heedlessly on, as in perfect security.

Amidst these terrors of nature, appeared suddenly, on all sides, occupying the heights, the Germans as foes, hurling forth their destructive weapons against the compressed masses of Romans. These could but little defend themselves in their heavy armor, upon a slippery ground, and with arms which were spoiled for use by the continued rain. They, however, continued their course under continual attacks, and arrived in the evening at a spot where a camp might be constructed. Fatigued as all were, they nevertheless exerted their utmost powers to raise defences which should keep the enemy off, in order to provide themselves with at least one quiet night, were it even to be their last. Thus they awaited the dawn of day between hope and fear. In the morning every thing unnecessary was burnt; the soldiers were thereby made lighter for battle, and the baggage was also diminished; this, together with the women and children, of whom there was a great number with the expedition, (as no war had been anticipated,) they placed in their centre, and commenced their retreat, probably in the direction of their fort *Aliso*. Their fate seemed to brighten; they came to a more open space, where they could muster and regulate their ranks, and where the Germans did not venture to attack them; but this was to be no resting-place for them, they were to resume their march forward, and the terrific forest once more received them. The enemy renewed and increased his attacks; the tempest still continued, at which the Germans exclaimed as they pursued the Romans: "Behold this is done by our God, who will this day revenge our wrongs upon our enemies." Many of the most valiant Romans sank beneath their wrathful, and unceasingly emboldened attacks.

In this desperate position night appeared a second time, and they again endeavored to construct defences. But the attacking enemy, with his cries of victory, left them no time, and then, when heaven and earth seemed to oppose them, and there was no hope of salvation, the courage of the bravest sank. Varus, seeing now that all was lost, and having already received several wounds, cast himself upon his sword; many of the leaders followed his example, while the whole army was either made prisoners or killed, very few escaping. This last battle took place, according to the most recent researches, very probably between the present Horn and Lippe spring, on the southern borders of the Lippe.* Thus was annihilated the finest and most valiant of all the Roman armies, with the auxiliaries, 40,000 men strong. This was the hour of the heavy retaliation that was to be expected upon some such day, from the fury of a severely oppressed, freedom loving, but still savage people. Many of the most distinguished prisoners bled as sacrifices upon the altars of the native divinities, others, who retained their lives, were used for the most degrading services; and as the Romans themselves inform us, several of their distinguished countrymen, to whom at home the gates of entrance into the senate were open, concluded their miserable lives as the herdsmen of German flocks, or as the keepers or porters of German gates. It is also related, how embittered the Germans showed themselves towards the Roman judicial functionaries, with the feeling, as it were, that it was by their arts that the greatest danger was prepared against freedom and independence; and further, that a German tore out the tongue of one of these functionaries with the caustic words, "Now cease hissing, adder!" Such is the account of the great German battle of freedom, according to the relation of our enemies themselves. In what a different light should we not behold it, had we the testimony thereupon of even *one* German historian!

But the opinion of all is unanimous and fixed, and it is confirmed by the confession of the Romans themselves, that our fatherland owes its freedom to this great victory in the Teutoburger forest, and we, the descendants of those races, are indebted to it for the unmixed German blood which flows in our veins, and for the pure German sounds pronounced by our tongue. But in Rome there was universal alarm and mourning;

* The three days of battle have been calculated by M. Schmidt, not without ingenuity, to have taken place about the 9th, 10th, and 11th of September.

while the Germans were full of rejoicing, and, storming the forts on this side of the Rhine,* cleared the whole country of the Romans. The Emperor Augustus was beside himself; in his fury he struck his head against the wall, and constantly exclaimed: "Oh, Varus, Varus, restore me my legions!" For some months he allowed his beard and hair to grow, the guards of the city were doubled, and that no riot might occur, the Germans were dispatched from Rome, and even the German body-guard was conveyed across the sea into the islands. At last Augustus vowed great festivals to his god Jupiter, "should his empire attain a more flourishing state."—Thus did it happen in the Cimbrian war.

In order to meet the more extensive incursions of the Germans which were now expected as certain, consequent upon this victory, Tiberius was hastily dispatched to the Rhine with a rapidly collected army; to his astonishment, however, he found every thing quiet. The Germans did not desire conquest, they wished only to protect their freedom, and according to the very nature of their alliance, after the danger was removed each returned to his home. Tiberius held the vacillating Gaul in obedience, and passed again across the Rhine, but without proceeding very far into the country; and as in a few years afterwards he succeeded Augustus in the empire, he transferred to his nephew, *Germanicus*, the son of Drusus, the management of the war against the Germans.

Germanicus, a young and ardent hero, had before his mind the great example of his father, and he resolved to revenge the defeat of Varus. He undertook three grand campaigns in Lower Germany, in the same districts where war had previously raged on the Lippe, and from the sea up the Ems towards the Weser and the Elbe. Germany was now again menaced with fresh danger, for Germanicus was a warrior worthy of the best ages of Rome. But equally as Arminius had obtained victory over bad leaders, so did he now with so much craft and valor resist those better chiefs who advanced with large armies, that although he was not always victorious in his battles, he obliged his opponent, at the end of every campaign, to withdraw to his fortresses on the Rhine. And thus, on these occasions, he did not less for the freedom of his fatherland than he had previously done in the annihilation of the legions of Varus.

Germanicus made his first campaign in the year 14 A. D., with 12,000 Romans and a multitude of allies from the Rhine, where Büderich and Wesel now lie, through the Cæsarean forest in the vicinity of the Marsi, and fell craftily from several sides upon the unprepared enemy, (who, thinking themselves in the midst of peace, were at the time celebrating a great festival,) and destroyed the country for fifty miles around with fire and sword. No age, no sex was spared, and a widely celebrated temple—that of Taufana—(according to some, in Tecklenburg, according to others, in the neighborhood of the present Münster)—was destroyed. He did not press farther into Lower Germany, for now the Brukteri, the Tubanti, and Usipeti, speedily collected themselves to revenge the misfortune of their friends. The retreat of the Romans was not unaccompanied by difficulties. It was only by prudence and strict order that Germanicus led his legions successfully back across the Rhine.

In the following year, after he had first attacked the Chatti, who had joined the confederation of the tribes under Arminius, he rescued Segestes, who was hated by his own tribe, and who applied to him for assistance and rescue from the hands of his opponents. The feud between the two hostile houses had again broke out. Arminius, who loved Thusnelda, third daughter of Segestes, and whom the father refused to give to him in marriage, had eloped with, and made her his wife. Her father, however, recaptured her, and brought her back to his castle. Here he was besieged by Arminius, in order to recover his wife; but Germanicus meantime delivered Segestes, and upon this occasion he took prisoner Arminius's consort, Thusnelda, and conducted her to Rome. But she never forgot her husband or her high rank, and in her sentiments she fortunately more resembled him than her father. Se-

* *Aliso* held out the longest. It was so strong, that the Germans, being without a knowledge of the art of besieging and the necessary instruments, could not conquer it by force. They had, therefore, recourse to famine; but the Roman garrison managed, in an unwatched moment, by a *ruse de guerre*, to slip out, and, although with loss, they nevertheless succeeded in reaching the Rhine.

gestes, on the contrary, who had now found a protector, addressed the Romans in the same sense as at all times is usual from such as have betrayed their country: "This is not the first day of my fidelity and constancy towards the Roman people!" he exclaimed. "Since I was made a Roman citizen by the divine Augustus, I have, in the selection of my friends and enemies, had solely your advantage in view; not from hatred towards my country—for traitors are hateful to those to whom they twin—but from the conviction that the same thing is beneficial to both Romans and Germans, and because I prefer peace to war, the old order of things to the new, and tranquillity to turmoil. And now that I am with you, I can become to the German people a useful advocate, should they choose repentance instead of ruin."

Thus spoke Segestes. Augustus promised him protection, and selected a dwelling for him on the Rhine. Arminius, however, felt the most violent rage and indignation, and above all, it pained him most deeply to think, that the child with which his consort was pregnant, must first behold the light of day in slavery among the Romans. Acting upon these feelings, he forthwith traversed the land of the Cherusci, summoning them all to the war against Segestes, and against the Romans. His words are rife with the most bitter energy: "The noble father! the great leader! the valiant army!" he exclaimed, ironically, "who all combined together to carry off a weak woman! Before *me* three legions, and as many leaders, have fallen; *I* do not conduct war by treachery, and against pregnant women, but openly against the armed; and in our German groves are now to be seen the Roman banners which I have there consecrated to our native divinities. Let Segestes continue to dwell upon the subjected banks of the Rhine. Let him there obtain the priestly dignity for his son; but let him know that the Germans will never forgive him, or forget that they have seen, between the Rhine and the Elbe, the Roman fasces and the Roman toga. If, therefore, my countrymen, your fatherland and families, and our ancient German manners, are dearer to you than alien rulers and their followers, then join Arminius, who will lead you to glory and freedom, rather than obey Segestes, who will only conduct you to disgrace and slavery!"

By such fiery language he excited and collected together the Cherusci and allied tribes, and at their head appeared at his side his uncle, Inguiomar, as the Romans call him, who stood in great respect and esteem among the people.

Germanicus had already retired with his legions to the Rhine: upon receiving intelligence, however, of this fresh and great rising of the German tribes, he resolved upon another expedition that same year, so as to prevent them from making an attack upon the Rhine. In order to pass more rapidly, and from several sides, into the heart of the country of the enemy, he, according to his father's example, led a portion of his army by sea to the estuary of the Ems; two other divisions, under Cœcina and Pedo, advanced from the Rhine through the interior of the country, and thus the infantry, cavalry, and the flotilla met together in Westphalia. Unfortunately the Romans were not without German auxiliaries; they had Batavian cavalry with them—and besides these, troops from the Tyrol and Salzburg, as also from the left bank of the Rhine. The country that lay between the Ems and the Lippe was devastated; the Brukteri destroyed their own country themselves, that a waste might lie before the Romans; but the latter pressed onward, recaptured, in their pursuit of the Brukteri, the eagle of the (19th) legion, which the latter had taken in the battle with Varus, and arrived in the neighborhood of the Teutoburger forest, where Varus had been destroyed. Germanicus glowed with the desire to show the last honor to the fallen leader and his army. He sent Cœcina forward to inspect the mountains and passes, and to lay bridges and dams over the deceptive morasses; and then he himself advanced and marched over the melancholy scene, ghastly and terrific in its appearance as well as in its associations. The vestiges of the first camp of Varus might still be recognised by the larger circuit of ground, capable of containing three complete legions; the second encampment was smaller, the wall half demolished, and the trench filled up and level. It was perceptible that the last remnant of the army had encamped itself there, until they were at length overpowered. In the middle of the plain heaps of whitening bones, the remains of the vanquished army, lay strewed around, and beside them were scattered about the fragments of lances, the bones of horses, and even heads transfixed to the trunks of trees. In the neighboring groves the altars still remained, upon which the commanders and most distinguished leaders had been sacrificed to the gods. And some few, who, having survived the battle and escaped from slavery, had joined the present army, pointed out, here a spot where a leader fell, there where an eagle was seized, yonder where Varus received his first wound, and finally, where, further on, he gave himself his death blow.

The Roman army then, in the sixth year after this defeat, buried the bones of the three legions without any one of them knowing whether he covered with earth the remains of his friend or enemy; the commander himself planting the first turf upon the mound. The army now advanced with increased fury against the enemy. Arminius had well understood his own advantage, and retired into the forests and morasses; and when the Romans incautiously followed him, he broke forth, repulsed the cavalry, and drove them back upon the infantry. But when Germanicus advanced with the disciplined legions, he retired, and the contest remained undecided. The results, however, were nevertheless those of a victory; the Romans commenced their retreat: Cœcina, one of the before mentioned leaders, serving under Germanicus, proceeded with four legions across the country towards the Rhine; Vitellius, another leader, marched with two legions towards the shores of the sea; and Germanicus himself, with the third body, embarked upon the ships.

The road taken by Cœcina was that of the formerly noticed *pontes longi*, or long bridges, a narrow dam road which ran across immense morasses. All around were gently rising wooded heights;* these heights Arminius now occupied, whence he courageously attacked the Romans, and but little was wanting for Cœcina to suffer the same fate as Varus. The dams and bridges had become so ruined with age, that it was found necessary to repair them, while at the same time a camp was formed, and efforts made to keep the enemy off. Many of the Romans sank into the morass, for the Cherusci, who knew the locality well, drove them to the most dangerous parts, and as these people were accustomed to fight among bogs, they, by their great length of body, and their monstrous javelins which they knew well how to cast from a distance, brought the Romans into great difficulties. Night alone saved the already wavering legions from the ruinous battle. But the Germans even then indulged in no repose, for they guided the courses of the springs which rose among those hills, direct upon the Romans encamped below.

This was the 40th year that Cœcina had either served or commanded as a Roman warrior; to him the chances of war were well known, and his mind, therefore, continued unalarmed in all situations. He accordingly gave his orders, and with presence of mind commanded what was most expedient in this necessity. The night was in a variety of ways most tumultuous. The Germans with their rejoicings and shouts made the very valleys below resound, so that even the ravines re-echoed with them; among the Romans there were only to be seen isolated small fires, and here and there was heard an abrupt voice, they themselves lying dispersed along the walls, or gliding about the tents, more because they were sleepless, than that they were watchful. Cœcina himself was alarmed by a bad dream. He thought he saw Varus rise, spotted with blood, from the morass, and beckon to him; but the Roman did not follow him, and when the former extended his hand towards him he struck it back.

At break of day the march was continued as Cœcina had arranged it, so that he was covered by two legions on each side. They, however, quitted their position upon the Germans attacking them with renewed fury, led by Arminius, who called out to them, "Here, Varus! here are the legions already conquered by a like fate!" The battle was severe and animated. Cœcina himself fell with his wounded horse, and must have been destroyed had not the first legion thrown themselves before him. The baggage and munition fell into the hands

* Probably the forest heights of *Mons Cæsius*, the so-called Baumberge, between Horstmar, Schapdetten, and Cæsfeld, where the sources of the Aa, Stewer, Berckel, and several rivulets are found.

of the enemy, and tne loss of these was the salvation of the Romans, for they enticed the booty-loving Germans from slaughter to pillage, and the legions thus at last arrived on the open plain, where they encamped.* Their condition was nevertheless deplorable, and the soldiers already began to complain aloud, that only one day was now left for so many thousands to live; and so great was their terror, that, when a horse which had escaped, ran towards a few soldiers standing in its way, they all thought the Germans had now broken into the camp, and they fled towards its back gates. Cœcina, to bring them to a stand, used entreaties, commands, and threats of punishment, but in vain; and as a last resource, he cast himself down across the gate, so that the fugitives could pass only over his body, and this desperate state of their old and honored leader, brought them at once to their senses and stopped their flight.

In the mean time the Germans had surrounded the camp. Arminius, who knew the firmness of a Roman encampment, would not venture to storm it, but preferred conquering the enemy by famine. His uncle, Inguiomar, on the contrary, insisted upon a speedy attack, and his advice, because it was bolder, pleased the Germans better. They stormed the camp accordingly, but just in the decisive moment Cœcina caused his troops to sally out, beat back the besiegers, and forced them to flight. Arminius left the battle without a wound, but Inguiomar, his uncle, was severely wounded, and the legions, as many as were left of them, arrived safely on the Rhine.

For the third campaign, in the 16th year, A. D., Germanicus made still greater preparations than he had for the former. A fleet of a thousand vessels, small and large, with deep and broad holds, and others with flat bottoms for landing, was collected to carry the whole army, without exposing it to the dangers previously experienced by an expedition by land, into the heart of northern Germany, and if necessary, so fitted as to bring them also back again. During these preparations Germanicus made a rapid expedition with six legions, probably upon the road from the Wesel towards Lippstadt, on the northern banks of the Lippe, as far as Aliso, to raise the siege of this fort, which had been retaken from the Germans and repaired, and which they were now again besieging. It succeeded, for the enemy dispersed on his approach, and he strengthened the highway between Aliso and the Rhine with new defences and dams. But as the chief attack was to be made from a different side, he marched back again to the Rhine, and thence embarked his whole army of not less than 90,000 men, and passing through the *fossa Drusiana* into the North Sea, landed at the mouth of the Ems. The Chauci were obliged to supply an auxiliary army, and the Angrivari were forced into subjection on the Lower Weser. The Roman army advanced as far as the present Minden. Arminius, at the head of the Cherusci confederation, opposed it, and a battle ensued at *Idistavisus*, on the Weser, (probably between Prussian Minden and Vlotho.) After a long and warm contest, the Germans were obliged to yield the field to the Romans, after the latter had gained the hills which commanded the plain. But the Romans could only attribute their victory chiefly to the German auxiliaries who were with them, from the North Sea and from the Danube; and thus, even at the very commencement of our history, it appears that Germans aided aliens in the subjection of their compatriots. But in those rude ages this must not be severely censured, for these tribes from the Danube had probably never heard of the name of the Cherusci. In this battle Arminius himself was wounded, and escaped only by the speed of his horse; and so great was the slaughter, that from mid-day to the very depth of night, the work of murder was continued, and the land was covered with bodies and arms to the extent of fifty thousand feet.

The subjected tribes of these districts had already determined to quit their seat between the Weser and the Elbe, and retire beyond the latter river, when they perceived the *trophies*, which the Romans had raised after the battle, and inscribed with the names of the conquered tribes; the sight of this inflamed their wrath more than their own wounds and the remembrance of their fallen friends. The populace, the nobles, the young and the old, all seized arms, and again advanced against the Romans. A second bloody battle took place in a wooded district between the Weser

* Possibly between Coesfeld and Velen.

and the Steinhuder Lake, which proved that the nations' force was not yet broken; for although the Romans ascribed the victory to themselves, they nevertheless immediately afterwards commenced their retreat, and Germany was saved. Henceforth the Weser never again saw a Roman army.

The greatest portion of his warriors, Germanicus led back by water down the Ems to the North Sea. But a tremendous storm overtook his fleet, destroyed a multitude of his vessels, and dispersed them on the coasts of Britain. He, himself, was shortly afterwards recalled from the command of the armies on the Rhine, by the emperor Tiberius, who was jealous of his military fame, and he was sent to Asia, where he was destroyed by poison in the bloom of manhood.

Thus did this truly German hero, Arminius, who was equally great whether in victory or in a doubtful battle, behold his country freed from the danger of a foreign yoke. The rapidity and strength with which he roused himself in misfortune, and instilled new courage into his people, produced its salvation. And be it remembered, he had not to contend merely with the rising or sinking power of the Romans, but while it stood in its highest perfection and extent. Such an army as fought against the German forces in most beautifully regulated military array at Idistavisus, and near the Steinhuder Lake, even the most powerful empires of the earth could not, up to that time, have resisted.

After he knew that the frontiers were secured, he turned against an internal enemy, who had remained indifferent to the contest for German liberty, and whose manners, aped from the Romans, together with his despotism, made him doubly hateful to his own tribe, as well as to his neighbors. This was Marbodius, the king of the Marcomanni. After the battle of the Teutoburger Forest, Arminius had sent the head of Varus to Marbodius, probably as a token of victory, to shame him, because he had not taken part in the league against Rome; perhaps, also, as an appeal to his patriotism to break forth, at this decisive moment, from his position, so favorable to the Germans, from its being so near and dangerous to the best Roman provinces. But Marbodius remained inert. The emperor Tiberius may likewise, perhaps, have employed his usual ingenuity—in order to conquer the Germans more by stratagem than arms—and have contributed his share also in this case, to produce a division between the two German princes.

The power of Arminius was now strengthened by the Senoni and Longobardi, who, wearied with the system of dominion exercised by Marbodius, at once renounced him, and joined the Cherusci; but, on the other hand, Arminius was forced to behold his uncle, Inguiomar, desert his own ranks, and pass over to those of the enemy. Hostilities appear to have been commenced by Marbodius, inasmuch as he was the first to advance beyond the frontiers; very probably in order to overtake and chastise the renegade Senoni and Longobardi. A severe and sanguinary battle was fought, in which, as Tacitus states, they did not fight in irregular array, but with perfect military order and discipline. The result of the action was against Marbodius; he was forced to retire back to his country, and thereby lost still more the confidence of his people; and finally, driven away by the Gothic prince, Katualda, he fled to the Romans. The latter granted him a pension, perhaps as a reward for having remained neutral instead of joining Arminius; and, eighteen years afterwards, he concluded his life—the means for prolonging which had been furnished by Roman charity—ingloriously at Ravenna.

We have no records of the last years of Arminius, except what Tacitus relates in a few words, viz.: that he himself having become suspected of indulging a desire to rule despotically, a conspiracy was formed against him, in which his relatives (possibly Segestes and Inguiomar) participated, and he was murdered in the year 21, in the thirty-seventh year of his age, and in the twelfth of his chief command. But we must not forget that the Romans had this tale, probably, from the assassins of Arminius, and, perhaps, from their old friend, Segestes, himself; for the whole spirit and tenor of his great life testify that he certainly desired nothing more for himself than what was justly his due. He may, however, have endeavored to have given to the north German confederacy—whose chief in war he was—a permanency and stability likewise during peace, and thus have drawn the confederation closer together, in order that a new enemy should not take them unprepared; and as his great object in this was misunderstood, his old enemy, Segestes, and his uncle, who was perhaps envious of the great fame of a nephew so much his junior in years, may have availed themselves of the general feeling to promote his downfall. The testimony of the great historian of his enemies, does especial honor to the memory of our hero; for, after the short narrative of his death, he thus speaks of him: "Arminius was, without dispute, the emancipator of Germany. In battles not always the victor, he nevertheless remained in war unconquered; and he is still celebrated in the heroic songs of the Germans. He is unknown in the chronicles of the Greeks, for they admire themselves alone; neither among us Romans does his fame stand high enough, for we elevate and dignify only that which is ancient, and have but too little regard for that which is modern."

Henceforth, the Romans thought no more of subduing Germany, but applied themselves solely to the means of securing their frontiers from the incursions of the German tribes. They therefore continued to add to the strength of the banks of the Rhine and the Danube, and kept a considerable army, consisting of their best legions, as a guard upon the borders. The emperor Claudius granted to the chief seat of the Ubi the distinction of a colony of veterans, and, subsequently, in honor of his consort Agrippina, born in that spot, it was called, Colonia Agrippina, (Cologne.) The strong camp upon the Taunus mountains, which the Romans likewise considered as one of the most important points in the district of the Rhine, was re-established also by Claudius.

In the year 69, another serious revolt again broke forth in the Low Rhine, under Claudius Civilis, a leader of the Batavian auxiliary tribes, and of royal birth. Like Hannibal, one-eyed, and of independent, haughty spirit, he nourished the greatest hatred towards the Romans, and, under Nero, had been dragged in chains to Rome, where he narrowly escaped death. When, therefore, now a tribute was demanded from the Batavians, although they were only bound to do military service, Civilis invited all the chiefs to a festival in the sacred grove, where he communicated to them his plans, and, by his eloquence, gained over the whole body to join in the revolt. Messengers were dispatched to all the neighboring tribes, nay, even across to Great Britain; and Civilis, without further delay, forthwith attacked and defeated a Roman encampment, and conquered the fleet on the Rhine; but not content with small results, he swore not to cut his beard, or the hair of his head, before he had gained a great and signal victory. He was now joined by the Caninefati, Friesi, and several tribes of the Saxon race; and as soon as he had conquered the *Castra Vetera*, and had destroyed or made captives several legions, the whole body of Germans, dwelling on the right bank of the Rhine, rose up and joined him, as well as the Brukteri and other tribes on the left bank; for their prophetess, Velleda, a Brukterian virgin of high rank, had predicted that the power of Rome was now approaching its end. Civilis sent her the most valuable portion of the booty he made; and from her isolated tower, in the forest near the Lippe, she herself directed the war. All the fortresses beyond Mentz were taken, Cologne was made to pledge itself to abolish the Rhenish dues, at the decree pronounced by Velleda, that the German trade should be open and free from taxation. Gallic tribes, also, joined the confederation. The emperor Vespasian, who had, meantime, succeeded to the imperial throne, now dispatched Cerealis, an experienced and active general, to the head-quarters, where, on his arrival, he at once proceeded to sow dissension, and produce suspicion among the army of Civilis against their leader; and the Gauls, in accordance with their usual changeable character, withdrew themselves; while Civilis, twice defeated, was forced to retreat among the marshes, and wade through the dikes. Numbers deserted him; Velleda was taken prisoner; and Cerealis, who gained over to him the passions of the majority, partly by mildness, partly by cunning, as well as by mysterious promises, offered terms of peace. Civilis then yielded; the generals met on a river, according to the ancient German custom, and peace was again restored under the old conditions of furnishing military service only. Of the subsequent fate of Claudius Civilis, nothing more is known.

After these fresh trials at superiority of arms, it was but occasionally that any emperor essayed to obtain military fame against his unconquered neighbors, and these endeavors were generally very unsuccessful, but in order to conceal the shame thereof, they were obliged to invent a variety of plausible excuses. No one, however, had conducted himself more shamelessly and ridiculously than the emperor Domitianus, who reigned between the years 80 and 90. He commenced a war with the Chatti, but did not venture to attack them seriously, for he quickly retired, leaving his purpose unfinished, and in order that he might not return to Rome with disgrace and obloquy, he purchased tall and strong-grown slaves in Gaul, dressed them like Germans, caused their hair to be dyed yellow and arranged in the German fashion, and then led them as if they had been German captives in triumph into Rome. In the second century after the birth of Christ, the Romans had to endure a very severe war with the Germans which they called the *Marcomannic war*, because the Marcomanni were best known to them from time immemorial, and because their attack, combined with that of the tribes of the Danube, most immediately threatened Italy. But a yet more extensive alliance of the tribes seems to have taken place, for also on the Rhine, and even on the coasts of the Baltic, the Romans had to endure hard contests. But, unfortunately, the accounts which we must collect from the later historians, (Jul. Capitolinus, Arl. Spartianus, Dio Cassius, as xtracted from Xiphilinus, Amm. Marcellinus, Orosius and others,) are very imperfect. The emperor Marcus Aurelius well understood the greatness of the danger; he caused the priests to be collected from all parts, prayers and large sacrifices to be made, and the oracles questioned respecting the issue of the war. It is also related by Lucian, that a wise man from Egypt, of the name of Alexander, who had acquired great fame, was questioned respecting the Marcomannic war. He replied that two lions, well anointed with fragrant herbs and spices, should be made to swim across the Danube into the enemy's country, and that victory would not then fail. His advice was followed. The Germans, however, who held these lions to be foreign dogs, killed them with clubs, and immediately afterwards gained a great victory over the Romans.

The war now became so desperate that the emperor was necessitated to receive into his army slaves, gladiators, and others, who were previously considered unworthy to bear arms. Even a band of robbers from Dalmatia were included in the service; and the emperor, that he might find means to carry on this severe war, sold every thing most precious in his treasury, together with his pictures, and his gold and silver vessels, the sale of which lasted two months.

The Marcomanni, nevertheless, pressed forward as far as Aquileja, which lies on the frontier of Italy, causing a similar panic and confusion in Rome as at the time when the Cimbri crossed the Alps.

Had a weak emperor then governed the Roman empire, its fate would probably have been decided. But Marcus Aurelius was a wise and valiant man, and saved Rome once more from great danger. He maintained a war for thirteen years against the allied tribes, and had to endure several sanguinary battles, being even obliged to maintain a warm skirmish with the *Jazygi* on the frozen Danube; and although he brought many of the tribes individually to peace and thereby weakened the enemy, and succeeded in irritating German tribes against each other, he, nevertheless, did not survive the end of the war, but died from his exertions during the campaign at *Windobona*, the present Vienna, in the year 180.

It now fell upon his son, Commodus, to lead the army against the enemy, and he made a speech to the soldiers, even over the body of his father, of what great things he purposed doing, and that the ocean alone should set limits to his conquests; but his heart longed for the pleasures of Italy and for the sensualities of his metropolis. This was well known to his flatterers and courtiers, and as they themselves were weary of the fatigues of the camp, they thus addressed him: "How much longer will you exchange Rome for the rude banks of the Danube, where nothing is to be met with but cold, rain, and eternal winter, where not a fruit-bearing tree is to be seen and nothing to be met with to exhilarate life? When will you cease to drink the frozen water of the Danube while others indulge in the warm wells and baths of Italy?" To such speeches Commodus listened eagerly and said, "It is true what you say, and if I preserve my life I can assuredly more effectually weaken the enemy than if I expose it to the dangers of war." Some of the tribes were so reduced by his father that they willingly concluded a peace with him, but from others he purchased it in a disgraceful manner by means of large presents, and then he hastened back to Rome. So valiantly, however, had these tribes fought, that, upon peace being concluded, the Quadi alone gave back 50,000, and the Jazygi 100,000 Roman prisoners; and all that the Romans had gained by the effusion of so much blood was, that things now remained for a short period tranquil upon these frontiers of their empire.

The proximity of the Romans on the Rhine, the Danube, and the Necker, had by degrees effected alterations in the manners of the Germans. They had become acquainted with many new things, both good and bad. By means of the former they became acquainted with money, and many luxuries. The Romans had planted the vine on the Rhine, and constructed roads, cities, manufactories, theatres, fortresses, temples, and altars; Roman merchants brought their wares to Germany, and fetched thence ambers, feathers,* furs, slaves, and the very hair of the Germans, for it was now the fashion to wear light flaxen wigs, instead of natural hair. Of the cities which the Romans built there are many yet remaining, as Salzburg, Ratisbonne, Augsburg, Basle, Strasburg, Baden, Spires, Worms, Mentz, Treves, Cologne, Bonn, &c. But in the interior of Germany, neither the Romans nor their habits and manners had found friends, nor were cities built there according to the Roman style.

The most important alteration that took place among the Germans at this period, was their concentration into several extensive confederations of the tribes. The more ancient example of the Suevi, the later combination of the Marcomanni and Cherusci, and perhaps various successful results in other German districts, chiefly, however, the character presented by the great Roman empire, which, notwithstanding its great corruption, was yet strong by its union: all this, as well as the predominant power of individual tribes, and perhaps many other unknown causes, produced four great confederations of the tribes, which probably arose from small beginnings, and had existed perhaps for some time, but had only become known and formidable to the Romans in the third century after Christ. Their origin will probably always remain obscure to us. The Roman writers here leave us entirely, or are so scanty and uncertain in their indications, that we cannot build upon them; and the historians who afterwards arose among the German tribes themselves, were so ignorant of their earlier history, that they were only able to produce old traditions, and often placed them in the most wonderful fashion in connection with the narratives of the ancient writers; and thus they connected the origin of the German tribes with the Trojan war, the expeditions of Alexander the Great, and other specially celebrated events of the ancient world. The confederations of the tribes as they occur in history, and as they are actually treated therein, are as follows:

1. The *Alamanni*, afterwards called the Alemanni, and Allemanni, between the Danube and the Maine; and subsequently, after they had won back the Roman tithe-land, also upon the Upper Rhine and Necker. They spread themselves later northward as far as the Lahn. They were a confederation of Suevic tribes, whose formation perhaps emanated from the Hermunduri, and, according to the opinion, erroneously formed, of some ancients, derived their name from their being composed of all kinds of men, or manni. But it is perhaps more correct to consider the name *Allemanni* as a warlike, confederative name, equally as the Marcomanni signifies the War-manni on the frontiers, Germani, the army or Ger-manni in general; the Allemanni may therefore mean the Manni, who formed the defence for the whole. They were warlike, wild, and valiant, and gave the Romans no little uneasiness. Dio Cassius first mentions them in the history of the emperor Caracalla; accordingly, at the beginning of the third century from this period—particularly after they had penetrated the *limes*, and towards the end of the third century, after the death of the emperor Probus, when they had conquered the tithe-land—they fell upon the effeminate Gauls (who henceforward, from terror, called all Germans *Allemands*,) at another time made incur-

* The Romans celebrated the white German goose, which they even called by its German name, *gans*.—Plin. Nat. H., x. 27.

sions across the Danube, and even across the Alps into Italy, and each time returned home with rich spoil. Northward from these dwelt:

2. The *Franks*, on the Lower Rhine, as far as the Netherlands and the North Sea; likewise a confederation collected from different tribes of the northwest of Germany: the Sigambri, on the Issel, which appears to have been the chief tribe, (the subsequent Salic Franks,) the Chamavi, Amsibari, Tenchteri, Usipeti, Brukteri, Chatti, Cherusci, Tubanti, and others. The Friesi and Chauci also joined them afterwards. The name of Frank is variously derived by ancient and modern learned men. The broadest derivation is that they wished to be *frank* and *free* people, and thence called their confederation. The name of Franks is much more probably supposed to be derived from their peculiar weapon, a javelin armed with a barbed hook, which writers call Franziska, (perhaps the ancient *framea* of the Germans.) History mentions the Franks to us for the first time distinctly about the middle of the third century, as a union of north German tribes. Flavius Vopiscus first names them in the life of the emperor Aurelian, about 242; after which the emperor Julian and other later writers. They were also very strong and bold. Their high opinion of themselves is expressed in the introduction to the Salic law, where it states: "The high-famed nation of the Franks, who have God for their judge, are brave in war, profound in council, firm in union, noble, manly in form, bold, prompt, firm; such is the nation, which, small in number, by strength and courage, burst the yoke of the Romans." They traversed many Roman countries, particularly Gaul, from one end to the other, whenever they were excited by the lust of prey and booty. They even crossed the Pyrenees into Spain, and conquered the city of Tarragona. The Romans in the third century had so frail a tenure of these countries, that the Franks and other German warlike hordes, among whom are named the Burgundians and Vandals, had possession of seventy considerable cities in Gaul. After a long period a hero again appeared among the Roman rulers, in the emperor Probus (276–282;) he drove the Germans beyond the Rhine, fell upon their country, and conquered so many of them, that in order to reduce them, he was enabled to transplant many thousands into other portions of his empire. He conveyed a body of the Franks, who had their seat upon the North Sea, more than a thousand miles into a distant country, to the coasts of the Black Sea. He expected the Germans would here forget their bleak fatherland, for here they dwelt in a most beautiful and warm climate, and in a rich and delightful country. They, however, could not banish from their recollection the cold shores of the stormy North Sea, but only planned how they could return. They attacked and took possession of several ships, and in them passed, amidst a thousand dangers and difficulties, through unknown waters, across the seas of Greece and Africa, and by the coasts of Italy, Spain, and France, towards their home. They were often obliged to land, and fight with the natives for provisions; they even conquered the large city of Syracuse in Sicily, which the Athenians in ancient times had vainly invested for three years; and they at last came through the great Ocean into the North Sea, and back to their German coasts. This took place in the year 280.*

3. The *Saxon confederation* is named, together with the Franks, as early as the year 288, by Eutropius, and was formed of the remaining Lower German tribes who had not joined the Franks, or had again separated themselves from them. Amm. Marcellinus next mentions the Saxons as the neighbors of the Franks about the middle of the fourth century, and after him they are named by many others. The greatest territorial extension which they attained in the course of the following centuries up to the time of Charlemagne, was from the Danes, from whom they were separated by the Eider, over Lower Saxony and the greatest portion of Westphalia, and in addition they occupied the banks of the Elbe, Weser, Aller, Seine, Ems, Lippe, and Ruhr. The history of this command of territory by the Saxons is entirely unknown to us. If we fix upon the name of the small tribe of the Saxons which is mentioned in the second century by Ptolemy alone, and who places them at the mouth of the Elbe, and towards Holstein, it then

* Zosimus, i., 71; Eumenius in Panegyr., iv., 18.

becomes probable that these, together with the Chauci, Brukteri, Cherusci, and Friesi, (who again detached themselves from the Franconian league,) the Angrivari, the Fosi, and other tribes, formed an alliance against the powerful confederation of the Franks, and drove these, who previously occupied the greater portion of Westphalia, farther towards the Rhine.

The Saxons appear subsequently divided into three circles: that of the *Eastphalians*, beyond the Weser, in the country of Hanover and Brunswick; the *Westphalians* on the Ems, and the Lippe in Münster, Osnabrück, &c., as far as the Rhine; and the *Engerians*, in the centre between both, in the vicinity of the Weser, continuing perhaps the name of the Angrivari in an abridged form.

The Saxons likewise well understood navigation, although in the earlier times they possessed but poor ships, formed as they were principally of twisted branches and boughs of trees lashed together, and then covered over with hides of oxen and bullocks—they were called by the name of *kiel.** They committed many piracies, and became first known to the Romans at the end of the third century as pirates on the Gallic coasts. We shall find, subsequently, that they crossed over to England, and there founded new kingdoms. They placed themselves only during the wars under the leadership of dukes, who afterwards immediately withdrew into the ranks of the nobility. In times of peace they legislated by representation, and sent from each of the three circles an equal number of chosen deputies to their assembly, whose decisions were valid for all. Thus the idea of a representative parliament, of which the ancient nations knew nothing, originated with the Germans.

But still more powerful than all these tribes were:

4. The *Goths*. Their name we have already found on the banks of the Vistula. Subsequently, however, it is mentioned from the shores of the Black Sea as far as the East Sea. They were evidently a union of many mixed nations, as it appears, belonging hereditarily to the Gothic race, and perhaps founded already at the period of the great war of the Eastern tribes against Mark Aurelius. And while on the one hand the Alemanni, Franks, and Saxons, attacked the country of the Romans, which lay towards the west, the Goths, on the other, turned their attacks towards the south and the east, the Black Sea and the Danube. Already, in the third century, the Romans had to maintain severe contests with them. The Gothic king Eniva, crossing the Danube, invaded Mœsia and Thracia, conquered several cities, laid the country waste, and when the emperor Decius advanced to meet him, he gained so great a victory over him at Abrutum, that the emperor himself and his son remained slain upon the field. From this battle, in the year 251, the superiority of the Germans, and the weakness of the Romans, became more and more evident, although several powerful emperors gained victories over them. Even the successor of Decius, the emperor Gallus, was obliged to purchase peace with the Goths, by leaving them all the booty, as well as all the distinguished prisoners, and promising them besides a yearly tribute. At a later period they made, in conjunction with the Herulians, several bold and dangerous piratic expeditions, from the northern coasts of the Black Sea, as well as beyond it, to those of the Mediterranean. Athens, with many monuments of its flourishing period, the vicinity of Troy, and the splendid temple of Diana at Ephesus, were overrun by them, and the latter wholly destroyed.

The great prince of the Goths, who, of all others, spread their dominion the most extensively, was Armanarich, or Hermanrich, who lived in the fourth century. He ruled over them for more than two generations, and attained himself the age of a hundred and ten years. His empire extended from the Black Sea and the Danube over Moldavia, Wallachia, Hungary, Poland, and Prussia, to the Baltic.

The Goths early divided themselves into two head divisions, which afterwards, after many changes, appear in the history under the titles of the *Eastern Goths* and the *Western Goths*. Kings of the race of the Amalians (probably the pure, without stain) ruled over the Eastern Goths; and the Western Goths were governed by the royal race of the Baltians, (from *balt*, bold.) Among the Eastern Goths, the Greuthungi, and among the Western Goths, the Thervingi, were the chief tribes.

The Goths belonged to the noblest and

* Kiel, a Danish port, still bears this sign in its city arms.

most civilized German tribes, and had adopted Christianity at a very early period. Their bishop, Ulphilas, or Wulfila, (Wölflein,) as early as the fourth century, undertook the truly wonderful task of translating the Bible* into their language, until then but little cultivated; and thus was speedily diffused among them, together with the belief in the Saviour of the world, both gentler feelings and manners.

Besides these confederations, there were other isolated tribes in Germany, particularly two, who will speedily appear among the rest, as distinguished for power and dignity, viz., the *Burgundi*, earlier on the Vistula, and the *Longobardi*, on the Elbe.

At the period that the German tribes flourished in their prime, and collected and combined their power in large unions, the Roman empire, in its declining strength, became daily more and more reduced within itself, and its magnitude was a burden to it. The majority of the Roman emperors, from the year 180 downward, became in a greater degree enervated, and with their effeminacy, grew likewise either more and more malignant and suspicious, or they were avowed tyrants, and shed the blood of the best men without reserve or shame. But even if a good ruler happened to appear, and sought to maintain right and order, he was speedily murdered by the wild horde of soldiers; for they it was who, in fact, ruled the empire. According to their pleasure, they elevated or deposed the emperors; and to such shameless extent did they carry their sway, that they publicly offered the imperial crown for sale, and placed it upon the head of him who gave them the most money. In the course of one hundred and twenty years, from 180–300, in which period, in the ordinary course of things, six rulers would have succeeded each other, no less than six and thirty emperors governed the Roman empire, of whom twenty-seven were murdered, three fell in war, and only six died a natural death.

It did not, however, suffice that an emperor was destroyed every moment, but the murderers slew all his adherents with him; so that blood was shed in streams, and the majority, in their selfishness, took especial care not to adhere too faithfully to their princes to the last. In such times, the Romans necessarily became a corrupted, reckless, and contemptible people, who only cared to pass their days in idleness, luxury, and sensuality. For when man beholds before him no security for the future, and knows not if the fruits of his industry will descend to his children, he then only considers how he himself shall enjoy the present moment; and thus, in his sensual voracity and brutality, he places himself upon a level with the irrational beasts, no longer thinking of a future judgment and a retribution.

It is true that the doctrine of Jesus had calmly diffused itself likewise among the Romans, and had certainly saved many from the general ruin. The emperor Constantine himself even, who removed the seat of empire from Rome to Constantinople, made it, in the year 311, the established religion of his empire; and, indeed, from that time Roman affairs took for a period a more favorable turn, but the improvement was not fundamental. The Romans, during the dominion of vice, had lost the higher moral power of the soul, in which alone the divine word can take deep root; the former sinfulness became intermixed with the modern doctrines, and thus, as pure spring-water, when flowing into a morass, becomes as bad as the stagnant pool itself, so did the admixture of the ancient wickedness with the new light of Christian virtue, destroy completely all beneficial results.

In this condition of the world, it is easy to understand that the attacks of the German nations upon the Roman empire, must necessarily have become daily more successful; and it also explains how they were urged by an irresistible natural impulse to overpower such miserable neighbors, by whom they themselves had been first attacked, and who, notwithstanding their enervation and corruption, considered themselves a nobler race than the unpolished Germans, whom they called barbarians. And thus in nature also it may be observed as a rule, that where there is a vacuum, the active, agitated powers of air and water forthwith strive to break in.

* This translation is the most ancient, and for us, an invaluable monument of our language. For a long period there only existed two MS. copies thereof: the so-called *Codex Argentius*, (of the silver letters,) in Upsala, and the *Codex Carolinus*, in Wolfenbüttel. These, however, contain only the four Evangelists and a portion of the Roman Epistles; while Ulphilas translated the whole Bible, with the exception of the books of Samuel and the Kings. In recent times, however, considerable portions of the remaining translation have been discovered and made known in Milan.

## CHAPTER III.

375—476.

The Hunns—Commencement of the Great Migration, 375—Irruption of the Western Goths, Vandals, Suevi, Burgundians, and other tribes, into the Western Roman Empire—Alaric—Attila, God's Scourge, 451—The Fall of the Roman Empire in the West, 476.

About the year 375, when the emperor Valens reigned in Constantinople, and the western empire was under the dominion of his nephew, the youthful Gratian, a new tribe, almost unknown and exceedingly savage, broke forth from Asia. They were not of German but of Mongolian origin, and were called Hunns. Terror and dread preceded them, and those who had seen them described them in the following terms:* "The tribe called Hunns surpass every degree of savageness. They have firm-set limbs and thick necks, and their whole figure is so misshapen and broad, that they might be considered as two-legged monsters, or as posts that have been roughly hewn to support the balustrades of bridges. And as, immediately after their birth, deep incisions are made in the cheeks of their children, so that the growth of hair may be hindered by cicatrizing the wounds, they remain beardless and most hateful to behold, even to the most advanced period of life. In addition to their ill-favored and repulsive shapes, they are so savage that they neither need fire, nor cook their victuals; but the roots of wild plants and the half-raw flesh of the first good animal they meet with, and which they place beneath them upon the backs of their horses and thus ride it somewhat tender, is their whole sustenance. They enter houses only when they are forced by the most extreme necessity; they avoid them as the separated graves of life, but wandering through mountains and valleys, they learn to endure, from their infancy, frost, hunger, and thirst. They clothe themselves in a linen garment or in furs, consisting of the skins of mice sewn together; they cover their heads with overhanging caps, and their legs with the skins of goats. Their rough and clumsy boots prevent them from walking freely, and therefore they cannot fight on foot; but are almost grown, as it were, to their horses, which are durable, but, in keeping with their masters, as characteristically ugly. All their business is transacted upon horseback, and thus this people buy and sell, eat and drink; and, leaning upon the neck of his swift animal, the rider sinks into a deep sleep, even to the very phantasma of dreams; and if a council is to be held upon serious matters, it is conducted in this same manner.

"They commence battle with a terrific howl; with the rapidity of lightning they advance and purposely disperse themselves in the same moment; return rapidly again, hover about in irregular array, destroying heedlessly whatever they meet with here and there; and from their extraordinary speed, almost before they are observed, they are already engaged in storming the wall, or plundering the camp of the enemy. At a distance they fight with javelins, whose points are furnished with polished bones, prepared with extraordinary skill; but in close combat with the sabre, while the enemy parries the thrust, they cast a noose over him and carry him off.

"Agriculture is not practised among them, and none touch the plough, for all roam about without a dwelling, without a home, without laws and fixed customs, always wanderers; the women dwell in wagons, where they weave their coarse garments and bring up their children. If the question be put to them, whence they come, none can return an answer; for they are begot at one place, born at another, and brought up again elsewhere. Adherence to contracts they know not, and like insensible animals, they scarcely know aught of justice or injustice, but they precipitate themselves with all the impetuosity of their desires upon an object, and they waver at every newly raised hope or prospect; nay, they are so changeable and irritable, that even sometimes in the same day, without the least offence, they fall out with their allies, and again, without any persuasion, they return and become friends with them again."

This lightly equipped and uncontrollable race, burning with a fearful and determined desire of booty, from strangers, broke forth from the sea of Asov, whither they were driven much earlier from their ancient pastures on the frontiers of China, and fell first upon the *Alani*, thought by some to be an Asiatic tribe, by others again considered to be a branch of the Goths; but it is probably a collective name, by which the Romans signify the tribes eastward of the Goths on the Wolga and the Don, who may possibly have been of different races. The

* Amm. Marcell. xxi., 2; Dordanis, 24

Hunns are said to have sacrificed their first European prisoners to the manes of their ancient princes. This immense swarm then rushed onward upon the Goths. Hermanrich, a brave old warrior, upwards of a hundred years of age, and still suffering from a severe wound received in battle, when he saw he could not resist the Hunns, would not survive his formerly acquired fame, and therefore, in despair, killed himself. His people were obliged to subject themselves to the power of these savages, and the Thervingians considering resistance useless, quitted their ancient seats, and sent messengers to the emperor Valens, at Constantinople, with a petition: "that if he would give them land and pasturage beyond the Danube, they would be the defenders of the frontiers." As mediator for the Thervingians, it is very probable, that much was effected by the Gothic Bishop Ulphilas, who, in a persecution made against the Christians by the pagan Gothic princes, had, some time previously, together with several Gothic Christians, taken refuge, and been granted an asylum on Roman ground, at the foot of the Hœmus. This pious and patriotic prelate had, indeed, during a space of forty years, been continually occupied in working for the benefit of his people. The emperor received them kindly. They were not pursued by the Hunns, who now followed pasturage, hunting, and pillage, for more than fifty years in the steppes and forests of the present southern Russia, Poland, and Hungary, by which means they came into frequent intercourse with the Romans, whom they often served in war; and, humanized by this communication with the latter and the Germans, much of the uncouthness in their manners was removed.

The new seat of the Western Goths in Mæsia became very soon too narrow for them; and as their herds did not supply them with sufficient support, they begged permission to barter for their necessary wants. The Roman rulers, however, Lupicinus and Maximus, took such shameful advantage of their necessities, that for a loaf and about ten pounds of miserable meat, (frequently the flesh of dogs,) they demanded a slave in return. The majority of their herds were consumed, their slaves gone, and famine induced many to give up even their children for bread. While the people suffered from these grievances, Fridigern, the Gothic prince, was invited as a guest by Lupicinus to Marcianopolis. He was a valiant youth, full of the heroic courage of his ancestors; and on this occasion many young men, his brethren in arms and other friends, accompanied him. While he was eating, the cries of his followers outside rose suddenly upon his ear, for the Romans had fallen upon them and were murdering them. With his eyes sparkling with vengeance, and his sword in hand, he sprang up, and rushing out, saved his friends, and hastened away with them.* The Goths, embittered at the treachery of the Romans, broke up, defeated Lupicinus, and traversed the nearest provinces with fire and sword; and from the walls of Constantinople were seen the flames of the villages and country-seats which they had lighted.

The emperor Valens advanced against Fridigern with an army; the assistance which his nephew, Gratian, was bringing to his aid from the west, he would not wait for, in order to retain alone the honor of victory; and he precipitately ventured a battle near Adrianople. It was severely contested; but the Gothic infantry repulsed at last the Roman cavalry, and then the legions. The emperor fled wounded; his horse falling, he had scarcely time to save himself in a neighboring peasant's hut. The Goths, far from thinking that the Roman emperor was concealed beneath a thatched roof, set fire to this as well as other huts; and Valens found his death in this miserable manner in the year 378.

In this pitiable state the empire was once more warded from its fall by the vigorous and prudent emperor Theodosius, a Spaniard by birth. He contrived to weaken the Goths by divisions, and made Fridigern's successor, Athanaric, conclude a peace. He promised the Goths a considerable supply of provisions, and they, in return, lent him 40,000 men as auxiliaries.

This emperor died in the year 395, and his two sons, Honorius and Arcadius, divided the empire between them; Arcadius took his seat at Constantinople, Honorius in Italy, and the first division was called the *eastern*, and the second the *western* empire.

The sons did not resemble the father

* Amm. Marcell., xxxi 5, and Jordanis, 26.

too indolent to undertake the government themselves, they allowed their chancellors, the Gaul, *Rufinius*, and the Vandal, *Stilicho,* to rule. Rufinius, who was chancellor in Constantinople, corrupt and selfish, thought by war and daring adventures to exalt himself and increase his power; accordingly he excited the Goths under Alaric to make an irruption. The presents promised them by Theodosius were not delivered, and Alaric devastated Thracia throughout; and Stilicho advanced against him, but was driven back by the jealous Rufinius, who was murdered by the embittered army. Upon this, Alaric turned against Greece, then quite defenceless, which he robbed of its last treasures and glories. Suddenly, Stilicho attacked and pressed hard upon the Goths; but Arcadius ordered him to retire, negotiated with Alaric, and made him general of Illyria, that is—gave it up to him in 396. The Goths broke up from here in the year 402, and advanced across the Alps. Stilicho, nevertheless, once more succeeded, by a determined resistance, in forcing his dangerous enemy to retire beyond the boundary line of mountains. And in the same manner he saved Italy in the year 405 from the attack of a large mixed army of German tribes, which, under Radagaisus, endeavored to break across the Alps from a different side, and were perhaps in alliance with Alaric. The history of these times is very confused, and it is therefore not clear if that body was destroyed near Fœsulæ, as some historians relate, or whether Stilicho was enabled to remove them by treaty, and direct them to Gaul. But it appears that Stilicho also pursued ambitious projects; for he had combined with Alaric to make an attack upon the eastern empire, but was accused of treachery by his enemies, and by command of the emperor Honorius, his own son-in-law, he was assassinated in the year 408. As soon as Alaric heard of the death of Stilicho, he once more advanced against Italy, pressed through the passes of the Alps, crossed the Po, and went direct to Rome; he left the emperor in Ravenna, for he despised this weak prince. In Rome all was terror and confusion; for since 600 years the Romans had seen no enemy before, nor during 800 years had they beheld an enemy within their walls, thence the city was called the eternal city. They, nevertheless, once more gave voice to their ancient haughtiness, and thus addressed Alaric:* "The Roman people are numerous and strong, and by their constant practice in arms are so bold and courageous that they have no dread of war." But Alaric only laughed aloud at this, and replied: "Thickly standing grass is much easier mowed than thin." The ambassadors then asked the conditions of peace. He demanded all the gold and silver, together with the whole of the rich plate contained in the city, and all the slaves of German origin. On which they asked, "What will you then leave us?" "Your souls!" said he. Thus insolently spoke a man, born among a barbaric tribe, upon the island of Peuce, (at the mouth of the Danube,) to that city which, for centuries, had ruled the habitable earth, and through the gates and streets of which the proudest heroes had marched in triumph, crowned with victories gained over foreign nations, and loaded with booty from Europe, Asia, and Africa!

At this moment, certain prophets from Tuscany, who were in the city, offered themselves to drive Alaric back from Rome by prophetic threats, if, in return, they might be allowed to institute feasts and sacrifices to their ancient divinities. Doubtless, when he heard of such weak and futile proposals being made, the valorous Alaric treated the matter with merited contempt and derision.

When now the Romans discovered no hopes of being rescued, they were obliged to fulfil the wishes of their enemy, and promise him 5,000 pounds of gold and 30,000 of silver, besides a multiplicity of rare and costly articles. But so much gold and silver was not to be found in the possession of the inhabitants. They were, therefore, obliged to have recourse to the ornaments and decorations of the ancient temples; and it is said that, among the statues of their divinities, that of *Valor* was also melted down—it thus appearing as if all that still remained in Rome of that noble quality in man was now annihilated for ever.

The emperor Honorius refused to enter into any negotiation whatever with Alaric, who, therefore, returned next year to Rome, and appointed another emperor, of the name of Attalus, as rival to Honorius; but as,

* Zosimus, v., 34.

after one year's trial, he also proved himself to be wholly worthless, Alaric reduced him again to the dust from which he had raised him, and the city of Rome, which held out against him, he now took by storm. This happened on the 23d of August, in the year 410. The Goths entered the imperial palace and plundered it, as well as the houses of the nobles; but they so far moderated their ire, that they did not burn the city. It was a happy thing for the Romans that the Goths were Christians; for those who fled to the churches were not molested or touched; nay, a singular occurrence, which is related to us, displays very evidently the pious feeling of these people. A warrior, who entered the house of a female, found gold and silver vessels there. She told him that they belonged to the holy apostle St. Peter, and were given to her in charge for the church; he might, therefore, act as he thought proper. The soldier communicated this to Alaric, who sent immediately thither, and caused the sacred vessels to be carried with solemnity back to the church. The Romans, animated by such generous tolerance, accompanied the train, chanting solemn hymns; and the Gothic warriors, astonished at the unexpected spectacle, ceased to plunder, joined the procession themselves, and thus was the fury of war transformed into genial peace by mere Christian emotion.

Alaric remained only a few days in Rome; he then advanced towards Lower Italy, indulging his imagination with magnificent plans, for, as it appears, he purposed embarking for the beautiful island of Sicily, and thence to proceed to Africa, in order to conquer likewise this granary of Italy. But death overtook him at Cosenza, in his 34th year. The entire Westro-Gothic nation bewailed his loss, and prepared a remarkable and memorable grave for him. They dug another bed for the river Busento, conducting the water through it, and then buried their king, fully armed and equipped, in the original bed of the river, accompanied by his war-horse and the trophies of his victories. They then conducted the course of the river back again, in order that neither Roman covetousness nor revenge should desecrate or disturb the great Alaric, in the grave where he reposed from his victories. Upon his death, the Goths elected for their king the most handsome of their young nobles, the youth *Athaulf*, or *Adolphus*, the brother-in-law of Alaric. He advanced from Lower Italy to Rome, where he obliged the emperor Honorius to give him his own sister, Placidia, as consort; he then quitted Italy, passed with his nation into Gaul and Spain, and he and his successor, *Wallia*, were the founders of the extensive Westro-Gothic kingdom, which comprised the south of France as far as the Loire, and speedily embraced Spain also, the metropolis of which was Toulouse, on the river Garonne. In the year 419, the Romans formally delivered Southern Gaul up to Wallia. The commencement of the fifth century was therefore in the highest degree turbulent, from the violent movements of the various nations. Almost all the German tribes sent out hordes of troops upon excursions of pillage or conquest; or they themselves, pressed forward by the superior attacks of other tribes, broke up their abode, that they might, arms in hand, seek elsewhere for new dwellings. The weak alone, who could or would not quit their paternal dwelling, remained behind, and became mingled with and lost amidst the immediately succeeding race. Besides the Goths, the Vandals and Alans were pressed forward by the Hunns, and advanced from the east gradually towards the west. In their advance, the Burgundians, who likewise had quitted their dwelling-place on the Vistula and had arrived as far as the Upper Danube, with a portion of the Suevi, namely, the Quadi, and other tribes joined them. It was probably a swarm of these mixed tribes which, under Radagaisus, or Radigast, made the attack upon Italy in the year 405, and which by great good fortune was warded off by Stilicho. This isolated horde disappears, as well as the name of its leader, without leaving a trace in history. But in their attacks upon Gaul and Spain the before-mentioned tribes were more fortunate. Stilicho had opened to them the road thither, by withdrawing the legions from the Rhine and from Gaul for the defence of Italy. They now desolated the country from Strasburg to Amiens. Treves was four times plundered, Mentz and Worms destroyed, the inhabitants of Strasburg, Spires, Rheims, and other cities driven forth as slaves. After these swarms had at last been driven back into the south of France by the Romans and the Franks, they, in the year 408, were called into

Spain by the rebellious Roman governor, Gervatius. Hitherto this country had been spared during these fearful times, but its turn came at last. The Vandals, Alani, and Suevi, crossed the Pyrenees, and speedily conquered the greatest part of the country. A portion of the Alani remained in Gaul, and are found later on the side of the Romans, in the great battle with Attila; after which they disappear. The Burgundians also remained under their king, Gundikar, (Günther,) and first founded their kingdom in Alsace, where it speedily extended towards the Rhone and Saone into Switzerland, and from thence it spread to Savoy. In Northern Gaul, however, the Franks appear about this time to have made themselves masters, so that all that lies towards the north, from Boulogne on one side, to Cologne on the other, was subject to their sway. Before the middle of that century Treves also, which they had four times conquered, remained in their power.

The Vandals, who with the Alani had taken their seat in the south of Spain, passed thence in the year 420, under their king, Geiserich or Genserich, upon the invitation of the discontented Roman governor, Bonifacius, over into Africa, and conquering there the whole of the northern coast, founded for a century a flourishing kingdom, the chief city of which was Carthage. What a migration, from the very shores of the Baltic, where these tribes first appear in history, even to the borders of the African deserts! Geiserich, one of the great men of his age, but of a savage disposition, ruled for 50 years, from 428–477. After him the kingdom of the Vandals fell, in the luxuriant climate of the country, produced by internal disturbances, and by the enervation of this otherwise powerful tribe. The emperor of Constantinople, Justinian, took advantage of their reduced state, and in the year 553 sent his general, Belisarius, to Africa with an army, who overcame them in eight months. Their last king, Gelimer, was led by him in chains on his triumphant entry into Constantinople.

The Suevi remained in Spain, but became, by degrees, more and more pressed upon by the Westro-Goths under Wallia and his successors, being soon limited to the northwestern portion of Spain and Portugal; and at last, in the year 585, they were entirely united with the Westro-Gothic kingdom.

In the middle of the fifth century, 449, the Angeli, Saxons and Futi, passed over into England, and there founded new dynasties. Under the emperor Honorius, and immediately after him, the Romans had entirely quitted Britain. The Britons had, however, become so enervated under their sway, that after the withdrawal of the Roman garrisons, they felt themselves incompetent to protect their freedom. Their neighbors in the Scotch Highlands, the warlike Picts and Scots, breaking forth from their mountains with undiminished power, pressed hard upon them; and they found no other alternative but to call strangers once more to their defence. Their choice fell upon the tribes of Saxon origin who inhabited the coasts of the North Sea, and whose valor they had often had occasion to know when these fell in with their piratic squadrons on the coasts of Britain. Two Saxon brothers, Hengist and Horst, or Horsa, heroes of a noble race, who derived their origin from Wodan, accepted the invitation of the British king, Vortigern, and with only three ships, which bore 1600 warriors, they landed. Their valor alone supplied the place of numbers; they beat the Picts near Stamford, and speedily afterwards large troops of their countrymen followed them over from the continent. The Britons then would willingly have been freed of their new guests; they, however, preferred remaining, subjected the whole of England as far as Wales, and founded the well-known Anglo-Saxon kingdoms or heptarchy, of which Kent, established by Hengist, formed the first.

In a large village, seated in a plain between the Danube and the Theiss, in Hungary, and surrounded by palisades, which had originated in a camp, there stood, in the midst of a spacious court, an extensive wooden mansion, adorned with many passages and halls, and which formed the dwelling of Attila or Etzel, king of the Hunns. He had united his people—until then dispersed under many leaders—under his own dominion; and in effecting this, had not hesitated even to slay his own brother, Bleda. All the tribes of the Hunns and their subjected nations, distributed from the Wolga to Hungary, reverenced his command. He was lord of the Gepidi,

Longobardi, Avari, Ostro-Goths, and many nations in the south of Germany; they, however, retained their languages, their customs, and their laws, and were ruled by their own princes; so that they were to be considered more as allies than subjects; and besides the language of the Hunns, that of the Goths, or German, was spoken at the court of Attila.

He himself was small of stature, had a large head, deeply-seated eyes, which he proudly cast around, a broad chest, much animation, and a manner and bearing which thoroughly displayed the ruler. His most favorite name, indeed, was Godegiesel, the scourge of God, for the punishment of the world.

But as it may be assumed generally with regard to rulers, the founders of mighty empires, that they have not alone to thank their conquering swords for their acquired power, so also on his part King Attila gave undoubted proofs that for governing he possessed capacities more mild and intellectual than the mere rude courage and skill of a warrior. For if he was terrible towards his enemies, and in his wrath severe and exterminating, still, on the other hand, he was gentle and kind to those he took under his protection. And if in war he himself always led on his people to battle, he was nevertheless, in times of peace, always to be found seated at their head before his palace gates, performing the office of mediator and judge between each and all who came to him, without distinction.

He loved splendor around him, but he himself lived in a simple and plain style, as if his greatness did not require this foil. The trappings of his horse were unadorned, and but little costly; at his banquets, gold and silver vessels were placed before his guests, while he alone had those of wood; he ate but little meat, despising, according to the custom of his nation, even bread. After each dish was served, the cup or wassail-bowl was handed round, and his health and prosperity drunk; while minstrels sang heroic songs in praise of his valorous deeds. The court jester then followed with his wit and fun, and hilarity and merriment ruled at the board of the royal host; but he alone never intermitted his strict seriousness. He remained throughout grave and thoughtful; and it was only when his youngest son, Irnack, entered the hall and approached him, that his features relaxed into a smile, and whom he greeted with affection; for of this son it had been prophesied, that he alone would be the means of preserving the succession of the race of Attila.*

This powerful ruler, of whom it has been said that, when with his mysterious sword—which had been found by a shepherd in the steppes of Scythia, and was considered to be the sword of the god of war—he struck the earth, a hundred nations trembled, and even Rome and Constantinople shook to their foundations, arose with his army in the year 451, and turned his course towards the west. He advanced with 700,000 men, all under him as chief ruler, and every tribe under its particular prince; and although the princes themselves trembled before him, his whole army had but one soul, and his nod alone directed every movement. His path was called destruction; for what could not fly, or was not destroyed, as he progressed in his road, was forced to follow in his train.

He advanced through Austria and the Allemannic country, across the Rhine, overcame the Burgundian king, Gundikar, (Günther,) even to the destruction of his whole tribe; conquered and plundered the cities of Strasburg, Spire, Worms, Mentz, Treves, and others, and vowed not to stop until he reached the ocean itself. The military portions of the countries he traversed joined him either spontaneously or by force, and the gigantic horde increased at every step like an avalanche.

But the Romans and several German nations had now armed themselves against the great danger which threatened the west; for it was now to be decided whether Europe should be German or Mongolian, whether German races were to found new kingdoms upon the tottering ruins of the Roman empire, or the great king of the Hunns. The Romans had at this time once again a good leader of the name of Ætius, who had formerly, when banished by Valentinian, sought refuge at the court of Attila; he collected an army in Gaul, and applied for aid to the Westro-Gothic king, Theodoric or Dieterich, who

* This description of Attila and his court is handed down to us by an eye-witness, the sophist, *Priscus*, who attended in the suite of an embassy from the emperor Theodosius II. at the court of Attila: Byzant. Hist. Script. i. Jordanis also describes Attila, cap. xxxv.—Both relate also about the sword of Mars

dwelt in Toulouse, and whose kingdom also was in great danger. To him Dieterich replied, although, in earlier times, Ætius had been his enemy: "A just war has never appeared to fall too heavy upon any king of the Westro-Goths; and never has any such king been known to fear when it depended upon a glorious deed. Even thus think the nobles of my kingdom also; and the entire nation of the Westro-Goths will, at the call, cheerfully seize their well-tried arms, at all times victorious." The Burgundians had also promised assistance, besides Sangipan, the Alanian, who ruled upon the Loire; a portion of the Franks also, together with the city of Paris itself, and even a branch of the Saxons, which had colonized, it is unknown at what period, at the mouths of the Loire, or perhaps had landed there direct from a maritime expedition—all these united together for the same purpose.

In the broad plain of France, through which the Marne flows, and which was called by the ancients the Catalaunian Plain, where the city of Chalons now lies, there rises near Mury, in the vicinity of Troyes, a moderately high hill, which commands the district. It was here that the army of the West met the forces of the Hunns, and a severe battle was fought. It may be called a battle of the nations, for the majority of the European nations stood here opposed to each other. The left wing of the Roman army was commanded by Ætius, the right by Theodoric; between them they posted king Sangipan, who was the least to be trusted. The hordes of the Hunns, on the opposite side, appeared innumerable; one wing was commanded by Arderic, the king of the Gepidi; the others by Theudimer, Widemir, and Walamir, the princes of the Ostro-Goths. Attila was in the centre of the whole. The multitude of petty kings obeyed his least nod, and they fulfilled his commands in silence and terror; he alone, the chief of all these kings, thought and acted for all. When the battle was about to begin, he summoned his leaders before him, and said, "It does not become me to say common-place things to you, or for you to listen to such. Be men; attack, break through, cast all down; despise the Roman array and their shields. Fall upon the Western Goths and Alani, in whom lies the strength of the enemy. If you must die, you will die even when you flee. Direct your eyes to me, for I shall go first; he who does not follow—shall be a corpse!"

Both armies strove to obtain the hill; the battle was very furious, and there was terrible slaughter. The Hunns soon broke through the centre, where the Romans were stationed, and whom they put to flight; and soon afterwards the Westro-Goths gave way before the Ostro-Goths. While the Westro-Gothic king was addressing his people he fell, but gloriously, for his death inflamed his nation to revenge it; and his son Thorismund leading them on, put the enemy to flight, and thus decided the battle. Upon the approach of night, Attila was obliged to retire within his camp of wagons. As he did not know but the enemy might pursue him, he caused innumerable saddles and wooden shields to be piled up, in case of necessity to set fire to them and die in the flames; at the same time, to terrify the enemy, he commanded a noise to be made all night with arms, drums, trumpets, and songs; but they did not attack him. Among the piled heaps of the slain, they sought the body of the Westro-Gothic king, and celebrated his funeral by a procession, amid laments and warlike instruments sounding, taking with them the spoils of the Hunns in their very presence, who however did not venture to interrupt the ceremony. Thorismund followed the body of his father, and wished to return and renew the attack; but he was dissuaded from this by Ætius, who advised him to return to his kingdom, that his brother might not take first possession of the crown. He was anxious not to destroy the power of the Hunns completely, in order, perhaps, to be enabled to use it subsequently against the Goths.

In the following year, Attila, who was thus enabled to recross the Rhine unpursued, made a second incursion into Italy, and destroyed in a terrible manner Aquileja, Milan,* and other cities. Rome itself was alone saved from a similar fate by the supplications of Pope Leo, and the rich ransom he offered to him. Want of supplies, and disease among his army, forced

* Sucibius relates that, at this place, Attila met with a picture, in which were represented some Scythian men kneeling before the Roman emperor; and that there, opposite to it, he had his own figure painted, seated upon the imperial throne, and at his feet the Roman emperors, throwing down before him bags of gold.

him to retreat across the Alps; he nevertheless threatened to return again, and had already prepared another expedition, but amidst his preparations he died, in the year 453. He was mourned over, and buried according to the customs of his people. The Hunns slashed their faces with wounds, and shaved away their hair, and upon a broad plain, beneath a silken tent, his body lay in state. About it coursed the cavalry, singing his deeds as they galloped around, and vaunting the good fortune, that the great Attila, after immortal victories, in the most glorious moment of his nation's history, and without pain, had closed his life, and had transferred himself to the spirits of the ancient heroes. In the night he was laid in a golden coffin; this was placed in a silver one, which was enclosed in an iron one; the caparison of his horses, his arms, and costly ornaments being buried with him. After the ceremony, the workmen were immediately slaughtered on his grave, that none of them might betray where the hero of the Hunns reposed.*

As soon as the terror of his name no longer bound the nations together, they separated; many refused obedience; and after his first-born son, Ellak, had fallen in a great battle against Arderic, the king of the Gepidi, the whole power of the Hunns disappeared, and they dispersed further towards the east. The head of one of the sons of Attila—such are the changes in human fate—was shortly afterwards seen held up for display, at one of the race-courses in Constantinople! Arderic occupied the country of the Lower Danube, and the Ostro-Goths took possession of Hungary, towards Vienna. The remaining portion of the German tribes who had been subject to the power of the Hunns, no doubt likewise took advantage of this moment of renewed independence, to return to their old, or to take possession of new dwelling-places. This period may therefore be considered as decisive of the form of the immediate future, until the entire destruction of the Roman power in Italy produced new revolutions for a portion of Europe.

The Western Roman Empire now consisting of Italy alone, declined more and more towards its utter extinction. The wretched emperor, Valentinian III., murdered with his own hand Ætius, who had been the support of the empire, and who had once more saved it in the Catalaunian plains, against Attila, because he had been made to suspect him. Valentinian himself was slain, at the instigation of Petronius Maximus, who now became emperor, and forced Eudocia, the widow of the murdered monarch, to marry him. She however, out of revenge, invited the Vandal king, Geiserich, from Africa. He came, conquered in 455 the city of Rome, plundered and devastated it in a dreadful manner for the space of fourteen days, as if, by him, Fate retaliated upon the Romans, for their terrible destruction of Carthage six hundred years before. He then embarked again for Africa, with a fleet of many ships, loaded with costly booty and prisoners of all classes, who were sold as slaves.

After Valentinian, nine sovereigns, in the short space of twenty years, bore the degraded title of Emperor of Rome. At last, in the year 476, Odoacer, a prince of Scyric descent, commander of an allied horde of Scyri, Herulians, Rugians, and Turcilingi, a man equally distinguished for his mental powers and physical strength, thrust the last of those shadowy emperors, Romulus Momyllus or Augustulus, as yet a boy, from the throne, and called himself King of Italy. The tender age of the young emperor when he laid aside the purple robes, the crown and arms, and came and deposited them in the camp, caused him to be spared, and he was sent by Odoacer to a castle in Campania. The above-named tribes, who doubtlessly belonged to the Gothic confederation, had gradually advanced from their earlier dwellings on the Baltic towards the south, until they found a dwelling on the Danube and the frontiers of Italy, and there served the Romans frequently for pay. This small band, therefore, at last extinguished the Roman empire, in the year 476, and in the 1230th year since the foundation of the capital.

About this period the following was the manner in which the countries of the western empire were divided among foreign tribes, the result of the great migration which had taken place a century before.

Italy was under the dominion of Odoa-

* The name of Attila, or Etzel, was afterwards mentioned in the German legends; he was there grouped with Hermanarich and the subsequent Theodoric, (Dieterich, of Berne.) He does not, however, appear there as an enemy to the Germans, but as a mighty valiant ruler in the east of Germany.

cer, and his kingdom extended itself towards the north, across the Alps, as far as the Danube. In Hungary the Ostro-Goths were powerful, and the Longobardi had long before advanced from their seats upon the Elbe, and fixed themselves to the north of the Danube, towards the Theiss. In Bavaria was formed by degrees, (without history giving a detailed account of it,) from remnants of the Rugi, Heruli, Scyri, Turcilingi, and certainly from Suevic tribes, particularly the Marcomanni—the nation of Bojoarians under the royal race of the Agilolfi. The name more particularly indicates the descent from the Marcomanni, coming from Bohemia, inasmuch as the more ancient name of this country, Boja or Bojos, has been transferred to Bojoheim, Baiheim, or Beheim. The Marcomanni, who had previously wandered back to this country, after the Danube districts had become free, fixed themselves in Franconia and Bavaria, and called themselves Bojoari or Bajovari.

The Allemanni dwelt in the eastern part of Switzerland, in Swabia, and down both banks of the Rhine, as far as the Lahn and Cologne. On the left bank of the Rhine they were afterwards called Alsatians. The name of Suevi also appears about this time among them, and has preserved itself to this day in the name of the country—Swabia.

In the centre of Germany, from the present Harz mountains to Franconia, the powerful Thuringians held their sway, whose earlier history is very obscure. They first appear noticed about the middle of the fifth century, without our author mentioning their origin or earlier state.

In Lower Saxony and Westphalia the Saxons retained their ancient seats and constitution, and close to them on the North Sea were the Friesi.

On the Lower Rhine, on the Maas and the Scheldt, as far as the Netherlands, and in the north of France, dwelt the branches of the Franks; the most considerable of which were the Salians, in the Netherlands, and the Ripuarians, dwelling along the coasts of the Rhine.

Close to them, on the Seine, a Roman governor, of the name of Syagrius, maintained his power for ten years longer, until the year 486, when already there was no longer an emperor in Rome. The northwestern point of France, the present Brittany, had already been occupied much earlier by fugitives from Britain, who had fled before the Picts, and then formed under the name of Armoricæ an alliance of free cities.

Southeastern France, Savoy, and western Switzerland belonged now to the Burgundians. Their chief cities were Geneva, Besançon, Lyons, and Vienne. The Burgundians were certainly the mildest of the conquering tribes of this period, being early attached to Christianity, cultivation, and art; and to them that portion of Franco is indebted for its many remains of ancient Roman works of art. In Switzerland the French language still marks its ancient boundaries against the Allemanni, for the Burgundians mixed more with the Romans, and adopted much of their language.

Southwestern France, from the Loire and Rhone to the Pyrenees, as well as a great portion of Spain, was subject to the Western Goths, but northwestern Spain to the Suevi.

The northwestern coast of Africa was Vandalian. In Britain the Angeli and Saxons by degrees retained their power and augmented it more and more.

The east and northeastern portion of Germany was left comparatively bare by the advance of the tribes towards the south and west, and Slavonic tribes migrated increasingly thither, who had been seated on those boundaries from time immemorial, and who had also, perhaps, been partly subject to the Germans. Those foreign branches now gained the superiority, and the remains of the Germans who would not quit their original dwelling-place, became subject to, and were dispersed among them.

# SECOND PERIOD.

## FROM THE CONQUESTS OF CLOVIS TO CHARLEMAGNE.

### 486—768.

The historical writers of this period form but a very limited class, and are of very unequal estimation. What they relate of the earlier times is mostly founded on tradition, and can scarcely be placed in conjunction with what has been furnished by the Roman authors: still, in reference to the history of their own period, and those immediately preceding, they are nevertheless of high importance:

1. For the "History of the Franks," we may consider as a principal writer, Gregory, bishop of Tours, (Gregorius Turonensis,) who died in the year 595. He calls his book an ecclesiastical history, but therein he describes generally the acts and proceedings of the Franks, in ten books, until the year 591. His language, characteristic of his time, is uncivilized, his description confused and interrupted by legendary wonders, going, however, very deeply into the details, and in reference to subsequent years, as the record of a contemporary, it is very exact, and thus renders him equally instructive; he likewise possesses the merit of being honest and a lover of truth. He has been styled the Herodotus of this period.

Fredegar, about the year 650, made from Gregory's work a short abridgment, interspersed with fables, ("Historia Francorum Epitomata,") which proceeds as far as the year 584, and then continues the history in a "Chronicum" until 641. This "Chronicum" was again taken up and resumed by three other men, but with certain chasms, until 768; very meager and without connection, but still important, because the writers were chiefly witnesses of the events described. The "Gesta Regum Francorum," are, likewise, in part extracted from Gregory, whose description they continue to the year 720, very briefly and not without many inaccuracies.

With these and later, are the "Annals," short sketches which were made annually in the monasteries, of the most important events, and thus, at least, in part originate from eye-witnesses. They were afterwards copied and communicated from the one monastery to the other, often augmented there, then subsequently various portions corrected and prepared, and thus they acquired greater extent and value. The most important are those which bear the simple title "Annalis Laurissenses," from a monastery in the Upper Rhine province, which go on from 741 to 788, and were continued by Eginhardt, from 788 to 829. They have been partially published in the older collections, but more completely given in the "Monumenta Germaniæ Historica," collected by Pertz.

2. For the "History of the Goths" are to be mentioned:

a. *Cassiodorus*, invested with high offices of state, under Odoacer, Theodoric, and their successors, and who died in the year 565, in the convent Vivarosa; he wrote a history of the Goths, which, unfortunately, was lost. There have, however, been preserved his "XII Libri Variarum," a very important work, because it contains edicts, instructions, and documents, which were written in the names of the kings; learned, elegant, but vain and verbose.

b. The monk *Jordanis*, (thus he is called, and not Jornandes, in the more ancient documents, and by himself likewise,) a Goth, living about the middle of the sixth century, has brought into an abridgment—de Rebus Geticis—the lost history of Cassiodorus, but has disfigured it by the interlineation of every thing he knew or heard of besides. Still, although without judgment and historical knowledge, his book is of the highest value, inasmuch as for many events that is nearly our only source. It extends to the year 540.

• The parallel of "Procopii Cæsarensis Vandalica et Gothica" may in the details explain much, because the Greek proceeds upon very different views to those of the western writers.

d. *Isidor*, bishop of Seville, (Isidorus Hispalensis,) who died in 636, wrote a short history of the Goths, Vandals, and Suevians, to the year 628, but which again explains nothing about the earlier history of these nations, and refers more properly to Spain alone.

3. The chief writer on the history of the Longobardi is *Paul Diaconus*, the son of Warnefried, one of the first men of his age, living at the courts of Desiderius and Charlemagne, and who died as a monk on Mount Cassino in the year 799. In his "De Gestis Langobardorum, libri vi.," he describes the deeds of his nation with a great predilection for tradition; the commencement is quite unhistorical, but subsequently he becomes more careful and exact, and presents us with detailed information extremely valuable.

4. For German history likewise are of great importance the biographies of the Roman Pontiffs, at least from the eighth century, composed by contemporary writers; they continue to the beginning of the ninth century.

5. Extremely important also are the letters of distinguished men which have been handed down to us from that period, especially those of Saint Boniface, as well as the biographies of him and other holy men, (Vitæ Sanctorum,) which often present the most faithful picture of their times, and have preserved for us the most valuable information.

6. And lastly; for our research into the relations of life, the manners, customs, and institutions, are very important, the "Laws of the German nations or tribes," who belonged to the Franconian empire: the Salians, Ripuarians, Allemannians, Burgundians, and Bavarians, and later, the Saxons and Thuringians. But there remains much therein which is very obscure, inasmuch as they contain principally only the penal law of these people, and cannot, therefore, yield us the desired information respecting the other relations, are not regulated according to general principles, contain nothing of the constitution of the empire beyond what refers to the administration of the law, and present even in that portion what to our eye appears very fragmentary.

## CHAPTER IV.

Clovis, king of the Franks, 482-511—Theodoric, surnamed Dieterich of Berne, 488-526—The Longobardi in Italy, 568—Changes in the Customs and Institutions of the Germans—The Language—Constitution—Feudal System—Laws—Pastimes—Christianity in Germany—The Grand Chamberlains—Charles Martel against the Arabs, 732—Pepin the Little—The Carlovingians.

During the great movements of the tribes, which we have just related, the Franks had not, like the Goths, Burgundians, and other nations, migrated from their dwellings to settle themselves elsewhere, but they remained in their own seat, and from thence conquered only that poition of Gaul which lies to the north of the Forest of Ardennes. And this forest also sheltered them from being drawn into the great stream of migration. Their division also into several branches, each of which had its own king or prince, prevented them from making extensive and general expeditions.

But their time came. About the year 482, Clovis, or as we should say, Lewis, the son of Gilderich, became prince of the Salian Franks; and he soon prepared himself to execute the plans of his bold and comprehensive mind, for the bent of his ardent spirit was to make war and conquest. Clovis belongs to that class of rulers in the history of the world, who think all ways good that lead to dominion. He has sullied the celebrity of his military fame by the most despicable want of faith to his relatives and allies. He at first concluded with the princes of the Franks, who were his equals, and for the majority his relatives, alliances of war against other tribes, and after he had conquered them by their assistance, and had become powerful, he then also dispatched those very friends out of his way by poison, the dagger, and treachery. By this means he became eventually king of all the Franks.

Of his foreign enemies, he first attacked, when only twenty, the Roman governor Syagrius, whom we mentioned above, effectually beat him at Soissons, (Suessiones,) and occupied the country as far as the Loire. Syagrius, who fled to the Western Goths, was obliged to be delivered up to Clovis and was executed. This commencement of the conquests of Clovis took place in the year 486, ten years after Romulus Augustulus was deposed.

He then advanced with his army against the Allemanni, who in the mean time had fallen upon the country of the Ripuarian Franks, for both nations having their boundaries upon the river Lahn, had been enemies for years. They met in the year 496, near Zulpich, in the district of Juliers, and fought bitterly against each other, and the victory already inclined to the side of the Allemanni, when in the heat of the battle, his soul excited by anxiety, Clovis fell upon his knees and vowed to become a Christian; and as victory now absolutely turned on his side, he caused himself and three thousand of his Franks to be baptized in Rheims, at the subsequent Easter festival, by the Bishop Remigius. This was the commencement of the introduction of the Christian faith among the Franks, and Clovis was henceforward called the eldest son of the church and the most Christian king. His consort Clotilda, the daughter of a Burgundian prince, had long wished to convert him to the better faith by the force of gentle persuasion; he, however, had always despised it until the necessity of the battle overpowered him, and it was indeed very evident both in him and in the Franks in general, that their conversion was a work of mere compulsion. For Clovis murdered his relatives *after* as well as *before*, and subdued one Christian nation after the other, while the Franks for several centuries bore the character of being the most treacherous of all the German nations.

After the Allemanni were reduced, and the kingdom of the Franks had spread itself along the Rhine to Switzerland, and after the Burgundians were obliged to promise tribute, Clovis bent his eyes towards the kingdom of the West Goths, who possessed the most beautiful portion of France in the south. Thus, although he had only shortly before had a conference with their king, Alaric, and had sworn friendship to him, he yet determined to attack him as an enemy.

The wise Ostro-Gothic king, Theodoric, who previously to this had founded his dominion in Italy, counselled the unruly Clovis, whose sister, Audofleda, was his consort, in the most urgent manner from his unjust expedition against Alaric, and reminded him that peace and union became Christian nations. But Clovis, who knew only the language of the sword and of rude force, gave no ear to him; he attacked the Westro-Gothic kingdom; and, in the year 507, in a plain of the river Vienne, near Vouglé or Vironne, fought and won a great battle in which Alaric himself fell, transpierced by the spear of Clovis, who took possession of the chief cities of his country, and would, no doubt, have destroyed the whole kingdom, had not the great Theodoric stepped between and driven him back with a strong hand. He was, therefore, obliged to content himself with the country between the Loire and the Garonne.

Clovis did not live long after this, but died at Paris, in the year 511, in the forty third year of his age, and his empire was divided between his four sons.

His successors to the throne of the Franks, who are called the Merovingians, were in general worthy of their founder. It appeared as if vice and tyranny, unheard of cruelty, and savage revenge were hereditary in this family, and as if a curse had from the beginning been poured over them. In the space of forty years six Merovingian kings were destroyed by poison or the sword; and the intrigues and revengeful passions of malicious women form an important feature in these horrid scenes. It cannot, therefore, suit the purport of this history to penetrate further into the details of these events, which are equally as unnourishing to the mind, as they are unfruitful in regard to the knowledge it is so desirable to obtain from the great entirety of our history. The nation of the Franks, under such princes, could not possibly be raised from its state of moral rudeness and degradation, but necessarily became plunged more deeply in vice. Their power, however, continued to extend itself more and more. They by degrees subjected the Burgundians, and in Germany the powerful nation of the Thuringians, and the dukes of Bavaria sought their protection. About the middle of the sixth century all the German nations from the frontiers of the Saxons to the Alps allied themselves with the kingdom of the Franks; Franks, Thuringians, Allemans or Swabians, and Bavarians. The Saxons alone and the Friesi still remained independent in their northwestern dwellings.

When, after king Attila's death, the kingdom of the Hunns fell asunder, the Ostro-Goths, as has been already mentioned, became again free, and dwelt in Hungary and the neighboring countries of the Danube. They had frequent disputes with the emperor, in Constantinople, and upon one of these occasions Theodoric or Dieterich, a son of one of their princes, was sent as hostage to that city, and there he saw, as had Marbodius and Arminius formerly, in Rome, the institutions of a great empire. He remained there ten years, and was instructed in the Grecian arts and sciences, so that no German prince of his time equalled him in accomplishments. After the death of his father, Theodemir, and of his uncles, he became sole king of the Ostro-Goths, and now resolved, like other rulers, to found for his people a large and beautiful kingdom, for they longed to be led to more desirable lands than the wastes near the Sau and the Danube. The Emperor of Constantinople, Zeno, who considered himself now as the sole inheritor of the entire ancient empire of the Romans, upon this presented him with the land of Italy as the reward for services rendered, and instead of his promised subsidies in money. Italy was still under the rule of Odoacer, but his kingdom was not properly to be considered German, because the Herulians and Rugians formed but a small portion of his people.

Theodoric broke up with his nation in the year 488, pressed through the passes of Italy, and encountered Odoacer near Aquileja and Verona. But the Italians fought with little zeal for their king, and he was both times obliged to fly. King Theodoric, from this last battle, was styled in legendary songs and ballads, in a multitude of which his fame was recorded, the great hero, *Dieterich of Berne*, (which signifies Verona.) Immediately after this, Odoacer was a third time defeated near the Adda, after his own city, Rome, had shut its gates against him, and for three years he was besieged in Ravenna, until, in the year 493, he was at last forced to yield, and his lands fell into the hands of Theodoric, by whom he was killed. His kingdom had lasted seventeen years. Theodoric became lord of Italy, and ruler over the countries beyond the Alps to the Danube, and in the wars of the Franks and Westro-Goths he made himself master of the provinces as far as the Rhone, an extensive and beautiful kingdom, which might have existed to the present day if his successors had equalled him in wisdom and virtue. His chief cities were Ravenna and Verona.

He himself reigned more than thirty years, and was not only a kind and mild master to his Goths, but also a gentle ruler over his Roman subjects and all who dwelt in Italy; so much so, that this country had not enjoyed so happy a time for many centuries as under him, the foreign prince. Agriculture and trade again flourished. Art and science found in him a protector, and ancient cities, lying in ruins, were rebuilt. Italy enjoyed under, and subsequent to his reign, for a period of forty years, continued peace, and was so diligently cultivated, that it not only grew sufficient grain for its own consumption, but could even export it to Gaul, while formerly, under the Roman emperors, it was always necessary to procure a supply from Sicily and Africa.

His wisdom and justice raised him above all the kings of his time. He stepped among them like the father of a large family and an institutor of peace; and the most distant tribes had recourse to his counsel, and honored him with presents. To the other kings of German origin, with almost all of whom he had allied himself by marriage, he wrote as a father, thus: "You all possess proofs of my good-will. You are young heroes, and it is my duty to counsel you. Your disorder and irregularities grieve me; it is not a matter of indifference to me to behold how you allow yourselves to be governed by your passions, for the passions of kings are the ruin of nations; while, on the contrary, your friendship and unity together are, as it were, the veins through which the wishes of nations flow into each other."

He placed such principles before their eyes, and showed thereby that his mind had formed the conception of a great alliance, founded upon justice and wisdom, between all the Christian nations of German origin, who had fixed their seat in Europe. An alliance, such as reason has depicted before the eyes of all ages as a ublime picture; and as it has displayed tself, from time to time, by the mouths of enlightened men, so that justice and order, and especially the spirit of Christian unity, should predominate, and hatred and thirst after prey be reined in—evils which, alas! through the want of such an alliance, have ravaged Europe from one end to the other. Had Theodoric been enabled to form such a noble union, he would have founded more of that which is truly grand than the ancient Romans, over whose possessions he had now become ruler, and whose empire he was anxious to restore, not by the rude force of arms, but in the form of a peaceful alliance of nations. But as the mild force of truth and justice always finds its enemy in the selfishness of those who only seek their own advantage and the indulgence of their passions, Theodoric consequently experienced that the world was not then yet rife enough for the fruction of his great ideas; for while he preached peace with earnestness and love, Clovis, the Frank, raged war with his sword, despising his doctrine, and seeking only tc bring a multitude of tribes under his dominion.

The great Theodoric died in the year 526. His monarchy had now no duration; for his son, Athalaric, was but just ten years old, and died shortly after his father. The nobles of his kingdom were no longer unanimous, but elevated and deposed several kings after each other. The Roman subjects, also, could not forget that their rulers were Goths, and attached to the Arian faith. They wished themselves again under the Greek emperors, who dwelt in Constantinople, and were members of the orthodox church, although the dominion of these emperors had become lamentably bad, and was in a ruinous state. It was then that the emperor Justinian, who was one of the best of the series, took advantage of this discontent, and sent his general, Belisarius, and after him Narses, into Italy, to subject this country again to his rule. A long and severe war arose, conducted by the Goths with their usual valor, but without success, and which destroyed the country, and almost depopulated Rome by several sieges, so that no trace was left of its ancient splendor.

The Goths raised themselves once more, after four of their sovereigns had been destroyed, under their king, Totilas, who was worthy of ruling the dominions of Theodoric; but as he also, after he had fought with fame for eleven years, was killed in the year 552, in a battle against Narses, and ten months afterwards, his successor, Tejas, fell likewise in the three days' desperate battle near Cuma, the Gothic kingdom sunk into such a ruinous state that twenty-seven years after the death of Theodoric, and in the year 553, the Ostro-Goths were not only vanquished, but also almost entirely annihilated. A few only escaped over the Alps to seek an asylum among other German nations.

Fifteen years after the fall of the Ostro-Goths, another valiant German nation, the Longobardi, who had taken possession of the earlier dwelling-places of the former on the Danube, executed an act of retaliation, justly timed for them, on the Greeks. The Greek general, Narses, upon falling under the displeasure of the emperor Justinian, had himself called forward their king, Alboni or Albwin, who had already overcome the Gepidi, and now ruled in Hungary, Austria, Carruthia, and even in a portion of Bavaria. This king possessed that heroic courage which graves itself deeply in the hearts of nations. Not only his own nation, but those of the Saxons and Bavarians sang his praise for centuries after his death.

On the second day of April, in the year 568, the king Alboni broke up from Hungary with all his Longobardian men, their women and children, accompanied by 20,000 Saxons. The country they hitherto possessed was left by them to their allies, the Avari, who were found still there by Charlemagne subsequently. It was a morning full of splendor when, from the heights of one of the advanced mountains of the Alps, which was afterwards called the King's Mountain, the astonished strangers cast their eyes down upon their new and beautiful country. Wherever Alboni passed he showed his veneration for the church, and sought, on every occasion, the affection of the people. By the conquest of Pavia, at the confluence of the Ticino and the Po, he founded his dominion in Upper Italy, which, to the present day, has been called Lombardy, from the Longobardi, and he made it the chief city of those districts. In Lower Italy, also, this nation conquered beautiful tracts of land, and founded the principality Benevento, which comprises the greatest portion of the present kingdom of Naples. But Rome and Ravenna remained in the hands of the Greeks, who gained the Franks to their side by presents, in order that they might, by their means, prevent the Longobardi from taking possession of the whole of Italy, and consolidating it into one powerful and strong kingdom. And, unfortunately for the country, in this object they succeeded. From that period to this day, Italy has remained disunited, and has endured the severe fate of a divided country, internally rent. Strangers have, from time immemorial, contested for its possession, and its ground has been deluged with streams of native and foreign blood.

The Longobardi cultivated their newly-acquired country so admirably, that the melancholy traces of former devastation became daily less discernible. The king also procured his supplies from the produce of his possessions; and from one farm to another he was regular in his visits of inspection; living, in fact, with all the simplicity of a patriarch, combined with the dignity of a great military leader. Their free-men, as among the ancient Romans, labored of their own accord to turn the desert and waste tracts into arable land, thus distinguishing themselves from other German nations. Agriculture flourished particularly around monasteries, whose chronicles, says a great German writer, contain the less dazzling but more satisfactory history, of the way in which they almost overcame, or, at least, assisted Nature, and how cheerful gardens and smiling fields covered the ruins of ancient Italy.

The majority of German nations, at the time of the great migration, had come into new countries wholly different from their former settlements, and there found inhabitants of a different race, with other languages, manners, and laws. They, consequently, could not themselves continue to exist stationary in their new country upon the same footing that they had been used to in their former homes; and it is important that we should place before our view, in its broad outline, the great difference presented between the tribes which had wandered forth as conquerors, and those which had remained behind adhering to their ancient simple customs.

The German conquerors found in Gaul, Spain, Italy, and England, inhabitants consisting of Romans and natives mixed. They left them, it is true, after they had appropriated to themselves a portion of their possessions, in their dwelling-places, but generally as an ignoble and degenerate race. By the laws of the Franks, the fine for killing a Roman or a Gaul was only the half, and in some cases but one fourth, of what it was for a free Frank. Afterwards, notwithstanding their original separation and distinctive character, it could not well be otherwise but that the Germans by degrees became mixed with the natives, and that many of the latter, who were superior to the Germans in knowledge, as well as in cunning and refinement, speedily obtained, under weak kings, distinguished offices, and now ruled their former lords. They even obtained, as services were paid only with land, grants of possession as feudal tenures, and became thereby partakers in the feudal rights. Romans and Gauls were seen to rank among the counts, dukes, and grand stewards, and thence arose, although perhaps but slowly, a mixture of nations, and accordingly of manners, languages, and forms of ideas.

The ancient vigorous nature of those Germans who came into warm and luxurious countries, became enervated by effeminacy and sensuality. Thus the Vandals in Africa, and the Ostro-Goths in Italy, in the course of twenty years after their arrival, had become so much transformed and degenerated, that they submitted to enemies who previously could scarcely bear their powerful glance. The tribes, however, which remained in Germany, continued as firm and vigorous as ever; and if afterwards they became by degrees more mild, like their climate, their forests were nevertheless cleared so gradually, that the change in the people took place without too rapid, and thereby injurious a transition.

But the greatest change that happened to the migrated German branches, was in reference to their language. For, as in the conquered countries, the Roman or Latin language was chiefly spoken, and as this was at that time much more cultivated than the German, it could not be supplanted by the latter; but there arose a mixture of both, whereby they became changed, and the indigenous language of the country before the Roman period, often formed a third component of this medley. Consequently in France, Spain, Portugal, Italy, and England, a language is spoken formed by a mixture with the Roman, which may perhaps fall more gently upon the ear than the German, which yet retains much of its former roughness from the ancient forests; while, however, the former tongue is neither so energetic, so hearty, and honest, nor so rich in peculiar words. The German language remains ever fresh and florid, and is open to continual improvement in beauty and richness. It is a language entirely original, the roots of which ramify into the aboriginal foundations of German national idiosyncrasy, and draws its nourishment from the rich fountain of life with which nature has endowed the nation; it may be compared to the living plant in a fruitful soil, and the labor bestowed upon it, is as that of the gardener who watches and carefully attends to the development of the favorite tree. But the language formed by a composition of many others, is but the work of man, like the artificial web which the hand of man prepares from the plants of the field. It is true this may be beautifully and richly worked; but it is then and for all times finished, and possesses no further internal power of life and growth.

The constitution of the conquering German nations necessarily became also essentially changed. At home, in their original condition, the power of royalty in peace was but insignificant. The elders or counts, as the appointed judges in every gau or district, regulated the usual affairs, adjudged disputes according to custom, and upon more important and general affairs the national assembly was convened. But in war the power of the leader surpassed every thing else, and justly so, as it then depended upon prompt decisions. The king or prince was the unlimited lord, and the most faithful of his suite or Gefolge ranked next to him. When such a war had speedily passed away, the prince again retired into the insignificance of a state of peace; but in the many years of the incursions, amidst constant warfare, his power became firmly established. The whole nation became an army, and it accustomed itself to the obedience necessary in war. The institutions of peace lost much of their force, and as in their incursive movements they had no country they could call their own, their whole confidence and attachment were necessarily concentrated in their leader, who led them to victory and pillage, and the forcible possession of a new country. He was the safeguard and hope of the nation; he stood to them in lieu of home and father-land, and those who stood next to him, as his suite, were the most prosperous.

To these latter, when conquest was completed, he apportioned first their share of booty and of land, as in ancient times he had given them only their horse, arms, and entertainment. But without doubt he took to himself the most desirable and considerable share, and particularly the lands of the conquered or slain princes; his power being thus founded by his possessions and strong adherents. The Goths, the Burgundians, and the Longobardi, who came as migrating nations, with their wives and children, must certainly have exacted from the conquered a considerable portion of their possessions. The Ostro-Goths in

Italy demanded one-third of the land, while the Westro-Goths and Burgundians required from the Gauls as much as two-thirds. The Franks, on the contrary, made their conquests in excursions from home, not only as a nation, but as the suite of their prince. Their numbers were not great, hence they did not require to take from the Gauls and Romans any portion of their land, although, according to their ideas of the rights of conquerors, they considered the whole as their property; and in many cases, no doubt, they seized much of private property, so that the chance of the Gauls became often much more fatal, inasmuch as they were more immediately exposed to the wild and arbitrary demands made.* But altogether, they still found in what the Romans had previously possessed as *national property*, a sufficiency of land; besides, in those portions of Gaul which they took from the Westro-Goths, the majority of those land possessions fell to them which the latter, upon the conquest, had appropriated to themselves; for many of them were killed in the war, and many likewise quitted the country and advanced into Spain, that they might not become slaves to the Franks. The whole mass of the conquered state-lands above mentioned (according to the Roman expression, *fiscus*) formed now, after the king had received his chief portion, the common property of the conquerors. It was thence, so long as they held together as an army, that their support was furnished; afterwards, when they began to domicile themselves among their new subjects, and, according to the original disposition of German nations, desired to obtain entire possession, they received this from the mass of fiscal lands, as a reward (*beneficium*) for the military services rendered; and for which they remained obligated to afford further military duty at the command of the king, holding, however, possession of the land merely as a fief, or loan, (*lehen*,) during their lives.

From this commencement was developed the entire constitution, afterwards so important and influential, and which was called the feudal state. In the following centuries it obtained, by degrees, its full perfection, particularly when it extended itself backward to the ancient seats of the Franks, and the other German nations subjected to them. The exertions to obtain fiefs, and procure appointment for the services connected therewith under the sovereign, became increasingly predominant, for thereby was attained influence and power; and to gain this many gave up their freedom. The feudatories took the name of liege subjects (*fideles*) and people (*leudes*) of the prince, or vassals, (*vassi*,) whence vasalli is derived. The feudal lord was called senior (whence seigneurs) or dominus. The name *antrustio* (confidential) signified the liege subject, leader of a troop, or arimanie of the escort or train, in which quality he had to take a particular oath of fidelity, and then stood *truste dominica*. Those liege subjects who stood in close service to the prince were called administrators.

The great vassals could distribute from their own land fiefs to other poorer individuals, who engaged in their service, and thus became after, or arrière vassals. They were obliged, with these their *fideles*, to follow the *heerbann* of the prince, while the common freeman, who had only an *allodial*, or free inheritance, (in contradistinction to *feudum*,*) was only obliged to attend in great national wars, and for which the heerbann, in the ancient German sense, was proclaimed. Notwithstanding which, the feudatories soon began to look down upon the freeman as upon one much their inferior, and to consider themselves, on the other hand, as the nobility of the nation—even when they were not descended from the *original* nobility of the nation, for Gauls were likewise enabled to receive fiefs; nay, already, under Clovis, these were elevated beyond the Franks in honors, for they more easily yielded obedience than the latter, and were thus more agreeable to the king. The law also made a distinction prejudicial to the free possessor. The liege subjects (*in truste dominica*) had a higher amount of fine-money allowed them; it amounted to three-fourths of that of the common freeman; and even when the liege subject was merely of Roman descent, the sum was higher than that of the free Frank, it being 300 solidis, while that of the latter was 200.

The feods, originally, were not heredi-

* "Nec ullus muttire coram iis audebat," says Gregory of Tours.

* The word *feudum*, however, does not present itself before the second century

tary; the lord could withdraw, and invest others with them; but in the course of time, and particularly under weak governments, the vassals found means, in one way or the other, to obtain hereditary possession, and make it nearly independent; the royal power being thus again restricted, by those whom it had previously elevated for its support. The majority of vassals were also powerful by their inherited property; and who would deprive the powerful man, or his son, of his feod? Property and feods became mixed, because he who inherited the property inherited also the feod.

The power of the kings was, therefore, not unlimited, and the ancient freedom not annihilated, inasmuch as the nation still participated in the decision of important national affairs. Regular assemblies were still held, and by the Franks at first, in March; afterwards, under Pepin the Little, in May; whence the names of March and May plains. But the greatest difference from ancient times was, that these assemblies consisted no longer of the majority of all the freemen, but chiefly of feudatories, so that the nobility gave the decision.

The laws of the German nations of this age show that their state was still very rude. The punishment of death was scarcely awarded to any crime except treason and infidelity. The German regarded personal liberty so highly, that he would not yield to any other the right to his life. Murder might be compounded for with money or goods, and the compensation obtained by relatives, who, according to the ancient right of the retribution of blood, could have demanded the blood of the offender. Accordingly, the injured family possessed the right of feud or hostility against the other, until satisfaction was given. Expiation for the non-exercised family revenge was, therefore, the original signification of the retribution, or fine-money. The punishment of death, however, would not have withheld these passionate nations, who instantly grasped the sword, and had but little fear of death, from the momentary satisfaction of revenge; the pecuniary penalty was, on the contrary, very high for that period, and therefore more felt; and he who could not pay it lost his freedom, and became the slave of the offended party. Many poor freemen thus lost their liberty, because their possessions were esteemed of but little value, as, for instance, an ox by the Salic laws was worth two gold shillings, a cow but one, a stallion six, and a mare three; therefore, an opprobrious word cost a considerable sum, for he who called another a liar, was obliged to give him six shillings, or two oxen; he who called him knave or scoundrel, as much as fifteen shillings. The extent of the punishment certainly conduced to their frequently making arrangements, in order that they might not, through the excitement of a passionate moment, involve each other in deep misfortune. As each went armed, and could always defend himself, the murder of a man, according to the Allemannic law, was only half as heavily punished as that of a woman, who was defenceless. But theft was more abhorred than murder, because a coward may also attack defenceless objects. According to the Saxon law, he who had stolen a horse was punished with death, but every murder, even that of a noble, money could buy off. The highest fines inflicted were, first, that of a Bavarian duke, of 960 shillings, and secondly, that of a bishop, of 900 shillings. There was no fine fixed for a king, for his person was considered sacred and unassailable. With the Franks, the fine-money of the royal *Antrustio*, if he was a Frank, was equal to that of a count, 600 shillings; of the freeman 200, and the *Litus* 100. For the Romans it was fixed at half these amounts, in the same proportion: so that the *Romanus conviva regis* paid 300 shillings, the *Romanus possessor* 100, but the *Romanus tributarius*, instead of 50, paid only 45. Among the other nations, according to their laws, there were many variations. Every corporeal wound was very precisely fixed by a money rate; the mutilation of the hand, for instance, cost 100 shillings, of a thumb 45; the nose the same, the fore finger 35, and any of the others 15 shillings.

Judgment was held under the open firmament, in an enclosed place, called Mallum, (Malstätte, or Malberg,) and before an elevated shield. The judges chosen under the presidency of the count were, in all cases, for freemen also freemen themselves, and called in judicial language *Rachimburgi*, or boni homines. These were nominated by counts, usually to the number of seven. In cases where the Rachimburgi could not find judgment, the so-called Sagibarones, who were appointed as special counsellors or magistrates, stepped in to decide. The regular tribunal which met at certain fixed periods, was called mallum legitimum. It was attended by the entire population, and the whole community gave its decision, and not the judges, (Rachimburgi,) who merely *found* the judgment. In the especial or summoned tribunals, however, at which only few assisted besides the counts and judges, the latter decided at once; the others present did not act as a community, but only attended as audience, and as such had nothing to say.

To arrive at the guilt or innocence of an accused person appeared to the Germans, with their acute feeling for the sacredness of justice, to be one of the most indispensable duties. When, therefore, the truth was not to be obtained by means of witnesses, they sought higher aid, by having recourse to the so-called judgments of God. The innocence of the accused party seemed confirmed if they remained unharmed upon being exposed to the dangers which, in the ordinary course of things, are injurious; if, for instance, upon exposing the hand or foot to boiling water or a glowing iron, it remained unmarked, or if in single combat he conquered his opponent. They had confidence that God would not allow innocence to fall, and no doubt in the single combat, at least, the consciousness of innocence would frequently give the victory.

Their chief pleasures were still the chase and war. The former they loved so much, and so highly prized all that pertained to it, that the Allemanni estimated a stolen lime hound at twelve shillings, while a horse could be compensated at six, and a cow at only one shilling. A common trained hawk was valued at three, and one that had taken a stork at six shillings.

The whole moral and civil condition of the German tribes, in the centuries immediately after the great migration, was in certain respects worse than their ancient simple state, when they followed the immediate impulses of their nature. They were now on the transit from the unconscious life of nature to a consequent progress in civilization, and this period of a nation is the worst, because the consciousness of moral dignity begins to awaken before the power of self-government is present to subdue the active impulses of passion.

The Goths, Burgundians, Longobardians, and Franks, had, as has been related, much earlier adopted Christianity; in Germany proper it made its appearance a couple of centuries later. For although the Allemanni, Thuringians, and Bavarians were subject to the Franks, the latter did not give themselves much trouble to disseminate the holy doctrines among them; although, by such a boon, they might have given them a compensation for the loss of liberty. It appeared, indeed, as if they, who had adopted Christianity in need and in the tumult of battle, sought and desired only to promulgate it with the sword. On the other hand, the apostles who planted these mild doctrines among the German forests, came from distant countries—from England, Scotland, and Ireland. The Angli and Saxons, who had landed there as heathens, were slowly converted to Christianity, not by force, but by instruction and conviction. And it, therefore, struck so deep a root in their minds, that speedily a multitude of inspired and Christian men travelled from those countries as teachers of the heathens. They had not to expect either rich abbeys or much honor and reward among them, but, on the contrary, ridicule, contempt, want, and the most extreme danger.

Such men were the holy Columban and Gallus, in the sixth century; Kilian, Emmeran, Rupertus, and Willibrod, in the seventh and eighth centuries; and, at last, the Englishman Winefred, who afterwards received the honorable name of Bonifacius, (the Beneficent.) He labored from the year 718 to 755 with inexhaustible courage for Christianity. In Franconia, Thuringia, on the Rhine, and among the Saxons and Friesi, his zeal planted the divine doctrines; and while he introduced and established the Christian worship, so humanizing to the manners, he collected the communities into villages, and this laid a foundation for towns. For the strengthening of the new faith, he fixed bishoprics here and there, or regulated those already existing, as in Salzburg, Passau, Freisingen, Ratisbonne, Wurtzburg, Eichstadt, and Erfurt; the celebrated abbey Fulda was founded by his follower Sturm, and at Ohrdruf he planted a school for future teachers, who, according to the rule of their institution, not only zealously propagated Christianity, but also the arts of agriculture and horticulture.

In addition to all this, he did not hesitate, although at great personal danger, to contend against the rude disposition of the people with the force of his faith. He overturned their altars, and cut down their sacred trees, beneath which they sacrificed to their gods. One among these, at Geissmar in Hessia, was particularly celebrated; but Boniface himself seized the axe and helped to hew it down. The surrounding heathens firmly believed that the god who dwelt in the tree would speedily come forth with fire, and consume the culprit and all his companions. But the tree fell without the fire coming, and with it dropped their former confidence in their god.

But Boniface complained even more of the bad Christian priests themselves, whom he found among the Franks, than of the savageness of the heathens. They lived in all kinds of vice, and made no conscience of sacrificing to the false gods, as well as to baptize howsoever was required from them for the money offered for so doing. And even the best among them took as much delight in arms and the chase as in the duties of their spiritual office. "Religion has now been prostrated full sixty or seventy years," says he in an epistle to Pope Zacharias; "and the Franks for more than eighty years have had neither an assembly in council of the church nor an archbishop. The bishoprics are in the hands chiefly of greedy laymen or criminal churchmen, who perceive profit in nothing but temporalities." Hence one of his chief cares was, that councils should be held by the Franconian clergy to restore good morals and the ancient church discipline, and that the clergy should participate in the assemblies of the March plains, (Martii Campi,) that the weal of the Church might also be there taken into consideration; and towards this he accomplished much, for which he made himself greatly distinguished.

In the year 746, Boniface was made archbishop of Mentz, and as such he stood at the head of the East-Franconian clergy, which he accustomed to unconditional obedience towards the Roman bishop, who now as pope stood uncontestedly at the head of the western church. Boniface, however, would not remain inactive and pass his later years in quiet, for the conversion of the heathens was now, as formerly, still the labor and aim of his life; and at last his zeal was rewarded with the martyr's fate. Upon his return to the Friesi, in order solemnly to consecrate some newly-baptized Christians, he was fallen upon by a troop of barbarians, who expected to gain booty from him. His servants seized their arms to repel the attack; he, however, forbade them to shed blood, and was therefore at once murdered with all his companions by the furious band.

The religious foundations, churches, and cloisters which Boniface and others built in Germany, became not only the sparks whence the light of religion and intellectual cultivation proceeded, but many of them formed also the nucleus of new towns and villages which, by degrees, arose around them. Not only the bondsmen built their huts close to them, but others also sought the protection of their walls, and merchants and traders proceeded thither in the hopes of making profit from the multitude of strangers who flocked there for the sake of worship. The name of the festival, Kirchmesse or Churchwake, derived thence its origin.

The kingdom of the Franks was divided into two great portions, Neustria and Austrasia, or the Western and Eastern kingdoms; and the former was again frequently divided into several parts. In the Western kingdom, the Roman manners and language maintained the superiority; but in the East those of the Germans were predominant. Both nations were frequently at war and discontented with each other.

In the year 613, Clothaire II. once again united the two divisions of the kingdom, but soon afterwards resigned that of Austrasia into the hands of his son Dagobert, who, on the death of his father, in the year 628, again combined the whole together. Under these two governments, which may be included in the series as the most happy, the kingdom became strengthened, and the internal relations, by the exertions of Arnolph, bishop of Metz, and the great chamberlain or prime minister, Pepin of Landen, (grandfather of Pepin of Heristal,) were greatly improved, and rendered more perfect and settled.

The judicial system now assumed more of the Christian character; for, according to the original pagan law, every act of murder, with the exception of that committed against the king, could be compounded for with money and land, whereas now it was decreed that each premeditated murder should be punished with death. The clergy likewise were placed upon a more elevated and distinct footing, and which, indeed, was extremely necessary and desirable, so that Christianity might not again sink and fall into neglect. In order that bishops should, as far as possible, consist of the most worthy men, the ecclesiastics received, with the co-operation of the people, the right of election, (clerus cum populo.) The jurisdiction of the clergy was likewise, at the great synod of Paris in 614, established upon a more firm and secure basis; and at the grand conferences its influence became more important, inasmuch as they appeared there almost alone with the great vassals or higher officers of the crown. The ancient assemblies of the people had, under Clovis, entirely ceased to exist.

Dagobert resided chiefly in Paris. We find that under him continual wars were carried on between the Franks and Slavi, which produced against them a friendly league between the Franks and Saxons. Dagobert released the Saxons from their tribute of five hundred cows.

After the death of Dagobert, in 637, the decline of the Merovingian dynasty commenced anew, and we find seven kings ruled like puppets by guardians, acting as prime ministers or mayors of the palace, thus producing the complete fall of the race. These mayors got the entire sway of the kingdom. Originally, the major-domus was only *steward;* he stood at the head of the royal house and of the royal people, (leudes,) and was leader of the feudal retinue in war, next to the king. The heerbann of freemen was not under him. But when the retinue obtained, by degrees, the precedence, and became properly the state, the heerbann fell into disuse, and the independent freemen becoming reduced in number, the grand steward then rose to be effectually the first officer of the kingdom, and under weak kings was their ruler. When a war was to be conducted, the grand steward placed himself at the head of the troops, and showed himself prepared for warlike feats; in peace also, he exercised privilege of mercy, disposed of offices, distributed vacant sinecures, and left to the king merely the honor of his name and that of the crown, and the indulgence of his sensuality in the inner apartments of the palace. It was only at the March assembly that the king appeared personally amidst his people. There he sat publicly upon the seat of his ancestors, greeted his nobles, and was saluted in return by them; he received the presents brought by the nation, and handed them over to the grand chamberlain or steward standing beside the throne, distributing, according to his recommendation, the vacant places, and confirming those he had already disposed of. He then mounted his chariot, which, according to ancient custom, was drawn by four oxen, drove to his palace, and remained there until the following March assembly.

Such was the condition of the great conqueror Clovis's descendants, before two hundred years had passed since his death. About the year 700, the grand steward over the whole kingdom of the Franks, Neustria as well as Austrasia, was Pepin of Heristal, (near Liège;) a very careful and prudent man, who restored order and justice, held the old March assemblies regularly, and won so much the love and confidence of the people, by restoring in this manner their rights against the encroachments of the hordes, that he was enabled to make the office hereditary to his family. His son, Charles Martel, who was grand steward after him, saved the whole of Christianity at this moment from a great impending danger.

A savage horde had arrived from the south, and had in a short time traversed extensive tracts with fire and sword, and subjected all to their dominion. No nation could set limits to them, their arm was irresistible, and struck their opponents like lightning. These strangers were the Arabs; they came from Asia, and they derived their great power from the new faith. For he whom they called their prophet, Mahomet, had announced to them much from the doctrines of Moses and of our Saviour; besides which he promised to this people, who were addicted to sensual pleasures beyond every thing, great rewards and an ever-during bliss in Paradise, if they fought zealously for their new faith, and extended it over all countries. Mahomet lived about the year 622. They had now rapidly conquered several lands in Asia and Africa, and in less than a hundred years after the death of Mahomet, in the year 711, they had already crossed the Straits of Gibraltar to Spain. Roderic, king of the West Goths, who ruled in Spain, opposed them near Xeres de la Frontera; he strove for his crown, for the freedom and religion of the West Goths; long and severe was the battle. Roderic fought heroically, until a treacherous count, who called the Arabs across the straits, passed over to the enemy. The king then fell, and with him the flower of his army. The kingdom of the West Goths was subjected to the Arabs, and they soon ruled from the sea to the Pyrenees, so that only a very small spot to the northwest of Spain, in the mountains of Gallicia, remained a free possession in the hands of the Goths.

After the Arabs had conquered Spain, they cast their eyes upon France, and, crossing the Pyrenees, fell upon that country. At the same time they showed themselves below Constantinople with a large army and a fleet: so that they embraced the whole of Europe from east to west, determined upon conquering it and extinguishing Christianity. And had they obtained the victory on both sides they would have advanced still farther, and the two great armies would have met and united in Germany and have completed the work. But Providence had determined otherwise. The city of Constantinople held firm against the attack, with its strong walls and Greek fire, which the inhabitants used against the ships of their enemy. But in France they were opposed by the powerful hero Charles Martel, the son of Pepin; he was called Martel or the hammer, because by his bravery he struck his enemies down, as it were, like a hammer. With his Franks he crossed the river Loire to meet the enemy, and came upon them between the cities of Tours and Poitiers, where a wide plain spread itself out. The battle here took place on a Saturday in October, in the year 732. Close and impassable, and covered with an advanced wall of shields, the Franks stood immoveable, and endured their first violent attack, for this was always the most furious. The Franks, however, then suddenly broke forth, precipitated themselves upon the Arabs, repulsed them, and it is said that more than 300,000 fell, together with their general, Abderachman, slaughtered by the swords of the Franks. Those who remained fled towards southern France, whence Charles soon drove them forth, and placed forever a boundary against them on this side. Charles, who, for this deed, was highly honored throughout all countries, died in the year 741.

His son was called Pepin the Little, or the Short; he was also grand steward until 752, and ruled the kingdom according to his pleasure, but with wisdom and justice, while king Childeric III. sat in his palace like a shadow, and took not the least care of his government. When Pepin saw the disposition of the Franks favorable to him, he caused an assembly of them to take place in the year 751, when it was determined to send an embassy to Rome, with this question: "Is he justly called king who has the royal power in his hands, or he who merely bears the name?" To which pope Zacharias replied, "He must also be called king, who possesses the royal power."

The holy Boniface had accustomed the Franks, in certain cases of conscience, to apply to the pope for advice as their spiritual father, and the papal reply is to be regarded as counsel and opinion, as an answer to such a question, but not as a deposal of king Childeric, by virtue of the power existing in the pope. Upon this, the Franks assembled again at Soissons, and took the crown from Childeric, the last of the Merovingians, cut off his long hair, the mark of honor with the Frankish kings, and had him removed to a cloister, there to end his days; while Pepin, the son of Charles Martel, and grandson of Pepin of Heristal, was in the year 752 solemnly anointed and crowned king of the Franks by the archbishop Boniface, 266 years after Clovis the Merovingian had, by his victory over Syagrius, upon this same field of Soissons, first founded the kingdom.

Pepin by his courage and wisdom augmented the power of his nation. At this time, in 753, pope Stephen crossed the Alps (he being the first pope who since the foundation of the church had undertaken this journey) to demand the assistance of Pepin against the Longobardian king Aistulph, who had conquered Ravenna, and demanded tribute and submission from the pope. Pepin promised him aid, and retained him through the winter at his court in Münster. Here the pope repeated the anointment of the king, as already performed by the holy Boniface, anointing also his two sons, Carloman and Charles, (after he had himself lifted the latter, then twelve years old, from the font,) and then presented to the Franks these members of the newly-created dynasty as alone legitimate. In the spring of the year 754 the king advanced against Italy, defeated Aistulph at Susa, reconquered Ravenna, with the surrounding country, which had previously belonged to the Greek emperors, and presented it to the pope. This formed the beginning of the papal states.

Pepin died in 768, in the fifty-fourth year of his age, and the Franks mourned his death as much as if he had sprung from the ancient royal race. In stature he was short, but very strong. It is related of him, that once, upon the occasion of a combat of wild beasts, some one jested about his size, upon which he stepped into the arena, drew his sword, and with one blow struck off the head of a lion: "I am not tall," said he, "but my arm is strong!"

His sons, Charles and Carloman, were elected kings by the nation of the Franks, in a solemn assembly, and regularly divided the kingdom between them.

# THIRD PERIOD.

## THE CARLOVINGIANS FROM CHARLEMAGNE TO HENRY I.

768—919.

THE events of the reign of Charlemagne called forth the energy of the historical writers:

1. The annals and chronicles, of which mention has been made previously, became augmented, and proved for this period more and more important; while education, so much promoted by Charlemagne, is therein displayed, both in the language and treatment of the subject.

2. In reference to the history of Charlemagne, the works of Einhard or Eginhard will always remain the most important, being written by a man who was in immediate communication with that sovereign. His "Annales," from 741–829, treat more particularly of this period than the continuation of the "Annal Laurissenses," before mentioned. The "Vita Caroli Magni," after giving a brief account of the wars of Charlemagne, describes especially every other particular connected with his life and its events; and must be read by all with pleasure. In addition to this we possess also his letters.

3. Theganus, bishop of Treves, who died in 848, wrote the life of Louis the Pious,—"De Gestis Ludovici Pii"—certainly not very impartially, and rather too briefly, yet written with sincerity and exact information.

4. The "Vita Hludovici Pii auctore anonymo," is much more complete, written by a member of the emperor's household; this is rich in facts, and is expressed with judgment.

5. Equally important is the poetical representation of a contemporary, Ermoldus Nigellus, in his elegiac poem, "in honorem Hludovici Cæsaris."

6. Nithard, grandson of the emperor, who died in 858, describes most completely the disputes among the sons of Louis, in his "IV Libris de dissensionibus filiorum Ludovici Pii;" he shows himself to be decidedly on the side of Charles the Bald.

7. The "Vita Sti-Anskarii," by Rimbert, Archbishop of Hamburg, written under Louis the German, treats more especially upon the North German relations.

8. Enhard's and Rudolphus's "Annals of Fulda," and their continuators, are, after the conclusion of Einhard, very important in German history. In his work, Rudolphus gives a very interesting description of the Saxons; he is the only writer who was acquainted with the writings of Tacitus, and from the latter's *Germania* he has quoted several chapters literally. With respect to the western moiety of the Frankish kingdom, the "Annales Bertiniani" (so called from the Abbey St. Bertinbei Gent) of 822, give the best information. The last moiety was perhaps written by the celebrated Archbishop Hincmar of Rheims.

9. A monk of St. Gallen, Monachus Sangallensis, has described in two books, "de Gestis Car. Magni," the life of the emperor in a peculiar fashion, according to communications received and popular legends, mostly without historical fidelity, but still not without grace.

10. Abbo, a monk of St. Germain, was present at the siege of Paris by the Normans in 885, and has described the events of that period in a poem, "de Bellis Pariiacis," in a very animated style.

11. The so-called Poëta Saxo, (900,) has rendered into verse what Einhard's Annals relate of the emperor, and has partly succeeded in his work, although he can never, or but rarely, be used as a reference.

12. The Chronicles of the Abbot Regino, who died in 915, and which extend to the year 907, are very important for the latter period of the Carlovingians.

13. The letters of the popes, sovereigns, princes, &c., of this period are also very important, particularly those which are contained in the Codex Carolinus; likewise the letters and works of Alcuin, as also the letters of Servatus Lupus, Eginhard's friend, and Hincmar, Archbishop of Rheims.

14. Finally, it is quite certain that the "Capitularia Regum Francorum," the laws of the realm, and general decrees of the kings, form a principal source of reference for our history. They were collected by Baluzius, and have been recently published by Pertz, in the third volume of the "Monumenta."

## CHAPTER V.

768—814.

Charlemagne, 768-814—The state in which Charlemagne found the Empire—The East-Roman or Grecian Empire—England—The North of Europe—

The Spanish Peninsula—Italy—Austria and Hungary—Germany—The Wars of Charlemagne—The Saxons—The Longobardi—The Arabs—The Bavarians—The Empire of Charlemagne—Charlemagne, Emperor of Rome, 800—The Death of Charlemagne, 814—His portraiture.

It has been the fate of Charlemagne, as well as of the majority of extraordinary historical characters, to be subjected to the ordeal of a very different, and frequently a very opposite criticism. By many he has been classed with the noblest heroes and sages of the human race, by some, however, he has been rejected as a bloodthirsty tyrant, whose whole object and desire was war and destruction. It is true that he led his armies from one end of his extensive empire to the other in constant warlike expeditions, and subjected many nations by force of arms to his dominion, thus giving Europe an entirely different form. The question therefore to be solved is, whether history shall bless or curse him for these extraordinary deeds.

A false judgment must necessarily be passed upon great men and the great events of nations, by those who cannot transport themselves from their own times back into those whereof the picture is to be drawn. In periods when society is in a ferment, and barbarism and civilization are in contest with each other; when from the existing component parts something new and great is to germinate, towards which the tranquil course of things, as handed down, will not suffice—Providence sends forth mighty individuals, who are destined to lead a whole age many steps onward in its development, and according to the object which they are to accomplish, it furnishes them with adequate vigor of intellect and strength of will. But because such chosen spirits do not follow the beaten track, and because, perhaps, while their eye is fixed upon the distant mountain summit, many a flower is crushed beneath their feet, and they in the impatient struggle, which in the short space of the life of one man is to determine the plan of the course of centuries, wound unconsciously many a sacred right; the easy, indolent spirit of the lover of repose, therefore, to which the sanctity of rights forms the foundation-stone of life, is loud in execration against the vessel in which was compressed such gigantic, mighty powers, and the judgment thence pronounced is frequently severe and unjust. But who shall censure the mountain stream because it flows not like the meadowy brook, but drags forth even stones and trees, bearing them onward with it in its course? It is true it tears forth by the roots the decayed and rotten stems, but thereby the light of heaven is opened to cheer the progress of the more young and tender plants.

Let this, however, by no means be considered as an apology for the violence of tyrannical rulers, whose actions flow from an impure source. Man is a free agent, and presents himself as the ready instrument of Providence in its great plans. The *manner* in which he executes his office depends upon himself, and either justifies or condemns him. It is not the great deeds he has performed, nor the thousands who have bled in battle, while others in the intoxication of victory have profanely worshipped him, that decide upon his merits or demerits, but it is the *object* by which he was governed, and the purpose for which he accomplished his extraordinary plans: whether he has been guided by great thoughts towards a worthy and noble end, or only by his own pride, his ambition, and vanity, or, to speak figuratively, whether in the mirror of his life the infinite creation and its worlds, or only his own proud image be reflected. This may be observed from many signs, but it is especially to be recognised therein, viz., when he has revered the dignity of humanity as a sacred object, even in its details, or not observing or acknowledging it, but despising men, he has merely used them as instruments to his purposes.

This should be our rule of judgment, in order that we may not allow ourselves on the one side to bestow admiration upon mere power without intrinsic goodness, nor on the other to prejudge unjustly all those names which are inscribed in the volume, too frequently perhaps in characters of blood and fire.

The work of a great man derives its proper light from the condition of the world when he appeared upon the stage; it is therefore necessary to take a short review of the state of Europe at the time Charles attained the empire.

1. The East-Roman, or Greek empire, still existed; but only in the strange mixture of old and new relations, of splendor and misery, of presumption and weakness, as it had existed for a thousand years—in

the history of the world a riddle. For it is scarcely to be conceived how the mere shadow of an ancient, great, and splendid state, or as it were the gaudily-decorated corpse of antiquity, as that empire has been happily called, should have preserved itself so long without internal life. The change of rulers and the inconstancy of all conditions were so great, that for an emperor of Constantinople no title was more flattering than being styled, "The imperial son of a father born in the purple robe," (porphyrogenitus porphyrogeniti.) For the throne came by turns to men who had been born among the dregs of society, and who owed their elevation to some crime. To Charlemagne this distant and extensive, but wealthy empire, could not be immediately either an object of dread or ambition. He maintained friendship with the Greek emperors, and they mutually honored each other with embassies and presents, for it was desirable to the Greeks to be upon good terms with him. "Retain the Frank for thy friend, but prevent him from being thy neighbor," was an established proverb among the Greeks.

2. England, at the commencement of Charlemagne's reign, was still divided among several Anglo-Saxon kings, and formed a secluded world of its own, without possessing any influence upon the nations of the continent. Charlemagne's name, however, was speedily known and highly esteemed. One of his most confidential friends, Alcuin, was an Englishman, and by his means he often caused the princes there to be written to, and persuaded them to be united and repel the attacks of the valiant Danes. Even the Thanes, or petty kings of Scotland, called him no otherwise than their lord.

3. The north of Europe was still but little known. It is true it was the cradle of valiant men, who knew how to wield the iron of their soil with a powerful arm, and who after the reign of Charlemagne, by their maritime expeditions gained themselves a terrific name upon all the coasts of Europe. They were yet, however, without importance to the Frankish empire. Nevertheless, with his comprehensive mind, Charlemagne perceived the danger which threatened from them. It is related that being once at a seaport, (it is said at Narbonne,) some ships approached the coast, but their crews were not known. Charlemagne's quick eye detected them to be Norman pirates by their shape and rapid motions. They hastily retired when they heard that the great emperor was there. After they had disappeared he turned sorrowfully from the window, shed tears, and at last said to those around him, "You would fain know, my friends, why I wept? Not from fear, no! but it vexes me that, during my life, they have ventured to this shore, and with grief do I foresee, alas! the mischief they will bring to my successors."

4. The Spanish Peninsula was subjected to the Arabians with the exception of some Westro-Gothic places among the mountains, but their religious zeal had already cooled, and their power was tamed by internal dissensions. Charlemagne's grandfather had deterred them from the conquest of Europe, and they thought only of maintaining their own existence in Spain. But Charlemagne could not behold with indifference the enemies of the Christian name as his neighbors.

5. Italy was divided into three dominions, the Longobardian in Upper and a portion of Lower Italy; the Grecian in Lower Italy and Sicily; and the Roman in Middle Italy. Rome was in a mixed state, for the power was divided between the pope, the senate, and the people, but the pope daily acquired more importance. The superior protective dominion of the city had passed from the Greek emperors to the kings of the Franks, for Pope Stephen, in the name of the Roman senate and people, had, in the year 754, conveyed the dignity of a Roman patrician to King Pepin and his sons. Between the Romans and the Longobards there arose a bitter hatred and implacable enmity, which were the immediate cause of Charlemagne interfering in the affairs of Italy. He had, indeed, endeavored to remove the ancient jealousy which prevailed between the Franks and the Longobards by marrying the daughter of King Desiderius, but upon this occasion Pope Stephen wrote to him thus: "What madness in the most excellent son of a great king to sully his noble Frankish race by an alliance with that most faithless and most fulsome nation, the Longobardi, who should not be named among the multitude of nations, and from whom doubtlessly the race of lepers had their origin. What community of feeling has light with darkness,

or a believer with an unbeliever?" The Longobards richly returned this hatred of the Romans; one of their bishops says of them: "Under the name of a Roman we comprehend all that is mean, cowardly, avaricious, and lying, nay, even all vices combined." Charlemagne's union with the royal house of the Longobards was not durable, for two years afterwards he sent back the daughter of King Desiderius: whether it arose from the ill-will of the pope to this marriage, or whether other unknown reasons urged him, we cannot say, but we shall speedily see that greater causes arose for the enmity between them.

6. To the southeast of Charles's possessions in Austria and Hungary, dwelt the Avari, a Mongolian nation from Asia, which had long warred with and plundered the provinces of the eastern empire, but now quietly but anxiously guarded the treasures amassed during two centuries. These lay heaped up in nine particular places, surrounded by walls and ditches, and which were called circles, appearing to invite, as it were, every one to retake them from their possessors, who themselves did not know how to enjoy them.

7. The remaining portion of the eastern German borders was occupied by the different branches of the Slavonians and Vandals, rude nations of a less noble, natural disposition than the Germans. In Germany they possessed Holstein, Mecklenburg, Brandenburg, Pomerania, a portion of Saxony, the Lausitz, Silesia, Bohemia, and Moravia. In Holstein were the Wagrians; in Mecklenburg, the Obotriti; in a portion of Brandenburg, the Wilzen; in another part the Hevellers and Ukerns; the Pomeranians in the province which has received their name—collective branches of the Vandals. In the district of Meissen, the Sclavonian Sorbi; in Lausitz, the Lausitzers; in Bohemia, the Ezechi; and the Moravians in Moravia.

8. In Germany itself Charlemagne found greater tranquillity. The Septs, who had been subjected to the Franks, the Allemanni, Bavarians, and Thuringians, had by degrees accustomed themselves to the foreign dominion, which was not only not oppressive, but had even left them their manners, laws, and peculiar customs. But with the exception of the Bavarians, they were no longer ruled according to ancient custom by their own dukes, but according to the Frankish institutions, by counts without hereditary power in distinct districts. Thence they wanted a central point of union, and the ancient love of independence survived most firmly among the Bavarians alone. The bishops in all these provinces were very much attached to the Carlovingian dynasty.

But on the borders of his empire, in the north of Germany, dwelt neighbors who offered the first object for the trial of his strength, namely, the Saxons, unconquered and free, fixed in their boundaries from the German Ocean to Thuringia, and from the Elbe to the vicinity of the Rhine. While among the Franks, the old German institutions had been much altered, and the warriors in the Gefolge or suite of the king, had assumed the order of nobility, and occupied the place of the freemen, the Saxons still lived in the ancient manners of their ancestors, without a common chieftain, each Gau or district under its own head, and only during war, under a self-elected leader. It was a community of freemen in free dwellings. The interior of their country was defended by forests and morasses, and strong places for the defence of the boundaries were erected on the Lippe, Ruhr, Weser, Dimel, and Elbe. In their groves of a thousand years' growth, they still sacrificed to the gods of their fathers, while the other German tribes had all adopted Christianity; nay, they were even accused of still celebrating human sacrifices. The Franks considered themselves so superior to them by reason of their Christianity, as well as the general superiority of their cultivation, that their historians can scarcely deprecate sufficiently the rudeness and wildness of the Saxons. But they were not so much dangerous as burdensome neighbors of the Franks, because, according to the ancient German practice, they did not wish to make conquests, but merely roved in predatory incursions into neighboring countries. But a well-guarded frontier would have been a sufficient protection against them, as well as against the Sclavonians and Avari, and we see from this sketched description, that Charles might have remained, like the Merovingians, in quiet possession of his inheritance without conducting such great external wars. The Frankish empire extended in self-sufficient strength, from the Pyrenees to the Lower Rhine, and from the English Channel to the Ens, in Austria, and had nothing to fear from any of its neighbors.

But a mind satisfied with mere tranquil possession was not accorded to Charles; its internal power was used to vent itself in new forms, for this was the law implanted in his nature. The condition of the world demanded great creative powers, in order not to remain for centuries longer waste and confused. We dare not censure Charles because he followed this impulse of his nature, but the way in which he followed it and modelled his new creation, gives the measure of judgment against him. Were high and noble thoughts his guide, and was his own genius great, or was it petty, and directed to vain things? Upon that the history of his life must decide.

After Charles (who ascended the throne in his twenty-sixth year) and his brother Carloman had reigned together some years, the latter died in 771. The nobles of Carloman's possessions desired his brother for their king also, and cast out the two sons of Carloman from succession to the throne, with whom the widow fled, and took refuge at the court of Desiderius, king of the Longobardi. Thus was Charles sole ruler of the Franks. Upon this he assembled at Worms an imperial diet in 772, where he represented to the assembly the repeated offences of the Saxons and the merit of their conversion to Christianity; upon which the nation declared war against the Saxons—the first and longest war that Charles was engaged in—for it continued with several interruptions to the year 803, consequently for thirty-two years. During this time Charles frequently conquered the Saxons in open field, and forced them to conclude peace, but when he again quitted their country, and was obliged to withdraw to the farther end of his empire, they broke the peace, rebelled against the obnoxious dominion, chased away the Frankish garrisons, and made incursions into the country of the Franks, until Charles again appeared and forced them anew to submission.

The first irruption made in their country, in the year 772, was successful and short. He proceeded from Worms, through Hessia to the Weser and the Dimel. He conquered the burg of Eresberg (the present Statberg, in the bishopric of Paderborn,) the Saxon place of retreat not far from the Weser, in a rude neighborhood, and upon a precipitous height; and destroyed the celebrated Irminsúl, (or statue of Irmin,) an object regarded with the most sacred veneration by the Saxons, but of which we do not precisely know whether it was an image of a god, or perhaps a monument of Arminius, thus revered with divine honors. The Saxons concluded peace upon the banks of the Weser, and gave twelve chiefs as hostages.

Charles was rejoiced at having so speedily concluded an advantageous peace, for already other affairs called him into Italy. Desiderius, who by the reception of the widow of Carloman had already shown himself as an enemy, required of the new pope, Adrian, that he should anoint the sons of Carloman as kings of the Franks; and upon Adrian's refusal, he threatened him with war. The pope demanded aid from Charles, who at once advanced, crossed the Alps, marched round the passes, of which the Longobardi had taken possession, and encamped before Pavia in the year 774. Desiderius purposed defending his metropolis until sickness and want should force the Franks to retire. But Charles was not of a disposition to be so soon fatigued; he let his army lie six months before Pavia, went himself to the Easter festival at Rome, which he for the first time witnessed, and there confirmed the deed of gift made by his father. He then returned to Pavia, which soon yielded to him, received Desiderius as a prisoner, and sent him, after shaving his head for the cowl, to the monastery at Corvey in France, where, after a short time, he died. Charles now called himself king of the Lombards, and caused himself to be crowned at Monza.

As the Saxons had in the mean time recommenced war, he on his return, and after he had held a diet at Düren, made in 775, a new incursion into their country, conquered Sigberg, restored the Eresberg destroyed by the Saxons, pressed onward over the Weser to the Oker, there receiving hostages from the Eastphalians, and on his return, near Buckeburg, (Buchi,) obtaining also those of the Angravarians. But as, in the mean time, the Longobardian, Duke Rotgaud, of Frioul, to whom, as vassal of the empire, he had intrusted the passes of the Alps, decided upon taking advantage of the moment, and rebelled, Charles was already again in Italy, (776,) and punished the seceders before they thought him even apprized of their plans. This time, also, he was about to advance to Rome, when a message arrived with intelligence that the Saxons had again revolted, had retaken Eresberg, and laid siege to Sigsberg. He speedily returned back into Germany, forced his way through all their forest-defences as far as Lippspring, when the Saxons again yielded, and many vowed to become Christians, and offered themselves to be baptized. He built a fortress on the Lippe, perhaps where Lippsstadt at present stands.

In the following year (777) he was already enabled to hold a diet at Paderborn, in the country of the Saxons, where the majority of the nation swore fidelity. Their boldest leader, however, Wittekind, (Saxon, Widukind,) had fled to the Danish king, Sigfried. It was at this diet that the ambassadors of the Arabian governors of Saragossa and Huesca, in Spain, appeared before Charles, and entreated his assistance against the king, Abderam. He considered it worthy of his dignity not to allow those who placed themselves under his protection to entreat in vain; besides, these unbelievers, who had pressed onward into Europe, were his most hated enemies. Accordingly he advanced in the following year (778) into Spain; the petty Christian princes in the mountains of Navarre, who had maintained themselves independent of the Moors, here joined him; he conquered Pampeluna, Saragossa, Barcelona, and Girona; and the country as far as the Ebro swore allegiance to him. Henceforward it formed part of his empire, under the name of the Spanish marches or limits, and was a land of protection for the Christians remaining in Spain.

Upon his return, however, with his army, winding itself, as it is poetically described, like a long brazen serpent among the rough rocks of the Pyrenees, and through the obscure forests and narrow paths, the rear-guard became separated from the main body, and in an ambuscade laid by the mountaineers, fell into the ravines of Roncesvalles. The Franks could not fight in their heavy armor, and they fell with their leader Rutland, the Count de la Manche. This is the celebrated knight, Roland, who later, as well as his king, Charles, is so much sung in the legends and heroic lays of Europe.

Meanwhile the Saxons, according to custom, when the king was at a distance, had again seized arms. Under Wittekind they fell upon the country of the Franks, and devastated it with fire and sword as far as Deuz, opposite Cologne. This, like the earlier revolts of the Saxons, was not so much a war of the nation and of the heads of families, but of individual leaders with their suite or Gefolge, who did not consider themselves bound by the treaties. Charles returned, drove the enemy far back into their country, and in 780 constructed fortresses on the Elbe to fix a strong rein upon them. And now thinking himself quite secured in that quarter, he made a journey in 781 to Rome, to cause his sons Pepin and Louis to be anointed by the pope, the former king of Italy, the latter king of Aquitaine, (South France.)

The Saxons in the interim had maintained themselves perfectly quiet, but the remembrance of their ancient freedom would not quite die within them, and Christianity, which had been brought to them with the sword by their hated neighbors, gained no power over their hearts. It appeared insupportable to them that a man should not himself revenge a contumely, and that a hero should not have a particular heaven. The impost of tithes which they were obliged to pay to the church, appeared also excessively oppressive to them. As Wittekind had, therefore, now returned and placed himself at their head, they thought the present was the best moment for them to shake off the yoke, and, the same as formerly, when their nation fell upon Varus in the Teutoburger forest, they now surrounded the Frankish leaders Geilo and Adalgis, upon Mount Suntel, on the Weser, just as they were about to march against the predatory Sorbians dwelling on the Saale, and destroyed them as well as the greatest portion of their army.

This deed inflamed the wrath of the king, (who was already excessively irritated at their repeated rebellion,) to the degree, that he broke into the country, desolated it far and wide, and caused 4,500 imprisoned Saxons to be beheaded near Verden on the Aller, as a terrible example to the rest, and as a sacrifice for his army destroyed—as it appeared to him, by treachery; a stain in his history which cannot be justified, but may partly be excused by the rash and turbulent manners of those times, and the excited passions of the king. As a consequence of this severe act, Charles, in 783, beheld the whole nation of the Saxons, under Wittekind and Alboin, rise simultaneously in such furious rage and madness as had never before been evinced. Two severe battles were fought near Thietmelle, now Detmold, and on the river Hase in Osnaburg; the first was undecided, but the second so unfortunate for the Saxons, that Charles advanced as far as the Elbe, and in this and the next year, when with his wife and children he passed the winter campaign at Eresburg, he progressively strengthened his power in their country. Wittekind and Alboin then saw that Heaven had decided the fate of their nation, and that a longer resistance would completely annihilate it. They promised submission to the powerful king, and took an oath to go themselves to France, and be there baptized; and they kept their word. In the year 785 they came to Attigny, and Charles himself was sponsor to the Saxon duke, Wittekind, and his wife Gera.

From this time henceforward Saxony became more tranquil, and submitted to the Frankish institutions as well as to those of Christianity. Charles, for the purpose of strengthening this doctrine among them, likewise founded, by degrees, several bishoprics and religious foundations, which continued to spread light around, viz: in Osnaburg, in 783; Verden, in 786; Bremen, in 788; Paderborn, in 795; Halberstadt; Elze, (which was removed in 822 to Hildesheim,) and Munster, in 806. Yet the seeds of disquiet were not quite destroyed; small disputes still frequently arose, and we shall shortly come to one of greater import.

Charles's next dispute was with Duke Tassilo of Bavaria, of the ancient race of the Agitolfingi. Tassilo had still old offences to answer for, inasmuch as he had never supplied Pepin or Charles with troops, and he was now charged with having incited the Avari of Hungary to war with the king. His consort Luitberga, a daughter of the Longobardian king, Desiderius, may have enacted her part likewise in these designs. Tassilo was condemned to death by the assembled nobles at the diet of Ingelheim, 778, but pardoned by Charles; and by his own wish, together with his son Theodore, banished to a monastery. Bavaria became now, like the other Frankish countries, ruled by royal counts or governors, and the bishopric of Salzburg was raised to an archbishopric over the whole of Bavaria.

In the year 787, Arechis, the Longobardian Duke of Benevento in Lower Italy, also yielded allegiance to the king as his superior feudal lord. He ruled that beautiful country as far as Naples and Brindisi. He made it a condition, however, that he himself should not come to Germany and appear before Charles, which was granted. The duke received the ambassadors of the king at Salerno; his army surrounded the palace, young nobles, with the falcon on their gauntlet, formed rows upon the grand steps leading up to the Burg, while the hall was filled with the provosts of cities, and their council in state dresses, &c. The duke, seated upon the gorgeous, golden chair of state, stood up, and swore to be faithful to the king, to maintain peace, and to perform feudal service to the extent of a league beyond the frontiers of Benevento.

After this, Charles formed the resolution to punish the Avari in Austria and Hungary for their earlier predatory expeditions. Accordingly, he marched against them in the year 791; the Franks advanced on the south side of the Danube; the Saxons, with the Friesi, who were both obliged to yield feudal service, advanced upon its northern bank; and upon the river itself a flotilla conveyed another portion of the army. Their appearance alone drove the Avari away full of terror; they left to the enemy the immense booty of their treasures, and Charles subjected the country to his dominion as far as the river Raab.

In the following years, he merely sent detached forces against them. His main army remained, meanwhile, in South Germany, and worked at a canal to form the junction of the Altmühl with the Rednitz rivers, between the Maine and the Danube, which, had it been completed, would have united the North Sea, by means of the Rhine, with the Danube to the Black Sea; an important work, replete with rich commercial prospects. Levantine merchandise would thus have found a direct course from their repository at Constantinople to the very heart of Charles's states. But unfavorable weather, and the difficulties of the ground, but chiefly the want of skill in his workmen, who knew not how to drain the water from the places that were dug, nor to secure the banks of the canal from falling in, rendered the work nugatory. Charles, therefore, abandoned the undertaking; but the honor of completing this great plan, originating with him, has been handed down and conferred in our days upon another sovereign of the German race. And the cause why he did not now again attack the Avari, and thus open to himself the road to Constantinople, was produced by a fresh rebellion of the Saxons, who, not liking long warlike expeditions, but only short excursions, found the hard marching feudal service in such distant parts particularly trying. They resisted it and mutinied, and induced the Friesi to do the same. The king was, therefore, obliged to make several incursions into their country, in the course of which, in 797, he advanced as far as the ocean between the mouths of the Elbe and Weser. Meantime, the war against the Avari was continued successfully by his generals, and then by his son Pepin, to the year 796; the seat of their Chagan or chief, the main circle of their land, with all its treasures were conquered, and the country thus wrested from them was taken possession of by fresh inhabitants, conveyed from other German states, but chiefly from Bavaria. Charles distributed the immense booty among his army, by which means the quantity of noble metals became suddenly very much increased in the Frankish country.

The object of Charles in this expedition against the Avari, as well as in those against the Sclavonian nations, was chiefly to secure the eastern frontiers of the kingdom. Thence arose a long line of frontier provinces, from the Adriatic Sea to the Elbe, along the ancient boundaries of the Longobardi, Bavarians, Swabians, Franks, Thuringians, and Saxons. To these were appointed margraves, who bore the title of marchio, (dux limitis,) and who had their seats originally fixed in the most strongly fortified burgs of the ancient districts. The inhabitants of these frontier provinces, through wars and repeated revolts, became gradually destroyed, and were replaced by German colonists, for whose protection the burgs were usefully adapted, as well as for bringing either into subjection or alliance the neighboring Slavonic princes. Several of these princes entered, subsequently, the ranks of the princes of the empire; for Charles's plans and regulations in these countries operated late in after years with beneficial effect.

The disputes with the Saxons continued until the ninth century; but the strength of these people became more and more weakened, and especially after Charles, forced, by their obstinate resistance, to adopt such extreme measures, transplanted some thousands of them from their native land into other parts of his kingdom. Thus they were gradually reduced to a state of peace, even without any formal treaty being concluded—the peace of Selz in 803, as hitherto accepted, not being admissible as a proof of treaty—and Charles was enabled to commence upon his plans and arrangements in Saxony. He proceeded at once to strengthen Christianity among them more firmly, while, however, he granted them greater independence than he had to the Allemanni and Bavarians. They retained their ancient privileges, and were chiefly governed by native counts, who were, it is true, chosen by Charles, and were placed under the imperial envoys. This, therefore, may rather be called a union of the Saxon nation with that of the Franks, as Einhard himself terms it, than a subjection; and, indeed, they well merited, by the persevering consistency with which they conducted it, so honorable a conclusion to their long struggle for freedom. But, on the other hand, Charles's perseverance is also to be admired; for although he had the advantage of numbers and great superiority in the art of war on his side, still the Saxons had the benefit of their country, and the forests and morasses, as formerly in their battles with the Romans.

Charles, to confirm tranquillity for ever among them, transplanted about 10,000 of the most violent from the Elbe and the coasts of the North Sea into the country of the Franks, as cultivators of the imperial farms; and from that transplantation, no doubt, is derived the names of Sachsenhausen near Frankfort, as well as Sachsenheim and Sachsenflur, in Franconia. The places left thus void on the Elbe he gave over to his allies the Vandal Obotriti, in Mecklenburg, and the Vagrian Sclavi, from whom this part of Holstein has received and preserved the name of Vagria.

If we cast back our glance upon these first thirty years of the reign of Charles, thus filled with wars, we must admire the great rapidity with which he marched from Saxony to Italy, from there back to the Weser, and then back again twice the same road; then into Spain along the Ebro, and back to the Elbe, proceeding on to Hungary, to the Raab, and again returning into his own country; and wherever he arrived, his presence immediately deciding the contest. Herein we have at once the true character of a hero; this boldness and rapidity of thought, resolution, and action; this impression of innate personal greatness, which nothing could resist, and which greatness nobody has sought to deny. But still more than all this, it was not absolutely the love of war and conquest, and the honor of his name, which inspired him to drive his armies on so breathlessly through the countries of Europe, but his plans were regulated by one grand creative idea for which he considered himself called upon to make these sacrifices.

What already the great Ostro-Gothic king, Theodoric, had in contemplation, prospective, as it were, of future times, but which it was not allowed him to accomplish, viz., the union of the Christian Germanic nations into one empire, Charlemagne executed; not certainly in Theodoric's manner, by the gentle force of persuasion and conviction, for by that means the end was not to be attained, but according to the custom of his nation and of his age, by the terror of arms. Yet, he cannot be charged with having capriciously sought war more urgently than was necessary for the attainment of his object.

The central point of this great Germanic empire was to be the beautiful country of the Rhine, and Ingelheim near Mentz was, therefore, made the royal seat, but which was afterwards transferred to Aix-la-Chapelle and Nimwegen. No doubt he might have found richer and more attractive spots in Italy and France, to induce him to fix his residence there, but his constant mind was more attached to his ancient fatherland than to the most beautiful countries of the earth. He was no Frankish king, as it has frequently been wished to represent him; but he belonged to the Austrasian Franks, which is the country of the Rhine, and where the Franks had their chief intercourse with the Germans still remaining there, and thus continuing most pure and unmixed. This country he intended should form the main and central seat of his empire, and the noble stream of his fatherland, as it were, its great vital artery, which should unite all its different sections. This is indicated by the canal by means of which he purposed connecting the Rhine and the Danube.

But if the Lower Rhine and Aix-la-Chapelle were to form the centre and seat of his empire, it becomes evident that his chief contest must be with the Saxons, who were here too close and unquiet neighbors of his residence for him to tolerate. He necessarily, therefore, extended the limits of his empire farther to the north and northeast. But his war with the Saxons had a still different but equally serious object; it being essentially a religious war, for the honor and diffusion of the Christian faith. Charles was eminently a champion of the church, and therein a type of the chivalric middle ages. It is true the mild doctrines of Christianity should not be diffused by fire and the sword; and Charles sufficiently experienced how little durable was the conversion when at his command hundreds at the same moment stepped into a river and had water poured over them in sign of baptism; but in this he followed less his own wishes than the character of his nation, which had itself been converted suddenly and during the external excitement of the tumult of battle. To him, however, belongs the fame and glory that he also knew and honored the right mode of igniting the light of faith. For besides this, he founded monasteries, churches, and bishoprics in Saxony, and that these doctrines might be more fully developed and propagated, he caused also all the young Saxons, received as hostages, to be assiduously instructed with others, that they might, as teachers, enlighten their nation. And so perfectly did he succeed in his plans, that this same Saxon nation, which had hitherto so obstinately resisted Christianity, was speedily filled with the greatest zeal for it, and made in every respect a flourishing progress.

The confidential and beloved friend of the king, Pope Adrian, died in 795. Charles mourned for him as for a father, and caused an inscription to be placed over his tomb which contains the expression of his veneration. His successor, Pope Leo III., was misused in a revolt of the Romans, and sought protection from Charles, who received him in solemn state at Paderborn,* whither the pope came in 799, amidst an almost incredible concourse of venerating people, when he gave him his promise to go himself to Rome to punish the evil-doers; and which promise he fulfilled in the year 800. At the Christmas festival of that same year, Charles was present at the service in St. Peter's church at Rome. On this great occasion individuals from almost every nation of the west were collected together in the metropolis of the Christian church, and an innumerable concourse of people filled the temple. After high mass, when Charles knelt at the altar, Pope Leo brought forth an imperial crown and placed it upon his head, when the whole assembled multitude exclaimed: "Charles Augustus, crowned by the Almighty, the great and peace-bringing emperor of the Romans. Hail, all hail, and victory!" At the same time the pope knelt down before him.†

Thus in 324, the year after Romulus Augustulus had lost the Roman imperial dignity, it was again renewed by Charlemagne, who, as a patrician, was already chief protector of Rome. He himself attributed so much importance to the imperial coronation, that all his subjects, from twelve years of age upwards, were obliged to renew their oath of allegiance. His power was now extended over Italy, France, Catalonia, the Balearic islands, and on the other side as far as the North Sea, the Elbe, the Bohemian forest, the Raab, and the mountains of Croatia, thus even over the greatest portion of the ancient Roman empire in Europe.

By this solemn act, Charles's grand undertaking was completed, according to its outward form. All the Christian nations of German origin, excepting England, were united in one large body, and Charles, as their temporal chief, was crowned under the ancient and, by God's guidance, renewed title of Roman emperor. As such, he was the chief protector of the church—by the Franconian synod he was styled the regent of true religion—as well as the guardian of justice and peace in Europe; and under his powerful protection, the recently planted germ of fresh life and new moral cultivation could safely develop itself, without being trampled upon by the destructive contention of nations. Accordingly, this was the great aim and purpose of the Roman imperial dignity, as renewed by the Germans, and as Theodoric had contemplated, which Charles alone, however, was enabled, by his power, to call into existence—an object which has ever continued to be fostered in the heart of every noble and magnanimous emperor succeeding to the throne of the Germanic empire.

Charles's empire was therefore not what it has been endeavored by a new name to call—a universal monarchy; not one empire wherein all the nations and countries within his reach were subject to his, the

* Pope Leo consecrated at Paderborn, among other objects, the altar of St. Stephen, which is still to be found in the vault under the choir of the cathedral.

† Eginhard, the biographer and friend of Charles, says indeed—and we may presume as received direct from the mouth of the emperor himself—that the latter had, at first, adopted the title, Augustus Imperator, with very great reluctance, and that he assured him he would not even have entered the walls of the church on that grand day of festival, had he foreseen the intention of the pope. Nevertheless, it is scarcely to be conceived that a proceeding so grave and highly important could have been arranged without the knowledge and concurrence of Charles, who, indeed, in all his actions never allowed himself to be led by others. Besides, it is already evident, from what is shown by other good testimonies,(Annul. Lauris. ham,) that the renewal of the imperial dignity had been discussed and resolved upon, for Alcuin himself knew of it beforehand, he having given to one of his pupils a Bible and a letter, both of which he was deputed to present to the emperor at the Christmas festival in Rome, and in which letter the learned master wished the mighty sovereign all happiness ad splendorem imperialis potentia. But what struck Charles, no doubt, with sudden surprise and momentary vexation was, that the pope should merely have *presented to him the imperial crown*, and that it had not been left to *him*, the sovereign, to place it upon his own head himself, or to *command* it to be done by the pope, (as his bishop,) as was the custom with the Greek emperors, who were crowned by their patriarchs; thence, there is little doubt, arose the expressions attributed to him by Eginhard. This, indeed, is clearly shown subsequently, when, at Aix-la-Chapelle, he ordered Louis to place the crown upon his own head Charles always considered himself as chief ruler over Rome, and styled the Romans in his decrees as his subjects, and included Rome in his will among the chief cities of his empire. The popes again, on their part, placed his own name, as well as those of his successors, on their coins, and included them in their bulls. In his letters, Charles henceforth calls himself: "Carolus serenissimus augustus a Deo coronatus magnus pacificus imperator Romanum gubernans imperium, qui et per misericordiam Dei rex Francorum et Langobardorum." To him it was important to hold dominion over those other nations which had not devolved upon him by hereditary right, by some other means than the mere sway of conquest, and he well knew that among the German tribes the title of Roman emperor always connected itself with the idea of supreme government. Besides, to the *emperor* all were equally bound to yield allegiance—counts, bishops, freemen, and servitors; while in obedience to the *king*, the freemen varied materially from the vassal, and the bishop from the layman. It likewise established his position towards the clergy, for the pope became now the first bishop of the empire, and Alcuin says distinctly, (cap ii.,) that the imperial power is higher than any other, even that of the pope.

individual's will, and by one law, custom, and language, united into one uniform, circumscribed whole. Such was not Charles's wish. He honored the peculiarities of nations, left them their laws, which were based upon their ancient customs and modes of living; he left them their manners and their language, which a nation could not be deprived of without inflicting the most grievous wound. He was even so widely distant from the idea of an empire strongly and despotically ruled by the will of one individual, that during his life, in the year 806, at Dietenhofen, he divided his countries between his three sons, so that Pepin should take Italy, Louis Aquitaine, and Charles the remainder, consisting chiefly of German countries. They and their successors were bound to consider themselves as the members of one race, and under the superior guidance of the emperor for the time being, or the head of the family, hold fraternally together, and accustom their nations to a similar unity.

His soul was full of such good and noble thoughts, that Europe would soon have flourished upon the basis he thus laid, had but a portion of his spirit fallen to the share of his descendants.

But Charles partially foresaw with his own eyes the destruction of his plans. Both of his most promising sons died shortly after each other, even before their father, and Louis, the weakest, alone remained. The eldest, Charles, had made several successful campaigns against the Sorbians beyond the Elbe. The father hoped every thing from this son, but unhappily these hopes were frustrated.

As Charles now felt his own end approaching more and more near, he sent for his son Louis to come to him in the year 813 to Aix-la-Chapelle, and there on a Sunday, when in the cathedral together, he reminded him of all the duties of a good monarch, and he then caused Louis to place the golden crown (which lay upon the altar) upon his head, and thus crowned, his venerable father presented him to the assembly as the future king of all the Franks. By this act Charles wished to show that his crown was independent of the papal chair, and the Franks were greatly pleased with this determination evinced by their prince at the close of his career.

The venerable emperor, however, remained still active; he continued to hold imperial diets and church convocations, and regulated all other affairs of the state.

In January of the year 814 he was attacked by a fever, which was followed by pleurisy. Charles, who up to his latter days had never been ill, and was always an enemy to medicine, wished to cure himself by his usual remedy of fasting, but his body had now become too weak. About five o'clock on the morning of the eighth day of his illness, (the 28th of January,) he felt the approach of death, and energetically raising his right hand, marked upon his forehead, bosom, and even to the feet, the sign of the cross. He then stretched forth his arms once more, folded them over his bosom, closed his eyes, and murmuring softly and in broken tones, "Lord, into thy hands do I commit my soul," he breathed his last sigh in the seventy-second year of his age, and the forty-sixth of his reign. On the very day of his death the body of the deceased emperor was solemnly cleansed, laid out, and anointed, and conveyed amidst the sorrow and mourning of the whole nation, to the vault of the church built by himself. He was there clothed in all the imperial robes, with a golden gospel spread out on his knees, a piece of the original holy cross upon his head, and a pilgrim's golden scrip around his loins, and placed thus in an upright position upon a marble chair; when, filling the vault with frankincense, spices, balsam, and many costly articles, they closed and sealed it up.

So much veneration for the emperor existed throughout all his dominions, and so much were all eyes directed upon him, that every thing which, during the last few years of his existence, had happened to him either wonderful or extraordinary, was considered as prophetic of his death. His biographer, Eginhard, mentions many such phenomena. During the three years preceding his death, there were frequent eclipses of the sun and moon; the arcade of columns, which Charles had caused to be erected between the minster and the imperial palace, sank by a sudden revolution of nature, upon Ascension Day, into the earth, and was destroyed to its very foundation. Besides which the Rhine bridge, near Mentz, which in the course of ten years he had built of wood with great ingenuity and art, so that it was rendered fit to last for ages, was entirely destroyed by fire in the short space of three hours. He himself in his last campaign against Godfrey, king of the Danes, upon marching forth one day before sunrise, beheld a fiery meteor fall suddenly from heaven, passing from the right to the left through the clear air. At this moment his horse plunged, and falling to the earth, overthrew him so violently that the clasp of his mantle broke, his sword-belt was torn asunder, so that he was lifted from the ground by his alarmed attendants without a mantle and without his sword. To which may be added a variety of other signs, equally alarming in their indication, but in which the great emperor was too wise to place any faith.

In order that we may completely comprehend the extraordinary man whose history thus calls forth our admiration, we necessarily desire to be acquainted with his outward form, wherein the mighty spirit was encased. We are anxious to know how the eye reflected the internal sentiments; whether the brow and countenance depicted dignity and repose, or whether they expressed the animated, impetuous emotions of the mind; and finally, whether the elevation and power of the spirit were equally displayed throughout the entire corporeal form. Eginhard, the friend of Charlemagne, and whom the latter had brought up in his palace as his adopted son, has drawn up for us a beautiful and affectionate description of his noble fosterfather:

"In person," he says, "the emperor was robust and strong, and of great height, for he measured seven of his own feet.* His head was round, his eyes large and animated; his nose somewhat exceeded moderate proportions; his gray hair was beautiful to behold, and his countenance joyous and cheerful, whence his figure derived peculiar dignity and charm. He had a firm step, and a perfect manly bearing. He practised riding and hunting incessantly, according to the customary habits of his nation, for scarcely a people existed upon earth that could rival the Franks in these arts. Besides this, he was such a skilful swimmer, that none could justly be said to surpass him.

"He enjoyed constant good health, with the exception of the last four years of his life, when he was frequently attacked by fever, which at last occasioned him to limp slightly on one foot. During these attacks, he continued nevertheless to follow his own counsel, rather than the advice of his doctors, with whom, in fact, he was sorely vexed, for they prohibited him from eating roasted meat, which he himself considered the most wholesome of all food.

"He was exceedingly temperate in both eating and drinking, but especially so in the latter, for intoxication was his abhorrence, in any person, and particularly in his own palace. His daily meal consisted of four dishes only, exclusive of the roasted joint, which his yägers or squires brought upon the spit, and which he preferred and relished before every other dish. During his meals he listened with great pleasure to the lays of his minstrels on the lute, or to a reader, the subjects sung or read being always the histories and events of heroic men. He also took much delight in the books of St. Augustine, particularly in those on the divine government of God.

"In summer it was his custom after dinner, to enjoy a little fruit, and to drink once; then to undress himself as at night, and thus repose for three or four hours. His nights were very restless, not merely by his awaking up several times, but likewise by his getting up from his couch and walking about. During his toilet, not only were his friends admitted, but likewise, if his Count Palatine had to present to him any appeal, which could not be decided without his opinion and determination thereupon, he forthwith caused the disputants to be brought before him, and then investigated the affair and gave judgment at once.

"His dress consisted of the national costume, and was but little different from that of the common people. He wore, next his skin, a linen shirt, over which a garment with a silken cord, and long hose. His feet were enclosed in laced shoes, and, in winter, for the protection of his shoulders and chest, he wore a waistcoat of otterskin. As upper garment, he wore a mantle, and had always his sword girded on, the haft and defence of which were of gold

* A staff or lance of iron has been preserved, which is said to give the exact height of Charlemagne, and according to which he measured six feet three inches by the Rhenish measurement

and silver; and at times he wore a sword inlaid with jewels, but only on particular festivals, or when he gave audience to foreign ambassadors. His raiment likewise, on these occasions, was of golden cloth, and he wore a crown adorned with gold and precious stones. *Foreign dress*, even the most beautiful, he disliked and despised, and would never clothe himself in such; except when at Rome, where, firstly at the express wish of Pope Adrian, and secondly, at the request of Leo, his successor, he wore a dress with a long train, and a broad mantle, with shoes made according to the Roman fashion.

"Charles possessed a style of rich and flowing eloquence, and whatever he wished, was expressed by him in the most clear and concise manner. He did not content himself with his mother tongue alone, but applied himself industriously to the acquirement of the classical and foreign languages generally. Of the former, he was so perfectly master of the Latin, that he spoke it equally as well as his native tongue; and the Greek, although he did not speak it, he nevertheless perfectly well understood, and was so proficient in it, that he could himself have become its teacher. He practised the superior arts very zealously, and was extremely liberal in the honors and rewards he conferred upon their professors. In learning grammar, he had the attendance of the venerable deacon, Peter of Pisa; and in other sciences, his instructor was Albin, with the surname of Alcuin, who was a native of Britain, but of Saxon origin; a very learned man, and Charles devoted much labor and time in acquiring from him a knowledge of astronomy. He also endeavored to attain the art of writing, and was even accustomed to have his tablets under his pillow in bed, so that when he had a leisure moment he might practise his hand in the imitation of letters. In this, however, owing to his commencing it at so late a period, he made but little progress.

"The minster at Aix-la-Chapelle, which is of extreme beauty, is a monument of his love for the arts, as also of his great piety, and which he caused after he had it built, to be ornamented with gold and silver, together with windows, lattices, and gates of solid brass. He had all the pillars and marble stones used for its construction, brought from Rome and Ravenna, as he could not obtain them in any other quarter.* His piety displayed itself in the support of the poor, and in gifts and donations which he sent to distant lands across the sea, and wherever he heard Christians to be in want; and thence it was that he sought the friendship of princes ruling in those distant countries, in order that some portion of nourishment might be dispensed to the Christians living under their dominion. It was thus he maintained a cordial friendship with Aaron, the king of the Persians, (Haroun al Raschid, caliph of Bagdad,) who ruled over nearly the whole of the east, with the exception of India. When, therefore, Charles sent his envoys with rich offerings to the holy tomb of our Lord and Saviour, they were not only very kindly received by Aaron, but, on their return, he sent with them his own ambassador to accompany them to the court of Charles, and who conveyed from him the choicest of the shawls, spices, and other costly rarities of the east, as presents to the emperor, to whom be it mentioned, he had already, in proof of their good understanding, sent some few years previously, the only elephant he then had in his possession."

From another source we learn that this elephant, which was called Abulabaz, or the destroyer, by its monstrous and unexampled size, amazed the whole world, and was Charles's especial favorite; and that among the presents sent with it there was a costly tent, together with a clock made of brass with astonishing skill and ingenuity. This latter contained a hand or indicator, moved round, during twelve hours, by the power of water, together with an equal quantity of brass balls, which, when the hours were completed, dropped into a brass cup placed beneath, by their fall indicating the hour, upon which mounted knights, fully armed, according to the number of hours, galloped forth from twelve windows—a work assuredly of great and extraordinary ingenuity for that period. Charles, on his part, made presents in return to the Persian ru-

* The church of the Virgin Mary and the imperial palace are, as far as we know, the first extensive buildings founded by a German prince. Charles's structures are based upon the Roman style of North Italy and South France, whence he procured his architects. The palace in Aix-la-Chapelle has, with the exception of a few remaining stones, entirely disappeared, but St. Mary's church still exists.

ler, of Spanish horses, mules, and Frisian mantles, which in the east were very rare and expensive, and finally, were added to these a number of dogs for hunting the lion and tiger, unsurpassed for swiftness and ferocity.

We have previously mentioned his friendly connection with the emperor in Constantinople, and his amicable relations with the princes of England and Scotland, by whom he was highly esteemed; and thus the impression of his personal greatness was reflected throughout the age in which he lived, as well in the descriptions given by those who were about him, as also in the veneration of distant nations. His own grandson, Nithard, who has described the disputes of the sons of Louis the Pious, says of him with great justice: "Charles, justly called by all nations the great emperor; a man who by true wisdom and virtue rises so high above the human race of his own age, that while he appears to all equally awe-striking and amiable, is at the same time universally acknowledged to be wonderful and admirable."

In the subsequent generations, still filled with veneration towards him, his figure became so irradiated by tradition and fiction, that its proportions appear gigantically magnified. Thus, for instance, in a legend of Low Germany he is described as follows: "The emperor Charles was a handsome, tall, strong man, with powerful arms and legs: his face was a span and a half long, and his beard a foot in length. His eyes, to those at whom he attentively looked, appeared so bright and searching, that the effect therefrom was to strike with awe and terror; while his strength was so mighty, that with one hand he could raise a fully-armed man above his head."

Another ancient Chronicle says of his expedition against Desiderius: "When the Longobardian king from his castle in Pavia observed the entire body of the Frankish army in full march against him, his eyes searched everywhere among the ranks to find the king. At length the majestic monarch appeared to view, mounted on his war-horse, (which both in durability and color resembled iron itself,) with a brazen helmet on his head, his entire lofty figure encased in iron armor, and a shining breast-plate spread over his chest. In his left hand he held his heavy iron spear and his right grasped his massive sword; and when at this moment Nosker, a noble, exiled by Charles, and who was standing near the king of the Longobardians, pointed to him, and said, 'Behold, O king, there is he whom thou hast sought,' Desiderius almost fell to the ground in wonder and dread, faintly exclaiming, 'Away, away! Let us descend and bury ourselves in the earth from the wrathful countenance of that terrible and mighty foe!'"

As a testimony that the admiration excited by true greatness extends far beyond the present and immediately succeeding periods, and maintains its estimation in all susceptible and glowing minds, even to the latest ages, we will here quote the opinion of a modern writer* upon the character of the great Charles: "The whole appearance and bearing of the emperor evince the true and *original* model of his energetic age—full of manly, yet cheerful virtue. Combined with the exuberance of power, which remodelled an entire world, were united mildness and placidity, and with all his dignity and elevation, we find consorted, simplicity, purity of mind, and a profound and noble fire of feeling. The mixture of serenity and childlike mildness in his deportment was the mystery whereby he filled all at the same time with veneration and love; retaining in faithful adherence to him even those who had been severely provoked, so exquisitely shown by the act of the noble Frank, Isenbart, who, although deprived by Charles of all honors and possessions, became, nevertheless, the unexpected but sole saviour of his life when threatened with great danger. There lay in the fire of his piercing eye so much power, that a punishing glance prostrated the object, so that to him might be applied the words of scripture: 'The king when he sits upon the throne of his majesty, chases by a glance of his countenance every evil thing;' while in the thunder of his voice there was such force, that it struck to the earth whomsoever he addressed in anger. On the other hand, again, we find that his countenance reflected such unutterable pleasure and gladness, and his voice was so harmonious and of such delightful clearness, that a writer styles him the joyful king of the Germans,

* M. Süvern: "Abhandlung über Karl der Grosse."

assuring us that he was always so full of grace and gentleness, that he who came before his presence in sorrowful mood, was by a mere look and a few words so completely changed, that he departed joyful and happy. In his countenance was reflected the full expression of a tranquil and clear mind, and in all these outlines of his character he is the perfect ideal of a true German hero and prince, worthy to be called, what he really was, the father and creator of the Germanic age, which he brought upon the stage of history, after it had attained ripeness and perfection in the womb of humanity. It was not merely in his works and external creations that he founded the Germanic age, but its greatness and simplicity, its heroism in war and friendship in peace, were ingrafted in his profound soul entire!"

We have already spoken of his friendship with Pope Adrian, founded on mutual esteem, and his paternal devotion to Einhard. But to none was he attached so affectionately as to Angilbert, or Engelbert, a young man of noble family, who was his constant companion in all his travels and campaigns, and to whom he confided his most important affairs. Engelbert was an excellent poet, and for some time appointed prime minister in Italy; he then became Charles's private secretary, and likewise married his daughter Bertha, from which marriage descended the before-named historian, Nithard. Charles was a reverential son to his mother Bertrande, a faithful brother to his only sister Gisla, and of his consorts he chiefly loved the second, Hildegarde, who bore him his three sons, besides three daughters. He caused his children to have the best education, and he even dedicated much of his own time to them with paternal watchfulness. His sons learned not only all chivalric accomplishments, but studied also the sciences. The daughters were taught to work in wool, sewing, and spinning, according to the prevalent simple German custom. He never took his meals without his children; they accompanied him in all his travels, his sons riding beside him, and his daughters following him. His heart was so attached to these, that he could never prevail upon himself to part with them. He superintended his domestic economy most carefully. To him even, the legislator of an extensive empire, it did not appear too trifling to overlook with prudent care his estates and farms, so that any father of a family might have learned from him how to regulate his household affairs. Some of his laws are still extant, and therein we find especially indicated, how many of every description of domestic animals, and how many peacocks and pheasants shall be reared and maintained for ornament on his farms; as likewise how wine and beer were to be prepared, and how the cultivation of bees, fisheries, orchards, and plantations, was to be pursued.

"If Charles's general greatness impresses us with reverence and admiration," so says the modern historian of his life, "this participation in the inferior concerns of life, not smothered by higher cares, brings him more closely in connection with us; this especial care of the domestic hearth, so peculiar to the genuine German, wherein he has grown up as the plant in the earth which bears and nourishes it, while his active power strives outward into the world of deeds and works, and his bold mind soars towards heaven, as the plant shoots its blossom forth towards the sun." And in truth, Charles's mind was directed towards the light of truth; he was animated with the love of the glorious and the beautiful, and planted both wherever he was able, and by all the means in his power.* He had formed with the wise Englishman, Alcuin, and other learned men a scientific society, and he maintained with them a regular correspondence, which was rendered more free and intellectual, inasmuch as a happy idea from Alcuin enabled it to be conducted without any interference with personal relations. The communications were not made in the ordinary names of the members, but in those of adoption, in which Charles himself bore the name of King David, his friend Engelbert that of Homer, Alcuin that of Horace, Eginhard that of Bezaleel, and the rest, other equally select names, whence the cheerful disposition of this union, breaking the restrictive chains of ordinary life, sufficiently displays itself.

* As regards the benefits produced by Charles's zeal for education and science, we find already that in the years 650 to 770, there were in Germany and France some twenty-six writers, while in the years 770 to 850, there were already in Charles's kingdom more than one hundred.

Its immediate purpose, besides the cultivation of both the ancient languages, may possibly have been to reanimate and draw forth from its obscurity the ancient German language and its poetry. Charles himself either sketched, or caused to be sketched, a German grammar, gave to the months and the seasons German names, and collected the aboriginal songs, wherein were recited the noble deeds and the wars of ancient heroes, (as formerly Lycurgus and Pisistratus collected the songs of Homer.) But there is not a more affecting trait of his own love for the sciences extant than that already related, when in extreme age he endeavored carefully to accustom his once powerful hand, which had been used only to wield the sword, to the practice of writing, and that even during the sleepless hours of the night. And how far he esteemed educated and scientific men is proved, besides the instances already cited, by his example shown towards the Longobardian historian, Paul Diaconus. He was private secretary to King Desiderius, and after the latter was conquered, the former participated in the subsequent revolt of the Lombards, upon which he was sentenced to have his hands chopped off. Charles, however, interfered and said, "If these hands are chopped off, who will, like him, be able to write us such charming histories?" and accordingly he pardoned him. The learned Alcuin already mentioned—in possessing whom at his court Charles felt more pride than in having a kingdom—had been previously provost of the high school of York in England, where almost all the learned men of that period had received their education and had imbibed their zeal for the sciences, and which contained one of the few then existing libraries of the west of Europe. In 793 he was induced by the repeated entreaties of the king to go over to France, where he founded the celebrated school of Tours. Charles esteemed him so much that he called him his beloved instructor in Christ, and presented him as his friend to the grand imperial diet and church convocation at Frankfort. And Alcuin proved himself worthy of this honor, for when all, from fear or doubt, were silent, he alone candidly told the king the truth. The correspondence of Charles with Alcuin is worthy of high estimation, and of which, happily, we still possess a considerable portion. Charles, on his part, there expresses the greatest respect and friendship for Alcuin, and the latter is full of true affection, nay, at times, of inspiration towards his king and friend. Charles's wife and his sons and daughters received instruction from Alcuin, and he was styled by them all their master and father, he, on his part, calling them his sons and daughters.

Combined with his anxiety for the affairs of the Church, Charles likewise, with proper foresight and penetration, felt deep interest for the instruction of the people; thence, wherever it was possible, he founded schools and investigated their progress with great solicitude himself. It is related that he once entered the school which was established at his own court, and examined the studies of the boys. The skilful he placed on his right and the unskilful on his left, and then it was found that the latter consisted chiefly of the sons of noble families. Charles then turned to the industrious class, praised them much, and assured them of his particular regard; the others he admonished and scolded severely, threatening them, notwithstanding their noble descent, to reduce them to the lowest rank in the school unless they speedily repaired, by zealous industry, the negligence shown.

The study of the Latin tongue was especially promoted by Charles for the sake of the church; but, at the same time, he acknowledged the value of the Greek language, as he proved by founding in Osnaburg a Greek school. In a royal decree addressed to all monasteries, in which he exhorts them to apply themselves to the sciences, he says expressly, that he has been led to make this exhortation, because their communications are written in such bad Latin. Another important result arising from the scientific labors of Charles and his friends, was the establishment of libraries in the chief schools. Alcuin laid the foundation of such a one in the school at Tours, by sending scholars to York for the purpose of making copies from the books there, and thus "transplanting the flowers of Britain to Franconia." This example was soon followed, the desire to possess books awoke, the office of extracting from writings now became a favorite occupation and duty in the monasteries and schools, and indeed, we have to thank this industry of the copyists for what has been preserved to us from ancient times.*

The sacred dignity of divine worship concerned him much; he gave himself particular trouble to introduce a good psalmody, and caused for that purpose organ players and singers to come from Italy; and at Soissons and Metz he instituted singing schools. Besides this, he ordered a number of good sermons by the Greek fathers to be translated into the Frankish tongue, and read to the people;† and he made a general regulation, that sermons should be preached in the national language, for King Charles well knew that civil order reposed upon the religious and moral dignity of the people, and without which it can have no solid basis. He considered church and state not as separated from, or inimical to each other, but conceived that they both had one great aim, that of the ennoblement and perfection of mankind. He, therefore, in his extensive empire, linked both these institutions still more closely together.

Even under the earlier Frankish kings, the clergy formed an essential portion of the constitution of the kingdom. The bishops, as well as the dukes, participated in state affairs, and had a seat and a voice in the national assembly. Charles made this a fixed principle, and this raised the clerical body to rank as one of the orders of the state. The constitution had already now formed two of its chief orders, that of the clergy and nobility; the civil order, as the third component, did not yet exist; later centuries brought it to perfection, and thereby completed the constitution of the state. But it was important for that period, that the feudal nobility, which had already become too powerful, should receive a counterbalance in the clerical order, which must necessarily become the preservation of Christian cultivation throughout Europe, and thereby unite Europe into one great whole. Besides, Charles felt himself sufficiently powerful to fear no misuse of such spiritual influence in his realms. Although he increased the possessions and the consideration of the clergy, he yet maintained his imperial power so much above them, that his quick eye was everywhere feared, so much so, that one of his historians calls him the bishop of bishops.

We frequently find in his decrees reproaches made against the clergy, when they commenced exceeding the limits of their power, and many of his laws generally allude to an ameliorated state of discipline among the ecclesiastical body, to a restraint being put to their worldliness, and commanding them to perform the duties of their office with zeal and activity. In fact, he may be regarded as the true reformer of the clergy, especially when we refer to the condition of that body under the Merovingians. Of the tithes which were to be paid to the church, he appointed for the bishops one fourth, for the inferior clergy one fourth, for the poor one fourth, and for the church itself one fourth, especially towards the building of fresh edifices. And as these taxes were altogether hateful alike both to the Franks and Saxons, he at once set the example himself of subscribing to them, by having them levied equally upon the royal estates. They were rendered less obnoxious and more moderate likewise by his subsequent decrees, that all church offices, such as baptisms, communions, and burials, should be performed gratuitously.

With respect to the administration of the state, Charles dispensed with the power of the grand dukes as governors of entire provinces, and divided the latter into smaller districts, causing them to be ruled by counts, whose chief occupation was the superintendence of the judicial office; but the dignity of count was not hereditary. The dukes, whom he himself appointed, were merely his lieutenant-generals in war and leaders of the arrière ban of a province. Besides which he dispatched, as often as he thought it necessary, royal en-

* Alcuin took especial pains to form and establish classes for the improvement and perfection of writing. In Tours, Fulda, and Treves, particular and distinct halls were appropriated for transcribers, provided with inscriptions, which impressed upon the mind the important duties of a writer. In fact, the art of writing in books and ancient documents appears, under Charles, to have undergone a change, completely sudden, in improvement. For, to the unsightly Merovingian style of italic character previously in use—even to the first years of Charles's reign—we find succeeding as it were, with one spring, a fine and legible form of round hand, called the Carolingian minuskel, or neatly reduced writing. This style became the legitimate source whence we derived all our present forms, both in writing and printing, in German as well as Latin. In the coins of the year 774, we likewise find displayed an improvement equally striking, thus showing that, even in minor objects, the great Charles operated efficaciously.

† He directed Paulus Diaconus to prepare extracts from the fathers, in the form of a collection of homilies throughout the year. This collection, from the usual opening of the pieces, "post illa," received, subsequently, the name postille.

voys (missi regii) into the provinces, who inspected their condition, and examined how they were governed, and were obliged to draw up written reports thereof. These envoys consisted generally of a bishop and a count, as the proceedings of the spiritual as well as temporal administrators were to be examined at the same time. The district of a *Missus* was called *Missaticum.* When any person believed he had experienced an avoidance in law from the count, he could appeal to the Missus; and again from this there was an appeal to the *Comes palatii.* The appointment of the judges in the courts was removed from the power of the counts by Charles, and transferred to the *Missus.*

He expressly and earnestly exhorted all his officials, and particularly the judges, to the fulfilment of their duties, as in fact the grand endeavor, shown throughout his entire government, had for its object the improvement of the administration of justice, and especially the protection of the poorer classes and the common free people, against the pressure of the higher ranks. It seemed as if in the latter period of his reign he had more and more perceived the danger with which the common freedom of his subjects was threatened by the feudal system. All administration of justice, however, was in vain. He was forced himself to attend in person, twice in the year, national assemblies or diets, the one in spring, called the May Field, (*Campus Madius,*) in which the king, with his estates, gave the decisions; the other in autumn, composed of the most distinguished of his nobles and confidential friends, with whom he regulated the most urgent matters, and prepared those affairs to be settled at the ensuing May meeting. The regulations made at these diets, particularly those passed in the Spring meetings, which, after their division into chapters, became known under the name of *capitulars,* produced for the entire kingdom a great combining power.

The envoys, each in their division, called together the communities four times every year, who, besides attending to their own matters, had to approve and confirm the resolutions passed at the grand assemblies, if they concerned the interests of the people: so little power had the king and his nobles to affect or alter their rights. Thus by means of all these institutions, Charles, who was still greater as a legislator than a warrior, was enabled to keep in order without garrisons and a standing army, all the people subjected to obedience, as well as his whole extensive empire, although composed of such a variety of nations. He himself remained within the boundaries of the constitution, honored the laws, listened willingly to the voice of his people, and showed in every thing, but especially in this, his noble genius and magnanimity, and the dignified superiority of his nature.

## CHAPTER VI.

### 814—918.

Louis the Pious, 814-840—Division of the Empire among his Sons, Louis, Lothaire, and Charles the Bald, 843—The German Sovereigns of the Race of the Carlovingians, 843-911—Louis, or Ludwig, the German—Charles the Fat—Arnulf—Louis the Child—The later and concluding period of the Carlovingians—Conrad I. of Franconia, 911-918.

After the race of the Carlovingians had produced consecutively four great men—a rare occurrence in history—its energy seemed to become exhausted. Louis the Pious did not resemble his ancestors. However, his personal appearance was by no means insignificant, for he is described as well made, with a prepossessing countenance, of a strong frame, and so well practised in archery and the wielding of the lance, that none about him equalled him. But he was weak in mind and will, and his by-name, "the Pious," implies not only that he was religious, but principally that he was so easy tempered, that it required much to displease him. A ruler of this description was not adapted to hold in union the vast empire of his father; nevertheless, the chief misfortunes of his whole life arose solely from his own sons.

He had three sons by the first marriage, Lothaire, Pepin, and Louis; and he very early divided his empire between these three, retaining for himself nothing but the title of emperor. He, however, soon afterwards espoused as second consort, Judith, of the family of the Guelfs, who bore to him his fourth son, Charles, and was a proud, ambitious woman, who would willingly have transferred all to her own child. Upon her persuasion Louis was induced to take a portion of the countries from his other sons, and give it to Charles. Whereupon open war arose between the emperor and his children, who took their father twice prisoner. The last time it occurred was near Colmar, in Alsace, and because most of the nobles of Louis's suite, who had sworn allegiance to him, passed over to his sons, the place has retained the name of Lügenfeld, or the Field of Lies. The good-natured Louis, turning to those who remained still with him, said, "Go ye, also, to my sons; I will not allow that even a single individual lose, on my account, life or limb." They wept and departed, and Louis fell again into the hands of his sons. Lothaire, who was the worst among them, had him conveyed to a cloister at Soissons in France, and urged him so incessantly, until he at last resolved to do public penance in the chapel. Lothaire's object in this was, that his father might thereby be made incompetent to take arms, for it was ordained by the canon law, that any one who had done penance was rendered incapable of bearing arms, and the Franks could not endure among them a king without a sword.

The pious Louis, who was easily persuaded that his own sins were the cause of all his misfortunes, absolutely allowed himself to be conducted into the chapel of the monastery, and after he had been divested of his sword and military accoutrements, he was clothed in a sack of penance, and was forced to read a paper aloud, whereon his son and his accomplices had inscribed all his sins, thus: "That he had unworthily filled his office, frequently offended God, vexed the church, was a perjurer, the originator of dissensions and turbulences, and, at last, had even wished to make war upon his sons." And while he made this confession, the clergy, consisting of the Archbishop Ebbo, of Rheims, whom Louis himself had raised from a servitor to an archbishop, and with him thirty bishops, spread out their hands over him, and chanted penitential psalms; Lothaire himself sitting close by upon a throne, and feasting his eyes upon the degradation of his father, who was immediately afterwards led away in the garment of repentance, and immured within a solitary cell, where he was left to remain, without any consolation.

This misusage of the emperor enraged his son, Louis of Bavaria, who was afterwards called Ludwig the German, and who was the best of the sons; he conferred with his brother Pepin, and they forced Lothaire to emancipate their father, who was formally absolved by the bishops, and received from their hands his sword and accoutrements back again.

But his misfortunes had not made him wiser, for, on the contrary, he allowed himself to be immediately persuaded by Judith to prefer his son Charles before the rest, and to give him his most beautiful countries, causing him to be crowned King of Neustria. He treated his best son, Louis, the worst, who consequently, in his irritation, seized arms against his father, and the old king could nowhere find a tranquil spot for his death-bed; for, as he was proceeding to Worms, to hold a diet there against his son, and was just passing over the Rhine, near Mentz, he suddenly felt his quickly-approaching end. He remained upon an island of the Rhine, near Ingelheim, caused a tent to be there pitched for him, and sank down upon his death-bed. He pardoned his son before his death, in these words: "As he cannot come to me to offer satisfaction, I acquit myself thus towards him, and take God and all of you to witness, that I forgive him every thing. But it will be your office to remind him, that although I have so often pardoned him, he must not forget that he has brought the gray hairs of his father to the grave in bitter grief." Thus died, in the year 840, King Louis, who was of a kind disposition, but whose life was one continued scene of trouble and affliction, because he knew not how to govern his own house, much less his empire.

The most celebrated acts of his life consist in the foundation of two religious institutions; viz., the monastery of Corvey, and the archbishopric of Hamburg. The first originated from the cloister of the same name, at Amiens in France. It was hither that Charlemagne caused many of the imprisoned Saxons to be brought, that they might be instructed in the Christian religion, and become thereby the future teachers of their fellow-countrymen in the same doctrines. Louis the Pious caused a religious colony of these Saxons to settle in their native country, on the Weser, and he commenced building the new monastery as early as the year 815. It was completed in 822, and the abby was enriched with many crown endowments. It speedily became the best school for education in that country.

Louis founded the archbishopric of Hamburg in 832, principally for the conversion of the heathens of the north. The first bishop was Ansgar, from the abbey of Corvey, one of the most zealous propagators of the Christian religion, and who had already taught the doctrine in Denmark and Sweden. But Hamburg, unfortunately, was destroyed by the Romans, in 845, on which account the archbishopric was transferred to Bremen.

The brothers, who had not hesitated to take up arms against their own father, could much less remain united among themselves. In particular, Lothaire assumed, as emperor, great privileges over his brothers. Louis and Charles, Pepin being already dead, consequently armed themselves against him; and as he would not agree to a treaty of peace, a battle was fought in 841, near Fontenay, in France. It was very sanguinary; forty thousand, according to others a hundred thousand, men were left on the field. Lothaire was conquered, and his great pretensions were thus dissipated, and in consequence, in the course of two years, an important treaty took place, which divided the great Frankish empire, and separated Germany forever from France. This is called the treaty of Verdun, concluded on the 11th of August, 843.

1. Louis received Germany as far as the Rhine; and across the Rhine, Mentz, Spires, and Worms, for the sake of the culture of the vine, (propter vini copiam,) as it is said in the original record. Thus were united all the countries wherein a pure German race, unmixed with the Romans, had remained, and the Germans may consider the treaty of Verdun as a great national benefit. For had that country remained united with France, and had the king made Paris, perhaps, the metropolis, or even changed about in the chief cities of that country, it is probable that, in the course of time, a ruinous mixture of the German and French languages, manners, modes of life, and idiosyncrasies of the two nations would have taken place.

2. Lothaire retained the imperial dignity and Italy, and acquired, besides, a long narrow strip of land between Germany and France, from the Alps as far as the Netherlands, namely, the country of Valais and Vaud in Switzerland, the south east of France, as far as the Rhone; and on the left bank of the Rhine, Alsace, and the districts of the Moselle, Meuse, and Scheldt. This long and narrow strip between the two other brothers was probably apportioned to the emperor that he might be near them both, and that, according to the wish of the father and grandfather, the imperial control might tend to preserve the unity of the whole. It likewise seemed that Italy and the ancient city of Rome, as well as ancient Austrasia, namely, the Rhenish districts, which Charlemagne had selected for his residence, with his capital, Aix-la-Chapelle, were not separable from the imperial dignity. But although Lothaire received beautiful and productive provinces, yet his portion was the weakest, for his empire on this side of the Alps had no natural frontiers, either in mountains or in a distinct national race. The inhabitants of his countries on the Rhone and down the Rhine were composed of very different tribes; thence as there was no natural necessity for this division of countries, it was merely produced by human caprice, consequently, there was no durability in it. On the contrary, it became the source of great misfortune. After the emperor Lothaire, pursued as it were by the spirit of his injured father, against whom he had chiefly offended, had laid down the sceptre and retired into a convent, where he died in 862, his three sons took up arms in contest for the land, and divided it among themselves; but neither of them transmitted it to his descendants. The countries of Burgundy, Alsace, and the province of Lorraine proper, which Lothaire II. had received, and which had from him received its name, were, after his early death, divided by his two uncles, Louis the German, and the French king, Charles; so that the land to the east of the Meuse, with the cities of Utrecht, Aix-la-Chapelle, Liège, Metz, Treves, Cologne, Strasburg, Basle, &c., fell to Germany. But this division did not terminate the dispute for the Lorraine inheritance, for it has remained through every century a bone of contention between the Germans and the French, and many sanguinary wars have taken place in consequence.

3. Charles the Bald received, lastly, the western division of the whole Frankish

kingdom, and which has continued to preserve its title.

Louis the German, (840–876,) who was an energetic prince, of lofty stature and noble figure, with a fiery eye and a penetrating mind, and who also possessed an active disposition for education and science, (which the schools of eloquence that he founded at Frankfort and Ratisbonne have proved,) had constantly to contend for the tranquillity of his realm; for the Slavonian tribes made incursions on the eastern frontiers, and the Normans on the north and northwest. These bold sailors, of ancient German origin, wild as their sea and its northern coasts, coming from the Norwegian, Swedish, and Danish waters, appeared with the rapidity of the wind, at the mouths of the rivers, and frequently advanced deep into the country. They ascended the Seine as far as Paris, flew along the Garonne to Toulouse, and sailed up the Rhine to Cologne and Bonn. And it was not the banks merely of these rivers which suffered from their devastations, but they knew also how to convey their vessels many thousand paces across the country into other rivers, so that no place afforded security against them. So great was the terror of their name, that the mere report of their coming drove to flight all before them. Their numbers were generally small, for a fleet of the small ships of that period could not convey large armies; but their courage, as well as their strength of body and their weapons, testified to their true northern origin; while in wielding the powerful spear, no race equalled them. A few ships, manned with valiant men, formed frequently the equipment of their royal princes; and as in ancient Germany, a noble leader with his company, in bold excursions, acquired honor and booty, and with his suite, even contested for the possession of a whole country; so, on the other hand, the squadron of the bold sea-hero, manned with warlike and pillage-seeking adventurers, was the source of his riches, forming often the moving basis upon which he erected his kingdom. It was thus they founded similar kingdoms in Normandy, France, Sicily, and in Russia. Louis the German succeeded in protecting his kingdom against them, and against the Slavonians; but not so his son, Louis the Fat, (876–887,) who, after the death of his brothers, Carloman and Louis, by the intervention of particular circumstances, again united for a short time the three portions of the Frankish empire, in Italy, Germany, and France. In France there was a minor king, Charles the Simple, six years of age, for whom he was to have protected the country against the Normans; but not possessing the qualifications necessary, this he was not able to do, and thence he was forced twice to purchase peace from them at the price of many pounds of gold: the first time when they had advanced upon the Meuse as far as Hasloff, and the second time when, with 700 vessels, they had ascended the Seine as far as Paris itself, and closely besieged that city. Such cowardly conduct, and the weakness of his whole government, brought him into contempt, and was the cause which produced his formal deposition, in a great and national assembly held at Tribur in the year 887. To his great good fortune, he died the following year.

In Germany he was succeeded (887–899) by Arnulf, a son of his brother Carloman, consequently a grandson of Louis the German, a valiant and worthy king. He beat the Normans at Louvain, in the Netherlands, where they had erected a fortified camp, which victory made him very celebrated, for those Normans formed the most valiant race of the north, and had never previously been known to fly before an enemy.*

Arnulf now marched also into Italy, to bring that disunited country—where many pretenders contested for supremacy—again under German dominion. He advanced, in 896, as far as Rome; but his army had been so much weakened by sickness and foul weather, that he dared not attempt to attack the strong walls of the city, and was

* About this time, in the southeastern frontiers of Germany, a Slavonic prince, Zwentibolt, had established a considerable dominion in Moravia. In order to gain his friendship, Arnulf gave him the vacant Duchy of Bohemia as a fief, and chose him as godfather to his son, whom he named after him. But the Moravian prince became unruly, and strove for independence; and Arnulf soon saw himself entangled in a severe war against him. In order, therefore, to gain allies, he had recourse to the Magyars, who rose against Zwentibolt, and, falling upon Moravia, completely overthrew his dominion, and established themselves there instead, while the late ruler withdrew, and sought refuge in a monastery. Arnulf, in order to extend the power of his house, now took advantage of some favorable circumstances presented in Lorraine, in order to procure for his son, Zwentibolt, the duchy of that country. In this he succeeded, after several encounters with the nobility; and in 895 his son took the title of king, but he held it but for a short time, being soon afterwards killed in a battle against his vassals, immediately after the death of his father.

about to turn back. Upon this, the Romans hooted and insulted the Germans so grossly, that, without awaiting the word of command, they turned back, advanced, and storming the gates, filled the ditches, mounted the walls, and carried the city. The Roman people were obliged to swear fidelity to him. But they knew not how to observe the oath they took; and as they had not been able to overcome the powerful Germans by open force, they had recourse to poison; thence Arnulf was, most probably, secretly drugged by them, for he returned ill to Germany, and died, after a long sickness, in the year 899, much too early for his kingdom, and mourned by all Germans; for he was yet young, and Germany never more than at that moment required his powerful arm.

A new savage tribe, in ferocity equal to the ancient Hunns, had now fixed themselves in Hungary, and extended their incursions to Germany. They were properly called Madschari or Magyars, and belonged to the Calmuc race of the Asiatic wanderers, but they were called Hunns, (also Hungarians, after the country they henceforward occupied,) because it was then customary to call all those tribes Hunns who were savage and terrible to behold, and who came from the east. They also, like the former Hunns, lived always on horseback, and suddenly appeared where they were not awaited. They unexpectedly attacked, and as suddenly fled, and in flying they always shot their arrows backward, and turned quickly round when all was considered safe. They shot their arrows from bows, formed of bone, with so much force and precision, that it was scarcely possible to avoid them; but they were ignorant of the art of fighting at close quarters, or of besieging cities. They were small in stature, ugly in countenance, with deep-sunken eyes, of barbaric manners, and with a coarse and discordant language; so that an ancient writer who lived at that period, says: "We must be astonished that Divine Providence should have given so delightful a country to be inhabited—not by such men, but by such monsters in human shape!"

These terrific enemies desolated in an unheard-of manner the German countries, during the period when Arnulf's son, Louis the Child, who was still a minor, was called King of Germany, from the year 899–911. These were probably the most miserable years that Germany had ever witnessed. With almost every year these Hungarians suddenly precipitated themselves in masses upon one or other of the provinces, desolated it with fire and sword, and drove thousands of the inhabitants back with them as slaves, while the Germans, valiant as they were, knew not the mode of conducting such a war, and could not defend themselves; besides which, they possessed as yet no walled towns wherein they might have sheltered their wives and children. Bavaria was first attacked by them, and made a prey to their devastations, and all the court and nobles cut to pieces. The following years the same happened to Saxony and Thuringia, and the two concluding years Franconia and Swabia were in turn devastated. The words of Solomon may be applied to these horrors of Germany: "Wo to the country whose king is a child." But, fortunately for the salvation of his own and other countries, this child now died early in the year 911.

After the race of the Carlovingians, which had commenced with so much lustre, became extinct in Germany, it still existed a short time longer, although but weak, and without any power or authority in France; it soon, however, disappeared there also—like a torrent which at first springs forth majestically, and dashes down all before it, but at last dividing itself into various isolated arms, its power becomes reduced, and gradually absorbed by the sand.

Meanwhile in Germany much had become changed that proved of great importance to futurity. Charles the Great, as we have seen, made the royal power superior to all other; he did away with the great dukes' reigning over entire provinces, and substituted royal officials, with smaller circuits of government; and had his successors followed his example in this, the system might have been established in Germany, as it was in France and other countries—namely, that but one lord should rule with unlimited power throughout the whole empire, and no prince besides. But fate ordered it otherwise, and caused many rulers to spring up among us, which has given an impulse to the development and cultivation of the German mind, and has been only then *not* dangerous to the country with respect to its exterior relations, when all who called themselves Germans held together in love and unity, and in that disposition constituted a firm and solid German empire.

The foundation of this polygarchy, or division of dominions, may be traced chiefly to the times subsequent to the treaty of Verdun. On almost all sides formidable enemies threatened the frontiers: the Hungarians, the Slavonians, the Venedians, and the Normans. The kings themselves were unfortunately too weak, and unable, like Charlemagne, to fly with assistance from one end of the realm to the other. They were therefore obliged to permit and authorize the German tribes, for the defence of the frontiers, to choose powerful chiefs raised among themselves, who continued to remain at the head of their troops, and led them against the enemy. The efforts made to establish a fresh foundation for the ducal power, become more and more visible in the last moiety of the ninth century, and very soon we find the royal Missi or Margraves, together with other proprietors of land, and influential men, raising themselves to the ducal dignity.

It lies in the nature of things, that the development of these relations could not be everywhere the same. We find often the governor of a province still called in the old records Graf, (*Comes*,) because he already possessed more of the ducal power than in another province was commanded by him who was ordinarily styled Dux. All research made into this subject is extremely difficult, and opinions thereupon are even yet not united. Thus much is certain, that if we consider and acknowledge in general those governors as owners of the ducal power, who possessed an overbalancing influence in their provinces, and who represented the king himself in war, and in the highest courts of jurisdiction, we find that, at the end of the ninth and commencement of the tenth century, they again appear, and gradually become dukes of Saxony, Thuringia, Franconia, Bavaria, Swabia, and Lorraine.

In Saxony, the Ludolphic race, as it appears, acquired at a very early date a power which we may call ducal. Eckbert, related to the house of Charlemagne, was placed by the latter at the head of all the Saxons between the Rhine and Vistula, as count and chief of the heerbann; his son Ludolph held also this rank, and possessed, in effect, already ducal power. His son Bruno, and, after his death, in 880, Otho, the father of King Henry, must be considered in every sense as dukes. Saxony became, by degrees, the most powerful and extensive duchy, for it embraced, at the time of its greatest development, the country from the Lower Rhine to the Oder, and from the North Sea and the Eider to the Fichtel mountains and the Wetterau.

Thuringia had, it is true, counts also, who at times were called herzöge, (duces limitis Sorabici;) but their power, owing to the frequent changes occurring among the owners, did not completely form itself into a ducal power. Burchard, whom we find mentioned as duke, fell in 908, against the Hungarians; his power was transferred to Otho of Saxony, who already possessed a province giving him the title of count, (Gaugrafschaft,) in the northern part of Thuringia. King Henry retained Thuringia united with his duchy.

In Franconia, which besides the ancient Frankish land on the Lower Rhine, comprised likewise Hessia and the countries of the Central Rhine, the title of duke could not otherwise appear than much later, because the country, as long as the kings continued of the Frankish family, was considered kings' land; still the administration of the country was performed by two powerful counts, and two families, the Babenbergerians in the eastern, and the Conradinians at Worms, in the western part, divided the power, until they broke out into a deadly dispute and fight, in which the former were completely defeated. Count Conrad, soon afterwards King Conrad I., became, therefore, potentissimus comes in Franconia, and possessed in reality ducal power. Widukind styles him likewise Duke of the Franks, although he, as well as his brother Eberhard, is called by others also comes. It cannot, however, be doubted but that under Henry I. Eberhard possessed the ducal dignity.

In Bavaria, Luitpold, who had to defend the eastern frontiers against the Slavonians and Hungarians, is styled dux in a diploma of King Louis, of the year 901, and his son Arnulf calls himself duke in the year 908.

In Swabia, where the defence of the frontiers was not so necessary, the ducal dignity appears to have connected itself gradually with the power of the royal missus, and to have developed itself later.

Burchard, however, under Conrad I. appears nevertheless as Duke of Swabia.

In Lorraine, finally, it became more easy to the nobles of the land by means of its doubtful and critical position between France and Germany in the later Carlovingian period, to maintain a state of greater independence, and we thus find upon record already in the year 901 a Duke Kebehart, and later, under King Henry, the Duke Gisilbrecht.

The dukes were not, it is true, regarded as lords of their people and lands, but as ministers and representatives of their king, in whose name they regulated in peace the affairs of justice and order, and in war led the army of their race to battle. But soon becoming large landed proprietors, and being no longer under the surveillance of royal envoys, the dukes took advantage of the weakness of the kings, and by degrees arrogated to themselves an increase of power, and brought the lesser vassals under their dominion; nay, they even gradually made their dignity, granted to them only as imperial crown officers, hereditary in their families, as well as the revenues of the crown lands, which they had only received as the salary for their service.

Like the great dukes, the inferior imperial officers, the counts, margraves, and others, established themselves more and more firmly in their dignities, and the estates attached thereto. The spiritual lords, archbishops, bishops, and abbots, were, like the temporal lords, members and vassals of the empire, and like them augmented their secular power and possessions; and all these became by degrees from the mere deputies of royal authority, independent princes of the German nation.

Besides this, in some individuals, the love of freedom and personal independence began already, as early as this period, to degenerate often into license. He who thought himself offended by another, and conceived he possessed sufficient strength to revenge himself, did not seek the establishment of his rights in the usual way, namely, through the judges of the land, but with arms and the strength of the fist. Thence that period wherein the appeal to the fist was so generally adopted, was called the period of the *faust-recht*, the fist or club law. It commenced, already, under the later Carlovingians, but it was long afterwards that it reached its highest extent.

The evil became necessarily great, for the manners of the nation were still rude. Arms and the chase remained their favorite occupations, and the sword and the falcon were the greatest treasures of the German. He could calmly see all taken from him, says an author, but if his sword and falcon came into any danger, he would not hesitate to save them even with a false oath. The hunting fêtes were superb, and were included among the highest festivities of life. Ladies, from gorgeously ornamented tents, beheld the destruction of the game. In the evening they feasted under tents in the forest, and the company, with their suites, returned amidst the music of the hunting horns. For the sake of the chase, the kings and nobles preferred remaining at their country seats, and on this account for a long time despised dwelling in cities.

During the later period of the Carlovingians, besides the wars within and beyond the land, which they so much desolated, what was greatly to be deplored was, that the germs of cultivation which Charlemagne, in his exertions for science, had planted in his schools for instruction, became again almost entirely destroyed. No period in the whole history of Germany is darker, more superstitious and ignorant, than that of Louis the German, to the end of the Carlovingian dynasty, and a short time beyond it—despite of the Germans being, from time immemorial, so susceptible of cultivation, and by their serious application and profound meditation so well adapted for the acquirement of art and science. An example of this is to be found even in that dark age. In the days of Pepin and Charlemagne the first organs were brought to Germany from Greece, and Charles took every pains to introduce the Latin psalmody and church music among his subjects. At first he had but little success; at least an Italian of that time complains that their natural rudeness was their great obstruction: "Great in body like mountains," says he, "their voice rolls forth like thunder, and cannot be modulated into gentler tones; and when their barbaric throats endeavor gently to produce the soft transitions and flexibilities of the music, the hard tones pour forth their volume in a rattling sound, like a coach rolling over the stones, so that the feelings of the hearer, which should be gently moved, are, on the contrary, completely startled and terrified." Thus was pronounced originally a criticism upon their disposition and qualification for harmony. And yet by industry and exercise they advanced so far in a short time, that Pope John VIII., who lived about the year 870, besought Anthony, bishop of Freisingen, to send him a good organ from Germany, and with it a person who was equally well able to *play* upon as to make it.

In this century a pupil of Rhabanus Maurus, the monk Otfried of Weissenburg, gave a very remarkable example of his love for his mother-tongue, by translating the gospel into German verse, in order that the people might be enabled to read it. Charlemagne had, indeed, commenced to improve and cultivate the German language, but after him no one thought further about it. Otfried now zealously endeavored to make it a written language, although it was very difficult to express by letters its hard and strange sounds. He strongly and justly contended against those who, indifferent towards their native-tongue, preferred learning, with excessive labor, and using the languages of the Latins and Greeks. "They call the German language," he says, "boorish, and yet do not endeavor by their writings or study to make it more perfect. They carefully avoid writing badly in Latin and Greek, and yet do not care for doing so in their own language; they are ashamed to offend against good taste by even a letter in those languages, but in their own tongue it happens with every word. Truly a singular fact this, that such great and learned men do all this for the honor of foreign languages, and yet cannot even write their own!"

The condition of the common freemen was the saddest of all in these times, and they, consequently, decreased so much that they scarcely formed a distinct order in the nation. Much earlier, already when the feudal system gradually developed itself, and elevated the vassals above all those who cultivated their own inheritance, their numbers had decreased considerably, but the worst time came after Charlemagne.

Charles knew well that the strength of a nation consists in the great preponderance of freemen, and that it is upon their courage and their animated love for their country that must depend the general weal and its security from all danger; he therefore applied great care and vigilance to the restoration of the arrière ban, which had also by the influence of the feudal system fallen into disuse. In this, however, he attained his aim but partially, because his wars, far from being real national wars, for the defence of the country, were only conquering excursions in distant countries. These were very oppressive to the common man, who, from the day that the army stepped upon the land of the enemy, was obliged to provide himself, at his own expense, for three months with provisions, as well as with clothes and arms. Many, therefore, endeavored to avoid the duties of this servile military service. They gave themselves up both in body and possessions to the service or guardianship of the church, or to the patronage of a noble, either as arrière or under vassals, because, as such, they were not bound to yield so much service as to the king in the arrière ban, or even as bondmen, and as such no longer belonging to the class of freemen. They were called the Lidi (Leute, people) of the seigneur, and remained, it is true, the possessors of their own inheritance, which they themselves cultivated, but they were subject to pay tax, and were held in soccage, and could neither quit the land nor sell it; but with their children and descendants they were bound to the soil, and were the property of their lord. This was severe; but they were at the same time exempted from doing any military service in distant expeditions; for, as bondsmen, they were not considered worthy of bearing arms, but remained all their lives in tranquillity with their families. At the most they were only obligated, under the most urgent circumstances, to repair to a short distance, within the immediate vicinity of their territory, there to fight, on foot, with stick or club; the lance and sword being forbidden to them. Had they rightly considered that men who are not allowed to bear arms, also speedily lose both courage and power, and if they are not absolutely called slaves, soon adopt slavish sentiments, they would, no doubt, much rather have remained poor and oppressed, but still freemen and warriors; but, alas! in necessity the nearest and most immediate aid appears the best to him who suffers, and the eye loses the power of perceiving the distant consequences.

Besides the oppressive service of the arrière ban, which brought many freemen into slavery, there were other causes which contributed to decrease their numbers, among which may be classed the terrific incursions of the Avari, the Normans, the Slavonians, and Hungarians, in which thousands of them were killed or carried off as slaves; and later, the disorders and oppressions of the *faust-recht*, or club-law, which likewise obliged many of the poor freemen to give themselves up to the service of some neighboring powerful noble, to secure themselves from the robberies of those who made a trade of pillage. Besides, in those times of disorder, when laying up magazines of provisions was not thought of, countries were often visited with desolating famine and pestilence; in such necessities many freemen, that they might not die of starvation, gave themselves up, with their children and property, to nobles or spiritual foundations for bread. And, lastly, many became servitors to cloisters and ecclesiastical establishments; and from piety, or for the salvation of their souls, they gave their all to the altar of God. For the church already, at this period, possessed and maintained the privileges, by which an individual might give to it his whole possessions, and thus entirely pass by the just inheritors. Thence, from all these causes, it happened that, at the end of this period, not only the ancient pride and courage, but also the majority of the freemen—accordingly the independence of the Germans—had disappeared, and scarcely any but noblemen and their feudatories remained, thus threatening the country with the sad prospect of decay and ruin. But whenever necessity has been great, God has always sent to the German nation unexpected aid and support. Accordingly, at this moment, it was precisely the devastation spread everywhere by the Hungarians which laid the foundation for the renewed elevation of the common freemen to a civic state, and re-established later the condition of the peasant.

After the death of Louis the Child, the principal German branches assembled, and looked about them for the most worthy among their princes to be their king. The election fell upon Otho the Illustrious, Duke of Saxony and Thuringia, who was related, on the maternal side, to the Carlovingians, and by the power of his house, as well as by age and wisdom, was held in great esteem by all. On the paternal side, he descended from Count Eckbert, whom Charlemagne had placed in Saxony against the Normans, in 810. Otho, however, refused the crown, because the cares of the empire were too great for his age, and advised rather that Conrad, the Duke of the Franks, (according to some writers, he was only a count,) be made king. For this act, Otho merits the greater praise, as Conrad was truly worthy to rule as king, and the race of the Franks still continued the most esteemed among the German nations; for hitherto it was from that race that the king had commanded over the whole of Germany. Otho, therefore, wisely considered it better that the rule of the empire should remain with them, and, in so doing, entirely dismissed from his mind the enmity which always had, and still partially existed between the Saxons and the Franks.

Conrad was accordingly elected king on the 8th of November, 911, at Pforzheim. He is described as being a man of great merit, both at home and abroad; valiant and prudent, kind and liberal. His first care was to elevate, from its sunken state, the royal authority, for upon it depended the order of the whole empire. But the confusion was too great, and Conrad's reign too short, to render his efforts completely successful. The Lothringians, or Lorrainers, who only, since the time of Louis the German, had belonged to Germany, were not contented with his election, and separated themselves, nor could Conrad bring them back again to the empire. After the death of Otho the Illustrious, he had to contend with his son, Henry of Saxony; for, misguided by the advice of Hatto, Archbishop of Mentz, he wished to deprive Henry of some great fiefs which he owned, besides his dukedom of Saxony, in order that no prince of the empire should be too powerful; probably these were the northern districts of Thuringia, which Otho had already possessed; but Henry was valiantly defended by his Saxons. He completely defeated the king's brother, Eberhard, who had advanced against him with an army, near Eresburg, (now Stadberg,) so that he retained the fiefs in the subsequent treaty, which terminated the war; nay, he even appears to have conquered also the southern portion of Thuringia, and to have maintained the ducal dignity over the whole of Thuringia.

Conrad confirmed Count Burkhard in Swabia, after some contest, as Duke of the Allemanni. Arnulf of Bavaria, however, who also revolted, and so far forgot himself as to call in the Hungarians to his assistance, was condemned to death by the princes of the empire as a traitor to the country, and was obliged to take refuge among the Hungarians.

Thus, by energetic measures and timely concessions, the general tranquillity and imperial dignity were re-established, and the unity of Germany maintained. But Conrad well felt how difficult the task was for him, and that the power of the Frankish dukes alone was not sufficient to curb the over-powerful nobles. It also required greater strength to protect the empire against the Slavonians and Hungarians, who still repeated, without ceasing, their incursions. At the same time, perhaps, he did not perceive in his brother, Eberhard, who pretended to possess the greatest claim to the crown, the proper qualities of a king; while, on the other hand, his earlier and now conciliated opponent, Henry of Saxony, was, in all respects, irreproachable, endowed with great energy of mind and body, and, by his power and influence, ranked at the head of all the German princes. When, therefore, Conrad lay sick of a wound at Limburg, on the Lahn, which he had received in his last expedition against the Hungarians, and felt death approaching, he thought of the example which Otho the Illustrious had given at his election, and forgetting all jealousy, and with his thoughts directed only for the weal of his country, he called his brother, Eberhard, to his bedside, and thus addressed him: "We command, it is true, great means, my dear Eberhard; we can collect great armies, and know how to lead them. We are not wanting in fortified cities and defences, nor in any of the attributes of royal dignity. Yet greater power, influence, and wisdom, dwell with Henry, and upon him alone depends the welfare of the empire. Take, therefore, these jewels, this lance and sword, together with the chain and crown of the ancient kings, and carry them to Henry the Saxon. Be at peace with him, that you may have him for your constant strong ally. Announce to him that Conrad, on his death-bed, has chosen and recommended *him* as king, in preference to all the other princes." He died in December, 918.

Eberhard did what his brother had commanded, and was the first who did fealty to King Henry. A kingdom wherein such sentiments were found, might truly and without danger remain electoral.

# FOURTH PERIOD.

## FROM HENRY I. TO RUDOLPHUS OF HAPSBURG.

### 919—1273.

THE tenth century is by no means rich in historical works:

1. The chronicle of Regino, already mentioned in the preceding epoch, was continued by another writer as far as the year 967, abridged, but mostly careful and exact, and altogether well written.

2. Luitprand of Pavia, private secretary to King Beranger II. of Italy, afterwards in the service of King Otho I., and finally bishop of Cremona, wrote the history of his time not without spirit, and, especially in his history of Italy, very instructive, although partial and enthusiastic. His style is far-fetched and bombastic, showing much of the courtier, and a great love for anecdote and illustration in his narrative. This history goes from c. 886-948, and a supplement from 961-964. He wrote also, in another distinct work, an account of his embassy to the court of the emperor Nicephorus.

3. Horoswitha, a nun of Gandersheim, wrote a poem, "De Gestis Ottonum Panegyris," from 919-964; as the title indicates, a poem in praise of Otho the Great, accordingly not always faithful to truth, and, of course, partial or one-sided; nevertheless, not without some proportionate merit here and there. She treats upon the later years rather fugitively.

4. Widukind, usually called Wittekind, a monk of Corvey, who died about the year 1000, wrote a history of the Saxons, (Rerum Saxinocarum, libri iii.,) as far as 973. As the first historian of his time, he presents his record of the events in a form equally agreeable and happy, devoted to the house of Saxony, but still with a desire after truth; and the second part of his work is of invaluable merit. The first portion is, in part, based upon the legends and traditions of the people.

5. Among the chronicles on the history of Germany, especially the relations of the Lotharingians, Flodoard of Rheims is particularly important, who wrote a history from 919 to 966.

6. Richer, a monk of St. Remy, near Rheims, studied medicine, and was a pupil of the celebrated Gesbert; and encouraged by his master to write history, he composed, in the years 995 to 998, his "Historiarum, libros iv.," from 888-995, which he dedicated to Gesbert. His history is, for France, partial, and he often

adapts the events to the advantage of that country. Nevertheless, amidst the dearth of historical source in his time, he is certainly of great value. His narrative is based upon a close study of the ancients. The middle ages being only taken up by Ekkehard, Richer was quite lost sight of, until Pertz discovered in Bamberg the only autographic document still existing by him, which has been published in the "Monumenta."

7. Detached and extremely interesting communications are given to us in the biographies of Bruno, archbishop of Cologne, the brother of Otho I.; of Udalrich, bishop of Augsburg; and other ecclesiastics of that time.

In the eleventh century, we find more important and a greater number of historians, who, in their descriptions, distinguish themselves especially:

1. The Life of Queen Matilda, written by command of king Henry II., by an unknown author, between the years 1002 and 1014; agreeably written, and not unimportant as regards the history of Henry I.

2. Ditmar, or Thietmar, bishop of Merseburg, who died in 1018, wrote a history of the German kings from 876–1018. His narrative is confused, his language obscure, being neither pure nor agreeable, and his description in the first books not impartial. Nevertheless, he is of great importance to us, rich in information of the most varied nature, and forms our principal source for the history of Otho III. and Henry II. He was a friend and relation of the Saxon emperors.

3. Besides the last-mentioned writer, we find the best detailed and correct information respecting the end of the tenth and commencement of the eleventh century in the "Annales Quedlinburgensis," to 1025.

4. The Life of Henry II. by Adelbold, bishop of Utrecht, is incomplete, and nearly all borrowed from Ditmar, but well written. The "Vitæ" of both the bishops of Hildesheim, Bernward and Godehard, are, as regards the history of Saxony, of great consequence; the Meinwercs of Paderborn merit being mentioned likewise.

5. Wippo, chaplain to the emperor Conrad II., whose life he has written in a pompous style, "Vita Conradi Salici." He was a man of science and letters, and of a remarkable mind.

6. Hermannus Contractus, (the lame,) of the family of the counts of Vehringen, and a Benedictine monk of Reichenau, who died in 1054. He wrote a chronicle from 1000–1054, continued to 1100 by Berthold and Bernold, of Constance.

7. Adam of Bremen, (born at Meissen, and canon and rector of the college of Bremen,) who died in 1076. He wrote a good ecclesiastical history of the North, from the middle of the eighth century to 1076; important for the history of North Germany, especially of the time of Henry IV.

8. Bruno of Corvey, (de Belle Saxonico,) a passionate adversary of Henry IV., and who exaggerates and disfigures much; yet he is important and indispensable for the history of the war.

9. Lambert of Aschaffenburg, a monk of Hersfeld, wrote a chronicle from the earlier times to 1077. A work of great genius, full of spirit, well written, and an important source for the period in which he lived; he is especially the best historian of the middle ages.

10. Marianus Scotus, who died in 1086; a monk of Fulda and Mentz, who wrote a chronicle to 1083, which was continued by Dodechin to 1200.

11. Sigbert, a monk of Gemblours, (Sigeb. Gemblacensis,) who died in 1112, wrote a chronicle; learned, written with great industry, and rich in information, but which is nevertheless confused and not altogether authentic. His work has been continued by several writers, and in the subsequent middle ages much resorted to.

12. Ekkehardus Uraugiensis wrote a chronicle to 1126, likewise very learned, carefully written, of great value in the particular history of his own times, and more impartial than most of the historians of that period, who all wrote for or against the emperors and popes. There are several continuations of this work, of which the most known is that by the abbot of Ursperg (Chron. Ursperg) to 1229.

13. The letters of the popes and other distinguished men, collected by an ecclesiastic, Ulrich of Bamberg, in the twelfth century, are extremely valuable.

14. It is likewise very interesting, in order to catch the spirit of those times when the dispute between Henry and Gregory excited the pens of various distinguished men to write in defence of both those parties, to know the various controversial productions which appeared on this subject, with the different opinions therein contained. The partisans of the pope had their central point in the monasteries of St. Blaise, Schaffhausen, and Hirschau; while, however, many learned and estimable men, of irreproachable character, wrote against the pope and in favor of the emperor. We cannot here give the names of these opposite writers, but their character will be found fully drawn in Stenzel's excellent work on the history of Germany under the Frankish emperors.*

15. The Biography of Benno, bishop of Osnaburg, a friend of Henry IV. by Norbert, abbot of the Convent of Iburg, which was built by Benno, contains important information.

16. The historians of the Crusades are more especially numerous; the importance of the subject, the universal interest taken therein, the peculiar nature of the expedition in a foreign country and at such a distance, together with the surprising and wonderful deeds performed, excited many, and particularly those who were present, to give their records of the scenes witnessed, for the perusal of those left behind at the time, and their successors. The majority of the chronicles have been collected by Bongars, under the title: "Gesta Dei per Francos, Hanoviæ, 1611, fol."

In the twelfth and thirteenth centuries, the impetus given by the Crusades produced its influence, and operated beneficially upon the historians. They became more particular in the selection and arrangement of the subject-matter, thus showing a commencement in the art of historical writing. Among the most distinguished writers are:

1. Otho, bishop of Freisingen, who died in 1158, son of the Margrave Leopold of Austria, a philosopher, of independent feeling, and full of eloquence. He wrote a universal history to the year 1152, well continued as far as 1209, by Otho of Sainte Blaise; and the life of the emperor Frederic I. to 1156, which was continued as far as 1160 by Radewich, canon of Freisingen; both works equally interesting and learned, and written with intelligence and discernment.

2. The History of Frederic I. receives important elucidations from the Chronicles of Vincenz of Prague, 1140–1167; the History of Lodi, 1153–1178, by Otho and Acerbus Morena; the History of Romuald, archbishop of Salerno, to 1168; the Poem of Günther: Ligurinus and the book of the so-called Sire Raul of Milan: "de Rebus gestis Frederici in Italia."

3. The Chronicle of the Slavi, by Helmold, an ecclesiastic of Lubeck, to 1170, and by Arnold to 1209; important for the history of Henry the Lion and the house of the Guelphs.

4. Valuable information is given upon the same subject by Gerhard, provost of Stederbuch, in his Chronicles of the Monastery, and by the Monk of Weingarten in his book "de Guelfis," and his Chronicles.

5. The so-called "Annalista Saxo" and "Chronagraphus Saxo," mostly compilations, but the former for the eleventh and the latter for the twelfth centuries, in the detail, are both very interesting.

Nearly all the bishoprics, churches, and monasteries of Germany, now received their appointed historians, who we find touch more or less upon general matters, and are often more important than the universal chronicles selected for general circulation. Such are for instance:

6. Albert von Stade, whose chronicle goes as far as 1256, and is continued by a stranger to 1324—also a compilation.

7. Gotfried von Viterbo to 1186; the monk Alberich, Joh. Vitoduranus, &c.

8. A collection of letters by celebrated men of that period is very important, especially those of Pope Innocent III. and Petrus de Vinea, chancellor of the emperor Frederic II., and who died in 1249.

9. The most complete collection of letters to and from the popes, of the transactions of their ambassadors and other similar documents, has been preserved in the archives of the Vatican in Rome, which, as may be easily conceived, are of the highest importance for the history of this period, but it is extremely difficult to gain

* Geschichte Deutschlands unter den Fränkischen Kaisern 1827–1828.

access to them. A great part of them, however, has been transcribed in Rome by Pertz, and already the commencement of their publication has been made in the fourth volume of the "Monumenta Germaniæ Historica."

10. A work of very great importance for the history of the emperor Frederic II., is the History of England, by Matthieu-Paris, who, together with the events of the English nation from 1066–1259, treats also occasionally upon the affairs of the other nations of Europe. So likewise various Italian historians, of whom we need only here refer especially to Richard de Saint Germano and Nicolas de Jamsilla, (both in the Collection of Muratori.)

11. All the great writers who form the source of history have been brought together in the great Collections of Duchesne, Bouquet, (for France,) Muratori, (for Italy,) Schard, Reuber, Urstisius, Pistorius, Freher, Goldast, Schilter, Meibom, Leibnitz, Ekkard, &c., (for Germany.)

12. Equally important as were for the history of the preceding epoch the collection of the ancient laws of the Franks and the nations subjected to them, are likewise, for the history of the middle ages, (although much abridged,) the collections of the later laws, known under the names of the *Sachsenspiegel*, or Mirror of Saxony, the *Schwabenspiegel*, or Mirror of Swabia, and *Kaiserrecht*, or the Imperial Law.

## CHAPTER VII.

### 919—1024.

Henry I., 919-936—His Wars—The Hungarians—The Slavonians—New Institutions—Otho I., 936-973—The Hungarians—Battle of the Lechfeld—The Western Empire renewed 962—Greece—Otho II., 973-983—Italy—Otho III., 983—1003—His Religious Devotion—His partiality for Roman and Grecian Manners and Customs—Henry II., 1003-1024—Italy—Pavia—Bamberg—His Death, 1024—End of the Saxon Dynasty.

THE accounts we possess respecting the election of Henry vary much, and are here and there very erroneous. If we follow—as is but just—the statements of the most ancient writers, Widukind and Ditmar, we shall find that the princes and elders of the Franks, yielding to the counsel of Conrad their king, given on his death-bed, assembled together at the summons of their duke, Eberhard, at Fritzlar, in the beginning of the year 919, and there, in the presence of the two nations, the Franks and the Saxons, elected Henry for their sovereign. The whole assembly with uplifted hands proclaimed and saluted with loud shouts their chosen king. Thus the choice was more properly made by the nobles of Franconia, while the Saxons naturally accepted the election made of their own duke. As yet, however, it could not be known what measures might be adopted by the other nations, and we shall soon learn in what way Henry speedily brought the Swabians and Bavarians to acknowledge his sovereignty.

Subsequent authorities relate that the envoys dispatched to offer the crown to Henry, met him on his estates of the Hartz Mountains, among his falcons, occupied in catching birds, whence he derived the by-name of the Fowler. It is possible that this tradition may have been preserved among the people, still the aforesaid earlier writers make no mention of it, while it is only in the middle of the eleventh century that we for the first time meet in the chronicles and other historical works, with this by-name Henricus auceps.

Henry's reign began, it is true, with some internal agitations, but these were soon quelled, for the anxious wish both of Otho the Illustrious and King Conrad became now fulfilled, and the Franks and the Saxons lived accordingly in harmony together. Duke Burkhard of Swabia, and Duke Arnulf of Bavaria, who had returned from the Hungarians, refused him homage; but he speedily brought them by the power of his arms and the gentler force of peaceful and friendly persuasion, back to their duty. Thus, from the year 921, the whole of Germany obeyed Henry, and no internal war disturbed the peace of his empire, although it was only after several battles that he conquered Lorraine, which had still wavered between France and Germany. Soon afterwards he strengthened his union with that country by giving his daughter Gerberga in marriage to its duke, Giselbert, and during seven centuries that beautiful land remained united with Germany.

Henry could now occupy himself with his foreign enemies, the Slavonians and Hungarians. The latter thought they could still continue their old system of destruction in the German countries, but they now found an opponent who arrested their progress. At first, indeed, Henry was obliged to yield to their furious attacks, (in 924,) and they advanced into the very heart of Saxony. He was, however, fortunate enough, in a sally he made from the fortified Castle of Werle, or Werlaon,* to capture one of their most distinguished princes; for his ransom and Henry's promise of a tribute the Hungarians concluded a truce for nine years, and engaged during that time not to attack Germany. They probably purposed after that to make doubly good the lost

* The position of Werle (called by Widukind, Werlaon) has been variously discussed; endeavors having been made to trace it in Westphalia, Brunswick, Hildesheim, and other districts; but most probably it was in the palatinate of the same name, near Goslar, as appears in the "Mirror of the Saxons."

time, but Henry profited so well by those nine years that when they did return they found a very different country to contend with.

He now commenced suppressing with much severity and justice internal turbulence and depredation, so that the greater zeal might be excited against foreign enemies. For under the reign of the last Carlovingians, as we have already seen, the spirit for war and rapine was cherished everywhere, even among the nobles. Henry pursued and punished these robbers wherever they were taken; but he pardoned those in whom he found the better spirit to exist, and gave them arms and land on the eastern frontiers of the empire, in order that they might thus have a fair opportunity for the exercise of their passion for war against his enemies. Merseburg, which served as one of the quarters for such a troop, thus became a sort of bulwark or protecting wall against the Slavonians, until Henry himself advanced farther into the country of that nation.

He then exercised his German soldiers, who until then only knew how to contend on foot, in the art of fighting on horseback, so that they might be better enabled to resist the hordes of mounted Hungarians; and as the Germans were always willing to learn, and were likewise skilful in the acquirement of the art of arms generally, they were speedily made perfect in the cavalry evolutions. He practised them to attack in close ranks; to await the first arrow of the enemy, and to receive it on the shield, and then suddenly to dash upon them before they had time to discharge the second. Combined with this reform in the cavalry exercise, he likewise introduced a more strict discipline; the eldest brother in every family, as it appears, was forced to do duty as a horse soldier, and all capable of bearing arms were obliged at the general summons (according to the ancient law, which he renewed) to join the ranks.

Finally, as he well saw that the enemy could still do much mischief, even if they were put to flight—for, like a flash of lightning, they appeared now here, now there, pillaging and murdering, and then vanished before they could be overtaken—he in this interval converted, with great industry, a number of unemployed buildings into fortified castles, placed at certain distances from each other, so that the inhabitants of the surrounding country, upon the first intelligence of the enemy's approach, might take refuge there with their property. The Hungarians knew nothing of besieging cities, and if they made but little booty in their incursions they did not very soon appear again. Henry's hereditary lands—as in fact generally the north of Germany—were very poor in those larger settlements which might be compared with towns; in those parts the custom of living in isolated localities was preserved later than elsewhere. Accordingly, as Widukind relates, all were busily occupied, day and night, with the construction of these burghs, and every one, without distinction of rank or other claims to independence, was forced to join in this grand work. Henry built these fortified castles and cities chiefly in his hereditary lands, Saxony and Thuringia, and among others Goslar, Duderstadt, Nordhausen, Quedlinburg, Merseburg, and Meissen are named. But that he might also have inhabitants and garrisons in these places, he ordered that of all the men who were bound to do service in war, every ninth man should dwell in the city, and these were obliged to occupy themselves with the building of houses, which might serve as places of refuge, upon the attacks of the enemy, and the others were bound to supply them yearly with the third portion of their produce, in order that they might have wherewith to live, and preserve the rest for all in time of danger.

When Henry had passed some years in making these preparations he resolved to exercise his warriors, by subduing the neighbors of the Germans in the east and north, who, although not so dangerous as the Hungarians, were still not less disposed to be hostile.

He attacked and beat the Slavonians (the Hevellers on the Havel) in the Marches of Brandenburg, and conquered their city Brennaburg, (Brandenburg,) which he besieged in the most severe winter, so severe that his army encamped on the ice of the river Havel. He then subjected the Daleminziens or Dalmatians, who inhabited the banks of the Elbe, from Meissen to Bohemia. He also undertook an expedition against the Bohemians, besieged Duke Wenzeslaus in Prague, the capital, and forced him to yield obedience. From this time the kings of Germany have continued to demand fealty from the dukes of Bohemia.

These events took place in all probability

in the years 928 and 929. But in this latter year a Slavonic race, the Redarians, encouraged no doubt by the absence of the king when on his Bohemian expedition, united with their neighboring tribes, and suddenly revolted, and it was necessary to summon together all the Saxons, in one entire mass, to advance against them. The king's generals laid siege to the town of Lukini, (Lenzen,) near the Elbe. A great army of the Slavonians advanced to its relief, and a grand battle was fought, in which they were completely annihilated. Widukind states their loss at 200,000; even if this number is exaggerated, it is quite certain that this victory of the Saxons produced the lasting subjection of the Slavonians.

No doubt it was in order to guaranty these new conquests against the Slavonians, that Henry extended the already existing defences on the Slavonian frontiers, and thence were formed gradually the Margraviate of Nordsachsen, (the present Altmark,) and the Margraviate Meissen, on the Elbe, where he founded the same-named city and fortification. Credit may not be given to him, it is true, for the complete establishment of both these margraviates, because that occurs in the time of the Ottonians; nevertheless they owe to him their foundation. Neither is it proved that in order to promulgate Christianity among the Slavonians, he had already founded bishoprics, the turbulence of the times may have prevented him during the rest of his reign from doing so; but his son Otho completed afterwards what his father projected, by introducing ecclesiastical institutions there.

Meantime the nine years' truce with the Hungarians having expired, they sent an embassy to Germany to demand the ancient tribute which that country had disgracefully been obliged to pay them. But Henry, to show them the contempt in which the Germans now held them, delivered to the ambassadors this time, in the form of a tribute, a mangy dog, deprived of its tail and ears, that being a very ancient symbol of the most utter contempt. At this the Hungarians were roused to fury, and prepared themselves to take bitter revenge for it; but King Henry now addressed his people thus:

"You know from what dangers our formerly-desolated kingdom is now free, for it was torn to pieces by internal dissensions, and external wars. But now, by the protection of God, by our efforts, and by your valor, one enemy, the Slavonians, being brought to subjection, nothing remains for us but to raise ourselves just as unitedly, and in one mass against the common enemy, the savage Avari, (thus he styled the Hungarians.) Hitherto we have been obliged to give up all our possessions to enrich them, and now to satisfy them further we must plunder our churches, for we have nothing else to give them. Choose now yourselves; will you admit that I shall take away what is appointed for the service of God to purchase our peace from the enemies of that God, or will you, as it beseems Germans, firmly confide that He will save us, who in truth is our Lord and Saviour?" On this the people raised their hands and voices to heaven, and swore to fight.

The Hungarians now advanced in two strong divisions. The first attacked Thuringia and devastated the country, to the Weser districts, as far as it was not defended by its fortified towns. But an army, formed of the Saxons and Thuringians, attacked this division, defeated it, destroyed its leaders, and pursuing it through the whole of Thuringia, annihilated it completely.

The other division of the Hungarians which had remained stationary in the eastern districts, received the tidings of the overthrow of their brethren at the moment they were laying siege to the seat of Henry's sister, married to Wido of Thuringia. What place this was, we have unfortunately not been able to learn. Some have thought it to be Merseburg, which Liutprand names as the enemy's place of encampment; others again pronounce it to be Wittenberg. The king, as Widukind relates, encamped near Riäde, the situation of which it is equally impossible to determine. Still it is extremely probable that the battle took place in the vicinity of the Saale, not far from Merseburg, in the Hassgau.

The enemy abandoned their camp, and according to their custom, lighted large fires as a signal to all the rest of their troops, dispersed around in plundering, to collect together. The following morning Henry advanced with his army, and exhorted his troops in the most glowing language on that day to take ample revenge for the wrongs of their country and their relations and friends slain, or carried off as slaves. Thus he marched through the ranks of his warriors, bearing in his hand the holy lance,* preceded by the banner of the army waving before him, which was consecrated as the angel's banner, it being decorated with the figure of the archangel Michael. Thence the German warriors felt within them the full confidence of victory, and awaited the signal for battle with impatience. The king, however, who already perceived by the motions of the enemy that they would not make a stand, sent forward a portion of the Thuringian militia, or Landwehr, with a few lightly-armed horsemen, in order that the enemy might pursue these almost unarmed troops, and then be seduced onward to attack his main body. And this took place; but they so speedily turned their backs upon viewing the well-armed ranks of the Germans, that it scarcely became a regular battle. They were pursued, and the greater part were either hewn down or taken prisoners; the camp of the enemy, with all the treasures stolen, was captured, and what to the feelings was most of all affecting and delightful was, that the prisoners whom the Hungarians had already forced along as slaves, now saw themselves so providentially freed from bondage. Henry then fell down on his knees, together with his whole army, and thanked God for the victory gained. The tribute which he had hitherto been forced to pay over to the enemy he now devoted to the service of the church, as well as to charitable gifts which he made to the poor; and the king himself, says Widukind, was henceforward called by his inspired warriors, "The father of his country," their "sovereign lord," and their "emperor;" while the fame of his great virtue and valor extended over the whole country.

This action took place in the year 933, in the neighborhood of Merseburg, and was what was usually styled the Merseburger engagement, or the battle of the Hassgau. In remembrance of the event, Henry, as is related by Liutprand, had a painting of the battle drawn in the dining hall of his palace in Merseburg, which represented the triumphant scene with nearly all the truth and animation of life itself.

The year 934 presented to King Henry another opportunity by which to gain great glory, by an expedition against the Danes, who were ravaging and laying waste the coasts of Friesland and Saxony. He marched into their own country, at the head of his army, forced their king, Gorm, (usually surnamed the old,) to conclude a peace, established at Silesia, on the frontiers of the empire, a fortified barrier, and founded there a margraviate, wherein he left a colony of Saxons. He also succeeded in converting one of the members of the royal family—probably Knud, the son of Gorm, but, according to others, his second son, Harold—to Christianity. Thus was re-established by Henry I. the Margraviate Schlei and Trenne, which had previously served as a bulwark for the imperial frontiers, and which the Danes had again possessed and destroyed. This good prince therefore had now the happiness to behold, when on the eve of his glorious life, these enemies of the north who, during an entire century, had spread terror throughout the countries of Europe, retire before him, and, confining themselves within the limits of their own territory, acknowledge his power.*

At home, in his own domestic circle, King Henry exercised the virtues and duties of an excellent husband and a good father. His queen, the pious and gentle Matilda, was the model of wives; for, possessing great influence over the king, she availed herself thereof, wherever it was possible, to obtain his grace and pardon for the guilty; and his kind and noble heart was always sadly pained when the stern command of public justice forced him to refuse her appeals for mercy. By her he had five children, Otho, Gerberga, Haduin, and subsequently Henry and Bruno. By his first wife, Hathberga, (who, having originally been destined for a convent, was never looked upon as his lawful wife, and soon left him,) he had a son, called Tancmar, but who was not acknowledged as a legitimate child.

He gave Otho, his eldest son and successor, in marriage to Edgetha, daughter

* This holy lance was handed to Henry by Rudolphus of Burgundy, as a present: it was furnished with a cross, formed of nails, with which, as was believed, the hands and feet of our Saviour had been fixed when crucified. King Henry and his successors held this sacred weapon in high veneration, and always used it on important occasions.

* This piece of land, between Schlei and Eider, remained thenceforward united with Germany for nearly a century, until the emperor, Conrad II., resigned it to King Knud.

of Edward, king of England; and by that act, set the first example which the kings of the Saxon dynasty followed so frequently afterwards, of seeking to unite themselves with all the other royal houses of Europe. This forms a distinguished feature in this noble race.

Towards the end of his life, according to Widukind, after having so gloriously succeeded in his devoted object, of producing for his country peace internally, and from all other nations respect externally, Henry had it in contemplation to proceed to Italy, in order to reunite that country with the empire of Germany. Whether or not this statement rests upon any good foundation, is not known; but the execution of this design, if really intended, was suddenly interrupted by sickness, he being attacked with a fit of apoplexy while staying at Bothfeld, in the autumn of 935, from which he suffered a long and severe illness. When he did recover sufficiently, he felt the necessity of at once attending to the means of securing the tranquillity of his empire, and he accordingly convoked an assembly of the nobles at Erfurt. He had long perceived in his eldest son Otho, all that energy and greatness of mind so suitable and necessary for a sovereign; but the mother was more in favor of Henry, the second son, because he was more mild than his passionate brother; besides which, she held him to possess a greater right to the succession of the crown, because he was the first-born son after his father had been invested with the imperial dignity. The will of the father, however, determined all the nobles to recognise Otho as successor.

More easy now in his mind, Henry left Erfurt and proceeded to Memleben. There he experienced a second attack of apoplexy, and, after having taken an affecting, but resigned farewell of his amiable wife, he died on Sunday the 2d of July, in the year 936, at the age of sixty, in the presence of his sons and different princes of the empire. His remains were buried in the church of St. Peter, before the altar, in Quedlinburg, the city he had himself founded.

Henry had reigned only eighteen years, and yet during that time he had not only raised the empire from a fallen state, but had elevated it to the highest degree of power and command. He was strong and mighty against his enemies, and towards his friends and subjects, kind, just, and mild. He is represented as having been of a handsome, chivalric form, skilful and bold as a hunter, and so adroit in all the exercises of the body and warlike arms, that he was the terror of his adversaries. He was extremely bland and affable in his manner, but still preserved so well his dignity that he kept every one within the bounds of respect.

Henry may, with justice, be styled one of the greatest of all German princes; for that which proves the greatness of a king is not so much the actions by which he astonishes the world, but the works he leaves behind him, and which bear in themselves the living germ of a new epoch.

Unfortunately, the most ancient and authentic writers in reference to King Henry are very imperfect and unsatisfactory, so much so, that it is impossible to place entire confidence in the subsequent statements. Still it is already much when we find at least, that all the writers of the middle ages agree in looking upon him as the institutor of chivalry and the ennobling reformer of the nobility, as well as being the founder of cities and citizenship, and, with one word, of all the noble institutions which became developed after him. This testimony proves that his works have had the greatest influence, and, accordingly, that his memory, as it has been, should continue to be honored among mankind. But even if we retain only what is clearly proved in history, enough will remain to establish his claims to glory and honor.

Henry became a still greater benefactor to Germany by founding, in the construction of cities, new municipalities. For although the immediate object of these strong places was to protect the country against the pillaging hordes of the Hungarians, it was one only secondary, inasmuch as they were far more important as the cradle of a new condition of life. The order of common freemen towards the end of the Carlovingian period was, as already stated, very much reduced or nearly extinct. The German people were upon the high road of becoming, like those other nations where there are but two classes, lords and slaves; two conditions between which that pride and energy given by freedom are never recovered. Already the country itself was chiefly cultivated by mere mercenaries.

and industrial employments as well as trade were almost entirely in the hands of the Jews. The nobles considered these occupations beneath their dignity; nay, they were very often dependent on the Jews, who had accumulated immense riches, because in their necessity they were forced to borrow money from them. As early as in the last period of the Roman empire the laws had already commenced to favor the Israelites, and by Honorius among others, they were entirely freed from all military service. Their chief dwelling-places were the cities on the Rhine and the Danube, which originated in the time of the Romans, (Cologne, Coblentz, Treves, Mentz, Worms, Spire, Strasburg, Basle, Constance, Augsburg, Ratisbonne, Passau, &c.,) and in these cities they lived in such great numbers, that they prevented all competition and obstructed all increase of trade and industry.

But King Henry now built, as we have seen, a number of cities in Saxony and Thuringia, and placed in them inhabitants from the country, to serve not merely, as has been supposed, during the time of war, but as constant dwelling-places; he also found means to overcome the ancient repugnance felt by the Saxons to living in towns. He promised to those who dwelt in them the security of justice; and it is not improbable that each town received its own count, who, in time of war was the leader, and in peace was the immediate judge and president, although in gradation he may have ranked under the count of the gau or district in which the town lay.

Afterwards he ordered, as is expressly stated by Widukind, that all councils, assemblies, and festivals of the inhabitants of the neighboring districts, should be held and celebrated in the cities; and that all trade-fairs in their turn, followed and joined in these regulations, and that industry and traffic found in the cities their central point of union, is to be inferred as a natural and important result. Whatever had been formerly executed in isolated dwellings, by the family or serfs, soon became, under the new order of things, worked and finished in quantities, and in a superior style, by the artisans and mechanics of the cities. And as the master and his men, in turns, prepared only one, to each allotted part of the work, wherein each was skilled and had been exercised from youth upward, such a division of labor proved, as it always must the foundation of all civilization among the people; and thence Henry was again the founder of industry, moral cultivation, and the development of the civil order of life.

And with the same motives that had caused him to give to chivalry a nobler aim and a more illustrious title for the exercise of arms, so did Henry now seek to introduce the practice of arms for the inhabitants of the cities, so that they might be skilled in the defence of their walls, and thus become a defensive and honorable body of the state. By this he succeeded in attracting inhabitants for his fortified places, in such great numbers, that as these, in their original state, soon became too narrow to hold them, the new-comers, as they arrived, built themselves houses around the fortified place, so that another city, as it were, was speedily completed, which was subsequently surrounded with strong walls, likewise as a defence against the attacks of the enemy.

By what, however, has just been said, it is not meant to convey that these institutions of King Henry had at once changed the whole course of existing customs and manners in Northern Germany, and substituted an extensive and independent order of civil institutions; on the contrary, owing to the ever-repugnant feelings of the Saxons against a confined life in towns, as is shown in subsequent times, this new order of things progressed but slowly. Yet he had laid the foundation, the commencement was made, he gave it an impetus, and more could not be demanded from him. His merit lies therein, that he perceived and acknowledged the necessary reforms required by the march of events, and he promoted their progress; but it was the course of human development which was to combine and complete, in an extended form, what was merely begun by him. This course, however, is not measured by years, but by centuries, and thus we shall find, that it is only in the subsequent period of the middle ages that the result of the great Henry's noble designs are made manifest in the flourishing state of the existence of the cities.

Already, before the death of Henry, the princes had promised him to recognise his son Otho as his successor to the empire; and this recognition was now confirmed in a great assembly at Aix-la-Chapelle, where

Otho was solemnly crowned. Two of the great archbishops on the Rhine contended for the honor of the coronation. He of Cologne claimed it from Aix-la-Chapelle being in his diocese; and the other, of Treves, because his archbishopric was the most ancient. However, it was at last concluded that neither of them, but that Hildebert, Archbishop of Mentz, should perform the ceremony. Giselbrecht, Duke of Lorraine, in whose duchy Aix-la-Chapelle lay, was charged, as high chamberlain, with the office of providing for the lodging and entertainment of the strangers, of whom a vast number attended. Eberhard, Duke of Franconia, as high steward, supplied the tables and the viands; Duke Herman of Swabia acted as high-seneschal, and Arnulf, Duke of Bavaria, as high-marshal, provided for the horses and the camp.

When the people were assembled in the grand cathedral of Aix-la-Chapelle, the archbishop led the young king forward by the hand, and spoke thus to the multitude: "Behold, I here present to you the king, Otho, elected by God, proposed by King Henry, and nominated by all the princes! If this choice be acceptable to you, you will signify it by raising your right hand towards heaven!"

The whole multitude then held up their hands and hailed the new king with loud and joyful acclamations. The archbishop then stepped with him to the altar, whereon the imperial insignia lay—the sword and belt, the imperial mantle, the armlets and the staff, together with the sceptre and the crown. The sword he handed to him with these words: "Take this sword, destined to repulse all the enemies of Christ, and to confirm, with most lasting power, the peace of all Christians;" and he handed to his majesty the other articles, with a similar address. He then placed the crown upon his head and led him to the throne, which was erected between two marble columns, where Otho continued to sit until the solemn ceremony was concluded. All eyes were turned with astonishment to the young king, whose countenance filled every one with veneration. His lofty, princely form, his broad manly chest, his large sparkling eyes, and beautiful flaxen hair, which flowed down to his shoulders in long locks—all seemed to announce him as being born to rule. The days of festival and ceremony having ended, Otho commenced his new reign with vigorous power, and it was speedily shown that outward appearances had not deceived.

But Otho did not gain over the hearts of men that same mild power which Henry his father had obtained. He has often been called a lion, from his proud and terrific look and manner, and because like the lion he cast all enemies down before him, whenever and however numerous in force they appeared against him, whether at home or abroad. He was a great and powerful monarch, and was soon considered the first prince in Christendom. He had placed upon his head the imperial crown of Charlemagne, and even rendered the Germanic empire and its name so celebrated among all nations, that none could venture to claim comparison with it. Such powerful results cannot be accomplished by a man of ordinary mind, and who lives only for tranquillity and peace, but by him alone, to whom, like Otho, the fame of his nation stands ever before his eyes as an elevated glory-beaming image; and if even the haughtiness of his soul raised many enemies against him, and even if in his wrath, with which his manly breast was often excited, he acted with harshness towards his adversaries, still in his noble dignity of mind, he may be compared with the lion, inasmuch as he pitied and spared many times those weaker enemies who besought his mercy and pardon. Anger and severity indeed never carried him beyond the limits of justice, for with him the law ever maintained its influence and authority.

Our country, which before these two great kings, Henry and Otho, was rapidly approaching its own ruin, being rent by internal anarchy, and surrounded externally by enemies who, in their contempt, according to their caprice, laid it desolate wherever they could, now rose again suddenly, and became as it were a new-born empire. Not only were the enemies struck to the ground, but even new countries were acquired, and all other nations which had previously mocked, now bent low before us. In the time of peace, when no danger threatens, and justice and order hold predominance everywhere, a nation may rejoice in a king who sits upon the throne of his fathers, intent upon continuing that state of peace; but when the world is violently agitated, and personal freedom and independence are in danger, or when a nation has become completely enervated by a long peace, and is thus rendered indifferent to honor and glory, then a king is required bold and proud as King Otho the First. His royal patriotic father had commenced the work, and he, the son, felt himself in possession of the power to perform its completion.

It is true that at the commencement of his reign many princes rose against him, as for instance: the Franks under Eberhard, and the Lothringians or Lorrainers under Giselbrecht, who still could not forget that a Saxon possessed the royal dignity; Tankmar, his step-brother, and even his own younger brother Henry, the mother's favorite, who considered he had a greater right to the crown than Otho, because he was born when his father was already a king, while Otho, on the contrary, was born while he was a duke. But the Franks and Lothringians were reduced by arms to tranquillity, after the dukes Eberhard and Giselbrecht were both slain; Tankmar was also killed in the contest; and Henry, who had been allied with them, repaired to Frankfurt, and at the Christmas festival, in 942, during mass in the night, cast himself at the feet of his brother, and received full pardon, although he had three times risen against him, and had even joined in a conspiracy to take his life. Nay, in 945, he was presented by Otho with the vacant duchy of Bavaria, and thenceforward they remained true friends until their death.

The king now turned his attention towards his external enemies. With his northeastern neighbors, the Slavonians, he had long and sanguinary wars, but he made them tributary as far as the Oder, and in order to confirm Christianity among them, he erected the bishoprics of Haselberg, Brandenberg, and Meissen, and subjected them later to the archbishopric of Magdeburg, which he had established in the year 968. The dukes of Bohemia and Poland were obliged to acknowledge his authority, and by the foundation of the bishopric of Posen he sought to extend the mild doctrines of Christianity to those distant countries. He drove back the Danes, who had shortly before desolated the Margraviate of Sleswig, founded by his father, as far as the point of Jutland; and an arm of the sea on this coast derived from him the name of the Otho-Sound, because he fixed his lance there in the ground, as a token of his arrival. Harold caused himself as well as his consort Gunelda and his son Sveno to be baptized, and bishoprics were erected in Sleswig, Ripen, and Aarhuus. Otho felt within himself that he was appointed to perform the part of a Christian German king, the same as Charles the Great; he spread Christianity around with a national feeling for its cultivation, by planting in the conquered countries German colonies.

Meanwhile, in Italy, circumstances had occurred which attracted the eyes of Otho to that country, longing as he did to perform great deeds there. Ever since the extinction of the Carlovingian branch numerous pretenders to its dominion had started up, scattering disorder and destruction throughout that beautiful land, in addition to which bands of plundering strangers had either taken up their quarters or made continual incursions throughout the country. Here and there the Saracens were found regularly housed among the rocks of the seacoast, while the hordes of the Hungarians or Magyars frequently overran the rich and fertile plains of Upper Italy. In the south of Italy, the dominion of the Greek emperors still maintained itself, and extended almost to Rome, and whose mercenaries, consisting of many nations, were a scourge to the land.

In Upper Italy, the native princes at one moment, and the kings of Burgundy in the next, took possession of the reins of government, and to a certain extent assumed the imperial title. Lothaire, the last king of the Burgundian race, died in the year 950, and the Margrave, Berengar of Ivrea, took forcible possession of the authority. In order to fix himself more securely in the government, he tried to force the young and beautiful widow of Lothaire, the Princess Adelaide, to marry his son Adelbert. But this she steadily and firmly refused, and was imprisoned by the king; but with the assistance of an ecclesiastic she escaped, and took refuge at the court of Adelhard, Bishop of Reggio. This event gave occasion for Otho to interfere with his influence, in order to adjust this sad state of confusion in that part of Italy, and especially as he was appealed to by many nobles of that land, as also by the persecuted Adelaide herself. Accordingly in 951 he crossed the Alps with a well-appointed army, besieged and took possession of Pavia, and as his first wife Edigatha had died in the year 946, he concluded by giving his hand to the beautiful Adelaide, whom he had thus so chivalrously delivered from her base persecutor. In the course of the following year he became reconciled with Berengar at Augsburg, and gave him Lombardy as a fief under German dominion. Verona and Aquislegia, however, he yielded to Henry of Bavaria.

These events, however, produced shortly afterwards great disputes in Germany. Otho was affectionately attached to his queen, Adelaide, and his brother Henry of Bavaria, and they both acquired great influence with him. Ludolf, Otho's son by his former marriage, felt himself, perhaps not unjustly, to be neglected, and was afraid he would be excluded from succession to the throne by the children his father might have by Adelaide. He was joined by Otho's son-in-law, Conrad, Duke of Lorraine, Frederic, Archbishop of Mentz, the Palatine Arnulf of Bavaria, and several other nobles, induced especially, as it would seem, by hatred to Henry of Bavaria, whose deceitful character had embittered them against him. It was only with the greatest trouble and difficulty that Otho was enabled, in the course of the years 953 and 954, to suppress the revolt. Obstinate and severe battles were fought in Saxony, Lorraine, Franconia, and Bavaria; and it was in vain that Otho besieged his adversaries in Mentz, as well as afterwards in Ratisbonne. Even the Hungarians renewed their destructive attacks, and were supported in them by the revolutionary forces; they pursued their incursions through Bavaria, Franconia, Lorraine, a part of France, and finally returned through Burgundy and Italy. But it was just these very devastations, committed by this arch-enemy of the empire, which at last put an end to the revolutionary war. Punished by their consciences, Conrad and the Archbishop of Mentz returned to their allegiance and humbled themselves before the king, by whom they were pardoned and received again into favor; and although in his obstinacy Ludolf for a time continued the contest, he nevertheless in the end, after the Palatine Arnulf had been killed before Ratisbonne, likewise yielded submission to his father, whose kindled wrath had been softened down by the intercession of the princes. Ludolf and Conrad, however, were not granted the restoration of their lost dukedoms, that of Lorraine being given to Otho's faithful brother Bruno, who had likewise been already appointed to the archbishopric of Cologne, while Burchard, Henry of Bavaria's son-in-law, was raised to the dukedom of Swabia.

Thus internal peace was happily restored, when in the year 955, the Hungarians in still greater force again invaded Bavaria, and besieged Augsburg. Udalrich, the bishop of that city, defended it heroically, until the king advanced to its assistance and encamped along the river Lech. His army was divided into eight battalions, of which the first three consisted of Bavarians; the fourth of the Franks under Conrad; the fifth of the élite troops of warriors, selected from the entire army, at the head of which noble division Otho himself commanded; the sixth and seventh were composed of the Swabians, and the eighth consisted of a thousand picked Bohemian horsemen in charge of the military stores and baggage, as from this side no attack was anticipated. Scarcely had the Hungarians, however, caught a glimpse of the army, when, with their usual rapidity, they spread out their innumerable hordes of cavalry, swam across the Lech, and attacked the camp behind the army; throwing the Bohemians and the Swabians into such disorder that the baggage became lost. The valiant Conrad, however, with his Franks, hastened to their assistance and restored order. The decisive battle was fixed to take place on the following day, it being the day of St. Lawrence. The whole army prepared itself for the contest by prayer; the king received the holy sacrament, and he and the entire army swore to remain true to each other unto death. Otho then raised the holy lance, the banner of the angel which had led to victory at Merseburg, waving also now in front; the king himself gave the signal for attack, and was the first to fall upon the enemy. He himself, with his chosen troop, and Conrad, who felt anxious to recover by splendid deeds the good name he had lost in his rebellion, decided the battle. Thus a great and glorious victory was gained; the enemy's troops completely defeated, and put to flight, nearly all being destroyed or made prisoners, and three of their leaders hung up like chiefs of robbers. Their own writer, Keza, assures us that out of both their large armies, consisting of 60,000 men, only seven stragglers returned —with their ears shorn.

But the victory of the Germans was dearly purchased. Many brave leaders fell; and the heroic Conrad, who, during the great heat, had loosened his armor to cool himself a little, was mortally wounded in the neck by a stray arrow, and died—thus repaying with his blood the debt he owed to his country. The Hungarians, however, after the battle, did not venture to appear again in Germany, and the whole of that beautiful country along the Danube, the subsequent Margraviate of Austria, was torn from them, and by degrees repopulated with Germans, so that eventually it flourished gloriously.

Otho gained in the same year, a victory not less important over the Slavonians, who, in conjunction with numerous discontented Saxons, renewed their attacks constantly. The Margrave Gero, one of the most important men under the reign of Otho I., and who had for many years continued to protect the eastern frontiers against the Slavonians, now, together with the valiant Hermann Bilburg, opposed them with great vigor and success, until the king himself was enabled to advance to their aid; and in a battle fought on the 16th of October, and which has been compared with that of Augsburg, he completely conquered them. The brave Hermann Bilburg was subsequently created a duke of Saxony by Otho, although, as it appears, without having attained the government of the entire country, and the full power of the other dukes.

Meanwhile, Berengar, the ungrateful King of Italy, to whom Otho had shown great kindness, again rebelled against him, and cruelly persecuted all who held with the King of Germany; and in their trouble they entreated assistance from Otho. He first sent his son, Ludolf, with an army across the Alps; its force was indeed but small, but the valiant son of Otho pressed the traitor so closely, that he must have been destroyed, if Ludolf had not suddenly died in the bloom of youth, and, as it is supposed, by poison, in the year 957. Some few years elapsed, when in the year 961, King Otho himself, invited by the pope, John XII., the Archbishop of Milan, and others, accompanied by Adelaide, his queen, marched himself a second time into Italy, after he had caused his son Otho, yet an infant, to be elected and crowned king. Berengar concealed himself among his castles, while his son Adelbert took refuge in Corsica; but Otho proceeded direct to Rome. During his progress towards the capital, the gates of every town were thrown open before the mighty King of the Germans, and everywhere the inhabitants were struck with amazement and admiration, when they beheld the powerful and lofty figures of the northern strangers.

Otho considered it worthy of his own glory, as well as of the dignity of the German nation, to replace upon his head, on the 2d of February, 962, the Roman imperial crown, which Charlemagne had transferred to the Germans, thereby testifying to the whole world, that strength and power were with that people, and that their monarch was the first of all Christian rulers. It was under his protection and support, that the church and its spiritual head, the pope, were to exercise their influence over the people; and in him, the emperor, every enemy of order and justice would find a stern and implacable judge. Thus had, likewise, Charles the Great founded anew the imperial dignity, and thus it was renewed by Otho I. It is true, the condition of Europe had changed since Charles's time; then almost all the Christian nations were under his dominion; while there were various independent kings who were not subject to him, the German king. Yet not one of them all could compare himself with him; the imperial crown had ever been justly regarded as belonging to the Germans, and the ancestors of Otho had none of them given up their claim to it. Otho was especially the protector of the Christian faith towards the north and east; he ruled in Burgundy; his authority was the ruling one in France, where his brother, Bruno, of Lorraine, acted as arbitrator and judge, and as which he was acknowledged by all; and now, having subjected Italy, to him alone belonged the dignity of Emperor of the Western Christendom.

Many have spoken against the renewal of the empire, and have particularly censured King Otho, that he cast this great burden upon Germany. The union of the two countries was the source of the greatest misfortune to Germany, which sacrificed so many men for the foreign ally, while at home it was itself entirely neglected by its own hereditary rulers. But what God had prepared as a great transition in the fate of a nation, and what a number of excellent men in former times acknowledged as necessary and good, cannot be rejected by the judgment of later descendants. It has been the same with the papacy; many have expended their gall against it, as having only contributed to the diffusion of darkness, superstition, and spiritual slavery. But those who thus express themselves, mix in their censure all ages, and are unable to transport themselves into those wherein the imperial throne and the papal chair were necessary links in the great chain of historical development.

It is not difficult for the unprejudiced and candid mind to perceive the grand idea which served as the foundation of both. In those times when rude force exercised its dominion, the emperor, with the scales of justice in his hand, presided as judge between Christian nations, and exerted himself for the peace of the world externally; while, on his part, the pope guided the empire of internal peace, piety, and virtue. As the condition of life was yet rude, and civil institutions still so imperfect, that the state could not of itself undertake to superintend mental cultivation; therefore, the church and schools, the clergy and teachers, necessarily stood under the supremacy of the head of the church, whose care it was that the truth and gentleness of the divine word should illumine all Christian nations, and unite them into one empire of faith.

With respect to the danger which might threaten—viz.: that, in the first place, the one of these two powers might bring under its dominion the body by means of the sword, and thence require what was unjust; and that, in the second place, the other would so bind the conscience, that it might force it not to put faith in truth itself, but merely in the word as given—a sufficient protection was provided, in either case, inasmuch as the said power, both of the emperor and the pope, was less an external than an internal power, founded solely upon the veneration of nations. Such an authority can never be lastingly misused without destroying itself.

It is true that not all emperors have truly seized the idea of their dignity, or else, perhaps, such great obstructions stood in their way that they could not execute it; and thus, also, the popes not having always retained themselves within the limits of those rights which were accorded to them alone in the dominion of the church, both powers, which should have worked in unity together, and the one have made the other perfect, have, in their enmity, at last destroyed each other. But—and this is the chief point—the grand idea itself must above all things be well distinguished from its execution. The more glorious it is, the greater is its contradiction to the fallibility of human nature, and the low bias of many ages; and the ill success of its accomplishment cannot detract from its own dignity or from the greatness of those who have contended for it.

With respect to the sacrifice of men in the Italian expedition, it depends upon the question, whether the object to be obtained was great and important or not. If it was so, the sacrifice must not be taken into consideration, if battle and war may be allowed for a high and necessary purpose. And the emperors who, with noble-minded dispositions and intentions, made this sacrifice for the idea of an empire, and the honor of their nation, are not, therefore, to be blamed.

The noble pride, however, felt by the Germans in the thought, that they and their rulers should be the central point of Christianity; the conviction of their strength, made manifest by the daring courage of the small forces, composed of their countrymen, in venturing across the Alps, and who, when reaching their destination, by the superiority of their nature gave laws to a numerous and populous nation; these recollections of the ancient glory of our nation, still existing in us the later descendants—all this is the reward for the sacrifice made.

Other advantages, becoming more and more immediately manifest, arising from the union of Germany with Italy, will be shown in the course of our history. We only mention in advance the great influence which the example of the free Italian cities, and, in particular, the flourishing state of commerce there, had upon the rise and successful progress of German towns, an advantage the importance of which cannot be too highly estimated.

Otho speedily exercised his right of protectorship over the church, and his office of superior Christian ruler, against the same pope who had crowned him. John XII. had recalled from Corsica the son of Berengar, for the purpose of placing him in opposition against the emperor; and, in addition to this, was charged by the Roman people, and the clergy, with the most serious crimes. John sprang from a very corrupt race, and had become pope as early as in his eighteenth year. Otho hereupon convoked a council, consisting of forty bishops and seventeen cardinals, and as John, upon the emperor's citation, refused to appear before these assembled fathers, he was deposed from his dignity, and Leo VIII. chosen instead. The Roman people, as well as the clergy, now swore to elect no pope in future without the consent of the emperor. The popes from this time again called the emperor their lord, and in acknowledgment of his supremacy, placed his name upon their coins, and marked the years of his reign upon their bulls.

But the Romans soon forgot their oath, drove away Pope Leo, and recalled the deposed John, after whose death, which speedily followed, they elected another pope, Benedict, in opposition. The patience of the emperor was now exhausted, and he exercised a heavy punishment upon the perjured Romans. He returned again with his army, laid waste the country around Rome, surrounded and besieged the city, and forced the inhabitants to surrender and open the gates, and to give up the pope, Benedict, into his hands. He then convoked a large assembly of the bishops and clergy, and in their presence Benedict was divested of his insignia, and at once banished, while Leo was replaced upon the throne.

Meantime Berengar, with his wife, Willa, had been taken prisoners by the emperor's generals, and were conveyed to Bamberg, where after their imprisonment they shortly died. The emperor himself, after he had thus established his dominion, returned in the beginning of the year, 965, to Germany, and celebrated at Cologne, with his beloved brother Bruno, his mother, his son Otho, and nephews, together with a numerous assemblage of the nobles of his empire, the joyful event of his return among them after a long and trying time of absence.

But already in the following year, 966, his presence was again required in Italy through the disturbances caused by Adelbert, the son of Berengar, and the revolt of the Romans against their pope. His appearance, however, once more produced order and peace; and he was now enabled to turn his attention to Lower Italy, where the emperor of Greece still had his governor, and then to Sicily, whence the Saracens threatened entire Italy. It was now Otho's wish to form an alliance with the family of the Greek emperor, in order, thereby, to open a prospect for his own house upon Lower Italy, as well as to become enabled to ward off more effectually the inroads of the unbelievers.

He sent for his son Otho from Germany, and had him crowned as future emperor by the pope, and then dispatched an embassy to Constantinople, for the purpose of demanding Theophania, the daughter of the emperor, in marriage for his son. Connected with this embassy, Luitprand, whom Otho had made bishop of Cremona, relates a singular circumstance, although, from his hatred of the Greeks, with evident exaggeration: "We arrived here," he says, "in June, and were immediately supplied with a guard of honor, so that we could not go anywhere without an escort. On the second day of our arrival we proceeded on horseback to the audience. The emperor Nicephorus is a short, stout man, so brown that, in a forest, he would strike us with terror. He said, 'he lamented that our lord and ruler had showed the daring boldness to assume and appropriate Rome to himself, and to destroy two such honorable men as Berengar and Adelbert, and then to carry fire and sword even into Grecian countries:' he added, 'that he knew we had counselled our lord to it.' We replied: 'Our lord, the emperor, has delivered Rome from tyranny and sinners, which he has come from the end of the earth into Italy to accomplish, while others have remained indolently sleeping upon their thrones, and deemed such great confusion and anarchy beneath their dignity to notice. Besides which,' we added, 'we have among us those brave and loyal knights, who are always ready and prepared to maintain, by single combat at arms, the justice and virtue of our master. Yet we have come here with views and intentions of peace, and for the purpose of demanding the Princess Theophania in marriage for Otho, our prince, and eldest son of our lord and emperor.' To which the emperor observed: 'It is now time to go to the procession. We will attend to this matter at a more convenient moment.' The grand procession, wherein the king appeared, attired in a long mantle, escorted by soldiers or city volunteers, without halberds, passed along slowly amid the acclamations of the people.

"When at table, he wished to censure our mode of warfare, saying our arms were much too heavy, while the Germans appeared to be only valiant when they were drunk; and that the true Romans were only now to be found in Constantinople. When he said this, he made a sign to me with his hand that I should be silent. At another time he spoke of the affairs of the church, and asked, mockingly, whether any council had ever been convoked in Saxony? I replied, 'that where there was most sickness, there was most need of the greatest number of doctors; that all heresies had originated with the Greeks, and therefore church councils were more necessary to be held among them. Nevertheless I knew of one council being assembled in Saxony, where it had been pronounced that it was more glorious to fight with the sword in hand than with the pen.'

"The emperor is surrounded with flatterers and sycophants; the whole city floats in sensuality, and even on holy days of festival there are plays performed. Their power reposes not in their own strength, but is dependent upon the mercenary forces of Amalfi, and upon Venetian and Russian sailors. I believe firmly that four hundred Germans in open field would put the whole Greek army completely to flight."

Nicephorus would not consent to the marriage, and Otho, as emperor, now sought to extend his dominion over the whole of Lower Italy, which was divided among the Greeks, Saracens, and native princes. The history of these expeditions is not clearly given; but altogether it appears the imperial arms were victorious, although it was not possible to gain any durable advantage in that difficult country. In December, 969, the emperor Nicephorus was murdered in a revolt, when his successor very willingly formed an alliance with the emperor of Germany. The Princess Theophania was crowned in Rome in the year 972, by the pope, John XIII., and united to the young prince, Otho. The emperor himself now returned to Germany, after an absence of six years, in order that he might enjoy some little peace at the close of a life so rich in striking events.

The great influence which Otho had acquired throughout the entire western world, was satisfactorily proved to the German nation during the last few months of his life. Having gone to Quedlinburg to visit the grave of his mother, Matilda, he was there waited upon by the rulers of the Poles and Bohemians, the chiefs Mjesko and Boleslas, in order to receive his opinion and judgment in their affairs; and these were immediately followed by the ambassadors of the Romans, Beneventanians, Greeks, Bulgarians, Slavonians, Danes, and Hungarians, and the whole completed by an embassy from the Saracens in Africa, which arrived shortly afterwards at Merseburg.

Just at this time, however, he was very much affected by the death of his faithful friend, Herman, duke of Saxony, who died in Quedlinburg on the 27th of March, 973. Grieved at the loss of that good man, says Widukind, he wandered solitary and dejected among the graves of those he had held so dear. Alas, how many of these had already preceded him in their departure from this life, reminding him of his own past career, so troubled, so eventful, but yet in many respects so glorious!

When on the 6th of May he arrived at his castle in Memleben, where his father had died, he felt himself extremely weak. Nevertheless he attended service in the chapel on the following morning, gave his usual alms to the poor, and then reposed again. At midday he again appeared, and at the appointed time he took his meal at dinner with cheerfulness and enjoyment, upon which he attended the evening service. It was then he suddenly felt overcome with a burning fever, and he was assisted to a chair by the princes in attendance. But his head sunk; he felt his approaching end, and indicating his wishes by signs, he was immediately assisted in the solemn service of the holy communion. Just after he had received it, and when the holy ceremony was over, as Widukind states, he ended his mortal career, and without a sigh tranquilly breathed his last, on the 7th of May, 973, aged sixty-one years, and in the thirty-eighth of his reign.

His body was conveyed to Magdeburg, his favorite city, and being deposited in a marble coffin, was placed as he had wished, on the side of his beloved Edgitha, in the church of St. Maurice.

Otho II., who, in the eighteenth year of his age, now succeeded to the throne, very soon had reason to find that the task which had thus early devolved upon his shoulders, of maintaining, in all its supremacy, the powerful empire of his father, extending, as it did, from the boundaries of the Danish country to nearly the extensive points of Lower Italy, was not a little arduous and difficult. For in the north and east, the Danes and Slavonians continued still unwilling subjects or neighbors; in the west, the French rulers were jealous rivals; in the south of Italy, the Greeks and Arabs were anxiously watching for an opportunity to extend their power; while, in the interior of Germany itself, many parties stood in a condition of direct hostility towards each other.

In this critical position, the necessary strength and energy of body was certainly not wanting in the young monarch, as was sufficiently shown by his figure, which, although rather short, was, nevertheless, strong and firmly knit together, while his healthy constitution was indicated by the florid, ruddy hue of his cheeks, and which, in fact, procured for him the by-name of Otho the Florid, or Red. But wisdom and forethought were not as yet at his command; and it was for him a misfortune that, even as a child, he had been designated as the sovereign; for he thus became proud and violent, extreme and unequal in his conduct; while mildness and severity were with him in constant interchange, and his liberality at times bordered upon extravagance itself. Had time, however, enabled him to moderate these strong passions of youth, and thus, by the experience of increased years, ripened and brought to perfection his nobler qualities, he might then have been included in the list of the most distinguished rulers of our country. But fate ordained otherwise; and he was struck down, in the bloom of manhood, at the age of twenty-eight years.

The very first years of his reign were already fully occupied with the different disputes and dissensions in the empire, but more especially with that produced by his cousin Henry, the second duke of Bavaria, or the Turbulent, who had revolted against the young emperor, but who, however, was taken prisoner, and deprived of his duchy; as likewise by the rising of Harold of Denmark against Otho, who was forced to march against him, and completely subdued him.

Soon afterwards, France made an attempt to acquire the Lorraine dominion, which, by the division of Verdun, was fixed in the centre between Germany and France, but had now become united with Germany. The king, Lothaire, secretly collected his army, and while Otho, completely unprepared, was holding a court on the occasion of the feast of St. John, in 978, in the ancient imperial palatinate at Aix-la-Chapelle, he suddenly advanced, and, by forced marches, without even announcing hostilities, hastened on to that city, in order to take the emperor prisoner. Fortunately, Otho received intelligence of the enemy's approach in time to enable him to quit the place on the day before his arrival. Lothaire took possession of Aix-la-Chapelle, and plundered it, while at the same time he commanded the eagle, erected in the grand square of Charles the Great, to be turned towards the west, in sign that Lorraine now belonged to France. But Otho forthwith held a diet of the princes and nobles at Dortmund, represented to them, with the most impressive eloquence, the faithlessness of the French king, and summoned them to march against the presumptuous enemy. They all unanimously promised their assistance, forgetting every internal dispute, for it now concerned the honor of the country.

Accordingly, on the 1st of October, 978, a considerable army marched into France, and without meeting with much opposition, advanced, by Rheims and Soissons, as far as Paris. Here, on the right bank of the Seine, around the Montmartre, the Germans encamped, and their mounted troops scoured the whole of the country around, committing devastation everywhere. The city itself was garrisoned by the duke, Hugo Capet; the Seine divided the two armies, but the French did not venture out to give battle. Otho, however, could not succeed in taking the city, which was strongly fortified; and as winter now advanced—it being the end of November—

and sickness very generally prevailed among the troops, he commenced a retreat. This expedition was one of the first undertaken by the Germans against Paris; the treacherous attack of the French king was now punished, nor did he venture to make another. In the treaty of peace subsequently concluded, Lorraine was secured to Germany forever.

In the year 980, Otho set out on his first expedition to Italy, from which, however, as it turned out, he was never to return. He was in hopes of being able to conquer the possessions in Lower Italy, which the Greek emperors still maintained, and to which Otho, by his marriage with Theophania, laid claim. The Greeks, however, called to their aid the Arabs, both of Africa and Sicily. At first, Otho gained some advantages, and, after a siege of nearly two months, he made himself master of Salerno. He then took Bari and Taranto, in Apulia, and pressed forward, in the spring of 982, to the mountains of Calabria. He beat the combined army of the Greeks and Arabs, first at Rossano, where they had waited for him in a strong position, and then overthrowing them at Coterna, pursued them as far as Squillace, where another decisive battle was fought on the 13th of July, 982. The imperial troops rushed with the greatest impetuosity upon the ranks of the Greeks, who held out bravely until mid-day, when they fell back upon Squillace. The successful troops, abandoning themselves now too eagerly to their elated hopes of victory and pillage, felt so secure, that they laid aside their arms, and marched leisurely and confidently along the banks of the river Corace. But here they were suddenly fallen upon by an ambuscade of the Arabs, hitherto concealed behind the rocks, and were speedily surrounded on every side by innumerable hordes of these swift warriors. The scattered troops were completely overpowered, and either cut to pieces or made prisoners by the enemy; and only a very small number of that army, but a short time before so triumphant, were enabled to save themselves. The emperor himself, as it were, by a miracle, escaped by plunging into the sea, mounted as he was on his trusty steed, and swimming towards a Greek vessel. The crew received him on board, not knowing the high rank of the imperial fugitive, yet hoping to receive a handsome ransom from him as a distinguished knight, for which they held him to be. By means of a slave on board, who had recognised, but not betrayed him, he saved himself a second time, near Rossano, by springing from this ship, and swimming on shore; and, after safely reaching land, he entered that city, and there joined his queen.

In this disastrous scene, many German and Italian princes and nobles perished, among whom were Udo, duke of Franconia, the margraves Berthold and Günther, Henry, bishop of Augsburg, (who had likewise fought in the ranks,) together with numerous others; and all the conquered portions of the country in Lower Italy fell again into the hands of the enemy.

Full of sorrow and vexation, the emperor proceeded to Upper Italy, in order to collect another army. He held a grand assembly in Verona, consisting of both German and Italian princes and nobles, and his mother, together with his queen and infant son, Otho, then only three years old, were likewise present; he succeeded in having the latter at once elected by all the princes as his successor. It was, at the same time, determined that the child should be taken back to Germany, under the charge of Willigis, archbishop of Mentz, and be crowned on the following Christmas, (983,) in the ancient imperial city of Aix-la-Chapelle.

The emperor himself, however, after he had regulated the affairs of Upper Italy, repaired to Rome. There he arranged to have his chancellor, Peter of Pavia, elected as pope, (John XIV.;) and this was his last public act. Overwhelmed with the important plans he nourished in his heart for his next campaign in Lower Italy, as well as with the excitement produced upon his impatient and nervous mind, by the sad reverses of the previous year, and the multifarious cares of his government, he was, in a few days, attacked by a raging fever, of which he died, in the presence of his queen, the pope, and several of his faithful adherents, on the 7th of December, [illegible], in the 28th year of his age. He was buried in the church of St. Peter, in Rome. The news of his death reached Aix-la-Chapelle the day after the coronation of his infant son had been celebrated in the assembly of all the princes.

The very tender age of the new sovereign, Otho III., would have been a great misfortune for Germany, had not his mother, Queen Theophania, a woman of extraordinary genius, been enabled to undertake, during his minority, the direction and control of the affairs of the imperial government with adequate spirit and energy, and if, likewise, among the greater portion of the German princes there had not existed a faithful adherence towards the imperial house, and a general desire for peace and order. For immediately after the death of Otho II., Henry, the deposed duke of Bavaria, after having been set at liberty by Poppo, bishop of Utrecht, into whose custody he had been given, came forward again with his pretensions, and even demanded, as nearest relation, to have the sole guardianship of the young king. The archbishop of Cologne, Warin, under whose protection the infant had been placed, actually delivered him up to Henry, who held him under his control during a whole year. The queen-mother, Theophania, who, according to her deceased husband's will, was to have the guardianship of the child, was still in Italy; and when she returned, Henry had already so strengthened his party, that he contemplated taking possession of the government himself. He had lost no time in forming a league with those nobles who were devoted to his interests, and had already agreed with them under what conditions they should give their assistance and support towards raising him to the throne. At the same time, the French king, Lothaire, availing himself of the disunion in Germany, had again stretched out his hand to grasp the Lorraine country, and had got possession of the important town and fortress of Verdun.

The Slavonians on the northern and eastern frontiers who, during the years that Otho II. was in Italy, had, by their united strength, almost entirely shaken off the German dominion, re-established paganism, and made many successful depredatory incursions in the various German possessions, now, together with the dukes of Poland and Bohemia on their part, promised the rebel, Henry of Bavaria, their assistance in his revolutionary plans. Thus the condition of the Germanic empire had at this moment become entirely critical.

But the alliance of Henry with the barbarians only served to bring back to their proper recollection all those nobles of Saxony and Thuringia who had hitherto formed the majority of the renegade's partisans, and they turned from him and joined the ranks of the legitimate party, headed by the Dukes Conrad of Swabia, Bernard of Saxony, and the newly created duke of Bavaria, (recently elected by Otho II.,) Henry the younger, of the house of Babenberg; the whole of whom, with Willigis, archbishop of Mentz, had still maintained their fidelity towards the young monarch and his royal mother. In Lorraine, also, a party rose up to defend the cause of Otho, the heart and soul of which was the distinguished ecclesiastic, Gerbert, the most learned man of his time; possessing a knowledge of all the sciences, but, more especially, so profoundly read in natural philosophy, that he was regarded as a magician. At the same time he possessed great powers of mind, with the necessary energetic and penetrating capacity for action in all political matters; and in his office of tutor to the young emperor, to which he was appointed subsequently, he continued to assist him with his valuable counsel until his death.

Thence, by means of this combined operation on the part of all his faithful friends and stanch adherents of the imperial house, Henry the Turbulent was forced, at a grand diet held at Rora,* in the month of June, 984, to surrender into the hands of the queen-mother and grandmother, who were both present, the infant emperor. In the same year, also, the desired union of peace and friendship between Henry and the guardians was completely restored and firmly established at the diet of Worms; Henry and his friends swearing fealty to the sovereign, and which he continued to hold sacred from that day; nay, through leading subsequently a life of peace, piety, and charity, he earned for himself the byname of the peaceful, instead of the turbulent Henry. In the following year he received again his long wished-for duchy of Bavaria, in return for resigning which, Henry the younger was indemnified with the duchy of Carinthia, which had become again separated from Bavaria, together with the Veronian marches. Other nobles were bound to the new government by presents and gifts of land. The margra-

* The exact site of this place cannot be traced.

viates, erected to oppose the Slavonians and Hungarians, were fortified anew, and supplied with faithful guards; the dukes Micislas of Poland and Boleslas of Bohemia returned to their allegiance, and thus, by wisdom, prudence, and firmness, both the empresses restored once more the order and tranquillity of the German empire internally, and again promoted and established its influential claims for respect externally.

In the year 987, after the death of Lothaire, France likewise concluded a treaty of peace, and his son and successor, Louis V., surrendered to Germany the bishopric of Verdun. He was the last of the race of the Carlovingians on the throne of France; and, after his death, in the same year, the house of the Capetingians followed in the person of Hugo Capet, his successor.

In Rome, after the Empress Theophania had returned to Germany, great disturbances broke out, and the patrician Crescentius, especially, exercised the greatest tyranny in the city. The empress, however, having beheld Germany tranquillized, and the dominion of her son established, returned in 988 to Rome, and with her innate power and wisdom, caused the authority of Crescentius to be checked and restricted within its proper limits. Unhappily, this distinguished woman died too soon for the times she lived in, her death taking place already in the year 991, at Nimwegen.

The education of the young emperor, now eleven years old, henceforward devolved more especially upon Bernward, of Hildesheim, a most excellent, and, for his time, a very learned man, into whose hands Queen Theophania had already confided her son. He treated the boy with mildness, but at the same time with firmness, and gained his entire good-will and confidence. Bernward's position became one of very great and decided importance, in connection with the relations of the government subsequently, particularly after he was appointed, in the year 993, bishop of Hildesheim; for in the northern frontiers of the empire there was continually fresh cause, even from year to year, for contention with the Slavonians or Normans, either by warding off their attacks at home, or in order to punish them, by sending expeditions into their own land.

When the youthful monarch had attained his sixteenth year, his grandmother, Queen Adelaide, expressed a desire to behold the head of her grandson decorated likewise with the imperial crown. Accordingly, in February, 996, he commenced his first Roman expedition, and all the nations of the Germans, Saxons, Franks, Bavarians, Swabians, and Lorrainians, yielded on this occasion military service, and joined in the ranks of the multitudinous train. He was crowned emperor on Ascension-day, the 21st of May in that year, by Gregory V., the first pope of German origin who had, as yet, presided on the papal chair, and who exerted himself with great perseverance to bring into order the confused state of the Roman relations. The patrician, Crescentius, was pardoned for the turbulent proceedings he had hitherto pursued; but scarcely had the emperor returned to Germany, when the ungrateful Roman again revolted, and banished Pope Gregory from the capital. Otho was forced, therefore, to march an army into Italy a second time in the year 997, and conducting the pope back again to Rome, he besieged Crescentius in the fortress of Engelsburg, which he took by storm, and the traitor was forthwith beheaded on the battlements of the burg, in view of the whole army and people.

Pope Gregory died in the year 999, and Otho caused his esteemed instructor and counsellor, Gerbert, to be elected to the papal chair, who adopted the title of Sylvester II.

Otho, who always felt a great preference for Rome and Italy generally, would fain have wished to remain longer there, but he was not able to bear the enervating effects of that hot climate. Altogether, he did not enjoy the strongest constitution, and his health was not always in the best condition; besides which, during the period between youth and manhood, he evinced a very marked expression of sadness and melancholy, and which often exercised upon his mind such an influence, that, completely overcome, he resorted to the most severe self-inflicted punishments and penalties. Thus he now made a pilgrimage to Monte Gargano, in Apulia, and sojourned for a considerable time in the monastery of St. Michael, undergoing the most severe exercise of expiatory penance. Thence he visited the holy abbot, Nilus, near Garta, who, with his monks, lived there in wretched cells, and in the most secluded state of strict devotion and humility. Here, likewise, Otho joined in the exercise of prayer, and severe and rigid repentance. Afterwards, we again find him following the same course of extreme self-punishment in Ravenna, for whole days together; and at one time he is said to have passed whole weeks with the hermits in the caves around, fasting and praying.

It was these Italian monks, and especially Nilus the holy, a venerable man, ninety years of age, who had succeeded in producing within the prince this melancholy view of life, and filled him with such continual desires to indulge in gloomy fits of abstinence and penitential sacrifices. He was particularly intimate with Adalbert, the apostle of the Prussians, who, after the period of the first Roman campaign, had become his constant companion, not quitting the imperial apartments either by night or day, and who, partly by the wish of Otho, proceeded to the north, in order to preach the holy gospel to the pagan Prussians, where he died a martyr's death, in the year 999. When the religious emperor returned, in the following year, to Germany, he was urged, by his affection towards this friend, to visit his grave in Gnesen. As soon as he came in view of the town, he dismounted from his steed, and continued the rest of his pilgrimage to the sacred spot barefooted. Deeply affected, he poured forth his devotions over the tomb of his much-lamented friend, and in recollection of the scene, he raised the bishopric of Gnesen, on the spot, into an archbishopric, placing under its authority the bishoprics of Breslaw, Cracovie, and Colberg, promoting Adalbert's brother, Gaudentius, to the sacred office.

Combined with the emotions originating in Christian humility and worldly sacrifice, we find, however, likewise excited within Otho's soul, (which appears to have been subjected to sensations of the most varied nature,) a high aspiring desire and aim, and, especially, an elevated idea of the supremacy of the imperial dignity. As the son of a Roman-Germanic emperor and the grandson of a Greek emperor; already chosen as reigning king from the first moment of self-consciousness, and, likewise, almost immediately afterwards decorated with the imperial crown; educated by the most learned and accomplished men of his time—a Gerbert, a Bernward, a Meinwerk, (of Paderborn,) and by the Calabrian Greek, John of Placentia—he held himself in high respect, and far beyond the Germans, who, in his opinion, were still uncouth and savage. He tried to persuade them to lay aside their Saxon barbarism, and exhorted them to imitate and adopt the more refined and elegant manners of the Greeks, and he even introduced the customs and usages of the latter; among the rest, which he himself adopted, that of dining alone from a table more elevated than the others, and to arrange the different places of honor according to rank and distinction. His tutor, Gerbert, had himself formed a high idea of the imperial dignity, which he had taken great pains to instil in the youthful mind of his pupil. "Thou art our Cæsar, Imperator, and Augustus," he wrote to him, "and descended from the noblest blood of the Greeks; thou art superior to them all in power and dominion," &c. Otho had indeed contemplated the restoration of the Roman empire, in its entire dominion, and no doubt he would have carried his intentions into effect, by making Rome the central point and the imperial seat of government, had he only been able to endure the climate.

He regarded the founder of the Germanic-Roman empire, the great Charles, as his model, and when, in the year 1000, he visited Aix-la-Chapelle, he felt a desire to elevate his mind by the contemplation of his ancestor's earthly remains. Accordingly he caused the vault to be unclosed, and descended its steps, accompanied by two bishops. He found the embalmed body still in the position it was placed, sitting in the marble chair, covered with the imperial robes, together with the sceptre and shield. Otho bent his knee in prayer, then took the golden cross from the breast of the emperor, and placed it upon his own. After which, before leaving, he had the body covered with fresh raiment, and then again solemnly closed the vault.*

Otho's strong predilection for Italy drew him once more into that country. Rome and the Romans appeared to him in all the splendor of their ancient dominion of the world; but they ill-returned the preference he showed for them. While he was sojourning in Rome, in the spring of the year 1001, the Romans revolted against him be-

* The emperor, Frederick I., caused the vault to be unclosed again in the year 1165, and had the body deposited in a superb tomb.

cause he had exercised his lenity towards the Tiburtinians, who, as in ancient times, still remained their hated enemies; they kept him a close prisoner in his own palace during three days, so that he could obtain neither food nor drink. Then it was that the emperor experienced that German fidelity and rude virtue were still better than the smooth but slippery words and more accomplished manners of his favorite Italians. Bernward, the bishop of Hildesheim, placed himself, with the sacred royal lance, under the portico of the palace, and, as his biographer states, thundered against it most dreadfully; and thus, through the bishop's resolution and the aid of his faithful adherents, the emperor was at length rescued from the Romans. Nevertheless, he looked over their bad conduct, and peace was resumed for a short time longer, but they soon again broke out against him. He then prepared at once to punish this false and treacherous people; but his spirits were now broken, and he weakened and reduced his body still more by nocturnal watchings and praying, often fasting, too, the entire week, with the single exception of the Thursday. He was attacked by a severe and inflammatory disease, (according to Dietmar, the small-pox,) and died on the 23d of January, 1002, at Paterno, in the twenty-second year of his age. The body was placed under the charge and protection of the few German princes and nobles who had accompanied the emperor, and they lost no time in conveying it away from that hateful country into their native land. In the course of its march, however, the funeral procession was frequently attacked by the Italians, who were eager to get possession of the corpse, and it was only by the united efforts of the brave and valiant band of noble warriors that formed its escort, that the enemy was successfully repulsed, and that, at length, after great difficulty, it arrived safely at its destination in Aix-la-Chapelle.

Thus all the male descendants of Otho the Great, his two sons, Ludolf and Otho II., and his two grandsons, Otho III. and Otho the son of Ludolf, died in Italy in the bloom of their youth; while of the imperial Saxon family, the great-grandson of Henry I., Duke Henry of Bavaria alone remained. The Germans were not at all inclined towards the Bavarian race; but Henry, who had, by means of his generous gifts, already enlisted the clergy on his side, and had, likewise, in his possession the crown jewels and insignia, succeeded by degrees in gaining over one by one the individual German states, so that, without a general electoral assembly taking place, each transferred to him the royal authority with the sacred lance.

Henry II. has received the title of saint from his strict and pious life, as also from his liberality towards the clergy, already mentioned. The latter had acquired extensive possessions under the Saxon emperors, who were all very generous towards them, and thence many of the leading members became powerful princes of the empire. Like Charlemagne, the kings saw with pleasure their increase of power, in order that they might use it as a counterpoise to that of the temporal lords, and at this period too, the spiritual power held chiefly with the kings. Otho I. had already begun to unite the lordships with the bishoprics, and Henry II. transferred to many churches two, even three lordships, and to that of Gandersheim he even made over seven. The partiality and attachment shown by the emperor towards the clergy was, no doubt, taken advantage of by many; still among that body there were likewise at this period many men who were perfectly sensible of the peculiar dignity of their calling, and zealously sought the spiritual welfare of their community, as well as the progress of the human mind in the arts and sciences, and all true cultivation; of which the tenth century, especially, presents us with several illustrious instances. Bishop Bernward, of Hildesheim, who, in the urgent danger of the emperor, Otho III., in Rome, displayed so much resolution, was a man of great intellectual mind, and nourished the most profound feeling for all that was good and beautiful. During his many voyages, chiefly in Italy, he took young persons with him for the purpose of exercising their taste in the observation of works of art, and in their imitation. He caused the pavements and churches to be decorated with mosaic embellishment, and costly vessels of a beautiful form to be cast in metal, with which he was furnished by the mines of gold and silver in the Hartz, discovered under the emperor Otho I. Thus did Bernward nobly exert himself for his diocese, and the school of Hildesheim was one of the most celebrated of that period.

When in Italy, the Emperor Henry received a second by-name—that of Huffeholz, or the lame. For fresh disturbances having arisen there after the death of Otho III., and the Italians having made a margrave, Ardovine, their king, Henry, in order to restore order, advanced thither in the year 1004, put Ardovine to flight, and caused himself to be crowned, with the iron crown, at Pavia. Out of regard for the city, and in order to show his confidence towards the citizens, he retained merely a small body-guard, and caused the rest of the army to remain outside the city in the camp. The capricious and inconstant disposition of the Italians immediately became manifest. They rose in revolt, stormed the palace of the emperor, and threatened his life. It was then, in springing from a window, that he lamed his foot. His companions, although but few, fought like valiant men, and successfully resisted the attacks of the enemy until the Germans beyond the city, hearing the tumult within, stormed the walls, and after severe fighting, broke through, paved their way to the palace and saved the king. The battle still continued most furiously in the streets and houses, whence the inhabitants hurled forth stones and other missiles upon the troops, who set fire to the whole city, and which destruction continued until the king put a stop to the fury of his soldiers, and saved the rest of the inhabitants. It was in this battle that the queen's brother, Giselbert, a valiant youth, being killed by the Lombards, a brave knight, Wolfram, his companion in arms, rushed upon the enemy, struck one of them such a powerful blow with his sword that, passing through the helmet, it separated his head and neck down to the shoulders; and having thus revenged the death of his noble friend, he returned, unwounded, back to his comrades.

This conduct of the Pavians produced great disgust upon the open-hearted and honest feelings of the king, and as nothing could induce him to remain longer in Italy, he returned to Germany as speedily as possible.

Here, also, many disturbances arose during his reign, for the emperor, who, with his good and pious qualities, was much too weak to hold the reins of his government, could not possibly maintain his authority. In particular the neighboring Polish duke, Boleslas, an ambitious, turbulent man, who had conquered and partially retained Bohemia and Silesia, gave him much trouble. For these countries, however, the usurper swore allegiance to the German emperor, but beyond this he maintained himself independently, and made himself feared on the other side even by the Russians and the Greek emperor.

Henry visited Italy a second time in 1013, and re-established the pope, Benedict VIII., in the papal chair; he swore to protect him faithfully, and was by him crowned emperor. Returning to Germany, he was especially occupied with founding the bishopric of Bamberg, his favorite seat, which he richly endowed, and had determined it should serve as a monument of his own piety as well as of that of his empress, Cunegunde. In the year 1020 he was much gratified by a journey which Pope Benedict made to Germany, who visited him in Bamberg, and consecrated his holy foundation.

The object of the pope's presence in Germany was more especially to induce the emperor to undertake another expedition to Italy, in order to prevent the Greeks, who threatened Rome from Lower Italy, from attacking and taking possession of that capital.

And Henry, who at once perceived the danger to which the church of Southern Italy was exposed of being robbed by the Greeks of its central point of operation, marched forth, for the third time, in the year 1021, for that country, drove the Greeks easily back to the most extreme points of their possessions in Lower Italy, conquered Benevento, Salerno, and Naples, and was everywhere greeted and hailed as king. But as he never liked to remain long in that country he returned to Germany in 1022, and devoted himself to the exercise of devotional and peaceful works.

Henry died in the year 1024, aged fifty-two, at his fortress, Grone, in the Leingau, (near Göttingen,) which had often been the seat of the Saxon emperors. His body was conveyed to Bamberg and there interred. Subsequently, 122 years after his death, he was added to the calendar of saints by Pope Eugene III. With him the house of Saxony became extinct, which, like that of the Carlovingians, had commenced powerfully but ended weakly. Germany now required once again a vigorous and great-minded ruler, in order to save it from internal dissolution, as well as to preserve it from losing its dignity among the other nations; for, during the minority of Otho III. and under Henry II., the imperial vassals had committed many usurpations based upon the imperial prerogatives. The sons of the nobles, endowed with imperial feods, retained them as if by right of inheritance, and many disputes were settled only by an appeal to the sword, without any regard being paid to the emperor's supreme judicial power. These wars devastated in particular the south of Germany.

Meanwhile the Christian countries wherein, together with the dominion of the church, a regard for the imperial dignity was disseminated, were now become considerably increased in number. Towards the year 1000 Christianity became still more deeply rooted in Hungary, Poland, Russia, Norway, Sweden, and Denmark.

## CHAPTER VIII.

### THE SALIC OR FRANCONIAN HOUSE, 1024–1125, TO LOTHAIRE THE SAXON—1137.

Assemblage of the Ducal States—The Election—Conrad II., 1024-1039—Re-establishes Internal Peace—Italy—Canute, King of England and Denmark—Burgundy—Ernest, Duke of Swabia—The Faust-Recht—Conrad's Death, 1039—Henry III., 1039-1056—The Popes—Henry's zeal for the Church—His Death, 1056—Henry IV., 1056-1106—His Minority—The Archbishops—Albert of Bremen—Henry and the Saxons—Their Hostility—Henry's Revenge—Pope Gregory VII.—His Ambition—The Right of Investiture—Rupture with the Emperor—Henry excommunicated—The Emperor a Fugitive—The rival Emperors and Popes—Rudolphus of Swabia and Pope Clement III.—Henry's Death, 1106—Henry V. 1106-1125—Rome—Pope Pascal II.—The Investiture Contest—Sanguinary Battle—Henry crowned Emperor—His Death, 1125—The First Crusade, 1096-1099—Lothaire the Saxon, 1125-1137.

THE Germanic states, each under its duke, assembled for the election of a new emperor, upon the vast plains along both banks of the Rhine, between Mentz and Worms, near Oppenheim. There were eight dukes; Conrad the Younger, who exercised the ducal power in Franconia in the name of the king—Franconia being still regarded as the king's country—Frederick of Upper Lorraine, Gozelo of Lower Lorraine, Bernard of Saxony, (of Herman Billung's race,) Henry of Bavaria, Adalbert of Carinthia, (the new duchy, separated under Otho II. from Bavaria, and which contained the passes into Italy,) young Ernest of Swabia, and Othelric or Ulric, of Bohemia. The Saxons, the eastern Franks, the Bavarians, and Swabians, together with the Bohemians, encamped themselves on this side of the Rhine; the Rhenish Franks, and those of Lower and Upper Lorraine on the other side. Thus a splendid and numerous assembly or diet of electors was here reflected in the waves of the great German stream.

The voices, after long deliberation, inclined in favor of the Frankish race, from which two Conrads, surpassing all the rest in virtue and consideration, presented themselves—Conrad the Elder or the Salian, and Conrad the Younger, the duke. They were kinsmen, being sons of two brothers, and descended from Conrad the Wise, the husband of the daughter of Otho I., who fell in the battle with the Hungarians on the Lech; both were worthy of their ancestors, and upon the female side related to the Saxon imperial branch. The choice balanced between them; the elder Conrad then advanced to the side of the younger one, and thus addressed him: "Do not let us allow our friendship and interest to be disturbed by the contest. If we dispute together the princes may elect a third, and posterity will then say we were both unworthy of the crown. Methinks that whether the election fall upon either you or me, we shall still both be honored, I in you and you in me. If the crown be awarded to you, I will be the first to do homage to you; vow, therefore, my friend and brother, to do the same by me." To this the younger prince agreed, and forthwith made the vow likewise.

When the election commenced, and the archbishop, Aribo of Mentz, was first to give his vote, he named Conrad the Elder; the archbishops and bishops followed. Among the temporal princes, the duke of the Franks was the first in rotation, and the younger Conrad arose, and with a loud voice gave his vote to his cousin, Conrad the Elder, who seized him by the hand, and placed him beside him. The remaining princes followed on the same side, and the people shouted their applause. Frederic of Lorraine and the archbishop of Cologne alone were discontented, and quitted the assembly; but when they beheld the unanimity of all the others, and that the younger Conrad had at once acceded to the choice made, they became reconciled, and returning, rendered homage with the rest of the princes.

The new king was now conducted to Mentz, to be there solemnly anointed and crowned. On the road to the church, the procession was stopped by the number of petitioners, who prayed for justice. The bishops became impatient, but Conrad listened tranquilly to their prayers and said, "To exercise justice, whether it be convenient to me or not, is my first duty." These words were heard with joy by all around; thence great hopes were formed of the new king, and Conrad did not disappoint them. He commenced his reign by visiting all parts of Germany; he practised justice, restored order, and showed so much strict judgment, combined with mercy, that all united in one opinion, that no king since Charlemagne had so well merited to occupy his seat upon the imperial throne. Robbers he punished so severely, that now there was more general security than had been known for a long period, while commerce flourished once again. He secured for himself and his race the voice of the people, by promoting the development of the municipal institutions by every possible means.

Thus did he govern his kingdom internally. In his foreign relations, he labored equally for the dignity and greatness of Germany. Shortly after the commencement of his reign, he advanced into Italy, where in Milan he was crowned king of Italy, and subsequently in Rome, emperor. The festival was rendered more august by the presence of two kings, Rudolphus of Burgundy, and the great Canute, king of England and Denmark. With the latter, Conrad formed a strict friendship; he united his son, Henry, with his daughter, Kunihilda, and regulated also with him the limits between Germany and Denmark, so that the river Eider, between Holstein and Silesia, became the boundary of both countries. He thus gave up, it is true, the margraviate of Silesia; but the country was difficult to defend, and Conrad was the gainer in other respects. Henry II. had already concluded an hereditary alliance with King Rudolphus of Burgundy, so that after his death Burgundy should fall to Germany. Conrad renewed the treaty, and after the death of Rudolphus he took actual possession of that country, although a portion of the Burgundians had called forward Count Odo, of Champagne, whom, however, Conrad drove back, and was forthwith recognised as king. This kingdom comprised the beautiful districts of the southeast of France, which were afterwards called Provence, Dauphiny, Franche-Comté, and Lyons, together with Savoy, and a portion of Switzerland, thus placing Germany, by means of the important sea-ports of Marseilles and Toulon, in connection with the Mediterranean: an important acquisition, which, however, afterwards, in the times of weaker emperors, became neglected, and fell into the hands of the French.

Conrad, however, was forced to experience, that this very acquisition of Burgundy became a subject of dissension in his own family, and thence a source of vexation to himself. His step-son, Ernest, duke of Swabia, (the son of his queen, Gisella, by her former husband Herman, duke of Swabia,) considered he possessed the first right to the crown of Burgundy, because his mother was the niece of Rudolphus, king of Burgundy. Dissatisfied with Conrad's conduct, in getting this territory annexed to the German empire, he deserted him in the Italian campaign, excited dissension against him in Germany, and was in hopes, by the aid of his friends, to invade and conquer Burgundy. Conrad, however, hastened back, disappointed him in his efforts, and as Ernest could not succeed in gaining over the Swabian vassals to his purpose, he was forced to surrender at discretion, and his step-father sent him a prisoner to the strong castle of Giebichenstein, in Thuringia. After an imprisonment of three years, he set him at liberty, and offered to restore him to his duchy, if he would deliver up to him his friend and principal accomplice, Count Werner, of Kyburg. This, however, Ernest hesitated and finally refused to do, and he was accordingly deposed; and at a diet of the princes and nobles of the empire, he was banished the country, together with all his partisans. He fled for refuge to his cousin, Count Odo, of Champagne, accompanied by Count Werner, and a few faithful friends; but soon afterwards returned, while his father was on an expedition against the Hungarians, concealed himself among the caverns of the Black Forest, and once more endeavored to gain adherents in Swabia. But the bishop of Constance, as administrator of the duchy for Gisella's second son Herman, (yet a minor,) to whom Conrad had transferred it, sent Count Mangold, of Vehringen, against him, when both armies met, (1030,) and fought a severe battle, until both Ernest and Werner, together with Mangold, were killed. The adventures of Duke Ernest became the subject of many heroic lays and legends; and the most wonderful deeds performed by his army were connected with his name, and eventually, collected together by later poets, formed one entire work. Meantime, the campaign undertaken by the emperor against the Hungarians proved triumphant, and he obliged Stephen, their king, to sign a favorable treaty of peace. He forced, also, to their former obedience the Slavonian and Vandalian tribes, who were still seated on the Oder, and northward on the Elbe; and Hamburg, which they had destroyed, raised itself by degrees from its ruins.

The emperor was also a zealous promoter of the institution whereby the church sought to set some limits to the rude force of the *faust-recht*—namely, that of the *Peace of God*. From Wednesday evening at sunset until sunrise on Monday morning, all feuds were to cease, no sword be raised, and universal security protect the affairs of life. He who should transgress against the peace of God, (treuga or treva Dei,) was to be punished with the heaviest ban. Odilo, of Clugny, is named as the originator of this institution, and the clergy of Burgundy and the Low Countries, where the most sanguinary feuds prevailed, with the consent of Conrad, first united themselves, in the year 1033, for this purpose.

Conrad returned sickly from his second expedition into Italy, wherein disease reduced his army; and his own step-son, Herman of Swabia, and Kunihilda, the young consort of his son Henry, the daughter of the Danish king, both died there. He himself never thoroughly recovered, and died at Utrecht, in 1039. His biographer, Wippo, thus speaks of him:—"I should expose myself to the charge of flattery, were I to relate how generous, how steadfast, how undaunted, how severe towards the bad, how good towards the virtuous, how firm against the enemy, and how unwearied and urgent in affairs he was, when the welfare of the empire demanded it."

His consort, Gisella, one of the most noble of German women, and who loved him most tenderly, refused every consolation, and mourned her husband in the convent of Kaufungen, near Cassel, until her death. The corpse of the emperor was brought to Spires, and deposited in the noble cathedral which he himself had founded.

This emperor had evidently formed the idea, which may be called the fundamental idea of the whole Salic imperial race—namely, to raise the imperial power of Germany to the most unlimited extent, to restrict the dominion of the princes within narrow bounds; and, in order to complete this, he endeavored to gain, by every favor, the assistance of the inferior vassals, who had almost become slaves to them. To this tended an important law, (constitutio de feudis,) which Conrad made in the year 1037, on his second expedition to Italy, for that country, and which was soon afterwards transferred to Germany, namely—that feudal estates, which had belonged to the father, should not be taken capriciously from the sons, but only in criminal cases, decided by tribunals composed of their co-vassals. Thereby he prepared for the lesser vassals the full right of property; so that from them there must necessarily have arisen a distinct, free order, for the support of the emperor against the greater vassals. These, on the contrary, and particularly the dukes, he sought to bring back to their old condition of mere imperial functionaries; and even gave the duchies of Swabia, Bavaria, and Franconia, to his son Henry, who seemed fully adapted to carry still farther his great and extensive plan. Had success attended it, Germany would have become earlier what France became later, an undivided, powerful empire. But the Salic race was stayed in its mid-career, partly by its own fault, and partly by the rapid rising of the papal chair, whose authority developed itself with astonishing energy, and whose victory over his grandson, Henry IV., the powerful Conrad certainly had not anticipated.

Conrad's son, Henry, or the black, whom the Germans had chosen during his father's life, was twenty-two years of age; but the hopes formed of him were great, and they proved not unfounded. Like his father, he was of a high mind and a determined will, obstinate and firm, and at the same time eloquent and well-informed, for the prudent Gisella had early induced him to cultivate his mind as much as possible by reading, although at that time books were very scarce. No emperor since Charlemagne maintained more vigorously the imperial dignity in Italy, Germany, and the neighboring lands, or ruled more powerfully within the limits of his extensive empire. What served to increase his great fame was, that he so humbled the wild Hungarians, who a hundred years before were the terror of Germany, that the Hungarian nobility, after a lost battle, took the oath of allegiance to him in the city of Stuhlweissen, in the year 1044, and that Peter, their king, re-established by Henry, received the country as a feud from him, by means of a golden lance. It is true this was no durable subjection; still the act of itself is sufficiently glorious for Henry, while thereby he gained a portion of Hungary, from Kahlenburg to Leitha, which he united with the marches of Austria.

The king then, in 1046, turned his attention towards Italy, to settle the great disorders existing there. There three popes held their sway at once: Benedict IX., Sylvester III., and Gregory IV. Henry, in order to be wholly impartial, convoked a council at Sutri. Here they were all three deposed, as irregularly elected; and then, in Rome, at the desire of the collective clergy and nobility, Henry, who, following the example of Charlemagne, had received the dignity of patrician for himself and successors, made a German, Suidger, bishop of Bamberg, pope, who took the name of Clement II.; and at the Christmas festival, 1046, he crowned Henry emperor. Subsequently, Henry gave the Romans three successive popes, for they were obliged to promise him, as they had done to Otho, to acknowledge no pope without the imperial sanction.

After these, the papal chair was filled by two more German popes, and these six pontiffs from Germany: Clement II., Damasus II., Leo IX., Victor II., Stephen X., and Nicholas II., who succeeded each other in very quick, but uninterrupted rotation, labored with one concurring mind for the good of the church, and raised it again from the ruinous state into which it had been thrown, through dissension in Rome itself, the immoral conduct practised by many of the clergy, and the purchase of spiritual offices for money. Thus they paved the way for the plans of that spiritual dominion of the world, which Hildebrand, or Pope Gregory VII., afterwards succeeded in executing. In our subsequent history of this celebrated pope, we shall allude farther to this question. Here, however, we must at once say, for the honor of these German pontiffs, that by their efforts, influenced by a noble and firm mind, and true zeal towards promoting the purity and dignity of the church, they must be classed as the precursors in the reforms eventually introduced. Leo. IX. (formerly Bruno, bishop of Toul, and a relation of the emperor Henry III.) was especially to be esteemed as a man of the most elevated moral virtue and true nobleness of mind. His humility was so great, that after he was elected pope, he left his bishopric of Toul for Rome on foot, and with the pilgrim's staff in hand, he journeyed all the distance thus lowly, accompanied by Hildebrand, then chaplain to the deposed pope, Gregory VI., in whom Leo had already recognised a man of extraordinary genius.

His zeal for the purification of the church urged him forthwith to operate against the prevailing system of Simonism, or the purchasing of spiritual offices with money, and the immoral life led by the clergy. He presided at three councils which were convoked for this purpose, in Rome, Rheims, and Mentz; and he succeeded in bringing to bear, within a year, the most important reforms. He then travelled from the one country of Christendom to the other, wherever his presence was most necessary, in order to promote and establish personally the purification of the church. He died in the year 1054, too soon for the great work he had in hand; but his successors continued to complete what he had commenced according to his grand plan.

Meantime, in Germany, Henry ruled as a wise and powerful sovereign. He abandoned, certainly, to other princes, the duchies which he himself formerly possessed, but only to such as were rulers of very limited power, and who received, it is true, the name but not the ancient prerogative of duke, as viz.: Bavaria to Henry of the house of Luxemburg, and, after him, to Conrad, of the Palatinate; Carinthia to

Guelf, son of Guelf, the Swabian count; Swabia itself to Otho, count palatine, on the Rhine. In Swabia, the Guelfic house was very powerful, and would therefore willingly have possessed the duchy; but it was precisely for that reason, that Henry placed Count Guelf in Carinthia, in order that the duke might not possess great hereditary lands in the country. Thus he acted as he pleased with the imperial dignities, while he favored the inheritance of the smaller fiefs. Upper Lorraine passed through him to Count Albert, of Longwy, an ancestor of the present Austrian house.

It was about this time that Henry gave a striking proof of his personal courage, for at an interview which took place between him and King Henry of France, near Mentz, in the year 1056, a dispute arose between them, and the latter king charged him with a breach of his word. As it beseemed, Henry replied only by casting his gauntlet down before the king, who, however, during the following night, retired within his frontiers. Nothing could be more pleasing to the Germans than this chivalrous bearing of their emperor.

Henry now returned to Saxony, where his favorite seat Goslar lay, in the Hartz, and which he raised to a considerable city. We must not wonder that a king of the Frankish race should fix his seat in Saxony, considering that he did so on account of its rich mines, which existed close to this said Goslar, in the Hartz. Mines, in those times, were the exclusive property of the emperor. In Goslar, Henry built a fortress, a palace, churches, and ramparts round the town, and he obliged the Saxons of the surrounding country to render excessive service. This increased the ill-will they felt at seeing an imperial fortress thus suddenly created in their country; and although under so severe and powerful an enemy, they could not give utterance to their thoughts, it nevertheless produced the more bitter fruits for his son. Henry died suddenly, in the year 1056, at Bothfeld, near Blankenburg, at the foot of the Hartz, (whither he had gone to hunt,) in the prime of life, being only thirty-seven years old, and in the midst of great plans which he formed for the future.

This emperor was strictly and bigotedly pious, notwithstanding his strong mind and sternness of will. He never placed his crown upon his head without having previously confessed, and received from his confessor permission to wear it. He likewise subjected himself to the expiatory penalties and punishments of the church, and often submitted his body to be scourged by his priests. Thus the rude and barbarous manners of those times held in no contempt corporeal chastisement—as practised among them to curb the violence of passion—even when inflicted upon the body by the sufferer's own lash.

Henry III. may, nevertheless, be named among those emperors who have proved the cultivation of their own mind, by their love for the sciences, by their predilection in favor of distinguished men, and by their promotion of intellectual perfection generally. Ever since he had received the poem addressed to him in Latin by Wippo, (the biographer of his father,) in which he encouraged him to have the children of the secular nobles educated in the sciences, he continued to evince the greatest interest in the erection of schools. Those of Liège, Lobbes, Gemblours, Fulda, Paderborn, St. Gallen, Reichenau, &c., flourished especially under his reign; and it was in the two last-mentioned schools that Herman le Contracte, one of the most learned men of that time, received his education. This extraordinary philosopher was, from his childhood, such a cripple, that he could only be conveyed from one place to another in a portable chair. He wrote also with the greatest difficulty, and stammered so painfully to hear, that his pupils required a long time before they could understand him; while, however, he was so admired and sought after by them, that they flocked to him in multitudes from all parts. His chronicles belong to the most distinguished historical sources, including the first division of the 11th century.

The sciences and the arts under Henry III. progressed to an extent by no means unimportant; and if much became neglected under the long and turbulent reign of his successor, Henry IV., still the foundation was then laid for that glorious developement which is presented to us in the after-times, under the reign of the Hohenstaufens.

The princes had already recognised the succession of Henry's son immediately on his birth. Unfortunately for the empire, upon the death of his father the young king was only a child six years old.

His education and the government of the realm were at first in the hands of his excellent mother Agnes, who, however, was not in a condition to retain the nobles of the empire in dependence, and thus complete the father's work. She sought rather by favoring some of them to acquire support for her government, and therefore gave Swabia, and at the same time the dominion of Burgundy, to Count Rudolphus of Rheinfelden, and Bavaria to Otho of Nordheim, confirming the grant with a dangerous clause, viz., that these dignities should remain hereditary in their houses. Henry, bishop of Augsburg, possessed especially her confidence, but this speedily caused envy and jealousy. At the head of the discontented stood the Archbishop Hanno of Cologne, an ambitious and prudent, but austere and severe man. In order to gain possession of the young king, and thereby of the government, he went at Easter in 1062 to Kaiserwerth on the Rhine, where at that moment the court of the empress was assembled, and after the dinner he persuaded the boy to go and view a particularly beautiful vessel, recently built. He had scarcely, however, got on board, when the sailors, at a signal given by the archbishop, loosened her moorings, and rowed to the middle of the Rhine, which so much terrified the youth, that he suddenly jumped into the river, and would certainly have been drowned had not Count Eckbert of Brunswick sprung after him and saved him at the hazard of his life. He was cheered up, and many fair promises being held out to him, he was thus decoyed away and taken to Cologne. His mother was much alarmed and grieved, and when she perceived that the German princes had no longer confidence in her, she determined to conclude her life in quiet retirement, and went to Rome.

The Archbishop Hanno, in order that it might not appear as if he wanted to retain the highest power in his own hands, made an order that the young king should dwell by turns in the different countries of Germany, and that the bishop, in whose diocese he dwelt, should, for the time being, have the protectorship and the chief government of the kingdom. His chief object, however, was to get the mind of the prince under his own control, but in this he could not succeed. His character and manner were not such as to gain the heart of the youth, for he was severe, haughty, and authoritative, and as it is related of him, that he even applied the scourge with severity to his father, the powerful Henry the Black, it may likewise be presumed that he often treated the youth very roughly. Among the remaining bishops there was one who was a very different man, as ambitious as Hanno, but subtle and flattering, and who gained the youth by granting all his wishes: this was the Archbishop Adalbert of Bremen. This ambitious man wished to unite the whole of the north of Germany into one great ecclesiastical dominion, and to place himself at its head as a second pope. In fact he was already invested almost with the authority and dignity of a patriarch of the north; for by his zealous efforts to propagate Christianity there, many bishoprics had been founded in the Slavonic countries, such as Ratzeburg and Mecklenburg, as well as several churches in Denmark, Norway, and Sweden. He hated the temporal princes, because they stood in the way of these objects, and in order to suppress them he wished to raise the imperial power to unlimited despotism. Hanno of Cologne and his confederates stood in the most decided opposition to him in this view, for they endeavored to raise the dignity of the princes upon the ruins of the empire; and thus both parties, without any reserve, went passionately to extremes. While Hanno was on a journey to Rome, where he remained some time, Adalbert obtained entire possession of the young prince. Nothing worse could have happened to the youth than to be subject to the influence of two such different men, and to this change of treatment so entirely opposite; for after having been treated with the greatest severity, he was now allowed to sink by too great lenity and indulgence into dissipation and sensuality.

Henry was distinguished for great mental as well as physical qualities; he was endowed with daring and ardent courage, quickness of resolve, and a chivalric mind which might have been directed to the most noble objects. But now his active and fiery nature became transformed into a revengeful and furious disposition, and his elevated mind degenerated into selfish pride and domination. Besides which, he loved sensual pleasures, and thence became often idle and careless. A good thought and a praiseworthy, honorable action in him changed speedily to an opposite character, because throughout his whole life he was wanting in a fixed leading principle whereon to base his actions. That steady calm repose and moderation, ever immutable, and which constitute the highest majesty of kings, were by him unattainable and never possessed; and thus are reflected in his whole existence the dissimilar and even contradictory sentiments and principles of those by whom he was educated.

It was strongly evinced and verified as a great truth in Henry IV., that according to our disposition and inward being, so is our fate. If the former be fixed and firm, our life as surely takes a fixed direction. But Henry's life was as unequal as his mind: the variation of good fortune with misfortune, elevation with abasement, and haughtiness with humiliation—such were the transitions of his life, even unto the moment of his death.

Adalbert had transplanted from his own soul to that of his pupil two feelings of the deepest aversion—the first was directed against all the princes generally, and the second against those of Saxony, and especially the ducal house of Billung, and the whole Saxon people, with whom he had previously had many disputes relative to his archbishopric of Bremen. He therefore impressed upon the mind of the young king, that as the princes, but chiefly those of Saxony, were striving for independence, he should reduce them by times to obedience and crush them. These principles embittered and destroyed the tranquillity of the king's whole life, for although the ambitious archbishop, after he had declared the king to be of age at Worms in 1065, was, by means of the princes, removed from Henry in the following year, his ward never forgot his instructions, and when, in 1069, Adalbert again visited the court of the young monarch, he used all his former influence to strengthen and confirm him in this hatred.

The Saxons speedily perceived the king's purpose of making their country immediately dependent on the crown; for he dwelt chiefly at Goslar, and commenced building in the mountains of the Hartz and in Thuringia a multitude of fortresses, and manned them with garrisons, to enable them to curb the natives more easily. The same Benno (afterwards bishop of Osnaburg) who, under Henry III., upon the building of Goslar itself had already forced the Saxons into service, now superintended these buildings. The chief of these fortresses was that of Hartzburg, near Goslar, Henry's favorite place, but an eyesore to the Saxons. Murmurs passed around, and the people complained that the freedom they enjoyed from their ancestors was about to be destroyed. It was also related, that while one day surveying the country around from a mountain in Saxony, the king exclaimed: "Saxony is indeed a beautiful country, but those who inhabit it are miserable serfs."

There were two other causes which increased the discontent. Henry, as a child, had already been betrothed by his father to Bertha, the daughter of the margrave of Susa, in Italy, and he had afterwards married her. Now, however, he wished to be divorced from her, and as for this purpose he required the assistance of the spiritual princes, he accordingly sought to conciliate before all others the friendship of Sigfried, archbishop of Mentz. But as his passions always drove him blindly on to the object he was so anxious to grasp, so likewise the means he now employed to attain it were equally bad. He commanded and forced the Thuringians to pay to the archbishop the tithe of their goods which he had formerly claimed, and they had refused. Thus he had now made the Thuringians doubly his enemies. Meantime, however, owing to the opposition shown on the part of the pope, he was not divorced from the queen; and subdued, shortly afterwards, by her noble and dignified conduct, his heart once more turned towards her, and she faithfully continued to share with him his good and bad fortune.

Besides this, Henry treated the Saxon count, Otho of Nordheim, to whom his mother had given the duchy of Bavaria, so badly, that all the nobles, but chiefly those of Saxony, were highly exasperated. This Duke Otho was a friend of the archbishop of Cologne, and might probably thereby have become obnoxious to the king, or the latter perhaps turned the hatred he had imbibed from Adalbert against all the nobles, more particularly against Otho, upon whose arm the Saxon people chiefly depended. And when at this moment an accuser appeared, named Egino, (probably employed for that purpose,) and charged the duke with having tried to persuade him to assassinate the king, and Otho refused to do battle with him because he was not of the same rank, and bore besides a bad character, Henry, by an unjust sentence, deposed him forthwith from his duchy of Bavaria, and destroyed with fire and sword all his hereditary lands in Saxony. He gave his duchy of Bavaria (in 1070) to Guelf the Young (IV.) the son of the Italian Margrave Azzo, and the founder of the junior Guelfic house, the elder house having become extinct by the death of Duke Guelf of Carinthia in 1055.

But in Otho of Nordheim he had now aroused for his whole life-time a most valiant and inveterate enemy. He joined Count Magnus of Saxony, son of Duke Ordulf, a noble youth, bold and valiant in arms, and united himself with him; but pressed by the royal forces, they were obliged to yield themselves both prisoners to Henry before they had hardly prepared themselves for battle. After the lapse of a year Henry set Otho at liberty, but he retained Magnus in prison in the Hartzburg, because he refused at his command to renounce his rights to his father's duchy; and although Otho nobly offered to take his friend's place in prison, he refused to listen to him. Thence arose the natural conclusion, that it was the king's intention to take possession of the duchy of Saxony himself, and leave the young prince to die in captivity.

These circumstances were the origin of that deep and violent enmity between Henry and the Saxons, and which prepared the most bitter and melancholy reverses for the king, and incited both parties to acts of the most implacable hatred and revenge.

The Saxons, with Otho of Nordheim at their head, concluded with each other a close alliance. All the Saxon and Thuringian nobles, temporal and spiritual, belonged to it, and among others, Burkhard, bishop of Halberstadt, who was a nephew of the archbishop of Cologne, and had imbibed from the latter his hatred against the imperial misrule and ascendency. This was still the time when the clergy themselves went into battle, and frequently fought at the head of their warlike hosts.

Quite unexpectedly, and while Henry was at Goslar, in the year 1073, a deputation from the Saxons came to him and demanded of him as follows: "That he should destroy his fortresses in their country; set Magnus, the heir of their Saxon duchy, free from his imprisonment; not always remain in Saxony; honor the ancient constitution of the country; and in imperial affairs not give ear to bad advisers, but take counsel of the states. If he would perform these conditions," they added, "no nation in Germany would be found more faithful and devoted to him than that of the Saxons." Henry, however, dismissed the deputation with contempt. The Saxons, accordingly, now brought into speedy effect and immediate execution the threatened consequences, and advanced towards Goslar with 60,000 men. Henry fled with his treasures to the strong fortress of Hartzburg, and as the enemy speedily followed him, he took to flight and sought refuge amid great danger in the Hartz mountains. He was obliged, for three days, to wander without food and drink, and with but few companions, under the guidance of a yäger, imagining in every whisper of the wind passing along the tops of the firs, to hear the steps of his pursuers. At last he reached Eschwege, on the river Werra. From thence he went to the Rhine, towards Tribur, and sent messengers throughout the whole empire, summoning all to arms against the Saxons. But the Saxons wisely profited by the interval, destroyed fortress after fortress, and took possession of the strong castle of Luneburg with its whole garrison; and which lucky circumstance they took advantage of to free their duke, Magnus, for they now demanded his freedom of the emperor under the threat, that, if not granted, they would hang up the whole garrison of Luneburg as robbers. Henry was obliged therefore, however unwillingly, to yield and set Magnus at liberty, together with seventy other nobles and knights. The monarch's humiliation, however, did not end here, for he was now likewise deserted by the princes of Southern Germany, and even the archbishop of Mentz, on whose account he had made so many enemies, left him. A circumstance also occurred at this moment which formed a parallel case with that of Egino and Otho of Nordheim, only that here the king was made out to be the assassin. Reginger, a knight and former favorite of Henry, now came forward and made public that "the king had employed him to murder the Dukes Rudolphus of Swabia and Berthold of Carinthia." This statement might possibly have been a mere manœuvre of the enemy, in order to prejudice public opinion against Henry, similar to that which he had himself previously employed against Otho of Nordheim. But it was equally successful, for it was even proposed to elect a new king, and the ungrateful Archbishop Sigfried convoked the princes for that purpose to hold a diet at Mentz.

In this emergency, when all his friends had deserted him, the citizens of Worms alone remained faithful to the king. They opened their gates to him against the will of their archbishop, offered him men and arms, and by their generous attachment and fidelity again restored his despondent mind, and as far as their means admitted they wholly supported him, no one else attempting to assist him. At this period, certain cities in Germany already began to have a voice in the imperial diets, and they became the chief support of imperial authority against the princes; thence we see how much, by industry and activity, they must have increased since the time of Henry I., both in the number and in the wealth of their inhabitants. But the faithful people of Worms could not defend him against the entire power of all the accumulated evils which now hung over his head. He was obliged, in order not to lose his crown, to make hard terms of peace with the Saxons in 1074, and to deliver up to them all his fortresses, even his beloved Hartzburg. After contemplating it with sorrow and regret for the last time, as, in the midst of the Saxons, he rode to Goslar, he once more, and even most earnestly entreated them to grant its preservation, but the proud fortress was doomed to fall, and in its destruction hatred raged so furiously, that the embittered populace, without even the knowledge or consent of the princes, plundered and burnt both its church and altar, tore open the imperial tombs, and desecrated the remains of Henry's brother and infant son.

But the Saxons very soon experienced that the most dangerous enemy to good fortune is the arrogance of our own heart; and one of those singular changes of fortune which distinguished Henry's entire reign now suddenly displayed itself. He had well learned by this time, that men must be differently treated to the fashion Adalbert had taught him, and that in order to conquer a people, something more is necessary than building isolated fortresses in their country. Accordingly he now began to address the German princes in a very opposite manner to what he had hitherto done; he sought to gain them individually, especially as their assemblies were in general prejudicially opposed to him, and for this purpose he employed a different but more suitably-adapted means with each of them separately. To all of them he complained bitterly of the shameful and revolting destruction of Hartzburg, and as soon as the public voice became more favorable towards him, he issued a general summons against the Saxons. This time obedience immediately followed, and a strong army was speedily collected both of knights and vassals, from all parts of the kingdom, even from Bohemia and Lorraine, an army such as had not been seen for a long time, while the Saxons, who had only hastily assembled a few troops, and by the artifices of the king had become disunited among themselves, were severely beaten, in 1075, near Hohenburg, not far from Langensalza, on the river Unstrut. Henry pursued the fugitives as far as Magdeburg and Halberstadt, and desolated their country with fire and sword. His vengeance was terrific, like all his ungovernable passions. But in the following year, the other princes, who would not suffer the poor people to be entirely destroyed, stepped between as mediators. Henry granted the Saxons a peace after their nobles had humbly knelt to him before all the army; but instead of effecting a complete reconciliation by a full pardon, he, contrary to the promise he gave through his ambassadors, retained many of the Saxon nobles as prisoners, and made over their fiefs to his vassals. The most dangerous of all their princes, however, Otho of Nordheim, he allowed to return to his estates, and even appointed him administrator over Saxony. He caused all the destroyed fortresses, including Hartzburg, to be rebuilt, erected additional ones, and had them garrisoned by his own troops, who, as before, oppressed the land by arrogance and extortion; thus the seeds of future revolt were again planted in this quarter, while from an opposite direction an enemy presented himself, far more powerful, and who fought against him with very different weapons to those of the Saxons.

Hildebrand (afterwards Gregory VII.) was the son of a carpenter at Saone, an Italian city. He entered the clerical state, and as he possessed extraordinary mental powers, he was taken by Pope Leo IV., in the reign of Henry III., from the monastery of Clugny to Rome, and there made sub-deacon of the Roman church, and afterwards chancellor; henceforward he alone directed the government of the popes, and became the soul of the pontifical court. His object was to raise the pope above all the princes and kings of the earth, and this aim he pursued during his whole life with so much prudence, constancy, power, and greatness of mind, that he must be placed among the most extraordinary men in the history of his times. When he first appeared great misuses had crept in among the higher and lower clergy; the majority purchased their holy offices with gold, whereby unworthy men could attain to high and important places. Immorality, dissipation, and vices of every kind were not rare among them, and as they were the slaves of their own sins, so also by their love for temporal possessions they attached themselves to temporal princes, who rewarded them with their possessions. Hildebrand therefore resolved, inspired as he was for the freedom of the church and the morality of the clerical order, to lay the axe to the root of these evils.

His first endeavors were very justly directed against the purchase of spiritual offices with gold, which was called the crime of simony (in reference to the history of Simon the magician, related in the Acts of the Apostles, viii. 18–24) and was considered a sin against the Holy Ghost. It is shown with what moral power and superiority of mind he knew how to influence men, in the example of an archbishop of France, who was charged with this crime, but had cunningly gained over the informers by gold. Hildebrand, so says the original document, sat as representative of the pope in judgment upon the affair. The archbishop then stepped boldly into the assembly and said, "Where are they who charge me? Let him step forth who will condemn me!" The bribed complainants were silent. Hildebrand then turned himself to him and said: "Dost thou believe that the Holy Ghost with Father and Son are one being?" To which the other replied: "I believe it." He now commanded him to repeat: "Honor the Father, the Son, and the Holy Ghost," and while the archbishop was pronouncing the words, he looked at him with such a piercing, penetrating glance, that the conscience of the convicted clergyman was so struck with his guilt, that he was unable to add "The Holy Ghost," although he several times tried it. This was considered a divine judgment. The archbishop fell at his judge's feet, acknowledged his crime, and confessed himself unworthy to hold the priestly office; after which confession he was enabled to repeat those words with a distinct voice. This circumstance worked so powerfully upon the minds of the people, that twenty-seven other churchmen and several bishops, as yet unaccused, laid down their offices, because they had acquired them with gold.

In order, therefore, that the clergy should now be made entirely free from the temporal power, it became essential that the head of the church should no longer be named by the emperor, but be appointed by a free election. This had been differently settled at the time that Henry III. caused the promise to be made to him, that the Romans should acknowledge no pope without the imperial sanction, and under this emperor Hildebrand probably would not have carried his object. But he now took advantage of the moment while the new emperor was still a child, and succeeded in the year 1059, under Pope Nicholas II., in having a law made, that every pope should be chosen by the cardinals, but with the clause that the sanction or confirmation of the emperor should be added, as it was only in subsequent times that endeavors were made even to abolish this decree, and to put a false construction upon the law of Pope Nicholas.

When Hildebrand as chancellor had, by this and other regulations, prepared every thing for his great object, he was himself elected pope in the year 1073, and called himself Gregory VII., in order thus to declare the deposition of Gregory VI. by Henry III. as invalid. The emperor Henry IV., who now ruled the empire himself, sent his faithful adherent, Count Eberhard, to Rome, to demand of the Romans why they had dared without the imperial permission to elect a pope. Gregory, who did not wish at this moment to commence the dispute with the emperor, excused himself by the plea that the people had forced him to receive the papal dignity, but that he had not allowed himself to be ordained before he had received the sanction of the emperor and of the German princes. With this excuse Henry was contented, and the pope was confirmed. Henry thus showed, that in the blindness of his fury against the Saxons, he had not at all perceived that all this time the degradation of all temporal dominion, and the elevation of a spiritual empire, was now being gradually prepared in Rome.

Gregory now stepped forth with new and very severe laws against simony, and against the marriage of priests. He desired, like the earlier popes and fathers, that the priests of the church should consecrate themselves wholly to the divine service, restrain themselves from all sensuality, and not even chain themselves to the love of the earth's possessions by the marriage tie. It is true that in Italy, as well as in France and Germany, this prohibition found at first great opposition among the clergy, for many of them, particularly among the lower clergy, were already married, but Gregory found in the people themselves the support necessary for the execution of his law. The populace, excited against the married priests, forced them, partly through the severest misusage, to separate themselves from their wives, but it lasted a full century before the celibacy of the clergy was fully established. The attainment of this object was of the greatest importance to Gregory for the completion of his extensive plans; for if the clergy throughout all Christian countries were no longer bound by their domestic cares and anxiety for their children, and were made independent of the temporal lords, the pope would thereby gain so many thousand more zealous servants, who would listen only to his command, and contribute to fix firmly the dominion of the church over all temporal power. But in order to possess such servants they must be rendered still more independent, and not receive, even in any shape, their temporal possessions from the hands of princes as a fief; for the same as the lay vassals received a banner as a mark of their services, so also the grand ecclesiastical dignitaries received from the princes as a similar sign, a ring and a shepherd's crook, which thus formed the investiture. Gregory, therefore, prohibited the clergy from receiving this said symbol of investiture from the hands of the nobles; and he insisted that for their elevation they were to be beholden to the papal chair alone, and only to the pope were they to swear the oath of obedience. According to this principle, the pontiff necessarily became sovereign lord of one third of all the property in the Catholic countries.

Such then is the commencement of the long and violent dispute of investiture, and especially of the contest between the emperor and the pope, the state and the church, and which by degrees weakened and destroyed both. We have already noticed previously that the peaceful co-operation of both the papal and imperial dignity might have formed a solid basis for the happiness of the people; but now the epoch commenced when both these powers strove singly to rise more elevated than the other. For if, on the one hand, the pope wished to reign not only in spiritual but also in temporal affairs over all princes and kings, and was anxious to take away as well as to provide crowns, so, on the other hand, the emperor would not admit in just and reasonable cases the authority of the pope, but insisted he could rule with the edge of the sword even over invisible and spiritual affairs and the conscience of man. Thus the two powers which in concord together might have made the world happy, destroyed each other, and after a contest of a century and a half, and after unutterable confusion and dissension in Germany and Italy, the imperial dignity lost its ancient splendor and its intrinsic power, while the head of the church became externally dependent upon a foreign power. In this schism great men stood opposed to each other, who might have exercised their energy and powers much more beneficially for society; but this very contest necessarily entered into the great plan of the history of the world, and it prepared those developments which otherwise would not have followed.

Pope Gregory continued to advance still farther in his principles. Not satisfied with having separated the church with all its endowments wholly from temporal dominion, he also now solemnly declared that emperors, kings, and princes, together with all their power, were subject to the pope. These principles are especially expressed in his own letters: "The world," he says in one of them, "is guided by two lights: by the sun, the larger, and the moon, the lesser light. Thus the apostolic power represents the sun, and the royal power the moon; for as the latter has its light from the former, so only do emperors, kings, and princes, receive their authority through the pope, because he receives his authority through God. Therefore, the power of the Roman chair is greater than the power of the throne, and the king is accordingly subject to the pope, and bound in obedience to him. If the apostles in heaven can bind and loosen, so may they also upon earth give and take, according to merit, empires, kingdoms, principalities, duchies, and every other kind of possession. And if they be appointed as sovereign judges over spiritual, they must likewise be so, and far more in proportion, over temporal affairs; and if, finally, they have the right to command angels, who are most assuredly placed above the most powerful monarchs, how much more may they not give judgment over the poor slaves of those angels. Besides, the pope is the successor of the apostles, and their representative upon the chair of St. Peter; he is the vicar of Christ, and consequently placed over all."

These principles Gregory resolved to exercise generally, and first of all upon the emperor himself, as the head of the kings and princes, in order thereby to prove his power before the whole world. At the same time, Henry, living as he did in continual dissension with his subjects, had less real power than any other king, while his name being greater, the victory over him must consequently become more glorious, and from the passionate character of this prince in all his proceedings, the pope soon found it easy to furnish a pretext. Complaints against the emperor came to Rome from every quarter, while the Saxons, likewise, bitterly complained because he still kept many of their princes prisoners. Gregory accordingly caused it to be signified to the emperor, "That at the ensuing fast he must appear before the synod at Rome, to answer for the crimes laid to his charge; otherwise, it was now made known to him, that he would be cast out from the bosom of the church by the apostolic ban."

Henry was more indignant than terrified at these words, for the invisible power of the papal ban of excommunication had hitherto been little proved. He assembled the German bishops at Worms, in the year 1076, and there, with equal precipitation and impatience, he caused to be pronounced at once against the pope the same sentence of deposition with which the latter had threatened him. He then wrote him a letter of the following contents:

"Henry, king, not by force, but by the sacred ordination of God, to Hildebrand—not the pope, but the false monk:

"This greeting hast thou merited by the confusion thou hast spread throughout all classes of the church. Thou hast trampled under thy feet the ministers of the holy church, as slaves who know not what their lord does; and by that desecration hast thou won favor from the lips of the common herd of people. We have long suffered this because we were desirous to maintain the honor of the Roman chair. But thou hast mistaken our forbearance for fear, and hast become emboldened to raise thyself above the royal power, bestowed upon us by God himself, and threatened to take it from us, as if we had received our dominion from thee. Thou hast raised thyself upon the steps which are called cunning and deception, and which are accursed. Thou hast gained favor by gold, won power by favor, and by that power thou hast gained the chair of peace, from whence thou hast banished peace itself by arming the inferior against the superior. St. Peter, the true pope, himself says: 'Fear God and honor the king!' but as thou dost not fear God, thou dost not honor me, his envoy. Descend, therefore, thou that liest under a curse of excommunication by our and all bishops' judgment, descend! Quit the apostolic seat thou hast usurped! And then shall the chair of St. Peter be ascended by one who does not conceal, under the divine word, his arrogance. I, Henry, by God's grace, king, and all our bishops, say to thee, 'Descend, descend!'"

Upon this the pope held a council also, and not only pronounced the sentence of excommunication against Henry, but he deposed him in the following words: "In the name of the Almighty God, I forbid to King Henry, the son of the Emperor Henry, who, with haughtiness unheard of, has arisen against the church, the government of the German and Italian empire, and absolve all Christians from the oath which they have made or will make to him, and forbid that any one serve him as king. And occupying thy office, holy Peter, I bind him with the bands of a curse, that all nations may learn that thou art the rock whereon the Son of God founded his church."

When, at the Easter festival of the year 1016, Henry received, at Utrecht, the news of his excommunication, he immediately pronounced, on his part, through the violent bishop, William of Utrecht, an anathema against Gregory; and the bishops of Lombardy, the enemies of the pope, renewed this anathema in a council assembled at Pavia, under the presidency of Wibert, archbishop of Ravenna.

The impression made by these unheard-of events was varied, according to the disposition and feelings of the people. The Saxons rejoiced, for their cause was now the cause of the church, and henceforward their usual shout of war was "Holy Peter!" while, throughout the empire generally, there was a division of parties; everywhere the cry was, "The pope for ever!" or, "The emperor for ever!" This was, indeed, a time of bitter contention, and hatred reigned throughout the whole country. Had the king been a good, irreproachable man, possessing the greatness of soul which can bind and rule the hearts, the power of the mere word would not have overcome him, for it was only from public opinion that this word received its force. But he had now numerous and bitter enemies, and his arrogance after conquering the Saxons had served to increase their number. Besides the Saxons, his conduct had likewise made Rudolphus, duke of Swabia, extremely hostile towards him, while the pope's legates exercised all their influence upon the minds of the people. Thence it happened that the majority of German princes assembled together at Tribur, on the Rhine, in order to elect a new emperor. Henry hastened to Oppenheim, in the vicinity, and at length, after many entreaties and vows of reform, he obtained from them an extension of one year's delay; and it was decided that, in the mean time, the pope should be requested to come to Augsburg, and himself closely investigate the affair; but if Henry, at the end of the year, was not freed from excommunication, they resolved to proceed immediately to a fresh election.

In this desperate state Henry formed quite an unexpected resolution. In the anxiety he experienced lest, in the diet at Augsburg, where his enemies constituted the majority of the members, nothing favorable towards him should be determined upon, he set off himself, notwithstanding he possessed no means, and was obliged almost to beg for his support, (while likewise the princes still occupied the passes between Italy and Germany,) and resolved to cross the Alps, accompanied only by his consort and one faithful companion. He passed through Savoy, where he was furnished by his mother-in-law, the margravine of Susa, with a few more attendants, and as it was winter, and indeed so severe a winter that the Rhine, from Martinmas until the first of April, was completely frozen, the journey over the mountains covered with snow and ice was, consequently, attended with immeasurable difficulties and danger, and the empress, wrapped up in an ox-hide, was obliged to be slidden down the precipitous paths of Mount Cenis by the guides of the country, hired for the purpose. He arrived at last in Italy, and his presence, to his astonishment, was hailed with joy; for the report had already spread "that the emperor was coming to humiliate the haughty pope by the power of the sword." In Upper Italy a strong hatred had long been cherished against Gregory; the temporal lords were indignant at his recent regulations, and among the clergy there were many whom his laws against simony and the marriage of priests had made his enemies. Besides, many Italians, even the archbishops of Milan and Ravenna, had shared in the sentence of excommunication. Had Henry, therefore, not been too much dejected and disheartened by what he had experienced in Germany, he might speedily have acquired a numerous train of adherents in Italy, to offer opposition to his mighty enemy, but he now had conciliation alone in view; the pope, too, was at this moment on his journey to Germany, to meet the diet at Augsburg, and there to sit in judgment upon the king. Upon hearing, however, of Henry's sudden arrival in Italy, and not knowing as yet whether he was to expect good or bad from him, he deviated from his direct route, and proceeded to the strong castle of Canossa, there to gain an asylum with the Countess Matilda, the daughter and heiress of the rich Margrave Boniface, of Tuscany, and who was a zealous friend of the papal chair; having even, at this moment, privately made over to it all her inheritance.

Matilda was the most powerful and influential princess in Italy, and reigned as queen throughout Tuscany and Lombardy, while she was likewise equally distinguished for her mental attainments and firmness of spirit, as well as for her piety and virtue. She contested with all her power, during a period of thirty years, for the elevation of the pontifical chair, having embraced this idea with all the strength of her natural character, and to which she was still more influenced by the new severe regulations adopted by Gregory VII., which so perfectly agreed with her own austere and rigid principles of virtue. She was married to Gozelo, duke of Lower Lorraine, but they lived separated from each other, owing to their opinions being so completely different; for while in Italy, where she ruled over the extensive possessions of her father and mother, she herself was busily occupied in the support of Gregory, her husband was doing all he could in aid of the emperor.

Henry now turned himself therefore to the Princess Matilda, in order to get her to speak to the pope in his favor. The latter, at first, would by no means hear of a reconciliation, but referred all to the decision of the diet; at last, however, upon much entreaty, he yielded permission that Henry, in the garb of a penitent, covered with a shirt of hair, and with naked feet, might be received in the castle. As the emperor advanced within the outer gate it was immediately closed, so that his escort was obliged to remain outside the fortress, and he himself was now alone in the outer court, where, in January, 1077, in the midst of a severe and rigorous winter, he was obliged to remain three whole days barefooted and shivering with the cold. All in the castle were moved. Gregory himself writes in a letter, "That every one present had severely censured him, and said that his conduct more resembled tyrannical ferocity than apostolic severity." The Countess Matilda, while vainly pleading for him, was affected even to burning tears of pity and grief, and Henry, in his distress, at length only prayed that he might at least be allowed to go out again. On the fourth of these dreadful days, the pope eventually admitted him before him and absolved him from excommunication; but Henry was still forced to subscribe to the most severe conditions. He was obliged to promise to present himself at the day and place the pope should appoint, in order to hear whether he might remain king or not, and, meanwhile, he was to abstain from all exercise of the royal attributes and monarchal power.

With shame and anger in his heart, Henry now withdrew, and as soon as the Italians and his old friends still under excommunication perceived the disposition he now evinced towards the pope, they assembled around him, and he remained during the winter in Italy.

His penetrating eye now perceived, during this his first visit to Italy, that the power of the pope was nowhere so weak as just in that very country of dissension and venal egotism; and that whoever only understood the art of creating adherents by money, promises, and cunning, would very soon succeed in collecting together a considerable party to aid him against the court of Rome. The illusory awe he had hitherto felt for the papal power now vanished; his former courage revived, and from this moment he commenced with the sword, as well as the pen, a war which he sustained, during thirty years, with the greatest skill and determination, and in which he very often experienced the most decisive success.

The German princes, however, were still his enemies, and availing themselves of his absence, held a diet at Forsheim in March, 1077, and elected Rudolphus, duke of Swabia, as rival emperor. Germany became now again divided by violent dissension; for Henry also commanded a strong party, chiefly among the cities and those of the clergy, who were discontented with Gregory's church laws. He returned now to Germany; war commenced, and for three years devastated many of the most beautiful countries of Germany. Rudolphus was obliged to retire from Swabia, and marched to Saxony, the Saxon people and the valiant Otho of Nordheim being his warm supporters. Henry gave the duchy of Swabia, together with his daughter, Agnes, to the bold and ambitious Count Frederic of Buren, who now removed his seat from the village of Buren, at the foot of the high Staufen, and fixed it upon the pinnacle of that mountain, where he built the Castle Hohenstaufen. Thus was laid the foundation of the greatness of this house, although, at the same time, it was a cause of enmity between the Hohenstaufens and the other noble houses in the vicinity, who envied the good fortune of this new race, and thought they had much greater right to the duchy of Swabia. The Hohenstaufens, however, remained henceforward faithful friends to the Salic-Imperial house.

Gregory acted with duplicity in this war between the two emperors; and it appeared as if he rejoiced in the destruction of Germany, and in the enervation of the temporal power by its own acts, for instead of supporting the Saxons and their king, Rudolphus, with all the power of his authority, in order that they might speedily gain the victory, he recognised neither of the emperors, but only continued to promise them that he would come to Germany and be himself the judge between them. "Nothing, however, took place," says Bruno, the historian of this war, "except that the pope's legates arrived and waited on both parties in each camp, promising at one moment to the Saxons, and in the next to Henry, the favor of the pope; while at the same time they conveyed away from both armies as much gold as they could obtain—according to Roman custom." The Saxons complained severely of this equivocal conduct of the pope, and they wrote to him among the rest as follows: "All our misfortunes would never have arisen, or at least have been but trivial, if upon having commenced your journey, you had turned neither to the right nor to the left. Through obedience to our shepherd we are exposed to the rapacity of the wolf, and if we are abandoned now by that shepherd, we shall be more unfortunate and miserable than all other people." This bold and reproachful address, however, did not please the pope; he returned no reply to it, nor did it produce more determination in his conduct than the subsequent desperate battle fought between the two armies at Melrichstadt, in Thuringia, in the year 1078; and it was only after Rudolphus had gained superior advantage in a second battle near Mühlhausen in 1080, that he declared for him, and even sent him the crown,* at the same time again excommunicating Henry. The latter, on the other hand, assembled a council at Brixen, again deposed the pope, and caused to be elected as pontiff against him the excommunicated Archbishop Wibert of Ravenna, or Clement III. Thus there were now two emperors and two popes. The victory, however, this time inclined on Henry's side.

Meantime, in 1080, he suffered a severe loss in a third battle, on the Elster, in Saxony, not far from Gera, through the valor of Otho of Nordheim, who there displayed the genius of a truly great leader, but unfortunately, Rudolphus himself was fatally wounded in the battle and died. His right hand was hewn off, and Godfrey, duke of Lower Lorraine, (Godefroy of Bouillon, the conqueror of the holy tomb,) as related in some records, thrust the spear of the imperial banner into his stomach. According to a later account, when his hand was shown to him, King Rudolphus is said to have remarked: "Behold, that is the hand with which I swore fidelity to King Henry!" His fall was considered as a judgment of God, and Henry's adherents increased in proportion; so that he was now enabled to undertake an expedition into Italy in order to make war upon his most violent opponent. He marched, therefore, with his army and came before Rome, which he besieged three times, in three successive years, and reduced Pope Gregory to such extremity that he was obliged to shut himself up in the castle of St. Angelo, where he was besieged by the Romans themselves; nevertheless, Gregory's spirit was too great, and his will too inflexible, to humiliate himself, and follow the example of Henry at Canossa. The emperor offered him reconciliation if he would crown him, but he replied firmly: "He could only communicate with him when he had given satisfaction to God and the church." Henry was obliged, therefore, with his consort, to be crowned by the rival pope, Clement, at Easter, 1084, after which he retired from Italy. Pope Gregory, however, was still besieged by the Romans, in the castle of St. Angelo, until he was freed by his friend, Robert Guiscard, duke of Normandy, who ruled in Lower Italy. The latter subjected the city to plunder, and then took with him the old and obstinate pope (who, even, in misfortune, would not renounce any of his views and pretensions) to Lower Italy,

* This crown bore the following inscription:—Petra, dedit Petro, Petrus diadema Rudolpho."

where he died the following year at Salerno. His party chose Victor to succeed him; but he possessed neither the genius nor the force of Gregory, for even Clement maintained the position he held, and continued to enjoy the chief authority in Rome.

Favorable and tranquil times now seemed to dawn upon the emperor Henry. The successor of Rudolphus of Swabia, Herman of Luxembourg, whom the princes had elevated to be his second opponent, could not maintain himself against him, and spontaneously laid down the dignity. A second, Egbert of Thuringia, died by assassination, and the Saxons, after Otho of Nordheim was dead, and the irreconcilable bishop, Burkhard, of Halberstadt, had been killed by his own people, (after he had tried, for the fourteenth time, to excite them to revolt,) wearied with constant war, voluntarily submitted themselves to the emperor—now made milder by the many painful trials he had undergone. But fate had reserved for him visitations still more severe. For he was obliged to behold revolt against him, even in the last years of his life; his eldest son, Conrad, and after his death in 1101, his second son, Henry, was gained over by the papal party. Both the successors of Gregory, Urban II. and Pascal II., renewed the papal ban against Henry the father; and his son now declared that he could hold no community with an excommunicated person. Nay, even when Henry, confiding in the apparent reconciliation with his son, was about to attend the great diet of princes at Mentz, the latter caused him, by cunning and treachery, to be disarmed, deprived him of the imperial insignia, by means of the archbishops of Mentz and Cologne, and placed him a prisoner at Ingelheim, where he forced him formally to abdicate the throne.

Henry, however, found an opportunity to escape from prison, and, full of grief and trouble, he went to his friend Otbert, the bishop of Liège. The latter, and Henry, duke of Lorraine, assembled an army for him, and beat back the degenerated son when crossing the Meuse in pursuit of his father. But the emperor died immediately afterwards at Liège, oppressed at length by a turbulent and vexatious career, in the year 1106. The number of battles he had fought during his life—being no less than sixty-five—sufficiently prove its agitated and anxious character.

The bishop of Liège buried the emperor as beseemed; but to such length did hatred go, that his body was again exhumed, conveyed to Spires, and there, for five years, it remained in a stone coffin above the earth, in an isolated, unconsecrated chapel, until at last, in the year 1111, Pope Pascal absolved him from excommunication. He was then interred with greater magnificence than any other emperor before him.

In the first years of the reign of Henry V., the ducal race of the Billungens, in Saxony, became extinct; and he bestowed the dukedom upon Lothaire, count of Supplingenburg.

Henry V., although he had previously revolted against his father, now acted according to his principles; and in defiance of the papal laws, he still continued to impart the investiture with ring and staff, a right, which, as he declared to the pope, his ancestors since Charles the Great had legitimately exercised for three centuries, under sixty-three popes; and as early as the year 1100, he marched with a large army of 30,000 horse-soldiers, besides infantry and servitors, for Italy, in order to be crowned with the imperial crown, and, in case of necessity, to maintain his rights with the sword. He was a much more dangerous enemy than his father, for, besides his physical force, he knew likewise how to avail himself of cunning and hypocrisy. Pope Pascal II. made a proposition to him, which would have ended the dispute for ever, could it have been executed. He caused the emperor to be apprized that—"As he founded his claims to the investiture only upon the donations which the emperors had presented to the church—the cities, duchies, counties, coins, tolls, farms, and castles—he might take them all back again; the church would only retain the presents of private individuals, and the tithes and sacrifices. For," said he, "it is commanded by the divine law, as well as by the law of the church, that the clergy shall not occupy themselves with temporal matters, nay, not even appear at court, except for the purpose of saving an oppressed person. But among you, however, in Germany, the bishops and abbots are so mixed up with worldly affairs, that the servants of the altar have become the servants of the court."

The pope might have been serious when making this proposition, for he was extremely strict in his principles, and thought, perhaps, in this manner to remedy the degeneration of the clergy, and to bring them back to their original simple condition. But Henry's penetrating mind foresaw well that the clergy themselves, particularly those who, by their possessions, were raised to the rank of imperial princes, would never consent to make such a restitution; therefore he promised to dispense with the investiture, if the pope would command the bishops to give back to him, the emperor, all those possessions which they had received from Charlemagne and his successors. He then advanced to Rome, and the solemn treaty upon this affair was to be ratified between him and the pope in a large assembly of the bishops, in the church of St. Peter, and then the coronation of the emperor was to be celebrated. But when the above condition became the subject of discussion, the most animated and violent opposition arose between the German and Italian bishops, and a long and angry contest ensued. At length one of the German knights present exclaimed: "Why do you all continue thus wrangling? Let it suffice for you to know that our lord, the emperor, is resolved to be crowned as formerly were Charlemagne, Louis, and the other emperors!" The pope replied once more—"That he could not perform the ceremony before King Henry had solemnly sworn to discontinue the right of investiture." Henry then, by the counsel of his chancellor, Adalbert, and Burchard, bishop of Münster, summoned his guards, and caused the pope, as well as the cardinals, to be made prisoners. The Romans, enraged and furious at this violent proceeding, on the following day attacked the Germans, who were encamped around the church of St. Peter. The king speedily mounted his steed, and boldly, but rashly, rushing into the midst of the enemy, pierced five Romans with his own lance, but was himself wounded and thrown from his horse. He was rescued by Count Otho, of Milan, who hastily assisted him to mount his own horse, which he gave up to the king, but for which service he was cut to pieces by the Romans. A murderous combat was continued throughout the whole day, until at length towards the evening the emperor cheered on his troops to make a final charge, the result of which was that the Romans were completely put to flight, and were driven partly into the Tiber, and partly across the bridges back into the city. The church of St. Peter, together with all that portion of the city, remained in the hands of the Germans, but which the emperor abandoned, together with all his prisoners, in order to scour the country around in the most dreadful manner. The Romans, now reduced to extreme necessity, urgently entreated the pope to conclude a treaty of peace with the emperor. He had now been a prisoner sixty-one days; and at length yielded to their prayers. He, accordingly, agreed that the emperor should retain the investiture with ring and staff, and promised, at the same time, that he would never excommunicate him on account of this proceeding. The treaty was signed by fourteen cardinals, and in the emperor's name by fourteen princes, and Henry himself was, on the 13th of April, 1111, solemnly crowned emperor by Pascal.

But scarcely were the Germans out of Rome when the whole clergy severely censured the pope, and persuaded him to assemble a council and excommunicate the agreement made between the king and him, as having been extorted by violence; for, according to the promise made by the pope, they durst not pronounce the ban against the emperor himself. The dispute thus commenced anew, and continued, also, under the following popes, Gelasius II. and Calixtus II., ten years longer. As long as Pascal lived, the emperor was not himself visited with the general excommunication of the church; but the legates and many of the heads of the church excommunicated him in their dioceses, and thereby gave occasion to fresh divisions and dissensions in Germany; and a great portion of the imperial princes accordingly refused obedience to the emperor and his laws. Arbitrary feuds, robbery, devastation, and murder took the upper hand. The most faithful allies of the emperor were his relations of the race of Hohenstaufen, and he raised their house accordingly still higher. When Frederic, the first duke to whom his father had given the duchy of

Swabia, died, he transferred it to his eldest son, Frederic, and, shortly afterwards, he gave the duchy of Franconia to his second son, Conrad.

His own sister Agnes, the widow of Duke Frederic, he married to the Margrave, Leopold of Austria, of the house of Babenberg, the father of that Leopold who was afterwards duke of Bavaria, and who also established on the place where Windobona then stood, the foundation of the present city of Vienna. Thus in the south of Germany the emperor gained the superiority, but in the north, on the contrary, he could acquire no lasting power. Here the Archbishop Adalbert of Mentz, who had been elevated by him, (and who was previously his own chancellor, and had advised him to imprison the pope, Pascal, but had now become his uncompromising enemy,) worked most strenuously against him, and excited one prince after the other to oppose him. Saxony, as in his father's time, became now the centre of opposition to him likewise. The emperor advanced in the year 1115 with an army into Saxony, but in a battle, not far from Eisleben, he was entirely defeated by the Saxon princes. An expedition, which he soon afterwards made to Italy, gave him for a short time the superiority in Rome, but brought upon him in 1118 the general excommunication of the new pope, Gelasius, which his successor Calixtus II. confirmed. The chief object of dispute was still the right of investiture. Finally, in the year 1122, both parties, tired of the long dispute, concluded a solemn treaty at the diet of Worms, where both yielded to each other. The emperor permitted the free choice of bishops, and gave up the investiture with the ring and staff, as signs of spiritual jurisdiction, but for which concession, on the other hand, the election was to take place in the presence of the king, or of his plenipotentiary, and he was to decide in doubtful cases, or in any disagreement of the electors, and lastly, confer fiefs of temporal possessions with his sceptre. The spiritual consecration of this bishop elect was to take place in Germany *after* the investiture with the sceptre; but in Italy it was to precede it.

After the records were publicly read, the legate of the pope gave the emperor the kiss of peace, and afterwards the communion. The joy expressed by the peacefully-minded members of the assembly upon this reconciliation was great; all separated, as the records say, with infinite pleasure.

The emperor reigned but a few years longer—in peace, it is true, with the church, but not without constant dissensions in the German empire. Amidst plans for strengthening the imperial power, in order to oppose more firmly those disorders, he died suddenly at Utrecht, in 1125, in the forty-fourth year of his age. He died childless, and with him the Salian house became extinct. Most of his hereditary possessions came to his nephews, the Dukes Frederic and Conrad of Hohenstaufen.

Henry did not acquire the love of his contemporaries; he was despotic, severe, and often cruel. On the other hand, however, it is not to be denied that he possessed many great qualities,—activity, boldness, perseverance in misfortune, and a noble-minded disposition. The maintenance of the imperial dignity against every enemy appeared to be with him the chief object of his life. He was entombed at Spires in the grave of his ancestors.

Meantime, while the two emperors, Henry IV. and V., were engaged in such warm and serious disputes with the pope, more than a hundred thousand Christians, summoned by the voice of the Church, and excited by their own immediate enthusiasm, assembled together, and abandoned their country in order to recover and secure from the power of the infidels the tomb of the Saviour in that Holy Land, wherein his divine footsteps remained imprinted.

Already, from the earliest ages, it had been a pious custom to make pilgrimages to the Holy Land, to pray at its sacred places, and to bathe in the waters of the Jordan, which had been consecrated by the baptism of our Lord. Constantine the Great, the first Roman emperor who embraced Christianity, as well as his mother Helena, issued orders for the purification and adornment of these holy places in Palestine, and the restoration of the sacred tomb at the foot of Mount Golgotha; and they erected over the tomb, at enormous outlay, a lofty dome, supported by beautiful pillars, with an adjoining oratory, richly adorned. Eastward of the sepulchre Constantine built a larger and still more magnificent temple. He celebrated the thirtieth anniversary of his reign by the consecration of this temple, on which occasion he was himself present; and the pious Helena, although in extreme old age, made a pilgrimage to the Holy Land at the same time, and built two churches, one at Bethlehem on the spot where our Saviour was born, and the other on the top of the Mount of Olives.

After this, pilgrimages to the Holy Land became more and more frequent; and even in the seventh century, when the land was under the dominion of the Arabs, the pilgrims were not obstructed or disturbed in their devotions. For the Arabs rejoiced in the advantage they derived from the visits of so many strangers, and took equal care not to molest either the patriarch of Jerusalem, or the Christian community. But when the Turks, a savage and barbarous people, seized upon the country in the year 1073, complaint after complaint reached Europe of the cruel treatment heaped upon the pious pilgrims, and of the shameful profanation committed by the infidels on the consecrated spots.

In the year 1094, a hermit, named Peter of Amiens, appeared before Pope Urban II. on his return from a pilgrimage to Palestine, with a letter of petition from the patriarch of Jerusalem, and gave a most affecting description of the unheard-of sufferings experienced by the Christians resident there, as well as by the pilgrims who repaired thither. The pope praised and encouraged his zeal, and sent him with letters of recommendation to all the princes in the various Christian countries, in order to arouse the minds of the people, and to prepare them for a great expedition. The enthusiastic language of the hermit, together with the fire which still shone from his deep-sunk eye, and his wasted, meager form, on which was imprinted the sufferings he had endured, made the deepest impression, and excited, wherever he went, equal enthusiasm among all classes, from the highest to the lowest. After this, in the year 1095, the pope convoked a great council of the Church, at Piacenza, in Italy, and another at Clermont, in France, at which were present fourteen archbishops, two hundred and twenty-five bishops, and four hundred abbots, besides numerous princes, nobles, and knights. And when Peter the Hermit and the pope advanced before them, and with words of overpowering fire and energy appealed to and called upon this assembly to come forward in deliverance of the sacred tomb, a thousand voices shouted aloud, "It is the will of God! It is the will of God!" When the pope and the hermit had concluded their eloquent appeal, Ademar, bishop of Puy, was the first to press forward, and throwing himself at the feet of the pontiff, begged from his holiness permission to proceed to the holy war. Many of the clergy and laity followed his example, and as a sign of their devotion to the pious undertaking, they sewed a red cross on their right shoulder. The final day of meeting for the great expedition was now fixed to take place on the 15th of August, 1096.

Accordingly, innumerable multitudes assembled, including warriors from Italy, France, Lorraine, Flanders, and particularly from Normandy, where the same love for distant and adventurous expeditions that had ever distinguished their heroic ancestors, was now evinced by the present natives. Not only the knights and nobles, but the whole people were set in motion, for as also in France the laboring classes experienced the severest oppression, many of these joined the expedition; because, according to the pope's decree, freedom was attained by dedication to the holy cross. Germany, which was then at variance with the pope, and agitated by internal discord, was least affected by this first movement. With the commencement of the spring, Peter the Hermit set out at the head of a crowd of people, whose impatience would not allow them to await the appointed time, in company with their commander, a knight named Walter the Pennyless; but their army was deficient in order and discipline, and especially in a supply of proper weapons. Before it reached Asia, the greater part, on account of the robberies committed, were cut off by the Bulgarians and Hungarians, and those who, under the guidance of Peter and Walter, reached and landed on the first Turkish territory, were so badly received and cut up by the Turks, that very few escaped; and Peter was forced to return home with the remnant in a very melancholy plight. A second and still ruder horde commenced its labors for the cross of Christ, by slaying the Jews in the cities on the Rhine; in Mentz alone nine hundred were in this way put to death.

In this was evinced the universal hatred of the people towards the Jews, who, by their usurious practices, and the immense wealth gained thereby, brought down upon their heads this full measure of vengeance. This party, and several other troops of crusaders, however, only reached Hungary.

So unpropitious a commencement might easily have crushed all inclinations for further attempts, had not these first adventurers, in great part, consisted of the lowest class of the people, and had not their leaders been deficient in prudence, experience, and noble zeal and energy. Accordingly, at the appointed time, in the middle of summer, a grand army, well appointed and disciplined, and burning with enthusiastic courage, was assembled, and on the 15th of August, 1096, set out for its destination. No king was present as leader of the assembled forces; but, among the princes and nobles, Godfrey, duke of Lower Lorraine, called, from his ancestral seat, Godefroy of Bouillon, stood proudly forward, conspicuous in every heroic virtue; having often fought in the armies of Henry IV. He was appointed the leader of a body of 90,000 men, and directed his course through Hungary and the dominions of the Greek emperor, while other princes proceeded through Italy to Constantinople. He conducted his army, with the most admirable order, through countries where so many of the crusaders had already perished, and having joined the other princes, entered the Turkish territories in the spring of 1097. The united forces of the crusaders consisted of 300,000 men, and with the women, children, and servants, made up a body of half a million. Unfortunately, however, they already found in the tribe of the Sedjoucidians, who first opposed their progress, an enemy equally cunning and active, while they met with still greater and more serious obstacles, in the deserts where the Turks had destroyed every thing which might have procured them some sustenance, and through which they had to pass from Asia Minor to Palestine. Hunger and disease carried off every day numbers of men and horses; even the bravest began to waver, and had it not been for the active genius and heroic firmness displayed by the brave Godfrey, this expedition would perhaps have experienced the same unfortunate result as those that preceded it.

At length, in May, 1099, the wearied feet of the remaining portion of the army which had escaped so many dangers, trod the cherished soil of that hallowed land, and on the 6th of July, they beheld from the top of a mountain near Emmaus, the object of their ardent hopes and desires—Jerusalem! One universal shout of joy filled the air, vibrating in undying echoes from hill to hill, while tears of rapture burst from every eye. Their noble leader could scarcely prevent them from rushing forward at once, in their wild enthusiasm, to storm the walls of the holy city. But Godfrey soon perceived that the conquest of the place was not easy, and could not be effected in a moment, especially as the garrison was much stronger in numbers than the crusaders, of whom out of 300,000, only 40,000 men were now left. At length every preparation being made, and warlike machines with storming-ladders provided, in spite of every existing difficulty—for the country around was deficient in wood—the first general assault was made on the 14th of July; but as the besieged defended themselves with the greatest bravery, this first attempt failed. On the following day, however, the Christians renewed the attack, and Godfrey was one of the first that mounted the enemy's ramparts. His sword opened a path for the rest; the walls were soon gained on all sides, the gates forced open, and the whole army rushed into the city. A dreadful scene of massacre now commenced; in their first fury the victors put all to the sword, and but few of the inhabitants escaped. When, however, reason at length resumed its sway, the warriors, wiping the blood from their swords, returned them to their scabbards, and then proceeded, bareheaded and barefooted, to prostrate themselves before the holy places; and the same city which just before had resounded in every part with the wild shrieks of the slaughtered, was now filled with prayers and hymns to the honor and glory of God.

The election of a sovereign for the new kingdom of Jerusalem became now an object of consideration, and Godefroy of Bouillon appeared to all as the most worthy to rule; but he refused to wear a crown of jewels on the spot where the Saviour of the world had bled beneath one of thorns, and would only take the title of "Defender of the Holy Sepulchre." As he died, however, in the following year, his brother Baldwin assumed at once the title of king.

Of the other crusades, which subsequently took place for the maintenance of the Christian dominion in Palestine, and in which the German emperors also took part, our history will speak hereafter.

After the extinction of the Franks, a moment had again arrived when the German princes, if they were desirous of becoming independent and sovereign rulers, were not obliged to place a new emperor above themselves; but such a thought was foreign to their minds, and they preferred paying homage to one, whom they had exalted to the highest step of honor, rather than behold Germany divided into numerous petty kingdoms.

Accordingly, in 1125 the German tribes again encamped on the banks of the Rhine, in the vicinity of Mentz, and ten princes selected from each of the four principal families, viz. Saxony, Franconia, Bavaria, and Swabia, assembled in Mentz for the first election. Three princes only were proposed: Duke Frederic of Swabia, (the mighty and courageous Hohenstaufen,) Lothaire of Saxony, and Leopold of Austria. The two latter on their knees, and almost in tears, entreated that they might be spared the infliction of such a heavy burden, while Frederic, in his proud mind, ambitiously thought that the crown could be destined for none other but himself; and such feeling of pretension indeed was too visibly expressed in his countenance. Adalbert, the archbishop of Mentz, however, who was himself not well inclined towards the Hohenstaufens, put to all three the question: "Whether each was willing and ready to yield and swear allegiance to him that should be elected?" The two former immediately answered in the affirmative; but Frederic hesitated and left the assembly, under the excuse that he must take counsel of his friends. The princes were all indignant at this conduct, and the archbishop persuaded them at length to make choice of Lothaire of Saxony, although against his own will.

But hostilities soon broke out between the two powerful Hohenstaufen dukes, Frederic of Swabia and Conrad of Franconia, and during nearly the entire reign of the new king, the beautiful lands of Swabia, Franconia, and Alsace, were laid waste and destroyed, until at last both the dukes found themselves compelled to bow before the imperial authority. In this dispute the emperor Lothaire, in order to strengthen his party, had recourse to means which produced agitation and dissension, and continued to do so for more than a hundred years afterwards. He gave his only daughter Gertrude in marriage to Henry the Proud, the powerful duke of Bavaria, (of the Guelfs,) and gave him, besides Bavaria, the duchy of Saxony likewise. This is the first instance of two dukedoms being governed by one person. Nay, with the acquiescence of the pope, and under the condition that after Henry's death they were to become the property of the Roman church, he even invested him with the valuable hereditary possessions of Matilda in Italy, as a fief, so that the duke's authority extended from the Elbe to far beyond the Alps, being much more powerful than even that of the emperor himself; for besides his patrimonial lands in Swabia and Bavaria, he had likewise inherited from his mother the moiety of the great ancestral possessions in Saxony, and in addition to all this his consort now brought him the entire lands of Supplinburg, Nordheim, and old Brunswick. Thus the foundation for the subsequent jealousy so destructive to Germany and Italy, between the Guelfs and Hohenstaufens—the latter, (styled by the Italians Ghibellini,) according to their castle Veibling, on the Rems, being called Veiblingers—was laid at this period, and the faction-names of the Guelfs and Ghibelins henceforward continued for centuries afterwards to resound from Mount Etna and Vesuvius to the coasts of the North and East Sea. Lothaire's reign became so shaken and troubled, partly by the dispute of the Hohenstaufens and partly by the Italian campaigns, that but very few, if any of the great hopes he had at first excited by his chivalric, wise, and pious character, were brought into effect.

During his second and rather successful campaign in Italy, in the year 1137, Lothaire was suddenly seized with illness, and died on his return, in the village of Breitenwang, between the rivers Inn and Lech, in the wildest part of the Tyrolese mountains. His body was conveyed to, and interred in the monastery of Königslutter, in Saxony, founded by himself.

However much the two princely houses of the Guelfs and Ghibelins may, from this time, have continued to attract and command attention, there was still a third, which, under this reign, excited not less interest. Lothaire had given the margraviate of North-Saxony, which then comprised the present Altmark, to Albert the Bear, of the house of Anhalt, one of the most distinguished princes of his time. He conquered from the Vandals the middle marches, as well as those on the Uker and Prignitz, together with the town of Brandenburg; and finally, in order to excite in these countries the desired industry, he procured from Flanders a great number of agricultural laborers. He may likewise be regarded as the founder of the Brandenburg territory; and it was also under his rule that, about the middle of the twelfth century, the name of Berlin appeared for the first time, which place, therefore, dates its origin from the same period that Leopold of Austria laid the foundation of Vienna.

## CHAPTER IX.

### THE SWABIAN OR HOHENSTAUFEN HOUSE, 1138–1254.

Conrad III., 1138-1152—The Guelfs and Ghibelins—Weinsberg—The Faithful Wives—Conrad's Crusade—Disastrous Results—His death, 1152—Frederick I., or Barbarossa, 1152-1190—His noble Character and distinguished qualities—Extends his dominions—The Cities of Lombardy and Milan—Pavia—Pope Adrian IV.—The Emperor's Homage—Otho of Wittelsbach—Dispute between the Pope and the Emperor—Milan taken and razed—The Confederation of the Lombardian Towns—The Battle of Lignano—Frederick defeated—Pope Alexander and Frederick—Venice—Henry the Lion of Brunswick—His Rise and Fall—Reconciliation and Peace—Lombardy—Frederick's Crusade and Death in Palestine, 1190.

The election even this time did not fall upon him who considered he had the greatest right to the crown, namely, the son-in-law of Lothaire, the powerful Henry (the Proud) of Bavaria and Saxony, although he had possession of the jewels of the crown; for the princes, repulsed by his pride, elected on the 22d of February, 1138, the Hohenstaufen duke, Conrad of Franconia, whom misfortune had made wise, and to whom his elder brother, Frederick, who contested with Lothaire for the crown, willingly gave up now the precedence. Henry the Proud would not bend before the new emperor, whereupon he was declared an outlaw, his two duchies taken from him, and Bavaria given to the margrave Leopold of Austria, the half-brother of the emperor Conrad by the maternal side, and Saxony to Albert the Bear, of Brandenburg. Henry died almost immediately afterwards, and left a son ten years of age, who became afterwards so celebrated under the title of Henry the Lion, to whom Albert, at the desire of the emperor, formally resigned the duchy of Saxony, which he had not been able to conquer, (so faithful did the Saxons remain attached to the Guelfic house;) and in return he was allowed to possess his hereditary estates in that country as a princely margraviate, independent of the duchy.

In Bavaria also, Count Guelf, of Altorf, the brother of Henry the Proud, still contended against the house of Austria, and not unsuccessfully. But when, in the year 1140, he ventured to march against the emperor, near Weinsberg, he was vanquished in the battle. It was in this action that the names "Guelfs and Ghibelins" were first heard as party names, for the battle-cry of the troops on one side was, "Strike for the Guelfs," and of those on the other, "Strike for the Ghibelins." After the battle, the long-besieged city of Weinsberg was obliged to yield. The emperor, irritated at its long resistance, had resolved to destroy it with fire and sword. He, however, permitted the females of the city previously to retire, and to carry with them their dearest jewels. And behold, when the day dawned, and the gates were opened, the women advanced in long rows, and the married bore each upon her back her husband, and the others each their dearest relative. This affecting scene so moved the emperor, that he not only spared the men, but also the whole city.*

The emperor Conrad was now about to proceed to Italy, to reconfirm and establish there the imperial dignity, when intelligence arrived in Europe that the unbelievers threatened the Holy Land, and had already conquered and destroyed the fortified city of Edessa, a frontier fortress; upon which, Pope Eugene III. sent letters

* This circumstance is recorded by a contemporary of that period in the chronicle of St. Pantaleonis

of exhortation to all the European kings and princes, that they might assist the Christians in the east; and a pious and zealous man, the holy Abbot Bernard of Clairvaux, in France, journeyed throughout Europe, preaching so powerfully, that many thousands took the cross. And when he addressed Louis VII. of France, the multitude of those who took the cross was so great, that St. Bernard (he being afterwards canonized) was obliged to cut up his own clothes to make crosses of them, and both the king and his consort Eleanor resolved upon the expedition. St. Bernard now turned his attention to Germany, and tried to stimulate the emperor Conrad, who long refused, and avoided the abbot, by proceeding from Frankfort to Spires, in order that he might take into consideration how much still remained to be put in order in his own empire. But St. Bernard would not quit him; he followed him to Spires, and there it was that Conrad, in the middle of the abbot's address, suddenly arose, and, with tearful eyes, exclaimed, "I acknowledge, holy father, the great goodness that God has shown me, and will no longer refuse, but am ready to serve him; for I feel urged to this expedition by Himself." St. Bernard immediately decorated him with the cross, and presented him with the holy banner lying upon the altar. Frederick, Conrad's nephew, who became afterwards the first emperor of that name, and even the old Duke Guelf, who had become reconciled with the emperor, both took the cross likewise, and a great army was assembled, which numbered 70,000 warriors alone. But in all human enterprises, a splendid commencement will not always secure a successful issue, and so, in this great expedition, nothing but misfortune followed. In the year 1147, while the army was encamped near Constantinople, on the banks of a river, in order to refresh themselves from the fatigues of the march, and to celebrate the festival of the birth of St. Mary, the waters so swelled in the night by a sudden rain, that the whole camp became overflowed, and great numbers of men and horses were drowned. And again, when the army was transported across the straits to Asia, treacherous guides led it into places which the Turks had previously devastated; the provisions they carried with them were soon consumed, and the cities which the expedition passed closed their gates against them. Many then entreated those upon the walls for bread, and showed their gold, which the people first let down ropes to possess themselves of, giving in return only as much as they pleased, frequently nothing at all, or only a little meal mixed with lime. Many thousands, consequently, died of hunger and disease, and still more were destroyed by the cimeters of the Turkish horsemen, who allowed the Germans no repose, either by night or day, never forming for a regular engagement with them, which the harassed troops so heartily desired. Thus, after a thousand dangers, Conrad arrived in the Holy Land with only the tenth part of his army. He entered Jerusalem and visited the holy spot of the cross, where he paid his worship; but these were the whole fruits of this crusade. The siege of Damascus was unsuccessful, and the French army was equally unfortunate. Conrad returned after an absence of two years, and died shortly afterwards, in the year 1152, at Bamberg. He was a valiant, high-minded, and noble-hearted man, and was universally esteemed. He recommended as his successor, not his own young son, Frederick, whose age would not as yet allow him to rule the nation, but his valiant nephew, Frederick Barbarossa, duke of Swabia, who had made the crusade with him, and who was unanimously elected at Frankfort.

Frederick I. was one of the most powerful of all the German emperors; high-minded, valiant, with a will firm as iron, and of a stern, energetic character. His very form displayed his lofty mind. His figure was manly and powerful; his limbs well formed and strong, auburn locks covered his high forehead, and beneath them sparkled his sharp and piercing eyes. His chin, according to the ancient custom, was covered with his beard, which being of a bright yellow, he thence derived his surname of Barbarossa. A youthful ruddiness of complexion and natural affability gave to his countenance that cheerful expression which attracts all hearts; but his firm, proud step, and the whole bearing of his presence, displayed the prince born to rule and command.

Already, even as a youth, he had performed deeds which announced the great man; besides which, he belonged to the Ghibelins on the paternal, and to the

Guelfs on the maternal side. It was hoped that he would cause the rivalship of both houses to be forgotten; and, indeed, one of his first acts in Germany was in favor of the Guelfic house. For, in the year 1154, he re-granted the duchy of Bavaria to Henry the Lion, the son of Henry the Proud, so that the duke again possessed Saxony and Bavaria in conjunction, by which means he became the most powerful prince in Germany. The Margrave Henry, called Jasomirgoth, of Austria, who, after his brother Leopold's death, had become duke of Bavaria, refused, indeed, to give up the country; but in 1156, Frederick induced him to renounce it, and compensated him by giving him the old Bavarian margraviate of Austria, and by making it independent of Bavaria, and raising it to a duchy, he presented him with great rights and privileges. The duchy was to be hereditary, not only in the male, but also in the female line, and the duke was to rank with the first imperial nobles.* He was only required to be invested in his own land, and to participate in the expeditions against the Hungarians, while, without his sanction, no foreign laws were available in Austria, &c. The reconciliation of the first princely houses in Germany caused universal satisfaction; and Frederick depended now more firmly than ever upon the assistance of the friend of his youth, Henry the Lion, for the execution of his enterprises. In the other affairs of the empire also, the new emperor exerted himself with vigor; he destroyed the castles of the freebooter-knights, whom he condemned to death; and proved himself to be, by all his acts, a protector of general order, and of the rights of the German people. A contemporary historian says, therefore, of him: "It appeared as if he gave to heaven and earth a new and more peaceful form."

The countries bordering upon Germany also presented him with an opportunity to give to the imperial name additional lustre. In his first diet, at Merseburg, in 1152, he decided the dispute of the two Danish princes, Sven and Knud, respecting the kingdom of Denmark. Knud received Zealand; but Sven the crown, which Frederick himself placed upon his head, and for which the Danish king swore allegiance to him. This also King Boleslaus, of Poland, was obliged to renew, and whom the emperor forced thereto by an effective campaign in Silesia. He gave to Duke Wladislas, of Bohemia, on account of his faithful adherence in this Polish campaign, the title of king, such titles the emperor alone being able to impart. King Geisa, of Hungary, renewed his allegiance, and fulfilled his duties as vassal in Frederick's second Italian expedition. And finally, in Burgundy, which had become almost estranged from the Germanic empire, Frederick re-established his influence by his own marriage with Beatrice, the heiress of High Burgundy, whereby his house acquired, at the same time, this portion of the kingdom of Burgundy. All the Burgundian nobles did homage to the emperor, and thus the ancient imperial dignity acquired additional splendor under the powerful monarch who now ruled in Germany.

It was only in Italy, the ancient seat of the dominion of the world, that the authority of the emperor had declined; and Frederick was not able to restore it entirely, even by the most glorious battles. The large towns in this country, since the weak government of Henry IV., had become overbearing, and submitted with great repugnance to the obedience due towards their superior feudal sovereign; above all the rest, the opulent city of Milan, the capital of Lombardy, was the most arrogant and independent. Milan, since the commencement of the 12th century, had, by the vigor and energy of its inhabitants, made such rapid progress, that one might almost have believed that ancient Rome had transplanted its spirit thither. It subjected, by degrees, several of the neighboring cities, especially Lodi and Como; and, at the same time, affected to treat the commands of the emperor with such contempt, that an imperial edict which Frederick issued in the year 1153, had even its seal torn off, and was trampled under foot. Upon this, the emperor, in 1154, crossed the Alps, and, according to the ancient custom of the Longobardian kings, held his first great diet in the Roncalian plains, on the banks of the river Po; and now that complaints from many

* "He shall rank equal with the ancient *Archiducibus*," stands recorded in the original statute. Thence, from this expression, originated the subsequent title of Archduke of Austria. This was first adopted by Frederick III. in the year 1453.

other places were urged against the oppression of this proud city, which even refused to meet or reply to them, his anger became excited, and he resolved to punish it severely. He did not venture this time to besiege it, as he was not prepared for such an important undertaking; but he destroyed several of its adjacent castles and forts, and conquered its allied cities, Asti and Tortona.

At Pavia he caused himself to be crowned king of Lombardy, and then rapidly advanced towards Rome. Here dissension existed between the pope and the people, who, in a revolutionary tumult, and under the guidance of a bold monk, Arnold of Brescia, wished to restore the ancient Roman republic. Neither of the parties knew in whose favor the emperor advanced. Pope Adrian IV. fled to a well-fortified castle called Castellana, but soon returned to the German camp, the emperor having promised him safety. Upon his arrival, Adrian (who had originally wandered from England, his native country, as a beggar boy, and had eventually raised himself to the papacy) expected that Frederick would hold his stirrup, as his predecessors had always done; as, however, he did not do it, the cardinals accompanying the pope fled hastily back to Castellana, for they regarded this omission as a bad omen of the imperial sentiments. Adrian, however, descended from his mule, and placed himself upon the seat prepared for him; and now Frederick cast himself before him, and kissed his feet. The pope now acquired fresh courage, and charged the emperor with the omission of the accustomed mark of deference; and the latter, who sought his glory in greater things, willingly yielded in this trifling affair, upon his princes assuring him that the emperor Lothaire had shown a similar sign of respect to Pope Innocent II. The ceremony of dismounting was consequently repeated on the following day, when the emperor met the pope and held his stirrup—thus it is related by the records of Rome. German writers, on the contrary—namely, Otho of Freissingen, and Helmold, inform us that the emperor, upon the first descending of the pope, had held the stirrup, but, from oversight, had seized the left instead of the right, and that the pope, in consequence, had refused him the kiss of peace. Upon the excuse of the emperor, that he had erred through ignorance, as he had not applied much attention to stirrup-holding, the pope replied: "If the emperor neglects trifles from ignorance, how will he show attention in important affairs?" The emperor, however, at the entreaty of the princes, yielded, and they both embraced each other as friends.

After this, Frederick went to Rome, and was crowned emperor in St. Peter's church, on the 18th of June, 1155. Meantime, a dispute ensued with the Romans, who would yield neither to the pope nor the emperor; the force of arms, however, soon reduced them to tranquillity.

In spite of these continual contests, however, with the perfidious and treacherous Italians, Frederick returned at length to Germany. But disputes speedily arose between him and the pope himself, who, confiding in the assistance of the Norman king, William of Naples and Sicily, wrote to the emperor a letter full of reproaches, and his legate, Cardinal Roland (afterwards Pope Alexander III.) uttered even in the assembly of the German princes, the arrogant words: "From whom, then, has the emperor the empire, if not from the pope?" The irritated count palatine, Otho of Wittelsbach, whose office it was to bear the naked sword before the emperor, upon hearing this raised the weapon, and was about to sunder the legate's head, for he considered the honor of the German prince deeply wounded by this language. Frederick, however, withheld him from this desperate act of indignation; but he commanded the ambassador to return early on the following morning to Rome. The German bishops, in reply to the reproaches of the pope, stated, that they had given themselves every possible trouble to mediate, but that the emperor had replied to them, firmly and gravely, thus: "There are two regulations, according to which our empire must be ruled—the laws of the emperors, and the good customs of our forefathers; these limits we will not, nor can we transgress. To our father, the pope, we will willingly pay all the homage we owe him; but our imperial crown is independent, and we ascribe its possession to divine goodness only." They then earnestly entreated the holy father no longer to excite the anger of their lord the emperor.

The dispute between the emperor and

the pope, after a short reconciliation, was, nevertheless, resumed, and lasted until the death of Adrian, in 1159. Thenceforward, affairs became still more entangled, for the imperial party chose Victor III., and the opposite party Alexander III., the same who, as cardinal legate, had uttered such bold words in the imperial assembly. Each pope excommunicated the other, and sought to strengthen his own party by all possible means.

The emperor Frederick, as early as the year 1158, had already prepared another more powerful expedition against Italy; the Milanese having in the preceding year reduced to ashes the city of Lodi, which had yielded allegiance to the emperor. All the princes of Germany, as well as the king of Hungary and the newly-elected king of Bohemia, performed feudal service; by which means such an army was collected as no emperor had previously led into Italy: consisting of 100,000 infantry and 15,000 cavalry. They broke up their camp near Augsburg, at Whitsuntide, and crossed the Alps. Almost all the cities of Northern Italy were humbled at the view of such a powerful force, and allied themselves with the emperor; but the rebellious city of Milan was declared outlawed, and, after a short siege, was obliged to submit to the irritated ruler. The Milanese appeared now before him, in humble supplication, forming a procession unusual to the Germans. First came both ecclesiastics and laymen barefooted, and dressed in tattered garments, the former holding up crosses in the air; then followed the consuls and patricians with swords hanging from their necks, and the rest with cords round their throats; and thus humbly they fell at the feet of the emperor. As he therefore only desired their submission, he pardoned them, saying: "You must now acknowledge that it is easier to conquer by obedience than with arms." Upon which he caused them to swear allegiance, and to promise that they would not interrupt the freedom of the smaller cities; and taking with him three hundred hostages, he placed the imperial eagle upon the spire of the cathedral.

But their humility was only feigned, and the effect of necessity; lasting only so long as the power of the emperor terrified them. For when, according to the imperial prerogative, he wished, in the following year, to appoint the civil functionaries, the citizens attacked Raynald, his chancellor, the count palatine, Otho, and the other ambassadors, with so much fury that they could scarcely save their lives. Upon being summoned, and an explanation demanded, they pleaded nothing but empty excuses; and at the second and third summons they did not appear at all. Upon which the emperor renewed the imperial edict of outlawry against Milan, and vowed, in his wrath, never to replace the crown upon his head until he had destroyed the arrogant city.

The war recommenced with all the bitter exasperation of that period. The Milanese sought even their salvation—such at least was the universal charge—in the assassination of the powerful emperor who thus menaced them. It is quite certain that a man of gigantic strength suddenly attacked the emperor while performing his morning devotions in a beautiful and solitary spot upon the Ada, and strove to throw him into the river. In the struggle both fell to the earth, and, upon the call of the emperor, his attendants rushed forward, and the assassin was himself cast into the stream. Shortly after this an old misshapen, squinting man glided into the camp with poisoned wares, the very touch of which was said to be mortal. The emperor being fortunately already warned, caused him to be seized and executed. His army, meanwhile, had become much strengthened, and with it he first besieged, in 1160, the city of Cremona, which was in alliance with Milan, and had obstinately refused submission; the inhabitants defended themselves for seven months with unexampled obstinacy, when they were at length obliged to yield. The city was razed to the ground, and the inhabitants were obliged to wander to other places.

It was only after a three years' siege, and after much blood had been spilled on both sides, that Frederick overcame the strong city of Milan. His patience was exhausted; the pardon he had once granted having only made the rash citizens more arrogant, he resolved therefore, by a severe punishment, to destroy their spirit of resistance. During three days, the 1st, 3d, and 6th of March, the consuls and chief men of the city, in increasing numbers, advanced to the imperial camp before Lodi, and on the third day, the whole people with them; they divided themselves into a hundred sections, and repeated thrice before that city, which had been so despised and ill-treated by them, the whole spectacle of their humiliation; with crosses, swords, and ropes hanging about the neck, and bare-footed. More than a hundred banners of the city were, upon the third day, laid down before the imperial throne, and, lastly, their chief banner, the CAROCIUM,* was drawn forward. Its lofty frame or tree, with its iron leaves, was bowed down before the emperor as a sign of the deepest humiliation; the princes and bishops, seated near him, sprang up, in dread of being killed by the weighty mass, but Frederick remained unmoved, and tore the fringe of the banner down. The whole of the people then cast themselves to the ground, with loud wailings, and implored mercy. The consuls and grandees of the city, and even the nobles of the emperor's suite, all supplicated his pardon for the capital, but the emperor remained inexorable, and desired his chancellor, Raynald, to read the law, whereby the city surrendered itself at discretion. He then said: "According to that law you have all merited death, but I will grant you your lives. As regards the fate of the city itself, I will so order it, that in future you shall be prevented from committing similar crimes therein." Upon which he retired to Pavia, to decide upon the fate of Milan in a large assembly of German and Italian bishops, lords, and deputies from the various other cities.

The sentence was, "that Milan should be levelled with the ground, and the inhabitants remove, within eight days, to four of their villages, two miles from each other, where they should live under the surveillance of the imperial functionaries." The city of Milan in its prosperity and arrogance, had so deeply injured many other cities—Cosmo, Lodi, Cremona, Pavia, Verrelli, Novarra, and others, that they all begged, as an especial favor, that they might themselves pull down the walls of the proud capital; so that, by the impulse of their hatred and revenge, they accomplished within six days what hired workmen would scarcely have executed in so many months: for, although the houses and churches were not pulled down, as later exaggerated records report, yet, the powerful walls and forts of the city were destroyed, the ditches filled up, and this once wealthy and splendid city, after the expulsion of the moaning inhabitants, became one dreadful scene of waste and desolation.* The emperor then, at a splendid banquet at Pavia, in the Easter festival, replaced his crown upon his head.

But Frederick was doomed to show to the world, by his example, that a change of fortune must ever produce its influence upon the most powerful monarchs, and that no force can check it but wisdom and moderation. The punishment of the city of Milan had been too severe, and if this may even be excused perhaps by the rudeness and strong passions of that period, still Frederick erred in not having treated that and the other cities of the north of Italy with mildness, and according to the laws of justice.

His deputies severely oppressed the country, and although, perhaps, without his concurrence, yet he did not sufficiently attend to the complaints which were made to him. At the same time he continued the contest with the still increasing party of Pope Alexander, and acted wrong in not taking advantage of the death of his own pope, Victor III., to reconcile himself with the former, instead of confirming the election of another rival pope, Pascal III. Frederick did not consider that his opponents, by their united inspiration, the one for civil freedom, and the other for their church-party, derived unconquerable power. The cities of Lombardy allied themselves still more closely together, and even those which had previously been the enemies of the Milanese became disinclined towards the emperor; for, now that their former oppressors were cast to the ground, they compassionated them. But the most dangerous enemy of the emperor was the bold and sagacious Pope Alexander, who had succeeded, after a two years' exile in France, in

* Upon a car strengthened with iron, a massive iron tree with iron leaves was fixed; a large cross adorned the top of the tree, in front of which was represented the holy Ambrosius, Milan's tutelary saint. The color of the car was red, and the eight oxen which drew it were also covered with red drapery. Before it was drawn away, high mass was celebrated on the car; the whole being an imitation of the ark of the Israelites.

* During this devastation of Milan, many relics were removed from the deserted churches. Among the rest, the archbishop Raynald conveyed the bones of the three kings with great solemnity across the Alps to the city of Cologne, and the king of Bohemia carried with him the candlesticks of the temple of Jerusalem.

gaining over the Romans to his side; and had now returned to his metropolis. Consequently, Frederick, after he had collected a new army, and had settled the most urgent affairs in Northern Italy, marched, in 1167, to Rome. The Romans were speedily beaten out of the field, and the city itself besieged. It was especially around the churches that the severest conflict took place, for they were defended like fortresses; and it was in the heat of combat that the Germans, having cast torches into the church of St. Mary, situated close to St. Peter's, the flames reached the latter edifice, which, in the general confusion, was taken possession of by the Swabian duke, Frederick. Pope Alexander, seeing that the Romans commenced murmuring at his obstinacy, fled secretly from the city, in the dress of a pilgrim. He was seen on the third day near a fountain, not far from Circello, whence he escaped to Benevento.

Frederick, however, together with his consort, was crowned by his pope, Pascal, on the first of August, 1167, in the metropolitan church of Christendom. But, immediately afterwards, an epidemic disease broke out among the Germans, of so terrific a nature that a great portion of the army and a multitude of the nobles and chief men were carried off. It was on a Wednesday, in August, that it first appeared; the heat had long been excessive and overpowering; on the morning of that day the sun was bright, after which rain suddenly fell, and a glowing heat succeeded; whence the vapor raised caused the sickness. Men died so suddenly, that often those who were perfectly well in the morning fell dead on the same day while walking in the street, and many, while even burying the dead, fell suddenly with them into the grave. The Archbishop Raynald, of Cologne, the emperor's able chancellor, four bishops, and eight dukes, and among these the emperor's cousin, Frederick of Rothenberg, and Guelf, the younger; besides many thousands of noble counts and lords who were numbered among the dead. The people everywhere exclaimed, "that this was a judgment of God for burning St. Peter's Church!" The emperor was obliged to retire to Pavia, and, in the following spring, he was forced, with only a few companions, to leave Italy like a fugitive, secretly and disguised.

The cities, however, now raised their heads. They had already, in that very year, 1167, and almost under the very eyes of the emperor, while he lay before Rome, concluded a formal alliance with each other; they even ventured to reconduct the Milanese back to their ancient city. The ditches, walls, and towers were speedily restored, and every one labored to reconstruct his habitation. For the capital had been so large and strong that, in its destruction, portions of the walls, most of the houses, and almost all the churches had remained standing. Thus, as Athens once, after its destruction by the Persians, so, also, Milan now raised itself by the aid of the other cities, more extensive and powerful than before. After this was done, the Lombard confederation built a new city, as an impregnable fortress against the emperor, in a beautiful and fertile spot surrounded by three rivers and deep marshes, and called it, in defiance of the emperor, and in honor of their pope, Alexandria. In the space of a year this city became inhabited, and garrisoned by 15,000 warriors. The most powerful cities participated in the Lombard confederation: Venice, Milan, Verona, Vicenza, Padua, Ferrara, Brescia, Cremona, Placenza, Parma, Modena, Bologna, &c.

Frederick, meanwhile, was not inactive in Germany; he remained there stationary nearly seven years; established more firmly the imperial dignity with all the strength of his high mind; regulated and adjusted internal disturbances, and, in particular, the great dispute in the north of Germany between Henry the Lion and his adversaries—upon which subject we shall enlarge as we proceed—and at the same time augmented the power of his house by various just and legitimate acquisitions for his five sons, still very young. Henry, the eldest, although only 15 years of age, was elected king of the Romans; Frederick received the duchy of Swabia and the lands of Guelf, the elder, who had bequeathed them, after the death of his only son, to the emperor, an example followed by many other counts and nobles in Swabia. Conrad, the third son, inherited the lands of the Duke of Rothenberg, who died childless. To the fourth son, Otho, Frederick gave the vice-regency of Burgundy and Arles; and to the youngest, Philip, who still lay in the cradle, he presented several confiscated crown possessions and clerical feods.

Thus the race of the Hohenstaufens stood firmly rooted like a vigorous and richly-branched tree of majestic oak.

But now Frederick again directed his attention to that still revolutionary country, Italy. The German princes were now, it is true, less easily induced to proceed to that intractable, unhealthy climate, but, by his persuasive eloquence and unwearied activity, he at length succeeded in again collecting an army, and appeared, in the autumn of 1174, for the fifth time, in that land. He besieged the new city of Alexandria, which had been built and fortified in order to check his course; and he was forced to remain seven months before it, during which his army suffered greatly in the winter from sickness and fatigue, in their camp, pitched upon marshy ground. Meanwhile the Lombard cities had collected an army to relieve the besieged, and which advanced at Easter, in 1175, fully prepared and equipped. The emperor resolved upon making a last attack against the place, and caused it to be stormed on the Thursday before Easter. The Germans, by means of a subterraneous passage, succeeded in advancing into the very heart of the city, as far as the middle of the market-place. Nevertheless the valiant garrison did not lose courage, and, to their great good fortune, this subterraneous passage fell in. Those of their enemy, who had thus entered the city, were overpowered, and the rest who were storming from without were beaten back. The emperor was therefore obliged to raise the siege, and to seek so hastily a different position, that he was forced to set fire to his own encampment.

It was then agreed, that a meeting of the belligerent parties should take place at Pavia, in order to conclude a treaty. The cardinal of Ostia, who appeared in the name of the pope, would not greet the emperor on account of the excommunication, but he evinced to him his regret, while he expressed his admiration of Frederick's great qualities. Both sides were, however, but little inclined to yield in any portion of their demands.

What tended much to increase the courage of the Lombards was, that precisely at this moment, Henry the Lion refused the emperor that assistance upon which Frederick had so much relied. The treaties were, consequently, broken off, and the Lombards, taking advantage of this favorable moment, advanced, under the protection of the grand and sacred banner of St. Ambrose, against the emperor, and fought the decisive battle of Lignano, on the 29th of May, 1176. Their force was far superior in numbers, and occupied a favorable position; while on one side they were flanked by a ditch which made all flight impossible. When they saw that the emperor had accepted their challenge, and now advanced against them, they immediately formed their line of battle. The Carocium of the Milanese was placed in their centre, surrounded by 300 youths who had sworn to defend it in life unto death, besides a body of 900 picked cavalry, styled the phalanx of death, who had, singly and collectively, likewise taken the oath of immolation. The battle commenced, and one of the Lombard wings beginning very soon to waver, the order of the Milanese ranks became confused. The emperor pressed directly upon the centre, to gain the Carocium, and, as now its band of defenders likewise faltered, the courage of the Germans increased, and at length they conquered the sacred banner, and tore down all its decorations. But at this moment the death-squadron recovered themselves, and again returned to the charge. Mortally wounded, the emperor's standard-bearer now sank at his side, and the imperial banner with him; but the brave Frederick, equipped in his splendid suit of armor, still fought on at the head of his warriors. Suddenly, however, he was seen to fall from his charger, and vanish from the view of the army. Terror and confusion now seized upon all, and Frederick's troops suffered an entire overthrow; he himself escaped with a few faithful friends in the wild tumult, and under the protection of the night. Almost all the citizens of Como, his allies, embittered by hatred and revenge against the Milanese on account of their ancient wars, fell a sacrifice and were left dead upon the field. For two whole days the emperor was mourned as slain, and even his consort put on a widow's robes; when, to the unexpected joy of all, he again appeared in Pavia.

After this the emperor wished and proposed a peace; when the pope, Alexander, said in reply: "That nothing was more desirable to him than to obtain peace from the greatest hero of Christendom; he entreated only, that the Lombards might participate in it, and he himself would proceed to that country." The two great opponents had now learned mutually to esteem each other, and Frederick having expressed a wish for an interview with the pope, the latter proceeded at once to Venice. His journey thither resembled a triumphal procession, for he was treated as the saviour of liberty, and as the father of the Italian free states. Frederick also came there in July, 1177, and, according to an ancient historian, "It pleased God so to guide his heart that he suddenly subjected the lion-like pride of his mind, and he became mild and gentle as a lamb, so that he cast himself at the feet of the pope, who awaited him at the entrance of the church of St. Mark, and kissed them; and the pope, with tears, raised him from the ground, and gave him the kiss of peace, at which the Germans exclaimed: 'Lord God, we praise thee!' The emperor then took the pope by the hand and led him into the church, where he bestowed upon him his benediction. On the following day, however, at the express desire of the emperor, the pope celebrated high mass, and Frederick, after he had himself, like an inferior of the church, humbly cleared the way for the pope through the crowd, took his place amid the train of the German archbishops and bishops, and devoutly assisted in the holy ceremony."

Thus, in those days, did mild, religious feelings moderate the severe and stern disposition of the emperor, without at all affecting the majesty of his presence, for his humility was voluntary, and thence acquired for him general esteem; while at the same time his conduct was sincere, and consequently his reconciliation with the pope was complete and lasting. But with the Lombards, as all the articles of the treaty could not be immediately settled, a truce of six years was concluded. All rights and customs were to be investigated; the demands of both sides equally weighed; and the relations of the Italian cities with the emperor and empire arranged afresh: all which demanded time.

In 1178 the emperor proceeded to Arles, where he was crowned king of Burgundy, and thence returned to Germany, where another important affair awaited his presence. While on the one hand the house of Hohenstaufen possessed at this period, in the person of its emperor, a powerful and high-minded chief, the house of Guelf enjoyed, on the other, an equal advantage in Henry the Lion, duke of Bavaria and Saxony. For, while Frederick, in the south, conducted his great wars against the Italian cities, Henry increased his power in the north by a successful war against the Vandals. Henry resembled the friend of his youth, Frederick, in valor, firmness, and chivalric sentiments. His outward appearance was also distinguished, and his powerful figure, strengthened by every corporeal exercise, displayed the bold courage of his mind. Yet, while Frederick, in his hair and complexion, bore the true impress of genuine German origin, Henry, on his part, presented in his whole appearance the evidence of his connection with the southern race of the Guelfs; his complexion being darker, his hair and beard black, and his eyes the same color. His name soon became terrible in the northern districts. He conquered a great portion of Holstein and Mecklenburg, as far as Pomerania, and populated the country, as Albert the Bear had done previously in the marches, with peasants from Brabant, Flanders, and Germany. He founded bishoprics and schools; distributed throughout these countries criminal courts and judges; transformed forests and marshes into fruitful fields; and, while he increased his own power, he became the promoter of civilization in the north of Germany. Lübeck, founded in 1140, and made the see of a bishop, soon developed itself and flourished nobly; and Hamburg, previously destroyed by the Vandals, was again restored. Thus his extensive possessions extended from the shores of the Baltic and the North Sea, as far as the Danube in the southern mountains, and were more considerable than the absolute dominions of the emperor; while, finally, he founded, in 1157, Munich, in Bavaria.

The object of Henry was to unite his two duchies under one entire political government, and thus to restrict throughout his territories, as much as possible, the rights of the nobles, both temporal and spiritual. At the same time, in so doing he laid himself open to the reproach of injustice; as, for instance, in the case of Count Adolphus III., of Holstein. This nobleman had labored greatly to advance the prosperity of his country, and having, among the rest, established some valuable salt works at Oldesloe, Henry now destroyed them by causing fresh water from the neighboring springs to flow into them, because his own salt works at Lüneburg were, as he thought, injured by the existence of those of Count Adolphus.

The jealousy of the neighboring German princes having now become excited against him, he, as a warning to them, caused a large lion, cast in bronze, to be placed before his castle in Brunswick. They understood what by this sign he meant to indicate, but although they trembled individually, they nevertheless tried once more to put a stop to his rapid progress by a great alliance, in which were included: the archbishops of Cologne, Bremen, and Magdeburg; the bishops of Hildesheim and Lübeck, the landgrave of Thuringia, and the margrave of Brandenburg, with several counts and knights. But Henry, sudden as the royal animal whose title he had chosen, broke loose, reconquered Bremen, devastated Thuringia and the archbishopric of Magdeburg with fire and sword, drove away Conrad, bishop of Lübeck, and thus overcame and crushed his enemies completely. Such was the state of affairs in Germany when the emperor Frederick returned from Italy, in 1168; his presence, however, restored tranquillity once more, and both parties were obliged to surrender to each other their conquests.

The noble Guelf, to whom repose was hateful, made now, in 1172, a pilgrimage to the Holy Land, but, upon his return, disputes were renewed, and he this time drew upon himself, in the person of the emperor, a far more powerful opponent. The latter, who had been hitherto his constant friend, and, in a series of years, had shown him nothing but kindness, considered he might with justice calculate especially upon him when, after raising the siege of Alexandria, in the year 1175, he collected all his forces together, in order to come to a decisive and final engagement with the Lombards. But it was just in that critical moment that Henry, to whom these distant expeditions were highly objectionable, and who preferred remaining at home with his army, for the purpose of increasing his own power, refused his assistance. He pleaded his age, although he was only forty-six years old, and thus younger than the emperor himself; pretending that too many necessary affairs required his presence in his own country. Frederick hoped, however, in an interview with him, to persuade him to change his mind, and invited him to the frontiers of Italy; the duke came, and the two rulers met at Chiavenna, on the Lake of Como. The emperor reminded his friend of their alliance, their close relationship, of his honor, and feudal duty as a prince; but Henry remained inflexible. The emperor then arose in great agitation, embraced the duke's knees, and entreated him still more earnestly—so important was his assistance to him at this moment. Henry was moved, and endeavored to raise the emperor, but did not waver in his determination. The empress then joined them, and said to her husband: "Pray rise, my dear friend, God will help you if, on some future day, you do but punish this arrogance!" The emperor arose, but the duke retired; and it was to his absence that Frederick might chiefly impute his subsequent bad success at Lignano. He could not forget this event, and upon his return to Germany, after the peace of Venice, in 1178, and fresh complaints resounded from all sides against the duke, he cited him to appear at a diet at Worms. Henry did not however attend. He was summoned a second time to Magdeburg; even there he did not appear; and, as he equally neglected a third and a fourth summons, at Geslar and Wurzburg, the emperor sat in judgment upon him, in the year 1180, and the princes confirmed his deposal from all his dignities and fiefs, as his punishment. Frederick then declared him outlawed, and divided his fiefs among other princes. The duchy of Saxony, to which he left but the shadow of preceding greatness—for he had himself already felt the danger resulting from too extensive duchies—he awarded to the second son of Albert the Bear, Bernard of Anhalt. The duchy in the western districts, as far as the dioceses of Cologne and Paderborn, comprising Limburg, Arnsberg, Westphalia, Paderborn, and a portion of Ravensberg, he gave to the archbishop of Cologne, who, however, only succeeded in holding possession of a portion of these countries. The bishops of Magdeburg, Hildesheim, Paderborn, Bremen, Verden, and Minden, took advantage of this opportunity to make themselves not only independent of the duchy, but also to increase their possessions. The duchy of Bavaria, which was somewhat decreased, was given to the valiant count palatine, Otho of Wittelsbach, the faithful companion of the emperor. The cities of Lübeck and Ratisbon became free imperial cities, and in Pomerania, which was now united with the empire, Frederick created the brothers, Casimir and Bogislaus, dukes.

After the emperor had passed judgment upon Henry, his enemies forthwith took up arms, to possess themselves of their portion of the booty; but the old Lion still defended himself valiantly. They could accomplish nothing against him, and were repeatedly beaten, until Frederick himself advanced with an army. Their reverence for the imperial name, and their natural repugnance to be allied with an outlaw, disarmed the duke's friends: he was obliged to quit his patrimonial estates, and was forced to see Brunswick, his capital, invested, one of his chief castles, Bardewick, taken; and finally, when the powerful city of Lübeck yielded to the emperor, he found himself left completely without any protection, even behind the Elbe. Driven, at last, to extremities, he cast himself at the feet of the emperor, at the diet of Erfurt, held in the year 1181. The humiliation of his old friend and companion in arms, whose proud soul was now broken, drew even tears of sympathy from the mighty Frederick, and he pardoned him. He counselled him, however, in order that, with time, the hatred of his enemies might become moderated, to absent himself for three years from Germany, and to remain, during that interval, with his father-in-law, Henry II., king of England; meanwhile his hereditary lands, Brunswick and Lüneburg, remained in his possession. Thus it was that, as it were by a singular reverse of fate, the duke dwelt as an exile for some time in the country where his descendants were subsequently to ascend a brilliant throne; for it was there that his consort, Matilda, gave birth to the same William who was afterwards the chief branch of the house of Hanover, which has placed the British kings upon the throne.

This great example of imperial superiority in Germany may possibly have worked upon the minds of the Italians; and as, in the following year, 1183, the truce of six years with the Lombards ceased, and the emperor, besides, showed himself a merciful ruler, they evinced a more satisfied disposition, and the peace of Kosnitz was accordingly signed with them, which henceforward stood as fundamental law between the emperor and Upper Italy. The emperor himself obtained great privileges: he had the right to appoint his own counts, as the burgomasters chosen by the citizens, and to renew their dignity every five years; he exercised the supreme judicial power, while he derived, besides, several imposts, particularly the subsidies for his army in the Italian campaigns; and all the citizens, from the age of 15 to 70, swore allegiance to him. Under these conditions the citizens, on their part, received the right of municipal freedom within their walls; were permitted to live according to their own manners and customs, and were even privileged to make such new regulations as they deemed just; and the confederation of their cities, already existing, was now confirmed.

Thus Frederick was enabled, now and for the last time, (in 1184,) to proceed to Italy in a state of peace, and, as he advanced, he was rendered more and more happy in witnessing the tranquillity and contentment that reigned throughout the land, while all around him was in a fever of joy and delight. The Lombards received him as if no enmity had ever existed between them. He caused the iron crown of the Lombards to be placed on the head of his son Henry, and gave him away in marriage, with great pomp and festivity, at Milan, in 1186, (which city had especially begged from the emperor that honor,) to Constanza, the last heiress of Naples and Sicily of the royal Norman race, and which allegiance gave the house of Hohenstaufen new and high expectations; for, being already in possession of Northern Italy, if it acquired in addition, Lower Italy, the whole peninsula would necessarily soon become subject to its dominion, and its subjection would accordingly lead to that of the whole of Germany. Such were the projects formed by the old yet youthfully-sanguine emperor, who was far from anticipating that by this last, and apparently splendid achievement of his glorious career, the seeds were sown for the fall and ruin of his house.

It appeared now as if fate, after having subjected the emperor to all its storms, had determined to prepare for him, in his venerable age, the glory of a noble death in a sacred cause; for, at this moment, intelligence arrived suddenly in Europe that Jerusalem, after the unfortunate battle of Hittin, or Tiberiad, in 1187, was again torn from the Christians by Saladin, the sultan of Egypt. Pope Urban III. died of grief at this news, and his successors, Gregory VIII. and Clement III., addressed urgent letters to the European princes, summoning them to rise and march forthwith to the deliverance of the Holy City; consequently, all the knights-templars and the knights of St. John, dispersed throughout Europe, were the first to embark; the Italians assembled together under the archbisnops of Ravenna and Pisa; the Normans furnished all their forces; a fleet of fifty vessels from Denmark and Friesland, and thirty-seven from Flanders, set sail, headed by their great leaders: Richard Cœur-de-Lion, king of England, Philip Augustus, of France, and the emperor Frederick Barbarossa, together with all the neighboring kings and princes, came likewise forward with their whole power for the sacred cause. Our venerable hero, Frederick Barbarossa, advanced, in the May of the year 1189, at the head of 150,000 well-armed combatants. The Greeks, who seemed disposed to practise similar treachery towards him as they had against Conrad III., he punished severely, and dismantled their cities. The Sultan Kilidish Arslan, of Cogni, or Iconium, in Asia Minor, who had offered him his friendship, and afterwards betrayed him, he attacked and put to flight, taking possession of his metropolis. Thus, in all these battles, Frederick, even as an old man, distinguished himself beyond all the rest by his heroic vigor and magnanimity, and he succeeded in leading his army through every danger as far as the frontiers of Syria, but here ended the term of his noble course. When, on the 10th of June, 1190, the army resumed its march from Sileucia, and traversed the river Cydnus, or Seleph, the bold and venturesome old warrior, to whom the passage over the bridge was much too slow, dashed at once with his war-horse into the river, in order thus to overtake more speedily his son Frederick, who led the van. But the rapid course of the stream overpowered and bore him away, and when, at length, assistance could be rendered him, the veteran was found already dead. The grief and lamentations of his son, of the princes, and of the whole army were indescribable. Fate nevertheless had by this means saved him from experiencing, subsequently, bitter pain and mortification, and his noble soul was not doomed to suffer by the unfortunate termination of so great an enterprise. For the German army, after his death, was almost entirely destroyed by sickness before the city of Antioch; and the emperor's second son Frederick, duke of Swabia, died at the siege of Acre, or Ptolemais, and Jerusalem was never reconquered.*

The grief which the emperor Frederick's death excited throughout the west of Europe, is testified by a French writer of that period, who, according to his peculiar style, thus speaks of it: "News so deadly piercing, even to the very marrow and bone, has wounded me so mortally, that all hope and desire of life have passed from me. For I have heard that that immoveable pillar of the empire, Germany's tower of strength and its very foundation, and that morning star which surpassed all other stars in splendor, Frederick the mighty, has ended his life in the east. Thus no longer exists that strong lion, whose majestic countenance and powerful arm frightened savage animals from devastation, subjected rebels, and made robbers live in peace and order." And the degree to which the imperial dignity in general was raised by him, is expressed in the words of his chancellor, Raynald, at a diet at Besançon, where he said, "Germany possesses an emperor, but the rest of Europe—only petty kings."

* This siege is one of the most remarkable and sanguinary on record. Both the kings of England and France were present, and took their share in the dangers. The city was eventually taken, after a long and vigorous resistance; but the sword and disease had combined to reduce the army of the Crusaders to such a degree, that it was in vain to contemplate any fresh enterprise. Several archbishops and patriarchs, twelve bishops, forty dukes and counts, five hundred of the principal nobility, together with a great number of knights, and an innumerable host of inferior officers and soldiers, became a sacrifice. Philip Augustus returned speedily to France; but Richard of England remained, and continuing on the war with the greatest activity, acquired the reputation of being the most valiant knight of his time; while Saladin likewise proved himself a brave and shrewd adversary. Richard, however, was recalled to Europe, through the dangers which threatened his own kingdom. He concluded a peace with the sultan, and gave up to him Jerusalem; and thus nothing more remained in the hands of the Christians than a narrow strip of land along the coast from Jaffa to Acre.

## CHAPTER X.

### FROM 1190 TO THE INTERREGNUM, 1273.

Henry VI., 1190-1197—His Mercenary and Cruel Character—Richard I. of England—Is seized and imprisoned by Henry—Naples and Sicily—The Grandees—Their Barbarous Treatment by the Emperor—His Death, 1197—The Rival Sovereigns—Philip of Swabia, 1197-1208, and Otho IV., 1197-1215—Their Death—Frederick II., 1215-1250—His Noble Qualities—Love for the Arts and Sciences—His Sarcastic Poetry—Preference for Italy—Disputes with the Popes—Is Excommunicated—His Crusade to the Holy Land—Crowned King of Jerusalem—Marries a Princess of England—Italy—Pope Gregory IX.—Frederick Denounced and Deposed—Dissensions in Germany—The Rival Kings—Death of Frederick II., 1250—His Extraordinary Genius and Talents—His Zeal for Science and Education—A Glance at the East and Northeastern Parts of Germany—Progress in Civilization—William of Holland, 1247-1256—Conrad IV., 1250-1254—Their Deaths—The Interregnum, 1256-1273—Progress of the Germanic Constitution.

Frederick's eldest son Henry, who, during his father's life, was named his successor, and in whose absence he had been invested with the government of the empire, was not dissimilar to his father in the power of his mind, in chivalric bearing, and in grand ideas and plans, but his disposition was extremely partial and severe, often cruel, and in order to execute great ambitious projects he betrayed feelings of a very mercenary nature. This was displayed in an occurrence which has not done him much honor. King Richard Cœur-de-Lion, of England, when in Palestine, had, at the siege of Akkon, or Acre, (of which we have already spoken,) a dispute with Duke Leopold of Austria ; inasmuch as the Germans, after the city was taken, being encamped in one of its quarters, Duke Leopold caused the German banner to be raised accordingly upon a tower, similar to the kings of England and France. But the proud Richard of England caused it to be torn down, and it was trampled in the mud by the English. This was an affront to the whole German army, and certainly deserved immediate and severe punishment. But the revenge which the duke and the emperor Henry took afterwards upon the king was of the most treacherous and ignoble character. Richard, namely, upon his return from Palestine in 1192, was cast by a storm upon the Italian coast, near Aquileja, and wished to continue his route through Germany ; but, although he had disguised himself as a pilgrim, he was recognised in Vienna by his expensive style of living, and by the imprudence of his servant. He was seized and delivered up to Duke Leopold, who had previously returned, and by whom he was surrendered to the emperor Henry. The noble chivalric king of England, and brother-in-law of Henry the Lion, was now detained at Trifels, in close confinement, above a year, until he was formally brought before the assembly of German princes at Hagenau, as a criminal, and had defended himself; nor was he liberated and allowed to return to his kingdom until the English had paid a ransom of a million of dollars—for that period an immense sum. In thus proceeding against Richard, Henry had, it is true, acted in conformity with the ancient right of the imperial dignity, according to which the emperor was authorized to cite before him all the kings of Christendom, and sit in judgment over them. But the manner in which he acted in this case was degrading, and unworthy of any ruling power.

The emperor concluded with Henry the Lion, who after his return from England had produced fresh wars, a permanent treaty of peace, and by the marriage which took place between the duke's son, Henry the Slender, and Agnes, princess palatine, and niece of Frederick I., the reconciliation of these two distinguished houses was confirmed.

The principal aim now of the emperor Henry, beyond every thing else, was to secure to his house Naples and Sicily, the inheritance of his consort Constanza ; but the avarice and cruelty with which he acted in his endeavors to gain his object, soon indisposed and rendered the feelings of his new subjects more and more adverse towards him, and increased their hatred against the Germans. For he not only conveyed away the gold and silver, together with all the costly ornaments of the ancient Norman kings, to such an extent that one hundred and sixty animals were loaded therewith, and proceeded with them to the castle of Trifels on the Rhine, but he caused the eyes of the grandees who had rebelled to be put out, and as an insult to their misfortunes, and in mockery of their efforts to get possession of the throne and wear the crown, he placed them upon seats of red-hot iron, and fastened upon their heads crowns formed equally of burning iron. The rest of their accomplices were, it is true, so much terrified thereby, that they vowed allegiance ; but this submission did not come from their hearts, and

Henry's successors paid severely for his cruelties.

He meditated the most important plans, which, had they been accomplished, would have given to the whole empire a completely different form. Among the rest, he offered to the German princes to render their fiefs hereditary, promised to renounce all imperial claims to the property left by bishops and the rest of the clergy; in return for which, however, he desired the imperial throne to be made likewise hereditary in his family. He even promised to unite Naples and Sicily wholly with the empire. Many princes voluntarily agreed to these propositions, which appeared advantageous to them; some of the greater ones, however, refused, and as the pope likewise withheld his consent, Henry was obliged to defer the execution of his great projects to a more convenient time. Affairs now called him again to Sicily, and there he died suddenly in 1197, in the 33d year of his age, and at the moment when he contemplated the conquest of the Greek empire, by which to prepare and secure a successful issue to the crusades.*

His son Frederick was but just eight years old, and the two parties in Germany, the Hohenstaufens and the Guelfs, became again so strongly divided, that the one side chose as emperor Philip, Henry's brother, and the other Otho, the second son of Henry the Lion, a prince distinguished for his strength and valor, and thus Germany had again two sovereigns at once.

Through this unfortunate division of parties the empire became for the space of more than ten years the scene of devastation, robbery, and murder, and both princes, who were equally endowed with good qualities, could do nothing for the country; on the contrary, in the endeavors made by each to gain over the pope to himself, they yielded to the subtle Innocent III., under whom the papacy attained its highest grade of power, many of their privileges. Otho IV. even acknowledged the pope's claim of authority to bestow the empire as he might appoint, and called himself in his letters to the pope a Roman king by the grace of God and the pope. For which concession, and because he was a Guelf, Innocent protected him with all his power, and when Philip in 1208 was assassinated at Bamberg by Otho of Wittelsbach, (a nephew of him to whom Frederick I. had given the duchy of Bavaria,) in revenge because he would not give him his daughter in marriage as he had promised, Otho IV. was universally acknowledged as emperor, and solemnly crowned at Rome. His friendship with the pope, however, did not last long, for Otho saw that he had gone too far in his submission, and ought not to sacrifice for his private interest all the privileges of the empire. The pontiff, therefore, opposed to him as king, the youthful Frederick, the son of Henry VI., who had meanwhile grown up in Sicily, and whose guardian he became after the death of his mother Constanza. Frederick soon gained adherents, and was crowned at Aix-la-Chapelle in 1215, and Otho lived henceforward deserted and inactive on his patrimonial lands until he died in 1218.

The emperor Frederick II., the grandson of Frederick I., by his heroism, firmness of will, and boldness of spirit, and combining with this majesty of character both mildness and grace, was worthy of his noble family, so that the impression of his personal greatness remained long after his demise. In addition to which, he was a friend of art and science, and was himself a poet: sentiment, animation, and euphony breathing in all his works. His bold and searching glance dwelt especially upon the follies of his age, and he frequently lashed them with bitter ridicule, while, on the contrary, he saw in every one, whence or of whatsoever faith he might be, merely the man, and honored him as such if he found him so worthy.

And yet this emperor executed but little that was great; his best powers were consumed in the renewed contest between the imperial and papal authority, which never had more ruinous consequences than under his reign, and Germany in particular found but little reason to rejoice in its sovereign, for his views, even beyond all the other Hohenstaufens, were directed to Italy. By birth and education more an Italian than a German, he was particularly attached to his beautiful inheritance of the Two Sicilies, and in Germany, thus neglected, the irresponsible dominion of the vassals took still deeper root, while, on the other hand, in France the royal power, by withdraw-

* Henry's tomb, at Palermo, was opened after nearly 600 years, and the body found well preserved. In the features of the face, the expression of imperious pride and despotic cruelty was still to be recognised.

ing considerable fiefs, commenced preparing its victory over the feudal system.

There were also three grand causes which served to excite the popes against Frederick. In the first place, they could not endure that, besides Northern Italy, he should possess Sicily and Naples, and was thus enabled to press upon their state from two sides; secondly, they were indignant because he would not yield to them, unconditionally, the great privileges which the weak Otho IV. had ceded to them; but, thirdly, what most excited their anger was, that, in the heat of their dispute, he frequently turned the sharpness of his sarcasm against them, and endeavored to make them both ridiculous and contemptible.

The commencement of the schism, however, arose from a particular circumstance. Frederick, at his coronation, in Aix-la-Chapelle, had spontaneously engaged to undertake a crusade for the deliverance of Jerusalem, and this promise he renewed when he was crowned emperor at Rome, in 1220. But he now found in his Italian inheritance, as well as in the opposition shown by the Lombard cities, which, after the death of Frederick I., had again become arrogant, so much to do, that he was continually obliged to require from the pope renewed delays. The peaceful and just Honorius III. granted them to him; and there existed between him and the emperor a friendly feeling, and even a mutual feeling of respect. But with the passionate Gregory IX., the old dispute between the spiritual and temporal power soon again broke forth, and Gregory strongly urged the crusade. In the year 1227, Frederick actually sailed with a fleet, but returned after a few days, under the pretext of illness, and the whole expedition ending in nothing, Gregory became irritated, and without listening to or admitting even the emperor's excuses, excommunicated him, for he maintained his sickness was a fiction. To contradict these charges by facts, the emperor actually went the ensuing year to Palestine. But upon this the pope censured him, even more strongly than before, declaring any one, under excommunication, to be an unfit instrument for the service of God. And in order that Frederick might accomplish nothing great in the Holy Land, he sent thither commands, that neither the clergy there, nor the orders of knighthood, should have community with him; nay, he himself even caused his troops to make an incursion into Frederick's Italian lands, and conquered a portion of Apulia.

But Frederick, in the mean time, speedily brought the war in Palestine to a successful termination. The sultan of Egypt, at Kameel, partly through the great fame which the imperial sovereignty enjoyed in the east, and partly from personal esteem for Frederick, (but weakened principally by family dissensions,) concluded with him a truce for ten years, and gave up Jerusalem, Bethlehem, and Nazareth. The emperor then entered the holy city, and visited the grave, but the patriarchs of Jerusalem and the priests, obedient to the commands of the pope, would celebrate no religious service in his presence. Notwithstanding which, he performed his devotions, and in the presence of his nobles, crowned himself with the crown of the kings of Jerusalem; a right he had acquired by his marriage with Iolontha, the daughter of King John of Jerusalem;* after which he returned quickly to Italy. His presence speedily repaired all that was lost, and the pope saw himself obliged, in 1230, to conclude a peace and remove the ban.

A tranquil moment seemed now to present itself in Frederick's life, but fate attacked him from another side. His own son Henry, whom he had left in Germany, as imperial viceroy, rebelled against him, excited, probably, by ambition and evil counsellors. After fifteen years absence, Frederick returned to Germany, and with a bleeding heart he was obliged to overpower his own son by force, take him prisoner, and place him in confinement in Apulia, where, seven years afterwards, he died.

Upon this occasion Frederick also held in 1235, a grand diet at Mentz, where 64 princes, and about 12,000 nobles and knights were present. Here written laws were made relative to the peace of the country, and other regulations adopted which showed the empire the prudence of its emperor. Before the diet assembled he celebrated, at Worms, his espousal with his second consort, the English princess Isabella. The imperial bride was received upon the frontiers by a splendid suite of nobles and knights; in all the cities through

* The kings of Naples and Sicily inherited the title of king of Jerusalem from Frederick

which she passed, the clergy met her, accompanied by choirs of sacred music, and the cheerful peals of the church-bells; and in Cologne, the streets of which were superbly decorated, she was received by ten thousand citizens on horseback, in rich clothing and arms. Carriages with organs, in the form of ships, their wheels and horses concealed by purple coverings, caused an harmonious music to resound, and throughout the whole night choirs of maidens serenaded beneath the windows of the emperor's bride. At the marriage in Worms, four kings, eleven dukes, and thirty counts and margraves, were present. Frederick made the most costly presents to the English ambassador; and among the rest, he sent rich gifts of curiosities from the east to the king of England, as well as three leopards, the leopards being included in the English coat of arms.

From these peaceful occupations, Frederick was obliged to turn, in the following year, to more serious affairs in Italy, where the Lombard cities more especially claimed his presence, they having renewed their ancient alliance among themselves and refusing to yield to him the obedience he required as emperor. With the assistance of his valiant leader, the knight Ezzelin de Romano, he conquered several of the allied cities, and so beat the Milanese in 1237, at Cortenuova, that they would willingly have humbled themselves, if he had granted only moderate conditions. But, unwarned by the example of his grandfather, he required them to submit at discretion: while the citizens, remembering earlier times, preferred dying under their shields, rather, they said, than by the rope, famine, or fire, and from this period commenced in reality the misfortunes of Frederick's life. According to the statement made by one of our writers, "he lost the favor of many men by his implacable severity." His old enemy also, Gregory IX., rose up again against him, joined henceforth the confederation of the cities, and excommunicated him a second time. Indeed, the enmity of both parties went so far, and degenerated so much into personal animosity, that the pope comparing the emperor, in a letter to the other princes, "to that Apocalyptic monster rising from the sea, which was full of blasphemous names, and in color checkered like a leopard," Frederick immediately replied with another passage from Scripture: "Another red horse arose from the sea, and he who sat thereon took peace from the earth, so that the living should kill each other."

But in that age there existed one great authority which operated powerfully on the side of the pope, and fought against Frederick—this was the power of *public opinion*. The pope now cast upon the emperor the heavy charge that he was a despiser of religion and of the holy church, and was inclined to the infidelity of the Saracens, (the fact that Frederick had employed, in the war with the Lombardians, 10,000 Saracens, appeared to justify this charge,) and although the emperor several times, both verbally and in writing, solemnly declared that he was a true Christian, and as such wished to live and die: nay, although he was formally examined in religion by several bishops, and caused a testimony of his orthodoxy to be published, this accusation of the pope still found belief among most men. In addition to which, Frederick's rash and capricious wit had too often thoughtlessly attacked sacred subjects; while his life also was not pure and blameless, but stained with the excesses of sensuality. Accordingly he sank more and more in general estimation, and it was this that embittered the latter period of his life, and at length entirely consumed him with vexation.

Gregory IX., who died in 1241, nearly one hundred years old, was succeeded by Innocent IV., who was a still more violent enemy of the emperor than even Gregory had been. As Frederick still continued to be powerful in Italy, and threatened him even in Rome itself, the pope retired to Genoa, and from thence to Lyons, in France. There he renewed, in 1245, in a large council, the ban against the emperor, although the latter offered himself in peace and friendship, and was willing to remove all points of complaint, while, in addition to all this, his ambassador, Thaddeus of Suessa, pleaded most powerfully for his lord. Indeed, the pope went so far as solemnly to pronounce the deposal of the emperor from all his states and dignities. When the bull of excommunication was circulated in Germany, many of the spiritual princes took advantage of the excitement produced thereby, and elected, in 1246, at Würzburg, the landgrave, Henry Raspe, of Thuringia, as rival emperor.

The latter, however, could gain no absolute authority, and died the following year. As Frederick, however, still remained in Italy, entangled in constant wars, the ecclesiastical princes elected another sovereign, Count William of Holland, a youth twenty years of age, who, in order that he might become the head of the order of knighthood, was forthwith solemnly promoted from his inferior rank of squire to that of a knight. The greatest confusion now existed in Germany, as well as in Italy. "After the emperor Frederick was excommunicated," says an ancient historian, "the robbers congratulated themselves, and rejoiced at the opportunities for pillage now presented to them. The ploughshares were transformed into swords, and the scythes into lances. Every one supplied himself with steel and flint, in order to be able to produce fire and spread incendiarism instantly."

In Italy, the war continued uninterruptedly and without any decisive result, especially with the Lombardian cities. The imperial arms were often successful, but the spirit of the emperor was bowed down, and at last his good fortune occasionally deserted him. In the year 1249, his own son, Enzius, whom he had made king of Sicily, and of all his sons the most chivalric and handsome, was taken prisoner by the Bolognese in an unsuccessful combat near Fossalta. The irritated citizens refused all offers of ransom for the emperor's son, and condemned him to perpetual imprisonment, in which he continued for two-and-twenty years, and survived all the sons and grandsons of Frederick, who perished every one by poison, the sword, and the axe of the executioner.

Exclusive of the bitter grief caused by his son's misfortune, the emperor, in his last years, was afflicted with additional pain and mortification at finding his long-tried friend and chancellor, Petrus de Vincis, to whom he had confided the most important affairs of his empire, charged with the crime of attempting to take the life of his master by poison. Matthieu of Paris, at least, relates as certain, that the physician de Vincis handed to the emperor a poisonous beverage as a medicine, but which the latter, having had his suspicions excited, did not drink. The chancellor was thrown into prison, and deprived of his eyesight, where he committed suicide by dashing his head against the wall. Whether de Vincis was guilty, or whether appearances were alone against him which he could not remove, is not to be decided, owing to the insufficiency of the information handed down to us. The emperor, however, did not long survive this painful event; he died in 1250, in the arms of his son Manfred, at the castle of Fiorentino or Firenzuolo, in the fifty-sixth year of his age.

If, after contemplating the stormy phases which convulsed this emperor's life, we turn our observation to his noble qualities, his acute and sensitive feeling for all that was beautiful and grand, and, above all, to what he did for science and enlightenment generally in Naples, his hereditary land, we feel penetrated with profound regret when we find that all this, like a transitory apparition, passed away without any lasting trace; but more especially are we pained to witness how he neglected to reign with affection and devotion over his German subjects. Since Charlemagne and Alfred of England, no potentate had existed who loved and promoted civilization, in its broadest sense, so much as Frederick II.. At his court, the same as at that of Charlemagne, were assembled the noblest and most intellectual minds of that age; through them he caused a multitude of Greek works, and in particular those of Aristotle, to be translated from the Arabic into Latin. He collected, for that period, a very considerable library, partly by researches made in his own states, partly during his stay in Syria, and through his alliance with the Arab princes. Besides, he did not retain these treasures jealously and covetously for himself, but imparted them to others; as, for instance, he presented the works of Aristotle to the university of Bologna, although that city was inimically disposed towards him, to which he added the following address: "Science must go hand in hand with government, legislation, and the pursuits of war, because these, otherwise subjected to the allurements of the world and to ignorance, either sink into indolence, or else, if unchecked, stray beyond all sanctioned limits. Wherefore, from youth upward, we have sought and loved science, whereby the soul of man becomes enlightened and strengthened, and without which his life is deprived of all regulation and innate freedom. Now that the noble possession of science is not diminished by being imparted, but, on the contrary, grows thereby still more fruitful, we accordingly will not conceal the produce of much exertion, but will only consider our own possessions as truly delightful when we shall have imparted so great a benefit to others. But none have a greater right to them than those great men who, from the original ancient and rich sources, have derived new streams, and thereby supply the thirsty with a sweet and healthy refreshment. Wherefore, receive these works as a present from your friend, the emperor," &c.

A splendid monument of his noble mind and genius is presented in his code of laws for his hereditary kingdom of Naples and Sicily, and which he caused to be composed chiefly by Peter de Vincis. According to the plan of a truly great legislator, he was not influenced by the idea of creating something entirely new, but he built upon the basis of what already existed, adapted whatsoever to him appeared good and necessary for his main object, and so formed a work which gave him as ruler the necessary power to establish a firm foundation for the welfare of his people. Unfortunately, the convulsions of his later reign and the following periods, never allowed this grand work to develop its results entirely.

Frederick himself possessed a knowledge unusual, and acquired by few men of his time. He understood Greek, Latin, Italian, French, German, and Arabic. Among the sciences, he loved chiefly natural history, and proved himself a master in that science by a work he composed upon the art of hawking; for it not only displays the most perfect and thorough investigation in the mode of life, nourishment, diseases, and the whole nature of those birds, but dwells also upon their construction generally, both internally and externally. This desire after a fundamental knowledge in natural science had the happiest influence, especially upon the medical sciences. Physicians were obliged to study anatomy before every thing else; they were referred to the enthusiastic application of Hippocrates and Galen, and not allowed to practise their profession until they had received from the board of faculty at Salerno or Naples, a satisfactory and honorable certificate; besides which, they were obliged to pass an examination before the imperial chamber, formed of a committee of competent members in the science.

The emperor founded the University of Naples in 1224, and he considerably improved and enlarged the medical school at Salerno. At both places also, through his zeal, were formed the first collections of art, which, unfortunately, in the tumults of the following ages, were eventually destroyed.*

Of Frederick II. it is related, as was already stated of Charlemagne, that the eastern princes emulated each other in sending him artistical works as signs of friendship. Among the rest, the sultan of Egypt presented him with an extraordinary tent. The sun and moon revolved, moved by invisible agents, and showed the hours of the day and night in just and exact relation.

At the court of the emperor, there were often contests in science and art, and victorious wreaths bestowed, in which scenes Frederick shone as a poet, and invented and practised many difficult measures of verse. His chief judge, Peter de Vincis, the composer of the code of laws, wrote also the first sonnet extant in Italian. Minds, in fact, developed themselves, and were in full action in the vicinity and presence of the great emperor, and there they commanded full scope for all their powers.

His own personal merit was so distinguished and universally recognised, that he was enabled to collect around him the most celebrated men of the age without feeling any jealousy towards them—always a proof of true greatness. His most violent enemies even could not withhold from him their admiration of his great qualities. His exterior was also both commanding and prepossessing. Like his grandfather he was fair, but not so tall, although well and strongly formed, and very skilful in all warlike and corporeal exercises. His forehead, nose, and mouth bore the impression of that delicate and yet firm character which we admire in the works of the

* On the bridge across the Vulturnus, in Capua, was erected a statue of the emperor Frederick II., with several others, and it continued there in a very good state of preservation until the most recent wars of modern times, when it became a prey to the devastation committed. The head of the emperor on this statue, however, has been copied and engraved upon a ring and it is after that, that the excellent portrait of Frederick has been drawn in the History of the Hohenstaufens, by M. F. de Raumer.

Greeks, and name after them; and his eye generally expressed the most serene cheerfulness, but on important and serious occasions it indicated gravity and severity. Thus, in general, the happy conjunction of mildness with seriousness was, throughout his life, the distinguishing feature of this emperor. His death produced great confusion in Italy, and still greater dissension in Germany. In the latter country two emperors again stood opposed to each other, throne against throne: the Hohenstaufen party acknowledging and upholding Conrad, Frederick's son, in opposition to William of Holland, the former having already, during his father's life, been elected king of the Romans.

But before we relate the history of these two rival emperors, it will be useful and interesting to cast our glance at the countries in the east and northeastern parts of Germany.

Europe was about this time threatened by a terrible enemy from the east, equally as dreadful as the Hunns were in earlier times. This enemy consisted of the Mongolians, who ever since the year 1206, under Dschinges-Khan, had continued to ravage Asia, and led by him had advanced as far as Moravia and Silesia. In the year 1241 they gained a great battle near Liegnitz over the Silesians, under the command of Henry II. of Liegnitz, who himself fell chivalrously fighting at the head of his troops; but by the valor with which he disputed the victory with the enemy, he destroyed the desire they had previously indulged in of penetrating farther westward, as they now turned towards Hungary. Thus, by his own death, Henry the Pious saved Europe; and indeed, upon the same spot (Wahlstadt) where, on the 26th of August, 1813, the action called the battle of Katzbach was so victoriously fought.

In this emergency Frederick well felt what his duty was as first Christian prince, and very urgently pressed the other kings for their immediate assistance against the common enemy; but at this moment the general disorder was too great, and his appeal for aid remained without any effect. As regards Silesia and Hungary the incursion of the Mongolians produced this result, that many German peasants migrated to the deserted and depopulated districts, and henceforward Lower Silesia became, indeed, more a German than Slavonic country. Other neighboring countries also were about this period occupied and populated by the Germans, consisting of the coasts of the Baltic, Prussia, Livonia, Esthland, and Courland. As early as at the end of the twelfth century, Meinhardt, a canon of the monastery of Legeberg, built a church at Exkälle, (in the vicinity of the present Riga,) where, shortly afterwards, Pope Clement III. founded a bishopric, and from this central point the diffusion of Christianity extended in that district. But temporal force soon mixed itself in these spiritual and peaceful exertions; the resistance of the heathen Livonians induced Pope Celestin III. to cause a crusade to be preached against them, and speedily a multitude of men from the north of Germany stormed towards these parts. A spiritual order of knighthood was formed under the name of the knights of the sword, and with the Christian doctrines the dominion of this order was by degrees extended over Livonia, Esthland, and Courland. The natives who remained after the sanguinary battles of this exterminating war were reduced to oppressive slavery, which was for the first time moderated in our own age by the emperor Alexander.

In Prussia also the sword established at the same time with Christianity the German dominion and superiority. About the year 1208 a monk of the monastery of Kolwitz, in Pomerania, of the name of Christian, crossed the Vistula, and preached Christianity to the heathen Prussians. But when the pope made him a bishop, and wished to establish a formal hierarchal government, they rose in contest against him, in which the knights of the sword, together with Duke Henry the Bearded of Breslau, and many warriors of the neighboring lands, immediately marched forth and gave warlike aid to the new bishop. But little was accomplished until the latter, upon the advice of Duke Henry, summoned to his assistance the knights of the Teutonic Order, which had originated in an institution of North Germany. Accordingly, in the year 1229, their first grand master, Herman Salza, with not more than twenty-eight knights and one hundred squires and attendants, advanced to Prussia; he proceeded in his work cautiously by establishing fortified places, among which Thorn, on the Vistula, serving, as it were, for the entrance gate of the country, was the first; and

Culm, Marienwerder, Elbing, Braunsberg, and others speedily followed. The dominion of the Teutonic Order was spread even in Livonia, as the Knights of the Sword, after a severe defeat by the Livonians, in 1273, were received in it; and in 1255, upon the advice of Ottocar of Bohemia, who had made a crusade against the Prussians, in which Rudolphus of Hapsburg joined, the present metropolis of the country was founded, and in honor of him was called Königsberg. The cities around, by their favorable situation for commerce, soon flourished again, and the peasants found themselves in a happier situation than their Livonian neighbors, for their services and imposts were rendered more moderate, and absolute slavery was only experienced by a few individuals as a punishment for their defection.

When we add to this the various emigrations which had commenced already much earlier, populating the Vandal countries as well as Brandenburg, Mecklenburg, and Pomerania, and take into consideration the many flourishing cities which were built there by German citizens, we may be inclined to style the twelfth and thirteenth centuries as the epoch of the migration of Germans towards the northeast, the same as that of the fourth and fifth centuries after Christ is called the period of migration towards the west and south. Indeed, if we reckon the hundreds of thousands which Germany at the same period sent with the crusades to the east, together with those sent with the Hohenstaufen emperors to Italy, we must really feel astonished at the population which that vast country produced, and assuredly cannot join with many other historians in calling a period presenting like this so much vigor and activity of life, an epoch of absolute misery, slavitude, and desolation.

Had the emperor Frederick rightly known the strength of Germany, and had he understood how to avail himself of the means to render it still more powerful by union, the whole of the east and north of Europe might then have become annexed to that country. But his eyes were turned exclusively upon Italy, and there he fruitlessly sacrificed all his strength.

Conrad, meanwhile, was likewise more occupied with his patrimonial inheritance than with Germany. He went as early as 1251 to Italy, and left his consort in the former country, who gave birth the following year to the unfortunate Conradin. Conrad, under the excommunication of the pope, like his father, conquered Naples, it is true, but made the inhabitants his most implacable enemies, by placing a bridle upon the horse, which stood as an emblem of the city upon the market-place. He died shortly after, in 1254, and said a few moments before his death: "Unhappy being that I am, why did my parents bring me into this world only to expose me to so much misfortune! The church, which should have shown both me and my father a maternal heart, has become much rather our stepmother; and this empire which flourished before the birth of Christ is now fading away and approaching its destruction!" And in this he prophesied too truly with respect to his own race, for he was the last king of the Hohenstaufens. Frederick II. had, it is true, left behind him a second son (Henry) by his marriage with Isabella, and a third (Manfred) by Blanca, his Italian consort, and two grandsons, the sons of his unfortunate eldest son Henry; but they all died in the flower of their age, and about the same time: so that at the death of Conrad IV., there only remained of the whole family of the Hohenstaufens, his son, the unfortunate Conradin, and his brother Manfred. We shall very shortly learn the fate of these two princes.

King William also lived but a few years after Conrad, and in so little esteem, that a common citizen of Utrecht cast a stone at him, and a nobleman plundered his consort upon the highway. When in the winter of the year 1256 he advanced against the Friesi, and crossed the ice near Medenblick, it broke under him, and he remained with his heavy war-horse sticking in the morass, where the Friesi killed him, although he offered a large sum for his life.

After his death the confused state of affairs in Germany became greater than ever.

Upon the demise of Conrad IV. and William of Holland, no German prince would accept the imperial crown, except, perhaps, Ottocar, king of Bohemia, but who, however, was not liked. Most of them preferred rather to occupy themselves in ruling over and extending their own hereditary lands, than to take upon themselves the heavy charge of restoring order and peace in those countries of Germany now become almost again savage, and thus renounce their own selfish interests, in order to consecrate all their powers to the common good. The spiritual electors now conceived the unworthy and degrading idea of electing a foreigner for emperor. Still they were by no means unanimous in their choice; the one party elected an Englishman, Richard, earl of Cornwall, the brother of King Henry III.; the other chose a Spaniard, Alphonso, king of Castile, who, on account of his knowledge in astronomy, was called the Sage, but who nevertheless was not wise enough to know how to rule even his own country. Both had offered the imperial princes considerable sums of money, and Richard, as some relate, came with thirty-two carriages to Germany, each drawn by eight horses, together with an immense tun filled with sterlings, an English coin of that period. He possessed extensive tin mines in Cornwall, then almost the only mines in the world, whence he acquired immense riches. With such arms as these, he speedily conquered many hearts, and was solemnly crowned at Aix-la-Chapelle, in 1257, after which he returned to England again, accompanied by several Germans of high rank. In England, however, the home of national pride, he was not treated otherwise than any other English prince or nobleman; and this so much vexed the Germans who were with him, that they returned to their country discontented. After that, Richard visited Germany at three different times, but on each occasion only for a short space. Alphonso, however, never came to that country at all. During this period, therefore, disorder and violence necessarily increased from day to day, so that the petty princes, counts, knights, and the cities themselves, lived in constant anarchy and warfare with each other, to an extent, that those who desired justice and tranquillity, wished most heartily for an emperor who might become their protection and shield.

Conradin of Swabia, the son of the emperor Conrad IV., the last descendant of the Hohenstaufen race, fell at this moment a victim to the most cruel fate. He was styled Conradin by the Italians, because he ended his career at so early an age. After his father's death, he had been brought up in Bavaria, and afterwards in Swabia, where he still retained some small inheritance; while his uncle Manfred, as regent, and subsequently as king, administered his hereditary estates in Naples and Sicily. The popes, however, who still remained the irreconcilable enemies of the Hohenstaufen house, sought to despoil him of these possessions; and as they could not effect this by their own power, it was determined by Clement IV. to bring another king in opposition to the hated Manfred. He applied, therefore, to Charles, duke of Anjou, who marched forth in 1266; he was accompanied by a numerous suite of French knights, who were ever happy to avail themselves of any expedition which promised them rich booty. King Manfred, who had unfortunately lost, in a storm, the whole of his fleet, with which he had set sail in order to prevent the French from landing, was defeated in an action at Benevento, on the 26th of February, 1266, principally through treachery, and preferred sacrificing himself by an heroic death, rather than to endure an ignominious life in prison; he therefore rushed into the midst of the enemy's ranks, and sank mortally wounded. His children, however, were seized by the conqueror, and remained in captivity during the rest of their lives.

When the youthful Conradin now became older, and bethought him of the lands which belonged to him, whereof one city alone was richer than his German possessions altogether, the bold disposition of his ancestors awoke within him, and he resolved to drive the robbers from his inheritance. In 1268, therefore, he went forth, accompanied by the faithful friend of his youth, Prince Frederick of Baden, and many faithful knights who followed him from Germany.

In Italy the numerous adherents of the Ghibelin party immediately flocked to him; the Romans, in defiance of their pope, Clement, who had called for the aid of the French, led him in triumph into their city, and he soon stood opposed to the enemy with a strong army near Tagliacozzo in Lower Italy. In battle, also, fortune at first favored him; the enemy was put to flight, but, unfortunately, in the pursuit his own army got into disorder, and in their eagerness for booty fell too soon upon the enemy's camp, for at that moment the French reserve returned and rushed upon the plunderers. The latter were wholly defeated, and Conradin, with his friend Frederick, after they had long fought most bravely, were forced to fly towards the sea. They had already got on board a ship at Astura, and were just setting sail for Pisa, when they were overtaken, made prisoners, and led before Charles of Anjou. And such was the insolence, perfidy, and cruelty of the tyrant, that he treated Conradin as a rebel against himself the legitimate and true king, and caused both the princes, at the age of sixteen, to be beheaded publicly in the market-place of Naples on the 28th of October, 1268.*

With the unfortunate Conradin ended the powerful house of the Hohenstaufens, and that was produced by means of the same possessions by which Frederick I. thought to elevate it to the highest degree of splendor and glory. But the Swabian patrimony now fell into so many divisions, that eventually no territory throughout Germany was divided into so many ownerships as Swabia. As the duchy was never restored, the whole of its states henceforward formed a part of the immediate possessions of the empire. Not only the bishops, counts, and superior free lords, but also the inferior ranks of the nobility, the cities, monasteries, and even the peasantry, which had been previously the vassals and subjects of the duke, became now emancipated; but they had not these rights and privileges individually, like the larger imperial lordships, but only as an entire combined body of the Swabian states, which they enjoyed as members thereof. The emperor derived from them important revenues, and the administration of these imperial possessions was transferred to seneschals; so that instead of the ancient Swabian dukes there were only now the imperial bailiwicks—Helvetia or Switzerland, Alsace, and Swabia, which were divided into cantons. These arrangements were adopted under the reign of the succeeding emperor, Rudolphus.

The fate of the duchy of Swabia leads us naturally to consider the circumstances which produced, especially in the interior of Germany, the dismemberment and abolition of the ancient national duchies. The basis for this important event was laid, as we have already seen, at the time of the deposition of Henry the Lion, in the year 1180. Although the plan and the limits of this general history of the empire will not permit us to trace more in detail all those princely houses which have arisen from the ruins of these ancient duchies, we may give at least a general outline of the changes as they occurred:

1. The duchy of Saxony had already become separated from the important margraviate of Brandenburg, which was transferred to Henry the Bear, who received therewith all the prerogatives of a duke in time of war, together with the rights of an elector, in his quality of arch-chamberlain. His son Bernard reunited subsequently, it is true, the duchy with the margraviate, and was created a duke; but his territory was of very little importance, and was, besides, divided into two portions between the two families of Lauenburg and Wittenberg, both of which disputed with each other for a long time for the possession of the office of grand marshal, and which question was not settled until the reign of Charles IV., who decided in favor of the Wittenberg house.

The ducal authority of the archbishop of Cologne in the western part of Saxony likewise could not recover its former elevation. The nobles in his jurisdiction made themselves gradually independent, after the example presented to them, especially by the spiritual princes of the ancient duchy. Besides which, the archbishop of Bremen came into possession of the lordship of Stade, in the territory of Detmarsh; the peasants took upon themselves the principal authority in that country; the count of Oldenburg refused to remain united with the duchy, and the important city of Lübeck was raised to the dignity of an imperial free city by Frederick II.; while at the celebrated diet of Mentz, in 1235, the emperor having conferred upon the Guelfic house new power and authority, by restoring to the infant duke, Otho, the duchies of Brunswick and Lüneburg, that powerful family likewise refused to recognise longer any rights claimed by the house of Saxe-Anhalt. Thuringia had already long since separated itself from the duchy, and had possessed its own particular counts from the time that the house of Saxony became imperial: we speak here of the north and

* The unfortunate Conradin, before his execution, transferred all his rights to Manfred's daughter Constanza; and this princess became afterwards the avenger of the Hohenstaufens. For, as the wife of Peter of Aragon, she favored the horrible conspiracy known under the name of the Sicilian Vespers, in the year 1282, by which Charles of Anjou lost his usurped kingdom of Sicily

southern parts of Thuringia, which became united under the valiant margrave, Eccard of Meissen. Under the Hohenstaufens, the margraviate was replaced by a landgraviate. The landgraves resided at Eisenach and in the castle of Wartburg. Their possessions extended, by means of certain allodial acquisitions, over Hesse and the towns of Münden, Cassel, Marburg, &c., as far even as the banks of the Rhine; such was the power commanded by Louis IV., landgrave of Thuringia, the husband of Elizabeth the Holy, at the commencement of the thirteenth century. With Henry Raspe, who died childless, in 1247, the masculine branch of the house of Thuringia became extinct. The female line contested together for the inheritance, and two of the descendants carried on a war against each other during a period of seven years. At length, in 1264, the fief of Thuringia was conferred upon Otho the Illustrious, of Meissen; but the allodial possessions, and especially the Hessian territory, fell to Henry, the son of Sophia, of Brabant. The aforesaid Henry of Meissen was the founder of the present Saxon house, and Henry of Hesse that of the house of the landgrave of Hesse.

In the north of Germany the counts of Holstein possessed claims to immediate imperial lordships: Mecklenburg, which belonged to the counts of Schwerin on the one part, and to the Obotrite princes on the other, had become an immediate fief of the empire, the same as the duchy of Pomerania.

2. The duchy of Bavaria, when it passed from the house of the Guelfs to that of Wittelsbach, possessed nothing more than the mere name of the ancient duchy. Carinthia, Austria, and Styria, had already since the year 1156, under the Saxon emperors, been separated from Bavaria.

Otho of Wittelsbach governed his duchy with much greater vigor certainly than Bernard of Saxony; but the bishops, nevertheless, withdrew from his sovereignty; Ratisbon became an imperial city; and in the south of Bavaria the count of Andechs, in his quality of heir to the house of the counts of Dachau, came in possession of the title of duke of Merau, (which this house had assumed from a tract of land on the coasts of Dalmatia,) which title he extended to the whole of his possessions in Franconia, and made it the basis for claiming his independence. In 1248, however, the house of Andechs became extinct, whence the greater portion of its possessions passed over to a house of Swabia, (the Hohenzoller branch,) the burgraves of Nuremberg, and laid the foundation for the duchies of Anspach and Baireuth.

Meantime the house of Wittelsbach, besides the acquisition of the duchy of Bavaria, came into possession of another territory extremely important—the county-palatine of the Rhine, which it received in 1227, by the marriage of Otho the Illustrious with the hereditary countess palatine of the house of Guelf. But the power of this house became considerably diminished by its dismemberment, after the death of Louis the Severe, in 1292, whose eldest son, Rudolphus, received the palatinate, and his second son, Louis, succeeded to the duchy. The count palatine of the Rhine possessed the title of arch-carver or steward, and consequently he commanded the first voice in the electoral college of the temporal princes. Bavaria contested with Bohemia for the office of arch cup-bearer, which Henry the Lion, or his father, who possessed two duchies, had been forced to abandon, and which it subsequently lost forever.

Those arch or grand offices fell gradually into the hands of those who possessed the right of election, after the original institution, which called together the principal heads of the people throughout the empire to take part in the meetings, had become altered. At the election of Otho I., there were present five of the principal nations: the Lorrainers, the Franks, the Swabians, the Bavarians, and the Saxons. When Otho of Saxony was elected, the dukes of the other four nations divided among themselves the offices of arch-chamberlain, arch-carver or steward, arch-cup-bearer, and arch-marshal. At the subsequent election of Otho III., however, the distribution of the offices had already become changed.

At the election of Conrad II. there appeared seven nations, because Lorraine was then divided in two portions, and Carinthia had likewise recently joined the rest. But at the election of Lothaire, the Saxons, the Lorrainers, and Carinthians, no longer attended, as the former had detached themselves from the empire, and the latter remained but a short time allied with the other chief nations. In earlier times the dukes did not possess this exclusive and positive right of election. All the princes, even the populace itself, took part in the choice of the sovereign: but subsequently, in proportion as the election assumed a more determined form, the elective right became more and more connected with the arch-offices, and was even transferred altogether with those dignities to other princes.

Thus Conrad III. indemnified the margrave, Albert the Bear, for the loss of the duchy of Saxony, by giving up in his favor the office of arch-chamberlain, which he held as a Hohenstaufen; while, on the other hand, the Hohenstaufens received the dignity of arch-carver or steward, when the remains of the duchy of Franconia passed over to their house. This office was then attached to the palatinate of the Rhine; and as, in ancient times, the duke of Franconia held the first rank among the temporal princes, so now, among the latter, the count palatine commanded the first voice.

We have already found that the office of grand cup-bearer was transferred from the Guelfs to the house of Bohemia; but with respect to that of grand marshal, it always remained with the Saxons. The right of Bohemia to a voice in the elections was a subject of long contest, inasmuch as the Germans would not admit the right of election to a Slavonic prince; and it was on this account that, at the period in question, the college of princes only possessed six votes: three ecclesiastical, consisting of those of the archbishops of Mentz, Treves, and Cologne, who, protected by the influence of the pope, were thus enabled to raise themselves to the highest rank in the empire; and three temporal votes, those of the dukes of Saxony, Brandenburg, and of the Palatinate.

3. In Swabia, we have seen that, at the fall of the Hohenstaufens, all their rights disappeared; their rich possessions had, in the latter period, been wasted or given away; and Conradin, at the time of his expedition to Italy, made over his remaining possessions to the house of Bavaria. We therefore naturally inquire who then, from that time, really ranked as the most important and influential family in Swabia? In answer to this, we find that the counts of Würtemberg stood at the head of all the rest of the nobility, and who had already chosen Stuttgard as their place of residence. After them, the rich counts of Baden, scions of the Hohenstaufen race, acquired from the house of Zähringen the territory of Breisgau, which was the commencement of the reign of the house of Baden. Another portion of the Zähringen inheritance, in Switzerland, fell to the counts of Kyburg, and after them to the counts of Hapsburg, who owed to this circumstance their subsequent importance. Of the counts of Hohenzollern, the burgraves of Nuremberg, we have spoken previously.

4. In Franconia, the duchy had already become extinct when the succession of the Salic house terminated. It had been divided equally between the ecclesiastical and temporal nobles; for the Hohenstaufens, who were called dukes of Franconia, possessed nothing of the authority of the ancient dukes; enjoying merely, as they were the most powerful lords of Franconia, and proprietors of the county-palatinate, a small portion of the ducal influence, and which was recognised by a few of those counts and knights who were dependent on them as feudatories. At the end of this period, besides the powerful counts palatine of the Rhine, we find in the ancient land of Franconia the landgraves of Hesse, who possessed a portion thereof, the counts of Nassau, the bishop of Würzburg, &c.

The general title of count palatine gradually vanished in Germany, leaving it only in the hands of the count palatine of the Rhine, while, on the other hand, the title of burgrave now came into use, and took rank immediately after that of the king.

5. Finally, with respect to Lorraine, it became divided into two portions: Upper Lorraine falling to the counts of Alsace, and Lower Lorraine to the counts of Lovain. They, however, did not possess the whole of Lorraine, and for this reason they were likewise styled counts of Brabant. Several other counts—of Holland, Zealand, Friesland, Juliers, Cleves, Guelder, Luxemburg, &c., ranked themselves as immediate imperial feudatories.

All the princes began now to consider themselves as feudatories, not only of the country of which they merely had the administration, but likewise of their hereditary lands, which they governed in their own name. Vassalage now received another meaning; it was no longer for their possessions, but their dignities, that the princes now held themselves bound to pay homage by the investiture; and as they had already raised themselves to the height of territorial power and sovereignty throughout their country—although they did not take to themselves the title—all the sovereign princes in the land became feudatories.

We will now proceed to give a sketch of the entire states existing in the empire, although we cannot pretend to present an exact detail thereof, on account of the confusion so prevalent in some of the dependencies.

Germany included, at this period, six archbishoprics; that of Mentz, (the most considerable and extensive,) having under its jurisdiction fourteen bishoprics, viz. Worms, Spires, Strasburg, Constance, Cour, Augsburg, Eichstadt, Würtzburg, Olmütz, Prague, Halberstadt, Hildesheim, Paderborn, and Verden; that of Cologne with five bishoprics—Liège, Utrecht, Münster, Osnaburg, and Minden; that of Treves with three bishoprics—Mentz, Toul, and Verdun; that of Magdeburg with five bishoprics—Brandenburg, Havelberg, Naumburg, Merseburg, and Meissen; that of Bremen with three bishoprics—Oldenburg, (afterwards Lübeck,) Mecklenburg, (afterwards Schwerin,) and Ratzburg; and, finally, that of Salzburg with five bishoprics—Ratisbon, Passau, Freisingen, Brixen, and Gurk. Besides which are to be added: Bamberg, which stood immediately under the pope, and Cambrai under the archbishop of Rheims. Altogether, therefore, they amounted to six archbishoprics and thirty-seven bishoprics. There existed, besides, seventy prelates, abbots, and abbesses, and three religious orders, thus forming, in the whole, more than a hundred ecclesiastical states.

The temporal estates were, viz.: four electors, (if we include Bohemia,) consisting of one king, one duke, one count palatine, and one margrave; six grand dukes—Bavaria, Austria, Carinthia, Brunswick, Lorraine, and Brabant-Limburg; about thirty counts with the title of prince, among whom some had also the title of duke, others of margrave, landgrave, and burgrave; about sixty imperial cities, of whom some, however, did not enjoy entirely the privileges of the imperial municipalities. Thus, altogether, these formed about a hundred temporal states; and, finally, both classes embraced more than two hundred members of the empire, spiritual and temporal.

Meantime, the dominion of the empire had, in certain respects, diminished in extent of government towards the end of the interregnum, inasmuch as it no longer held under its sway either Denmark, Hungary, or Poland; while Burgundy and Lombardy had both withdrawn themselves from the imperial rule, Prussia alone having joined in alliance.

We will now avail ourselves of this short interval, and cursorily review the chief features presented in the Middle Ages, which immediately succeed this period of the interregnum; for every thing that has been said, whether favorable or unfavorable, upon the character of this barbarous and yet glorious epoch, is especially appropriate at the present moment.

## CHAPTER XI.

### THE MIDDLE AGES.

Chivalry—The Cities—The Peasantry—The Arts and Sciences—The Clergy and Ecclesiastical Institutions—The Monasteries and Convents—The Faust-Recht—The Administration of Justice—The Vehm-Gericht or Secret Tribunal.

The period of the Middle Ages has also been called the period of Chivalry, and it was knighthood indeed which chiefly gave to it its great and peculiar lustre. By the diffusion of the feudal system over the whole of Germany, as has already been shown, the nobility became the influential portion of the empire, to the extent that, beyond the cities, few common freemen were to be found. War was conducted principally by the nobles and their vassals. The former fought only on horseback, were equipped in heavy iron armor, and were so inured to the exercise of arms from youth upward, that they could not only bear them with ease, but were enabled to use them freely and powerfully. A man thus encased in armor and arms, on horseback, was infinitely superior to the common warriors, who served on foot, and who were badly armed; and thence an army was speedily counted solely by the multitude of its knights. In order to maintain these privileges, the education of the nobility was necessarily entirely warlike. An ancient writer says—"The boys born in Germany, in their quality as pages, prefer learning to ride rather than to read; their horses may run and gallop as they please, still they remain immoveably fixed in the saddle. They carry after their lords their long lances; and inured to cold and heat, they are not to be fatigued by any toilsome exercise. The bearing of arms is as easy to the Germans as carrying their own limbs, and it is surprising, and almost incredible, how skilful they are in governing their horses, using their bows and arrows, and wielding the lance, shield, and sword."

By their exclusive attention to the improvement of their corporeal strength, while the intellectual occupations which in later centuries began to be treated as the chief portion of education were then entirely unknown, this generation must have sunk into a state of complete barbarism, had not the happy nature and noble capacities of the German races, and the development of the grand institutions of chivalry, produced a preponderating power by their beneficial effects. But in order to comprehend the details, it is necessary we should know more exactly the institutions of the middle ages.

These various grades of condition and rank were particularly distinguished by the changes introduced in military service from the time of Henry I.; for from that period the cavalry department especially underwent such reforms that, in the course of a short time, it came exclusively into the hands of the nobility and their own vassals, to the extent that the honor of this warlike arm of the service belonged to them alone. It was made to form two divisions or classes, the *Semper-freien*, or available freemen, (always free,) and the *Mittel-freien*, or mediate freemen. The former, who, in ancient times, consisted merely of the nobility, and were called *ingenui* in the codes of law, were the immediate nobility, which, after the dismemberment of the early duchies, retained their independence of every prince, and were only subjected to the empire. Of this class, the high clergy formed part, with this exception, however, that the nobility acquired by birth what the former received by their office.

The second class was composed of mediate freemen; firstly, of those freemen who were originally bound by their possessions to do service as cavaliers, but who could not disengage themselves from the authority of the princes, and were forced to follow them to the wars; and secondly, of those who were employed by the higher nobility of the empire, and who served as cavaliers under their orders with the title of *milites minores*. These mediate freemen very soon advanced their claims to titles of nobility, especially after Conrad II. had been the means of raising them to higher importance and consideration by making the lowest fiefs hereditary. Thus was created by degrees a higher and lower class of nobility.

But for both these grades it was strictly necessary that the descent of families should be from parents of equal rank; and in case of unequal unions, the children were forced to remain in the inferior condition of the one or the other parent.

The king, however, always retained the right of power to elevate any subject from this lower grade to the rank of a nobleman.

Thence the nobility formed two distinct classes from the moment that the art of war became wholly based upon its cavalry service; and it was in this sense that the knighthood already existed under the Saxon and Salian emperors. But it was not until the twelfth century that it formed itself into one especial institution, which served as a connecting link between the higher and lesser nobility, inasmuch as it thus brought into union by military and religious vows, and under especial discipline, *militaris ordo*, both the Semper-freie and Mittel-freie. The Crusades had the most important influence and shed the greatest lustre upon chivalry, for it was in the sacred service of God and the Saviour that the swords of the knights obtained for them the greatest glory on earth. The goal which was to be attained lay far distant from home, and in other climes; the imagination became more enthusiastically excited, and the descriptions given by such as had returned from those eastern countries were perfectly adapted to heighten and render still more vivid the glowing colors of the picture their heated fancy had already formed. Thence this period was inspired by such daring and fanatic enthusiasm, that no enterprise was deemed too difficult to undertake, and such heroic deeds were actually achieved, that in modern times they have been regarded almost in the light of fabulous creations of the mind. Three religious orders of knighthood, which owed their origin exclusively to the Crusades, served especially to attach the warriors to the cause of Christianity by a sacred and solemn vow. The first of these was the order of the Templar-Knights, which originally only consisted of a small body of French cavaliers, for the purpose of protecting the pilgrims on their journey to the Holy Land; they took the three religious vows—obedience, poverty, and chastity; adding a fourth, which was altogether military, viz. to protect travellers, *stratos publicas custodire*. Baldwin II., king of Jerusalem, granted them as quarters a portion of his palace, next to the temple of Solomon; and it is from this circumstance that they adopted the title of Templars. Two years afterwards originated the order of the Knights of the Hospital, who devoted themselves to the charge of the sick pilgrims, subsequently adopting the name of St. John, from their tutelary saint, John the Baptist; their vows were exclusively religious. To these followed shortly after the order of the Teutonic Knights.

These examples operated with a very great effect upon the continent; and as the entire spirit of the times produced a closer union between individuals of equal habits and condition, the result was that chivalry in the middle of the twelfth century became more and more extended, and formed one grand body of alliance, to which access could only be obtained after passing through certain ordeals in which the religious vows of chastity and poverty were, however, exempted, but religious consecration was retained.

Thus the entire education of the nobility connected itself with the sole object of attaining knighthood by passing through all its various gradations. As soon as the boy had escaped from his maternal guide, he was transferred to the charge of some esteemed knight and friend, whom he served as page; and, subsequently, after he had become versed in arms, and received his sword, he attended him as his esquire, (famulus, armiger,) regarding him as the model of his future life. He accompanied his lord at all hours, and in every occupation. In the pleasures of the chase, the festival, the tournament and military jousts, as well as in the dangers of the battle. His first duty was the most faithful attachment to and vigilant care of his lord; and if, in the heat of the battle, he had defended him with sword and shield, and had saved his life, he thence acquired the highest degree of fame that could be earned by a young nobleman. Thus fidelity was the first virtue which, by hourly and daily exercise, became so deeply impressed upon the memory of the youth, that it grew up in indissoluble connection with his mind. After several years of honorable service as a squire, the youth (generally in his twenty-first year) was made a knight, and received into military companionship under the consecration of religion. Solemn occasions, grand festivals, coronation days, and such scenes, were diligently sought for the purpose, and frequently many were dubbed knights at the same time. Fasting and prayer preceded, and after the youth had partaken of the sacrament he received from the hands of a knight, or noble lady, the spurs, breast-plate, and gauntlets. He then knelt down, and one of the knights (often, however, the reigning king or prince) gave him, with a naked sword, three gentle blows across the shoulder, upon which he vowed with a solemn oath, to faithfully fulfil all the duties of an honorable knight, to speak the truth, to defend the laws, and to draw his sword for the defence of religion, of widows and orphans, and of persecuted innocence, but, above all, against every unbeliever; finally, he received the helmet, shield, lance, and sword. Thus, in the most inspired hour of the youth's early career, the practice of manly virtues: truth, justice, and religion, were again, by solemn oath, elevated to become the inviolable law of his whole life. Honor stood before the eyes of the youthful knight like a brilliant star—an emblem to which he was to remain faithful to his last breath—as the noble object of, and, at the same time, the reward for the due observance of the oath he took. So highly was this solemn consecration of the noble warrior esteemed, that Count William of Holland, as we have already seen in his history, was necessarily made a knight before his coronation.

The prerogative of the knight was to belong henceforward to a select body of his equals, which none could join but by the especial reception he himself had experienced, and to be enabled to confer knighthood himself; as also to take his share in the tournaments, which in the twelfth century were introduced from France into Germany. These had the most important influence on the education of the nobility; for as none could take part in them whose honor had suffered the least stain, and the whole imagination of the boy and youth was from earliest infancy devoted to the glory and high reputation these contests conferred, chivalry thenceforth became the school of honor and morality, as well as of every other heroic virtue. Thence this period presents us with the most complete and undeniable evidence of the principle—that in order to disseminate a love for virtue in a generation, it is not enough to try to promote it by instruction, but it is likewise necessary to encourage and give an impulse to the practice thereof by the irresistible force of example.

Such is the light in which the design and object of chivalry must present itself before us in the most flourishing period of its existence; for although a system may not be carried out so completely as to render it possible to say, that it is in every respect perfect, and, consequently, although in the most happy times of chivalry, much barbarism and uncouth violence too often appeared, still it cannot be denied that it laid the foundation for that elevation of thought which eventually, in a moral point of view, exercised its influence upon the community at large.

The noble institution of chivalry was, in fact, of the highest importance in its results to the whole of the Christian nations, inasmuch as even when the imperial dignity lost its powerful influence, and the authority of the church began to totter on its base, the principles of honor and rectitude, together with the irresistible force commanded by the manly, chivalric word, in all cases of need and succor, operated so beneficially upon all classes, that this grand and illustrious foundation of knighthood served as a tower of strength, impregnable against all subsequent attacks attempted by uncivilized and barbarous assailants.

While the aristocracy of the German nation thus vigorously cultivated itself, and wore the sword equally for the honor of their faith and defence of their country, the citizens in the towns labored with industry and activity for their commercial prosperity. The German cities during this period daily increased in population and riches, and the source of all was commerce, for which also the crusades operated very advantageously. The spirit for great undertakings and speculations was aroused, the costly wares of southern countries were brought more frequently and in greater abundance to Europe. The Italian maritime cities, particularly Venice, Genoa, and Pisa, introduced the merchandise of the east, and then it was conveyed the same as the produce of Italy itself along the ancient commercial roads, through the passes of the Alps to Germany, there extending its transit upon the high roads and rivers, and what was not consumed in the country itself was carried still farther towards the territories bordering upon the North Sea and the Baltic. All that was brought to the northern countries from across the ocean was forwarded through Germany, and by means of this extensive commercial agency, to which was added the produce of native German industry, the ancient cities of the empire progressed and flourished in all their wealth and prosperity. Augsburg, Strasburg, Ratisbon, Nuremberg, Bamberg, Worms, Spires, and Mentz, in the south of Germany; in the north, Cologne, Erfurt, Brunswick, Lüneburg, Hamburg, Bremen, and Lübeck, and many others proudly raised and extended their walls and towers, and an increasing and active, but equally industrious population, animated their streets. Their riches soon gave them the means to purchase their freedom and independence from the princes who held them in dominion, for as in those ancient times, when but few or no regular imposts were levied, the privileges of those princes and lords were not so productive as now, no large sum was required to obtain this emancipation. The cities then acknowledged the emperor alone as their superior feudal lord, and thence were called free imperial cities.

This progress, however, was only made by degrees, and was not everywhere attended with the same favorable results. The first step was made in the tenth century, when Henry I. encouraged the foundation and extension of cities, and improved their internal condition in eastern Germany, and when afterwards the episcopal cities in the south and western parts of the country, according to the ancient Roman cities, were raised to a state of immunity, and the authority of the count was substituted by that of the episcopal intendant, or *advocatus casæ*. After their example, a number of other cities received also imperial governors, and were thus freed from the jurisdiction of the count.

Subsequently the cities advanced still farther, and sought to elevate themselves from their state of immunity, in order to become their own governors; for the intendants, replacing the counts in their quality as judges, selected their assessors from the municipal council, who, previous to the twelfth century, were called *cives*, in its more distinguished acceptation, and later, in imitation of the Lombardian cities, they were styled *consules*, or counsellors; and their president, *proconsul*, or *magister consolum*, burgomaster. Those families among whom the counsellors were usually chosen, formed a civic or urban nobility, and were called patrician families. As this council was intrusted with the administration of the commercial property and the magisterial authority of the city, it is easy to conceive what increasing influence it must have had at its command, and how it must have extended its power in the administration of affairs beyond, as well as within the city, and the burgomaster, consequently, in the course of time, left little or nothing for the intendant to perform. In fact, this latter functionary in the end had reason to congratulate himself if he was only allowed to retain the administration of justice; and, even then, means were not wanting on the part of the council to arrogate this department to themselves when they found it favorable for their object to do so.

But the authority did not rest exclusively in the hands of the council; the various guilds and trade associations had also their share in the government. Their influence derived strength from the increasing activity among the industrial and working classes, and consequent prosperity in trade; and thence their claims to a portion of power they enjoyed were based upon the interest they took and shared individually and among themselves in the municipal institutions. The extent to which they gradually succeeded in establishing their united dominion is made evident by their generally triumphant contests with the patrician families in many of the cities.

If commerce and gain had alone been the objects of the inhabitants of the cities, they would soon have become subject to all those evils which necessarily arise when the mind of man becomes wholly occupied and absorbed in his mercenary pursuits; the citizens would have been rendered timid and cowardly, and would have sacrificed both their liberty and pride in their efforts after worldly possessions. But in those times, when the Faustrecht or club-law existed in all its violence, they found opposed to them the entire nobility of the empire—princes, counts, and knights, as well as bishops and abbots, who, jealous of the riches of the cities, closely observed their deeds and acts, and waited only for an opportunity to overturn and destroy their freedom.

If the cities, therefore, desired to submit no longer to these powerful enemies, they found they must necessarily bear arms themselves, and preserve inviolate in their breasts that manly courage which is the shield of freedom. In an ancient chronicle we find the following account of the Nuremberg patricians: "The furniture of their houses consists chiefly of gold and silver, but amidst all that meets the eye nothing is more conspicuous than their swords, armor, battle-axes, and horses, which they particularly display as the chief signs of their nobility, and the ancient rank of their families. But the simple citizen also keeps his arms ready and in good order in his house, so that on the first movement he may appear fully equipped immediately at the appointed place of assembly." The whole of the internal regulations of the city had war in view; the citizens were divided into companies according to their trade and dwelling-place; and when the city was in danger, each of the different bodies assembled in its appointed quarter, and under its particular banner, and thus all marched forth together, and fought united in battle. This was a beautiful union, firmly bound by warlike and peaceful occupations, and the rivalry and emulation evinced by all in valor have frequently obtained the victory for cities in time of danger. The citizens collectively did not lose their time in a love for petty things and trifles, nor in the effeminacy of a sedentary life in the close rooms of their houses, but they were both in body and soul good men and true, as well as independent. And, notwithstanding their riches, notwithstanding their extraordinary expenditure upon great festivals, which honor demanded in those more ancient and better times, their daily ordinary life was very simple and temperate, and not sophisticated by artificial wants. Thence their bodies remained strong, and their prosperity lasting; for the source and guarantee of prosperity do not so much consist in rich acquisitions as in that moderation which knows how to preserve them. "That the Germans are rich," says Machiavelli, in his treatise, *Ritratti della Alamagna*, "arises from their living as if they were poor. It suffices for them to have a superfluity in bread and meat, and a room, whither they may retreat from the cold. Thus little or no money quits their country; on the contrary, far more comes into the land in payment for the wares they manufacture themselves. The power of Germany is based upon its cities; they are the nerves of the provinces, for in them there exist both wealth and good order."

At this glorious period of the municipal institutions, many German cities united together for the protection of their freedom, their independence, and their commerce generally. Thus, in the year 1254, seventy cities in the south of Germany formed the Rhenish league, for offence and defence, and powerfully opposed themselves to the encroachments and pretensions of the nobility. Afterwards arose the Swabian cities'-union, which was also very numerous and strong.

But the most powerful confederation among all was that of the Hanse towns. Already early in the middle ages, the trading cities of Germany had formed alliances in the large commercial towns of other countries, and there established warehouses and factories. These factories bore the name of Hanse, probably from the word Hansa, which signifies trade imposts, (confounded subsequently with the Italian word *Ansaria*,) and as several such houses were united in foreign cities, there consequently arose a general Hanse, which was termed German Hanse. Very early we find in London, German Hanses from Cologne, Hamburg, Lübeck, Bremen, and other cities, and, perhaps, their union was a chief cause for the establishment of the whole alliance. In the history of its formation also it is important to notice the league which in 1241 the cities of Lübeck and Hamburg concluded together, and which is commonly but incorrectly considered as the first commencement of the whole confederation. It was agreed that both cities should prepare ships and supply troops to protect from all robbery the highway between the Trave and the Elbe, and the rivers themselves, down which both sent their merchandise to the sea. Several northern cities soon joined this alliance; about the year 1300 it numbered already sixty cities from the Lower Rhine as far as Prussia and Livonia; later it included as many as a hundred, and in the middle of the fourteenth century we find the name Hansa universally distributed. In Germany there belonged to it, besides Lübeck and Hamburg—Bremen, Stade, Kiel, Wismar, Rostock, Stralsund, Greifswalde, Stettin, Colberg, Stargard, Salzwedel, Magdeburg, Brunswick, Hildesheim, Hanover, Lüneburg, Osnaburg, Münster, Coesfeld, Dortmund, Soest, Wesel, Duisburg, Cologne, and many others besides; and out of Germany—Thorn, Dantzig, Königsberg, Riga, Reval, Narva, Whisby, Stockholm, &c. They wholly monopolized the trade in the Baltic, and chiefly that in the North Sea, and had four grand depots: at Novogorod in Russia, Bergen in Norway, Bruges in Flanders, and in London.

The establishment of these emporia called forth the greatest possible development in trade, and produced the most glorious results in commercial intercourse. From the northern regions they shipped timber for building vessels, flax, hemp, tar, furs, and smoked and dried fish, the consumption of which was extremely great on account of the rigorous observance of the periods for fasting practised by the Catholics; and they maintained the herring fishery exclusively in their own hands. From England they procured raw wool and cloths, which they had dyed and prepared in Germany. Bruges at this epoch was one of the most important of the commercial cities, and formed a depot for the merchandise of Asia, Italy, and Western Europe, which the Hanseatic towns conveyed thence to the north of Europe: spices of every sort, silks, gold and silver wares, fruit, &c. This traffic exercised, likewise, the most happy influence upon the sale of the produce of Germany: linen, cloth, metal wares, corn, flour, beer, Rhenish wine, and woad, (so much sought for before the introduction of indigo, and much planted in Germany,) and many other articles which, by means of the Hanse, found a market in foreign countries. It is, therefore, not surprising that when uniting its strength the confederation was richer and more powerful than the northern kingdoms. It was enabled to collect together whole fleets and armies whenever it chose, even if only a portion of the cities united, and its friendship was universally sought. It forced King Philip IV. of France to forbid the English all traffic on his coast, and obliged England to purchase peace for 10,000*l.* sterling. It conquered, in 1369, even Copenhagen and Helsengoer, commanding the mouth of the Sound, and offered the kingdom of Denmark for sale; to such an extent did it hold the northern kingdoms generally in its dependence, and the city of Lübeck might well be proud of being the head of such an alliance. It was divided into four classes: 1. The Wendish, of which Lübeck was particularly the head; 2. The Westphalian, with Cologne at its head, (Cologne emulated Lübeck for precedency; it carried on an extensive commerce by sea, and founded in London a celebrated German factory; its maritime commerce, however, fell when Dortrecht received its oppressive staple-right;) 3. The Saxon, of which Brunswick was the head; and 4. The Prussian and Livonian, with Dantzig at the head.

Many records testify how extensive and populous the cities were precisely at a time when violence through the Faustrecht raged most wildly. In the fourteenth century, for instance, Aix-la-Chapelle had 19,826 men who could bear arms, and Strasburg 20,000 more; Nuremberg had 52,000 citizens; and increased annually by 4000 male born children. Upon a revolt of the citizens of Lübeck, the council alone armed 5000 merchants and their servants. And besides these and other large places Germany was covered with a multitude of towns of middling size, which likewise flourished in trade and population, but which now retain only the shadow of their former importance; as, for instance, the many imperial cities in Swabia.

Æneas Sylvius, (afterwards Pius II.,) in the fifteenth century, speaks with great admiration of the riches of the German cities, although even then their splendor began to sink: "The kings of Scotland might envy," he says, "the state of the meaner citizens of Nuremberg. Where is there a tavern among you where you do not drink out of silver? What married woman, I will not say of rank, but the wife of merely a simple citizen, do we not find decorated with gold? What shall I say of the neck-chains of the men, and the bridles of the horses, which are made of the purest gold, and of the spurs and scabbards, which are covered with jewels?"

The source of such especial riches in precious metals, possessed by Germany, originated not only in the commerce, but also in the recently discovered mines of the country. In the year 1477, for instance, when Duke Albert of Saxony dined in the mine of Schneeberg, in the Hartz mountains, the viands were laid out upon a solid block of silver, whence afterwards 400 quintals of silver were produced.

The flourishing state and increasing power of the German cities was also a chief motive for the peasantry to recover their freedom; for the inhabitants also of the rural districts, who, under the oppression of slavery, were obliged to cultivate their own land, as serfs, for a master, at the view of the flourishing free cities were aroused to the love of liberty and independence, and when this desire is once properly reawoke in an enslaved people, it rests no more until it has cast its oppressive and degrading burden from its shoulders. Not that the gradual rise of the rural population is to be attributed to one source only, but, on the contrary, as in this case, it must be a consequence of the collective working of many causes, which here earlier, there later, supplied an individual, a family, or a whole community with freedom and possession of the soil. In this view also the crusades now produced the most important and beneficial results.

By command of the pope, every serf who took the cross to proceed into the Holy Land was obliged to be made free by his lord, and thousands of them proceeded thither and became free accordingly. In other cases, the lord, previous to setting out upon the crusade, animated by pious zeal, gave his serfs their freedom at once, or perhaps he did not return at all; and if he had no heirs, many of his feudal servitors, in the consequent dispute for the inheritance, faithful until then, now made themselves free. This method of disfranchisement was the more easily put into effect when they belonged to a noble, and if they dwelt near large cities. For they put themselves under the protection of the latter, and continued to live within their walls, or remained upon their own inheritance, and were called then Pfahlbürger or suburban citizens, and in case their lord sought to force them to return to his service, it became the affair of the powerful city itself, and even of the entire league to which it belonged.

It is not to be denied, that under such circumstances many cities in their municipal arrogance were unjust towards their noble neighbors, inasmuch as they, without having one justifying cause, received and harbored their subjects in opposition to him; but what incited them chiefly to do this was the recollection of the injustice which these lords or their predecessors had done to them—for injustice provokes injustice—or they were perhaps at open variance with them, and they thought they were justified in injuring them in every way. When now the nobles saw themselves in danger of thus losing all their subjects, one after the other, if they persisted in retaining them in their service by force, they preferred emancipating them themselves, under certain conditions, for lighter services and a fixed yearly impost. Finally, many from a kindliness of disposition, and influenced by the enlightenment of the period, may possibly have seen that it was more honorable as well as more lucrative, to cause their land to be cultivated by free laborers, who in the feeling that they were toiling for themselves and their descendants, now devoted all their powers of mind and body to that occupation which formerly as slaves they were forced to be driven to perform.

It was in this manner, particularly at the period of which we now speak, that by a hundred different causes, a basis was laid in Germany for the establishment of the important class of common free peasantry, which by degrees became the fundamental strength of the more modern states of Europe.

When man is raised to a certain degree of prosperity, in which his mind is no longer absorbed in acquiring the more immediate and pressing means to satisfy the necessary cares and wants of life, he then applies and devotes the powers of his genius towards producing the beautiful and grand—to that, the creation of which must shed over his whole life and memory, an enduring halo of glory and honor—and accordingly all those gifts of intellectual greatness are promoted by their cultivation, and enjoy the free independent action they demand. Thence the cities with their increasing riches necessarily became the cradle of German art and science; to which the excitement of the imagination, and the impulse which the crusades produced in all minds, contributed not a little. Ideas both novel and of vast and extraordinary character spread over the world, elevated the powers of the mind beyond the ordinary condition of life, and filled it with images which it found itself excited to represent and embody in beautiful productions of art. If we had no other evidence of the splendor of the middle ages than that displayed in the works of art of all kinds which that period has handed down to us, we should even then have ample proof wherewith to refute those opinions which, without any modification, pronounce that epoch to have been dark, barbarous, and miserable. A period of ignorance and calamity could not have produced such sublime works as the minsters of Strasburg, Vienna, and Ulm, together with the cathedrals of Cologne, Magdeburg, Spires, Freiburg, and so many other churches in the cities of Germany and the Low Countries. For art flourishes solely in the light of freedom and in the genial warmth of prosperity and human happiness.

We have here taken our examples from architecture, because there is scarcely any other art which, like this, so peculiarly expresses the genuine German genius. What we call Gothic architecture,—and which would be better expressed with the general name of the nation, Teutonic architecture—is a combination of the greatest boldness and sublimity of idea, produced by religious inspiration and deep natural feeling, with the most admirable industry and perfection in the execution of the detail. In the contemplation of those wonderful structures, our heart swells and the breast expands with reverential awe and emotion; we become completely lost, and forget ourselves in the presence of so much grandeur, while we feel as we continue gazing as if with those bold ideas our mind was conveyed upward towards heaven, leaving its earthly infirmities behind it—such is precisely the expression which characterizes the truly sublime and grand in all the creations of nature, as also in the works of man. And when the eye, after it has recovered from this first and overpowering impression of the whole, contemplates the detail, it observes that there is scarcely a solitary stone throughout the gigantic edifice which is introduced in its rough state, but each bears some artistical labor which makes it share in the embellishment of the whole. Thus it might be almost said, that as in the works of the wide creation itself there is not a blade of grass but possesses its own peculiar beauty and ornament, and this blade with its millions of semblant companions, combined with the trees, rocks, and lakes, present a rich and magnificent picture of nature—so, likewise, these works of German industry and art, faithful in the detail, and sublime in the idea of the whole, are in this union of both, objects surpassed by no other nation. We will only remark of the Minster of Strasburg, that it has the loftiest tower in Europe, being 594 feet high. Bishop Werner began to lay the foundation of the church in 1015, but it was not completed until 1275. After which the eminent architect, Erwin of Steinbach, sketched the plan of the tower in 1277; this was begun and completed in 1439 by John Hulz, of Cologne, so that 424 years were consumed in the entire construction. Of the Cathedral of Cologne, which in its design, commenced by archbishop Conrad, of Hochstedt, in 1248, is still more noble, not even the church itself, not to name its tower, has been completed, although its construction has lasted 250 years. But we shall not wonder at this, when we consider the thousands of images which are carved in the stone.*

It tends to the eternal fame of our nation and of those times that the industry, patience, and outlay of capital so necessary for the construction of such works were not spared, while later generations have but too often wasted their powers upon undertakings which have left no trace behind.

In order to comprehend the origin, and especially the successful execution of those miracles of architecture, according to one great plan, we must remark that it was not individual architects, who, with sometimes good, sometimes bad workmen, as in our times, undertook such works, but they were accomplished by an association of masons, distributed over the whole of Germany, and indeed over the whole of Europe, who were bound together by religion, honor, and discipline. Even among the Romans there were building societies of great extent, the remaining members of which retired to the monasteries, and there occupied themselves chiefly with the construction of churches, and created the more sublime style of Christian architecture. Regular but temporal builders were also received into the society, and when, in the eleventh century, the vigor of the monachal system began to slumber in the indolence and satiety of acquired riches, these temporal builders obtained by degrees the superiority, and eventually formed the grand associations by means of which those wonderful works were executed. They possessed and followed mysterious signs and customs, by which the members of the body forming the class of the more sublime architecture were distinguished from the more simple artisans. Every society had its protecting patron, from whom it was named; and wherever a grand undertaking was to be executed, they all came from their various districts and assembled on the spot, so that their art, like a common possession, was beneficially distributed throughout most Christian countries. These important societies received from the reigning emperor and princes letters of license, and even their own exclusive judicial courts, at which the chief architect presided as judge. Close to the spot on which was to be erected the large building they were engaged upon, and which edifice perhaps took centuries to construct, a wooden house or *Hütte* was generally built, neatly adorned inside, in which the said chief architect, with the sword of justice in his hand, sat under a canopy and pronounced

* It is, however, gratifying to observe as one among the many existing signs of the progress made in our time in the fine arts, that the completion of this noble edifice has been recently determined and commenced upon.

judgment. This hütte or courthouse, in Strasburg, derived a peculiar importance during the period of the construction of the minster. It was soon regarded as the most distinguished among all in Germany; its institutions were imitated, and the other courthouses frequently derived counsel and decision from it.*

But the noble principle of these associations ended with the decline of the general spirit of the middle ages. The great architectural undertakings ceased; the energies of men were divided in all directions. War monopolized so entirely the resources of states, that for great monuments of art but little more could be done, as will be more particularly developed as we proceed in the course of our history.

Painting was also zealously practised for the decoration of churches and other holy places, and our old cities are full of splendid specimens of this art. German art in its entire character is grave, chaste, and moral, abounding with depth of thought and expression, like the nation itself. In the figures of the holy apostles and saints, as well as of pious men and women generally, who are represented in devout contemplation and prayer, we find expressed the profound sublimity of thought and sentiment which would be vainly sought for in the works of art produced by any other nation, although they may, and do possess a superiority in finish, richness of color, and skilfully-deceptive representation. In their pictures, also, the Germans display that untiring industry which does not consider it too trifling to carefully represent, with truth and fidelity, the smallest and most minute decorations of the walls, furniture, or garments. It is true that painting attained its culminating point much later, and the names of the most celebrated German and Flemish painters, who worked in the same spirit, belong to the fifteenth and sixteenth centuries; although in earlier times, and by masters whose names are unknown, splendid pictures of subjects taken from sacred history were executed for the churches. The most celebrated of the later artists were John Van Eyck, of Bruges, who died in 1441, and who is considered as the inventor of oil painting; his countrymen, Hans (John) Hemling, Martin Schön of Culmbach, in Franconia, Michael Wohlgemuth of Nuremberg, but above all others Albert Dürer, who was born in 1471 and died in 1521, and whose works are characterized by vigorous feeling and profound seriousness of expression; and, finally, Lucas Cranach, who was born in 1470, and died in 1553.

As a third art in the list of the middle ages, poetry was one which particularly flourished in the time of the Swabian emperors. This derived its vigor from the inspiration of the whole period of the crusades, and was in high estimation among the higher and lower classes. The celebrated singers who knew how to elevate the hearts of men by their songs of the great deeds of ancient heroes, or by their tender lays of lament—here and there, however, refreshed by encouraging and energetic strains—were hospitably welcomed at every festival, and, richly rewarded, proceeded from the courts of emperors, princes, and counts, to flourishing cities, throughout the whole of Germany. Sometimes a contest of art was instituted, similar to those wherein the knights disputed for the prize of arms, and, before an assembly of selected and competent judges, songs resounded of the most inspiring and admirable nature. Some of the most celebrated poets and troubadours of this period are Henry of Vildeck, about 1170, Wolfram of Eschenbach, Hartman of the Aue, Henry of Ofterdingen, Godfrey of Strasburg, Walter of the Vogelweide, and Conrad of Würzburg. But also emperors, princes, and noble knights themselves practised poetry. All the Hohenstaufens from Frederick I. have left us poems, besides Margrave Otho with the Arrow, of Brandenburg, Duke Henry of Breslaw, Henry of Meissen, Duke John of Brabant, Count Rodolph of Neuenburg, Kraft of Toggenburg, and many others. One of the greatest and most splendid collections of German poems is that of the *Niebelungen* or Legends of Chivalry, which although not originally composed in this period, still at that time was collected together and formed into one entire work; a poem as sublime and grand as it is sweet and touching, and may be justly compared with the Homeric lays themselves. The *Heldenbuch*,

* After Strasburg came, in 1681, under the dominion of France, all connection between this principal *Hütte* and the others of Germany gradually ceased to exist; and the consequent disputes which arose between these latter on the subject of each other's claims to superiority were eventually put an end to in 1731 by an imperial decree, by which all distinctions of privilege between these associations and the common class of architects were abolished.

or great book of heroes, which is derived from the Swabian period, likewise contains the most beautiful poems; and, about the year 1300, a counsellor of Zürich, Rüdger of Manesse, collected the metrical lays of one hundred and forty *Minnesingers*, or troubadours.

In the sciences, the period of the middle ages cannot, probably, be compared with those of later times, however superior, on the other hand, it may rank in the fine arts, inasmuch as the sciences are a fruit of serious reflection and of long experience, and one age can build upon the foundation laid by a preceding one; while art, on the contrary, is more a free blossom of nature, and a work of happy inspiration, being not so much the result of deep research as it is of the impressions aroused by an excited epoch. The sciences, however, were not despised, but, on the contrary, zealously promoted by the Hohenstaufen emperors. When Otho, bishop of Freisingen, handed to the emperor Frederick I. his Chronicles, the emperor said: "I receive with extreme pleasure the chronicles which you have compiled so wisely in such good order, and which, hitherto obscured and concealed, you have brought to light and harmonized; and I rejoice always, when freed from the labors of war, to read them, for I guide myself to excellence by the splendid deeds of the emperors." We have already seen in the life of the emperor Frederick II. how much he esteemed science. And although herein his care was directed chiefly to his Italian states and universities, yet we must take into consideration its subsequent reaction upon Germany; for all that we trace proves that Germany itself was occupied in the most active development of science and art. No period of the middle ages can in this respect be compared with that of the Hohenstaufens. The mind of Frederick II., without doubt, worked both powerfully and effectually among us for the promotion of this object.

Science, at this period, was chiefly confined to the ecclesiastical body, the members of which, by their state of indepen dence, were called to be its true preservers. It has been customary to consider monasteries as the seat of indolence and ignorance, hypocrisy and sensuality, and, in fact, of many other vices. But this is an unjust opinion, confounding the thing itself with its abuse; and what, in the course of years, by the change of all things, was forced to pass away, has been at the same time wholly misunderstood in its earlier and more active form. In times when rude force held its sway in the world, and every one who could not defend himself was obliged to succumb, or was cast to the ground, the cloisters were places of refuge and retreat for thousands of men, who found therein, not only desirable asylums for security and repose, but also that necessary leisure for the calm and contemplative occupations of the mind, which silently and progressively produced the sciences. Without the monasteries, we should have possessed but little of the treasures of ancient literature, which they chiefly preserved for us; indeed, but for them we should know almost nothing of our earlier records, and possess but a very meager and brief history of the events of former times. Before the invention of printing, it was so difficult and laborious to multiply copies of works, that without the leisure and the industry of the monks in cloisters, who, with astonishing and admirable patience, transcribed entire works in elaborate characters and with illuminated letters, almost all traces would have been lost of the primitive and the middle ages. Besides which, the authors of nearly all the historical works were clergymen. Their names have been mentioned at the commencement of this period, and when we read their productions, we must be filled with equal esteem and admiration for the ecclesiastics of the middle ages.

The warlike spirit of that epoch, however, had an important effect upon the manners of the clergy. Christian, the archbishop of Mentz, who was frequently at the head of the armies of Frederick I., in his expeditions to Italy, and conducted the very obstinate siege of Ancona, in 1174, was as valiant a warrior as he was a zealous priest and skilful statesman. He could speak six languages—the German, Latin, French, Brabant, Greek, and Italian. When, as a clergyman, he stood before the altar, he was the true representative of the minister of peace, in full priestly dignity; but when, again, he was mounted on his warlike steed, he displayed an equally commanding and elevated mien as a leader of the church militant. Under his sacerdotal robe he wore a coat of iron armor, upon his head a splendid helmet of gold, and in his hand a massive three-edged club. It is related of him that, in the different battles in which he fought, he killed nine enemies with his own hand.

The monasteries, of the importance of which for the middle ages we have already spoken, merit here still closer observation. They owe their first origin to that pious spirit which prizes, by far, the heavenly above all earthly possessions; and which, by severe self-denial, repentance, and mortification, in all sensual gratifications, seeks to make itself worthy of the blessings of a purer life. At first, minds thus tutored sought to fly from the tumult of the world, and retired into solitary and isolated places; and when several thus disposed were collected together, they united themselves into brotherhoods, with the resolution of practising, in a body, similar penance and mortification. Thus those holy men, Antonius and Pachonius, founded in this manner, in the middle of the fourth century, in the deserts of Upper Egypt, the first monasteries. By degrees, their example was followed in several places; and also in Europe monasteries were founded, after the holy Athanasius brought the first monks from Egypt into Rome.

In the commencement of the sixth century, (515,) St. Benedict, of Nursia, gave, by the rule he formed for his monastery at Monte Cassino, and which was everywhere followed, an entire new form to monastic life; and this monastery, seated upon a high mountain in the most beautiful part of Lower Italy, may be considered as the model of all the others in western Christendom. It has existed and operated during a space of thirteen hundred years, and above thirty popes, and a great number of cardinals, bishops, and ecclesiastics of the highest rank, have sprung from the order of Benedictines. Everywhere now arose monasteries; partly because active monks settled themselves in previously uncultivated districts, made them arable, and thus acquired a right to the land around; partly because emperors, kings, and princes, the high clergy, and noble families, as a pleasing work to God, built abbeys, and endowed them with the ground upon which they were erected. Monasteries also arose in cities and villages, and cities formed and settled themselves around monasteries. The enthusiastic zeal excited in ancient times for a monastic life, and the donations which these institutions received, are incredible; the monastery of Ebersberg, in Austria, alone received, as many as two hundred and twenty-eight such gifts. It was thought that no better use could be made of earthly possessions, than to give them to a monastery; and the monks had, besides, at sick-beds, opportunities enough to foster and maintain this opinion. Economical management, and cheap and advantageous purchases made at a convenient time, augmented these possessions, and especially so at the period of the crusades. The nobles who were not able to command the necessary means for the expeditions to those distant countries, sold their estates, or borrowed money upon them; and if they did not return, or could not pay back what they had borrowed, the property remained in the hands of the monastery. Subsequently too, in the time of violence or the Faustrecht, many freemen gave themselves up, together with their possessions, into the hands of the monasteries, to enjoy their protection. And finally, the monasteries received from the pope, in the thirteenth century, the privilege to retain for their own possession, the bequeathed property of the deceased relatives of the brethren—a productive source of wealth; while, likewise, it was made into a law, that neither nuns nor monks could ever bequeath any thing to a third party, but were forced to leave their whole inheritance to the monastery they belonged to. The cloisters even bestowed upon many rich persons the title of monk, in order to inherit their property, and permitted them afterwards to live beyond the monastery, the same as before. If we consider all this, it is very easy to comprehend how the convents, by degrees, acquired such large, and some even immense riches. The example produced stimulation, and their number increased incredibly. St. Bernard, of Clairvaux, who lived at the period of the second grand crusade, founded alone one hundred and sixty, and some cities contained even several hundred monasteries.

The urgency displayed by applicants to be received in them was extraordinary; many sought admission from a true spontaneous impulse of the soul, many in order to find the means of living, and, lastly, many were persuaded and forced into them.

by their relatives. It is true, in order to remedy and prevent this latter abuse, the canon law forbid expressly that any one should be forced to take the vow, either by imprisonment or any other measure of compulsion; besides which, it was ordained that a year's novitiate should always precede taking the habit; and, finally, that no male should take the vow of monk before his fourteenth year, nor any female before her twelfth year; but this age was evidently too early, for many certainly took the vow without knowing what they were doing. Many orders fixed, also, a more advanced age.

The occupation of the lay brothers, according to the rule of St. Benedict, consisted in agricultural labor, the sciences, instruction of youth, transcribing of books, attendance on the sick, and the exercise of prayer and religious worship. Their mode of life was very severe, their dress very simple, while their food was restricted to merely the most necessary diet, and frequent fasting was strictly enjoined. Later orders, which took that rule as their foundation, but increased its severity, imposed upon their members the most rigid penances, including corporeal castigation. The order of the Carthusians, which was founded by a German, St. Bruno, previously a canon at Rheims, in an inhospitable and desert valley near Grenoble, was considered the most severe. Their raiment consisted not only of a rough hair skin worn next the flesh, as in many of the other orders, but the rule commanded expressly that it should be a prickly one; and they were forbidden any covering for the head or the use of shoes and stockings. They fasted three times in the week, and during the eight holy weeks they took nothing but bread and water, while fat of all kinds, butter, oil, &c., were wholly prohibited. The religious exercises were not interrupted either by night or day, and solitude and melancholy silence increased the rigidness of this mode of life. And yet who could believe that notwithstanding this severity of the order, it numbered, two hundred years after its origin, no less than two hundred and eleven monasteries and nunneries? Such examples may serve us as a proof that the spirit of monastic life, far from being in contradiction with the manners, was much rather a necessary feature of that age. Their subsequent degeneration into worldly views, and the whole changed spirit of the period, must not cause the judgment of history to err in its consideration of the origin of these institutions.

The head of the monastery, to whom a blind and unconditional obedience belonged, was the abbot; under him stood next the prior, then the deacon, the butler, the steward, the cantor, &c. In the convents there were under the abbess similar female dignities. But every convent of nuns had a prior for religious worship, for preaching, confession, &c., because these functions could not be transferred to women. Lay-brothers were also found in monasteries, who, without having taken the entire vow of monks, attended to the external business of the monastery, in order that the others might not be obliged to quit the cloister or enclosed space of the monastery.

The monasteries, according to the ancient order of church government, stood originally under the jurisdiction of the archbishops and bishops of the diocese, and the abbots were consecrated by them; they gave permission for the foundation of those institutions, authorized donations, the purchase and sale of land, &c. But ambition and a desire for greater independence became excited by degrees in the cloisters; they soon wished to be dependent only upon the popes, and the latter were not unwilling to increase in this manner their immediate and extended influence. The same as with the cities in Germany and Italy, who sought to make themselves free from the domination of princes, and would only be subject to the emperor, so it was with the cloisters, with respect to the bishops and the pope. With the temporal clergy also, the patrons and curators, the monasteries by degrees stood in direct opposition. Originally they had nothing to do with the cure of souls. Shortly, however, many individuals turned to the monastery to confess, to have children christened, &c. The clergy complained of it, and several popes prohibited these incursions upon the diocese. But in the course of time the monks, by the favor of the bishops, and subsequently of the popes, gained in this respect also greater freedom, and exercised the clerical duties in a far more extended circle around them.

A third great extension of their power originated in the circumstance, that from the tenth century the previously solitary standing monasteries became gradually united into large societies or congregations, belonging to the different principal orders. In the year 910, arose that of Cluny, from the monastery of that name in Burgundy, founded by St. Odo ; in 1018, that of the Camaldulensians, by Romuald ; in 1086, that of the Carthusians ; in 1098, that of the Cistercians ; in 1122, that of the Premontratensians, &c. These orders received from the chief monastery one common central and superior direction. All monasteries sent their deputies to the chief assembly held in this head cloister, and here their common affairs were deliberated upon and arranged, and resolutions fixed. The abbot of this head cloister, to whom the remaining abbots vowed obedience, was charged with the execution of these regulations, inspected the cloisters, regulated them, and thus exercised episcopal rights and privileges.

These congregations were in reality very powerful associations, and infused into the monastic life fresh vigor and strength. In the beginning of the twelfth century, consequently two hundred years after its foundation, there were 2000 other monasteries subject to the parent monastery of Cluny. Its abbot received all the privileges of a bishop, and placed in all the dependent monasteries priors only from his own monks ; and he himself was elected by them. In Cluny itself there lived four hundred and sixty monks, and yet not one was obliged to remove from his own cell, nor was any chamber appointed for public use required to be cleared when, in 1245, Pope Innocent IV., with several cardinals and bishops, the king of France, with his mother, sister, and brother, the emperor of Constantinople, the sons of the kings of Castile and Aragon, all with their suites were entertained as guests in this splendid and spacious monastery. The order of Premontratensians, founded by St. Norbert of Xante, at Premontré near Laon in France, numbered, eighty years after its origin, twenty-four provincial or district directors, one thousand abbots, three hundred friars, and five hundred convents of nuns. Norbert was afterwards archbishop of Magdeburg, and introduced his rule into the monasteries of Magdeburg, Havelberg, Brandenburg, &c., and the order spread to Bohemia and Silesia.

In opposition and as a contrast to these rich orders, which by their very wealth had developed the germ of degeneration and indolence, there was established at the commencement of the thirteenth century the order of beggar-monks, whose first law was to acquire no fixed property beyond their monastic walls, and to seek their support by receiving small gifts. Thus, they could never be troubled with a desire after temporal possessions in their practice of self-denial, poverty, and mortification—three essential virtues in this new order. Francis of Assissi, an Italian, founded, in 1210, the order of the Franciscans, and Dominique Guzman, a Spaniard, that of the Dominicans, in 1215, and it was to this Guzman that the pope afterwards transferred in particular the inquisition. In 1238, the Carmelites, who had previously had their original seat upon Mount Carmel, in the east, came to Europe, and about this time, under Pope Gregory IX., they assumed the rule of St. Augustine, and founded the order of the Augustines. All these orders speedily, and at once, spread themselves, but it was only in the following centuries that their activity came into full operation.

In this manner the whole empire of the church had divided itself into two portions ; on the one side the whole of the monastic clergy, and upon the other the secular clergy. It is true they were both united in their several grades, under their superior and supreme head, the pope ; but this division of the church was not beneficial. Envy, jealousy, and many vexatious disputes were thereby produced. The closer inspection of the bishops might have kept the monasteries in a better state of discipline and order. St. Bernard of Clairvaux, who belonged to the order of the Cistercians, the only order which recognised the jurisdiction of the bishops, writes upon this subject thus: "The pope can by virtue of his power withdraw the bishop from the jurisdiction of the archbishop, and the abbot from that of the bishop, but it ought not to take place, for the bishops would thereby only become more arrogant, and the monks less restrainable. All superiority, all fear, would be removed, and the whole structure of the hierarchy, which in wise order ascends to the pope, would be undermined. Beneath their humble demeanor and expressions are concealed the haughty dispositions of the abbots ; they plunder the church in order to free themselves from the superiority of the bishops, and they purchase their independence so that they may escape from that obedience which should be their richest ornament. Thence this desire of each to rank next to and as immediately as possible after the pope, dissolves the entire bonds of the hierarchy."

It has been shown how in the course of time these institutions which had grown from, and were adapted to the necessities of the age, and which, retained in proper limits, might afterwards, as at first, have continued to fulfil their object, degenerated from the moment that their temporal exertions entirely outweighed their intellectual efforts, their multiplicity having thus become ten, nay, a hundred times too great. For a proportionate number of men of really inspired minds, who, disgusted with the world, desired the retirement of a monastic life, could not possibly be found to inhabit the cloisters thus numerously distributed. Thence thousands against their wills, or urged by base motives, had adopted the cowl, to which they were now forever bound, and this majority thus introduced the germ of ruin into every institution they entered. Complaints of the degeneration of the monks, of their continued life of sensuality, dissipation, and other vices, became more and more frequent. The ancient reverence which had hitherto surrounded and hovered over these places of repose and pious meditation, now gradually disappeared. The inhabitants of cities, who, formerly by presents and grants, had contributed to build and endow the cloisters within their walls, became now their enemies, when they beheld them stretch their arms too widely around them, and when among other rights, they found them arrogate to themselves that of a freedom from all civil impost, not only for themselves, but likewise for their laborers and mechanics. Between the princes and nobles on one side, and the monasteries on the other, there arose jealousy, contention, and unjust reprisals. In order to protect themselves against external power, as well as to exercise their rights of freedom, which alone depended on the empire, the monasteries were obliged to procure and establish an authorized governor and protector (*Schutz* or *Kast-vogt*) selected chiefly from among the powerful nobility of the neighborhood, and for which service they paid him a considerable tax. But between the Vogt and the monastery disputes often arose, and thus many a monastery was severely oppressed by the Vogt, its own chosen defender. The contest often forced itself within the very walls of the monastery itself. The monks rebelled against their superiors, misused and drove them away; the lay brothers revolted against the whole monastic brotherhood, and consequently violence and murderous scenes of blood desecrated those walls originally consecrated to peace. Such is the fate of every human institution as soon as it steps beyond the true limits assigned to it for the legitimate attainment of its appointed object.

Nevertheless, we must here observe, that this sad degeneration in the monastic life occurred less in the age of the Hohenstaufens than in the following centuries, when it becomes evident that all the institutions of the middle ages inclined, and in fact were hastening towards their fall and ruin.

It remains now for us in this description of the middle ages to speak of that which is made its greatest objection, the misuse of power to obtain justice, or even without the least justice, to offend. Upon this account these times are called those of the *Faust-recht*, (fist or club law,) because the fist so generally decided instead of the word, and force had all the validity of law. Every prince had his fortified castle, every knight his strong tower, frequently upon an inaccessible rock, and every city its protecting walls; and confiding in these places of retreat, every one mocked the demands of the other, often when he was wrong, until he was obliged to yield to force, or was himself destroyed. Little attention was paid to the sentence of judges, and, frequently, even the emperor's word was not heeded, and thus it was that while the empire enjoyed profound peace with its neighbors, internally the most violent contests, small and great, raged in different places at once, so that in what they called the most ordinary state of these fatal times of anarchy in Germany, thousands of individuals perished by the sword annually. Such a condition appears fearful to us, and we cannot comprehend how men could, in such a state, be easy and cheerful as if in perfect security. For it would seem that only those who were violently and rapaciously inclined held dominion, while peaceful, tranquil men must have lived in constant fear and dread of destruction. So severe a judgment, however, would again be based upon a misconception of the spirit of that age, while closer observation will only serve to soften and mellow down the harsh and hideous colors of this sad picture.

The noble lived amidst his warlike arms, and was always ready at a moment's notice to resist force by force whenever he was attacked; and in so doing, he did not consider himself verging at all beyond his ordinary sphere; it often, indeed, afforded him pleasure to be thus occasionally aroused from a temporary state of lethargy. It was a realizing proof of that glory he was bound to sustain, and as it was for honor's sake that the very best friends broke a lance together—often in serious contest—in the tournaments, so likewise in the most violent feuds honor was constantly the guiding star. They did not oppose each other in battle with the animosity and absolute hatred excited in enemies of later times, for very frequently their encounter was only a more serious joust at arms, in which the opponents measured their strength with each other for life and death. It was an ordeal of God, an open and energetic mode of deciding the quarrel which reason and argument could no longer terminate, and this decision was regarded as that of justice and good right.

We have already seen that besides this, the cities excited by these continual wars of the *Fehde*, or *Faustrecht*, between the princes and nobility, were aroused to a full development of their powers, and that, together with industrial activity, both manly virtue and the feeling of civil honor had become firmly united, and more and more energetically brought into action. When, therefore, the citizen was at home, within the walls of his own city, he lived in perfect security and full of confidence in the courage of his fellow-citizens; and when he was travelling he protected and defended himself with his own arms, assisted by his numerous suite, with which, whenever possible, he took care to provide himself.

The peasant was forced to suffer most in these feuds, and his condition was sadly deplorable during this period. The battle was most generally fought upon his ground, and thus his plantations became destroyed, while he himself was defenceless and without arms, not having even the right to bear them; being held unworthy of such honor unless he was wholly or at least half freed. But, again, in many cases he found a protection in the point of honor established in chivalry, which did not permit an injury or offence being offered to a defenceless man, while he likewise derived considerable compensation from the security he possessed in being, with his sons, exempt from military service. Besides which, the evils of war were less in extent, and left much fewer and less disastrous traces behind than in our days; for what are all those minor mischances of the battle-field compared with the misery so inexpressible and incalculable which a single war in the present time disseminates!

We should also err very much if we thought that in this period of the Faustrecht the law had no effect, that no judges were appointed, or tribunals held, and that all was left to arbitrary will. On the contrary, the *Fehde-recht*, in its peculiar sense, was connected with the dispensation of justice and the infliction of punishment conformably with the spirit of the age. But to perceive and comprehend this better, we must refer back to the primitive judicial system of the Germans, and prosecute its entire development in the middle ages.

The German judicial system like every other, the object of which is to furnish a civil community with order and well being, was based upon the principle that peace should reign between all its members. Thus, whosoever had broken the peace by murder, fire, robbery, &c., (so did nature interpret and decree to the Germans—who desired not only justice but speedy justice,) it was not necessary to cite the criminal before a tribunal, but the offended party was at liberty to prosecute retaliation until the former made compensation, either by money or otherwise. Thence this ancient and original right of the freed man served to found the collective feudal system. The individual who had committed the crime might be himself attacked on the same day and immediately after it occurred; but subsequently, when the feudal code became better regulated, a previous announcement of three days was necessary. When, however, the offender offered reparation of honor and right, that is to say, a just restitution, there was then no longer cause to seek justice by force of arms.

In the earlier periods of German antiquity, when all justice proceeded directly from, and rested in the grand and mighty union of all the freed men, there existed no other law but the common law practised by the count, together with the community of his Gau or district, the *Centgrave* or centenary, and the *Decanus* or tything man, at the head of the communities of their jurisdiction. Every judge held regularly, and at certain periods of the year, his *Echte Ding*, or court of session. Every defendant was compelled to appear, the complaints were made, the judge required the verdict of the community, and what these decided by their foreman, who was called on for that purpose by the judge, the latter declared as sentence. The community consequently founded the law which became absolute for all similar cases subsequently, and every freeman took a part in its legislation. Charlemagne first introduced the *Schöffen*, whose office it was to attend at every court held, in order to refer to ancient precedents. If the condemned refused to submit to the sentence, the judge himself, together with the whole judicial community, were obliged to see the sentence executed. Thus the whole system was based upon the equalized strength of the individuals, and the firm union of the collective community. Charlemagne by his power knew how to maintain order, and prevent each from taking the law in his own hands. Under his reign no private or distinct feud was heard of. But Louis the Pious, with his sons, soon afterwards gave already an example of violence, and under the later Carlovingians the count lost all his judicial authority, and with it, likewise, vanished more and more the power of the communities; for, on the one hand, the clergy, the monasteries, and the high nobility, with their vassals, began to assume to themselves particular privileges which removed them from the ordinary jurisdiction of the communities, and, at the same time, exempted them from the duty of making the disobedient attend to the sentence pronounced thereby; and, on the other, the necessary general equality of the community was destroyed by the preponderating authority acquired by the princes, counts, and lords.

A superior power—that of a duke—became then requisite in order to restore the vigor of the courts. Ever since the first emperors of the house of Saxony, Henry and Otho, had created dukes and raised them to their proper position, the judicial courts became also restrengthened and improved; inasmuch as they by their summons issued to all their officials in the districts they ruled, and by the aid of their own vassals, were enabled to command the necessary respect being shown to their authority. The first Salic emperors strove, it is true, to weaken and overthrow the ducal authority in order to procure a more immediate influence for the imperial power, but it was exactly in the powerful authority invested in these emperors that justice and order found their support. But the long and unfortunate reign of Henry IV., who was continually at war with the Saxons, as well as with his rivals to the imperial throne, and finally with his own sons, was the cause of the abandonment of justice once more and of its becoming a prey to violence.

Not but that the majority of the Hohenstaufens possessed dignity and personal authority enough to re-establish order, but all their energies being directed towards Italy, the inclination so general in Germany for the Faustrecht could therefore be put into practice more easily, especially as the power of the dukes, by the jealousy of the emperors, and of Frederick I. in particular, was now destroyed. The emperors, indeed, now sought to place themselves more immediately at the head of the judicial power, and by maintaining its dispensation themselves, endeavored to cause its authority to be respected by their princes and counts. For this purpose Frederick I. established the Landfriede, or peace of the country, which was re-established by Frederick II., in 1235; but the confusion in the rights and possessions of the princes being already too great, the individual princes and nobles opposed each other in constant feuds. Those wars had acquired even a more regular form by the ordinance of Frederick I., which decreed that the declaration of war should be announced three days previously, and thus each knight was enabled to find greater opportunity to secure himself against the judicial power of his superior.

After this law, opposition to justice, and private feuds which, in earlier times, owing to the vigor and strength of the institutions, existed only as exceptions, became now of regular and established occurrence. The baneful spirit of disorder took the upper hand at the period of the Interregnum, and spread its dominion everywhere around, while the noble chivalric feeling of honor and virtue which was still maintained under the Hohenstaufens, gradually disappeared, and rude and brutal violence became more and more intolerant and oppressive.

Several of the emperors, whom the next division of our history will name, endeavored to remove and overcome these evils. Rudolphus, or Rodolph of Hapsburg, renewed, in several diets, the law for the *Landfrieden*, (or peace of the country,) and strove to strengthen it by the association of several districts, as, for instance, Westphalia, Lower Saxony, Thuringia, Hessia, Bavaria, and Swabia. This was, in reality, a new mode of giving strength to justice, after it was found that the authority of the courts, the dukes, and even that of the emperors had successively lost all power. But in a country which was divided into so many petty dominions, these unions only fostered too easily a party spirit, and consequently led to much injustice. The temporal nobles and knights, especially in the southwest of Germany, took advantage thereof, to oppose and make war against all those powerful cities, which had also concluded alliances together. To which followed very speedily, continued dissensions and disputes upon the subject of the election of the emperors, and claims to inheritance in several countries: in Lüneburg, Hessia, the Tyrol, &c.; during which the nobility received greater weight, and could arrogate to themselves the right of justice. The emperor Wenceslas and his successors endeavored to unite all these various associations into one grand alliance of a *Reichsfriede*, (or peace of the empire,) and thus restore a superior authority, but in vain. It was not until towards the fifteenth century, when the nobility were obliged by degrees to yield to the power of the territorial princes, and when, especially, the vigor of chivalry was broken by the development of a new epoch, that, at length, a solid and durable foundation was laid for the dominion of justice, by the emperor Maximilian's fixed law of the *Reichsfriede*, which secured the public peace forever.

We will now trace the prominent features of the forms of judicial proceedings, and of the laws in the middle ages. Originally, the superior court of jurisdiction was held only in the particular county which, in the name of the king, or under the *Königsbann*, exercised high judicial authority over real property and life. In the centgraviates (which were called, in Lower Saxony and in Westphalia, *Gogerichte*) there was only a petty court of justice, to which the nobles (Semperfreien) were not subject; for, throughout the whole of the middle ages, we find maintained the rule, that every one, to whatsoever class he belonged, could be adjudged only by his equals; so that the general grand principle of the administration of justice by the communities, from the highest to the lowest, continued to form the basis of all judicial proceedings throughout Germany. The emperor could pass no sentence which the princes and nobles had not approved; and in the class of peasants, even in the courts of law, among feudatories and vassals, no lord and no superior authority could adjudge capriciously and arbitrarily, inasmuch as it was necessary to have the approbation of the community. Justice, therefore, remained the living property of the people, and its code was formed by custom and descent, from among themselves. Written laws, indeed, were held in dread and suspicion, for then the proceedings would have fallen into the hands of those learned in jurisprudence. The church alone was ruled by written laws, and almost in every thing by the Roman code. Wherever solitary written laws were found, such as privileges, principles of jurisprudence and rights, for cities or particular districts, they were of such trifling import in their incomplete state, that, far from being so constituted as to form sources of right and fountains of justice, they only served as testimonies to prove that the true law lived exclusively in the people.

The first collection of German laws was formed by a Saxon nobleman, Epke or Eike von Repgow, between 1215–18, and which is known under the name of *Sachsenspiegel* or Saxon Mirror. It was a mere private labor; but as the collection was more complete than the hitherto so-called laws, it came by degrees into general practice, particularly in the fourteenth and fifteenth centuries. The compiler was totally ignorant of the Roman code, and did not therefore adapt his composition to it, either in form or matter; but those who revised it subsequently, introduced much of the Roman canon law. Among the compilations, we must include the *Schwabenspiegel* or Swabian Mirror, and the *Kaiserrecht* or Imperial Code, the latter of which, in particular, contains the feudal system.

The Roman law was evidently introduced by the clergy into Germany, and was adopted in the ecclesiastical courts. It was only in the fifteenth century that the municipal courts commenced referring to it. The reawakened taste for the study of Roman antiquity, in general, brought with it also a desire to investigate and make researches into the Roman law-books, particularly in the universities; and they commenced, in doubtful cases, to procure opinions and legal decisions, as well from the doctors of the universities as from the superior courts. The influence which the gradual introduction of the Roman law had upon the public affairs of Germany, will become more and more evident as we proceed in the course of our history.

Before we conclude our description of the state of judicial affairs in the middle ages, we will contemplate one of its most remarkable institutions, namely, that of the *Vehm* or *Femgericht*, (secret executive tribunal,) which formed itself in Westphalia, and which gives us a profound view of the spirit of that period. But for the sake of connection, we must previously enter upon and anticipate the limits of the immediate succeeding period.

In Westphalia the jurisdiction of the princes and nobles was wholly founded upon the *Gogerichte* or Centgraviates. The ancient tribunal, however, of the Graf or count had also maintained itself, although much diminished in authority, as the supreme and royal court. The high nobility and the families comprising the original free land proprietors, who had continued free from fiefs and had never become the vassals of the dominant lords, could alone be chosen as *Schöffen* or ministers in this court; they being called on that account *Freischöffen*, or free ministers and judges, and the court was styled a free court or tribunal.

Again, as the rights of the free tribunals were attached to the primitive rights of the ancient jurisdiction of the counties, so also those of the *Stuhlherr* were connected with the *Freistuhls* or free courts; for the term Stuhlherr was applied to every prince, noble, and knight, who as judicial lord possessed a jurisdiction which did not depend upon the emperor. The Stuhlherr was appointed to watch especially that justice was done. For this purpose he created a *Freigraf* or free count, who was invested with authority by the emperors, or dukes, and, after the fall of Henry the Lion, he was appointed by the archbishop of Cologne, as inheritor of the duchy of Westphalia. The free count stood in the same affinity to the Stuhlherr as the judge or judicial lord; the Freischöffen, however, were not servants of the judge, but they represented the ancient community or jury, and the free count was only the president or foreman who maintained order in the assembly. All the Freischöffen present possessed the right to participate in pronouncing judgment; a less number than seven members could not form a court, and if there were too many to enable all to take an immediate part in the proceedings, the remainder formed the audience, of whom, in the later and more splendid periods of this tribunal, there were assembled hundreds and even thousands. Besides this, every free count had his clerks, who were called *Fronboten*, and were appointed to serve him especially, taking no share in the decisions of the court.

The superior Freistuhl or tribunal was at Dortmund, that city being a free city of the empire, and acknowledging no Stuhlherr or judicial lord, owing, perhaps, to the antiquity and celebrity of its tribunal, as well as the aboriginal privileges it had acquired in the time of Charlemagne. In Dortmund all the free counts assembled every year to meet a general chapter, where they founded *Weisthümer*, or principles of law, examined the judgments of the free courts, and confirmed or put them aside when an appeal was entered.

As these tribunals drew their origin from those of the ancient county courts, it will be readily perceived that they exercised a jurisdiction over ordinary legal disputes which we call civil actions, as also over penal cases, which presuppose a crime. But this last division of their office, at that time so important, became still more so in the course of time, in order to enable them to exercise their whole power, in suppressing as much as possible the savage spirit existing so universally and among all classes, to commit the most serious crimes against life, honor, and property. And as they adjudged in the name of the emperor, and by the law of life and death, they thought that in all criminal affairs they could extend their jurisdiction beyond the limits of Westphalia, more especially as not another tribunal existed throughout the empire so authorized, from which to obtain justice against criminals. In fact, such influence did this tribunal command, that at length no cases of contention, nor even purely civil disputes arose which could not be brought before them for decision, if the defendant refused to do justice and honor to the plaintiff; for thence the crime became one absolutely confirmed against the sanctity of the law.

Thus in the fourteenth and fifteenth centuries the power of the *Freigerichte* extended over all parts of Germany, as far as Prussia and Livonia; while all complaints, even from the most distant districts, were obliged to be brought before a Westphalian superior tribunal, and it was upon Westphalian ground (styled in the judicial language the red earth) that the cited person was forced to appear. Beyond Westphalia no such Freistuhl could exist, and when the emperor Wenceslas endeavored to introduce one into Bohemia, the free counts declared that any one participating in such a Freistuhl incurred the penalty of death. Thus originally it was Westphalians alone, and of these only the ancient free-born *Schöffen* or *Stuhlfreien* that could be constituted judges in the tribunal; but in the thirteenth century it was the custom to receive also other free, irreproachable, and honorable men as *Schöffen*, and when the court itself extended its jurisdiction beyond the boundaries of Westphalia, every free German could become a Freischöffe, and princes, counts, knights, and citizens, strove to attain the honor of participating in the privileges of Freischöffen. A Freischöffe could be cited only before a Freigericht or free tribunal, and great weight was laid upon his word and oath. But they were very careful and strict in their election of a Freischöffe; he was obliged to prove that he was free born, of a good family, not suspected of any misdeeds, and was in the enjoyment of all his rights, and finally two Freischöffen were obliged to become his security. The reception could take place only in Westphalia. Even the emperor himself could make Freischöffen only upon the so-called red earth, in this superior court. They had among them a very ancient secret sign and peculiar greeting, whereby they recognised each other; whence, or perhaps from their knowledge of the laws, they were called the initiated, and in order to make any one knowing or wise implied receiving him among the Schöffen of the superior tribunal; even emperors were subjected to this reception, for in the year 1429 the emperor Sigismund was solemnly received among the initiated, at the Freistuhl of Dortmund. We may consider these courts of justice in Westphalia at this brilliant moment of their existence, when almost all the princes, nobles, and knights, became Freischöffen, as an absolute and important association, which in all its ramifications spread over the whole of Germany, and which, at a time when all the other courts had lost their power, acted as a substitute, and constituted a barrier against the rude and brutal force of crime. A solemn oath held all the members united, and not even in the confessional were they suffered to reveal a secret of the *Vehm* tribunal; neither were the clergy themselves admitted into it.

Originally the non-initiated were not taken at once before the secret tribunal, but before the ancient tribunal of the community or jury court, (the *Echte Ding*,) but that was formed by the same individuals; the forms only were less severe, and likewise there every one could be present. But if the cited individual did not appear, he was then taken before the closed or secret court, so called because only those initiated could be present, and any non-initiated one venturing to introduce himself was immediately hanged. The term *secret* here, therefore, implies *closed* court, and does not indicate those terrible mysteries which dared not be exhibited before the light of day.

It is equally as fabulous that these tribunals were held at night in woods, caverns, and subterranean vaults, although in later times, when this court had become degenerated, it may have occurred in isolated cases. But the place of meeting was the ancient palace court of the grafs or counts, generally upon a mountain or hill, whence the eye could command a view of the entire country around, under the shade of lime-trees, and by the light of the sun. The free graf or count ascended and presided on the seat of justice; before him lay the sword, the symbol of supreme justice, at the same time representing in the form of its handle the cross of Christ, and the next to it the *Wyd*, or cord, as a sign of right over life and death. The count then opened and closed the court, that is, he called the Schöffen around him and assigned to them their places. They were obliged to appear bareheaded and without arms or armor. Upon the judges' declaration that the court was opened, peace was commanded for the first, second, and third time. From that moment the deepest silence reigned throughout the assembly, no one ventured to argue or converse, for by so doing he transgressed against the solemn decreed peace of the tribunal. The cited person, who was also obliged to appear without arms, stepped forward, accompanied by his two sureties or bail, if he had any. The complaint made against him was stated to him by the judge, and if he swore upon the cross of the sword, the legal oath of purification, he was free: "He shall then take a *Kreuzpfennig*, or farthing piece," says an ancient work on jurisprudence, "throw it at the feet of the court, turn round and go his way. Whoever attacks or touches him, has then, which all freemen know, broken the king's peace." Such was the ancient proceeding with the genuine Freischöffen, who enjoyed particular privileges, and who were presumed to have a strict love for truth and honor. In later times that simple straightforward way seems to have become quite changed, for we read in other ancient codes that the plaintiff was entitled to oppose and destroy the validity of the purifying oath of the defendant by three witnesses, which, however, the latter could again oppose with six; if the accuser appeared with fourteen, the defendant could swear himself free with twenty-one, which was the highest testimony. If the defendant acknowledged the crime, or if the plaintiff convicted him by oath and witnesses, the *Schöffen* then gave judgment. If the criminal received sentence of death he was executed immediately and hanged on the next tree; the minor punishments were exile and fine.

But if the defendant did not appear upon the third citation, and could produce no satisfactory cause of absence within a stipulated period, he was considered as having confessed his crime, or as one despising justice and peace, and, therefore, having placed himself beyond the pale of either, the sentence of the *Vehm*, which was equivalent to condemnation, was pronounced against him; and thence these courts received the name of *Vehmgerichte*.

The sentence pronounced by the court was dreadful: "As now N. has been cited, prosecuted, and adjudged before me, and who, on account of his misdeeds, I summoned before me, and who is so hardened in evil, that he will obey neither honor nor justice, and despises the highest tribunal of the holy empire, I *verfeme*, or denounce him here, by all the royal power and force, as is but just, and as is commanded by the Königsbann, or royal ban. I deprive him, as outcast and expelled, of all the peace, justice, and freedom he has ever enjoyed since he was baptized; and I deprive him, henceforward, of the enjoyment of the four elements, which God made and gave as a consolation to man, and denounce him as without right, without law, without peace, without honor, without security; I declare him condemned and lost, so that any man may act towards him as with any other banished criminal. And he shall henceforward be considered unworthy, and shall enjoy neither law nor justice, nor have either freedom in, or guidance to any castles or cities, excepting consecrated places. And I herewith curse his flesh and his blood; and may his body never receive burial, but may it be borne away by the wind, and may the ravens and crows, and wild birds of prey consume and destroy him. And I adjudge his neck to the rope, and his body to be devoured by the birds and beasts of the air, sea, and land; but his soul I commend to our dear Lord God, if He will receive it."

According to some customs, after he had cast forth the rope beyond the walls of the court, the count was obliged to pronounce these words three times, and every time to spit on the earth with the collective Schöffen, as was the usage when any one was actually executed. The name of the condemned criminal was then inserted in the book of blood, and the count then concluded the sentence as follows: "I command all kings, princes, lords, knights, and squires, all free counts, and all free, true Schöffen, and all those who belong to the holy empire, that they shall help with all their power to fulfil this sentence upon this banished criminal, as is but just to the secret tribunal of the holy empire. And nothing shall cause them to withhold from so doing, neither love nor affection, relationship, friendship, nor any thing whatever in this world."

The banished man was now in the condition of the criminal condemned to death, over whom execution lowered. Whosoever received or even warned him, was also taken before the tribunal of the free count. The assisting members of the court were bound by a terrible oath, and by a heavy sentence of death, to conceal the judgment which had been passed against any one; that is to say, to make it known to nobody but one initiated; and even if the condemned man was a brother or father, the member durst not warn him thereof. Besides which, each initiated one to whom the sentence was authentically conveyed, was bound to help to put it in execution. Generally a letter of outlawry was given to the plaintiff, with the seal of the free count and seven Schöffen, that he might pursue the guilty party; the oath of three Freischöffen sufficed to confirm the sentence. Wherever the Verfemte, or banished man was found, whether in a house, in the open street, the high road, or in the forest, he was hanged at the next tree or post, if the servants of the secret court could obtain possession of him. As a sign that he was put to death in execution of the holy Vehm, and was not murdered by robbers, they left him all that he bore about him, and stuck a knife in the ground close beside him. Besides this, the Schöffen of this secret court possessed the privilege of hanging without a trial every criminal *taken in the fact*, if, faithful to the laws of honor, they took nothing from him which they found about him, and left behind the sign of the Vehm.

We are astonished when we contemplate this terrific and mighty power of the Schöffen alliance, and can at the same time easily comprehend how the most extraordinary traditions of this *Vehmgericht*, or secret tribunal, based upon their nocturnal assemblies, their mysterious customs, their initiation and course of justice, together with their condemnation and execution of the criminal, have been preserved in the mouths of the people, for even the plain historical descriptions thereof are sufficiently striking. An association of several thousand men spread throughout the whole of Germany, from the highest to the lowest classes, (for we find examples of common freemen, mechanics, and citizens, being clothed with the dignity of a free count, and that even princes and knights did not disdain to assist as Schöffen under their presidency,) such a society whose members recognised each other by secret signs, and by a solemn oath were bound to support each other, who adjudged and punished in the name of the emperor and the empire, who reached the criminal even after an elapse of years, and in whatever corner he might seek refuge, and finally who were not subjected to give any account for what they did if only the terrific knife was present as evidence: what power, we repeat, did not this alliance command against the evil-minded, and what a powerful support and guarantee might it not have been for the peace and justice of the empire? The prince or knight who easily escaped the judgment of the imperial court, and from behind his fortified walls defied even the emperor himself, trembled when in the silence of the night he heard the voices of the Freischöffen at the gate of his castle, and when the free count summoned him to appear at the ancient malplatz or plain, under the lime-tree, or on the bank of a rivulet upon that dreaded soil, the Westphalian or red ground.* And that the power of these free counts was not exaggerated by the mere imagination, excited by terror, nor in reality by any means insignificant, is proved by a hundred undeniable examples, supported by records and testimonies, that numerous princes, counts, knights, and wealthy citizens, were seized by these Schöffen of the secret tribunal, and in execution of its sentence, perished by their hands.

Such power placed in human hands without the protecting check of publicity and responsibility could not long exist without

* We must add here, that the summons was executed by two Schöffen who were the bearers of the free count's letter. If they did not succeed in finding the accused, because he was living either in a city or a fortress, where they could not safely enter, they were authorized to execute the summons in the night. They stuck the letter, enclosing a farthing piece, in the panel of the gate of the castle, and cut off three chips from the same gate, which they handed to the free count as a testimony that they had delivered the summons, having, when leaving the gate, cried out to the sentinel on the walls that they had deposited there a letter for his lord. If the accused was a man without any regular place of residence, and if he could not be met with, he was summoned at four different cross roads, where at each point, the east, west, north, and south, they attached a summons, enclosing in each the royal petty coin.

misuse. In the great development and extension of the association, it could not be avoided, but that unworthy individuals should be received as members, who used the power confided to them for the sole satisfaction of their revengeful and baser passions. At the end of the fifteenth century many complaints arose in several parts of the empire, and particularly on the part of the clergy, against these free courts; and we find that the whole spirit of modern times began to work against them far more than these charges upon isolated events. The power of the lords of the soil had now become increased and confirmed; they could not endure that their subjects should be judged by a strange, although originally imperial tribunal. Thence arose alliances of princes, nobles, knights, and cities, against the Westphalian courts, and when the law for the lasting peace of the land, the new imperial chamber of justice, and a new criminal court were introduced, the study of law and jurisprudence became substituted for a knowledge of the ancient customs; and when crimes against the peace of the land and against obedience to the authorities ceased, then did the power of the secret tribunal evaporate of itself without any formal abrogation, so that it is equally difficult to trace the last as it is to fix the first year of its existence.*

* In the sixteenth century, the association contended for its rights and privileges, and the struggle still continued in the seventeenth century, although much weakened and the scene confined to Westphalia. In the eighteenth century there were left only a few traces, the ruins of the past; its recollections and its signs, however, still continue to exist among the peasants of certain provinces in Westphalia. At Gehmen, in Münster, the secret tribunal was only extinguished entirely by the French legislation in 1811; and even to the present day, some of the free peasants who have taken the oath of the Schöffen, meet annually at a particular spot around the *Freistuhl*, and it has been impossible to extract from them the secret oath. The principal signs are indicated by the letters S. S. G. G., which signify stock (stick,) stein (stone,) gras (grass,) grein (tears;) but we cannot trace the mysterious meaning these words convey in connection with the *Vehmgericht*.

# FIFTH PERIOD.

### FROM RUDOLPHUS I. OF HAPSBURG TO CHARLES V.

### 1273—1520

THE sources of the history of this period are again still more scanty than in that of the Hohenstaufens, consisting chiefly of special chronicles rather than of general historical works, constituting one entire and continuous representation of events, added to which they are all, or for the greater portion, written in the Latin tongue. The first we have to mention are those works of general history which appear in the form of chronicles or annals, and which present but a meager portion of German history. The most important are:

1. Hermann, a monk of Attaich, known under the name of Henricus Sterv; Chronicle 1147-1300.
2. Annales Colmarienses, 1211-1303; in the collection of Urstisius.
3. Matthias of Neuenburg; Chronicle as far as 1353, continued by Albert of Strasburg (Albertus Argentinensis) to 1378; in Urstisius.
4. John Vitoduranus; Chron. 1215-1348; in Eccard.
5. Gobelinus Persona, deacon of Birkefeld; Review of the World (Cosmodromium) to 1418; in Meebom.
6. Dieterich Engelhusen; Chronicle to the year 1420; in Leibnitz and Menken.
7. Andreas, a Presbyterian of Ratisbon; Chronicle to 1442; in Eccard.
8. Werner Rolewink of Laer, a Carthusian monk in Cologne; Chronicle to 1476, continued by Hans Lindner to 1514; in Pistorius.
9. Hermann Korner, Domin, in Lübeck; Chronicle to 1435; in Eccard.
10. Hartmann Schedel, a doctor in Nuremberg; Chronicle to 1492; printed separately.
11. John Nauklerus, professor in Tübigen; Universal History, to 1500; printed separately.
12. John of Trittenheim, (Joannes Trithemius,) from the vicinity of Treves, abbot of Sponheim and Würzburg, who died in 1516: his works are very important, and have been edited by Freher. The most valuable among them is the Chronicle of the Monastery of Hirschau in Wurtemberg (published at St. Gallen in 1630; Chronic. Hirsaugiense) 830-1514; in which the historian has interwoven the whole history of Germany.
13. Albert Kranz, canon in Hamburg, who died in 1517, wrote the history of Northern Germany, in three parts: Metropolis, Saxonia, et Vandalia; a learned man, and, for his time, an independent thinker.

As especial and entire works on Germany may be mentioned:

14. The State letters of the Emperor Rudolphus I. edited by Gerbert, 1772, and Bodmann, 1806.
15. The Biography, &c., of the Emperors Rudolphus I., and Albert I., written by Gottfried of Ensningen, by desire of Magnus Engelhard, a citizen of Strasburg.
16. Albert Mussatus, professor in Padua, and who died in 1330, wrote De Gestis Henrici VII. Imp., and History of Italy, after the death of Henry VII.
17. Caroli IV., Commentarius de vita sua ad filios.
18. Æneas Sylvius Piccolomini, subsequently Pope Pius II., and who died in the year 1464, produced:
   a. The history of his own times from 1405-63, which he caused to be written by his own private secretary J. Gobelin, of Bonn.
   b. The history of the ecclesiastical council of Basle written by himself; as also
   c. The history of the Emperor Frederick III., and
   d. Various minor works, among which the Descrip

tio de Ritu, Situ, Moribus et Conditione Germaniæ, and numerous letters, all of which have been collected and repeatedly printed.

19. Pertz's Scripta rerum Austriac. contains many valuable sources for the history of the Austrian emperors.

20. J. Joach. Müller has collected the most important transactions of the diets of the Germanic empire, especially of those under Frederick III. and Maximilian I., published in Jena, 1709, and subsequently.

In the fourteenth and fifteenth centuries we find historical works in the German language become more frequent:

21. Ottocar of Hornegk wrote a Chronicle in rhyme, which contains the entire epoch of the Interregnum and the history of the Emperors Rudolphus, Adolphus, Albert, and Henry VII., as far as 1309; a work which although not strictly historical, is nevertheless worthy to be referred to as a history of those times. It is reprinted in Pertz's History of Austria.

22. Jacob of Königshoven, an ecclesiastic in Strasburg, who died in 1420, wrote a Chronicle of Alsace and Strasburg in the Swabian dialect, which was edited by Schilter, and published with his notes in 1698.

23. Eberhard Windeck, of Mentz, private secretary to the Emperor Sigismund, wrote a biography of that monarch; in Menken.

24. J. Rothe, domin. in Eisenach, wrote a Chronicle of Thuringia, in the low Saxon dialect, as far as 1434; continued by an anonymous writer to 1440.

25. The Limpurgian Chronicle from 1336–89, which contains much, especially of the history of manners, customs, &c., and has been several times reprinted.

26. Conrad Bothe, chronicler of the Saxons to 1489, in the low German dialect; in Leibnitz.

27. Diebold Schilling, about 1480, history of the wars of Burgundy; very well written.

28. Melchior Pfinzing (of Nuremberg, born in 1481, Imperial Counsellor, and subsequently Provost in Mentz) sang the history of the Emperor Maximilian I., under an adopted title: "Geuerlichkeiten and Geschichten des löblichen streitbaren Helds und Ritters Tewrdanks." Nuremberg, 1517, and subsequently often reprinted.

29. Marcus Treizsauerwein, private secretary to the Emperor Maximilian I., has presented us likewise with a description of that monarch's great deeds in his work: der Weiskunig, 1514; and for which the emperor himself furnished much of the materials.

30. Bilibald Pirkheimer (of Eichstädt, born 1470, Counsellor in Nuremberg, and subsequently Imperial Counsellor, died in 1530) wrote his: Hist. belli Helvetici, and Currus triumphalis, honori Max. I. inventus; together with many other works.

31. Finally, we must mention two works by Sebastian Franks, (born 1500, died 1545,) the Zeitbuch, 1531, and Teutsche Chronik, 1538.

## CHAPTER XII.

### EMPERORS OF DIFFERENT HOUSES.—1273–1347.

Rudolphus I. of Hapsburg, 1273-91—Adolphus I. of Nassau, 1292-98—Albert I. of Austria, 1298-1308—Switzerland—Confederation of the Swiss—Gessler—William Tell—Henry VII. of Luxemburg, 1308-13—Frederick of Austria, 1314-30, and Lewis of Bavaria, 1314-47—Switzerland—the Battle of Morgarten, 1315—The Battle of Mühldorf, 1322—The First Electoral Alliance, 1338—Death of Lewis, 1347.

THE state of commotion in Germany continued to grow daily more violent; and when, in 1272, Richard of England died, and Alphonso took not the least interest in the German empire, the princes at length, in the year 1273, held an imperial diet at Frankfort, in order to choose an emperor who should meet the views of every one. It was necessary that he should be great and wise, in order that he might restore the imperial dignity; but at the same time not powerful, lest the princes should have reason of apprehension for the security of their own power. To unite both requisites was a difficult matter; however, good fortune determined the election to the advantage of the country. In Switzerland lived Count Rudolphus of Hapsburg, whose territories and subjects were not very extensive or numerous, but who by his valor, prudence, and integrity, had obtained the respect of the higher orders, and of the people generally. He had been formerly the companion and friend of the emperor Frederick II., who in the year 1218, had personally stood godfather to him, and in one of his campaigns in Italy, possibly after the glorious battle at Cortenuova, had conferred upon him the order of knighthood. During the turbulent time of the Interregnum, he lived on his family estates, and defended, to the utmost of his power, all who required his assistance against the oppression and injustice of the rapacious knights. He was for a long time the protector and governor of the cities of Zürich and Strasburg, and of the towns situated at the foot of the Alps of St. Gotthard. In his manners he displayed the natural simplicity and frankness of a good and noble man; and in a letter addressed to the pope, the archbishop of Cologne, when speaking of him, says: "He reveres the church, he is a lover of justice, a man of prudent counsels and piety, beloved of God and man, possessing an agreeable form and countenance, and which although of a stern expression, still when he speaks is invested with an air of affability which inspires confidence; he possesses besides, a hardy constitution, and in his wars against the faithless he has always been successful."

He was more especially held in high esteem by Werner, archbishop of Mentz, for when on one occasion this prelate took a journey to Rome for the purpose of receiving his archbishop's robe, deeming the passage through the mountains of Switzerland unsafe, he besought Count Rudolphus to escort him from Strasburg to the Alps and back. This Rudolphus did with all the chivalric faith of a true knight. During the journey the archbishop became gradually acquainted with his great and rare virtues, and when he was about to leave his noble defender, he said, that he only wished to live long enough to be able in some degree to reward him for his services; and this opportunity had now arrived. He so urgently recommended Count Rudolphus of Hapsburg for the imperial dignity, that the German princes elected him at once to the throne of the empire.

Rudolphus, who little expected such an elevation, was at that moment engaged in war with the city of Basle, in order to reinstate in that city, that portion of the nobility who called themselves the "Sterners," and who had been expelled by the other party, the "Psittichers." It was at midnight that the burgrave of Nuremberg, Frederick of Hohenzollern, Rudolphus's brother-in-law, arrived at the camp, and brought the unexpected intelligence. Rudolphus, at first, did not believe it; but when the marshal of the empire, Henry of Pappenheim, arrived, he sent the burgrave into the city, with an offer of peace to the citizens, he being now, as he said, the more powerful party. They accepted it with gladness, and were the first to congratulate him upon his elevation. He then went to Frankfort, and thence to Aix-la-Chapelle, where he was publicly crowned. After the coronation the princes present, according to the ancient custom, rendered homage to the new emperor for their estates. It so happened, that there was no sceptre at hand, probably because, owing to the many foreign emperors, and the consequent changes in the government, the state jewels were dispersed; great concern was, therefore, manifested, as to what the emperor could possibly use for performing the ceremony of enfeoffment. Rudolphus thereupon removed the difficulty, and snatching up a crucifix, he employed that instead of the sceptre: "For," said he, "a symbol by which the world was redeemed, may well supply the place of a sceptre;" language which pleased all present.

The new emperor began his reign with great rigor, but at the same time with such paternal benevolence, that the meanest of his subjects experienced the good results therefrom: his new dignity effecting no change in the greatness and firmness of his character; and even in his outward appearance he remained as simple and unostentatious as before. So little did he regard external display and magnificent apparel, that he did not hesitate, especially in his great expeditions, to wear, equally with his companions in arms, an inferior cloak, and even with his own hands to repair his own doublet. Once only we find, by his accounts, that he bestowed a large sum of money upon dress for himself, his consort, and children, which occurred on the occasion of his first interview with the pope.

In order that he might at once heal and eradicate the disorders of the kingdom, he sent the following communication to all the vassals and loyal subjects of his realm: "I now intend, by the blessing of God, to reestablish peace throughout this country so long distracted, and to take under my protection against farther tyranny all those who have hitherto groaned under oppression; to promote which object I confide in the efficient co-operation of my estates."

He suited the action to the word, and travelled throughout the countries of Franconia, Swabia, and the borders of the Rhine, and wherever he met with a peace-breaker who would not conform to order, he punished him with all the severity of the law. This was the case especially with regard to the more petty robbers and disturbers; but Rudolphus clearly perceived, that if the imperial dignity was to be clothed with its original and proper importance, the great princes must likewise be compelled to perform their duties, and pay him due homage. King Ottocar, of Bohemia, however, would hear nothing of any such subjection to the emperor; he was a much more powerful prince than the count of Hapsburg, possessing in addition to Bohemia, also the Austrian estates, which, after the extinction of the ducal house of Babenberg, he had obtained partly by inheritance and partly by money and force of arms, and he by no means felt bound to yield. Moreover, the Austrian estates complained bitterly of his tyranny and oppression. Rudolphus, therefore, commenced by summoning Ottocar to appear at the imperial diet of Nuremberg, in 1274, there to take the usual oath of allegiance. But the king came neither then nor to a second diet at Würzberg; and to a third held at Augsburg, in the year 1275, he only sent Bernard, bishop of Seckau, as his representative, who was, however, so daring as to begin a Latin speech in the presence of the assembled princes; in which he endeavored to prove that the emperor Rudolphus's election was not legitimate. Rudolphus however interrupted him, saying, "My lord bishop, if you have any affairs to settle with my clergy, speak by all means in Latin, but if you have to say ought touching me or the privileges of my empire, speak as is the custom, in the language of the country," and the princes, when they understood that he intended to impeach Rudolphus's election to the empire, could scarcely refrain from turning him out; but the bishop saved them the trouble by departing of his own accord, and he hastened away from Nuremberg.

The ban of the empire was now pronounced against the rebellious Ottocar; but he was so insolent and faithless, that he ordered the heralds who had brought to him the declaration of the ban, to be tied up at the gates of Prague. He, however, soon suffered the punishment due to him. Rudolphus, in the year 1276, suddenly made an attack upon Austria, and subdued the country as far as Vienna, which he besieged. Ottocar encamped on the opposite side of the Danube, thinking himself secured by the width of the river; but Rudolphus, to the astonishment of all, so quickly threw a bridge across, in order to attack and capture the king in his stronghold, that the latter, being greatly alarmed, immediately offered peace. He was obliged to resign Austria, Styria, Carinthia, and Carniola. And for the ratification of peace a marriage was contracted between the Bohemian crown prince, Wenzeslas, and one of the six daughters of Rudolphus, and another between the son of the emperor and a Bohemian princess. Ottocar then came to Rudolphus, in his encampment, to obtain the feoffment of his estates. This scene did not pass without the humiliation and shame of the proud king. He had hoped by the splendor of his royal retinue to eclipse the unostentatious emperor, but Rudolphus availed himself of this very circumstance in order to humble him: "The king of Bohemia has often laughed at my gray doublet," said he, "but to-day my gray doublet shall laugh at him." Accordingly, arrayed in his plain and simple attire, and seated upon the imperial throne, he received the king, who, glittering in gold and purple, was now obliged, in the presence of all the bishops and princes, to humbly supplicate on his knees for pardon, and to do homage for his kingdom of Bohemia and Moravia.

Hereupon the princes of the empire, as usual after a terminated campaign, returned home; but Rudolphus, who by no means trusted the proud king, remained in Austria with his faithful Alsatian and Swabian knights, who continued attached to him from the time when, under his orders as count of Hapsburg, they fought with him in so many battles. And, in reality, very shortly afterwards Ottocar recommenced hostilities, thinking that Rudolphus had now no competent forces with him. But the emperor with his small but valiant band boldly marched against his adversary, and maintained a most sanguinary battle, on the 26th of August, 1278, at Marchfeld, on the other side of the Danube. The victory was long doubtful, and Rudolphus himself was in great danger, for among the Bohemian knights several had agreed and sworn to attack and destroy him. One of them, Henry of Fullenstein, sprang upon him with his couched lance, but the emperor avoided the stroke, and dexterously thrusting the point of his own spear through the aperture of his antagonist's helmet, he pierced his head, and he fell dead from his horse. At the same moment, however, a gigantic Thuringian knight, who also belonged to the conspirators, stabbed the horse of Rudolphus, which fell to the ground, and its royal rider with difficulty protected himself with his shield from being trampled under foot, until one of his own knights brought him another horse. Being again mounted, and his general, Berthold Kappler, bringing up now the rear-guard, he once more dashed against the enemy, who could no longer resist the attack, but was completely put to flight. Nevertheless, although deserted by his army, Ottocar, as Rudolphus himself testifies, fought bravely to the last; until, with his horse, he was struck to the earth and killed by a knight of Styria, whom he had formerly much injured and oppressed. When peace was restored, the marriage between the two royal houses was celebrated, and Bohemia was governed in trust for the children of Ottocar by the margrave of Brandenburg.

Rudolphus, however, with the consent of the German princes, transferred Austria, as imperial fief, to his own house; it was, in fact, a country reconquered by his arms for the German empire; and one of the electoral princes, in a letter he wrote in approbation of this arrangement, said—"That it was only just that Rudolphus should convey over to his children, if he thought fit, that principality which he had reconquered for the empire with so much sacrifice of his own blood." Accordingly, at an imperial diet held in Augsburg in 1282, the emperor took solemn possession thereof, and in the presence of all the princes and nobles of the empire, he gave to his sons Albert and Rudolphus, the countries of Austria, Styria, Carniola, and Vienna; but Carinthia he gave to Meinhard, count of Tyrol, whose daughter his son Albert had married. Thus the emperor Rudolphus became the founder of the powerful house of Austria.

These affairs being settled, he was again, although far advanced in years, zealously engaged in seeking to promote the tranquillity of the empire. He required the counts, nobles, and cities of the several countries throughout the empire to take an oath to preserve the public peace for the term of five years; and knowing well that all who nourish evil intentions are never sufficiently bound by their word, he himself journeyed through all the provinces, and routing the freebooter knights from their castles and strongholds, completely destroyed them. Thus, on one expedition to Thuringia, he razed sixty-six such places, and executed twenty-nine of these brigand nobles; among those of the most troublesome princes whom he punished was Count Eberhard of Wurtemberg, and whose motto was, "The friend of God and enemy of the world;" him he besieged in his own city of Stuttgard, and forced him to yield and to raze with his own hands the walls of that his actual place of residence. On the other hand, he suffered other persons of rank to build fortresses for their defence against the freebooters, as in the case of the bishop of Paderborn, who in 1290 was permitted to build two castles upon his domain.

Hence the emperor Rudolphus was so fully employed in Germany, that he never seriously contemplated going to Italy in order to be crowned king. He was also accustomed to say that "Italy resembled a lion's den, in which it was true many traces might be found of those emperors who had entered it, but very few, if any, of those who had quitted it." Nay, so little did he follow out the plans of former kings with regard to Italy, that in a negotiation with the pope, Gregory X., he ceded all the imperial right of interference within the domain of the Church as in the present day. Hence he could congratulate himself in beholding that destructive cause of incitement removed which impelled the emperors to make their expeditions into Italy.

Towards the latter end of his reign, Rudolphus was anxious, at an imperial diet held at Frankfort in 1291, to have his own son Albert recognised by the princes as emperor of Germany; but the nobles, jealous and tired of the government of Rudolphus, which had already become too vigorous and firm for them—inasmuch as it prevented them from following their own selfish interests—thinking that Germany would cease to be an elective kingdom if the son were allowed to succeed his father, refused their consent to the proposal. Displeased with this ingratitude Rudolphus took his departure in disgust, and proceeded to Basle.

He had now attained a great age, and suffered much from infirmity and disease; so much so that, during the last year of his life, his physicians had only prolonged his existence by artificial means. One day, while he was sitting at the chess-board, they announced to him the near approach of his death. "Well then," he said, "let us away, my friends, to Spires, to the tomb of the kings!" Accordingly he was carefully conveyed to the travelling equipage, and with his train set off and journeyed along the Rhine; he did not, however, reach Spires, but died on the road, at Germersheim, on the 30th of September, 1291, aged seventy-four.

His memory was so universally revered throughout Germany, that for a long time after his death it was common to say: "No, no, that is not acting with the honesty of Rudolphus!" He was a warrior from his boyhood, and one of his dearest wishes as a youth was that he might have the command of a German army of 40,000 infantry and 4000 cavalry, for with such a force, he said, he would have marched against and faced the whole world.

Several of the princes were not unfavorable to Albert of Austria, the son of Rudolphus, but Archbishop Gerhard of Mentz understood so to arrange matters that his own cousin, Count Adolphus of Nassau, was chosen emperor. Adolphus was indeed a brave and valiant knight, and possessed many amiable qualities, but for such a station he had neither sufficient tact, nor adequate power and influence. He held only the moiety of the territory of Nassau, and his property was so insignificant that he could not even cover the expenses attending the coronation; and when he tried to extricate himself from this difficulty by imposing a tax upon the Jews in Frankfort, he was opposed by the mayor of that city; Archbishop Gerhard, therefore, was obliged to mortgage his ecclesiastical estates in his favor.

As emperor, he sought to follow in the footsteps of Rudolphus, by maintaining the peace of the land, and at the same time endeavoring to aggrandize his own house; but it was impossible for him to succeed in either of these objects, and in the latter especially he employed such means as produced disaffection and disgust in the public mind. In the first place, in order to obtain money, he promised King Edward I. of England his aid in troops against Philip of France, in return for a considerable sum. This aid, however, although the money was paid, was not required, as the war between the two kings was suspended for that time. The money, however, Adolphus devoted to the purchase of fresh lands. Just at this period a profligate margrave, Albert the Base, held his sway in Thuringia, and abandoned his amiable and virtuous wife Margaret, the daughter of the emperor Frederick II., in order to marry Cunigunde of Isenburg. The unhappy mother, when obliged to take leave of her children, in the anguish of separation, bit the cheek of her son Frederick, who from this circumstance is styled in history "Frederick with the bitten cheek." This unnatural and truly base father sold the hereditary estates of his two sons by the first marriage, to the emperor Adolphus, and presented the money to Albert, the son of Cunigunde. Subsequently, however, Frederick and Dietzmann, the two sons of Margaret, having come to manhood, fought bravely for their inheritance, their people having remained faithful to them; so that the emperor found himself obliged to wage an unrighteous war against them—he whose primary duty it was to maintain with all his power and influence right and justice towards all. The brothers, however, regained a portion of their lands.

Such unworthy proceedings had brought down upon Adolphus the hatred of Germany; besides this, the fickle-minded archbishop, Gerhard of Mentz, was also dissatisfied with him, because he found that he was deceived in the hopes he had cherished of making him subservient to his own interests. At his suggestion, therefore, a new diet of all the princes and nobles was held, and Adolphus was there deposed: inasmuch as he had desolated the churches, received pay from a prince (the king of England) inferior to himself, and had likewise diminished the empire instead of extending it, and finally had not promoted and maintained the peace of the country. Albert of Austria was therefore chosen to replace him. This was the first instance in which the electoral princes, without the instigation of the pope, dethroned an emperor of their own accord. The two rival sovereigns appealed to arms, marched against each other, and met at Worms, where, in 1298, they fought the decisive battle. Adolphus was completely overthrown, and fell in the contest mortally wounded—as some say, by the hand of Albert himself.

This Albert was by no means of a kind, friendly disposition like his father; on the contrary, he was a severe, austere, and despotic ruler; besides, even in his external appearance he was disfigured by the loss of an eye. It is true his severity towards the archbishop of Mentz was just, for the emperor not being disposed to consult his will in every thing, the archbishop had menacingly said, "that he had yet more emperors in his pocket;" and actually adopted means for the election of another. But Albert very soon brought him to reason, and obliged him to sue for mercy. In other matters, however, his actions were not always guided by justice. His aim was to bring under his subjection several other countries, in which he partly succeeded; and his eyes were now turned towards Thuringia, Bohemia, and Holland, when all his enterprises were suddenly annihilated by death. In the spring of the year 1308, he went to his hereditary estates on the borders of Switzerland, in order to re-establish peace among the insurgent

Swiss, and to levy great forces to enable him to carry on the contemplated war against Bohemia. He had with him also his young nephew, John of Swabia, the son of his brother Rudolphus, from whom, although he was now out of his minority, he withheld the share he inherited of the Hapsburg estates. In vain did the ambitious youth repeatedly beg for his patrimony; the king always refused. Finding, therefore, all his just demands in vain, he, with four knights, who also nourished a secret hatred against Albert, determined at length to assassinate him. On the 1st of May, 1308, and in the tenth year of his reign, the emperor set out from Stein near Baden through Argau, in order to return to the camp at Reinfeld, where his court was assembled. They came through the deep valleys to the ferry across the Reuss at Windisch. Here the conspirators pressed forward with a view of entering the same boat with the emperor; and thus, having separated him from his attendants, they crossed the stream together. Having reached the shore, they remounted their steeds and proceeded for some distance, through the vast cornfields, at the base of the hills, on the highest of which towered the mighty castle of Hapsburg, when suddenly rushing upon the emperor, Duke John of Swabia buried his lance in his neck, loudly exclaiming: "Such is the reward of injustice!" At the same time Rudolphus of Balm stabbed him with his dagger, and Walter of Esehenbach divided his head with his sword. The king sunk to the earth powerless and bathed in his blood. A poor woman, who had witnessed the deed, hurried to the spot, and in her arms the emperor Albert breathed his last. The conspirators decamped and separated from each other immediately after the tragedy; and, tormented by their guilty consciences, never afterwards met or saw each other again. One of them, Rudolphus of Wart, was taken and broken upon the wheel on the spot where the deed of blood was committed; the others, as well as the duke himself, ended their days in obscurity and misery.

It was during the year in which King Albert was murdered, that the foundation of the Swiss confederacy was laid. The history of this vigorous, industrious, and freedom-loving people, who inhabit many greater and smaller tracts of country at the foot of, and amidst the lofty chains of mountains which run between Germany, France, and Italy, belongs also to the history of Germany; for the origin of the Swiss nation is entirely German, and it is only on the borders of this country and France that the French language is spoken. The chief cities in the districts towards Swabia, Berne, Zurich, Freiburg, Soleure, &c., were originally, and continued for a long period to be imperial free cities; and the Waldstädte, or forest towns, Schwyz, Uri, and Unterwald, were likewise under the immediate protection of the empire. Their form of government was very ancient, and seemed, as it were, fresh from the hand of nature. The same as among the ancient Germans, the whole community of freemen exercised, under their *Landammann* or president, the greatest power; and the strength of their constitution lay entirely in the combined will of the people. The emperor of Germany however, as they belonged to the empire, had among them his Vogts or intendants, who attended to the collection of taxes, the coinage and stamping of money, and matters by no means burdensome.

Albert, who was anxious to extend the power of his house, proposed that they should renounce their connection with the imperial state, and place themselves under the protection of his powerful house, possessing as it did such extensive patrimonial possessions in their immediate vicinity, which meant, in other words, that, instead of remaining longer Germans, they should become Hapsburgians, or Austrians. They, however, regarding his acts with a suspicious eye, refused to agree to his proposal; upon which the emperor, in his turn, renounced them, permitting, and even encouraging the intendants to oppress and levy upon the people severe and cruelly unjust exactions. He treated these comparatively little known and obscure mountaineers with derision and contempt. He appointed as his representatives two Vogts: Hermann Gessler of Bruneck, a haughty, overbearing nobleman, who possessed, near the town of Altorf, in Uri, a castle or strong fortress, in which he used to force the inhabitants of the neighborhood to obedience; and Beringer of Landenberg, who dwelt at the castle of Sarnen, in Unterwald; to those Albert added several other officers, who performed the functions of unter-vogts or sub-intendants.

But three patriotic and noble-minded Swiss, who felt and deeply participated in the misery endured by their native land, while deprived of its ancient freedom, united together in order to overthrow and crush the tyrannical power of these imperial Vogts.

The names of these fearless and magnanimous men were: Werner Stauffacher of Schwyz, Walter Fürst of Attinghausen in Uri, and Arnold of Melchthal in Unterwald. They knew well that their hardy countrymen, bold and undismayed in the defence of their rights, would readily take part with them. Arnold of Melchthal especially, however, had grievous cause for resentment, inasmuch as the intendant, Landenberg, for some very trifling circumstance, had most unjustly taken from him a team of fine oxen, and when his father complained of it, Landenberg's officer replied, contemptuously: "If peasants wish to eat bread, let them draw the plough themselves." Arnold, incensed at the shameful act itself, as well as indignant at the fellow's insolence, broke the servant's arm with the stick he held in his hand, and knowing but too well the cruel character of the Vogt, took flight and secreted himself. The tyrant, unable to find him, ordered the eyes of his venerable father to be plucked out—an instance of savage cruelty but too frequently presented at that time in this oppressed country.

These three patriots now uniting together, met regularly during the silent hour of night at Rütli, a small meadow in a lonely place, between high rocks on the banks of the Lake of Lucerne. At the same time they were busily engaged in enlisting their friends into the noble cause, and on the night of the Wednesday before Martinmas, in the year 1307, each brought with him to this place ten fellow-patriots, men of upright, resolute mind. When these thirty-three good and true men were assembled at the Rütli, filled with the recollection of their former liberty, and united together by the perils of the times in the closest bonds of friendship, the three leaders lifted up their hands to heaven, and swore in the name of the Supreme Being that they would manfully combine in defence of their common liberty. The other thirty members, following the example of their chief, and raising their hands to heaven with equal ardor and enthusiasm, pronounced the same oath. The execution of their plan, however, was reserved for the first day of the ensuing new year; and separating now, they each returned to their cottages, where in the mean time they preserved the most strict silence, and put up their cattle for the winter.

Meanwhile, the Vogt or Governor, Hermann Gessler, was shot by William Tell, a citizen of Uri, and a native of Burglen, son-in-law of Walter Fürst. How that free and brave man refused, at the command of the cruel Vogt, to do homage to a hat, the symbol of his tyranny, how he was obliged to shoot an apple from the top of his son's head, and how he escaped from the threatened incarceration by leaping out of a boat in the midst of a heavy storm, on the Lake of Lucerne, and finally of his shooting Gessler at Küssnacht—all this is well known, and having continued to form the theme of universal praise, has been celebrated by the poet and painter, both in ancient and modern times, down to the present moment. And although this event took place before the hour destined to liberate the country, and without the interference of the oppressed people, it nevertheless strengthened the courage of the confederates, and was hailed as the harbinger of their emancipation by all the sturdy natives of that noble and majestic country.

Early in the morning of the first day of the year 1308, when Landenberg, the Vogt, was proceeding from the castle to attend mass at Sarnen, he was met by twenty men of Unterwald with calves, goats, sheep, fowls, and hares, which, according to the custom of the mountaineers, they brought for his acceptance as a new year's gift. The Vogt, pleased with their present, desired the men to convey the animals into the court of the castle. As soon, however, as these twenty patriots had entered within the gates, one of them blew a horn, at which signal each of them drew forth a steel blade concealed beneath his doublet, and fixed it upon the end of his stick, while thirty more of their comrades rushed down the hill through the wood of Erlen, and joining them in the castle, they all took possession of the place, and made the whole garrison prisoners. Landenberg, who having heard the tumult, had fled from Sarnen, across the fields, towards Alpnach, was pursued and taken; but as the confederates had agreed to shed no blood, they having first made him swear to quit Switzerland forever, and never return to it, allowed him to depart and seek refuge at the court of his emperor.

By similar stratagems to that employed in the taking of the castle of Sarnen, many others were captured and demolished, and the various imperial Vogts, with their dependents, sent beyond the borders; so that messengers arrived from every quarter at the Lake of Lucerne, with the good news of success. On the following Sunday, the 7th of January, the Swiss met together, and again pledged themselves to the ancient oath of confederacy. The next and most immediate danger which threatened them was from King Albert, who was resolved to avenge himself upon them for their conduct. From this, however, they were in a few months rescued by the arm of Duke John of Swabia, and his confederates. Nevertheless, they had still to sustain some dreadful struggles for their newly-acquired freedom.

After the death of Albert I. the German princes remained true to their principle, not to choose several emperors from the same house in succession, and therefore as chivalric virtues in their estimation surpassed all other, they elected Count Henry of Luxemburg, who was known to be a valiant, manly hero and knight. His reign in Germany was too short to permit him to do much for its welfare; nevertheless, brief as it was, he showed by his conduct that he possessed sufficient courage and nobleness of mind to render himself worthy of the ancient imperial crown. He likewise made an expedition to Italy,* whither no emperor had gone since Conrad IV.; and there he testified his noble and chivalric principles by effecting a reconciliation between the Guelfs and the Ghibelins, thus again uniting together, under the ascendency of the government, those whose minds had been distracted with hatred and discord; but the violence of the parties soon again broke forth, and Henry himself sunk, probably their sacrifice. After being crowned at Rome, he died suddenly in the midst of their contention, in an expedition against Robert, king of Naples, at Buonconventi, near Sienna, on the 24th of August, 1313, as was thought by poison.

He acquired for his house the kingdom of Bohemia, and by this means laid the foundation of its greatness. In Bohemia, Ottocar's grand-daughter Elizabeth was left as the last survivor of the ancient royal race. In a spirit of hatred to the Hapsburgian house, which, after this princess, possessed the next claim upon Bohemia, the nobility gave this heiress in marriage to John, the son of the emperor, and with her the house of Luxemburg obtained the royal crown of Bohemia, to which was afterwards added also the imperial crown.

In the new election of emperor the princes were far from being unanimous; the one party, with the archbishop of Mentz at their head, chose Lewis of Upper Bavaria; the other, led by the archbishop of Cologne, selected Duke Frederick of Austria, surnamed the handsome, because of his fine and noble form. Lewis was crowned at Aix-la-Chapelle and Frederick at Bonn, with the real insignia of the empire. Thence a new war broke out in Germany; everywhere there was violent opposition. The greatest number of towns, especially those in Swabia, were for Lewis, and, as might be expected, the Swiss people also; on the other hand, the nobility were chiefly for Frederick of Austria. Moreover, Frederick had a powerful ally in the person of his brother, Duke Leopold, who was a brave knight and a good general. This prince resolved in the first place to avenge the honor of the Austrian house upon the Swiss people, and he forthwith advanced into their country, accompanied by a numerous retinue of knights. He threatened to trample these boors under his feet, and provided himself with an abundant supply of ropes for the execution of their rebellious chiefs; for he had no idea of the astonishing feats which an oppressed people are capable of performing in the cause of their freedom, however unskilled in the ordinary tactics of war.

The duke divided his army into two divisions, and advanced from Aegeri to Morgarten, towards the mountains of Schwyz. The heavy cavalry, consisting of knights clad in complete iron armor, the pride and flower of the army, formed the van-guard, for the known heroism of the duke had attracted the whole of the ancient nobility of Hapsburg, Lenzburg, and Kyburg, to

* Dante was among the first to do homage to him on his arrival, and presented him with a letter and a Latin discourse upon the imperial dominion, in which he, as a Ghibelin, highly extolled it, and invited Henry to make a vigorous use of his power

join his ranks, together with the Vogt of Landenberg, and the male branches of Gessler's family, all burning to revenge his death.

But the confederates, when they received the news that the enemy was approaching, did not in the least waver in their courage and heroism, but prepared at once for battle. On that same night four hundred men from Uri landed at Brunnen, in Schwyz, and a few hours afterwards they were joined by three hundred men from Unterwald; they then all marched across the fields, and joined the main body in Schwyz. There they were gladly welcomed by a venerable patriot, Rudolphus Redin, of Biberegg, so aged and infirm that he could scarcely totter, yet so skilled and prudent in war, that the people, as he now drew up their plan of attack, gladly listened to his sage advice, which they scrupulously followed: "Our grand aim, my sons, must be," said he, "as we are so inferior in numbers, to prevent the duke from gaining any advantage by his superior force." He then showed them how they must occupy the heights of Morgarten and the Sattel mountain, in order to surprise the duke's army in the narrow pass, and falling upon its flank, thus divide and cut it off.

The small but united band of patriots, after they had knelt down, and implored the help of God, according to ancient custom, went forth to the number of thirteen hundred, and gained the summit of the Sattel mountain, near the Einsiedeln boundary. Here they were joined by an unexpected body of fifty men, who on account of some dispute had been banished from Schwyz, but who on being made acquainted with the danger that threatened their country, forgot their quarrel, and repaired to Morgarten, resolved to sacrifice their lives for their native land.

On the 16th of November, 1315, the host of well-accoutred horsemen commenced the ascent of the mountains under the ruddy rays of a morning's sun, in the reflection of which their forest of glittering spears and lances extended as far as the eye could reach. The van now entered the pass, and the avenue, which was hedged in with mountains and water, soon became filled with the close ranks of the cavalry. At this moment the aforesaid fifty exiled Schwyzers, shouting aloud, rolled down from the heights of Morgarten huge fragments of rock in quick succession on the enemy. When the 1300 Swiss who were posted on the summit of the Sattel mountain, beheld the confusion now produced among the ranks of the horsemen in the pass beneath, (near the Lake of Aegeri,) they quickly descended, and in a firm, united body, made an overwhelming attack upon the enemy's flank, committing everywhere the most sanguinary execution with their iron-pointed clubs and halberbs. Many of the nobles and knights, the flower of the Austrian nobility, fell, two of the Gesslers were slain, and Landenberg was pierced to death. Duke Leopold himself narrowly escaped from the vengeance of those hardy mountaineers, previously held by him in such contempt, but now become his victorious pursuers, and was with difficulty saved by a peasant acquainted with the roads, who conducted him through narrow by-passes as far as Winterthur, where he at length safely arrived in the greatest dejection and fatigue of mind and body.

Thus the whole Austrian army, in spite of all its chivalric bravery and superior discipline, was completely annihilated by a small body of peasantry, who, however, although simple and rude by nature and condition, aroused at length from their former state of slavery and oppression, became at once ennobled by their innate love of liberty and patriotism; so that already within the short space of an hour and a half, by their united courage and tact, they succeeded in trampling upon their haughty and tyrannic foe, and obtaining over him a glorious triumph. After this happy day the confederates renewed their ancient bond of amity, whose basis was, that all should be ready in defence of one, and one in defence of all; and the emperor Lewis in several letters confirmed the liberty of the Swiss.

In Germany, however, the war between Frederick of Austria and Lewis of Bavaria still continued with undiminished fierceness. Many provinces were desolated with fire and sword, until at length, in the year 1322, a decisive action was fought at Mühldorf in Bavaria. Frederick very indiscreetly allowed himself to be drawn into that battle, without awaiting the arrival of his brother Leopold, who was advancing to the spot with assistance. The battle commenced at sunrise, and lasted ten hours. Frederick himself fought bravely at the head of his body-guard, equipped in a splendid suit of gold armor, and bearing aloft upon his helmet, glittering in the sun's rays, the imperial eagle; while Lewis, on the contrary, did not appear at all on the field of battle. At noon, Lewis's brave and experienced general, Seyfried Schweppermann of Nuremberg, ordered his army to wheel round, and thus the Austrians had the sun, dust, and wind full in their face, while at the same time, as directed by Schweppermann, the burgrave of Nuremberg fell upon them from behind with five hundred cavalry. This body, for the purpose of deceiving the enemy, carried Austrian colors and banners, so that Frederick and those with him were so deceived that they felt assured Duke Leopold had at that critical moment arrived with his desired aid. When, however, they discovered their mistake, they were speedily thrown into disorder and put to flight, and Frederick, whose horse was stabbed, was, with his brother Henry, taken prisoner. When he was presented by the burgrave of Nuremberg to Lewis, he was received by the latter with the words: "My cousin, we are glad to see you." Frederick, however, made no reply, but with his eyes fixed upon the ground remained completely silent. He was conveyed to the strong fortress of Traussnitz, in the Upper Palatinate.* Lewis was now the sole ruler of Germany, but Frederick's brother Leopold, and other princes, would not recognise him, but still carried on war against him; while in addition to this, Pope John XXII. excommunicated him for having taken part with the duke of Milan, against him. Lewis determined, therefore, in this emergency, to effect a reconciliation between himself and the house of Austria. Accordingly he went in 1325 to Frederick, who was still imprisoned in the castle of Traussnitz, and concluded a treaty with him, in which Frederick renounced all claim to the empire, and agreed to some other severe conditions, after which he was set at liberty, having, however, through his imprisonment become so much changed in his appearance, that his relations scarcely recognised him, while his wife Elizabeth of Aragon had, during this interval of two years and a half, so incessantly wept tears of grief and lamentation on his account, that she had become totally blind. Frederick on his part employed every means to carry into effect the stipulations of the treaty; he made his abdication known throughout the empire by public documents, and exhorted every one to submit to Lewis. Neither the pope nor Leopold, however, felt themselves bound by the contract, but, on the contrary, proceeded in every possible way to show their hostility to Lewis. The two princes then gave an example of fidelity and friendship, which redounds to their honor. Frederick maintained his friendship with Lewis, paying no regard either to the representations of his brother, nor to those of the pope, who even offered to release him from the obligations of his oath to Lewis, the latter being excommunicated; while Lewis, appreciating this magnanimity of character in Frederick, and remembering their mutual friendship in early life, they having grown up together, resolved formally to share the empire of Germany with him. Frederick came to him at Munich, and Lewis offered, as he was just on the point of making an expedition on behalf of his son Lewis in Brandenburg against the Poles, to intrust the defence of his own country against Leopold to his hands. That expedition, however, was not made, and the two kings, on the 5th of September, 1325, at Munich, entered publicly into an alliance: "They would both conjointly bear the title of a Roman king, call and regard themselves as brothers, and in their dispatches and other documents their signatures and seals should be affixed alternately. They would grant enfeoffments in their joint capacity, and would both together as one person preside over and govern the Roman empire, over which they had been appointed and set apart." The two friends pledged themselves anew, ate at one table, and lived affectionately together, as they had done in their childhood.

Pope John, who knew nothing of the German character, and who considered such good faith unprecedented, wrote to King Charles of France, to whom it might appear equally novel: "This incredible example of friendship and confidence was confided to me on the best authority, in a communication from Germany."

* It is related that the victorious army, after the battle, were without any provisions, having merely a small supply of eggs, which, on being distributed among them, left but one for each man. The emperor Lewis on hearing this exclaimed: "Well, give to every soldier his egg, but to the brave Schweppermann give two!" as a proof that to him alone was due the honor of the victory.

Frederick, however, did not long continue to take a part in the government; for, greatly depressed by his many sufferings, he retired into solitude, and spent the remainder of his life in quiet meditation, at the castle of Guttenstein, where he died in the year 1330, his amiable and afflicted consort having preceded him a short time before.

The house of Austria, as well as the pope, remained still inimical to Lewis of Bavaria, and did all in their power to oppose him; so that his whole reign presented one scene of confusion and anarchy, and this emperor, whose kind and noble, although less powerful mind, would in happier times have rendered him an excellent ruler, was not able, in the rage of such distraction, to direct the helm. It is difficult to say what degree of blame attaches to him, or how much was owing to the perplexity of his situation; but his measures appear to have been often indeterminate. At one time he adopted the language of entreaty, at another he employed the means of resistance; now, he united with the king of Bohemia, then with the king of England, and at last even with the king of France; and, in order to get rid of the anathema, he sent to the pope more than seven ambassadors; but all was in vain. For the popes resided no longer at Rome, having for a considerable time held their seat at Avignon in France; they were therefore in subjection to the kings of France, who, not being upon good terms with Germany, were rejoiced at the disunion which there prevailed, and prevented a reconciliation taking place between the pope and the emperor, as Pope Benedict XII. himself privately acknowledged, with tears in his eyes, to the German princes. In like manner, King John of Bohemia, when he had secured himself against Austria, showed himself hostile to the house of Bavaria, whose growing greatness he sought to oppose as much as possible. This daring and adventurous prince, who was incessantly traversing Europe on horseback, like a courier, used his influence in throwing the torch of discord into Italy, producing there the most sad dissensions, while he likewise succeeded in confirming both the pope and the king of France still more strongly in their hatred against the emperor Lewis.

In the year 1388 the German electoral princes, in order to preserve the security of the empire, held a diet at Reuse, on the Rhine, and made there the famous treaty known by the name of the first electoral alliance. In this they solemnly declared that as the holy Roman empire had been, and still continued to be attacked in its honor, burdened and oppressed in its rights and possessions, they would unite to defend it, and courageously support it with all their strength and power against every aggressor. Besides which, this protest was solemnly approved by all the other estates in an imperial diet, when it was declared: "That the imperial dignity and power were immediately derived from and depended upon God, and that as a matter of right and ancient custom, the moment an individual was elected emperor, that moment he must, by reason of his election, be regarded as a true king and Roman emperor, without any need of confirmation by the papal see." This imperial decision was made known to the pope in a special communication, and from this moment commenced the strong opposition made against the papal see.

Had Lewis now possessed sufficient firmness of character to have availed himself of this declaration made by the diet, and thereupon have based his power; if, above all, he had understood how to confide in the fidelity and constancy of all his subjects, as did in ancient times his imperial predecessors, he might still, notwithstanding all the hostility of foreigners, have enjoyed a prosperous reign. But as he was deficient in that greatness of soul, so necessary to bring into happy realization the great objects in view, the princes became more and more inimical towards him, so that, at a diet held at Reuse in 1344, they again brought heavy complaints against him, and censured his maladministration of the affairs of the empire. This ill-will, however, of the princes towards the emperor originated chiefly in the jealousy with which they regarded the gradual aggrandizement of his house. For by his marriage with the daughter of the count of Hennegau, Holland, Zealand, and Friesland, he had acquired a title to all these countries, inasmuch as there was no male heir; and, again, when the line of male descendants to the territory of Anhalt-Brandenburg became extinct, he made over, in 1323, to his son Lewis, the Brandenburg possessions, and afterwards gave this same son in marriage to Margaret, of Maultasch, the heiress of Tyrol. By this last acquisition he made the house of Austria still more hostile towards him, while in the two previous cases he brought down upon him the enmity of the Luxemburg-Bohemian house, and that of the king of France.

The opponents of Lewis, especially Pope Clement VI., carried their animosity at length to such an extent that a number of the princes, at an assembly held in the year 1346, chose as German emperor, Charles, the son of John, king of Bohemia, who was also margrave of Moravia; a prince who was brought up at the French court, his father having a great predilection for France. This emperor, however, proved to be no blessing to Germany. When after being proclaimed at Reuse, he mounted the so-called imperial throne erected there, in order to present himself before the people for the first time, and while the *Vivat Rex* resounded on every side, the imperial banner, which had been elevated on the bank of the Rhine, fell into its waters, and, in spite of every exertion made to save it, sunk to the bottom—an event which was regarded by all as an evil omen. Neither did he enjoy any popularity while Lewis lived; the latter, however, in the following year, 1347, died of apoplexy while hunting a bear. The spot where he fell from his horse, in the vicinity of Fürstenfeld, near Munich, is still called the *Kaiserwiese* or emperor's meadow, in recollection of the event. Lewis was the last emperor excommunicated by the popes.

## CHAPTER XIII.

### EMPERORS OF DIFFERENT HOUSES—1347–1437.

Charles IV. 1347-1378—Wenceslas, 1378-1400—Switzerland—The Battle of Sempach, 1386—Leopold of Austria—Arnold of Winkelried—His Heroism and Self-Devotion—Wenceslas deposed—Rupert of the Palatinate, 1400-1410—Sigismund, 1410-1437—Grand Council of Constance—John Huss and the Hussite Wars—Death of Sigismund, 1437.

At this time there were in Germany three powerful houses, which, if they had been united, could easily have subdued all the others; but they were so far from acting in concert together, that they, on the contrary, opposed each other. These were the house of Luxemburg, which possessed, in addition to Bohemia and Moravia, also part of Silesia and Lusatia; that of Bavaria, which had acquired Brandenburg, Holland, and the Tyrol; and that of Austria, which, besides its hereditary estates, possessed likewise much of the Swabian territory.

The house of Bavaria could not forget that Charles IV. had been the enemy of Lewis; accordingly, in conjunction with the archbishop of Mentz and other princes, it sought to procure and establish a rival king in opposition, and at length, after King Edward of England, and the Margrave Frederick of Meissen, had rejected the crown, it found in the person of Count Günther of Schwarzburg, a brave, powerful, and upright man, who accepted it, as he declared, solely for the welfare of the empire, and who would have been a very important rival to Charles, if he had not suddenly fallen sick, and soon after died—as he himself thought, of poison. Charles, therefore, now reigned alone and for a lengthened period. Much was expected from him, as he was cunning and skilful in his enterprises, and was likewise master of many languages. Nevertheless, however well he succeeded in promoting the interests of his hereditary lands by various useful regulations, still he was, as it were, but a step-father of the German empire, and his heart was not devoted to it. The last existing remains of the imperial estates, which in some degree still contributed to preserve the dignity of the empire, were sold by him similar to the unworthy head of a family, who turns his real property into money, in order that he may the more readily enjoy it.

His reign presented a series of many great calamities, which certainly could not be imputed to him, and were in fact beyond his control. Already at its commencement, Germany, like many other countries of Europe, was visited with the most terrible disasters. The same as in the summer of 1338, ten years previously, innumerable hosts of locusts had flocked from the east, and covered a part of Europe so dreadfully, that they completely obscured the light of the sun, and Hungary, Poland, Austria, and other places, became entirely desolated, and famine raged among mankind; so likewise in the year 1348, a succession of even still greater afflictions followed. On the 17th of January in this year the sun was eclipsed, and on the 25th a great earthquake was felt over nearly the whole of Europe. Cities and villages were overwhelmed, and buried their inhabitants under their ruins. The shocks during this year were several times repeated, and in the following one, a great plague, which was brought into Italy by the ships trading in the east, raged throughout that country, and soon extended its desolation over the whole of France and Germany. History presents no parallel to the terrible scenes of misery presented in this epoch. In the large cities the dead were numbered by hundreds of thousands, and in many cases the survivors scarcely amounted to a tenth part of the previously-existing population. Thousands of families became wholly extinct, whole streets uninhabited and laid waste, and no living being, nor even domestic animal was to be found: nay, some travellers who were going from Italy to Bohemia, found whole cities and villages without a single living inhabitant of any sort.

These calamities had the effect of awakening to reflection many who were previously sunk in sin; for the age which had preceded this had been extremely corrupt. In this state of despair, penances of every description were again put into force, and especially the use of the scourge was again put in requisition. Hundreds and even thousands went in procession from city to city, and practised their flagellations in the market-places, walking with their backs bare, singing, and at the same time flogging themselves and each other with knotty thorny whips. The leaders of the procession were often obliged themselves even to check by stern command the rage with which the infatuated penitents lacerated their flesh. Even children were infected with a passion for these inflictions, and took part in these scenes. As these proceedings were found to be the result of mere fanaticism and madness, accompanied by extravagances of every description, the pope at last interdicted them on pain of excommunication; but it was only with difficulty that they could be suppressed.

Meantime, as if that epoch was to be one distinguished alone for its wild disorders and excesses, the former persecution of the Jews was also renewed. Among the people the opinion had become more and more prevalent that the Jews had been the originators of the late great plague, by poisoning the springs and rivers, for the purpose of exterminating the whole o. Christendom. The ancient animosity was revived, and became more and more embittered; the authorities were unable tc restrain the fury of the people, and throughout Switzerland, in all the cities along the Rhine, and generally throughout Germany, the massacre of the Jews was so dreadful, that many of them in their despair destroyed themselves in their own houses. The mildest treatment they received was that of having their property confiscated, and being banished the country. The princes, and especially the pope and bishops, at last interested themselves in behalf of this persecuted people, and saved the small remnant of those as yet left untouched. History, however, leaves unmentioned whether the emperor Charles contributed his share towards the general good during this time of distress.

The most important work effected by him for Germany was published in an imperial edict called the Golden Bull, (thus called from the seal of gold affixed to it,) the institution of a fundamental law of the empire, enacted in the year 1356, which determined and regulated the rights and privileges of the seven electors, the mode of precedence in electing the emperor in the diet of Frankfort, and at the coronation at Aix-la-Chapelle, and some other regulations; among the rest it was decreed that after a proclamation made three days previously, the right of warfare should be declared and enforced.

But it was not by such regulations affecting the external and less essential objects, that the dignity of the empire could be restored; on the contrary, division, jealousy, and selfishness were excited more than ever by the advantages which he secured especially to the electoral houses; so that from the time of the Golden Bull may be dated the dissolution of the imperial dominion, rather than its re-establishment. The seven electoral princes who had already, for nearly an entire century, exercised the right of voting, included the archbishops of Mentz, Treves, and Cologne, together with the king of Bohemia, the duke of Saxe-Wittenberg, the margrave of Brandenburg, and the count palatine of the Rhine.

Charles labored with ability and extraordinary success for the aggrandizement of his own house. By his first consort Anna, princess palatine, he secured to his house the upper palatinate, and by his second wife Anna, of Schweidnitz and Jauer, he again transferred to it the possession of the entire southwest line of the beautiful territory in Silesia, along the borders of Bohemia; while already his father John and himself subsequently, having both gradually succeeded, partly by fraud and partly by force, in subjecting all the other princes of Silesia to the dominion of Bohemia, he, by a royal decree in 1355, united the whole of Silesia and Lower Lusatia to Bohemia. In like manner he became possessed of the margraviate of Brandenburg from the house of Bavaria, by which it had been only shortly before acquired under the emperor Lewis; for, availing himself of their weakness and total want of energy, he induced the Margraves Lewis the Roman, and Otho, to conclude a treaty, according to the terms of which, passing over their cousins of the house of Bavaria, the margraviate should be transferred to the house of Luxemburg in the event of both margraves dying without any heir. Soon after Lewis died, and the imbecile Otho made over, even during his life, in 1373, the government of his own country into the hands of the emperor, shortly after which, in 1379, the former died, despised and forgotten. Thus Charles, solely bent upon the aggrandizement of his house, united Brandenburg to the kingdom of Bohemia, and by this means, quite contrary to all the institutions of Germany, he made one German electorate dependent upon another. Henceforth likewise, he took as warm and paternal an interest in the newly acquired country as he did in his own hereditary estates; ruling over a range of beautiful tracts of country, extending from the confines of Austria, near the Danube, to Pomerania. Nevertheless, Charles, as so often happens to the selfish, was all this time working for strangers. His son Sigismund already mortgaged the margraviate of Brandenburg to the family of Hohenzollern, and by that laid the foundation for the greatness of that house; while the greater part of his other lands fell to the house of Austria, which was destined to rise still higher, after having been so much injured by him. At this time also that house obtained a great increase of territory in the county of Tyrol, where the Bavarian lineage, introduced by the emperor Lewis, had become extinct, and the house of Wittelsbach approached its end.

Charles proceeded also to Italy, but not as it became the successor of the great emperors, who had by their bravery obtained the sovereignty of that country; for he was obliged, in order that the pope might confirm his election to the Germanic empire, to submit to the disgraceful stipulation, that when he came to Rome in order to be crowned, he would only remain one day in that city, and quitting it before night, forthwith retire from the pope's territories. Accordingly he made his entry into Rome on Easter day, 1355, was crowned, and under pretence of going out to hunt, left the city on the same day and hastened out of the country. The Romans, not knowing the cause, were not a little astonished at his abrupt departure, and Petrarca, the celebrated poet, who by his animated letters had called upon him to reassume the ancient glorious imperial sway, now wrote to him: "What would his ancestors, the ancient German emperors, have said, if they had met him on the Alps retreating so ignobly?"

Towards the close of his life, his great fondness for France induced him to visit that country once more; and, immediately after his return to Germany, he died in the year 1378.

Charles IV. had already induced the princes to nominate as emperor after his death his son Wenceslas. But actuated in like manner, as his father had been, by that egotism and avarice, which ever aimed at his own interest, the son, although naturally endowed with good qualities, but without energy, and wholly given up to sensual gratification, especially to drinking and the chase, achieved nothing important either for Germany or even for his own hereditary lands.

The times were, at this moment, in a state of dreadful anarchy. The imperial government had lost all its dignity. Religion was at its lowest ebb, and Christendom was divided into parties; instead of one, there were two popes, one at Rome, the other at Avignon; both thundered forth against each other their bans of excommunication; and in their wrath, each anathematized whole communities and countries that happened to adhere to his opponent. Long and vainly did the most upright and judicious men of the day raise their voices against the destructive vices of their time, which were spreading far and wide, and all urged a general assembly of the Christian council; but Wenceslas, whose business it was as emperor to convoke such an assembly, had neither the will nor energy of mind sufficient to enforce it.

Under his reign there arose throughout Germany an increasing number of confederations among individual members of the empire for mutual protection; which was a proof of the prostration of the supreme power, and served still more to weaken and destroy it. The most powerful of these associations was that of Swabia, which consisted of thirty-four, and afterwards, even of forty-one cities, including likewise several princes. On the other hand, various similar societies, formed of the nobles, were not less flourishing, when, as a matter of course, contests and battles upon a large as well as small scale were the order of the day. The Swabian towns followed the example of the Swiss confederacy, which became more and more extensive, including even in its alliance several of the chief towns of Switzerland, Berne, Zürich, Soleure, and Zug, and already adopted the name of confederates. Thence, as in times of discord and hatred, no class keeps within the bounds of moderation, or adheres to justice, it is to be presumed that the complaints made by the princes and nobility, viz. that the towns had unlawfully deprived them of the services of such of their people as were bound to serve them, by affording them protection and granting them the privileges of citizens, were in many cases reasonable and well-founded. In consequence, therefore, of these grievances, a new war broke out between the nobility of Austria and the Swiss.

Duke Leopold of Austria, in heroism and arrogance equal to the Leopold who fought at Morgarten, was incensed against the Swiss, because in their alliance they had included several towns and villages which were subject to him, as for instance: Entlibuch, Sempach, Meyenberg, and Reichensee. There was certainly good foundation for complaint, but Austria likewise was not free from blame; for these places had been severely oppressed by its avaricious and inhuman agents; while the duke, contrary to the stipulations made, had imposed taxes on the frontiers of the Swiss, which checked their commercial intercourse. Duke Leopold vowed he would chastise the whole of the inhabitants, the originators and promoters of, as he styled it, unrighteous and unlawful warfare, and swore to destroy their offensive alliance. The hatred towards the free peasantry and citizens became so generally violent among the nobility, that within a few days no less than one hundred and sixty-seven of the nobles, both spiritual and secular, joined in denunciations of war, breathing utter destruction against the confederates. The letters of war were brought to the assembled confederacy by twenty distinct expresses, that their terror might be perpetually renewed. On the evening of the day of St. John the Baptist, a messenger from the court of Wurtemberg arrived with fifteen declarations of war; these letters were scarcely read when the messenger of John Ulric of Pfirt, and of eight other nobles arrived with letters to the same purpose, and he had scarcely finished when the letters of the lords of Thurn and of all the nobles of Schaffhausen came to hand. Finally, on the following day eight more messengers arrived with forty-three such declarations of war.

The confederates had no other aid to look or hope for but that of their own faithful union and persevering courage; undismayed, however, they awaited the commencement of the contest with indescribable impatience. The cry of war and the din of hostile preparation resounded throughout the country, and already four days previously all the population capable of bearing arms were equipped and ready. The term of the armistice having expired, the war between the federal peasantry and their nobles now burst forth, and within a week or two many a strong castle—so long the terror of the frontiers—was levelled and razed to the ground by the brave confederates.

Duke Leopold now, with a numerous force, including many distinguished knights and auxiliaries from all his states, marched from Baden through Aargau by Sursee for Sempach, in order to punish, as he said, with the rod of iron its citizens for their inflexible adherence to the confederates. But on his arrival there he found the confederates already collected on the heights, prepared and burning with impatience to receive him. Unwilling to await the arrival of his foot-soldiers, and afraid lest the cavalry might be thrown into confusion in a mountain engagement, he commanded all the nobles, knights, and the entire body of horsemen to dismount to the number of several thousands, and joining their ranks as closely as possible, like an impenetrable wall of iron, he ordered them to rush forward and charge the confederates spear in hand. When the baron of Hasenburg, a veteran warrior, perceived this order of battle, and contrasted it with the position commanded by the Swiss, he at once tried to dissuade the proud duke and his nobles from adopting this plan of attack, adding, as he cautioned them, that pride never served any good purpose, "that they had better wait until the infantry marched up." They, however, only derided him, and cried aloud, "Der Hasenburg hat ein Hasenherz!"* (Literally, "Hasenburg has a hare's-heart.") Some of his nobles having represented to the duke how necessary it was that he should restrain his ardor, while they tried to persuade him to keep in the rear of the army, he only smiled a reply; but when they continued to urge him to adopt their suggestions, he exclaimed impatiently: "What! shall Leopold be a mere looker-on and calmly behold his knights die around him in his own cause? Never! here on my native soil with you, I will conquer or perish for my people!" Saying which, he placed himself at the head of his troops.

As long as the enemy remained on horseback, it appeared too dangerous to the confederates to descend and stand the charge of such a body of cavalry on level ground; but when they beheld them quit their saddles, and form in ranks as foot-soldiers, the mountaineers forthwith abandoned their elevated position, and marched down into the plain below. Their numbers were: 400 men from Lucerne, 900 from the Waldstädten, and about 100 from Glaris, Zug, Entlibuch, and Rotenburg. Some were armed with short weapons, others carried halberds, with which their forefathers had fought in the pass at Morgarten; and some again, instead of a shield, had only a small board bound to their left arm.

This small, but firm and united body of brave men, now fell upon their knees and prayed to God, according to their custom. while the nobles on the opposite side buckled on their helmets, and the duke then created several knights. It was then the season of harvest, when the sun shone with full power, and the day was extremely sultry. The confederates now precipitated themselves with great impetuosity upon the impregnable phalanx of shields; but not a man yielded to the shock. The Swiss fell one after another; and the company of Lucerners, especially, fought with impatient and enthusiastic rage, seeking to make a road between the forest of spears, but in vain. Numbers lay bleeding around, and their force began to waver. The enemy then moved his extended body of men round in the form of a half-moon, thinking to encircle the few courageous Swiss. But the scene of this dreadful moment of approaching destruction to the confederates was unexpectedly changed, by a brave knight, Arnold of Winkelried, in Unterwald, who suddenly, in a voice of thunder, exclaimed to his comrades: "I will open a passage, to freedom, faithful and beloved confederates! Protect only my wife and children!" And with these words, rushing from his ranks he threw himself upon the enemy, and seized with both arms as many of the enemy's spears as he was able, buried them in his body, and sank dead to the ground, while the confederates rushed forward through the breach, over the body of their heroic and self-devoted compatriot. The Austrians gave way; and, in endeavoring to stop the breach, became, in their confusion, so crowded, that many of them died in their armor, unwounded, but suffocated and overwhelmed with heat and terror. Meantime, the chief banner of Austria was sinking for the third time to the ground, when Ulric, a knight of Aarburg, seized it, bore it aloft, and defended it, until, after a desperate struggle, he was mortally wounded, crying out with his last breath: "Save Austria, rescue!" At this moment, Duke Leopold, pushing through the crowd, received the banner from his dying hand; it once again appeared aloft, covered with blood, waving in the hand of the duke. But he was now surrounded by the Swiss, who pressing close upon him, he

* A play upon the baron's name, *Hasenburg*, hare's-stronghold, literally interpreted; Hase, hare; Burg, fort, or stronghold; and Herz, heart *Hasenherz*, hare's-heart or heart of a hare.

exclaimed, as he saw all his brave warriors falling around him: "Since, then, so many nobles and knights have ended their days in my cause, thus let me also honorably follow them!" and, vanishing from the sight of his few remaining adherents, he plunged, in the madness of grief and despair, amidst the hostile ranks, seeking his death. In the pressure of the crowd he fell to the earth; and while he was struggling in his heavy armor to raise himself upon his feet, he was discovered by a citizen of Schwyz, to whom Leopold, quite helpless, called out, "I am the prince of Austria!" The man, however, either did not hear or believe him, or, perhaps, thinking that, in war, all distinctions cease, forthwith killed him. The body of the duke was found by a knight, Martin Malterer, who bore the banner of Freiburg in Breisgau; he stood petrified, and the banner fell from his hand. He threw himself upon the body of the prince, in order that it might not be trampled upon by friends and enemies, and in this situation he awaited and received his own death.

The Austrian troops, in a state of utter dismay and terror, now gave the signal for retreat, and all the cavaliers flew to regain their horses. But they were too late; their attendants had already mounted them, and saved themselves by flight. All therefore that remained for them now, oppressed with their ponderous armor, rendered still more intolerable by the scorching rays of the sun, and exhausted with thirst and fatigue, was to avenge their prince, and sell their lives at as dear a rate as possible. Thus, there perished altogether six hundred and fifty-six counts, barons, and knights, together with thousands of their vassals.

Such was the issue of the great battle of Sempach, fought on the 9th of July, 1386; by this victory, and another at Näfels, the confederates of Switzerland so weakened the power of Austria, that in the year 1389, by the mediation of tne imperial cities on the Lake of Constance, a seven years' peace was agreed to, by which means the Swiss preserved all they had acquired, while Austria retained only its chief possessions in Aargau and Thurgau.

In the cities of Germany the passion for war was again awakened by the successes of the Swiss. The ancient hostility between the nobles and citizens was resumed, particularly in Swabia, on the Rhine, and in the Wetteraw. But these cities did not command the favorable passes of the mountains, neither were the citizens equal to the peasants of Switzerland. They were beaten in several contests, among others by Count Eberhard of Wurtemberg, between Weil and Döffingen, also by the Count Palatine Rupert, near Worms. In 1389 tranquillity was in some degree restored by the peace proclaimed at Eger. This was a sad period of disaster for Bavaria, Swabia, Franconia, and the whole of the Upper Rhine. It is related in the Chronicle of Königshoven, that more persons were destroyed at that time than had been for several centuries before. Most of the country people were obliged to remain throughout the winter in the fortresses and cities. In many parts not a single village or house was to be found within ten miles of the cities and strong castles: so much desolation had been produced by fire and sword.

The emperor Wenceslas had not sufficient energy and authority to settle, by the imperial decision, the existing differences between the nobility and the cities; besides which he came but seldom to Germany, and after the year 1391, he only visited it at the end of six years. The Bohemians, who were likewise dissatisfied with him, owing to the cruel acts he had committed at various times, which together with his other infirmities, made him only the more hated and despised, imprisoned him in the castle of Prague, where he remained until he was liberated by his younger brother John. This was an additional cause of his downfall in Germany, and at length, in the year 1400, the princes proceeded to depose him. The charges against him were: "that the holy Roman empire, the holy church, and all Christendom, instead of finding in him comfort, protection, and succor, had, on the contrary, been rent asunder, abused and shamefully abandoned by him; that all this had been repeatedly and fearlessly represented to him, but he had neither restored peace to the church, nor had he felt any concern at the many feuds and tumults of the empire, so that no one knew where to seek redress, protection, and security. Since, therefore, all remonstrances had failed, the princes could not do otherwise than conclude that he no longer cared for the welfare of the empire, and thence they, the princes, necessarily forbade him henceforward to have any share in the government of the Germanic nation, and accordingly they deposed him, the said Emperor Wenceslas, as negligent and unworthy." On the following day they elected Rupert of the palatinate, as emperor.

In the succeeding year, Wenceslas, who still held possession of Bohemia, was again taken prisoner by his brother Sigismund, and confined for nineteen months at Vienna.

Rupert, an active and brave man, endeavored to re-establish the imperial dignity; but the existing state of disorder was already too great, and his government of too short a duration to allow him to gain this object. He was likewise unsuccessful in an expedition to Italy, and he died, without having effected any thing of importance, in 1410.

The princes now elected Sigismund, the brother of Wenceslas, to fill the imperial throne, and in certain respects, this emperor was the most distinguished of the house of Luxemburg. His appearance was majestic and graceful. He was tall and well-formed, and his manly countenance, shaded by light brown ringlets, rendered him one of the handsomest princes of his day. He possessed a lively spirit and an acute mind, and being master of six languages, may be considered altogether as a monarch of superior intellectual acquirements. He had a degree of open honesty and true heartedness in his disposition, which won the hearts of all; combined with a genuine love for all that was good and meritorious. Nevertheless, with all these good qualities and brilliant endowments, his resolution and power of action did not correspond in proportion. He was changeable and undecided, and wholly incapable of realizing and maintaining the great designs he contemplated. Besides all this, however, he was a bad economist, always squandering away what he possessed, and consequently, perpetually in difficulties. Sigismund directed his first attention to the great schism existing in the church; there being one pope in Italy, another in France, and a third in Spain, whence each pronounced the ban of excommunication against his opponent, and those who sided with him. Finally, in the year 1414, the celebrated council of the church was held at Constance, and perhaps there never was a council more numerous and brilliant. Besides the pope, there were present the patriarchs of Constantinople, Grado and Antioch, twenty-two cardinals, twenty archbishops, ninety-two bishops, one hundred and twenty-four abbots, one thousand eight hundred of the lower clergy, numerous doctors of science and masters of arts; as likewise the graduates of the universities of Paris, Orleans, Cologne, Vienna, and others; about one thousand six hundred princes, nobles, counts, and knights, with their retinues; so that altogether the number that attended this grand council exceeded 100,000.

Of the three popes, the only one present was John XXIII., from Rome, who had convoked the assembly in the hope that his two opponents would be deposed, and he himself confirmed. The council, however, notwithstanding the opposition of the Italians, determined at once to dispense with all three, that the evil might be struck at the root. It was agreed that not only bishops and abbots should have a vote, as had been hitherto the custom, but that likewise doctors of divinity, as well as of the canon and civil law, together with the princes and their ambassadors, and lastly, all the priests present, should share in this privilege; and that the votes should not be given individually, as formerly, but according to the nation; so that each of the four principal nations—Germany, England, France, and Italy, should have each one vote; (the Spaniards had not yet arrived.) For if the votes had been taken individually, the Italians, whose number was by far the most considerable, would have outvoted all the others. The Germans, as is stated by a contemporary of that period, were distinguished on this important occasion, for their determination, vehemence, and persevering remonstrances in support of their claims; the English for their boldness and acuteness; the French for their ostentation and self-importance; and the Italians for their finesse, stratagem, and partiality.

But the English and the Germans were united in their decision upon the deposition of the popes, and the French soon afterwards joined with them. John XXIII., being present, was the first to sign the abdication; he tried to avoid it, but at length he yielded, and, kneeling before the altar, publicly read his consent to abdicate. The emperor Sigismund and all present were filled with joy; the emperor even rose and kissed the feet of the pope, and thanked him in the name of the Christian world, for setting such a glorious example of self-control. But John had only yielded *in appearance;* for he had already conferred with his friend, Duke Frederick of Austria, and concerted with him the necessary measures for his flight. Accordingly, the duke made arrangements for a grand tournament, which took place on the 20th of March, 1415; and, while the attention of all present was directed to the festival, the pope hastened away, disguised as a postilion, to Schaffhausen, which still belonged to Austria. The duke followed him quickly afterwards; and, during the night, several hundreds of Italian and Austrian prelates likewise arrived. The pope hoped to retain possession of his authority, even against the will of the council. But the assembled fathers of the church from Germany, England, and France, together with the emperor Sigismund himself, were too serious in their decision. The council, under the presidency of the emperor Sigismund, declared: "That its power being derived immediately from Christ, and being *superior to the pope*, its decrees, without the authority of the pope, should reunite and reform the church." The greatest severity was shown to all those who had taken their departure; Duke Frederick was excommunicated by the council, and outlawed by the emperor; and, finally, at his command, the imperial troops under Burgrave Frederick of Nuremberg, and the Swiss, seized the hereditary estates of the duke, and deprived him of the chief portion of them. Aargau, and the ancient castle of Hapsburg, were conquered by the Bernese. About ten years after this, however, the emperor again received the duke into his favor, and returned to him such of the lands as were at the control of the empire; the Swiss, however, never restored the territories they had gained, but retained possession of Aargau and all the rest.

The pope, who had been deprived of the protection of the emperor, was obliged to submit to the decrees of the council; he was brought back from Freiburg in Breisgau, whither he had fled, to the small town of Ratolfszell, near Constance, there to receive his final sentence, as follows: "That as he had publicly and criminally availed himself of the privileges and estates of the Roman church, and as he had, moreover, brought down scandal upon Christianity by his immorality, he was thenceforth deposed from the papal chair." John submitted to his sentence, was kept in custody until the year 1419 at the castle of Heidelberg, and then at Mannheim, where he was liberated, and soon afterwards died as cardinal-bishop of Frascati.

The second pope, Gregory XII., who was eighty-eight years of age, and whose seat was in France, immediately declared his readiness to resign his office, if the peace of the church required it; and accordingly he voluntarily resigned in that same year, 1415, and was made cardinal-bishop of Porto.

But Benedict XIII. was not to be persuaded; his seat was in Spain. The emperor Sigismund himself undertook, at the request of the council, a journey to Spain for the purpose of inducing the old man to yield; but he failed. King Ferdinand of Aragon, however, who had hitherto adhered to him, withdrew his protection, and now the council without further ceremony deposed him.

Thence was accomplished the grand and principal design of the ecclesiastical council, and thus terminated the ruinous schism of the church, which had lasted during forty years; and they were now able to proceed to the election of a new pope. But the assembled fathers had another important object in view, viz., the reformation of the church itself. Complaints were made about many abuses which had crept in: the immorality of the clergy, simony, and especially the increasing pretensions of the papal chair, had now become excessive. These abuses the assembled heads of the church were anxious in the name of their several countries to sweep away, while, at the same time, they were ready to secure to the pope all due respect, obedience, and also many just revenues from all countries.

The Germans, and at their head the emperor himself, were extremely anxious for a thorough reformation of the church. But the Italians, who derived the greatest benefit from the large sums of money which poured into Rome from the other countries, endeavored to frustrate their design, and thought the best course they could adopt for that purpose would be to induce the council, in the first place, to choose a pope who might afterwards, as he thought fit, undertake the reform of the church. The Germans, on the contrary, who perceived what was meant by this artful proposal, very justly required that the new pope should be chosen afterwards, and that the first condition of his election should be, that he would abide by and confirm the new constitution of the church. Their reasons were perfectly just and rightly founded; nevertheless, the Italians succeeded in winning over to their party the French and the Spaniards, who had in the mean time arrived, and as the English had received command from their king to support the cardinals, the Germans stood alone, and were of course at last obliged to yield.

The new pope was accordingly elected; he was by birth an Italian, Otho of Colonna, and took the name Martin V. He was an extremely clever man, and understood how to evade most ingeniously almost all the regulations which the council had contemplated for the curtailment of the papal power. The other powers now awakened from their slumber, and the French, in particular, applied to the emperor Sigismund to take up the matter. But he answered them: "When we Germans desired the reformation to take place *before* the pope was elected, you Frenchmen were not satisfied, but were determined first to have a pope. Now you have one, as we have; go and require from him your reformation of the church."

The pope, who knew well that in order to be conquered, enemies must be first divided among themselves, began to negotiate with the nations separately, since each nation had made its own proposals for the reformation, and hence arose the particular concordates.

Thus the great object which the council had in view, viz., to effect the reformation of the entire constitution and administration of the church and its clergy, was in a great measure defeated. How much more happy would have been the results if the desired reform could have been effected! People consoled themselves with the expectation that henceforth every ten years general councils would be held; but what is not done at the right time remains forever undone—the projected decennial councils were never held.

When Pope Martin had thus obtained all his wishes, he, on the 22d of April, 1418, closed the council, and on the 16th of May, clothed in a golden papal robe, with a white mitre, rode out of the city upon a horse covered with scarlet, under a splendid canopy. Sigismund went before, leading the horse by the bridle, and three princes, who walked on either side of and behind the horse, bore its covering. Such was the termination of the great Council of Constance, which had continued nearly three years and a half.

This council also judged in another matter, and by its decision produced the most important results.

The emperor Charles IV. had founded the University of Prague, and it was soon attended by students from all the neighboring countries. But Charles had granted to the Germans especially many and great privileges there, with which preference the Bohemians became dissatisfied, and thence King Wenceslas was induced, in the year 1409, (he being then still king of Bohemia,) to deprive the Germans of those privileges. Exasperated at this, thousands of foreign students with their teachers abandoned Prague, and established or enlarged other high schools; among others Leipzig, Ingolstadt, and Cracow. John Huss, the most zealous and learned of the Bohemian professors, was at this time rector of the university. He soon embraced and promulgated principles at variance with those hitherto held, being those maintained by the celebrated divine, John Wycliffe, who lived about thirty years before Huss. He preached against the corrupt state of the morals of the clergy, and maintained that it was contrary to scripture that they should have temporal riches; he also rejected all monastic orders, and in his zeal condemned them severely. These and similar doctrines were propounded by Huss; he also resolutely opposed indulgences, and being accordingly charged with heresy, he was cited to appear before the judicial chair of the pope at Rome. He did not obey the summons, and was excommunicated. But he had already gained a large party of adherents, even the king, Wenceslas himself, had for a time taken him under his protection; and in Prague, as in other parts of Bohemia, great contention arose, ending in scenes of bloodshed; among others who took a prominent share therein was Jerome, a professor of theology in Prague, and a strong adherent and associate of Huss. Huss was now summoned before the council at Constance, and this time he obeyed the call: the emperor Sigismund having, at the request of his brother Wenceslas, furnished him with a safe conduct. But the emperor did not act in this case as Charles V. in that of Luther at Worms did, a century later; on the contrary, he suffered himself to be persuaded that there was no necessity for him to keep his imperial word, being told that his word must not prejudice the interests of the Catholic faith, and interrupt the spiritual judge in the performance of his functions; also that he who opposed that faith forfeited every claim to protection. Sigismund accordingly suffered Huss to be arrested, and promised not to meddle with the affair at all.

They required Huss to recant all his doctrines on pain of being condemned to die at the stake as a heretic. He chose the latter, and was, on the 6th of July, 1415, like his friend Jerome of Prague, eleven months afterwards, publicly burnt at Constance. They both died with a fortitude admired even by their enemies. Their ashes were cast into the Rhine, in order that they might not serve as an object of veneration for the Bohemians.

The news of these proceedings created great excitement and tumult in Prague, for the Bohemians attributed the execution of Huss to the hatred of the Germans, and became only the more attached to his principles. They even went still farther; fresh teachers published new doctrines to those advanced by Huss, and a certain Jacob of Miess, in particular, who maintained that the sacrament must be distributed in both forms, obtained many followers. The partisans of this new doctrine met together upon a mountain, which was afterwards called Mount Tabor, and whence they assumed the name of Taborites. King Wenceslas did not venture to interfere with these assemblies, for their members sometimes amounted to as many as 40,000; and, as usually happens in similar cases, their zeal increased in proportion to their growing numbers, and according to the violence with which they were condemned as heretics by the pope and church. Shortly afterwards they went in solemn procession through Prague, with the chalice carried before them, and Wenceslas, who thought himself no longer safe, abandoned the city, and died almost immediately after he had left, in 1419.

On one occasion, when the Hussites were marching through Prague, and were just passing the senate-house, some one having thrown a stone thence which struck one of their priests, they furiously stormed the house, and threw out of the window thirteen of the senators, who were received by the enraged mob on their pikes, and murdered: such was the sanguinary signal of the revolt. Under the guidance of Ziska, who had acted as leader in the storming of the senate-house, the multitude roamed about the country, pillaging and destroying the monasteries, torturing the priests, and laying waste the possessions of the Catholics.

Sigismund, who, after the death of Wenceslas, had become the legitimate king of Bohemia, demanded the assistance of the German empire against the Hussites, and collected a considerable army. He entered Bohemia in 1420, and besieged Prague; Ziska, however, repelled the attack bravely, and the king was obliged to conclude an armistice and quit the country. In 1427, the German princes made another attack with four bodies of troops; but their dread of the Hussites—rendered by their religious enthusiasm almost unconquerable—had become so great, that the soldiers no sooner saw them than they fell into confusion and retreated. Another army, which was estimated at 100,000 men, and advanced upon them in 1431, met with the same fate; it was so completely beaten at Riesenberg, that 10,000 men were killed upon the spot, all the artillery and baggage lost, and Cardinal Julian himself with difficulty saved his life; being minus his cardinal's hat, his insignia, and the papal bull against the Hussites. The Hussites, on the other hand, made attacks upon Meissen, Saxony, Brandenburg, Franconia, Bavaria, and Austria, and their career of desolation became more and more fearful. One of the dogmas held by the Taborites was, viz.: "That when all the cities o the earth should be burnt down and reduced to the number of five, then would come the new kingdom of the Lord; therefore, it was now the time of vengeance, and God was a God of wrath."

At length, however, affairs changed for the better. Great endeavors were used to bring about an accommodation between the church and the Hussites, and this was at length effected at a council held at Basle. The Hussites were allowed to partake of the sacrament in both kinds of form, yet on condition that the priests should teach the people that Christ was perfect in each.

The greater part of the Bohemian people cheerfully entered into this arrangement; but two parties, more exalted and fanatic, namely, the Taborites and the Waisen, under the direction of Procopius the Great and Procopius the Little, would hear nothing of moderation or of any agreement. It came eventually to open war between them and the moderate ones, when the latter gained a great victory, in which the two leaders of the former perished, and the emperor Sigismund succeeded at length in obtaining his recognition as king of Bohemia; an event, however, accomplished only a few months before his death, which took place in 1437, he being sixty-nine years of age: having reigned fifty-one years as king of Hungary, and twenty-eight years as emperor of Germany.

This emperor, notwithstanding his numerous and wealthy possessions, was often in the greatest pecuniary embarrassment, produced chiefly by his frequent journeys, which were enormously expensive. On this account he mortgaged, in 1417, the territory of Brandenburg, (which, under Charles IV., had fallen to the house of Luxemburg,) together with the elective franchise and the office of archchamberlain, connected therewith, to the burgrave of Nuremberg, Frederick of Hohenzollern, for 400,000 gold florins, which sum the latter had lent to him at various times. On the 8th of April, 1517, the ceremony of enfeoffment was performed at Constance; by which the house of Hohenzollern became possessed of that country, and included among the great electorates. By similar means, Frederick the Warlike, margrave of Meissen and landgrave of Thuringia, obtained from the emperor Sigismund, for 100,000 marks, the Saxon electoral dignity, and the circle of Wittenberg, after that branch of the house of Anhalt, which had possessed Saxony, Wittenberg, and the electoral crown, had become **extinct.**

## CHAPTER XIV.

### THE HOUSE OF AUSTRIA.

Albert II., 1438-1439—His Death—Frederick III., 1440-1493—The Council of Basle, 1448—Æneas Sylvius—The Turks—Belgrade—Defeat of the Turks—The Diets—The Emperor besieged in Vienna—His Resolution—His Brother, Duke Albert—The Count Palatine of the Rhine—His Hostility—Defeats the Imperialists—Albert of Brandenburg, the Achilles of Germany—Feuds of the Nobles and Cities—Nuremberg—The Nobles Defeated—Austria and Burgundy—Charles the Rash—His Ambition—Attacks the Swiss—Defeated at Murten—The Battle of Nancy—His Death—Mary of Burgundy—Marries Maximilian of Austria—Her Death—The Emperor Frederick a Fugitive—His Return—Maximilian, Roman King—The Laws—Their Improvement—Frederick's Obstinacy and Refusal—Maximilian Appealed to—The Swabian League—Death of Frederick III., 1493—Prussia—The Teutonic Knights—Their Decline and Fall—Prussia under Polish Sway, 1466.

After the death of Sigismund, the princes, in 1438, elected an emperor from the house of Austria, which, with scarcely any intermission, has ever since occupied the ancient throne of Germany. Albert II. of Austria, who, as son-in-law of the late emperor Sigismund, had become at the same time king of Hungary and Bohemia, was a well-meaning, distinguished prince, and would, without doubt, have proved of great benefit to the empire; but he died already in the second year of his reign, after his return from an expedition against the Turks. Perhaps there never was a sovereign so lamented by high and low, rich and poor, as was Albert II.

In the year 1431, during the reign of Sigismund, a new council was assembled at Basle, in order to carry on the work of reforming the church as already commenced at Constance.

But this council soon became engaged in many perplexing controversies with Pope Eugene IV., whom they even deposed, and instead of whom they appointed Duke Felix of Savoy, under the title of pope Felix V. The principle that a general ecclesiastical convocation was above the pope, and was the supreme legislative authority in the church, was most solemnly maintained at Basle, as it had before been at Constance. The Germans, for a time, took no part in the dispute; at length, however, under the emperor Albert II., they formally adopted the chief decrees of the council of Basle, at a diet held at Mentz in the year 1439. From the imperial states there were present, the three spiritual electors in person, with the ambassadors from the emperor and the remaining states; besides these came ambassadors from the kings of France, Castile, Aragon, and Portugal, to advise with the Germans upon the constitution of the church. The patriarch of Aquileja appeared as representative of the council.

Among the resolutions then adopted were such as materially circumscribed the existing privileges of the pope. Instead of the enormous sums of money which were annually paid by all the higher clergy to Rome,* the pope was to receive a fixed income, (provisio;) and the German princes contributed, as voluntary aid, only the eighth part of that which had hitherto been paid into the papal treasury on a vacancy occurring among the clergy. In like manner, the pope in future was not to make any clerical appointments beyond his own territory, while the free elections were restored to the chapters. Finally, the council made regulations for the election of the pope, fixed the number of cardinals, and determined the qualifications necessary. The principle laid down was, that proportionally from every country in relation with Rome, the pope should be surrounded by an equal number of cardinals, who, being especially acquainted with the peculiarities of each nation, would be able to place the point in debate in its proper light, "in order that," as the council expresses it, "the cardinals may, in fact, be, what their name imports, the hinges (*cardines*) upon which the doors of the church may rest and move." At that time a great obstacle was already presented against the establishment of peace between the people and the church, inasmuch as the cardinals, whose office it was to act as counsellors of the pope in the direction of the Christian republic, were in the majority chosen from among the Italians.

These and other decisions, calculated to give important privileges and considerable independence to the German church, were, in a great measure, annulled by Albert's cousin and successor, Duke Frederick of Austria, who was elected by the princes after him in the year 1440, as Frederick III., and by the Vienna Concordate (formerly falsely called the Aschaffenburg Concordate) with Pope Nicholas V., in the year 1448; whence the council of Basle broke up in the same year, after it had been assembled seventeen years, without having accomplished its original object. The antipope, Felix V., voluntarily abdicated his office. The man who was chiefly instrumental in giving this turn to the affairs of the church, was the former secretary of the emperor Frederick, Æneas Sylvius, of the house of Piccolomini, in Sienna, one of the most distinguished men of his day. He had himself been formerly secretary of the council of Basle, and the most zealous vindicator of the rights of the councils; but if, when his ambition was flattered by the prospect of a more splendid career in attaching himself to the papal chair, he asserted its dignity against the danger which threatened it, he showed himself well able to induce his emperor and several German princes to favor the interests of the pope. He himself afterwards became Pope Pius II., but soon after died in 1462.

Frederick, the emperor, was a prince who meant well, but, at the same time, was ot too quiet and easy a nature; his long reign presents but little that was calculated to distinguish Germany or add to its renown. From the east the empire was endangered by the approach of an enemy—the Turks, against whom no precautionary measures were adopted. They, on the 29th of May, 1453, conquered Constantinople, and put an end to the Grecian dominion, after it had maintained its sway nearly 1000 years longer than that of the Romans had endured in the west. They then made their way towards the Danube, and very nearly succeeded also in taking Hungary. Frederick, as well as the pope, tried to raise a crusade against them, but these enthusiastic times had gone by, and none would now take the cross.

That any measures were at all taken against the enemies of the Christian name, was to be attributed solely to the pope, Calixtus III., who fitted out, at his own expense, a fleet of 16 galiots, and for that purpose did not even spare the riches of his treasury; while his legate, John Capistran, a man who, in appearance and glowing eloquence, resembled Peter the Hermit, the preacher of the first crusade, succeeded in inspiring with holy zeal for the common cause of Christendom, at least some thousands of poor citizens, peasants, and monks, and appeared with them in 1456, at that most critical moment, when

* The emperor Maximilian I. maintained, even in subsequent times, that the pope drew from the German empire an income exceeding a hundred-fold that received by the emperor himself.

the sultan Mahomet II., with 160,000 men, was besieging the fortress of Belgrade. This fortress, once taken by the enemy, Hungary must be lost, and the passage to Vienna opened for him, as the young king, Wladislas of Hungary, as well as the emperor Frederick and the German princes, were not prepared for war, and instead of acting were deliberating. Then it was that Capistran, with his forces very inadequately provided with pikes, flails, and hay forks, which he had brought in boats, attacked the Turkish fleet on the Danube, which surrounded Belgrade, and made his way into the city. The Hungarian commander-in-chief, John Hunnyades Corvinus, had also collected some forces, and with the crusaders repelled the furious attacks of the Turks. However, he did not venture to touch their well-intrenched camp, and even forbade every attack upon it under pain of death; but the ardent zeal of the crusaders was not to be restrained, and Capistran, when he saw this, placed himself at their head with a staff in one hand and a crucifix in the other, and stormed three Turkish intrenchments one after the other, while Hunnyades now coming up with the cavalry, fell upon the rear of the enemy who was completely put to rout. Their intrenchments were after a severe contest taken, together with all their artillery and an immense booty, and Mahomet being wounded, fled with such of his army as remained. Upwards of 20,000 Turks fell in the battle, and the sultan's power was for many years crippled.

This deliverance Christendom owed to the enthusiastic courage and the patriotic valor of a monk and a Hungarian nobleman, while the kings and princes remained inactive or engaged in petty negotiations. If this victory had been followed up by the union of vigorous force, the Turkish power might, perhaps, have been wholly destroyed; but nothing was done, and even the two heroes who might have achieved something more, died in the same year, 1456, exhausted by their super-human exertions.

The Hungarians, on the death of the son of the emperor Albert II., Wladislas Posthumus, in the year 1457, without leaving an heir to the throne, chose Matthias, the son of John Corvinus, as king, being resolved not to elect one from among the Austrian princes. The Bohemians likewise selected a private nobleman for their king, George Padriabrad, and thus the Austrian house found itself for a time rejected from holding possession of either of these countries. "Singular is the fact," says Æneas Sylvius in his Bohemian history, "that both those kingdoms should have become transferred from the most noble princely houses to those of common noblemen?"

In Germany, meantime, there existed numberless contests and feuds, each party considered only his own personal quarrels, or pursued his own private interest, and when a diet was resolved upon and assembled for determining an expedition against the Turks, they were for some months discussing how much money and how many troops each was to contribute, ultimately postponing the whole affair until the next year. Generally, at the German diets, little was done of any importance. The emperor and princes were seldom personally present, but sent their ambassadors, whose chief concern was not to forego any thing for the interests of their masters. Frequently many of those were sent who were well versed in the Roman law, which was now very extensively studied; these came with their specious speeches, and already prepared with a hundred different reasons, by which to prove that too great a portion of the burden of the whole was laid upon the particular prince or imperial city they represented. They were engaged in discussing who should contribute least towards the welfare of Germany; and, therefore, nothing that was great or noble could be accomplished. Then began, also, the unhappy practice of no longer speaking intelligibly, briefly, and pithily; but communicating by tedious writings and counter-statements. And when it was thought that an affair was at length settled, perhaps an ambassador would rise and say, as an excuse for not concluding the business, that he had no farther instructions, and thus, until his new instructions were received, a delay of many months might intervene. Thence it happened, that from that time, scarcely at any diet a single valid, conclusive resolution was adopted; they were always postponing the business in hand for the decision of a future assembly, and even then another final meeting was adjudged necessary. How different, and far better was it, when the princes in former times were present in person, and when more was done in one hour's cordial conference than in after years in weeks and months. What, however, had operated much to change the form of the diets was, that instead of that equalized right enjoyed by those who formerly attended, there were now introduced three gradations of form: that of the electors, the princes, and the cities. By the Golden Bull, the first college had acquired very important privileges, and was wholly separated from that of the princes and cities; while the latter, for a long period, commanded only a vote in the council, but no co-determinating voice.

The emperor could not give any weight to public measures; scarcely could he maintain his dignity among his own subjects. The Austrian nobility were even bold enough to send challenges to their sovereign; while the city of Vienna revolted, and his brother Albert, taking pleasure in this disorder, was not backward in adding to it. Things even went to such an extremity, that, in 1462, the emperor Frederick, together with his consort and son, Maximilian, then four years of age, was besieged by his subjects in his own castle of Vienna. A plebeian burgher, named Holzer, had placed himself at the head of the insurgents, and was made burgomaster, while Duke Albert came to Vienna personally to superintend the siege of the castle, which was intrenched and bombarded.

The emperor, on this occasion, showed himself firm and resolute; he encouraged his small garrison of 400 men to make the bravest resistance, and called aloud from the walls, "This spot will I defend until it becomes my grave!"

The German princes, however, could not witness with indifference such disgraceful treatment of their emperor, and they assembled to liberate him. George Padriabrad, king of Bohemia, was the first who hastened to the spot with assistance, set the emperor at liberty, and effected a reconciliation between him and his brother. The emperor, however, was obliged to resign to him, for eight years, Lower Austria and Vienna. Albert died in the following year, after he had inflicted the merited punishment upon the burgomaster Holzer, who had endeavored to betray him to the emperor; the traitor was quartered alive.

In the Germanic empire, the voice of the emperor was as little heeded, as in his hereditary lands. Frederick the Conqueror, count palatine of the Rhine, who, by success of arms, had enlarged the palatinate by one third, after Frederick had pronounced the ban of the empire upon him, was suffered to build at his castle at Heidelberg, a strong tower, which he called his "Defiance to the emperor." (*Trutz Kaiser.*) This very count palatine ventured publicly to take under his protection, Diether, archbishop of Mentz, the head of the party in Germany who sought to curtail the privileges of the pontiff, after Pope Pius II. had deposed and excommunicated him. The emperor Federick, on the contrary, wished to carry into effect the sentence of the pope, and committed to the Margrave Albert of Brandenburg, and Count Ulric of Wurtemberg, as his generals, the direction of the imperial war against the count palatine and his confederates; the two generals, however, failed. The army of the Wurtembergian chief was totally routed by the count palatine, near the village of Seckenheim, and Ulric himself, with the margrave of Baden, taken prisoner; and in the same year, the ally of the count palatine, Duke Lewis of Bavaria, attacked Albert of Brandenburg with equal success not far from Giengen, in Swabia, and captured the imperial banner. The Archbishop Diether, however, subsequently submitted of his own accord to the sentence of the pope, and resigned the archbishopric into the hands of Adolphus of Nassau, who had been nominated by the pontiff.

Another memorable feud during the reign of Frederick, was that of many princes and nobles, under the leadership of the aforementioned Margrave Albert of Brandenburg, (who from his strength and prowess, was called the German Achilles,) against the city of Nuremberg in Franconia.

Nuremberg was then one of the most flourishing and powerful cities of entire Germany; the ancient animosity between the free citizens and knights broke out, in the year 1449, into a great war. Seventeen of the greatest princes of the empire, the electors of Brandenburg and Mentz, William of Saxony, Otho of Bavaria, Albert of Austria, &c., declared war against the city. On the other hand, seventy-two imperial towns took part with Nuremberg, and the Swiss also sent 800 men. This desolating war—which especially affected the rural districts, wherein two hundred villages were burnt to the ground—lasted eight years. Eight times were the nobility victorious; but in March, 1456, the army of the margrave was totally beaten near Pillerent; the victory being mainly gained by the Swiss; and the margrave, who now saw that even princely power availed not against the strong walls and opulence of the cities, gladly made peace with Nuremberg.*

The feudal system raged under Frederick's reign to such an extent, that it was pursued even by the lower classes. Thus, in 1471, the shoeblacks in Leipsic sent a challenge to the university of that place; and the bakers of the Count Palatine Lewis, and those of the margrave of Baden defied several imperial cities in Swabia.

The most important transaction in the reign of Frederick, was the union which he formed with the house of Burgundy, and which laid the foundation for the greatness of Austria.

Charles the Rash, duke of Burgundy, was one of the richest and most celebrated princes of his time. He governed the beautiful countries which are situated at the mouths of the rivers Rhine and Scheldt, and which are known by the common name of the Netherlands; he also held dominion over the territory and dukedom of Burgundy. This prince might have rendered himself the most happy of all his royal contemporaries. But his proud, ambitious mind aimed at greater things, even the imperial crown itself; he was glad, therefore, when the emperor Frederick III. proposed to give his own son, Maximilian, in marriage to his only daughter, Mary, who afterwards became the heiress of the beautiful lands of Burgundy. But when he perceived that the emperor did not intend to sacrifice to him the succession to the empire, he demanded of him, at least, the royal title; preceding emperors having also made kings of the dukes of Bohemia, as feodal-princes of the empire. For the purpose of negotiating this matter, they agreed upon a conference at Treves, in the year 1473. The rich duke appeared with more than imperial splendor, and Frederick, who, through the disordered state of his finances, was reduced almost to penury, met him in a very poor and mean condition. This striking contrast in their appearance was, no doubt, mortifying to the emperor; and he, especially, was displeased with the proud, assuming behavior of the duke; for so certain did the latter feel of obtaining the royal title, that he had actually brought with him the jewels for his coronation, and had made great preparations for the august festival. But how must he have been shocked, when the emperor suddenly, without having crowned, nay, without even having taken leave of him, took his departure from Treves, under the cool pretext that his presence was urgently required at Cologne, on account of the disagreement there existing between the archbishop and his chapter. Full of indignation, and now by no means disposed for the projected marriage with the house of Austria, the duke likewise left Treves immediately afterwards.

Nevertheless, this meeting was not attended without its important effects. Charles had, on this occasion, become much prepossessed in favor of the young, chivalrous son of the emperor; and on his return he gave his daughter a description of his merits, in the most glowing colors: her heart was so captivated, that without having even seen Maximilian, she, from this time, cherished a secret attachment for him, and soon afterwards, in a letter she sent direct to the young prince, she betrothed herself to him.

The dispute between Archbishop Rupert of Cologne, and his chapter, had become so serious, that the latter now fixed its seat in the city of Neuss, and openly opposed him. The archbishop sought the assistance of Charles the Rash, and he, gladly embracing the opportunity, and no doubt already considering himself as prince of the Rhine, marched forth with an army of 60,000 men, and encamped before Neuss. The city, however, defended itself with the greatest heroism and glory: eleven months did the duke remain before it, during which he made fifty-six vain assaults, and lost upwards of 15,000 men; and, at last, when the emperor Frederick approached

* This battle is celebrated in a poem, called "The Battle of Nuremberg," written by Hans Rosenplüt, an heraldic painter of Nuremberg. The warlike, intrepid spirit of the free citizens is there vividly expressed, and the description of the princes taking to flight, does not want for point and ridicule. A Low-German poem of the time commemorates the celebrated battle of Soest, in 1444, when Dietrich, the archbishop of Cologne, with 70,000 men, made an attack upon that city but was at last obliged to retreat in disgrace.

with an imperial army to succor the city, and Charles was unable to effect any thing by nine more assaults, which he made in one day, he was obliged to conclude a treaty through the means of the pope's legate, which, although unattended with any advantage, brought him nevertheless no disgrace. Neuss yielded to him, but only in appearance; for he withdrew the same day he entered, and resigned it into the hands of the legate of the pope, who was to hold dominion over it until affairs were settled between the archbishop and the chapter.

The restless duke soon afterwards attacked René, duke of Lorraine, whose country he wished to annex to his own. He conquered the chief city, Nancy, was there acknowledged, and wished now to direct his arms against the Swiss, so that his dominions might descend from the sources of the Rhine to its mouth. In vain did the Swiss represent to him that their entire country was not so valuable as the trappings of his horses; regardless of their remonstrances, he invaded Switzerland, and made so sure of a victory, that he ordered the garrison of Granson, which he had taken, to be suspended on the trees. The Swiss then advanced against him, and took heavy vengeance for this act; for although his army was three times more numerous than their own, they totally defeated it, and captured his entire camp, filled as it was with implements of war and immense treasures.* He fled from the field, accompanied by only five of his remaining attendants. Enraged at this defeat, he equipped a new army of 60,000, and in the same year, 1476 he marched a second time against them.

The armies met at Murten. Hans of Hallwyl, who led the confederates, ordered them, before the battle, to kneel down and offer up their prayer, as their fathers had been accustomed to do; and while they were praying, the dense clouds which had hitherto overhung the sky with blackness, now parted, and the sun cast its bright genial beams on the suppliant multitude. This luminary appeared to them, at this awful hour, as a messenger from Heaven, and a sure pledge of victory; and in this assurance, rendered more strong and intrepid in the cause, they fell so bravely upon the enemy that he was put to the rout, and the field was covered with the bodies of 20,000 Burgundians, which were collected and deposited in the charnel-house of Murten, with the superscription, "This memorial has been left behind by the martial host of the mighty duke of Burgundy."

In the following year, 1477, on the 5th of January, a cold winter's day, there was another sanguinary battle at Nancy, in which the warlike duke at last met with his death.

The united armies of Lorraine and Switzerland completely defeated his troops; and he himself, who, in the din of war, after fighting bravely and honorably for his house, had been struck down, was found, scarcely known, among the slain, late on the following day.

His death inspired the crafty French king, Louis XI., with the hope of acquiring new and more glorious countries; he employed every means to gain for his eldest son, Mary, the heiress of Burgundy; but the people of the Netherlands held in bitter dislike every thing French; and when the ambassadors from the emperor Frederick arrived, and, to the astonishment of every one, presented the autograph letter and ring, which the Princess Mary had previously sent to the Archduke Maximilian, the people were delighted, and Mary declared openly and freely: "*Him* have I fixed upon in my mind, *him* will I have for my husband, and none other." Thereupon, Maximilian went to the Netherlands and was united to Mary of Burgundy. He soon found opportunity to prove to his new subjects his valor and discretion in their wars against the French king; for the lat-

* In order to show the wealth of the proud duke, we will just specify some of the principal spoils made by the Swiss. In his tent, which on the outside was hung with armorial shields of gold and pearls, they found the golden throne upon which he sat on solemn occasions; his ducal hat of yellow velvet, thickly studded with the most precious jewels and pearls; the golden fleece, the order which his father had instituted; the great seal of Burgundy, in gold, weighing a pound; together with the golden chaplet of his father, having jewel drops, cabinets of relics, a valuable prayer-book, &c. The dining-room was well stored with golden and silver goblets, dishes, and plates, besides four hundred travelling trunks, containing the most precious golden and silver embroidery, which the soldiers sold for a few pence. The gold was distributed in hats. The largest of the duke's jewels, equal in size to the half of a walnut, and the value of which he estimated at the price of an entire province, was picked up on the road by a Swiss, and sold by him for a florin. Pope Julius II. purchased it afterwards of the citizens of Berne for 20,000 ducats, and it yet shines as the chief jewel in the papal crown. A second jewel of the duke, which was taken, is in the French crown, and a third is in the imperial treasury at Vienna.

ter, who regarded the young prince as an insignificant adversary, and relied upon his own superior power, had by force of arms made a conquest of various parts of Burgundy. Maximilian, however, bravely made head against him, and defeated his avaricious enemy at Guinegast, in 1479, and would to a certainty have reconquered from him every portion of the estates of Burgundy still in his possession, but for the sad loss he sustained in his beloved Mary, who died in the year 1482, in consequence of a fall from her horse while chasing herons. The zeal of the Netherlanders then grew cold in the protracted war, and Maximilian was obliged to leave his beautiful inheritance in the hands of the French.

In these battles the emperor Frederick could afford his son no assistance; he was hard pressed in his own hereditary lands, partly by the Turks, who made their way into Carinthia and Carniola, and even to Salzburg; and partly by Matthias, king of Hungary, who, in 1485, took possession of Vienna itself; and all regard for public honor being now diminished, the Germanic empire could with great difficulty be induced to make any exertions on behalf of its emperor. The latter having made his escape, was compelled to wander a fugitive through his land, seeking a temporary asylum in some of the convents and cities, where he was charitably furnished with the necessities of life; nay, sometimes he was glad to beg a lift on the high road from some peasant driving his team of oxen. Nevertheless, even in this state of degradation, his feeling of dignity never forsook him; by himself, and those few scattered sympathizing subjects by whom his sovereignty was still acknowledged, he was regarded as the source of justice and authority in his extensive empire. This undauntedness of opinion and conviction now gradually operated in his favor, and produced once more a union of the princes of the empire, while he succeeded in effecting what his great ancestor in all the fulness of his power had been unable to accomplish; inasmuch, as in the year 1486, the whole of the assembled princes, influenced especially by the representations of the faithful and now venerable Albert, called the Achilles of Brandenburg, elected Maximilian, the emperor's son, king of Rome.

Indeed, about this period a changed and improved spirit began to show itself in a remarkable degree in the minds of many throughout the empire, so that the profound contemplator of coming events might easily see the dawn of a new era. Universally was it felt that the time was come for the re-establishment of the imperial power on stronger foundations. But as this power could alone no longer subsist as a central point of dominion over the Christian world, it was necessary to rest it upon the basis of a constitution, for which indeed all the elements of a grand system of community were already at hand, could they only be brought to bear in happy combination.

The diets were regarded as the focus of jurisdiction and administration; an imperial court of justice was already established; a register, by which every member of the empire was bound to give his name for the general defence of the empire, had been established in the war against the Hussites. Thus, if these institutions could only be brought into thorough operation, good order, and the proper government of the empire would be secured.

In order to promote this grand object great activity was shown, especially towards the latter part of the reign of the emperor Frederick. In the year 1486, the decree of the *Landfriede*, or peace of the country, was renewed, although still accompanied with certain clauses which in many cases sanctioned self-defence or private warfare. In the year 1489, the forms of council at the diets were more firmly regulated and fixed, according to the three colleges in rotation, viz. the electors, princes, and cities.

It was held desirable likewise, that to the imperial tribunal there should be added another imperial chamber, furnished with the vigorous power of the executive, in order to maintain the law of the *Landfriede*, possessing equally with the emperor himself the right of pronouncing the imperial ban against all disturbers of the peace of the country, with authority to adopt and regulate the necessary measures for its execution. But on this point the old emperor, who clung to the ancient system, remained extremely obstinate, being determined not to yield any portion of his own power and authority. The colleges were therefore forced for the present to wait and be satisfied with receiving from his son Maximilian, the recently elected king of Rome, the promise that he would use every exertion with his father to bring into operation the proposed institution. It was well known, of course, that he would not succeed in gaining the object desired; but it was believed, that by this expression of feeling, he himself would, when he came into power, feel bound to bring it into effect. How he acted in this respect we shall find in the history of his reign; all, at least, were satisfied in having only gained something.

It was at this period, likewise, that in another respect, a very powerful alliance was formed, by which in the municipal territories of Germany the preservation of peace would be materially promoted. This was the Swabian league, which, in 1488, under the mediation of the emperor, was effected with the more immediate object of opposing the violent and overbearing power of the dukes of Bavaria, who had seized and held possession of Ratisbon, and by whom several other imperial cities were now threatened. At first, a considerable body of knights and many of the cities combined together, under the direction of a select council of the confederates, for common defence against every enemy, and for the preservation of the peace of the country. These were soon joined and headed by the neighboring princes, especially Wurtemberg and Brandenburg. Against this formidable body Albert of Munich soon found he was unable to contend, and accordingly, he was forced to give up Ratisbon, and, indeed, soon afterwards joined the league himself.

These last years were the best in the whole life of the emperor, and yielded to him in return for his many sufferings, that tranquillity which was so well merited by his faithful, generous disposition. He died on the 19th of August, 1493, after a reign of 54 years.

The emperor lived long enough to obtain, in the year 1490, the restoration of his hereditary estates by the death of King Matthias, by means of a compact made with Wladislas, his successor.

Frederick was the last emperor who was in person invested with the Roman imperial crown in Rome; this took place on the 19th of March, 1452.

During the reign of Frederick III., a neighboring country, which was conquered and peopled by the Germans, and which subsequently became more closely united with the German empire; viz., Prussia, became subject to the sovereignty of Poland. How, during the reign of Frederick II., the knights of the Teutonic order entered Prussia, and there founded a government under which the cities and country gloriously flourished, we have already seen.

This prosperity continued until the fifteenth century. The commercial towns of Danzig, Thorn, and Elbing, obtained such greatness, that the first-mentioned town could (according to Æneas Sylvius) command a force of 50,000 men, and the chronicles also relate of a peasant, who when, about the year 1400, he entertained the grand-master of the order, Conrad of Jungingen, placed round the table as seats, twelve tuns, of which eleven were completely, but the twelfth only half filled with gold. He even offered them to the grand-master as a present, who, however, ordered the twelfth to be quite filled, in order that it might be said, that in Prussia there existed a peasant who possessed twelve tuns filled with gold.

But already, under this grand-master, the dominion of the order began to fall into decay. It had become too rich—luxury and vice enervated the prowess of its members; injustice and oppression estranged the people from their rulers, and when now the rising power of the Polish kings was directed against the order, they exhibited a total relaxation of their ancient power. In a great battle at Tannenberg, in 1410, the knights were completely beaten by King Wladislas Jagello. It is true they obtained moderate terms at the peace of Thorn, in 1416; yet the old evils continued. Besides this there were internal broils; the nobility and cities of the country entered into an alliance against the knights, and chose, in 1454, Casimir III. king of Poland for their protector. After a war of twelve years, at the second peace of Thorn, in 1466, the order was obliged to resign to Poland part of the country, together with Culm, Marienburg, Elbing, and other places; and to acknowledge for the portion left to them the feodal right of the Polish crown. The country had suffered indescribably from the desolating war; of twenty-one thousand large villages, only three thousand were left, and the order had become reduced to a mere shadow of its former greatness.

## CHAPTER XV.

Maximilian I., 1493-1519—His Mental Acquirements and Chivalric Character—His Government—Italy—Charles VIII. and Lewis XII. of France—Switzerland—The Venetian Republic—The League of Cambray—Maximilian's Honorable and Consistent Conduct—The Battle of the Spurs—Union of Hungary and Bohemia—Internal Administration of Affairs—Perpetual Peace of the Land—End of the Faust-Recht—The Imperial Chamber and Aulic Council—Opposition of the States—The Emperor Triumphant—State of the Country—The Nobles, Cities, and Peasantry—Götz of Berlichingen, &c.—Death of the Emperor Maximilian, 1519—Events of his Reign, and End of the Middle Ages—Discovery and Use of Gunpowder—Artillery and Fire-arms—Invention of Printing, 1457.

During the preceding century Europe had become fully prepared for great changes, which, when they had once unfolded their results, would produce a complete revolution in the condition of nations. The invention of gunpowder had already begun so to alter the science of war, that chivalry, which for centuries had predominated throughout the middle ages, was now approaching its end. The art of printing, in connection with the invention of paper, had created a new medium for the communication of thought, by which, with the rapidity of lightning, the human mind might be agitated from one end of Europe to the other. The discovery of a new quarter of the globe, and a sea passage to the East Indies, altered entirely the former course of commerce, and transferred the great power thereby gained to nations, which, among the rest, had hitherto been but little mentioned or known. Finally, political economy, as it now arose, and came especially from France and Italy, assumed quite another form—it made honor and good faith give way to interest; and this was now the principle upon which states acted in their alliances, so that in the conduct of nations towards each other there appeared to prevail a law different to that which is recognised by individuals.

During this period of fermentation, so fertile in invention, it may be said of the emperor Maximilian, that he stood forth amid the new forms as a dignified image of olden time, since in him again, and for the last time, was personified chivalry in all its glory. As this in its great features was equally elevated and amiable, so did Maximilian unite with bravery, dignity, and decision of character, the gentleness of a child; and as the warm imagination of the middle ages prompted to the most astonishing and unprecedented adventures, so also in the exploits of Maximilian we find predominating valor, enthusiasm, and sometimes temerity.

One of his most favorite, because the most daring, pastimes, was that of hunting the chamois, and on these excursions he often ran into such hazard that his friends trembled for his life; in like manner did he sport with danger in wrestling-matches, where, with his own hand, he conquered the very lion itself, the same as on the field of battle, where many an antagonist was doomed to lie at his feet. At the same time, the emperor, amid his other avocations, found time for the arts and sciences, and acquired knowledge to a degree which would excite admiration, even from those whose whole life is directed to such pursuits. He spoke nearly all the European languages then in vogue, and left behind him several works which he had written in German. He acquired the art of forging armor, which he did with his own hand; was much attached to all that was learned and scientific, and in conversation he was so intellectual, affable, and kind, that every one recognised in him the accomplished man. He was never known to allow an oath or a blasphemous word to pass his lips, while his noble mind and heart were constantly, even amid the most bitter insults, inclined towards mercy. His outward appearance was also in perfect keeping with the character here depicted, being tall and muscular, and of a truly royal carriage. In his younger years his flaxen hair flowed in ringlets down to his shoulders, his blue eyes expressed glowing ardor, mixed with kindness, and his high forehead and aquiline nose finished the expression of majesty in his features. His natural fervor and vivacity of character Maximilian derived from his mother, Eleanor of Portugal, a princess endowed with an amiable and noble disposition, but who died unhappily too soon, being scarcely thirty years of age. It must also be said to the honor of his father, that he bestowed great care upon the education of his son from childhood upward, by providing for him excellent masters, as well as by his own personal instructions.

Maximilian's first appearance in public life resembles the opening of a romance of chivalry. Love and honor called him forth, while yet a youth, to the field, and he then already gave signs of his noble and courageous disposition in a contest at arms which he maintained in the most honorable manner, with the artful and more experienced king of France, Lewis XI. But in the course of his career, all did not succeed as this his first essay in life. The time was gone by, when a bold chivalric venture brought with it the necessary successful results. Instead of, as in ancient times, rushing into an enemy's country, accompanied by vassals, summoned at a moment's notice, and after the termination of a short but glorious campaign, speedily returning home, it was necessary now to keep up a mercenary army. It was no longer the preponderance of spirit and individual strength, which ensured success to great enterprises, but all was decided by the superior command of external resources; and our valiant, noble-minded emperor, who at an earlier epoch would have governed as gloriously as the most renowned and powerful of his ancestors, now, for want of these advantages, stood far behind the artful, cold-calculating kings of France and Spain. He knew not, as they did, the importance of such external resources, and especially money; he wasted large sums away without reflection, so that whenever a critical and decisive moment arrived, these means were wanting, and his troops for lack of pay were disbanded.*

These observations explain Maximilian's life, and his incongruity with the age in which he lived; nevertheless, mindful, however, of the ancient honor of the imperial dignity, he pursued the grand object of maintaining, so far as he was able, justice, peace, and order throughout Europe, and that, too, less by force of arms, than by the dictates of wisdom and reason; of protecting the church, and finally, directing the united power of Christendom against the universal enemy, the Turks. And truly did he succeed in adding more influence to the imperial dignity than it had possessed for centuries: he even contemplated the bold design of attaining the papal crown, and thus, by uniting in his own person the two chief dignities of Christianity, promote the peace and welfare of the world. This is no fiction, for it is proved by documents and the autograph letters of the emperor, which show that in the year 1511 he had made serious preparations for his election as pope in the event of the death of Pope Julius II., who was then dangerously ill, but who afterwards recovered. And if we duly consider the actual state of the world at that time, the idea of the emperor was not so chimerical and impossible as it might at first appear; besides which, a main difficulty that might have presented itself from the fact of his marriage, was obviated by the recent death of his second consort Bianca. Maximilian, however, in this case, as in fact in almost all the other acts of his life, did not duly estimate the extent of his external resources; the idea was too grand in contrast with the limited means of accomplishment, and thus his enterprises generally did not succeed, as the history of his life will now more particularly show.

The external operations of Maximilian were directed almost exclusively to Italy. Here the French kings, whose power had materially increased by the total expulsion of the English from the French territory, as well as by annexing to the crown the great fiefs of Burgundy, Brittany, Provence, and Anjou, persisted in their efforts to withdraw that country, broken up already by factions, from its allegiance to the emperor, and, as much as possible, to bring it under French subjection.

Hence Charles VIII. sought out and produced the ancient claims of the house of Anjou to the kingdom of Naples, where a collateral lineage of the Aragonian family reigned. With an army which he had levied hastily he invaded Italy, and in 1495 speedily gained possession of Naples. This success was greatly owing to the use of metal cannons, which, drawn by horses, followed the troops; those hitherto used being only of heavy iron, employed merely in sieges.

As soon, however, as the Italians had somewhat recovered from their first alarm they united together, friends and foes, against the French; the emperor, the pope, and the king of Aragon, Ferdinand the Catholic, promised also their aid; so that

* While yet a boy, Maximilian once expressed this disposition, when his father presented him with a plate of fruit and a purse of money. Maximilian kept the fruit, and gave the money away to his servants. "That boy will become a spendthrift!" sighed his father. But Maximilian replied: "I wish not to be a king over money, but over the people, and all those who possess money."

the king of France was forced to abandon his conquest as quickly as he had made it. It was on this occasion that the emperor Maximilian negotiated and settled definitively the highly important marriage of his son Philip, who already possessed the Netherlands, with Joanna, the daughter of the king of Spain. This son, Philip, had been born to him by his beloved Mary of Burgundy, and the issue of Philip's marriage with Joanna of Spain, was the subsequent emperor, Charles V., who reunited and held the half of Europe under his sway.

The French, however, would not allow themselves to be entirely discomfited by the failure of their first attempt upon Italy. The successor of Charles VIII., Lewis XII., resolved to conquer Milan, to make up for the loss of Naples. He founded his claims upon ancient family alliances with the house of Visconti, and made a hostile attack upon the reigning duke, Louis Moroni. With the aid of the Venetians, to whom he promised a portion of the booty, he, in the year 1500, soon made a conquest of the entire duchy, and the unfortunate duke was obliged, after ten years confinement, to end his days in a dungeon in France. The king now directed his attention again to Naples, united with Ferdinand of Aragon, and both shared together that kingdom, to which neither had any right. On this occasion, however, Lewis was forced to experience that one artful man may be cheated by another more artful than himself, inasmuch as the Spanish king, by means of his general, Gonsalvo of Cordova, soon expelled the French from Naples, and retained the kingdom for himself.

The emperor was wrong to allow foreign nations thus to run loose upon Italy; that unhappy country, unable to maintain its independence, ought at least, under imperial protection, to have been secured against such arbitrary treatment. And, indeed, Maximilian would gladly have asserted his ancient rights of sovereignty, but unhappily he was not supported by the Germanic empire, and his power was too much restricted. He was compelled, therefor, to allow King Lewis to hold possession of Milan, who, however, so far honored the imperial dignity as to consent to retain the duchy as a fief of the empire.

While the French established themselves in Italy, Maximilian made another attempt —the last that was made—to bring the Swiss once more under the dominion of the empire. The ancient hatred of the nobility, especially in Swabia, became now again manifested against the Swiss peasantry. This time it was called forth by an insignificant quarrel of the Austrian government in Tyrol with the confederates of the Grisons. The chief cause, however, was, viz., that the Swiss had become the allies of the French kings, and gave them assistance in their expeditions against Italy—an act regarded as a breach of their obligations to the empire, they having always been looked upon as included in the imperial alliance. But the war which was waged against them, in 1499, was disgraceful to Germany. The Swabian nobility were in several skirmishes severely beaten; a numerous and well-appointed army, which Maximilian himself collected in Constance, was, in consequence of the reluctance of the princes to join in a battle among the dangerous mountains of Switzerland, forced to turn back, retreating through the passes on the confines of the country of Berne. The grand marshal of the emperor, Count von Fürstenberg, who was ordered to conduct the army of the princes of the Rhine, through Alsace, by Basle, into Switzerland, was surprised and overthrown by the Swiss at Dorneck, with the loss of 3000 killed, and all his ammunition. They were obliged to make peace and leave to the Swiss their independence, although the latter did not as yet expressly dissolve their connection with the empire. Soon afterwards, Basle and Schaffhausen, which had hitherto remained imperial cities, were included in the Swiss confederation.

Maximilian very soon again found employment in Italy. Here, at this time, no state was more flourishing than that of the Venetians. By their extended commerce they had acquired immense wealth, a great part of Upper Italy had by degrees become subject to them, and they aimed at still greater power.

But their pride and insolence excited the hatred of their powerful neighbors, who besides laid claim to various parts of their territories; the principal portion of what they possessed in Upper Italy, excepting their old country, having formerly belonged to the empire, and other portions to the papal dominions; while in Lower Italy they had taken places to which Ferdinand the Catholic, as king of Naples, laid just claims; and finally, France wished to obtain those possessions immediately bordering upon Milan.

Hence arose, in 1508, the famous league between Spain, France, the warlike Pope Julius II., and the emperor, against the republic of Venice, known under the name of the league of Cambray, threatening instantly to crush that free state, which although rich, was still insignificant when compared with such great powers opposed to it. But as this is the first great league of the kind in the history of the more modern states of Europe, it has also become the prefigure of most of those which have succeeded it, and seems as a sort of mirror in which is reflected the instability of the political relations of these states, which being grounded in selfishness and self-aggrandizement, without having a hold in the moral dignity of the people, again dissolved like an empty vapor, as soon as the cards of fortune were reshuffled, and thus became an object of derision for the whole of Europe. For the artful republicans so well knew how to divide the allies by dazzling before the eyes of each the tempting bait of self-interest, that those who were friends before became hostile to each other, while they themselves retired unhurt from their conflict with the most powerful princes.

Of the emperor Maximilian himself history records, that he was most sincere in his dealings with his allies, and maintained the honor of his word. Louis XII. was the first to hasten to the scene of action, in the year 1509, and in a few weeks made a conquest of all that the league had promised him as part of the booty; and when Maximilian also arrived, and with his troops took one place after another, the Venetians begged from him peace, offering to make over to him all that they had ever taken from the house of Austria or the empire; thus an opportunity was presented by which he might have made a very advantageous treaty with them. But he refused; the allies having solemnly agreed only to grant peace conjointly. The others, however, did not act equally conscientious. Ferdinand the Catholic, as he was sure of his possessions in Lower Italy, took no farther part in the war, and Pope Julius II. abandoned the league altogether, out of hatred to the French, and joined the Venetians. Ferdinand soon afterwards did the same, and the three allies called their union the holy league. The French were now expelled from Milan. Their policy then quickly took a turn; the first calculation having failed, they entered into an alliance with their former enemies, the Venetians; while, on the other hand, the Spaniards again united with the emperor and with the king of England, Henry VIII., against both the others. Thus, in the course of a few years, friendship gave way to hostility, and the latter again yielded to the former; Spain, for instance, from being first hostile, had become allied with, but was now again hostile to Venice; and throughout the whole of this game treachery appeared to pass for wisdom, while honor was treated as nothing.

The French, however, were not benefited by this new calculation; in the battle of Novarre, in 1513, they were driven completely out of Italy, in which affair the Swiss fought against them; as they were hard pressed also in their own country by the imperial and the English troops, who in the same year, under the personal command of Maximilian, gained the battle of Guinegate, (which on account of the hasty retreat of the French was called the Battle of the Spurs,) Louis found it necessary to renounce for a time his claims to Milan. Maximilian gave Milan as a fief of the empire to Maximilian Sforza, the son of Louis Moro; but he did not possess it long.

When Louis XII. died in the year 1515, he was succeeded to the French throne by the youthful, daring, and ambitious Francis I., and in order that he might commence his reign with some brilliant act, he sallied forth, in the same year, with an army to Italy, and recaptured Milan. The Swiss who came to the assistance of the city, and incautiously attacked the enemy, were after a severe engagement, which lasted two days, completely defeated at Marignano. This was the first great battle in which they had lost the field.

The French artillery and the German lanciers, who served on French pay, and were ever after considered the best infantry, gained the victory. The emperor, indeed, made an expedition once again in the following year into Italy, and besieged Milan, but increasing age and so many futile efforts made him disposed for peace;

moreover, his forces soon dwindled away for want of pay. By a treaty made at Brussels in 1516, he resigned to the king of France the duchy of Milan, and, what was still more galling to his feelings, he gave back to the detested republic of Venice the important city of Verona.

Thus was concluded, after a great variety of changes, the war of Italy, in which the best exertions of the emperor had been required. This contest had withheld him from pursuing that object so important to the empire, and for which his chivalric spirit so naturally disposed him, namely, in making war against the Turks, and if possible banishing them from Europe. This wish he constantly cherished, and even expressed most ardently but a few months before his death, at his last diet held in Augsburg, in a proposition he made to the states of the empire, to undertake an expedition against the Turks; but the petty and selfish spirit of the day was not favorable to such an enterprise.

Among the other external arrangements of the emperor, one most worthy of remark was the ratification of the reunion with Hungary and Bohemia. Besides the grandson, who afterwards became emperor Charles V., he had of his son Philip, who was already dead, and Joanna of Spain, another grandson, afterwards Ferdinand I.; him he gave in 1515 in marriage to the daughter of Wladislas, king of Hungary, and thereby laid the foundation for the direct connection of Hungary and Bohemia with the countries of Austria.

Already during the last few years of the reign of the emperor Frederick III., as before mentioned, great efforts had been made by the states of the empire to establish public tranquillity, and to render it secure by a legislative institution. Immediately after the commencement of the reign of the new emperor, these exertions were perseveringly continued. The most active and zealous promoter of this grand object was Bertold, the elector of Mentz, and count of Hanneberg, one of the most extraordinary men of his day. From the period when, under Frederick III., in 1486, as first spiritual elector, he stood at the head of the states of the empire, down to the present moment, he had continued to be the advocate and warm supporter of all the operations tending to improve the institutions of the country; indefatigable, free from all personal motive, and having the cause of his country alone in mind and heart, he was continually at work to promote its welfare.

At the first diet held by the new emperor at Worms, in 1495, the subject of the *Landfriede*, or peace of the country, and the proposed *Kammergericht*, or imperial chamber, were immediately taken into discussion. The emperor, who likewise heartily desired that peace should at length reign throughout the empire, in order that its strength might be more effectually brought to bear against the hostile power of France, zealously joined in the grand undertaking, and thus was completed and brought into operation the institution for the perpetual peace of the country—a work which gained for this diet the greatest praise and renown. And although this *Landfriede* was still shackled with certain restrictive clauses, and the feudal system did not altogether cease its operations, still the new law possessed this advantage, viz., that *legally* club-law must henceforth entirely terminate, and the authority of the law in its normal form take its place; a system which, in the course of time, after it had come more and more into operation, was universally adopted. When we consider the incalculably important consequences which attended this change of things among the middle and lower classes of the people, we must assuredly acknowledge the year 1495 to be one of the most momentary and striking in our history, while we must regard the emperor Maximilian as one of the greatest benefactors of the nation.

Still in respect to the more enlarged plan of the Elector Bertold and the states, which embraced the strengthening of the imperial government and the imperial chamber, Maximilian did not so easily yield his sanction; like his father, he was very reluctant to give up any portion of the imperial rights, however incapable he might be, through his important affairs abroad, of fulfilling the duties they imposed upon him. He was, however, at length prevailed upon by the states to yield in the main to the general desire, especially when he was reminded of the former promise he had partially made when they elected him king of Rome in 1489, and which he could not retract. The imperial chamber was to be permanently established for the purpose of equitably deciding the disputes between the states of the empire, which had hitherto always been settled by an appeal to arms, and what is still more important, it was authorized to pronounce in the name of the emperor the imperial ban of excommunication against all who opposed it. In its entire construction, likewise, it was no longer to form merely an especial *imperial* tribunal, but in reality a tribunal of the empire. The emperor appointed only the president or chief judge; the fifty assessors were presented by the states, while the cities, likewise, were allowed to nominate a few. The emperor opened the court himself, and handed to Count Eitelfried von Zollern the judicial sceptre, as chief judge of the chamber. The first court was held on the 3d of November, 1495, in Frankfort.

The progress, however, made by this institution, was equally slow with that of the *Landfriede;* the idea was good, and the plan laid out with great wisdom; but in respect to the execution thereof, many difficulties and insurmountable obstacles stepped in to prevent a successful issue. Many would not attend to the decrees pronounced, and the power of enforcing them was wanting, inasmuch as the emperor was occupied in foreign countries, and besides which he felt but little real desire to promote a tribunal rendered independent of his own especial sway. Then followed the non-payment of the necessary fees and salaries, as the contributions from the various members of the empire came in very irregularly or perhaps not at all; so that the court often sat and broke up without effecting any thing. At last it became so neglected, that the emperor was himself forced to reconstruct it, and supply the necessary funds; and thus made it, as in former times, wholly dependent upon himself. The discontent thence produced between the emperor and the states increased more and more, until at length the elector of Mentz brought forward twenty-two points of accusation against Maximilian, to which the latter replied by twenty-three articles in opposition. A most angry and bitter correspondence ensued between the emperor and the elector; but the scale of balance on the side of the former became only more and more on the ascent, and turned completely against him.

But, as often happened in Maximilian's varied career, the scale dropped once more in his favor. He contrived, although the body of electors were inimical towards him, to enlist friends on his side from among the temporal and spiritual princes. He filled up various vacant bishoprics, with the co-operation of the then friendly papal authority, with his friends. Among the temporal princes were at that time many young, warlike lords, who all glowed with military ardor under his command; and the gay, chivalric emperor, continually engaged in some enterprise, perfect master in all military exercises, combining true genius with a generous and friendly disposition, knew well how to enchain them to him. We have already seen how Duke Eric of Calenberg fought with so much glory in the wars of Austria, and that the entire house of the Guelfs adhered to that dynasty. So likewise did the dukes of Saxony, Mecklenburg, Pomerania, and Cleves; while the emperor gained Wurtemberg, by granting the earl's claims, and conferring upon him the title of duke. The margraves of Brandenburg were secured by the faithful adherence of their ancestor Albert, the German Achilles. Thus by rewards and promotions of various kinds, the emperor, in order to augment his party, availed himself of the remnant left of imperial privileges. Indeed he had become in the year 1504 so strong, that he was enabled to bring to a successful issue, and according to his own wishes, a very important contest originating in the inheritance of George, duke of Bavaria-Landshut. The dukes of Bavaria, Munich, and the Palatine Rupert stood opposed to each other; and Maximilian himself laid claim to a portion of the lands. As the palatine refused most obstinately to submit to the decree pronounced by the imperial chamber, the emperor at once adjudged the ban of excommunication against him. With the aid of the afore-mentioned allied princes, together with the Swabian league and his own immediate adherents, he executed the sentence successfully; the palatine was forced to submit, and Maximilian himself gained no inconsiderable portion of the possessions.

His position in judicial affairs was rendered still more favorable by the death of the leader of the electoral opposition party, Bertold of Mentz, who died in the year 1504. He was now enabled, in the two following years, at the diets held at Cologne and Constance, to bring into effect the preponderating power he possessed, inasmuch as he substituted the organic regulations of the empire in accordance with *his* views for those which had previously existed and had originated in the visionary project of realizing a national unity. It was not now simply a question of combining the regulation of the empire with almost imperial power; but, also, of restoring the imperial chamber according to the resolutions fixed at Worms; together with the establishment of a register, by which the contributions for the expenditure of the country and the contingent of troops in the wars of the empire were divided among the states according to their power: these were the two important results of the diet of Constance in 1507. Both continued in force during a period of three centuries, and, in spite of the independent territories, represented the unity of the Germanic empire.

It was after the foundation of these happy internal regulations of the empire, that Maximilian proceeded into Italy, as before mentioned, on his great campaign against the Venetians; and his hopes were so strong, that in the February of 1508, in Trieste, he assumed the title of Roman king elect, without waiting to be crowned in Rome. This act was of great importance to future times, Maximilian's successors having afterwards assumed the imperial title, immediately after their coronation in Aix-la-Chapelle; and during the whole of the subsequent periods, only one emperor was crowned by the pope.

At the diet held in Cologne, in 1512, the emperor introduced an important proposition, touching the internal peace of the empire, viz., that the decisions of the imperial chamber should, by a definite authority, be enforced and carried into effect in every part of the empire; without which they were of little or no avail. It was proposed, therefore, that the division of the circles, which had been hitherto brought into operation for the purpose of returning deputies to officiate in the imperial chamber, should now be made available in this case, and be rendered efficient accordingly. At first they consisted of six circles—Bavaria, Swabia, Franconia, the Rhine, Westphalia, and Lower Saxony; now, however, it was resolved to add four more—the Lower Rhine, including the four electorates, Upper Saxony, embracing its electorate and Brandenburg, Austria, and Burgundy.

Each circle was to be regarded as one distinctly organized and comprehensive body, and all matters of peace and war to be superintended by a military chief. Notwithstanding great contention ensued between the emperor and the states upon this question, a resolution was passed, and accordingly a decree for its adoption was agreed to by the states of the empire. Its execution, however, was not brought into force immediately, for it was only after some ten years had elapsed, that this division of circles was at length effectually established.

Besides the foundation thus laid for these organic institutions, which, if not emanating from Maximilian alone, were at least produced with his co-operation, Germany has to thank him especially for the introduction of an entire new system of discipline in the army, which he remodelled completely, by dividing it into regiments; and finally, it was by him that a system of posting was first introduced.

We must not, however, deceive ourselves in the character of this period, which is more especially distinguished in our history as a period of transition. Such epochs are marked by the most contradictory phenomena, more especially, however, by a universal rupture and fermentation of all relations, calling forth at every moment the feeling that we are, as it were, standing upon undermined ground, where are raging in all their unrestricted fury the elements of new creations. As yet the seeds only were strewed, the full growth and fruit of which were reserved for after times.

At present on neither side was contentment to be found; the mutual privileges and duties of the ruler and the states had become more than ever fluctuating. Innumerable representations (*reclamationen*) were made against the assessments of the register; princes had been included who were no longer in existence; many states had been inscribed as immediate which had become mediate, and were now claimed back again by the sovereign lord, especially among cities. Thus, it was urged by the ambassador of Denmark and Holstein, that among others, a city (Hamburg) had been marked as an imperial city, but that, as it was situated in Holstein, it must be reclaimed by his sovereign and restored, as part of his patrimonial possessions, he being lord of the manor by natural succession. He, however, did not succeed in his claim, as the imperial freedom of the city was nevertheless acknowledged.

The aulic council of the imperial chamber, with its decrees, met with great opposition from all sides. It roused, generally, a desire for independence, and which, in fact, broke forth in such a series of cruel and barbarous acts, that the commencement of the fifteenth century again presented scenes of sanguinary contention in many parts of the empire.

1. The princes resorted to open war in order to extend their territorial dignity. The countship of Hoya, among the rest, was, in 1511, invaded by Brunswick, Lüneburg, Bremen, and Minden; while the remaining body of free Fresians were, in 1514, also attacked by Brunswick, Lüneburg, Calenberg, Oldenburg, and George, duke of Saxony; and in these, as in all other cases, the superior power triumphed.

2. The whole body of knights in every quarter feeling themselves, as it were, penned in by the princes, formed a close alliance, and declared open war. The depredations of the freebooter-knights, on the high roads, and their attacks upon the merchants and dealers to and from the fairs, were again resumed, and continual scenes of robbery and murder, by day and night, occurred throughout the land. It was about this time that the celebrated Götz of Berlichingen, Franz of Selbitz, but more especially the noted Franz of Sickingen, who was enabled to collect and march whole armies against the princes, were actively engaged in the cause they espoused.

3. The cities, although overrun and oppressed on every side, still retained their ancient strength to a certain extent; they now defended themselves against the assaults of the knights with the same success as when formerly attacked by the princes; and wo to the nobleman or knight who once fell into their hands! For no petition, either from his family or friends, nor even the intercession or remonstrances of any of the princes, were of any avail to save him from the axe of the executioner. In the north, Lübeck especially stood most prominently at the head of the Hanse Towns. In the year 1509 they attacked John, king of Denmark, captured all his ships at Elsinore, returning home loaded with booty. In the battle of Bornholm a Lübeck vessel beat off three Danish ships by which she had been grappled, and even made one of them a prize.

At the diets the cities still maintained a very important position. Their commercial associations, by which they were enabled to transact the most extensive business and embark in the most profitable enterprises, produced for them such opulence, and with it its preponderating influence, that the jealousy and envy of the princes became more excited, until, at length, they combined together in proposing at several diets, held about this time, such resolutions as should, if not wholly destroy, at least reduce the great power they possessed by taxation, and certainly there was great foundation for these measures, inasmuch as the complaints made against the enormous prices demanded by the merchants for the goods supplied became more and more general.

Within the cities themselves the turbulent spirit of the times was not less conspicuously shown. The municipal authorities became seriously oppressed and overpowered by the communities and the heads of the various guilds and societies—now considerably augmented in number and influence—who would no longer submit either to be governed by a select and limited body of patricians, or to be taxed at the high rate hitherto levied. The records of many of these cities, at the commencement of the sixteenth century, are filled with the most sanguinary scenes of discord and civil war.

4. But the state of the peasantry and the rural districts presented at this period a far more melancholy and serious spectacle than that of either of the classes mentioned. With them reigned universal fermentation throughout the whole empire. The demands of the territorial lord, as well as those of the lord of the manor, were increased, because each sought to transfer the burdens of the empire to the shoulders of the lower orders. On the other hand, the latter had now learned to know their strength in the use of arms, and soon from among them issued the formidable bodies of the *Landsknechte*, or foot-soldiers. The example presented by the Swiss peasants, who had now almost entirely thrown off the yoke of the empire, and made themselves independent, produced its exciting

effects among the German peasantry, and more especially in Upper Germany.

Towards the end of the fifteenth century, in 1493, there was formed in Alsace, near Selestadt, a secret union of discontented peasantry, who, in the depth of night, journeying along almost impassable roads among the mountains, assembled together in a retired spot, and there, by a solemn vow, swore, under heavy threats to him who proved a traitor, as follows: "That they would be taxed only according to their own free will and consent; that the imposts should be removed altogether, as likewise all spiritual jurisdiction; that no ecclesiastic should receive a higher salary than forty florins; that the Jews should be put to death, and their possessions divided equally among the confederates," &c. &c. This confederacy, which adopted the sign of the shoe (the shoe of the common German peasant) upon their banner, extended its operations very considerably.

A similar union arose in Wurtemberg in 1514, under the name of the Poor Conrad league. Both originated in a hatred towards the nobility and clergy, and which, in fact, appeared to be the principle upon which they acted. It is true, the Shoe-league was, by force of arms, eventually destroyed in 1502, as was likewise the Poor Conrad league soon after its formation; but the seeds of revolt were left behind, and at the diets the subject of a revolution among the peasantry was often discussed with some anxiety and dread. At the diet of Mentz, in 1517, in which several of the members advised, on account of the disordered state of the empire, that a summons should be issued for every fiftieth man to take up arms in its defence, the states would not venture to adopt a measure which must be so generally felt as tyrannical: "The common peasant, already sufficiently suffering from dearth and hunger, would, in his present discontent, only be still farther excited to the most desperate acts, and thence the glimmering sparks of private indignation would burst forth into one universal flame throughout the whole country." Such was the opinion expressed by the states, and the general feeling was in favor of rather quelling by mild means the turbulence which already began to agitate the empire. Nevertheless, we shall shortly read in the history of the Reformation, how, after the lapse of another year, the destructive elements did break forth in all their fury.

The emperor, however, was not doomed to witness or share in these revolutions; the course of his career was nearly ended, and his powers of mind and body, exercised in so many toilsome and, to a certain extent, fruitless struggles, became now gradually exhausted and consumed.

At the diet of Augsburg, in 1518, he used every endeavor to prevail upon the states to elect, as king of Rome, his son Charles, already seated on the Spanish throne; his anxious wish, however, was not fulfilled, inasmuch as the pope, and a portion of the electoral princes, in their fear to bestow too great a power upon his son, hesitated and refused to yield to his wishes. Indignant and mortified, Maximilian quitted Augsburg, and died on his journey at Wels, in Upper Austria, on the 12th of January, 1519, in the 59th year of his age, and was buried, according to his wish, beneath the altar-stone of the church at Neustadt, by the side of his beloved mother, Eleanora.

It is said, that he had for several years carried about with him his coffin. Thus, as in his earlier life, when in all his vigor, he had often bid defiance to death, so now in the latter years of his existence, did he hold familiar counsel with it, and view its approach with religious confidence and resignation.

We have already had occasion to consider, in the preceding chapters, various important changes, for which Germany had been ripening during the last century. With Maximilian, as their last representative, the middle ages had passed away; a new period, of which the germ had long been sown, now gradually developed itself and became established. We will just glance at the signs which characterized this new age, and at those great discoveries which contributed chiefly in producing it.

Where and when gunpowder was first invented cannot be positively ascertained, it appears probable that the Chinese were very early acquainted with it, and that it came from them to the Arabians, and thence to Europe. But it was not as yet employed in war, and could not, therefore, with strictness be called *gun*-powder. It is not found to have been used for that purpose earlier than in 1350, and the discovery of this application of it is ascribed to a German monk, Bertold Schwarz. He had, it is said, pounded a mixture of saltpetre, sulphur, and coals, in a mortar, when by accident a spark dropped into it, the mass ignited, and forced with great violence the pestle into the air. This accident led to the thought of making great metal mortars for the purpose of war, from which stones and balls might be thrown against a hostile city, and thus was produced the heavy artillery, which about the year 1400 was pretty generally used. The first time we hear of its being practised, is at the battle of Crecy, between the French and English, in 1346. The smaller fire-arm, or arquebus, was invented somewhat later; this weapon, however, is mentioned in a record of 1381, when the city of Augsburg undertook to send thirty men armed with guns to the war which the cities then waged against the nobility.*

By these newly-discovered instruments of destruction the whole system of war and military tactics became changed. In ancient times the hostile encounter was almost always maintained man to man, and hand to hand, with lance and sword; whence individual force, dexterity, and prowess decided the victory. In case either one of the armies did not at an early stage cowardly turn round and flee, the battle was never decided before the field was strewed with the bodies of the greater portion of the combatants. The contests were sanguinary and decisive. But since the new plan now adopted was to fight at a distance, and the individual no longer had his antagonist face to face—leaving it to chance to decide whether his ball should contribute towards the success of the action, or waste itself in the air—and as the warrior had thus become more and more the mere simple machine employed by the calculations of the general, whose genius and judgment were now rendered sufficient to decide the battle—accordingly, by this new method of war the spirit of chivalry became gradually annihilated. The latter, in fact, was based upon the greatest development of personal strength, which gave to the individual such a superiority that a whole troop of common foot-soldiers were not able to resist the attack of the knight when, mounted on his barbed steed, and armed at all points, he dashed among them; while now the most cowardly disposed man might, with his firelock, bring down the bravest warrior at a distance. The nobility for a length of time continued to oppose and contend against the use of this new arm of war, which they characterized as dishonorable, degrading, and perfidious to employ; but when it finally obtained the superiority, the cavalier of the martial field of olden times was forced to succumb, and resign his battle-axe and lance.

This change, however, did not come into operation all at once; for long after the invention of fire-arms, while those who bore them formed but a small part of the army, and heavy cannon was only employed in sieges, the mailed cavalry continued to compose the *élite* of the troops, and the nobility still preserved and maintained their military discipline. The tournaments still continued to form their principal festivals, where the youth of the nobility learned at an early age to play with danger; and all the prohibitions of the popes and ecclesiastical councils issued against those who took part in them, on account of the danger attending them, (for they frequently ran with pointed lances,) and all the punishments which the Church inflicted upon those who engaged therein—as, viz., that none who died in a tournament should receive Christian burial—were not sufficient to eradicate the enthusiastic attachment to these festivals. And even down to the fifteenth century, there was scarcely a single princely family in Germany which had not lost some of its members in these essays at arms. Of Albert, margrave of Brandenburg, the German Achilles, it is related that he had thus tilted at more than seventeen tournaments with the pointed lance, and even the emperor Maximilian had entered the arena several times. Thus the historian of the house of Austria, Fugger, relates, that at a diet at Worms, in 1495, a French knight, Claudius Barre, appeared and challenged the whole German nation to a trial of arms in single combat. The emperor

* These guns, however, were merely simple tubes, which, like the cannons, were ignited by a match. But as this was tedious and troublesome, and impeded the power of taking aim, German ingenuity discovered, in 1551, at Nuremberg, the improved arquebus, in which the spark was produced by a steel wheel being made to strike in its revolution the flint; and afterwards, in France, this invention was brought to the perfection of the present musket.

Maximilian on this occasion took upon himself the right to fight for the honor of his people, and which he maintained by eventually overcoming the foreign knight with the sword, after their lances had left the combat undecided. While this emperor is, properly so called, the last of the chivalric emperors, and as the period of his reign concludes the middle ages, we find in some of his contemporaries, such as Götz of Berlichingen, Franz of Sickingen, and Ulric of Hutten, the contest for the ancient splendor of their order against the mighty revolutions of time, again maintained, until their death. Even among the clergy of these chivalric times the warlike disposition of knighthood is occasionally apparent. When Frederick III. went forth against Charles the Rash, to deliver Neuss, the valiant bishop of Münster, Count Henry of Schwarzburg, was the first to land an army, consisting of Westphalians, Netherlanders, and Lower Saxons, and exhibited a greater degree of warlike zeal than even was shown by the imperial general, the margrave Albert (or Achilles) of Brandenburg himself; nay, he even cherished the hope of meeting the proud duke of Burgundy in battle, and engaging with him hand to hand in mortal combat. But as no battle took place, a truce having been determined upon, during which the Münsterians had a hot engagement with the duke's Picardians, the bishop, who could obtain no satisfaction for the insult offered to his army, challenged Duke Charles to fight a duel, but which the emperor Frederick prohibited. The army, however, adjudged that in this expedition it was not the margrave of Brandenburg, but the bishop of Münster, who had merited the title of the German Achilles.

Meantime the whole system of military tactics underwent the most important changes. Instead of the ancient levies of the ban, there were now introduced Lanzknechte, or mercenary troops, and thus, with this change arose the entire distinction made between the martial and the civil order. In former times the imperial vogt, or intendant, who administered the judicial and civil affairs of a district, was, at the same time, the military chief or commandant of the city and burgh, and the leader in the field, as were all the counsellors and officials of the princes. All the departments so administered throughout the land harmonized and were conducted with equal energy in every part. Now, however, they were separated, and war became a distinct mercenary profession.

But the worst part of this change was, that when the princes could not maintain their mercenaries in times of peace, the latter then, having neither the disposition nor ability to return to the employments of civil life, became a pest to society. The chronicle of Sebastian Frank complains bitterly against this: "The destructive lanciers," he says, "are a shameless race, and of use to nobody; when they are not in pay or enrolled they run loose upon society, demanding war and misery. An unchristian and lost set, whose employment is murder, rapine, incendiarism, gaming, drinking, blaspheming, wantonly making widows and orphans, yea, whose only delight is in the calamities of the people, feeding upon the vitals of mankind, and whether in or out of war, tormenting the peasantry. The state of matters, alas! is come to this, that as soon as a man becomes a lancier, and from the moment he has taken the oath, and places a lance on his shoulder, henceforth to the end of his life he abandons all other work. Formerly, when a prince carried on a war, he fought with his own people; now, that these worthless fellows are employed, each adversary strives to outdo the other in the number of his soldiers and extent of his preparations for the war, so that it now costs more before it is begun and these hirelings are equipped, than formerly it cost to commence and finish it altogether. Were it not for these mercenary troops, there would be much less war, and although a prince might be forced to fight with but as many hundreds as there are now thousands employed, he would still effect more glorious results; for these rascals do all in their power to protract the war, and sorry would they be, indeed, if they beheld it terminate and peace restored. Thus the country is exhausted to an extent that there is scarcely a prince or peasant who has any more money."

The same chronicle makes honorable and clear distinction between these mercenary troops who served anybody that would give them pay, and those warriors who fought only for their country. "Those subjects," he says, "who in obedience to their princes enlist at their summons, and when the battle is over return to their work, I do not call mercenary Lanzknechte, but brave and faithful warriors." Meantime, however, these lanciers, whose insubordination has called forth such complaints, were excellent soldiers in battle. Armed with lances eighteen feet in length, and protected by a helmet and cuirass, they stood like a firm wall, and their presented lances resembled an impassable forest, whence their battle array was called by the French the *Herisson*, or porcupine-phalanx. The emperor Maximilian greatly improved their discipline. They eclipsed even the glory acquired by the Swiss, and now completely destroyed the superiority hitherto commanded by the chivalric cavalry, whose importance had already been diminished by the Hussite and Swiss infantry.

Equally as important as the invention of gunpowder was for war, was also the discovery of the art of printing for the objects of peace. This also is the work of German ingenuity; not, however, originating in accident, inasmuch as it was found out by a process of profound study, and became perfected by degrees.

There had been in use long previously, after the manner of the little figures which were carved in wood, and printed, a certain description of wooden boards, upon which were cut all the letters necessary for the page of a book, there being as many such boards as pages in the books from which impressions were taken, whence the entire book was completed. Although this operation was much more troublesome than copying, yet with these boards they were enabled to print a book many hundred times, which repaid their labor. Great improvements, however, could yet be made; and thus thought John Guttenberg. Born in 1401, at Mentz, of an ancient noble family, he, with all the powers of his mind, prosecuted the idea of cutting out the letters singly, of an equal size, on the end of small wooden sticks; and after composing these into words, taking therefrom an impression, when he again took them to pieces, and used them for composing the next page. After many experiments, he succeeded. He entered into partnership with his townsmen, John Faust and Peter Schöffer, of Gernsheim;* and this association enlarged the discovery by composing the letters of a mixture of metals, inventing the press, and preparing printers' ink. Thus they were prepared to print. Their first attempt was the Bible; but the real inventor, Guttenberg, did not enjoy that fruit of his labors which he so richly deserved, inasmuch as Faust, the goldsmith, who had advanced him money, after he had spent his fortune in making the necessary experiments, deprived him, by legal process, of all his instruments and property, and excluded him from the concern. Thus the inventor of the most important and valuable art of ancient and modern times, was obliged to spend the remainder of his days dependent upon the bounty of the elector of Mentz, and died in 1468.

In the year 1457, the first book, the Latin Psalms, was completed by Faust and his associates, and in 1462 the entire Bible. So great a difference was even then perceptible between the price of such a work and the expense of transcribing, that a Bible, which, when transcribed, cost from 400 to 500 florins, was to be had for 30 florins. And thus did these men lay the foundation for the immense advantages subsequently derived by this great discovery, and by which every degree of knowledge which raises the intellectual character of man is no longer the peculiar privilege of the few, but may become not only the possession of whole nations, but of the entire world. Thence it is that the art of printing exerts a most wonderful influence in the development of mankind. The law of this development, as is most evident from the observation deduced from all history, down to the present day, is, that the cultivation and intelligence of the human mind progressively enlarges its boundaries, and in its widening circle embraces an increasing number of our fellow-creatures. Although it may admit of dispute whether, upon the whole, we are further advanced in the arts and sciences than many nations of antiquity and the middle ages, the progress in the more universal spread of knowledge can admit of no question, and it is the noble art of printing, which, as the great lever, has effected this glorious object.

Of great importance to the extraordinary results of the art of printing was also the previous discovery of linen-paper.

* The prevailing opinion that Schöffer was a clergyman is incorrect. The name of Clericus, which he took, signifies also calligraphist, or one who devoted himself to the copying of books.

Formerly, parchment was used, which, however, was too expensive and too thick; then cotton-paper, which was not sufficiently durable. Paper made of linen, which is also probably a German discovery, first appears in a document of the year 1318, at Kauffbeuren.

We close our general reflections upon the age just passed, with a few words upon the results produced by the discovery of America and a sea passage to the East Indies.

They did not indeed originate in Germany, but they exerted a great influence upon that country; not only by enlarging the empire of the mind, which must be one result, but also more particularly in producing a change in commerce. Until that time East Indian produce, of which Europe required annually a vast supply, had been brought by various channels through Asia to the Mediterranean sea, and thence taken especially by the maritime states of Italy and conveyed farther. The transit by land to the north was made, as has been before stated, through Germany. But now that the Portuguese, in 1498, had found a passage by sea round Africa, they were able, from the great profits of freightage, soon to monopolize the whole East Indian trade; Venice and the other Italian maritime states declined, and Germany also very soon indirectly felt the effects. Its trade became depressed in proportion as that of Portugal and Spain rose; and, in consequence of this great reverse, the Hanseatic League was dissolved, although their commerce extended to many other wares. The German cities were from the sixteenth century no longer able to maintain their ancient elevation in wealth and power, and thus also in this respect the way was paved for the rising power of the princes.

# SIXTH PERIOD.

## FROM CHARLES V. TO THE PEACE OF WESTPHALIA.

### 1520—1648.

AMONG the MS. documents relating to this period, the "Transactions of the Imperial Diets," as preserved in the archives of the various individual states, are the most important, inasmuch as the diets never exercised so much influence at any period of our history as from the commencement of the fifteenth century until the war of thirty years. Meantime, the newly discovered art of printing promoted especially the composition and circulation of historical works, and we find that, with every ten years, their number increased accordingly to a considerable extent. At the same time, the awakened desire for scientific research, and the taste for the study of ancient authors, became more and more generally diffused and appreciated.

Among the writers, who treat upon the general history of this period, are included:

1. Paul Jovius, (born at Como, 1482, died as bishop of Nucerie, 1552,) Historia sui Temporis, from 1494 to 1546.

2. J. A. Thuames, or de Thou, (born in Paris, 1553, died 1617, as president of the parliament and chief librarian to Henry IV.; very learned and esteemed,) wrote likewise a Historia sui Temporis, 1543 to 1607.

3. John Genesius de Sepulveda, (a Spaniard, born 1491, died 1572, historian of Charles V.,) De rebus gestis Caroli V., Colon, 1657.

4. Among the Spanish historians may be added: Petrus Salazar, Prudentius de Sandoval, Alphonso de Ultoa, and Antonius de Vera et Zunniga.

5. Among the Italians: Louis Dolce, Gianbattista Adriani, and Gregorius Leti. Adriani is especially important.

6. Several separate and, in part, important writings, referring to the time of Charles V., in number about sixty-two, have been collected together by Simon Schard, in the second volume of his Script. rer. Germ., and by Freher, in the third volume of his Script.

For the History of the Reformation we have:

7. The writings of the reformers themselves and of their partisans, which are of the highest importance; containing, at the same time, much in explanation of the political history of their time. The works of Luther, Melanchthon, Zwingli, and Calvin, need not be here especially enumerated.

8. The works of Erasmus of Rotterdam, (born in 1467, died in 1536,) partly in accordance with, partly against the sense of the Reformation, are likewise important; also—

9. The writings of Ulric of Hutten, (born in 1480, died in 1523,) who came forth with glowing zeal and acute mind in the cause of the new ideas advanced.

10. John Sleidanus, (born in 1506 at Sleida, died in 1556; professor of laws at Strasburg, and historian of the league of Schmalkald,) Commentarius de Statu Religionis et Reipublicæ Carolo V., Cæsare. An important work; continued by Londorp from 1555–64.

11. George Spalatin, (born in 1482, died in 1545, court-chaplain and secretary to the Elector Frederick the Wise, who took a great share in the diet at Augsburg in 1530,) Annales Reformationis, besides his Lives of the various Popes of his times, and some minor works, collected together in Menken's Script. rer. Germ.

12. Veit Lewis of Seckendorf, (born in 1626, died in 1692; who, although not a contemporary, is, nevertheless, a source of good authority, inasmuch as in his office as minister of Saxe-Gotha, he collected largely from the documents in the archives of Gotha,) Com-

ment. Hist. et Apologeticus de Lutheranismo, in reply to the Hist. Lutheranismi of the Jesuit Lewis Maimburg, (born at Nancy in 1610, died in 1686,) which merits observation also.

13. The acts relating to the History of the Reformation were completed subsequently, at the commencement of the eighteenth century, from manuscripts preserved in the archives, by J. J. Muller, Valentin Löscher, C. Lehmann, &c., &c.

The History of the Confession of Augsburg is especially treated upon by—

14. David Chiträus, (born in 1530, died in 1600, professor at Wittenberg, Rostock, and Helmstadt, who was commissioned by Maximilian II. to establish a plan of discipline for the Protestant church in Austria, and contributed towards the Formula Concordiæ,) in his Hist. Confess. Augustanæ. He wrote, likewise, Lectures upon Charles V., Ferdinand I., and Maximilian II.

15. George Cœlestin (senior court chaplain to the elector of Brandenburg, died 1576) wrote Hist. Comitior Augustæ, 1530, celebratorum.

Upon the War of Schmalkald:

16. Louis d'Avila, a Spaniard, and general of Charles V., wrote his Comment. de Bello Germanico a Carolo V. gesto, 2 vols. Antwerp, 1550. He writes very much in favor of Charles V. On the other hand—

17. Fred. Hartleder (born in 1579, died in 1640, a privy counsellor of Weimar) in his Transactions and Development of the Causes of the War against the League of Schmalkald, Frankfort, 1617, and Gotha, 1645, embraces warmly the Protestant cause. His work is based upon the documents contained in the archives of Weimar.

Upon the Council of Trent:

18. Paul Sarpi, (born at Venice 1552, died in 1626, a monk and counsellor of that city,) History of the Council of Trent, written in Italian, and published in London in 1619, under the title of Petrus Suavis; translated into German by Rambach, Halle, 1761.

19. In reply to Sarpi, whose writing is too free, appeared another History of the Council of Trent, by the Jesuit Sfortia Pallavicini, (born at Rome in 1607, died in 1667.)

Biographies of celebrated men of that period:

20. Adami Reisneri Comm. de vita et reb. gest. Georgii et Casp. Frundsbergiorum. Frankfort, 1568.

21. Joach. Camerarius, (born in 1500, died in 1547, a friend of Melanchthon, and professor of Tübingen and Leipsic,) Vita Melanchthonis and Vita Mauritii Electoris.

22. Götz of Berlichingen, (died in 1562,) Memoirs by himself; edited by Pistorius, Nuremberg, 1731; and by Büsching and Van der Hagen, 1813.

23. Sebast. Schärtlin of Burtenbach, (general of the cities in the war of Schmalkald,) Memoirs by himself.

Original sources for the History of the Reigns of Ferdinand I. and Maximilian II. may be found in:

24. Script. rer. Germ. by Schard; vols. 3 and 4.

In reference to the period continued beyond the reign of Ferdinand II., and especially the Thirty Years' War:

25. F. C. Count Khevenhüller, (imperial counsellor and grand master of the court, died in 1650,) Annales Ferdinandei, from 1578 to 1637.

26. N. Bellus, Affairs of Germany in peace and war, under Matthias and Ferdinand II., from 1617–40.

27. W. Lamormain, (a Jesuit and confessor of Ferdinand II., died 1648,) Virtutes Ferdinandei; Vienna, 1637.

28. P. B. Burgus, (of Genoa, and a witness of the deeds of Gustavus Adolphus, accordingly in his favor,) Comment de Bello Suecico, from 1618–32.

29. Eberh. Wassenberg, (of Emmerich, Historian of Wladislas, king of Poland,) Florus Germanicus de Bello inter Ferd. II. et III., et eorum hostes ab ann. 1618–40 gesto; very zealous against the Protestants; as likewise—

30. The Italian Historians of the War of Thirty Years; viz., J. Ricci, J. Damiani, Galeazzo Gualdo, and others.

On the other hand, in favor of the Protestant party, are:

31 P. von Chemnitz, (Swedish counsellor and historian, died 1678,) who wrote the Swedish-German war, in nine parts, but of which only two were printed. The others, preserved in the royal archives of Stockholm, have, no doubt, been used by:

32. The celebrated Samuel Puffendorf, (counsellor and historian at Stockholm, subsequently privy counsellor, died in 1694,) in his work De rebus Suecicis sub Gust. Adolpho usque ad abdicationem Christinæ.

33. Tobias Pfanner, (counsellor of Saxony, born in 1640,) in his Hist. Pacis Westph.

34. And, commencing with the year 1617, the voluminous work, Theatrum Europæum, in 19 vols., by various authors, and of very unequal, sometimes inferior, merit.

Finally, in reference to the lives of two other distinguished men of this period, Bernhard, duke of Weimar, and Wallenstein, duke of Friedland, we have:

35. The Achievements of Bernhard, duke of Weimar, collected from the archives by E. S. Cyprian. Gotha, 1729.

36. The Life of Wallenstein, by G. Gualdo. Lyon, 1643, and

37. The Original Letters of Wallenstein, from the year 1627 to 1634, throwing a new light upon his life and character. Edited by Fr. Förster; Berlin, 1828.

## CHAPTER XVI.

State of the Empire—Internal Anarchy—Charles V. of Spain, and Francis I. of France—Frederick the Wise, elector of Saxony—Charles V. elected emperor of Germany—His Character—Jealousy and Discontent of the Spaniards—Try to dissuade Charles from accepting the Imperial Crown—New Spain—Discovery of Mexico—Arrival of Charles in Germany—His Coronation, 1520—Schism in the Church—Causes which produced it—Ignorance of the Clergy—Their Vices—Murmurs and Discontent of the People—A Reformation in the Church universally demanded—Scholastic Wisdom—Theology—Enlightenment of Science—John Reuchlin.

The imperial throne, now vacant by the death of Maximilian, required a successor. The general agitation throughout Europe, as well as the confusion prevalent in Germany itself, where the Faustrecht appeared immediately after the death of the emperor to resume its sway, demanded a monarch, endowed with energy and consequent power, in order to maintain the necessary equilibrium between the internal and external government. The war still continued between Spain and France upon the subject of Italy, although neither of these powers possessed the right of decision in the cause of a country which knew not how to govern or even help itself, such decision being vested in the hands of the emperor alone. In the east the Turks again threatened to devastate the country; and Hungary, reduced by mal-administration as well as by the luxury and effeminacy of the people, was no longer able to serve as a bulwark against this formidable enemy; hence from this quarter likewise the emperor was called upon to come forth as the protector of Europe. In Germany itself, and in the very heart of the empire, two grand contentions arose at this moment, and raged with all their ungovernable fury. Duke Ulric of Wurtemberg, having cause to revenge himself upon the free town of Reutlingen for some offence, fell suddenly upon that place, in the winter of 1519, and having made himself master of it, he continued to hold it in possession as his own. The Swabian league, however, which had been established by the emperor Maximilian, in order to maintain the tranquillity of the land, finding the duke paid no respect or attention to their repeated summons to surrender the town, advanced at once against him, and by their superior force not only regained possession of the place, but pursued the duke throughout his own territories so closely that he was compelled to quit them for safety.

In Lower Saxony again another still more sanguinary struggle raged—the so-called bishop's feud of Hildesheim. Two noblemen, lords of Saldern, but vassals to John, bishop of Hildesheim, proclaimed war against him, in which they were supported by the dukes of Wolfenbüttel and Calenberg; while, on his side, the bishop found assistance from the duke of Lüneburg, and the counts of Lippe, Hoya, and Diepholtz. On the 28th of January, 1519, both parties met on the plain of Soltau in Lüneburg, and after a most obstinate and sanguinary battle, the victory was gained by the bishop, although severely purchased, while on the other side the valiant duke of Calenberg with other nobles were taken prisoners, and four thousand of their men were left dead on the field of battle. The continued repetition of such scenes could not but produce the most dangerous consequences, since, although the Landfriede had happily succeeded in putting an end to the feuds and robberies of the lesser nobility and freebooter knights, it became more and more evident that in order to prevent the princes from following in the same steps, and thus by force of arms seeking to add by conquest to their possessions, it was rendered necessary to elect an active and strong-minded emperor, who should maintain and protect the authority of the laws.

Maximilian had, in the course of his reign, gained several voices in favor of his grandson Charles, already king of Spain; many princes, however, still thought consideration requisite before they could undertake to place the imperial power in the hands of a sovereign who already reigned over the half of Europe; for, as inheritor of the houses of Spain and Austria, Charles possessed, besides Spain and the kingdom of Naples and Sicily, the beautiful Austrian provinces, and all the patrimonial territories of Burgundy in the Low Countries. If to so much splendid power the additional lustre acquired by the possession of the imperial crown were to be added, it was to be feared—thus the princes thought—that his house might become too powerful, and thence conceive the proud and ambitious project of invading and destroying the liberty of the German princes, and seek accordingly to render the empire, without limitation, hereditary and independent.

From another side again, as his competitor for the imperial crown, came forth to oppose him the king of France, Francis I. The pope was in favor of his election, at least he appeared to be so; in addition to which, this young sovereign had gained a great reputation by his first expedition to Italy, where, for his valiant and chivalric bearing, especially in the victorious battle of Marengo, he was extolled—particularly by his own nation—to the very skies. The ambassadors from France presented to the assembled princes at Frankfort a document laudatory of their royal master, in which they thus alluded to the danger threatened by the incursions of the Turks:—"He must indeed be wanting in understanding who, at a time when the storm has broken forth, should still hesitate to confide the steerage of the vessel to the most skilful helmsman."

Nevertheless, in spite of the confidence with which the envoys spoke, the princes felt the danger of electing a French king to be emperor of Germany; and as the elector of Saxony, Frederick the Wise, to whom they had offered the crown, declined it with the magnanimous observation in excuse—"That the inferior power of his house was not equal to contend with the difficulties of the times," adding even his recommendation to them to elect the young Spanish king instead, the princes, after further consideration, remembered and admitted that at least he was a German prince, and the grandson of their late revered emperor Maximilian; they decided accordingly in his favor, and elected him to the imperial throne on the 28th of June, 1519. Before the election, however, his ambassadors were obliged by the princes to sign the following conditions, viz.: "That the emperor shall not make any alliance, nor carry on any war with a foreign nation, without the approbation of the princes, neither shall he introduce any foreign troops whatever into the empire; that he shall hold no diets beyond Germany; that all offices at the imperial court and throughout the empire shall be conferred upon native Germans; that in all the affairs of the empire no other language but German or Latin shall be employed; that in conjunction with the estates, he shall put an end to all the commercial leagues which, by means of their capital, have hitherto held so much sway, and maintained so much independence; that he shall not pronounce the imperial ban against any state of the empire without urgent reasons, nor without a proper form of judgment; and, finally, that he shall come to Germany as speedily as possible, and make that country his principal residence."

These and other articles being sworn to by the ambassadors in the name of their royal master, they proceeded at once to hasten his arrival in the Germanic empire.

The youthful monarch had occupied the Spanish throne about two years; but as yet he was unknown to the world. Hitherto the majority hoped but little from him. The premature death of his noble and chivalric father, Philip the Handsome, the insanity of his mother Joanna, his separation from his brother Ferdinand, who had been educated in Spain, while he himself had been brought up entirely among strangers in the Netherlands—all these circumstances acted unfavorably upon his mind, and produced that retiring, exclusive disposition which made him shrink from the world and live in the privacy of his own mind. Added to this, it was but slowly that he arrived at that clearsightedness and independence of action which subsequently produced his greatness; it appeared indeed, as if he were to be guided and ruled entirely by his counsellors. Those alone who commanded a profound knowledge of human nature were capable of observing and interpreting the movements by which his soul was actuated. At a grand tournament in Valladolid, the young king, who from his childhood was warmly attached to chivalric exercises, entered the lists completely equipped, and exchanged a few courses at arms with his chief master of the horse. He broke three lances with him, and each time the air was filled with shouts of applause from the assembled multitude; for the youth, who had not attained his eighteenth year, and had always been considered as weak, both in body and mind, and of easy persuasion, appeared here in the most undaunted and noble character, and with all the vigor of a knight, while on his shield he bore the motto: "Nondum!" (not yet.) Those who knew and understood the meaning of the word, awaited with impatience the moment when he would be enabled to come forth before the world uncontrolled and independent.

That moment had now arrived. He was chosen emperor of Germany, and it was for him now to decide promptly whether or not he would abandon Spain in order to seize the reins of government in his new empire. The important announcement appeared to produce no change whatever in our young prince of twenty years: "Our king, who is now emperor," says an eye-witness, "seems to regard this, the greatest fortune that can happen to mortal, as nothing; his greatness of mind and gravity of expression are so extraordinary, that any one would suppose from his appearance, that he was playing at football with the universal globe." The resolution he was called upon to adopt would have proved to any ordinary mind a matter of extreme difficulty. Spain at that time was in a state of great fermentation, and almost ready to burst into full flame; for strong and influential parties stood opposed to each other face to face: the royal authority, a powerful nobility, and proud and wealthy cities. In Germany again he would find an agitated empire in complete anarchy, and above all, the grand contest which raged upon the subject of religion, and to which all eyes were at present directed. The Spaniards themselves were discontented at beholding their sovereign invested with the imperial dignity; they feared they might in consequence be reduced to the form of a secondary kingdom, subject to the rule of arbitrary governors. "What else had the empire now become," they said, "but the mere shadow of an immensely overgrown tree?" In such poor estimation was the ancient and, formerly, so venerated imperial crown now held in foreign countries.

The majority of his counsellors advised and warned Charles not to abandon his hereditary kingdom for the sake of a possession so uncertain, and at least difficult to maintain; but his genius saw and acknowledged that this very circumstance paved the way for bold and independent action; he found himself summoned as it were to a career of glory, and he followed his destiny without fear or hesitation. It was at this time, while he was on his journey to Germany, there to take possession of the crown offered to him, that the important news arrived announcing the acquisition made in his name of a second empire, that of Mexico, then just discovered in the new world. A more common mind would have been overcome with the weight of such great events; but the effect they produced upon the young and mighty emperor was only such as to accelerate the maturing of his mind. His care and solicitude were now claimed by one entire moiety of the universe, and from that moment he showed in all his actions the character of a clear-sighted, truly energetic, and comprehensive-minded ruler.

Charles landed in the Netherlands and continued his journey on to Germany. He was crowned on the 22d of October, 1520, at Aix-la-Chapelle, with great pomp and magnificence, and he then appointed the 17th of April of the following year as the day for holding the first imperial diet at Worms. This diet was one of the most brilliant that had ever been held; it was attended by six electors and a numerous body of spiritual and temporal princes. The most important transaction that occurred on this occasion was the trial of Martin Luther.

The church had for centuries been subject to violent agitation and disorder in every shape, and the reckless abandonment of all external discipline had operated materially to shake the faith of numerous Christians, as well as to corrupt the morals of the people generally. Complaints of the decline of the church, and the desire for its general reform, had long been growing loud and more urgent in expression. There are none, let them belong to whatever doctrine or sect they may, who, knowing the history of those times, will not admit that these complaints were at that period too well founded. They were raised in the name of entire nations, and proceeded more especially from the mouths of the faithful adherents of the ancient church, as well as the venerable bishops themselves, together with the most learned and profoundly-minded men of the church and state.

At the time of the great schism, from the year 1378 to 1414, when several popes disputed the possession of the holy chair of St. Peter, each rival claimant excommunicated the other in turn, together with all his partisans; so that all the countries of Christendom found themselves subject to the ban of the church, either by the one pope or the other, and all religious and pacific minds were at a loss to know where in reality they should seek and find the true peace of God. At such a period, and under the influence of such violent and furious passions, it was to be expected that that veneration hitherto felt for the name of the pope would be sensibly weakened, and the invisible and sacred bonds gradually loosened.

To this was added a state of ignorance which prevailed throughout the spiritual body, or at least among the majority of its members; for it was not possible for a few individual men of learning to succeed in dissipating the darkness that overspread the mass. And as darkness of the mind always brings with it its consequent vices, which can alone be extirpated by divine light, a number of the clergy were at that time clothed in sin, an abomination in the eyes of the good, and a scandal to the people generally. In the year 1503, accordingly, some time before the appearance of Luther in the field, one of the first theologians of Germany represented this degenerated, fallen state of the church in strong terms:

"The study of theology," he says, "is despised among us, and the gospel of Christ, as well as the excellent writings of the holy fathers, are completely neglected; faith, piety, moderation, and all the other virtues, so much praised and valued by even the pagans themselves, the wonders of God's grace and the merits of Jesus, all these are doctrines upon which the most profound silence is maintained by them. And such people too, who understand nothing of either theology or philosophy, are elevated to the highest dignities of the church, and become the guardians of our souls! Thence the melancholy decline of the Christian church, the hatred towards the clergy, and the total absence of all good and salutary instruction! The profligate life led by the ecclesiastics, shocks the feelings of well-minded parents, and prevents them from allowing their sons to devote their lives to that once holy service. They omit entirely all search into the Holy Scriptures, and they corrupt their taste to such an extent, that they no longer feel their beauty and force; they become lukewarm and lazy in their duty, and are only too glad when the service is speedily at an end, the chant and sermon hurriedly concluded, and their presence no longer required! They discourse more gravely and impressively with the mortal upon whom they may have a claim for money, than with their divine Master and Creator. Instead of devoting their leisure time to study, they pass it in gambling, debauchery, and licentiousness, without caring in the least, or having any consideration for the disgust their conduct everywhere produces. How then is it possible that in this shameful state of things, the laity can feel respect for them or religion itself? The gospel tells us that the path to Heaven is narrow and difficult, but they only strive to make it broad and easy."

That this description is not too strongly colored, is proved by a hundred other undoubted witnesses; and although the monks accused the learned professor, who, as we have just seen, reprimanded them so severely before the pope, Julius II., still he had truth so much on his side, that the papal commissioners themselves pronounced in his favor. The pious bishop of Augsburg, Christopher of Stadion, in a synodal charge to his clergy, coincides exactly in all these complaints, and reproaches them bitterly for their vices, which, he says, could not fail to produce the most corrupt and destructive effects upon the church and the public; and Hugo, bishop of Constance, although inimical to the doctrine of Martin Luther, complains equally in the same strain, together with many others of the chief members of the Catholic church of that time.

But how could it be otherwise, when the investiture of the spiritual offices was regulated by the amount of purchase-money, without any regard to the qualifications and real character of the individual chosen, and when, as has already been shown, only the smallest portion of the clergy in reality possessed any knowledge of the word of God? To such a degraded state indeed had the church become reduced, that according to well-authenticated evidence, we are assured that out of all the principal leading members of the clerical body throughout the Swiss confederation, at the commencement of the sixteenth century, there were not three who had ever read the Bible; and when the people of Valais received about this time a letter from Zürich, in which was quoted a sentence from the sacred volume, only one man was to be found who knew the book, and even what he knew was by hearsay!

How deplorably great and universal must have been the ignorance existing at this period through the negligence of the clergy, when we find not only that men were unacquainted with the source itself of religious devotion and Christian virtue, but that its very name was scarcely known to them!

In Italy, and especially in Rome, this want of faith and knowledge in divine matters was still more strikingly evident and notorious. Under the pontificate of the accomplished Leo X., from 1513 to 1521, the arts certainly flourished in the capital to a remarkable degree; but while these ripened forth from their rich and fertile soil, they smothered the simple germs of the true religion of God. The enjoyment of the senses was valued above every thing as the greatest treasure; the belief placed in the existence of a higher invisible world, could not coexist with such principles, and the calm and silent piety of the heart became in the eyes of the world a subject of ridicule and contempt. The usages and forms of divine worship appeared to be retained and practised in order to serve rather as a check upon the mass of the people, whence they soon became regarded in the character of purely external ceremonies.

In proof of this we will refer to the opinion expressed by the pious Pope Adrian VI., in his letter addressed to his nuncio at the diet held at Nuremberg, in 1522: "We know," says he, "that in this holy see much corruption has continued to abound during many years, great abuse in all ecclesiastical affairs, as likewise in all that has emanated from our chair, and in one word, a depravation in every thing. Thence it is no wonder if the disease has transferred itself from the head to the other members—from the pope to the priests;

therefore, we promise, as far as lies in us, to devote all our attention and care towards reforming first of all our chair, whence perhaps all this evil has originated, in order that as the destruction has issued thence to descend to the inferior grades, the cure and renewed enjoyment of health may likewise find their source there."

The feeling of the necessity existing for a thorough reform in the church, had long since become so generally acknowledged throughout all ranks of society, that the lower orders had continued, even from the middle of the fourteenth century to the present time, to nourish the false hope of the return of the emperor Frederick II., (then dead since more than a hundred years,) assured that he would come forth as the desired reformer. We have also observed what urgent representations were made by the Germans, the English, and French, when assembled at the councils of Constance and Basle; and in the year 1510, the diet at Augsburg raised once more its voice against the state of the church, having drawn up and established ten heavy charges, in reply to the pretended and assumed rights of the popes, and by which the schism of the church was already proclaimed: "For if the causes for these complaints," said the diet, "are not removed or remedied, there is good reason to believe that a general persecution against the priests must shortly arise, or, according to the example already set by the Bohemians, one universal abandonment of the Roman church will, perhaps, inevitably take place."

Thence we perceive that, at this time, the ancient sacred edifice of the hierarchy, which had existed during so many centuries, and which, according to its fundamental object, was well and indispensably calculated for the unity of the Christian nations, was now undermining itself, and produced, by its own means, its tottering condition; inasmuch as it had lost all respect and consideration among the people, because its leading members, living in proud and haughty security, paid no regard to the spirit of the times.

However evident all we have just related must appear to the minds of all men, we must, nevertheless, once more strictly examine the operating causes of the mighty change produced in the world, in order to perfectly comprehend it.

A little good-will and gradual amelioration would have sufficed to satisfy and remove all the charges referred to—inasmuch as they related chiefly to the external forms and administration of the church—had there only been, at the head of religion itself, a genius in possession of clear-minded views, an active spirit, and energetic powers. But such a leading genius was no longer to be found in the clerical body; religion itself no longer maintaining its pure spirit. Not only the ignorance of which we have before spoken, but a completely *perverted* system prevailed in almost all the doctrines of religion. They set a great value upon a certain class of school wisdom, which they styled scholastic science, and which, in ancient times, had originated in the mixture of philosophic principles with the doctrines of Christianity. The plain and simple truths of the Holy Scriptures, so intelligible and clear, even to the mind of the most ignorant and juvenile reader, were clothed in obscure and erudite words, and these words were regarded as the principal object; they soon proceeded to discuss their interpretation, and of the disputants he who carried on the contest in the most sharp and refined style of language was held to be the most learned. Thence, as it often happens, that both spirit and truth become lost in the crowd of many words, so likewise the gentle, simple, and beneficent light of Christian faith vanished more and more from the science which they called their theology. With the fifteenth century, however, a new epoch opened upon the sciences, and the human mind became increasingly enlightened; the darkness in which it had hitherto been enveloped, now yielded before the divine light of knowledge. Before its overpowering rays, the scholastic sophism, with all its shallow pretensions to its important interpretation of words, could no longer maintain its ground; a few select and distinguished men of the day now came forth and attacked it with the irresistible weapons of reason and sarcasm, exposing it to the world in all its bareness. Its disciples, however, on the other hand, while thus overwhelmed by the force of their adversaries, would not in their retreat endeavor to redeem their character, by seeking to find the necessary light even in their own doctrine—which might have operated in their favor, and have served as their only protection—but with blind zeal and defiance they sought to extinguish and destroy at once the dawning rays which announced the coming of the glorious day—a vain and futile effort, which has, at all times, only been attended with disgraceful defeat, and ever fallen powerless to the ground.

In Germany this new light in the sciences was more especially promulgated by John Reuchlin, (born at Pforzheim in the year 1455,) one of the first and most distinguished men of learning that our country ever produced, possessing the most erudite knowledge of the Latin, together with the Greek and Hebrew languages—a man endowed with a mind so vast and comprehensive, that it was said of him, that in his mind was combined all the scholarship, all the knowledge of the arts and sciences, together with all the learning then to be found in the Christian world. Many of the theologians vented all their rancorous passions against him, although he lived before the time of the Reformation, and accordingly took no share in it. We must not, however, include all the leading members of the clergy among those so plunged in darkness, for the before-mentioned Christopher of Stadion, bishop of Augsburg, did not think it beneath his dignity to undertake a journey of seven days to Freiburg, in order there to become acquainted with the celebrated Erasmus of Rotterdam, while John of Dalberg, bishop of Worms, formed a library containing the works of the most distinguished writers, and was so attached to the sciences, that he became a member of the Rhenish society of learned men, founded by the poet Conrad Celtes. But the number of these better-minded men was too limited to cope with those whose blind and furious zeal, in their hatred to all enlightenment, confounded together the good with the bad, and produced, accordingly, the destruction of their own empire.

## CHAPTER XVII.

**Outbreak of the Reformation, 1517—Abuses in the Church—Letters of Indulgence—Martin Luther the Reformer—His exposure and condemnation of these proceedings—Is summoned to appear in Rome—Withheld from going by the Elector of Saxony—The Pope's Nuncio, Cardinal Cajetan, and Luther at the Diet of Augsburg, 1518—Refusal of Luther to retract—Luther's Appeal to the Pope for a fair hearing—Controversial Discussion between Luther and Dr. Eck—Luther maintains his ground—The Pope's Bull against Luther—The Reformer burns the Bull with the Canon Law and Eck's Writings—Propagation of the New Doctrine—Luther addresses the People—Ulrick of Hütten and Francis of Sickingen—Frederick the Wise of Saxony and the Princes in favor of Reform—The Grand Diet at Worms, 1521—Charles V.—The Pope's Legate, Cardinal Alexander—Luther's appearance and Examination there—Solemn Refusal to Retract—The Emperor's Declaration—Luther Excommunicated and his Writings burnt—Conveyed by the Elector of Saxony for Safety to the Castle of Wartburg—His translation of the New Testament—Tumults and Revolutions of the Peasantry—Münzer the Fanatic—Battle of Frankenhausen—Münzer's Death—Tranquillity restored.**

We have in the preceding chapter endeavored to develop the causes which during several centuries had prepared the way for the schism of the church; but that which more immediately hastened its accomplishment, was the abuse so universally practised, in the declaration and distribution of indulgences.

The agents of the papal court were authorized to offer letters of the indulgence in every country that recognised the pope, by which those who obtained them received from the church remission of the punishment they had merited by their sins. Such letters of indulgence, however, were not of recent origin, inasmuch as in the early ages of the church, when it punished public crime by severe and public penitence, by exclusion from divine worship, often for the space of years, &c., there were many penitents, especially those who distinguished themselves by their zeal in the practice of repentance, whose term of trial was abridged by the bishop, or the punishment altogether remitted, and the performance of pious acts of gifts or endowments substituted. At the time of the crusades, the popes accorded to all who undertook to encounter the dangers and fatigues of these expeditions, the remission from all the punishment of the church to which they would otherwise have been obliged to submit. Subsequently, the same indulgence was granted to all those who, in lieu of taking part in these holy wars personally, contributed their aid in money instead. After this period, the object of these expiatory acknowledgments was extended to other pious works, such as the building of churches, schools, &c.; and when Europe was threatened by the Turks, the expeditions against their armies presented numerous opportunities to the popes to distribute their letters of indulgence. Very soon, however, the belief that these letters of indulgence absolved their possessors from sin itself—an error quite in keeping with the coarse and depraved state of feeling in those times—became more and more promulgated among the people, and was supported generally by the prelates themselves; while, on the other hand, suspicions were increasingly nourished and murmurs loudly expressed, with respect to the employment of the sums professedly collected for the exclusive object of works of piety. Thence, at length, both the princes and the people united their voices in complaint against the existing abuse of indulgences, and subsequently the council of Trent issued a decree against the criminal agents of the church, "who availed themselves of the word of God in order to fill their own pockets with lucre."

In order to draw from these indulgences as much profit as possible, the sale thereof in entire provinces was let out to the highest bidders or farmers-general, and these again appointed several sub-farmers, who, for the sake of gain, committed the most shameful abuses. To promote the sale of these letters of indulgence, they selected men who, possessing eloquence and impudence, might succeed in exciting the minds of the people and induce them to purchase them by wholesale; and truly, the shameless proceedings of some of these men exceed all belief. They sold indulgences for the most heavy crimes committed: for pillage of churches, perjury, and murder; nay, the promise of indulgence could even be obtained *before* the commission of the contemplated crime.

But additional evidence to prove the destructive influence with which such an abuse of religion must operate upon the morality of mankind, is superfluous. Suffice it, that the long-nourished feeling of discontent at length burst forth. Leo X. having, in the year 1516, announced fresh indulgences in order to complete the building of the church of St. Peter in Rome, commenced by his predecessor, Julius II., it was generally believed that an important share of the money collected, viz., that contributed in Saxony and the countries as far as the Baltic, was not to be devoted to the building of the church of St. Peter, but was intended for the pope's sister. In addition to which, the clerical agents employed on this occasion, especially a certain Bernard Samson, and John Tetzel, the former in Switzerland, and the latter in Saxony, excited by their shameful conduct the greatest indignation.

It was at this moment that Martin Luther, born in 1483, at Eisleben in Thuringia, an Augustinian friar, and professor of theology in the university of Wittenberg, came forth and publicly condemned these indulgences; and on the eve of All Saints' day, (the 31st of October, 1517,) in the church of the palace of Wittenberg, he read ninety-five theses in which he bitterly inveighed against the traffic of indulgences, and challenged all the most learned men of the day to contest them with him in a public examination. Similar public assertions on certain articles of faith were not of unusual occurrence, but those expressed by Luther were conveyed in a language so bold, and in a spirit of such independence, that they excited forthwith the greatest sensation, and were read throughout Germany with the most eager curiosity and interest. Therein he maintained, "that the pope possessed no power to remit sins himself, but only to pronounce their remission by God; that whatever power herein the pope might possess was equally shared by every bishop and prelate; that whoever sincerely repented of his sins would receive remission from punishment without the indulgences; that the treasures of the Saviour and the church were so equally distributed and shared in by the faithful, that the pope could not impart to them any fresh claim," &c. At the same time he did not at all contemplate attacking either the authority of the pope or that of the ancient church. The doctrine, however, which he published upon the indulgences could not but excite the most violent opposition on the part of Tetzel and his friends, especially the Dominicans, who for a long time had been opposed to the order of the Augustinians; they denounced him as a heretic, and they already threatened him with the sword and burning pile.

Meantime in Rome itself the most strict silence was maintained, although the disputes had now continued for nearly nine months. The whole matter, however, was not the less known there, but the pope perhaps regarded it merely in the light of a monkish dispute; besides which, in Rome they were totally unacquainted with Ger many. They considered it to be still a half-savage country, its population patient, accustomed to obedience, and slow in forming a resolution. But this ignorance and depreciation of our nation proved fatal to the pontifical chair, and brought down likewise upon ourselves the most disastrous consequences.

At length, in the month of August, 1518, Luther was summoned to appear at Rome, there to justify himself before the tribunal of the Holy See. But the elector of Saxony, as well as the University of Wittenberg, which, but recently founded, owed its rapidly flourishing state entirely to Luther, would not suffer him to make the dangerous journey. By their mediation he received permission to adjust the affair in Germany, and with this object to present himself at the end of October, 1518, before the pope's nuncio, Cardinal Thomas de Vio of Gaeta, (usually known under the name of Cajetan,) at the diet of Augsburg. The latter, who, as a Dominican friar, had already been an opponent of the theological views and opinions of Luther, demanded from him a retraction of his sentiments. Luther declared his willingness to make it, provided what he had advanced could be refuted by the Holy Scriptures. The cardinal, however, who considered it beneath his dignity to hold argument or dispute with a monk, abruptly dismissed him with the words: "Retire hence, nor come again before us, unless it be that thou wilt retract."

Luther now composed and handed in to the nuncio a letter of justification, in which he acknowledged he had acted too impetuously, and had not spoken of the pope with sufficient respect, promising henceforth to maintain complete silence, if on their side his opponents were subjected to the same restraint towards him. As, however, he received no reply to this document, he held himself bound to address the pope personally, and with the aid of a notary, in the presence of witnesses, drew up in Latin an appeal against the unjust judgment pronounced, requiring that a more fair and just inquiry and decision should take place before the pope himself; this paper he caused to be affixed publicly on the gate of the cathedral church in Augsburg, and immediately afterwards quitted that city. This document proves, that Luther at that time had not yet formed the resolution to separate himself from the Romish church; but the pressure of circumstances, and the warmth of controversy with his adversaries, impelled him from one step to the other.

A professor of theology at Ingolstadt, in Bavaria, Dr. John Mayer of Eck, usually called Dr. Eck, one of the most zealous and talented partisans of his church, a man of comprehensive scientific knowledge, the exercise of which he always had at command, and to which he added an imposing figure and a powerful, penetrating voice, challenged Luther and another professor of Wittenberg, Andrew Carlstadt, in the year 1519, to meet him at a public dissertation upon subjects of faith in Leipsic, which formed part of the territory of George, duke of Saxony. They both appeared there, accompanied by a pupil of Reuchlin, Philip Melanchthon, afterwards so celebrated, and at that time professor of Greek at Wittenberg; the meeting was likewise honored with the presence of the duke of Saxony himself. The controversial trial lasted from the 27th of June to the 13th of July, 1519. They discussed at great length the subjects of the principal articles of faith and the respect due to the pope; but as always happens in all disputes, when carried on with zealous spirit, words of bitter and acrimonious import were exchanged between the two parties, while, however, it became more and more evident in the course of the contest that Luther successfully maintained his position, in not only rejecting the infallible authority of the pope, but likewise that of the councils, until at length Eck exclaimed: "Reverend father, if you then really do believe that a lawfully-assembled council can err, then must I regard you as a gentile and publican."* Saying which he quitted the assembly, and proceeded at once to Rome, and demanded that the heretic should be

* In this celebrated controversy at Leipsic, which forms a critical point in the great development of the history of those times—Duke George of Saxony himself regarding it as such, he having proposed that the decision of the dispute should be transferred to the consideration of other universities—two peasants' sons represented the conflicting ideas that characterized the present and future times, and their unity or still greater division could not but produce the most important consequences. While Luther on the one hand was the descendant of a peasant family, living at the foot of the Thuringian forest in Moravia, Eck, on the other was the son of Michael Mayer of Eck, a peasant, and afterwards mayor of that place, (similar to Luther's father, who became a counsellor of Mansfeld,) whither he had wandered to work in the mines—he, as younger son, not having any patrimonial claim to the farm.

visited with the utmost rigor of the apostolic power.

Accordingly, he soon reappeared in Germany armed with a bull from the pope, in which forty-one propositions selected from Luther's writings were designated as heretical, while he himself, unless he publicly retracted them within sixty days, was declared under the ban of the church; and which the zealous agent endeavored to circulate throughout all the cities of Germany. But it found admission only in a very few places; the magistrates generally forbidding it to be made public, and where the document did find a place upon the walls of any town, it was immediately torn down by the people—such was the respect in which the principles of the new doctrine were already held. Luther now proceeded without farther hesitation to perform an act which rent asunder forever the ties which bound him to the ancient church. He convoked by public summons the whole of the members of the University of Wittenberg, to meet on the 10th of December, 1520, before the Elster gate of the town, when all the students having erected a funeral pile, one of the magistrates set fire to it, and Luther, amid the loud acclamations of the assembly, cast into the burning mass the popish bull, together with the canon law and Eck's writings.

It is impossible to describe the rapidity with which the new doctrine spread from one end of Germany to the other, extending even far beyond the frontiers of the empire.* Such celerity cannot be conceived by those who form their calculation by the scale of sensuality; for it is only the vivid flash communicated by the lightning of the mind which ignites in millions the inflammable materials already prepared, that can produce such mighty results.

When an age is ripe for great changes, the signal alone is wanted to rouse the whole community into action, as if struck by the wand of magic; and he who has thus supplied that want, and proclaimed it aloud, is appreciated by all as the great author, although he has only pronounced with his voice that which has long since existed in the lap of time, and has become already matured within the souls of all. Meantime we have seen in the preceding chapters, how the progress that science had already made, together with the great inventions of the preceding century, more especially the art of printing, now the means of at once communicating to thousands information that otherwise had remained limited to the possession of a few—perhaps locked up within the walls of the monasteries—how, we say, all this combined to prepare the world for the coming changes we have already seen. On the other hand again, this very rapidity shown in the propagation of the new doctrine is an irrefragable proof of the great fall of the religious and moral spirit of that epoch. For attachment to the customs, more especially to the faith of his fathers, is so powerfully and deeply rooted in the heart of man, that to separate himself from this as long as he at all sincerely feels its inspiration, is contrary to the laws of human nature; it can only occur when that which should constitute the most ardent and fervent feeling of the heart has become cold and torpid, and reduced to a state of mere external display.

Many other causes existed among the citizens and the people generally, which throughout the empire operated materially to hasten the crisis. Up to the present moment the great majority of the common free people had been completely neglected and despised; nothing had been done to raise them from their state of ignorance, and thus all their mental energy was left to perish in uninterrupted barbarism. Luther now came among them as their great national teacher; promising them instruction, nay, making them his arbitrator in his dispute. And this he undertook and performed in a language so energetic and penetrating, that it struck upon the ears of the people in tones hitherto unknown to them.

The external condition of the people likewise promoted Luther's exertions. The peasantry, it is true, had gradually acquired a state of greater freedom than had existed in former times; but the services

* The ninety-five propositions of Luther against the indulgences were distributed throughout Germany within a fortnight, in the course of from four to six weeks they were known by the whole of Europe, and the universal excitement they must have produced may be easily conceived. In 1520, Luther's writings were translated in the Netherlands into Spanish, and in 1521, a traveller found and purchased them in Jerusalem. When Herr von Miltitz, a distinguished Saxon, travelled, in 1519, from Italy to Wittenberg, deputed by the pope to prevail upon Luther to make concession and to promise to maintain silence, he himself acknowledged to the great reformer that throughout his journey in Germany he had found on the average three voices to one in his favor, and at this time Luther had only been two years upon the scene.

they were condemned to perform were nevertheless even now very oppressive. They were still forced to bend under the weight of burdens inflicted upon them by all the other states, and hitherto their rights as men continued, generally speaking, unrecognised by knights, lords, and princes, and by many of these they were overwhelmed with the most unjust severity. Now, however, the word—"Christian liberty!" resounded and was echoed forth even to the huts of these oppressed peasants. This magic word, which was not interpreted by them in its spiritual and moral sense, but in that of its action upon their external condition, excited within them new and great hopes, producing, unhappily at first, as we shall learn, the most calamitous disorders and turbulence. For, in the universal commotion of one entire generation, as is demonstrated in the history of all nations, it is difficult to preserve the just limits of moderation.

Equally prompt with the people, the nobility of Germany were soon forced to join in the newly-created excitement. They were still animated with enthusiasm for the liberty and honor of their country; and as Germany was now regarded and treated with open contempt by Rome, this was cause sufficient to enlist them on the side of him who came forth to attack the power of the Romish see. On the other hand, the revived love for science had also made considerable progress among the greater and better portion of the nobility; and since the invention and introduction of gunpowder had given a death-blow to chivalry, the practice of the sword was no longer the only occupation of the young nobleman; the more noble exercise of the mind enlarged his views, and prepared him for new and more elevated thoughts; and, finally, Luther in his celebrated work, addressed "To the Nobility of Germany," had more especially made an appeal to them, and called upon them to devote themselves to his cause.

Among the most zealous of his proselytes was included Ulric of Hutten, a leader of the people, such as are ever produced in an age of excitement and revolution; keen and energetic either with the sword or pen, at once a warrior and a scholar, full of wit and persuasive eloquence, he was ever ready for the most perilous enterprise. Once when in his presence he heard four Frenchmen speak in dishonorable terms of the emperor, he forthwith threw down his gauntlet at their feet, and challenged them in the name of German chivalry to mortal combat; he fought and overthrew them all. He was equally successful with his pen as with his sword, when he employed it in condemnation of the monks, the abuses of religion, and against all those who opposed enlightenment and civilization. A satire which he wrote in the Latin tongue, now more and more generally cultivated, created so much interest that it was soon circulated throughout the principal cities of Europe. This extraordinary man, possessing a soul of fire, joined Luther's party, less perhaps from a zeal for religion than from an interest excited by the bold and dangerous character of the reformer's cause; he wrote upon, and devoted all his eloquence to the subject, and would have gladly promoted it with his sword as well, had he been permitted.

Another man of rank, and equally important, Francis of Sickingen, in Franconia, warmly espoused the principles of Luther. His character was so highly estimated, and he was so much distinguished for his valor and noble qualities, that he was at one time considered by many of the princes and nobles, even worthy to wear the imperial crown itself. He generously offered his friend Luther an asylum in his castle, and the protection of himself and friends against any persecution he might experience. Luther, however, gratefully declined his proffered aid; and when the ambitious nobleman—whose active mind would not allow him to remain quiet, but urged him continually to carry out some great project—commenced hostilities against Richard, archbishop of Treves, and declared open war against that prelate, Luther in vain endeavored formally to oppose it. This enterprise was one of the last demonstrations made of the effects produced by the Faustrecht in Germany, inasmuch as, on this special occasion, this single knight, with his friends, raised an army of twelve thousand men, and, in defiance of the interdictions of the imperial diet, marched forth against a powerful prince of the empire, fell upon his territories, devastating with fire and sword the entire land, and only withdrew therefrom, and slowly marched back to his own strong castle, after two other princes, Lewis, elector of the Palatinate, and Philip, landgrave of Hesse, having come to the aid of the archbishop, were seen advancing with their united forces against him.

In the following year, however, the valiant knight was himself closely besieged by these same troops in his fortress of Landshut, and, after defending himself bravely for a considerable time, he was mortally wounded and taken prisoner. He died a few days afterwards, and even his enemies could not withhold from him their admiration, while they joined in the regret so universally felt, that such great powers of mind and body as those possessed by the fallen hero, should thus have sunk without having been able to develop themselves in a more extensive sphere of action.

The death of Sickingen, however, produced nothing unfavorable to the cause of Luther, inasmuch as he was strictly careful in maintaining it exclusively independent, and free of all those external political demonstrations with which that knight and others were so desirous to invest it. And this, indeed, was the principal reason for the duration of its institutions; for had it been abandoned to the chances of this outward struggle, all the active, zealous strength of the nation would have consumed itself, and the whole excitement of the times would have passed away, and left but little or no trace of the contest.

Among the princes of Germany, Frederick the Wise, elector of Saxony, took the most active part in, and supported with great zeal the cause of Luther. He did not at first advance to his aid, neither did he defend him; nevertheless, he would not let him be delivered up to his enemies before he had been brought to a conviction of his error. After the diet of Worms, however, he decided at once in his favor: "The affairs of Germany," said he, in 1523, in Nuremberg, "have advanced so far, that it is no longer in the power of man to lead them in a good direction; God is alone capable of performing this, and to Him we must commit this important controversy, which is beyond our strength."

By degrees several of the other princes declared in favor of the new doctrine; some no doubt from sincere conviction, while others were charged by their adversaries with being allured to their conversion by the spoil they obtained from the ecclesiastical territories. Still, even such inducements would not have sufficed to explain such great and important results. The principal motive which operated so powerfully in the cause of reform, originated in the spirit now roused throughout the German nation, which sought to strike out a new and more level course in each of the three principal elements of life—the state, the sciences, and in religion, in substitution for that which had grown old and obsolete. The leaders and promoters of this new epoch felt conscious that in it was involved the commencement of a grand change in the world. On the other hand, however, the friends of the old system armed themselves more and more zealously to battle for its protection and preservation.

It was resolved that at the grand diet of Worms these religious disputes, which at this moment kept the minds of all throughout the empire in great suspense, should be brought to a termination. There the pope had now sent his legate, Cardinal Alexander, in order to prevail upon the emperor and the princes to employ the arm of temporal authority against Luther. To his great astonishment, however, the nuncio on his arrival discovered that all classes of the people were universal in their declarations of antipathy against the pope. Everywhere he found distributed, writings, songs, and pictures, in mockery and contempt of the pope; and he himself, although in the suite of the emperor, was compelled to witness his appearance greeted with every mark of derision, and at times even his own life endangered. At the diet he demanded, in accordance with his instructions, the adoption of the most severe measures against the man who was already condemned as a heretic, laying, at the same time, before the princes, a long list of propositions selected from Luther's works, in order to prove how much he really deviated in the articles of faith from the doctrines of the church, and especially in those of the council of Constance. The elector of Saxony now, however, rose in opposition to the legate, and insisted that Luther himself should be heard, in order to learn from his own lips whether these propositions were or were not correctly and faithfully copied from his writings, and whether he acknowledged them as such. In this opinion he was supported by the emperor and all the princes;

the cardinal, however, opposed it, saying, "that what had been already decided by the pope, could not be subjected to examination before a diet composed of spiritual and temporal members." In reply it was stated to him, that they did not desire to examine the faith of Luther, but merely to hear from his own mouth whether or not he had actually written and taught that for which he was condemned; therefore, for this reason, it was necessary he should be summoned before the diet. This, in fact, was one of the most important acts in the history of the Reformation; for thence the cause of Luther had become an open and national affair.

His friends, and especially the elector of Saxony, now demanded for him the imperial and inviolable safe-conduct; this was granted, and Luther immediately set out from Wittenberg on his journey to Worms. As he proceeded on his route, he soon learned to know the strength of his party; for the people flocked in thousands from every quarter to behold and welcome him; and when, on the day after his arrival at Worms, (the 17th of April,) he was conducted to the diet, the grand-marshal of the empire was obliged to lead him a by-way, across gardens and obscure parts; so numerously thronged was the whole town. His appearance, on entering the hall in which the diet was held, produced no great effect; the emperor himself is recorded to have said, as he turned to his neighbor: "This man would never succeed in making a heretic of *me*." And truly, Luther was at this moment very pale, and, as he was only just recovering from a severe fever, presented a rather emaciated and feeble appearance. In this weak state, his feelings were at first not a little affected when he found himself unsupported by a single friend, standing alone in the august presence of the emperor himself, and so numerous a body of the princes and nobles of the empire.

A vicar of the archbishop of Treves now put to him the question in the name of the emperor and the diet there assembled, whether he acknowledged as his own the writings then shown to him, and if he persisted in maintaining the propositions therein contained? To the first part he replied, yes; but with respect to the latter, he begged to have a short time granted him for consideration before he returned an answer. Accordingly he was allowed until the following day. He then reappeared before the assembly, and publicly declared: "That his writings were of three kinds; some treated upon the subject of articles of faith and good works, which his enemies did not in any respect find offensive—he could not, therefore, retract them without injury to his conscience; that others attacked the power of the popes and their decrees, and if he retracted them he should only thereby confirm their tyranny in the face of the whole world; the rest were directed against those who defended papacy, and had attacked him in their writings; he confessed that therein he had used severe and bitter language, but which must be ascribed alone to the treatment he himself had received from his adversaries." He then concluded, saying: "If they could convince him from the Holy Scriptures that he was in error, he was ready forthwith with his own hands to cast the whole of his writings into the flames."

The chancellor replied, that they were not there to dispute with him, but to hear from his own lips whether or not he would retract. Upon which Luther declared with the most solemn determination, that his conscience forbade him doing so; whereupon he was dismissed.

On the following day an especial conference took place with Luther, in which the elector of Treves himself took a very active share; but all attempts to bring him to a retraction were in vain; and when eventually the elector demanded of him whether he knew of any means by which all might be restored to order and tranquillity, his last words in reply were: "If this work is a human work, then it will disappear of itself; but if it comes from God, then you cannot disturb or arrest its progress."

The emperor, on the other hand, declared to the princes in decided and serious terms: "That he was resolved to consecrate all he possessed, his empires, kingdoms, states, friends, his body and blood, nay, life itself, to check at once all farther progress of that impious and ungodly spirit, which otherwise must involve himself and the whole German nation in eternal shame and disgrace; that his ancestors, the Christian German emperors, the Catholic kings of Spain, and the dukes of Austria and Burgundy, continued, to the latest period of their lives, faithfully attached to the Roman church; that he had received from them as an inheritance the Catholic doctrine and discipline of the church, in the faith of which he would live and die; that, consequently, he would no longer listen to Luther, but dismiss him at once from his presence, and treat him as he would a heretic."

This declaration of the emperor was of grave and serious import. If the question had been limited to the mere curtailment of the pontifical power, he might not, perhaps, have beheld this generally increasing agitation without some degree of pleasure; but when he had reason to believe that it involved the apostacy of the ancient and eternal faith, to which he was so much and so sincerely attached, and that thence the unity of the church was menaced, he felt himself justified in expressing, in the strongest terms, his fixed determination to oppose it. His penetrating, comprehensive glance, which embraced and recognised acutely the great relations of the world, quickly beheld and measured in advance the mighty consequences of these changes: he foresaw the dissension and irritation that must be produced in all minds, and the contest of opinion which, so soon and so easily converted into a contest of arms, would terminate in the dreadful realities of a religious war. All this danger it was Charles's firm opinion he could smother in its birth, and he felt that his dignity of emperor and protector of the church imposed upon him this duty. And, assuredly, had he been supported everywhere by the same invariable and firm will, had not so many impure, worldly views been brought into operation against it, and produced their baneful influence; but more especially, had the truly honest and sincerely disposed Pope Adrian VI.—who reigned in the years 1522 and 1523, and whose serious wish and intention it was to reform the church—lived but a short time longer, then, perhaps, our country would have been spared the infliction of the dreadful scenes it was doomed to endure.

In his hereditary lands, where he was sole master, Charles certainly did endeavor to extirpate with great rigor the new doctrine; he considered it was here especially his right and duty to do so; and the decrees of his council, the voice of his people, and particularly of the Spanish nation, together with the Neapolitans, all combined to demand this severity from him. But in Germany, on the other hand, where he had to treat with a number of independent princes and a nation in a state of general excitement, where he was bound by the stipulations of his election, and where every violent act was regarded as an attempt to acquire the independence of the imperial power, he proceeded for a considerable time to act with the greatest moderation. The preservation of peace appeared to him of paramount importance, and he was very desirous to bring the parties to mutual concessions. For this very reason he was closely watched by the Spaniards throughout his whole existence, from a fear that he might be infused with heretical principles by his connection with the Germans.

Several of Luther's bitterest enemies sought to persuade the emperor to the adoption of violent measures against him, grounding their arguments upon the same principles which had operated in bringing Huss to the stake; but Charles replied, that his imperial word was inviolable, and he granted Luther an extension of his safe conduct for twenty-one days, during the period of his return home. Nevertheless, many of his friends still trembled for his life, dreading some secret treachery; and on his arrival in Thuringia, his royal protector, the elector of Saxony, caused him to be removed from his carriage, as if by violence, by several disguised knights, and conveyed at night, through a deep wood, to the strong castle of Wartburg, near Eisenach. There it was arranged he should remain concealed, until the fury of his enemies became appeased.

Meantime, in Worms, the imperial ban of excommunication was pronounced against him, as well as against his adherents and protectors. His books were condemned to be burned wherever they were found, and he himself was adjudged to be taken prisoner, and delivered up to the emperor; such was the edict of Worms, dated the 8th (26th) of May, 1521. In Rome, great rejoicings took place; and even in Germany itself it was generally believed that the whole affair was now settled and at an end. But a Spaniard, Valdez, wrote from the diet itself to one of his friends thus: "Far from beholding the termination of this tragedy, I only see its commencement; for I find that the minds of the Germans are especially excited against the pontifical chair." And even while the emperor was still in Worms, after the writings of Luther had been publicly burned, some copies which had escaped that fate were openly offered for sale.

Luther himself continued solitary and uninterrupted in his isolated, but secure asylum in the castle of Wartburg, and devoted those tranquil moments to translating the New Testament into German, so that it might be read and understood by every one throughout the empire. While thus employed, he was informed that, through mistaken zeal, serious riots had broken out in Wittenberg, where the people had forced open the churches, committing the most serious injury by destroying all the holy figures and pictures contained therein, together with their altars and confessionals; and he was grieved to find that these furious and blindly zealous rioters were led on by his friend, but violent enthusiast, Carlstadt. Casting aside all fear, Luther at once abandoned his place of refuge, and, without having waited until he received the permission of the elector, he appeared in Wittenberg, in March, 1522, where he preached to, and remonstrated in severe terms with the people, upon their outrageous conduct, and succeeded in again restoring peace and order.

Shortly afterwards, however, events of a far more serious nature occurred, which threatened to destroy all order in the civil state of Germany. We have already shown, at the close of the government of Maximilian I., what discontent existed among the peasantry throughout the empire, and that the leagues formed in Alsace and Swabia were only put down by force of arms. Some sparks, however, still glimmered amid the ashes, and, in the course of a short time, combining their whole force, burst forth once more into one universal flame. The rural population considered themselves entitled to an equality of rights with those hitherto their lords and masters, and in south Germany especially, where the sight of the prosperity and independence enjoyed by their neighbors, the Swiss—strikingly contrasting with their own condition—acted powerfully upon the mind, the indignation of the people was first roused, and the flame of discord and revolt again produced its devastating effects.

The first that rebelled were the peasantry of the abbot of Kempten and those of the archbishop of Augsburg. Twelve articles, containing all the rights and demands made by the whole body, were drawn up in Swabia, and distributed and made known throughout the whole of Germany with astonishing and almost incredible rapidity, viz.: "That the peasants should be allowed to choose for themselves the ministers who were to preach to them the word of God, pure and without the introduction of any worldly matter; that in future they should not pay any other tithes but that of corn; that they had hitherto been treated as slaves, although by the blood of our Saviour all men had been made free, and, although they desired not to live independent of all superior authority, they were, nevertheless, resolved no longer to continue in this state of slavery, unless it could be proved to them by the Holy Scriptures that they were in error. That, finally, they had to complain of many things, but that they would observe silence in the hope that what they claimed would be yielded, and that their lords would treat them in accordance with the counsel and precepts of the gospel, and while they moderated the oppression they had exercised from the earliest times down to the present moment, they, their lords, should likewise abstain from adding thereto daily fresh burdens."

There can be no doubt but these demands were just, and, at the same time, moderate; but when the accomplishment of the object demanded was left to the charge of the brutal mass, then the passions soon overcame the weak and subdued voice of moderation, and bursting through every barrier, became deaf to reason, and their fury knew no bounds. As is the case in all such riotous proceedings, the complainant became the judge in his own cause, and exercised the very same injustice by which he himself had been previously oppressed. The peasantry, collected together in various strong bodies, commenced with attacking the castles of the nobles and the rich possessions of the clergy, burning and destroying every thing, and often putting to death the owners. These troops soon increased to armies, of which Swabia alone supplied three. In Franconia the riots grew more and more serious, extending even to Würtzburg, which city combined with the peasantry against its bishop and the rest of the Franconian nobility. Already, indeed, a great number of the cities throughout Upper Germany had joined in league with the peasants, while several princes and nobles, such as the elector palatine, the counts of Hohenlohe, the bishops of Bamberg and Spires, &c., had entered into negotiation with the rioters, and had been forced to promise a removal of their burdens based upon the twelve articles aforesaid.

In Thuringia the hallucination of this excited period was shown in another form, although not altogether dissimilar in spirit, inasmuch as it was founded upon religious enthusiasm. A secular preacher, Thomas Münzer, formerly one of Luther's first adherents, pretended that he was gifted with especial divine visions from God, by which he was enabled to reveal the essence of Christian liberty with much more clearness than Luther. "God," he said, "had created the earth as an inheritance of the believers, and all government must be regulated only by the Bible and divine revelations. There was no necessity whatever for the princes, superior authorities, the nobility, or the priests, and the distinction which existed between the rich and the poor was altogether unchristian; inasmuch, as in the kingdom of God all men must be equal." Such doctrine, however, caused Münzer to be banished from Saxony, and he repaired to Mühlhausen in Thuringia, where he gained over the people, and caused them to upset all authority, and make him their preacher and governor of the town. His principles of the equality of all men, and of the community of possessions, which he introduced after he had driven all the more wealthy inhabitants from the town, augmented the number of his partisans considerably, and extended his influence to a great distance beyond his seat of government.

The whole of Thuringia, Hesse, and Lower Saxony, were in danger, and as now the war of the peasantry raged likewise in the south of Germany, there was too much reason to fear that the fanatics of every part would combine their forces, and thus, like a rushing torrent, march through the whole empire, destroying and sweeping all before them. In this state of peril into which the whole community was about to be ingulfed, a deputation from the peasantry waited upon Luther, and submitted to him the twelve articles for his approbation; at first he agreed that several of their demands were just, and condemned the oppression of the princes and nobility; he then, however, reproached the people for their violent and riotous proceedings, representing to them that Christian liberty was a spiritual liberty; and when now the Münzer revolution arose, he himself, in order to remove at once every impression that such outrages were at all connected with his doctrine, called upon the princes to draw the sword against the revolters. And truly it was high time to make this appeal; inasmuch as the castles of the nobles, and the monasteries in Thuringia, Franconia, Swabia, and along the banks of the Rhine as far as Lorraine itself, were now already demolished, and presented one universal mass of smoking ruins.

Accordingly the princes, at Luther's urgent exhortation, united their forces against the rebels in Thuringia, led on by the Elector John of Saxony—Frederick the Wise having recently died, after having beheld with sorrow the commencement of these sad scenes—George, duke of Saxony, the Landgrave Philip of Hesse, and Henry, duke of Brunswick. A division of their army, under Philip of Hesse, marched at once against a body of the peasantry near Frankenhausen in Thuringia, on the 15th of May, 1525.

The princes, in order to bring the rioters to terms by lenient measures, promised them pardon if they would retire peaceably and give up their leaders. Münzer, however, in order to avert the danger from his own person, took advantage of the appearance of a rainbow which at the moment presented itself in the heavens, in order to excite anew the mad enthusiasm of his partisans, declaring to them that it came as a messenger to him from God. For the moment he succeeded in his object, for, roused by his inflammatory language, the fanatics rushed upon the ambassadors of the elector and stabbed them with their daggers; and fortifying themselves in their intrenchments, they prepared for a vigorous defence. In a very short time, however, their blind and desperate courage sunk, and they looked in vain for the appearance of the troops of angels which had been promised to them by Münzer; he himself was one of the first who fled, while the greater part of his army was put to the sword. The fugitive leader took refuge in the loft of a house in Frankenhausen, but was soon afterwards discovered, dragged forth and beheaded, dying without evincing the slightest courage or fortitude.

Just about the same time, the wars of the peasantry in the south of Germany were likewise brought to an end. The Swabian league, which had been renewed, collected an army, and under the leadership of George Truchsess of Waldburg, attacked and destroyed the various troops of peasants in Swabia and Franconia with the same success as in Thuringia. Everywhere the most dreadful retribution was now inflicted by the conquerors upon all those who had taken a share in the revolutionary scenes, and the most revolting cruelties were perpetrated.

Thus these terrible and sanguinary commotions, which might have produced the complete overthrow and destruction of the institutions of Germany, had these excited powers been brought into effect by the influential direction of skilful men, were once again promptly subdued. As it was, however, they occasioned a sacrifice of much blood; it being calculated that more than 100,000 of the peasantry perished in these contentions.

## CHAPTER XVIII.

Foreign Relations of Charles V.—Francis I. of France —War between these two rival Monarchs—Italy—Milan—The Duke of Bourbon—The Chevalier Bayard —The Battle of Pavia, 1525—Defeat of the French—Francis I. taken Prisoner—Madrid—The King of France liberated—His dishonorable Breach of Stipulation—The Imperialists in Rome—The Pope a Prisoner—His Ransom—War with France resumed—Andrew Doria—Peace of Cambray, 1529—Charles V. crowned Emperor and King of Lombardy in Bologna —His Generosity—Return to Germany—First League of the Protestant Princes, 1526—The Augsburg Confession, 1530—Melanchthon—His Character of Charles V.—John, Elector of Saxony—His determination—The Imperial Council—The Emperor's Declaration—Reply of the Protestant Princes—Ferdinand, King of Rome, 1531—Religious Peace—The Turks in Hungary—Their Defeat—Ulric, Duke of Wurtemberg—Restored to his Possessions by Philip of Hesse—Insurrection of the Anabaptists—Their Defeat—The Emperor in Africa—Tunis—His Triumph and Liberation of 22,000 Christian Slaves—Francis I. attacks Italy—Charles V. enters France—Suspension of Arms —Interview between the two Monarchs at Aigues-Martes—Revolt in Ghent—Progress of Charles V. through France and Ghent—Hospitality received—Peace restored in Ghent—The Diet at Ratisbon, 1541 —Charles V. in Algiers—Disastrous Expedition—His Fortitude—Return to Italy—Francis I. resumes Hostilities—His Ill Success—Charles V. on the Rhine—Attacks the Duke of Cleves—Overcomes and pardons him—Marches into France—Advance upon Paris—The Peace of Crepi, 1544.

During this interval the emperor Charles had not been without occupation abroad. He had proceeded from the diet in Worms to the Netherlands and thence revisited Spain, where he remained nearly eight years; his penetrating glance embraced the whole of Europe. His immediate attention, however, was more especially directed to the movements of Francis, king of France, who, as a dangerous neighbor and rival, availed himself of every opportunity to gain some advantage over him.

It would be useless to investigate the particular causes of jealousy between these two monarchs; in their character as men, and their political relations to each other as rulers, ample foundation existed for this rivalship. Charles, like Francis, was ruled by ambition and pride, but in him, these passions assumed a more ennobling character. Both had been rivals for the imperial throne, and Francis, who claimed superiority not only in years but in reputation as a knight, and in personal endowments, was highly mortified when he found the latter elected in preference to himself. At the same time the duchy of Milan, which had been conquered by Francis and held by him as a fief of the empire, served as an inevitable cause of dispute, inasmuch as Charles felt himself bound to recover it by force of arms, and restore it under the imperial sway; while, on the other hand, the preponderance of Charles's power in Europe, now assuming a more threatening aspect, excited the fears of the other rulers, and Francis, who, next to the emperor, possessed the most powerful dominion, considered himself called upon before any other to enter the field against him. He had turned his attention more especially towards Italy, in which country he had already made one successful expedition; and it was there that Charles's power should be weakened and destroyed, for which purpose the French king sought to revive all the claims he derived from his ancestors to the kingdom of Naples in that quarter. Charles meantime had augmented his power by an alliance with Henry VIII. of England, whose vanity had been offended by Francis, and thus the war, which had already commenced in the year 1521, was carried on by the English and Flemish troops from the Netherlands as far as Spain; but in Italy more especially the contest was maintained with the greatest obstinacy. What operated much to Charles's disadvantage was the wide dispersion of his possessions, which produced a necessary division of his forces; while Francis, on the other hand, from the central point on which he had rallied his troops and formed them into one united mass, was enabled to dash forward and at once strike the blow in whatever direction he pleased. But that which principally characterized the superiority of Charles, and which, in reality, constituted his power and shed over him so brilliant a lustre, was that he had been enabled to collect around him a body of the most distinguished men of the day, from among whom his penetrating eye at once singled out the general best qualified to lead his army against the foe, the ambassador whose diplomatic talent could best loosen the complicated knot of political intrigue, and the counsellor whose prudence and superior judgment rendered him the most efficient adviser. It is by the intellectual powers that the world should be governed, and Charles knew how to enlist them in his service.

Charles, duke of Bourbon, a valiant and distinguished general of the French army, having been deeply injured by Francis, came over to the emperor's side. He was received by that monarch with open arms, and was at once appointed leader, in conjunction with the viceroy of Naples, Launoy, and the marquis of Pescara, at that time the most distinguished warrior of the imperial army in Italy. The king of France, on the other hand, lost about this time (in the year 1524) one of his most brave and loyal knights, the Chevalier Bayard, who, in the retreat from Italy, saved the army by his heroic courage on the bridge of Sesia, but receiving a mortal wound, fell a sacrifice to his patriotic devotion. The advantages of the war appeared now wholly on the side of the emperor; Milan was retaken, and the French driven out of Italy. But Charles having resolved to attack France itself, marched with his army into Provence, and laid siege to Marseilles; there, however, he nearly lost the superiority he had gained. He found that to take France from this side was more difficult than he had calculated; the city itself was not to be conquered, and the whole country around having been laid waste by the enemy himself, Pescara was forced to retreat. It required, indeed, all the ingenuity of that great general to save the army in its dangerous march back, for the French monarch followed at his heels, and again taking possession of Milan, proceeded to attack Pavia. The imperial generals found their situation at this moment very embarrassing; for in front of them was an enemy of superior force, who threatened one of the chief cities; behind them was the terror of the pope, who had just formed an alliance with Francis; and finally, their own army was in a most distressed condition, a feeling of languor and depression, produced by the late retreat, pervading the spirits of all. Nevertheless, the courage, wisdom, and good fortune of the leaders, soon effected a change for the better.

The commandant who defended Pavia, Don Antonio de Leyva, not discouraged for a moment, most obstinately maintained his position against the besiegers during the entire winter until the February of 1525. By this time the imperial army was reinforced by a strong body of 15,000 lancers, who marched to their aid from Germany, under the command of the brave warrior, George of Freundsberg, or Frundsberg, and a combined attack was made upon the French king near Pavia. The quick, experienced eye of Pescara selected the point of attack in a quarter least expected by the king, who was consequently wholly unprepared for it. He fancied his rear to be perfectly secured by a wood enclosed by an extensive strong wall: Pescara, however, caused a road to be cut through the entire forest during the night, and with the dawn of morning his troops rushed upon the surprised enemy, and completely overthrew them at this point. At the same moment Leyva made a sally from the citadel itself, while Launoy and Bourbon made an attack in another quarter, and the entire French army, thus overwhelmed, was soon put to rout. The Swiss auxiliaries, a circumstance unusual with them, were the first to yield and take to flight, while the German mercenaries, although they fought with great courage, were overmatched by the valor of the Germans under their brave leader, George of Freundsberg, and to whom in fact the imperialists were chiefly indebted for the victory, for burning with indignation to find their fellow-countrymen fighting in the ranks of the French army, they cut them down almost to a man. Francis had his horse killed under him, and he continued fighting on foot, defending himself against a host of Spaniards who had surrounded him without knowing the royal, chivalric warrior they endeavored to overcome. Fortunately for the king, a French nobleman, Pomperant, belonging to the suite of the duke of Bourbon, came up at this moment, and recognising the sinking monarch, summoned him to yield himself a prisoner to the duke, his master; this he refused to do, but with reluctance ordered him to send Launoy to him. The combatants paused until the general arrived, when the king resigned his sword into his hands. Launoy received it kneeling, and giving the monarch his own in exchange, said: "It suits not that so great a king should stand unarmed before a subject of the emperor." A fortnight after this decisive battle no enemy remained in Italy.

Charles was almost discontented with his too great fortune which left him without an object to pursue: "Since you have made a prisoner of the king of France for me," he says in a letter to Launoy, "I find nothing more to do but to fight against the infidels. This I have always felt a great desire to do, and now more than ever. Arrange matters, therefore, so that I may be enabled before I grow too old to perform deeds that may promote the service of God, and not be unattended with glory to myself."

The king of France was conveyed a captive to Madrid and closely guarded. Great difference of opinion was expressed by the council of the emperor respecting the manner in which he was to be treated, and the means of availing themselves of their present good fortune. One party, at the head of which was Launoy, advised the emperor to act with generosity towards the king, and thus destroy, perhaps forever, the seeds of discord and enmity between the two monarchs; while another party, headed by the Chancellor Mercurinus Gattinara, sought to derive every possible advantage from the circumstance. The emperor chose the middle path between the two parties, and lost the entire fruit of his good fortune. He approved of the plan proposed by the chancellor, viz.: to demand from the captive monarch, as the price of his liberty, the restoration of the duchy of Burgundy, which France had unjustly wrested from his grandmother, and to which he attached great and especial value; but he considered the detention of the king as prisoner until the fulfilment of this condition—as advised by his chancellor—too harsh, and unworthy of the imperial dignity. He trusted, therefore, to the promise of the king; but that promise, with whatever chivalric importance Francis may have invested it, was never sincerely given nor eventually performed. Before he signed the treaty, he secretly summoned to his presence some confidential agents in Madrid, and before them, in the presence of the pope's nuncio, declared that he was not bound to perform the promise he should make as a prisoner, and that the pope, Clement VII. himself, had absolved him from the performance of any engagement into which he might enter. The voice of conscience being thus quieted, he knelt before the altar and swore on the Holy Bible itself faithfully to fulfil the conditions to which he had agreed. At the same time he pledged his royal word to return and surrender himself again a prisoner within six months from that time in the event of his not being able to execute the said conditions.

Francis I. was accordingly set at liberty, in the year 1526, after an imprisonment of one year—but never kept his word. The excuse he made for such a breach of honor was, that his states would not by any means admit the abandonment of Burgundy, while at the same time he offered a considerable sum as a ransom for his two eldest sons whom he had sent to Spain as hostages. Charles, however, returned for answer: "That he had violated faith and truth, both of which he had solemnly and publicly sworn to maintain; that he had not acted as became a man of noble birth and a sovereign prince; and that he, Charles, was ready to support the charge with the sword in single combat." Francis accepted the challenge, but only with words; for subsequently he avoided the meeting under various pretexts, and thus the people were once more forced to terminate with their own blood the contest produced by the ambition and folly of their monarch, and war was once more declared between Charles V. and Francis I.

Just at the commencement of this war, however, a most unheard-of event took place in Italy. The duke of Bourbon had succeeded to the chief command of the imperial army in Milan, after the death of General Pescara. The country was completely devastated, and the generals without money, while the troops became more and more loud in their demands for their pay. All means having been employed in vain to appease them, the army suddenly broke up in the month of January, 1527, and advanced in forced marches against Rome, without, however, having received any commands from the emperor; neither is it known for certain whether it was by the order of the duke of Bourbon, who, perhaps, may have formed some grand projects of ambition, or whether it was the result of some sudden determination of the army itself, which calculated on finding in Rome abundance of supplies and a rich booty besides. Be this as it may, Bourbon arrived with the army before the city, after a most difficult march. On the 6th of May the command was given for a general assault against the ancient capital of the world, and Bourbon was one of the first upon the walls, his example serving to inspire the whole of the besiegers; but he had scarcely got his footing on the ramparts when he was mortally wounded by a shot from an arquebusier. His troops, nevertheless, forced their way into the city, and, for several days, a scene of pillage and devastation was continued, equalled only in the time of the Vandals. The pope, Clement VII., with his court, had taken refuge in the Castle of St. Angelo, where he was besieged for several months, until, forced by necessity, he promised the imperialists a sum of 400,000 ducats, in order that the whole army might be paid their full arrears.

Meantime the emperor Charles sent letters to all the princes of Christendom, in which he took especial care to exonerate himself in their eyes in respect to these excesses, which took place without his wish or knowledge; nay, during the time that his generals kept the pope a prisoner in the castle of St. Angelo, and laid siege to that place, he ordered public prayers to be offered in all the churches throughout Spain for his deliverance. He has been reproached with hypocrisy for doing this; but it is, no doubt, a fact, that his mutinous troops would no longer obey his orders until they had received the arrears due to them. It was only then, at the end of eighteen months, that the army was once again brought into a state of discipline, and, at his command, marched towards Naples. But owing to the excesses committed in Rome, it had become so reduced, that when the king of France, in the year 1527, once more invaded Italy, his army, under the command of Lautrec, was enabled to penetrate, without opposition, as far as Naples itself, to which place it laid siege. The sudden defection of the celebrated naval hero, Andrew Doria, who, with his fleet, came over to the emperor's side, together with the sickness which prevailed throughout the French army, combined, however, to turn the scale in Charles's favor; the French were forced to give up the siege, and also to abandon Milan. Both parties, equally tired and worn out by the war, agreed to sign a treaty of peace at Cambray, in the year 1529, and which was styled the ladies' peace, inasmuch as it was negotiated by the emperor's aunt and the king's mother. Francis paid two millions of crowns for the deliverance of his two sons in Spain, renounced all claims to Milan, Genoa, Naples, and all the other countries beyond the Alps, and married Eleonora, the sister of Charles; while the emperor, on his part, without requiring the immediate secession of Burgundy, still retained his ancient rights.

The time had now arrived when the emperor was enabled to appear with dignity in his Italian states, where, in fact, he had hitherto never shown himself. He landed in August, 1529, in Genoa, and continued his progress on to Bologna with the pomp worthy of an emperor. Here he had appointed a meeting with Pope Clement, which took place in great solemnity. The former enmity was altogether forgotten; the emperor, following the example of his ancestors, dropped on his knee and kissed the foot of the holy father, and the latter solemnly crowned him emperor and king of Lombardy.

Thus was celebrated the coronation of the greatest and most powerful monarch who had borne the crown since Charlemagne, and who was, likewise, the last emperor who visited Italy. Charles appeared now to the Italians, who had only known him hitherto as a prince to be dreaded, in the character of a mild and noble ruler, and their fear was changed into the most sincere veneration. The emperor would not even retain Milan for himself, but, before he left Italy, restored it into the hands of Francis Sforza, who received it as a fief of the empire. **Hav-**

ing accomplished this, Charles now hastened to return to Germany to preside at the grand diet of Augsburg.

In Germany many of the princes had now openly introduced the new doctrine into their various territories. One of the most zealous among them was the young landgrave of Hesse, Philip the Generous; he urged the other princes who joined with him in opinion, to form an alliance for mutual defence, in the event of the adverse parties seeking by violent measures to execute the edict of Worms. Nor was his anxiety without foundation. Several of the Catholic princes had already held a meeting at Leipsic, and had deliberated together upon the necessity of making common defence against the dissemination of the new faith; and for this purpose they had claimed the assistance of the emperor, who in his reply promised the extirpation of all the errors of the Lutheran sect. Accordingly a league was formed at Dessau by these princes, at the head of which were the electors of Mentz and of Brandenburg, and the dukes of Wolfenbüttel and Calenberg. On the other hand an alliance was formed on the 4th of May, 1526, at Torgau, between the elector of Saxony, John the Steadfast, Philip of Hesse, the dukes of Grubenhagen and Celle, Duke Henry of Mecklenberg, Prince Wolfgang of Anhalt, Counts Gebhard and Albert of Mansfeld, together with the imperial free city of Magdeburg. Albert, margrave of Brandenburg, formerly grand master of the Teutonic order, but who on embracing the new faith, and with the sanction of the king of Poland as chief feudal lord, secularized the territory of the order into a dukedom of Prussia, concluded an especial alliance with the elector of Saxony. The firm position maintained by the allies at the diet held in Spires in 1526, presided over by Ferdinand, produced for them the favorable resolution: "That the states of the empire in affairs referring to the edict of Worms, should so decide and rule among their subjects as to be able to render good account of their conduct before God and the imperial majesty." Thence it was left to the conscience of each authority to proceed in religious affairs as far as he might deem requisite.

During this time the emperor had been occupied with his royal prisoner, Francis I., against whom, however, he afterwards had to maintain another war, but now was urgently appealed to by the German princes to exert his authority in settling their differences; and only succeeded in allaying their impatience by promising them to hold a new diet as soon as he was at liberty to come to them. Meantime he summoned a provisional diet at Spires, in 1529. The result of this meeting, however, was only still more to widen the breach between the two parties by giving a permanent name to the partisans of the new doctrine, inasmuch as the majority of the states being Catholic, decreed: "That the essential edicts of the diet of Worms should be retained; that the celebration of mass should be preserved; that all those who had been gained over to the new doctrine should abstain from further innovations; and that no subject of the empire should be permitted to give protection to a co-religionist against the authorities." The Lutheran party, dissatisfied with these resolutions of the diet, drew up accordingly an instrument in opposition, in which they protested against them, whence they took the name of Protestants, declaring at the same time that they would continue in all their proceedings to act up to the decree of the year 1526. The Protestant party included the whole of the princes who joined the league of Torgau, together with George, margrave of Brandenburg, of the Salian house, and the cities of Strasburg, Nuremberg, Ulm, Constance, Reutlingen, Windsheim, Memmingen, Lindau, Kempten, Heilbronn, Issny, Weissenburg, Nördlingen, and St. Gallen.

In the following year, 1530, the grand diet was held in Augsburg, to which the emperor himself repaired from Italy as he had announced. Even before he arrived, he was met on the road by several deputies from both parties, who sought to gain his preference; he referred them, however, to the approaching diet itself, without declaring his sentiments on the subject. On the 22d of June, in the evening, he made his entry into the city with great pomp, surrounded by the numerous electoral and other princes and nobles. No longer now the young and inexperienced prince as when ten years before he first appeared in Germany, the emperor at this moment stood unrivalled by any cotemporary monarch, unsurpassed by his predecessors since the dominion of the great Charlemagne, and admired universally for his distinguished qualities. In Francis I. of France he had humbled one of the most haughty and ambitious of his foreign enemies, and Rome itself had not been able to withstand his mighty power. His noble figure and dignified carriage produced their imposing effect upon all—whether friends or foes—who approached his presence.

Melanchthon, who had come to Augsburg in the suite of the elector of Saxony, thus expresses himself in a confidential letter upon the subject of the emperor: "But the individual most worthy of remark in this assembly, is certainly the emperor himself. His uninterrupted success has no doubt excited wonder even in your country; but far more to be admired is his great moderation, amidst all this good fortune, which seems to come at his bidding; for neither by action nor word does he indicate in the slightest degree the effect it may have upon his feelings. What emperor or king can you show me in the records of their reign in whom success has not produced some change? With him, on the other hand, nothing appears to operate upon his feelings; no trace of passion, hauteur, or cruelty, is ever visible in him. To omit other examples, I will instance what has occurred in our case. Although in these religious disputes our enemies have employed every art to render him hostile to us, he has ever condescended to listen attentively to the arguments of our party. His domestic life abounds with instances of abstinence, moderation, and temperance. That system of household discipline, so rigidly exercised in former times among the German princes, is now confined exclusively to the imperial palace. Neither are the traces of vicious or licentious men to be found within its walls; while as friends he selects among his court only those distinguished for their genius and virtues. Whenever I behold him, methinks I see before me one of those heroes or demi-gods who in ancient times were wont to mix with men. Who, therefore, ought not to rejoice in witnessing such a combination of noble qualities in one man?"

In spite, however, of the veneration with which the emperor's personal character was regarded, the preponderance of his own power, and that of the Catholic princes nerally, the Protestant princes, who were l present, maintained their ground of opposition with so much determination and firmness, that they succeeded in effecting their object even in matters of merely external ceremonies of worship, and obliged him to revoke several of his edicts. Thus when he had ordered that all the princes present should join in the celebration of the festival of Corpus-Christi-day, (the day after his arrival,) the whole number of German princes, mounting their horses at dawn of day, proceeded in solemn state to the palace, where, demanding an audience of the emperor, they firmly declared they would not attend, and he found it expedient to abandon his purpose. With equal resolution they protested against the ordinance, prohibiting their clergy from preaching in Augsburg, and withdrew only after he had revoked it and substituted another, in which he ordered that no sermon should be preached on either side, and that on Sundays the gospel and epistles alone should be read. At the head of the rest of the Protestant princes was John, elector of Saxony, a man whose remarkable zeal and firmness in the cause of reform acquired for him the surname by which posterity has distinguished him. When even threatened by the emperor with his refusal to invest him with the enfeoffment of the electorate of Saxony, as yet not conferred, he still maintained his position. This prince, the last of the four excellent sons of Ernest, possessed a simple but resolute mind, which, when once under the influence of conviction, was impressed by no fear, regardful of no sacrifice. At the same time, he did not conceal from himself the fact, that with his inferior power it must be impossible for him to contend against the mighty and preponderating force of the emperor; but the question he put to himself was: "Whether he should renounce the almighty power of God or the world?" and the answer to which removed all doubt from his mind and heart. He was likewise much encouraged and confirmed in his conviction by the letters of Luther, who, on account of the ban still in force against him, was able to proceed only as far as Coburg, from which place he watched the important proceedings that were taking place in Augsburg with the greatest anxiety and expectation; but, at the same time, with an indomitable resolution inspired by his faith and zeal in the great cause. It is said that at this time he composed his beautiful hymn, "Eine starke

Burg ist unser Gott," (A mighty rock is our God.) When now the question of the religious disputes was at length discussed before the diet at Augsburg, the Protestant princes laid before the assembly their confession of faith, exhibiting in succinct, but comprehensive language all the articles in which the new church differed from the old. This was completed by Melanchthon from the seventeen articles prepared by Luther at Schwabach, and from other writings which the Protestant princes had brought with them; thus was produced the Augsburg confession, which from that moment has formed the basis of the Protestant church. It was read publicly before the diet by Bayer, the chancellor of Saxony, on the 25th of June, and its reading occupied several hours. The emperor then replied to the Protestant princes, through Frederick, the count palatine, "That he would take into consideration that important and remarkable document, and make known to them his determination."

In the council of Charles, as well as in that of the Catholic princes, opinions were very much divided. The popish legate, as well as George, duke of Saxony, William, duke of Bavaria, and the majority of the bishops, required that Charles should force the Protestants to abjure at once their doctrine; others again, among whom was the cardinal-archbishop of Mentz, were more moderate. They observed that such a proceeding must inevitably be attended with great bloodshed, and produce civil war; they referred to the dangers to be dreaded from the Turks, who only recently, in 1529, had ventured to attack Vienna itself, although happily without success; and they recommended either that the Protestants should be brought to return to the church through conviction, produced by mild treatment, or that the question should be settled with a view to preserve, at least, the internal tranquillity of the empire.

In accordance, therefore, with this latter opinion, a refutation of the Augsburg confession was drawn up by several Catholic theologians, headed by the celebrated Dr. Eck, which was forthwith read to the Protestants with the intimation that they should quietly acquiesce therein; and when they declared at once that they could not do so conscientiously, various other attempts at reconciliation and accommodation were made, for many of the more moderate of both parties still thought this result attainable. Melanchthon himself wrote to the pope's legate to this effect: "There still remains a slight difference only in the usages and forms of the church which appears to interfere with the accomplishment of a reunion, and the ecclesiastical canons themselves admit that, notwithstanding this discrepancy of opinion, the unity of the church may yet be maintained." But the more zealous partisans of both sides opposed many obstacles in the way of a conciliatory investigation, and what was conceded did not at all affect the principal points of dispute. In addition to this, various Protestant princes and free cities became influenced by worldly considerations when they found the question arise: whether or not the episcopal power should be re-established in their different territories; while on the Catholic side they now, more obstinately than ever, held to the strict performance of the articles in respect to which indulgence had formerly been granted, for instance, to the Greek church and the Hussites; these articles had reference to the prohibition of the marriage of priests, and of the administration of the holy communion to the laity under both forms. Thus were defeated all those attempts to produce the desired reconciliation, and the two parties, instead of approaching each other more closely on terms of mutual peace and concord, became now more and more widely estranged. The emperor, at length, issued the following declaration to the Protestants: "That they should consider and determine by the ensuing 15th day of the month of April, whether or not they would unite in favor of the articles in discussion with the Christian church, with the pope, the emperor, and the other princes, until they were more amply explained in a council to be assembled at an early future day; that during this period of peace, they should not print any thing new in their various territories, nor seek to strengthen their party by receiving fresh adherents from among their own subjects or strangers; that, as many abuses and irregularities of every kind had, for many years down to the present moment, become more and more prevalent throughout Christendom, the emperor would use all his endeavors, with the pope and the other princes of Europe, in order that a general council should be convoked within a period of six months, or at latest within a year from the present time."

To this the Protestants replied, as usual, that their dogmas had not as yet been refuted by the Scriptures, that their conscience would not, therefore, permit them to consent to this decree of the diet, by which they were prohibited from propagating their faith. At the same time they handed over to the emperor a defence of their confession, and all who still remained in Augsburg immediately departed. The rupture between the two parties was now formally declared. In the resolutions of the diet subsequently made public, the Lutheran doctrine was treated as heresy, and characterized as such in the most severe and condemnatory language; the restoration of all the confiscated convents and religious establishments strictly ordered; a censorship over all writings on subjects of religion was rigidly enforced; and all those who contumaciously acted against these decrees were threatened with the severest punishment.

The Protestant princes, at the end of this year, assembled together in the city of Schmalkald, and there renewed their alliance more firmly. Some among them were even anxious to commence the struggle, and appeal to arms at once; but others again still retained their ancient religious dread of civil war, and veneration for the sacred person of the emperor, as expressed by themselves; whence, as this feeling of the majority exercised its predominating influence upon all, their league was saved from incurring the reproach of having been, without necessity, the first to kindle the flame of a religious war. The Catholic electors and princes likewise, on their part, and with equal merit, checked the feeling so prevalent among them for warlike measures—a desire so much encouraged in Rome, and by which the emperor himself already appeared to be somewhat influenced. They would not allow the ban of the empire to be pronounced against the Protestant party, because they were reluctant to furnish the emperor with full powers for war; they wished, as they expressed themselves, to contend, but not with the sword's point, and they hoped, by means of the imperial chamber of justice, which with this object had been cleansed of all its anti-Catholic elements, and strengthened by the addition of six assessors, to bring the decree of the grand diet into full operation. But we shall very soon see tha these means likewise proved totally inadequate.

The emperor, on leaving the diet of Augsburg, had proceeded to Cologne, where he summoned the electoral princes to meet him. He there proposed to them that they should select, as king of the Romans, his brother Ferdinand, to whom he had already ceded his hereditary lands in Austria—and who, since the extinction of the royal house of Bohemia and Hungary in the person of Lewis II., who was killed when fighting against Soliman II. in the battle of Mohacz, in 1526, had acquired the crowns of Bohemia and Hungary, by the rights founded upon ancient treaties of inheritance—in order that he might be enabled to maintain good order throughout the empire during the frequent absence of the emperor. The electors consented, and Ferdinand was crowned at Aix-la-Chapelle; the elector of Saxony, who caused his protestation against this election to be handed in by his son, and the dukes of Bavaria, who had for a long time been jealous of the power of the Austrian house, and who on this occasion joined in alliance with their enemies in matters of religion, the princes of the Schmalkaldian league, were the only two parties who made any opposition, and refused to acknowledge Ferdinand.

The new king of the Romans was extremely desirous of preserving tranquillity in Germany, as his new kingdom of Hungary was at this time hard pressed by the Turks, and his chief source of assistance must be derived from the German princes. The Protestants, however, refused to give their co-operation until peace had been secured to them in their own country, and its continuance sworn to be maintained. The emperor accordingly now concerted fresn measures, in order to promote a state of union, and at length, after the most warm and urgent exhortations from Luther in favor thereof, they produced the provisionary religious peace of Nuremberg, in 1532. The emperor declared, in contradiction to the opinion of the Catholic majority: "That, in virtue of his imperiai power, he would establish a general peace, according to which no person should be attacked or condemned on account of his faith, or any other religious matter, until the approaching assembly of the council, or the meeting of the estates of the empire." Nay, he promised likewise to suspend all proceedings taken by his imperial chancellor in matters of faith, against the elector of Saxony, until the next council.

The subsidiary troops against the Turks were now collected, and formed an army of such force as had not been produced for a length of time, the Protestant princes and cities themselves sending very large contributions. The danger appeared, indeed, extremely urgent, for the sultan had advanced with a force of three hundred thousand men to attack the Austrian territories from four points; and to oppose him, the emperor had only seventy-six thousand men at command. However, the first attempts they made very soon showed the Turks with what men they had to deal. Ibrahim Pasha, who led the vanguard, considered he was bound for honor's sake to punish the little town of Gunz, in Hungary, which to his mortification had closed its gates against him, thinking that it would easily fall into his hands on the first assault; but its brave commandant, Jurischtisch, with his small garrison repulsed all his attacks, and kept him before the walls for the space of a fortnight. At this sudden and unexpected check upon his march, Soliman calculated what the great city of Vienna might cost him, especially as now the emperor had come to its aid; and perceiving, in addition, that the German princes, whom he thought to find in a state of dissension, had now become reunited, he resolved at once to sound a retreat. Thus the whole of Europe, to their great surprise, found the great Soliman quickly abandon an expedition which it had cost him three years to prepare.

The emperor was now enabled to turn his attention to other affairs, and proceeded, first of all, to Italy, for the purpose of arranging with the pope upon the subject of the convocation of the grand council. But he found that the pope was by no means in earnest about the matter, neither was it, at this time, at all desired by the papal court; and Charles accordingly departed for Spain without doing any thing.

During the absence of the emperor in Spain, and while Ferdinand was engaged in employing all his means to establish his dominion in Hungary, the doctrine of the reformers spread more and more in Germany, and party spirit daily increased. The Protestants went so far, in the year 1534, as to declare to the imperial chamber that they would no longer obey its decrees: because, contrary to the conditions of the treaty of Nuremberg, it pronounced judgment against them in cases which referred to the restitution of confiscated church property; and which proceeding rendered completely invalid the laws for the perpetual peace of the country, as established by the emperor Maximilian. Another subject of dispute was the territory of Wurtemberg. We have already had occasion to refer to the circumstance of Ulric, duke of Wurtemberg, having, just after the death of Maximilian, and before the election of Charles V., been driven out of his country by the Swabian league, on account of a feud which had existed between him and the town of Reutlingen. The league ceded the land, which was burdened with a heavy debt, to the emperor, and the latter transferred it, in 1530, to his brother Ferdinand, together with his Austrian states. It appeared now as if that country was destined to form forever a portion of the Austrian possessions; but the deposed duke, who was now wandering through the empire a fugitive, seeking to enlist his friends in his cause, found at length a protector in his relation Philip, landgrave of Hesse. Ulric had already adopted the Lutheran faith, and Philip now formed the determination to re-establish him in his possessions even by force of arms. He accordingly raised an army of twenty thousand men, marched unexpectedly into the very heart of Wurtemberg, defeated the Austrian governor of the country at Lauffen, in 1534, and restored the reconquered duchy to Ulric. It was expected that this bold act would have produced a sanguinary war; but this time the storm passed over. Charles and Ferdinand were both too much occupied elsewhere, and perhaps they may have felt it ungenerous and unworthy to augment their already extensive power, by the addition of a foreign country, while, on the contrary, the other members of the Schmalkaldian league, who had taken no share in this act of the landgrave, endeavored to bring the matter to a peaceful adjustment. Thence was effected, under the mediation of the elector of Saxony, the peace of Cadan in Bohemia, by which Duke Ulric received back his land as an arriere fief of Austria;

the religious peace as signed at Nuremberg was confirmed, and Ferdinand was formally acknowledged king of Rome by the elector of Saxony and all his family. And in order to maintain at least the imperial sovereignty, it was decided that the landgrave and Duke Ulric should ask pardon of the emperor personally, and of the king of Rome by deputy, for having disturbed the peace of the land.

Another circumstance occurred which threatened important and serious results, but still did not interrupt definitively the peace of the empire, viz., the contentions of the anabaptists in Münster, in 1534 and 1535. The principles of Thomas Münzer upon Christian liberty and equality, and upon the community of possessions, as well as upon his faith in immediate divine revelations, were not as yet eradicated, and had still been preserved, especially in Holland, among the so-called anabaptists. They demanded that mankind should do penance and be baptized anew in order to avert the wrath of God. Two of their fanatic preachers, Jan Matthys, a baker of Harlem, and a tailor, Jan Bockhold or Bockelsohn, of Leyden, proceeded, in the early part of the year 1534, to Münster, at the time that an ecclesiastic, called Rothmann, had just introduced the doctrine of Luther; they gained him over to their sect likewise, and with the aid of the populace and other anabaptists from the vicinity, drove out of the city all the wealthy citizens, created fresh magistrates, and established a community of possessions. Each person was required to deposite in a general treasury all he possessed, whether in gold, silver, or other precious articles, while the churches were despoiled of their ornaments, pictures, and images, and all the books they contained, except the Bible, were publicly burnt. Everywhere, as in all such scenes of fanaticism, the most licentious acts were committed, and passions, the most violent and brutal, raged throughout the city. Under the sanction of their creed of Christian liberty, each man was authorized to take to himself several wives, and their chief, John of Leyden, set the example by marrying three at once. Finally, one of his partisans, who made a boast of having especially received a divine communication, John Dusentschur of Warendorf, saluted him as king of the whole globe, and as such, appointed to restore the throne of David; and twenty-eight apostles were selected and sent forth to preach this doctrine to the whole world, and to bring the inhabitants thereof to acknowledge the newly-appointed king. These agents, however, wherever they arrived, were immediately seized as rebels and executed.

The bishop of Münster, supported by the landgrave of Hesse, and several other princes, advanced, in the year 1534, with a large army against the city. In the first assault, however, that they made on the 30th of August, they were repulsed most valiantly by the fanatic anabaptists; but the more slow and not less fatal attacks of famine, to which the latter were gradually reduced by the besiegers, who cut off the supplies, could not be overcome. Want increased from day to day, and diminished more and more the zeal of the people. The new king resolved to establish his royal authority more firmly by terror, and even beheaded one of his wives with his own hand in the public market-place, because she gave vent to the expression, that she could not possibly believe that God had condemned such a mass of people to die of hunger, while the king himself was living in abundance. At length, however, after a great number had really perished through starvation, two citizens led the bishop's troops, on the night of the 25th of June, 1535, into the city; and after a sanguinary battle, John of Leyden, and his executioner, Knipperdolling, together with his chancellor, Krechting, were made prisoners, and having been publicly exhibited in several cities of Germany as a spectacle, they were tortured with burning pincers and put to death by piercing their hearts with a red-hot dagger. Their bodies were then placed in iron cages, and suspended from the steeple of the church of St. Lambert, in the market-place of Münster, and the form of Catholic worship, and the authority of the bishop, were immediately re-established in that city.

Meantime the emperor had proceeded upon an expedition, the results of which crowned him with lasting honor and fame. A pirate, Haradin Barbarossa, born of obscure parents in the island of Lesbos, but one of the most daring and extraordinary men of his day, had established himself on the north coast of Africa. To join him in his depredations he had gained over a numerous body of Moors, who, driven out of

Spain by King Ferdinand the Catholic, burned with the desire of revenging themselves upon the Christians, and thus strengthened, this desperate pirate infested the Mediterranean seas in every direction. His cruelty and audacity rendered him the terror of all the inhabitants along the coasts; while in the African peninsula he held in his possession Algiers and Tunis, and the Turkish sultan, Soliman, himself had confided to his charge the whole of his fleet, in order to employ it against the Christians, of whom already some thousands languished as captives in the hands of the barbarians.

As protector of entire Christendom, Charles felt he could no longer endure the existence of such outrage and cruelty, especially as the fugitive and rightful king of Tunis, Hascen, had come to him for protection. He embarked, therefore, with an army of thirty thousand men, including eight thousand German troops, under the command of Count Max of Eberstein, and a fleet of five hundred vessels; the latter being under the orders of Doria, and the army commanded by the emperor himself in person and the Marquis de Vaston. They arrived before Tunis in the summer of 1535, and captured the citadel of Goleta, which defended the port, on the first assault; all the ammunition was seized, and more than two thousand Turks put to the sword. The army of Haradin Barbarossa, which was drawn up ready for battle on the plain in front of the city, was attacked at once and completely put to rout. The victorious troops now took possession of the city, and proceeded immediately to open the prisons of their suffering fellow-Christians; and Charles, to his inexpressible joy, was enabled to set at liberty no less than twenty-two thousand of these objects of severe oppression, who now, with tears of joy and gratitude, were restored to their relations and friends. The emperor himself declared that glorious day to be one of the most happy and delightful of his entire life. His fame spread far and wide throughout every country; and this he truly merited by the courage and perseverance he had evinced in this perilous but heroic undertaking; while, at the same time, he proved by his example how easily these barbarian corsairs of the African coasts might, with a bold and resolute spirit, be overcome. He restored the fugitive king, Hascen, to his throne of Tunis, but, at the same time, he prohibited him from all capture or imprisonment of Christian slaves, and as a pledge of his obedience, the emperor retained possession of the citadel of Goleta. Haradin, after his defeat, had flown to Algiers, whither Charles resolved to pursue him in the ensuing year.

A fresh war, however, with the king of France prevented him from executing this intention. This prince, on the death of Francis Sforza, had renewed his claims to Milan, and in order to ensure for himself an open road to Italy, he unexpectedly attacked and took possession of the duchy of Savoy, upon whose duke he also made claims. Charles saw at once the necessity of war, and resolved to fix the scene of contest in the south of France. Unwarned by the disastrous results which attended his first expedition, under the duke of Bourbon, he undertook another in 1536, and having advanced as far as Marseilles, he once more laid siege to that city. He however found that it was much too strongly fortified to hold out any chance of success, while the whole of the neighboring country was laid waste by the French themselves; whence want of supplies and disease forced the emperor, after having remained two months before the place, to withdraw his troops and make as good a retreat as he could, but in which he nevertheless lost much of his ammunition and luggage.

By the mediation of the pope, a suspension of arms, during ten years, took place in Nice, in the year 1538, and soon afterwards the two monarchs had an interview at Aigues-Mortes, on the Rhone. The proposal for this meeting was first made by the king of France; and although the imperial council considered it unsafe for the emperor to trust himself upon French ground, Charles, notwithstanding the doubts they expressed, resolved, were it even for the novel and extraordinary nature of the project—to him so pleasing—to accept the invitation. When he arrived in the harbor the king himself embarked in his state barge to receive him, and conducted him ashore. Here a splendid dinner was prepared and served up, which was followed by a grand fête, at which the royal personages presided until midnight. On the following morning the dauphin himself attended upon the emperor and handed him the water and towel for his toilet, and, indeed, both sides rivalled each other in marks of mutual friendship and civility. And in all this there was no hypocrisy; they were both desirous of a lasting peace, and in the following year, 1539, Francis gave an additional proof of his good intentions and sincere wishes. The city of Ghent, in Flanders, owing to some new impost, had risen in revolt against the emperor Charles, and offered to place itself under the protection of the king of France; but the latter immediately communicated the circumstance to the emperor himself, and proposed at the same time, in order to reach the scene of contention in Flanders with more expedition, that he should take the shortest route from Spain through France.

This offer was accepted by Charles without any mistrust, and as he proceeded on his journey through the kingdom he was everywhere received with the greatest honors, and at every city or town he entered the keys of each place were presented to him, while in Fontainebleau, where the king had previously arrived, he was detained by magnificent fêtes during the space of an entire fortnight, and when he reached Paris he was equally well entertained during another week.

His presence in Ghent very soon appeased the rioters; and while he was still there, Charles received the most urgent appeals from Germany, hoping that he would quickly reappear in that country, where his presence was become more necessary than ever, in order to put down the disorders which had daily increased.

He acceded to their wishes, and, in the year 1541, presided at the diet of Ratisbon. We shall relate in the succeeding chapter how, on this occasion, and subsequently for several years, he endeavored by writings, religious discussions, and his own persuasive eloquence, to reunite the contending parties; and how, at the same time, the maintenance of internal peace in Germany was the desire and aim of his government, as well as the necessary principle of his reign, threatened as he was, on the one hand, by invasions from the Turks, and forced, on the other hand, to carry on wars with the French. Here it only remains for us to throw a glance at the progress made by the emperor in his foreign relations, until the period when, at length, he found his entire thoughts and labors absorbed in the interests of his Germanic empire.

Charles quitted the diet at Ratisbon, and proceeded to Italy, whence he set out on his expedition to Algiers, as previously determined upon. His enterprising mind, ever delighting in new and brilliant exploits, aspired to the realization of a project, at once grand and commensurate with his powers—the annihilation of the corsairs of the barbarian states of Africa; the accomplishment of which he now felt himself especially called upon to effect, inasmuch as the audacious Barbarossa had again excited general indignation by his recent piracies on the coast of Spain. This new expedition, however, commenced under very unfavorable circumstances; the season for the navigation of the Mediterranean had already become extremely tempestuous, and the experienced admiral, Andreas Doria himself, prognosticated a disastrous voyage. Charles, however, would not consent to its being postponed, and they accordingly set sail. The fleet arrived on the 20th of October, 1541, before Algiers, and the troops were forthwith landed. Towards evening, however, before the artillery, baggage, and provisions could be brought on shore, a tremendous gale arose, and did much damage to the ships, several of which were wrecked on the coast.

All thoughts of conquering Algiers were of course abandoned, and the grand object now was the preservation of the army; for the light cavalry of the Turks made their appearance on the following day and pressed hard upon the ranks of the jaded troops. In this trying and dangerous moment, however, the emperor Charles displayed the energy and perseverance for which, as a warrior, he was ever distinguished. During a march of three entire days, through water and mud, he led his troops, amidst the harassing attacks of the enemy, along the whole extent of the coast as far as the Bay of Metafuz, where the remnant of the dispersed fleet had assembled. Without distinction he shared with his common soldiers the most severe privations and fatigue, and thence it was that he succeeded in reviving their spirits and stimulating their courage, till at length they reached their destination and re-embarked. The emperor set sail for Italy, where, having arrived safely, he disembarked, and proceeded at once to Spain.

The king of France had availed himself of Charles's absence in order to renew hostilities. All his experiments of friendly understanding with Charles would not suffice to banish from his recollection the duchy of Milan; and now he thought the moment had arrived when he must succeed in reconquering it, and for this purpose he renewed his alliance with the Turks. While, therefore, Charles, after his return from Algiers, sought a little repose from the fatigues of that sad expedition, Francis forthwith entered the field against him; the incapacity of his generals, however, when brought to compete with the experience and superiority of the Spanish leaders, combined with disease and the scarcity of supplies for the troops, operated so much against him, that the whole of his five armies could effect nothing in the first campaign, and were forced to return home dispirited and disappointed.

In the following year, 1543, Charles set out for Italy, and thence, suddenly crossing the Alps, proceeded to the Lower Rhine, where the duke of Cleves had made an alliance with Francis I.; and this prince, who had recently begun to encourage the doctrines of Luther, was selected as the first to feel the imperial authority. The appearance of the emperor in this country was quite unexpected. It was reported among the people that he had been shipwrecked on his return from Algiers and had perished. Believing this statement, they treated the news of his arrival in Germany as a mere fable. The garrison of the small town of Düren, on being summoned by Charles to surrender, replied: "They were no longer in dread of the emperor, as he had long since become food for the fishes." When, however, the Spaniards scaled the walls, cut down all before them, and set fire to the town, alarm and terror spread throughout the whole country. They said the emperor had brought with him a species of wild men, half black and half brown, with long sharp nails at their fingers' ends, which enabled them to climb the loftiest walls, together with huge teeth with which they tore every thing asunder.

It is unnecessary to say that the beings thus marvellously described, were no other than the old warriors of Charles, who, by constant exposure to the sun, had become dyed completely brown, and, reckless of all danger, when making an assault on a fortified town usually fixed their daggers or lances in the fissures of the walls, and thus formed for themselves the means of ascent to the ramparts. The terror, however, which their appearance created very soon brought under subjection the entire country; and the duke of Cleves was obliged humbly to sue for pardon on bended knee. This was granted to him by the emperor, but under the condition that he should not forswear his religion; that whatever changes he had introduced should be immediately abolished, and the original regulations re-established, and that he should not enter upon any alliance in opposition to the emperor.

No action or engagement of any importance took place with the French this year; but for the ensuing one Charles collected a very large army, and after he had held a new diet in Spires, in the winter of 1543, and had secured to himself the co-operation of all the German princes, he marched in the following spring into the enemy's country at the head of a numerous body of chosen troops. The flower of this army consisted of thirty thousand Germans, the result of the good understanding which the emperor had established at this last diet between himself and the Protestant princes, and more especially the elector of Saxony and the Landgrave Philip. The first place he took was Saint Dizier, whence he marched direct for Paris, and having taken possession of Epernay and Château-Thierry, he was within a march of only two days from the capital, whence the inhabitants, already alarmed at his approach, took to flight. Now, however, Francis made proposals of peace, which the emperor accepted at once, being anxious for a reconciliation with his rival, as affairs in Germany grew more and more complicate, and, on the 24th of September, 1544, the peace of Crepi was signed—the last that Charles signed with the king of France. By this treaty little alteration was made in the main points of dispute; as before, Burgundy remained in the possession of France, and Milan was retained by the emperor. Francis, however, pledged himself this time to support the emperor not only in checking the Turks, but in restoring the unity of faith.

## CHAPTER XIX.

State of Religious Affairs in Germany, from 1534 to 1546—Vain Attempts at Reconciliation—Rapid Propagation of the New Doctrine—Henry, Duke of Brunswick—Death of Martin Luther, 1546—Charles V. and the Pope—Their Alliance—Preparations for War—The League of Schmalkald—The Elector of Saxony and the Landgrave of Hesse—Their characters contrasted—Maurice, Duke of Saxony—His extraordinary Genius—His Adherence to the Emperor—The Pope's Bull—The Holy War—The Schmalkaldian Army, 1546-1547—General Schärtlin—Division among the Protestant Leaders—Inglorious Results—The Imperial Camp besieged—Charles triumphant—Duke Maurice and the Elector of Saxony—Treachery of Duke Maurice—The Emperor in Upper Germany—Conquers the Imperial Free Cities—Saxony—The Battle of Mühlberg—The Saxons defeated—The Elector taken Prisoner—Deposed and condemned to Death—The Game of Chess—The Elector's Firmness and Resignation—His Life spared—Duke Maurice made Elector of Saxony—Wittenberg—Charles V. and Philip of Hesse—The Landgrave's Submission and Humiliation—Detained a Prisoner, and his Lands seized by the Emperor—The Elector Maurice—His Mortification, and Projects against the Emperor—The Spanish Troops in Germany—Their Insolence and Oppression.

In Saxony, the Elector John the Steadfast, since the year 1532, had been succeeded by his son John Frederick, a prince of just and honorable principles, but of a reserved mind, and in this respect quite the opposite of the bold and active Landgrave Philip of Hesse, who continued to march at the head of the Protestant princes as one of the most energetic and effective among them. Not only this contrast of character presented in the two leaders, but other causes had operated to produce a division among the body of Protestants themselves. Already, in the tenth year of the Reformation, a dispute had arisen among them with respect to the doctrine of the communion, in which at first Luther stepped forward to resist Carlstadt, and afterwards extended his opposition to the reformer of Switzerland, Ulric Zwingli, with whom he had a religious conference at Marburg, in 1529, but which led to no satisfactory result. They parted, it is true, with an improved opinion of each other's merit, and Luther himself was in hopes that the violence of spirit, which had hitherto breathed throughout their controversial writings, would now become softened down; but the primary subject of division still retained its influence, and presented an obstacle even to the external union of the parties in a common alliance; so that in fact it might have led to the total destruction of the new church, if the Catholics had availed themselves of the existing schism between them.

But among the latter, likewise, dissension prevailed to such an extent that, as we have already seen, the dukes of Bavaria had even joined the Schmalkaldian league. And, subsequently, when these princes separated from it, and the new church was thus threatened with greater danger, the strict Lutheran party, by the advice of their chief himself, became reconciled, for a time, with the Swiss, by a concordate of Wittenberg, and the towns of Switzerland as well as several others of Upper Germany, joined the league. This was one of the most important events towards the development of the evangelical church.

The propagation of the new doctrine increased rapidly from day to day. Several bishops even, including those of Lübeck, Camin, and Schwerin, embraced the new form of worship, and the venerable Hermann, elector of Cologne, of whom we shall speak more in detail as we proceed, made serious preparations to follow their example.

One of the most important changes, however, took place at this time in the Saxon territories. The moiety of these provinces, together with the cities of Dresden and Leipsic, belonged to Duke George, (by-named "the bearded,") who was a zealous adherent and defender of the old church, and who employed every means in his power to prevent the introduction of the new doctrine into his estates. His two sons, however, died before him, and his brother, Henry of Altenburg, (father of Maurice, the subsequent duke and elector,) his immediate inheritor, was, on the other hand, devoted with his whole soul to the doctrines of Luther. When, therefore, his brother George died, in April, 1539, the first act of Henry's government was to introduce the Reformation everywhere throughout his land. The majority of his subjects submitted willingly; the university of Leipsic itself, after a slight opposition, became completely changed, and the most zealous of the Catholic theologian professors, having been removed and discharged from their offices, were replaced by the partisans of the new doctrine.

A similar change took place in Brandenburg, nearly about the same time. Prince Joachim I., a zealous Catholic, having died in 1534, was succeeded by his son Joachim II., who had been educated by his mother, a princess of Denmark, in the principles of Luther. Encouraged by the example set by the bishop of Brandenburg, Matthias Jagow, this prince subscribed to the Augsburg confession, and introduced into his country a church service which retained some portion of the old form of worship, but in the chief points was strictly conformable with the principles of the reformed church.

The superiority which the new doctrine was now gaining in the north of Germany, induced the venerable Cardinal Albert, archbishop of Mentz, a prince of the house of Brandenburg, to abstain from making farther opposition to its progress in his two bishoprics of Magdeburg and Halberstadt, and withdrawing to Mentz, he granted permission to the states and cities of those provinces, in return for the payment of a considerable sum of money, to establish their new doctrine and build churches, as they might deem best and most advantageous.

After this, the more evil the state of things became, the more strenuous were both the emperor and his brother Ferdinand in their endeavors to reunite both parties, and for this object they established from time to time successive religious conferences: at Hagenau, in 1540; at Worms, in 1541, where Melanchthon and Eck stood opposed to each other; and in the same year likewise at Ratisbon, at which the emperor himself presided and took an active part therein. All, however, was in vain; the new doctrine was too widely separated from the old, and in it were now involved too many interests: on all sides too many worldly considerations were brought into operation, and amidst the wild party passions and distractions of that period, it was impossible to obtain for the subject that calm and profound investigation so necessary and so desirable.

These attempts at reconciliation producing little or no result, the emperor, as usual, had recourse either to a general council, confirming in the interval the treaty of Nuremberg; or, of his own authority, issuing, even against the voice of the Catholic majority, decrees by which all the Protestant churches in the land were recognised by the state. Thus it occurred at the diet of Ratisbon, in 1541, before Charles's expedition to Algiers; thus likewise at Spires, in 1542, by the mediation of Ferdinand and the elector of Brandenburg, in order to collect together all the forces of the empire against the Turks, and finally, in 1544, at the second grand diet in the same city, at which the emperor and all the seven electors were present, when he prepared his second expedition against Francis I. of France, and of which we have already spoken. The personal relations between the emperor and the two Protestant leaders, John Frederick of Saxony and Philip of Hesse, had never been upon a more favorable footing, so much so indeed, that the question of a marriage between a son of the elector and a daughter of Ferdinand had already formed a subject of discussion, while the landgrave received from the emperor a promise that in the next campaign against the Turks he should be appointed commander-in-chief in lieu of himself. And yet in spite of all this, the Protestants about this time sought to aid themselves by force of arms. Duke Henry the younger, of Brunswick, a zealous Catholic, and of impatient and violent spirit, was at enmity with the elector of Saxony and the landgrave of Hesse, more particularly on account of their religion; and each party attacked the other in fierce pamphlets abounding in passionate invective and furious abuse. In addition to this the two towns of Brunswick and Goslar, which formed a part of the league of Schmalkald, invoked the protection of the Protestant provinces against their own duke, who oppressed them in every possible way, and whom the emperor himself as well as King Ferdinand had repeatedly, although in vain, reproached for his unjust violence against those towns. At length, in 1542, the league raised an army, invaded the territory of the duke, conquered and drove him from the country, and held possession thereof. The duke appealed to the emperor for succor; he, however, only referred the matter to the consideration of the next diet.

Accordingly at the diet of Worms, held in 1545, it was decided that, until the affair was equitably adjusted, the emperor should hold the estates of Brunswick under his own immediate dominion. This arrangement, however, by no means accorded with the demands of the impatient and haughty duke, who would willingly have found himself at the head of the Catholic party: "To pretend to make use of threats in the name of the emperor, was," he said, "just like hunting with a dead falcon." In his zeal he was misled into an act for which he stood committed in the eyes of Francis I., king of France. This monarch had confided to his charge a considerable sum of money, for the purpose of collecting a body of troops for his service; as soon, however, as the duke had succeeded in this object he marched them into his own duchy, in the autumn of 1545, in order to regain it from his enemies. The no less bold and energetic Landgrave Philip, however, was soon on the alert with his army, and the elector of Saxony with Duke Maurice having joined him with their forces, they surrounded the duke so completely in his camp of Calefeld, near Nordheim, that he was forced to yield himself a prisoner, together with his son. The landgrave led them away as captives to the castle of Ziegenhain, and the emperor took no farther interest in the matter beyond advising him to treat his prisoners with lenity, and according to their rank as princes.

Meantime the before-mentioned diet of Worms, although it operated once more towards the maintenance of religious peace, presented, nevertheless, stronger indications of the growing schism, and the complaints of both parties became more and more urgent. The Catholics did not fail to complain of the confiscation of their ecclesiastical possessions in the Protestant countries, and the Protestants on their side refused to acknowledge the decrees pronounced by the imperial chamber in these and similar matters, inasmuch as the Catholics would only permit judges of the ancient faith to preside there. Distrust had now increased to such an extent that but a small number of Protestant princes appeared at all at the diet. The grand medium for reconciliation, from which Charles had formerly hoped so much, viz., a general council of the church, was now ineffectually employed, for it was now too late to resort to it, neither was it regulated in a just and equitable form. The court of Rome had eventually given its consent to such an assembly, and had convoked the council for the 15th of March, 1545, at Trent, in Tyrol, which was solemnly opened on the 13th of December of the same year. The Protestants, however, refused to recognise its authority for deciding in their affairs, giving as their reasons—that the council was convoked on the frontiers of Italy, in a country totally unacquainted with the customs of Germany, and which consequently could not fail to have an injuriously preponderating influence; and farther, that the pope, who had already condemned them as heretics, or at least had treated them as accused of heresy, presided at the said council as their judge. If, therefore, this council was to be regarded as an independent one, they must enjoy equal rights with the others.

Some time previously, Frederick, the elector palatine, who had then recently gone over to the new church doctrine, made a proposition which might have produced advantageous results if every one had been animated with good faith and influenced by pure principles. He proposed, viz., "to convoke a national or general council of Germany, and to transmit to Trent the convention therein concluded between all parties, as being the opinion of the entire body of the German nation." The same idea had been vainly suggested, even prior to this, by John Frederick of Saxony, who proposed that the said council should meet in Augsburg. This expedient, free from all foreign influence, and by which the nation would have been so represented as to express its wants fairly and directly, appeared the only one which must have proved beneficial and have led to a conclusion of religious disputes.

The anxiety felt by the emperor and the Catholics, lest the Protestants should acquire a superiority throughout the empire, was not without foundation. Three out of the four lay-electorate princes in the imperial council, had already adopted the new doctrine, (although the elector palatine and the elector of Brandenburg had not as yet joined the league of Schmalkald,) and now even one of the three prelates, Hermann, the venerable elector of Cologne, declared himself more and more decidedly in favor of the new cause. He was desirous, with the sanction of his states and a portion of his chapter, to introduce into his bishopric the most searching and important reforms, and had already entered upon the grand work himself, having invited Melanchthon from Wittenberg to aid him therein. The university and the corporation of Cologne, however, together with the opposition party of the chapter, were against all such reforms, and appealed to the emperor and the pope for their authority against these measures. This university had, previously to the Reformation, in the time of Jacob Hoogstraten, taken an active part in the dispute against the humanists, the professors and restorers of the study of the ancient languages, and especially against Reuchlin; while it was one of the first to condemn the dogmas of Luther.

In this increasing complication of affairs, where no longer the least hope of conciliation remained, the emperor, more and more urged to hostile measures by Rome and Spain, (the duke of Alba having now arrived in Germany from the latter country,) considered himself at length called upon—however much, hitherto, an inward warning voice might have restrained him—to employ, as a last resource, the force of arms, and thus promptly and definitively to decide the question. His chancellor, Granvella, held, therefore, secret council with the pope's legate, Cardinal Farnese, on the possibility of carrying on a war against the Protestants; he gave him to understand that the pope must necessarily join in active co-operation, as the emperor himself was exhausted, and the Catholic princes without energy; and the cardinal, in his joy to find the emperor now seriously determined to proceed to extremities, made the most flattering promises. In order to be unoccupied with any foreign enemy, Charles now concluded a truce with the sultan, and with Francis I. he likewise made peace.

We are now arrived at a critical period of Charles's life. In forming the resolution to accomplish with the sword that which he had so long endeavored to effect by peaceful means, he fell into a great error; falsely imagining that the mighty agitations of the mind could be checked and held in chains by external power. From that moment, on the contrary, he was himself vanquished by that very overwhelming epoch, the course of which, until then, he had appeared to direct and hold in rein; it was henceforward no longer in his power to restrain its career. His genius, impaired with increasing years, and over which, about this time, the Jesuits had gained an influence not to be mistaken, became more and more clouded and prejudiced against all that was new and vigorous in life, and thus, in his gloomy and morose spirit, he thought he was able to cut with the sharp edge of his sword the knot he found it so difficult to loosen. This mistaken idea of the emperor Charles at the closing period of his reign resembles a tragedy, in which we find a noble mind forced to bend and sink beneath the heavy burden to which fate has subjected it. These latter years, it is true, may be included among the most brilliant of his life, by their external successes produced so rapidly; but it was precisely this good fortune which made him lose sight of the exact point of moderation which, down to this moment, he had so happily maintained, and whence he was soon laid low by the iron hand of destiny, and all his plans, formed with so much trouble and anxiety, completely annihilated. Nothing else now remained for him, but to collect his reduced powers in order to withdraw in time from the whirlpool before him, and, while he threw aside the shining brilliancy of earthly grandeur, to preserve at least the independence of his spirit. And, assuredly, by this last resolution, of which subsequently we shall speak more fully, the emperor Charles secured to himself his dignity as a man while he conciliated the voice of posterity.

Shortly previous to the commencement of the sanguinary war of religion, Luther, the founder of the grand struggle, breathed his last. He had used all the weight of his power and influence in order to dissuade his party from mixing external force with that which ought only to have its seat within the calm profundity of the soul; and, indeed, as long as he lived, this energetic reformer was the warm advocate for the maintenance of peace. He repeatedly reminded the princes that his doctrine was foreign to their warlike weapons, and he beheld with pain and distress, in the latter years of his life, the growing temporal direction given to the holy cause, and the increasing hostility of parties, whence he augured nothing good. Providence, however, spared him from witnessing the final and disastrous course of events. He had suffered from severe illness for several years, and during a journey he had undertaken, in the year 1546, to Eisleben, in order to settle a dispute between the earls of Mansfeld, he was seized with a fresh stroke of illness, and died on the 16th of

February of that year, at the age of sixty-three after having repeated once more, with his dying breath, that he had lived and now died in the firm belief of Christ, the Saviour of the world. His body was conveyed in solemn state to Wittenberg, where it was placed in the vault of the royal chapel of the castle.

While the diet of Ratisbon was still sitting, in 1546, where for the last time the Protestants urged, viz. "A lasting peace and equal rights for the evangelical and Catholic estates, together with an equitable council of the German nation," the emperor had already collected an army, and concluded a treaty of alliance with the pope. He determined, in combination with the Holy See, to adopt extreme measures against Hermann, the archbishop of Cologne, who was at once formally deposed from his electorate. This and other acts alarmed the confederates of Schmalkald; and they demanded from the emperor the object of his military preparations. He replied briefly: "That all those who submitted to his authority would find him influenced by the same gracious, paternal, and good intentions he had hitherto shown; but on the other hand, all such as acted in opposition to him must expect to be treated with the greatest severity." And shortly after this, when the messenger returned from Rome with the treaty signed by the pope, he issued his declaration of the 26th of June, 1546: "That as hitherto all the diets had produced no effect, it was his desire that all should await with patience the determination he might adopt upon the subject of religion, whether for peace or war." This declaration showed evidently that it was the emperor's intention to have recourse to war, and the Schmalkaldian league immediately prepared to take up arms in their defence. The marked contrast, however, between the two great leaders held out but little prospect of brilliant results.

The elector of Saxony, who adhered to his faith with his whole soul, and was but little influenced by any thing external beyond it, would not for a moment admit any political calculation to connect itself with his cause, but rested solely upon his conviction, "That God would not forsake His gospel." Previously, he had already refused the alliance of the kings of England and France, because they both appeared to him unworthy to defend the doctrines he held to be the most pure, and he even considered that he was bound to refuse the co-operation of the Swiss, because they deviated from him in their belief of the doctrine of the Eucharist. The elector, whose ideas were extremely circumscribed, had never for a moment suspected the existence of the plans so long contemplated by the emperor; on the contrary, he always continued to nourish in his heart, even to the last moment, the most sincere and genuine veneration for the ancient sacred name and person of the emperor. And, indeed, had it not been for his able chancellor, Bruck, to whom he confided every thing, and who, fortunately, knew better than himself how to bring into connection the maxims of state policy with the strict principles of religion, so firmly advocated by his master, the league would have suffered still more severely.

Philip of Hesse was not wanting either in attachment and zeal for his faith; but there were other motives besides of an external character by which he was influenced in the part he had chosen. He had from the first been excited by the most burning ambition, and had it not so happened that a combination of events had cut him off from all friendly connection with the imperial throne, he would doubtless have occupied a distinguished position among the counsellors and generals of the emperor. Finding himself, however, placed by fate at the head of the opposite party, his bold and enterprising genius prompted him to employ every expedient against the emperor; and for which purpose he was gifted with powers far more comprehensive than the elector of Saxony. He would willingly, in several cases, have taken up arms where the circumstances were favorable, in order to obtain for himself and his co-religionists at once those rights for which they were otherwise forced to wait until granted them by the emperor. We have seen already how he twice boldly took the field at all hazards, at one time in favor of Ulric of Wurtemberg, and at another against the duke of Brunswick; but whenever he urged the policy of undertaking more extensive expeditions, he found himself always checked by the elector, who was ever anxious not to infringe the laws; whence it was alone the common danger which held in union two minds so different in character, and almost wholly opposed to each other. This inequality of thought and feeling, however, could not fail to produce necessarily great confusion and opposition in moments of decisive action.

This was the weak side of the Schmalkaldian league; but for this, its power under good and wisely-concerted direction, would have been sufficiently effective to have obtained complete success in a legitimate defence against the emperor. And in such case, to have proceeded upon the principle and feeling with which the elector of Saxony acted, would have been highly praiseworthy and honorable; for thence the Protestant party would have been able to defend its liberty of faith with advantage, without the interference of foreigners, which was always destructive to Germany; it would have preserved the respect and reverence due to the imperial majesty so long, at least, as the latter did not transgress the limits of justice, and without having recourse to the dishonest artifices of that policy which honors truth in proportion only as it accords with its own interest. But the league was unhappily devoid of unity of action and cordial cooperation, as well as in fixity of purpose in the execution of its plans. A considerable number of princes had refused to join its ranks, and even opposed it by attaching themselves to the emperor's party. Maurice, the young duke of Saxony, although himself a Protestant and cousin of the elector, as well as heir to the Landgrave Philip, was in secret communication with the emperor; while the margrave of Brandenburg, John of Küstrin, abandoned the league, and Albert of Baireuth also openly entering the service of the emperor, acted with him in concert against it.

Maurice of Saxony was one of the most remarkable and distinguished men of his day. Young, bold, and active, he already possessed the keen glance and quick conception of the more experienced warrior, and had at command that searching, comprehensive view of circumstances which enabled him to execute his purposes with characteristic promptitude. His whole appearance, likewise, displayed the perfect man; and his eye of fire and penetration, together with the entire expression of his noble, daring countenance, indicated his heroic character. The emperor Charles himself, who always ranked the Germans far behind his subjects of the southern climes, and accordingly held but few of them in much respect, soon learned to know the young duke's character, and quickly penetrating into all that was grand and noble in his nature, he singled him out at once as worthy of especial regard and esteem beyond all his other courtiers.

Maurice, whose keen glance penetrated far more deeply into future events than that of his cousin the elector, discovered very soon that the latter could not possibly maintain the contest against the superior address and tact of the emperor, and he accordingly formed at once the resolution of making himself the chief of the house of Saxony. In doing this, he may, perhaps, have justified himself by the plea, that there was no other means of saving it; still his justice and truth were put thereby severely to the test. He would not join the league of Schmalkald because he wished to attach himself to the emperor and preserve his alliance until, by the attainment of his object, he should be at liberty to act with independence.

On the formation of the league he gave his advice against it, and when invited to join it, he refused and declared that he would only take up arms in defence of his own lands. He was, however, already, at the moment he made this declaration, in secret understanding with the emperor; but to what extent and how closely he was allied, and under what stipulations, has not been clearly shown: unfortunately, however, there is every probability to suppose that the reward held out to him was the prospect of receiving the electorate. Such being the case, what an inward struggle must it have cost him, and how painfully must it have agitated his whole soul, when the unsuspecting elector, just before he set out on his expedition against the emperor, confided into his hands the whole of his lands, in order to protect and watch over them as his substitute during his absence, to be faithfully restored to him on his return! Nevertheless, no external sign betrayed this inward contention, and wisdom triumphed over truth; and in order not to betray himself, he accepted the protectorate of the electoral territories.

The emperor exerted every effort in order that the approaching war should not assume the character of a purely religious war. In a proclamation to the principal Protestant cities, Strasburg, Nuremberg,

Augsburg, and Ulm, printed in Ratisbon, he assures them positively: "That the preparations for war made by his imperial majesty, were by no means adopted for the purpose of oppressing either religion or liberty, but solely in order to bring to submission a few obstinate princes, who, under the cloak of religion, sought to seduce over to their party other members of the holy empire, and who had lost all sense of justice and order, as well as respect for the imperial dignity."

The straightforward good sense of the German citizens, told them plainly that a part of this proclamation was nothing but mere empty words, while they felt the danger with which they were themselves threatened by the overthrow of the princes. They held themselves, therefore, firmly attached to their league with the Protestant states. An unexpected event which now took place rendered perfectly useless all the pains that Charles had taken to conceal the object in view. He had scarcely concluded his alliance with the pope, the nature of which was exactly the opposite of what he had so lately assured the cities in question, when the pope made it publicly known, and issued a bull throughout Germany, in which he represented the emperor's expedition as a holy undertaking for the cause of religion: "The vineyard of the Lord," it says therein, "shall now be purified, by fire and sword, of all the weeds which have been sown by the heretics throughout the Germanic empire." By the terms of the compact itself, the pope promised to assist the emperor with twelve thousand Italian foot-soldiers, and fifteen hundred light cavalry troops, which he undertook to maintain at his own cost for the space of six months. Besides this, he gave two hundred thousand crowns towards the general outlay of the war, and authorized the emperor to draw the moiety of the revenues from the ecclesiastical possessions in Spain, and to dispose of Spanish monastic property to the amount of five hundred thousand scudi. In return for which Charles promised: "That he would compel, by force of arms, all the rebels in Germany to return to their obedience to the holy chair of Rome; that he would restore the ancient religion, and that, without the consent of the holy father, he would enter into no treaty with those of the new heresy, that might be disadvantageous or injurious to the Romish church."

Thus this manifesto, contrary to the wish of Charles, gave a religious character to the war, and such was the pope's desire. In the Protestant countries, however, the most bitter and indescribable exasperation was excited, and if the leaders had only known how to avail themselves of that moment, by directing the entire strength of the mass thus aroused, the emperor, with his Spaniards and Italians, must have been completely overcome. For the other German princes, and even the Catholic princes, held themselves generally quiet; dreading lest, after overthrowing the Protestants, the emperor would exercise sole dominion over the whole empire.

The army furnished by the cities of Upper Germany marched first into the field; a well-appointed and select body of troops under the command of a man distinguished for his military skill and well-tried experience, Sebastian Schärtlin of Burtenbach, near Augsburg. This brave officer and knight was remarkable for his resolution and firm, undeviating principles of action; he would never brook half measures, but always manœuvred for the total defeat and destruction of his enemy. He had served in all the campaigns against the Turks and the French, and had shared in the battle of Pavia and the storming of Rome under the duke of Bourbon. He was now soon joined by the corps of Ulric, duke of Wurtemberg, under the command of the brave John of Heydeck. Schärtlin speedily drew up his plan of the war, according to which he commenced operations by at once seeking to annihilate the emperor's forces at the very onset of their formation; for Charles, who still remained stationary in Ratisbon, had as yet at the utmost only from eight to ten thousand men, while he still awaited the troops collecting in Germany and those that were marching to his aid from Italy and the Netherlands.

Schärtlin advanced against the town of Fuessen on the river Lech, in Swabia, one of the principal military depôts of the emperor; but the troops on his approach evacuated the place, and retired into Bavaria, and just as he was about to march in pursuit of them, a messenger arrived from the council of the city of Augsburg, in whose service he was more especially engaged, with instructions not to enter the territory of the duke of Bavaria, who was a neutral power.

The house of Bavaria had threatened to join the emperor in case they did not leave his country unmolested; at the same time it may be observed, that if it was resolved to remain entirely neutral, it ought assuredly not to have permitted the troops of the emperor to pass through its territory. But there was at that moment a secret compact concluded between the Bavarian house and the emperor, by which the former agreed to furnish at least a certain contribution in money. It was, therefore, with no little pain and mortification that Schärtlin found himself thus suddenly checked and forced to make a halt on the very banks of the river Lech, without being permitted to cross it and destroy the enemy thus slipping through his fingers; especially as his plans embraced far more important and decisive results, it being his determination, after having defeated the troops now before him, to have proceeded by forced marches on to Ratisbon itself. The army there collected being but small, the emperor would have been forced to take to flight, in which case he must have lost the whole of Upper Germany. Referring to this subject Schärtlin wrote: "That assuredly Hannibal himself had not experienced greater regret and mortification, when compelled to withdraw from Italy, than he had endured when forced at that moment to retire from the Bavarian territory."

The brave Schärtlin now proceeded at once to carry into execution the plan he had formed immediately after the failure of his first project, and which was to oppose the march of the pope's troops across the Tyrolese mountains into Germany.

Never had such a well-appointed army been formed in Italy as that which now marched forth to join the emperor's force; the soldiers, under chiefs long distinguished for courage and experience, being all united in one zealous, enthusiastic feeling against the Protestants. Schärtlin, by forced marches, soon gained the passes and made himself master of the important defile of Ehrenberg. Thence he marched against Inspruck, and had he been allowed to proceed, would have obtained his object and commanded the whole country; but here he received fresh orders from the leaders of the league, by whom he was now instructed to evacuate the land, inasmuch as King Ferdinand, to whom it belonged, had not as yet declared war against the Schmalkaldian league. Thus was evinced already, even at the commencement of operations, all that doubt and fear among the confederates whence might easily be foreseen the most unfortunate and disastrous results. For it was the height of folly and madness, after the war had become inevitable, to show consideration towards those who, although as yet not declared enemies, were nevertheless known to be decidedly hostile. Nevertheless, the general was obliged again to obey superior orders, and was thus unable to avail himself of the advantages he already possessed, or might at any future period gain.

Meantime, the Saxon and Hessian troops were brought into the field, and directed their march towards Upper Germany. The two chiefs of the league addressed, on the 4th of July, a letter to the emperor as follows: "That they were not conscious of having committed any act of disobedience, for which they had been accused by the emperor. If, however, they had laid themselves open to such reproach, it was only just and equitable that they should be heard beforehand; and if this did take place, then they would make it clear in the eyes of all, that the emperor undertook the war merely at the instigation of the pope, in order to oppress and crush the doctrine of the evangelists, and the liberty of the Germanic empire." This last and most grave accusation, now made for the first time against the emperor by his opponents, was soon eagerly caught at and disseminated throughout the world. This one sentence, if it was held to be truly expressed, must have produced a startling change even in the Roman Catholics themselves, have subdued all their zeal, and rendered them less desirous to behold the emperor succeed in overcoming his adversaries.

Charles, indeed, immediately afterwards, by committing a most rash act, appeared to confirm the accusation thus made against him; for when the document from the leaders of the league was laid before him, he would not even touch it, but proceeded at once, on the 20th of July, to reply to it by a declaration of the imperial ban against the two princes of Saxony and Hesse. He therein charged them with disobedience to the imperial authority, and a design to "deprive him of his crown, his sceptre, and all authority, in order to invest themselves therewith, and finally to subjugate every one to their tyrannical power." He called them "rebels, perjurers, and traitors," and absolved their subjects from all obligation of homage and obedience to them. Thus severely did he express himself in reply to their address, although quite in conformity with the excitement and violence of that turbulent period. By this, his last act, however, the emperor violated the ancient rights of the empire, according to which he was not empowered to declare the ban against any state, without the council and judgment of the princes. No exact estimate, therefore, can be made of the extent to which the emperor might have been carried, had circumstances continued favorable; for to minds like his, which subject themselves entirely to the dictates and guidance of prudence, circumstances constitute the only measure of restriction. They undertake only what appears to them practicable, and Charles accordingly was cautious in not attempting to do that which he could not complete. He held the sway over so many extensive states, and had opposed to him so many powerful adversaries in Europe, that he felt it quite impossible to devote that continual and exclusive care to Germany, which a plan of absolute sovereignty, to be carried out successfully, strictly demanded; whence he wisely abstained from the attempt. Nevertheless, Charles gave ample evidence of his character as a proud and mighty emperor, and the ruler of half the world, by acting in particular circumstances, when every thing depended upon prompt measures of execution, independent of all forms of law; whence it may be said that the violation of the rights and privileges of the empire rested more in his intentions than in his plans.

Meantime he entered upon this opening scene of the Schmalkaldian war in conscious superiority of mind and true heroic independence. Although having at command but a small body of troops, and threatened by an army of at least fifty thousand men, the most complete and formidable force that Germany had produced for several years, he only replied to the declaration of the princes by the said document of excommunication, and then proceeded from Ratisbon to Landshut in order to be more immediately at hand to receive the succors marching from Italy. To remove, however, all doubt or fear from the minds of his partisans, he declared to them that he would never abandon the German soil, but would adhere to it living or dead. His best guarantee was the state of dissension existing in the camp of the allies. Schärtlin with the municipal troops had now joined the army of the two disunited princes. The citizen-general now advised that they should march with their combined forces against Landshut, and there surround the emperor at once; but, as usual, they could come to no determination, and the valuable opportunity was lost once more. The emperor, on the contrary, lost no time in making the most of these valuable moments; he collected around him all the reinforcements as they arrived from Italy and Spain, as well as the auxiliary troops from Germany, and when he found himself in sufficient strength, he ascended the banks of the Danube as far as Ingolstadt. There he encamped, and strongly fortified himself; for as yet he could not venture to enter the open field and attack the enemy, preferring to wait the arrival of Count Buren, who was advancing to join him with a considerable body of troops from the Netherlands. The allies had followed him to his present position, and now they at length determined to attack his camp, as yet not quite secured, with their artillery, and thus force him to draw up in line of battle.

Accordingly, on the 31st of August, they advanced at break of day, and forming themselves into a half circle, occupied all the heights in the rear of the camp with their planted cannon. The allied troops were animated with courage and a desire for battle; and at this favorable moment, a bold and decisive assault, conducted with prompt and energetic effect, would have produced for the allies an easy, but complete and glorious victory. For the emperor was far inferior in force, and his camp was as yet only defended by a simple trench. The idea of such an assault was not unthought of by the allies; according to some accounts the Landgrave Philip, according to others General Schärtlin, had suggested it at the very moment when the fire from his twelve heavy cannons was dealing destruction among the emperor's Spanish arquebusiers, and sent them back flying into the camp. But again this time irresolution and disunion among the leaders rendered futile the decision which ought to have been put into force immediately. The emperor, who with the greatest *sang froid* encouraged his troops, and himself defied all danger, now gained time to complete the fortifications of his camp, and was soon enabled to witness in perfect security how vain were the efforts of the enemy to point their cannon with any effect against him. From this moment Schärtlin, as he himself relates, placed no longer faith in this war, "for he saw no serious efforts made to render it an honorable and legitimate war."

The princes continued during five entire days to cannonade the imperial camp, without producing any desired result; and when they heard that Count Buren, with his auxiliary troops from the Netherlands had already crossed the Rhine, they raised the siege, and suddenly retired with their whole army in order to march against him. The emperor could scarcely believe his eyes, when he beheld the powerful army of his enemy thus retire without having effected any thing, and mounting his horse he rode out of his camp escorted by the duke of Alba and others of his staff, to observe their retreat more closely.

Meantime the princes, notwithstanding their rapid march, were unable to prevent the junction of Count Buren with the emperor, who being now so much reinforced, proceeded at once to march in advance, taking possession of one place after another along the Danube, and making himself complete master of that river. When at length he approached and threatened Augsburg, the citizens summoned their general, Schärtlin, to their aid and protection. The allies, however, notwithstanding they had not understood properly how to avail themselves of their superiority, maintained the war by an obstinate resistance until November, so that the emperor could not bring them to a general action; while, in the mean time, the Spaniards and Italians of his army already suffered greatly from disease and fatigue.

The allies suffered likewise from severe weather, to which was added the want of supplies, both in provisions and money, and the army now began to show signs of discouragement and dejection, because the leaders were incapable of inspiring confidence; the Swabian division of the army was more especially disgusted with the war, because the whole burden was thrown upon its shoulders, while the two armies had now been encamped face to face for more than six weeks, without doing any thing. The princes at length sent a dispatch to the imperial camp, in which they declared themselves ready to negotiate for peace, or at least a suspension of arms. By this act, however, they only betrayed and acknowledged at once their weakness, and yielded themselves as conquered without striking a blow. Rejoicing triumphantly, the emperor commanded the document to be read before the whole army drawn up in order of battle, and in full of all reply, he briefly announced to the princes, through the margrave of Brandenburg: "That his majesty knew of no other way by which peace was to be restored, except by the submission of the electors themselves, and their adherents to the imperial authority, together with their entire army, their lands, and subjects."

Upon receiving this reply, the allied princes broke up and separated on the 22d of November, at Giengen, and each returned to his own territories.

The presence of the elector of Saxony had been more especially claimed by his country through a message dispatched to him in his camp, announcing that Duke Maurice had, with the exception of a few small places, taken entire possession of the whole land. For the emperor had authorized his brother Ferdinand, as king of Bohemia, to execute, in conjunction with Duke Maurice, the sentence of the ban adjudged against the elector; and such was the position of affairs, that it appeared, if Maurice did not himself take immediate possession of the electorate, it would most probably be lost forever. Such at least was the representation made by Maurice when he summoned together the states of the country, in order to obtain their sanction for such proceeding; for without that he could not have commenced upon such an important undertaking. He employed all his powers of speech and argument, in order to give his conduct and wishes the semblance of right and justice. The sudden arrival, however, of Ferdinand, with his Hungarian light cavalry, which he had brought with him from Bohemia, produced the decided effect; their savage appearance spread universal terror, and it was regarded as a happy relief to yield to the

Saxon warriors of Maurice. The entire electorate, therefore, with the exception of Wittenberg, Eisenach, and Gotha, was speedily in the hands of the ambitious duke. The voice of the people, nevertheless, loudly condemned his proceedings; he was looked upon by them as a renegade in the cause of the new doctrine of faith; and by the clergy, both in the pulpit and in their various writings, he was most severely censured and lashed.

The elector himself now, in December, 1546, returned to Saxony, full of sadness and dejection. He soon succeeded, however, in reconquering his lands, and in seizing a portion of the duke's territory, after he had overthrown and taken prisoner in Rochlitz, Albert, margrave of Brandenburg, who had been sent to the aid of his friend, Duke Maurice, by the emperor. Maurice was likewise left without any assistance from Bohemia, as the estates of that country refused to fight against their co-religionists in Saxony, referring, at the same time, to a treaty of inheritance which existed between the crown of Bohemia and the electoral house of Saxony; while Ferdinand himself began to feel rather uneasy on account of his own kingdom. That country had already ripened into a state of open revolt, and the states had even proceedec to collect together a considerable army, in order, as they pretended, to protect the Bohemian territory against the attack of the unchristian Spanish and Italian forces. Whence it resulted that Maurice, of his own land, only retained possession of the towns of Dresden, Pirna, Zwickau, and Leipsic, and he was reduced to place all his hopes in the emperor Charles.

Meantime Charles was occupied in bringing to subjection the Protestant cities in the south of Germany. This, however, was deemed no easy undertaking, these places being exceedingly strong, and might have resisted his arms for a length of time; while, in the interval, the princes of the north could avail themselves of the opportunity, and make their preparations for a fresh campaign. It seemed, however, as if both courage and resolution had suddenly deserted them altogether; for wherever the emperor presented himself the cities submitted to him at once without offering any resistance. Bopfingen, Nördlingen, Dunkelsbühl, and Rothenburg, threw open their gates without its being necessary for him to unsheath the sword at all; while Ulm itself, powerful as that city was, dispatched messengers tc meet him, who on their knees, and in the open field, besought his pardon in the Spanish tongue, (this act was especially, and with justice, most severely condemned by the allies,) and paid over to him as a fine 100,000 florins. Frankfort paid likewise a sum of 80,000 florins, Memmingen 50,000 florins, and the smaller towns paid sums in proportion; and now the turn came for Augsburg. This city was protected by walls almost invulnerable, mounted with two hundred pieces of artillery, and provided with a strong garrison, and a warlike population; if, therefore, it had only maintained its ground with determined bravery, it must thereby have revived once more the sinking courage of the entire body of the allied forces. But the rich members of the municipality took fright when they found the danger so close to their own door; and one of them, Anthony Fugger, proceeded as deputy to wait upon the emperor in his camp, and returned with the conditions exacted, viz.: that the city should pay a sum of 150,000 gold florins; that it should receive a Spanish garrison, and banish its brave commandant Schärtlin. The latter employed every effort to prevail upon them to defend the place, but all his eloquence was in vain, he could not infuse courage into them; finally, he reminded them of their contract with himself, according to which they had engaged to retain him in their service, and could not banish or discharge him. They, however, only replied, by begging him with tears in their eyes, for God's sake, to leave the city; accordingly the brave old warrior quitted the place in disgust and indignation, and retired to Switzerland—the Spanish troops taking immediate possession. The cities, indeed, had reason to congratulate themselves upon having the permission granted them to retain the same privileges in respect to religion as were enjoyed by Duke Maurice and the house of Brandenburg; although this arrangement did not certainly accord with the promise made to the pope.

Besides the cities, two princes in Upper Germany had taken an active part in the war: Ulric, duke of Wurtemberg, and Frederick, elector of the palatinate. The latter was not a member of the Schmalkaldian league, and had only, in accordance with an hereditary treaty between him and Duke Ulric, furnished the latter with a subsidiary force of three hundred cavalry and six hundred foot soldiers; added to this, he had been a juvenile companion and playmate of the emperor when together in Brussels as boys, whence he easily obtained a pardon. The duke of Wurtemberg, however, was obliged, together with his council, to beg for pardon on their knees, as likewise to give up his strongest castles with all the cannon, and to pay a fine of 300,000 gold florins, after having sworn to obey the emperor in all things.

Thus the Schmalkaldian league in Upper Germany was speedily destroyed, and the emperor resolved at once not to allow his army any repose, but to bring matters in the north of Germany to an equally prompt and decisive termination. He himself stood, indeed, much in need of rest; his hair during this war had become quite gray, his limbs were completely lamed from gout, while his countenance was so deathly pale, and his voice so weak and tremulous, that he could hardly be recognised or understood. His spirit, however, still reigned with all its original power within that infirm body; and he was now urged on by necessity to obtain his object, inasmuch as he was anxiously expected at Eger by King Ferdinand and Duke Maurice, who there tarried like two fugitives driven from their possessions until he came. He joined them at length, on the 15th of April, and they celebrated together the Easter festival; they then forthwith proceeded on their march, and on the 22d of April, Charles found himself already encamped within a short distance of the walls of Meissen on the Elbe.

The elector could not, for a long time, believe it possible that Charles was marching against him; but now, when to his no little surprise, he found he was actually within sight and close upon him, he gave hasty orders to destroy the bridge near Meissen, and marched with his army along the right bank of the Elbe, in order to reach Wittenberg, his capital, where he would have at command all the means necessary to maintain a long and vigorous resistance. The emperor, on the other hand, held it most important that an immediate attack should take place, by which to bring the war to a speedy end; especially as his army was four times as strong as that of the elector. Accordingly, he lost not a moment, but pursued his march along the opposite shore, almost in a line with the elector's troops, and searched along the river for a spot to ford it and ge his army safely and expeditiously across The elector halted near the small town of Mühlberg, while the emperor, very late a night, once more rode with his brother and Duke Maurice along the shore, seeking in vain for a favorable spot by which to cross over; for the Elbe here was at least three hundred feet wide, and the opposite shore was considerably higher than on his side. At length his general, the duke of Alba, brought from a neighboring village a young miller, (his name—preserved by history—was Strauch,) who promised to lead them to a fording-place. He was induced to commit this act of treachery by a feeling of revenge towards his fellow-countrymen, who, as they marched in the course of the day through his village, had taken with them two of his horses—this circumstance, and the tempting offer of a hundred crowns, made him by Duke Maurice, with the promise of two other horses to replace those taken from him, determined him to serve the enemies of his country.

At the dawn of morning, and under favor of a very thick fog, several thousands of Spanish arquebusiers now commenced crossing the river, and a select troop among them having cast aside their guns, and thrown off their armor, placing their swords in their mouths, holding them tight between their teeth, plunged into the stream, and swimming to the other side, seized the remains of the bridge which had been destroyed by the Saxons. This they succeeded in repairing while the cavalry forded the river, each horseman taking with him on his saddle a foot-soldier. Lastly followed the emperor, his horse guided by the said miller, King Ferdinand, Duke Maurice, and the Duke of Alba, with the rest of the imperial suite.

On the morning of this eventful day—the sabbath—the elector attended divine service in Mühlberg, and when, in the midst of his devotions, a messenger arrived in breathless haste and announced to him that the enemy had crossed the river and was in full march in pursuit of him, he could not, would not believe it, but desired the service of God not to be interrupted. When it was over he found the news was too true, and he had scarcely time to retire with his army. He ordered his infantry to march in all haste for Wittenberg, but he directed the cavalry to keep the enemy at bay by skirmishing; the artillery having already been sent in advance to Wittenberg. The imperialists, however, pursued the Saxons with such speed that they overtook them on the plain of Lochau; and although his artillery and the greater portion of the infantry still remained behind, the emperor, nevertheless, by the advice of the duke of Alba, gave orders for an immediate attack. The Spanish and Neapolitan troopers dashed with impetuous force against the Saxons, Maurice himself leading the attack. The elector's cavalry was soon thrown into confusion, and fell back upon the ranks of their own infantry, which was hastily drawn up in battle array on the borders of a deep forest. The elector gave his orders from a carriage, his weight of body not permitting him to mount on horseback; the emperor, on the other hand, in whom the signs of illness were less than ever perceptible on this day, rode an Andalusian charger, holding in his right hand a lance, and wearing a helmet and cuirass gorgeously decorated with gold, his eye beaming with warlike ardor. The imperial cavalry, with their terrific shout of "Hispania! Hispania!" broke now through the ranks of the Saxon infantry, which were completely put to rout. All now took to flight; everywhere was confusion and terror. As they flew across the plain, the fugitives were overtaken and struck down by their pursuers, covering with their bodies the whole line of road from Kossdorf to Falkenburg and Beiersdorf. One of the elector's sons was overtaken by some troopers of the enemy; he defended himself with great courage, and shot one of them dead at the moment when, having received two sword-cuts, he was sinking from his horse; some of his own men just coming up in time, rescued and bore him away in safety. But his father was not so successful; he could not escape. He had been urgently entreated by his faithful adherents to seek safety in flight, and gain a secure asylum in Wittenberg; but his only observation was, "What will become of my faithful infantry?" and he remained on the field of battle. In the heat of action he had quitted his carriage and mounted a powerful Friesian charger; he was, however, very soon surrounded by the enemy's cavalry, and as he valiantly defended himself, he received a cut on his left cheek from the sabre of an Hungarian trooper. The blood streamed all over his face, but even in this sad condition the undaunted warrior would not yield, until a Saxon knight in the suite of Duke Maurice, Thilo of Trodt, penetrated through the Hungarians that surrounded him, and called out to him in German to save his life. To him, as he was a German, the elector gave himself up a prisoner, and in token thereof he drew from his finger two rings which he presented to him; while to the Hungarian he gave his sword and dagger. The knight conducted his royal prisoner to the duke of Alba, and the latter, at the earnest and repeated persuasion of the elector, led him before the emperor, who still continued mounted on his horse in the centre of the plain. The elector, as he approached, sighed deeply, and raising his eyes up to Heaven, said, mournfully, "Heavenly Father, have pity on me, for behold I am a prisoner!" His sad condition and appearance excited the compassion and sympathy of all around; his wounded face still streaming with blood, and his cuirass likewise being covered with spots of gore. He was assisted to dismount by the duke of Alba, and was about to drop on his knees before the emperor, taking off the gauntlet from his right hand, in order, according to German custom, to present it to his majesty; but the latter refused to take it, and with a stern and haughty look turned from him. The mortified prince now addressed him with the words: "Mighty, gracious emperor!" "Ay, now I am your gracious emperor, am I?" returned Charles, haughtily. "It is long since you styled me thus!" The elector continued: "I am your imperial majesty's prisoner, and beg to receive the treatment due to me as a prince." "You shall receive the respect you merit," concluded the emperor. The elector was now conducted to the camp by the duke of Alba, together with Ernest, duke of Brunswick-Lüneburg, who had also been taken prisoner.

Thus was that day brought to a successful close for the emperor, on the subject of which, in the style of Cæsar, he writes: "I appeared, I fought, and God vanquished."

After a repose of two days, Charles

marched on to Torgau, which surrendered forthwith, and thence he proceeded to Wittenberg, the capital of the country. The place was defended by a strong fort and a good garrison, while the citizens themselves assisted with determined courage and loyalty; had they continued to make resistance for any length of time, the emperor would have been forced to withdraw from Saxony without having completed his work, as he was not at all prepared for a long campaign. Thence, in his impatience, and by the urgent persuasion of his confessor and others around him, he had recourse to an expedient which completely transgressed the limits of his prerogative, and was contrary to the constitutional rights of the empire. He summoned a council of war, and pronounced sentence of death upon the unfortunate prince; an act which, however just the sentence, could not legitimately take place, except in a diet held by the German princes of the empire. Probably he may not seriously have contemplated the execution of the sentence, but only sought to use it as a means to terrify the friends and faithful adherents of the elector within the walls of the city, and thus induce them to surrender the place; but the violation of the law was based in the form of the judgment, and in case it did not operate in the way, perhaps, originally intended by Charles, there was too much reason to fear from his stern nature, which never allowed him to waver or recede, that execution would follow.

The elector, who, when in prosperity, was too often wanting in resolution and fixity of purpose, evinced at this moment all the heroic courage of a firm and energetic soul founded upon unchanging and indomitable faith. The sentence of death pronounced upon him, was announced to him at the moment he was engaged in a game of chess with his fellow-prisoner, Duke Ernest of Brunswick-Lüneburg. His appearance and manner betrayed neither alarm nor despondency, but as he resumed his game, he calmly replied: "I can never believe that the emperor will proceed to such extremes in his treatment of me; if, however, his majesty has truly and definitively thus resolved, then I demand to be informed thereof in such positive and legitimate form as will allow me to proceed to fix and arrange my affairs in regard to my wife and children."



It is not known whether Duke Maurice did at all interest himself on this occasion with the emperor in favor of the elector; but, on the other hand, it is known for certain, that the Elector Joachim of Brandenburg hastened immediately to the imperial camp, where he strenuously exerted all his powers of eloquence with the emperor to prevent, by some mediatory accommodation, the fulfilment of the sentence. He succeeded at length in his object, but under conditions most severe and painfully humiliating to the elector of Saxony. He was obliged to renounce for himself and descendants all claim to the electoral dignity, as well as the possession of the territory, which were transferred to Duke Maurice. His castles of Wittenberg and Gotha were surrendered to the emperor, while he himself remained his prisoner during imperial pleasure; so that if deemed proper and necessary by Charles, he might even have been sent to Spain itself, and there placed under the immediate charge of the Infant Don Philip. The necessary provision for him and his family was to be furnished by Maurice, produced by the revenues derived from the towns of Eisenach, Gotha, Weimar, and Jena. In one article of the conditions it was proposed, that the elector should even promise in advance to accept of every thing that might be decreed by the council of Trent and the imperial power in religious matters—but to that the resolute prince would by no means be brought to agree, and on this point he remained so firm and immoveable, that the emperor was obliged to yield; he struck out the passage with his own hand, and the Spaniards themselves even acknowledged the firmness of the elector to be both honorable and praiseworthy.

When it became known in Wittenberg, that its city was to be delivered up to the emperor, although in religious worship it was guarantied the free exercise of the Augsburg confession, considerable indignation and consequent opposition and confusion arose. At first the citizens resolved to defend themselves to the last man, because they found it impossible to place any confidence in the promise made that they should have their religious liberty; particularly after the cruel manner in which the Spaniards had acted towards their land. The elector, however, commanded them not to make any further resistance, as the emperor would, he assured them, faithfully keep the promise he had given; especially as the latter granted them permission to receive only German troops as a rrison. Accordingly on the 23d of May, 1547, the Saxon soldiers marched out and the imperialists took possession of the town. In the course of a very short period an interchange of a more peaceful and friendly feeling arose between the camp and the city, and mutual distrust disappeared more and more. The Saxons, to their great wonderment and admiration, beheld their deposed lord and prince comfortably lodged and entertained in the tent of the duke of Alba, where he was waited upon and treated with the greatest distinction and reverence by the Spaniards. The electress herself and her children, dressed in complete mourning, were led before the emperor by the sons of the Roman king and paid him their homage; Charles assisted the princess to rise, and consoled her in her sorrow and affliction with words of sympathy and encouragement, granting permission to the elector to pass an entire week with his family in his castle of Wittenberg, and there celebrate with them the festival of Whitsuntide. In addition to this, he himself repaired to the castle and returned the visit of the princess. The impression produced by his noble and exalted spirit, now so much softened, diminished and almost extinguished that feeling of antipathy hitherto existing against him throughout the country; while, on his part, he formed a much more favorable opinion of the people of the north of Germany than the enemies of the new doctrine had led him to conceive: "Things and people appear far different in this evangelical country to what I fancied and believed them to be before I came among them," was his expression now. And when he learned, that on his arrival the Lutheran form of divine service had been prohibited and had ceased, he exclaimed: "Whence has that proceeded? By whose authority? If it be in our name that the service of God has been interdicted here, then does it incur our high displeasure! We have not altered aught touching religious matters in High Germany, why should we do so here?" He then visited the royal chapel of the castle, and examined the tomb of Luther. One or two of his suite—it is said the duke of Alba and the bishop of Arras, the son of Granvella—advised him "to have the remains of the heretic resuscitated and publicly burnt;" but Charles replied: "Let him repose in peace, he has already found his judge; I war only with the living, not with the dead."

Maurice, the new elector, showed himself equally friendly and indulgent towards the Wittenbergians: "You have been so faithful to my cousin that I shall always remember and think well of you," were his words to the corporation as he left them. On the 6th of June the imperialists withdrew from Wittenberg, and, immediately afterwards, the soldiers of the new elector marched in and took up their quarters in the city.

On the same day that the emperor Charles entered Wittenberg, his former rival, Francis I. of France, was borne to the tomb, as if fortune had resolved to remove at once from before his path every obstacle to the plans he had formed. From Wittenberg he marched on to Halle, in order to attack the second leader of the Schmalkaldian league, the landgrave of Hesse, and the latter having now no longer any hope of deliverance but through the grace and pardon of the now all-powerful emperor, employed every effort by means of his son-in-law Duke Maurice, and the margrave of Brandenburg, to obtain both.

Both these princes exerted themselves most actively and zealously for him, and at length they succeeded; the emperor declaring, through his chancellor, Granvella: "That if the landgrave came to him in person, surrendered himself at discretion, and signed the conditions which would be submitted to him, he promised not to seize his lands, neither would he take his life nor punish him with lasting imprisonment." Thus it is expressed in a copy, recently discovered, of the transactions of that period. The mediators, however, either did not well weigh the last sentence of the declaration, and imagined it was meant to convey that the prince should suffer no imprisonment, or, as they themselves admitted, some months afterwards, at the diet of Augsburg, "In their verbal negotiations with his majesty's counsellors too great confusion and misunderstanding existed through ignorance or misconception of language;" enough, they pledged their word of honor with the landgrave to give themselves up prisoners to his sons in case the emperor did not give him full liberty to return. Accordingly, on the 18th of June, Philip, in full reliance on their word, came to Halle, and on the following day he was led before the emperor. Charles was seated on his throne, surrounded by a crowd of Spanish grandees and Italian and German nobles, and among them stood conspicuous Henry, duke of Brunswick, lately the landgrave's prisoner, but whom he had been forced to release, and who now triumphed in his late conqueror's humiliation. With dejected and mortified mien the landgrave humbly knelt at the foot of the throne, while his chancellor, Güntherode, kneeling behind him, read aloud to the emperor the petition for pardon. It was expressed in the most humble terms, and an eye-witness relates, that in the excess of shame and confusion with which the prince was overwhelmed at this moment, in the presence of such a large and august assembly, a slight smile played about his mouth, as if produced by an unconscious effort of nature to repress the feeling of shame by which he was so painfully tried. But this expression did not escape the lynx-eyed monarch; he held up his finger menacingly, and said in his Netherland dialect—for he spoke the German very badly—"Wöl, ick soll di lachen lehren!" (Ay, ay, I will teach you to laugh.) The imperial chancellor, Dr. Seld, then read the emperor's reply: "That, although the landgrave, as he himself acknowledged, deserved the heaviest punishment, the emperor, nevertheless, in his innate goodness, and in consideration of the intercession made in his favor, would allow mercy to take the precedence of justice; he therefore removed the ban of excommunication pronounced against him, and granted him the life he had by his acts forfeited." After this document had been read, the landgrave was about to rise as a free prince from his humble posture, but waited in vain for the signal from the emperor; finding, therefore, that this was withheld, and that the clear and solemn promise of pardon was likewise refused to him, he rose of his own accord and withdrew from the assembly.

In the evening he supped with the Elector Maurice and the margrave of Brandenburg, in the quarters of the duke of Alba; after the meal, he was about to retire, when the duke informed him he must consider himself his prisoner. He was seized at once with astonishment and indignation, as were also the two princes who had guarantied his liberty. They immediately appealed to the emperor, and represented to him that they had pledged their princely word for the landgrave's liberty; but Charles denied having promised him remission from all imprisonment—as the mediators had falsely understood—although he declared at the same time that he would not punish him with perpetual captivity. And indeed it is very possible that his counsellors promised more than he himself intended to grant; or that in the ignorance of the chancellor Granvella and his son of the German, and of the two electors of the Spanish and French languages, an error may have arisen in the correspondence.

Still it would have been more noble and manly to have fulfilled the engagement to which the two princes had pledged themselves towards the landgrave. On the other hand, it was certainly very important to the emperor that he should hold the leaders of the Schmalkaldian alliance his prisoners until he had completed the whole of his contemplated arrangements for the settlement of the religious affairs of Germany; for he still believed in the possibility of effecting a reunion of parties, and these two imprisoned princes were the most obstinate and violent opponents to such a measure. But Charles did not consider that honesty and generosity became much more the sovereign, and led more securely to the attainment of the object in view than cold, calculating caution; and forgot that when this is once established as a law, the ingenious and clever politician may, in the course of time, be overreached by one still more cunning, and thus all his gains slip through his fingers. Duke Maurice, who was now unable to fulfil his engagement, and appeared in the character of a perjurer towards the landgrave, felt, no doubt, from the moment that the emperor would not acknowledge the pledge he had given to the landgrave in such good and confiding faith, that he was himself released from all obligations of gratitude and fidelity towards that monarch; and thenceforth he considered that in their relations together they must be governed alone by skilful and sagacious policy, and in this respect, at least, the duke needed not to yield in any thing to the emperor.

The deposed elector and the landgrave were therefore obliged to follow as prisoners the court and camp of the emperor wherever he proceeded. Besides this, all the Hessian castles and strongholds, from Cassel to Ziegenhain, were razed, all the cannon and ammunition seized and taken away, and the states of that country forced to pay a fine of 150,000 florins. The emperor Charles, in his treaties with his adversaries, followed the principle of the Romans in the time when they contemplated the conquest and sovereignty of the whole world. For in the same way as they had then exacted from the Carthaginians, and the kings of Macedonia and Syria large sums of money, together with the extradition of all their ships of war, warlike machines, and elephants, so also now Charles disarmed and rendered powerless his enemies, by forcing them to dismantle and raze their fortifications, to surrender all their heavy artillery, which at that period it was seldom possible to replace, and finally to pay him heavy sums of money to enable him to undertake new enterprises. In his treaties with the cities of Upper Germany, the duke of Wurtemberg, the elector of Saxony, and the landgrave of Hesse, he gained more than five hundred pieces of cannon, which he caused to be conveyed to Italy, Spain, and the Netherlands. The Spanish garrisons which he quartered wherever he found it possible, and especially in the cities of Upper Germany, excited everywhere the greatest discontent. The overbearing pride and shameful treatment displayed and exercised by these haughty foreigners, animated as they were by their religious hatred, were insupportable, while it was not forgotten that the emperor, in the stipulations of his election, had promised not to bring or introduce any foreign troops into the empire.

---

## CHAPTER XX.

**The Council of Trent—Rupture between the Emperor and the Pope—The Interim or Temporary Code of Doctrines—Its Condemnation by both Parties—The Captive Elector of Saxony—Refuses to adhere to the Interim—His Declaration—Shameful Treatment in consequence—The Elector Maurice—Magdeburg—Maurice marches against that City—The Emperor and Maurice—Maurice deserts the Emperor, and with Albert of Brandenburg joins the Protestants—Their Declaration against the Emperor—His Reply—Albert's Depredations—Maurice's Separation from him—Charles V. at Inspruck—Pursued by Maurice—The Emperor a Fugitive in the Mountains of the Tyrol—His desolate and forlorn Condition—His return to Augsburg—Release of the Elector John Frederick—His Welcome Home—Jena—Treaty of Passau—Liberation of Philip of Hesse—Charles V. in France—Metz—Unsuccessful Campaign—Albert of Brandenburg—Defeated at Lüneburg by Maurice—Death of Maurice and Albert—Religious Peace of Augsburg—Final Separation of the two Religious Parties—Abdication of Charles V.—Retreat to a Hermit's Cell—Rehearsal of his Funeral Procession—His Death, 1558.**

It now became more and more evident that peace in matters of religion would not emanate from the council of Trent, for as its members consisted altogether of Italians and Spaniards, they could not possibly be regarded as the representatives of the Christian world in the sense of the former convocations of the church. The Protestants now, as well as previously, refused not only to acknowledge their authority, but, on the contrary, insisted upon a council "in which the pope should not have the presidency, and where the Protestant theologians should enjoy the privilege of voting with and on the side of the bishops, and where the decrees recently made should undergo fresh examination and revision."

The papal party, on the other hand, would not consent to these demands, although the princes of Germany, including even the Catholics, urgently demanded that the states who had assisted at the confession of Augsburg should be admitted to join the council. Nay, the cardinals themselves viewed the circumstance of its being held at Trent with a very unfavorable eye, and they strenuously endeavored to have it transferred to the interior of Italy; for they were afraid that if the aged Pope Paul III. died during the period of its being assembled, the council, supported by Charles, would take upon itself the office of electing a new pope in opposition to the rights enjoyed by the college of cardinals, and by which the interests of that institution must be materially affected. At length, a case of fever came fortunately to their aid and seconded their wishes; and although it was feared that the disease would have proved more generally fatal, still one only of the bishops became its victim. This, however, was sufficient to produce the accomplishment of their object, and on the 9th of March, 1547, the council was removed from Trent to Bologna. The emperor, on hearing it, was highly indignant, and flew into a most violent passion, while the pope approved of the step taken by his legate; whence the division already existing between him and the emperor—owing, on the one part, to the former having withdrawn his troops from Germany immediately after the expiration of the agreed term of six months' service, and on the other, to the latter not having availed himself of the triumph he had obtained in his empire by forthwith extirpating the Protestant party—became more confirmed. The emperor told the pope's nuncio in plain language: "It could not be expected that the Protestants, who were willing to submit to the council, would themselves repair to Bologna, or even pay attention to what might be concluded there; while the rest did not require this motive for refusing to attend. If, therefore, Rome did not furnish him with a council, he himself would speedily have one assembled which should be so formed as to satisfy every one, and produce all the reforms required;" adding, "that the pope was an obstinate old man, whose only desire was to ruin and demolish the church to its foundation." Such were the angry terms in which Charles, against his usual manner, addressed the prelate, and by that we have another proof of his anxiety and zeal to promote the peace of the church. The German bishops, on their part, now likewise most urgently besought the pope to remove the seat of council to Trent, but their efforts remained for a length of time without producing any effect.

In consequence, Charles now proceeded to re-establish of his own accord, at a diet held in Augsburg, in 1548, order and peace in religious matters in Germany, and with this view, he opened a new conference, to which, on the side of the Catholics, two moderate men were appointed—the bishop of Naumburg, Julius Pflug, and the grand-vicar of Mentz, Michael Helding; while the court-chaplain of the elector of Brandenburg, John Agricola of Berlin, was selected on the part of the Protestants. They applied themselves to the subject with great industry and zeal, and marked out a plan of reunion which they laid before the emperor. Agricola, however, from his too great anxiety to establish the desired peace, had deviated in several essential points from the original principles of his faith. He had succeeded, it is true, in gaining for his own party the admission of the two articles, viz., of the marriage of clergymen, and the celebration of the Lord's Supper in both forms, but to continue valid only until the council should have given its decision upon the subject. As to the rest, he recognised the authority of the pope, the celebration of mass, and the Catholic church and its signs of faith generally; whence it was easy to foresee that great discontent and opposition must arise. As, however, the elector of Brandenburg, and likewise the elector palatine, engaged both to sanction and adopt it, Charles considered he should now be able to compile therefrom his code of doctrines, called the "Interim." He convoked his states on the 15th of May, and then caused to be read to them the work in question, which was entitled: "Declaration of his imperial and royal majesty, which determines how religion shall be exercised and maintained within the holy empire until the decision of the general council shall be pronounced." After the reading, and a short discussion had taken place between a few individual members, but which led to no result, the elector of Mentz rose, and in the name of the states returned thanks to the emperor for the trouble, labor, industry, and love he had taken and shown for the sake of the country; and as none ventured to make any objection, the emperor concluded that the sanction of the entire body of the states was given to the measure, and regarded it now as the law of the empire.

While the emperor Charles thus sought, on the one hand, to make himself independent of the proceedings of the pope, and, on the other, to maintain the unity of the German church—by which that of the Germanic empire itself must be rendered still more firm—he was guided by the one grand and fundamental principle observed throughout his entire reign; viz., to restore the importance and dignity of the ancient empire, as had formerly been projected, and in part effected by the great Charlemagne, the Othos, and other high-minded emperors. His aim was to render the empire replete with spiritual and temporal power. The emperor, according to Charles's plan, was to be made in reality the chief authority of entire Christendom; with his temporal power he was to unite a material and effective influence over the church, and not only protect, as a machine of the spiritual power, the order of the church, and assist in enforcing duty to its commands, but he was to have an important share and interest in its councils and resolutions. Like Charles the Great, who presided at the synods of his bishops, and whose decrees were sanctioned by his signature, so, likewise, it was the desire of Charles V. to partake in the direction of the general council, or at least maintain next the pope, and as the central point of the ecclesiastical order of the Germanic empire, the dignity with which he was invested.

The emperor was well aware that a most grand and important step would be gained towards the establishment of his "Interim," if the imprisoned elector of Saxony, whose spiritual influence in the Saxon territories had recently very much increased—he being now regarded as a martyr to his faith—could be persuaded to give it his approval. Accordingly, he sent his chancellor Granvella, and his son, the bishop of Arras, together with the vice-chancellor Selb, to submit to him the proposals to accept that code of doctrines, and likewise to recommend its adoption to his sons. The elector, however, in reply to their request, handed over to them a declaration which, in anticipation of such a visit, he had already prepared and written with his own hand; viz., "That the education he had received from his youth upward at the hands of the servants of the divine word, together with the profound researches he had himself since made in the writings of the prophets and apostles, had united to convince him that the true Christian doctrine was to be recognised in the Augsburg confession, and his conscientious belief therein remained unshaken. If he accepted the 'Interim' as a Christian and divine doctrine, he should be forced, against his conscience, to deny and condemn the Augsburg confession in many articles upon which his immortal happiness depended, and sanction with his lips what in his heart he held to be completely contrary to the doctrines of the Holy Scripture; in doing this, he should consider he was shamelessly abusing and blaspheming the holy name of God, for which sin he must severely and bitterly suffer in his soul. His imperial majesty, therefore, would not, he hoped, feel ungracious towards him, if he refused to accede to the 'Interim,' and persisted in adhering strictly to the Augsburg confession."

The ministers refused to accept of this declaration, and reminded the elector, "that the emperor was empowered to make laws and decrees even in religious matters, and that several Roman emperors, ancestors of his present majesty, had created such, which even to that day were obeyed by all the subjects of the Roman empire." The elector, however, remained immoveable; and as during the discussion they were interrupted by a loud peal of thunder, the elector felt rejoiced and strengthened by the conviction that this was sent as an indication from Heaven that his conduct met with divine approbation, and that he should be guided by the judgment of God alone, and not by that of mortals.

The act committed against the elector, immediately after this interview—although it is believed to have been done without the sanction of the emperor himself—was both petty and unjustifiable. He was deprived at once of the society of his chaplain, Christopher Hoffmann, and a seizure was made of all his books, among the rest, of his own especially-treasured copy of the Bible, beautifully illuminated; but amid the painful mortification he endured, while forced to submit to this trial, his firmness did not forsake him, for as the minions quitted the place with these, to him, invaluable treasures, he said, resignedly: "You may take the books; but that which I have learned from them you can never take or even tear from my heart."

The sons, following the example of their father, refused to introduce the "Interim" into their territory, and, in fact, the emperor soon found himself deceived in his hopes of succeeding to bring his code into general use. The Protestant theologians rose in one body against the measure, and many were forced to vacate and abandon their offices, and take up the pilgrim's staff as wanderers; viz., in Augsburg, Nuremberg, Regensburg, Ulm, Frankfort, and other cities: the number of banished ecclesiastics in the upper countries alone amounted to four hundred. What, however, is still more astonishing is, that the Catholics themselves disapproved of this "Interim," although it was by no means pretended that it should be put into practice among them. The Catholic church would have reaped the greatest advantage therefrom; for if the emperor had succeeded in his plan, the reunion of both would have been a necessary consequence. Thence their opposition can only be interpreted into a declaration, that they would not regard as valid any regulation in matters of religion coming from him as a layman.

Thus, during his sojourn of two years in the Netherlands, whither he had repaired after the diet of Augsburg, the emperor was forced to receive continual complaints from Germany; his "Interim" was only acknowledged outwardly in a few places, while, generally, in all parts of the empire much bitter feeling was expressed against it, and even the Elector Maurice himself gave it but a very limited reception in his land. He had commissioned several theologians, including Melanchthon, to prepare a church formulary for his own subjects, and with great trouble, and not without incurring severe censure from the more rigid of the Lutheran clergymen, they completed what was called "the Leipsic Interim," and which, certainly, deviated in many points from, but as a whole adhered to, the Protestant faith. It was introduced in several parts of the north of Germany, although here and there with considerable alterations; but, on the other hand, in many other parts of the country the greatest stand was made against any change whatever. The cities of Constance, Bremen, and Magdeburg especially, declared themselves most firmly opposed to it, and refused to submit to the imperial order; whereupon the emperor pronounced the ban of the empire against them, and the two former places returned to their obedience. But Magdeburg continued obstinate, being influenced in a great measure by several theologians who had taken refuge there after their banishment from Wittenberg on account of the "Interim;" among whom a certain Flacius, with the by-name of Illyricus, was the most violent and zealous. The Elector Maurice received at the new diet of Augsburg, in 1550, orders to execute forthwith the sentence of the ban pronounced against that city. He accordingly marched with his army at the commencement of the autumn in the same year, and laid siege to the place.

At this diet Charles sought to gain for his son Philip, whom he had sent for from Spain, the title of king of the Romans. However, neither his brother Ferdinand, nor the latter's son, Maximilian, nor, in fact, any of the electors or princes, would give their consent; for, besides other causes, the haughty, gloomy, repulsive appearance and manner of the prince could not possibly operate in his favor among the Germans. His father, therefore, saw himself obliged to send him back to Spain, whither Philip indeed was too glad to return, for he was more attached to that country than any other.

The emperor, at the conclusion of the diet, left Augsburg for Inspruck, as the new pope, Julius III., having now removed the seat of the council from Bologna to Trent, Charles was anxious to be in its vicinity.

Meantime the new elector of Saxony nourished in his heart a most bold and determined design against the emperor, the immediate motives for which, however, we are not able to define, inasmuch as the whole of this man's thoughts and actions have remained an enigma in all historical research. Still there is no doubt he was influenced in his conduct by at least two grand causes: firstly, the severe and unjust confinement of his father-in-law, the landgrave of Hesse, towards whom he considered he was still bound to redeem the word and guarantee he had given for his liberty, while neither the arguments nor prayers resorted to by him had the least effect upon the emperor; and, secondly, the sad condition of the Protestants in Germany. These latter felt more and more convinced that the emperor only waited now for the resolutions of the council of Trent, in order to establish them as the laws of religion throughout the empire; and as he had already commenced hostilities against Magdeburg, on account of the "Interim," so likewise, as soon as he had collected fresh troops, it might be expected that he would force all the states of the land to submit to all those decrees of the church. Indeed, at this moment, the whole body of the Protestants were in a state of anxious expectation and suspense. Those who dreaded the worst results condemned the Elector Maurice as the most culpable party: inasmuch as he had betrayed the league of Schmalkald, and it was through him that John Frederick of Saxony and the landgrave of Hesse were now suffering imprisonment. Those, on the other hand, who still cherished some hope of relief, turned their eyes towards him, for to them he appeared the only one now left capable of protecting the new faith. The moment had now, indeed, arrived, when with one grand and mighty stroke he might expunge all recollection of the past and regain the public opinion. Maurice was not long in deciding the course he should take, and he determined to put his plan into execution at once. He availed himself of the opportunity presented in the expedition against Magdeburg, to collect, without exciting suspicion, a numerous body of troops, while at the same time, in accordance with the object in view, the siege of the city itself was conducted as tardily as possible. At length, in September of the following year, 1551, he, of his own authority, agreed to a suspension of arms, and in the succeeding November, he concluded a treaty with the city—the terms of which were extremely mild. and favorable for the latter—while, however, he took care not to discharge his troops on this account. He secretly dispatched his early friend and companion, Albert, margrave of Brandenburg-Culmbach, to the court of Henry II., king of France, the son of Francis I., in order to conclude an alliance with him, and he immediately engaged in his service the leader of the Wurtemberg troops, John of Heydeck, who, together with Schärtlin, had been previously placed under the imperial ban. These proceedings, however, had not escaped observation, and were communicated to the emperor; but Charles remained deaf to all the warnings given to him. He placed the greatest confidence in the man whom he thought he had thoroughly tested, and when thus cautioned against him, he replied: "That as he had never, to his knowledge, given cause, either to Maurice or the Margrave Albert, to act inimically towards him, but, on the contrary, had shown to both great proofs of his favor and consideration, he could not believe it possible that they would be guilty of such ingratitude; and he was convinced that with them their acts would go hand in hand with their words, and that they would not swerve from that honorable line of conduct for which the German nation had ever distinguished itself." And thus, while, on the one hand, the emperor placed his firm reliance upon German fidelity, his minister, Granvella the younger, calculated upon the simplicity of the Germans, for the observation he made in reply was: "That it was wholly impossible for a phlegmatic German to conceive a plan and endeavor secretly to bring it to bear, without its being immediately discovered and known in all its details."

Both the emperor and his minister, however, were struck as it were with a clap of thunder, when Maurice, in the month of March, 1552, suddenly appeared with his whole army and invaded Franconia, augmenting his forces with those of the landgrave of Hesse and the troops of the Margrave Albert. At the same time both these princes drew up a declaration against the emperor, which they made public, wherein they sought to justify the war they commenced. They complained of the prolonged imprisonment of the landgrave, as likewise of the attacks made by the emperor upon the liberty of Germany. They reproached him with having confided the seals of the empire to foreigners, who were totally unacquainted both with the language and laws of Germany, so that the Germans themselves were actually forced to learn a foreign tongue before they were allowed to make known their demands to the imperial government. "Contrary to the oath he took, he had," they said, "introduced into the country foreign troops, who pillaged and ruined the unfortunate inhabitants, whom they likewise abused and ill-treated in every possible way; nay, he had gone to such extremes, that he had clearly shown he was swayed by no other thought or feeling than that of subjecting all and each to the most shameful servitude, whence his conduct had been such, that if the sweeping torrent of destruction was not speedily and effectually checked, posterity itself would have too great reason to abominate the negligence and cowardice of the present generation, during which the liberty of our fatherland—its greatest and most precious treasure—had been allowed to fall a sacrifice."

Although in many of these reproaches there was much exaggeration, still we find therein reflected, in the most striking and glaring colors, the great and especial evil in Charles's character, and to which his unjust treatment of the Germans is to be undeniably traced. This great error he evinced in the contempt he expressed for the nation, while on the other hand he showed the greatest preference and favor towards his Spaniards and Netherlanders, of whom the former, more especially, by their proud and overbearing conduct, together with the cruelty practised by their common soldiers, brought down upon themselves the just indignation and hatred of the country. The love of the nation Charles never could possess, for he himself cherished none towards the people; condescension was the utmost his pride would allow him to vouchsafe to the Germans. But this cold and formal display of affability is more insupportable to a brave and loyal nation than even arrogance and tyranny; while the discontent and mortification expressed by the princes when they saw that a haughty foreigner, like Granvella, was installed in his office as chancellor, and had thus confided to his charge the entire control of the government, were but too well founded. It was, however, less the *acts* than the *disposition* of the emperor as evinced against the Germans, which drew upon him this humiliating war with Maurice. The Margrave Albert, in his declaration to the emperor, introduces an accusation, the nature of which appears still more striking, but which had its origin in that very arrogance then so openly and directly displayed by these foreigners towards the nation. Albert, in his furious indignation against the historian of the Schmalkaldian war, Louis d'Avila, bestows upon him the epithets of "liar and villain," inasmuch as in his work he speaks of the Germans being a savage and unknown people, "devoid of all honorable, manly, and noble virtue, and of whose descent and origin nothing was known."

The emperor again, whose actions were better than as in these declarations they were represented, in the feeling of his dignity made no other reply than: "That the accusations of the two princes being so childish, unconnected, and absurd, they only contained in themselves their own falsehood and want of foundation, while they laid bare in ample evidence the mischievous character of those who had invented them."

The enterprise of the two princes, however, very soon lost character in public opinion through the conduct of the margrave himself, who, with his people, committed violence and devastation, equalled only by the most lawless band of freebooters and incendiarists, everywhere throughout the flat portions of the country. Thence Maurice and the young Landgrave William of Hesse, both of whom had nobler objects in view, were forced to separate from him and leave him to act for himself.

The emperor was now in a state of great embarrassment; he was in want both of troops and money, which latter, to his mortification, the money-lenders of Augsburg refused to advance him, and he was reduced to the extremity of deputing his brother Ferdinand to open negotiations with Maurice. As, however, they led to no result, and Maurice easily perceived that the design of Charles was to gain time, he broke up at once from Swabia and marched his troops into the Tyrol, in order, if possible, to fall upon him unprepared. His progress was so rapid, that he actually preceded in person the announcement of his advance; he marched on to Ehrenberg, which fell into his hands, and had he not been detained an entire day by a mutiny which broke out in one of his regiments, he would have succeeded in gaining Inspruck in time to have surprised the emperor there and taken him prisoner. Charles, however, was thus enabled to escape on the previous night, (of the 19th May,) during a most dreadful thunderstorm, and arrived in safety at Trent; he himself was conveyed there upon a litter, being at the time extremely ill, and his brother Ferdinand, the captive elector of Saxony, and the rest of the suite followed, some on horseback, others even on foot, while servants with torches lighted them on their road through the narrow passes of the Tyrolese mountains—such had been their haste. But even Trent itself was no longer secure, and after a few hours of repose, Charles was again forced to resume his flight across the most difficult and dangerous roads as far as the village of Villach, in Carinthia; the assembled council at Trent having also in their alarm broken up and taken flight on every side. Maurice, however, on finding that Inspruck was evacuated, turned back again, after he had distributed among his troops the imperial booty collected, and marched on to Passau, whither an assembly of the princes had been convoked.

Meantime it cannot be doubted but that these reverses of fortune, which, together with his bodily afflictions, had humbled the proud heart of Charles in these days of disgraceful flight, were sent by Providence for his justification. It was, no doubt, during this trying period that he formed the resolution of voluntarily laying down his crown as soon as ever he had quelled this new war, and, renouncing the world's pomp, to retire into solitude, and devote his remaining days to the exclusive service of the eternal and immutable Creator.

He now gave the imprisoned elector of Saxony his liberty once more; stipulating only that he should remain with the court a short time longer. And truly, the sight alone of this suffering prince must have produced within him bitter and painful feelings; for it was only five years previously that, on the plain of Lochau, the elector, with bleeding form, appealed to him on his knees for grace; while now the same prince beheld him, the former conqueror, sick and helpless, traversing almost impassable mountains as a fugitive, and pursued, too, by another elector of Saxony, whom he in his days of pride and glory had himself promoted and rendered powerful. What, however, afflicted the emperor more than any thing else, was to find himself deserted by all his states—not even being aided by the Catholics—while they all preferred submitting patiently to be plundered by the Margrave Albert, rather than uniting together for the succor and protection of their emperor. Then it was that he but too truly felt the conviction at heart, that it is only in the love of his people that a sovereign can hope to find a sure protection in the hour of danger.

In Augsburg, the Elector John Frederick took leave of the emperor, who, in their parting scene, testified much respect and even emotion towards the prince. The latter left Augsburg immediately, and hastened to return to his own lands. As he proceeded he was everywhere welcomed and received with sincere and hearty respect and congratulation; and when he approached Nuremberg, he was met on the road by a train of fifty deputies from the magistrates of that city on horseback, and the whole populace greeted him with shouts of joy, while at the same time many were affected even to tears. When, at length, he arrived at his own town of Coburg, his beloved wife Sibella—who had now thrown aside the mourning robes she had worn during the entire five years—on finding that the wish she had so often expressed had now become fulfilled, viz., that before she died she might see her husband released from his captivity, was so overpowered that she fell into his arms completely insensible. On his arrival at Jena, where his sons had built a university in lieu of that taken from them at Wittenberg, he was especially rejoiced in meeting and once more holding communion with the learned professors and their students. His old and faithful friend, Lucas Cranach, the painter, together with the eldest of the princes, sat in the same carriage with him: "Behold!" exclaimed the delighted elector to his son; "this is the true fraternal study of the sciences;" and the entire body of professors having now advanced to welcome him with an address of congratulation, the gratified prince listened to it with uncovered head. Such was the reception experienced, and such were the feelings produced on the reappearance of this truly German prince among his subjects, by whom he was regarded in the light of a father. Charles V., however, was unfortunately never so received in Germany.

The emperor meantime left it to his brother Ferdinand to negotiate with Maurice at Passau. He himself had a great objection to the whole transaction, but he was nevertheless very desirous to make peace with Maurice, in order to be enabled to turn all the power of his arms against the enemy he most hated—the French; who, during this interval, had invaded Lorraine and taken one city after another. Under such circumstances, the treaty of Passau was concluded on the 31st of July, 1552. Therein it was stipulated: "That the Landgrave Philip of Hesse should at once be set at liberty, and that the ban of the empire pronounced against all who had joined in the war of Schmalkald should be withdrawn. That with respect to the other religious grievances, a new diet should be convoked, and that until then the imperial chamber of justice should exercise its judgment with equal impartiality for both parties, but that the imperial council should be composed of Germans only."

After the conclusion of this peace, Maurice, in order to prove the justice of his intentions, disbanded all the foreign troops of his army, and marched with his own soldiers to Hungary in aid of King Ferdinand. Philip of Hesse was liberated, and returned to his family and country. The long and severe imprisonment he had endured had humbled and depressed his independent spirit, and destroyed all farther inclination for great undertakings; he employed the remaining years of his life in the praiseworthy task of healing, as far as possible, the wounds inflicted during the previous unhappy period of anarchy throughout his dominions.

The emperor having, in the mean time, collected an army from Italy and Hungary, marched against Henry II., king of France, and sick and enfeebled as he was, he followed it in a litter and commanded it at the siege of Mentz. But it appeared now as if fortune had abandoned him entirely; the city defended itself with great obstinacy, and however determined the emperor and his army might have been to carry on the siege, they were nevertheless compelled to yield to the severe effects of the winter, and to withdraw from its walls. Much discontented, Charles returned to the Netherlands, and commenced making preparations for the next campaign, 1553. This, however, as well as the two following expeditions of 1554 and 1555, produced nothing decisive for the two nations: the French, when Charles sought to bring them to an open engagement in the field, fortified themselves in their strongholds, and the entire war limited its operations to merely devastating the provinces of the frontiers. Charles was accordingly forced to transfer its achievement to his son Philip II.

The treaty of Passau had produced in Germany a happy state of repose; one man alone appeared determined not to allow its uninterrupted enjoyment—the turbulent Margrave Albert of Brandenburg. He pursued his war of pillage and incendiarism against the bishops and several cities in Franconia, Swabia, on the Rhine and Moselle, with unheard of impudence and daring, and as at length all the warnings given to him were of no avail, Duke Maurice, to whom the peace of Germany had now become more and more dear, united with Henry, duke of Brunswick, and both made a combined attack upon the margrave, in 1553, on the plain of Lüneburg, near Silvershausen; he having by this time extended his depredations even to Lower Saxony. The battle was severe and bloody; the margrave, however, was completely beaten; but two sons of the duke of Brunswick, a prince of Lüneburg, fourteen counts, and nearly three hundred of the nobility besides, were left dead on the field, while Maurice of Saxony himself was mortally wounded. He was conveyed to a tent erected close to a hedge, and there he received the captured banners and papers of the margrave, which latter he examined with all the eager curiosity his sinking state would permit. Two days afterwards he expired, exclaiming with his dying breath: "God will come—!" the rest of the sentence was unintelligible. Although only thirty-two years of age, he had already acquired greater authority and commanded more influence in Germany than any one of his contemporaries. Hence any farther testimony is unnecessary in order to prove the preponderating power of his genius. The final efforts he so patriotically made for the promotion and establishment of general tranquillity, and his love for peace and order, which he sealed with his own blood, have in a great degree served to throw the mantle of oblivion over his earlier proceedings, and conciliated the critical voice of public opinion. He was succeeded in the electorate by his brother Augustus.

Albert, the restless margrave, in whom the turbulent spirit of the times of the Faustrecht was revived in all its destructive form, still continued, in spite of the severe defeat he had suffered, to harass the country. Completely reduced after this last battle, he, in his extremity, sought the aid of the king of France, and supported by the money he received from that monarch, he immediately began, in 1556, to collect fresh troops and make arrangements for another campaign—or rather series of depredations. Happily, however, his death, which occurred suddenly amid his warlike preparations, prevented him from committing further devastation. He was likewise a prince of extraordinary powers, and resembled very much his ancestor Albert, the Achilles of Germany; but the innate wildness of his disposition and character generally, combined with the disordered state of those times, which destroyed all principle, however firmly based, had operated to give to his energies a direction fatally destructive.

In the treaty of Passau it had been fixed that a diet should be held in order to regulate the affairs of religion, and to investigate the accusations of the Elector Maurice against the emperor. Charles himself urged its assembling with great zeal, in order that it might not appear as if he stood in any fear of the inquiry; but the affairs of Germany having now become altogether equally indifferent to him, nay—and who could blame him—even odious, he confided their direction to his brother Ferdinand, who devoted all his energies with noble and praiseworthy zeal to the undertaking. In spite of the lethargy and indolence of the German princes, and not discouraged by several vain attempts to effect his object, he at length succeeded, in 1554, in forming a diet at Augsburg. A committee was immediately named to examine and settle the various matters of religious contention, composed of the ambassadors of Austria, Bavaria, Brandenburg, Wurtemberg, Eichstädt, Strasburg, Juliers, Augsburg, and Weingarten, and they all worked with sincere and laudable industry in the great cause. The Roman king aided them therein most strenuously; he removed every external difficulty presenting itself in the progress of their task, and when he learned, among other things, as is related by his chancellor Zasius, "that several of the spiritual princes were engaged in fruitless disputes, that they were occupied in strewing the path with every sort of disquisition and difficulty, adapted more to destroy altogether even to the foundation the building they were engaged to reconstruct, while such proceedings must produce, on the other side, bitter and inimical feelings," he dispatched Zasius and his vice-chancellor Jonas to them, and warned them, in most grave and solemn terms, to desist from such a line of conduct; and in thus acting he effected his object.

And by proceeding, in another circumstance, to act with equal firmness towards the Protestants, he caused them likewise to yield to his wishes. The point was one of great importance, inasmuch as they demanded that the ecclesiastical body of Germany should be at liberty to adopt the Augsburg confession, and retain at the same time their offices and lands; but the Catholic party rose in strong opposition against it: "If this demand," they declared, "was conceded, the whole of the ecclesiastical possessions in Germany would very soon be transferred into the hands of the Protestants. Much rather, on the contrary, ought the law to be thus: that as soon as a spiritual prince, in his own person, passed over to the new doctrine, he should be forthwith succeeded by a Catholic." Eventu ally the Protestants were obliged to cede the point for the moment, but they held it in reserve, meantime, to be discussed on a future occasion: a subject of dispute which became important under the title of the "Ecclesiastical Reservation." Thus was concluded at length, on the 26th of September, 1555, at Augsburg, the religious peace which for a time put an end to the long contest. Free exercise of religion was granted legally to the Protestants throughout the whole of Germany, and they retained possession of all the revenues hitherto received from the ecclesiastical institutions. Neither Protestants nor Catholics were allowed to seek proselytes at the expense of either party, but every person was permitted to freely follow his own faith. And while every reigning prince was privileged to fix and establish the religion of his dominions, he was not at liberty to force any of his subjects to adhere to any one church beyond another; on the contrary, it was left open to any one, who might desire to do so from religious motives, to remove from one territory into another. Hence, in this respect, the progress of reform had not as yet attained that degree of tolerance which allowed the subject professing a faith different to the established creed of the country, equal rights to those enjoyed by all the rest of his fellow-subjects. Another law, however, by which the interests of the Protestants were beneficially promoted, was that their co-religionists became now likewise members of the imperial chamber of justice.

After the conclusion of this religious peace, the subject-matter of the accusations brought by Prince Maurice against the emperor came on for discussion in the college of the electoral princes; but, to the satisfaction of Charles, none of the other states of the empire would join in the investigation, and consequently the whole question was abandoned.

The division of the two religious parties in Germany was now established forever by this peace. Charles, who had devoted a great portion of his existence and power towards their reunion, experienced little or no satisfaction when he contemplated the present state of things—so different to the objects he had in view; and consequently

Germany had now become to him a country more and more indifferent and estranged. Meantime, the war with France proceeded at a very slow and unsatisfactory pace, and Charles was forced to witness how increasingly that power interfered in the affairs of Germany, while his genius saw beforehand the influence that government—to him so hateful—would gain over Europe, when once the power of the Spanish-Austrian house became divided, and which even now, while united under his reign, had scarcely been able to confine that ambitious nation within its boundaries. Hence he already beheld all the grand plans created within his comprehensive mind, either incompletely executed or altogether destroyed, and accordingly, the greater his desire to bring them to bear, the greater was the mortification he was forced to experience in the contemplation of their failure, and more especially did he feel this in his present afflicted state of body. On the other hand, the country towards which he had ever turned his eye with pleasurable, genial feelings—Spain—had now found in his son, Philip, a protector who possessed the general confidence of the nation. Accordingly, every thing now combined to strengthen the motives for the plan determined upon by Charles, and which, in imitation of Diocletian, he had some time had in contemplation, viz., to abdicate his throne, and end his days in the retirement of a monastic life.

In the autumn of 1555, he summoned his son Philip, who had shortly before married Mary, queen of England, to Brussels, and on the 25th of October of the same year, he solemnly transferred into his hands the dominion of the Netherlands. This ceremony took place in the same hall in which forty years before Charles had been declared of age. Here, when all were assembled, the invalid emperor, having with great difficulty risen from his seat, and supporting himself upon the shoulders of Prince William of Orange, addressed the princes and nobles in a speech so touching, that all were deeply affected, some even to tears. He declared, "that since the seventeenth year of his age, his whole thoughts had been occupied in promoting the glory of his empire; that he had been always anxious to be personally present in all his undertakings, that he might be an eye-witness of their progress and results, for which reason his entire reign had been almost one uninterrupted scene of pilgrimage and travelling; that he had been nine times to Germany, six to Spain, four to France, seven to Italy, ten to the Netherlands, twice to England, twice to Africa, and, finally, that he had made eleven voyages by sea. That now, however, his sinking body warned him to withdraw from the tumult and vexation of temporal affairs, and to transfer the burden of all these cares to younger shoulders. That if, during his many long-tried efforts, he had neglected or imperfectly settled any matters of importance, he earnestly besought the pardon of those who might thereby have suffered; and that, finally, he himself should always remember his faithful Netherlanders with love and affection to the end of his life, and continue to pray to God for their prosperity."—He then turned to his son Philip, who had dropped upon his knees and kissed the emperor's hand, and exhorted him in the most urgent and impressive manner to seek by every effort in his power to render his reign one replete with glory; and overcome with fatigue and emotion, he sunk down exhausted upon his chair.

On the 15th of January, in the ensuing year, 1556, his abdication of the crowns of Spain and Italy, in favor of his son Philip, took place in Brussels with equal solemnity; and in the following August, that of the Germanic empire, in favor of his brother Ferdinand, was effected by an embassy, at the head of which was Prince William of Orange. Ferdinand assumed the government from that moment on his own authority, but was only formally acknowledged by the body of electoral princes in the beginning of the year 1558, at Frankfort, where he swore to the stipulated terms of his election, and the imperial crown was solemnly placed on his head by the archchancellor of the empire, the Elector Joachim of Brandenburg, which, together with the sceptre, had been brought from Brussels at Charles's desire, by the imperial deputation.

Charles embarked with his two sisters for Spain, on the 17th of September, 1556, and he kept them with him until he reached Valladolid; there he parted from them, and now left entirely alone, he proceeded to a small building near the convent of St. Just, belonging to the order of St. Jerome, situated in the beautiful country of Estremadura, and which he had caused to be built expressly for himself. Here he now dwelt until his death, two years afterwards; living quite alone, not even seeing his sisters. His hours were divided between pious meditation and mechanical inventions, to which latter occupation he was much attached; he, however, still continued in correspondence with his son, and interested himself in the affairs of Spain. He, likewise, employed himself in his garden, which he took great pleasure in cultivating. It is related of him that he once made two watches, upon which he bestowed much ingenuity and labor, and placing them together on the table, he endeavored to make them go exactly alike. Several times he thought he had succeeded in his object, but all in vain—the one went too fast, the other too slow. At length he exclaimed: "Behold, not even two watches, the work of my own hands, can I bring to agree with each other according to a law, and yet, fool that I was, I thought I should be able to govern, like the works of a watch, so many nations, all living under a different sky, in different climes, and speaking a different language!"

Finally, shortly before his death, in order to celebrate in the most awe-striking manner the renouncement of life, and the mortification and corruption of all sense and feeling, he caused a solemn rehearsal to be made of his own funeral. Being placed in the coffin he had already prepared, the monks of the neighboring convent carried him in solemn procession to the church, where they performed over him the service of the dead. It was now that the mortal fever which had been so long raging in his body broke out. Medicine it was useless to offer him, his only desire being now to take the holy sacrament, which he received from the hands of the archbishop of Toledo. Shortly afterwards he died, on the 21st of September, 1558, in the fifty-sixth year of his age.

In his youth, and before he was bowed down with illness, Charles was of a noble manly figure, full of majesty and dignity. He spoke but little, and a laugh or smile was rarely seen upon his countenance, which was extremely pale; the color of his hair was blond, and his eyes blue; and in his whole appearance there was a mixture of the Flemish and Spanish character.

## CHAPTER XXI.

Ferdinand I., 1556-1564—His industrious Habits—Moderation and Tolerance—The Calvinists and Lutherans—Their Hostility towards each other—Ferdinand and Protestantism—The Foundation of the Order of Jesuits by Ignatius Loyola, 1540—Its rapid and universal Dissemination—The Council of Trent—Ferdinand's Ambassadors—Their Propositions refused—Their Letter to the Emperor—Death of Ferdinand I., 1564—Maximilian II., 1564-1576—His Qualifications and good Character—Bohemia—Poland—State of Tranquillity—William of Grumbach in Franconia—His Revolt and Excommunication—Gotha—The young Prince of Saxony—Joins Grumbach—His perpetual Captivity and Death in Styria—Grumbach's Execution—The mercenary Troops—Evils they produce—German Soldiers in Foreign Service—Death of Maximilian II., 1576—Rudolphus II., 1576-1612—His Indolence and Irresolution—Bad Counsellors—Religious Excitement renewed—The Netherlands—The Duke of Alba—The Elector Gebhard of Cologne and Agnes of Mansfeld, Canoness of Gerresheim—Gebhard excommunicated—John Casimir the Count Palatine—Calvinism—Donauwerth—Austria—Rudolphus against the Protestants—Deprives them of their Churches—Hungary—Revolt of Stephen Botschkai—The Emperor an Astrologist and Alchymist—Neglects his Government more and more—Tycho Brahe and Keppler—Rudolphus resigns Hungary to his brother Matthias—Bohemia—The Letter of Majesty—The Palatinate—The Evangelical Union—Juliers—Henry IV. of France joins the Union—The Catholic League—Prague—Revolt—The Emperor a Prisoner—His Death, 1612.

Ferdinand, when he became sovereign, continued to exhibit the same spirit of peace and justice he had shown during the reign of Charles V. All his actions and his whole character expressed a special goodness of heart, and the most kindly inclinations. Experience had rendered his mind more and more mature and settled, while he never swerved from his word, and occupation and activity were to him so necessary, that his vice-chancellor, Waldersdorf, says of him: "His club might have been more easily wrested from the hands of Hercules, than affairs of business from the emperor." He had read with great attention when a youth, the celebrated work by Erasmus on the education of princes; and he knew almost by heart the treatise of Cicero on our duties.

This excellent prince, who was a Catholic with his whole soul, and in his last will addressed the most urgent exhortations to his sons, to be firm and constant to the ancient and true religion, as their ancestors had been before them, including the Roman emperors and kings, as likewise the glorious princes of Austria and Burgundy, together with the kings of Spain—whence they had drawn down upon themselves the blessing of God—this prince, nevertheless, maintained and cherished within his heart a firm and unchanged tol erance and generosity towards those of a different opinion, which is innate in every well-disposed mind. In his own hereditary lands the new doctrine spread more and more, owing principally to the great want felt there for educational institutions, which obliged all those who were desirous of giving education to their children, more especially the nobility and higher classes, to send them in foreign countries, and generally in preference to the university of Wittenberg, which was distinguished above all the rest for its learning and science. Nevertheless, it never for a moment entered the mind of the emperor that it was necessary to prevent this from taking place; on the contrary, he only sought the means to produce reconciliation and union, and for this purpose he was especially anxious to avail himself of the council of Trent.

Religious peace had, it is true, restored the tranquillity of the empire externally; but internally, after such mighty storms, it could only proceed with difficulty and by slow degrees. The two parties continued to watch each other with fear and doubt; and the most absurd reports as to their hostile intentions were eagerly caught at and believed by either side. "If a prince happens to take into his service," says Zasius, the emperor's chancellor, "either a general or a cavalier, then distrust is immediately awakened; and every rustling leaf gives rise to suspicion."

The division among the Protestant party added materially to that already existing in Germany. The Calvinists, who, coming from Switzerland and France, became more and more distributed throughout the empire, gained increasing numbers of adherents, and were objects of hatred to the Lutherans, while the latter were equally so to the former. Among the princes the elector palatine was the first to declare in their favor. The Lutherans, however, divided themselves into two parties, that of the moderate and that of the extreme party. The former followed the spirit and principles of Melanchthon, the latter held to the very letter the doctrine of Luther, for which they battled with fiery zeal, because they venerated that alone, and believed they possessed its whole nature in words and forms. All those who at this time raised their voices so loudly in the Protestant church, only gave another proof how difficult it is for the human mind to maintain itself within the strict limits of moderation, and when it has exceeded them to resume its former equanimity. Instead of entering upon those calm and peaceful researches so desirable to enlighten the mind, or those Christian discussions in which the first principle is to pay homage to truth, they rendered Christianity the vehicle of the most furious passion, and employed it as a vent of the severest language against each other—produced often by the criticism of a sentence and even of a word. The emperor Ferdinand was but too correct, too well justified when, in his will, to which we have already referred, he thus expressed himself to his sons upon the subject of the numerous Protestants of his time: "While, instead of being of one mind among each other, they are so disunited, so unenlightened in their opinions and feelings, how can they be assured that what they put so much faith in is good and just? It is not the many beliefs, but only the one that can hold good. As they themselves, therefore, do not deny that they have among them so many different beliefs, the God of truth cannot surely be with them."

It has often been matter of astonishment, that the Protestant doctrine did not spread with equal rapidity throughout the whole of Germany, considering the favorable disposition evinced by the people to receive it; but the enigma is in a great measure explained by the speedy degeneration of Protestantism itself. How was it to be expected that a doctrine which so soon dissolved into a frivolous, spiritless dispute of words, and the converts to which overwhelmed each other with maledictions, could possibly succeed in gaining the hearts of the multitude? On the contrary, many parties were found in various directions, who, having gone over to the cause, in the course of a short time abandoned it, and returned to their ancient faith.

Another great obstacle to the rapid progress of the stream was, at this moment, presented in the institution of the order of Jesuits, founded in 1540 by a Spaniard, Ignatius Loyola, a man glowing with zeal, and of a very profound mind. This order, which was established more properly with the object of supporting the pontifical chair, spread its principles more and more widely throughout the whole of Europe.

Its constitution was based upon the unity and powerful co-operation of its members, and the most rigid obedience was its law. The head of the order lived in Rome; to him were addressed, with the most minute detail, the reports made by the directors or chief agents established in the provinces, and who again had under their control many sub-agents: thus descending gradually to the last member, whence the entire fraternity were governed by one spirit. The superiors examined each member's qualifications strictly, and during a sufficient length of time to enable them to place him in the office considered by the order as the most calculated to promote its views. Thus was formed a finely woven net, the meshes of which were laid with cunning and sagacity, and extended all over Europe. When, in 1540, Loyola received the approbation of the pope, he had ten disciples; in 1608, they numbered more than ten millions, and in 1700, they had augmented to twenty millions. As the members of the order were exempt from all ecclesiastical functions, and, indeed, even from clerical duties altogether, they were enabled to devote their whole time to science, and thus it resulted that they soon included in their ranks a considerable number of excellent teachers and writers, distinguished preachers, enthusiastic missionaries, and professors of every department of science. It was they who were enabled to enter the lists against the Protestants, defending the Catholic system with all their zeal, and rivalling them in powers of spiritual eloquence from the pulpit. All their efforts were directed against the new doctrine; they worked against it, whether in the character of confessors and governors of princes, or teachers among the people; and the efficient management, produced by the cordial co-operation so zealously exercised by the order, rendered their exertions successful. This institution, indeed, promoted materially the development of modern ages. It must not be forgotten that, in its day, this order rendered essential service in the education of youth; and if the civilization of the Catholic world in subsequent times has become far more perfect, and has ranked far above that existing at the end of the middle ages, it is to be ascribed alone to the exertions of the society or order of Jesuits. If, therefore, the operations of its members had been less devoted to external matters; if they had been more limited to the dominion of the mind; if the morality of the order had been equally simple and sincere in proportion as its wisdom was great and comprehensive; and if it had not attempted to grasp with invisible hand at the direction and government of states, then the entire world of Catholicism would have had just cause to bless unanimously its memory. We shall have occasion more than once in the course of our history to refer to the influential actors belonging to this order, whose operations in important moments produced great effect.

The emperor Ferdinand already learned to know their influence in the most clear and decided manner at the Council of Trent, although to his disadvantage. Matters did not proceed here as he wished. In order to appease the minds of his subjects in his hereditary lands, and in the hope, perhaps, of being able to avoid all division, he caused his ambassadors at the council to argue with great zeal in favor of certain propositions, whence he anticipated the most happy results. These points embraced the service of the holy communion under both forms and the marriage of priests, the sanction of which depended, as he said, only upon the indulgence of the church. The ambassadors, likewise, of France and Bavaria spoke on the same side, and the latter especially, concluded their arguments thus: "We can assure this assembly, with the most sincere and conscientious feeling, that nothing could or would prove more serviceable and beneficial at the present moment, towards reconciling the minds of Christians with each other, terminating the disputes of religion, preserving our own party in their faith, and restoring to it those that may have deserted from it, than the accordance of these legitimate and Christian demands of the emperor's ambassadors." But an equitable and acute judgment upon the subject of our affairs was not to be expected from an assembly composed for the greater part of foreigners and men totally unconversant with that which was peculiar to Germany, and what was best adapted for it under those circumstances; this, indeed, is sufficiently confirmed by the reports made to the emperor by his ambassadors, among whom were four bishops: "We now behold quite clearly," they write, "and the facts stare us in the face, although we can scarcely bring ourselves to acknowledge it without real pain and mortification, that nothing can be effected here without having recourse to intrigue. The Spaniards will not swerve an inch from the instructions of their king, while the Italians watch with eager eye the slightest signification made by the pope and his cardinals. The bishops from the other countries, who perchance are best aware of the present state of things, comprise the minority, and consequently can do nothing; because the majority of voices decide all things. From Germany itself we have only had the bishop of Louvaine, who attends in the name of the archbishop of Salzburg, and a few days since he was joined by the grand-vicar of Eichstädt. On the other hand, the Italian archbishops and bishops continue to arrive in troops, especially such as are highborn and wealthy. All, however, are dependent upon the nod of the pope's legate Simonetta; while it is generally known that a few good and pious bishops who spoke warmly in favor of a reform in the church, have, in consequence, been marked down in Rome on the condemned list. If, therefore, no end be put to these secret machinations and human passions, truly we know not what good can be expected from this quarter."

Such complaints were repeatedly made, and thence this last effort made by the emperor Ferdinand to restore the peace of Christendom by a searching investigation of ecclesiastical affairs, made under the sanction of the Church, completely failed. The cause of this ill success, however, was the same as that which had prevailed at Constance, and which rendered all attempts of the same kind—suggested by the German representatives with the most sincere and honest intentions—perfectly useless. This evil consisted in the mixture of foreigners presiding at these councils, whose knowledge of our nation was little or nothing, but whose influence, from the commencement of our history, in all external as well as internal affairs, always deprived us of peace.

Meantime, however, the council of Trent, besides a great number of dogmatical decisions, has pronounced some most excellent principles upon the morals of Christianity, which operate even to this day as rules in the doctrine of the Catholic church. It is in this field of the service of God that all parties are united; it is the same for all, and indicates equally to all the means by which they may show themselves to be true Christians in mind, word, and deed.

The council closed its sitting on the 9th of December, 1563; and shortly afterwards the emperor Ferdinand died, on the 15th of July, 1564, in the sixty-second year of his age. The convincing testimony in his favor recorded in history is, that during the difficult period when hatred and violence so often decided opinions, he, nevertheless, carried with him to his grave the glory of being praised as an excellent monarch by all parties, Catholics as well as Protestants.

Ferdinand had already proposed his eldest son, Maximilian, as his successor, at the assembly of electoral princes in Frankfort, in 1560, and they had acknowledged him as such. The father recommended his son in language worthy of record: "Endowed," he says, "with considerable intellectual powers, great address, mildness, and goodness of heart, he is likewise gifted with all the other princely virtues and good morals; possessing a disposition open to all that is truly just, good, and honorable, together with a sincere love for the holy empire of the German nation, the glory and prosperity of which it was his earnest desire to promote. Finally, he was master of the six principal languages usually spoken in Christendom, and was consequently enabled to regulate in person all transactions with foreign powers." Another honorable testimonial was rendered him by his Bohemian subjects when they recommended him to the Poles as their king: "Our Bohemia," they said, "is far better under his government than if it were ruled even by a father born among us; our rights, our liberties, and our laws are protected by him; he allows every thing to take its course without making any change. And what we justly regard as almost a work of miracle, is the generous impartiality and tolerance he evinces towards all classes of believers, by which he leads them to reciprocal love and harmony." And let it be remembered, that he exercised this spirit of peace in a period when the word tolerance was scarcely understood or perhaps known; nay, he publicly avowed the principle, "that God alone could hold dominion over the conscience." Such was the glorious character of this emperor, and it was by meritorious and praiseworthy conduct such as this, after the example of his good father, that he happily succeeded in establishing generally, throughout Germany, that tranquillity which, until that moment, it had never enjoyed since the religious divisions; a circumstance rendered still more striking, as it was effected at a period when, in the cause of religion, violent and sanguinary scenes were taking place in the Netherlands, and more especially in France, where the most dreadful acts were committed, and the universal massacre (on the eve of St. Bartholomew) of the Protestants, excited a feeling of horror throughout Europe.

The imperial chamber of justice, originally instituted for the purpose of eradicating the system of the Faustrecht, now succeeded completely in gaining the upper hand, and abolishing forever that brutal law. We find that the last expiring effort made to exercise its power was attempted about this time by a Franconian knight, William of Grumbach, who, with the remains of the savage horde formerly collected by Albert of Brandenburg, resumed operations in Franconia and spread devastation in different parts of that country. His attacks were more especially directed against the territory of the bishop of Wurzburg, and which prelate he actually shot in his own city. The imperial chamber pronounced the ban of the empire against the murderer, who took to flight and sought refuge in Gotha at the hands of the son of the unfortunate Elector John Frederick. He had succeeded, it appears, in filling that young and weak-minded prince with hopes of being able to reconquer for him the electorate of Saxony, and he was thus the means of leading the young duke to experience a fate far more distressing than that undergone by his father. The Elector Augustus, the brother of Maurice, marched with his army to execute the imperial ban, laid siege to Gotha during the entire winter, until both the duke and Grumbach were reduced to the necessity of surrendering themselves. The young prince was conveyed a prisoner to Vienna, where, on his arrival, a straw hat was placed on his head, and he was led through the streets in an open cart as a show, amid the mockery and derision of the populace. He was then taken to Styria, in Austria, where he died after a close imprisonment of twenty-eight years; Grumbach, however, was executed at once by being torn into quarters by four horses, after having previously undergone the most dreadful torture.

In lieu, however, of the Faustrecht, which contributed so much to degenerate the art of war under the feudal system, other evils, caused by those who regarded war merely in the light of a lucrative employment, now produced much calamity throughout the empire, as if to make the people feel the injurious results of all military institutions in which every free man is not required to arm and fight for his country. Those troops of mercenaries whose reckless ravages commence the moment they have sold themselves to a particular standard; the numerous depots established for recruiting and mustering the men; the continual marching to and fro in all parts of the land; together with the billeting of the wild and uncouth men thus suddenly collected together—all combined to create great discontent and irritation. The same complaints were now made as in the time of Maximilian I. In the representations made by Maximilian II. to the diet, he says: "The present system pursued by our German soldiers—in former times, distinguished beyond those of any other nation for their discipline, loyalty, and devotion—renders them more fit to be regarded in the character of barbarous savages; so much so that in the end their wanton and dissolute conduct will be carried on to such an extent that no honest man will be able to remain in his dwelling, nor will either house or farm be left longer in possession of their owner."

These complaints were met by creating new and more stringent laws for the discipline of the army; but the adoption of the most essential means of reform, and which had been suggested by the emperor himself, viz., the prohibition against the enlistment of troops in Germany by foreign princes, was not agreed to. The princes maintained: "That from time immemorial to serve for the honor and distinction of accomplishing chivalrous feats at arms in the armies of foreign princes, had ever continued to be regarded as an honorable privilege of national liberty, so long as such practice caused no injury to their native country; and that if this custom was abolished, the warlike spirit of the empire would be annihilated at once, and in the moment of danger no warriors would be at hand to aid in the general defence." In this language may be traced that of the time of Tacitus, when the youth of Germany, during the period of peace in their own tribe, incited to deeds of valor, entered the ranks of such other races as at that moment were engaged in war with each other.

In 1575 the emperor Maximilian succeeded in having his son Rudolphus elected king of the Romans, and he died in the following year in Ratisbon, on the same day and in the same hour that the conclusion of the imperial diet was made public.

The long reign of his successor, Rudolphus II., whose government accumulated over Germany fresh tempests and violent disorder, serves as another melancholy proof, that in difficult times irresolution and indolence may operate with greater evil than is produced even by a disposition the most wicked. The emperor Rudolphus cannot certainly be reproached with the latter feeling, neither can he be charged with ignorance or mental incapacity, but his mind was much more occupied with other subjects than the duties he had to fulfil as emperor, and consequently, almost every thing that occurred took place without his knowledge, and often against his wish. He was in fact in the hands, and entirely under the influence of bad counsellors.

The state of excitement on the subject of religion, which had recently become somewhat allayed, began now to resume its former violence when the Catholic princes, by the advice of the Jesuits, commenced the task of reforming their own dominions by forcing their Protestant subjects either to return to their ancient faith or quit the country. According to the treaty of the Augsburg peace of religion, the other princes could not venture to reproach or condemn them for this proceeding; at the same time, however, the Protestants perceived but too clearly that in so acting the Catholics had made a violent attack upon their liberty of conscience, and had given a fresh proof of their hostile intentions towards the Protestant party. France and the Netherlands presented a melancholy instance of the result to which these inimical acts must lead. The contest carried on by the latter country against Philip and the merciless duke of Alba,* for the sake of its religious liberty, produced not only the greatest excitement throughout Germany, on the frontiers of which the most dreadful scenes took place, but transferred by degrees the horrors of war and rapine to the empire itself, whither the Spanish army, impelled by disease and want, took refuge, and retreating from the Netherlands, marched into the Westphalian territory, where it extended its devastation throughout the land.

In addition to this, serious events took place at this moment in the German portion of the frontier countries. At Aix-la-Chapelle a body of emigrants from the Netherlands, with their Protestant minister, had augmented the number of their adherents to such an extent, that, emboldened by their success, they considered themselves justified in claiming the same rights as those enjoyed by the Catholics. They chose from among their number two burgomasters, and when their adversaries refused to acknowledge their authority, they flew to arms, and making themselves masters of the arsenal, they succeeded in obtaining what they demanded by force. In the neighboring district of Cologne scenes of still greater revolt took place. The Elector Gebhard was at this time enamored with the beautiful Agnes of Mansfeld, canoness of Gerresheim, and in order to make her his wife, he adopted the Protestant religion, a proceeding insisted upon by the counts, her brothers. The chapter of the cathedral and the corporation of Cologne, immediately appealed to Rome and the emperor, and obtained from both the ban of excommunication against the archbishop. As his successor, the chapter selected Prince Ernest of Bavaria, who, by means of the Bavarian and Spanish troops, took immediate possession of the land.

Gebhard took refuge at first in the Netherlands, and subsequently he removed to Strasburg, where he became dean of the chapter, and died in 1601. The Protestant princes quietly submitted to his deposition and expulsion, although the acquisition of a new vote in the electoral council

* The duke of Alba boasted, on his return to Spain, that he had put to death with the sword more than eighteen thousand men in the Netherlands, and he vowed that he would willingly, old as he was, sacrifice one of his own legs if the king—who was not endowed with too much indulgence—would only show a greater desire for war and its sanguinary accompaniments.

would have been to them of the utmost consequence. Possibly, they may have been induced to act this neutral part from their respect for religious peace, a principle both honorable and noble; but the public voice reproached them with having refused to assist Gebhard, because being themselves strict Lutherans they disapproved of his adopting the Calvinistic doctrine, which they hated almost as much as Catholicism itself. However this may be, it is quite certain that only one prince—a Calvinist—stepped forward to assist Gebhard: John Casimir, the count palatine, who advanced with a few troops against Cologne, and blockaded that city for a short time, but the return of the Bavarians and the want of money to pay the men very soon produced their dispersion.

This prince, John Casimir, was a zealous partisan of his church, and would hear nothing of the Lutheran doctrine, refusing it admission altogether into his territory; whence no part of Germany suffered so much from the melancholy effects of the hatred of the Protestant parties as this palatinate. The Elector Frederick III. had, previous to his decease, gone over to the Calvinists; and of his two sons, the younger and before-mentioned palatine, John Casimir, adhered to his father's principles, while the elder, Lewis the elector, was so devoted to the Augsburg confession, that he would not even allow the Calvinistic chaplain of his late father to pronounce the funeral oration over his remains. In accordance with this hostile feeling, he deprived the Calvinists of all their churches, and sent all their clergymen as well as teachers out of the country: their number amounting to more than two hundred. At the premature death, however, of Lewis, the guardianship of his son Frederick IV. devolved upon John Casimir, whence every thing underwent an entire change; the Lutherans in their turn were treated as his brother had treated the Calvinists, and young Frederick, then only nine years old, was forthwith removed from all connection with Lutheranism, and strictly educated in the catechism of Calvin. This was called Christian zeal of faith! Through such zeal, however, the palatinate was forced to change its religion three times in the course of sixty years. No wonder, therefore, if the old church felt itself justified in proceeding as it did against the new one, since the latter was so zealous against its own disciples. Subsequently, indeed, this very dissension of Cologne produced a similar contest in Strasburg, whither Gebhard had withdrawn with three canons of his chapter, Protestants like himself; and the town of Donauwerth, which until then had remained a free imperial town, and had adopted the reformed principles of faith, brought upon itself the ban of the empire on account of its religious disputes, and, in 1607, fell into the hands of the duke of Bavaria, who executed the sentence of excommunication pronounced against it.

But, during the reign of Rudolphus II., Austria itself was more especially the scene of great agitation and discord. Maximilian II. had granted to the Protestant states the free exercise of their religion, and even allowed them to supply themselves with a form of church service which was prepared for them by a theologian of Rostock, David Chyträus; as, however, the emperor wished at the same time to exclude their style of worship from Vienna altogether, he furnished them with various churches situated in the vicinity of that city. Their number became very soon considerbaly augmented, several of their teachers, particularly a certain Doctor Opicius, were, very unjustifiably, most zealous in their endeavors to gain over to their side all they could of such as were of an opposite or different faith; and the complaints against them growing more and more numerous, Rudolphus, swayed as he always was by the influence of party counsellors, proceeded in his measures against the Protestants to such extremes, as to deprive them altogether of the churches so recently given to them, and withdrew from them even their right of citizenship throughout all the towns of Austria. These proceedings, however, very soon excited so much discontent and indignation, while, on the other hand, the internal disorders of Hungary, together with the troubles produced by the presence of the Turks in that country, were so great, that he was forced to return to measures of a more mild and pacific nature.

In Hungary itself great discontent was produced by his government, partly because he paid little or no attention to the affairs of that country, but more especially because he not only never attended in person at any of the states' assemblies, and had never even once visited that kingdom, but permitted his German soldiers to commit every sort of insolence and violence without control. Thence, at the commencement of the seventeenth century, a most serious revolt took place there, at the head of which was a nobleman, Stephen Botschkai, who united with the Turks, and took possession of the greater portion of the country. Nevertheless, in spite of this dangerous state of his kingdom, the emperor grew more and more indifferent and negligent, and took no longer the least interest in its government. Celestial and natural science occupied his attention much more than the affairs of his dominion, and this application very soon brought him into the association of those who pretended to teach him the prophecies of the stars and the art of making gold. Thence, while his court comprised a mixture of such deceivers, and the most learned men of the day—such as Tycho Brahe and Keppler—so likewise in the mind of the emperor, trivial and puerile indications became proportionably confounded with sentiments of a nobler nature. Productions of ancient art, statues, chiselled stone work, as well as pictures, were objects of his greatest delight, and he devoted large sums of money in their collection; while, however, on the other hand, his alchymical laboratory, where he sought to produce his manufacture of gold, possessed no less attraction for him, and such members of his government as wished to communicate with him upon important and pressing affairs connected with the empire, were often forced to extend their researches after him to the retirement of his stables, where he was accustomed to pass a portion of the day. This inactivity and carelessness, the revolution in Hungary, together with the disorders prevailing in the hereditary Austrian provinces themselves, could not be regarded with an eye of indifference by the brothers and cousins of the emperor, more especially as he himself had no family. They accordingly deliberated together what was best to be done for the well-being of their house, and they finally concluded a treaty, in 1606, according to the terms of which Matthias, the eldest brother of the emperor, was empowered to restore order forthwith both in Hungary and Austria. At first, the emperor was much dissatisfied with this arrangement; after a few years, however, he yielded his consent, and voluntarily resigned to Matthias the upper and lower portions of the Austrian territory along the Ens, together with the kingdom of Hungary: "in order that this country which, in the absence of the emperor, had endured so much during a war of sixteen years, might, under the government of Matthias, recover its tranquillity and prosperity." And, in reality, this prince did succeed in restoring peace in Hungary, and shortly afterwards, on the death of Botschkai, in subjecting it altogether to his authority.

Beyond his imperial dignity, nothing was now left to the emperor Rudolphus but the kingdom of Bohemia. The Protestant states of this country, anxious to avail themselves of the favorable moment in which their sovereign was placed without power, and at variance with the other members of his family, left him no peace until they at length obtained from him, in 1609, the permission for the free exercise of their religion, the establishment of their own consistory, the surrender of the academy of Prague, together with the right of building fresh churches and schools in Bohemia, in addition to those they already possessed. This important document is called the letter of majesty, and it was this said document which formed the first pretext for the thirty years' war.

Feelings of distrust and doubt had now gradually resumed their sway among the religious parties of Germany. At the same time, the division existing in the house of Austria, which had been the support of the Catholics, produced a more immediate alliance between the Protestant states, and urged them to form a new league, offensive and defensive. The palatine house was more especially active in the promotion of this object, and zealously contributed all its influence; their efforts in the cause, however, only produced a fatal result to the league, for as the palatinate adhered so closely to the Calvanistic doctrine, the Lutherans were induced to think unfavorably of the alliance, and the majority of their party refused to join it. When, therefore, Frederick, the elector palatine, succeeded in the year 1608, after great exertion, in constituting a new alliance, to which the name of the *Evangelical Union* was given, he found himself joined only by the margraves of Brandenburg, the Count Palatine Philip Lewis, of Neuburg, the duke of Wurtemberg, and the margrave of

Baden, together with the three principal cities: Strasburg, Nüremberg, and Ulm. This union was based upon the principle of mutual support in council and arms, and its especial object was to protect religion; the palatine to have the direction of affairs during peace, and its term to extend to ten years. Endeavors were made to enrol several other members, and the elector of Brandenburg was not altogether unwilling to join it, but Saxony was most decided in its refusal to do so, replying, "That if the nature of the affair was gravely considered, it would be found on the one hand, that the union was not at all necessary; and on the other, that in reality its results must be nothing else but a separation and dissolution of the whole empire." In truth, if the palatine house was really influenced in the affair by ambitous and impure motives, it had, subsequently, but too much reason to regret it, for it suffered severely in consequence.

In the following year, 1609, an event took place in which the Evangelical Union took an immediate and active share. Duke John William of Juliers, who possessed the beautiful lands of the Lower Rhine, Juliers, Cleves, Berg, and Mark, died the 25th of March in that year, without leaving any children. He had four sisters, who were all married to German princes, and not only their husbands, but likewise other distant relations, laid claim to the inheritance. Two of the claimants, however, the elector of Brandenburg, and the count palatine of Neuburg, took first possession and signed a treaty at Düsseldorf, by which they agreed to govern the country in conjunction until the matter was definitively settled. The emperor, however, displeased with the arbitrary conduct of these two princes, sent his brother, the Archduke Leopold, bishop of Passau, in order to take possession of the land as a vacant fief of the empire. He arrived with some troops, but could gain nothing more of the country than the city and fortress of Juliers, where he was admitted by the governor; he, however, caused fresh bodies of soldiers to be raised in Alsace, and resolved to maintain the rights of the emperor by force. The Evangelical Union, finding the house of Austria mixing itself up in this affair, came forward and prepared to march to the aid of the two princes thus threatened; while Henry IV. of France now joined the league, and promised to give the cause his support. It is well known with what grand projects this monarch was constantly occupied, even to the entire transformation of the whole of Europe, and how desirous he was to reduce the Austrian house in order to form Europe into a federative republic, which it was his intention should furnish one common army wherewith to drive the Turks out of Europe. His alliance with the Evangelical Union had these objects in view; and he fixed the year 1610 for the commencement of his plans against Austria. The army of the union accordingly marched into Alsace in the spring of this same year, attacked and defeated the few thousands collected there by the Archduke Leopold, and, in order to justify these proceedings, accused the emperor of having acted illegally in the affair of Juliers. The emperor, it was said, according to the ancient right of the empire, ought not to have attempted to decide this matter alone, but in conjunction with an appointed number of electoral and other princes.

The sudden assumption of arms, and the hostile measures pursued by the union wherever their army appeared throughout the territories of the spiritual princes, excited the most bitter feeling among the Catholics; for their troops had now distributed themselves throughout all the sees of the Rhine: Mentz, Treves, Cologne, Worms, Spires, and others, levying contributions, and exercising the greatest violence in every direction. The Catholics, however, now determined to unite together likewise, and concluded an alliance at Würzburg, in 1610, for nine years against the union, which they called the Catholic League. The members it comprised included all the spiritual princes, together with the princes of the house of Bavaria; and in order to ensure uninterrupted unity among them, the chief direction over the entire body was confided into the hands of Maximilian, duke of Bavaria. Thus this Catholic League was rendered much more firm than the Evangelical Union, which, not having any especially chosen head during the war, was forced to appoint a general, to which honor, as they all consisted of lay princes, each considered himself entitled. In other respects the Catholic League was based nearly upon the same principles as the Evangelical Union.

This league now took to arms likewise;

but as Henry IV. of France was assassinated about this time, the members of the union showed themselves more disposed to terminate matters in an amicable way, and both parties shortly afterwards laid down their arms.

The old emperor embittered his few remaining years with vexatious quarrels with his family. He was much dissatisfied with his brother Matthias, nor was he indeed attached to any other of his relations except the aforesaid Archduke Leopold, bishop of Passau. He felt, therefore, desirous of giving him his kingdom of Bohemia—the last in his possession—and in the year 1611, according to a plan calculated very badly for the promotion of his object, he empowered him to march with his troops from Passau and enter Bohemia at their head. The states of the kingdom, who naturally imagined that in this proceeding hostile intentions were directed against their religion, took to arms, and making the emperor a prisoner in his own castle of Prague, they summoned to their aid Matthias, who for a considerable time had calculated upon the crown of Bohemia. He obeyed their call at once, and entered the city amidst their acclamations, while Rudolphus was obliged, after a bitter and mortifying negotiation, to yield the crown to his brother. It is said, that during this time of trouble, and in the irritation of the moment, he burst open the window of his room and exclaimed, in words fatally prophetic—as they turned out: "Prague, ungrateful Prague! through me you became elevated, and to-day you ungratefully desert and turn your back upon your benefactor! May you be pursued by the vengeance of God, and may His curse fall upon you and throughout Bohemia!"

Of all his crowns, the last and only one remaining to him now was that of the empire; death, however, which soon afterwards delivered him from all his troubles, saved him likewise from the final disgrace of resigning this, which mortification, it is but too probable, he would have been forced to undergo; he died on the 20th of January, 1612, aged sixty years.

## CHAPTER XXII.

**Matthias I., 1612-1619—His Coronation—Its Pomp and Splendor deceptive—The Protestants—Increase of General Discontent—Austria—Aix-la-Chapelle—Cologne—The Prince-Palatine Wolfgang William, and the Elector of Brandenburg—Their Quarrel—Box on the Ear—Baneful Consequences—Foreign Allies—The young Archduke Ferdinand—Elected King of Bohemia—His Character—His Devotion to Catholicism and Hatred of the Protestants—Banishes the New Faith from his Lands—The Electoral Princes—Ferdinand warned against his Proceedings by the Elector of Saxony—Bohemia—The Letter of Majesty shamefully infringed—The Protestant Churches destroyed—Indignation and Revolt of the Protestants—Their Defender, Count Matthias of Thurn—Counts Martinitz and Slavata—Their Hostility to the Protestants—Prague—The Council-Hall—Martinitz and Slavata thrown out of the Window—General Revolution—The Emperor's Alarm and Desire for Peace—Ferdinand's Declaration in Reply—Commencement of the Thirty Years' War—Count Ernest of Mansfeld, the Leader of the Protestants—His great Military Genius and Heroic Character—Death of Matthias I., 1619—Ferdinand II., 1619 to 1637—Count Thurn and the Bohemians in Vienna—Surround the Emperor in his Palace—Ferdinand unexpectedly rescued—The Bohemians depose him—The Elector-Palatine Frederick V., Son-in-law of James I. of England, King of Bohemia, 1619—His Irresolution and Pusillanimity—Ferdinand and Maximilian of Bavaria—Their Alliance—Superiority of the Imperialists over the Bohemians—Battle of Weissenberg, near Prague, 1620—The Bohemians defeated and their King put to flight—His Abdication—Prague capitulates—Bohemia severely punished by Ferdinand—Thirty thousand Families banished the Country.**

MATTHIAS, the eldest brother of the late emperor, was now chosen successor to the imperial crown, and was crowned at Frankfort, on the 24th of June, 1612. The ceremony was performed amid a display of stately pomp and splendor such as had not been witnessed for a length of time—if, perhaps, at all. All the electors, except the elector of Brandenburg, were present, and a host of the other princes of the empire. "It seemed," says an historian, "as if they had assembled in such numbers in order to take a final leave of each other, for after this occasion they never again collected in a body so numerous." Matthias himself had in his suite alone three thousand persons, two thousand horses, and one hundred carriages, drawn each by four horses; and the other princes appeared equally well attended, in proportion to their means. Festival succeeded festival, and foreigners, witnessing all the grand and brilliant scenes that passed, and all the joy and hilarity that everywhere prevailed, must have regarded Germany as the first country in the world, especially when they beheld this assemblage of all its princes thus met in, apparently, friendly association. But behind this galaxy of royal and noble personages hovered the spirit of dissension; the profound observer might have recognised in the joy expressed by the Catholics the hopes they entertained for their party, based upon the activity and firmness of the new emperor; and in the delight evinced by the Protestants, he might have perceived the expectations they formed, founded upon the illness expressed in his appearance. Prince Christian of Anhalt, one of the most active among the latter party, made rather a humorous observation in reference to the double meaning in which this festival must be regarded: "If it should come to a dance, our emperor Matthias will make no very high springs."

In truth, the new emperor did not by any means show the activity and energy which had been anticipated from him; it appeared as if he had only compelled his late brother to resign his crowns in order to perpetuate his indolence and irresolution. On the other hand, the passions of the multitude continued to operate more and more seriously, and prepared the way for those violent and disastrous eruptions which burst forth again even during the reign of Matthias. In the Austrian territories, the religious parties, excited by their preachers from the pulpit, resumed their violence towards each other with redoubled fury, all human relationship between the contending parties disappeared and became annihilated, for such hatred as adheres to that which is held most sacred in man remains the most implacable of all.

In other parts of Germany, some very serious occurrences took place about this time. Fresh disturbances broke out in Aix-la-Chapelle as well as in Cologne, between its inhabitants and the two princes, governors of the territory of Juliers, because the latter, to the injury of the former, had raised the small town of Mühlheim, on the Rhine, to the rank of a city. In both these cases, the emperor decided in favor of the Catholic party, and consequently excited fresh anxiety in the minds of the Protestants. His judgment, however, in the cause of the Mühlheim dispute would have produced but little effect, had not both the princely houses who had possession of the patrimonial estates of Juliers, become divided with each other. The prince-palatine, Wolfgang William, had been accepted as the future husband of a princess of the house of Brandenburg, and he paid a visit to the court of Berlin upon business connected with this affair. There, however, while at dinner, and heated with wine, a dispute arose between him and the elector; both forgot each other, and the latter gave the prince-palatine a blow on the ear. Never, perhaps, did such an insignificant circumstance produce more grave and serious results in the history of the country; they operated upon the whole system of the empire down to the latest period of its records. The indignant prince quitted Berlin immediately; and out of hatred to the house of Brandenburg, he allied himself with the house of Bavaria, by marrying one of its princesses, and adopted the Catholic religion. The elector of Brandenburg, on the other hand, who was in dread lest Wolfgang William, with the aid of the league or the Spaniards, should attack his portion of the Juliers territory and wrest it from him, claimed the assistance of the Netherlanders, who were still at war with the Spaniards; and in order to satisfy them and ensure their aid, he abandoned the Lutheran church and adopted that of the Calvinists. Accordingly, the Juliers possessions were attacked by the allies of both sides; the Netherlanders occupied Juliers itself, and the Spaniards, commanded by Spinola, held possession of Wesel; and thus both these armies brought into effect the decree of the emperor pronounced against Aix-la-Chapelle and Mühlheim. Accordingly, the dissensions throughout the empire became more and more confirmed in their hostility, and the German states commenced forming alliances with foreign countries.

The uneasiness and anxiety of the Protestants became now much increased by the selection which was made of a successor to the imperial throne. Matthias himself, as well as his two brothers, Maximilian and Albert, were without any children, and as the affairs of the empire presented no attraction sufficiently great to induce the latter princes to undertake the government, they renounced all claim to the succession of the Austrian states, and proposed as their substitute their cousin, the young Archduke Ferdinand, who already possessed Styria, Carinthia, and Carniola. The emperor was very much opposed to this arrangement, but his brothers were so urgent in their representations that he was obliged finally to yield. Accordingly, Ferdinand was acknowledged at the diet of 1617 as future king of Bohemia, and three weeks afterwards he was crowned as such with great pomp at Vienna. The states demanded nothing beyond the confirmation of the rights they had hitherto enjoyed, and the non-interference of the new king with the affairs of government during the lifetime of the emperor.

This Ferdinand, in the course of his reign, became a principal cause of all the violent commotions and revolutions that were produced in his time, and as he has at all times been more or less subjected to severe condemnation or impassioned praise, his acts merit here a more impartial investigation and equitable judgment. His education, which he received in the university of Ingolstadt, in Bavaria, was superintended more especially by the Jesuits, under the eyes of William, duke of Bavaria, a zealous Catholic, and, from his boyhood upward, the most strict principles of Catholicism were instilled into his mind. Consequently he firmly believed in that one church, by which alone he could hope to obtain salvation, and he held it to be the first duty of his life to use every means at his command, whether by the gentle power of reason, or by the more definite argument of the sword to bring back those who had renounced the faith, and support all who adhered to it—for the salvation of the soul, as he had been taught, "took the precedence of every other human consideration." Whence the faithful maintenance of these principles constituted the aim and direction of his whole life; he looked upon himself as appointed by God to be the champion of the Catholic church and the restorer of the ancient faith. And of this conscientious belief he never attempted to make the least mystery; he entered the arena openly and honestly, and herein is presented a grand and noble feature in his history. For every man who undeviatingly and obstinately pursues, with all the power and energy of his nature, that which he has recognised as just and sacred, is assuredly worthy of honorable appreciation. And if Ferdinand, throughout his entire career, and in the error of his conviction, did continue to believe that that same God who vouchsafes to spread the light of his sun with equal mercy over nations of every faith, was only to be worshipped in one exclusive form, and persisted in his efforts to establish with fire and sword this said form of devotion all over the world, those alone were answerable for such results who filled his mind while yet a child with such intolerant doctrines, and which they only strengthened more and more in the youth, and matured in the man.

The young prince had no sooner become lord over his states than he commenced reforming them, by reintroducing the ancient form of divine service. He maintained the principle, that the sovereign of a country, in order to promote one uninterrupted unity of thought and action, ought not to tolerate more than one established religion in his dominions; and as, by the treaty of the Augsburg religious peace, no other resource was left to the Protestants but expatriation, he compelled those who would not join the ancient faith to leave the country. These measures were very severe, as nothing can be more trying to the feelings of a truly sincere and conscientious man, than to be forced to quit the soil of his ancestors and the home rendered so dear to him from childhood by the ties of love and affection. Such harsh proceedings necessarily produced most serious consequences throughout the territories of Ferdinand. Above all others of his subjects, the inhabitants of the mountainous districts were the first to rise in opposition; accustomed as they were to live uninterruptedly amidst their mountains, and existing in a state of complete isolation from the rest of their fellow-subjects in the lowlands—wholly occupied as they were with the grand and eternal creations of nature around them—they scarcely troubled themselves with the scenes of human contention and dissension occurring beyond their native hills. They adhered, therefore, with far greater obstinacy and firmness to their peculiar habits and opinions, which they regarded, like the soil they dwelt upon, as their hereditary birthright. Nevertheless, in the measures adopted by the young prince, so much resolution was combined with temper, and he evinced so much determined seriousness, that he succeeded in quelling the disturbances excited by this discontent almost before their outbreak; and although, as a warning, he had caused to be erected in various parts places of execution for the most turbulent, still tranquillity was effected without its being necessary to have recourse to them, or even to shed a drop of blood. Thence, within a few short years, as if produced by a miracle, not a single

Protestant church was left standing, nor a Protestant sermon allowed to be preached throughout the whole of those dominions in which, until then, the majority of the inhabitants had professed the Protestant faith. Such persevering energy displayed by so young a prince, very naturally excited great hopes in the one party, while it produced serious alarm in the other. The united states of Germany, and especially the electoral-palatinate, beholding now, in the elevation of Ferdinand as chief of the Austrian house, fresh cause for exertion, renewed and strengthened their bond of union. They endeavored, by every means in their power, to gain over to their party the elector of Saxony; but all in vain. His unwillingness to join the union was, no doubt, produced principally by his dislike to the Calvinistic doctrine; but in this resolution he was also influenced by his sincere desire for the preservation of peace throughout the empire—a desire participated in by all the Lutheran princes, more particularly since the death of Maurice. A letter from the elector of Saxony to the Archduke Ferdinand proves, at least, that this feeling was sincerely cherished by him; he therein exhorts him thus: "That as things had reached that sad state that little or no good understanding could be found to exist any longer among the states of Germany, and all confidence had nearly vanished, he would earnestly recommend him to do his utmost towards the re-establishment of both, if only in a partial degree. For if matters continued to remain in their present dangerous condition, when recourse was had to measures of extreme severity rather than to those of a more mild and simple nature, it was evident these attempts to effect a cure of the evils existing must lead either to the total ruin of the one or the other of the two parties; or, after having caused much sacrifice of blood, and produced the destruction of the country and its inhabitants, end in adopting that middle course which might now still be made available without any violent or dangerous means." The import of these words was like an announcement of future events, and might have opened the eyes even of Ferdinand himself to the contemplation of the coming struggles, if he had not held them immoveably fixed upon one point. Circumstances, however, very soon indicated, in still more expressive and forcible colors, the danger which threatened even the proximity of his own house.

Since the nomination of Ferdinand as future king of Bohemia, the whole body of Protestants in that country very soon had reason to observe much greater activity and assurance among the Catholics. Report, which in extraordinary times is ever more active in spreading alarm and terror than in ordinary periods, was now busily occupied in announcing the most arbitrary measures against the Protestants. "The letter of majesty which guarantied their security and liberty, was now no longer valid, it having been extorted from King Rudolphus,"—such was the language of the Catholics. "When King Ferdinand arrived," they said, "it would be found that with their new king they would receive likewise new laws;" while some again exclaimed, "Then more heads must be decapitated, and property transferred into other hands, and many a beggar would be made rich therewith," &c. In addition to this, when Ferdinand did homage in Moravia, pictures were everywhere circulated in which the Bohemian lion and the Moravian eagle were represented bound in chains, while a sleeping hare, with eyes open, was introduced to indicate that the states, with their eyes widely opened as they were, were still not able to perceive the fate that threatened them: these, and many similar demonstrations, augmenting in number as they progressed from place to place and mouth to mouth, excited increasing terror and dismay in the minds of all.

At length a cause was soon presented whereupon to base the foundation of open hostility. In the aforesaid letter of majesty the Protestants of Bohemia were granted the privilege of building new churches, but the present government restricted its meaning to the Protestant provinces of the kingdom, and refused its application to the Catholic provinces. The Protestant party, nevertheless, insisted that the article included all their co-religionists throughout the land. Accordingly, in 1617, the Protestants residing in the jurisdiction of the archbishop of Prague, built for themselves a church in the small town of Clostergrab, while those in the territory of the abbot of Braunau also erected one in the latter place. The archbishop and abbot would neither of them tolerate their existence, and they both appealed to the emperor; and as soon as ever the buildings were completed, the archbishop put into execution an imperial decree, according to which the church in Clostergrab was razed to the very foundation, and that in Braunau was closed; and as in consequence of this arbitrary act the inhabitants of the town rose up in opposition against it, several of them were cast into prison.

The Protestants, however, now loudly complained of this violation of the letter of majesty, and they found a determined champion for their cause in Count Matthias of Thurn. This nobleman, who was a native of Gratz, on the borders of Italy, but who had long since resided in Bohemia, supported their cause and its privileges with all the warmth and zeal of his Italian blood, and being chosen at once as defender of the Evangelists in Bohemia, he, as such, convoked the Protestant states to meet in Prague. Several petitions were forwarded to the emperor, in which his majesty was earnestly besought to remove the causes of complaint, and to order the liberation of the imprisoned citizens of Braunau.

The emperor's reply was very harshly worded. Therein he characterized the resistance made by the inhabitants of Braunau and Clostergrab as a revolt, and he condemned the states for having occupied themselves with the affairs of citizens who to them were strangers, and for having held illegal meetings, and seeking, by the false reports they made of the danger to which the letter of majesty was exposed, to alienate from his majesty the love and fidelity of his subjects, &c.; while the threat with which it concluded, "that the matter should be investigated, and each should be treated according to his merits," sufficed to produce in the minds of all, excited as they already were, still greater cause to anticipate and prepare for the worst results. To this was now added the report that the said document had not issued from Vienna, but had been prepared in Prague itself, in the office of the imperial governors, and more especially superintended by two Catholic privy-counsellors, Martinitz and Slavata. The indignation of the Protestants was now directed at once against them, as the more immediate objects. Both these noblemen had long been hated, because they refused to take any part in the procuration of the letter of majesty nine years previously; while many cruel acts were laid to their charge, by which they had at various times displayed their zeal for the Catholic church. Among the rest, it was related of Martinitz, that he had caused his Protestant dependents to be hunted out of the Catholic church on his estate, with his own dogs; while of Slavata it was said, that he had compelled his people to adopt the Catholic faith by refusing to allow them the service of baptism in the church, or burial in consecrated ground.

Rendered more indignant and furious by these reports, the deputies of the states, armed to the teeth, presented themselves, on the 23d of May, 1618, before the imperial governors and such of the council as were then assembled in the council-hall of the castle of Prague, and demanded whether or not they had been present in council when the imperial document in question, so harshly and inimically worded, had been deliberated upon, and if they had voted for it? And when the governors replied, that in order to decide upon the answer to be given to such an important question, it would be necessary to have the presence of the absent members of the council, several of the deputies stepped forward and exclaimed: "We know full well that the head burgraves, Adam von Sternberg, and Diphold von Lobkowitz, now present, did attend during the composition of that hated writing, but we are likewise aware that they did so unwillingly, and did not sanction its adoption." Saying which they advanced and conducted them into another room for safety. The other deputies meantime rushed upon Count Martinitz, and dragging him to the window, ejected him forthwith into the court below. All stood now aghast and trembling; when Count Thurn, pointing to Slavata, exclaimed to his confederates: "Noble friends, yonder you behold the other!" upon which they immediately seized him and precipitated him after his colleague. The next doomed to the same fate was the private secretary, Fabricius, who was known to be the sycophant of the two preceding victims. Wonderful to relate, however, although the depth of their fall was more than fifty-six feet, they escaped with life, because, in their descent, they fell, happily for them, upon an immense pile of paper shavings and other soft materials; and even afterwards, when they were assisted to their homes, they were no less fortunate in getting clear of the shots that were fired at them as they were led away.

The Bohemians endeavored to justify this act by referring to several examples of the same kind in ancient history; among the rest to the period when the Romans precipitated traitors from the Tarpeïan rock, and to the portion of the Old Testament in which it is found recorded that Queen Jezebel was thrown from a high window for having persecuted the people of God. Nevertheless, they were well aware that such a plea of justification would not secure them against the punishment that must follow, unless they made immediate preparations for self-defence. Accordingly, the castle was garrisoned with their own troops; all persons in office took the oath of fidelity to the states; all the Jesuits, who were considered as the main cause of the hostile feeling evinced against the Protestants, were banished from the country; and, finally, a council of thirty noblemen was established for the government of the land. All this indicated the determination of the people to defend themselves to the last, and in all these preparations the chief mover and director was Count Thurn, whose whole soul was devoted to the cause.

The emperor was not a little disconcerted when he received the news of what was passing. For whence could he receive the aid necessary to put down these revolutionary acts and restore order in Bohemia? Discontent, indeed, was scarcely less formidably expressed even in his Austrian territories, while in Hungary its demonstration was equally as serious.

Conciliation appeared to be the only means of preserving to the house of Austria that important country, and even the confessor and usual counsellor of the emperor, Cardinal Klesel, the most zealous opponent of the Protestants, advised that course. But such considerations were most strenuously opposed by young Ferdinand: "It is of the utmost importance that men should know," says he, in writing to the emperor, "that God himself has appointed the troubles of Bohemia; for he has manifestly struck the Bohemians with blindness, that by means of the direful deed, which to every rational being, whatever his religion, must appear to be hateful, unchristian, and culpable, the grand pretext of the rebels, that they were engaged in the cause of religion, might be completely frustrated. For under this pretext they have hitherto only sought to rob their rulers of all their rights, all their revenues, and all their subjects. If, therefore, government is of divine authority, the conduct of these men must originate with the devil, and it is impossible that God should approve of the concessions heretofore made by the government. Possibly He may have permitted these extremities to come to pass in order that the rulers may at once break loose from this state of bondage to their own subjects." Accordingly, it was his opinion, that nothing remained but to have recourse to arms.

From this epistle of Ferdinand we at once perceive the firmness of his principles. From words he immediately proceeded to action, levied soldiers in every quarter, and manifested such determination, that it was evident he would not suffer the indecision of the emperor to thwart his career. And at his instigation, and that of the other archdukes, backed by the pope, the pacific Cardinal Klesel was unexpectedly arrested, and charged with a variety of crimes. The intention was to remove him from the presence of the old and weak emperor, who was now without support, and obliged to resign all to the archdukes. From this moment the impotency of the emperor was complete, and all hopes of an amicable pacification of Bohemia lost.

The Bohemians, likewise, took to arms, and possessed themselves of every city in their country as far as Budweis and Pilsen, which were still occupied by the imperial troops. They obtained assistance, quite unlooked-for, in the person of one who may be regarded as one of the most remarkable heroes of that day, and furnishes a distinguished example of a single individual, who, without territory and people, by the mere celebrity of his name, gathered round him legions of brave soldiers, and, like the ancient warrior-princes of Germany in the time of the Romans, conducted them as his *Gefolge* or retinue, for hire and booty, whithersoever his prowess was needed. Men of this character came forth at this period likewise, as the signs of an extraordinary age thrown out of its usual course. Their armies were maintained and furnished by the war; the war had to sustain itself; and therein is the mystery explained how it continued to rage on upon the German soil for thirty years. Count Ernest of Mansfeld, a warrior from his youth, was of a bold and enterprising spirit; he had already encountered many dangers, and had just been raising some troops for the duke of Savoy against the Spaniards. The duke, who now no longer required them, gave him permission to serve in the cause of the Evangelical Union of Germany; and by that body he was dispatched with 3000 men to Bohemia, as having apparently received his appointment from that country. He appeared there quite unexpectedly, and immediately took from the imperial army the important city of Pilsen.

Meanwhile the emperor Matthias died on the 10th of March, 1619, after having witnessed in quick succession the interment of his brother Maximilian and his consort; and the Bohemians, who acknowledged his sovereignty while living, now resolved to renounce his successor Ferdinand, whose hostile intentions were already too clearly expressed.

Ferdinand attained the throne under circumstances the most perplexing. Bohemia in arms, and threatening Vienna itself with invasion; Silesia and Moravia in alliance with them; Austria much disposed to unite with them; Hungary by no means firmly attached, and externally menaced by the Turks; besides which, encountering in every direction the hatred of the Protestants, against whom his zeal was undisguised. But in these circumstances Ferdinand manifested his undaunted firmness and courage: "Notwithstanding these imminent perils," says Khevenhüller, "this illustrious prince never desponded; he still retained his religion and confidence in God, who took him under His protection, and, contrary to all human expectation, delivered him through this Red sea."

Count Thurn advanced upon Vienna with a Bohemian army, and when he was questioned respecting the purpose of his expedition, he answered, "That he marched in search of any collected bodies of troops or people, and wherever he found them he would forthwith disperse them. That in future there must be perfect equality between Catholics and Protestants, and the former must not, as heretofore, hold the ascendency, and, as it were, float on the surface like oil." He came before Vienna, and his men fired even upon the imperial castle itself, where Ferdinand, surrounded by open and secret foes, had taken up his quarters. He dared not leave his capital, for by so doing, Austria, and with it the preservation of the empire itself, must have been sacrificed. But his enemies looked upon him as lost; and they already spoke of confining him in a convent, and educating his children in the Protestant faith. At this most critical moment, when Thurn was in the suburbs of Vienna, encamped before the gate of Stuben, on the 10th of June, 1619, sixteen members of the Austrian states appeared before Ferdinand, and vehemently demanded his consent to their taking arms, and to the treaty which they wished to conclude with Bohemia. Nay, their leader, Thonradel, went even so far as to hold the king by the button of his coat, urging their demand, that he would put his signature to the proposed articles, in the most impressive manner. But just then, as if by miraculous interference, five hundred of the imperial cavalry arrived in the city from Krems, and, ignorant of what was passing in the castle, with a flourish of trumpets marched into the court-yard. The deputies immediately retired and made their exit in the greatest consternation and alarm, imagining that the arrival of the cavalry was preconcerted, and thus Ferdinand was extricated from his distressing situation.*

Count Thurn was obliged soon to return to Bohemia, as Prague was menaced by the armies of Austria, and Ferdinand availed himself of this moment in order to undertake another hazardous and daring project. Although the Austrian provinces had not yet declared their allegiance, and during his absence much that was untoward might occur, he nevertheless resolved to proceed to Frankfort to attend the election of emperor. The spiritual electors had been gained over; Saxony also adhered closely to the house of Austria; Brandenburg was not unfriendly; hence the opposition of the palatinate alone against him could accomplish nothing; accordingly Ferdinand was unanimously chosen emperor on the 28th of August, 1619. By a strange reverse

* Since this period, in commemoration of that important event, this regiment of cavalry has permission, in passing through Vienna, to ride over the Burgplatz, which others are not allowed to do.

of fortune it happened, that at the very moment when, after the conclusion of the election, he, with the electoral princes, was retiring from the hall to proceed in procession to the church of St. Bartholomew, he received the intelligence of his deposition in Bohemia, and which had just been made public among the people.

The Bohemians having, on the 26th of August, 1619, at a general assembly of the states, deposed Ferdinand, "for having, in opposition to the fundamental compact which he had entered into with them before the emperor's death, intermeddled with the administration of state affairs, introduced war into Bohemia, and concluded a treaty of alliance with Spain to the prejudice of the liberty of the country;" they proceeded at once to another election. The Catholics proposed the duke of Savoy and Maximilian of Bavaria, while, in the Protestant interest, the Elector John George of Saxony, and Frederick V. of the palatinate, were put forward. The latter obtained the election, being a son-in-law of King James I. of England, from whom they expected assistance, and who personally was regarded as resolute, magnanimous, and generous. The incorporated provinces of Moravia, Silesia, and Lusatia, supported the election, and even the Catholic states of Bohemia pledged their fidelity and obedience. Frederick was warned against accepting so dangerous a crown by Saxony, Bavaria, and even by his father-in-law; but his chaplain Scultetus, and his own consort Elizabeth, who as the daughter of a king aspired to a royal crown, persuaded him with all their influence to accept it. Frederick was accordingly ruled by them, received the regal dignity in Bohemia, and was crowned at Prague with great pomp on the 25th of October, 1619. He considered it to be his duty, as he himself says, not to desert those of his own faith by whom he had been appointed. If this youthful king of twenty-three years of age had possessed the strength of mind requisite for a successful prosecution and accomplishment of the work, history would have ranked him among those daring men, who, relying upon their own internal resources, never hesitated to venture upon great and noble enterprises; but fate had decided against him, and in adversity he failed to show that energy and presence of mind which must ever be at the command of him who has resolved to wear a hazardous crown.

Ferdinand in returning from Frankfort passed on to Munich, and there concluded with the duke of Bavaria that important treaty which secured to him the possession of Bohemia. These two princes had been companions in youth, and the Evangelical Union had by several incautious proceedings irritated the duke. Maximilian undertook the chief command in the cause of the Catholic party, and stipulated with the house of Austria that he should be indemnified for every outlay and loss incurred, to the extent even, if necessary, of the surrender of the territories of Austria itself into his hands.

With Spain also the emperor succeeded in forming an alliance, and the Spanish general, Spinola, received orders to invade the countries of the palatinate from the Netherlands.

Subsequently the elector of Mentz arranged a convention at Mühlhausen with the Elector John George of Saxony, the elector of Cologne, and the Landgrave Lewis of Darmstadt, wherein it was determined to render all possible assistance to the emperor for the maintenance of his kingdom, and the imperial dignity.

Frederick, the new Bohemian king, was now left with no other auxiliary but the Evangelical Union; for the Transylvanian prince, Bethlen Gabor, was, notwithstanding all his promises, a very dubious and uncertain ally, while the troops he sent into Moravia and Bohemia were not unlike a horde of savage banditti. Meanwhile the union commenced its preparations for war as well as the league. The whole of Germany resembled a grand depôt for recruiting. Every eye was directed to the Swabian district, where the two armies were to meet; there, however, at Ulm, on the 3d of July, 1620, they unexpectedly entered into a compact, in which the forces of the union engaged to lay down their arms, and both parties pledged each other to preserve peace and tranquillity. The unionists felt themselves too weak to maintain the contest, since Saxony was now likewise against them, and Spinola threatened them from the Netherlands. It was, however, a great advantage for the emperor, that Bohemia was excluded from this treaty, for now the forces of the league were at liberty to aid him in subjugating his royal adversary. Maximilian of Bavaria, therefore, immediately took his departure, and on his way reduced the states of Upper Austria to the obedience due to Ferdinand, joined the imperial army, and made a spirited attack upon Bohemia. On the other side, the elector of Saxony took possession of Lusatia in the name of the emperor, after lying four weeks before Bautzen, which he subdued after a smart resistance.

Frederick of Bohemia felt now the difficulty of his situation; nevertheless, with the aid of a faithful and courageous people, who had already two hundred years before defended their country in the Hussite wars against the combined power of Germany, he might still have maintained his ground. But, either from ignorance or indifference, he failed completely in gaining the confidence of the nation. His life was careless and his time wasted in extraneous matters, and his mind without that inward dignity of self-possession and calm reflection so necessary at a moment so portentous; while he even made the Bohemians subservient to his German counsellors and generals. The Bohemian nobility, who had in fact brought about and directed the entire movement, availed themselves of their preponderating influence for their own advantage, inflicted great injury upon the citizens in their trade, and transferred to them and the rural districts the whole weight of taxation. There was one general complaint against the imposts and the burden and oppression of the soldiery, besides which the Calvinistic party, by their ecclesiastical domination, annoyed no less the Lutherans than the Catholics. Frederick was not able to govern these conflicting elements, and this weakness effected his ruin.

As the imperialists advanced, the Bohemian forces marched into Prague and intrenched themselves on the Weissenberg (white mountain) near the city. But before the intrenchments were concluded, the Austrians and Bavarians advanced and gave battle at once, as Maximilian's impatience would not suffer the event to remain undetermined for a single hour. And in less than an hour the fate of Bohemia was decided. Frederick's troops, in spite of the bold resistance made by several companies, were beaten, and the whole of his artillery, together with one hundred standards, were taken by the enemy. Frederick himself, who, at the commencement of the battle, was quietly seated at his dinner-table, which he would not leave, saw its termination only at a distance from the ramparts of the city, and with it lost all the little resolution he still retained. Against the advice of a few of his more intrepid friends, he on the following night, with Count Thurn and some others of his suite, fled from Prague—which otherwise might still have defended itself—into Silesia; there, however, he could not resolve to stay, although he might have rallied his friends around him, but fled still farther into Holland, and dwelt there without a kingdom, and without courage to reconquer it—maintained at the expense of his father-in-law, the king of England. The emperor, however, pronounced the imperial ban of excommunication against him, in consequence of which all his estates were confiscated.

Prague at once yielded submission; the whole of Bohemia, except Pilsen, which Mansfeld bravely defended, followed the example; the countries of the palatinate were occupied by the Spaniards, under Spinola, and the union, alarmed at their proximity, was, in 1622, quite dissolved. Like the Schmalkaldian league it terminated ingloriously, and both were, through a concurrent fatality, destroyed by the influence of the Netherlands; for it was by means of the Netherland troops under Count Buren that formerly Charles V. became the vanquisher of that league.

Sad for Bohemia was the punishment which the emperor now inflicted upon the country. During the first three months nothing took place, but many of the fugitives having meantime returned, forty-eight leaders of the Protestant party were suddenly taken prisoners, on the same day and in the same hour, and, after a judicial investigation, twenty-seven of their number were condemned to death; of whom three belonged to the nobility, seven were knights, and the others citizens. The property of those condemned was confiscated, as well as that of the absentees, who were declared traitors, among whom Count Thurn was included. Afterwards by degrees all the Protestant clergymen were banished from the country, and finally, in 1627, it was declared to all nobles, knights, and citizens, that no subject would be tolerated in Bohemia who did not adhere to the Catholic church. It is calculated that the number of families who at this time were forced to leave Bohemia amounted to thirty thousand; they for the most part resorted to Saxony and Brandenburg. The lot of Silesia was much more fortunate, for through the intervention of the elector of Saxony it obtained the establishment of its religious and civil liberties and a general amnesty, securing Protestantism within its borders.

## CHAPTER XXIII.

Military Expeditions in Germany, 1621-1624—Generals Mansfeld and Tilly—Successes of Mansfeld—Joined by the Margrave of Baden-Durlach and Christian, Duke of Brunswick—Tilly—The Palatinate—The Heidelberg Library—Ferdinand resolves to continue the War—The Duke of Bavaria made Elector-Palatine—Tilly defeats the Duke of Brunswick in Münster—War with Denmark, 1624-1629—The Protestant forces under Christian IV. of Denmark, the Duke of Brunswick and Mansfeld—The Emperor without a Leader—Count Wallenstein—His extraordinary Character—Ambition—Astrological Studies—Faith in Destiny—His Bravery—Weissenberg—Wallenstein Duke of Friedland—His stately Palace and royal style of living—Raises an Imperial Army—His Appearance—Pursues Mansfeld—Death of Mansfeld, 1626—Death of the Duke of Brunswick—Christian IV. of Denmark—His Flight—Dukes Adolphus and John of Mecklenburg banished—Their Estates seized by Wallenstein—Created Duke of Mecklenburg and a Prince of the Empire, 1628—Pomerania—Stralsund—Besieged by Wallenstein—Its Brave Resistance—Forces Wallenstein to retire—Peace between the King of Denmark and the Emperor, 1629—The Edict of Restitution, 1639—Its Effect—Augsburg—The Catholic League—Tyranny and Cruelty of Wallenstein and his Army—Complaints of the Catholics and Protestants against Wallenstein to the Emperor—The Princes and the Nation insist upon his Dismissal—His Resignation.

According to all human calculation, the contest appeared now decided; Bohemia was subjugated, the Evangelical Union dissolved, the palatine house overthrown, and the elector a mere fugitive. Whence, therefore, could resistance be apprehended? And yet it came, and that, too, from the restless activity of Count Mansfeld, who would not abandon victory at so easy a price, and who knew the age in which he lived too well, not to calculate upon those unexpected means which a change of fortune must present to men of a daring and confident disposition. He knew how highly the minds of the people were excited, and that they were only waiting for leaders in order to recommence the obstinate struggle in favor of their faith. Whoever commanded their confidence might venture upon the adoption of extraordinary measures.

Accordingly, he collected quite unexpectedly, after having left Pilsen, new troops, and declared that he would still farther maintain the cause of Frederick against the emperor. In a short time he had an army of about 20,000 men, and obliged the forces of the league, under the Bavarian general, John Tserklas Tilly, (raised by the emperor, since 1623, to the dignity of count,) to keep the field against him. By rapid and well-planned marches he deluded his antagonist, and in his course spread desolation among the Catholic bishoprics of Franconia, Würzburg, Bamberg, and Eichstadt, together with those of Spires, Worms, and Mentz on the Rhine; and, finally, in the beautiful and flourishing provinces of Alsace.

His example was followed by others. First of all, George Frederick, margrave of Baden-Durlach, took the field in favor of the palatine house, collected a strong army and united with Mansfeld. He would not fight as a prince of the German empire, lest his land should be made to suffer for it, but as a knight and champion in that cause which, to him, appeared the most just; accordingly, before he entered into action, he transferred into his son's hands the government of his country. For him, united with Mansfeld, Tilly was no equal match; but when, however, they separated, he defeated the margrave at Wimpfen on the 8th of May, 1622.

Mansfeld next found an ally in Christian, duke of Brunswick, brother of the reigning duke, who, full of youthful ardor, likewise came forward in the cause of the banished electoral prince. After a variety of adventures, he at length joined Mansfeld with a considerable body of men, and, thus united, they entered Alsace once more, extending their march to the provinces of Lorraine, and, in fact, made even Paris itself tremble for the moment, as they threatened to advance thither to the aid of the Huguenots. After devastating all the neighboring provinces, they finally marched into Holland, where they joined the Netherlanders in their struggle against the Spaniards.

Tilly, meantime, retained possession of the entire palatinate, and it was on this occasion that he seized upon the magnificent library of Heidelberg, of which the duke of Bavaria made a present to the pope,

Gregory XV.; it was conveyed to Rome, and placed in the Vatican.*

It appeared now as if the moment had once more arrived when peace might have been restored to Germany, if the victors had been at all inclined to act with moderation. But Ferdinand had no idea of halting in the midst of all his revolutionary movements. He considered himself, as he states in a letter written by himself and sent to Spain, as called upon by Providence "to crush all the seditious factions, which had been supported chiefly by the heresy of Calvinism, and he recognised in the success which had hitherto rewarded his efforts, an intimation from God that he ought to persevere in the course he had entered upon."

A grand step would be gained towards the promotion of his plans, if he could arrange the investiture of his friend the duke of Bavaria as electoral-palatine, and as a recompense for his faithful services; a matter upon which they both agreed in secret together. In the aforesaid letter of Ferdinand, he says: "If we could gain one more vote in the electoral college, we should be forever secured in our object of placing the empire in the hands of the Catholics, and ensuring its possession to the house of Austria."

But this step was one of great danger, as it was likely to bring upon him the most determined opposition of all the Protestants, and more especially might make an enemy of the electoral house of Saxony, hitherto a friend so faithful. Nevertheless, Ferdinand accomplished his wish; he hastened to summon together the electors at Ratisbon in 1623, in order to confer the investiture upon Maximilian, and after many negotiations Saxony was induced to give its consent by the concession of Lusatia.

In the same year, Duke Christian of Brunswick was routed by Tilly near Stadlov in Münster, at the moment when he was about to recommence operations, and thus fortune appeared to realize the anticipations of the emperor, and crown his confidence with continued success. Nevertheless, many links were still necessary to form the chain of this war.

The Protestants, meantime, considered that they could not remain in a state of inactive expectation of the fate to which they might be subjected, but felt themselves bound to exercise forthwith the little energy and self-possession still at their command. The first movement was made in the states of the circle of Lower Saxony, on the frontiers of which Tilly, the terror-striking general of the Bavarians, had taken up his position with his formidable army. After having made in vain their representations for his recall, they took to arms, and chose the king of Denmark, Christian IV., as duke of Holstein, for their commander-in-chief. He promised them considerable aid, and England on its part did the same. Christian of Brunswick and Mansfeld reappeared, and enlisted troops with English money. Hitherto the war in Germany, on the Catholic side, had been carried on almost wholly by the army of the league; but as the preparations of the Protestants became now more extensive, they demanded from the emperor supplies of troops accordingly. At the same time it was likewise the emperor's wish to furnish an imperial army himself, in order that the house of Bavaria might not claim the merit of performing every thing alone; but he was in want of the necessary means to effect this object, and he was at a loss how to raise and equip the number of men required. Under these circumstances, however, an individual presented himself to his notice, who contemplated carrying on the war by means of his own resources, and single-handed—similarly to Mansfeld; and offering at once to relieve the emperor from his difficulties, he lost no time in bringing his plans into operation.

Albert of Wallenstein—more properly Waldstein—the descendant of a noble family in Bohemia, was born in the year 1583, in Prague, of Lutheran parents; as they died when he was young, he was sent by a maternal uncle to a celebrated convent of Jesuits at Olmütz, and was thus educated in the Catholic religion. Later he travelled with a wealthy nobleman from Moravia through a great part of Europe, and became acquainted with Germany, Holland, England, France, and Italy. The learned companion of the illustrious pair, the mathematician and astrologer Peter Verdungus, (subsequently a friend of Keppler,) encouraged Wallenstein's predilection for astrology, and in Padua he was initiated in cabalistic lore and the other occult sciences of the stars by Professor Argoli. A mysterious

* This library, at the intercession of the emperor of Austria and the king of Prussia, was restored to Heidelberg in the year 1815

inclination of his nature led him to this dangerous study, which at that time was universally pursued, and occupied even great minds like that of Keppler; his soul was lost in its dark labyrinths; but this much he saw with the greatest certainty in the stars, since he intuitively felt it, viz., that he was destined to effect something extraordinary. An unbounded ambition possessed his whole soul, and he was conscious of an energy sufficient to carry the entire age with him; whence he regarded as within his reach the accomplishment of the greatest enterprise.

He attached himself to the Archduke Ferdinand, whose firmness and determination he recognised, and set out in 1617, accompanied by 200 cavalry, raised at his own expense, to render him aid in an expedition against Venice. By way of remuneration, Ferdinand assigned to him the rank of a commander of the militia in Moravia. During the troubles of Bohemia he aided the Viennese in their defence against the Bohemians, fought against Bethlen Gabor of Transylvania, who raised his pretensions to the crown of Hungary, and filled the situation of quarter-master-general in the imperial forces under Boucquoi, when he, with Maximilian of Bavaria, gained the battle of Weissenberg near Prague. After this battle he had another engagement with Bethlen, by whom the imperial generals Dampierre and Boucquoi had been defeated, made him retreat, and obliged him to accede to terms of peace, and to relinquish his claims to the Hungarian crown. For these services, and at the same time as an indemnification for the devastation of his estates in this war and the expenses he had incurred —having at his own cost furnished and supported several regiments—Wallenstein received, in 1622, the territory of Friedland in Bohemia, together with the title of prince, and later that of duke. In addition to this, he purchased for a large sum of money about sixty estates of the Bohemian nobility, which had been confiscated by the emperor after the battle near Prague, and thus came into possession of more than princely wealth. The duchy of Friedland alone comprised nine towns and fifty-seven castles and villages. Subsequently, and while Tilly was in command at the head of the league, he lived retired on his estates, although at the same time he felt much discontented at finding the war carried on without him. Now, however, when he found the emperor was anxious to raise for himself an army, he, as we have already seen, offered his services to levy troops of his own for the imperial service, taking upon himself nearly the whole cost. He stipulated only that he should be allowed to exercise unlimited control over them, and possess the exclusive power of appointing officers, and collecting a force, not of 20,000 but of 50,000 men—as such an army, he said, would soon be enabled to maintain itself. He obtained, accordingly, the full authority required, and in a few months afterwards the army was raised and completely equipped—such was the influence his very name already produced.

Wallenstein was born to command; his acute eye distinguished at the first glance, from among the multitude, such as were competent, and he assigned to each his proper place. His praise, from being but rarely bestowed, animated and brought into full operation every faculty, while his steady, reserved, and earnest demeanor secured obedience and discipline. His very appearance inspired reverence and awe; his figure was lofty, proud, and truly warlike; his jet-black hair was cut close above his high and commanding forehead, while in his bright piercing eye was expressed profundity of thought, combined with gravity and mystery—the characteristics of his favorite studies and researches in the language of the stars and the labyrinths of the planets.

He marched with his new army, in the autumn of 1625, through Swabia and Franconia into Lower Saxony. Tilly withheld from joining a rival whose ambition he saw was to excel him, and both conducted the war apart. Wallenstein, after having put to rout a body of armed peasantry who had attempted to intercept his march near Göttingen, advanced to the districts of Halberstadt and Magdeburg, which had not as yet been subjected to the devastations of the war. The campaign of 1626 commenced with more serious deeds of arms. Count Mansfeld, who advanced along the Elbe against Wallenstein, having been defeated on the bridge of Dessau, directed his course with a bold determination towards Silesia, in order to join Prince Bethlen Gabor, and carry the war into the Austrian dominions, whither Wallenstein, to his great regret, was forced to follow him. After a most harassing and difficult march, Mansfeld arrived in Hungary; he was, however, very badly received there, because he had not brought with him the sums of money expected by the prince. Pursued by Wallenstein, his retreat cut off, and without the means of procuring supplies in such a remote country, he was forced to sell his artillery and ammunition, and disband his soldiers; and then crossing Bosnia and Dalmatia, he proceeded with a small suite along the road to Venice. Thence it was his intention to repair to England, in order to procure the necessary supply of money; but on arriving in the village of Urakowitz, near Zara, his nature, already completely overwhelmed by the superhuman struggles and fatigues undergone, finally sank beneath these heavy trials, and the noble warrior breathed his last on the 20th of November, 1626, in the forty-sixth year of his age. When the dying man felt at length the approach of death, he had himself clothed in his military coat, his sword buckled on, and thus equipped, and standing supported by the arms of two friends, he patiently awaited the final moment of his mortal career. His remains were interred in Spalatro.

In this same year died likewise his friend, Duke Christian of Brunswick, who was only twenty-nine years of age; and thus the Protestants were deprived of their best generals. Christian, king of Denmark, was not able to replace them, for in him was wanting all that warlike spirit and energy so necessary in a commander; added to this, there was no union between the princes of the circle of Lower Saxony, and one of whom, indeed, George, duke of Celle, a general of the Saxon army, passed over to the emperor, whose service he entered. Thence, although Lower Saxony was much relieved by the retreat of Wallenstein, King Christian was, nevertheless, not only unable to defend it against Tilly, but he was completely defeated by him on the 27th of August at Lutter near Barenberg, in Hanover, and lost all his artillery, together with sixty ensigns.

In the year 1627, Wallenstein marched back again through Silesia, whence he drove all his enemies before him into the north of Germany, crossed Brandenburg and Mecklenburg, and with Tilly entered Holstein, in order to force the king of Denmark to abandon Germany altogether. The whole of that country, with the exception of a few fortifications, was speedily conquered. Silesia and Jutland were next invaded and fearfully devastated. The king was obliged to take refuge in his islands, and some letters of Wallenstein even mention that he seriously contemplated causing the emperor Ferdinand to be chosen king of Denmark, having been informed that the states were dissatisfied with their own king. It was in this same year that Wallenstein added to his immense possessions the duchy of Sagan and the territory of Priebus in Silesia, which he purchased of the emperor for 150,000 florins.

Meantime the army of Wallenstein had gradually increased to 100,000 men, and this mysterious and incomprehensible man continued enlisting fresh troops with still greater zeal in proportion as the numbers of the enemy diminished and disappeared. It was not known whether it was for himself or for his sovereign that he was thus paving the way for the attainment of unlimited dominion. The Catholic princes themselves regarded him with suspicion and doubt, for it became more and more evident that his grand object was to abolish their league, while Tilly especially hated him because he monopolized for himself all the fruits produced by their victories. The princes of Mecklenburg, Pomerania, and Brandenburg, appealed to the emperor to remove the heavy and oppressive burden of war from their lands; but the will of his general was more powerful than that of the emperor himself, and the whole of North Germany obeyed his slightest nod, and trembled beneath his wrath. He himself lived in a style of pomp and splendor far beyond his imperial master, in which example he was imitated by all his officers in proportion; while around him thousands of human beings were forced to languish in inexpressible misery, and without exaggeration, literally died through starvation. In addition to all this, the general brought against the emperor a heavy account of the sums he had advanced out of his own funds for the expenses of the war, and which he calculated at more than three millions of florins. This sum the emperor found it impossible to pay, and resolved, therefore, to seize the territories of the dukes Adolphus

Frederick and John Albert of Mecklenburg, and transfer them into the hands of his general, in consideration of the debt. Thus Wallenstein was made a prince of the empire, and while on a visit at the castle of Brandeis, in Bohemia, put into immediate practice the privilege he now commanded of appearing with covered head in the imperial presence.

In vain did the inhabitants supplicate to have their rightful dukes, whose family had reigned in their dominions for nearly a thousand years, restored to them, and who, they said, had not committed themselves more than the princes of the other provinces in the circle of Lower Saxony. Ferdinand forgot again, this time, the laws of moderation in victory, and shamefully violated the constitution of the empire in thus banishing these princes from their territories without legally impeaching them before the electoral princes, and without giving them a hearing or pronouncing judgment against them. On the contrary, it was to him an object of great importance to secure for himself the presence of a Catholic prince of the empire on the coast of the Baltic Sea, who would thus be enabled to keep in check the north of Germany, and form a protective power to watch the proceedings of the Protestant kings of Denmark and Sweden; while from this point he confidently hoped to be enabled to re-establish the Catholic faith throughout the north. He also appears to have contemplated holding complete dominion over the maritime commerce of the Baltic from this quarter, for Wallenstein even assumed the title of admiral of the north and eastern seas, and it is seen by his letters addressed to Arnim, general-in-chief of the army in the north of Germany, during his absence, that the desire he had most at heart was to burn all the Swedish and Danish vessels that sailed within the range of his dominion, and to collect and establish a fleet of his own.

From Mecklenburg Wallenstein now turned his looks towards its neighboring territory, Pomerania. The old duke, Bogislas, was without any family, and after his death his duchy might be very conveniently united with that of Mecklenburg. What, however, was to this ambitious man of the utmost importance, was the possession of Stralsund, which, it is true, was in the dominion of the duke of Pomerania, but which, at the same time, as forming part of the Hanseatic league, enjoyed many privileges, and an independent administration in all its internal affairs. This city, as well as the whole country, had contributed very large sums towards the maintenance of the imperial troops; and now it was intended to furnish it with a garrison. This the citizens refused to receive; and in the spring of the year 1628, Wallenstein gave orders to General Arnim to march against, and lay siege to the place. The citizens, however, defended their walls with determined courage and perseverance, while the kings of Sweden and Denmark furnished them with liberal supplies of troops, together with ammunition and provisions from the sea-side. Their obstinate resistance excited the furious wrath and indignation of the imperious general, and he exclaimed: "Even if this Stralsund be linked by chains to the very heavens above, still I swear it shall fall!" He then advanced in person against the city, and repeatedly assaulted it; but he now learned to know what the heroic courage of citizens can effect under prudent guidance; for after having remained before the walls for several weeks, and suffered a loss of at least twelve thousand men in the various desperate assaults made, he was forced, to his no little mortification, to withdraw without accomplishing his object.

Meantime, the king of Denmark had demanded peace, which, contrary to all expectation, the emperor was advised by Wallenstein to conclude; from which it may be presumed that as he was now a prince of the empire himself, he no longer considered it desirable to destroy farther the power of the German princes. The king, through the mediation of the general, made on the 12th of May, 1629, in Lübeck, a very advantageous peace, and he received back all his lands, without paying the expenses of the war. But this peace did not add much to the glory of the king, inasmuch as for his own preservation, he sacrificed in the dukes of Mecklenburg two faithful allies. He promised not to take any share in the affairs of Germany, otherwise than as a member of the imperial states, and thus resigned the right he possessed to protect the two dukes. Wallenstein now received from the emperor the investiture of the duchy of Mecklenburg, and was thus confirmed in his rank among the princes of the empire.

How rejoiced must the peacefully disposed inhabitants of Germany have been, after their long persecution, when they received the happy tidings of peace! The contest, indeed, could not now be continued any longer, for no enemy was left to oppose the emperor; while the duke of Bavaria had obtained quiet possession of the electoral dignity, and that portion of the palatinate which had been promised to him as an indemnification for his expenses in the war. The Protestants were now so completely reduced and subdued, that there was no longer cause to dread fresh hostilities on their part. The war had now reached its twelfth year, and every year had left behind it fresh traces of the ravages produced throughout the whole empire, turning flourishing provinces into deserts, and rendering once opulent citizens beggars and fugitives. The war, indeed, might now have easily been brought to a termination, had the victorious party only known when to fix the just limits of their course, and if the emperor, after having thus completely purified his states of the new doctrines, and reestablished his authority therein with all its original power, had secured religious peace in all its plenitude to all the other independent states of the empire, disbanded his army, and thus delivered the reduced and miserable country from that especially heavy burden. But nothing is more difficult to the human mind than to restrain itself in its course amid prosperity. The Catholic party imagined this was a moment too favorable for them to neglect, and they determined, accordingly, to draw all the advantages they could from the fortunate state of circumstances in which they were placed. They demanded of the Protestants the restitution of all the ecclesiastical benefices, of which they had taken possession since the treaty of Passau, in 1552: being no less than two archbishoprics, Bremen and Magdeburg, twelve bishoprics, and a multitude of inferior benefices and convents. Until this moment, the restitution of what it had been so long the acknowledged right of the Protestants to hold possession, had never been for an instant contemplated; but now, however, urged on by the Catholics, the emperor published a solemn edict, known under the title of the Edict of Restitution, dated the 6th of March, 1629. "The Protestants," says a distinguished historian, "were completely paralyzed, while the more short-sighted portion of their adversaries hailed it with exultation." The cause, however, for such exultation, produced eventually unutterable calamity all over Germany.

Under these circumstances, therefore, it was determined not to disband either of the two grand armies at this moment engaged in their devastations throughout the empire; their services were retained in order to bring into effect the execution of the edict of restitution, and orders were accordingly issued, that they should assist if necessary, with the force of their arms, the various imperial deputies authorized by the government to witness the due accomplishment of its decrees. Operations were immediately commenced, and the south of Germany was selected as the spot to receive the first visitation. The city of Augsburg—where only shortly before the treaty of religious peace had been signed—was forced, among the rest, to acknowledge the ecclesiastical jurisdiction of the bishop, and renounce the Protestant form of worship, while the duke of Wurtemberg was obliged to restore all his monasteries. In addition to all this, the Catholic league, in a meeting which took place in Heidelberg, made a resolution "not to restore any of the possessions conquered by their arms, whether spiritual or temporal, unless they were indemnified beforehand for all their war expenses." Thence the Protestants were threatened with still greater danger from the league party than even from the emperor himself.

But the intolerable tyranny exercised by Wallenstein's army produced increasing indignation, and excited still more loudly the complaints and murmurs of both parties, which attained at length that degree of irresistible power, that the emperor could no longer shut his eyes against the universal ruin—no respect being shown for either party, friends or foes, Catholics or Protestants—caused by those overbearing, ruthless violators of right and justice. The emperor's own brother, Leopold himself, wrote him a long letter, in which he gave a dreadful and harrowing description of the pillage, incendiarisms, murderous outrages, and other shameful oppressions inflicted by the imperial troops upon the peaceful inhabitants. Such testimony overbalanced all the arguments to which, hitherto, the friends of Wallenstein had had recourse, and successfully brought to bear in his defence; while, finally, at the assembly of the electoral princes held in Ratisbon in the summer of 1630, the emperor found himself overwhelmed with petitions from every quarter. "The imperial soldiers," complained the Pomeranian deputies, "marched into our country, and were received as friends, and yet they have already exacted from the principality of Stettin alone, ten millions of dollars as a contribution, while in spite of this they have nevertheless reduced to ashes seven of our towns, and completely devastated the whole country around. And yet in the moment that they were scattering such dreadful ruin and misery everywhere around, they themselves lived in such an expensive style, that every captain and even his lieutenant exercised more princely extravagance than their own Duke Bogislas himself. Besides all this, the innkeepers and landlords upon whom the troops were billeted experienced the most brutal treatment, and many men were constantly being murdered in cold blood, and their bodies thrown to the dogs; in short, no act of cruelty could be mentioned or even thought of that these savages had not exercised, and many hundreds of the wretched inhabitants, in order to prevent these horrible acts from being inflicted upon themselves, and to escape from dying through starvation, had committed suicide."

This frightful picture shows us the exact nature of the war carried on by these troops serving for pay, and presents us with a description of the misery existing at this period of our history: nor in this is there any exaggeration. Count Mansfeld, the original projector of this system for the promotion of the war, has himself given us his testimony in a defence he was called upon to make against similar accusations upon the subject of the license given to and practised by his own army: "When the soldiers do not receive their pay," he says, "it is wholly impossible to maintain them in their discipline. Neither they themselves nor their horses can live upon air; while what they wear, both in clothing and arms, soon becomes ragged and useless. Thence they take whatever they can find, although not in proportion with what may be due to them; for they neither calculate the number nor weigh the amount of the articles they seize. The gate once opened to them, they rush through and proceed to act upon the plan they have laid down with unlicensed fury, and from which they are not to be deterred. They seize upon every thing, they overcome every thing, and strike down all and every thing that may oppose them. In short, it is impossible to imagine the disorder and riot thus produced; for, constituted as the army is of all nations, they all vie with each other in their exercise of the most monstrous acts. The German, the Netherlander, the Frenchman, the Italian, and the Hungarian, each contributes something peculiar to his own nation in violence and cruelty, as well as in cunning, deceit, and invention. I am aware of this, and have, I confess, even been forced to witness all these infamous acts, while my heart has grieved at the sight. But what is to be done? It is not enough to know and deplore these things; if we wish to remove the evil, we must adopt such measures as will ensure strict discipline in the army, but which cannot exist unless the troops receive their pay regularly."

Ferdinand could no longer resist the unanimous voice of complaint thus urged, and as now the whole body of princes insisted that Wallenstein—whom they all hated without exception—should be deprived of the chief command, and more especially as at their head Maximilian of Bavaria expressed himself most warmly in favor of it, the emperor, after some hesitation, gave his consent, and yielded to their wishes. It was, however, still left to be seen whether or not the proud and mighty chief would obey the summons: to the surprise of all, however, he did so. His astronomical calculations appeared to have produced their tranquillizing effects, and mollified his haughty spirit. "He by no means complained against or reproached the emperor," he said calmly to the imperial deputies, Count Werdenberg and Baron Questenberg, "for the stars had already indicated to him that the spirit of the elector of Bavaria held its sway over that of the emperor; but," he added, "in discharging his troops, his imperial majesty was rejecting the most precious jewel of his crown." He now withdrew to his duchy of Friedland, establishing his seat of government at Gitschen, which he considerably enlarged and beautified. This dismissal of Wallenstein took place in September, 1630.

Such of the imperial troops as did not

receive their discharge, joined those of the league, and the united army was placed under the command of Tilly.

## CHAPTER XXIV.

Gustavus Adolphus, king of Sweden, in Germany, 1630–1632—His Character—Motives and Plans in favor of Protestantism—Stralsund—Gustavus declares War against Ferdinand—Lands with his Army in Pomerania—Stettin—The Protestant Princes hesitate to join Gustavus—Cüstrin and Spandau—The Elector of Brandenburg—The Elector of Saxony—Siege of Magdeburg—Count Tilly—Conquers and burns the City—Dreadful Massacre—Gustavus and Tilly—Battle of Leipsic—Defeat of the Imperialists—Glorious Results to Gustavus—Surrender of the Cities—Ingolstadt—Tilly wounded—His Death—Munich—Prague—Ferdinand and Wallenstein—Regal Splendor of Wallenstein—His Palace—Reassembles an Army for the Emperor—Extravagant Conditions—Appointed Generalissimo—The Camp of Nuremberg—The Swedish and Imperial Armies—Gustavus in Saxony—Battle of Lützen, 1632—Gustavus killed—His Death revenged by the Swedes—Total Defeat of Wallenstein—Portraiture of Gustavus Adolphus.

The power of the Protestant princes had now become much weakened, and the edict of restitution was carried into effect generally. Those who knew the character of Ferdinand might easily foresee what were his designs against the new church, and it was scarcely necessary to question whether or not his grand object was to annihilate its entire existence, for the proceedings adopted throughout the empire clearly showed what its party had to expect. But amid this growing danger, and indeed almost in the very moment itself when the minds of the Protestants, as they beheld the crisis gradually approaching, had sunk into that state of despondency and settled gloom, which the sad succession of events must naturally produce, they received, most unexpectedly, assistance from a nation hitherto but little known, and living in uninterrupted seclusion within the frontiers of their northern territory. This people—the Swedes—were nevertheless distinguished for their bravery, while they were steadfast and faithful in their religious principles, being the descendants of the Goths, the noblest of all those nations most justly entitled to boast of their German origin. In the year 1611, Gustavus Adolphus succeeded to the Swedish throne, and he it was who was destined to lead his people upon the grand scene of this eventful period. It was this firm conviction, so deeply implanted in his mind, by which Gustavus felt inspired to undertake the mighty contest against the powerful house of Austria.

Opinions equally contrary and inconsistent have been pronounced upon the character of this great monarch, because, living at a period when party spirit raged so furiously, it was not to be expected that his actions could undergo a more impartial review than those accomplished by his contemporaries. On the one hand he has been regarded only as a conqueror, compelled by the excitement produced by burning ambition to cross the ocean in order to vanquish foreign lands, which he sought to effect more securely under the cloak of religion, and whence he was enabled to conceal his desire for war; and again, on the other hand, he has been viewed only as an enthusiastic champion in the cause of his faith, while the existence of all the ambitious motives attributed to him, and by which his adversaries have insisted he was alone influenced, has been denied, and the charge thus made condemned. In either case there is a mixture of truth and falsehood. Gustavus was by no means influenced by a feeling of ambition, which in its usual sense means the vain passion of personal and selfish glory, although assuredly the love for that reputation which is inherent in all men, and which in the mouths of people adorns the object with immortal life, occupied likewise a space within his heart; neither, on the other hand, was it solely in order to rescue his fellow Protestants in Germany that he took up arms, although faith and piety exercised sufficient influence over his soul to inspire him to fight in such a cause. Both these motives, however, acted in concert together upon his mind, united by another law of his nature—that which inspired him with the feeling and conviction of being destined to perform a conspicuous part in that eventful epoch of the history of the world. He felt he was called upon to lead forth from their seclusion and obscurity his noble people—who, although limited in number, were inferior to none in courage and virtue—and to place them in the ranks of the other nations of Europe. Hitherto, in connection with the other states of Europe, Sweden's position had been similar to that of Macedonia before Philip and Alexander in the ancient world, and as subsequently that of Russia was, previous to Peter the Great, in mdoern history; and as the lives of those great men can only be thoroughly comprehended when they are viewed in connection with the historical facts alluded to, so likewise in the same point of view must the life of Gustavus Adolphus of Sweden be regarded. For although this monarch left behind but very inconsiderable results when placed in contrast with those effected by the sovereigns with whom we have compared him, it must, at the same time, be remembered that he was snatched away by death at the age of thirty-eight years only, and at the very moment when he had commenced to lay the foundation of his grand work.

His great plan was immediately demonstrated in the first moment of his appearance upon the scene. Previous to the war in Germany he had already conquered from the Russians and Poles the provinces along the coast, Ingria, Carelia, and Livonia, together with a portion of Prussia. Various important motives compelled him now to take a share in the affairs of Germany. He had been very seriously provoked and mortified by the emperor Ferdinand; his intercession in favor of the Protestants and his cousins the dukes of Mecklenburg, as well as his mediation for peace with Denmark, had been treated with great contempt, and disdainfully rejected; while, in addition to this, Wallenstein had even sent 10,000 imperial troops to the aid of the Poles against him. Beyond all these causes of complaint, however, which might perhaps still have been peacefully adjusted by negotiation, his presence was summoned by the danger which now hovered over the Protestant church, and the fear he entertained lest, in the person of Wallenstein, a fresh power might usurp the coast of the Baltic sea, and thus strengthen and extend the cause of Austria and Catholicism.

The danger to which the city of Stralsund was exposed had already, as we have before shown, produced his co-operation in favor of that place. He not only yielded to its wishes in this respect, but formed an alliance with it, by which it placed itself under his protection, and it was indebted to the succor he afforded especially for its preservation when besieged by Wallenstein. Now, however, when he beheld that the cause of Protestantism was menaced more seriously than ever throughout the whole of Germany, he took the decisive step, and formally declaring war against the emperor, he, on the 24th of June, 1630, landed on the coast of Pomerania with 15,000 Swedes. As soon as he stepped upon shore, he dropped on his knees in prayer, while his example was immediately followed by his whole army. Truly he had undertaken, with but small and limited means, a great and mighty enterprise!

When the emperor was informed of his landing, he, in his feeling of confidence, inspired by his continual success, appeared to treat the affair with so much indifference that the news had no influence whatever in the dismissal of Wallenstein, which just at this moment formed the subject of discussion in the diet of Ratisbon. All the Catholic party throughout the empire turned the fact of the arrival of the petty king of the north, as they termed him, into ridicule, and styled him, in contempt, the snow-king, who would speedily melt beneath the rays of the imperial sun. But these 15,000 men constituted an army of heroes, a phalanx of hardy warriors, belonging as it were to another world; their ranks were regulated by strict discipline and religious principles, while those opposed to them knew nothing of war but its barbarism, and that licentious exercise of its worst passions which under no circumstances would be curbed or submit to reason. The imperialists were a mixture of all nations and creeds, and bound together by no other ties but those of mutual warfare and pillage; the Swedes, on the other hand, were strengthened in the confidence they felt that God fought on their side, and to him they offered up their prayers regularly twice a day, each regiment possessing its own chaplain. Besides this, the inventive genius of Gustavus had introduced the exercise of some new military tactics in his army; and in this he may bear comparison with many great men of antiquity, inasmuch as he surprised his enemies by the novelty and boldness of his positions, order of battle attacks, and thus he was soon enabled to throw all those who still adhered to the old system into confusion. Hitherto they had made a practice of forming their line of battle ten rows deep, but Gustavus reduced it to six in the infantry, and four in the cavalry; whence his little army gained considerably in extension, and was more easy and rapid in its movements when in battle; while the balls from the enemy's artillery committed less damage among their ranks, thus less densely crowded. The Swedish troops, especially the foot-soldiers, were likewise less heavily supplied with armor and other accoutrements, by which they were enabled to fire off their muskets with much more ease and dispatch, and which were constructed too of far lighter materials than those of the imperialists.

The imperialists, whose forces were by no means strong in the vicinity of the coast, were soon driven out of Rügen and the smaller islands at the mouth of the Oder, and Gustavus now marched against Stettin, the capital of the duchy of Pomerania. The duke, who was both old and timid, would not venture to decide upon joining the king of Sweden, and yet he could not resolve to oppose him. After long hesitation, during which Gustavus used every means of persuasion in firm but mild and consoling language, he at length surrendered to him the city, which the king intended at once to convert into a principal military depôt during the war.

The Protestant princes of the empire, like the duke of Pomerania, appeared quite undetermined how to receive their new ally. The king had invited them all to unite and form one grand alliance; but many felt too much afraid, and dreaded the vengeance of the emperor: others again were jealous of all foreign dominion in case of success, while the rest felt disposed rather to remain faithful in their allegiance to the empire and government, than to risk any change whatever. Gustavus was by no means pleased with the disposition thus shown: "We evangelists," he said, in his address to the inhabitants of Erfurt, "are placed in a position similar to a vessel when in a storm. In such a moment it does not suffice for a few only to labor with zeal for the general safety, while the rest of the crew look quietly on with their arms folded; all ought to work together, and each ought to assist with all his might in the particular part assigned to him." The Protestants, however, possessed no such spirit of union, neither did they cherish that conscientiousness of purpose so necessary. As usual, they were divided among themselves by jealousy and prejudice. The palatinate was entirely subjected; and Saxony, which for a length of time had kept aloof from the Evangelists, and at times, during the period of the palatine's influence, had even adhered to Austria, was now vacillating between its dread of Austria and a foreign prince. George William, the elector of Brandenburg, a weak prince, was guided by his minister Schwarzenberg, who was opposed altogether to an alliance with Sweden. Among the petty princes, of whom many were in truth much more determined, but were at the same time dependent upon the power of Austria, there were only two who joined the king, the landgrave of Hesse Cassel and the duke of Saxe-Weimar. The others, together with Saxony and Brandenburg, held a meeting in April, 1631, at Leipsic, and resolved to raise an army for themselves in defence of their territories against any attack, whether proceeding from the Swedes or Austrians. The emperor, who perceived clearly that the grand struggle must be decided by the sword, and would not for a moment entertain the idea of submitting his will to the diet, commanded the immediate dissolution of the Leipsic alliance, and commenced forthwith disarming all the princes and cities in the south of Germany forming a portion thereof.

The king of Sweden, now reinforced by a large number of enlisted troops, advanced with rapid marches direct through Pomerania, and completely beat and put to flight the whole of the imperialists before him. The latter in their retreat devastated the country, pillaged all the towns, many of which they burnt, and ill-treated and murdered the inhabitants. This dreadful war now resumed all its horrors. The Swedes, so steady and strict in their discipline, appeared as protecting angels, and as the king advanced, the belief spread far and near throughout the land, that he was sent from heaven as its preserver.

Gustavus was desirous to march in security step by step, and not to leave any fortified place in his rear; whence, after he had carried by assault Frankfort on the Oder, which contained a garrison of 8000 imperialists, he desired the elector of Brandenburg to surrender into his hands the fortified towns of Cüstrin and Spandau. The latter, although related by marriage to Gustavus, who had married his sister, hesitated; but the king marched on towards Berlin, and invited him to a conference on the plain between Berlin and Cospenik. Here, however, the prince still continued to hold out, when, at length, the king exclaimed with warmth: "My road leads to Magdeburg—at this moment closely besieged by Tilly—whither I must hasten, although not for my own advantage, but solely for that of the Evangelists. If none, however, will lend me their aid, I will free myself from all reproach and return to Stockholm; but bear in mind, prince, that on the last day of judgment you yourself will be condemned for refusing to do aught in the cause of the gospel, and, perhaps, even in this world you may receive the punishment due from God. For if Magdeburg *be* taken, and I withdraw, imagine to yourself what must happen to you!" This appeal produced its effects; the elector surrendered Spandau into his hands at once. The distance thence to Magdeburg was but short, and the inhabitants of that hard pressed city were most urgent in their prayers for assistance; unhappily, however, Gustavus found it quite impossible to cross the Elbe in face of the enemy so as to proceed by the direct road. Accordingly he requested permission from the elector of Saxony to pass through his territory, his object being to proceed to Wittenberg; but the prince refused to grant the accommodation desired. While, however, the king was engaged in endeavoring to prevail upon the elector to accede to his request, the dreadful, fatal day of conquest arrived—and the devoted city was lost.

The city of Magdeburg, which, from the commencement, had continued to distinguish itself for its zeal in the cause of the Protestant faith, was likewise the first in the list to throw itself into the arms of the preserver of religious liberty. They urgently invited him to direct his march towards the Elbe, and promised not only to throw open their gates to him, but enlisted at once a number of soldiers for his service; while Gustavus, who perceived the great importance of such a grand depôt, accepted their offers with eagerness, and lost no time in endeavoring to meet their wishes. Tilly, however, who was equally aware of the advantage to be derived by his adversary from the occupation of such an important place, used all diligence to make himself master of i. before the king's arrival. He commenced the siege in the month of March, 1631, seconded by General Pappenheim, a brave and determined officer. In the city itself there were only two hundred Swedes, under the command of Melcher of Falkenberg, whom Gustavus had shortly before dispatched as commandant of the city; but the inhabitants, full of courage and religious zeal, united in defending the place with determined perseverance. They had even erected two strong intrenchments in front of the city walls, which, in testimony of their undaunted resolution, they styled Trutz-Tilly, (defiance to Tilly,) and Trutz-Pappenheim, (defiance to Pappenheim.)

But in the mean time, unhappily, the want of provisions increased the distress with each succeeding day more and more, for the old general left no means untried to bring them to a surrender. Their only hope now was in the succor they expected to receive from the king, who, they knew, was close at hand; and on the 19th of May, when the thunder of the enemy's artillery ceased, and the guns were actually wheeled away from the trenches, they firmly believed their deliverer had now arrived. This, however, was only the signal for their destruction, and the prelude to preparations that were being made by the iron-hearted general for the final assault he had now determined upon making. In the silence of the night the scaling ladders were all fixed ready, and the attack ordered to be made at five o'clock in the morning. The sentinels on the walls having kept watch until the dawn of day, now finding all quiet, and, as they unsuspectingly thought, every thing secure, retired to get a brief half hour's repose.

Shortly afterwards the dreadful, fatal hour struck. The signal for the assault was given, and the division of the imperialists under Pappenheim scaled that portion of the wall next to the new town, and the artillery again thundered forth against the walls, which here and there were now soon shattered to pieces. The enemy speedily succeeded in mounting the ramparts, and while the brave commandant, Falkenberg, was hastening to the most dangerous part, he was shot dead. The terrified citizens, now deprived of their commander, and completely deadened with the sound of the roaring cannon, abandoned their walls and hurried to their homes. Many were mad enough to imagine that they would be enabled to defend themselves more securely there, and fired upon the enemy from their windows, while the females themselves hurled stones and other missiles from the roofs of the houses. But this only served to increase the rage of the imperialists, and neither mercy nor pity was shown. Men, women, children, the aged and the young, all were massacred alike, the very infants at the breast of their mothers being seized, stabbed, and hurled into the flaming mass beside them: a scene of horror which these monsters in human shape continued from ten o'clock in the morning and during the whole day until night. Every possible cruelty, and torments of every description were put into practice on this direful day—the insatiable imperialists devoting all their energies to the performance of their sanguinary and destructive work. It is related that a few of his officers, touched with a little remorse, repaired to Tilly, who had remained in the camp, and inquired whether he would not, perhaps, give orders to close the scene of pillage and murder? But he replied: "No, no; let them go on for another hour, and then come to me again. The men must have some reward for the danger and fatigue they have undergone."

By ten o'clock in the evening, nothing more was left of this ancient and magnificent city but the cathedral, one solitary convent, and a few stray fishermen's cabins on the Elbe; all else was reduced to cinders and ashes. More than twenty thousand human beings perished, either by the sword or in the flames, and when, two days afterwards, the cathedral was opened, more than a thousand miserable beings were found heaped together, who, having taken refuge there, were now sinking and dying around from starvation and mental agony. Such as were still to be saved, Tilly supplied with food; his wrath was now appeased, but all glory and good fortune, hitherto so faithful to him, abandoned him from this day, and his name henceforward was never pronounced without a malediction.

After the conquest of Magdeburg, Tilly was very desirous of having a drawn battle with the king of Sweden, for his troops suffered much in that ravaged district from want of supplies; Gustavus, however, considered he was not yet in sufficient force to risk a meeting, and he continued to keep himself intrenched in his camp of Werben, in Altmark. He was likewise extremely anxious to restore his cousins, the banished dukes of Mecklenburg, to their hereditary possessions. Accordingly, he furnished them with the necessary quantity of troops with which they reconquered their dominions, and made their solemn entry in their town of Güstrow, in which Wallenstein had previously established his court residence. The king heightened the interest of the grand festival given upon the occasion by attending it in person, and he ordered that every mother with a suckling child should attend in the open square, and that each infant should receive some of the wine there generally distributed, in order that the children of their children might forever remember the day of the return of their own legitimate princes.

Tilly, meantime, now turned his eyes towards the rich provinces of Saxony which had hitherto escaped the devastation of war, and in the vicinity of which he had now taken up his position. At the same time, however, it was certainly an act of injustice and ingratitude to inflict the burden of war upon the elector of Saxony, who had shown so much fidelity towards the house of Austria; but Tilly very soon found a pretext for such proceeding. He referred to the imperial decree, which ordered that all the members of the Leipsic league should throw down their arms; and, as he found that the elector, in spite of this command, still continued on the defensive, he immediately marched into Saxony without even making any declaration of war, and taking possession of and pillaging the cities of Merseburg, Zeiz, Naumburg, and Weissenfels, he advanced to Leipsic itself. This unjust act of violence effected more than all the persuasive eloquence of the king might have produced, for the elector threw himself immediately, and without any reserve, into his arms, concluded with him a firm and definitive alliance, offensive and defensive, and joined him with his army at Düben on the 3d of September, 1631.

On this same day, the imperial general made his attack upon Leipsic, which had closed its gates against him, and he took possession of it the next day; but the king now advanced with his united forces to recover the city, and the day had at length arrived on which the decisive trial was to take place between the old and hitherto unconquered general of the emperor, and the royal and youthful hero of Sweden. Gustavus, who knew how necessary it was that he should succeed by a grand action to secure and command the confidence of Germany, based upon his genius and good fortune, felt deeply the importance of this day, and wavered in his determination. He still doubted the prudence of staking the fate of the war upon a single battle; for there was too much reason to believe that the loss of this action must put an end to all his hopes on that side of the ocean, while it would produce the ruin of the electors of Saxony and Brandenburg, together with the complete and final destruction of the Protestant church throughout the whole empire.

The elector of Saxony, however, who could no longer endure to behold his country thus demolished by the hands of a pitiless and ruthless foe, urged the king in the most forcible language to give battle, and Gustavus accordingly yielded and marched on to Leipsic. The two armies met in the fields of the village of Breitenfeld, on the 7th of September, 1631, and there fought the decisive battle. Gustavus divided the Saxons from the rest of his troops, and posted them on his left wing, for as they were only recently enlisted, he could not put entire trust in them. The cannonading on both sides commenced about midday, and the shots told with far greater precision and consequent effect among the crowded ranks of the imperialists than on the other side; and, in order to put an end at once to this opening scene of destruction, the right wing of the imperialists fell upon the Saxons with such force that they were soon overthrown and put to flight, when, having partially rallied again at some distance from the scene of action, they reassembled round their elector, who had withdrawn to Eilenburg, where, according to Chemnitz's account, he fell into a state of despondency.

At the same moment that this first attack was made, Pappenheim, who was distinguished as the best cavalrist of his day, with the *élite* of his cavalry, threw himself upon the right wing of the Swedes, in order to break through their line. Here, however, he found himself opposed by an invulnerable wall; seven times were his attacks repulsed by the brave Swedish general, Banner. Tilly, who had abandoned the pursuit of the Saxons, now directed his attack upon the exposed flank of the Swedes; but, here again, the royal hero promptly turned his efforts in good time against the old warrior, whose troops were forced to expend all their fury in vain against the invincible firmness of their Swedish adversaries. The imperial general found himself completely puzzled and put out of his way by this new order of battle; the system was entirely changed, and against all expectation the confidence he usually placed in all his plans and calculations now deserted him for the first time; he found he had to deal with a superior genius, and while he was thus struck with embarrassment and mortification, Gustavus availed himself of this moment of hesitation, and making an attack upon the enemy's artillery, took possession of it, and turned the muzzles of the guns against the imperialists themselves.

This moment was decisive; the ranks of the enemy fell into disorder and were put to rout; 7000 were left dead on the field of battle, and Tilly himself was in great danger of his life. He was pursued by a captain of the Swedish cavalry, who struck him several times upon the head with the handle of his pistol; but was himself shot dead by an imperial officer who came to the rescue of his distressed leader. The sexagenarian general escaped, at length, with several wounds, and, completely exhausted in body and spirits, reached Halle, where he was joined by Pappenheim, who was the last to quit the field, having killed with his own hand, as Tilly relates in his bulletin of the battle, fourteen of the enemy. Of all his own brave squadrons of cavalry, formerly so dreaded, he had now only a small troop left.

This victory proved for Gustavus the grand foundation upon which was based his great reputation as a warrior throughout Germany, and from that moment was excited that veneration—almost amounting to adoration—for his person and character For this was a period, as in all extraordinary epochs of history, when, properly speaking, public opinion was all-powerful; when the faith, confidence, respect, an enthusiasm produced in the minds of the people by the actions of one man, were sufficient to establish him in their favor, and whoever knew how to avail himself of this moral force must be certain of success. All now turned towards the star thus ascending from the north; and he was enthusiastically received by zealots both in religious and superstitious faith. Prophecies, miracles, and dreams, were all made to refer to the great Gustavus; and wherever he appeared the Protestants received him as their deliverer, with indescribable transports of joy, and truly, during the whole period of the world's existence, the royal presence of a king was never so gratefully honored and reverenced as was that of the heroic and nobly-born champion of the Protestant faith, Gustavus Adolphus of Sweden.

Gustavus possessed a glance too keen and comprehensive not to perceive and fully understand the power which was now contributing all possible strength to his cause; and, although formerly he exercised the greatest and most anxious caution in the steps he took, marching his army slowly through the country, and securing his safe retreat by making himself master of all the fortified places in his route, he now pressed boldly onward through the empire, his progress presenting one triumphant march. Proceeding through Thuringia and across the Thuringian forest, he arrived in Franconia, and thence continued his course to the Rhine; where, having fixed his quarters during a short winter's rest, he resumed his progress, and, returning to Franconia, marched on direct to Bavaria. The most important cities fell into his hands, some after a slight resistance, and most of them yielded themselves voluntarily, including Halle, Erfurt, Würzburg, Frankfort, Mentz, Nüremberg, &c. Tilly, whose army was now so reinforced, that he found himself at the head of a much more numerous body of troops than the king himself had under his command, nevertheless would not venture to oppose his march; for since the battle of Leipsic he found it impossible to recover that confidence within himself which, until then, he had always had at his command.

The Elector Maximilian of Bavaria having, however, summoned him to march to his aid in order to protect his own hereditary estates, the old general advanced to the river Lech, in the passage across which he was to oppose the king, and to assist in which object Maximilian himself joined him near Rain. But Gustavus, before whom every thing now yielded, surmounted likewise this obstacle. After a vigorous cannonade, the imperial army being forced to quit the position it had taken, the king crossed the river and marched in pursuit of the enemy. But in the early part of the action, Tilly himself was struck in his right knee by a cannon-ball weighing three pounds, and fell from his horse; he was conveyed to Ingolstadt, followed by Maximilian. Thither, after he had taken and placed a garrison in Augsburg, Gustavus repaired and immediately laid siege to that town. The garrison defended the place bravely, and the king himself narrowly escaped, his horse being shot dead, and overthrowing its royal rider. Tilly, although sinking fast, still encouraged the garrison to the last; he died twenty-five days after he received his mortal wound, in the seventy-third year of his age. He was a stern, iron-hearted man, who made a merit of boasting that he had never once known the feeling of love or affection; at the same time he was of a firm and incorruptible character, and a good general. In personal appearance he bore a great resemblance to the duke of Alba, under whom he had served in the Netherlands. He was of middle height, and very thin; his eyes were large, but their expression, together with the contour of his whole countenance, indicated the stern and rigid nature of the man. He was the descendant of a noble family in Liege.

The Swedish king raised the siege of Ingolstadt and marched to Munich, which trembled at his approach. The inhabitants, and the Bavarian people generally, in their hatred against the Swedes, had treated many of that nation with great cruelty, putting them to death and then mangling their remains; by which inhuman conduct they had excited the greatest indignation in the king. Nevertheless, he received the deputies of the city graciously when they presented the keys to him: "You have done well," he said, "and your submission has disarmed me. I should have been justified in making an example of your city in revenge for the unhappy fate of Magdeburg; however, fear nothing, depart in peace, and fear not for your property or religion. My word is more valuable than all the signed capitulations in the world."

The greater portion of the Bavarian territory was now in the hands of Gustavus, and the elector was forced to seek refuge in Ratisbon.

The Saxons, meantime, agreeably to the plan of war drawn up by Gustavus, had marched into Bohemia, under the command of Field-marshal Arnim—who had quitted the service of the emperor and passed over into that of the elector of Saxony—and very easily made themselves masters of Prague, which was but slightly defended; there, on the 11th of November, 1631, the elector made his solemn entry.

Thus that single battle of Leipsic snatched from the hands of the emperor the entire fruits of a twelve years' war, and he now saw himself threatened even in his own patrimonial estates; this was a crisis for which he was by no means prepared, and which came upon him like a clap of thunder. In such a critical moment he, with his council, saw but one means of extrication, and this was the recall of that proud and ambitious man, Wallenstein, who, offended and indignant at being dismissed from the imperial service, now lived in mortified retirement brooding on the past. No other was now left who could venture to enter the lists against the powerful king; no other who was capable of again raising an army for the emperor's service.

But the task of winning him over to the imperial cause, seemed now more difficult than ever. He lived upon his estates in Bohemia in a style of luxury truly royal, and appeared to bid defiance to emperor and kings; and it was thus the millions he had gained in the war enabled him to live. His palace in Prague was erected with royal magnificence, and which even at the present day bears the stamp of its original character. While his enemies congratulated themselves upon having reduced him to this condition of a private individual, he had his own figure represented in fresco on the walls of the state saloon of his palace, by artists whom he procured from Italy and Germany, in the character of a conqueror seated on a triumphant car borne along by four milk-white steeds, while over his laurel-crowned head was placed a star. Sixty pages, each of noble family, in their rich costume of blue and gold velvet, attended upon him, and some of his officers and chamberlains had even previously served the emperor himself in the same rank they held under Wallenstein. Three hundred horses of choice breed filled his magnificent stables, and the assemblies in his palace rivalled in character the imperial court itself, for he was always visited by the most distinguished men of the day, too eager to seek and enjoy intercourse with such extraordinary genius. Outwardly he observed the greatest ease and tranquillity of manner, but internally he was still agitated with burning ambition. He had beheld the progress made by Gustavus with inward joy, because therein was satiated his revenge against the emperor and the hated elector of Bavaria, and all eyes would soon again be directed towards him as the only friend in need. And in reality, as he expected, the imperial deputies did arrive.

Wallenstein received them coldly, and it was only after being most urgently pressed by them that he yielded the promise to raise for the emperor an army of 30,000 men; but he would not engage to take command of it. And now the mighty man sent forth his followers in all directions to erect his recruiting standard. Thousands rallied around it, for it had ever led to pillage and fortune; and in this stormy age it was easier to gain a livelihood in war than in the workshop or behind the plough. The heavy horsemen under Wallenstein received each nine florins monthly pay, the light cavalry six, the infantry four, besides daily rations of meat, bread, and wine. The 30,000 men were collected together already by March in the year 1632; but he alone who had raised them was capable of conducting them.

Of this the emperor was well aware, and he accordingly submitted to the incredible degradation of permitting Wallenstein to dictate to him the following conditions: "The duke of Friedland, generalissimo of the emperor, shall have the supreme command of the whole archducal house, and of the crown of Spain without any limitation whatever, (in absolutissima forma;) neither the emperor, nor king Ferdinand (son of the emperor, whom the adverse party would fain have made general-in-chief) shall appear in person with the troops; to secure the remuneration of his services he shall receive as a guarantee a portion of the Austrian patrimonial estates, and with it he shall be entitled to exercise an exclusive and irresponsible control over the conquests he shall make in the empire, and command the privilege of conferring distinctions as he may deem best. Mecklenburg or some other indemnification shall be made over to him during peace, and during the war, if necessary, he shall be at liberty to choose any of the hereditary provinces of the empire for his seat of retirement."

Clothed with such—almost imperial—power, Wallenstein again appeared upon the stage, increased his army to 40,000 men, conquered Prague once more on the 4th of May in the year 1632, and with little difficulty expelled the Saxons from Bohemia.

The elector of Bavaria, who, in the mean while, was sorely pressed at home, applied to Wallenstein in the most urgent terms for help, which the latter, appearing to enjoy thoroughly his distress and humiliation, for a long time hesitated to afford; at length, after the elector had engaged to comply in an unqualified manner with all his instructions in the conduct of the war, he sent him an invitation to join him at Eger, intending thence to make an advance upon Nüremberg, one of the most considerable places of defence the king possessed. But Gustavus, who perceived the design, anticipated him, and made his appearance quite unexpectedly with an army near the city, which he intrenched, being vigorously aided by the devoted and enthusiastic inhabitants, whose youths filled the ranks of his army, and thus he was prepared for the enemy. The latter advanced and likewise made an intrenchment on the heights of Zirndorf and Altenberg, in full view of the Swedish encampment. Both parties had formed the plan of forcing each other by famine and disease to leave their strong-hold. They maintained this position eleven weeks, and neither would stir. But the distress of the whole surrounding country had now become very great; every thing was consumed or laid waste. In Wallenstein's camp alone, in addition to the large army itself, there were about 15,000 servants and attendants upon the baggage, and an equal number of women whom he had permitted to follow their husbands, together with 30,000 horses, which had been employed chiefly in removing the immense quantity of baggage. The licentiousness of this vast multitude increased daily, for they subsisted upon rapine and plunder. In Gustavus's army, likewise, strict order was no longer maintained as at first, it being now considerably increased by recruits and German auxiliaries. These he could not restrain as he wished, although he adopted the severest measures for that purpose. The disorder however was produced mainly through their own leaders, who were negligent of all discipline. The pious mind of the king was sorely pained and indignant when he heard of the outrages perpetrated by his troops upon the poor inhabitants of the country. He called the leaders together, sharply rebuked them, and exclaimed: "They made him so miserable, that he was weary of having longer any thing to do with such a perverse set." Unfortunately his eye could not be everywhere, and the mischief had already become too deeply rooted. He then resolved to bring this undecided and ruinous state of affairs to a conclusion by making a daring attempt. On the 24th of August he stormed the heights of Wallenstein, but found the undertaking too formidable; the most determined courage availed nothing against these fastnesses defended by their thundering artillery; the king was therefore obliged, after serious loss, to give up the assault. He waited fourteen days longer in his encampment, and as Wallenstein still continued immoveable, he retired and returned to Bavaria on the 8th of September, marching with sounding trumpets past the enemy, who would not venture to attack him.

Wallenstein now abandoned his encampment likewise, set fire to it, and unexpectedly formed the resolution of carrying a determined war once more into northern Protestant Germany; he marched at once for Saxony, and his approach was indicated by carnage and conflagration. The king hastened to afford relief, and reached Naumburg on the 11th of November. The people welcomed him as their guardian angel, gathered around him as he entered, and kissed his feet. A sad misgiving possessed his soul at this excessive veneration: "Our cause is good," said he to his chaplain Fabricius, "but I fear that God will punish me for the folly of these people. Does it not seem as if these people were actually making an idol of me? How easily could that God, who abases the proud, cause them and myself to feel, that I am nothing but a feeble and mortal man!"

As just about this time the weather was intensely cold, and the king had intrenched himself near Naumburg, Wallenstein did not deem it advisable to commence hostilities before the spring, and dispatched Count Pappenheim to the Rhine with instructions, first of all to drive the Swedes out of Halle and the contiguous town of Moritzburg. Gustavus immediately took his departure, advanced to Weissenfels, and in the evening of the 15th of November took his position in front of Wallenstein's army near Lützen. Both made immediate preparation for battle, and the imperial general summoned Pappenheim, who was still engaged in the siege of Moritzburg, to return with all possible speed.

The king spent the cold autumnal night in his carriage, and advised with his generals about the battle. The morning dawned, and a thick fog covered the entire plain; the troops were drawn up in battle array, and the Swedes sang, accompanied by trumpets and drums, Luther's hymn: "Eine feste Burg ist unser Gott," (A mighty rock is our God;) together with the hymn composed by the king himself: "Verzage nicht, du Häuflein klein," (Fear not, thou little flock.) Just after eleven o'clock, when the sun was emerging from behind the clouds, and after a short prayer, the king mounted his horse, placed himself at the head of the right wing,—the left being conducted by Bernard of Weimar,—and cried, "Now, onward! May our God direct us! Lord! Lord! Help me this day to fight for the glory of thy name!" and throwing aside his cuirass with the words, "God is my shield!" he led his troops to the front of the imperials, who were well intrenched on the paved road which leads from Lützen to Leipsic, and stationed in the deep trenches on either side. A deadly cannonade saluted the Swedes; many here met their death, but their places were taken by others, who leaped over the trench, and the troops of Wallenstein made a retreat. In the mean while, Pappenheim had come up with his cavalry from Halle, and the battle was renewed with the utmost fury. The Swedish infantry fled in trepidation behind the trenches. In order to render them assistance, the king hastened to the spot with a company of horse, and rode in full speed considerably in advance to descry the weak points of the enemy; a few of his attendants only, and Francis, duke of Saxe-Lauenburg, followed him. His short sightedness led him too near a squadron of imperial horse; he received a shot in his arm, so that he nearly fell to the ground powerless; and just as he was turning round to be led away from the tumultuous scene, he received a second shot in the back. With the exclamation, "My God! my God!" he fell from his horse, which had likewise been shot in the neck, and hanging by the stirrup he was dragged some distance along the ground. The duke of Lauenburg abandoned him, but a faithful page, Leubelfing, endeavored to raise him up: the imperial horsemen, however, shot him also, killed the king with several wounds, and completely plundered him; the page died of his wounds five days after at Naumburg.

The corpse of the king was so much trampled upon by the hoofs of the horses that it was quite disfigured. His bleeding horse returning without its rider, conveyed to his friends the sad news; this kindled in their breast a feeling which thirsted for revenge, and under the leadership of Duke Bernard of Weimar, who with heroic firmness now rallied and cheered on the troops afresh, they again pushed forward over the trenches and rushed upon the ranks of the enemy. These could no longer make resistance; Piccolomini, already covered with blood, mounted his fifth horse, and Pappenheim, who had fought nobly, fell mortally wounded by a ball. Many fled, and disorder prevailed: "The battle is lost, Pappenheim is dead, the Swedes are upon us!" was the cry. Wallenstein gave orders to sound a retreat. A thick fog, together with night coming on, prevented the Swedes, no less than their own weariness, from making pursuit; they spent the night on the field of battle, and kept possession of the imperial artillery. Wallenstein marched with the remains of his army to Bohemia, although he had formerly determined to winter in Saxony. Thus the issue unequivocally declared the Swedes victorious, although Wallenstein represented the battle as undecided, and the emperor ordered a Te Deum to be sung in all his cities.

On the following day the Swedes made a search for the body of their beloved king, among the thousands which covered the wide battle-field; they found it at length, among many others, so disfigured by the hoofs of the horses, and covered with the blood issuing from eleven wounds, that they could hardly recognise it. It was carried to Weissenfels, and thence by the desire of the queen, Maria Eleanor, who had followed her consort to Germany, attended by weeping multitudes, it was removed to Stockholm, where it was interred.

The collar, also saturated with blood, and which the king had worn in battle, was brought to the emperor Ferdinand at Vienna; it is said, that when he saw it he shed tears, by which he did honor to his fallen enemy and himself. Ferdinand's soul was great enough to admire heroism even in a foe.

Thus, in the thirty-eighth year of his life, in the midst of a career of victory, was Gustavus Adolphus called away; the preponderating influence of his mind gave another character to the constitution of Germany and the progress of our development. He had already conceived the idea of getting himself nominated king of Rome, and his design, the extent of which is known to none, may also have comprehended other countries of Europe. He often expressed his astonishment that the present age did not produce generals like those of antiquity; and when he was told that the altered character of the weapons and tactics of war, and the existence of strong fortifications were the cause, he replied: "The difference is not in the nature of the weapons, but in the degeneration of men; if we could again meet with the heart of an Alexander, the courage of a Hannibal, and the enterprising spirit of a Cæsar, we should see renewed the deeds of Alexander, the conquests of Hannibal, and the successes of Cæsar." Such lofty conceptions of human life, such a thorough acquaintance with the agencies which govern the world, and with history, did he possess; and who will venture to determine what limits a mind like this had prescribed to itself? A contemporary, whose judgment may be regarded as impartial, Count Galeazzo Gualdo, a Venetian and a Catholic, who spent several years in the imperial as well as in the Swedish armies, describes the personal and mental qualifications of the king thus: "Gustavus was tall, stout, and of such a truly royal demeanor, that he universally commanded veneration, admiration, love, and fear. His hair and beard were of a light brown color, his eye large, but not far-sighted. War had great charms for him, and from his earliest youth honor and glory were his passion. Eloquence dwelt upon his tongue, (he spoke—in addition to the German, the native language of his mother—the Swedish, Latin, French, and Italian languages;) and in discourse he was agreeable and lively. There never was a general who was served with so much cheerfulness and devotion as was Gustavus. He was of an affable and friendly disposition, readily expressed commendation, and noble actions were indelibly fixed in his memory; on the other hand, excessive politeness and flattery he hated, and if any person approached him in this way, he never trusted him."

He was severe against all the excesses of the soldiery, and was greatly concerned for the security of the citizens and peasantry. When, after taking a Catholic town, some sought to induce him to treat the burghers with harshness, and to give them new laws, he made answer: "The city is now mine, and no longer the enemy's. I am come to loosen the fetters of freedom and not to rivet them afresh. Let them live as they have lived heretofore; I give no new laws to them who know how to live as their religion teaches." "In dealing with Protestants and Catholics he made no distinction. His maxim was, that every one is orthodox who conforms to the laws, and to keep men from going to hell was not the calling of princes, but that of the ministers of religion."

Thus he carried out these sentiments during his stay at Munich, as well as on other occasions. On Ascension-day, in the year 1632, he went to the chapel of Our Lady, to be present at a mass celebrated with all the solemnity of the Catholic worship; he then visited the college of the Jesuits, replied to the rector's Latin address in the same language, and conversed with him for nearly an hour on the subject of the Lord's Supper. In magnanimity and liberality of sentiment he occupies a position strikingly in advance of his generation, no less for the respect he paid to the religious feeling of others, however it might differ in form from that which he conscientiously preferred, than for the homage he paid to greatness and truth in general. How natural it was that the affections of mankind should be gained by a character like this, by the side of such narrow-minded and prejudiced rulers of the day as Ferdinand II., Maximilian of Bavaria, or even the well-meaning but weak John George of Saxony! Besides Gualdo, other Catholic writers, such as Khevenhüller, Riccius, Burgus, &c., do not conceal their veneration for Gustavus Adolphus.

The monument of Gustavus Adolphus in Germany was for a long time a mere stone land-mark, placed in the battle-field of Lützen, upon the spot where he fell; more recently, however, an admirer of his character has erected in the same place another plain but more worthy memorial.

## CHAPTER XXV.

Continuation of the War, 1632–1635—Chancellor Oxenstiern—Wallenstein's Inaction—Court Martial over his Officers—Military Executions—Count of Thurn taken Prisoner and released by Wallenstein—The Emperor's Remonstrance and Wallenstein's Reply—The Swedes in Bavaria—Wallenstein withholds Assistance—Prohibits his Officers from obeying the Imperial Commands—Pilsen—Military Council and Compact between Wallenstein and his Officers—Counts Terzka, Illo, and Piccolomini—The Emperor divests Wallenstein of all Command—Italian-Spanish Conspiracy against Wallenstein—Piccolomini marches against Wallenstein—Wallenstein negotiates with France and Sweden for his Services—The Crown of Bohemia offered to him—Retreats to Eger—The Supper in the Citadel—Murder of Counts Terzka, Illo, and Kinsky by Deveroux and Geraldin—Assassination of Wallenstein, 1634—His Estates confiscated—Succeeded in Command by Ferdinand, King of Rome—The Battle of Nördlingen—The Elector of Saxony—Peace of Prague, 1635—Dreadful Condition of Germany—Cardinal Richelieu and Chancellor Oxenstiern—French and Swedish Alliance against the Emperor—Inglorious Character of the War—Death of Ferdinand II., 1637.

It now became a question whether or not the Swedes, after the death of their king, would continue to carry on the war. If they did not, the Protestant allies had good reason to be apprehensive that Wallenstein would visit them with a heavy retribution. The Swedish council, however, to whom the guardianship of Christina, the daughter of Gustavus, was intrusted, resolved to continue the war which might entitle Sweden to some of the provinces of Germany, and the late king's friend, the Chancellor Axel Oxenstiern, was determined to fill his place; a man whose comprehensive and prudent mind knew how to hold the strength of his party together. Nevertheless, he had not the suavity and generous magnanimity of his late master. The electoral princes, especially Saxony, found it irksome to yield obedience to the dictates of a Swedish nobleman, and although he succeeded in uniting the Protestant states of the four upper circles—Swabia, Franconia, and the Upper and Lower Rhine, in the treaty of Heilbronn in the spring of 1633, it was soon manifested, by the indecision of some, the opposition of others, and the want of union among the leaders of the army, that the genius of Gustavus Adolphus no longer presided over the whole.

Wallenstein alone, whose genius surpassed all others, might have availed himself of this moment of doubt and hesitation by bringing the war to a decision, and making the emperor triumphant, but he was occupied with other cares, and remained in a state of incomprehensible inaction. After the battle of Lützen he summoned a court-martial, in order to remove from his own shoulders all responsibility for the loss of that action; and as he possessed the power of life and death over all those under his orders, he forthwith condemned several of his generals and superior officers to the axe, and adjudged a great number of private soldiers to be hung; finally, he ordered more than fifty names of absent officers to be nailed to the gallows in Prague, as those of traitors and cowards. He then enlisted fresh troops, replaced his artillery by melting down the bells of the churches, and was soon in possession of an army equally as powerful as his former one. Instead, however, of directing his march through the imperial states, and advancing against the Swedes under Gustavus Horn and Duke Bernard of Weimar, who were masters of the frontiers of Germany, he marched on to Silesia, where such a large army was not at all required, and negotiated with the Saxons for a length of time upon the subject of a separate treaty of peace, after he had already concluded an armistice with General Arnim, in command of the Saxon army. At the same time, according to the subsequent accusations brought against him, he endeavored to ascertain what amount of indemnification the enemy would allow him in case he went over to their side, for he had long since believed to have read in the stars that it was his destiny to reign and hold unlimited sway as king. Meantime, in order, by more active proceedings, to prevent the emperor from suspecting his intentions, he attacked the Saxons and the Swedes, and drove them out of Silesia, taking prisoner the old count of Thurn, the originator of the war. The whole of Vienna was in a state of excitement, and fully expected that the man they so much hated would be led through their streets as the most culpable of all those connected with the dreadful scenes of the revolution; Wallenstein, however, to the astonishment of all, gave him his liberty, and when he was remonstrated with by the emperor for releasing his prisoner he replied: "What use was I to make of such a fool? I wish the Swedes possessed no better generals than this Thurn, for at the head of the Swedes he will do more service for the imperial cause than he could if in prison."

During this interval Bavaria was very hard pressed by Horn and Bernard of Weimar, and, urged by the elector's earnest demands for aid, the emperor had already repeatedly summoned his general to march to the relief of that country. Wallenstein, however, delayed doing so for a considerable time; at length he advanced slowly through Bohemia, arrived in the upper palatinate and marched back again into Bohemia, where he fixed his winter quarters. He gave strict orders to all his generals, in command of distinct divisions of the army, under the most severe penalties, not to obey the orders of the emperor; and when the latter caused a Spanish army to march from Italy into Germany without placing it under the orders of Wallenstein, and even commanded that a portion of the grand army should be detached from the main body in order to form a junction with the Spanish division, the generalissimo complained loudly and indignantly at this violation of the treaty made between himself and the emperor.

Wearied with these mortifications, and tormented by his attacks of gout, to such an extent that he was obliged to have pieces of raw flesh cut out of the excoriated foot, he resolved to resign the supreme command; but he was determined to do so in such a manner as to place himself in a position to command the fulfilment of the promises originally made to him. He endeavored, therefore, to attach the leaders of his army still more closely to himself, and to that end summoned them all to assemble, at the commencement of the year 1634, at Pilsen. It was by no means difficult for him to gain them over to his exclusive interest, for it was upon his promise, and in the hope of being completely indemnified through his recommendation, that they had all raised and equipped regiments at their own expense, and, in some, instances, staked their whole fortune. If, therefore, he fell, they were in danger of losing all compensation. Consequently, on the 12th of January, 1634, forty superior officers, having at their head, Field-marshals Illo and Count Terzka, assembled at a dinner—at which, however, through severe illness, Wallenstein himself could not preside—and entered into a solemn compact "to adhere faithfully to the duke in life and death as long as he should remain in the emperor's service, or as long as the latter should require his services in the war;" and they at the same time made him promise them "to remain with them for some time longer, and not to withdraw from the supreme command without their privity and consent." Field-marshal Piccolomini, who subsequently betrayed his general, attached his signature to this agreement, likewise, with the rest.

Wallenstein's enemies availed themselves of this certainly important circumstance to bring him more and more under the emperor's suspicion, and carried out their designs to such an extent as to make Ferdinand resolve, at length, to divest him of the supreme command, and to transfer it into the hands of Gallas. It is not to be at all doubted but that an Italian-Spanish conspiracy was firmly established against Wallenstein in the imperial court, and which was joined by the elector of Bavaria, who continually complained, in most bitter terms, against the general. The principal agent in these secret proceedings was an Italian, Colonel Caretta, marquis of Grana.

These intrigues against Wallenstein were conducted so secretly—the emperor Ferdinand himself being in actual correspondence with him on official business twenty days subsequently to that of the 24th of January, when he had issued the instrument for Wallenstein's dismissal—that the latter only first learned it when Gallas, Piccolomini, and Aldringen published their ordinances, in the name of the emperor, in which they interdicted all the leading officers of the army from accepting farther orders from Wallenstein, Illo, and Terzka. Wallenstein drew up immediately a solemn declaration, signed by himself and twenty-nine of his generals and colonels, in Pilsen, in which it was stated that the compact entered into between himself and officers on the 12th of January, contained nothing whatever that was hostile to the emperor or the Catholic religion. He also dispatched two officers to the emperor with the declaration that he was ready to resign his office of generalissimo, and would appear to justify himself before any tribunal the emperor might be pleased to appoint. These two officers, however, were met and detained on the road by Piccolomini, and the message they bore only reached the emperor after the death of Wallenstein.

Piccolomini marched with his own troops against Pilsen, and Wallenstein was obliged to withdraw to the citadel of Eger, of which the commandant, Colonel Gordon, was especially attached to him from motives of gratitude for favors he had conferred upon him. Here, three days previously to his death, having too much reason to feel assured of the hostile intentions of his enemies, he was impelled by necessity to seek for aid from the Duke Bernard of Weimar, who was now encamped in Ratisbon, and whom he urgently requested to advance with some of his troops towards the Bohemian frontiers. It is historically proved that Wallenstein's brother-in-law, Count Kinsky, banished from Bohemia on account of his Protestant faith, was in treaty with the French ambassador, Feuquières, for the engagement of his relative's services in the cause of France and against the emperor, and that Cardinal Richelieu promised Wallenstein the crown of Bohemia as a recompense; and, according to the Swedish writers, similar negotiations were carried on with their party. But no written document, nor any direct act of Wallenstein himself corroborates these statements, or proves that he did charge Count Kinsky with the execution of such commission, while both the French and the Swedes remained to the last moment in doubt whether or not Wallenstein was merely playing with them in order to gain their confidence. At the same time it is not unlikely that this extraordinary and incomprehensible man, anticipating the probable loss of the emperor's favor, was desirous not to refuse altogether the propositions of the enemy, but rather to hold this resource in reserve in case of being again overturned, as he was before at the diet of Ratisbon.

Wallenstein quitted Pilsen on the morning of the 22d of February, borne along in a litter, and suffering excruciatingly from the gout; he was accompanied by only ten followers, including Colonel Butler, by whom he was subsequently murdered; and at the end of the second day's journey he reached Eger, taking up his quarters in the house of the burgomaster, Pechhelbel, in the market-place. On the following evening, Terzka, Illo, and Kinsky proceeded to the citadel to sup with Colonel Gordon, the commandant. While they were dining, thirty dragoons, commanded by Captains Deveroux and Geraldin, suddenly burst into the hall from the ante-room in which they had been waiting, and, falling upon their victims, pierced them to death; not, however, before Terzka, who bravely defended himself, had killed two of the band of assassins. Immediately after this murderous act, Deveroux proceeded with six dragoons to complete the sanguinary plot by assassinating Wallenstein himself. It was now midnight, and the duke had already retired to rest. Having, however, been roused by the shrieks of the Countesses Terzka and Kinsky, who had just learned the fate of their husbands, he rose, and opening the window, asked the sentinel what had happened? At the same moment, Deveroux forced open the door of the chamber, and, rushing upon him, exclaimed, as he stood at the window: "Death to Wallenstein!" The latter, without uttering a word, laid bare his breast, and received the fatal blow.

Thus silent and reserved to the hour of his death, all the profound and mysterious thoughts and sentiments of his soul remained hidden from the world, and a veil of obscurity was cast over his whole life and actions. He was one of those men whose deep-laid plans and motives it was impossible to fathom, and of whom little or nothing can be said in explanation of their views or ideas.

After his death his estates were confiscated, and a great portion of them were transferred as a reward into the hands of his enemies, and even to those by whom he had been murdered. Gallas received the duchy of Friedland, Piccolomini had the principality of Nachod, while Butler, and the actual assassins, were rewarded with others of his estates and large sums of his money. The major part of his possessions, however, was retained by the emperor himself. The value of Wallenstein's landed property alone was estimated at fifty millions of florins. His widow received the principality of Neuschloss; and his only surviving child, Maria Elizabeth, became shortly afterwards the wife of Count Caunitz.

In order to justify Wallenstein's assassination, a lengthy document was drawn up by the especial command of the emperor himself, containing all the accusations brought against the duke, and which, for a long time, continued to convey the most false and unjust ideas and opinions of the character of that extraordinary man.

After the death of Wallenstein, Ferdinand, king of Rome, and son of the emperor, obtained the chief command of the imperial army, and fortune opened the commencement of his career with the most brilliant success. After having followed the Swedes beyond the frontiers of Bavaria, he overtook them near Nördlingen, in Franconia. His own army was composed of the most choice troops, and augmented by 15,000 Spaniards; while that of the Swedes was by no means in a state of union and discipline. The command was devided between General Horn and Duke Bernard of Weimar; the more experienced and prudent counsel of the former chief, in anticipation of defeat, opposed giving battle altogether, while the more young and daring spirit of the latter insisted upon making a stand, and receiving the enemy's attack. Accordingly the action took place on the 6th of September, 1634; but the reduced number of the Swedes, their bad position, the disunion existing between the leaders, and the misunderstanding and confusion arising therefrom, combined altogether to act against them; and, in spite of all their courage, they, after a combat of eight hours, were completely defeated and nearly cut to pieces. Twenty thousand of their troops were either slain or made prisoners, and among the latter was General Horn himself, while Duke Bernard with the remnant of his army retreated towards the Rhine.

This battle might have proved as favorable in its results for the Catholic party as that of Leipsic had been for the Protestants. The Swedish power seemed annihilated in Germany, and this produced at once the secession of the Saxons from the Swedes. Their elector, John George, had for a length of time beheld with pain and mortification the province of Lusatia continue in the hands of the imperialists, and apprehended that he should not only never recover that, but perhaps might lose still more; accordingly, in the spring of 1635, he made peace with the emperor at Prague. He received back Lusatia, together with a portion of the province of Magdeburg, and full liberty of religious worship for forty years. The evangelical portion of Germany was extremely irritated against the elector, but several other states soon followed his example and made terms with the emperor, such as, Brandenburg, Mecklenburg, Weimar, Lüneburg, and others; and it appeared as if this sanguinary war would find its termination by the enervation of the factions. In truth, unhappy Germany, which had been overwhelmed by warriors from almost every part of Europe, presented a sad and mournful picture at the present moment; everywhere the land devastated, the population frightfully diminished, the corn-fields trodden down or uncultivated, the towns laid waste, and piles of ruins and ashes, where formerly blooming regions had everywhere greeted the eye. What had escaped the sword was destroyed by famine, misery, and disease, while the pen itself refuses to describe the horrible extent to which the sanguinary and cruel scenes of this war were carried.

In such a state of general distress and misery, when the German states everywhere showed an inclination for peace, and the emperor himself was disposed to revoke at least a portion of the Edict of Restitution—as he had already proved by his treaty of peace with the Saxons—the oppressed nation found at length some foundation to hope that the period when its sufferings would terminate was close at hand.

But once again did the fatal hand of destiny, which during so many years had already collected over us so many clouds of disaster, repeat its withering blow. The French minister, Richelieu, had long observed with secret satisfaction the misfortunes of the house of Austria, and of the empire generally. The French government regarded it as the most wise and prudent motive of state policy, to torture and execute, on the one hand, the Protestants of France throughout the entire kingdom; while, on the other, it lent its aid to those of Germany, and thus rendered that faith a means by which it might serve to conceal its thirst after conquest. The moment had now arrived when the cardinal thought he was able to vend the services of France at a dear rate. Accordingly he offered them to the Chancellor Oxenstiern, stipulating for the fortress of Philipsburg on the Rhine as a recompense; while, at the same time, he indicated that his designs extended to the still more important territory of Alsace. This was the first time that foreigners had ever negotiated for the frontiers of our country. With this treaty between Richelieu and Oxenstiern affairs at once assumed a character both ignoble and degrading; for from that moment the Swedish minister sought only to transfer a portion of Germany to his own nation. They found in Duke Bernard of Weimar, otherwise a brave and noble prince, the arm so desirable to second their measures, more especially as he himself was anxious to gain possession of a province on the Rhine. Accordingly, a powerful and well-equipped army was soon collected with French money, and placed under the duke's orders, with which he marched against the imperialists and Bavarians, and from this moment the Rhenish provinces became the scene of war, being pillaged and devastated the same as those along the Oder, Elbe, and Weser, had been previously. The Swedes, however, possessed likewise a brave and active general in Field-marshal Banner; and reinforced by French troops from Sweden, he marched in all haste from Pomerania—whither the remnant of his army had fled after the battle of Nördlingen—against the Saxons, now the allies of the emperor, and on the 4th of October, 1634, gave the elector battle at Wittstock, near Mecklenburg, and completely defeated him.

This war, however, from this moment, only presents a continuation of gloomy and disheartening scenes; for wanting, as it did, a leader of noble genius, and uninfluenced, as its agents were, by motives of a worthy and honorable nature, its whole character assumed an ignoble and mercenary stamp. The royal hero, whose elevation of soul shed a brilliant lustre over all around him, and who was inspired by his religious faith, combined with the glory and honor of his nation, was now no more; the impenetrable, mysterious, and all-powerful general, who alone could venture to make a stand against the forces of Sweden, had also been snatched from the realization of his dark projects; while those who now had the command of the imperial armies, although brave and not without distinction, were only second in rank of genius, and wholly incapable of aspiring to the elevated thoughts and feelings of their predecessors. In this war it was egotism alone by which the parties were swayed; consequently, however remarkable its operations may appear, they must still be regarded in the light of ordinary events.

The emperor Ferdinand himself, who ranked among the most distinguished spirits of his age, now also disappeared from the great scene of contention without living to witness its termination, and died on the 15th of February, 1637, aged fifty-nine years, after having had the satisfaction of seeing his son Ferdinand unanimously acknowledged, at the diet of Ratisbon, as his successor.

## CHAPTER XXVI.

Ferdinand III., 1637-1657—Continuation of the War—Duke Bernard of Weimar on the Rhine—His Death—Cardinal Richelieu—The Swedish Generals—Banner—Torstenson—Wrangel—Negotiations for Peace—Tedious Progress—French and Swedish Claims of Indemnification—Humiliation and Dismemberment of the Empire—Territorial Sovereignty of the Princes—Switzerland—The Netherlands—Final Arrangement and Conclusion of the Peace of Westphalia, 1648.

In the year 1637 and 1638, Duke Bernard of Weimar pursued his victorious career along the Rhine; he surprised the army of the league at Rhinefeld, attacked and overthrew it, taking prisoners four generals, including the brave leader, John of Werth, and Rhinefeld, Röteln, and Friburg, surrendered to his arms. But the chief object of his wishes was to gain the important fortification of Brisach, which he was anxious to make the principal seat of his dominion along the Rhine. He accordingly laid siege to it, and once more defeating the Catholic army which came to its relief, he conquered that stronghold after it had become completely reduced by famine and disease, and caused himself to be solemnly acknowledged by the inhabitants as their ruler. But he remained only a short time in the enjoyment of his conquest; for just as he was about to prepare for another expedition, he was seized with sudden illness, and died on the 18th of July, 1639, in the thirty-sixth year of his age, being the youngest of eight equally brave and warlike brothers. He himself declared his belief that he was poisoned, and his chaplain at once confirmed this suspicion in the sermon he preached over his remains. If this was, indeed, the case, the act can be attributed to no other source but France, for immediately after the duke's death, the army was visited by several French agents who negotiated for the services of the army, which they purchased for large sums, together with all the places in its possession. Three regiments of Swedes alone refused to sell themselves to the French, and they marched out of the place with beat of drum and unfurled banners to join the main body of their army; and thus Brisach was conquered for the French by the valor of the German troops.

Already in the year 1636, the appeal made by thousands of those unhappy beings who suffered so much from the disastrous state of the country, for that peace so much wished by all, had at length produced some effect, and some attempts were made for this purpose; but Richelieu was far from wishing for pacification, inasmuch as war made France an indispensable ally, and the hostile views of its state policy were promoted by seeing Germany cut to pieces by its own people as well as foreigners. Still, in the year 1640, fresh and more serious attempts were commenced to establish peace, and in 1643 the ambassadors of the various powers assembled in Münster and Osnaburg. These negotiations, however, continued during a space of nearly five years; while, meantime, the war was carried on with all its sanguinary results.

Banner, the Swedish general, died in the year 1641, at Hallerstadt, after he had committed dreadful devastation in Bohemia and other lands. He sent to Stockholm more than 600 standards he had captured from the imperialists; but although he possessed talents as a leader, his heart was cruel and without the least mercy, and his campaigns were attended with more bloodshed and oppression than all the others during this war. While he was quartered in Bohemia, there were often more than 100 villages, small towns, and castles, burnt during the night; and one of his principal officers, Adam Pfuhl, boasted that he had, with his own hands, set on fire about 800 different places in that unhappy country. And when soon afterwards, on an expedition he made against Thuringia, this same officer felt his end approaching, and desired the last services of a minister of religion, such was the wasted and forlorn state of the country, that none could be found within the distance of many leagues.

Banner was succeeded in command by Leonard Torstenson, who, although so weak in body that he was always forced to be carried in a litter, was nevertheless the most active and talented of all the generals in this war. He commenced, in 1642, by invading Silesia, attacked and defeated Francis Albert, duke of Saxe-Lauenburg —the same general at whose side the great Gustavus fell at Lützen, and who had now gone over to the Austrians, and conquered Schweidnitz. Thence he marched on to Moravia, took Olmütz, and made Vienna itself already begin to tremble. Disease in his army, however, forced him to retreat; but in the autumn of this year, he attacked the imperial general Piccolomini at Leipsic, who had followed him in his retreat, and completely overthrew him. This was the greatest battle fought in this last period of the war; Piccolomini having lost 20,000 men, forty-six pieces of artillery, and nearly two hundred ensigns.

In the beginning of the following year Torstenson resumed his march through Moravia, advancing as far as Olmütz, so that his light cavalry approached the vicinity of Vienna; and then, while it was thought he was occupied in this quarter, he suddenly appeared, as if by magic, hundreds of miles distant on the coasts of the Baltic sea, in Holstein and Schleswig, the territories of the king of Denmark.

These territories, which had long continued untouched by the destructive arm of war, presented the Swedes with every thing valuable and desirable wherewith to enable them to fix their winter quarters there; while it was easy to find a pretext for making war with Denmark in the jealousy with which that kingdom had always regarded the victories gained by the Swedes. Accordingly, in the ensuing spring of 1644, the Swedes, who had received considerable reinforcements, advanced again into Germany, attacked and completely overthrew the imperial army under Gallas, and in the spring of the succeeding year, 1645, Torstenson defeated the imperial troops, under Generals Götz and Hatzfeld, at Jankau, in Silesia, which he entirely destroyed; Götz himself fell, mortally wounded, Hatzfeld was taken prisoner, and the whole of the ammunition and provisions fell into the hands of the Swedes. The victorious army now marched through Moravia, and advanced to Vienna itself, and had not the city of Brünn, by its most obstinate and heroic defence, arrested the progress of the Swedish general, there is little doubt but that capital must have been taken. But his army was so much reduced by disease before the walls of Brünn, that Torstenson was forced to make a retreat, and as he himself was completely worn out with illness and debility, he was compelled to give up the command of the army.

He was succeeded by Gustavus Wrangel, who continued the war with considerable success. The French armies, under their distinguished generals, Turenne and Condé, fought against the imperialists and Bavarians along the Rhine, and in conjunction witn them Wrangel soon afterwards conquered and subjected the whole land of Bavaria, so that the elector was forced to abandon all further hostilities; and, in 1647, concluded an armistice. Brandenburg had already been obliged to do the same in the year 1641, and Denmark and Saxony followed the example in 1645 and 1646: thus the emperor was left alone to contend with his successful enemies. The grand cause of the ill success he experienced at this period, emanated from his want of efficient leaders; his two best generals, Werth and Merci, having been killed, he was forced to confide the chief command of his troops to General Melander of Holzapfel, a Protestant, who had deserted the Hessian party and gone over to the imperialists.

The allies now once more attacked the hereditary states of the empire; the Swedish general, Königsmark, laid siege to Prague, and had already made himself master of that portion of the city, called the Kleinseite, while Wrangel was in full march to support him with his whole army —when the happy tidings of peace were announced from Westphalia.

The conferences for the settlement of peace had already been opened in the summer of the year 1643: with the Swedes in Osnaburg, and with the French in Münster. The imperial envoys arrived even before the time fixed, but those from Sweden only appeared at the end of the autumn of that year, while those from France presented themselves as late as the month of April, in the following year, 1644: an ominous sign for the progress of those measures of pacification, towards which the eyes of the oppressed empire were turned with anxious and painful longing. And, in truth, these congresses commenced with the discussion of such numberless details, that there appeared little or no chance of any prompt decision being effected. Many months were lost in petty and miserable disputes of precedence, and the French ambassadors, with all imaginable pride and pomp, more especially insisted upon taking the first rank, and assumed all the state and ceremony of a royal court. Subsequently, much time was again sacrificed in deciding whether or not the deputies for all the petty states of the empire should be convoked, and which was, at length, determined in the affirmative, so that the French were enabled to produce still greater discord among us.

The chief subject of negotiation ought to have been the re-establishment of order upon a solid basis in all the provinces of Germany, and more especially among the various religious parties, for through their contentions the war had originated; but the two foreign powers insisted upon receiving first of all their indemnification for the expenses and losses incurred by them during the war, and in the degraded state of necessity to which they were reduced, and at the urgent persuasion of the elector of Bavaria, the Germans were forced to satisfy the demands of these foreigners before they ventured upon the arrangement of their own affairs.

France, which had contributed so little

of its own powers, and which had only mixed itself up in the war for its own advantage, and the pleasure it derived from producing evil as a Catholic state for a Protestant cause—France, we say, demanded enormous sacrifices; and her ambassadors, d'Avaux and Servien, well practised in the art of verbosity, political cunning, and deception, intruding themselves with all the authority and command of masters, insisted upon their claims. The Swedes, although rather more moderate, nevertheless grasped at and tore asunder large portions of the empire, and the friends and well-wishers of the country felt as if cut to the heart when they thus beheld the mortifying treatment it was forced to undergo: "On the same soil where, in former times, our noble ancestors hurled defiance against the insolent Varus and his legions," says a contemporary, "we are now doomed to behold foreigners without arms insult us and triumph over Germania. They summon us, and we humbly obey the call; they speak, and we listen with humility and attention as to an oracle; they promise, and we place faith in them as in God; they menace us, and we tremble like slaves. A sheet of paper filled up by a woman, whether at Paris or Stockholm,* makes the whole Germanic empire tremble or rejoice. They already, in the very heart of Germany, discuss and dispute together over Germany, as to what they shall take from, and what they shall condescend to leave us, what feathers they shall pluck from the Roman eagle, and therewith decorate the Gallic cock. And we ourselves, divided continually among each other, abandon our tutelary divinity for the idols of foreign nations—to whom we sacrifice life, liberty, and honor!"

The imperial envoys acted with firmness and dignity; Count Trautmannsdorf and Doctor Volmar sought, with all the strength of reason and principle, to grapple with the pretensions set forth by foreign powers, while they endeavored, by mildness and patience, to conciliate the discordant feelings existing in the German states. They did not, however, find themselves sufficiently seconded by the other members of the empire, especially in the latter period of the war, when Bavaria became so vacillating; while every dispatch they received announced the success of the enemy, and overturned all the advantages they might otherwise have effected by their conferences. Hence they were obliged to make the following arrangements:

1. France received the bishoprics of Metz, Toul, and Verden, as much of Alsace as had belonged to Austria, the Sundgau, and the important fortresses of Brisach and Philipsburg; besides which, it forced Germany to destroy a great number of fortifications along the Upper Rhine, in order that the French army might have an open and free passage into Germany. Thus all those places which had served as the bulwarks of the south of Germany, fell, through this peace, into the hands of the hereditary enemy of the empire. The French envoys themselves, in the excess of their joy, declared loudly that France had never concluded a peace upon such advantageous terms.

2. Sweden, which had likewise made great claims for compensation, but whose interests were but too inadequately and unfavorably represented by the grand chancellor's son, John of Oxenstiern, a proud but inexperienced statesman, together with the counsellor Adler Salvius, a man too much open to bribery, was forced to content herself with Western Pomerania and Stettin, the island of Rügen, the city of Wismar in Mecklenburg, together with the sees of Bremen and Verden on the Weser; a territory the major portion of which was very poor and much devastated. On the other hand, Sweden never availed herself of these possessions to act inimically towards Germany. As an indemnification for the expenses of the war, the Swedes received five millions of dollars extracted from the already exhausted sources of the empire.

3. The elector of Brandenburg, who had just claims to the whole of Pomerania, only received the eastern portion of that country, and, as an indemnification for the western division, he received the archbishopric of Magdeburg, and the bishoprics of Halberstadt, Minden, and Kanim, as lay-principalities.

4. Mecklenburg received, in lieu of Wismar, the sees of Schwerin and Ratzeburg.

5. Hesse Cassel, which from the com-

* In Sweden the throne was occupied by Christiana, daughter of Gustavus Adolphus, and, during the minority of Louis XIV., his mother, Queen Anne, reigned as regent in France.

mencement of the war had adhered firmly to Sweden, and whose beautiful and talented landgravine, Amelia, succeeded in captivating all hearts, received through the mediation of Sweden and France, although it had suffered no loss, the abbey of Hersfeld, a portion of the country of Schaumburg, and six hundred thousand rix-dollars.

6. Brunswick-Lüneberg, which extended its claims to Magdeburg and Minden, and subsequently to Osnaburg, received the privilege by which one of its princes should hold possession of this latter country alternately with a Catholic bishop.

7. The eldest son of the unfortunate Frederick V., of the palatinate, Charles Lewis—Frederick himself having died thirteen days after Gustavus Adolphus—received back all his patrimonial estates, except the upper palatinate, which the elector of Bavaria retained; and as he likewise would not yield the title of the electoral dignity—the fifth—a privilege which belonged to the palatine house, a fresh title—the eighth—was created for it purposely.

8. The negotiations for the adjustment of religious affairs in Germany were attended with extreme difficulty and considerable delay. The Protestants demanded religious liberty, not only for themselves, but likewise for all the Protestant subjects of the emperor; while on this point, the latter was equally firm and inflexible in withholding his consent. They were obliged, therefore, to restrict the operation of this measure to the empire itself, and, after a deliberation which lasted six months, the decree of the religious peace of Passau was eventually renewed and fixed as the fundamental basis of the present measure, and it was resolved that the Protestants should retain all the ecclesiastical property they possessed in the year 1624, in land and churches. This year was henceforth styled the normal year, and from that time the question of the edict of Restitution was altogether abandoned. The Protestants accordingly retained the archbishoprics of Magdeburg and Bremen; the bishoprics of Lübeck, Osnaburg, (alternately,) Halberstadt, Verden, Meissen, Naumburg, Merseburg, Lebus, Brandenburg, Havelberg, Minden, Kanim, Schwerin, and Ratzeburg; the abbeys of Hirschfeld, Walkenried, Gandersheim, Quedlinburg, Hervorden, and Gernrode. It was likewise ordered and approved, that no sovereign prince should oppress any of those of his subjects whose faith in religious matters deviated from his own; while it was also decreed that the imperial chamber should be composed of an equal number of counsellors and members –Protestant and Catholic. By these regulations the peace of Westphalia became a fundamental law of the empire, and although some causes for dispute and discontent were not altogether removed, the minds of the people in general were more tranquillized. Feelings of hatred were no longer cherished, the principles of tolerance became more and more widely disseminated, and gradually exerted their beneficial influence in the hearts of all; so that very soon the bigotry of parties disappeared, and the hand of fraternity was held out between those who, although differing in their faith from each other, nevertheless now acknowledged themselves to have an equal claim to rank as fellow Germans and Christians. Difference in religion now no longer formed an insurmountable wall of separation between men; and certainly in this point of view the peace of Westphalia, by establishing fixed laws in the external affairs of the Church, produced highly satisfactory and beneficial results.

9. Respecting the rights of sovereignty due to the princes, and the relations of the states of the empire with the emperor, the peace of Westphalia contained such regulations as must in the course of time produce a still greater relaxation of those ties, already partially loosened, which held together the empire in one entirety. In earlier times the constitution of the empire contained already many defects: great disorder, abuse of power in defiance of the laws, nay, the evils produced by the existence of an entire century, during which force prevailed over justice—all this was sufficient evidence of the corrupt state of things. The main cause, however, of these results originated in the want of fixed written laws, whence, as we have already seen, after the edict of the golden bull, various measures were adopted in order to establish in Germany, by imperial laws, a more determined form of constitution. Nevertheless, there existed in earlier times a bond of union which operated with more success in periods of disorder than even

the written laws might have done, and this consisted in those ancient characteristics for which Germany was ever distinguished: sincere and faithful loyalty, antipathy to foreigners, a holy veneration for the imperial majesty of the sovereign, produced by the conviction that the dignity of emperor was derived from God as a divine favor for the homage of mankind. In such light was the imperial presence regarded by the princes themselves, as expressed by them in various authentic documents. Subsequently it was the feudal system, based upon the ancient customs and manners, and springing from the essential condition of the people, which served on great occasions, in spite of the want of written laws, to hold together the various portions of the empire.

When in ancient times the prince, the nobles, and the people, assembled together, and when later the emperor himself presided at the head of the princes of the empire at the diets, it was then the prompt and decisive power of the sovereign's voice and animated eye which decreed the means of remedying existing evils; and if at times disputes arose, his regular presence, the attention with which he observed with eye and ear all that passed before him, and the confidence he accordingly produced and established between himself and those around him, placed him at once in a position to command the reconciliation of the disputants. At the same time, this proximity of the imperial dignity, and the respect it inspired in all sensible and well-minded men, operated for the benefit of the entire nation, while the emperor himself, by the high consideration he commanded throughout Christendom, represented and maintained its honor.

Now, however, for a length of time, as we are already aware, the princes but rarely attended personally at the diets; but were satisfied with sending their envoys, or merely their written communications. The negotiations were often carried on at a most tedious rate upon subjects of the most trivial nature, and only under pressing and extreme cases of necessity were the decisions pronounced. Meantime this state of legislation was not at all sanctioned by any law of the empire; but at the peace of Westphalia the independence of the princes was made completely legal. They received the entire right of sovereignty over their territory, together with the power of making war, concluding peace, and forming alliances among themselves, as well as with foreign powers, provided such alliances were not to the injury of the empire. But what a feeble obstacle must this clause have presented? For henceforward, if a prince of the empire, having formed an alliance with a foreign power, became hostile to the emperor, he could immediately avail himself of the pretext that it was for the benefit of the empire, the maintenance of his rights, and the liberty of Germany. And in order that the said pretext might, with some appearance of right, be made available on every occasion, foreigners established themselves as the guardians of the empire; and accordingly France and Sweden took upon themselves the responsibility of legislating as guarantees, not only for the Germanic constitution, but for every thing else that was concluded in the peace of Westphalia at Münster and Osnaburg.

Added to this, in reference to the imperial cities whose rights had hitherto never been definitively fixed, it was now declared that they should always be included under the head of the other states, and that they should command a decisive voice in the diets; thenceforth, therefore, their votes and those of the other states—the electoral and other princes—should be of equal validity.

10. By an article in the treaty of Westphalia, French cunning likewise separated the Swiss confederation from the Germanic empire, and acknowledged it as an independent state. It is true it had long since discontinued rendering homage to the empire, but its dismemberment therefrom had never been legally declared, whence the way for its return to the imperial dominion always lay open and feasible, in case any of the confederates might have felt a desire to renew their alliance.

11. In the same moment that the empire thus sacrificed one of its most secure defences on the frontiers of the south, the loss of the Netherlands left it completely bare in the northwest: for in this peace Spain was forced to acknowledge the independence of that country, and Germany was equally obliged to free it from all obligation of fealty. That country had likewise originally belonged to the same race as ourselves, it forming, from the period of Charles V., part of our confederation, and commanding the mouth of our national

river—the Rhine. Thence Germany was left equally exposed to the attacks of its enemies in the north from the Netherlands, as it was in the south from Switzerland.

It was only after great care and exertion that the intricate work of pacification was at length brought into operation, and it could only be perfected by slow degrees and at much additional sacrifice. The French obstinately refused to evacuate the conquered fortifications until the most petty details of the conditions had been fulfilled; while the Swedes remained two years longer in Germany, distributed in seven circles of the empire, determined not to withdraw until they received the five millions of dollars they demanded as indemnification for the war expenses, and which, in the already reduced and miserable state of our unhappy country, could only be collected with great trouble and difficulty. In addition to this, it has been calculated that during these two ruinous years, the maintenance of the foreign soldiers quartered throughout the empire, cost at the rate of 170,000 dollars per day. Nay, even six years after the settlement of peace, a certain number of Swedish regiments levied contributions in the bishopric of Münster, and Duke Charles of Lorraine, who had been driven out of his territory by the French, continued for a considerable time to hold possession of several fortifications on the Rhine.

---

# SEVENTH PERIOD.

## FROM THE PEACE OF WESTPHALIA IN 1648 TO THE PRESENT TIME.

In the first portion of this period, from 1648 to 1740, the art of historical research made but little progress in Germany: we find the sources of record to consist chiefly of compilations made from public acts, collected together in numerous and heavy masses, interspersed with the lives of the emperors, written in the most partial and inflated style. Any regular and critical statement or investigation of facts, presenting in their treatment elevation of thought and originality of genius, is not to be found among them. In France, however, among the numerous memoirs of the time of Louis XIV., we meet at least with that peculiar style of representation, by which the connecting links in the chain of state policy are far more clearly traced, and the ideas and motives of individuals more strikingly developed.

As collections embodying especially public transactions and political events we find included:

1. Records of the Imperial Chancery, 1657–1714.
2. Diarium Europæum, 1659–1681, 45 vols.
3. Sylloge Publicorum Negotiarum, 1674–1697, by Lunig., (died in 1740.)
4. European Court of Chancery; commenced by Leucht, and continued by Faber and König, 1697–1760, 115 vols. Resumed by Faber under the title of New Court of Chancery, 1760–1783, 17 vols.
5. European Fame, 1703–1734, 350 parts in 30 vols., and New European Fame, 1735–1756, 192 parts in 17 vols.
6. Mercure Historique et Politique, commenced by G. Sandras, tom. I., Parma, 1686; from 1688 to 1782, at the Hague, in more than 200 vols.
7. The History of the Emperor Leopold I., has been written in a very good historical style in Italian by Galeazzo Gualdi, Bapt. Comazzi, and Jos. Maria Reina; and in German by J. J. Schmauss, C. B. Menkin, G. Rink, and best of all in Latin, by F Wagner, but only to the year 1689.
8. S. von Puffendorf, Res gestæ Frid. Guil. Magni, Elect. Brand. Berlin, 1695, and Lips. et Berol., 1733.
9. Camill. Contarinus, History of the Turkish war in 1683, in Italian; Venice, 1710.
10. L. de St. Simon, Œuvres, 13 vols. Especially valuable in reference to the time of Louis XIV.
11. The Life of Joseph I., by Wagner, Zshackwitz, Nink, and Herchenhahn.
12. The Life of Charles VI., by Zshackwitz, Schwarz, Schmauss, and Schirach.

On the history of the War of Succession to the Spanish throne, the principal works are:

13. De Lamberty, Mémoires pour servir à l'histoire du 18me siècle; 1700–1718, La Hague, 14 vols., and
14. History of the War of Succession to the Spanish throne, by two anonymous writers. Two Editions; one in French, printed at Cologne in 1708; the other in English, printed in London in 1707.
15. Mémoires du Prince Eugene de Savoie écrits par lui-même. Weimar, 1810.
16. W. Coxe, Memoirs of John, Duke of Marlborough, 6 vols., 1820.

The great events which took place during the period of 1740 to 1789, especially those of the Seven Years' War, and the enthusiasm with which Frederick the Great inspired all his contemporaries, excited a spirit for historical composition which, although it may not have produced works of the first order, is nevertheless entitled to place its writings in the second rank. The great Frederick himself devoted his pen to the task of writing a history of his own times and actions, his—

17. Frederick II., Histoire de mon Tems, and Histoire de la Guerre de Sept Ans; and other works relating to history and politics, together with his correspondence with many distinguished persons, are valuable documents in our historical collection.
18. Adelung, History of the States of Europe from 1740 to 1798, 6 vols., treats especially upon the history of the succession of the house of Austria.

The following works give especial details of the Seven Years' War:

19. War-office reports, (Deutsche Kriegskanzlei,) 1757–1763, 18 vols.
20. Contributions to the more recent History of War and State Policy, (Beiträge zur Neueren Staats- und Kriegs Geschichte,) 1756–1762, 13 vols.
21. Lloyd, Histoire de la Dernière Guerre en Allemagne; traduit de l'Anglais par Templehof, 5 vols.
22. Archenholz, History of the Seven Years' War, 2 vols.
23. Retzow, Criticism of the important events of the Seven Years' War.

24. De Mauvillon, Histoire de Ferdinand de Brunswick, 1790.
25. Campaigns of the Allied Armies, 1757-1762, from the journal of Major-General von Rheden, 1805.
26. History of the Battle of Künersdorf, by Kriele, pastor of Künersdorf. Berlin, 1801.
27. The Life of Frederick II. has been written by several historians, including Koester, Seiffart, Zimmermann, Funke, Garve, Stein, Thibault, Förster, Preuss, and Nicolai, the latter of whom has added numerous anecdotes in Frederick's life.

On State Politics we have:
28. Count Hersberg, Recueil des Deductions, Manifestes, Declarations, Traités, &c., publiés par la Cour de Prusse depuis l'année 1756-1790, 3 vols.

The following are the works which treat upon the period subsequent to the Seven Years' War:
29. Manso, Geschichte des Preuss. Staats vom Hubertusburger Frieden bis zur zweiten Pariser Abkunft, 3 vols.
30. Dohm, Memoirs of my Times, 1778-1806, 5 vols. A work of great importance connected with the latter period of the reign of Frederick the Great and the French Revolution, but more especially valuable for the impartiality displayed by the author.
31. Büsching, Magazine of History and Geography, 1761-1781, 15 vols., Hamburg; and 1781-1793, 23 vols., Halle.
32. Schlözer, Historical Correspondence, 1775-1782, 10 vols., and Political Advertiser, 1782-1793, 18 vols.
33. Schirachs, Political Journal, 1781-1804, continued by his son to the present day.
34. Archenholz, Minerva, 1792-1809, continued to the present time by A. Bran.
35. Girtanner, Political Annals, 1793-1794.
36. Posselt, European Annals, 1795-1804, and continued to the present time by other authors.
37. Review of the Prussian Monarchy under Frederick William III., 1798-1801.

From the commencement of the 19th century we have:
38. The Times, by C. D. Voss, 1805-1820.
39. Bredow, Chronicle of the 19th century, 1801-1808, continued by Venturini as a history of our times, from 1809 to the present moment.

On the History of the French Revolution, the following are the principal works in Germany:
40. Girtanner, Historical Revelations of the French Revolution, continued by Buchholz, 17 vols.
41. Von Eggers, Memoirs of the French Revolution, 6 vols.
42. J. G. Eichhorn, The French Revolution at one View, 2 vols.
43. Rehberg, Researches into the French Revolution, with a critical notice of the most distinguished works upon the subject.

The following treat upon the wars of the French Revolution:
44. Scharnhorst, Military Memoirs of our Time, 6 vols.
45. Charles, Archduke of Austria, History of the Campaign of 1799 in Germany and Switzerland, 2 vols.

On the Negotiations of the Peace of Rastadt:
46. Von Haller, Private History of the Rastadt Negotiations of Peace in connection with the political transactions of this period. Germania, 6 vols.
47. Münch von Bellinghausen, Protocol of the Deputation for the Peace of the Empire at Rastadt, compared exactly with the original documents, with notes, 6 vols.

On the Wars of the 19th Century:
48. Von Bülow, The Campaign of 1805 in a military and political point of view, 2 vols.
49. The Battle of Austerlitz, by an officer present.
50. K. von Plotho, Journal of the Military Operations in the years 1806 and 1807.
51. Von Valentini, Essay upon the History of the Campaign of 1809.
52. Von Hormayr, the Austrian army in the war of 1809, in Italy, the Tyrol, and Hungary, from official sources.
53. Bertholdy, The War of the Tyrolese in 1809.
54. History of Andreas Hofer, from original sources. Leipsic and Altenburg, 1817.
55. Lüders, The War of 1812, between France and Russia.
56. K. von Plotho, The War in Germany and France, 1813-1815.
57. Odeleben, Napoleon's Campaign in Saxony in the year 1813.
58. Aster, The Battle of Leipsic, with plans; with many other works upon the same subject.
59. The Central Administration of the Allies under Baron Stein.
60. General Müffling, History of the Campaign of 1815, under Wellington and Blücher.
61. F. Förster, Field-marshal Blücher and his operations, 1821.
62. Saalfeld, History of Napoleon Bonaparte, 2 vols.
63. Klüber, View of the Diplomatic Transactions at the Congress of Vienna, 1816.
64. Protocol of the German Diet, 1816.
65. G. von Meyer, Repertory of the Transactions of the German Diet, 1822.
66. Monumenta Germaniæ Historica, ed. G. H. Pertz.
67. J. Schmidt, History of Germany, continued by Milbiller and Dresch, 27 vols.
68. Heinrich, ditto, ditto, 3 vols.
69. A. Menzel, History of Germany, 9 vols.
70. Luden, History of the German Nation, 12 vols.

---

## CHAPTER XXVII.

General Observations—State of the Empire—Agriculture—Commerce—The Nobility—French Language, Fashions, and Customs—Decline of National Feeling in Germany—Death of Ferdinand III., 1657—Leopold I., 1658-1705—The Rhenish League—Louis XIV. of France—His ambitious and aggrandizing Spirit—Conquers the Netherlands—The Elector Frederick William of Brandenburg—Westphalia—The Rhine—War between France and Germany—Battle of Fehrbellin, 1675—Successes of the Elector of Brandenburg—His energetic Character—Extends and improves his Territories—Berlin—Königsberg—Generals Montecuculi and Turenne—Peace of Nimwegen, 1678—The Four French Chambers of *Reunion*—Treachery and Dishonesty of Louis XIV. towards Germany—Claims and takes possession of Strasburg and other German Towns on the Rhine—Enters Strasburg in Triumph, 1681—Pusillanimity and Disgraceful Inertness of the Germans—The Turks in Hungary—Advance and lay Siege to Vienna, 1683—Flight of Leopold and his Court—Brave Defence of the Viennese under Count Rüdiger of Stahrenberg—Relieved by Duke Charles of Lorraine and Sobieski, King of Poland—Heroism of Sobieski—Battle of Naussdorf—Total Overthrow and Flight of the Turks by Sobieski—His Letter to his Queen—Description of the Battle.

It will not require many words, nor will it prove a task of much difficulty to represent the sadly depressed state of the country after a war of such devastation, and which had continued during half the period of that existence commonly allotted to man. Two thirds of the population had perished, not so much by the sword itself, as by those more lingering and painful sufferings which such a dreadful war brings in its train: contagion, plague, famine, and all the other attendant horrors. For death on the field of battle itself is not the evil of war; such a death, on the contrary, is often the most glorious, inasmuch as the individual is taken off in a moment of enthusiastic ardor, and while he is inspired with the whole force of his vital power; thus he is relieved from the anxious and painful contemplation of the gradual approach of his last moments. But the true curse of war is based in the horrors and miseries it spreads among, and with which it overwhelms, those who can take no active share in it—women, children, and aged men, and from whom it snatches all the enjoyments, all the hopes of life; thence the germ of a new generation becomes poisoned in its very principle, and can only unfold itself with struggling pain and sorrow, without strength or courage.

Nevertheless, in Germany the natural energy of the people speedily aroused itself among them, and a life of activity and serious application very soon succeeded in a proportionate degree to that which had so long been characterized by disorder and negligence: and it is thus that the two extremes often meet. The demoralization so generally existing—produced on the one hand by the warriors who, on their return home from the camp, introduced there much of the licentiousness they had previously indulged in, and, on the other hand, through the juvenile classes having grown up and become matured without education, and being by force of example in almost a savage state—obliged the princes now to devote all their attention and care towards re-establishing the exercise of religious worship, and restoring the schools and ecclesiastical institutions; measures which never fail to produce beneficial results. But it was agriculture which more especially made rapid strides in the improvements introduced, and which was pursued with an activity hitherto unexampled. As a great number of the landowners had perished during the war, land generally became materially reduced in price, and the population accordingly showed everywhere the most active industry in the cultivation of the soil; so that within a short space of time the barren fields were replaced by fertile meadows, and fruitful gardens amidst smiling villages greeted the eye in every part. The moment had now arrived, likewise, when the claims of the peasantry to the rights of freeborn men were acknowledged more and more, and the chains by which they had been hitherto bound were gradually relaxed, until at length the final link which held them fell to the ground. Thus Germany might have become more flourishing than ever by the prosperous state of its agriculture, for it is from the maternal earth that a nation draws its source and strength of life, when it devotes its powers to that object; but essential and general causes interfered, unhappily, to prevent the fulfilment of this desirable object.

In the first place, the declining state of the cities operated in a special degree to destroy the beneficial results of agriculture. The prosperity of the cities had received a vital blow, as already shown, by the complete change which had been introduced in the whole system of commerce; its decline, however, was only partial until the period of the war of thirty years. Shortly previous to the commencement of this war, a foreign writer placed Germany still at the head of every other country, in respect to the extent and number of its cities, and the genius, talent, and activity of its artists and artisans. They were sent for from every part of Europe. At Venice, for instance, the most ingenious goldsmiths, clockmakers, carpenters, as well as even the most distinguished painters, sculptors, and engravers, were, at the end of the sixteenth century, all natives of Germany. But it will suffice to mention the names of such celebrated artists as Albert Dürer, Hans Holbein, and Lucas Cranach, to form an idea of the prosperous state of the arts in the cities of Germany at the commencement of the sixteenth century. This terrible war, however, gave them their mortal blow; numerous free cities, previously in a flourishing state, were completely reduced to ashes, others nearly depopulated altogether, and all those extensive factories and institutions which gave to Germany the superiority over other nations, were, through loss of the workmen, completely deserted and left in a state of inactivity. Thence, at a meeting of the Hanseatic league in Lübeck, in 1630, those few cities which still remained in existence declared they were no longer able to contribute towards the expenses of the league. Economy and strict industry might perhaps have raised them gradually from the state of misery into which they had thus fallen, but their ancient prosperity and importance were both forever gone; and, as is stated by one of our early writers, on the foreheads of these once wealthy citizens might be traced in characters too clearly expressed, how fallen was their state, reduced as they now were to endure a painful and laborious existence. Many of the cities, some voluntarily, others through the necessity of the times, saw themselves compelled to submit to the power of the princes, as for instance, Christopher, bishop of Gahlen, made himself master of Münster, in 1661; the elector of Mentz, of the city of Erfurt, in 1664; the elector of Brandenburg, of the city of Magdeburg, in 1666; and the duke of Brunswick, of the city of Brunswick, in 1671; while those which retained the title of free cities, how poor and miserably did they drag on their existence, until at length, in more recent times, they likewise lost their privilege altogether.

The nobility had likewise lost much of their ancient dignity and lustre. Ever since they no longer formed more especially the military state of the empire, and their noble cavaliers no longer conferred exclusively glory upon the nation; ever since they had abandoned their independence, by attaching themselves to the court, or wasted all their strength in a life spent in indolence, and without any noble object in view; and, finally, ever since they had commenced imitating and adopting the manners, customs, and languages of foreign nations, and substituted their effeminacy and refinement for the ancient energy and sincerity for which Germany had ever been so renowned—ever since, we say, these changes and innovations had been introduced, the nobles of the empire had gradually degenerated and lost all their consequence and dignity. Thus were eclipsed two of the most important and essential states of the empire, and which above every other had both contributed to give to the middle ages, in spite of all their other defects, that grand and vigorous character for which that period was so much distinguished.

It is true, that during the last few centuries changes of a similar nature had taken place in other countries of Europe, and which, by thus substituting a new order of things, obliterated all that which had characterized the middle ages. But with all this, ample compensation was found in the wealth and prosperity commanded by commerce, while in this respect Germany was now deprived of all such resources. The share which a few of the cities still took in the commerce of the world could not establish or effect a balance of the whole; while, on the other hand, instead of restricting themselves to that simple order of life—so especially necessary among an agricultural people—and thus trying to avert the coming indigence, they launched out more and more into a luxurious state of living; and accordingly, in exchange for precious and exotic articles of merchandise, they gave up to foreign nations all the rich fruits of agriculture and industry produced at home at the expense of so much toil and anxiety. For, however fertile the soil of our country, and however varied its produce, it could not possibly equal in value the rich wares imported from all parts of the world. When, however, the love of luxury and sensual pleasure has gained the upperhand, nothing can restrict or check its extravagant and insatiable demands.

This evil, however, was not one originally implanted in our nature, it was communicated to us by those foreigners whom we sought to imitate in every thing—even in their degeneracy. The excursions now made beyond Germany, and especially to France and its metropolis; the imitation more and more indulged in of the fashions and manners of the French, and even of their immorality itself; the introduction and reception of French professors and governesses into various German families for the education of the juvenile branches; the contempt more and more shown and felt for our own native language; the enthusiasm indulged in for that French philosophy, so superficial, and yet at the same time so easily adapted to render the individual wholly indifferent to his religious, moral, and social duties; all these causes, we repeat, had operated more and more injuriously among the higher, as well as the middling classes of society, and thence, at the present period, their influence presented the most baneful effects.

On the other hand, however, it is not to be denied but that our relations with foreign countries have materially promoted the civilization of Germany; and it is impossible not to recognise in the course of modern history a tendency to render more and more firm and durable the bond of union between all the nations of Christendom. Placed as we are in the centre of the principal nations of Europe, we have ever warmly sympathized with, and the forms of our political constitution have ever encouraged the movement of moral and intellectual progress. For in most other countries, each of which was constituted into one homogeneous kingdom, the chief city was the first to set the example in the adoption of all that it might judge worthy of patronage and dissemination, and thence it established the rule or law for the co-optation thereof generally throughout the provinces: by this means, however, the progress made became gradually subjected to certain fixed forms, whence it could not be exempt from partiality. In Germany, on the contrary, science and art have marched together full of activity and independence as in a free dominion. The superior, equally with the lesser states, rivalled each other in their patronage; no single town, no particular individual, was empowered to impose laws; and, finally, no favoritism, no exception of person, was shown, but every thing bearing within it essential and sterling merit, was sure sooner or later to meet with due acknowledgment and appreciation; and thence it is that our nation has made such progress in all the sciences.

Nevertheless, this moment must be regarded as teeming with dangerous error. Nothing is more difficult for human nature than to maintain the one direct and central path without diverging to one side or the other; nothing more difficult than to combine civilization and enlightenment with religious and moral strictness, to unite an acute sensibility for all that is really good and valuable in genius, wherever found, with honesty and constancy of principle, and to conjoin independence of spirit with self-denial and submission. This medium course ought, therefore, to be the main object of the endeavors of all, both of individuals and nations. The period we are about to trace will show us in what degree this object was alternately approached by or receded from our nation; while, at the same time, it will present us with all those vicissitudes to which mankind is subject.

This series of good and bad fortune is, we shall find, more especially shown in our external relations: days of prosperity and peace were succeeded by those of distress; but the latter down to and during this period, continued in their degree to outweigh the former. In no period of our history do we find presented such melancholy pictures as during the long reign of Louis XIV. of France, nor has our state policy ever shown so much weakness and pusillanimity as when suffering from his ambitious designs. During the short interval of tranquillity from the time of his death to the war of the Austrian succession, the arts of peace once more revived a little, but the progress of their development was again checked by the storms of that contest, and more especially by the still more ruinous war of seven years, which immediately succeeded. The interval of twenty-five years, from the conclusion of this war to the commencement of the French revolution, was the longest period of tranquillity we had hitherto enjoyed; and during this space of time, art and science once more came into activity, and made such flourishing progress, that in spite of the war of twenty-five years by which the French revolution was succeeded, this progress, although much checked, was not altogether destroyed. Let us hope that the state of peace we at present enjoy, may long continue to heal the wounds so bitterly inflicted upon our country, and thus encourage more and more the growth and development of the intellectual resources of the German nation.

The emperor Ferdinand III. lived nine years after the peace of Westphalia; he reigned with moderation and wisdom, and until his death the peace of Germany remained undisturbed. He had already procured the decision of the princes in favor of his son Ferdinand, as his successor to the imperial throne, when unfortunately that young man, who had excited the most sanguine hopes, and towards whom all eyes were turned with confidence, died in 1654 of the small-pox. Ferdinand was, therefore, forced to resume his efforts with the princes in favor of his second son, Leopold—although he was far from possessing the capacity of his deceased brother—but he himself died on the 2d of April, 1657, before the desired object was fully obtained.

The election of the new emperor met with considerable difficulty, because the government of France was anxious to avail itself of this moment to obtain possession of the imperial dignity, to which it had long aspired. It had in fact already succeeded in gaining over the electoral princes of the Rhine; but all the rest of the German princes felt the shame and disgrace such a choice must bring upon the nation, and decided at once in favor of Leopold, archduke of Austria, although this prince was only eighteen years of age; and he was accordingly elected at Frankfort on the 18th of July, 1658.

Meantime Cardinal Mazarin, the prime minister of France, had already formed an alliance, which, under the name of the Rhenish league, had for its object the total annihilation of the house of Austria, although *apparently* its only aim was the conservation of the peace of Westphalia. The parties included in the union were France, Sweden, the electors of Mentz, Cologne, and Treves, the bishop of Münster, the palatine of Neuburg, the elector of Hesse-Cassel, and the three dukes of Brunswick-Lüneburg; a singularly mixed alliance of Catholic spiritual and lay princes with the Protestant princes and Swedes, who had only so recently before stood opposed to each other in open warfare. A learned historian of that period unfolds to us what were the real intentions of France in forming this league, as well as the motives by which she was guided throughout her proceedings against Germany: "Instead of resorting to open force, as in the war of thirty years, it appeared more expedient to France to hold attached to her side a few of the German princes, and especially those along the Rhine, by a bond of union—and, as it is said, by the additional obligation of an annual subsidy—and, above all things, to *appear* to take great interest in the affairs of Germany; thus, the princes might be brought to believe that the protection of France would be more secure than that of the emperor and the laws of the empire. This means of paving the way for the destruction of all liberty in Germany was, as may be easily judged, by no means badly conceived."

France very soon showed that she only waited for an opportunity of seizing her prey with the same hand which she had so recently held out in friendship. The long reign of Leopold I. was almost wholly filled up with wars against France and her arrogant prince, Louis XIV.; and our poor country was again made the scene of sanguinary violence and devastation. Leopold, who was a prince of a mild and religious disposition, but, on the other hand, of an equally inactive and pusillanimous character, was by no means calculated to enter the field against the French king, in whom were united great cunning with unlimited ambition and insolent pride. France now pursued, with persevering determination, the grand object she had in view, of making the Rhine her frontiers, and of gaining possession of the Spanish Netherlands—which, under the name of the Burgundian circle, belonged to the Germanic empire—Lorraine, the remaining portion of Alsace, not yet in its occupation, together with all the lands of the German princes situated on the left bank of the Rhine. This spirit of aggrandizement was shared in equally by the king and the people, and it is an error to suppose this feeling was only first brought into existence in our time through the revolution, and the wild ambition of a few individuals. Already, during the reign of Louis XIV., the French authors began to write in strong and forcible language upon the subject of conquest, and one among them, a certain d'Aubry, even went so far as to express in a pamphlet his opinions founded on the question—at that moment a novel one, but which afterwards became of serious consideration, and was nearly carried into execution—that, viz. "The Roman-Germanic empire, such as was possessed by Charlemagne, belonged to his king and his descendants;" and the Abbé Colbert, in an address to the king, in the name of the clergy, adds the words: "Oh, king, who givest laws to the seas as well as to all lands; who sendest thy lightning wherever it pleasest thee, even to the shores of Africa itself; who subjectest the pride of nations, and forcest their sovereigns to bend their knee in all humility before thee in acknowledgment of the power of thy sceptre, and to implore thy mercy," &c. Such was the language used already in 1668, and in the face of Europe, by a state which ought to have surpassed all others in moderation and truth.

Accordingly, Louis now commenced operations by conquering the Netherlands, pleading his ancient hereditary right to the possession of that country. The Spaniards appealed for aid to the other circles of the Germanic empire, but not one of the princes came forward to assist them; some through indifference, others from fear, and the rest again from being disgracefully bought over by French money: such were the results of the Rhenish league. Abandoned thus by all, the Netherlands fell into the hands of the king, and at the peace of

Aix-la-Chapelle, in 1688, the Spaniards saw themselves forced to surrender a whole line of frontier towns to France, in order to save a portion only of the country.

In addition to this, in the year 1672, France, with equal injustice, invaded Holland itself, and had she succeeded in her plans, she would very soon have been in a condition to hold dominion over the European seas. This new danger, however, produced as little effect upon the princes of Germany as the preceding one; they paid little or no attention to it, nay, the elector of Cologne, and the warlike bishop of Münster, Bernard of Gahlen, one of the most distinguished men of his day, actually concluded an alliance with France. One only of the princes of Germany, the elector Frederick William of Brandenburg, known likewise under the title of the great elector, acted with the energy so necessary; and, completely aware of the exact condition of the nation, felt the necessity of preventing the total subversion of the equilibrium of Europe. Accordingly, he made immediate preparations for placing his territories of Westphalia in a state of defence, exposed as they were in the immediate vicinity of the scene of action; for by the definitive arrangement of the inheritance of Juliers, in 1656, he had received the duchy of Cleves, and the provinces of Mark and Ravensberg, while to the prince-palatine of Neuberg had been allotted the duchies of Juliers and Berg. Frederick William induced likewise the emperor Leopold to adopt measures for opposing the farther progress of the French invaders; and both together raised an army which they placed under the orders of the imperial general, Montecuculli; but the co-operation of the Austrians became almost nullified through the influence of Prince Lobkowitz, the emperor's privy-counsellor, who, gained over by France, opposed all the plans of the imperial general. Thence the elector beheld his fine army harassed and worn out by hunger and sickness, and in order to prevent the French from completely destroying his territories in Westphalia, in 1673, he concluded with them a peace in their camp of Vossem near Louvain. His possessions were restored to him with the exception of the castles of Wesel and Rees, which the enemy resolved to retain until a general pacification was permanently established.

Now, however, the emperor, after having lost his best allies, determined to pursue the war with more vigor. Montecuculli gained some advantages along the Lower Rhine, and, among the rest, he succeeded in making himself master of Bonn; but all along the Upper Rhine and in Franconia, the French redoubled their ravages, and more especially in the palatinate, which was now made the most sanguinary scene of the whole war, as in fact it was subsequently, where the French have left eternal monuments of their cruel proceedings. As they thus continued to invade even the very empire itself, the princes now united to resist them, and the elector of Brandenburg renewed his alliance with the emperor. On this occasion, Austria was distinguished especially for her energy and activity. At the diet of Ratisbon, long discussions were held upon the subject of the war, but nothing was concluded; and Austria, having discovered that this delay was produced by the French ambassador, who there endeavored by every means to deceive, first one and then another of the princes, that power immediately commanded him, without waiting for any other formality, to quit Ratisbon within three days, and on his departure a declaration of war was forthwith made by the emperor against the king of France.

The war was carried on with varied success and loss, but altogether the advantage was on the side of the French, whose generals were completely successful in their object of making the German soil alone the field for their operations; while, on the other hand, the leaders of the allied forces were without activity or union. In order to furnish occupation in his own land for the most powerful of the German princes, the elector of Brandenburg, Louis XIV. concluded an alliance with the Swedes, in 1674, showing them the great advantage they would derive by the invasion of that territory. This they accordingly did, severely handling that country; nevertheless, the elector would not abandon the Rhine, but contributed his assistance, and remained as long as his presence was necessary, and it was only in the following year, 1675, that he at length did withdraw from that seat of war, and by forced marches hastened to the aid of his suffering country.

To the astonishment of both friends and

foes, the elector suddenly arrived before the city of Magdeburg, and passing through it, continued on his march, until he came right in front of the Swedes, who believed him to be still in Franconia. They immediately retired, and sought to form themselves into one body, but he pursued them, and came up with them on the 28th of June, 1675, at Ferbellin. He had only his cavalry with him, his infantry not being able to follow quick enough; nevertheless he determined to attack the enemy at once. His generals advised him to await the arrival of his foot-soldiers before he gave battle; but every moment of delay appeared to him as lost, and the action began forthwith. It was attended with the most brilliant success; the Swedes, who ever since the Thirty Years' War had been regarded as invincible, were now completely overthrown and put to flight, directing their course towards their Pomerania. Thither they were pursued by the elector, who conquered the greater portion of that province.

This elector may be regarded as the founder of the Prussian monarchy, and his successors only built upon the basis he laid down. Besides acquiring the Westphalian territories from the Cleve inheritance, he made the duchy of Prussia independent, and wisely availing himself of the peculiar circumstances of the times, obtained, in 1675, the treaty of Welau, by which Prussia was declared free of all enfeoffment to Poland. Berlin, its capital city, he enlarged by the Werder and Neustadt; while in Frankfort and Königsburg he promoted the progress of the universities, and had already formed a plan for the erection of an additional one in Halle. He encouraged all kinds of art and industrial invention throughout his lands, and hospitably received and employed a considerable number of refugee artisans from France. Frederick William always thought and acted for himself, pursuing his own independent course, and we shall again find him on various occasions successfully producing that respect for the power and dignity of his small dominion which he was determined to maintain with all his influence, not only as a German prince, but with all the authority of one who ranked among the rest of the monarchs of Europe. Such is the true sign which indicates the hereditary princely grandeur of a ruler who desires that his people shall be inferior to none of all the other nations, and whose sole object is nobly to raise it in their estimation. And who can reproach him for acting with such energy and determination, at a moment, too, when the German alliance had lost all its strength, when the power of the emperor himself was reduced almost to a mere shadow, and when many of the princes of the empire had actually already entered into a league with foreigners? Had he himself joined in such treaties to the injury of the empire, and thus inflicted the final blow upon the small remnant of hope still left, he might assuredly have merited severe and just condemnation; but, on the contrary, the whole aim of his life was to oppose as much as possible the aggressions of the French, and to protect, as far as was in his power, the liberties of the German and European nations generally.

In the year 1675 the imperial general, Montecuculli, an old and experienced soldier, received a second time orders to march to the Rhine, and he commenced operations with more favorable results. Opposed to him was the celebrated French general, Vicomte de Turenne, one of the greatest men of his time. They advanced against each other with extreme caution, for they were already well known to each other. At length Turenne fixed upon a favorable spot for giving battle, combining every advantage necessary, near the village of Sasbach and in the vicinity of Oppenheim. But while he had advanced in front of the enemy in order to make his observations, and form his army in line of battle, he was mortally wounded by a cannon-ball which struck him off his horse. His death produced the greatest alarm and dismay among his troops, who immediately retreated and took to flight, in which they suffered severe loss.

Nevertheless, very little advantage was gained by this affair. The French, in order to drive the imperialists out of their country, had recourse to the most extreme measures. As they were unable to defend their frontiers with troops, they proceeded to adopt other means of protection; and, accordingly, in the following year they laid waste the whole of the country along the river Saar to such an extent that, throughout a space of more than seventy miles, nothing else was to be seen but burning villages and fields. Thence the German troops could no longer remain encamped in a country thus destitute of the means of supply, and they were forced to turn back, while the unfortunate inhabitants were obliged to seek refuge in the forests, where a great number of them perished through famine and disease.

All eyes were now directed with anxious hope and expectation towards Nimwegen, where now, in 1679, a conference was being held for the establishment of peace. The French, it appears, were forced at length to hasten the conclusion of a peace, were it even disadvantageous to themselves, because they were at this moment surrounded with enemies. Nevertheless, they were at all times extremely happy in their attempts to produce division among their adversaries, and in this instance they were equally successful. By making large and advantageous offers they induced the Netherlanders, for whom the war had been principally undertaken, and who owed their safety to the imperialists, to withdraw from the empire, and concluded with them exclusively a treaty of peace, and by this they received the citadel of Maestricht. They were succeeded by the Spaniards, who, in order to make peace, were obliged to make good most of what the Netherlanders had been relieved from paying; accordingly they ceded a great extent of territory in the Netherlands, together with the whole of the Franche-Comté. Finally, the emperor, who was not disposed to carry on the war alone, was forced to make terms of peace likewise, and to give up the important fortress of Friburg in Breisgau. Thus the elector of Brandenburg, who had conquered nearly the whole of Pomerania from the Swedes, and was in hopes of making an advantageous peace, abandoned as he was now by all, even by the Netherlands—for whom he had fought, but who now refused their assistance, was forced to restore nearly the whole of his conquests. At this conference of Nimwegen it was easy to observe the preponderance now commanded by France over Europe, even by the circumstance of the language itself; for among those ambassadors assembled thirty years previously at Münster and Osnaburg, only very few understood French at all; while now, at Nimwegen, every one present knew and spoke it fluently. Nevertheless, the articles of peace themselves were still written in the Latin tongue.

The oppressed provinces began now again to breathe more freely and enjoy the blessings of peace, after the insatiable ambition of the French became at length satisfied. But our enemy was ever ready, even in the very bosom of peace, to pursue his prey. A member of the French parliament from Metz, a certain Rolland de Revaulx, laid before the king a plan by which he might extend his dominion far beyond the Upper Rhine, if he only gave the right interpretation to the words used in the article of the Westphalian treaty: "That Alsace and the other territories shall be ceded to him *with all their dependencies.*" It was, therefore, he said, only necessary to seek out what territories and places had *formerly* belonged to that country, and in the course of a short time many possessions might be found, of which, under this pretext, he might make himself master without any difficulty. This suggestion was approved of, and it was taken into further consideration; and, in order to give it an appearance of justice, the French government instituted, in 1680, four courts of council under the title of *Chambres de Réunions,* at Metz, Dornick, Brisach, and Besançon; these were appointed to examine what lands and subjects might still belong to the king, according to the wording of the article referred to. It is easy to be conceived that these judges were not long in making their discoveries; the most trifling foundation was laid hold of in order to carry out their plans. The convent of Weissenburg, for instance, although situated beyond Alsace, was declared attached to it, and as such belonging to the king, because it had been founded by King Dagobert, more than one thousand years previously; and the acquisition of Weissenburg served them as a pretext to demand that of Germesheim, inasmuch as it had formerly belonged to Weissenburg. In this way the four chambers extended their claims for the restoration of Zweibrücken, (Deux-Ponts,) Saarbrück, (Sarre-Louis,) Veldenz, Sponnheim, Mumpelgard, Lautenburg, and many other places, more particularly, however, the free imperial cities of Alsace, and among the rest Strasburg especially. These places had not been given in the Westphalian treaty, as Austria could only then cede in Alsace her own hereditary possessions.

The princes and nobles whose property was thus suddenly to be transferred from German into French hands, exclaimed loudly against it. The emperor himself protested against it, and Louis XIV., in order to observe at least appearances—such was his cunning policy—and to shut the mouths of his adversaries, promised to examine their counter claims, and summoned a congress at Frankfort.

Meantime he resolved, beforehand, to make himself master of the citadel of Strasburg, which to him was of more value than all the rest, and which had always been regarded as the key to the Upper Rhine. Charles V. considered it of such importance, that he said, should ever Vienna and Strasburg be both threatened at the same moment, he would hasten first to save Strasburg. In the month of September, 1681, and while the principal citizens were absent at the Frankfort fair, several regiments were secretly assembled in the vicinity of that place, and, to the astonishment and alarm of the inhabitants, suddenly surrounded its walls. In a day or two afterwards, Louvois, the minister of war and confidential adviser of the king, appeared with a numerous army and a train of artillery, and with heavy threats summoned the citizens to surrender. Not being at all prepared to resist this attack, and urged on by a party in the city bribed by the king, they were forced to yield, and opened their gates on the 30th of September, 1681. The troops took immediate possession of the arsenal and the citizens' arms, the Protestants were obliged to vacate the cathedral of which they had enjoyed possession for more than a hundred and fifty years, and immediately afterwards Louis XIV. arrived himself, and, as in triumph, made his solemn entry in the city. No sign of shame at this act was visible in the countenance of that king, who had, nevertheless, already loudly boasted that he made *honor* the law of his life.

The conference at Frankfort, meantime, produced no change in the plans of the king; his deputies evaded with much address all serious discussion upon the inquiries made, and continued to maintain their principles; while on this occasion, for the first time, they introduced as a law the use of their own language in all diplomatic transactions. Hitherto, as with other nations, they had written all their state documents in the Latin tongue; but at Frankfort they were composed in French, and all the arguments used by the imperial ambassadors against this innovation were perfectly useless; the only reply made was: "It is by command of our king." Thence they were forced to succumb, and from this moment the French language was adopted as the established medium of communication between France and all other countries. Men of intelligence and enlarged views easily foresaw the danger to be dreaded from this arrangement, and prophesied the gradual estrangement which must be produced in a country imitating the language and customs of a nation like France, so anxious to hold it under dominion.

The disputes which arose between the different imperial envoys themselves were sufficient to show how weak and futile must be the attempts they made to seek indemnification from the usurpers; for here again at Frankfort all those old and contemptible questions of pre-eminence, the madness of which exceeds all belief, were renewed, and while they thus wasted away their precious time in a war of words, the French took advantage of their miserable neglect, and fortified themselves more and more strongly in the lands they had usurped. At length, however, Austria succeeded in forming an alliance with several princes in order to repulse force with force; but a revolt which at this moment arose in Hungary, together with a fresh invasion of the Turks there, which had been promoted by Louis himself to suit his own purposes, prevented any result arising therefrom.

Ever since the year 1670, Hungary had been continually agitated by dissension. That country was extremely annoyed and indignant at beholding its constitution violated, and all its cities garrisoned by German soldiers, whom they thoroughly hated; while, in addition to this, the Protestants complained loudly against the persecutions they endured at the instigation of the Jesuits. Accordingly, the discontented portion of the nation having, in the year 1678, found a determined leader in Count Emmeric of Toeckly, they rose *en masse*, and even formed an alliance with the Turks. The warlike and ambitious grand vizier, Kara Mustapha, prepared at once for the invasion of Hungary at the head of an army far exceeding any in strength since the conquest of Constantinople. Fortunately for the emperor Leopold, he found in the Polish king, John Sobieski, a brave and determined ally, while the German princes now faithfully, and contrary to their custom, speedily came to his aid, and Charles, duke of Lorraine, was appointed chief in command of the imperial army. This heroic prince, the conqueror of the Turks, and the instructor of the subsequently distinguished Prince Eugene, was equally great and magnanimous in his character as a man, as he was in that of a warrior and a supporter of the house of Austria.

Nevertheless, the spring of the year 1683 had commenced before the preparations were completed, while the Turks, who were never accustomed to open a campaign before the summer season, had already begun their march in the winter of the preceding year, and on the 12th of June they crossed the bridge of Esseck. The imperial army was hastily formed and reviewed in Presburg, and consisted of 22,000 foot and 11,000 cavalry; while that of the Turks exceeded 200,000 men. The latter continued on their march direct for Vienna, without halting to lay siege to any of the towns in Hungary, as it was hoped they would have done. Consternation and alarm filled the whole city; and the emperor with his court fled, and sought refuge in Linz. Many of the inhabitants followed him; but the majority, after the first moment of terror was over, armed in defence of their city, while the slow progress made by the Turks who, as they proceeded, occupied themselves with pillaging all the villages and castles along their march, left time for the duke of Lorraine to send a body of 12,000 men into the city as a garrison; and as he could not venture to advance with his small army in order to cut off the passage of the enemy, he drew off his troops from the high road, and awaited the arrival of the Polish king.

Count Rüdiger of Stahrenberg was appointed by the council of war commandant of the city, and he showed all activity and haste in doing every thing possible to place it in a state of defence, and every man capable of working or bearing arms assisted cheerfully. On the 14th of June the vizier appeared with his immense army before the walls, occupying a space of the country around them to an extent of six leagues. Two days afterwards the trenches were opened, the cannon fired upon the city, and the siege commenced; the walls were undermined, and every preparation was made by the Turks for blowing up the bastions in order to rush pell mell into the devoted place, where they hoped to make a glorious booty. The besieged, however, made an heroic defence, and repaired in the night what had been damaged during the day. Every step of ground was obstinately disputed, and thus a struggle equally desperate and determined was maintained by the assailants and the assailed. The most fierce and sanguinary scene of contest was at the Löbel bastion, where scarcely any part of the ground was left unstained with the blood of friend and foe. Meantime the Turks gained a footing more and more; at the end of August they were already in possession of the moat of the city walls, and on the 4th of September they sprung a mine under the Burg bastion; the explosion made half the city shake and totter, the bastion itself was rent asunder to an extent of more than thirty feet, and pieces of its walls scattered around in all directions. The breach was so great that the enemy made an immediate assault, but they were repulsed. On the following morning, they made another attack and were again driven back by the brave defenders. On the 10th of September another and final mine was sprung under the same bastion, and this time the breach was so extensive that a whole battalion of the enemy's troops was enabled to penetrate through it. This was now a moment of most extreme danger; the garrison was completely exhausted by constant fighting and fatigue, and sickness had reduced their number considerably, while the commandant had sent courier after courier to the duke of Lorraine in vain. At length on the 11th, while the whole city was in momentary expectation and dread of the enemy's assault, the Viennese observed from their walls that, by the movements in the enemy's camp, the expected and so much longed-for succor must be near at hand; and soon afterwards, to the joy of all, the Christian army showed itself on the Kalen Hill, and announced its presence by discharges from the artillery. The brave Sobieski had now arrived at the head of his valiant army; and he was immediately followed by the electors of Bavaria and Saxony, Prince Waldeck with the troops of the circle of Franconia, the duke of Saxe-Lauenburg, the margraves of Baden and

Baireuth, the landgrave of Hesse, the princes of Anhalt, and many other princes and nobles of the empire, who all brought with them a numerous body of their own troops. With such a select body of leaders Charles of Lorraine felt he might venture to advance against the enemy, although his entire force amounted only to 40,000 men.

On the morning of the 12th of September, the Christian army descended the Kalen Hill in order of battle. The village of Nussdorf, situated on the banks of the Danube, was first attacked by the imperialists and Saxons, who occupied the left wing, and was taken after an obstinate resistance. Meantime, towards mid-day, the king of Poland had descended into the plain with the right wing, and at the head of his cavalry dashed against the innumerable battalions of the Turkish horsemen, and with irresistible force penetrated through the very centre of their ranks, spreading before him confusion and dismay; his daring courage, however, carried him a little too far, for he was speedily surrounded by the Turks, who now closed upon him and his few companions, and he must soon have been overcome and destroyed, had he not summoned the German cavaliers who were in his rear to the rescue, and who, galloping up with lightning's speed, fell with tremendous force upon his turbaned captors, and delivering him from their hands, put them to flight, and soon the whole of this body of the Turkish army was overthrown and sent flying in all directions.

This action, however, only served as an introductory scene to the grand battle which was to decide the fate of the war; for the immeasurable camp of the Turks, covered with thousands of tents, still maintained its position, while their artillery continued to bombard the city.

The imperial commander-in-chief held a council of war whether the battle should be commenced that evening, or whether the soldiers should rest until the following morning, when he was informed that the enemy appeared to be already running away in every direction. And such was the case in reality. An irresistible terror had come over them; they fled, abandoning their camp and all their baggage and ammunition, and very soon even those who had fired upon the town followed the example and decamped with the whole army.

The booty made in the camp was immense; it was estimated at 15,000,000 dollars, and the tent of the grand vizier alone was valued at 400,000 dollars; in the military chest were found 2,000,000 of dollars. The king of Poland obtained 4,000,000 of florins for his portion, and in a letter to his consort, he writes respecting the battle and the great joy felt by the delivered inhabitants of Vienna, in the following terms: "The whole of the enemy's camp, together with their artillery and an incalculable amount of property, has fallen into our hands. The camels and mules, together with the captive Turks, are driven away in herds, while I myself am become the heir of the grand vizier. The banner which was usually borne before him, together with the standard of Mahomet, with which the sultan had honored him in this campaign, and the tents, wagons, and baggage, are all fallen to my share; even some of the quivers captured among the rest, are alone worth several thousand dollars. It would take too long to describe all the other objects of luxury found in his tents, as for instance his baths, fountains, gardens, and a variety of rare animals. This morning I was in the city and found that it could hardly have held out more than five days. Never before did the eye of man see a work of equal magnitude dispatched with a vigor like that with which they blew up, and shattered to pieces huge masses of stone and rocks. I myself had to sustain a long contest with the vizier's troops before the left wing came up to my aid, but after the battle I was surrounded by the elector of Bavaria, Prince Waldeck, and several other princes of the empire, who embraced me with warm affection. The generals took hold of my hands and feet, the colonels with their regiments of horse and foot saluted me with, 'Long live our brave king!' This morning the elector of Saxony, together with the duke of Lorraine came to me; and, finally, the governor of Vienna, Count Stahrenberg, with a multitude of the people, rich and poor, came to meet me; all greeted me most cordially, and called me their deliverer. In the streets were loud rejoicings and cries of 'Long live the king!' When I rode out into the encampment after dinner, the populace with uplifted hands accompanied me out of the city gate. Let us, for this most glorious victory, render to the Most High, praise, honor, and thanksgiving, for ever!"

The Austrians had good cause to feel grateful for this deliverance. For this formidable foe not only plundered and slaughtered the people according to his usual practice in war, but without making any distinction, dragged after him all he could seize as slaves. It has been calculated that altogether, Austria lost in this way 87,000 individuals, among whom were 50,000 children and 26,000 women and young females, and of the latter alone 204 belonged to the families of counts and others of the nobility.

The whole of Europe took an interest in the deliverance of Vienna; Louis XIV. alone was greatly confounded, and none of his ministers could command sufficient courage to bear the intelligence to him; nay, credible writers assert that, in the tent of the grand vizier, letters were found from the king, containing the entire plan for the siege of Vienna.

The war with the Turks continued with a few intermissions fifteen years longer, ending gloriously for the imperial arms. The terror felt for their name ceased, and their military fame had now declined. In the year 1687 they were totally defeated at Mohacz by the duke of Lorraine and Prince Eugene of Savoy, and as a consequence of this victory the whole of Hungary submitted to the imperial dominion, and even made its regal dignity hereditary, instead of being, as hitherto, only elective. After the great victory of Prince Eugene at Zeutha, in 1697, an armistice for twenty-five years was concluded with the Turks at Carlowitz.

## CHAPTER XXVIII.

Fresh War with France, 1688-1697—Alliance of England, Holland, and Spain, against Louis XIV.—The French in Germany—Dreadful Devastation and unheard-of Cruelties committed by orders of Louis XIV.—Conflagration and complete Destruction of Heidelberg, Worms, and Spires—Deplorable Condition of the Inhabitants—The Tombs of the Emperors pillaged—Peace of Ryswick, 1697—Compensation demanded for Germany—Insolence of the French Ambassadors—Elevation of the German Princes—The First Elector of Hanover—Frederick, Elector of Saxony, ascends the Throne of Poland, 1696—Frederick, Elector of Brandenburg, places the Crown on his own Head as King of Prussia, 1701—War of the Spanish Succession between France and the House of Austria, 1701-1714—William III. of England—Louis XIV proclaims his Grandson, Philip of Anjou, King of Spain—Prince Eugene—His Military Genius and Private Character—Appointed Commander-in-Chief of the Imperial Army—His Reply to Louis XIV.—Marches into Italy—Defeats the French at Carpi and Chiari—England—Louis XIV. and the exiled Stuarts—The Duke of Marlborough, General of the Allied Army—The Elector of Bavaria—The Bavarians in the Tyrol—Their Overthrow by the Tyrolese—Battle of Hochstadt—Blenheim—Triumphant Victory gained by the Duke of Marlborough and Prince Eugene, 1704—The Duke of Marlborough created a Prince of the Empire—Death of Leopold I., 1705.

Louis XIV. had employed the interval, while Austria and the German princes were subjugating their formidable enemy in the southeast, in gathering new forces, for he did not deem the usurped possessions already in his hands sufficient. And as he thought the present to be the most favorable moment, he availed himself of certain insignificant disputes respecting the hereditary title of Charles, the electoral prince of the palatinate, and the succession to the electorate of Cologne, after the death of Maximilian Henry; and pretending that it devolved upon him to protect the constitution of Germany, he issued a fresh declaration of war against the emperor in 1688. Before it was even made known, his troops invaded the Netherlands and began to lay waste as before. Summoned by this danger, numerous armies from Northern Germany, Saxony, Hanover, and Hesse, hastened to the Rhine on the defensive. This was the more praiseworthy, as at Ratisbon they were yet discussing the question whether or not there should be a war. However, even here, things began to wear a more determined aspect; an imperial war was declared, without allowing any one of the states to remain neutral, and the emperor added to the declaration: "The government of France is not to be considered simply as the enemy of the empire, but, like the Turks, the enemy of all Christendom."

The arrogance of France and the violations of the Nimwegen treaty of peace excited also the indignation of the other European states; soon England, Holland, Spain, and subsequently Savoy, took part in the war, and the new king of England, William III., who was at the same time stadtholder of the Netherlands, in his declaration of war, likewise calls King Louis—"A disturber of the peace and the common enemy of all Christendom."

In order that France might wage a successful war against so many adversaries, unhappy Germany was again subjected to the inhuman treatment which the minister Louvois had suggested: the flourishing banks of the Rhine were reduced to a state of complete desolation, and the recital of the cruelties inflicted excites but one feeling of horror.

As early as January, 1689, the cavalry of General Melac surrounded the country around Heidelberg and set fire to the towns of Rohrbach, Nuszloch, Wisloch, Kirchheim, Eppenheim, Neckarhausen, and many others, while the poor defenceless people, who supplicated for mercy on their knees, were stripped and hunted naked into the fields, then covered with snow, where many perished through the cold. Heidelberg itself was set on fire in several different places. The towns of Mannheim, Offenburg, Creuznach, Oppenheim, Bruchsal, Frankenthal, Baden, Rastadt, and many other small towns and villages, met the same fate. The inhabitants were not even permitted, after being plundered and ill-treated, to take refuge in the German districts, but were obliged to betake themselves to the French territory. The ancient free cities of the empire, Spires and Worms, underwent a lingering and truly pitiable state of suffering. After innumerable calamities, after the inhabitants had for seven months endured all and sacrificed all, and now thought that at least their cities would be saved, it was announced to them that the interest of the king required that both these cities should be razed to the ground. The unhappy people were compelled to wander forth out of their gates, as mendicants and destitute of all means of subsistence, into the nearest French cities, and Spires and Worms were both set in flames and reduced to ashes. On this occasion French avarice violated and sacrilegiously broke open the very graves of the ancient Salic emperors in the cathedral of Spires; several silver coffins deposited there were removed, and the venerated bones they contained scattered upon the ground. In Worms alone, fifteen Catholic churches and convents, besides those of the Jesuits and Dominicans, were reduced to ashes. When the young duke of Crequi, who had the chief command in these operations, was asked why he visited these cities with such severity, he merely replied, "It is the king's pleasure,"—and produced a list of 1200 towns and villages which were yet to be destroyed. These enormities were perpetrated by a nation, calling itself the most civilized and polished in the world, and just at that period of its history too, which it denominated the golden age of its refinement; they were the commands of a king, who wished to assume the character of a protector of the arts and sciences wherever he found them. Before he made known the designs which his thirst for conquest had led him to form, he sent presents to sixty foreign savants, accompanied with the following letter from his minister, Colbert: "Although the king," he says, "is not your sovereign, he is desirous of being your benefactor; he sends this present as a token of his regard." In this way he succeeded in attaching to himself partisans amidst the most learned men of other nations; but now none had longer confidence in the honesty of his intentions, and those who formerly wished success to his arms, broke out into execrations and curses against him and his people.

This animosity against France, and the excellent generalship of the old duke of Lorraine, rendered the German arms, during the first years of the war, tolerably successful; and several fortified towns on the Rhine were recovered from the French. After the duke's death, however, and when the zeal of the first moment had cooled down, the advantage turned in favor of the indefatigable enemy, especially after the great French general, the marshal of Luxemburg, had in 1690 routed a German legion at Fleurus. Subsequently, however, in 1693, they in some measure regained their former position under a new German general, Prince Louis of Baden, a pupil of the duke of Lorraine, who ably defended the banks of the Neckar; and with an army of inferior numbers, he made such an admirable stand at Heilbronn, that the enemy would not again venture to invade Swabia.

All the belligerent nations being wearied out, a congress of peace was at length convened at Ryswick, a small village with a castle near the Hague, in Holland. Louis XIV. was desirous of peace this time, in order to prepare for a new war which he anticipated as near at hand. The death of Charles II. the king of Spain, was expected shortly to take place, and as he had no children, Louis wished to obtain that country for himself. Accordingly, he now offered to deliver up many places, and among the rest the important citadel of Strasburg. But the negotiations were hardly entered upon before he succeeded, with his usual cunning, in disuniting the allies, by promising especial advantages to England, Holland, and Spain. They therefore concluded a separate peace for themselves, and abandoned the emperor and empire altogether. And now the ambassadors resumed their high and haughty tone.

When the question was discussed respecting the compensation to be made for the excessive losses produced by the war, and when the cities of Worms and Spires alone demanded, as an indemnification, 9,000,000 florins, while the duchy of Baden claimed 8,000,000, and Wurtemberg 10,000,000, they replied in an ironical tone: "War brings with it many evils; if the Germans are determined to have satisfaction, let them lead their army into the centre of France, and there plunder or conquer as much as they please." At last they engaged, out of all they had conquered, to deliver up Freiburg, Brisach, and Philipsburg, together with those places reunited by the four chambers beyond Alsace. On the evening before the ratification of peace, and just when all considered that every thing was arranged for signature, the French ministers came forward with an additional stipulation, insisting upon its being acceded to, viz., "That in all the reunited places now about to be restored, the Catholic religion should remain as it was;" that is, in 1922 German townships which had been previously Protestant, and into which the French garrisons had introduced, with a high hand, the Catholic worship, the latter should remain the state religion. The Protestant ambassadors of Germany strenuously resisted this clause; but their remonstrances were not attended to, and the treaty of peace was signed. The worst feature of the case, and what Louis undoubtedly aimed at, was that the Protestants looked upon the emperor himself as the secret mover of this so-called Ryswickian clause, whence it produced in Germany fresh distrusts on the subject of religion; and, in truth, the imperial ambassadors by no means showed themselves vigilant against the designs of France, nor were they sufficiently determined in their opposition.

Another cause also of the discord which at this period prevailed in Germany, was the creation of a new electoral dignity, on behalf of the house of Hanover, or Brunswick-Lüneburg. That princely house had rendered the emperor very important service in the wars against the Turks and the French; Leopold, therefore, was desirous of rewarding it with the said electoral dignity, and a majority of the other electors, even those of the Catholic party, became by degrees agreeable to this proceeding, although it would, at the same time, add a new Protestant vote to the electoral college; still, to them, this appeared not unreasonable, since the Protestants had lost a vote through the elector-palatine having gone over to the Catholic religion. But the princes, especially Brunswick-Wolfenbüttel, struggled vehemently against this elevation of one of their number, for thereby one of their most valuable votes would be withdrawn from them. When, therefore, the emperor, notwithstanding their opposition, conferred, in 1692, the investiture of the new electorate on Ernest Augustus of Hanover, it produced so much contention and general discontent in the college of princes, that it was deemed advisable, for the present, that Hanover should not be permitted to occupy a place in the electoral assembly. The new electorate was not inconsiderable; the elder brother, George William of Lüneburg, had transferred his dukedom to his younger brother Ernest Augustus, so that now Lüneburg, Calenburg, and Grubenhagen, with the provinces of Hoya and Diepholz, formed together one of the largest of the German territories. The new elector was also chief standard-bearer of the empire, and he promised, in all cases of the election of an emperor, always to give his vote to the house of Austria, and to grant the Catholics in his own dominions the free exercise of their religion, as well as to furnish in aid of the war 500,000 dollars, together with 6000 men to Hungary, and 3000 to the Rhine. When Ernest Augustus died in 1698, even those of the electoral princes who had not heretofore approved of the creation of a ninth electorate, now voted for the investiture of his son George Lewis; the college of princes, on the other hand, protested anew against it; nor did they recognise it till the year 1705. The house of Hanover, however, was soon to rise yet higher, for in the year 1714, George Lewis ascended the English throne by inheritance, on the demise of Queen Anne, who had survived the whole of her thirteen children.

The year 1696 also witnessed the elevation of a German prince to a royal throne; the Elector Frederick Augustus of Saxony, after the death of the gallant Sobieski, was elected king by the Poles, and took the title of Augustus I. He was obliged to change his creed and conform to the Catholic church; in his Saxon dominions, however, no alteration was attempted in the constitution of the church. The Polish crown, however, proved no boon to the Saxon house, and was soon lost again.

This was a period of aggrandizing effort among the princes, and these examples influenced several. A prince of Orange had just become king of England, and the elector of Saxony was king of Poland; this prompted Frederick III., elector of Brandenburg, who was at the same time duke of Prussia, likewise to assume the royal title. His territories were indeed small, but Frederick loved splendor and outward show more than any thing else; he caused himself to be proclaimed king at Königsberg, on the 17th of January, 1701, and on the following day he solemnly placed the crown on his own head and that of his consort; henceforth he was known as Frederick I. of Prussia.

The circumstances of the times were exceedingly favorable for these self-promotions; at another period they might have encountered much opposition. The Spanish war of succession was on the eve of breaking out, and the powers which were implicated in it hastened to obtain allies. The emperor Leopold was the first to acknowledge the new Prussian royal title, and he received in return assistance in the war, and the assurance that the imperial dignity should continue in the house of Austria. Sweden, England, Holland, Poland, Denmark, and Russia, also soon followed, all equally from motives of state policy. On the other hand, France and Spain, together with the pope, finding their adversaries had already gained over the king, delayed their recognition until the peace of Utrecht.

The curse of our history since the Thirty Years' War, has been that our country was drawn into all the quarrels of the nations of Europe, even such as were foreign to her, and her soil was the principal arena on which others spent their rage in war. Hence it is that the plains of Saxony, Swabia, and Bavaria, are distinguished by the names of so many battles, and this is the reason why the banks of the Elbe, the Saale, and the Elster, as well as those of the Danube, the Lech, the Inn, and the Neckar, have been so severely trodden down by the burning foot of war.

In like manner, at the commencement of the eighteenth century, that shock which convulsed the southern half of Europe, was, to a great extent, fought out on the plains of Germany. This was occasioned by the death of Charles II., king of Spain.

Two sovereign families, at that period, had the government of the greater part of Europe—the houses of Austria and Bourbon: the former had separated into two branches, the Austrian proper and the Austro-Spanish branch; but the moment had now arrived when both could again blend together in one. Louis XIV. had, it is true, married the eldest sister of the deceased king of Spain, but she had, by a solemn covenant, renounced her right to the Spanish succession. The second sister was married to the emperor Leopold; she had made no such renunciation. Her daughter, however, consort of Maximilian Emanuel, elector of Bavaria, was obliged before her marriage, like her aunt, to renounce all her hereditary claims to Spain. The emperor Leopold, however, by a second marriage with a princess of the palatine house of Neuberg, had two sons, Joseph and Charles; Leopold demanded the crown of Spain on behalf of the latter, on the ground that Leopold's mother was an aunt of Charles II. France, however, as well as Bavaria, refused to allow that the renunciations of these princesses affected their families, because they had given up only their own claims, and had no power to renounce the rights of their posterity. Each of these powers now endeavored, through their ambassadors, to induce King Charles II., during his lifetime, to make a will in their favor; and Charles, with the view of maintaining the independence of Spain as much as possible, named Joseph Ferdinand, elector of Bavaria, his successor. This youth, however, died of the small-pox, even before the king, in the year 1699, and the contest between the houses of Bourbon and Austria commenced afresh. Leopold could easily have obtained the victory if he had been represented by a more able envoy at Madrid, and if he himself had possessed more decision of character; for both the Spanish queen and Cardinal Portocarraro, archbishop of Toledo, the most influential man at the court, were favorably disposed towards Austria. But Leopold's ambassador, Count von Harrach, a haughty, avaricious blunderer, left the field quite clear for the adroitness and cunning of the French agent, the Marquis d'Harcourt; this man gained over the most considerable of the Spaniards one after another, and, at last, even the cardinal, and through him the king himself. Charles made a secret will, and when he died, on the 1st of November, 1700, it was discovered that he had named therein the grandson of Louis XIV., Philip, duke of Anjou, heir to the whole Spanish monarchy. The emperor was thoroughly confounded by this unexpected blow; but he had to thank himself alone for it, for previously, when the Spanish court had repeatedly pressed him to let his son, the Archduke Charles, come into Spain with a small army—during the continuance of the former war with France—the emperor, owing to his want of resolution, refused to give his consent.

Louis XIV. knew well that, notwithstanding the will of the late king, to take possession of Spain for his grandson without war was not possible; for Austria had been too severely injured; while the other states of Europe likewise viewed, with great jealousy, the excessive power of the house of Bourbon. William III., king of England and stadtholder of the Netherlands, an active and very able man, who considered it his province to preserve the due balance of the powers of Europe, and therefore had always been the enemy of Louis, concluded an alliance between both of his dominions and Austria; this was the more important, as England and Holland were the wealthiest and most powerful rulers of the sea. Hence Louis considered awhile whether he should accept of the Spanish king's will; he then called his council together, and as they unanimously concurred, he resolved to do so; accordingly, he proclaimed his grandson king of Spain and both the Indies, in the presence of a brilliant assembly of his court. When he entered from his cabinet, leading the prince by the hand, he exclaimed, as stated by a French writer, with the air of a lord of the universe: "My lords, you see here the king of Spain. Nature has formed him for it; the deceased king has nominated him, the people desire him, and I consent."

This was the signal for a new and direful struggle in Europe. Germany was, alas! divided in itself; Prussia, Hanover, the palatinate, and a few other states were, from the beginning, for the emperor. Maximilian Emanuel, elector of Bavaria and also stadtholder of the Spanish Netherlands, was on the side of the French, and Louis, in consideration of his claims to the Spanish succession, had already made a secret promise to him of the Netherlands; whether seriously, it is difficult to say. The brother of Maximilian, the elector of Cologne, followed his example and received French troops into his territory, "for the good of the Germanic empire and the preservation of its peace, (!)" as it is expressed in the official declarations.

The emperor Leopold determined without delay on sending an army into Italy, to take possession of the Spanish territories in that country, Milan and Naples. He placed at its head Francis Eugene, prince of Savoy, one of the first of the warriors and statesmen of his time, as well as of all history. He sprang from a collateral branch of the house of Savoy, and was intended in his youth for the clerical profession; but his genius led him to the study of history and its great examples, and this again impelled him into the rapid current of active life, where the skill of such as aspire to glory is put to the test in sight of waving laurels. When in his twentieth year, he offered his services to Louis XIV. The latter, not deeming him worthy of notice on account of his diminutiveness, treated his offer with ridicule, and advised him to continue in the clerical profession. Eugene immediately turned to Austria, where the Turkish war seemed to favor his wishes, and he soon distinguished himself so greatly, that, after the deliverance of Vienna in 1683, on which occasion he fought gallantly, the emperor gave him the command of a cavalry regiment. Charles, duke of Lorraine, already recognised him as a hero, and predicted what he would one day become in relation to the imperial house; and, in 1693, Leopold appointed him field-marshal. Louis would now gladly have gained him over to himself, and for which object he sent to him an offer of the stadtholdership of Champaign, and the dignity of a marshal of France; but Eugene answered the person deputed: "Tell your king that I am an imperial field-marshal, which is worth quite as much as the staff of a French marshal."

Eugene was in every respect a great general; his mind embraced at once the most important enterprise, together with all its details, and while engaged in forming his plan of battle, and all its accompanying operations, he never neglected to provide for the most minute wants of his army, which consequently placed the greatest confidence in their commander. His eagle eye eagerly seized with the greatest promptitude the advantages of the moment, and the errors of his adversary were speedily caught at and made available for his own object. He was, however, not less distinguished in his private character as a man; for his spirit rose superior to the religious and political prejudices of his day, and he esteemed more highly the arts of peace than the dazzling glories of war; while, at the same time, he was so modest and unpretending, and estimated his own qualifications with so much moderation, that he not only regarded the promotion of others without envy, but, on the contrary, he willingly occupied a subordinate post, if by so doing he could promote the general good. In person Prince Eugene was under the middle size, and as he walked amidst the tents of his camp, enveloped in his gray military cloak, it may be supposed that few would recognise in his small figure the renowned leader of armies, except those to whom the brilliant fire of his dark eye betrayed his presence.

In the month of March, 1701, Eugene marched against Italy with the imperial army, together with ten thousand auxiliary troops from Prussia, and a division of Hanoverians. The forces assembled at Roveredo, and ascended the mountain chain; but all the passes on the other side were already occupied by the French, so that it appeared impossible to descend. The imperial general, however, ordered his men, who always obeyed him with enthusiastic ardor and alacrity, to cut a passage over the rocks and precipices to the extent of thirty miles, in which they marched, and thus, before the enemy could be at all aware of it, his army poured forth from the terrific passes of the mountains, and encamped on the plains of Verona. By two victories gained at Carpi and Chiari, Eugene drove the French from a part of Upper Italy, and established his winter quarters there.

As early as the autumn of 1701, an alliance was formed between England, Holland, and Austria. The maritime powers stipulated that they should retain possession of all the conquests they might make in the Spanish Indies; and in return, they promised the emperor to assist him in conquering the Spanish Netherlands, Milan, Naples, and Sicily. The English would not have taken so active a part in the war, if Louis XIV. himself had not foolishly and impudently provoked their exasperation. England had just succeeded in driving from the throne the family of the Stuarts, on account of their zeal for the Catholic religion, and had transferred it to William of Orange. Louis received the exiled family and gave them his protection, and in 1701, on the death of James II., (who died at Saint Germain,) he recognised his son James III. as king of Great Britain; and it was even reported that this prince was about to effect a landing in England at the head of a French army. The English were so incensed that a stranger should thus presume to dispose of their throne, that king William, instead of 10,000 men, now obtained from parliament a vote for 40,000.

William placed at the head of this army the earl of Marlborough, created afterwards a duke. He had not deceived himself in making this selection of his commander-in-chief; Marlborough had learned the art of war in the school of the great Turenne, and, as a general, stood second to none of his day. Nature had formed him for a martial leader; being tall, handsome, energetic, and of such noble deportment and superior genius, that the most elevated in rank and distinguished men of every country involuntarily did homage to him. In individual feeling, he stood inferior to Eugene; he did not possess that integrity and nobleness of mind which in the contemplation of grand objects loses sight of self; while he is also accused of an immoderate thirst for gain.

In March, 1702, Marlborough landed in the Netherlands and placed himself at the head of the Anglo-Dutch army; his immediate object was to drive the French out of the electorate of Cologne. King William III. died the same month in consequence of a violent fall from his horse while hunting; but his successor, Queen Anne, implicitly adhered to all his plans, and the war was continued.

With this firm determination shown on the part of foreigners, the states of the Germanic empire resolved upon taking a decisive part in this war of vengeance against their hereditary enemy. The declaration of war followed on the 6th of October, 1702, and it concluded thus:—"France has done every thing in her power to humble and crush the German nation, in order that she might the more easily effect, what she has so long and zealously been aiming at, viz., the establishment of a universal monarchy." The conduct of the elector of Bavaria had likewise provoked the decision of the other members of the empire in favor of the same cause; for, obstinately adhering to France, he had collected a considerable force with which he suddenly attacked and took possession of the free imperial city of Ulm, on the 3d of September; an act severely condemned by the other states.

The dukes of Brunswick also, in consequence of their continued indignation against the elector of Hanover, forgot themselves so far as to raise troops for the service of France; and as they paid no regard to the reiterated warnings given to them, they were forcibly disarmed, in 1702, by the elector of Hanover, and thenceforth compelled to submit to the will of the emperor and the nation.

The fortress of Landau on the Rhine was also this year besieged and captured by the imperial general, Lewis of Baden. The Roman king, Joseph, came himself into the camp, and evinced great courage and resolution. In Italy, Eugene was as yet too weak to attempt any thing of importance; and it appeared as though the hostile parties had determined to test each other's strength merely in skirmishes.

The following year was one more rich in exploits. Marlborough employed it in the conquest of several fortified places on the borders of the Netherlands, and captured Bonn, Tongern, Huy, Limburg, and Guelders.

In Southern Germany affairs were not so prosperous, for the emperor was obliged to withdraw a considerable part of his army from the Rhine, in order to suppress the dangerous insurrection headed by Count Ragoczi, which had been raised in Hungary by French influence. The protracted struggle in that country had the effect generally of greatly hindering the Austrian powers from making any thing like a demonstration against France. In the year 1703, the French field-marshal, Villars, succeeded in crossing the Rhine and uniting with the elector of Bavaria. The latter now devised the plan of making an incursion into the Tyrol, and possessing himself of that country, situated for him so conveniently. He marched thither with about 16,000 of the flower of his army, and the French marshal remained behind to cover Bavaria. Owing to a fire which unfortunately broke out in Kufstein, that strong mountain fortress fell immediately into the hands of the elector, and in their first terror several other places surrendered, and among the rest even Inspruck itself. Thence the Bavarians ascended the Brenner mountain to make their way into Italy. Here, however, they were anticipated by the brave Tyrolese, a people ever ready to lay down their lives and their all in the cause of their beloved country, who on the present occasion were strengthened by a large reinforcement of Austrian soldiers, under the leadership of the gallant amtmann, Martin Sterzing. They climbed up the rugged heights on the sides of the passes, and hurled trees and rocks down upon their foes, as they defiled beneath them, who, finding it impossible to continue their march, retreated in all haste. A Tyrolese sharpshooter in a ravine lay in ambuscade for the elector himself, but, deceived by his rich uniform, he shot the count of Arco in his stead. The Bavarian army suffered still greater loss on its retreat, and, after two months, the elector returned to his territory with only half the forces he had taken with him.

As a sort of indemnification he succeeded, during the winter of the same year, in taking possession of the opulent town of Augsburg, as well as of that of Passau, the frontier fortress of Austria, and on the Rhine the French had in the mean time conquered the strong fortresses of Brisach and Landau.

To counterbalance these losses, the allies proposed the following year to try with all their forces united for better success, and according to the plan laid down it was determined that the three generals, Marlborough, Eugene, and Lewis of Baden, should fight in conjunction in Southern Germany, and that General Stahrenberg should remain in Italy to carry on a defensive war. The three generals met at Heilbronn on the Neckar, and Marlborough, with the margrave of Baden, directed his course to the Danube, and Eugene marched along the Rhine. The Bavarians had stationed a part of their army in an advantageous position on the Schellen mountain, near Donauwerth, to dispute the passage of the imperialists over the Danube; but they were attacked there themselves, and after a brave defence compelled to fly, their entire camp falling into the hands of the enemy.

After this engagement the united powers made overtures of peace to the elector, and promised him considerable advantages if he would withdraw from the alliance of France. He began to waver, and was on the point of signing the articles of peace, when a messenger informed him that Marshal Tallard was advancing with a fresh army to his assistance. On receiving this news, the elector threw the pen out of his hand and refused to sign the treaty. The marshal came, but with him came likewise Prince Eugene, who had followed at his heels and now joined Marlborough. They sent the old unyielding prince of Baden away to the siege of Ingolstadt, lest he should derange their plans of battle; and the English general cordially fought hand-in-hand with the unpretending Eugene, as the latter was ever ready to sacrifice his own personal renown for the success of the common cause.

On the 12th of October both generals took up their position immediately in front of the French, and the Bavarians near the small town of Hochstädt; and on the 13th they began the battle. The enemy was far superior in numbers, and commanded a highly advantageous situation, while they were well defended by morasses. Marlborough led the right wing, composed of the English, Dutch, and Hessians, against the French; Eugene with the left advanced against the Bavarians. The battle was most fierce, and the assailants were several times driven back by a most terrible fire from the enemy's artillery. The contest was most severe on the left wing, where Maximilian fought with the utmost bravery, skilfully availing himself of his covered position in the bog. Eugene perceived that something extraordinary must be hazarded; careless of his own life, he rushed forward animating his men, when a Bavarian dragoon close by levelled his piece at him, but one of the prince's orderlies cut him down. At that moment Prince Leopold of Dessau, with a number of Prussian infantry, pressed forward to his aid, and to him Eugene himself ascribes the determination of the contest in favor of this wing. Meanwhile Marlborough likewise had with his wing routed the French, and when the elector saw them flying from the field, he also retreated with his division. Twenty-eight battalions and twelve squadrons of French still sought to defend themselves in the village of Blenheim, but they were surrounded and forced to yield themselves prisoners. Thus a great and decisive victory was gained by the allies; 20,000 French and Bavarians lay on the field of battle, 15,200 were taken prisoners, among whom was Marshal Tallard himself, with his son and 818 officers. As to booty, the victors had won a rich military chest, 117 cannon, 24 mortars, and 300 stand of colors; and besides this, 5000 wagons, 3600 tents, and two pontoon bridges. From this day the name of Marlborough became the theme of heroic song throughout Germany, and the emperor created him a prince of the empire.

The elector of Bavaria saw himself compelled to cross the Rhine with the French, and take up his position in Brussels; his territory was occupied by the imperialists, and his consort retained for her support only the town and revenue of Munich. Thus, unhappily for him, terminated the campaign of 1704.

In the following year, 1705, the emperor Leopold I. died of dropsy on the chest, in the sixty-fifth year of his age; few of his subjects mourned for him, for he by no means possessed that affability with which princes so easily win the hearts of those who surround them, and what rendered him still more unpopular, was that he was too fond of intrenching himself behind the bulwark of the severest Spanish court etiquette then still in practice. His dress was always black, while the color of his stockings and the plume of his hat were of scarlet, and on his head he wore a peruke with long descending ringlets. His form was insignificant, his deportment serious and frequently gloomy, while his countenance was disfigured by a large projecting under lip. The most marked trait in his character was a severe, austere tone of piety, but it was of such a nature that it placed him completely under the direction and sway of the will of his clergy. In other respects he was conscientious, good-natured, and very charitable to the poor, but from want of judgment, his liberality was severely imposed upon. Leopold I. was not a sovereign equal to the times in which he lived, neither was he at all a match for an antagonist like Louis XIV. He was succeeded by his eldest son Joseph, in his twenty-seventh year.

## CHAPTER XXIX.

Joseph I., 1705-1711—Continuation of the War—Riots in Bavaria—The Elector outlawed—Marshal Villeroi—Battles of Ramillies and Turin, 1706—Triumph of Marlborough and Eugene—Complete overthrow of the French—General Capitulation—Naples—Spain—Battles of Oudenarde and Malplaquet, 1708-1709—Defeat of the French under Bourgoyne, Vendome, and Villars—Humiliation of Louis XIV.—England—Queen Anne—Marlborough recalled and dismissed—Death of Joseph I., 1711—Charles VI., 1711-1740—Peace of Utrecht, 1713—Peace of Rastadt and Baden, 1714—Death of Louis XIV., 1715—The House of Austria in its Relations with the Germanic Empire—Peaceful Reign of Charles VI.—His Death, 1740—Maria Theresa of Austria—Her Title to the Imperial Throne disputed by Charles Albert of Bavaria—Frederick II. of Prussia—His extraordinary Genius and energetic Character—His Army—Invades Austria—The first Silesian War, 1740-1742—Glogau—Sanguinary Battle of Molwitz—Defeat of the Austrians—Alliance of France, Spain, Bavaria, and Saxony, against Austria, in support of Charles Albert—Hanover—George II. of England—Charles Albert, King of Poland—Election of Emperor in Frankfort.

Leopold I. was succeeded by his eldest son Joseph, in his twenty-seventh year, who was endowed with an energetic and aspiring mind. During a short period it was doubtful whether or not the new emperor would continue the war with equal energy in favor of his brother Charles, who had proceeded to Spain in 1704, where he had since continued, and had been actually acknowledged as king in Aragon, Catalonia, and Valencia. Joseph, however, declared his determination to prosecute the war with vigor, and he kept his word.

Nevertheless, there was nothing of importance accomplished anywhere during the campaign of 1705. Eugene was sent to Italy, in order to reorganize the army there, which had fallen into great disorder; but more than this he was not able to do this year. Marlborough had returned to the Netherlands, where he was obliged to collect fresh forces. In Bavaria, meantime, a violent tumult broke out, in consequence of the oppressive measures adopted by the Austrian officers and garrisons. They forced the youth of the country into the Austrian service, and this outrage led to a revolt on the part of the sturdy and independent Bavarians. They took up arms, liberated the young men who had been pressed into service, attacked several bodies of the Austrian troops, and encouraged by their first success, they collected together about 20,000 of the bold peasantry under the orders of a young and fiery student named Mainl. They proceeded at once to make an assault upon the fortresses of Braunau and Schärding, and forced the small garrisons to surrender. The Austrians were obliged to negotiate with them and to conclude an armistice, not as with rebels, but as with men defending their independence. They, however, availed themselves of this circumstance by collecting together a small imperial army from the neighboring districts, and with this assistance they routed the peasants, recovered from them one town after another, and in some measure re-established order. This, however, was attended with many acts of severity, and the feeling of bitter animosity between the two parties increased more and more. The elector himself, being looked upon as the first mover in the insurrection, and an enemy of the empire, was, together with his brother, the elector of Cologne, now formally declared an outlaw, and his territory escheated as a fief of the empire. At the urgent request of the elector palatine, the emperor restored to him the upper palatinate which his family had lost in the Thirty Years' War, and which had been transferred to Bavaria, together with its ancient seat in the assembly of electors. About this time also the princes, who had hitherto disputed the electoral dignity of Hanover, at length yielded; it was universally acknowledged, and the elector palatine resigned to the new elector of Hanover the office of grand treasurer.

France had determined to turn her chief force in the succeeding campaign against the Netherlands, in order that she might, if possible, obtain in wealthy Holland the means of continuing the war. Accordingly she sent into the field the finest army that had as yet appeared in this war; but its general, Marshal Villeroi, was no match for the daring Marlborough. Actuated by vain confidence, he left his strong position at Louvain on the 22d of May, in order to attack the enemy on the plains of Ramillies.* This was exactly what Marlborough desired; his position was excellently defended by a morass and some ditches filled with water, so that when the enemy advanced to the attack, it was impossible for them to approach the weaker and more exposed points in his order of battle, protected as they were by a natural defence; while he, on the other hand, could turn his whole force upon their separate points and break through them. Before the battle, a French officer declared their army to be so superior, that if they did not conquer that day, they ought never again to show their faces before the enemy. Nevertheless they were defeated; for no bravery can atone for the faults of a general. More than 20,000 men were lost, and eighty standards, together with the drums and colors of the royal guard itself; and two months elapsed before the French army was able to repair its losses.

On the other hand the conqueror marched through Brabant and Flanders, took possession of all the towns, made them swear allegiance to Charles III. as their rightful sovereign, and a council of state was established at Brussels in the name of the new king.

Prince Eugene, on his part, would not allow this year to pass without some great action in Italy. He undertook one of the most daring expeditions to be found in the annals of war. With not more than 24,000 German troops he completed a march of more than two hundred miles, ascending mountains and crossing rivers, and through a country wholly occupied by the enemy, in order to effect a junction with the duke of Savoy, who was closely pressed, and whose capital city, Turin, was at that moment besieged by the enemy. To the astonishment of every one, the expedition succeeded. Eugene arrived in time to aid the duke, and hastened to the relief of Turin. Although his army was much inferior in strength, and only indifferently equipped, he nevertheless ventured an attack upon the French lines on the 7th of September, at four o'clock in the morning. He was received by a terrific cannonade, which, however, did not prevent his men from bravely rushing forward. Prince Leopold of Dessau, subsequently known by the name of the old Dessauer, led the Prussians on the left wing against the intrenchments, followed in the centre by the Würtembergers and the troops of the palatinate, and those of Gotha on the right wing; at the same time Count Daun made a sally with his men from the citadel. The battle was extremely obstinate; two assaults made by the Germans were repulsed, when at length, after two hours' fighting, the Prussians* succeeded in mounting the ramparts first, and were soon followed by the others.

The confusion of the enemy was greatly increased through their rear line being attacked by the garrison of Turin, and the loss of both their chief generals, the duke of Orleans and Count Marsin, who were severely wounded and obliged to leave the field of battle. Marsin was taken prisoner and died next day at Turin; 5,000 dead, and a yet greater number of wounded covered the field of battle, and the rest fled in such disorder over the mountains into France, that of the whole army, originally 80,000 strong, scarcely 16,000 men escaped. All the immense supplies they had brought with them, 213 pieces of cannon, 80,000 barrels of gunpowder, together with a vast quantity of ammunition, fell into the hands of the victors. The results of the battle, however, presented still greater advantages than all this booty, for

* This field is almost identical with that on which the great battle of La Belle Alliance and Waterloo was fought, and the latter name already was employed to designate the engagement above referred to more than a century ago.

* In a letter to Count Singendorf, Prince Eugene himself says: "The prince of Anhalt has once more done wonders with his troops at Turin. I met him twice in the thickest fire, and in the very front of it, and I cannot conceal it, that in bravery, and especially in discipline, his troops have far surpassed mine." The emperor Joseph himself wrote to Prince Leopold, as well as to Prince William of Saxe-Gotha, very honorable letters of thanks.

the French lost rapidly one place after another in Italy, and were forced to conclude a general capitulation, according to the terms of which they evacuated Italy entirely, and engaged to send no more troops there during the whole war. The heroic conduct of Prince Eugene during this memorable campaign had produced such glorious results, that his fame resounded from one end of Europe to the other, and in token of his high regard for his great and distinguished merits, the emperor presented him with a valuable sword, and appointed him governor-general of Milan.

In the year 1707 France lost a third portion of the Spanish inheritance, which fell into the hands of the emperor; Lombardy and the Netherlands had already been secured to him by the two great battles of the preceding year. Naples, where only a small body of Spanish troops was quartered, was taken possession of without any difficulty, and thus France lost its last hold in Italy; while in the Netherlands not a single place was now left for Marlborough to take. The only compensation left to Louis XIV. was in the Upper Rhine, where he availed himself of the slow progress made by the imperialists in their operations. The old general, Lewis of Baden, who died in 1707, was succeeded by the margrave of Baireuth, who was equally as inactive in his movements as his predecessor, and who, by his irresolution, allowed the French to cross the Rhine at Strasburg, and to resume their whole system of relentless devastation in Franconia and Swabia. It has been calculated that, in the space of only two months, they levied contributions to the amount of nine millions of florins. The margrave, to the satisfaction of all, did not long delay giving in his resignation as commander-in-chief, and he was replaced by a more active leader, George Lewis, elector of Hanover. The ill condition of the imperial army, however, prevented him from undertaking any thing important; he was obliged to content himself with forcing the French, through want of supplies, to recross the Rhine, and with opposing their passage a second time in the following year.

An expedition which Prince Eugene had to make, by desire of the maritime powers, in the same year, 1707, from Italy to the south of France, in order to take possession of Toulon, succeeded no better than those previously undertaken by Charles V. in the same quarter, while King Louis had the satisfaction to see his grandson Philip V. once more master of nearly the whole of Spain. The Archduke Charles had been, it is true, extremely fortunate in his operations in Spain the preceding year; his army, which chiefly consisted of Portuguese auxiliaries, had succeeded in taking the capital, Madrid, and he had there been proclaimed king of Spain; but his own natural indolence, the dissension existing among his generals, the hatred of the Castilians towards him and the Aragonians, as well as to the English and Portuguese, together with other causes, assisted gradually to deprive him of his conquests, so that in the year 1707 he retained nothing more beyond Catalonia.

Meantime Louis XIV. had already suffered such severe losses in this war, and his country was so exhausted, that he most anxiously longed for peace, and by controlling his innate feeling of pride, he made attempts to purchase it even at great sacrifices. His adversaries, however, determined to punish him severely this time for all his former arrogance; Eugene and Marlborough especially, being hostilely disposed towards the vain monarch, used all their influence equally both in Austria and England to prevent any pacificatory measures, being resolved to reduce him to the most humiliating condition, and in which object they succeeded.

Both these generals, after Eugene had regulated affairs in Italy, formed a junction once more in the Netherlands; and thus united, they gave battle to, and completely defeated the dukes of Bourgoyne and Vendôme—between whom there was great disunion—on the 11th of June, 1708, at Oudenarde. After this victory, Eugene boldly attacked the citadel of Ryssel, which was regarded as impregnable, and of which he made himself master.

The ill success experienced by France in this campaign, was made still more grievous by its being followed by an unparalleled severely cold winter, 1708, and the consequently serious injury produced thereby. The cold was so intense that the very animals in the forests and the birds in the air were frozen to death, and the vines and fruit-trees completely destroyed—while the inhabitants themselves, already suffering so acutely from the war, were driv en completely to despair by this terrible visitation of nature; their lamentations were heart-rending, and all resources for the supplies of the army in the next campaign were entirely destroyed. Thence the king, being now completely discouraged and crestfallen, was obliged to humble himself once more, and make overtures of peace; he declared, accordingly, that he was willing to renounce Spain, India, Milan, and the Netherlands, if they would leave to Philip V. Naples and Sicily. But the two generals, who appeared at the Hague in the midst of these negotiations, declared briefly that the house of Austria should not lose even a single village of the Spanish monarchy, and when this severe exaction was at length agreed to, they demanded still farther concessions from the territory of France itself: "Alsace," they said, "must be given up, and an entire line of strong places in the Netherlands, as well as in Savoy, must be surrendered, to secure these countries for the future against the crafty proceedings of France." All this the French envoys successively conceded; they only refused their consent to one proposal of their enemies, and which was in truth of a character highly derogatory and dishonorable, viz.: that in case his grandson Philip would not resign Spain of his own accord, Louis should himself assist in expelling him therefrom by force of arms. To such an indignity the French monarch would not submit, and the war was commenced again.

Part of the summer of 1709 had already passed away in these negotiations, and Eugene and Marlborough hastened to avail themselves of the remaining portion of the season. They took possession of Tournay, and marched against Mons. This place Marshal Villars wished to protect, and had accordingly taken up a strong position at Malplaquet, in front of the city. The two victorious generals, however, attacked him in his intrenchments without delay, on the 11th of September, and after a battle, the most obstinate and sanguinary during the whole war, victory declared in favor of the allies. Eugene himself, at the very outset of the action, received a grazing shot in the head; but he very calmly folded his pocket-handkerchief round his head, and led on his troops into the very hottest fire. Mons was now closely besieged, and shortly afterwards taken.

Another campaign was now lost, and Louis XIV. was again forced to renew his offers of peace. He agreed to every thing that was demanded, excepting that in order not to be obliged to send an army to assist in the expulsion of his grandson from Spain, he promised to furnish the allied powers with a sum of money instead for that purpose. But Louis was now to experience in his own person what others had but too often felt through him, viz., how acutely severe the haughty insolence of the conqueror pierces the heart of him whom misfortune has laid prostrate at his feet. He was now forced to witness what was but too clearly manifested, how by the duplicity he had himself formerly practised in all his negotiations, he had alienated from him the confidence of all the other European nations; he was answered that, as long as Philip V. remained in Spain, they could put no trust in the promises of his cabinet; and if he seriously desired peace, he must commence by satisfying all the demands made by the allied powers, and fulfil all the conditions of the treaty within the period of two months.

After such a declaration, expressed in terms so haughty and overbearing, the humbled monarch was forced to recommence war, at whatever sacrifice, and Eugene and Marlborough succeeded without much difficulty in capturing one town after the other on the frontiers of France; while in addition to this the news now arrived from Spain, that Count Stahrenberg, Charles's general, had completely defeated the army of Philip V., and that on the 28th of September, 1710, Charles had made his triumphal entry into Madrid.

Louis XIV., already old and feeble, was now reduced to the last extremity, and was left without one resource. After so many wars, and the consequent sacrifice of so many thousands of lives, together with such large sums of money, he was forced to behold the destruction of the whole of that fabric built to perpetuate the grandeur of his name and government, and he was even called upon to offer up a portion of his own ancient patrimonial realm.

Never did fate appear to have dealt more hardly with one who felt secure in the conviction that he had elevated himself to the highest pinnacle of monarchal greatness and imperial glory. But his adversaries had themselves now lost sight of that moderation in the moment when its influence would have saved them; they had likewise become arrogant through their good fortune, whence they lost a great portion of the fruits of their victories. Three favorable circumstances at once rescued France from the great extremity to which she was reduced, and gained for her more liberal conditions of peace. These fortunate events were: the recall and dismissal of the duke of Marlborough, the triumph of the French partisans in Spain, and the death of the emperor Joseph I.

In England, where the friends of Marlborough had hitherto governed the state, an opposite party had, during his absence, gradually and secretly formed itself into a powerful body, and adopted the term Tories or Royalists, in contrast to the other—the Marlborough party, which represented the Whigs or friends of the people. The efforts made by Marlborough in the war were now regarded as suspicious by Queen Anne, and his wife, who had hitherto held great sway over her mind, was now supplanted by another influential party, Lady Masham; a new parliament was elected in 1710, of which the Tories formed the majority, and thence measures for peace were loudly advocated in substitution for those of war. Marlborough was allowed to hold command for a short time longer, but with such restrictions that he almost immediately afterwards resigned it altogether.

The death of the emperor Joseph I., on the 17th of April, 1711, contributed not a little to establish a peace. He died of the small-pox, in his thirty-third year, and is represented in history as a prince of an active and prompt character, and far superior to his father and brother. His mind was capable of entertaining the most noble and enlarged ideas, and thence it was that his penetrating eye selected Eugene, with his extraordinary genius, as worthy of his entire confidence. As the emperor died without heirs, he was succeeded to the throne by his brother, the Archduke Charles. The question now arose respecting the equilibrium of the powers of Europe, as in the time of Charles V.: whether it were advisable that the present Charles, if elected by the Germans as their emperor, under the title of Charles VI., should be allowed to preside over the half of Europe, and the power of the house of Austria thus become so preponderating? For Charles VI. would have possessed the same domination as Charles V., if he united the whole of Austria to the Spanish monarchy. Such a predominance appeared dangerous to the other states, especially to the maritime powers, and they accordingly promoted the election of Charles as emperor, with the view of afterwards depriving him of a portion of the Spanish succession. He was therefore crowned at Frankfort, on the 22d of December, 1711.

Charles, however, had in the mean time lost all he had gained in Spain. Defeated several times by the able French general, the duke of Vendôme, all his possessions there were reconquered, and Philip V. was re-established in his kingdom.

During this interval the English ministers had been secretly negotiating with France, and the preliminary conditions of peace were already signed; so that the allies found themselves forced to agree to stipulations by no means advantageous to them—so little honorable had been the conduct of England in her proceedings with regard to her confederates. The conferences for a general peace now commenced, and Utrecht was chosen as the place of assembly.

Upon the subject of the main point to be discussed—the Spanish inheritance—they, notwithstanding the protestations of the emperor, were soon agreed. Philip V. was to have Spain and India, and Charles the remainder; at the same time Philip was to renounce all claim to the throne of France, so that the two crowns of Spain and France could never be placed upon the same head.

France ceded to England Hudson's Bay and Newfoundland, and moreover, by desire of that power, she demolished the whole of the fortified works of Dunkirk. To Portugal she gave up likewise various territories in South America; to Prussia the possession of Spanish Guelderland, and the sovereignty of Neufchatel and Valengin, and she acknowledged its prince as king of Prussia. Savoy obtained important fortresses on the French frontiers, and as that country could also lay claim to the Spanish crown, the island of Sicily was resigned to her as an indemnification. Holland, which had adhered to the league more faithfully than all the others, and had always refused the advantages offered by a separate peace with France, received but very poor amends, while she was forced to relinquish the strongest fortresses she had conquered, only being allowed to retain a few of the weaker places, to her of little service. Spain eventually surrendered to England the stronghold of Gibraltar and the island of Minorca, and thus England reaped the greatest benefit from this treaty of pacification.

The emperor and the imperial states, deserted now by their allies, found themselves obliged either to negotiate a peace or prosecute the war alone. The stipulations made by the French were of the most shameful and humiliating nature; inasmuch as Louis, in order no doubt to prove himself extremely generous towards his ally, the elector of Bavaria, demanded that all the estates of that prince should be restored to him, and that the territories of Burgau and Nollenburg, together with the island of Sardinia, as a kingdom, should likewise be ceded to him: a truly royal recompense for him who had been the faithful ally of the empire's foe! To have agreed to such conditions would have been too dishonorable; accordingly the war was resumed—but with what chances of success? Eugene with his forces, now reduced to a mere handful of imperialists, was not in a condition to face the entire French army under the command of Villars, nor even to maintain his ground in defence of the banks of the Rhine; whence the adjacent circles of that territory were again devastated, and the important fortresses of Landau and Friburg again fell into the hands of the French.

In this state of things, Eugene and Villars, in November, 1713, met in the castle of Rastadt, and recommenced negotiations. These two great generals, who had already more than once confronted each other on the field of battle, were now equally desirous of being distinguished as the promoters of peace, and after overcoming the difficulties thrown in their way, and which in one or two instances were produced by the overbearing pride of Louis himself, they at length signed the treaty of peace on the 7th of March, 1714. The emperor received the Spanish Netherlands, Milan, Sardinia, Mantua, and the sea-ports of Tuscany; and France restored all the conquered places she had gained on the Rhine, as far as Landau. The electors of Bavaria and Cologne were freed from the imperial ban, and were reinstated in all their possessions and dignities.

These were the principal conditions of peace, but there were many other points, especially relative to the Germanic empire, which were definitively agreed to on the 7th of September, 1714, at Baden, in Aarau.

And thus, once more, a violent tempest had passed over our heads. Meantime, the great war in the north, and which at this moment convulsed the other moiety of Europe, north and east, although not much felt in Germany, pursued its course until the death of the Swedish monarch, Charles XII., in December, 1718. During the ill fortunes of Sweden, Brandenburg took possession of a portion of Swedish Pomerania, and Hanover secured to itself by purchase, the bishoprics of Bremen and Verden, and both retained their acquisitions during the peace. On the death of Louis XIV. in 1715, Europe, after these two great wars, was suffered to enjoy for some time a state of repose.

We have described the important war just concluded more in detail, because therein France lost her ascendency; while for Austria and Germany in general, it produced that favorable moment by which they were enabled to occupy, once more, their ancient honorable position in the world's history. As it was to be feared, since Louis XIV. had manifested such desire for conquest, that if left to itself, a single state must be too weak to resist the preponderating power of France, King William III. of England strenuously labored, single-handed, to oppose, by means of a convention of several states, a barrier to that ambition, so that in future the laws of justice and equity should alone govern nations among themselves. Thence he was the founder of the new system of political equilibrium, and merits the appreciation due to a great man; for he effected great things with small means, and was, in truth, the shield of Europe. Beyond every thing else, however, he founded his hopes for the maintenance of lasting peace and security upon the union of England with Austria—an alliance, to use the expression of that period, of the most independent Protestantism with the most legitimate Catholicism. This union, in fact, produced an entire new form in the development of all the relations of the different European states. But one of its most important results has been to render the principles of tolerance, reciprocal esteem, and moral dignity, more prevalent among nations; and it is in this respect especially that the first moiety of the eighteenth century distinguished itself, in spite of its many imperfections. Thence, by this means, Austria was placed once again in the centre of Europe, as the power destined to establish relationship between all other nations, and to maintain among them order and union; while with respect to Germany itself, she was called upon to defend, with still greater power, the pristine dignity and the ancient constitution of that empire. The glory and the acquisitions that had fallen to her share through the late war, appeared indeed as an indication of the favor of divine providence, and as a ratification of the rank she was to hold in order to bring into operation the objects she was destined to realize. She was, in fact, more powerful now than even if she had succeeded in uniting the Spanish crown with that of Austria; for the reign of Charles V. himself had already shown that such an extension of dominion is any thing but real augmentation of power. Austria was chiefly indebted for her present state of elevation to the great genius of Prince Eugene, and to the sovereign she lost too soon, the emperor Joseph I., who entered completely into the exalted ideas of that distinguished man.

Had the emperor Charles VI. possessed sufficient penetration of mind to perceive the position he was called upon to secure to Austria and Germany in the history of European policy, and of which he might have made himself master forthwith, he would have been enabled to establish the greatness and renown not only of his own portion of the empire, but of the whole of Germany, and have laid the foundation for a long and glorious peace throughout Europe. But Charles's genius, as well as that of the age he lived in, was not capable of comprehending, much less executing such an important plan. The idea of the equilibrium of the states became more and more materialized into a careful estimation of the physical powers, a measurement of the produce of countries, and an exact census of their subjects and soldiers. Thence one of the greatest evils originating in the reign of Louis XIV., became now more universally adopted, inasmuch as sovereigns sought for the security of their independence, not in the love of their subjects, where alone it rests, but in the great number of their soldiers, ever ready to strike the blow. Whenever one state augmented its mercenaries, its neighbor followed the example, and this was almost the only scale of proportion between nations; while, at the same time, all moral and intellectual power was accounted as nothing, because it could not be reduced to measurement. Such a state of things must bring with it a heavy judgment; intellect thus misprized, abandoned altogether the structure, the formation of which had cost so much labor and pain, and which it alone could uphold, and thence this system of equipoise, after a short duration of splendor in the time of Eugene and William, and an extended period of doubtful existence, finally fell its own sacrifice at the end of the same century in which it took its rise.

In consequence of this system, and the position therein occupied by the house of Austria, Germany found itself implicated in the wars of that dominion; besides which, it was forced to share in all the commotions of Europe, without reaping any advantage by them, until the venerable and tottering fabric of the empire, completely overcome by continual concussion, fell to pieces. For in the existence of nations, as in that of individuals, there is no pause; if they do not press onward they retrograde incessantly, and Germany had just shown itself frigidly indifferent and unwilling to embrace a favorable opportunity for its elevation.

Meantime, the last twenty years of the reign of Charles VI. were, with trifling exceptions, a period of peace. He more especially devoted himself to the internal administration of his extensive and beautiful provinces; and this, after an epoch of so much suffering and calamity, operated gratefully and beneficially. As he had no male issue, he had drawn up a solemn law, called the Pragmatic Sanction, according to which he transferred to his daughter, Maria Theresa, the peaceful possession of his hereditary lands. This he was extremely anxious to have confirmed by the leading states of Europe, and in this object, after many abortive endeavors, he succeeded; but this sanction, nevertheless, did not serve to secure his daughter, after his death, from the attacks of a host of enemies, who hoped to make good their pretensions by force of arms.

The emperor himself carried on a war from the year 1733 to 1735, on behalf of Augustus III. of Saxony—who had been elected king of Poland—against the French, who were desirous of dethroning him, and substituting in his place Stanislaus Leczinski, father-in-law to the French monarch, Louis XV. This war, however, was not favorable to Austria and Germany; Augustus III. continued, indeed, by the subsequent treaty of peace, king of Poland, but in return for this, Germany was obliged to sacrifice to its rapacious neighbor a new province: Lorraine being ceded to Stanislaus, and through him it came into the hands of France; Francis Stephen, then duke of Lorraine, being made grand-duke of Tuscany, while the Spanish infante, Don Carlos, was indemnified for Tuscany by the cession of Naples and Sicily. The Austrian army was equally unsuccessful against the Turks, and at the conclusion of peace in 1739, the government was forced to give back the important fortress of Belgrade, which Prince Eugene had conquered, and which had served as a frontier stronghold in that quarter.

The emperor Charles VI. died October 26, 1740, and his daughter, Maria Theresa, by virtue of the Pragmatic Sanction, took possession of the government in all his dominions. But immediately after the decease of the emperor, an envoy of the elector of Bavaria arrived, furnished with a declaration from his master, in which he said: "He could not acknowledge the young queen as the inheritress and successor of her father, because the house of Bavaria had legitimate claims to the hereditary Austrian provinces." These pretensions the elector founded upon his descent from the eldest daughter of the emperor Ferdinand I., whose posterity ought to insist upon their title to those possessions, seeing that the male line of the house of Austria was now extinct. This claim, however, it was evident, could only be made valid in case the late emperor had not left a daughter; but as he had done so, she must take precedence of all collateral female relations. The law advisers of the elector attempted to justify the claims of their sovereign upon several grounds; but what, however, influenced the elector in his proceedings beyond every thing else was, the encouragement he received from France, who secretly promised him her aid in the dismemberment of the Austrian inheritance.

Before, however, the dispute in this quarter was brought to a decision by force of arms, another enemy presented himself to oppose Maria Theresa, and whose appearance was still more unexpected, viz: the young king of Prussia, Frederick II., who only having just mounted the throne in the same year, 1740, marched suddenly into Silesia, and took possession of that country. In his manifesto, which he published at the same time, he laid claims to various principalities of Silesia, viz., to Jägerndorf, Liegnitz, Brieg, and Wohlau respectively. With regard to the first territory, he traced his rights from the period of the Thirty Years' War, when the margrave of Brandenburg-Jägerndorf was placed under the ban of the empire, and his principality confiscated by the emperor Ferdinand II., because he had formed an alliance with the Bohemian king, Frederick V. The king of Prussia maintained, that even supposing the said act of outlawry against that prince was just, still the land in fee simple ought not to have been withheld from his kindred, when they were not implicated in the offence he committed. But his claims to the principalities of Liegnitz, Brieg, and Wohlau, Frederick based upon a covenant of a much earlier date, viz., upon that of Duke Frederick of Liegnitz with Joachim II. in the year 1507. What, however, more especially worked and operated in the soul of the young and ambitious king, and which, in the very first year of his reign, made him take up arms so eagerly, in order to seize the opportunity by which he might renew those claims—which but for his appearance in the world might have remained perhaps in abeyance forever—this incentive he himself discloses to us in a very few words. After having recorded, in his History of the house of Brandenburg, the elevation of Prussia into a kingdom by Frederick I., he gives the following explanation: "This act of Frederick I. served as a stimulus to all his successors, for by that he seemed to indicate to them the grand object by which he was swayed, and to address them thus: 'I have gained now a title for you, and it is for you to render yourselves worthy of it; I have laid the foundation for your greatness, and it is for you to complete the work I have commenced.'" These words are the key which throws open to our view the motives by which Frederick the Great was actuated throughout his whole reign. The same sentiments by which Charlemagne had been incited, and which, brought by him so successfully into operation, made him a conqueror; the same ideas by which Gustavus was urged on to the most daring enterprises, even to the sacrifice of his life on the field of battle, worked likewise in the mind of Frederick. Thence he held himself to be the chosen instrument appointed by fate to raise his people to the rank which, in his strength of mind, he regarded as completely feasible, and to embody in the title of king the more substantial possession of royal power and aggrandized dominion. Nature had endowed him with a genius so bold and aspiring, that he felt his present sphere of action much too contracted for the exercise of his vast plans, and he accordingly lost little time in extending his field of operations. In energy and activity of character Frederick has never been surpassed by even the most distinguished and enterprising men in the pages of history, and none ever acted with such commanding influence upon his age. But again, the greatest man is an evidence of his age, reflecting in a clear mirror its virtues and defects. We must not, therefore, be surprised if Frederick II., notwithstanding the greatness of character inherent in him, does not in many points maintain his superiority when placed in comparison with the great men to whom we have alluded, and if even in certain circumstances he may appear mean and ignoble, when, perhaps, in ordinary times his acts might have merited a more noble interpretation; neither must we be astonished that the evils he produced in his country called forth the severe and bitter complaints against him.

At the death of Frederick William I., on the 21st of May, 1740, Frederick was only twenty-eight years of age; his essentially active mind, excited still more by incessant application to the sciences, and by constant communication with learned men, was adapted for the most profound subjects of research. The study of history had transported his thoughts far beyond the narrow confines of his own times, and had instilled within him the most elevated ideas of the dignity of kings, of which his first acts as sovereign gave immediate evidence. It was soon shown that he was resolved to be his own ruler; his activity in the administration of affairs, the attention he devoted to all subjects, from those of the most grave import down to those of the most trivial nature, his sacrifice of rest and pleasure, the strict distribution of his hours, so that not one should be lost in inactivity—all this excited the greatest astonishment in those of his court, who had never heard of, or been accustomed to witness their sovereigns imposing upon themselves so many sacrifices for the government of their dominions. The extraordinary effect thus produced is very aptly described by a resident ambassador when writing to his own court: "In order to give you a correct idea of the new reign," he says, "it is only necessary to state that the king positively does all the work himself, while his prime minister has nothing to do but to issue forth immediately from the cabinet the commands he receives, without ever being consulted upon the subject. Unfortunately, there is not one at the king's court who possesses his confidence, and of whose influence one might avail one's self in order to follow up with success the necessary preliminaries; consequently, an ambassador is more embarrassed here than at any other court." In truth, the policy introduced by France into Europe, which consisted in envenoming all relations of sovereigns between each other, by employing every art of cunning and espionage in order to discover the projects of foreign courts, even before they had been matured by those courts themselves, could not be brought to bear against Frederick II.; for he weighed over every plan within the silence of his own breast, and it was only in the moment of its execution that his resolution was made known.

Thus it was that he proceeded with his invasion of one of the Austrian provinces on the death of Charles VI. Some preparations for war were observed being made, it is true, but these were only partially necessary, inasmuch as the system of economy and good order pursued by Frederick William I. had enabled him to leave to his son an excellent army of 80,000 men, and a treasury of more than eight millions of dollars; besides which, every thing was arranged with so much silence and secrecy, that none could penetrate into the real intentions of the young king. Usually, before undertaking a war, it was necessary to seek an alliance with other powers; but in this case Frederick communicated with no ambassador, nor would he enter upon or contract any treaty with any one sovereign. He knew full well that the best help lies in ourselves; and he likewise calculated upon the strict discipline and activity of his army, upon which, devoted to it as he was with his whole soul, he never failed to rely during his entire reign.

"When the king resolves to make a journey," says the afore-mentioned ambassador, "it is his custom never to announce his intention to those around him, nor to those even who are to accompany him, until a few hours before his departure, when he finds them all ready in waiting, for his retinue consists neither of court nor courtiers, but is formed of the *élite* of his princes, generals, and adjutants." Thence, by means of such expedition and secrecy, he was enabled to augment the power of his states and to supply the wants of the mass.

The emperor Charles VI. died on the 20th of October, 1740, and on the 13th of December of the same year Frederick II. marched already into Silesia. While his army however was *en route* for Silesia, his ambassador appeared simultaneously at the court of Vienna with proposals for a convention. Frederick offered the queen of Hungary, if she would give up peacefully the principality of Silesia, the aid of his arms in the maintenance of her other dominions, and his vote at the electoral college for her husband, Francis Stephen of Tuscany, on electing the future emperor of Germany; but these proposals were rejected. The few Austrian troops quartered in Silesia were very soon routed; the fortified places alone made resistance and were closely besieged; the following spring, however, was to decide whether the possession of this country, thus so easily subjected, could be maintained against an Austrian army. Field-marshal Neuperg, an Austrian general of the school of Eugene, advanced with a numerous body of troops to reconquer Silesia, and the younger soldiers of Prussia, who were as yet only acquainted with the theory of war and not with its realities, stood now front to front opposed to those who ranked unquestionably among the first warriors of Europe. But the first essay of the Prussian arms crowned them with glory. In the night of the 9th of March the hereditary prince of Dessau scaled and carried the walls of the fortress of Glogau, and on the 10th of April the king, with the main army, came up with the Austrians at Molwitz, where he was not at all expected by them; they, however, gained sufficient time to form their line of battle, and the action commenced about two o'clock in the afternoon. It remained for a long time undecided, for the Austrian cavalry fought with the greatest bravery, and throwing the right wing of the Prussians into confusion, rushed on to their train of battery, of which they took possession, and turned the muzzles of the cannon against the Prussians themselves. The king, who now for the first time beheld war in all its fearful reality, lost his self-command; Schwerin, his experienced field-marshal, who viewed all that passed with the greatest coolness and resolution, being well acquainted with and depending upon the chances of war, advised his sovereign to fall back upon the division commanded by the duke of Holstein-Beck, in order with him to cover the retreat if necessary. This advice, after considerable hesitation, the king followed, and towards dusk he withdrew with a small retinue, and rode to the little town of Oppeln. He imagined the place was still occupied by the Prussians, but they had been driven from it the previous evening, and when in answer to the sentinel's "Who goes there?" he replied, "Prussians!" the king and his small party were forthwith greeted with a discharge from the muskets of the Austrians behind the grated gate. The king quickly turned round and galloped off to the small town of Löwen, and was only saved by the darkness of the night from being taken prisoner. Meanwhile, scarcely had he quitted the field of battle before fortune changed in favor of the Prussians; Field-marshal Schwerin, by a dexterous attack on the enemy's flank, turned the success of the day to the side of his sovereign; and the sharp-shooting of the Prussians, to which the Austrians were as yet unaccustomed, completely decided the battle. The king received the happy tidings on the following morning at Löwen, and hastened to congratulate his brave general and his army upon their success.

This sanguinary and dearly-purchased victory turned the eyes of all his contemporaries upon the young sovereign of Prussia; and this enterprise, because it was successful, was applauded as being the decision of fate in his favor. Had however Frederick been unfortunate, a thousand voices would have condemned and ridiculed him as a fool, for having undertaken the realization of projects without having calculated upon the power necessary to ensure their success; similar to the judgment pronounced upon Charles Albert of Bavaria, who with equal ambition advanced and stretched out his hand to seize the royal and imperial crown. And in truth, the daring power which attempts aught of a nature uncommon and extraordinary in the grand theatre of the world, is only appreciated in proportion to the success with which the execution of its design may be crowned.

The ill success of the Austrian arms in Silesia encouraged the French government to avail itself of the moment now offered to promote the dismemberment of the Austrian states. Cardinal Fleury, who now ruled in France at the head of the government, and found in Marshal Belle-Isle a clever diplomatist, succeeded in concluding with that view an alliance between France, Prussia, Spain, Bavaria, and Saxony; for the elector of Saxony, Augustus III., although he was likewise king of Poland, came forth with his claims to the Austrian inheritance, originating in a preceding marriage of the house of Saxony, and Spain was anxious to appropriate to herself the duchies of Parma and Placenza. Besides which, the plan of this coalition was to elevate the electoral prince of Bavaria, Charles Albert, to the imperial throne; and although he at first hesitated, he, nevertheless, eventually decided to accept of the heavy burden attached to such an important election. It was agreed that the choice should be made in Frankfort.

Accordingly, two French armies marched in the summer of 1741 across the Rhine; the one advanced against the frontiers of Hanover, whereby Maria Theresa lost her last ally, George II. of England, who, anxious to preserve his electorate, concluded a treaty by which he engaged to remain neutral. The other French army marched on direct to Austria, and joined the elector of Bavaria in the month of September. This prince, who, since the month of June, had already taken by surprise the important city of Brunau on the frontiers, now no longer hesitated to march upon Lintz, which he took and entered, causing himself to be acknowledged there as hereditary duke of Austria. Vienna, the capital, began now to feel alarmed, and every thing valuable and precious was forthwith transported to Presburg in Hungaria; the elector being only within three days' march of the city. But quite suddenly and unexpectedly he altered his line of march and proceeded to Bohemia. This change of resolution excited universal astonishment, more especially as, by the taking of Vienna, Maria Theresa must have lost every thing, as she was without an army to oppose the elector. But it was his jealousy of Saxony which made him alter his plans, and removed him from the heart of Austria. A Saxon force had entered Bohemia; and Charles Albert, who was anxious likewise to gain possession of that country, and dreaded lest the Saxons might wrest it from him, preferred abandoning Vienna for the moment, and determined to conquer Bohemia. Accordingly he marched at once against Prague, and was favored so much by fortune that this important place was surprised and fell into his hands, with scarcely any resistance, on the 29th of November. Immediately afterwards he caused himself to be declared king of Bohemia, and received from all the civil and military estates the oath of fealty. Thence he marched to Mannheim, where he resolved to await the result of the election of emperor. Thus the house of Bavaria appeared to attain an elevation more and more splendid and glorious.

## CHAPTER XXX.

Charles VII., Emperor of Germany, 1742-1745—Maria Theresa in Hungary—Her Appeal to the Nobles—Their Devotion to her Cause—March into Bavaria—Seize that Country and banish its Elector—Charles VII. a Fugitive—Battle of Czaslau between the Austrians and Prussians, 1742—Treaty of Peace between Maria Theresa and Frederick II.—Continuation of the Austrian Succession War, 1742-1744—The French in Prague under Marshal Belle-Isle—Prague besieged by the Austrians—Abandoned by the French—Charles VII. in Bavaria—Again a Fugitive—George II. of England in Germany—Battle of Dettingen, 1743—Defeat of the French—Alliance of Saxony and Austria—Second Silesian War, 1744-1745—Ill Success of Frederick—Death of Charles VII., 1745—Silesia—Battle of Hohenfriedberg—Frederick victorious—Battle of Sorr—The Princes of Brunswick—Frederick triumphant—Battle of Kesseldorf—Frederick conquers and enters Dresden—Peace of Dresden and End of the Second Silesian War—Francis I. elected Emperor, 1745-1765—Austria and France—Peace of Aix-la-Chapelle, 1748—Brief Interval of

Repose, 1748-1756—State of Affairs—Alliance of England and Prussia, 1756—Alliance between France and Austria, 1756—Saxony—Russia—Sweden—Combination of Powers against Prussia—The Seven Years' War, 1756-1763—Frederick in Saxony—Battle of Losowitz, 1756—Frederick victorious—The Saxons lay down their Arms—Frederick Conqueror of Saxony—Immense Armies opposed to Frederick—His Presence of Mind—Desperate Battle of Prague—Charles of Lorraine—Death of the Prussian General Schwerin, and the Austrian General Brown—Frederick victorious—Battle of Kollin—General Daun—Frederick's grand Manœuvre—Generals Ziethen and Hulsen—Frederick and Prince Maurice of Dessau—Defeat of Frederick—Shameful Conduct of the Duke of Cumberland—Convention of Closter-Seven between him and the French—Battle between the Russians and Prussians at Grossjägersdorf—Defeat of the Prussians—Withdrawal of the Russians—The Empress Elizabeth of Russia—The Grand Chancellor Bestuschef—Retreat of the Swedes.

Charles Albert succeeded in his designs upon the imperial crown, and was elected at Frankfort on the 22d of January, 1742, his cause being seconded by France and Prussia; but his reign was short and agitated. It already commenced under very unfavorable auspices, for on the very day that Charles was crowned emperor at Frankfort, the Austrian general, Bärenklau, took possession of Munich, his capital.

Maria Theresa was indebted to the energy of her own mind alone for this happy change in her fortunes. She knew perfectly well wherein was based the power of the sovereign, and she accordingly availed herself of this advantage. She lost no time in exciting in a high degree the affection and enthusiasm of the nation over which she still held sway, and which adhered to her with the greatest fidelity; and this it was that saved her. She convoked a grand imperial diet of the Hungarians at Presburg in the autumn of 1742; here, overwhelmed as she was with affliction at the persecutions of her enemies, the princess presented herself before the assembled nobles of Hungary, and holding in her arms her infant son, as yet unweaned—subsequently Joseph II.—she presented the child to them, and with her eyes filled with tears, which operated with irresistible force upon the audience, she addressed and appealed to them for aid against her enemies in language thus expressed: "To your valor and heroic fidelity we confide ourself and infant; and in you alone will we put our whole trust." At these words the Hungarian warriors exclaimed with enthusiasm, "We will die for our Queen Maria Theresa; our lives and every drop of our blood shall be devoted to her!" In a very brief space of time more than 15,000 nobles and chiefs were assembled, mounted and completely armed, and collected together numerous bodies of troops on every side, in Croatia, Slavonia, Wallachia, as well as in Austria and the Tyrol. And thus what official commands would only have produced after long intervals of delay, attachment and devoted courage completed in a few weeks. The whole of Upper Austria was delivered from its enemies in six days, when the victorious army marched on to Bavaria, and, as we have seen, took possession of Munich, and the new emperor was forced to live in retirement at Frankfort, far from his own dominions.

In another quarter, however, fortune was not equally favorable to Austria. Prince Charles of Lorraine had received orders from the council of war at Vienna to give battle to the Prussian army, in order to check the further success of Frederick II., who still maintained his position in the beautiful territory of Silesia, and was now penetrating into Moravia. Prince Charles followed him to Bohemia, and their armies met at Czaslau. They were nearly equal in force, and the position each occupied had its advantages and disadvantages, and the troops on both sides fought valiantly, whence the fate of the battle wavered on either side, until the king, who here displayed his generalship, caused an adjacent eminence to be suddenly taken possession of, whence he attacked the entire flank of the Austrians. This manœuvre, added to the disorder caused among the Austrian cavalry by the pillage of the Prussian camp, decided the contest, and Charles sounded the retreat. The loss sustained, however, was nearly equal on either side, and eighteen pieces of cannon were all the trophies gained by the Prussians.

The results of this battle, however, were more important than the battle itself, for it brought to maturity a treaty of peace between Maria Theresa and Frederick, by the terms of which, severe as they were, the former nevertheless agreed to resign all claim to the conquests made by the young king, and which was all the latter desired. Negotiations of peace, therefore, were quickly commenced, and on the 28th of June the treaty was signed by both powers at Berlin. The king retained Upper and Lower Silesia and the province of Glatz, with the exception of the towns of Troppau, Jägerndorf, and the mountains of Silesia on the other side of the Oppa; being an extension of territory measuring seven hundred German square miles. On the other hand he paid over 1,700,000 dollars to the English, who had previously advanced that sum to the country he had thus conquered.

Thus freed from such a formidable enemy, the Austrians were now enabled to turn all their force against the French and Bavarians, for the Saxons, following the example of the Prussians, had withdrawn from the war. The French army was still in Bohemia, and held possession of Prague. The prince of Lorraine marched against that place and besieged it, and very soon reduced it to a state of famine, which, however, as is generally the case, pressed more heavily upon the inhabitants, for the military seized upon all provisions by force of arms. When, however, all was consumed, and after more than a thousand unhappy beings had fallen a sacrifice to starvation, the whole city resembling a large infirmary, Marshal Belle-Isle put into operation a plan he had determined upon in the last extremity. He collected all the troops still available, amounting to about 14,000 men, abandoned the city in the night of the 17th of December, 1742, and marched forth in the most bitter cold weather, through mountain regions and across pathless, snow-covered ravines to Eger, where after a toilsome march of eleven days he arrived. But in those eleven days more than four thousand men had perished, besides those left behind in Prague. Thus ended the dominion of France in Bohemia; nor was Charles VII. more fortunate than his allies. While the Austrians had marched their whole force against Bohemia, he had availed himself of the moment, and retook possession of the whole of Bavaria in the course of the autumn; in the subsequent spring, however, he was forced to abandon his territory once more as a fugitive, and took refuge again in Frankfort, an Austrian administration being organized meantime in Bavaria.

In the year 1742, England likewise took an active part in the war against France; she captured all her ships at sea, took possession of her colonies; while King George II. landed in Germany with an army of English troops, reinforcing it with Hanoverians and Hessians, with which he attacked and overthrew the French on the 27th of June, at Dettingen, pursuing them across the Rhine. In addition to this the court of Vienna succeeded in gaining over the Saxon minister Brühl, whose influence over his sovereign was all-powerful, and through him an alliance was formed between Saxony and Maria Theresa. Thus fortune had now crowned her firmness, and transferred the victory to her side, while the only loss she sustained was that of the Silesian possessions; this, however, she hoped either to recover or find compensated by some other acquisition.

Meantime, Frederick had not beheld without some anxiety and alarm the successful progress made by Austria, and more especially her treaty of alliance with Saxony; for how easily might they now, when no longer occupied with France and Bavaria, turn their combined power against him? At the same time he felt it due to his own dignity not to allow the emperor, whose election he had promoted, to be overthrown; accordingly, the urgent appeals made to him by Charles VII. prevailed. The king of Prussia forthwith made preparations for a fresh campaign, in 1744, entered the field with 100,000 men, "imperial auxiliaries" as he termed them, marched into Bohemia, and took Prague; the duke of Lorraine, however, advanced against him with a numerous army, and forced him to retreat from Bohemia into Silesia. This was an unfortunate campaign for the king; he suffered great losses in men, ammunition, and provisions, exhausted all his military stores and money, and found to his cost that no faith was to be placed in his French allies; while, finally, he lost the emperor Charles VII., who died suddenly, on the 20th of January, 1745.

The aid of Frederick came only in time to afford the emperor the consolation of dying in his own palace at Munich, which city he had reconquered for the third and last time, but which immediately after his death fell once more into the hands of the enemy. With his death the principal motive urged by the French for carrying on the war vanished, and Frederick now found himself abandoned by his ally. Meantime, Maria Theresa declared publicly that, inasmuch as the king of Prussia had broken the treaty of peace concluded at Berlin, Silesia must revert to the house of Austria. Upper Silesia, accordingly, was overrun with Austrian troops, several of the principal fortresses fell into their hands, and it required all the firmness and strength of soul at his command to prevent the hard-pressed king from sinking under the weight of his difficulties. Full of confidence, however, in his army, and in the chances of fortune in his favor, he, on the 4th of June, attacked the prince of Lorraine at Hohenfriedberg. The prince was by no means prepared for such an unexpected and sudden attack, and the victory was soon decided in favor of the king of Prussia; thus he retained Silesia, while the Austrians made a hasty retreat back to Bohemia.

In the ensuing year, however, they reappeared in Silesia; the prince of Lorraine having received orders to advance at the head of 40,000 men, and give battle to the king, whom he surprised in his camp near Sorr of only 18,000 men. This was a hard-fought battle for this small body of Prussians, and lasted more than five hours; but, eventually, they gained it. The Austrian general committed many important blunders; while the generals in Frederick's service were, on the other hand, perfect masters in all the tactics of the war. One of them, Prince Ferdinand of Brunswick, afterwards so celebrated, took possession of an important height, which by a singular accident was defended by his brother Lewis, at the head of a party of Austrians.

Nevertheless, this victory had not removed all the danger with which Frederick was threatened; for it was now resolved that the Austrians should form a junction with the Saxons, and the army thus united should march direct to Berlin, in order to force the king, by the capture of his capital, to abandon Silesia; and by this means, Saxony was in hopes of gaining from him the duchy of Magdeburg. But as soon as Frederick perceived this movement, he speedily collected together his whole army and marched to Lusatia. At the same time he gave orders to the old duke of Dessau to collect his forces near Halle, and marching into the electorate, to proceed direct to Dresden. He overtook the Saxons and a division of the Austrians on the heights near the village of Kesseldorf, attacked them at once, and, in spite of their favorable position, gained a complete victory over them. This triumph gained for Frederick the capital city, Dresden, which he entered on the 18th of December, and procured the peace of Dresden, which terminated the second Silesian war, and confirmed the Prussians in their possessions.

In the beginning of the year 1745 Maria Theresa had already concluded a treaty of peace at Füssen, with the son of the late emperor Charles VII., by which Maximilian Joseph recovered his principality, on renouncing for himself and his descendants all claims to the succession of Austria, and promising to give his vote for the election of emperor to the grand-duke of Tuscany, Maria Theresa's husband. Meanwhile, the other electors also, with the exception of the elector of the palatinate and Frederick II., gave their votes to the same duke, and Francis I. was elected at Frankfort on the 15th of September, 1745, and crowned on the 4th of October following. The king of Prussia, likewise, formally acknowledged him in the treaty of peace concluded at Dresden.

The war with France continued some years longer without any successful results to Austria; for since the celebrated general, marshal of Saxe, commanded the French army, he had continually been gaining ground in the Netherlands. This general obtained two victories over the Austrians in the year 1745, one at Fontenoi, and another at Raucour, and took both the Austrian Netherlands and Dutch Flanders. These victories gained by the French army tended more and more to increase the inclination for peace, and in April, 1748, the ambassadors met at Aix-la-Chapelle. The peace drew nearer and nearer to its conclusion during the whole course of the summer, and followed on the 18th of October. Austria gave up in Italy, Parma and Piacenza to Don Philip, the youngest son of the king of Spain; France, however, got nothing for the great sacrifice she had made, both of men and money, in this war, and was obliged to see the house of Austria, which she wished to destroy, secured afresh, and put in possession of the imperial dignity.

The period of eight years which had been allowed to the different states of Europe, from the peace of Aix-la-Chapelle until a new war broke out, did not produce in them the desired feeling of united firmness and security; but, on the contrary, all seemed unsettled and in dread of the new commotions which hovered over this brief state of repose. For it was but too evident that the inimical powers so recently roused up—not having as yet found their equilibrium—had only made a pause for the purpose of soon resuming hostilities against each other with renewed vigor. The empress-queen could not brook the loss of Silesia, and she felt this loss the more acutely, inasmuch as she was obliged to undergo the mortification of knowing that the king of Prussia, by adopting a proper course of administration, had been able to double the revenue of that beautiful country. Frederick, on the other hand, was too clear-sighted not to foresee that a third struggle with her was inevitable. Among the other European powers, too, there was a restless spirit at work; they entered into alliances, looked about them—now here, now there—for friends, and increased their strength by land and sea. Europe was at this moment divided by two leading parties—France, Prussia, and Sweden adhered to the one, Austria, England, and Saxony to the other; the rest had not yet come to any conclusion as to which party they should support, but their assistance was eagerly sought by both. Maria Theresa at first cast her eye upon the powerful state of Russia, whose empress, Elizabeth, appeared inclined to hurl back her bold northern neighbor into his former insignificance; and eventually both parties concluded an alliance by means of the grand-chancellor of Russia, Bestuschef, who had a personal dislike to the king of Prussia, because the latter refused to gratify his avaricious disposition. In order to induce Russia to take active measures against Prussia, England found it necessary to act upon the grand-chancellor with her money, and by this means a war was all but declared already between Russia and Prussia. George II. of England more especially desired this, in order that he might by such war be relieved of the anxiety he felt for his principality of Hanover; for, as he was already engaged in a maritime war with France, with the view of acquiring new territories in other parts of the world, it was to be expected that France in union with Prussia would forthwith attack his electorate. Maria Theresa, however, on her part, saw this storm preparing in the north of Europe without fear or inquietude, as she nourished strong hopes that it would give her an opportunity of reconquering her Silesian territory.

This, indeed, was the period of that cunning and refined diplomacy which has been termed state wisdom; an epoch which established between sovereigns false and artificial relations, but never inspired noble and exalted ideas and principles. Frederick the Great, although he understood well how to calculate after the manner of his contemporaries, was, nevertheless, so far superior to them in the feeling of his own strength and resources, that he placed his whole and exclusive reliance on himself and people. The others sought assistance chiefly from among each other; and, as a necessary consequence, were often in great difficulties; while Frederick, inasmuch as his calculations were far more simple, attained with greater certainty the object in view. Thence it was that he now formed and put into immediate execution a plan no less unexpected than extraordinary. Abandoning the lukewarm aid of France, which lay, as it were, in a state of political lethargy, and had afforded him but very trifling assistance in his two Silesian wars, he suddenly turned to England, now so much increasing in power and enterprising boldness, and claimed her alliance; and the English nation, which has always shown a preference for engaging in a cause backed by patriotic and straightforward principles, readily acceded to his proposal: nor, perhaps, was an alliance ever accepted in England with more universal enthusiasm and cordial feelings than this. Both nations, which in their essential endeavors could not become dangerous to each other, needed this reciprocal aid against other adversaries; and, at the time, required the mutual confidence of each other in order that England might be at ease with regard to Hanover. Hence the alliance between England and Prussia, which based its security in the sympathy of both nations, might be truly termed a natural alliance, and was founded upon firmer grounds than those of mere state policy.

By this single turn the relations which had hitherto existed between the different states of Europe were altogether changed. Prussia had declared itself independent of France, and England of Austria; and, through a singular capricious sport of fortune, France and Austria, who had been enemies for three hundred years, now found themselves, to their own astonishment, placed in close proximity, and called upon to give each other their hands; and all the rules of political calculation hitherto held as immutable, were at one blow demolished. Luckily for Austria, she possessed in her prime minister, Prince Kaunitz, and in the empress Maria Theresa herself, two whose power of mind enabled them at once to perceive and avail themselves of the altered position of affairs, and did not suffer themselves to be held in check by ancient custom. They sought for an alliance with France, and obtained it. On the 1st of May, 1756, the treaty of Versailles was drawn up, after that between England and Prussia had been already concluded at Westminster in the month of January of the same year.

The elector of Saxony and king of Poland, Augustus III., was guided in every thing by his minister, Count Brühl; he himself was fond of ease and a life devoted to sensual pleasure; but his minister, who, without any true merit, had raised himself from the office of page to that of minister of state, was full of secret designs. He hated King Frederick, because he himself was despised by him, and allied himself with Prince Kaunitz for the purpose of ruining Prussia, and both found in the Russian chancellor, Bestuschef, the third associate in their alliance. The empress Elizabeth of Russia was also personally an enemy to King Frederick, inasmuch as he made her the subject of his satire; and various malicious members of her court had even laid before her some of the king's productions, containing much mockery and scandal.

With respect to Sweden, she, this time, adhered so much to France and her interests, and followed in her footsteps so closely, that the king of Prussia could not but expect to find an enemy in this otherwise so honorable a nation, when it came to a general war.

Thus Austria, Russia, France, Sweden, and Saxony, had now all united against one king, whose dominions scarcely contained five millions of inhabitants, and who was deprived of all foreign aid, with the exception of England, who, however, in a continental war, could not ensure much resource. Accordingly, the three ministers felt secure within themselves of the fate of Silesia; and already they beheld, in imagination, the bold and enterprising king reduced to the government of his single duchy of Brandenburg. In this calculation, however, they had altogether lost sight of that power of mind with which this prince was endowed, and the prodigies of courage and endurance a nation can perform when inspired with pride and confidence by their ruler.

The king was already acquainted with their designs, for through a secretary of the Saxon government, whom he had bribed, he received copies of all the documents and treaties between the courts of Vienna, Petersburg, and Dresden, and by these means saw what storms were gathering over his head. In this trying position the great Frederick had recourse to those extraordinary means suggested at once by his bold and undaunted spirit. Determined not to lose a moment by preparing only for his defence, and thus quietly await the coming danger, he forthwith rushed to meet and face it as it advanced; for, however unfortunate might be the result produced by adopting this daring and immediate course, still it could not equal, much less exceed, the evil he beheld in the distance, and which could only grow more and more serious and fatal by tardy measures.

Frederick made his preparations for the campaign with so much secrecy and order that none could observe his design; and thus, in the month of August, 1756, seventy thousand Prussians suddenly made their appearance in Saxony, and demanded a free passage to Bohemia. The object of the king was not so much to proceed to hostilities against the Saxons, as to force them, by a bold manœuvre, to join him, as had previously been done by Gustavus Adolphus; for, in order to attack Bohemia, as he hoped, with success, it was necessary that he should make sure of Saxony in order to serve him as a *point d'appui.* Accordingly, he endeavored by every possible means of persuasion, through his envoys and negotiations, to bring Augustus III. to form an alliance with him; when, however, he found he could not succeed, and all he could gain from Count Brühl was a promise of remaining neutral, Frederick felt he could not with safety allow a doubtful and armed power to remain in his rear, and proceeded at once to act upon the offensive. The Saxons, amounting to seventeen thousand men, thus surprised, gave way, and leaving behind their baggage and provisions, hastily retreated to the narrow valley of the Elbe, between Pirna and the fortress of Königstein, and encamped there, where they raised up strong and almost impregnable intrenchments. This plan was the best for them to adopt; while for Frederick it was more disadvantageous than if they had crossed the mountains and formed a junction with the Austrian army; for this army, still in a disordered and weak state, could not, even when reinforced by the Saxons, have succeeded in resisting the first attack of the Prussians in Bohemia, in addition to which, the latter now saw themselves forced to lose much precious time in blockading the Saxons, and cutting off their supplies; while the imperial army availed itself of this interval, and recovered its organization and strength, and would be enabled, by a successful battle, to relieve the Saxons. Such, indeed, was the course taken by the imperial general after the king had been four weeks quartered in Saxony.

On the 30th of September Field-marshal Brown, commander-in-chief of the imperial troops, advanced to Budin on the Eger, and directed his march against the position taken up by the Prussians on the mountains which separate Saxony from Bohemia. Meantime, the king advanced against him with a portion of his army, consisting, however, only of 24,000 men against 70,000, being compelled to leave the rest behind to keep the Saxons at bay, while the Austrians were commanded by the best officers in the service; nevertheless, he did not hesitate to risk making a desperate attack, and he succeeded. The two armies met on the 1st of October, close to the little town of Lowositz. The country around was mountainous, and the Austrian general, accordingly, was unable to draw up the whole of his army in line of battle, especially his cavalry, which consequently could not take its share in the action; while, on that account, the fire from the artillery and small arms was much more severe, and in which latter the Prussians excelled the Austrians. But it was now no longer by the Austrians of the Silesian wars that they were opposed, but by men who, for ten years, had undergone severe practice, were better disciplined, more active than ever before, and were well supplied with excellent artillery. Mid-day had now arrived, but the Prussians, in spite of their skill and bravery, were not able to gain any advantage over the firmness of the Austrian ranks.

After six hours' incessant firing, the left wing of the Prussians at length expended all their ammunition, and began now to lose courage on finding they could receive no fresh supply. "What!" exclaimed the duke of Bevern, who commanded this division, "have you not been taught to attack the enemy with the point of the bayonet?" At these words they closed their ranks, and rushed in full charge against the Austrians; all resistance was in vain, for like an impetuous, sweeping torrent, they threw down all before them, and took the little town of Lowositz by storm. This was the decisive moment; and although but a small portion of his troops had been engaged in the action, General Brown nevertheless sounded a retreat and withdrew to Budin, on the opposite side of the Eger.

Frederick in this battle learned to know the new and improved system of warfare now exercised by the Austrians, and already felt how severe must henceforth be the struggle he should have to maintain with them. On the other hand again, the heroic courage and devotion displayed by his own troops had excited within him the greatest admiration, and on this point he addressed them thus: "I have now seen what my warriors can do; never, indeed, since I have had the honor to lead them on to battle, have they performed such prodigies of valor."

Frederick now saw how urgently necessary it was that he should put an end to the delay so long produced by the Saxon army, which, indeed, although placed in a most distressing position, nevertheless endured every privation with the most heroic firmness. Both men and horses had long been in want of the most necessary supplies, and all were now so much reduced that if succor did not quickly arrive, they must perish. They had received intelligence in their camp that Field-marshal Brown was on his march, and they were all buoying themselves up with the hope of soon seeing his colors waving on the mountains instead of those of the Prussians, when all at once loud shouts of victory proclaimed the success gained by the Prussians in the battle of Lowositz, and resounding through valley and mountain, were echoed forth in the Prussian camp. The impression produced by this event upon the distressed Saxons was truly painful, reduced as they were to the last extremity of suffering and want. The only chance of deliverance now left to them was by making a desperate effort to fight their way through into Bohemia; this they accordingly attempted, but opposed by the very elements themselves, for they were overwhelmed by a complete hurricane of wind and drenching rain, and harassed by the Prussians, they failed in their object, and thus these brave men, who having now been three days and nights without food or rest, were nearly dropping down from exhaustion and disease, were forced to lay down their arms, their number now reduced to 14,000, and with their general, Count Rutowski, gave themselves up prisoners to the Prussians on the 14th of October.

The officers were set at liberty on their parole of honor, but the men were forced to enter the Prussian service. Frederick calculated that these 14,000 men, if he gave them their liberty, would serve as a considerable reinforcement in the ranks of the enemy, and if he detained them as prisoners of war they would cost him annually some millions of dollars to support; thence he determined to derive some advantage for the expense they incurred for their maintenance. For at this period the soldier was considered less as a citizen of the state than as a man who equally sold over both body and spirit to the military service for a certain period, and could, therefore, soon accustom himself to serve in the ranks of him against whom he may even have previously fought: military honor was distinct from civil honor, and the oath of the soldier was held to be more sacred than the word of the citizen. Nevertheless Frederick derived but little service from the Saxons; they deserted his colors in troops on the first favorable opportunity, and hastened to return to their king in Poland, whither he had repaired after the loss of his army, or they went over to the Austrians. Such were the results of the first campaign: Saxony remained in the hands of Frederick II.

The preparations made for the ensuing campaign presented to the eyes of Frederick an aspect in prospective affairs of a character any thing but encouraging. The great powers of Europe, infuriated by the stand he made, had now become more firmly united than ever in their determination to destroy him, and combined together with all their armies to overwhelm him. Austria came forth with all the troops, together with all the wealth and resources furnished by her extensive territories; Russia contributed no less than 100,000 men; France supplied even a greater number; Sweden came forward with 20,000 men; while the Germanic empire generally, regarding the invasion of Saxony by Frederick as a violation of the peace of the country, offered to the imperial court an additional aid of 60,000 men. Thus a combined army of at least 500,000 men stood under arms ready to march against the king of Prussia; while he, on the other hand, could only oppose to this mighty and overwhelming force 200,000 men, and those collected together only at the sacrifice of every resource at his command. As allies he only possessed England, the landgrave of Hesse, and the dukes of Brunswick and Gotha, and he was obliged to leave them alone to carry on the war with France; and, with respect to the other powers, he hoped to make up for his inferior force by the ability of his great generals and doubling his strength by rapid marches, and thus swiftly passing with the same army from one point to another, be enabled to fight his enemies one after the other. Thence, he resolved to direct his first and principal effort against Austria, whom he regarded as his chief enemy, while in the mean time he left behind 14,000 men under the command of his old Field-marshal Lehwald, for the defence of Prussia itself against the attack of the Russians, leaving only 4000 men for the protection of Berlin against the Swedes; fortunately, however, for Prussia, the Swedish portion of the allies took no very serious share in the war.

Maria Theresa, influenced by an extraordinary predilection for her husband's brother, Prince Charles of Lorraine, appointed him, although he had already been twice beaten by Frederick, commander-in-chief of the imperial army; while, under his orders she placed the talented and experienced soldier, General Brown. This arrangement proved of great service to the king. Brown, with his usual prudence and forethought, advised Prince Charles to anticipate the quick movements of the Prussians in the attack they contemplated, and penetrating into Saxony and Silesia, thus remove the seat of war from the hereditary states of Austria ; Charles of Lorraine, however, although on other occasions too precipitate, resolved in this case to be the very opposite, preferring to adopt the defensive, and was anxious to wait until he had drawn around him all the forces he could collect. This was exactly what Frederick most anxiously desired, and he contrived to strengthen the prince in the belief that he himself, overmatched by so many powerful enemies, thought it most prudent to assume the defensive likewise. Suddenly, however, and while the Austrians imagined themselves in perfect security, the Prussians broke up, and dividing themselves into four divisions, poured forth in rapid marches across the mountains into Bohemia, and, like so many mighty and impetuous mountain rivers, swept all before them, taking possession of all the supplies of the imperialists, which served to furnish themselves with provisions during several months, and reunited their forces at a certain hour in the morning of the 6th of May, at the appointed quarters in the vicinity of Prague.

The prince of Lorraine, hastily collecting together all his troops, had now taken a strong, intrenched position in the mountains, near Prague, where he considered himself secured against every attack. Frederick, however, to whom every hour which delayed the execution of the final blow appeared as lost, resolved to give battle at once now that the enemy was within sight, and in this determination he was cordially seconded by his favorite officer, General Winterfeld, a bold and undaunted warrior, whose ardor nothing could withstand. Accordingly the latter received orders to reconnoitre the enemy's position, and he reported that their right wing might be easily attacked, as in front of it were several green meadows, which would facilitate the advance of the troops. But these—as he thought—meadows, were nothing else but deep dried-up ponds, with slimy bottoms, which had been sown with oats, and after the harvest, were again to serve as fish ponds. This error served ultimately to produce much injury to the Prussians in their attack. The venerable Field-marshal Schwerin, who had only arrived at head-quarters that morning with his fatigued troops, and was altogether unacquainted with the spot chosen for the scene of action, suggested that they should postpone operations until the following day ; but the king, whose impetuosity was not to be restrained, and who, having now formed in his mind completely the plan of a glorious battle, was impatient to put it into execution, would not listen for a moment to any further delay. Upon this the old warrior, who, in his seventy-third year, retained still a great portion of his youthful fire, exclaimed, as he pressed his hat over his eyes: "Well, then, if the battle shall and must be fought this day, I will attack the enemy there on the spot where I see him!"

The battle only commenced at ten o'clock in the morning ; so much time having been taken up in making the necessary preparations, as the ground turned out to be generally swampy and hilly. As the Prussians worked their way through and approached the enemy, they were received with a terrific cannonade ; the carnage was dreadful, and whole ranks were levelled with the ground ; indeed, it seemed impossible for human courage to hold out against such tremendously destructive odds. Each attack made was unsuccessful, and the ranks of the Prussians began to waver. At this moment the brave old marshal, Schwerin, seized an ensign, and calling upon his troops to follow him, rushed into the thickest of the fire, where, however, pierced with four balls, the veteran warrior fell and died the death of a hero. General Manteufel released the gory standard from the firm grasp of the dead old soldier, and led on the troops, now burning with revenge at the loss of their brave commander. The king's brother, Prince Henry, sprang from his horse, and led on his men against a battery, which he conquered ; and Duke Ferdinand of Brunswick attacked and overthrew with the greatest courage the left wing of the Austrians, pursuing the enemy from mountain to mountain, and conquering seven intrenchments. Nevertheless, the victory remained undecided as long as Field-marshal Brown was able, by his influence and command, to maintain order among the ranks of the Austrians ; at length, however, he fell, mortally wounded, and with his fall vanished all success from the Austrian side. King Frederick, who with his keen eye surveyed the field of battle, quickly perceived the enemy begin to give way, and seeing a large gap in the centre of their ranks, he at once advanced, with some of his chosen troops, and, dashing into it, completely destroyed all communication between them, and put them entirely to rout. Thus the victory was gained: the Austrians fled in every direction, the greater portion of the fugitives throwing themselves into Prague, and the rest hastening to join Marshal Daun, who was posted in Küttenberg with an army of reserve.

Dearly, however, was this victory purchased! Twelve thousand five hundred Prussians lay dead or wounded on the battle-field, and among them was included one precious corpse—that of Field-marshal Schwerin; but the remembrance of his heroic death, and the blood-stained flag he bore in his nervous grasp, were regarded by the Prussian army as the most sacred legacy, serving them as a continual source of excitement to follow in the same path of glory. The Austrians, likewise, suffered an irreparable loss in the death of Field-marshal Brown; he had grown gray in the wars of his country, and the experience he had undergone rendered him the most distinguished general of his day.

The struggle in Bohemia was by no means decided by this battle, although the actual position of the parties was such that the campaign bid fair to terminate gloriously in favor of Frederick, for he now kept the prince of Lorraine a prisoner in Prague, together with 46,000 men, without any resources left to enable them to hold out for any length of time. Their only hopes of relief rested in Field-marshal Daun, who was then in the immediate vicinity with a considerable body of troops; but if he himself should be defeated by the king, the army hemmed in within the walls of Prague must be lost, the campaign itself won in the most glorious manner by the Prussians, and, perhaps, peace obtained, already in the second year of the war; for Frederick desired nothing more than what he obtained at the end of the war—the retention of Silesia. Fate, however, had not decreed that he should obtain this object so easily, and it was decided that his career of success should receive a check, while his spirit was doomed to undergo bitter and painful trials.

He determined not to wait for the attack of Daun, but to anticipate it; and after he had remained five weeks before Prague, he withdrew, with twelve thousand men, in order to join Prince Bevern, who had kept the army of Daun in observation, and which Frederick forthwith attacked, near Kollin, on the 18th of June. The plan of the order of battle adopted by the king was excellent; and had it been followed out entirely it would have given him the victory. Frederick decided upon this occasion to employ the same order of battle as that used in ancient times by Epaminondas, and by which he overcame the invincible Spartans: this was termed the oblique line of battle. By this plan, the weakest force, by promptitude of action, was enabled to operate with advantage over a superior body; for instance, if the general in command has recourse to such a bold manœuvre it is very rare if he does not succeed, but to ensure this victory he must be certain of the perfect co-operation of his army, so that by the celerity and exactitude of its movements the enemy may be completely deceived and vanquished before he has even had time to perceive the plan of attack by which it has been accomplished. Such was the manœuvre practised by the Prussians at Kollin, and the first onset made by Generals Ziethen and Hulsen upon the right wing of the Austrians put them entirely to rout. The centre and the other wing of the Prussian army had now only to follow it up forthwith, by falling upon the enemy's flank, battalion after battalion in succession, and thus complete its entire annihilation. While, however, every thing was thus operating in the right direction, the king himself, as if the usual clearness of his mind became suddenly clouded in impenetrable gloom, gave orders for the rest of the army to make a halt! In truth, throughout the whole of this important day, Frederick presented in his own person and manner something so unaccountably gloomy and repulsive that it rendered him totally incapable of attending to the ideas and observations suggested by those around him; he rejected every thing they advised, and his sinister look, together with his bitter remarks, only made them shun his presence.

When, at the most important and decisive moment, Prince Maurice of Dessau ventured to represent to the monarch the serious consequences that must result from the change he had commanded to take place in the plan of the order of battle, and reiterated his observations and arguments in the most urgent manner possible, Frederick rode up close to his side, and with uplifted sword, demanded, in a loud and threatening tone of voice, whether he would or would not obey orders? The prince at once desisted and withdrew; but from that moment the fate of the day was decided. Through the halt thus made so ill-timed, the Prussian lines found themselves right in front of the position held by the Austrians, and which they had strongly intrenched and made completely insurmountable; and when they made an attempt to take it by assault, the regiments were swept away one after the other by the destructive fire of the Austrian artillery. No exertion, no desperate effort, could now obtain the victory; fortune had now changed sides. General Daun, already despairing of success at the commencement of the battle, had marked down with a pencil the order to sound a retreat, when, just at that moment, the colonel of a Saxon regiment of cavalry having perceived that the ranks of the Prussians changed their order of battle, resolved to delay execution of orders, and placed the official paper in his pocket. The Austrians now renewed their attack, and the Saxon regiments of horse were more especially distinguished for the desperate charges they made, as if determined to revenge themselves for the injuries endured by their country. In order that all might not be sacrificed, orders were issued to make a retreat, and Daun, too well pleased to gain this, his first victory over Frederick the Great, did not follow in pursuit. The Prussians lost on this day 14,000 men, in either killed, wounded, or prisoners, and forty-five pieces of artillery. This formed nearly the moiety of the Prussian army, for in this battle 32,000 Prussians had fought against 60,000 Austrians.

What a change of fortune was this to Frederick! After having been on the point of capturing an entire army in the very capital of the country, and thus extinguishing, at the first moment of its commencement, and in the short space of eight months, the most dreadful war, he found himself forced to raise the siege of Prague, and abandon Bohemia altogether; having, in addition to these reverses of fortune, to lament, with sincere grief, the death of his beloved mother, who died ten days after the sad battle of Kollin. The allies of Austria, after this unexpected victory, resumed operations with greater activity than ever. The Russians invaded the kingdom of Prussia, the Swedes pursued their preparations more vigorously, and two French armies crossed the Rhine in order to attack the territory of Hesse, Hanover, and thence to march against the hereditary states of Prussia. One of these armies, under the command of Prince Soubise, advanced towards Thuringia, in order to form a junction with the imperial forces under the orders of the prince of Hilburghausen; while Marshal d'Estrée, who commanded the leading French army, on entering Hanover, fought and beat the duke of Cumberland at the head of the Anglo-Germanic troops, on the 26th of July, near Hastenbeck, on the Weser. This defeat was produced through the inexperience and imbecility of the English general; for his army, although limited in force, had, nevertheless, obtained considerable advantages through the courage and good generalship of the hereditary prince of Brunswick, and had forced the French general to sound a retreat, when the duke, to the no little surprise and indignation of every one, abandoned the field of battle, nor halted in his shameful retreat until he reached the Elbe near Stade. Nay, to complete the disgrace, he was forced shortly afterwards to conclude at Closterseven, on the 9th of September, a convention by which he engaged to disband his troops, and give up to the French Hanover, Hesse, the duchy of Brunswick, and the whole of the country situated between the Weser and the Rhine.

The duke of Richelieu, who succeeded Marshal d'Estrée in the command of the French troops, was a man of a most overbearing and prodigal character, devoid of all conscientious feeling or principle, and gloried in draining the country by every possible means of cruel exaction; and as all around him followed his example, and made the gain of money and licentiousness their all-ruling passion, this degrading practice spread more and more widely throughout the ranks of the entire army, until there was no excess to which it did not resort. In their system of devastation, indeed, the French, although belonging to a more polished nation, surpassed even the Cossacks and Calmucks, who, at this moment, were similarly occupied in the kingdom of Prussia itself. The destruction of morals is more surely to be dreaded from a civilized than a barbarous people; because, under the charm of seduction, it leaves behind a consuming poison in every city and village generally, and especially in the more sacred bosom of domestic life. The bad reputation of the French army, and the hatred felt and shown by the Germans, naturally more plain and simple in their manners and customs, against the smooth and polished mask of vice, contributed not a little to gain over the hearts of the majority of the people throughout Germany in favor of the cause of Frederick. Indeed, it was almost inconceivable, with what joy the people generally received the news of the victories he gained, although perhaps at the same moment their own princes, as members of the imperial states, were in arms against him. Such is the commanding influence exercised by a superior mind over his age; such the sympathy which a generous heart can rarely withhold from him who by strength and courage is enabled to battle with an overpowering and inflexible destiny! But much of this feeling was produced, likewise, through beholding how Frederick, with the aid only of his own Prussians, had to contend against hordes of barbarians from the east, as well as the hated and most formidable enemy from the west; while in the interior, he had to face the Austrian armies composed of soldiers all differing in language, customs, and manners, but all equally eager after pillage, including Hungarians, Croatians, and Pandurians. Had Frederick carried on the war merely against the Austrians and other Germans, true patriots would only have deplored the blindness of the hostile parties in thus contending against each other when they ought, on the contrary, to have sheathed the sword and held out to each other the hand of fraternal peace and friendship. The north of Germany was more especially attached to Frederick, ranking itself on the side of his own people, and participating in their joys and sorrows; for as that was the seat of war against the French, the cause of Frederick was regarded as that of Germany.

The convention of Closterseven paved the way for the French as far as the Elbe and Magdeburg itself; and their second army, now united with the imperial troops, was already in Thuringia, and made preparations for depriving the Prussians of the whole of Saxony, whence the latter received their stores and supplies of provisions.

This was not the only side by which Frederick was hard pressed. The Swedes spread themselves throughout the whole of Pomerania and Ukermark, and laid those countries under heavy contributions, while they had only to avail themselves of their whole force in order to advance direct upon Berlin itself, and make themselves, with scarcely any opposition, masters of that city. The Russian general, Apraxin, had already entered Prussia with 100,000 men, and to oppose him, Field-marshal Lehwald had only 24,000 men; nevertheless, he was forced to give the Russians battle, however great the sacrifice, as Frederick sent him strict orders to drive out these barbarians and put an end to their devastations. Accordingly the action took place at Grossjägerndorf, near Welau; but the most undaunted and desperate courage displayed by the Prussians was employed in vain against a force so overwhelming. Lehwald was forced to retreat, after a loss of several thousand men, and thus Prussia now appeared irretrievably lost—when, to the astonishment of all, Apraxin, instead of advancing, withdrew to the Russian frontiers ten days after the battle he had gained.

Thus we find, from time to time, the troubled path of Frederick illumined by a glimmering ray of hope, which appeared to lead him on to better fortune. This time it originated in the serious illness of the empress Elizabeth of Russia; and the grand-chancellor Bestuschef, believing her death close at hand, and having his eye directed to her successor, Peter III.—an admirer and friend of the Prussian hero—lost not a moment in commanding General Apraxin to withdraw his troops from the Prussian dominions. This enabled the army under Lehwald to march against the Swedes, who, on the approach of the Prussians, evacuated the entire country and retreated as far as Stralsund and Rügen.

## CHAPTER XXXI.

Continuation of the Seven Years' War, 1757-1760—Battle of Rossbach, 1757—Total Defeat of the French—General Seidlitz and the Prussian Cavalry—Reverses of Frederick—Silesia—Battle of Leuthen, 1757—Frederick's Appeal to his Officers and Army—Their Enthusiasm—Complete Overthrow of the Austrians—Glorious Results to Frederick—His Proposals of Peace rejected by Maria Theresa—France—Russia—England's Enthusiasm for Frederick—William Pitt—England supports Frederick—Treaty of Closterseven disavowed—Duke Ferdinand of Brunswick General-in-Chief of the Allied Army—Defeats and drives away the French from Germany—Frederick in Silesia—Schweidnitz—Frederick's rapid March into Moravia—Olmütz—Bohemia—Pomerania—Battle between the Russians and Prussians at Zorndorf, 1758—Dreadful Slaughter and Defeat of the Russians—The Prussians attacked and defeated by the Austrians at Hochkirch, 1758—Frederick's Presence of Mind—The Prussian Army—The Imperial Diet—The Prince of Mecklenburg—The Imperial Ban against Frederick proposed—Negatived—The Allied and French Armies—Battle of Bergen, 1759—Partial Success of the French—Battle of Minden—Shameful Conduct of the English General, Sackville—Defeat of the French—Battle of Kay and Künersdorf, 1759—Total Defeat of the Prussians—Frederick's Misfortunes—His Despair—Prince Henry of Prussia—Continued Reverses of Frederick—Battle of Liegnitz, 1760—The Prussians defeat the Austrians—Beneficial Results to Frederick—Battle of Torgau, 1760—Total Defeat of the Austrians—Frederick in Leipsic.

Frederick, after having endeavored for a considerable time, but in vain, to give battle to the Austrians in Lusatia, broke up his army, and in the month of August advanced up the Saale into Saxony, in order to drive the French out of that country. After various marches and counter-marches he at length came up with them and the imperial army on the 5th of November, in the village of Rossbach, close to the Saale. Frederick had only 22,000 men, while the enemy had 60,000; and they already began to triumph in anticipation of his overthrow, being determined that the king, with his handful of troops, should not escape them this time. He encamped his army upon a height, and the French advanced by forced marches, with sound of trumpet, towards his camp, curious to see whether or not he would have the courage to make a stand against them, for their object was to surround him completely, and thus, by making him prisoner, put an end to the war at once. The Prussians, however, fired not a single shot, but remained perfectly quiet, apparently unprepared for, or not taking any notice of the movements of the enemy; the smoke ascending from their cooking fires indicated their present occupation, while Frederick himself took his meal with his general officers and staff with the appearance of the greatest coolness and indifference. But when the favorable moment arrived, about half-past two o'clock in the afternoon, he gave his orders accordingly, and in an instant, as if by magic, the tents were struck, the army drawn up in battle array, the artillery opened its tremendous fire, and Seidlitz, at the head of his brave cavalry, dashed among the battalions of the enemy as they arrived. The French had never, hitherto, encountered such rapidity of action from the Germans, and they found it totally impossible to form into line; for they were completely overwhelmed and routed before they could even attempt it, and in the course of less than half an hour the action was decided, and the entire French army put *hors de combat.* They were seized with such a panic that they never halted until they reached the middle states of the empire, while many, even, deeming themselves still insecure, only paused when they reached the opposite banks of the Rhine. Seven thousand prisoners fell into the hands of the king, including nine generals and three hundred and twenty officers of every rank, together with sixty-three pieces of cannon and twenty-two standards; while this glorious victory only cost the Prussians one hundred and sixty-five in killed, and three hundred and fifty wounded. The king was indebted for this great triumph to the excellent state of discipline and order maintained throughout his whole army, which was thus enabled, at such momentary notice, to execute so successfully the daring plans formed often so suddenly and unexpectedly by their royal chief; above all, however, he owed much of this victory to the rapid and overwhelming courage of General Seidlitz and his cavalry.

Saxony was now rescued and secured on this side, while the moral effect of the battle of Rossbach produced much benefit to the king; nevertheless, his military labors and fatigues, for this year, were not yet completed. For, during his absence, his favorite and confidential friend, General Winterfeld, had perished in an action near Moyes; the duke of Bevern had retreated with his army into Silesia as far as the walls of Breslau, and as he could not undertake any thing against the united forces of the prince of Lorraine and Field-marshal Daun, the important fortress of Schweidnitz fell, on the 11th of November, into the hands of General Nadasti. On the 22d, the entire Austrian army attacked the Prussians at

Breslau, and vanquished them after a vigorous defence; the duke of Bevern, dreading his sovereign's wrath, yielded himself prisoner—according to all appearance voluntarily so—to the Austrians; and, finally, the capital, Breslau, with all its rich supplies of provisions and ammunition, was given up to the imperialists through the cowardice of General Lestwitz. Thus Silesia appeared now to be lost for Frederick; for, if it should be allowed to remain only one winter in the hands of the enemy, they would fortify it in every possible way, so as to make it totally impossible for him ever to reconquer it. On the other hand, it appeared equally impossible, unless by a miracle, to recapture it with the 14,000 men he brought with him from Saxony, and the 16,000 forming the remnant of the vanquished army under the duke of Bevern.

It was in moments like this, when all around him assumed that gloomy character, such as must naturally produce despair and desolation in the mind, that King Frederick displayed in the most striking manner the greatness of his genius, the treasure of mental resources at his command, and the irresistible power with which he operated upon the feelings of all under him. He summoned a council of his generals and chief officers, and addressed them in such soul-inspiring language, that they were aroused to a state of the most ardent and zealous enthusiasm. He represented to them the difficult, and even desperate condition in which their country was at that moment placed, and under which it must inevitably sink, if he could not calculate upon their courage to save it. "I know you all feel that you are Prussians," he added, in conclusion; "nevertheless, if there be one among you who fears to share such dangers with me, he is at liberty to resign his command from this very day, without having the slightest reason to dread any reproach from me for so doing." And when in reply to this he beheld in the eyes of all around him the expression of the one universal determined feeling—that they would all rally around their brave sovereign, and devote their lives to his and their country's cause, he exclaimed, with gratified mien: "I was well convinced, beforehand, that not one of you all would desert me in this trying moment; whence I am sanguine in my hopes of victory. Should I fall, and thus be prevented from rewarding you for your courage, be assured our country will not neglect to do so. Farewell then, my friends and comrades; in a short time we shall either have driven away the enemy now before us, or this will have proved our eternal adieu!"

The enthusiasm called forth by this inspiring language soon produced its good effects throughout the entire army, and all awaited with eager impatience the moment for marching against the foe. The latter had taken up an equally strong and advantageous position behind the river Lohe, where it was extremely difficult for the king to attack him. The cautious leader, Field-marshal Daun, was desirous of holding possession of it, for he had already learned to know at Kollin how necessary it was to command a good position in order to check and hold at bay the impetuosity of the king. But General Luchesi and others of the imperialists, who held it degrading to a victorious army to seek to intrench itself in a position against a force so much inferior in numbers, persuaded Prince Charles to march at once and meet the king, assuring him, "that the *parade guard of Berlin*," as they thus styled the Prussian army, "would never be able to make a stand against them." This advice was most acceptable to the prince, naturally of a more impetuous than reflective disposition, and he marched forth. The two armies accordingly met on the vast plain in the vicinity of Leuthen, on the 5th of December, exactly one month after the battle of Rossbach. The imperial army, in its plan of attack, extended its lines over a space of nearly five miles; while Frederick was forced to have recourse to those means by which he was enabled to double his power by the celerity of his manœuvres, and adopted, on this occasion, his former oblique order of battle. He caused a false attack to be made on the right, while his principal attack was directed against the left wing; and having overcome this completely, the consequent disorder was communicated to the whole of the Austrian army. Resistance had now become useless, and in the course of three hours Frederick gained the most complete victory. The field of battle was covered with the slain, and whole battalions surrendered themselves prisoners, amounting altogether to 21,000 men. Added to this, the Prussians captured one hundred and thirty cannon, and three thousand ammunition and other wagons. This is one of the most extraordinary victories met with in history, where 30,000 men only were opposed to 80,000, and by which it was amply proved how superior genius may sometimes triumph over superior numbers, and more especially when the ideas and plans formed, are seconded and carried out with that proportionate activity and firmness, so gloriously displayed on this occasion by the Prussians.

Meantime, Frederick and his army, however great had been their efforts, would not allow themselves time for repose, although so much needed, but followed up without the least delay the fruits of their victory, until they had completely driven out the Austrians from the Silesian territories beyond the Bohemian mountains. This was undertaken by the ever-active and indefatigable General Ziethen, and was accomplished by him with his usual success, making immense booty and numerous prisoners; while, meantime, the king himself attacked Breslau, which he captured with its garrison of 17,000 men, and in the same month, December, Liegnitz likewise surrendered to his conquering arms. Thus, by one bold stroke, upon which he risked his all, cost what it may, Frederick reconquered the whole of Silesia—where he was enabled to take up his winter quarters as far as Schweidnitz—as well as Saxony; and, what was more than all, he gained for himself that immortal renown in the annals of his country which will continue to be handed down to the latest posterity. The Austrian army, however, which so shortly before was so powerful in numbers, exceeding 80,000 men, and so perfect in its appointments, had suffered so much that its relics when collected in Bohemia, scarcely mustered 17,000 fighting men. All the Prussian territories, as far as Westphalia, were now completely freed of the enemy.

Four grand battles, and numerous actions more or less important, had combined to make the preceding year, 1757, one of the most sanguinary to be found in history. Both parties had sufficiently tested their strength against each other; and Frederick now offered at the court of Vienna terms of peace, manifesting by this the principles of ancient Rome—not to propose peace until after he had gained a victory. But the empress Maria Theresa still continued too much embittered against the conqueror of Silesia to admit of the acceptance of his proposals; and, in addition to this, every care had been taken to conceal from her the heavy losses sustained by her army at the battle of Leuthen, as well as the distressed condition to which the war had reduced her states. She was likewise influenced in her resolution by France, which insisted upon the continuation of the war in Germany, otherwise that power would be obliged to contend alone against England. Thence the offers of Frederick were rejected, and preparations for a fresh campaign renewed on a more extensive scale than ever. Prince Charles of Lorraine, who had lost the confidence both of the army and the country, was forced to resign the chief command. It was found, however, extremely difficult to meet with his substitute, for the brave Field-marshal Nadasti, owing to the jealousy and intrigue excited against him, was completely supplanted, and eventually the choice was fixed upon Field-marshal Daun, for whose reputation the victory of Kollin had effected far more than his otherwise natural tardiness of action and irresolution merited.

The French armies were likewise reinforced, and another general-in-chief, Count Clermont, was appointed instead of the duke of Richelieu. The latter, accordingly, returned to France with all the millions he had exacted, during the period of his service, upon which he lived in the most extravagant, gorgeous style, in the face of the whole world, and in defiance of all shame and disgust. Russia also joined in the desire for a continuation of the war, and the chancellor Bestuschef, who had in the previous year recalled the army from Prussia, was removed from office, and another leader, General Fermor, was placed at the head of the Russian troops; he, in fact, lost not a moment, but marched at once against Prussia, in the month of January, and conquered the kingdom without any resistance, owing to the absence of General Lehwald, who with the army was then in Pomerania, contending against the Swedes.

In order to oppose and make a stand against such serious and overwhelming danger, Frederick was forced to summon together the entire and extreme resources of his own dominions, as well as those of the Saxon territories. Levies in money and troops were forthwith made with equal activity and rigor, and the king found himself reduced to the necessity of coining counterfeit money for the payment of his troops: a measure which such a case of extreme necessity alone can justify or excuse. He knew, however, too well that, since the feudal system of war had been succeeded by that of modern times, the grand principle upon which war must now be carried on was founded upon the employment of its influential agent—money. For as regarded allies upon whom he might place dependence, he possessed only England and a few princes in the north of Germany, and these were already paralyzed by the disgraceful convention of Closterseven. Fortune, however, served him very favorably at this moment in England; the British nation, always ready to acknowledge and appreciate patriotic achievements in every quarter, was inspired by the battle of Rossbach with the greatest enthusiasm for Frederick; while the most complete disgust was generally excited against the shameful convention of Closterseven. In accordance with these feelings, the celebrated William Pitt, who had just been appointed prime minister, caused this treaty, which had not as yet been confirmed, to be at once disavowed, and determined to continue the war with renewed vigor. The army was forthwith augmented, and the appointment of its leader was intrusted to Frederick himself. His eagle eye soon fixed upon the genius best adapted for its extraordinary powers to be chosen to co-operate with himself, and he accordingly furnished the allied army with a truly distinguished chief, Ferdinand, duke of Brunswick, who, by his good generalship, so well justified Frederick's choice, that his name will ever continue to maintain its brilliant position on the side of that of the great king, in the records of this sanguinary war.

According to a plan agreed upon between Frederick and himself, the duke already opened the campaign in the month of February, and, marching at the head of his small army, he surprised the French in their winter quarters, where they were living in abundance and luxury at the expense of the Hanoverians and Hessians; the odds between the two armies were great, for the duke had only 30,000 men against their 100,000. But with him all his measures were so well calculated, while on the part of his adversaries so much negligence and frivolity existed, in combination with the incapacity of their general, that in a very few weeks the duke completely succeeded in driving them out of the entire country situated between the Aller and Weser, and the Weser and the Rhine; their haste being such that they abandoned all their provisions and ammunition, and more than 11,000 were taken prisoners by the allied army. They recrossed the Rhine near Düsseldorf, hoping there to be secure; in this however they deceived themselves. Duke Ferdinand pursued them to the other side of the Rhine, attacked them at Crefeld, and, in spite of their superiority in numbers, he put them completely to rout, causing them a loss of seven thousand slain. After this battle the city of Düsseldorf surrendered to the duke, and his light cavalry scoured the country throughout the Austrian Netherlands, even to the very gates of Brussels itself.

Frederick, during this interval, had not been idle. He commenced with laying siege to Schweidnitz, which strong and important place still remained in the hands of the Austrians, and carried it by assault on the 18th of April. Field-marshal Daun meantime remained stationary in Bohemia, and used every exertion to cut off the march of Frederick into that country, for he fully expected to be attacked there by the king. But while he imagined himself perfectly secure, Frederick suddenly broke up with his army, and instead of proceeding to Bohemia, advanced, by forced marches, to Moravia, and laid siege to Olmütz. In this expedition was shown the peculiarity of Frederick's genius, which led him to undertake the most bold, extraordinary, and perilous enterprises, while his constant aim and glory was to take his enemy by surprise; and on this occasion he was more especially influenced by the idea, that if he once became master of Olmütz, he would then have the command of the most important position in an Austrian territory hitherto perfectly undisturbed, and thus be enabled to threaten the immediate vicinity of Vienna itself. Fortune, however, did not this time second his bold design; the place defended itself with the greatest bravery, the inhabitants of the country, faithful to their empress, annoyed the Prussians as far as was in their power, and conveyed intelligence to the imperial army of all their movements. By this means Daun was enabled to intercept and seize upon a convoy of three thousand wagons, upon the arrival of which the entire success of the siege depended; whence it was obliged to be given up. But now the retreat into Silesia was blocked up; and Daun, having taken possession of every road, felt certain that he had caught the enemy within his own net. Frederick, however, suddenly turned back, and marching across the mountains, arrived in Bohemia—where the Austrian general did not at all expect him—without the loss of a single wagon; and he would not have been forced to leave this country so soon again had not the invasion of the Russians recalled him to Pomerania and Neumark. Accordingly he recrossed the mountains from Bohemia into Silesia, and leaving Marshal Keith behind to protect the country, he hastened with 14,000 men to attack the Russians.

At every step he took as he marched through the provinces he met with the sad effects of the devastation committed by these barbarians, who spared neither women, children, the young, nor the old. The town of Cüstrin was burnt to ashes, with the exception of three houses, and the land around presented one vast desert. When the king, as well as his entire army, beheld these melancholy scenes, they were overwhelmed with burning rage, and the moment they came in sight of the enemy they commenced the attack, when one of the most sanguinary battles of the entire Seven Years' War was fought, and which raged from nine o'clock in the morning until ten at night. Thirty-seven thousand Prussians were opposed to sixty thousand Russians, fighting hand to hand in the manner of the ancient Germans, each combatant resolved to perish rather than yield in the fatal struggle—and in which the Prussians, after what they had seen, were more especially excited to wreak their vengeance upon the savage invaders—giving by their sovereign's command no quarter, but fighting for life or death. On the evening of this sanguinary day more than 19,000 Russians lay dead or wounded on the field of battle; but, on the other hand, nearly 11,000 Prussians were slain or disabled, for the Russians, finding they were completely edged in, and to all appearance without any hope of escape, sold their lives dearly, and fought, likewise, with desperate courage. If, indeed, it had not been for the invincible cavalry of Seidlitz, which flew in every direction where the danger was greatest, to the support of their sinking comrades, and thus, by efforts almost superhuman, overthrew whole battalions of the enemy, the victory would still have remained doubtful, as indeed was acknowledged by Frederick himself. As it was, however, the Russian general, Fermor, abandoned Prussia entirely, and retreated into Poland; while Frederick marched into Saxony, where his brother Henry was hard pressed by the superior forces of the Austrians.

General Daun, on the approach of the king, retired to a strong position he had selected in Lusatia. His object was to cut off the passage of the king into Silesia, in order that his general, Harsch, might have time to conquer the fortress of Neisse. Frederick, however, who perceived his aim, hastened to occupy the route to Silesia through Bautzen and Görlitz, and marched close past the lines of the Austrian army, in order to encamp himself upon an open plain situated between the villages of Hochkirch and Cotitz. This plan was any thing but wise, although it showed great contempt for the enemy. His quarter-master, Marwitz, and at the same time a confidential favorite, represented to him the great danger to which he was exposed by taking up this position, and, hesitating at first, he finally refused to pitch the camp there, in spite of the king's commands. He was, however, forthwith placed under arrest, and his duties transferred into the hands of another. The army continued here encamped three days, completely exposed to the attacks of the enemy, so much superior in numbers; while Frederick remained obstinately deaf to all the representations of his generals. He considered that as the Austrians had never attacked him first, he might easily calculate that Field-marshal Daun would never think, and was quite incapable of undertaking such a bold step; while, in addition to this self-deception, he was betrayed by an Austrian spy, whom the enemy had bought over, and who accordingly furnished him with false reports of their plans and proceedings.

On the morning of the 14th of October, and before the dawn of day, the Prussian army was aroused by a discharge of artillery; the Austrians having, during the night, silently advanced to the village of

Hochkirch, and exactly as the church-clock chimed the hour of five, they fell upon the Prussian advanced posts, took possession of the strong intrenchment at the entrance of the village, turned the muzzles of the cannon against their adversaries, and, by a murderous fire, destroyed all the Prussians that attempted to make a stand in its defence. The slaughter committed was dreadful, for the troops poured forth in thousands to assemble in the principal street of the village as head-quarters. The generals and principal officers endeavored in vain, amid the darkness, to form them in regular line of battle; the brave Prince Francis of Brunswick had his head carried away by a cannon-ball, in the very moment he was about to attack the enemy on the heights of Hochkirch; Field-marshal Keith, a venerable but equally brave and well-tried warrior, fell pierced with two bullets, and Prince Maurice of Dessau was likewise dangerously wounded. Generals Seidlitz and Ziethen formed their squadrons of cavalry on the open plain, and threw themselves with all their usual bravery upon the Austrians; but the advantages they gained could not compensate for the serious loss already sustained. Hochkirch, the camp, together with all the baggage and ammunition fell into the hands of the enemy. The dawn of day brought with it no advantage, for an impenetrable fog prevented the king from reconnoitring the enemy's position as well as his own, so as to be enabled, perhaps, by a prompt movement, to bring back to his colors that good fortune which had thus so unexpectedly abandoned him. Nevertheless, his regiments had now through that discipline which was never so admirably displayed as at this moment, succeeded in forming themselves into regular order, and when, towards nine o'clock, the sun made its appearance, he perceived that the Austrian army had already nearly surrounded him on every side, and he accordingly gave orders for a retreat. This took place in such good order, that the Austrian general was taken so much by surprise that he found it impossible to attempt to oppose it, and returned to his old quarters. The king, however, had suffered a loss of several of his best generals, nine thousand good soldiers, and more than one hundred pieces of cannon; and, as he had lost all his baggage, nothing was left wherewith to supply his troops with clothing for the approaching winter.

Meantime, the king maintained the utmost tranquillity and firmness of mind throughout this period of trial, and his appearance inspired his troops with the same feeling. And, in truth, if Frederick ever showed himself great in misfortune, he did so especially after this serious loss; for, although deprived of all the necessary provisions and supplies for his army, he nevertheless was not less successful in accomplishing by hasty marches and masterly manœuvres his original plan; and thus, deceiving the enemy, and circuiting his position, forced General Harsch in all haste to raise the siege of Neisse. Silesia was now entirely freed from the enemy; while Daun, conqueror as he was, after being unable to prevent Frederick from entering Silesia, and obtaining, by his attack upon Dresden, no other result but that of forcing the Prussian general, Count Schmettau, in his defence to set fire to the beautiful suburbs of that capital, returned in mortification to Bohemia, where he established his winter-quarters. Thus superiority of genius produced those results for the conquered, which otherwise might have fallen to the share of the conqueror.

At the end of this year Frederick found himself, in spite of the vicissitudes he had undergone, in possession of the same countries as in the preceding year, in addition to which he now had Schweidnitz, which was not in his hands previously; while in Westphalia all his provinces which had been captured by the French were now reconquered by the valor of Prince Ferdinand. The latter had not certainly been able to maintain, with his small army, his position on the other side of the Rhine; but, at the end of the campaign, he forced the French to abandon the whole right bank of that river, and to establish their winter-quarters between the Rhine and the Meuse.

The following year, however, in spite of the perils he had already undergone and battled against, the heroic king found himself destined to encounter vicissitudes, which rendered this period of the war more trying than perhaps any other. The hope of being at length enabled to crush him, excited his enemies to strain every effort in order to effect this object. The Austrian army was completely reorganized and reinforced to its full complement, and indeed, with every coming year, it marched into the field with increased vigor and augmented numbers, because the ranks were filled up with the hardy peasantry of the hereditary lands, who were well drilled, and who being intermingled with the more experienced and well-tried veterans of many a hard-fought battle—of whom, notwithstanding the heavy losses sustained, the army still retained a powerful body—were soon initiated in the rough and perilous scenes of the camp. In Frederick's small army, on the other hand, which had to contend equally with Austrians, Russians, Frenchmen, and Swedes, as well as with other troops of the empire itself, the number of those who had escaped the sword and disease, formed but a small body, and consequently its ranks were principally filled with newly-levied and inexperienced recruits. And however speedily these young soldiers, who often joined the army at the early age of boyhood, entered into the spirit and honor of the cause for which they fought, and in which they emulated, as much as possible, the acts of their more veteran comrades—sometimes, perhaps, even surpassing them in daring courage—still their number was far inferior compared with those levied in Saxony, Anhalt, Mecklenburg, and such as were collected in various other parts, consisting chiefly of deserters. Thênce, although the Prussian army was soon completed in all its numbers and appointments, it fell far short when compared with the Austrians in internal organization and united strength.* Besides this, Frederick's own estates, as well as those of Saxony and Mecklenburg, suffered so much by oppressive taxation, and the continual conscription, which thus seriously diminished the male population, that it seemed as if they never could recover from the sad effects. The duke of Mecklenburg, indeed, in his indignation, acted with such imprudence at the diet of Ratisbon, as to place himself at the head of those princes who were most loud and bitter in their complaints against Frederick, and demanded nothing less than that the ban of the empire should be at once pronounced against him; for which act the duke's land was subjected to the most extreme severity of treatment, and, in fact, dealt with rather as that of an enemy than an ally. The imperial ban, however, was not adjudged against the king, for as the same sentence must have been pronounced against the elector of Hanover, the evangelic states refused to condemn two such distinguished members of their body. Besides which, this word, which in ancient times was more fatally annihilating in its effects than the sharp edge of the sword itself, had, unfortunately, long since become void of power and effect, and if pronounced, would only have exposed more degradingly the dissolution of the Germanic confederation.

Maria Theresa, however, by her urgent appeals to the sovereigns of France and Russia to carry on the war, endeavored to effect the destruction of Frederick with far more certainty than could have been accomplished by all the bans pronounced against him by the imperial diet. The empress of Russia, in order to obliterate the stain of the battle of Zorndorf, sent fresh troops under the command of General Soltikow, a brave and active officer. In Paris, the duke of Choiseul, hitherto French ambassador at Vienna, and the chief promoter of the war against Frederick, was now chosen prime-minister, and he determined to employ all the forces at command, in order to reconquer Westphalia, Hanover, and Hesse. Had this design been brought into execution, these countries would have experienced the most dreadful persecution, and Hanover more especially would have been singled out by France upon which to wreak her vengeance, for the losses she had sustained both at sea and on her coasts, from the naval expeditions of Great Britain. For the glorious victories obtained by the British men-of-war had completely diminished the maritime force of France, while both in North America and the East Indies

* A foreigner of rank and great wealth, having requested to be permitted to serve in the campaign of 1757 as a volunteer, Frederick granted his wish, and the noble recruit arrived in a splendid carriage, and attended by several servants; in fact, displaying an unusual lavishment of expense and luxury. He received, however, no mark of distinction, and, indeed, very little or no attention, being generally stationed in the wagon-train. He bore no part in any engagement, much less in any general battle, and had to experience the mortification of not sharing in the victorious action of Rossbach. He had often sent a written complaint to the king, but without any effect; at length, however, he had an opportunity of addressing the king in person, when, in reply to his representations upon the subject, Frederick said, "Your style of living, sir, is not the fashion in my army; in fact, it is highly objectionable and offensive. Without the greatest moderation, it is impossible to learn to bear the fatigues which accompany every war, and if you cannot determine to submit to the strict discipline my officers and troops are forced to undergo, I would advise you, in a friendly way, to return to your own country."—*Mülcher*.

all her settlements and possessions were reduced or captured. Prince Ferdinand, with his small army, was, however, the only disposable power at command to oppose the enemy in his designs against Germany from this quarter.

Ferdinand was menaced upon two sides: on that of the Maine by the army of the duke of Broglio, whose head-quarters were at Frankfort, which he had taken by surprise—for, in spite of its being an imperial free city, and although it had accordingly furnished, without hesitation, its quota of contributions to the confederation in men and money for the war against Frederick, it was not the less exposed to attack; and from the point of the Lower Rhine, Marshal de Contade advanced with the main body of the army, to invade and overrun Hanover. Ferdinand was in hopes of being able, like Frederick, to make a successful stand against both armies through the celerity of his movements, and marching at once against the duke of Broglio at the opening of the campaign, came up with him on the 12th of April at Bergen, near Frankfort. He immediately attacked him with his brave Hessians, but the position occupied by the French was too strong, while they were enabled to replace the troops they lost by continual fresh supplies, whence the Hessians were repulsed in three attacks. Ferdinand now prudently resolved not to expose his army to the chances of a total defeat, and accordingly made a retreat in good order. It required, however, the exercise of all the genius and experience he possessed to enable him to protect Lower Saxony against the attack of Marshal de Contade. This general had succeeded in crossing the Rhine near Düsseldorf, and, marching through the Weser forest towards Giessen, formed a junction with Broglio, and took Cassel, Paderborn, Münster, and Minden, on the Weser. In all his operations thus far he was equally prompt and successful, and Ferdinand found himself forced to withdraw as far back as the mouth of the Weser near Bremen, while the French general now regarded Hanover as already within his grasp.

In Paris all were in high glee at this glorious beginning—but the German hero soon changed that exultation into the opposite feelings of sorrow and depression by gaining a brilliant victory. Ferdinand, placing full confidence in his resources, marched to meet the French army, and found it, on the 1st of August, near Minden, occupying a position, the nature of which offered him every advantage for the attack. Contade was forced to fight, inasmuch as his supplies were cut off, but he calculated upon his superiority in numbers; he, however, gave very few proofs on this day of his talent and experience, although at other times he had not shown himself wanting in ability. Contrary to all military practice hitherto, he placed his cavalry in the centre, and this very error in his tactics, and which, no doubt, he expected must operate to his advantage, produced his defeat and Ferdinand's triumph. He ordered the British and Hanoverian infantry, whose steady firmness he had already tested, to advance and charge the enemy's cavalry—a bold and happy idea, and which by the results effected, was through its realization an additional evidence of Ferdinand's superior genius, which at such a moment directed him to swerve from the ordinary course of operations. The French cavalry, forming the *élite* of the whole army, astounded at this daring attack of the allied infantry, met the charge with tolerable firmness at first, and endeavored to force the ranks of their bold opponents and gallop over them; but every attempt they made against these solid and invulnerable ranks of bayonets was completely defeated, and at length the sweeping discharges of the artillery, together with the destructive execution made by the well-aimed muskets of the infantry, produced the greatest confusion among them, and put them completely to flight. Ferdinand now gave orders to General Sackville to dash through the hollow space thus left in the centre of the French line with his British cavalry, and to pursue the flying enemy; by obeying which orders he would have completely divided the two wings of the French army, and thus overpowered by the allies, its entire destruction must inevitably have followed. But whether it was through jealousy or cowardice—for his unaccountable behavior has never been clearly explained—the English general turned traitor, disobeyed the order given by the duke, and thus allowed the French time to reassemble and make good their retreat. As it was, however, they lost eight thousand men and thirty pieces of cannon. But the results of this battle were still more important. Contade, being now continually pursued, withdrew along the Weser to Cassel, and thence continued his retreat southward to Giessen; while the army of Ferdinand captured successively Marburg, Fulda, and Münster, in Westphalia, so that, by the end of the year, this distinguished general found himself once more in possession of the same territories he occupied at its commencement.

King Frederick had not shown his usual eagerness to open the campaign this year, inasmuch as his advantage did not now, so much as at the commencement of the war, depend upon the results of prompt measures; but the main object of his plans at this moment was rather if possible to prevent the junction of the Russian and Austrian armies. He encamped himself in a strong position near Landshut, whence, by sudden incursions directed equally against the Russians in Poland and the Austrians in Bohemia, he wrested from them their most valuable magazines, and thus prevented both armies, for a considerable time, from undertaking any important enterprise; for when, according to the system pursued by the belligerent parties at this period, the armies remained quartered in a country for any length of time, they abstained as much as possible from depriving the inhabitants of all their provisions; whence much greater supplies were rendered necessary for the troops.

At length, however, the Russians, consisting of 40,000 men, crossed the Oder, and Laudon was waiting ready to join them with his 20,000 Austrians. Frederick, in such an extremity, resolved, in order to save himself, to have recourse to extraordinary measures. Among his generals he had one, young it is true, but at the same time distinguished beyond any other for his daring courage in difficult circumstances: this was General Wedel. Him he held as best qualified to be intrusted with the command against the Russians, but he was doubtful whether or not, perhaps, the senior generals would submit to his orders. The king, however, decided at once to adopt the plan of the Romans—who in extreme danger made it a rule to place the whole authority and direction of affairs in the hands of one man, whom they styled their dictator—and accordingly appointed General Wedel dictator over the army opposed to the Russians. According to the royal instructions he received, he was to attack the enemy wherever he came up with them. These instructions the young dictator obeyed to the letter, but without reflecting upon what such orders presupposed. Accordingly he attacked the Russians on the 23d of June, at the village of Kay, near Züllichau, but planned his attack so badly that, in order to make it, his army was forced to cross a bridge and march through a long narrow line of road, in single files, so that the battalions were only able to reach the field of battle in successive bodies; where, as they arrived, they were received by a murderous discharge of grape-shot, and were thus destroyed in detail by the Russians. The Prussians lost more than 5000 men, and the enemy being thus no longer opposed, effected a junction with Laudon without any further delay.

It was necessary now that Frederick himself should hasten with his 43,000 men to meet the combined forces of the enemy. He knew and felt the great danger to which he was about to expose himself personally, and summoning his brother Henry from his camp at Schmottseifen, gave him strict charge to watch the movements of Field-marshal Daun, and besides this, appointed him regent of the Prussian dominions, in case he himself should be either killed or taken prisoner in this expedition. At the same time, however, in the event of such a misfortune, he demanded from him the most solemn promise, never to submit to a peace which in the slightest degree might bring shame or disgrace upon the house of Prussia. Frederick well knew how to live and die as a king, and he would willingly have lost his life rather than be made a prisoner; for he was too well aware what great sacrifice his enemies would have demanded for his ransom.

On the 12th of August, he found the united forces of the Russians and Austrians, amounting to 60,000 men, strongly intrenched upon the heights of Künersdorf, near Frankfort on the Oder. After reconnoitring their position, he formed his plan of battle, and which was so drawn out as to ensure not only a complete victory, but likewise the entire annihilation of the enemy. Many have condemned the king for conceiving his plan upon such desperate and cruel principles; but this very plan is a characteristic evidence of the greatness of a general, who prefers terminating the war with one blow rather than tediously prolonging it by a succession of insignificant actions, and which, nevertheless, when summed together, prove by their results still more murderous in the lives sacrificed. And, again, why should such a reproach be made against Frederick, seeing how many enemies he had to battle with at once, and how much reason he had rather, if possible, to bring hostilities to an end with each, by contending with them separately? But the plan of the battle of Künersdorf was not the cause of the misfortune of the day; it was produced, firstly, through ignorance of the different localities around—for although the king had collected information from those who knew the country, he was still left without an exact knowledge of the field of battle; and, secondly, through the too great confidence he placed in human strength. For after having succeeded, by the most extraordinary exertions of his troops, in his attack against the left wing of the Russians, capturing ninety pieces of cannon, and putting the whole of this left wing to flight—so that the king, in his elated hopes, had already dispatched a courier to Berlin with the announcement of victory—and the day now declining, his generals advised him to pause and spare his worn-out soldiers, especially as the Austrians had not as yet taken any share in the battle, and the right wing of the Russians still remained immoveable. They likewise added their expectations, that the enemy would withdraw from the field in the course of the night of his own accord. The king, however, who would not hear of any work being half done, paid no attention to their representations; while at the same time, no doubt, he perceived how dangerous it would be to break off the fight in the immediate vicinity of the Austrian army, ready prepared and waiting for battle; accordingly, he gave immediate orders to make a fresh attack. Thus the soldiers, already faint and exhausted with the great exertions they had made during the whole of that hot day, were again doomed to scale the heights and conquer the strongest positions, whence the batteries of heavy artillery scattered the most dreadful havoc among their ranks. The greatest courage could not possibly hold out before such superiority of force; each time that their generals, and the king himself, led them on to the attack, they were repulsed, until at last the entire army was seized with terror and dismay, and took to flight. The Austrian cavalry now pursued and fell upon the fugitives, causing the most dreadful carnage, and all hopes of making a retreat in good order were out of question. Frederick himself, when he witnessed the defeat of his troops, a defeat such as he had never before experienced, was seized with such overpowering feelings of depression and despair, that he renounced all thought of saving his own life; there he was seen amidst the dead, the dying, and the wounded, in every part of the field, during which he had two horses killed under him, and he himself received a bullet in his left side which penetrated through his coat to his waistcoat pocket, where fortunately its dangerous course was stopped by his gold snuff-box. At length, as he continued utterly regardless of all that passed around him, paying no attention to the warnings of those near him to save his life, and as at that moment several squadrons of the Austrian cavalry were galloping towards him, some of his suite seized the bridle of his horse and led him away almost by force from the field of battle. He was conveyed under the escort of Captain Prittwitz and his troop of hussars to a temporary place of security. Here the king wrote with his pencil a hasty note to his minister, Finkenstein, saying, "All is lost! save the royal family!" and a few hours afterwards he sent another note with the words: "The consequences of this lost battle will be still more dreadful than the battle itself. I shall not survive the ruin of my country. Farewell forever!"

Such was the depressed and gloomy state of Frederick's mind and heart; and when on the evening of that dreadful day, as he lay stretched sleepless upon his bed of straw, in the almost roofless hut of a poor peasant, in the village of Oetscher, and while his small retinue were asleep on the stone floor around him, he was thus abandoned to his own thoughts, he felt more acutely than ever how little it is that man, with all his strength, can accomplish when left to himself, and how vain are all his calculations. For, in his present reverses, he saw and acknowledged that if he and his nation were not rescued by a higher power, they must be irretrievably lost. The road to Berlin was now left completely open for the invasion of the conquering enemy, and he would be enabled to penetrate without opposition into the very heart of the kingdom. Of the Prussian army the king, on the morning after the battle, was only able to collect together about 10,000 men, and it was only after some time had elapsed, when a considerable body of the fugitives had returned, and he had been joined by all the stray troops he could muster, that his whole force was increased to 20,000 men; while with great difficulty he partially replaced the 165 pieces of cannon he had lost at Künersdorf, by a fresh supply from Berlin. Nevertheless, his capital was saved; for the Russian general—influenced either by some secret consideration towards his hereditary prince, Peter, or perhaps, by the indignation excited against the Austrians for their inactivity, did not follow up his victory. For when he was summoned by Field-marshal Daun to advance with his forces, Soltikow wrote to him in reply: "I have already gained two battles, and now I only wait to march in advance until I receive news that you have gained two victories likewise. It is not just that the troops of my empress should be expected to do every thing alone." This jealousy and discontent between the leaders of both nations continued during the whole war, and produced more than once the salvation of the Prussian monarch in moments of extreme difficulty and danger.

Meantime the Austrian general was detained in Lusatia by the king's brother, Prince Henry, who on this occasion employed every stratagem in the art of war to gain his object, and by continual marching and counter-marching, without risking a single battle, forced his enemy to retreat across the mountains of Bohemia. The prudence and caution exercised by the prince in conducting this war were such, that he effected, without shedding a drop of blood, that which the impetuosity and rash courage of his brother would only have accomplished after a sanguinary battle; and it appeared as if fate had brought the two together, in order that the one brother might repair the faults of the other. Frederick himself has avowed this character of his brother, when he says: "He was the only general throughout the entire war who committed no faults."

Nevertheless, Prince Henry could not prevent the king from suffering at the end of this campaign two severe losses. The first was the evacuation of Dresden, the most important place for the Prussians during the whole war, and which was surrendered to the Austrians. Frederick, after the battle of Künersdorf, had sent orders to Count Schmettau, the governor of that city, in case he was seriously attacked, to save, before every thing else, the military chest which contained seven millions of dollars. Following but too exactly these commands, General Schmettau gave up the city to the imperial army the same day (the 4th of September) on which General Wunsch—sent too late by the king to the succor of the city—arrived in the vicinity. The chest was saved, but all the provisions, together with the place itself, were sacrificed: a loss which enabled General Daun to establish his winter quarters for the first time in Saxony. Frederick used all his efforts in order to dislodge him from this position. He dispatched General Fink with 13,000 men to attack the rear of the Austrian army near Maxen; but, in his desire to see the idea he had formed brought into operation, the king lost sight of the danger of the enterprise. The general, who, however, at once perceived this peril, but who, in spite of his representations, was forced to proceed to action, lost, immediately on being attacked, all confidence and presence of mind, and, after a brief but sanguinary combat, surrendered, together with the remains of his army, about 5000 fighting men, to the Austrians. Such an event was hitherto unheard-of in the Prussian army, and it served as an expiation for the 14,000 Saxons who, at the commencement of the war, were made prisoners by the Prussians nearly on the very same spot. Daun entered the city of Dresden with his prisoners in triumph, and nothing could now alter his determination to take up his winter quarters in Saxony. The king, who could not endure the idea, resolved to harass him by his firmness, and remained encamped, in the open plain, and in spite of the most severe frost, near Wildsruf, during the space of six weeks; through which he forced Daun to do the same, and to suffer equally from the inclemency of the season. Finally, however, in the month of January, 1760, the excessive, rigorously cold weather forced both leaders to afford their armies some repose, and the king, determined not to abandon that portion of Saxony which still belonged to him, established his head-quarters in Freiburg.

The situation of King Frederick became more and more difficult at the opening of every fresh campaign. The sphere of independence which he could still call his own, and in which he could move freely, had not been much, if at all, circumscribed; but the resources upon which he depended for life and strength to carry on the war, declined materially. His army was considerably diminished in numbers, and was very deficient in its appointments; while, on the other hand, the forces of the enemy appeared to increase more numerously after each successive loss. His ever bold and enterprising spirit, which indeed was only brought into full operation when on the attack, was now forced to submit to a war of defence; and even this, at the commencement, yielded him but little advantage. In this campaign he determined to protect Saxony himself, while his brother Henry was to maintain the Marches against the Russians, and General Fouquet was to defend Silesia against the Austrians, under Laudon. But the latter, the most distinguished of all the Austrian generals, had under his command an army thrice the strength of that of the Prussians, and was enabled to hold it in a state of perfect inactivity, while a detachment of his own forces laid siege to the important town and citadel of Glatz. Fouquet, therefore, now relinquished his position in the Silesian mountains, in order to afford more immediate succor wherever it might be required. But now the towns and villages in the mountains, inhabited by an active and industrious people, were forthwith most severely and cruelly handled by the Austrian troopers, and their urgent appeals determined the king to give his general orders to resume his former post in the mountains near Landshut. Fouquet, who was of a severe and austere disposition, whence he was by no means liked in Silesia, although at the same time he was a most brave and determined soldier, perceived the peril he was in; but, as his representations were quite ineffectual, he resolved, at any rate, to meet his fate, not, like Fink at Maxen, by a surrender, but by defending himself to the last. Accordingly, when on the 23d of June, he, with his 8000 Prussians, was attacked and surrounded on all sides by 30,000 Austrians, he bravely maintained the unequal contest for more than eight hours, and in order to resist the charges of the Austrian cavalry, he formed his infantry into squares, and thus, as long as strength prevailed, they disputed every inch of ground. At length, however, the brave general's charger having received a shot, fell and overthrew his rider, who must have been cut to pieces by the enemy, had not his faithful yäger rushed forward, and, shielding him with his own body, received the thrusts aimed at his master. The general was then recognised by an Austrian officer, who, seeing his wounded state, took him under his own charge and saved him. The Prussian cavalry cut their way through, but the whole of the infantry, with the exception of four thousand prisoners, were put to the sword.

This was a severe blow to Frederick; Fouquet was his friend, and Silesia now lay open before the enemy. Nevertheless, he soon rallied, and with the view of obliterating, by one bold act, the impression of this defeat, he deceived Field-marshal Daun by simulated marches, got considerably in advance of him, and appeared suddenly before the walls of Dresden, which he immediately bombarded. It would have been of great advantage to him, had he been able to make himself master of that place; but its brave commandant, General Macquire, although a third portion of that handsome city was completely laid in ashes by the vigorous firing of the Prussians, would not for a moment think of a surrender, knowing, as he did, that the grand Austrian army was following close in the rear of the king, and must shortly relieve the place. And, as he expected, Daun did come up just in time before the city was forced to surrender; and had that tardy general only been more prompt in his measures, he might have averted the whole of the injuries inflicted upon Dresden. The king abandoned the siege and hurried on, in hasty marches, to Silesia, where a fresh disaster had summoned his presence: General Laudon, having, through the treachery and cowardice of the commandant, Oo, an Italian, made himself, in one day, master of Glatz—after Magdeburg, the most important fortification of the Prussian states, and the key to the whole of Silesia. For tunately, Laudon found in the governor of Breslaw (the capital) General Tauenzien, a most determined opponent, whom nothing could dismay, and who was soon relieved by Prince Henry.

The king had now likewise arrived in Silesia, followed, or rather accompanied, by the Austrian army; for, on one side of him marched Field-marshal Daun, and on the other, General Lasci; and, at length, amidst constant fighting by day and night, being incessantly attacked by the lighter troops, his army took up its position at Liegnitz. Beyond this, Frederick was unable to proceed; for Daun, who had now formed a junction with the army of Laudon, blocked up his passage towards Breslaw and Schweidnitz, which contained all his magazines; while, on the other side, Prince Henry was detained by the Russians on the Oder. The king had only enough provisions to serve his army for a few days, and the Austrians were as near to him as at Hochkirch, so that he was forced to change his quarters every night, in order to secure himself against a surprise. At length the Austrians thought they had found the favorable moment for giving battle, and accordingly, on the night preceding the 15th of August, Laudon marched in advance, in order to gain possession of the heights of Puffendorf, and thus take the Prussians in the rear. It was resolved to attack the king on every side, and, if possible, to completely annihilate him. But it happened that on this very night the king had ordered his army to remove their camp in the greatest order and silence, inasmuch as, on the preceding day, the Austrians had caused his position to be too closely reconnoitred, and accordingly he encamped his troops on those very eminences of Puffendorf towards which Laudon was now advancing. The watch-fires, kept up by peasants, were still seen burning in the old forsaken camp, and patrols of Prussian hussars continued to cry out the challenge every quarter of an hour; but the king and his troops were already established in their new quarters. The soldiers lay with their arms in their hands; while the king himself, wrapped in his military cloak and seated by the fire, with his brave and faithful Ziethen and a few others of his principal officers around him, had gradually fallen asleep. A solemn stillness reigned throughout the whole army; all noise, the slightest sound was interdicted, and either slumbering upon their arms, or softly whispering together as they lay in groups, the warriors awaited the approach of day. Towards two o'clock, however, the officer in command of the patrol of hussars arrived at the royal tent in full gallop, and awoke the king with the unexpected report that the foe was at hand, and within a hundred yards only of the camp! This announcement acted like an electric shock; in a few moments, however, the generals were already mounted in their saddles, the troops under arms and drawn up in line of battle, and the cannon poured forth its destruction. The astonished Laudon soon perceived, as the day dawned, that he had before him the greater part of the Prussian army, but far from being discouraged by that, he redoubled the ardor of his attack, in hopes that Daun might hear the thunder of the cannon and march to his aid; but this was prevented by an adverse wind, which turned aside the echo, and that general heard nothing. After a conflict of three hours, the battle was decided. Laudon had lost four thousand killed, six thousand wounded, together with eighty-two pieces of artillery, and was forced to retreat in all haste across Katzbach. Daun, who advanced on his side against the king's army, fell in with the right wing of the Prussians, commanded by General Ziethen, and was received by a heavy discharge of artillery, and having then found that Laudon had been defeated, he likewise made a retreat.

This victory, with which the king was so opportunely favored by his good fortune, ameliorated his condition materially, and he proceeded at once to profit by it with his usual promptitude. Three hours after the termination of the battle, he was already on his march, the prisoners in the centre, the wounded, both friends and foes, being conveyed in wagons, in the rear, and the captured cannon added to the train of artillery. The main body of the army marched that day more than fifteen miles, and the road to Breslaw was now no longer obstructed, neither was there any fear of the supplies being cut off.

Silesia was now in a great measure delivered; but, meantime, sad reverses had taken place in the Marches and in Saxony. The Russians had retreated from Breslaw, in order to advance along the Oder, and they resolved to march on with 20,000 men, in junction with 15,000 Austrians under General Lasci, to Berlin itself. This city was unable, with its feeble garrison, to make any stand against such a formidable force, and on the 4th of October it surrendered to the Russian general, Totleben. Fortunately for Berlin, this general was of a mild and humane disposition, and preserved the place from pillage, with the exception of the royal summer residences in the vicinity, and several monuments of art, which were despoiled by the Saxons. The allies held possession of the city during the space of an entire week, and large sums of money were extracted from the citizens; however, it being reported that the king was on his march to the relief of his capital, the enemy immediately abandoned their conquest, and retired into Saxony and across the Oder.

Frederick came not merely on account of his captured city, but more especially on account of Saxony. While he was occupied in Silesia the imperial army had entered that territory, and, meeting with no resistance, had taken possession of the entire country. Daun had now arrived likewise with his army and encamped near Torgau, in a very strong position. It was now necessary for Frederick, if he did not wish to lose that beautiful country altogether, nor renounce the hope of fixing his winter quarters, for the first time, on his own soil, to reconquer it before the coming winter. No alternative was left him; and, as had happened several times already at the end of a campaign, he was once more forced to stake a great loss against a great gain, and, in truth, this time his destruction appeared inevitable should this perilous chance miscarry. Nevertheless, he appears in such case to have made up his mind to die—and as it proved, he was this time once again nearly on the point of losing the battle.

The attack upon the strongly-intrenched lines of the enemy on the heights of Torgau, was to be made on the 3d of November from two sides by two separate divisions of the army, one headed by the king in person, the other by Ziethen, who was to lead his men round towards the Siptitzer heights, and thus fall upon the rear of the Austrians. A thick forest concealed the king's approach, but his troops became more and more bewildered in the wood as they advanced, and were obliged to halt several times, which produced considerable delay; as soon, however, as the king with the advanced guard emerged therefrom, he heard a heavy firing proceed, as he thought, from Ziethen's division, and concluded that he was now fully engaged with the enemy. This, however, was not the case, as the firing only proceeded from the advanced posts, and Daun was enabled to turn his whole force against the king; accordingly, when the latter in his impetuous haste, and without waiting for the rest of his infantry and cavalry, led on his grenadiers against the Austrian intrenchments, he was received with such a destructive cannonade from more than two hundred pieces of artillery that whole lines of his men were swept away as if by a thunderbolt, and their bodies, thus stretched in rows upon the ground, prevented his cannoniers from bringing their guns to bear against the foe, and they themselves, with their horses, were laid prostrate by the murderous fire, which continued without ceasing. The king himself declared to those around him that he had never witnessed such a scene of carnage; while the loud, thundering peals of the artillery instantaneously deprived many of those who survived this dreadful day of their hearing. A grazing shot struck the king on his breast, but, happily, without producing any material effect. Fresh battalions of the Prussian infantry came up and gained some ground, but they were beaten back by the Austrian cavalry, who, however, were repulsed in their turn by the Prussian horse, which had at length arrived on the field of battle, and now the conflict was kept up with varying success until night. But the heart of the king was bowed down with grief and affliction; the flower of his infantry lay before him on the field, and yet the Austrian bulwarks were not gained, while Field-marshal Daun had even dispatched a courier to his empress with the announcement of victory. Fortune, however, had ordained otherwise.

While, on the king's side, the contest was still carried on in the darkness of the night, and often friend against friend, owing to the number of troops who had lost their way; and while, on account of the bitter coldness of the night, innumerable fires were kept burning on the heath of Torgau, to which both the unwounded as well as the wounded were glad to creep, including even enemies as well as friends, and again, just as the disheartened king, seated on the lowest step of the altar of the little church in the village of Elsnig, was occupied in writing his dispatches, his veteran general, Ziethen, had gained the summit of the Siptitzer heights, after having fought his way through until ten o'clock at night, and finally formed a junction with General Saldern. By this the position of the Austrians became broken; they were unable to resume the action next morning, and Daun, who had himself received a wound in the heat of the battle, retreated during the night, in the greatest silence, through Torgau across the Elbe to Dresden. This retreat was effected so secretly that the Prussians were even preparing for a fresh action on the following morning, completely unconscious of the withdrawal of the enemy. When, however, Frederick rode out of the village at early dawn, he, to his no little surprise, found the field of battle abandoned by the Austrians, and he was hailed as victor by his troops. By this sanguinary battle he reconquered the greater part of Saxony, and he accordingly fixed the winter quarters of his army there, and established his own head-quarters in Leipsic itself.

## CHAPTER XXXII.

Conclusion of the Seven Years' War, 1761-1762—The Austrian and Russian Armies—The Camp of Bunzelwitz—Frederick's difficult Position—Jealousy between Generals Butterlin and Laudon—Schweidnitz, Glatz, and Colberg—Saxony—Berlin threatened by the Russians—The Prussians rise *en masse* to expel them—Death of Elizabeth of Russia—Peter III.—Peace and Alliance between Russia and Prussia—Sweden—Battle of Reichenbach—Frederick victorious—Schweidnitz—Final Battle and Defeat of the Austrians at Freiberg—Peace between France and England, 1763—Peace between Prussia and Austria at Hubertsburg, 1763—Observations—The Age of Frederick the Great—His Army—Exerts himself to repair the Calamities of his Country—His indefatigable Industry—His Labors and Recreations—Genius for Poetry and Music—His Early Years—His Father's Tyranny—Its sad effects eventually proved—His Predilection for French Education and Literature—Voltaire—Helvetius, &c.—His Anti-German Feelings and neglect of National Genius—Lessing—Klopstock—Goethe—Kant—Fichte—Jacobi, &c.—Joseph II., 1765-1790—Dismemberment of Poland, 1773—Prussia and Russia—Stanislaus Poniatowski—Bavarian War of Succession, 1778—Death of Maria Theresa, 1780—Innovations and intolerant Measures of Joseph II.—Frederick and the Allied Princes of Germany against Joseph II.—Death of Frederick the Great, 1786—Death of Joseph II., 1790—Leopold II., 1790-1792.

THE concluding years of the war are less distinguished for great and striking events. The exhaustion of the troops became more and more apparent, and Frederick, who had usually been the foremost in enterprising vigor and activity, was forced to act on the defensive, and to devote all his strength in protecting what he still possessed, which truly was no easy task. In 1761 he himself took the command in Silesia, and employed every stratagem in order to prevent the junction of the Russian army under Butterlin with Laudon, who alone led on 72,000 Austrians; and in this the king succeeded for a time, by which a great portion of the summer passed away in inaction, an advantage Frederick was anxious to avail himself of. At length, however, the two armies united together on the 12th of August, in the environs of Strigau, and thus combined formed a force of 130,000 men, by which Frederick found himself forced with his 50,000 men to retire to a strong position. Accordingly he fixed his quarters near Bunzelwitz, where, for the space of twenty days, he was kept completely shut in by the enemy, and was forced to employ so much vigilance that his men were kept under arms and formed in battle array during the night, being only able to take their rest in the day-time.* And his adversaries being, as they were, nearly three times his superior in number, by falling upon and overwhelming the weakest points of his intrenchments, might have completely conquered the king, had they been under the guidance of a genius capable of acting with the energy so necessary; but the two generals not being of accord, either in feeling or principle, and jealous of each other's claims to distinctions, they

* In the intrenched camp near Bunzelwitz Frederick shared in all the fatigues and sufferings of his common soldiers. Many nights he slept on one of the batteries, reposing on a bundle of straw among his men. One night he rose and thoughtfully proceeded with General Ziethen between the lines of watchfires, around which his worn-out men were lying asleep. One trooper, however, was very busy baking a cake, made of bacon and flour. The fragrant smell reached the king's nose; he halted, and addressing the busy soldier in a friendly tone, said: "That cake, comrade, smells very nice!" "Yes," returned the man, without looking up from his cake, "I believe you, but you won't catch any more than a *smell* of it—that I can tell you!" "Hush, for heaven's sake!" exclaimed one or two of his comrades, who had started up at the king's voice. "What are you about? Why, don't you see that is the king himself?" The soldier, believing they were only joking, and still attending to his cake without allowing himself to be disturbed, exclaimed laughingly: "Ha! ha! Well, and suppose it really was old Fritz, why what would that matter?" "Come along, Ziethen," said the king to his companion, "I see we shan't be invited to supper *here* to-night!"—*Mächler.*

refused to co-operate either for the renown of the one or the other. Each imagined he was burdened with the most heavy portion of the common labor, and, as was usual in this war, the Russians not being able to act in unison with the Austrians, they again on this occasion separated without having effected any thing. Thus Frederick with his army was now left in greater freedom, and in order to secure himself against all pursuit from the Russians—at least for this year—he caused all their magazines in Poland to be pillaged and destroyed by a bold expedition he placed under the orders of General Platen; in the execution of which commission that brave commander so well succeeded, that the Russian army was completely paralyzed for this campaign.

Nevertheless, this year was not to pass away without some misfortune for the king. When he abandoned his camp of Bunzelwitz, in order to allure the Austrians down to the plains of Silesia, Laudon suddenly descended the mountains, and instead of following the king, he directed his march at once to Schweidnitz, which he surprised, and it being but slightly garrisoned, he took it by assault in the night of the 1st of October. Thus, by the occupation of Schweidnitz and Glatz, the Austrians had now at command the entire moiety of Silesia, and were enabled to pass the winter there. In addition to this the Russians, on their part, took possession of Colberg on the 13th of December, after a siege of four months, by which they were enabled to establish their winter quarters for once at least in Pomerania.

The king had never before been so completely hemmed in. Prince Henry, it is true, had, during the summer, succeeded against all the attacks of Daun's forces, in maintaining possession of the whole of that portion of Saxony still remaining in his brother's hands, but this only formed the moiety of that country, and thus the Russians, in the course of the coming spring, would be enabled to advance within a few yards of Berlin itself. Reduced to such extremity, it might have been expected that the Prussian nation would have at length resigned all hope; on the contrary, however, they did not abandon themselves to despair, but, showing themselves worthy of their king, they cheered and supported him in this adversity by one enthusiastic, ardent expression of that confidence with which he inspired all classes; a cordiality of feeling which was echoed forth in strains of loyalty and patriotism by the youth of all ranks throughout the land, as they hastened to join the standard of their heroic leader. Thence it was clearly manifested that as long as they continued to be thus strengthened by the zealous co-operation of the inhabitants themselves, both the king and his army might still bid defiance to the invaders: for king, army, and people, being firmly united by one indissoluble bond, the ruin with which all were threatened, should it prove inevitable, must at least be gloriously shared by all.

The new year, however, unexpectedly brought with it a bright ray of hope; for on the 5th of January, 1762, the Russian empress, Elizabeth, died, and in her Frederick was relieved of one of his bitterest foes. Her nephew, Peter III., now ascended the throne, and being an enthusiastic admirer of Frederick the Great, he obeyed at once the impulse of his mind, and forthwith discharged all the Prussian prisoners without any ransom, and not only signed on the 5th of May, at St. Petersburg, a treaty of so disinterested a character, that he relinquished the whole of Prussia without any indemnity whatever, but likewise immediately formed an alliance with Frederick, and caused his own general, Czernitschef, to march with 20,000 Russians to the aid of the Prussians in Silesia.

Sweden followed the example of Russia; for, weary of a campaign producing so little honor and glory, she made peace likewise with Prussia, at Hamburg, on the 22d of May.

Frederick was now enabled to employ all his energies against the Austrians, and calculated upon speedily recovering Silesia from them. He resolved to commence with Schweidnitz itself; and as Field-marshal Daun protected it from a very strong position he occupied near Burkersdorf, Frederick decided accordingly to attack him at this point immediately after being joined by his Russian allies. He was already on his march, when suddenly the discouraging report reached him that the Russian emperor, Peter III., had been murdered, and his consort Catherine proclaimed empress, news almost immediately confirmed by the commands received from St. Petersburg by Czernitschef, to return with his army to Poland forthwith. The young emperor, on coming to the throne, had imprudently and most prematurely commenced introducing many innovations into Russia, by which he produced great irritation and disgust among the clergy and nobility, in addition to which he had ill-used his wife, and by various ill-judged acts, evinced a striking partiality for the Germans around him, whence he was deprived of his throne and life within six months after the commencement of his reign.

Frederick beheld himself now again threatened with danger .from a quarter whence he had vainly hoped to receive important aid in his war against Austria; for he could not but anticipate that Catherine would be similarly disposed towards him as had been her predecessor, Elizabeth. Nevertheless he took courage, and arranging his plans, resolved at any rate to derive all the advantage he could from the presence of the Russians. And so great was the influence of Frederick's genius over other men, that he soon prevailed upon General Czernitschef to withhold from the knowledge of his army, at least for three days, the orders he had received for his return; and marching with him against the Austrians on the day of attack, thus succeeded by his presence in holding a portion of the enemy's troops in check—a service which Czernitschef, although he could not resist the king's persuasion, felt he yielded at the risk of his head. Frederick gave battle on the following day and gained it. The Russian army next day separated from the king, and retired. Czernitschef, however, was not called to account for his conduct in this affair, inasmuch as the opinions and feelings of the empress towards Frederick had now undergone a favorable change. She had at first imagined that Frederick himself had excited her husband to adopt the harsh measures he had pursued against her; but when, after the death of Peter, she looked through his papers, and unexpectedly found several letters addressed to him by Frederick, in which he exhorted him most earnestly to exercise prudence in all the measures he adopted, and more especially to act with kind and gentle feelings towards his wife, the empress immediately changed the course of her policies against Frederick, and ratified the peace made between her late husband and the king, yet without committing herself by promising him her aid in the prosecution of the war against Austria.

Frederick now commenced the siege of Schweidnitz, which, however, occupied the entire summer; for badly as the Russians themselves had, on the one hand, on two previous occasions defended this important place, it was now determined by the Austrians, on their part, to maintain its possession as long as they possibly could, and with which object, General Guasco, the commandant, and Gribauval, its engineer, exerted all their courage and skill. The siege lasted nine weeks, the king himself superintending the operations with unabated zeal to the last moment; and it was not until they had lost all hopes of relief, and were left completely without provisions, that the Austrians at length, on the 9th of October, surrendered the place with its garrison of 10,000 men to Frederick.

This year Prince Henry, with his usual measures of prudence, conducted the war in Saxony so successfully, that he retained possession of the whole country with the exception of Dresden, while he at the same time was equally fortunate in the expeditions he made into Bohemia and the imperial states, in which he was ably seconded by the brave generals under his orders, Seidlitz, Kleist, and Belling. When finally the Austrians, with the imperial auxiliaries, attempted by superiority of numbers to drive him from the advantageous position he held in Freiberg, he attacked them at once on the 29th of October, and completely routed them. This was the last and concluding engagement in the Seven Years' War. The king, on the 24th of November, signed an armistice with Austria, and distributed his troops in their winter quarters, extending through the country from Thuringia to Silesia; General Kleist, however, was left with 10,000 men to keep the field against the princes of the empire, and penetrating into Franconia, forced each prince, one after the other, to conclude a peace.

Duke Ferdinand of Brunswick, meantime, during the last three years of the war, had well and gloriously maintained his reputation in defending Lower Saxony and Westphalia. France employed all her powers to reconquer these countries, and preserve the honor of her arms; fresh commanders were continually appointed, and her army in 1761 was reinforced to the number of 150,000 men, but which, although only opposed by a force of 80,000 men, could effect nothing but the occupation of Hesse, which it was impossible for Ferdinand to defend, inasmuch as he was threatened from two quarters at once, viz., from the Lower Rhine and the Maine. On the other hand, neither stratagem nor menace could make him quit his position on the left bank of the Weser and on the Dimel, whence he protected Lower Saxony and Westphalia simultaneously. The generals under his command—the hereditary prince of Brunswick, Spörken, Kielmannsegge, and Luckner, distinguished themselves in many separate engagements. At the close of the last campaign, a successful battle near Wilhelmsthal placed the duke in a position by which he was enabled to act on the offensive, and by a second engagement near Lutterberg, which terminated equally to his advantage, he succeeded in driving the French from the vicinity of Cassel, and thus completed the campaign of the year 1762, as well as the entire war, by the conquest of this city, on the 1st of November. An armistice was now likewise concluded with the imperial powers in this quarter.

The whole of the belligerent nations were now exhausted and longed for repose. England had made great and important conquests beyond the seas, but had at the same time increased her national debt by at least one hundred and twenty millions sterling, and, since the demise of George II., and after the earl of Bute, the preceptor of the new sovereign, had become prime-minister instead of Pitt, a desire for peace was more and more strongly felt, a feeling in which France likewise joined. Thus Frederick and Maria Theresa were now left to carry on the war alone; but Austria, although amply provided with troops, being, nevertheless, without money to furnish the necessary supplies, was not in a condition to continue hostilities unaided, and as Frederick's only object from the first was to retain possession of Silesia, he agreed accordingly, upon having that territory secured to him, to sign a treaty of peace. Austria having, therefore, yielded to him this point, he at once ratified the convention as framed by his own plenipotentiary and those of Austria and Saxony, in the castle of Hubertsburg in Saxony. A restitution of conquests was made—the prisoners exchanged—and neither party claimed indemnification for the expenses or losses incurred. Frederick remained, therefore, in possession of Silesia, and he restored to the elector of Saxony his estates. Thus this severe and sanguinary war had in its results produced no change in the external state of things, although it had at least inculcated certain great lessons, and to which it cannot be denied but that Europe was indebted for the happy state of tranquillity she enjoyed after the conclusion of this peace, during the space of nearly thirty years. Agitation in public affairs, suspicion and jealousy, productive of so much hostility among states, were now at an end, and all were sincere in the conviction that the actual condition of affairs would be lasting. Fate had pronounced its decree in favor of Prussia, that, viz., its power rested upon a sure and solid basis as long as it was guided and governed by united thought and action, however limited might be its sphere. An earnest, industrious, and warlike feeling evinced both by king and people, justice and economy in the administration of affairs, a progressive spirit of research for all that the age brings with it and yields of the really good and noble—such were the means which enabled Frederick and his nation to maintain single-handed the war against the moiety of Europe, and such means must ever continue to operate for the preservation of Prussia, as long as she knows how to treasure up and avail herself of these resources.

Austria indicated at this time, likewise, as on every former occasion when threatened with the danger of vicissitude, that her power was not so easily destroyed, that her rich and beautiful domains, the faithful adherence and co-operation of her inhabitants, their attachment to a mild and paternal government, nourished within themselves a germ of life, unchangeable and unsurpassed. And equally on their parts the Hessians, Hanoverians, and the troops of Lower Saxony, when fighting against the French invaders, evinced enduring perseverance and courage to such a degree as to add greatly to the glory of the German name; and, in fact, the fame of this war conduced especially to the honor of the Germans generally.

And when it was inquired who had shown a superiority of mind in the tumult of bat tle, and had given undeniable proofs of that rapidity of thought which knows how to seize the immediate moment for action, all mouths proclaimed and referred to the names of Frederick the Great and Duke Ferdinand of Brunswick. Nor was it forgotten to include, as equally worthy of distinction, that of Prince Henry, who, as the model of what a prudent and wary general should be, well knew how to keep an enemy of far superior force in constant exercise, while at the same time, by wisely-laid plans, he adroitly maintained his own ground without exposing his little band to that destruction otherwise so inevitable. Finally, in the list of heroic names, those of Ziethen* and Seidlitz, who so especially distinguished themselves at the head of their cavalry, appeared conspicuous with the rest. On the other hand, all who wished to study the art of selecting good and masterly positions for an army, or of choosing the critical, well-timed moment for bringing the guns to work with fatal and unerring effect, were referred to the Austrians, and the names of Generals Brown, Laudon, Nadasti, Lacsi, and others, were justly registered on the side of the older celebrated generals of Austria.

It is consoling to reflect that such great renown was calculated to mitigate at least the sorrow and pain arising from the state of embittered strife existing between the rival nations of a country with which all were equally allied as its children, and who, forgetting all distinctions, and considering themselves as one people, ought rather to have joined in the grasp of fraternal friendship and peace; while these warlike achievements served in some measure to throw into the shade the bad system pursued by the internal government of the empire. The condition, in fact, of the deliberative and influential portion of our constitution was so imperfect; the forms established for the direction of affairs were so antiquated; the course of proceedings so tedious and inefficient—that unless both heart and arm had done their duty so well, and thus shown to other lands that the martial spirit of ancient Germany had not yet vanished, the country must long ere this have become the spoil of the stranger.

France gained but little honor in this war; her feeble, unsystematic government had clearly shown that its administration was in the hands of women and their favorites, and thence it languished in mortal throes. Nevertheless, that country did not lose so much by the peace of Paris, which was signed five days previous to that of Hubertsburg, as might have been expected after the success of the English at sea; but this peace was brought about by the not over-sagacious statesman, the earl of Bute, while Pitt, on the contrary, when presiding at the head of the administration, had in the course of the war made manifest in the most brilliant manner what extraordinary energy dwelt in the English nation, and which only waited for the proper moment to be brought into full operation.

During the period of repose, which continued for nearly thirty years, consequent upon the peace of Hubertsburg, various new developments, the germs of which had been planted at an earlier date, now began to attain a degree of perfection. With the view of characterizing this era by one term, we have denominated it the Age of Frederick the Great, because in him was embodied the spirit of the age, and in him were seen on a grand scale both the good and the evil of his contemporaries. It remains for us, in order to become thoroughly acquainted with the man, to contemplate his character in peace as well as during the continuance of war.

The first and most immediate object of Frederick's attention and anxiety was the re-establishment of his army, in order that no enemy might hope to reap advantage from a sudden renewal of hostilities. In order to bring the recently-levied troops upon a par with his veteran well-trained warriors—of whom, however, but a very small number still remained—military exercise and drilling were enforced with the most rigorous exactness. But in this instance

* Once Frederick marched at the head of the grenadiers of his guard until the depth of night. At length he made halt, dismounted, and said: "Grenadiers, it is cold to-night. Come, light a fire and let us warm ourselves."—Saying which, he wrappe[illegible]s blue mantle around him and seated himself upon some bundles of wood, while some of his grenadiers laid themselves down around him. At length General Ziethen came up and sat himself down next to the king, and both, extremely tired and worn out, soon fell asleep. The king, however, was the first to awake, and observing that Ziethen in his sleep had slipped off from one of the bundles of wood, and that a grenadier was replacing it under him, he exclaimed softly: "Ah, the old man is indeed knocked up!" Just afterwards another grenadier, only half awake, sprang up, and proceeding to light his pipe, happened to touch against the old warrior's foot. Frederick rose up suddenly, and holding up his finger to the soldier, said, in a whisper, "Hush, grenadier! Take care, don't wake up our old Ziethen, he is tired enough. Let him sleep on; he has watched long and often enough for us!"—*Müchler.*

it happened, as is too frequently the case in the generality of human affairs, when endeavors are made to preserve entire and perpetuate an institution which in the moment of its most glorious development appeared perfect, that the form which then belonged to it becomes essential, while the spirit, which can never assume a second time the same mode, abandons that form, and gradually puts on another which is new and strange; but men continue for a length of time to respect that which is merely the envelope, equally as much as if they possessed the reality it encloses. The illustrious monarch himself, when he beheld the whole of Europe adopt his military tactics, was deceived in the over-estimation of their value. The system of maintaining standing armies was carried to its highest point, and became the principal object in the administration of every state; grave utility degenerated into mere display, until a grand convulsion of the world made its vanity and puerility but too apparent.

The care taken by Frederick to effect the restoration of his overwhelmed country was a much more beneficent employment of his energies, and was productive of incalculable good, while it formed the most imperishable leaf in his wreath of glory. The corn which was already bought up for the next campaign he bestowed upon the most destitute of his people, as seed for sowing, together with all his superfluous horses. The taxes were remitted for six months in Silesia, and for two years in Pomerania and Neumark, which were completely devastated. Nay, the king, in order to encourage agriculture and industry, appropriated large sums of money for that purpose in proportion to the greatness of the exigency, and these various sums amounted altogether during the four-and-twenty years of his reign after the peace of Hubertsburg, to no less than twenty-four millions of dollars. Such noble generosity redounds still more to the glory of Frederick, inasmuch as it was only practicable through the exercise of great economy, and to promote which, he subjected himself to every personal sacrifice. His maxim was that his treasure belonged not to himself, but to the people who supplied it; and while many other princes—not bearing in mind the heavy drops of sweat which adhered to each of the numerous gold pieces wrung from their subjects—only thought of dissipating the entire mass in the most unlicensed prodigality and waste, he lived in a style so simple and frugal, that out of the sum appropriated to the maintenance of his court, he saved annually nearly a million of dollars

He explained on one occasion to M. de Launay, the assessor of indirect taxes, the principles by which he was actuated in this respect, in clear and distinct terms: "Louis XV. and I," he said, "are born more needy than the poorest of our subjects; for there are but few among them who do not possess a small inheritance, or who cannot at least earn it by their labor and industry; while he and I possess nothing, neither can we earn any thing but what must belong to the state. We are merely the stewards appointed for the administration of the general fund; and if, as such, we were to apply to our own personal expenditure more than is reasonably necessary, we should, by such proceeding, not only bring down upon ourselves severe condemnation in the first place for extravagance, but likewise for having fraudulently taken possession of that which was confided to our charge for the public weal."

The particular care and interest shown by the king in the cultivation of the soil, produced its speedy improvement. Large tracts of land were rendered arable, fresh supplies of laborers were procured from other countries, and where formerly marsh and moor were generally prevalent, fertile, flourishing corn-fields were substituted instead. These happy results, which greeted the eye of Frederick whenever he took his regularly-appointed journeys throughout his dominions, were highly grateful to his feelings; while during these tours of survey nothing escaped his acutely-observing mind; so much so, that few sovereigns could boast of such a thorough knowledge of their domains—even to the most trifling details—as the king of Prussia acquired of his own estates through continual and indefatigable application to this one object. Silesia, which had suffered so much, was especially dear to his feelings, and to that territory he devoted particular attention; when, therefore, upon a general census in the year 1777, he found it contained 180,000 more inhabitants than in the year 1756, when the war commenced; and when he perceived the losses sustained during that war thus amply repaired, and the glorious results produced by agricultural labor and commercial enterprise, he, in the gladness of his heart, expressed, in a letter to his friend Jordan, the sensations he felt at beholding the flourishing state of a province, the condition of which was but a short time before so sadly depressed and miserable.

Industry is indispensable in a people who depend on their energy and activity for their rank among nations; but this rank is not the only attendant advantage: a benefit far greater is the fresh, healthy vigor it imparts to the people. And in this respect Frederick the Great was a striking example, truly worthy of imitation by all his subjects; for even during the early period of his life, he already wrote to his friend Jordan thus: "You are quite right in believing that I work hard; I do so to enable me *to live,* for nothing so nearly approaches the likeness of death, as the half-slumbering, listless state of idleness." And, subsequently, when he had become old and feeble, this feeling still retained its power, and operated with all its original influence upon his mind, for in another letter to the same friend, he says: "I still feel as formerly the same anxiety for action; as then, I now still long to work and be busy, and my mind and body are in continual contention. It is no longer requisite that I should live, unless I can live—and work."

And truly in making a profitable use of his time, King Frederick displayed a perseverance which left him without a rival, and even in his old age he never swerved from the original plan he had laid down and followed from his earliest manhood, for even on the very day before his death he was to be seen occupied with the business of his government. Each hour had its occupation, and the one grand principle which is the soul of all industry, viz., *to leave over from to-day nothing for the morrow,* passed with Frederick as the inviolable law of his whole life. The entire day—commencing at the hour of four in the morning and continuing until midnight, accordingly five-sixths of the day—was devoted to some occupation of the mind or heart, for in order that even the hour of repast might not be wholly monopolized by the mere gratification of the stomach, Frederick assembled around him at mid-day and in the evening, a circle of intellectual men, and these *conversaziones*—in which the king himself took an important share—were of such an animated and enlivening nature, that they were not inaptly compared to the entertainments of Socrates himself. Unfortunately, however, according to the taste of that age, nothing but witticisms and humorous sallies were made the subject of due appreciation and applause. Vivacity of idea promptly expressed, and strikingly *apropos* allusions, were the order of the day, while profundity of thought, and subjects of more grave and serious discussion, were banished as ill-timed and uncalled-for: a necessary consequence, arising from the exclusive adoption of the French language which formed the medium of communication at these *réunions* of Frederick the Great. The rest of the day was passed in the perusal of official dispatches, private correspondence, and ministerial documents, to each of which he added his replies and observations in the margin. After having gone through this all-important business-routine of the day, he directed his attention to the more recreative occupations of his pleasure-grounds and literary compositions—of which latter Frederick has left behind him a rich collection; and finally, as a last resource of amusement, he occasionally devoted a few stolen moments to his flute, upon which he was an accomplished performer.* This, his favorite instrument indeed, like an intimate and faithful friend, served often to allay the violent excitements of his spirit, and while he strolled

* In the course of a journey which Frederick once made into Holland, quite *incognito,* giving himself out as a musician, he arrived at a small tavern in Amsterdam, especially celebrated for the rich cakes produced there. Feeling a desire to taste one, he commanded his travelling companion and aide-de-camp, Colonel Von Balby, to order one of the landlady. The colonel obeyed the command, but the landlady, rather suspicious of her plainly-dressed guests, measured the messenger from top to toe, and exclaimed, "Why, it is all very well for you to order it, but pray, sir, can you pay for it when it is made? Do you know that such a cake as you order will cost more than six or seven guilders?" To this the colonel replied by assuring her that the gentleman with whom he travelled was immensely rich, that he played the flute so beautifully, that whenever he performed in public a considerable sum was collected in a very short time. "Indeed! Oh, then," said the landlady, "I must certainly hear him directly, I am so very fond of music." Saying which, she hurried on before the colonel to the king's chamber, and said very politely: "I understand, sir, that you play a tune very well; oblige me by warbling something for me to hear!" Frederick could not, at first, imagine what she meant, but the colonel explaining to him in French the origin of this singular request, he laughed, and seizing his flute from the table, played in such a masterly style, that the listener was struck with admiration, and when, to her sorrow, he ceased, she exclaimed, "Excellent! You do, indeed, play sweetly, and I dare say can earn a few guilders. Well, you shal have your cake, at any rate!"—*Müchler*

with it through his suite of rooms, often for hours together, his thoughts, as he himself relates, became more and more collected, and his mind better prepared for calm and serious meditation. Nevertheless, he never permitted affairs of state to be neglected for the sake of the enjoyments he sought both in music and in poetry, and in this point of view Frederick's character must ever command respect and admiration. Hence how glorious might have been the reign of this monarch, and overwhelming every intervening obstacle, how nobly might he have exalted the age he lived in, and by his acts have identified himself with the elevated position to which his nation might have aspired, had his mind, when in its infancy, received from the cherishing hand of his parents that encouraging and unerring direction by which those noble, honest, and upright feelings implanted in him by nature must have become more and more developed and confirmed.

Unhappily, however, the bad education Frederick received left many a noble germ within him neglected. His father, Frederick William I., was a man of a stern and forbidding character, for whom the muses had no charms, neither did he ever show the least affection for his son Frederick, who from his earliest age evinced a strong desire to cultivate habits of a more refined nature than those indulged in by his father, whence the latter subjected him to the most harsh and despotic treatment. He placed no confidence in him as his successor to the throne, and he even projected substituting his second son, Augustus William, instead; and by this means the heart of Frederick became more and more estranged from the paternal roof, until it was rendered cold and dead to all the ties of filial affection. At length this state of things operated with such influence upon his mind, that in the year 1730 the prince, when on a journey to Wesel with his father, made a desperate attempt to escape from the oppression he endured under the paternal control; but being discovered and retaken, it was with great difficulty that he escaped being made a sacrifice to the indignant, ungovernable rage of his ruthless father, who would but too willingly have sentenced his persecuted, although perhaps imprudent, son to the guillotine. Thus Frederick grew up to manhood without experiencing the true warmth of affection, which alone is capable of developing the tender feelings of youth, and this want he continued to evince unhappily throughout his entire after-life to the day of his death. In the fire of youth his heart was open to impressions of the most enthusiastic friendship; but this ardor of feeling, however sincere and pure, gradually dissolved into icy indifference and misanthropy under the rigor of discipline to which he was subjected; so that, finally, the great king saw himself abandoned and, anchorite-like, left to the solitary enjoyment of his own thoughts and feelings.

The injurious and baneful custom of the age required that French preceptors and French books should furnish the means by which to direct the sphere of thought both of the boy and youth; and already, in the earlier period of his youth, Frederick unhappily became acquainted with the writings of a man, whose influence upon the age he lived in produced no little evil, and whose acute mind and satirical, cutting wit, left nothing sacred undefiled. This man—Voltaire—was to the youthful and susceptible mind of the prince, a model worthy of imitation. The productions of this writer were daily studied by him, and they so completely fascinated his mind, that he regarded him as exalted above all other men, and impelled by his enthusiasm, he sought the friendship of that dangerous individual as a treasure far beyond appreciation. The vain and selfish Frenchman well knew how to profit by this feeling, so clearly expressed in the letters he received from the young prince. He flattered his royal friend in return, and in this game of reciprocal egotism, Frederick imagined he had succeeded in forming the basis of a friendship which should prove to be not only sincere, but lasting. But as friendship can only subsist on a foundation of truth, and in connection with joint and zealous efforts for the attainment of virtue, the union of these two men, resting upon so unstable a basis, could not withstand the force of any severe test. In their subsequent intercourse, after Voltaire, in 1750, had taken up his residence at the court of the king, the coldness, jealousy, and malignity of the favorite became more and more manifest; the film of fascination dropped from before the king's eyes, the sentiments of friendship between the two declined with each day, and becoming eventually estranged from, and inimically inclined towards each other, they parted as enemies. Voltaire, however, on his return to France, gave vent to his revengeful feelings by writing the most bitter satires against the king.*

Such mortifying results closed the heart of Frederick more and more against all amicable impressions, and produced a misanthropy, which previously formed no part of his character, and the necessary effect of which is to overshadow the path of life with the clouds of gloom.

The government of the king itself was impressed with this mark of the reserved and isolated state of his soul; for it was a *despotic government* in the most strict sense of the word; every thing emanated from the king, and every thing reverted to him again. He never accorded any share in the administration to an assembly of states, nor even to the state council—which, composed of the most enlightened men, would have been able to have presented to their sovereign, in a clear and comprehensive light, the bearings of the intricate questions connected with government. Nevertheless, however penetrating his eagle eye that individual survey was not sufficiently comprehensive to command a knowledge of every thing, whence many essential circumstances must have remained concealed from his view.

Thence it is, that a government supported by the states of the kingdom is difficult to be overturned, while its power increases in proportion; inasmuch as according to the form of such government, the voice of the most enlightened and well-intentioned of the public may be heard by the whole nation through legitimate means, and thus every active member of the state may, although he holds no office, aid his country with his opinions and advice.

But such views and principles were altogether unknown at this period, which deviated from the simple course of nature, and only endeavored to elevate itself upon the basis of the subtlety of the mind; the object then sought was to found the stability of a government upon the ground-work of mere external forms, while, on the contrary, its security rests upon the hearty co-operation of all for the common weal of the country, to the exclusion of all individual power. These magnanimous principles of government would, no doubt, have operated with happy results upon the naturally vigorous and clear mind of Frederick, had they been at all brought forward during his time; but they could not originate with him, inasmuch as he felt in himself the power to govern alone, seconded by the strongest desire of making his people happy and great. Thence it appeared to his mind, that the predominant strength of a state was based upon the means which are the readiest and most efficacious in the hands of one person, viz.: in his army, and in the treasury. His chief aim, therefore, was to manage that these two powerful implements of government should be placed in the most favorable condition possible; and thus we find, that Frederick often sought the means to obtain this, his grand object, without sufficiently taking into consideration the effect they might subsequently produce upon the disposition and morality of the nation. In accordance with this principle, he, in the year 1764, invited a distinguished fermier-general of France, Helvetius, to Berlin, in order to consult him

* In 1752 an Englishman was received at court who possessed an extraordinary memory, so much so, that after some fifty, nay, a hundred pages of a work had been read to him, he could forthwith repeat the whole, word for word, from recollection. Frederick was much struck with this person's gift of memory, and putting it one evening to the proof, found by the result a confirmation of the statement. Just as he was about to dismiss the Englishman, Voltaire sent to inquire if his majesty had half an hour's leisure time to hear him read a poem he had just completed? Frederick, struck with the inquiry coming so *apropos*, determined upon passing a joke at that vain man's expense, and sent a reply in the affirmative. He ordered the Englishman to take his station behind a screen, and requested him to treasure up in his memory every line and word that Voltaire might recite. The great poet arrived and read through the whole of his verses with great declamation and evident self-satisfaction. The king listened with apparent coolness and indifference, and then said, "Why, I must candidly confess, my dear Voltaire, that it strikes me you appropriate as your *own* the productions of *others!* I have noticed it more than once before; this poem is again another instance." His indignation at being thought a plagiarist produced upon Voltaire's countenance—always a subject for the caricaturist—an expression more than usually harsh and bitter. He expressed himself highly offended and mortified; his majesty had been misled by his treacherous memory to commit a great error, and he had acted with still greater injustice. "But how if I prove to you that these verses are already well-known to an Englishman at my court here?" "All that your majesty may bring forward in contradiction, all assurances are to me mere empty words, for I can disprove all and every thing!" Upon this Frederick ordered the Englishman (who had just before glided away from his screen into the next room) to be introduced. He was commanded by the king to recite the verses he had shortly before heard repeated, and accordingly gave the whole of Voltaire's poem word for word, without a single omission. Almost mad with rage, the poet rose and exclaimed: "Heaven! destroy with thy thunder this robber of my verses! Here is some magic in play which will drive me to desperation!" With these words he rushed from the king's presence in the greatest agitation. Frederick was, however, delighted with this mystification, a proof how little he esteemed Voltaire at heart.—*Müchler.*

upon the means of augmenting the revenues of the state, and in consequence of his suggestions, measures were adopted which were extremely obnoxious to the public, and caused many to defraud, instead of co-operating with, the government. At the same time, however, by these and other means resorted to by the king, the revenues of the kingdom were increased considerably. It must, however, be advanced in Frederick's vindication, firstly, that he adopted these measures, not for his own individual advantage, but for the benefit of all; and, secondly—we must again repeat it—that the great errors of the age completely obscured his own view. With what eagerness would not his clear mind have caught at the enlightenment produced by reform, had he but lived in a time when freedom of thought was more appreciated, for to him this freedom of thought was so dear, that he never attacked the public expression of opinion. His subjects enjoyed under his reign, among other privileges, that of the liberty of the press; and he himself gave free scope to the shafts of censure and ridicule aimed against his public and private character: for the consciousness of his own persevering endeavors in the service of his country, and of his sincere devotion to his duties, elevated him beyond all petty susceptibility. The chief object of the king's care was a search into truth and enlightenment, as it was then understood. But this enlightenment consisted in a desire to understand every thing: to analyze, dissect, and—demolish. Whatever appeared inexplicable was at once rejected; faith, love, hope, and filial respect—all those feelings which have their seat in the inmost recesses of the soul, were destroyed in their germination.

But this annihilating agency was not confined to the state; it manifested itself also in science, in art, and even in religion. The French were the promoters of this phenomenon, and in this they were eventually imitated throughout the world, but more especially in Germany. Superficial ornament passed for profound wisdom, and witty, sarcastic phraseology assumed the place of soundness and sincerity of expression. Nevertheless, even at this time, there were a few chosen men who were able to recognise that which was true and just, and raised their voices accordingly; and, in the world of intellect, the names of Lessing, Klopstock, Goethe, &c., need alone be mentioned, being, as they were, the founders of a more sterling age. They were joined by many others, and thus united, they constituted an intellectual phalanx in opposition to the progress made by the sensual French school. These intellectual reformers were soon strengthened by such auxiliaries as Kant, Fichte, Jacobi, &c., who advanced firmly under the banner of science, and from such beginnings grew, by degrees, that powerful mental reaction, which has already achieved such mighty things, and led the way to greater results still.

This awakening of the German mind was unnoticed by King Frederick; he lived in the world of French refinement, separate and solitary, as on an island. The waves of the new rushing stream of life passed without approaching him, and struck against the barriers by which he was enclosed. His over-appreciation and patronage of foreigners, however, impelled the higher classes of society to share in his sentiments, equally as much as his system of administration had served as a model for other rulers to imitate. Several among his contemporaries resolved, like him, to reign independently, but without possessing the same commanding genius, whence, however well-intentioned, they were wrecked in their career; among whom, may be more especially included, Peter III. of Russia, Gustavus III. of Sweden, and Joseph II. of Germany.

In the year 1765, Joseph II. was acknowledged as successor to his father, Francis I., who died in the same year, but whose acts as emperor present little or nothing worthy of record. His son, however, was, on this very account, the more anxious to effect great changes, to transform ancient into modern institutions, and to devote the great and predominating power with which he was endowed towards remodelling the entire condition of his states. All his projects, however, were held in abeyance until the death of his mother, Maria Theresa, in 1780, who, ever wise and active, had, even to the last moments of her existence, exercised all her power and influence in the administration of affairs, and, accordingly, her maternal authority operated effectually upon his feelings as a son, and served for a time to suspend the accomplishment of his desires. Meantime, in the interval between the year 1765 and 1780, various events took place, which exercised an important influence upon the last ten years of his reign. Among the rest may be more especially mentioned the *dismemberment of Poland* in 1773, and the war of the *Bavarian succession* in 1778.

Augustus III., king of Poland, died in the year 1765, leaving behind him a grandson, only as yet a minor; consequently the house of Saxony, which had held possession of the throne of Poland during a space of sixty-six years, now lost it. Both Russia and Prussia stepped forward forthwith, and took upon themselves the arrangement of the affairs of Poland: an interference which that nation was now unable to resist, for strong and redoubtable as it had been formerly, dissension had so much reduced its resources, that it was, at this moment, wholly incapable of maintaining, or even acting for itself. Both powers required that Poland should choose for her sovereign a native-born prince, and an army of 10,000 Russians which suddenly advanced upon Warsaw, and an equal number of Prussian troops assembled upon the frontiers, produced the election of Stanislaus Poniatowski to the throne. Henceforth there was no longer an imperial diet held at which foreigners did not endeavor to bring into effect all their influence.

Shortly after this event, a war took place between Russia and Turkey, in which the former took possession of Moldavia and Wallachia, which that power was extremely desirous of retaining. This, however, Austria opposed most strenuously, lest Russia should become too powerful, and Frederick the Great found himself in a dilemma how to maintain the balance between the two parties. The most expedient means of adjustment appeared in the end to be the spoliation of a country which was the least able to oppose it, viz., Poland; and, accordingly, a portion of its territory was seized and shared between the three powers—Russia, Prussia, and Austria. With whom this idea first originated has not been clearly ascertained, but it is easy to see that it was quite in accordance with the character of the times. For as the wisdom of that age only based its calculations upon the standard of the senses, and estimated the power of states merely by their square miles, amount of population, soldiers, and revenue, the grand aim of the then state-policy was to devote every effort towards aggrandizement; nothing was held more desirable than some fresh conquest, which might advantageously round off a kingdom, while all consideration of equity and justice was forced tc yield before this imperious principle. When one of the larger states effected such an acquisition, the others, alarmed, considered the balance of Europe compromised and endangered.

In this case, however, the three kingdoms bordering upon Poland, having shared between them the spoil, were each augmented in proportion, whence all fear of danger was removed. This system had become so superficial, so miserable and absurd, that they lost sight altogether of the principle that a just equilibrium and the permanent safety of all can only be secured by the inviolable preservation of the rights of nations. The partition of Poland was the formal renunciation itself of that system of equipoise, and served as the precursor of all those great revolutions, dismemberments, and transformations, together with all those ambitious attempts at universal monarchy, which, during a space of five-and-twenty years, were the means of convulsing Europe to her very foundations.

The people of Poland, menaced as they were in three quarters, were forced in the autumn of 1773 to submit to the dismemberment of their country, of which, accordingly, three thousand square miles were forthwith divided between Russia, Prussia, and Austria.

Maximilian Joseph, elector of Bavaria, having died in 1777 without issue, the inheritance of his estates and electoral dignity came into the hands of the elector palatine. The emperor Joseph, however, with his usual rashness, resolved to avail himself of this inheritance in favor of Austria; he accordingly raked up old claims, and marched suddenly with his army into Bavaria, of which he took immediate possession. The pacific palatine, Charles Theodore, thus surprised and overawed, signed a treaty, by which he ceded two thirds of Bavaria to the house of Austria, in order to secure to himself possession of at least the other third portion. The conduct of Austria on this occasion, together with the part she had previously taken in the dismemberment of ill-fated Poland, was the more unexpected, inasmuch as she was the only one of all the superior states which had hitherto abstained from similar acts of aggression. But the mutability of the age had now destroyed likewise in Austria the uniform pacific bearing for which she had so long been distinguished.

These proceedings gave rise to serious commotions in various parts of the empire, and Frederick the Great more especially felt he could not and ought not to remain an inactive observer of what was passing. Accordingly he entered the lists against Austria at once, and commenced operations as protector of the heir of Charles Theodore, the duke of Deux-Ponts, who protested against the compact signed by the former with Austria, and claimed the assistance of the king of Prussia. The young and hot-headed emperor Joseph accepted the challenge forthwith, and taking up a position in Bohemia, he there awaited the king; the latter, who had already crossed the mountains, finding him, however, so strongly intrenched, was reluctant to hazard an attack under such difficult circumstances, and withdrew from Bohemia. After a few unimportant skirmishes between the light troops of both sides, peace was signed by the mediation of France and Russia, at Teschen, on the 13th of May, 1779, even before the end of the first year of the war. The empress Maria Theresa, now advanced in years, by no means shared in her son's taste for war, but, on the contrary, earnestly desired peace; while Frederick himself, who had nothing to gain personally by this campaign, was equally anxious for a reconciliation. Moreover, he was likewise far advanced in years, and possessed an eye sufficiently penetrating to perceive that the former original spirit and energy of the army, which had performed such prodigies of valor in the war of Seven Years, had now almost disappeared, although the discipline under which it was still placed was equally severe and tyrannical as in former times. Under these and other circumstances, therefore, peace was preferable to war. By the treaty now concluded, Austria restored to the palatine house all the estates of Bavaria, except the circle of Burgau, and the succession was secured to the duke of Deux-Ponts.

After the death of Maria Theresa, in 1780, Joseph II. strove, with all the impetuosity of his fiery and enterprising nature, to bring into immediate execution the great and ambitious plans he had formed, and to give to the various nations spread over the boundless surface of his vast possessions, one unique and equal form of government, after a model such as he had himself formed within his own mind. Indeed, from the daring, reckless character he displayed, and the conduct he pursued, he might with justice have been regarded as one only anxious, by the changes he made, to pave the way for the most unprecedented revolution in the annals of Europe. But this prince, together with others of the age he lived in and that which followed, beheld all their creations destroyed almost as suddenly as they had been formed, inasmuch as they had involved themselves in the error of believing that they could change, in the short space of a man's life, or perhaps of only a few years, that which the human race was only able to bring into operation in the slow growth of centuries. This arrogant presumption evinced by a man, who would thus pretend to realize the ideas he has conceived solely because he deems their realization *possible*—however opposed they may be to reason—was manifested in Joseph in the highest degree, and hence he was frustrated and disappointed in all his expectations and good intentions. He himself was influenced, it is true, by a mere desire for all that is just and good, for the prosperity of his dominions, for the progress of enlightenment and liberty of spirit; but he neglected to search strictly but calmly into human nature, and thus make himself thoroughly acquainted with the peculiar character of his variously-disposed subjects. What he undertook to effect was too often altogether unsuited to their actual condition, and what was acceptable to one was repugnant to another. In the feeling of his good intentions, Joseph adopted as his model the absolute principles of Frederick in his system of government; but Frederick occupied himself more with external arrangements, with the administration of the state, the promotion of industry, and the increase of the revenue, interfering very little with the progress of intellectual culture, which followed its particular course, often altogether without his knowledge; while in this respect Joseph, by his new measures, often encroached upon the dearest privileges of his subjects. He insisted certainly upon liberty of conscience and freedom of thought; but he did not bear in mind, at the same time, that the acknowledgment of this principle depended upon that close conviction which cannot be forced, and can only exist in reality when the light of truth has gradually penetrated to the depth of the heart.

The greatest obstacles, however, thrown in the way of Joseph's innovations proceeded from the church; for his grand object was to confiscate numerous monasteries and spiritual institutions, and to change at once the whole ecclesiastical constitution: that is, he contemplated obtaining during the first year of his reign, what would of itself have occurred in the space of half a century.

By this confiscation of ecclesiastical possessions more than one neighboring prince of the empire, such as the bishop of Passau and the archbishop of Salzburg, found themselves attacked in their rights, and did not hesitate to complain loudly; and in the same way in other matters, various other princes found too much reason to condemn the emperor for treating with contempt the constitution of the empire. Their apprehensions were more especially increased when the emperor, in the year 1785, negotiated a treaty of exchange of territory with the electoral prince-palatine of Bavaria, according to which, the latter was to resign his country to Austria, for which he was to receive in return the Austrian Netherlands under the title of a new kingdom of Burgundy: an arrangement by which the entire south of Germany would have come into the exclusive possession of Austria. The prince-palatine was not at all indisposed to make the exchange, and France, as well as Russia, at first favored it in its principle; but Frederick II. once more stepped forward and disconcerted their plans, in which he succeeded likewise in bringing Russia to coöperate with him.

The commotions, however, produced by these efforts made by Joseph to bring his rash projects into immediate operation, caused the old king of Prussia to form the idea of establishing an alliance of the German princes for the preservation of the imperial constitution, similar in character to the unions formed in previous times for mutual defence. Such at least was to be the unique object of this alliance according to the king's own words; and this league was accordingly effected in the year 1785, between Prussia, Saxony, Hanover, the dukes of Saxony, Brunswick, Mecklenburg, and Deux-Ponts, the landgrave of Hesse, and several other princes, who were soon joined by the elector of Mentz. This alliance was based upon principles in their nature less inimical than strictly surveillant; nevertheless, it effected the object contemplated, by acting as a check upon the house of Austria in the various innovations threatened by the emperor, while it operated as a lesson indicating to that house that its real distinction among the other nations of Europe was to preserve the present order of things, to protect all rights and privileges, to oppose the spirit of conquest, and thus to constitute itself the bulwark of universal liberty; but failing in all this, it must inevitably lose at once all public confidence. This alliance of princes, however, produced little or no important results for the advantage of Germany, owing partly to the death of Frederick II., which took place in the following year, and partly to the circumstance of the successors of Joseph II. happily returning to the ancient hereditary principles of the house, both in its moderation and circumspection; and finally, owing to the unheard-of events which transpired in Europe during the last ten years of this century, and which soon produced too much cause for forgetting all previous minor grievances.

This alliance of the princes of the empire was the last public act of the great Frederick of any consequence; and he died in the following year. He continued active and full of enterprise to the last, in spite of his advanced age, but his condition became gradually more isolated, inasmuch as all the companions of his former days had in turns disappeared and sunk into their last resting-place before himself, the last among them being the brave old warrior, Ziethen, who died in the January previous of the same year as his royal master, at the age of eighty-seven; and, on the other hand, heaven had not blessed him with any family, and thus he was debarred from the endearing enjoyment experienced by a father, when he sees himself growing young again, and revivified in his posterity. At the same time, he was wanting in all those feelings conducive to this state of life—a state against which his whole nature recoiled.

His mind, with scarcely any interruption, retained all its power during the long space of seventy-four years, although his body had latterly become much reduced and enfeebled. Through the extravagant use he had always made of strong spices and French dishes, he dried up the springs of life, and after suffering severely from dropsy, he departed this life on the 17th of August, 1786, and was buried in Potsdam, under the pulpit of the church belonging to the garrison.*

Although the news of Frederick's death at such an advanced age excited no very great astonishment, it nevertheless produced a considerable sensation throughout the whole of Europe. He left to his successor a well-regulated state, containing a population of six millions of inhabitants; a powerful, strictly-organized army, and a treasury well provided; the greatest treasure however he left, was the recollection of his heroic and glorious acts, which in subsequent times has continued to operate upon his nation with all its awakening power and heart-stirring influence.

The emperor Joseph, meantime, had engaged, in 1788, in a war with the Turks, which did not produce the results he had been led to anticipate. His army suffered very considerable losses, more especially through sickness, and, although he himself was present in person, his troops effected nothing, for he was wholly without those necessary qualifications—firmness and presence of mind; characteristics so highly requisite in a general, in order to ensure success. About this time also the Hungarians began to show strong symptoms of discontent, caused by the unjust treatment they received at the hands of him they had formerly saved when appealed to by his mother, Maria Theresa. In the Netherlands, however, the whole population broke out into open rebellion at once; the clergy, the nobility, the people, and the cities altogether, perceiving, by the reforms too precipitately enforced upon them by the emperor, the attacks that were being made upon their ancient rights and privileges. They seized arms, and on the 22d of October, 1789, the provinces of Brabant declared themselves independent in a grand meeting held at Breda. Nearly all the cities took part with the revolters, who had at their head a barrister, named Van der Noot, and the Austrian officials were forced to take their flight. This was, in fact, a kind of introductory scene to that which was being prepared, about the same time, in France itself. During the period of these contentions Joseph died in his forty-ninth year, on the 20th of February, 1790, an event greatly hastened by the fatigues he had undergone in the Turkish war, and more especially promoted through bitter mortification at finding all his mad and ill-timed projects fall to the ground, and the pain he felt at the state of anarchy and revolt existing among his subjects.

As he left no family behind him, his brother, Peter Leopold, hitherto grand-duke of Tuscany, succeeded him in his hereditary estates of Austria. The task undertaken by the new sovereign was by no means the most easy one, inasmuch as he found everywhere dissatisfaction, contention, and sedition. He perceived that in order to steer the vessel safely through the raging tempest he must employ moderate and reconciliatory measures, and, happily, Peter Leopold possessed the necessary disposition and ability to effect this object. The dangerous innovations introduced by his predecessor were at once abolished, Hungary pacified, and the Netherlands, partly by the necessary force of arms, and partly by the confirmation of their rights and constitutions, were restored to a state of tranquillity; and, finally, in the following year, a treaty of peace was concluded with the Turks. On the 20th of September, 1790, the hereditary prince of the house of Austria was chosen emperor of Germany, under the title of Leopold II. He, however, died on the 1st of March, 1792, and thus his short reign of two years ended at the moment when a new and eventful era commenced in the history of Europe, teeming with scenes of intrigue, anarchy, and atrocious outrage,

* In his last illness Frederick displayed great mildness and patience, and acknowledged with gratitude the trouble and pain he caused those around him. During one of his sleepless nights he called to the page who kept watch in the room, and asked him what o'clock it was? The man replied it had just struck two. "Ah, then it is still too soon!" exclaimed the king, "but I cannot sleep. See whether any of the other attendants are awake, but do not disturb them if they are still sleeping, for, poor fellows, they are tired enough. But if you find Neuman (his favorite yäger) stirring, say to him, you believe the king wishes soon to rise. But mind, do not awaken any one!"—*Müchler.*

already but too well known in the annals of that disastrous period to require much farther comment or description in the present work.

---

## CHAPTER XXXIII.

Leopold II. and the State of France—France declares War against Austria, the Imperial States, Holland, Spain, &c., 1792—Francis II., Emperor of Germany, 1792-1806—Prussia—Successes of the Allies—General Dumouriez and the Republican Army—The Austrians defeated at Jemappes—The Netherlands Republicanized—Defeat of Dumouriez at Neerwinden, 1793—Joins the Allies—Continued Successes of the Allies under the Dukes of York and Coburg—Carnot—Generals Pichegru and Jourdan—Battles of Tournay and Fleurus—Jourdan's Aerial Reconnoitring Messenger, or the Adjutant in the Balloon—Defeat of the Allies—Successes of the French—Conquests in Flanders, Holland, and the Rhine—Kaiserslautern—Peace of Basle, 1795—England and Austria—France—The Austrian Generals, Beaulieu, Wurmser, and Archduke Charles—Napoleon Bonaparte, 1796—Appointed General in Italy—His Army—His Conquests and rich Booty made in Italy—The French in Germany—Archduke Charles—Moreau—His famous Retreat—Mantua—Bonaparte in Germany—His rapid Marches—Vienna—Peace of Campo-Formio, 1797—Shameful Conditions—State of Europe—Alliance of England, Russia, Austria, and Turkey—Hostilities resumed, 1798—Bonaparte in Egypt—Cairo—Aboukir—His Fleet destroyed by Nelson—Italy—General Suwaroff—His Successes in Italy—Genoa—Switzerland—Suwaroff's Passage across the Alps—His desperate Appeal to his Soldiers—His recall—The Emperor Paul and England—Bonaparte First Consul, 1799—Genoa—Battle of Marengo, 1800—General Desaix—Moreau in Germany—Peace of Luné-ville, 1801—Sad Results to, and Sacrifices made by Germany—Resignation of William Pitt—Peace of Amiens, 1802—England declares war against France, 1803—Bonaparte takes possession of Hanover—The German Legion.

The emperor Leopold II. remained faithful to his system of pacification, although he could not but feel serious apprehensions when he beheld the alarming state of affairs in France. Several of the princes of the empire had already expressed a strong desire to take up arms against that revolutionary country, in favor of the emigrated princes and nobles, who, making the banks of the Rhine their place of refuge, collected together in numerous bodies at Coblentz, and finally prevailed upon the princes of the land to maintain their rights, and commence hostilities. The revolution had, in fact, affected and seriously injured a number of the German princes in the privileges they enjoyed from the earliest times in France, and more especially in Alsace—and now, when they demanded an indemnification for these losses, they only met with the same arrogant and scornful reception in the language which it had been the practice of France to express during the last five-and-twenty years. The imperialists, however, should have borne in mind that to a country in a state of revolution, a war with a foreign power is both desirable and beneficial, inasmuch as it acts as a check upon internal divisions, and by promoting a more united feeling, furnishes it with still greater power against the common enemy.

The new emperor, Francis II., formed now an alliance with Frederick-William II. of Prussia, against France, but which the latter government anticipated by declaring war against Austria in 1792. The attack of the Prussians took the young republic—which still retained the king, although powerless, at its head—completely by surprise. The country was not as yet prepared for war, and the first invasion was accordingly attended with successful results. The armies of the imperialists continued to march in advance, and took possession of all the towns along their route. Valenciennes, Longwy, and Verdun, were conquered, all the passes of the forest of Ardennes occupied, together with the plains of Champagne; and even Paris itself began to tremble. But the people now aroused themselves, and this was promoted, in fact, by their enemy himself. For, misled no doubt by the presumption and mad hopes cherished by the emigrants, the duke of Brunswick, who commanded the Prussian army, issued a manifesto, which was distributed everywhere throughout the entire kingdom, and which was so insultingly and cruelly worded, as to make the heart of every Frenchman recoil and tremble within him, and of those more especially who refused to acknowledge the ancient rights of royalty; for, among the other threats it contained, the document declared that Paris should be burned to the ground, and the inhabitants put to the sword, and not a single stone of the metropolis should be left standing. These dreadful words acted upon the people with all the power of an electric shock, and forthwith, from every part of the country, were to be seen both young and old hastening in shoals with all possible speed to join voluntarily the standard of General Dumouriez, and under which they burned to conquer or die in the defence of their country's freedom. The army was soon in a condition to face the invaders, and it marched forth and took up an advantageous position on the high-road near Sainte-Menehould; but, as the Prussians now began to suffer greatly from the want of supplies in that impoverished part of the country, as also from the sickness and disease produced through the continual heavy rains which, badly clothed as the troops were, thinned their ranks sadly, they were forced, after a slight cannonade at Valmy, to make a retreat; this they were happy enough to succeed in effecting in good time, and they gained the banks of the Rhine, which they lost no time in crossing.

At Jemappes, however, Dumouriez came up with the Austrians, and giving them battle at once, on the 5th of November, 1792—the first under the republican government—gained a decisive victory. His force was greatly superior in numbers to the Austrian army, while he was likewise in possession of an overwhelming train of heavy artillery, which at each discharge mowed down whole ranks of the enemy, and made the very earth tremble. The Austrians, nevertheless, fought with a courage truly heroic for two entire days against their formidable adversaries, but were eventually forced to yield the field of battle. By this single battle, the house of Austria lost the whole of the Netherlands, for the victorious army, like a rushing torrent, carried all before them, and the inhabitants, already dissatisfied with the dominion of Austria ever since the reign of Joseph II., and seduced by the thoughts of liberty, threw off the imperial yoke and received the French with open arms. They planted everywhere the tree of liberty, established a national convention, and adopted all the republican principles and institutions of their conquerors.

At the same time General Custine had marched against the Rhenish provinces, and through treachery made himself master of the important imperial city of Mentz. The mania for liberty now held its sway in that place, and the republican institutions of Paris were likewise introduced there. Frankfort, however, its neighboring city, maintained itself firmly against all the influence of these insinuating and destructive principles, and when invited to follow the example set by those around, the citizens replied, that they were contented with the liberty they had thus far enjoyed all along.

The sanguinary proceedings—but more especially the dreadful and revolting fate of Louis XVI., on the 21st of January, 1793, excited universal indignation and horror; and England and Spain, together with Holland, armed at once against the French republic, which had declared war against them. Germany was not long in joining these powers, and as Naples, Rome, Tuscany, and Portugal, came forward likewise, a coalition of the governments of the moiety of Europe was brought to bear against that of France.

The commencement of the campaign of 1793 was distinguished by a series of brilliant victories gained by the allies in the Netherlands. Dumouriez was defeated at Aldenhoven, and he was again overthrown on the 18th of March in a grand battle near Neerwinden; and, dreading lest he might be summoned to Paris and thus fall into the hands of the Jacobins, of whom he was no friend, and who, he knew too well, were the last to treat misfortune with mercy, he passed over to the ranks of the allies. The latter now pressed forward in rapid marches; their united army comprised the Austrians, the Prussians, the English, the Hanoverians, and the Dutch, commanded by the duke of Coburg and the duke of York. Dumouriez's successor, General Dampierre, was again defeated on the 8th of May on the plains of Famars, being himself killed in the action; and the allies having now made themselves masters of Valenciennes and Condé, the road to Paris lay open before them.

Meantime the Prussians and Austrians, on the Rhine, reconquered Mentz, and having forced the lines of the hill of Weissenberg, they commenced the siege of Landau under the command of the crown prince of Prussia.

In the Pyrenees a Spanish army crossed the Alps and marched into France, where the progress made was attended with considerable success; in conjunction with the English they took possession of the important seaport of Toulon, which, having declared itself opposed to the convention of Paris, they defended against the republican forces.

Towards the end of the year, however, the republican forces were more successful along the frontiers of the kingdom. On the Upper Rhine, Landau and the whole of Alsace, after continued and most sanguinary fighting, fell again into their hands, and the republican flag was everywhere planted along that portion of the banks of the Rhine; while, in the Netherlands, Dunkirk was delivered, and many severe actions gained by the French. In this quarter the forces were commanded by Houchard and Jourdan; while on the Rhine the troops were headed by Pichegru and Hoche—names elevated from their original obscurity by the rushing tide of the revolution. On the 30th of September a grand fête was held in Paris, on which occasion *fourteen* different armies were represented in a triumphal procession, in honor of the victories they had gained.

At the commencement of the year 1794 the allies united all their forces in the Netherlands, under the orders of the duke of Coburg, and the emperor Francis himself joined the camp, in order by his presence to encourage the troops. On the 7th of April they gained a complete victory near Cateau-Cambresis, and on the 30th of the same month they made themselves masters of the town of Landrecies. Fortune, however, now changed. Carnot, who properly understood how to employ the system of war by which a nation in arms might obtain victory, issued his orders forthwith to the grand armies, commanded by Pichegru and Jourdan, to attack the allied army with the most daring impetuosity and without ceasing, so that not a single day might pass without constant hard fighting. With respect to the number of French troops that were slain, that was a matter of no consideration; fresh battalions were marched up to replace those that had fallen, and thus the allied generals, finding themselves so hard pressed, looked in vain for an opportunity where and how to form their principal point of defence. All their ordinary tactics of war were perfectly useless; for when whole battalions, on being repulsed, fell back upon each other, and instead of taking to flight rallied again and renewed the attack, and fought on without yielding an inch as long as life gave them the power, and when neither the fear of death nor any thing else, however formidable its nature, could make them quit the field of battle, then necessarily at the end of the action victory remained with the greatest number. Thence the Austrians and their allies, the English, Dutch, and Hanoverians, harassed and overcome with fatigue, were ultimately defeated on the 22d of May near Tournay by Pichegru, and on the 26th of June at Fleurus, by Jourdan, in two sanguinary battles. At Fleurus the French general turned the course of the contest, which was going against him, eventually in his favor by adopting an expedient completely novel and hitherto unknown in war; he caused, namely, one of his aides-de-camp to get into a balloon in which he ascended, and this enabled him to observe exactly the position of the allied army, and on this officer's return from his aerial expedition he gave his report accordingly to the general, who renewed the action, and, guided by the instructions he had received, gained the battle.

After this victory the success of the French arms continued without interruption; nothing could check their progress either in Holland or on the Rhine. All the places taken from them in France—Landrecies, Le Quesnoy, Valenciennes, and Condé, were reconquered one after the other; besides which, the republicans took possession of Brussels on the 9th of June, and in the autumn they commanded the rivers Meuse and Vahal. These successes, however, appeared to have now reached the term of their duration, and more especially as the sluices of all the canals throughout Holland had been opened, in order, by a general inundation, to rescue that country from the French arms. But nature herself came to the aid of the invaders, by converting these very waters into a secure passage for their troops, inasmuch as the winter of this year, 1794, becoming extremely severe, they were all completely frozen, and to such a depth was the ice, that, by means of these natural, seasonable bridges, soldiers, artillery, and baggage-trains, were enabled to advance, and penetrate into the very heart of Holland; thus, on the 17th of January, 1795, they were in possession of Utrecht, and on the 19th they took Amsterdam. The stadtholder was forced to seek refuge with his family in England, and Holland was forthwith converted into a republic.

Meantime Jourdan, in the autumn of 1794, had driven the Austrians out of Brabant towards the Lower Rhine, and completely defeated them in several encounters; and eventually he forced them to cross the Rhine to Cologne. Liége, Aix-la-Chapelle, Juliers, Cologne, Bonn, and Coblentz, fell into the hands of the French; Luxemburg alone holding out by a brave and determined defence until the month of June, 1795.

In the circle of the Upper Rhine the campaign of 1794 took almost the same direction as in the northern provinces. At the commencement, on the 22d of May, a great victory was obtained by the Austrians and Prussians at Kaiserslautern; this was succeeded by continuous attacks made upon the allies by the republican army, now considerably reinforced by levies *en masse* produced through the national summons, and finally, on the 15th of June, by another battle fought at Kaiserslautern, in which the French, although repulsed eight times with great loss, returned to the attack for the ninth time, and gained the victory. After a short cessation of hostilities, the allies retired at this point, to the right bank of the Rhine.

The success of the French arms had now become so great, and produced so much alarm, that whoever attentively considered the condition of Europe, and especially Germany, could easily perceive that it could not do otherwise but unite all its forces, in order to carry on the war for its own preservation. The French already made no mystery of their intention to retain possession of the whole of Germany situated along the left bank of the Rhine, to the extent of the entire course of that river. Were we then, through the unfavorable results of one campaign, to allow our dangerous neighbor to remain master over those territories, which to gain he had been striving in vain for centuries? No; Germany ought never to have permitted such a disgrace; but where in such times was to be found that ancient, hereditary, and noble feeling of independence, coupled with that inborn magnanimity to uphold and defend the honor of our common fatherland? Jealousy and envy among the commanders-in-chief and the first ministers of the empire had paralyzed the powers of the army, and obstructed the success of every operation; and now the entire confederation allowed itself to be dissolved by its crafty enemy. On the 5th of April, Prussia concluded at Basle a separate treaty of peace with the French republic, and Hanover, as well as Hesse Cassel, concurred therein likewise. A line of demarcation was drawn for the north of Germany, which exempted the Prussian territories in Westphalia, including Hesse and Lower Saxony.

Shortly afterwards Spain, through want of means wherewith to pay her troops, as well as of that firm, determined will so necessary under the circumstances, likewise separated herself from the coalition against France; whence, of the higher powers, Austria and England alone remained in the grand arena, and thus it has always happened with Austria ever since the time of Maximilian I., whenever that power formed an alliance to maintain a war in conjunction with several other states.

During the conferences of peace with Prussia, and even afterwards, in the summer of 1795, as Austria and the Germanic empire appeared equally desirous for a pacification, both parties agreed to a cessation of arms, and the two armies retained their position in front of each other on the opposite banks of the Rhine, separated only by the waters of that noble river. This short repose was of great benefit to France, for the general scarcity of provisions which prevailed throughout this year—producing almost a state of famine—would otherwise have completely prevented the army from accomplishing any extraordinary operations. But as the harvest was now safely gathered in, Jourdan, on the night of the 6th of September, crossed the Rhine between Duesburg and Düsseldorf, which latter town he forthwith invested, and pursuing his impetuous course of victory, drove the Austrians from the banks of the rivers Wupper—the commencement of the Prussian line of demarcation—the Sieg, and the Lahn, over the Maine. Field-marshal Clairfait, however, had reassembled his troops behind the latter river, and he now attacked the French at Höchst, near Frankfort, completely routed them, and sent them back over the Rhine with the same expedition that they had used in advancing across it; thus Mentz was delivered from its state of siege, and Mannheim retaken. The summer armistice had reduced the strength and spirit of the republican armies, and their zeal had become considerably diminished. A war conducted on the opposite bank of the Rhine was no longer regarded as a war in the cause of liberty, and many volunteers of the higher classes had now returned to their homes.

When, in 1796, the new order of things had become gradually consolidated in France, the directory resolved to force Austria and the Germanic empire to conclude a treaty of peace by one general overwhelming invasion. It was determined that the armies should, in the ensuing spring, cross to the other side of the Rhine and the Alps, and penetrate from every point into the heart of Germany. Moreau was to march through Swabia, Jourdan through Franconia, and a third army was to overrun Italy. In the latter country, the Austrian troops were commanded by the old general, Beaulieu; in the Upper Rhine, the old veteran, Wurmser, held the chief command; and in the Lower Rhine, the general-in-chief was the Arch-duke Charles of Austria; to the two latter armies were united the troops of the imperial states. The war commenced in Italy. But there the old and experienced general found himself confronted with a young daring leader, filled with the most gigantic projects, and who now on this occasion first came forth to develop his marvellous powers and indomitable perseverance before the eyes of astonished Europe.

Napoleon Bonaparte, born at Ajaccio in Corsica—where his father was an advocate, and subsequently promoted to the French procuratorship of Corsica—educated in the military schools of France, and inured to the most extraordinary scenes and enterprises by all the horrors of the revolution, in which he had been a participator, was only six-and-twenty years of age when he received his appointment as general of the Italian army. Barras, one of the five directors of the executive power, and who had taken him into his especial favor, concerted a marriage between him and the widowed Princess Josephine de Beauharnais, and had now caused his promotion to the rank beforementioned. The post he held was one of great difficulty and danger; the army over which he was placed, was in such a disorganized state, being without supplies of provisions and clothing, and even without ammunition, that its condition could only be improved when under the direction of a resolute and daring general, and who, by judicious management, might perhaps succeed in making even that very unfavorable condition itself serve as a means to lead to victories all the more glorious, for, in their present desperate state, the soldiers had no other choice but conquest or death.

And truly the newly-appointed leader soon succeeded in gaining the most extraordinary influence and sway over his troops, and in infusing among them no small share of his own daring and undaunted spirit. This indeed formed the spirit of his military tactics, and the means by which he was led on to adopt the most ambitious plans, and sought to make himself the conqueror of the entire world. By his bulletins, couched in the most concise and forcible language, in the style of the ancient Romans, thoroughly adapted to the French character; by the distribution of marks of honor and distinction, of colors and eagles, to those regiments which he at the same moment was about to place in the most dangerous part of the battle, together with other similar incentives to honor and glory, Bonaparte well understood how to generate the highest enthusiasm at the decisive moment. He even had the temerity to announce in advance the result of the battles, and fortune verified his words; people speedily believed what he had predicted, and this very faith produced the accomplishment of the event. He more especially confounded his enemies by never doing what might have been anticipated and calculated upon, but by performing exactly what was completely opposed to these expectations, and was the most bold and perilous in its nature. All experience and practice, therefore, in the science of war, were nugatory against him; a defensive war with him must be unsuccessfully carried on, for the blow always came before it could be preceived, or even anticipated, and he never allowed his adversary to commence the attack, because no one was so prompt in his measures and resolves as himself.

The opening of this campaign was followed by the most brilliant success. By the promptitude of his manœuvres and suddenness of his attacks, he completely overcame and separated the army of the Sardinians from that of the Austrians, and forced the king of Sardinia to sign a treaty of peace; and this he followed up by turning his arms against the Austrians, and pursuing them to the north of the river Po. Thus the whole of central Italy lay now open before him, and all the princes of that country trembled at his vengeance. They alternately demanded peace and obtained it, but at the sacrifice of millions in money, numerous invaluable paintings, together with other treasures of art and precious manuscripts. It was with these spoils that he intended to decorate Paris, in order subsequently to make it the metropolis of the entire world. The duke of Parma was the first who bound himself by a treaty of the 9th of May, to furnish in payment for peace, a large collection of the most rare paintings; and from this moment the example of ancient Rome towards Greece was emulated in every part where the French armies got a footing. Vanity, combined with the eager desire to collect together and concentrate in their capital, and thereby render it the counterpart of ancient Rome and the central point of nations, urged the invaders to pillage the sanctuaries and monuments of art and science of every country they marched through. The pope was obliged to purchase neutrality by the payment of 21,000,000, francs, and by giving up to them 100 costly pictures, and 200 rare manuscripts. Naples obtained peace without any sacrifice; because it lay at too great a distance, and because, likewise, its hour, according to Bonaparte's calculation, had not yet arrived.

Meantime great events had likewise transpired in Germany. The forces there had scarcely commenced operations, when already the principal blow was struck in Italy, and the brave old warrior, Wurmser, was summoned from Germany with 30,000 men to the relief of Mantua, the last stronghold of the Austrians in Italy. The French armies, according to the plan of the campaign drawn up by the French directory, were now enabled to penetrate into the heart of the Germanic empire. About the middle of August, Jourdan was only within a few days march of Ratisbon, and Moreau was close to Munich, with the army of the Rhine and Moselle; the latter general declared openly that his object was to give his right hand to the army under Bonaparte in Italy, and his left to that of Jourdan. This junction of such overwhelming masses of troops brought with it the most alarming appearances, and this was one of the most critical and dangerous moments for Austria. Nevertheless, the peril thus threatened was once more diverted by the youthful hero of that imperial house. The nearer the war approached the Austrian frontiers, so much the more did the danger thus menacing their native soil spur on the imperial troops; while at the same time their numbers were augmented more and more by fresh reinforcements from the interior. The Archduke Charles now came forth, and suddenly marching with his troops against Jourdan, attacking him at Neumark on the 22d of August, and at Amberg on the 24th, beat him so completely that the whole army of the Sambre and Meuse took to flight, and never halted till it gained the Lower Rhine. Jourdan rallied them at Mühlheim on the Rhine, marched thence to Düsseldorf, and shortly afterwards resigned the command. By this disaster of the other army, Moreau was forced likewise to make a retreat to the Upper Rhine; and this he effected in such masterly style, that after marching over the most perilous roads through Swabia and the Black Forest, and being continually pursued and hemmed in by the enemy, as well as exposed to the attacks of the enraged mountaineers, he gained the banks of the Rhine well provided with booty, and bringing with him even a number of prisoners taken on his march. By this admirable retreat, the fame of Moreau as a general was permanently established. The leaders on both sides now agreed upon an armistice being concluded on the Rhine during the winter.

The Archduke Charles, on whom the eyes of all were now turned with admiration, received a hasty summons to repair to Italy, in order to reorganize the Austrian army. Wurmser, although successful in several attacks, was only able to throw himself, with a subsidy of 10,000 men, into Mantua; but Bonaparte had now arrived, and renewing the siege, forced them, on the 6th of February, 1797, to surrender.

The Archduke Charles, with a broken-down and dispirited army, was not in a condition to check the progress made by Bonaparte. The latter, after the fall of Mantua, penetrated more and more northward, crossed the Alps which separate Italy from Carinthia, and, marching into Styria, took possession of Clagenfurth, and advanced as far as Judenburg, on the river Mur, whence he threatened Vienna itself. But his course, this time, had been pursued with too much impetuosity, and the situation in which he now found himself was extremely critical. In his front he had the imperial army, which, at every retrogressive step became more and more formidable, as Vienna had already armed itself, and Hungary was now rising *en masse;* on his left flank, the imperial general, Laudon, was marching in advance against him from the Tyrol; and, in his rear, in the vicinity of Trieste, another numerous body of troops, together with the whole of the inhabitants of the Venetian territory were under arms; while, in order to gain the first and nearest garrisoned town, Mantua, he would have to march a distance of more than two hundred miles, over rugged hills, and an impoverished and naked country: in addition to all which evils, his army had scarcely sufficient supplies for ten days longer. In this state of things, it is almost certain, that if Austria had been willing to stake the chances, she might have succeeded in annihilating her dangerous adversary at once, and with one blow. But this, it appears, was not at all contemplated, for when, with his usual cunning, Bonaparte, with the arrogance of a conqueror, now offered peace, she accepted it, and concluded the principal conditions on the 18th of April, at Leoben, and the definitive treaty was signed on the 17th of October, 1797, at Campo-Formio, a nobleman's castle in the neighborhood of Udine. Thus Bonaparte, in two campaigns, subjugated Italy; gained fourteen battles; wrested the arms from the grasp of all the states in that quarter; and, finally, brought over Austria to sign a peace.

The emperor, by this treaty, ceded the Austrian Netherlands to France, and renounced his Italian possessions, including the capital city of Milan, together with several other Italian provinces, which were to form a Cisalpine republic, under the protectorship of France. In return for this, Austria received Venice, the Venetian Isles, Istria, and Dalmatia, and engaged to deliver up Breisgau to the duke of Modena, and to summon, forthwith, a congress at Rastadt, in order to treat more fully the several conditions of the peace concluded between the republic and the Germanic empire.

But this peace of Rastadt was in every respect humiliating and disgraceful to Germany. The empire was wholly abandoned and sacrificed by the emperor, as it had previously been by Prussia. Austria having, in a secret article, consented to surrender the whole of the left bank of the Rhine, as the limits of the Germanic empire, who had we now left as its shield, when its most powerful protectors had thus deserted it? And yet no one individual state can be condemned, inasmuch as *all* committed themselves; and, having withdrawn from the general co-operation as soon as they found the danger approaching them closely, it could not be required of Austria that she alone should make herself the sacrifice. It is only with painful feelings that we can dwell upon these sad results, and we willingly hurry over the close of the eighteenth and the opening of the nineteenth century, when Germany lay in its deepest humiliation; nevertheless, these times ought not to be passed over in silence, for it is necessary that we should know the sad condition to which the discord, schism, and egotism of individuals, as well as the total want of patriotic feeling, could bring the German nation.

The congress of peace was accordingly convened at Rastadt, and Bonaparte appeared there himself as negotiator. But in what style of insult and contempt was not the empire treated in these negotiations? With what arrogance were our princes met by the French envoys, who exercised the authority of masters over them? Nevertheless, ill-used and imposed upon as they were, the states were forced to submit and agree to every thing, viz.: to the cession of the left bank of the Rhine, to the secularization of the right bank, as an indemnity for what had been lost on the left, and to the destruction of the fortress of Ehrenbreitstein, together with various other equally humiliating demands. These negotiations had continued until the end of the year 1798, when they were brought to a termination; but, in the mean time, Europe itself had undergone a material change.

The members of the French directory, in their arrogance, had undertaken to revolutionize and overturn the governments of other countries, and the measures they adopted made it very soon manifest that the French republic was even more dangerous in a time of peace than during a war. In the beginning of 1798, they, in scornful defiance of the pope, remodelled the states of the church into a Roman republic, and shortly afterwards, they transformed the government of Switzerland, after several sanguinary contests, into an Helvetic republic; and under the pretext of securing these new advantages, they left their armies in possession of the countries which they drained by unheard-of exactions. Austria, who still considered herself called upon to watch over the safety of Europe, could not sanction such proceedings, and she found in the emperor Paul of Russia, who had succeeded to the imperial throne on the death of his mother Catherine, in 1796, a co-operative spirit. He was a decided enemy to all the principles professed and followed out by the French; and his mother had already denounced and threatened those "regicides" and "atheists." Paul at this moment was more especially excited against France, because the knights of the order of St. John had elected him their grand-master, after the French had taken possession of the island of Malta. This circumstance was well adapted to act as a spur to his ambition. Accordingly, a coalition of powers was now formed against France, such as had never before been brought into operation: being a union of Russia, England, Austria, and even Turkey, which, until now, had always cherished the greatest enmity towards two of these powers; France herself, however, had forced Turkey, hitherto her old ally, to a war, by the formidable expedition she sent against Egypt in May, 1798.

The republic of France had never conceived a more grand and stupendous design, of which they contemplated the realization by this enterprise. At the moment when the negotiations with the Germanic empire had as yet made but little progress, and consequently, the peace of continental Europe was not yet secured, and when England was maintaining a gloriously victorious struggle on the seas, the flower of the French army, headed by Bonaparte and their best and most successful leaders, suddenly embarked, and set sail towards a distant land, "in order," as stated in the French manifesto, "to deliver Egypt from the tyranny of the Mamelukes, and to avenge the Porte upon those overbearing and insolent vassals." A plan more strange and unexpected could not have been thought of, only that behind these words was concealed a deep-laid scheme, which events very soon made clearly manifest, but which likewise fell to the ground.

Bonaparte, after a prosperous voyage, and after having made himself master of the island of Malta, landed in the bay of Aboukir, on the 2d of July, 1798, and having taken Alexandria by storm, continued his march, and took up his position near Cairo, the capital of that country. Here, at the foot of the great pyramids, he found himself opposed by twenty-three Mameluke Beys at the head of their cavalry, drawn up in battle array. Having made his preparations for the attack, Bonaparte turned to his troops, and exclaimed, as he pointed with his sword to the pyramids: "Behold, and remember, that four thousand years are looking down upon you from those monuments!" After this short address, so well adapted to the French national character, the troops attacked the enemy, and completely overthrowing their whole army, advanced against the capital, which they captured, and now looked upon Egypt as a conquered country. But this success was very speedily changed into disaster. France had imagined that the Turks, who were rather in name than in fact the masters of Egypt, would view her successes with indifference—not so, however; for on the contrary, they regarded the matter more seriously, and renouncing their alliance of three hundred years with that country, united with the other states against that power. England now clearly perceiving the great importance arising from this expedition, strained every nerve to defeat and destroy it; Admiral Nelson, the great naval hero, after a long search, came up with the French fleet on the 1st of August, in the bay of Aboukir, and although the sun had already set, he nevertheless, with his usual undaunted valor, formed his plan of battle and commenced the action, broke through the enemy's line of battle, and gained a glorious victory; having completely annihilated the French fleet, of which the admiral's ship itself, L'Orient, was blown up with more than one thousand of her crew. By this victory, Bonaparte found himself completely separated from Europe, and cut off from all succor; while, in the mean time, the most formidable preparations were being made by the coalesced powers for the war against France.

The emperor of Austria now, at the commencement of the year 1799, recalled his ambassador from the congress at Rastadt, and the meeting of plenipotentiaries was dissolved. On the 6th of March, the

French republic, according to its system of always anticipating the measures of its enemies, declared war once more against the emperor of Austria, for having allowed the Russian army to enter the Austrian territory.

In Italy the war had commenced a few months sooner; for the queen of Naples, a violent enemy of the French, would not wait for the moment of general attack, but caused the Neapolitan troops, in November, 1798, to advance against the Roman territories; an impatience, however, which produced very bad results. The French, with their usual celerity, directed their whole operations against that quarter, and driving the king of Naples with his family out of Sicily, they took possession of Lower Italy, as far as Calabria. The kingdom of Naples was now changed into a Parthenopian republic, and in order to transform the whole of Italy into one entire republic, the states of Genoa and Tuscany were declared free states.

This time, however, these new creations had but a short existence, for the armies of the allies now marched forth from every side to open the campaign, led on by able and well-tried generals. The French directory had lost much of its former influence and power even in France itself: La Vendée had again taken up arms, the French armies were for the greater part badly conducted, and in the government of the state, as well as in the administration of war, the greatest lethargy and disorder prevailed. Added to this, Archduke Charles completely overthrew General Jourdan at Stockach, as well as in several other encounters, and drove him out of Germany; while from General Masséna he reconquered the whole of the western portion of Switzerland beyond Zurich itself, and then awaited on the banks of the Rhine the results of the war in Italy.

There the French army was under the orders of General Scherer, a man of a licentious character and addicted to drink. Defeated by the Austrian general, Kray, at Verona and at Magnano, he resigned the command into the hands of Moreau, when the latter found the army reduced to a state of the greatest disorganization and confusion. At this moment Marshal Suwaroff, an old but active, daring warrior, with his Russians, formed a junction with the Austrian army in Italy. Against such an adversary Moreau found it impossible to make head with the ill-conditioned troops under his command. Accordingly Suwaroff completely defeated him on the 27th of April, near Cassano, and on the day following entered Milan in triumph. By this victory the whole of Lombardy was reconquered, the Cisalpine republic destroyed, and the north of Italy restored to the house of Austria. After this the Russian general marched against Macdonald, who had returned with the French army from Naples, and beat him, in the month of June, in several sanguinary actions on the banks of the Trebia, nearly on the same spot where Hannibal vanquished the Romans. The whole of Italy as far as the states of Genoa was retaken from the French, all the fortresses were besieged and captured, the republican governments disappeared one after the other, and the ancient duchies were restored.

Meantime General Joubert had collected another army; but he met with the same fate as his predecessors. On the 15th of August the hard-fought battle of Novi, which continued for twenty hours, was fought, in which Joubert himself fell mortally wounded. Genoa was now the only city that remained in the hands of the French. Leaving the siege of this place to be conducted by the Austrians alone, Suwaroff directed his march towards the Alps, in order to penetrate into Switzerland and to make himself master of that gigantic fortress of nature—the bulwark of France. When he arrived at the foot of those vast mountains, the summits of which, towering to the very heavens above, became lost in the mist of the clouds, his warriors were struck with awe and dread at a scene of such majestic grandeur, by them wholly unknown amidst their own vast plains, and they hesitated for a moment before they ventured to ascend the rocky, precipitous heights. Beholding this, the veteran general, who commanded the entire devotion of his soldiers, threw himself upon the ground before them, and exclaimed: "Behold, comrades! rather than return, my body shall be buried here at the foot of these mountains, so that the world may know that you have abandoned your leader, Suwaroff, on this spot!" The soldiers, struck with shame and confusion at these words, delayed no longer, but marching forth with reanimated vigor and courage, they commenced the ascent of St. Gothard, and passing onward through its intricate defiles amidst constant fighting, gained the Devil's bridge, and thence descended into the valley of Luzern.

During this interval, however, Masséna having by a successful manœuvre taken the Russian general, Korsakow, by surprise, completely overthrew him; while General Soult defeated the Austrians under Hotze in the neighborhood of Zurich. Suwaroff's object was to join the Austrians; but after their defeat it became impossible to save Switzerland, and the war could not be protracted in a country so poor that no supplies were to be obtained for the troops. Accordingly, Suwaroff retreated to Feldkirch in Swabia, directing his march through Graubündten, across such narrow passes that his soldiers were only able to march in single file: a retreat accomplished in such a masterly style that he lost not a single man. Shortly afterwards he was recalled with his whole army, and he returned to Russia. The Russians had only shared in this one campaign with the Austrians; but it was a campaign almost unparalleled in the annals of war, both in respect to the deeds accomplished, and the profitable results produced. For, besides the several battles gained, eight strong fortresses, and no less than five thousand pieces of artillery, had been taken.

The restless and false character of the emperor Paul, who pretended that he was neglected and insulted by his allies, was the cause of the sudden termination of the alliance. An attempt had been made in the autumn of this year to invade Holland with a combined force of English and Russian troops; but through various blunders which occurred in the expedition, it turned out unsuccessful, and this result produced more especially the discontent of the emperor of Russia. Thence France, through this ill success of her adversaries in Holland, and by her repossession of Switzerland, was delivered from the great and more immediate danger with which she had been threatened. Nevertheless, she was not yet altogether free from difficulty; for the victorious troops of Austria, after having reconquered Italy, maintained their position on the banks of the Rhine, which they made preparations for crossing in conjunction with the rest of the imperial forces, which had at length resolved to join in the war; while, in addition to this, the government of France itself was in a state of disunion, and had lost public confidence. Bonaparte, however, now arrived to extricate the nation from its embarrassed condition.

When this general, who had during this interval been actively engaged in Egypt and Syria, learned the dangers that threatened France, the unsuccessful battles fought, and the loss of Italy, he quitted his then scene of action in the east, without waiting to be recalled, and, with only a few followers, hoisted sail homeward. Having, with daring courage, miraculously escaped the vigilance of the British fleet, he landed on the 9th of October at Frejus, and appeared suddenly, and to the wonderment of all, in Paris itself. His presence, thus unexpectedly, produced considerable alarm among those to whom his arrival was any thing but welcome, and to whom his ambition was well known; others again, who had already witnessed and appreciated the victories he had gained, and by which he had been the means of producing peace, hailed his reappearance as the harbinger of a beneficial change in the state of affairs; while the majority congratulated themselves with the sanguine hope that by his means their personal interests would be promoted. And truly he did very soon succeed in reforming the government of the country, which at once placed in his hands the predominating power, and he was chosen consul.

His first word was peace; and at this moment this was his principal object in order to fix himself more securely in the new power he commanded; but all the other nations, doubtful of his faith, refused to receive his offers of peace. "Well then!" he exclaimed, "we must conquer peace ourselves." And these striking words were soon re-echoed throughout the country, operating with such powerful influence, that a numerous and well-appointed army was already assembled for action in the spring of the year 1800, at Dijon.

The Austrian army closely besieged Genoa on every side, and however bravely defended by Masséna, still, owing to the want of provisions, disease and misery prevailed to such a dreadful extent throughout that populous city, that great numbers of the wretched inhabitants perished daily. The idea of any aid being furnished across the Alps, did not for a moment enter the minds of the members of the war-council in Vienna, and so far were they from entertaining such a suspicion, that General Melas received instructions to march across Nizza, and from this point enter the south of France. But at this moment the first consul suddenly marched from Dijon with the army of reserve, and leading his troops, with all his cavalry and heavy artillery, in spite of every obstacle, over the great mountains of St. Bernard, the Simplon, and St. Gothard, he descended to the other side, and arrived in safety on the plains of Lombardy before even Melas had been informed of his expedition; for had he known it, it would have been extremely easy for him to have annihilated the troops, corps after corps, as they descended the mountains. On the 2d of June Bonaparte made his public entry into Milan; and on the same day Masséna surrendered to the imperialists the city of Genoa, in which both garrison and inhabitants were suffering all the horrors of famine. The Austrians allowed him and such of his troops as were fit for active service to march out with flying colors.

Shortly after this, on the 14th of June, a grand battle was fought near the village of Marengo, on the vast plains between Alexandria and Tortona; a battle the most obstinate and sanguinary of all those hitherto fought in the war of the revolution, and in which all the destructive powers at man's command were employed to hurl forth their murderous effects during a space of thirteen hours. Both armies fought with great spirit and determination, and victory was already inclining towards the Austrian side—their valorous battalions having beat back the French in four different attacks, until their retreat was becoming more and more general—when, most opportunely for Bonaparte, Desaix, one of the bravest of all the French generals, and especially esteemed as a man by all, arrived at this moment on the field of battle with the *corps-de-reserve*. The battle was forthwith resumed by Desaix, and he was followed by the rest of the army, who rallied around him. He himself was mortally wounded by a cannon-ball; but his soldiers, rendered more furious by this, fought with such desperation, that they eventually gained the victory, which, after such great efforts, had now become decisive.

Thus was lost in one day the fruits of all the successes gained by the Austrians during the campaign; while the French acquired possession of the whole of Italy. Melas, who by this defeat lost all self-command, as all retreat into Austria was now completely cut off, abandoned all the Italian fortresses he held, except Mantua and Ferrara, on condition of being allowed to retire without molestation.

General Moreau pursued hostilities in Germany during the interval between the months of April and December, 1800, with a boldness and good fortune almost unexampled. On the 25th of April he crossed the Rhine, and already a fortnight afterwards he gained the banks of the Iller, having made himself master of the entire country between that river, the Rhine, the Danube, and the lake of Constance, and fought two successful battles at Stockach and Moskirch; thence he penetrated farther into Bavaria, and conquered the whole line of territory as far as Munich. The Austrian general, Kray, having now proposed a suspension of arms, Moreau consented, and negotiations were commenced; as, however, Austria would not treat without the co-operation of England, and as France refused to receive the English envoys at the conference, hostilities were resumed on the 1st of December. At the commencement the Austrians appeared to have the advantage, but on the 3d of December they met with a complete defeat at Hohenlinden. Moreau, after this great victory, advanced with hasty marches, and crossing the Inn to Salzburg, he proceeded by Linz and arrived to within twenty leagues of Vienna itself. Another proposal for a suspension of arms was agreed to, and the negotiations for peace were now resumed with greater determination at Lunéville. This subsequent treaty of peace concluded at Lunéville, owed its origin entirely to the exploits of Moreau in this campaign; for, in the short space of eight months, of which four had been devoted to a suspension of arms, he had crossed the Rhine, the Danube, the Lech, the Iller, the Inn, the Salza, and the Ens; he had been conqueror in six grand battles, and had enriched the treasury of the republic with 40,000,000 francs.

After the losses of the year 1800, England absolved the emperor of Germany from all his obligations previously entered into not to make a separate peace; whence the negotiations between the Austrian envoy, Count Cobenzl, and Joseph Bonaparte, the eldest brother of the first consul, were carried on with such dispatch, that the treaty of peace was signed on the 9th of February, 1801; which treaty confirmed that of Campo-Formio in all its points, and Austria acknowledged therein the Batavian, Helvetic, Ligurian, and Cisalpine republics. A fresh condition which had not been included in the treaty of Campo-Formio was now added, inasmuch as it was agreed that the duke of Parma, a near relation of the king of Spain, should be elevated to the rank of a king, with the title of king of Etruria, such being the name into which that of Tuscany had now become changed; the grand-duke, on the other hand, in return for his duchy, received in Germany the archbishopric of Salzburg as a temporal principality, together with other frontier territories, and the title of elector. The duke of Modena likewise received, as had been already agreed upon at Campo-Formio, the margraviate of Breisgau as an indemnity for the losses he had suffered in Italy.

Besides these concessions made by Germany to the princes of Italy, who were thus transplanted among us, great changes were effected within the empire itself; for Germany ceded to France the whole of the left bank of the Rhine, consisting of twelve hundred square miles of territory, and four millions of inhabitants; while all those princes, who were losers on that side of the river, were to be indemnified with the ecclesiastical possessions and the imperial cities, situated on the right bank. A diet, appointed for the regulation and adjustment of the rights of all interested, was assembled under the mediation of France and Russia. Its sittings were opened on the 24th of August, 1802, and terminated on the 10th of May, 1803. In these conferences, France dictated the law with even still greater authority and arrogant arbitrariness than formerly at the peace of Westphalia. She granted or refused her favor according to her caprice, and thus established her influence over dependent Germany more firmly than ever.

The peace of Lunéville deprived the ecclesiastics of all their domains in Germany, even to the very last in the list; of forty-eight imperial cities only six now remained: Lübeck, Hamburg, Bremen, Frankfort, Augsburg, and Nuremberg; the counts and knights were made only mediately dependent on the empire, and of all the lay princes, four only received the electoral power, a power which, a few years later, lost all its ancient and venerating signification; for these newly-created princes were not allowed even the time to exercise their noble privileges. This was regarded as the prognostication of the approaching downfall of every thing; for, comparatively speaking, the changes introduced in consequence of the Westphalian treaty, in the administrative forms of the empire, were nothing. What had then been cautiously brought into operation, merely for a trial, the peace of Lunéville accomplished at once, without any fear or dread of the ruinous results entailed upon institutions existing for more than a thousand years. Such acts of spoliation could not but fill the hearts of all patriots with profound grief; for who could contemplate, without bitter feelings, the scattered heaps of ruins into which the raging storm had converted the once-beloved home? But, although the columns of the ancient edifice were torn asunder, and razed to their very foundation, still, on the walls were to be traced the symbols of its ancient majestic grandeur, and the remains of a powerful and prosperous nation, such as are recorded of few other nations.

A short period of tranquillity now reappeared once more on the continent, after the long war; but the maritime war still continued: for the great statesman who was at the helm of the British government, and who penetrated into the very depths of Bonaparte's designs and motives, knew full well that peace could never exist between the latter and England. The position of France and England towards each other, at this period, has been compared to Rome and Carthage in ancient times: a comparison equally just and happy. For, between these two powers existed a mortal hatred, and thence Pitt was resolved, similar to Hannibal, to fight a war of life and death. At the same time, however, many voices in England were in favor of peace, inasmuch as commerce was in a very depressed state; the embargo laid by France on the exportation of corn had produced a considerable augmentation in its price in England; and, finally, the national debt had increased to the enormous amount of five hundred and fifty-eight millions sterling. Consequently, Pitt gave in his resignation, in order not to throw any obstacle in the way of the said peace, although he could not, conscientiously, sign the treaty himself.

The peace of Amiens was concluded on the 27th of March, 1802, by the terms of which England restored all she had conquered from France, Spain, and Holland, except Trinidad and Ceylon, resigning even Malta, and her conquests in Egypt under General Abercromby; the former being restored to the knights, and the latter to the Turks. Such a peace, however, the terms of which, after the great victories gained at sea, were held to be both unfavorable and highly disadvantageous, could not last long, and in less than a year it terminated. England very soon perceived that Bonaparte's object, in desiring peace, had only been to increase his naval power, and, if possible, to raise it to a level with that of Great Britain, and make himself master of the Mediterranean. He formed alliances with the Porte, the bey of Egypt, and with the piratical states; and, soon afterwards, he prohibited all introduction of English produce into France and Holland. Thus England found she had no less cause to dread a state of peace than she had that of war; for, assuredly, she was as little inclined to submit to a rival on the seas, as France was to endure one on the continent. Other causes, however, soon operated to add to this discontent. It became more and more evident, that the new regulations and institutions, already brought to bear in Europe by Bonaparte, formed merely the introduction to those other grand plans of usurpation he had still in contemplation. The Cisalpine republic was made to acknowledge the first consul of France as its president; while Holland remained in the occupation of the French army, and was placed completely under the control of the French government. Switzerland, which could not be brought to agree unanimously to the new constitution forced upon her, was at once disarmed, and changed into a federative republic, it being declared, "that she was left to the free administration of her internal affairs, but, in all external matters, she was henceforth dependent upon France."

England, after these events, preferring open war to an insecure peace, determined upon the course she should take, and demanded from Bonaparte the evacuation of Holland and Switzerland, which being refused, she declared war against him, in May, 1803. Bonaparte had only waited for this opportunity, in order to take immediate possession of the territory belonging to the English crown on the continent, and already, in the following month of June, the French armies marched into Hanover, and made themselves masters of the entire country, wholly indifferent to the fact, and slighting, altogether, the consideration that it formed a portion of the Germanic empire, and, as such, could not be held or bound to take any share with England in the war. The moment was deemed too opportune not to be made available, and thus a new source was presented for visiting us with fresh exactions, for maintaining a strict watch over the maritime commerce of the neighboring cities, and restricting their trade with England. All the Hanoverian troops were disarmed; but thousands of them successively passed over to the British shores, and, forming themselves into a select battalion, fought, under the title of the "King's German Legion," against the enemy with the greatest courage, and sustained the ancient glory of the Hanoverian arms in many subsequent battles, sieges, and expeditions, in Portugal, Spain, Italy, France, and Germany itself; while at Salamanca, especially, the brilliant services of this corps obtained for the officers a permanent rank in the English army, as was afterwards confirmed by act of parliament, in 1812.

## CHAPTER XXXIV.

Napoleon's Consulship—Gains the Nation's Confidence—Restores internal Tranquillity and improves the Institutions—Napoleon Emperor of the French, 1804—His Usurpations—Alliance of Austria, Russia, and England—War declared—Napoleon in Germany, 1805—Defeats the Austrians—Ulm—General Mack—Battle of Austerlitz—The Allies defeated—Peace of Presburg—Dismemberment of the States of Germany—Naples—Joseph Bonaparte—Holland—Louis Bonaparte—Rhenish Confederation, or League of the German Princes—Their Degeneration—The Emperor of Austria lays down his title of Emperor of Germany, 1806—Prussia—Declares War against France—The Prussian Army—Battle of Saalfeld—Death of Prince Lewis Ferdinand of Prussia—Battles of Jena and Auerstädt—Defeat of the Prussians—Napoleon enters Berlin—The Russian and Prussian Alliance—Battles of Eylau and Friedland—Defeat of the Allies—Peace of Tilsit between Russia and France, 1807—Prussia's Dismemberment—Westphalia—Hesse—Jerome Bonaparte—Prussia—Lieutenant Schill—Napoleon's Triumphant Return to Paris.

The first years of the consulship were for France a period of repose, and marked by order, industry, and prosperity throughout the country; the most turbulent, as well as the most timid, were now tranquillized and breathed more freely, while the name of the first consul was repeated everywhere with praises and blessings. And even beyond France many looked towards him with sanguine hopes and expectations, as the only one who, after the recent period of savage and inhuman crime, could re-establish order upon a solid basis: nor did he want the ability and energy necessary to effect this desirable object. The power with which he made every thing yield to his will was truly astounding, whether we regard the promptitude displayed in his measures of administration, or the indefatigable zeal with which he undertook to condense into a single code the results of multiplied experience in public life. All that was held most valuable in the civil institutions of his period—the recognition of the rights of man in every thing; equality of the citizen in the eye of the law; abrogation of all feudal rights; liberty of conscience in all invisible matters; and a government which, in an eminent degree, combined the force of union in the execution of laws, with the advantages of variety of counsel in their formation—all these, and many other institutions, under the fostering care of that extraordinary man, were seen to grow, in the now genial soil of France, and to ripen into maturity, as a striking and praiseworthy example for other nations.

What might not this man have been to Europe, how different his history in the annals of the world, had he made real and complete this beautiful and noble picture, of which his zeal, thus far pure, in the cause of truth and justice, already presented, before the eyes of all, a glorious sketch! How might he not have been enabled, for centuries to come, to have led on the way to enlightenment, and having carried all with him, have merited the blessings, instead of the curses of all mankind!

Napoleon Bonaparte was now elected emperor of France, and thus, in the 11th year of the republic, his imperial throne was erected upon the ruins of the royal and legitimate dynasty; nevertheless, his ambition was not yet satisfied. Immediately afterwards, he changed the Cisalpine republic into a kingdom, and created himself king of Italy, together with all his descendants; and as a proof of his moderation, as he said, he appointed his son-in-law, Eugene de Beauharnais, viceroy of Italy. Parma, Piacenza, and Guastella, were now altogether united with France, as also the Ligurian republic. All these changes were contrary to the treaty of peace concluded at Lunéville, and gave great offence to Austria, who found sympathy in the emperor Alexander of Russia, now so much exasperated by the execution of the duke d'Enghien—shortly before effected by the cruelty of Bonaparte—and who already felt himself called upon to aid in the protection of Europe. Accordingly these two powers now came forward and made known to William Pitt, the prime minister, their wish—by him long desired—to renew their alliance with England against France. A coalition was immediately formed between these three governments, to which Sweden was added; and, according to their plan of war, the French power was to be attacked at every point, in Italy, Switzerland, Holland, and in France itself. Napoleon, however, overthrew this design, in his usual way, and by the celerity of his movements he was enabled to anticipate the allies in all their operations, and was already in advance of them when and where least expected. Since 1803 he had stationed nearly the whole of his army along the northern coasts of France, in order to operate as a check upon England, and where, indeed, he contemplated making a landing; now, however, the troops received marching orders, and suddenly abandoning their present quarters, they proceeded by hasty marches to the Rhine, which they speedily crossed, and forced the princes of South Germany to form an alliance with France; while the Austrian army, now under the command of general Mack, remained completely inactive in its quarters near Ulm.

General Mack, otherwise an efficient leader, was on this occasion entirely deserted by his good fortune, and evinced a total want of resolution and judgment; for, imagining the enemy would advance upon him direct from the side of Swabia, he quietly awaited his coming. On his right flank he had at command the Franconian territories belonging to the king of Prussia, who took no share in the war, and he accordingly considered himself completely covered in that quarter. But such a bulwark furnished but a poor means of defence in front of an army led on by Napoleon. Bernadotte, Marmont, and the Bavarians, disregarding the neutrality of Prussia, very soon advanced direct through Franconia towards the Danube, and attacking the Austrian general in the rear, cut him off from all communication with Austria. Surprised and stupified, he, after a sanguinary battle, threw himself into Ulm, where, instead of forcing for himself a passage with his sword through the very centre of his enemies, as any other brave and determined spirit would have done—and which indeed had been previously accomplished by Duke Ferdinand in Bohemia, at the head of only a few squadrons of cavalry—he surrendered himself prisoner, together with the whole of his army, on the 17th of October, 1805. Napoleon, after this first part of the campaign, during which he had almost annihilated 80,000 men, sent to the senate in Paris forty standards he had taken, saying, "They were a present from the children to their fathers."

The French army marched on without any obstacle to the capital of Austria, and took possession of it on the 11th of November, 1805. The Russians and Austrians had retreated to Moravia, and on the 2d of December the allied and French armies stood front to front near Austerlitz, resolved to hazard a decisive engagement. The battle—called by Napoleon the three emperors' battle—commenced on a beautifully sunbright, frosty morning. The allies, however, were not well supplied with leaders, and their movements, therefore, were not made in the best order; in addition to which, they were unacquainted with the strength and position of the French army, whence the Russian line of battle was very soon broken through; and, in spite of all their bravery, the troops were put to rout. The left wing sought to save themselves by crossing a frozen lake, but Napoleon ordered the artillery to play upon the ice, which speedily dissolved and immersed the whole of the fugitives within its deep waters, where they perished. Nevertheless this victory was not so easily gained, nor would its results have been so decisive, had not the emperor Francis, in his anxiety for his subjects, hastened to conclude a peace, and demanded, for this purpose, a rather premature conference with Napoleon in the mill of Saroschitz, for on the following day a body of 12,000 Russians arrived to reinforce the army, which had now rallied. In addition to this, too, the Archduke Ferdinand had collected an army of 20,000 men in Bohemia, and completely routed the Bavarians, taking possession of the whole country; Hungary was arming everywhere; Archduke Charles was now in full march from Italy with his victorious army to the aid of his country, and would arrive in a few days to deliver Vienna and harass the enemy's rear; while the Russians and English had now landed at Naples, and the Russian, Swedish, and English troops had already entered Hanover; finally, however, what was more important than all this, the Prussian troops were now assembling in order to revenge themselves for the violation of their territory of Anspach. Nevertheless the emperor of Austria, very anxious for peace, signed a treaty for a suspension of arms. The misfortunes of his country were a source of great pain to him, and he flattered himself with the hope that a peace, purchased as it must be from such an enemy at such heavy sacrifices, might still be rendered permanent; as if sacrifices, however great, could ever satiate the latter's inordinate love of conquest!

The Prussian ambassador, Count von Haugwitz, who had been deputed by his government to prescribe either the terms of peace or to declare war, found himself placed in a very embarrassing position after the resolution expressed by Austria, and, under the circumstances, he deemed it most prudent, instead of giving vent to the menaces as instructed by his sovereign, to adopt a more moderate and pacific style of language. The French, when they found this, expressed themselves thus: "That they could not but praise the wisdom shown by the Prussian government, which had never possessed a more faithful and disinterested friend than France; although, at the same time, the French nation was wholly independent of every other, and that 150,000 enemies more in the war would only have tended to prolong it a little longer." The Prussian ambassador ought to have given the right interpretation to this language, and feeling the dignity of his country wounded thereby, he was bound forthwith and on the spot to have made known the resolution he conveyed from his government—especially as Austria had not yet signed the treaty—a resolution which, nevertheless, six months afterwards, his king was forced to carry into execution. And Austria, had she seen that Prussia was really in earnest, would, without doubt, have preferred even a continuation of the war to a disgraceful peace. Instead of this, however, Haugwitz, without even possessing the necessary power, signed the treaty of Vienna, by which Prussia gave up the province of Anspach to Bavaria, Cleves and Neufchatel to France, receiving in exchange Hanover, to which England by no means renounced her claim. Thus Napoleon strewed the seeds of division between Prussia and England, well knowing that if united those two powers must be too formidable for him.

Five days after, the treaty being drawn up, it was signed by Austria, at Presburg, on the 25th of December, 1805; and by this peace, the terms of which were more severe than any hitherto made, Austria lost one thousand square miles of territory, and three millions of subjects—constituting its most valuable possessions. The Tyrol—ever faithful, and which had shown its attachment to the house of Austria, more especially in the last war—Burgau, Eichstädt, a portion of Passau, Voralberg, together with other lands in eastern Austria, were ceded to Bavaria; what Austria possessed in Swabia was given up to Würtemberg and Baden, and the Venetian states were yielded to Italy. In compensation for all this Austria received but a trifling indemnification, viz., Salzburg; the electoral prince of Salzburg being forced to leave that territory, which he had only recently received, and accept of Wurzburg, which Bavaria renounced. All these countries with their inhabitants were treated like so much merchandise, passing from the hands of one into those of another, according to the state of the market. Such were the principles of the despotic conqueror, by which he sought to eradicate all love and attachment towards the ancient hereditary princes of the empire, and thus, by destroying all national patriotic feeling, his object was to reduce the subject to a complete state of submission, alive only to the mortifying conviction of the service he had to render to whatever master he was placed under—whether native or foreign, of to-day or yesterday—and whom he was born only to obey.

In order to complete the ruin of the Germanic empire, the electors of Bavaria and Würtemberg were created kings, and they, as well as the elector of Baden, were granted the uncontrolled government, or rather—to use the more favorite expression of that period—the sovereignty of their lands. The emperor himself renounced all claim to the exercise of supreme power over their states, and thus the empire by this act paved the way for its eventual dissolution, and the storm gathered more and more fiercely, until it finally burst forth in all its fury, producing those sad effects which sealed the doom of our country.

The first word pronounced by Bonaparte after the peace of Presburg, was, as usual with him, the sentence of confiscation. The king of Naples having received into his territories an allied body of English and Russian troops, the French emperor immediately ordered his brother Joseph and Masséna, with 60,000 men, to march into and take possession of the whole of Italy; adding, in the manifesto he sent with them, "That the Bourbon dynasty had ceased to reign in Naples." This dreadful word produced so much alarm in the royal family of that house, that the king abandoned his capital and fled to Sicily, while Napoleon declared his brother Joseph king of Naples. This new throne, nevertheless, was not gained without the sacrifice of much blood, for the inhabitants of Lower Italy rose up *en masse* against the invaders, and defended themselves with great courage; but they were at length forced to submit to the French, who poured large bodies of troops into the country, and both Calabria and Abrazza were conquered and completely devastated.

Holland was next on the list, being likewise changed into a kingdom, and given to another brother, Louis Bonaparte, as his portion. That country, however, did not suffer by the change, as the new sovereign anxiously promoted its prosperity, feeling it his duty rather to reign for the good of his people than be controlled by the will of his brother. Immediately afterwards, the brother-in-law of the emperor, Joachim Murat, received the duchies of Cleves and Berg, on the Rhine, the former having been ceded by Prussia, and the latter by Bavaria for Anspach; and, finally, to

Alexander Berthier, who was the emperor's confidential adviser, was allotted the principality of Westphalia.

It was in the middle of this eventful year that the last blow was inflicted upon the constitution of the Germanic empire ; its dissolution, which already existed in the act, was now clearly and definitively confirmed. On the 12th of July a Rhenish league was formed, by which the kings of Bavaria and Würtemberg, the electoral arch-chancellor, the elector of Baden, the landgrave of Hesse Darmstadt, and the duke of Berg, (the last four as grand-dukes,) together with the princes of Nassau and Hohenzollern, and other petty princes and nobles, separated themselves from the imperial alliance, and acknowledged the emperor of France as the protector of their confederation. He commanded the right of naming the prince-primate of the league, who presided at the assembly ; of deciding upon the question of war and peace, and fixing the contingent to be furnished ; so that each war of France must become a war of the Rhenish confederation, and thus forcing its members to take up arms in her cause, even against their compatriots of Germany. By such sacrifices the princes obtained unlimited authority, without being dependent upon any tribunal to which their subjects in case of necessity might appeal, and without being bound to adopt any ameliorated measures of government. On all these points, the resolutions of the league were clear and precise ; but in all the rest, every thing was obscure and equivocal, in order that the protector's will might operate with all the effect of a law. It is unnecessary to pronounce an opinion upon this confederation ; its fate was very soon decided, and posterity will no doubt seek to obliterate all traces of its existence from our history.

The emperor of Germany, deposing the degraded crown of the ancient empire more than a thousand years after Charlemagne had placed it upon his own head, declared himself, on the 6th of August, 1806, hereditary emperor of Austria.

What protection, however, Germany had to expect from her new self-made guardian, when compared with that afforded her by the house of Austria, was immediately shown. For, at the very moment itself, when the French envoy, Bacher, renewed the assurance that France would never extend her frontiers beyond the Rhine, the fortress of Wesel was arbitrarily taken possession of by the French, and chosen as the head-quarters of the seventy-fifth division of their army.

The hostile designs contemplated by the formation of the Rhenish confederation were directed against Prussia as well as Austria ; for both powers beheld those who had remained their natural allies during the existence of the imperial government, now changed into enemies, ready to declare their hostility towards them at the first outbreak with France. Napoleon had up to this moment tantalized the king of Prussia with the prospect of being able to form, under his protection, an alliance in the north, embracing the whole of that portion of Germany, after the model of that of the Rhine ; now, however, such alliance was completely repudiated, and even the restoration of Hanover to England was not withheld by France. Every thing, indeed, was done to mortify Prussia, and make it evident that the French emperor was resolved not to endure the existence of any independent nation beside his own. At length the indignant king felt himself called upon to protect his country against farther insult and humiliation from the hands of the insolent invader, and in this determination he was supported by the voice of his army and the nation throughout. Accordingly he demanded that France should withdraw her troops from Germany, that she should no longer oppose the formation of a northern alliance, and that Wesel should be at once evacuated by the French troops. Compliance with these demands having been refused, Prussia forthwith declared war.

When he received this declaration Napoleon said : " His heart grieved to see that the genius of evil swayed continually, and ever frustrated his plans for the promotion of the peace of Europe and the happiness of his contemporaries." He now assembled his armies, which were all ready for action, in France and Swabia, and he advanced with rapid marches towards the Thuringian forest. On the north side of this forest was posted the grand Prussian army under the orders of the duke of Brunswick, an intrepid but old soldier of seventy-two years of age, and whose principal officers were in a state of disunion. Only a very small portion of the Prussian army had taken any share in the war of the Revolution, and thus been enabled to make themselves acquainted with the lightning-like celerity of movement now practised by the French armies in all their operations; the majority had abandoned themselves to ease and indifference during the long peace of three-and-forty years, and it was because the outward form of the institutions of Frederick the Great still existed, that their continued reliance upon themselves became the more dangerous. Not that either courage or capacity was wanting in many individuals, but they were altogether without that energetic genius so necessary to unite the whole. Thence they were forced to experience—what indeed the most pusillanimous among them could never have thought possible—that, as in the wars of the ancient world, one unlucky day decided the fate of an entire kingdom.

On the 10th of October, Prince Lewis of Prussia, the king's cousin, in his impetuous warlike ardor, imprudently engaged the enemy in an equal contest near Saalfeld, and was mortally wounded on the spot. This unfortunate affair laid open for the French the entire route of the Saale, and advancing now with a superior force, they surrounded the left flank of the Prussian army, and cut off all communication with Saxony; hence, on the 13th of October, Davoust was already in possession of Naumburg. The supplies of the Prussians were lost, which reduced the whole army to a state of the greatest want, unavoidably producing depression and disorganization, and in this condition the troops were called upon to fight, having the Saale and the Elbe in front of them instead of in their rear: thus the army was vanquished already before the battle.

A portion of the Prussian army was at Auerstädt, under the command of the duke of Brunswick; and the other, under the orders of the prince of Hohenlohe, was stationed at Jena and Vierzehnheiligen, but both without at all acting in combination with each other; and they were accordingly attacked and defeated on the same day. Marshal Davoust fought at Auerstädt, and Napoleon at Jena. The duke of Brunswick at the very commencement of the battle was killed by a cannon-ball; his death disarranged the plan of the battle and threw the army into confusion. The desperate courage of a few scattered regiments could neither compensate for the want of the co-operation of the whole army, nor effect a general restoration of confidence. Surrounded on every side, the Prussians retreated in the direction of Weimar, where they hoped to find themselves reinforced by the corps under the command of the prince of Hohenlohe, not being aware that his army had experienced a similar fate at the same moment. They were, however, very soon undeceived; for the disorder was so general in both armies, that in the course of the night, while the one army was retreating in all haste from Auerstädt to Weimar, it met a portion of the other which was in full flight from Weimar to Auerstädt.

Ten days after the battle of Jena, Napoleon marched into Berlin itself; and in less than six weeks from the commencement of the war, he had already advanced as far as the Vistula and made himself master of nearly the entire kingdom, containing nearly nine millions of inhabitants and numerous fortified towns—the fruits of a single battle, in which an army, which had hitherto maintained its character as the most distinguished body of troops in Europe, was completely annihilated.

This speedy conquest of the Prussian states—a conquest far beyond the expectations even of the emperor himself—had completely banished from the heart of the conqueror every feeling of moderation, and only served to excite within his ambitious soul a greater desire for unlimited dominion. Encouraged by his success, he declared in Berlin, that he would never give up that city until he had conquered a general peace; and it was from the same city that he issued the decree of the 21st of November, 1806, against the English, by which the British islands were declared in a state of blockade, British manufactures excluded from all the continental ports, all British property on the continent, and vessels that had only even touched on the shores of Albion, were to be seized. This unheard-of system might have crushed the commercial prosperity of England; but the results, as it turned out, were more injurious to the continent. For England, now taking possession of all the colonies of Europe, cultivated their soil with great care and industry, and instead of importing the timber for the construction of her ships from the north of Europe, supplied herself therewith from Canada and Ireland; while Europe itself found its commerce languish and sink, and although its industry furnished many articles which it would otherwise have imported from England, it could not compensate for the loss of its commerce on the seas.

The remains of the Prussian army under Kalkreuth and Lestocq, now made more wise by the bitter experience of the few last months, and rendered a more select and organized body of troops, formed a junction with the Russians, who now entered once more the field of battle. After several skirmishes in Poland, all without any important results, the two armies, amounting to nearly 200,000 men, again met in Prussia, and on the 7th and 8th of February, 1807, during the most severe frost and amidst a continuous fall of snow, they fought another sanguinary battle at Eylau, near Königsberg. The *élite* of the French guard were here completely annihilated, and the battle still remained undecided. The Russians fought with the most determined and unshaken courage, and the Prussians under the orders of Lestocq, arriving just in time to the aid of the right wing, which was hard pressed, bravely repulsed the final attack of the French with complete success. Both armies maintained the field, each claiming the victory; the advantage, however, was on the side of the allies, and it was generally believed that a fresh attack on the third day must force the French to make a retreat. But Beningsen, the Russian general, did not hold himself bound to exact from his army, already so much fatigued, such superhuman efforts, and he therefore retired to Königsberg. The French likewise withdrew to their old position on the Passarge, and an uninterrupted cessation of hostilities was preserved for the space of four months, during which the two armies strengthened their forces as much as possible; while, meantime, this overwhelming burden of several hundred thousand foreign troops dispersed all over her kingdom, inflicted upon ill-fated Prussia incalculable suffering and distress.

Napoleon, during this interval, hastened, with all possible activity, to lay siege to Dantzic; this strong fortification was commanded by General Kalkreuth, and was bravely defended by him, until, finding all communication with the sea cut off, by which he was deprived of all hopes of relief, he was forced to a surrender on the 24th of May, although upon honorable terms of capitulation. The Russians and Prussians, after having neglected to avail themselves of the former favorable and decisive moment, now advanced and attacked the French intrenchments on the Passarge. They fought with the greatest bravery, but the enemy having been reinforced by the 30,000 men who had just returned from the siege of Dantzic, and being likewise well protected by their strong intrenchments, they repulsed the allies, and were now, in their turn, enabled to act upon the offensive. A succession of severe and obstinate fighting took place from the 5th to the 12th of June, on which day the decisive battle of Friedland was fought. This hard-contested action lasted from the dawn of day to the middle of night. The Russians fought with great bravery, and the victory was decidedly on their side; but in their elated feelings, they neglected to exercise that caution which should always be observed, even by a conqueror. Thus, towards the afternoon, the divisions under Ney and Victor, together with Bonaparte's guard, marched into the field, and the fate of this sanguinary day was at once decided; the Russians were overthrown on all sides, and retreating across the river Alle, they fell back upon their own frontiers, and gained the river Niemen. On the 19th of June, Napoleon took and entered Tilsit, the last of the Prussian towns, and on the 16th of the same month, his army took possession of Königsberg.

A conference now took place between the emperors of France and Russia, on a raft erected on the river Niemen, at which a peace was speedily agreed upon, the dismemberment of Prussia was decided, and a compact for mutual support in the relations of Europe concluded for a fixed period. Napoleon, always so happy in the employment of cunning and specious language, of which he was a perfect master, succeeded this time, likewise, in persuading the emperor Alexander, that his sole object was the pacification of the continent; while all his plans were uniquely directed towards protecting the coasts against the insolent arrogance of the English nation, and to secure eventually the free dominion of the seas. He then pretended that his chief desire was to form a bond of lasting friendship with Russia, in order that, both united, they might be enabled to establish the prosperity and happiness of Europe, inasmuch as then, without their concurrence, no war could arise to interrupt the union of nations.

Accordingly, in this peace, Cattaro, Ragusa, and the seven isles (of the Ionian seas) were given up to France by Russia, who received in return, as compensation, large tracts of land, together with 400,000 subjects belonging to Prussian Poland; while Frederick William, who was scarcely able to call any part of his kingdom his own, was forced to submit to the most degrading and painful sacrifices, and ceded eventually the moiety of his possessions with 5,000,000 of subjects, including, among the rest, the city of Dantzic, which was now declared a free city, and the Polish territory, which was changed into a grand-duchy of Warsaw, of which the king of Saxony was chosen grand-duke. Thus, Frederick Augustus, who had declared himself a neutral power three days after the battle of Jena, and soon afterwards joined in alliance with France, was now king of Saxony and a member of the Rhenish Confederation.

In addition to all this, Prussia lost the whole of her territories between the Elbe and the Rhine, the greater part of which Bonaparte converted into a new kingdom—Westphalia—which he gave to his youngest brother, Jerome; to which he added a portion of Hanover, the duchy of Brunswick—because its duke had been leader of the Prussian army—and the principality of Hesse-Cassel. Thus the terrible ban was now at once pronounced and executed against the house of Hesse, viz.: "That it should cease to reign, for having," as he said, "always shown itself inimical to France, and for having farther, in this war with Prussia, maintained so equivocal a position." Such was termed the neutrality which Hesse had so strictly observed of her own accord throughout the war. The entire country was forthwith invaded and conquered, and the elector driven from his capital and made a fugitive; while the new king, a complete stranger, entered its gates in triumph, followed by a train of French officials, and, to the shame of Germany, mounted the throne of this ancient princely family, the descendants of the Saxons and Chatti.

King Frederick William was now left with only a small portion of his states and subjects, yet in the latter he found himself surrounded by a firm and devoted body of men; while he had the additional gratification of knowing that at least three of his fortified cities in Prussia—Colberg, Graudenz, and Pillau, bravely refused to accept terms of surrender from the enemy, and that two others in Silesia—Kosel and Glatz—likewise maintained a successful defence. Graudenz was commanded by a veteran, General Courbiere, who, when summoned by the French to surrender, and who represented to him that the king had now lost his kingdom and had crossed the Niemen, replied: "Well then, I will be king in Graudenz."

The king had placed Colberg under the command of Colonel Gneisenau, well assured beforehand that in him he sent a pillar of strength to that city, and one who would never yield. In addition to this, a free corps of light hussars had been formed in the neighborhood, under the sanction of the king, by a young heroic officer, Lieutenant Schill, assisted by others of equally daring character, which continually harassed and fell upon the enemy's troops everywhere around.

Meantime Napoleon returned to Paris, and brought with him, as tokens of triumph, the car of victory which he had removed from one of the gates of Berlin, together with the sword of Frederick the Great; while he caused two bridges to be erected in the capital, bearing the names of the two great battles of Jena and Austerlitz. His domination, indeed, was by this new peace raised to such a pinnacle of glory, and appeared in the eyes of all men to be so firmly established, that whoever would have predicted that ere the elapse of a few more years those very Prussians, then trodden under foot, would march into Paris itself, and, arms in hand, retake possession of their car of victory, would only have been laughed at and treated as a maniac. But those who could penetrate into Napoleon's character, might have easily foreseen that his restless ambition must soon hurry him on to contend for fresh conquests; but which, although acquired, only produced his eventual overthrow.

## CHAPTER XXXV.

Austria declares War against France, 1809—Battles of Gross-Aspern and Esslingen—Archduke Charles—The Austrians Victorious—Lieutenant Schill killed—Execution of Palm, the Bookseller—The Tyrolese—Battle of Wagram—Defeat of the Austrians—Peace of Vienna—The French in the Tyrol—The Mountaineers overpowered—Execution of Hofer, the Tyrolese Patriot—The Duke of Brunswick—His territory seized—His bold March—Embarks for England—His Heroic Death—Napoleon at the Height of his Power—Marriage with the Archduchess Maria Louisa of Austria, 1810—His continued Usurpations in Germany—His Campaign in Russia in 1812—Conflagration of Moscow—The French Army destroyed—Napoleon's Flight and Return to Paris—The King of Prussia's Declaration and General Arming of his Nation against the Invaders, 1813—Napoleon's Preparations—The French in Germany.

Austria was once more roused, and actuated by the same motives of honor as influenced Prussia in the year 1806, she determined at any sacrifice to revenge herself for the insolent arrogance and menaces of her detested enemy; accordingly she took up arms again, and recommenced war in 1809. Her own immediate territory, it is true, had not undergone the same treatment as that of her neighbor, but it was this very state of suffering and degradation in which she beheld those around her, that induced her to take this step. In addition to this, Napoleon had in the preceding summer held a meeting with the emperor Alexander at Erfurt, and there had renewed more firmly his alliance with that monarch, by which it appeared as if Russia and France had resolved to arrogate to themselves the right of assuming the character of arbitrators of Europe, and thus treat Austria, which for so many centuries had been the central point of the European powers, as no longer worthy of consideration. This conduct could no longer be tolerated with patience, for beyond a certain degree, patience itself degenerates into pusillanimity. Thence Austria's declaration of war was in all respects honorable, noble, and generous, for she came forth and entered the field of battle unsupported by any other power, trusting alone to her own resources.

At the same time, however, Austria, well knowing that on the present occasion she must not depend upon her regular army alone for her safety, resolved upon carrying on the war in all its extent and making it national. She issued proclamations for a general rising of the people to rally under her banners as volunteers; formed numerous bodies of them into regular regiments of Landwehr or patriotic defenders, appealed to the nation in the most eloquent and heart-stirring language, placed the princes of her own royal house at the head of the troops, and finally availed herself of, and brought at once into operation, all the powers and resources of her rich and beautiful possessions, to an extent never before effected: productive altogether of such determined co-operation throughout the entire nation, that if ever its immediate deliverance and permanent liberty might be looked upon as secured through its own united strength, such glorious results might be justly anticipated on the present occasion.

But now in 1809, as previously in 1806, Europe was not yet ripe for her deliverance; it was still necessary that the fire of purification should penetrate in all parts, and that the misery, already so general, should be rendered infinitely greater, in order that every feeling of egotism should be renounced, and the history of the entire world present the grand and unusual spectacle of a holy war, in which all nations of the east and west, north and south, should rise up as one single individual, animated by one spirit only, and, united by one common bond, fight for liberty, honor, and virtue.

What German patriot, to whom his native country is more dear and precious than all other possessions, can ever forget the fluctuating feelings of hope and fear by which he was agitated during this war of 1809, or the indignation aroused within him when he beheld the enemy he so hated and loathed advancing with his army, the flower of which was composed of his fellow-countrymen, the federalists of the Rhine? Who can ever forget how with this brave body of Germans he forced the Austrians by furious and incessant attacks to retreat from Bavaria, into which territory they had only just penetrated, and how in his arrogance he declared, that ere the lapse of another month he would march into Vienna itself? Truly, this was a disastrous period for Austria, and the actions fought at Pfaffenhofen, Tann, Abensberg, Landshut, Eckmühl, and Ratisbon, from the 19th to the 23d of April, although maintained with the greatest bravery and determination, ended in the complete discomfiture of the Austrian army; these sad results, however, were more especially produced through the fault committed by the Austrians in extending their line of forces to too great a length, and thus Napoleon, with his usual celerity of movement, brought his entire force against one single point. He was then enabled to advance with the *élite* of his army, and especially his cavalry, and by throwing himself now against one division, then against another, he succeeded by these overwhelming attacks in throwing the Austrian line into complete disorder. And it must certainly be admitted that on this occasion especially, he gave remarkable proofs of his military genius and talents. He appeared everywhere, and in the thickest of every danger at the moment he was required, his presence and example inspiring his soldiers with the greatest enthusiasm. Indeed, it appeared as if he had determined to devote all his strength and power this time towards the total annihilation of the Austrian army, for he followed up his victory without a moment's loss of time, resting neither night nor day.

The Archduke Charles retreated with his troops, which, in spite of the sanguinary days of April, still formed a powerful army, to the left bank of the Danube, towards Bohemia; while Napoleon advanced along the right bank to Vienna. The Archduke Maximilian defended this city for a few days successfully; but owing to its great extent, and the want of necessary means of defence, it was impossible to hold out a siege, and the place accordingly surrendered to Bonaparte, who entered it on the 12th of May; immediately after which conquest the French army resumed its march, and crossing the Danube, pursued the Archduke Charles, in order to inflict the last annihilating blow upon Austria. On the 21st and 22d of May, a severe battle was fought on the immense plains of Aspern and Esslingen, close to the spot where in former times Rudolphus of Hapsburg overthrew Ottacar, king of Bohemia. Napoleon, however, found that the Austrian army was more difficult to contend with now than previously, and he found it animated with a far more active and energetic spirit than when last he met it at Ratisbon. The heroic Charles, during the short interval that had elapsed since the reverses of April, had applied himself more especially to perfect his infantry in the improved system of forming themselves into squares, and thus present an invulnerable wall against all attacks from the enemy's cavalry; and in this object he succeeded completely, as was evinced on the present occasion. Every attempt made by the French cuirassiers to penetrate these masses was in vain; firm as rocks, they maintained their ground in the most cool and undaunted manner, and the furious horsemen were repulsed at each renewed attack, until at length, receiving the reserved fire of the Austrians, they were completely overthrown, and taking to flight, were pursued in all directions by the Austrian cavalry.

This firm and unshaken courage displayed by the Austrian infantry, the personal bravery for which the Lichtenstein cavalry were so much distinguished, together with the excellent generalship and heroism shown by Prince Charles himself, who was in every part where danger threatened, most combined on this great day, the 21st day of May, to paralyze all efforts made by the French, who were fairly beaten. The village of Aspern, of which the enemy had taken possession as the central point of operations, was now retaken by the Austrians. And now the archduke, availing himself of every resource, brought to his aid another powerful ally, by which still more to incapacitate the enemy. Thus turning to advantage the present swollen state of the waters of the mighty Danube, he caused heavy barges and other loaded craft to be launched down its course against the bridge of boats, recently constructed by Bonaparte. And in this he likewise completely succeeded. The bridge was torn asunder, and thus the French leader found himself on the left bank of the river, cut off from Vienna and the rest of his army; being now forced in that position to renew the battle on the following day, the 22d. All his efforts and tactics were, however, on this occasion futile; neither his cavalry, infantry, nor artillery could hold out against the Austrian forces. The battle was lost, and if Masséna had not succeeded in capturing the small town of Esslingen, the walls of which served as a rampart to cover and secure their retreat, the entire French army would have been annihilated. Nay—as it has subsequently been asserted—independently of this, it must have still been destroyed had the archduke followed up his victory, and immediately attacked the island of Lobau, where Napoleon had taken refuge, and awaited in the greatest anxiety, until the bridge was repaired on the other arm of the Danube; but being left unmolested, he recrossed the river, by which means he was enabled to return to Vienna. The field of battle, however, was covered with his slaughtered troops, of which the Austrians counted three thousand cuirassiers alone.

This decisive battle excited fresh hope in all hearts. Already, in various districts throughout the land, the people now emulated each other in evincing their hatred and fury towards the invaders, and shaking off their yoke. In the north, the bold patriot Schill again came forth at the head of his hussars and a numerous body of brave volunteers, and directed all his energies against the common enemy; while in Hesse another daring leader, Dörnberg, united with several others for the purpose of driving from the throne of their legitimate prince, the foreign usurper who had fixed his seat of government in Cassel, and thus the work of deliverance commenced in that quarter. Nevertheless, owing to the universal respect in which the law and spirit of public order were held by the people, there was a want of that co-operation so necessary, and the attempts thus made turned out unsuccessful. Schill, who had unfortunately found himself less supported than the cause he fought for merited, was forced eventually to throw himself into Stralsund. Thence he hoped to be enabled to set sail for England, in order subsequently to return at a more favorable moment to Germany, and recommence operations upon a more effective plan. Stralsund, however, was besieged and taken by the united forces of France, Holland, and Denmark, and Schill, with his little band of heroes, was unhappily cut to pieces. From this moment, terror and dismay produced their disheartening effects in every part of Germany, and deterred all from attempting to free themselves from the despotic sway of the ruling powers. They were, indeed, not only fettered in their liberty of action, but also in that of speech, inasmuch as Napoleon condemned an innocent bookseller—Palm of Erlangen—to be shot for having published a pamphlet containing remarks upon the humiliating state of Germany, and refusing to give up the name of its author. This tyrannical act produced such revolting effects upon the minds of all throughout Germany, that the feeling of bitter hatred, already excited so universally against him, became more and more confirmed and deep-rooted, and the cry of vengeance for the innocent blood thus shed did not long remain unsatisfied.

An event of a more serious character than those alluded to in the north of Germany, was the revolt of the faithful Tyrolese under Hofer, Straub, and Speckbacher. These bold and hardy men of the mountain had already driven away the French invaders twice from their land, adopting the same system of warfare formerly pursued with such overwhelming effect by the Swiss, and by which the latter so completely succeeded in humbling the pride of their Austrian rulers, and the flower of their nobility and cavaliers. All Germany rejoiced when it beheld on the summit of these majestic mountains that liberty still maintained her sway in the bosom of that home where all spoke the national tongue, and fervent was the hope that victory would crown those efforts devoted to so noble and sacred a cause Other hopes were now likewise excited, by encouraging events in another quarter, inasmuch as the English had, at this time, sent a numerous fleet to the island of Walcheren, on the coast of Holland, and thence it was expected a grand blow would be inflicted upon the power of France—all these hopes and anticipations, however, only proved once more illusive.

Bonaparte, after the battle of Aspern, collected reinforcements from Bavaria, Würtemberg, Saxony, Italy, and Illyria, so that he was now enabled to recross the Danube, and advance against the Archduke Charles with a very superior force. The passage across the river was effected during a most tempestuous night, and amidst the continual roaring of cannon; and on the 5th and 6th of July, was fought the grand and decisive battle of Wagram. From the towers of Vienna the inhabitants beheld the two armies drawn up in battle, and were enabled to observe clearly the movements of the right wing of the Austrians; when they saw these troops gaining upon the enemy and in full pursuit, one universal shout of joy was echoed forth from every quarter. But this welcome, grateful feeling of elation had but a brief existence; for, in the mean time, the left wing of the Austrian army had been completely surrounded—the auxiliary troops from Hungary not having marched up in time—and the Archduke Charles was forced to retreat. Thence, only six days after the battle, an armistice was concluded, and negotiations for peace were commenced.

The news of this unexpected reverse was very disheartening to the Tyrolese. Nevertheless, they once more united all their efforts, and expelled the French under Marshal Lefevre from their country, in the hope that, stimulated by such patriotic devotion, the Austrians would recommence war. But the misfortunes and deprivations endured by his subjects operated too strongly upon the feelings of the emperor Francis; while, in addition to his own depressed condition, the news arrived of the disastrous results of the English expedition to Holland. Accordingly, the negotiations were continued, and a peace was finally concluded. Meantime, the Tyrolese were again assailed by the French, now united with the Bavarians, and this time the invaders were triumphant. The entire country was surrounded on every side, and, in spite of the desperate resistance made by the brave mountaineers, and the consequent losses sustained by their foes, pass after pass, mountain after mountain, were conquered, and the whole land devastated with fire and sword—the brave defenders being either killed or made prisoners. Their heroic and devoted chief, Hofer, was seized, and dragged to the other side of the Alps, in Italy, and cruelly shot, as a traitor, in the citadel of Mantua.

Another hero, the duke of Brunswick, likewise made a brave attempt to reconquer his own possessions; but his efforts were in vain. However, by a bold and successful march he made with his devoted corps of twelve hundred men—the black hussars—commencing at the frontiers of Bohemia, and continuing his course over a space of nearly four hundred miles, and in the midst of the enemy's troops—he crossed the territories of Leipsic, Halle, Halberstadt, his own hereditary duchy—whence the usurpers had driven him—and Hanover, and paved his way to the mouth of the Weser at Elsfleth; there, with his brave legion, he embarked and set sail for England, where he safely landed, and was received with that hospitality and admiration due to him as an exile and a hero.*

Austria, by the peace of Vienna, was forced to yield Salzburg and several other territories to Bavaria; the major part of her possessions in Poland she gave up to the grand-duke of Warsaw and to Russia; and she was likewise deprived of her remaining provinces in Italy, together with the whole of Illyria; and thus she was forced to sacrifice, on the one side, all her possessions annexed to the sea; and, on the other, all her frontier line of fortified places, together with the mighty bulwarks of her mountains. These latter sacrifices were even more severely felt than the loss she now again sustained of two thousand square miles of territory, and more than three millions of her subjects.

The emperor Napoleon, by the peace of Vienna, had now raised himself to such an eminence, that all hope of reducing his power was nearly extinguished. In order to fix himself more securely in the position he commanded, and to exalt himself in the eyes of the world by an alliance with the most ancient of all the princely houses of Europe, he compelled his wife, the empress Josephine, to sign a divorce, and offered his hand to the Archduchess Maria Louisa, daughter of the emperor Francis. The latter consented to make this great sacrifice: "It was in order to promote," as was stated in a subsequent declaration of Austria, "the most sacred interests of the monarchy and of humanity itself, and as a bulwark against evils the extent of which could not be seen, and as a pledge for the maintenance of order, that his majesty resigned one of the most precious objects of his affections: and thus he formed an alliance, the object of which was to console and relieve his oppressed and unhappy subjects; to restore and make permanent the long-desired feeling of security after the sufferings and calamities produced in a struggle so unequal; to incline the powerful and overbearing to act with moderation and justice,

* The subsequent history of this heroic man may be summed up in a few words. He died as he had lived, the bravest of the brave, in the desperate action of Quatre Bras, on the evening before the never-to-be-forgotten day of Waterloo, at the head of his Black Hussars.

and thus establish an equilibrium, without which the community of states could only form a community of misery." The emperor Napoleon had now attained that point in his career, when the object of his desire should be rather to confirm, than with insatiable ambition to extend the conquests already obtained. By his alliance with this, the most ancient imperial house in Christendom, the edifice of his grandeur would acquire in the eyes of the French nation and the whole world such solidity, that farther attempts to augment it, especially by wars, would only have the effect of impairing it, and ultimately, perhaps, bringing about its total destruction. After so many years of futile efforts and incalculable sacrifices made by Germany for the establishment of peace, it was hoped that now the confidence and good faith thus shown and proved on the part of Austria towards France, must produce prosperous and happy results.

But how much was the noble-minded Francis deceived in the confidence he thus so generously and naturally expressed! In the same year that the new alliance was formed—the marriage having taken place on the 2d of April, 1810—the viceroy of Italy was elected successor to the prince-primate, now grand-duke of Frankfort; Holland, after Lewis had resigned the crown because he would not allow his brother to make him his agent in the destruction of the people, was now annexed as a province to the kingdom of France, "that country being," as was pretended, "nothing else but an alluvion of the Rhine, the Meuse, and the Scheldt, the principal arteries of France." And, finally, in order to show the power he possessed of doing as he pleased, and that no consideration should operate as a check upon his designs, Napoleon suddenly determined to unite with France the whole of the northwest of Germany, situated at the mouth of the Weser, the Ems, and the Elbe, together with the ancient free cities of Hamburg, Bremen, and Lübeck. His pretext for this was, "that a system of contraband trading with England was pursued along these coasts, and by those cities." Thus Germany found herself wholly deprived of her coasts and maritime commerce; the great river which had hitherto formed the natural division of territory between France and Germany, was now wholly under French dominion. In fact, an arbitrary line of demarcation was marked out across countries and rivers, as it suited the conqueror's caprice, so that it was easy to perceive that this was only the introduction to that which was to follow upon a much more extensive scale, and that the whole of Germany must gradually, and part by part, be drawn into and ingulfed in the one universal, final abyss.

Meantime, Napoleon was far from comprehending the legitimate means by which he would have been enabled to secure to his power, so newly established, and originally produced by the violation of all sacred and human rights, that fixed duration extending beyond the existence even of the founder himself; he was ignorant of the method by which to inculcate in the minds of his people the necessary faith in this lasting power, and all that he did only tended to produce the opposite of this impression. Already, in 1809, while in Vienna, he caused the pope, the venerable father of the Catholic community, to be made a prisoner like a criminal in his own ancient capital; and now he followed up this act of tyranny by annexing Rome itself to his own vast empire, and decided that his son, newly born, as well as all eldest sons of future emperors, should receive the title of king of Rome. Such acts called forth the most bitter hatred against him in the hearts of millions of men in all countries, and his name was pronounced with curses; but upon his iron-hearted nature neither curses nor blessings left any impression. His empire appeared to him immoveably fixed, and based, as it was, upon the strength of 500,000 soldiers, and an auxiliary force of innumerable spies, he felt secure in all his power. Nevertheless, scarcely had two years passed over his head, before the colossus of this mighty power was overturned, and the emperor of France forced to sign his abdication.

Napoleon now turned upon the emperor Alexander, and accusing him of maintaining a secret understanding with England, and encouraging the people of Germany to revolt against him, he forthwith declared war against Russia; he accordingly commenced preparations for this campaign, the results of which produced his ruin, and enabled the Germanic empire to throw off the yoke imposed upon it by the ruthless invader.

In the summer of the year 1812, Napoleon commenced his march for the invasion of the gigantic empire of Russia, with an army of 400,000 infantry and 60,000 horse, together with a train of twelve hundred pieces of artillery. The preparations for this great expedition had occupied him full two years; having collected together the most choice troops from all parts of Europe, and supplied and equipped them with every necessary *matériel* for the campaign. The first and immediate object in view was the destruction of the Russian empire; but there is no doubt that it was the intention of Napoleon, if he succeeded in forcing the Russians to conclude a peace, to extend his progress even to Asia itself, in order, if possible, to expel his greatest enemies, the English, from their vast possessions in the East Indies. He crossed the Niemen, and directed his march towards Moscow, where he arrived, and made his triumphal entry on the 14th of September, taking up his residence in the Kremlin, the ancient palace of the czars. Here, however, Providence fixed the term of his victorious career, for, scarcely had he established himself in his quarters before the entire city was a mass of flames, having been set on fire in more than a hundred different parts, and very soon this place, so shortly before the magnificent metropolis of the country, was completely reduced to a heap of ruins and ashes, and all the supplies upon which Napoleon had calculated, so necessary for his troops during the five months of winter, became likewise a prey to the flames. He had now only sufficient provisions to last for a few weeks, and as the emperor Alexander refused to come to any terms of peace, he was forced, at the end of October, to make a retreat; instead, however, of taking the route across Caluga, as the most wise and prudent course, inasmuch as the war had not touched that territory, he returned by the road of Smolensko, along the whole of which all the magazines had been sacked, and every thing laid waste by both the French and the Russians themselves. Thence the fugitives, amid the rigors of this particularly bitter winter, very soon experienced all the horrors of famine; which, added to the want of clothing and shelter, completed their misery. Disorder and insubordination spread throughout the ranks, and the light cavalry of the Russians now harassing them in every direction, night and day, their numbers diminished more and more. Nevertheless the common danger held together great numbers of the retreating army, and out of such an immense body hundreds of thousands might still have escaped had it not been for their more destructive and mighty enemy—the dreadful winter—which sealed their inevitable doom. But the pen refuses longer to dwell upon the horrors resulting from this campaign, which, in truth, were beyond all description. Suffice it, that out of half a million of human beings, who were led into this war by their arrogant chief, scarcely 30,000 returned capable of bearing arms.

Germany now saw the favorable moment arrive of which she must avail herself at once in order to throw off the tyrant's yoke, and reconquer her liberty. Prussia was the first to set the example. Her army, which had been compelled to follow in the ranks of the French in the Russian expedition, was, fortunately, in good condition to fight for the liberty of its country, inasmuch as the position it had occupied in the invader's forces having been the extreme left, it had scarcely suffered at all. General York, the Prussian commander, who was equally well acquainted with the sentiments of the king as he was with the feelings of the people, had no sooner gained the frontiers of Prussia than he abandoned the French, and hastened to demand of his king whether he should form a junction with the Russians. Frederick William, who was still in Berlin, which was garrisoned by the French, decided in the affirmative, and repaired immediately to Breslaw, whence, on the 3d of February, 1813, he called upon the youth of his dominions to come forth and assemble around him in defence of their fatherland. His appeal penetrated the hearts of all, and thousands of young men poured in and ranged themselves under his banner; Berlin itself contributing a force of 10,000 men.

In addition to this, the king summoned together the Landwehr or militia of the country, and on the 17th of March, 1813, he declared war against France. This bold and determined step, however, was not unattended with danger, for the French still possessed in Prussia and Poland eight strong fortifications, and more than 65,000 of their troops were in occupation of the Prussian dominions; nevertheless, Prussia was soon enabled to develop her entire strength. For the king, in conjunction with those around him, had not allowed the short interval to pass away idly, and the most prudent measures were adopted in secret in order to be ready at the desired moment. The youth had been kept in the continual practice of arms, mustering alternately in small bodies, at the appointed places, and thus the country was supplied with its brave defenders, uniting the power with the will to exterminate their hated invaders.

Napoleon, in the mean time, having determined to provide for his own personal security, had abandoned the remnant of his army in Russia and fled to Paris, travelling night and day, and arrived there on the 18th of December.

He immediately ordered a fresh levy of 350,000 men to be made, in order to replace, as he said, the loss, mentioned in his twenty-ninth bulletin, of 30,000 men and great part of his artillery and baggage; and when the king of Prussia's declaration of war was published, he ordered an additional levy of 180,000 men. The French nation, accordingly, accustomed as it was to obey the emperor's commands without a murmur, did not hesitate a moment to pour forth its youth, and to the astonishment of the whole of Europe, a numerically superior and well-appointed army was collected, which forthwith marched to and crossed the Rhine and advanced into Germany to fight for and maintain the glory of the French emperor.

At the same time, in order to secure himself a guarantee for the tranquillity of his empire, he appointed a guard of honor, consisting of young men of the most distinguished families, who served as volunteers, armed and equipped at their own expense. And as he had lost the whole of his cavalry in Russia, he collected together all the gendarmerie throughout France, out of which he formed a body of 16,000 cavalry; while to serve as artillerymen he collected together 30,000 of his marines. In addition to these troops, he received 50,000 auxiliaries from Italy, and the Rhenish confederation furnished him with a considerable contingent of soldiers. Thence he was enabled, in the month of April, to march into Saxony with several hundred thousand men, and as his army was continually augmented, he eventually entered the field with the gigantic force of 500,000 men. Completely blinded by his success in raising such an army, in which he placed his entire reliance, he would not listen for a moment to any proposal for peace. Austria took great pains in endeavoring to promote this object, and if his proud and obstinate mind had only partially yielded to the dictates of reason, he might have succeeded in retaining possession at least of all the territories along the Rhine. On the 31st of March, shortly after he had received the king of Prussia's declaration of war, he caused to be inserted in the government journal of that day, his determination, viz.: "that if even the enemy were to march into Paris, and take up his position on Montmartre itself, still he would not give up a single village out of all the conquered territories in his possession!" and on the following day, the 1st of April, he published a counter-declaration of war against the king of Prussia, and resolved in his heart this time to completely annihilate the kingdom as well as the very name of Prussia.

## CHAPTER XXXVI.

Successes of the Prussians—The Duke of Mecklenburg-Strelitz—His Daughter, the Queen of Prussia—Erfurt—Russia unites with Prussia—Battle of Lützen—Napoleon in Dresden—The King of Saxony—Battle of Bautzen—Hamburg taken by Marshal Davoust—Heavy Contributions—The Armistice—Prussia—The Lützow Free Corps—Theodore Körner—Austria endeavors to negotiate a Peace between France and the Allies—The Congress at Prague—Napoleon refuses all Concession—The Emperor of Austria declares War, and joins Russia and Prussia—Dresden—Renewal of Hostilities—Strength and Position of the Allied Forces—Bernadotte—Blücher—Prince Schwartzenberg—Marshal Oudinot—Battle of Gross-Beeren—Defeat of the French.

THE Viceroy Eugene was encamped with the remnant of the French army which had escaped from Russia, and a few additional troops, under the walls of Magdeburg, and found himself forced to leave the river Elbe completely open. The French were, nevertheless, anxious to maintain, at least, possession of its mouth, together with the important city of Hamburg, and General Morand advanced accordingly with the four thousand men who had held possession of the coasts of Mecklenburg and Pomerania; but he was pursued by the light troops under the command of three brave leaders, Tettenborn, Czernitschef, and Doernberg, who prevented him completely from gaining any footing on the right bank of the Elbe, and thus forced him to recross the river and retire to Bremen. The people throughout the whole north of Germany greeted their deliverers with the greatest joy and delight. The duke of Mecklenburg-Strelitz was the first to follow the example of the king of Prussia, and shake off the French yoke, exclaiming that "with the help of God, he would at any rate show himself worthy of the honor of being a German prince."* The citizens of Lübeck and Hamburg were not a little rejoiced at the change, and united together in order to promote the general cause of liberty. Doernberg, at the head of four thousand men, advanced against General Morand, who was now quartered in Lüneburg, and scaling the walls of that town, took it by assault, and mortally wounding their leader, either slew or made prisoners of the whole garrison. With this brilliant feat of arms General Doernberg opened the second campaign.

About the same time, the Viceroy Eugene suddenly attempted to advance from Magdeburg with his 30,000 men upon Berlin, imagining that on his march he should only have to contend against an insignificant force; but Generals Wittgenstein, Bulow, and York, having forthwith mustered together all the troops at hand, attacked him with a far inferior force on the 5th of April near Moeckern with so much fury, that he was compelled to renounce his design of marching to Berlin, and retreated to Magdeburg with heavy loss. In this, their first encounter with the French, the young Prussian foot-soldiers, after firing a few volleys, cast aside their firelocks altogether, and rushed upon the enemy, *club in hand*, deeming that the most expeditious mode of warfare.

As soon as the new forces of France had assembled on our side of the Rhine, Napoleon himself set out from Paris, and on the evening of the 25th of April he arrived at Erfurt. Thence he proceeded towards the Saale, and forced the allied cavalry to retreat behind this river. Both armies now approached each other and prepared for a grand and decisive battle.

When, on the 29th of April, Napoleon reached the shores of the Saale, he beheld the allied army immediately facing him, in the vicinity of Pegau. The Russians were commanded by General Count Wittgenstein, and the Prussians by Generals Blücher, York, and Kleist; while both the emperor Alexander and King Frederick William cheered on their warriors by sharing in the campaign. The French army, after a few skirmishes, advanced by different routes towards the plains of Leipsic, which Bonaparte had fixed upon as the spot to give the grand battle. On the 1st of May,

* This noble-minded prince was the father-in-law of the king of Prussia, who married his amiable daughter Louisa. The sad reverses and heavy afflictions it was the fate of this virtuous woman to undergo, on the invasion of the French, may be too visibly traced in the following pathetic letter she wrote to her affectionate father. Overwhelmed with the misfortunes inflicted upon her, her delicate constitution gradually sunk under their effects, and she died on the 19th of July, 1810, aged 34, to the great grief of her beloved husband, and the universal regret of the whole country:

"Memel, June 17, 1807.

"My dearest Father,—I have perused your letter of April last with the deepest emotion, and amid tears of the most grateful sensations. How shall I thank you, dearest, kindest of fathers, for the many proofs you have shown me of your paternal love, your gracious favor, and indescribable benevolence! What secret consolation is not this for me in my sufferings—how strengthening to my spirits! When one is thus beloved, to be completely unhappy is impossible.

"We are again threatened with another dire calamity, and are about to abandon the kingdom. Imagine my state of mind at this juncture; but I solemnly beseech you not to mistake the feelings of your daughter. There are two grand principles by which I feel myself strengthened and elevated above every thing: first, the recollection that we are not led blindly onward by chance, but are guided by the hand of God; and secondly, that if we *must* sink, we, at all events, will do so with honor. The king has shown, and to the whole world he has proved it, that he prefers honor to disgrace; Prussia would never voluntarily wear the chains of slavery. The king, therefore, could not deviate one step without becoming unfaithful to his character and a traitor to his people. But to the point. By the unfortunate battle of Friedland, Königsberg has fallen into the hands of the French. We are surrounded on every side by the enemy, and as the danger advances I shall be forced to fly with my infants from Memel, and then endeavor to reach Riga, trusting to Heaven to assist me in the dreaded moment when I have to pass the frontiers of the empire. And truly my strength and courage will then be required; but I will look towards God with hope and confidence; for, according to my firm persuasion, we are not suffered to endure more than we can. Once more, then, be assured, my dear father, that we yield only with honor, and respected as we shall be, we cannot be without friends, inasmuch as we have merited them. The consolation I experience by this conviction I cannot express to you; and, consequently, I endure all my trials with that tranquillity and resignation of mind which can only be produced by a good conscience and a firm faith. Therefore, my dear father, be convinced that we can never be completely unhappy, while many, perhaps, whose brows are oppressed with the weight of crowns and wreaths are as unhappy as ourselves; for as long as we are blessed by Heaven with peace in our hearts, we must ever find cause to rejoice. I remain, forever, your faithfully dutiful and loving daughter, and, God be praised that your gracious favor permits me to add—friend, LOUISA."

after having proceeded towards Weissenfels, he was met, near Poserna, by the artillery and cavalry of the Russians, who resolved to dispute his passage. This corps was under the command of General Winzingerode, who had been sent forward for the purpose of attacking the French, and ascertaining whether the entire army was *en route*. Marshal Bessière, commander of the emperor's guards, having advanced to meet the attack, was killed by a cannon-ball. The position was carried, and Napoleon continued his march on to Lützen, the same field of battle on which, two hundred years previously, Gustavus Adolphus met his death when fighting against Wallenstein. Here the French halted for the night; but when in the morning Napoleon was about to resume his march for Leipsic, he suddenly heard heavy discharges of artillery in his rear and on his left flank.

The Prussians and Russians had already well perceived that it was Napoleon's intention to gain possession of Leipsic in order to cut them off from the Elbe; and as they resolved not to leave him the liberty of forming as usual his own dispositions, and choosing the field of battle himself, they anticipated his movements this time and attacked him, on the 2d of May, when he least expected it, and imagined they could not possibly be prepared to give battle before the following day. Towards mid-day they pressed onward with all their strength through the villages of Gross-Görschen and Klein-Görschen, Rhano and Kaja, of which Marshal Ney still held possession. The emperor Alexander and the king of Prussia ascended an eminence in the rear of Gross-Görschen whence they commanded a full view of the scene of engagement, while their presence, now so visible to all, inspired the troops with the greatest courage. The brave and dauntless Blücher with his Prussians commenced by carrying the village of Gross-Görschen by assault, and immediately afterwards a most obstinate and sanguinary contest took place around the other villages, terminating in favor of the allies, who remained masters of the ground, and forced the French to fall back in the rear. It was just at this moment that Napoleon arrived on the field of battle with his guards and the rest of the troops he brought with him; and he lost not a moment in pushing them forward to reinforce Ney's corps, while he himself rode through their ranks and cheered them on, regardless of his own danger; for he knew too well that the loss of this battle must necessarily produce discouragement among his troops, and deprive him of his hold in Germany. The action was accordingly renewed on both sides with still greater fury around the villages, which were taken and retaken several times. For the fourth time the allies united all their strength and made a final attack, and were successful; they retook the whole of the villages and completely defeated the French, who retreated in great confusion as far as Weissenfels and Naumburg. When informed of this, Napoleon, according to the testimony of an eye-witness, turned round, and with a look of fury at his officers, exclaimed: "What, do *you* believe then that my star is on the descent?" He however soon recovered his presence of mind, and adopting one of those sudden resolutions, which, when brought into operation, disconcerted all the plans of his adversaries, he gave immediate orders to his general of artillery, Drouet, to bring together the whole of his cannon—eighty pieces—and planting them on one spot, thence scatter destruction amidst the ranks of his enemies: for such operations he always held in reserve the guns belonging to his guard—at the same time he posted sixteen battalions of the guard upon the heights in the rear of the village of Kaja. The artillery, with volcano-like fury, swept every thing before it, whole ranks of the allied forces were mowed down, the villages were reduced to cinders, and consequently they were abandoned entirely. At the same moment the Russians were hard pressed on their right flank by the Viceroy Eugene, who had now arrived from Mark-Ranstädt with 30,000 fresh troops.

Napoleon, urged on by his impatient desire to see the victory decided, continued to advance, protected by the unceasing fire of his sixty to eighty pieces of artillery, planted in his centre. Nevertheless, the Russians and Prussians, although almost overcome with heat and fatigue, only retired slowly, and step by step, and bravely maintained every inch of ground capable of defence, until the fall of night.

Profound darkness now enveloped the sanguinary field of battle; nothing else was visible except the alternate flashes of the cannon which were still discharged at long and irregular intervals, and the flames of the villages, which were gradually becoming more and more faint. Napoleon, having issued his orders for the operations of the next morning, had retired to his quarters, within the strong bulwark of the regiments of his guards; when, suddenly, the silence of the night was broken in upon by the clashing of swords, and a desperate attack, as if by magic, was made upon the French, even to the very guards of the emperor himself. This bold assault was made by a corps of Prussian hussars, led on by the heroic Blücher, who, with his usual intrepidity, resolved to make a last attempt, in order to serve as a warning to the French, that the allies were not yet beaten. He succeeded in his object; for the enemy did not venture a pursuit, but passed the entire night under arms.

This first battle may be truly characterized as a battle of *honor*, and, as such, it was a *won battle*. For, in spite of the great numerical superiority of the French, the allies had not lost a single color or cannon, nor had they, notwithstanding the heavy fire kept up by the French artillery, turned their back upon the enemy—while the force of the latter was 120,000 men, and that of the allied army was only 70,000. The amount altogether, on both sides, in killed and wounded, was about 30,000 men. The Prussians, especially, fought with such a desperate defiance of death, that several of their heroic leaders fell a sacrifice on the field, including the prince of Hesse-Homburg himself—and Generals Blücher and Scharnhorst were both severely wounded.

On the following morning, Napoleon expected to be again attacked; but the allies having taken into consideration the loss already sustained, and their great inferiority compared with the French army, determined to retreat, and, accordingly, withdrew across Borna and Altenburg on the Elbe, and took up a strong position at Bautzen: the Prussians crossing the Elbe at Meissen—the Russians at Dresden, and both the emperor Alexander and the king of Prussia quitted that city on the morning of the 8th of May.

On this same day, the 8th of May, Napoleon marched into Dresden, whence he immediately dispatched an envoy to the king of Saxony, in Prague, in order to demand his immediate return to his capital, and threatened to treat Saxony as a conquered country if he refused compliance with his order, and did not give up for his service the fortress of Torgau, and supply them with all his Saxon army for the reinforcement of the French army—granting the king only two hours for his decision. The dread he entertained lest the emperor, who now already occupied the major portion of his territory, should carry his threats into execution, operated upon his feelings more than any other consideration; and not daring to form an alliance with Austria, as he would have wished, he returned to Dresden on the 12th of May. The emperor met him at a short distance beyond the gates of the city, and they both made their triumphal entry—as ordered by Napoleon—the latter addressing the municipal authorities who were waiting to receive them, as follows: "Behold, here I bring to you your deliverer; for if your sovereign had not thus shown himself a faithful ally, I should assuredly have treated your country as a conquered state. Henceforth, however, my armies shall only march through it, and protect it against all its enemies."

On the previous day, the 11th of May, the French army having hastily rebuilt the bridge over the Elbe, crossed that river, the passage having occupied seven hours; during the whole of which time, Napoleon remained seated on a bench, watching the troops—French, Italians, and Germans—as they marched by, a sight which produced in him feelings of exultation. He now determined to attack the allies a second time in the strong position they occupied near Bautzen and Hochkirch, and whose force now consisted of 100,000 men, while that of their enemy amounted to 150,000. The emperor sent Marshal Ney and General Lauriston from Hoyerswerda to turn the right flank of the allies, which being perceived by the latter, they detached several battalions under York and Barclai de Tolly as far as Königswartha to meet them. They came up with and surprised an Italian division of 9000 men, whom they immediately routed, and captured all their cannon and ammunition wagons. But as the main body of the French was now advancing they retired, and fell back upon their own lines.

On the following day, the 20th of May, after a sanguinary combat on the heights of Burg and near Bautzen, Napoleon forced a passage to the Spree, which he crossed with his whole army; while the allies retired in the greatest order to their head-quarters near Gleina and Kreckwitz, as far as the mountains. The Russians formed the two wings, and the Prussians under Blücher occupied the centre. Although the movement effected by Ney had weakened their position, still they resolved not to leave it without a battle. Napoleon's plan was to cause the left wing of the allies to be attacked by Marshals Oudinot and Macdonald, in order to draw their whole attention to that side; while at the same time, according to his original instructions, Marshal Ney was to gradually surround their right flank. Early in the morning of the 21st of May, and before sunrise, the emperor mounted his charger, and with the attack of the left wing of the Russians, commanded by the prince of Würtemberg and General Milloradowitsch, the battle commenced. The charge was bravely met and sustained by the Russians, who being masters of the heights, had great advantage over the enemy, so that after an obstinate and severe action, the French were obliged to give way. The battle did not become general until about mid-day, as Napoleon waited patiently until Ney had made himself master of the position he was to take. The latter succeeded in his manœuvre, and forcing General Barclai de Tolly to retreat, he captured the heights of the Gleiner windmill, as well as the village of Preititz. This was a most critical moment for the allies, as this village lay completely behind them; Blücher, however, hastened to dispatch General Kleist to its aid, and it was retaken. Napoleon now saw that it was necessary to bring up his fresh troops, which he had held in reserve. He placed at their head his best general, Marshal Soult, and at the very moment that the Prussians had weakened their centre by the corps they sent to support the right wing, Soult was ordered to make an attack upon it. This was done with so much fury, seconded by the heavy cannonade kept up by the French artillery, that the Prussian infantry were forced to give way before the overpowering enemy, who remained masters of the heights of Kreckwitz. The allies now saw that they were placed in such a predicament, that they must either sacrifice every thing, and collect all their remaining strength to storm and regain these heights, or end the battle at once, as their present position could no longer be maintained. The same reasons by which they were influenced to retreat from Lützen, operated upon them in the present instance. The moment had not yet arrived in which it was advisable to risk extreme measures; as yet, they were not supplied with the reinforcements which were *en route* to join them, both from Russia and Prussia; and they felt certain that the emperor of Austria must very soon abandon his son-in-law and join their cause. Accordingly, they determined upon a retreat, and this they commenced about three o'clock in the afternoon, effecting it in such good order, that the French found it useless to attempt a pursuit, whence they suffered little or no loss. Napoleon, who was at that moment on a high hill, near Niederkuyna, had mounted one of the drums belonging to his guards, and thence observed the allies as they retreated; he then sent some of his troops to harass their rear, but the light cavalry of both the Russians and Prussians, which covered their retreat, kept them at bay, and he was forced to content himself with remaining master of the field of battle—an advantage gained very dearly, for his loss in this action was more than 20,000 men, while that of the allies altogether was not more than 12,000.

The allied forces retired into Silesia, and Napoleon marched in rapid pursuit of them. Each time, however, that the French advanced too closely upon the heels of their rear-guard, the latter turned upon their pursuers, and after hard fighting, drove them back. Napoleon, vexed at finding that his generals took so few prisoners from a retreating army, took upon himself the command of the advanced guard, and attacked the rear of the allies on the 22d of May, at Reichenbach. But his cavalry was completely beaten back, and a cannon-ball killed close by his side his generals Kirgener, Labruyère, and Marshal Duroc, his especial friend and favorite, and whose loss was acutely felt by Napoleon, for the marshal, possessing his entire confidence, never hesitated to express his opinions openly and sincerely, and they had both been school-fellows together.

On the 26th of May, Blücher gave orders to Ziethen to wait in ambush with his cavalry until the French arrived close to Haynau; and when, according to agreement, the windmill of Baudmannsdorf was set on fire as a signal, the 3000 troopers rushed from behind the heights, and falling on the enemy's squares with loud hurrahs, put them to flight, after making 300 prisoners. Colonel Dolfs, however, the leader of this brave squadron, fell gloriously while fighting in the midst of the enemy.

Napoleon now plainly saw that the allies were not to be overcome, and accordingly he proposed a suspension of arms, to which the allies having consented, a truce for six weeks was signed on the 8th of June. The French abandoned Breslaw, of which they had shortly before made themselves masters, and retained only a portion of Silesia; while, however, Hamburg, through unfortunate circumstances, now fell into their hands. For at the very commencement of May, when Napoleon opened the campaign, Marshal Davoust marched with 14,000 men to lay siege to that place, which contained but a very feeble garrison commanded by General Tettenburg, by no means sufficient to defend so large a city. The citizens, however, calculated upon the aid of their Danish neighbors in Altona, as well as upon that of the Swedes, who had collected in considerable force under their crown-prince in Pomerania and Mecklenburg. The latter, however, were anxious to possess Norway, and had already stipulated with England and Russia to have it transferred into their hands as the price of their aid in the war; and as Denmark on her part resolved not to submit to this loss of half her territory, she formed an alliance with France; and accordingly, on the 30th of May, the very day they entered the ill-fated city, the Danes gave it up to the enemy. Thus Hamburg was sacrificed through the jealousy of these two powers. Napoleon, embittered against the inhabitants for their independent principles, and the opposition shown against him, imposed upon them a contribution of no less than 48,000,000 of francs.

The news of the armistice reached Berlin on Whit-Monday. The public were by no means tranquillized by this information, but on the contrary, when they beheld the present unguarded position of their city, which was no longer in a condition to defend itself against the attack of the enemy, much disappointment and alarm was expressed—far more so than if the war had been continued. The king, however, soon succeeded in restoring confidence, by publishing a declaration, in which he assured his people "that this armistice was only concluded in order to afford time for the perfect development of the whole strength of the country. As yet the enemy was much too powerful to be overcome, and what the nation had thus far accomplished, had only served to uphold once again its ancient honor and heroic courage; now, however, they must become so strong as to be enabled to reconquer their independence and permanent liberty. He conjured his subjects to maintain their firmness, to confide in him, their devoted king, and the object so much desired must be attained."

Meantime, whenever he could, Napoleon did not hesitate to increase by his treacherous acts, the bitter feeling already existing against him, and the following instance presents another proof of his revengeful disposition. Major Lützow, with his squadron of hussars, had boldly advanced to the rear of the French troops far into Saxony, and even beyond, into Franconia, harassing them continually, and cutting to pieces or making prisoners of whole detachments, so that Napoleon was much exasperated against this brave, intrepid band. According to an article of the armistice, the Lützow corps was to have crossed the Elbe by the 12th of June, but it was not till the 14th that their commander received official intelligence of this condition, which it was thus impossible for him strictly to fulfil. On this, Napoleon gave orders "to destroy these robbers wherever they might be met with," and on the evening of the 17th of June, as they were proceeding to pass the Elbe, they were suddenly attacked in the village of Kitzen, near Leipsic, in a most treacherous manner by the enemy's cavalry, who were to escort them. The little band was easily dispersed, many were cut down, wounded, and taken, and a part only, with their brave leader, succeeded in fighting their way through.*

* This free corps, it may be observed, was an association formed of youths chiefly of the middle and superior classes, who united themselves under the command of a military officer of great gallantry and experience, the above-mentioned Major von Lützow, for the freedom of their fatherland. Their exploits were of the most daring and heroic character, partaking rather of the bold and chivalrous spirit of the middle ages than the

Meantime, the emperor of Austria came forward as a mediatory power, and endeavored to effect a peace; a congress assembled in Prague, and the emperor Francis proceeded to Gitschen, near Prague, in order to assist in person towards the promotion of the object he so much desired. Napoleon, however, felt his pride hurt when he beheld another power attempt to dictate terms to him, and refused to abandon any of the conquests he had made. Thence, although the armistice had been prolonged to the 17th of August, the negotiations were attended with no results affording any hopes for peace; while, in the interval, both sides were occupied in making their preparations for renewed hostilities. Napoleon's army received continual reinforcements from France, so that he was soon enabled once more to bring into the field a force of no less than 350,000 men, besides which, his faithful adherent, the Viceroy Eugene, collected in Italy another army of 60,000 men to defend that country against Austria—in case a rupture should occur between that power and France; and, on the frontiers of Austria, Bavaria was forced to support him with another army of 30,000 men, under General Wrede.

The emperor of Austria, finding that all his efforts to bring his son-in-law to agree to any terms of peace were made in vain, now resolved, without further delay, to join the emperor of Russia and the king of Prussia, and to take an active part in the confederation for the overthrow of the usurper. Meantime, the latter had been anxiously waiting in Dresden for the declaration of Austria, although he continued confident in his expectations, that by means of his cunning management, he would continue to hold that power in a state of inactivity. At length, on the 15th of August, his envoy, Count de Narbonne, arrived from Prague, and Napoleon, summoning his minister Marat, had a long conference with both soon after. They were seen, all three, engaged in earnest conversation, walking, with hasty strides, to and fro in the garden of the Marcolini Palace, the residence of the emperor; his suite, which was at a considerable distance off, watching their master with anxious looks, and waiting the result of this meeting, upon which the fate of so many thousands of human beings depended. Suddenly, Napoleon was seen to stop, and by a hasty and indignant movement of his hand, seemed to reject at once the offered terms of peace. War again! now sounded from every side, and spread from mouth to mouth. The emperor, however, his eyes still sparkling with fury, returned to the palace, and proceeding with hasty steps across the hall of marshals, entered his carriage, and galloped off for Bautzen and Görlitz, towards Silesia.

cold and calculating nature of modern warfare. Among those who joined its standard were many who are highly distinguished in letters and the arts, as for instance, the Baron de la Motte Fouqué, (the author of *Undine*, &c.,) Frederick Förster, (the historian of *Wallenstein*,) and more especially the gifted poet and gallant soldier, Körner, who fell mortally wounded. Even women, inspired with the prevailing spirit of patriotism, served in their ranks undiscovered.

The allies had, during the interval of the armistice, strengthened their forces to such an extent, that they were far superior, even in numbers, to the French; for Austria alone, when joining them, brought an addition of 200,000 men, and which was rendered the more necessary, as their immense army being distributed at various points, they were forced to advance against the French in extended circles; while Napoleon, who concentrated his forces into one circle, was enabled to attack first one point, then another, and thus decide the contest at once with the same body of men. The position of the allied army was as follows:

1. The crown-prince of Sweden, Bernadotte, who had likewise entered the field with 24,000 Swedes, was appointed commander of the whole of the northern army, and was instructed to defend, with a force of 125,000 men, Berlin and the whole of Brandenburg. Besides his own troops, he had under his orders the Prussian divisions under Bülow and Tauenzien, the Russian divisions under Winzingerode and Wallmoden. The latter general, with 25,000 men, consisting of Russians, English, Hanoverians, Mecklenburgers, the Russian-German legion, and the corps of Lützow, was appointed to oppose Marshal Davoust and the Danes on the frontiers of Mecklenburg.

2. Marshal Blücher commanded the Silesian army of 95,000 men, and he had with him General York, at the head of the first Prussian division, and the Russian divisions under Generals Sacken, Langeron, and St. Priest. The first general of his staff, however, was Gneisenau, who, from this time, became more and more distinguished in the field.

3. The main division of the allied army

in Bohemia, consisting principally of Austrians, but reinforced by a Prussian division under Kleist, a Russian division commanded by Wittgenstein, and the Russian guard under the orders of the Grand-duke Constantine, was commanded by the Austrian field-marshal, Prince Schwartzenberg, who, together with great courage and experience, possessed all that calmness and decision of character so necessary in the commander of such numerous armies of mixed nations. This division of the allied forces amounted to 230,000 men.

This position and the division of the allied forces into three armies were well planned, for whichever of these forces Napoleon might attack, he was sure to have the other two in his rear or in the flank. When, with his grand army, he pressed forward from Dresden and Lusatia towards Silesia, Blücher retired in order to draw him towards the Oder; but during this interval the main army of the allies advanced from Bohemia, and, taking possession of Dresden in his rear, caught him completely in their net; so that if he turned to the right along the Elbe, in order to penetrate into Bohemia, Blücher must meet him in the front, and pursuing him into the passes of the Bohemian mountains, thus place him between two fires. Finally, Napoleon advanced with a superior force direct against Bernadotte towards Berlin; the latter, however, followed the example of Blücher and retreated, leaving the Prussian capital exposed, it is true, although only for a moment; for, in the mean time, the army of Bohemia conquered Dresden and Leipsic, together with all the supplies of the French in Saxony.

The French emperor had little imagined the allies would have been capable of forming such a grand plan; and especially of bringing it into operation so unobservedly and successfully. On the contrary, he had calculated, as usual, upon availing himself of the happy chances thrown in his way by the errors of his adversaries, and in this he was supported by his generals around him. Fully confiding in the lightning-like celerity of their emperor's plans and movements, they comforted themselves with the assurance to which they repeatedly gave utterance, that their enemies must commit blunders which they would take advantage of, and falling upon their whole army, completely annihilate it.

The more wise and prudent, however, not coinciding with the majority, counselled their leader to abandon his position on the Elbe, which was too seriously menaced on its right from the Bohemian side. Marshal Oudinot, among other things, wrote to him, "That if he withdrew his garrisons from the fortifications he held, reinforced his army with them, and then retreated to the Rhine, distributing his invalided troops in good cantonments, and establishing the rest of his army in suitable positions, it might still be in his power to dictate to the allies his terms of peace." But such advice, however wise and discreet, appeared madness itself to that mighty and all-violent man, who held himself so much beyond all others in thought and action; and thus it was ordained that his obstinate pride and egotism should eventually produce the deliverance of Germany.

In order not to lose the advantage of making the first attack, he determined to turn all his strength against the Silesian army, and fall upon that division separately; while, meantime, to prevent the Austrians from advancing from Bohemia and harassing his rear, he posted Marshal Gouvion St. Cyr with 40,000 men at the entrance of the mountains near Giesshübel. At the same time Marshal Oudinot received orders to march, with his 80,000 men, direct against and capture the city of Berlin. If his plan had succeeded, his complete triumph must have been infallibly secured; but the old and expert general in Silesia was too much on his guard. For when he perceived, after several encounters between the 18th and 23d of August, that the main army of the French was now in full march, and was gaining upon him near Löwenburg on the Bober river, he refused to give battle, and according to the previously arranged plan, retreated to Jauer. Napoleon, who in the mean time had received hasty news of the advance of the Schwartzenberg forces upon Dresden, could not venture to pursue him; but on the 23d of August he, with his guards and the sixth corps of his army, commenced his retreat back to Dresden.

On the same day the brave Bülow came up with the French army *en route* for Berlin, and attacked it near Gross-Beeren. They had already advanced to within eight or nine miles of the capital, and Napoleon had already publicly announced that Oudinot would be there on the 23d of August. General Regnier had, by Marshal Oudinot's orders, already taken possession of Gross-Beeren on the 23d of August, and thus the road to Berlin being secured, he made sure of making his triumphal entry there on the following morning. But his hopes of the attainment of this grand object were completely destroyed, even on the very night before; for scarcely had the day declined and evening set in, before Bülow with his brave Prussians attacked the French with such fury in Gross-Beeren itself, that they were completely routed, and obliged to abandon the village in the greatest disorder, the darkness of the night alone protecting them from total destruction. In another quarter, on the extreme left wing and with a very small force, General Tauenzien had bravely resisted, and finally repulsed, the attack made by General Bertrand.

The French marshal now clearly seeing that he had to contend with a superior enemy, would not venture upon a general battle, but retreated in all haste as far as the Elbe, having suffered a loss of twenty-six cannon, and several thousands of his men made prisoners. Berlin, which had been in a state of fearful suspense, was now full of joy and rapture when the news arrived of the glorious victory by which it was delivered from the invaders, and thousands of the citizens poured out of its walls, and eagerly sought the battle-field, in order to cheer and rescue their wounded preservers, conveying all back with them to the city, where they were carefully attended to. Just about the same time, on the 27th of August, the French general, Gerard, who had made a sally with the flower of his troops forming the garrison of Magdeburg, in order to assist in the taking of Berlin, was attacked by the brave veteran, General Hirschfeld, near Lübnitz and Hagelsberg, and completely routed, being forced to shut himself up within the walls of Magdeburg.

## CHAPTER XXXVII.

**Glorious Victory of the Prussians under Blücher at Katzbach—Blücher created Prince of Wahlstadt—Battle of Dresden—Defeat of the Austrians—Death of General Moreau—Battle of Kulm—General Kleist—Generals Vandamme and Haxo made prisoners—Battle of Dennewitz—Battle of Wartenburg—General York—Preparations for the Battle of Leipsic—The French Army—Honors and Promotions conferred by Napoleon—The Allied Forces—Prince Schwartzenberg.**

Napoleon, on quitting Silesia for Dresden, had left behind him Marshal Macdonald with a body of 80,000 men, in order to hold at bay the Prussians and Russians. But no sooner did Blücher perceive who was now his opponent, than he forthwith advanced against him—for it was not his system to keep the enemy waiting long. He soon learned that Marshal Macdonald, with his whole army, was in full march across the mountains on the left bank of the river Katzbach, in order himself to make an attack upon the allies. The wary veteran allowed his enemy to proceed without interruption until he knew him to be secured amidst the ravines and narrow passes, when, the favorable moment having now arrived, he exclaimed to his soldiers: "Now, lads, there are enough Frenchmen passed over—come on—forwards!" And on the Prussians rushed after their leader, with re-echoed shouts, and soon the battle became general. This attack took place on the 26th of August between Brechtelshof and Groitsch, amidst torrents of rain. The right wing was commanded by Sacken, the centre by York, and the left by Langeron; while the heroic Blücher, as commander-in-chief, with all the fire of his youthful days, led on the cavalry himself, and, at their head, dashed among the paralyzed foe. Such an unexpected, overwhelming attack the French could not withstand, and, consequently, they were everywhere put to flight. One entire division, under General Puthod, which attempted to attack the Prussians in the rear, was, at Löwenberg, either cut to pieces or taken prisoners. Terror and dismay seized upon the whole of the French army, and they were pursued in every direction by the embittered Prussians. At length Blücher sounded the recall, and, in an address, congratulated his troops upon the laurels they had gained, and so truly merited, by their courage displayed in this grand battle. The results of this victory are thus described by him in the conclusion of his address:

"By this great victory we have forced the French to abandon the whole of Silesia; we have captured one hundred and three pieces of cannon, two hundred and fifty ammunition-wagons, two French eagles, together with numerous other trophies, and we have made 18,000 prisoners, including many of their superior officers."*

Henceforth from the day of this triumphant battle of Katzbach, the great Prussian general was called, by his army, Marshal *Forwards*, and in honor thereof, and as a mark of his own and the nation's gratitude and esteem, the king of Prussia shortly afterwards made him a field-marshal, and created him a prince by the title of Prince of Wahlstadt.†

On the same day that the battle of Katzbach was gained, and also on the following day, the two grand armies met and fought with great obstinacy near Dresden; but the results were not yet ordained to be decisive. Prince Schwartzenberg and the three allied sovereigns, after having marched with their grand army across the mountains which separate Saxony from Bohemia, and driven the French from their position at Giesshübel, arrived before Dresden on the 25th of August. The city, during the armistice, had been strongly fortified and supplied with a numerous garrison; nevertheless, it might have been taken if the attack had been made a day sooner. But the roads across the mountains were, in some parts, so impassable that twenty and even a greater number of horses were scarcely able to drag along a single cannon, while the convoys of provisions for this army of 100,000 men were obliged to remain behind, and the troops were reduced to the greatest possible want. Thence the allies were only able to assemble before Dresden in the night of the 25th of August; while Napoleon arrived in that city on the following morning, followed by a great portion of his army. His presence was quite unexpected, as it was generally believed that he was in the depths of Silesia. He had a short conference with the king of Saxony, and then gave directions for the defence of the city. The grand garden of his palace was already in possession of the Prussian sharp-shooters, one of whom shot a page dead close to the side of his imperial master. The principal attack was made about four o'clock in the afternoon, the allies occupying the whole range of heights along the left bank of the Elbe to the extent of three miles around the city. The signal being announced by three cannon-shots, the allied troops descended from their position on the heights in six separate divisions of attack, each preceded by fifty pieces of cannon. Having arrived in the plain, they drew up in line of battle, and the infantry advanced and stormed the French intrenchments, upon which their artillery, at the same time, poured forth the most destructive fire. One brave corps of Austrians succeeded in making themselves masters of an intrenchment defended by eight pieces of artillery, and pressed forward to the very walls of the city; but they were not sufficiently strong to maintain their ground, while Napoleon now kept sending forth from the city gates, and under shelter of his batteries, large bodies of infantry and cavalry. Both sides fought with great courage, and the city itself was much injured and many of the inhabitants killed by the artillery of the allies. The latter, however, who were forced to contend against intrenchments, ramparts, and masses of the enemy's troops, continually increasing in number, could not succeed in gaining their object, and accordingly, night having set in, they retreated and fell back upon their former position on the hills.

During the whole of this night reinforcements of French troops kept incessantly arriving at Dresden from the opposite shore of the Elbe, and on the next morning, at about seven o'clock, they were marched forth from their intrenchments. Napoleon's object as to force the allies to abandon altogether the neighborhood of Dresden, where he had established his head-quarters, and to drive them back across the Bohemian mountains. He had now assembled together the flower of his army, and even his guards, which were only employed in extreme and decisive moments, were now selected to share in the battle. His plan of battle was to occupy the attention of the enemy's right wing and centre by a well-sustained fire from his heavy guns, as if intending to direct his entire force against that quarter; while, meantime, the king of Naples, with a numerous body of infantry, and the *élite* of the cavalry, was to march on to Freiberg and fall upon the left wing of the Austrians; and, as the latter portion of the allied army was divided from the main body by the

* Once when Blücher's heroic deeds were lauded in his own presence, he exclaimed: "What is it my friends you are praising? What I did was accomplished through my own natural temerity, seconded by Gneisenau's presence of mind, but above all, through the Almighty's mercy!"

† Wahlstadt is a princely but spiritual domain in Silesia, founded by St. Hedwig in remembrance of Duke Henry of Lower Saxony, who lost his life on this spot in the year 1241, in a great battle against the Mongolians.

valley of Plauen, and the rain poured down in such torrents that every thing around was obscured, the French were completely successful, and came up close to the Austrians before they could be discovered. The attack commenced, and the heavy cavalry of the assailants dashed among the Austrian newly-levied foot-soldiers, and as the latter, owing to the deluging rain, found their firelocks perfectly useless, they were all either killed or made prisoners, of which the latter, amounting to 12,000, including their general, Mezko, were all marched into Dresden.

Among those who lost their lives on this sad day was General Moreau, who had just returned from America, whither he had been banished by Napoleon, and who had engaged to aid the emperor Alexander with all his knowledge and experience for the deliverance of Germany and Europe, in the cause of which he entered most heartily. Both his legs were shot off by a cannon-ball on the morning after his arrival at head-quarters, and while he was in conversation with the emperor Alexander. He underwent the painful operation of amputation of both thighs with the firmness and resignation of a hero accustomed to meet death in any form; but he, nevertheless, sunk under it, and died at Laun in Bohemia, on the 2d of September. He was an excellent general, an upright and noble-minded man, and one whose whole soul was so devoted to liberty that it was universally regretted he was not spared to witness as well as to assist in its restoration.

The want of supplies and of the means of their conveyance, together with the overthrow of the left wing, by which the high road to Freiberg was completely cut off, induced the allies to withdraw their forces and retire into Bohemia, more especially as news now reached them that General Vandamme, with a chosen body of troops, was advancing by hasty marches from the opposite side across Pirna, in order to cut off likewise the second grand route. Napoleon's chief aim was to annihilate the allied army, by forcing it to retreat across bad roads, and thus, by entangling it in the difficult passes of the mountains, destroy it by famine and disease, or, having thus reduced the whole of the forces to the last extreme, oblige them to lay down their arms and give themselves up prisoners. And truly the dangers to which they were exposed might have produced what he so much wished—but all his plans very soon rebounded against himself.

Presumption, ambition, and especially the sanguine hopes he entertained of obtaining the marshal's baton by a brilliant action, stimulated General Vandamme to march boldly forward, and he well nigh succeeded in giving the allies a decisive blow. But on the 20th of August, when he arrived at the entrance of the valley of Töplitz, he found his passage opposed by the Russian guard, amounting to 8000 men, commanded by General Ostermann—a phalanx of heroes, who firmly planted themselves across his path like an impenetrable wall of adamant. His own force consisted of 30,000 picked men, but who were, nevertheless, held at bay by these 8000 guards the entire day, who at length slowly retired, and disputed every inch of ground before the superior numbers of their foe; nor did they retreat indeed, until half their force was either killed or wounded, and their brave leader, Ostermann, had lost an arm.

Nevertheless, it was determined that Vandamme should not maintain the position he commanded, which was so dangerous to the allies, and he was again attacked upon the heights of Kulm and Arbesau, on the 30th, by the Russians and two divisions of the Austrians, who had come up during the night. His right flank was protected by the Geiers mountain, and by the road across the hill of Nollendorf he expected aid from the forces under Marmont, St. Cyr, or Mortier, who were likewise in pursuit of the allies, and were only distant a few hours' march. Both armies fought with great obstinacy, and the rocks and precipices around vibrated a thousand-fold with the cries of the combatants, the clashing of their swords, and the fire of their guns. Suddenly, however, appeared upon the heights, in his rear, what Vandamme at first thought was the very aid he expected, but he soon found out his mistake, it being, on the contrary, several battalions of Prussians led on by Kleist, and who were now descending upon the French in all haste. The latter were struck as with a clap of thunder, and no longer thought of victory, but only of their own safety, and a portion of the cavalry unexpectedly rushing upon the Prussians with the greatest fury, succeeded in cutting their way through and escaping. But the Austrians and Russians coming up now joined the Prussians, and they completely surrounded Vandamme and the rest of his army. From ten to twelve thousand men were made prisoners, together with Vandamme himself and General Haxo; in addition to which, eighty pieces of artillery, all their ammunition-wagons, two eagles, and three standards, fell into the hands of the victors.

This was an unexpected blow to Bonaparte; and while he praised the courage displayed by his general, he condemned him for his want of prudence. On the other hand, the brave Prussian general, Kleist, was honored by his sovereign with the title of "Kleist von Nollendorf."

Nearly about the same time that these glorious achievements were effected in the presence, as it were, of the three sovereigns themselves, the news arrived of the victories gained at Katzbach and Gross-Beeren; which was immediately followed by the announcement of the triumphant battle fought at Vittoria by the British troops under their heroic leader, Wellington. In gratitude to Heaven for these glorious results, the three monarchs ordered a solemn *Te Deum* to be celebrated at Töplitz on the 3d of September, in the presence of themselves and the whole of the allied army.

Napoleon now resolved to make up for the losses he had sustained by gaining advantages in another quarter, and appointed Marshal Ney, whom he had created Prince de la Moskwa, to succeed General Oudinot in command of the army which was to take possession of Berlin. The crown-prince of Sweden, Bernadotte, managed very successfully to deceive and draw him into the net, by pretending to detach 25,000 men from his army in aid of General Wallmoden against Davoust, taking care, however, to allow his preparations to be made known to the watchful spies of Napoleon, to whom the information thereof was very speedily conveyed. Ney received immediate orders to march from the Elbe with his 80,000 men, and attack all before him —under the idea that the aforesaid 25,000 men were *en route* for Mecklenburg.

Ney succeeded, nevertheless, in deceiving the crown-prince as to his intentions, by counter-marches, and on the 6th of September he fell all at once, with the whole of his army, upon the Prussians commanded by Bülow and Tauenzien, at Dennewitz near Jüterbogk. The Prussian army, which consisted of only 40,000 men, suffered a severe shock from this overwhelming force, against which they had to contend the whole day, until the arrival of the Russian and Swedish troops. The French generals used all their efforts in order to gain the battle; Ney exposed himself so much that half of his staff officers were killed around him, and his example was followed by Oudinot, who attacked the corps under Tauenzien at the head of his men; while Regnier continued for a long time fighting amidst the enemy's sharpshooters, as if seeking his death at their hands. But the courage of the Prussians was not to be overcome, although more than a third of their number became a sacrifice; and at length, towards the evening, when fifty battalions of the Swedish and Russian infantry, together with 6000 cavalry and 120 pieces of artillery, marched into the field and joined in the battle, the French were forced to yield, and were put to rout at once, pursued by the allied cavalry to the very banks of the Elbe, losing from 18,000 to 20,000 men in killed, wounded, and prisoners, together with eighty pieces of cannon and other trophies.

After such repeated reverses experienced by his generals, Napoleon gave up planning any fresh attacks, and had he only given ear to the voice of reason and moderation, he would, at the same time, have perceived at once that he could only defend himself for a short time longer in Saxony. But the presumption, wrath, and the thirst after vengeance with which his heart was filled, completely blinded him, and like the gambler, who in his despair stakes his all upon the last throw, Napoleon madly resolved to lose or gain all, and obstinately determined not to move from the spot.

Throughout the whole of September he was continually marching either between Dresden and Lusatia on the one side, or towards the mountains of Bohemia on the other, in order to inflict a decisive blow upon the Silesian army, or to keep at bay the main body of the allied forces in the latter country. The allies, however, took good care not to venture an action in an unfavorable position, and as he advanced they secured themselves in such a locality as completely prevented him from attacking or drawing them into a general battle. This continual marching and counter-marching harassed and depressed his soldiers so much, that they began now to murmur and express disgust at the war which but a short time previously they entered upon with such enthusiasm.

He now advanced once more from Dresden with his guards, apparently for the purpose of gaining upon Blücher, who neared the Elbe more and more; but he changed his plan, and irritated and furious at being so often foiled, he turned his march against the allied army in Bohemia, and on the 17th attacked them in a narrow valley of the mountains near Nollendorf, in order to force a passage on to Töplitz. Once again, and for the last time, the thunder of artillery vibrated here from rock to rock, and the sanguinary struggle was resumed; but Napoleon was again unsuccessful, and was forced to fall back with the loss of ten cannon and 2000 prisoners taken by the Austrians under General Kolloredo. On the 22d he advanced once more against Blücher, who took up a strong position on the river Spree, and on the 24th Napoleon was forced to return to Dresden.

This was a losing game at war, which the longer it lasted must turn the tide of fortune more and more against him; while, in addition to this, the want of supplies was felt increasingly by his whole army. He was now almost surrounded on every side, and only a narrow road across Leipsic was still left open for him, by which to keep up his communication with France. And even of this he was very soon deprived, for several daring leaders at the head of their light squadrons were now constantly harassing his troops in that quarter; among these was more especially Colonel Mensdorf, who more than once advanced to the very gates of Leipsic itself; General Thielmann, who, having abandoned the Saxon service, now devoted his arm to the allied cause, and made frequent incursions in Weissenfels, Lützen, Naumburg, and Merseburg; and, finally, the Russian general Czernitschef, who, with his daring flying cossacks, penetrated even as far as Cassel, and, driving before them the effeminate and voluptuous Jerome from his usurped kingdom of Westphalia, returned to the Elbe loaded with rich booty.

These bold operations were extremely annoying and injurious to Napoleon. All his convoys were seized, and the guards killed or made prisoners; every passage being so unsafe that he could neither receive or dispatch messengers, for they were sure to be attacked and robbed of their letters. He determined to put these daring intruders to rout, and accordingly gave orders to General Lefebvre-Desnouettes to march with eight thousand infantry and cavalry of the guard against them, and exterminate them. But he was met at Zeitz, on the 28th of September, by the Hettmann Platoff and General Thielmann, who so completely defeated him that he never ventured to show himself before them a second time.

Those events, however favorable to the allied powers, or disastrous to the French, effected, nevertheless, nothing decisive; while unhappy Saxony was suffering dreadfully from the presence of such large armies. Blücher, who in spite of his age still evinced all the fire and activity of youth, could no longer endure this state of uncertainty, and he resolved to form a junction with the army of the north, which had already shown the example by throwing a bridge across the Elbe, near Dessau, and making other preparations for more active measures. Suddenly, by a rapid counter-march, equally bold and unexpected, he arrived at Jessen on the Elbe, at the moment he was thought to be at Bautzen; and while, in order to deceive the enemy, he ordered music and dancing to be continually performed in his camp, he caused two bridges to be constructed during the night on the river, and on the following morning the Silesian army was already marching along its left bank. This was a bold and dangerous undertaking, for the army was exposed to the fire of two fortifications in front and rear, Torgau and Wittenberg; General Bertrand had likewise just marched into that country with 20,000 men, and had taken up a very strong position near Wartenburg. Scarcely had he established himself there before he beheld advancing upon him the veteran marshal and his Prussians, whom he little expected, and who themselves were equally surprised by the presence of so strong a French force. General York, however, at the head of the vanguard, immediately attacked the advanced posts, and an obstinate and sanguinary battle took place. The French, however, were forced to retreat after a loss of 1000 prisoners, and thirteen pieces of cannon; and the Prussians suffered likewise considerably, especially the Landwehr or militia of Silesia, commanded by General Horn, which eminently distinguished itself. Shortly afterwards, in honor of this victory, the king of Prussia conferred upon General York the title of "York von Wartenburg."

Blücher marched thence to Düben, and joined the army of the north, which had crossed the Elbe, and arrived at Dessau. At the same time the grand allied army broke up from Bohemia, and leaving Napoleon in Dresden, to the right, advanced across the passes of the Hartz mountains, and reached the large plains of Saxony. On the 5th of October, the army established its head-quarters at Marienberg.

Napoleon could now no longer remain in Dresden; the allied forces threatened to close upon his rear, and to cut off his road back to France. Accordingly, he marched away on the 7th of October, accompanied by the king of Saxony. He left in Dresden itself a corps of the army amounting to 28,000 men, under the command of Marshal Gouvion Saint-Cyr, and this circumstance shows clearly, that he had not as yet decided upon abandoning the Elbe.

He now directed his march against Blücher; but what was his astonishment when, on arriving on the 10th of October at Duben, he found the Prussian general was no longer there, and learned that instead of withdrawing to the Elbe, he had marched behind the Saale, there to be ready to form a junction with the Bohemian army, as soon as it arrived in the neighborhood of Leipsic. Under these circumstances there remained nothing else for him to do but to march to Leipsic himself, and to assemble there all the forces he could command. But before this could be effected, and every thing be prepared for action, he was forced to pass four tedious days of supense at Düben itself.

The whole of the French army had now collected at Leipsic, and Marshal Augereau having arrived from Naumburg with 15,000 of the old troops, including a corps of cavalry from Spain, Napoleon immediately followed, and entered Leipsic on the 14th of October. The greater part of his army was encamped near Wachau, about four miles southeastward of Leipsic, where they awaited the appearance of Prince Schwartzenberg with the main body of the allied army, for whom, however, they had not long to wait. His cavalry had already come up, and caused the French to feel their presence on that day at Liebertwolkwitz. Murat had placed himself at the head of six squadrons of the old cavalry from Spain, and was determined to give the allies some farther proofs that the former bravery of the French horsemen could still be maintained; but he had to deal with those who sat yet more firmly in their saddles. The Russian, Prussian, and Austrian cavalry fell upon them with such fury, that they were completely overthrown and put to flight, and Murat himself nearly taken prisoner.

According to official statements made at the time, the French army, originally 300,000 strong, now amounted to 208,000; the rest having been already swept off by the war. If from this number are deducted the 28,000 men forming the garrison of Dresden, it will be found that the numerical force of the entire army at Leipsic was 180,000 men. These forces Napoleon, on the 15th of October, drew up in a circle around the city, an action being now inevitable. The army was still strong and select, for all those of its ranks who had become tired and disgusted with the war had returned to France, and such again as were of weakly constitution had been carried off by famine and the severity of the weather, or had sunk under the infirmities and illness produced by their continual marching. The troops that now remained formed a firm and hardy body of men, defying all danger, and well aware that, surrounded as they were at every point by an embittered and vengeance-seeking foe, their united strength and courage alone could save them. At the same time the confidence they continued to place in their master was so strong and unchangeable that they regarded victory as certain, and themselves as invincible in his presence. At the same time Napoleon sought still more by every possible means to inflame the courage of his men. He created new leaders, made fresh promotions, distributed crosses of the Legion of Honor and other marks of distinction, while several regiments were furnished with the imperial eagle. Thus he celebrated a grand military fête throughout the entire camp, as was his custom on the eve of any great and decisive event.

On his part, Prince Schwartzenberg, the commander-in-chief of the allied army neglected nothing in order to encourage his troops, and in his address pointed out to them, that the moment had now arrived, when by their valor and firmness they must reconquer and establish, once more and forever, the liberty of their country.

## CHAPTER XXXVIII.

The Three Days' Battle of Leipsic—Murat—The Austrian General Meerveldt taken prisoner—Battle of Moeckern—Marshals Marmont and Blücher—General Horn—Total Defeat of the French—Bonaparte's Offers to Negotiate rejected—Breitenfeld—Bernadotte—Bennigsen—The Prince of Hesse Homburg—Prince Poniatowsky—Probstheyda—The Saxon Army deserts Bonaparte and joins the Allies—The Allied Sovereigns—Night Scene on the Field of Battle—Bonaparte's Slumber—Retreat of the French—Destruction of the Elster Bridge—Prince Poniatowsky's Death—Triumphant Entry of the Allies into Leipsic.

THE French army had so encamped itself around Leipsic that it commanded all the approaches to it within a distance of four miles, except on the west side near Lindenau, whence Napoleon felt secured from any serious attack, and where, about two miles from the city, General Bertrand was posted with the fourth division of the army.

During the night of the 15th of October, Prince Schwartzenberg ordered three rockets to be fired off as the agreed signal to the Silesian army on the other side of Leipsic, which was immediately answered by the ascension of four rockets in that quarter, an acknowledgment producing universal joy and confidence among the allied forces.

The morning of the 16th was at first extremely misty and gloomy, but towards nine o'clock, after a second signal had been given by the discharge of three cannon-shots, which was succeeded by the thunder of artillery on both sides, the clouds of vapor gradually disappeared, the sky became serene, and during the whole of this sanguinary day the sun shone upon the field of battle. The cannonading kept up on both sides was so terrific that the very earth trembled with the continued concussion, and the oldest warriors present declared never until that moment to have witnessed such awful discharges of artillery: for on the side of the French alone the number of cannon employed in this destructive work was 600 pieces, and that on the part of the allies amounted to between 800 and 1000.

The battle raged with great fury at three principal points, but the most serious engagement was southwest of the city, near Markleeberg, Wachau, and Liebertwolkwitz, where the main body of the allied army fought; next, to the west near Lindenau, between Bertrand and the Austrian general, Giulay; and, finally, towards the north, near Moeckern and Lindenthal, between Blücher and Marshal Marmont. This last action assumed a more distinct form, and was called the battle of Moeckern.

Prince Schwartzenberg had posted at his extreme left, on the other side of the Pleisse, General Meerveldt, who was to attack the flank of the right wing of the French; at this point was stationed Prince Poniatowsky with his Poles, who, as usual, fought with the greatest bravery for Napoleon. The centre was occupied by the Russians and Prussians, commanded by Wittgenstein and Kleist; and at the right wing were the Austrians under Klenau. All these divisions of the allied army had arrived in the morning, prepared for the attack. General Kleist took possession of Markleeberg; to the left, the prince of Würtemberg penetrated through the centre into Wachau with the Russians and Prussians; and the Austrians under Klenau made themselves masters of Kolmberg near Liebertwolkwitz to the right. The whole battle-line of the French army fell back, and Napoleon himself with his guards was so close to the fire of the allies, that several of his staff were killed around him; but he was not the man to abandon the field of battle on the first assault.

In the midst of the battle's rage, he had with his keen eye examined the whole range of contention around him, and to the right and left of Wachau had prepared meantime two strong columns of attack, composed of the flower of his infantry, cavalry, and artillery; which he now, seeing it the most favorable moment, pushed forward against the centre. This attack, ordered by himself and effected under his own eyes, was so impetuous that the allies were forced to abandon the villages they occupied, and to retreat within the lines they had quitted in the morning. The French now succeeded in capturing several of the heights on the opposite side of these villages, and penetrating as far as the village of Güldengossa, took possession of the hills called the Swedish intrenchments, which command the country many miles round.

Victory appeared now as if inclined to pronounce in favor of Napoleon; already the left and right wings of the allies were nearly both cut off from their centre, and at three o'clock in the afternoon Napoleon dispatched a courier to Leipsic to announce his triumph to the king of Saxony, with the command that all the bells should be rung in honor of the glorious event. These sounds brought with them but gloomy prospects to our fellow-Germans shut up within the walls of their city—but circumstances very speedily produced a more cheerful state of feeling, for the cannonading had not yet discontinued, nor had its echo become more distant; nay, it appeared, on the contrary, to approach more and more closely. This changed aspect in affairs was produced by the following happy circumstance:

Some officers of Prince Schwartzenberg's army stationed in Gautsch, having observed from the tower of the church, whence they commanded a full view of the field of battle, the dangerous turn events had taken, made their report to the prince forthwith, who saw at once that this was now the decisive moment. It was of the last importance not to allow the enemy, against whom the powers of Europe were assembled in arms, to retain even a momentary advantage. Accordingly he ordered forth the Austrian reserve under the command of the hereditary prince of Hesse-Homburg, and these troops, consisting of the various regiments of cuirassiers denominated those of Albert, Lorraine, Francis, Ferdinand, and Sommarina, advanced across difficult roads, crossed the Pleisse, and attacking the French division, which had established itself to the right of Wachau, dislodged it; whence the junction of the left wing with the centre was reformed. Thus Kleist, who with his Prussians had maintained possession of Markleeberg against every attack, was, at five o'clock, relieved from his arduous duty by the arrival of the Austrians, and was permitted, after his hard-fought defence, to take a little breath.

On the other side, the left column of Napoleon's attack, led on by the impetuous Murat, had already reached Güldengossa, and used every effort to take possession of the place; and had they succeeded, the allied army would have been thrown into the utmost confusion, and its centre forced into the marshes of the valley of Gosel. The enemy's battalions of infantry had already penetrated into the middle of the village, their cuirassiers attacked and carried by a desperate assault a battery of twenty-six cannon, cutting down all before them, and pushing on, they had nearly gained the height where the monarchs of Russia and Prussia were attentively surveying the battle, when the emperor Alexander immediately ordered his body-guard of Don Cossacks, under the command of Count Orloff-Denissow, to attack the daring intruders, and he was immediately obeyed; with their usual loud and savage shouts they rushed down like lightning with their lances, and completely overthrew their mailed and more heavily accoutred adversaries, whose principal leader, Latour-Maubourg, in a charge he made, had his leg completely smashed.

The danger was now over; the enemy lost all the advantages previously obtained. It was now five o'clock, and the day was drawing to a close, when Murat ventured upon another attack against Güldengossa; but it was valiantly met and repulsed by Prince Eugene of Würtemberg with his Russian grenadiers, and the Prussians under Pirch and Jagow, and the enemy was forced to give it up. This was the last effort made on this side; night broke in and terminated the contest.

Thus, after a struggle of ten hours, during which so much blood had been shed, both armies at this point remained in the same position as in the morning; excepting that the French retained possession of the Swedish intrenchments on their left wing; while, on the other side, the moiety of the village of Markleeberg remained in the hands of the Prussians and Austrians.

By this plan of battle the allies did not realize their expectations, and in this respect, therefore, Napoleon was a gainer by this sanguinary day: their object having been to cut off his retreat to the Saale. An Austrian division had been dispatched in advance to Weissenfels; General Giulay was to make himself master of Lindenau, and General Meerveldt with the left wing was to advance along the Pleisse against

Leipsic, and form a junction with General Giulay. Had these objects been effected, and had Blücher at the same time advanced from the northwest as far as Leipsic, the French army must have been completely cut off and lost. But Giulay endeavored in vain throughout the entire day to gain possession of Lindenau, which was defended by General Bertrand; the strong intrenchments were gained for a moment by the Austrians, but were almost immediately afterwards recaptured by the French, and the former were eventually forced to withdraw. General Meerveldt was still more unfortunate; he made various attempts to advance from the other side of the Pleisse and dislodge the Poles from Dölitz, Lösnig, and Connewitz; but, owing to the marshy ground and the incessant fire kept up by the enemy, he failed in his object altogether for a length of time, and when, finally, at five o'clock in the afternoon, he did succeed in taking Dölitz with a portion of his troops, he was immediately followed by a large body of the guards which Napoleon dispatched to relieve the Poles, and thus the Austrians being pressed on all sides, were completely overthrown and their brave leader himself made prisoner, at the moment when his horse was shot under him in a final charge he made. This was a fortunate event for Napoleon, and he determined to avail himself of the circumstance by getting General Meerveldt to use all his influence with the emperor of Austria, and persuade that monarch to abandon the other allied powers.

But Napoleon lost at Moeckern against Blücher three times over the benefits he derived from the action gained at Lindenau and the capture of General Meerveldt; for at the very moment that he made known his victory at Leipsic, and the bells were set ringing in order to stimulate the courage of his soldiers by their deceptive sound, Blücher by one well-timed blow, entirely disappointed his premature calculations. He had not been prepared for this promptitude displayed by the old warrior, however willing he was to acknowledge the celerity of his movements generally. That general had arrived about mid-day, and immediately ordered the attack to be made, with the entire force under York, against Marshal Marmont in Moeckern, simultaneously with that executed by Langeron against Gross and Klein Wiederitsch; and as the two points of attack were widely apart from each other, Sacken was stationed in the centre with the reserve, to furnish aid either to the right or left.

Glorious recollections were attached to this field of battle, inasmuch as it was the same spot on which the great Gustavus Adolphus had, in former times, completely defeated Tilly, the ruthless destroyer of Magdeburg.

The Prussians had to sustain the most obstinate and hard-fought contest of all in Moeckern and its neighborhood; nevertheless they did not flinch, although their numbers diminished very seriously; and the reserve, consisting of General Horn's brigade, was all now left to them. Field-marshal Blücher now sent orders to General Sacken to advance with his troops; but the distance was too great, and York saw well that at this critical moment he had no time to lose, but must depend upon his own resources. Accordingly, he dispatched one of his aides-de-camp to General Horn, who was stationed in the open plain, and announced to him the pressing danger in which he was placed: "Eh! is it so, Captain —— ?" exclaimed the brave general.* "Well, then," addressing his soldiers, "let us in our turn, comrades, advance to the rescue with our cheers!" Saying which, he led on his troops amidst loud shouts to the attack, and, penetrating to the left of the village, charged the enemy with the bayonet, and before the latter were enabled to load their cannon a third time, they were captured and their ranks overthrown. Happily arrived also, just at this moment, the entire corps of Mecklenburg hussars, who, dashing upon the French squares of infantry, completely overpowered them, and putting them to flight, pursued them as far as the Partha, thus coming up just in time to terminate gloriously the fate of the day, without awaiting the arrival of Sacken and the Russian reserve. More than fifty pieces of artillery, besides ammunition, were captured.

Langeron, on his part, had fought at the

* By a singular coincidence of good fortune, it was ordained that General Horn should thus essentially contribute to the glorious decision of this day, on the very same spot where, in 1631, his ancestor, Gustavus Horn, leader of the left wing of the Swedes, fought so valiantly at the head of his foot-soldiers against Pappenheim's cavalry that he produced the most triumphant results in that great battle.

head of the Russians with no less courage, and carried the villages of Gross and Klein Wiederitsch, taking thirteen cannon; so that Marmont found himself, on the evening of this day, pursued as far as the left bank of the Partha, close to Leipsic.

On the following day, the 17th, Napoleon used every effort in order to divide the allied parties, and obtain a suspension of arms, during which he hoped to recover from his present dilemma. But the proposals he caused to be made to the emperor Francis through the medium of Count Meerveldt were not listened to for a moment; for his character was now too well known not to see that his object was only to gain time. If, as he declared, his only motive was to save all farther effusion of blood, it was only necessary for him to withdraw and make the retreat, which, after all, he was forced to effect two days later, and after an additional sacrifice of 50,000 men. He might have known by the actions already fought on the 10th, that he could never succeed in beating the brave forces of the allies. He himself could expect no more reinforcements, all the troops he commanded were now assembled around him; while the allies, on the other hand, still had large corps of reserve. Bernadotte arrived during the night, driving before him General Regnier, whose troops were chiefly composed of Saxons; while Bennigsen marched up in the morning with a fresh army of Russians, and at mid-day Kolloredo advanced with an Austrian division.

Napoleon, however, could not summon up resolution to quit the field of battle as long as there was the least shadow of hope remaining; and yet, at the same time, he lost all that activity he had on former occasions so frequently shown, and which had so often crowned him with victory.

The French army which Napoleon had drawn up in the form of a crescent, was to be attacked from three sides: from the north by Bernadotte and the Silesian army; from the east by Bennigsen, who, with the Russians, had also under his command the Austrians under Klenau, and a division of the Prussians under Ziethen; and from the south, whence, however, the grand attack was to be made, as that was the enemy's strongest point. Here, accordingly, the general-in-chief divided his army into two grand divisions, of which one composed of Russians and Prussians under Wittgenstein and Kleist was to attack the central point of the French, and the other constituting the flower of the Austrian army, under the hereditary prince of Hesse-Homburg, was to fall upon Prince Poniatowsky, who had defended himself so obstinately on the Pleisse, and force him to retreat to Leipsic.

Napoleon, on his part, had drawn together more closely his half circle in order to render it more firm. He had abandoned Wachau and Lieberwolkwitz, where so much blood had been spilt on the 16th, and made Probstheyda the central point of operations; he himself, however, with his guards, took up his position between this village and the right wing on the Pleisse, establishing his head-quarters upon a hill close to a wind-mill, pierced through and through with cannon-balls and half in ruins.

Exactly as the clock struck eight the battle commenced. The hereditary prince of Hesse-Homburg advanced towards the Pleisse against Dölitz, which he stormed. The Poles and the French under Poniatowsky defended themselves with desperation, and the struggle was extremely fierce and sanguinary. The Austrians were several times repulsed, and their brave commander himself receiving two wounds, his place was immediately filled by Kolloredo. Finally, being supported by Bianki, he succeeded in conquering Dölitz, Dösen, and the heights on the right bank, and maintained his position the whole day in spite of Marshal Oudinot and the guards, who came up to the aid of the Poles.

To the right, the Russians and Prussians had likewise been successful, and drove the enemy before them as far as Probstheyda, where, at mid-day, they came right in front of Napoleon. Here was fought the most obstinate battle; for upon the retention of this village depended the fate of the whole French army. Thence Napoleon had assembled within and around it, large bodies of troops of all arms, and had erected besides several strong intrenchments; while he himself remained on the spot with his guards, in order to furnish aid without a moment's loss of time, every house in the village being converted into a kind of citadel. The Prussians, nevertheless, under the command of Prince Augustus and Pirch, penetrated into the place after a fierce and heroic combat; but it was only for a moment, for they were unable to maintain their ground. A strong division of Russians now advanced to the attack, but they were likewise repulsed, and were equally unable with all their courage to make themselves masters of the village. The carnage was so great that the allied troops could scarcely move along, the bodies of their slain comrades completely choking up every passage. At length the three allied sovereigns, having from a neighboring height where they were assembled in order to watch the progress of the battle, observed the superhuman efforts made by their brave troops in that quarter, gave orders at five o'clock to give up the contest for the place, and spare the lives of the men; especially as the victory was now made decisive in different parts of the field, and Napoleon had, in fact, already given orders to Marshal Bertrand to retire with his troops from Lindenau towards the Saale—an undeniable proof that he had decided upon the retreat of his whole army.

Such were the results produced in this part of the field of battle. On the west side Bennigsen attacked Marshal Macdonald, who was ordered to defend the French lines in this direction. The marshal maintained his position with great bravery, especially in Holzhausen, which was taken and retaken several times. At length, however, about two o'clock, the Austrians and Russians made themselves masters of this place; while the Prussians took Zückelhausen, and now Macdonald retired to Stötteritz, close to Probstheyda. The whole of the troops which had formed the centre were now concentrated around these two villages, and they maintained their position there until night.

On the left wing, however, Marshal Ney experienced the most severe defeat of the whole day. He had under his charge the defence of the entire line of country from Macdonald's position to the Partha; but he found it impossible to hold out against the two armies—the Northern and Silesian—which now advanced against him, and he was forced to retreat to within a short distance of Leipsic itself. The two armies crossed the Partha in two directions, Blücher, with the Russians, fording the river at once near Mockau, although up to the waist in water, because he found it would take up too much time to cross over by Taucha. The French, under Marmont, made no resistance, but retreated in all haste to Schönfeld; while the Saxon regiments of hussars and lancers, together with several battalions of infantry, received the allies with open arms and joined their ranks at once.

About mid-day the army of the north, which had remained to cross the river at Taucha, advanced to fill up the gap left between Blücher to the right and Bennigsen to the left, thus making the line perfect to its whole extent, and by which the French were gradually surrounded more and more closely. Langeron, at the head of the Russians, took possession of Schönfeld, on the Partha, which, however, was defended with the greatest obstinacy by Marmont. The contest lasted four hours, and fresh troops on both sides were continually brought forward; until, at length, between five and six o'clock, when the village and its church were completely in flames, the French quitted the place and retreated by Reudnitz and Volkmansdorf to Leipsic. Ney and Regnier, who had to maintain possession of the open country beyond Paunsdorf, being attacked, in the afternoon, by the army of the north and the Prussians under Bülow, were driven altogether out of Paunsdorf, and when they attempted to defend themselves in the plain the Russian and Prussian cavalry, which had all this time been unemployed, as the fighting had been confined to the villages, dashed with all their fury among them, seconded by several congreve-rockets, which were fired into their squares, and spread death and destruction in every part. They were completely overthrown and put to flight, never stopping until they reached Volkmansdorf, and the villages were recaptured.

It was at this moment that the entire army of the Saxons, which had been led forth, very unwillingly, to draw the sword in the cause of Napoleon, resolved to abandon him; and forthwith marched over in a body to the ranks of the allies, under their various commanders, and with their ensigns flying, accompanied by the music of their different bands, and followed by all their cannon, ammunition, and baggage-wagons.

Napoleon, completely disconcerted by this event, hastened to send the cavalry of the guard, under the command of Nausouty, to fill up the vacant ranks. These troops had no sooner arrived than, accompanied by a heavy train of artillery, they advanced to attack the flank of Būlow's division; but the Austrians, under Būlow, who were close by, marched forward themselves to meet the enemy's assault; while from another quarter the Swedes, by Bernadotte's orders, discharged among their ranks the artillery just brought over by the Saxons. The old French guard was accordingly forced to retire and abandon possession of the country to the allies.

At length the sanguinary day approached its end; the last rays of the sun shed their parting genial lustre over the heads of the three sovereigns and their distinguished companions, as, standing upon the hill, they contemplated the gradual termination of this memorable scene of action. Thither also Prince Schwartzenberg summoned a council of war, including the principal leaders of the allied army, and arrangements were forthwith made for the operations of the ensuing day.

Napoleon, on his part, awaited the appearance of night with impatience and anxiety, for then the remainder of his troops might hope to be rescued from the farther fury of the enemy. He had lost a great deal of ground, and had reduced considerably his crescent-formed army of the morning, so that it was now diminished into the form of a triangle, of which one point was at Probstheyda, whence the line joining Connewitz and the Pleisse composed one side, and that joining Stötteritz and Volkmansdorf formed the other. Had not his army fought with the greatest courage, and, notwithstanding the difficulties with which they were beset, retreated in perfect order—for this praise cannot be withheld from them—one of these lines of the triangle would inevitably have been destroyed before the evening, Leipsic taken, and the entire army lost. Napoleon this day fought only for a retreat, and already, at ten o'clock in the morning, immense trains of baggage-wagons and others of every description, together with innumerable horses, had quitted Leipsic under an escort of troops, belonging to General Bertrand's division.

When darkness covered the wide field of battle, Napoleon still remained at his station on the hill near the windmill, where he sat gazing on the watch-fire he had ordered to be lighted. He had confided the charge of the retreat to his superior general, Berthier, who gave the necessary orders to his aides-de-camp before another watch-fire which appeared behind his master; during which a profound silence reigned around. The French emperor, overcome at length by the extraordinary exertions of the present and preceding days, as well as by the agitations of his mind, now gradually sunk into a slumber; with his elbows upon his knees and his head resting between his hands, he thus for a short time reposed amid the horrors of the gory scene around him—of that field covered with the lifeless bodies of those who had fallen the victims of his inordinate ambition and pride. His generals near him preserved a deep and gloomy silence, which was interrupted at intervals by the low murmuring noise of the retreating columns as they marched underneath at the base of the hill, or pursued their course in the distant plain. At the end of a quarter of an hour Napoleon awoke, and cast around him a look of inquietude and wonder. The present reality may have struck him for a moment as a dream, for, starting up from his chair, he mounted his horse and galloped on to Leipsic, which he re-entered at nine o'clock.

The retreat of the whole army through Leipsic commenced immediately after midnight; but as the various regiments, marching from all parts of the field of battle, could arrive by one route alone—the narrow paved road of Ranstadt—considerable obstruction and confusion was unavoidable; wagons and cannons were mingled and clogged together, while the foot-soldiers with difficulty extricated themselves from this scene of disorder. The rear-guard was ordered to remain behind and defend Leipsic as long as was possible, and although the place was not fortified, the utmost was done to render it strong by forming intrenchments, barricading the gates, and putting in a state of defence the moats and garden-walls.

Meantime the allied army, by no means inclined to permit the French to retire so quietly, and carry away with them the spoils and supplies of ammunition they had accumulated in Germany, advanced at eight o'clock in the morning and stormed the gates of the city. This sudden attack increased the disorder still reigning, and Napoleon himself was forced to quit the place by a by-path. The allies might have added to this embarrassment considerably, and have caused more extensive destruction, if they had brought their artillery to bear against the gates and walls of the city. But such a proceeding, which must have involved the innocent as well as the guilty in one common ruin, would have been too cruel, and they, accordingly, confined themselves to storming the gates. The French and the Poles made an obstinate resistance and disputed every inch of ground; the victory, however, was not long doubtful, and the allied troops made themselves masters of the city.

It was just at this moment that the bridge on the other side of the city, that of the Elster-Mühlengraben, the only one left for the French to cross over, was blown up in the air, without its being known positively by what cause: whether by command of Napoleon to secure his army from the pursuit of the allied troops, or whether it originated in the too precipitate alarm of the officer in charge of it. An exclamation of horror arose from the crowds as they hastened to reach the spot in time to cross. A great number threw themselves into the Elster, in order to swim to the other side, but the majority were either drowned or perished in the mud-banks. Several of the generals sprang likewise with their horses into the river, in order to escape being made prisoners; but they nearly all lost their lives, and among the sufferers was Prince Poniatowsky, whom but three days before, Napoleon had created a field-marshal of France; Macdonald fortunately escaped, whilst Regnier, Bertrand, and Lauriston were taken prisoners.

Napoleon lost more men on this day than on the day of battle itself. More than 15,000 well-armed soldiers were taken prisoners after the bridge was blown up, and more than 25,000 sick and wounded were abandoned and left to the discretion of the conquerors. In the city, and on the road leading to it, an incredible quantity of cannon and ammunition-wagons were everywhere scattered, of which more than 300 of the former, and 1000 of the latter, fell into the hands of the allies.

At one o'clock, the emperor Alexander and the king of Prussia, attended by their numerous staff of generals, entered the city of Leipsic, the acclamations of their own brave troops mingling with those of the happy inhabitants, who greeted with joy the appearance of their deliverers; the emperor Francis arrived a few days later, and participated in this glorious scene.

## CHAPTER XXXIX.

Napoleon's Retreat across the Rhine—Bavaria—General Wrede—Hanau—The Allied Forces invade France—The Minister Von Stein—Their rapid March—Napoleon against Blücher—Battle of Brienne—Battle of Rothière—Repulse of the French—Temporary Successes of Napoleon—The Congress of Chatillon—Napoleon's Confidence restored—His Declaration—Blücher's bold Movement—Soissons—Laon—Napoleon against Schwartzenberg—Rheims—Arcis—Napoleon's desperate Courage and final Charge with his Cavalry.

Bavaria, by the treaty of Ried, had already joined the grand alliance before the battle of Leipsic; and she now sent her general, Marshal Wrede, to the provinces on the Maine, with a large army, to which were united some Austrian and Würtemberg troops, in order to oppose the passage of the French across the Rhine, and effect their total annihilation. Wrede directed his march to Hanau and Frankfort, while the grand army of the allies pursued the fugitives from another side, and York especially overtook and attacked them at Freiberg on the Unstrut, causing them great loss. In front and on each side of them, they were harassed by Czernitschef and other light troops, and all who detached themselves from the main body were made prisoners. Thus they proceeded along the route from Leipsic to Erfurt, and thence to the Rhine, abandoning at every moment all that could not follow in their train, cannons, baggage, and such of their comrades as were too ill to proceed along with them; for the march was so rapid and continuous, that at the end of eleven days, the army had already reached Frankfort.

Napoleon arrived with the remnant of his forces of from 70,000 to 80,000 men before Hanau, where he encountered Marshal Wrede, who determined to oppose his passage, although his army was inferior in numbers; for if he succeeded in detaining him until the arrival of the allied grand army, his ruin was certain. This Napoleon well knowing, he employed his guard, as yet in good condition, to force their passage onward. During three entire days, the 29th, 30th, and 31st of October, the contest was carried on with the greatest obstinacy before and within the town of Hanau, Marshal Wrede himself being severely wounded. Finally, however, the French succeeded in cutting their way through, although at a great loss.

On the 2d of November Napoleon gained the banks of the Rhine, which he now saw for the last time; he was immediately followed in all haste by his troops over the bridge of Mentz, while General Bertrand intrenched himself on the heights of Hochheim. This, however, was not tolerated by the allies, who would not suffer the French to possess an inch of ground on this side of the Rhine; accordingly, on the 9th of November, Prince Schwartzenberg caused him to be attacked by General Giulay, and he was forced to retreat to Mentz. The three allied sovereigns were now reunited in Frankfort, where they determined together upon the continuation of the war.

With the commencement of the new year, 1814, the allied powers, seeing clearly that nothing but the sword could decide between them and their obstinate adversary, redoubled their efforts, confiding in their superior strength and in the justice of their cause. The Russians brought at least 200,000 men into the field; the Prussians 160,000; and Austria 230,000, equally divided on the Rhine, in Italy, and in the interior of Germany. In addition to these forces, the brave Field-marshal Wellington had already placed his foot on the French territory with the British army of 80,000 men. Finally, the other states of Germany furnished their contingent of troops of 150,000 to 160,000 men.

These were divided into eight distinct corps, viz: the first comprised 36,000 Bavarians under General Wrede; the second was under the command of the duke of Brunswick, and consisted of 33,000 Brunswickers, Hanoverians, Oldenburgers and Mecklenburgers, together with some Hanseatic troops; the third, amounting to 23,000 men from the Saxon territories, was commanded by the duke of Saxe-Weimar; the fourth, consisting of 14,000 Hessians, was led on by the elector of Hesse-Cassel himself; the fifth, comprising 10,000 men from the provinces of Waldeck, Lippe, Nassau, Coburg, Meiningen, Hildburghausen, and Strelitz, was under the orders of the duke of Saxe-Coburg; the sixth was commanded by the prince of Hesse-Homburg, and formed the contingent furnished by Darmstadt, Würzburg, Frankfort-on-the-Maine, Isenburg, and Reuss; the seventh consisted of 12,000 Würtembergers under the leadership of their own crown-prince himself; and, lastly, the eighth was placed under the command of the Baden general, Count von Hochberg, which included the troops of Baden, Hohenzollern, and Lichtenstein.

Although the entire mass of these troops could not be sent into the field all at once, and there was a necessity for continuing to retain possession of a great extent of country, while many thousands of troops were required to invest the numerously fortified towns which the allies would not lose time in laying formal siege to, it is, nevertheless, certain, that an army consisting of at least 500,000 men was now in full march against France, and which would surround the enemy's forces, not amounting now to half that number. At the same time, in the rear of the allied army every preparation was made necessary to ensure its complete equipment and organization, for which purpose, and in order that operations might be carried on with all possible order and uninterrupted unanimity, a sort of central administration or council of war was established and presided over by a man who might truly be characterized as a hero, and one, too, who worked indefatigably for the liberty of our country, although not actually marching at the head of her armies. This noble-minded patriot and persevering champion was the minister Baron von Stein. He was one of those who, while Germany was sighing under the yoke of the usurper, indignantly and resolutely spurned every attempt made to render him subservient; for, on the contrary, he never ceased, as before stated, devoting his superior genius as well as all his thoughts and actions towards the emancipation of his country, and gaining thus the confidence of his fellow-countrymen, he was looked up to as a tower of strength in their cause. When the war of 1812 broke out against Russia, he repaired thither at the head of many others of an equally bold and dauntless mind, in order to assist in annihilating the expedition thus directed against a nation whose energy was well known to, and appreciated by him. The emperor Alexander found in him all the support he so much needed at that all-important, trying moment, and it must ever be acknowledged that it is to the bold and active genius of Von Stein that Germany owes her complete deliverance from the yoke of foreign despotism.

During the first twenty days of January, the allies had already traversed Switzerland, Franche-Comté, Alsace, Lorraine, and Burgundy, without meeting with any obstacle; and the mountains of the Jura, the Waldensis, the Hundsruck, and the forest of Ardennes, together with numerous rivers and a triple line of fortifications on the frontiers, were all happily captured and cleared, and the armies of Schwartzenberg and Blücher were already, within a short distance of each other, in full march along the banks of the Seine and the Aube, and within some ninety or a hundred miles of Paris itself. Now, however, Napoleon entered the field at the head of his army. His object was to penetrate between his enemies, prevent their junction, drive them back one after the other to the mountains they had just left, where the effects of the winter and the armed inhabitants would combine together to render their retreat one equally disastrous and fatal. Blücher had established his head-quarters in Brienne, a small town near the Aube, with a castle which had served as a military-school for young Frenchmen, and where Napoleon had himself learned that science in which he afterwards so distinguished himself. Suddenly the French appeared and attacked the town. The assault was repulsed, but as soon as it was dusk, the French general, Chateau, who was well acquainted with the localities of the place, penetrated with his grenadiers into the gardens of the castle as far as the terrace itself, without being observed. Blücher was in great danger of being taken, and had scarcely time to mount his horse and escape by a private road. He immediately placed himself at the head of his troops, and inspiring them with the most undaunted courage, he warned them not to let the enemy boast of having put them to flight on their first encounter upon French ground, and he maintained the contest until midnight, and completely drove back the left wing of the enemy, not abandoning the place before it was set on fire by the French, "in order," as he wrote in his dispatch, "that Napoleon might set fire to his cradle with his own hand." Nevertheless, the latter did not succeed in cutting off Blücher's army from that of Schwartzenberg.

The battle of Brienne took place on the 29th of January, and on the 1st of February the intrepid Blücher was already again on the same spot, drawn up in battle array. He had not as yet assembled all his troops, for Langeron was still at Mentz, and York and Kleist were *en route;* but Schwartzenberg had furnished him with the greater part of his army—the divisions of Giulay and the prince of Würtemberg—together with the Russian reserve corps: by which means he found himself sufficiently strong to advance against Napoleon. The latter had taken up a strong position in the neighborhood of Brienne, and established his centre in the village of Rothière, about four miles distant. The battle began at mid-day at all points. To the right the prince of Würtemberg, having paved his way through the forest of Eclance, took possession of the villages of Lagibrie and Petit-Mesnil. On the side of the Würtembergers, General Wrede, at the head of the Bavarians and Austrians, advanced likewise and conquered the villages of Morvilliers and Chauménil, and thus laid bare the whole of Napoleon's left wing. The latter now came up himself with the artillery of his guard, and fired upon Morvilliers, whence he succeeded in dislodging the Bavarians. Wrede now detached his best regiment of cavalry, commanded by the brave Diez, which forthwith threw itself upon the French and completely routed them.

Meantime the battle was continued with the utmost fury in the village of Rothière, which formed the principal point in the position held by the French. Here Napoleon commanded in person, and continually brought up fresh troops against the Russians. On the other side, the emperor Alexander and the king of Prussia encouraged on their troops by their presence, whence prodigies of valor were performed At length Marshal Blücher placed himself at the head of his troops, and threw himself into the village, exclaiming, "Forwards!" The village was carried and taken definitively. The right wing of the enemy, which had defended the village of Dieuville against Giulay, was likewise forced to retreat at midnight, and the victory was now decisive at all points.

The allies finding that Napoleon's force was not so extensive as they imagined, and knowing that the late actions must have reduced it still more, deemed a combined plan of operations unnecessary, and determined therefore to divide their armies: that of Blücher to take the route towards the Marne, while that of Schwartzenberg was to proceed along the Seine. This was exactly what Napoleon wished; for by this separation he should be enabled to resort to his former promptitude of manœuvring. He maintained his position between the two armies, and watching his opportunity, alternately attacked the one or the other division as his prey, and overpowered it by the superiority of his forces. By this means, he succeeded in obtaining those temporary successes which enabled him to detain them on their march to Paris several months.

The Silesian army, accordingly, advanced towards the capital by the route of Champagne, in detached bodies; Sacken to the rear, Kleist the centre, and Blücher, the general-in-chief, brought up the rear-division of Kleist. The Russian advanced-guard had now arrived to within fifteen leagues of Paris, which many of the inhabitants were now abandoning in all haste, believing the emperor's reign completely at an end. Suddenly, however, the latter, being now reinforced with 20,000 men of the old troops, which he had conveyed from Spain in coaches and light wagons, obliquely traversed the immense plains between the Seine and the Marne, in spite of the representations of his generals, who held the execution of his plan to be impossible; and, although forced to leave his cannons in the mud behind him, he came in front of the enemy, and seeking his opportunity, fell upon the rear-guard of Sacken, commanded by General Olsufiew, cutting the moiety of them in pieces, or making them prisoners. This was the first ray of good fortune which once more shone upon Napoleon, and reproduced confidence within him. He wrote to the duke of Vicenza, his plenipotentiary at the congress of Chatillon, then sitting, that his arms had been once more crowned with a brilliant victory, and that the French government might now reassume its independent, dictatorial tone.

Meantime, Field-marshal Blücher, when news reached him of the danger threatened, marched with all possible haste *en route* for Champaubert with Kleist's division, and the Russians under General Kapczewitsch, in all about 20,000 men. But the generals whom he wished to join had already recrossed the Marne, and on the 14th he found himself attacked by the French, with a far superior force. Their cavalry threw itself upon the two wings, while the infantry and artillery attacked the centre with such desperate fury, that on the first onset several of the Prussian battalions were completely destroyed. In addition to this force, the allies found another body of French cavalry advancing upon them in their rear upon the high road between Champaubert and Etoges. No other resource was left them now but to trust to their courage and resolution and cut their way through. They formed themselves into solid squares, and advanced with charged bayonet against the cavalry, which gave way before them. The enemy now attacked them in the flank, and harassed them in every direction, in order to bring their ranks into disorder; but by the able management of the brave and prudent general, Gneisenau, the furious attacks were received with firm and unshaken courage and order, and to this alone is the preservation of the army to be attributed.

At length night arrived, and promised the Prussians the repose they so much needed. They, however, were forced to encounter some hard fighting when they arrived at Etoges; but they once more opened for themselves a road at the point of the bayonet, and gained at length their former position at Vergères. The divisions of the Silesian army united together behind the Marne, and shortly after marched towards the Aube, in order to form a junction with the grand army.

Napoleon was delighted beyond all measure in being able once again to boast of his victories in his bulletins and gazettes; but these triumphant strains were very speedily hushed when it was known as a certainty, that the advanced guard of Schwartzenberg was only ten leagues distant from the capital, while the French army was fighting on the Marne. Napoleon gave up at once all farther pursuit of the Silesian troops, in order to turn his force against Schwartzenberg. The latter had detached Wrede and Wittgenstein to the rear of the French army, in order to relieve the Silesian army; but as all the operations in that quarter had been extremely rapid, the aid came too late, and these two generals found themselves opposed to Napoleon, who with his superior army forced them, after a severe action, to retreat to the Seine. The brave prince of Würtemberg, who led the advanced guard of the grand army, had taken up his position with his Würtembergers and Austrians, in the village of Montereau. Napoleon, after pursuing Wittgenstein, on the 17th of February, as far as Nangis, made a violent attack on the prince's troops on the 18th. The latter, nevertheless, maintained themselves firmly throughout the whole day; but having expended all their ammunition, and finding themselves taken in the flank by the French, they were forced to give way and to recross the river.

These ten days of success restored to Napoleon all his former presumption, especially as just at this moment Marshal Augereau sent him a message from Lyons, that he had driven back the Austrian general, Bubna, as far as Geneva, and was penetrating into Switzerland with a powerful body of troops. If the French general succeeded in reconquering that country, then the retreat of the allied army must be completely cut off, and already calculating upon this conquest, Napoleon's imagination foresaw Alsace and Lorraine rising *en masse* against the allies, and all the numerous garrisons along the frontiers uniting with the national guard to annihilate the enemy. Thence, although the conference at Chatillon was still continued, he would no longer hear of peace; and when, among the terms stipulated, it was required that he should resign Holland and Italy, he exclaimed: "What are our enemies thinking of? Tell them, I am at this moment closer to Vienna than they are to Paris!"

Paris was in a state of joyful excitement, and the whole of France shared in the hopes of the emperor. At the same time any acute observer could easily see that it was merely a moment of illusion; for although the grand army did partially withdraw, still it was in accordance with the plan of the campaign, and not after any general defeat, nor because there was any discouragement in the soldiers, who, on the contrary, were more eager than ever to march to Paris.

Meantime, at head-quarters, the question of a peace was seriously discussed, and it was already suggested, that the allied forces should gradually retire to the Rhine, in order to await the result of the conference held at Chatillon. The veteran Blücher, however, opposed this with his whole force. He offered, in a dispatch he sent to the allied sovereigns, from his quarters at Merry, to march direct to Paris, and thus draw off Napoleon from the grand army, if they would place under his orders the divisions of Bülow and Winzengerode. He would then find himself again at the head of an excellent army of 100,000 men, and with that alone he would venture to threaten the capital without any farther delay. His wish was accorded. This unexpected movement—pronounced by a French historian to be the boldest throughout the campaign—completely disconcerted the French emperor, who was at this moment in Troyes. He had just refused the offer of an armistice, and already beheld himself in imagination once again on the banks of the Rhine, whereas he found himself now forced to abandon the grand allied army, and devote all his attention to the bold adversary he thought he had completely beaten.

Napoleon's object was to come up with the old marshal before he had formed a junction with the other corps of the army, from which he was separated by the river Aisne. But Bülow and Winzengerode had already laid siege to Soissons, situated on this river, where an excellent bridge formed a desirable point of reunion for the two armies. This strongly fortified city contained a numerous garrison, but Bülow forthwith made preparations for an assault. Already, towards night, the scaling-ladders were fixed and the assailants about to mount them, when the commandant of the place, not aware of Napoleon's presence in the vicinity, surrendered the city, and retired with his garrison. Blücher immediately crossed the river and advanced northward as far as Laon, where he united all his forces and took up a strong position near that city. Napoleon, in order to grapple with and overthrow this daring opponent, pursued him closely to the other side of the river, although by so doing he left more and more distant in his rear both the grand army of the allies and Paris itself, which was three-and-thirty leagues off.

On the 7th of March he attacked Winzengerode and Woronzow in their intrenched position on the heights of Craone, and only forced them to retreat to Laon after he himself had suffered a great loss. Here Blücher awaited him, having made the city, which was situated upon an almost impregnable height, the central point of his position. On the 9th of March, at break of day, the French attacked and took the village of Semilly, at the base of the hill, which, however, they retained only a short time, being driven from it by Bülow's troops, and Napoleon did not venture to ascend the height. The contest, at both wings, lasted the entire day, Napoleon's object being especially to drive the Prussians from the high road to Belgium. Towards mid-day he succeeded in obtaining the advantage, and the Prussian advanced-guard was forced to abandon the village of Athis; but, in the evening, Generals Kleist and York resolved to annihilate his plan at once by a *coup de main*. As soon as it was completely dark, and the enemy, believing the sanguinary day at an end, had already lighted their fires in the camp, the Prussians returned to the attack. Every thing succeeded; the enemy was utterly overthrown and forty-six pieces of artillery captured. This complete victory was gained with scarcely any loss on the side of the Prussians; while that of the corps of Marmont, which had suffered this defeat, was very considerable.

Napoleon was not a little mortified at finding this attack upon the Silesian army so unsuccessful. Nothing now remained for him but to turn his arms against Schwartzenberg, surprise the grand army, and, endeavoring to separate it, attack and destroy each detached corps.

The commander-in-chief had again taken up his position on the Aube, whither he had marched immediately after the departure of Napoleon in pursuit of the Silesian army. The issue of operations between Blücher and Napoleon he soon learned by the sudden appearance of the latter himself, who returned from Laon to commence his movements against the grand army. He had scarcely arrived before he, on the 13th of March, suddenly attacked and took the town of Rheims, which was occupied by General Saint-Priest and the Russians, killed that general, and on the 20th he was in front of the grand army, and took possession of Arcis-sur-Aube. He hoped by a prompt manœuvre to bring the allies into confusion, and thus be enabled to make the attack contemplated; but he found their ranks too firmly knit together, and he was thus, a second time, defeated in his design. The emperor Alexander and the king of Prussia themselves, who were resolved not to defer longer a decisive battle, had hastened by forced marches to rejoin the army, and on this day, the 20th of March, a most serious engagement took place near Arcis. The regiments of French guard were repulsed with so much force, that Napoleon, in order not to lose such an important place, drew his own sword, and rallying the flying squadrons, placed himself at their head, and led them on to the attack again. In this charge he exposed himself so much that, in order to defend himself against a cossack who rushed upon him with his lance, he was forced to fire at him one of his own pistols. A great number of his staff were killed and wounded around him, and his own horse was shot under him; nevertheless, instead of shunning danger, he appeared only to court it. It was only by these extraordinary exertions, and the arrival of a reinforcement of infantry, that he was enabled to save the town.

## CHAPTER XL.

The French and Allied Armies in Battle Array—Napoleon's sudden and mysterious Retreat before Action—His secret Designs for the Destruction of the Allies—His Plot Discovered—The Allies before Paris—Its Capitulation—Triumphant Entry of the Allies in that City—Napoleon Deposed—Louis XVIII. King of France—Napoleon at Fontainebleau—His Abdication—Banishment to Elba—Peace signed in Paris—Conclusion.

The allied army prepared for a grand and final action on the following day; Napoleon himself formed his line of battle in front of Arcis, and the two armies thus facing each other waited a considerable time—extending even to several hours—for each other's attack. In truth, it was a solemn moment, and one portending the most important and decisive results to the whole world. It was during this interval that Napoleon brought into operation a plan he had long contemplated, and upon which he based all hopes; but which, nevertheless, produced his ruin. While, therefore, the eyes of the allied army were anxiously fixed upon his movements, it was observed, to their no little astonishment, that the ranks of the enemy were broken up, and the troops, crossing over the Aube in confused masses, were seen ascending the opposite hills, and the field of battle was abandoned by them without a blow being struck. After long consideration, Napoleon felt he had already good reason to remember how often he had met the allied armies in the open field, and he accordingly determined now to change the plan of battle.

His manœuvre this time was to gain the rear of Schwartzenberg by forced marches, and as the allies would doubtless fall back in order to secure for themselves a safe retreat, he was in good hopes they might fall into the various ambuscades, which he would take good care, with the aid of the different garrisons and the inhabitants themselves, to have planted ready to meet them in Lorraine and Alsace. He had, in fact, long since made his preparations for the execution of this design ; all his commandants throughout those countries having received his instructions to this effect through secret messengers and spies. The inhabitants entered most cordially into the spirit of the plot, and had already commenced operations by concealing themselves in the woods, narrow passes, and cross roads, and attacking all the couriers and small detachments of soldiers proceeding in those directions. All the convoys were stopped, and the allies already began to experience the want of ammunition; and thus a retreat must have produced the total ruin of the allied armies.

Meantime, a letter addressed by Napoleon to the empress, in which he detailed to her the whole of his plan, was found upon one of his messengers who was taken prisoner, and was the means of making the whole plot known to the allies. This then was a most important moment for them. One party held it advisable to secure their retreat and march back to the Rhine; the other again, more confident, deemed it preferable to proceed direct to Paris, which could not resist: and this last counsel was adopted. It was resolved to leave Napoleon in the rear, and that the grand army should forthwith march in advance, in order to form a junction with Blücher on the Marne.

On the following day, the 24th of March, it was found that the Silesian army was already in the vicinity, and the council of war, assembled at Vitry, resolved at once that the two united armies should march for Paris, and that General Winzengerode should remain behind to meet Napoleon with 10,000 cavalry and flying artillery, in order to make him believe that the main body of the allied army followed them in the rear.

After various victories, the allied armies marched forward in conjunction, and arrived at length, on the 29th of March towards evening, before the gates of the proud city which had styled itself the capital of the whole world. Joseph, Napoleon's brother, and formerly king of Spain, was there with numerous partisans, and he continued to deceive the inhabitants, by assuring them that it was merely a detachment of the allied army, which had advanced for the purpose of frightening the city. Marshals Marmont and Mortier had assembled all the troops they could muster, and posted them on the heights outside the city, with all their artillery ; their army thus distributed on the Montmartre and other hills, consisted altogether of 25,000 men, and 150 pieces of cannon. Their object was to hold the allies at bay until the emperor marched up to their relief.

Napoleon was in truth advancing with all speed to their aid, but he was at too great a distance to arrive in time. He had been the victim of his blind confidence, and had thus given the allied army the advantage of four days' march in advance of him. Generals Winzengerode and Czernitschef had completely deceived him, in making him believe they were the advanced guard of the allied army in pursuit of him, and he already congratulated himself upon the successful results of his *ruse*. Nevertheless, finding the troops consisted of nothing else but cavalry, and that not a single foot-soldier was visible, he became suspicious, and, determined to convince himself, he attacked General Winzengerode, who was accordingly forced to give way before him. Still he could ascertain nothing certain, until the 29th of March, when an estafette arrived from Paris and met him at Doulancourt, on the Aube. He hastened to peruse the contents of these mysterious dispatches, and was struck as by a clap of thunder, when he found that the allies were before the gates of the capital, while he himself was at that moment more than forty leagues distant! He lost not a moment, but abandoning his army at once, departed with a few followers in hopes of still arriving in time; but he urged his postilions on in vain, for in spite of all the efforts made, he was forced to content himself with only hearing at a distance the heavy cannonading before his capital; and on the 30th, at six o'clock in the evening, on reaching Fromenteau, five leagues from the metropolis, he learned he had arrived a few hours too late—Paris had surrendered. Napoleon was only separated by the Seine from the advanced posts of the allied army; the fires from their bivouacs lighted up the whole length of the left bank, while the darkness of the night concealed from observation the presence of himself, a few companions, and the two post-chaises. At four o'clock on the following morning, when he was convinced positively that the capitulation was signed, he turned his horses' heads and drove off to Fontainebleau.

On the morning of the 30th of March, General Barclai de Tolly, who commanded the Russians and Prussians, under the orders of Prince Schwartzenberg, commander-in-chief, attacked the heights of Belleville, which formed the central point of defence. The contest was extremely obstinate, and at the same time indecisive; because the gardens, vineyards, and shrubberies everywhere around greatly facilitated the means of defence, but more especially because the troops of the prince of Würtemberg and Blücher, who ought to have aided on the right and left, did not arrive before mid-day. The French artillery, which commanded a good position, did great execution in the ranks of the brave assailants; but, finally, the heights of Belleville were carried, and the cannon taken. Then it was that the Parisians perceived that the troops before the place formed a more numerous and powerful body than a mere detachment, and they soon had too much reason to know the real state of things. At mid-day, the Silesian army stormed the heights of Montmartre. York, Kleist, and Langeron, drove the French before them out of all the villages, and on this occasion, the cavalry bore a principal part in the achievements of this day; the black hussars, and those of Brandenburg especially, making a most valiant attack upon the enemy—who defended the village of La Villette to the last—and forced them to evacuate it, and thence Montmartre fell forthwith into the hands of the allies.

At the extreme left, the prince of Würtemberg had, likewise, in spite of the vigorous defence maintained by the various troops posted in the quarter of Vincennes, forced them to give way and advanced to the gates of the city on that side. Thus the entire army of the allies was now assembled on and around the heights they had conquered, ready to follow up their victory by penetrating at once into the capital. But the two marshals, and the authorities of the city, having come forward and offered to capitulate, it was accordingly agreed that the place should be surrendered to the allies on the following day, the 31st of March, and that the said Marshals Marmont and Mortier should retire with the remnant of their troops.

Accordingly, as arranged, and on the day fixed, the emperor Alexander and the king of Prussia—the emperor Francis having remained behind at Lyons with his army—accompanied by their staff, and followed by a portion of their army, made their triumphant entry into the city.

On the 1st of April the emperor Alexander published, in the name of himself and allies, a declaration, "That he would, in no way whatever, treat either with Napoleon or any one of his family; and the French were at liberty to choose another government."

In consequence of this decree, the municipal council of the metropolis declared itself absolved from its oath of fealty to Napoleon, and demanding the restoration of the ancient royal house, that body, on the 2d of April, in the name of France, declared the deposition of Napoleon.

This event acted with the force of a thunder-stroke upon Napoleon, who had continually flattered himself with the certainty of reassembling his army, and once more trying the chances of war. He was still at Fontainebleau, twelve leagues from Paris, where he remained a prey to his feelings, and alternately excited by disappointment and hope; at length he resolved on marching to Paris, being full of confidence in his army. The 3d of April was fixed for his departure, and already a crowd of warriors assembled to follow him; but just at that moment his marshals refused to act in co-operation with him for the promotion of his design. Ney and Lefebvre followed him into his chamber, and made known to him the fact of his deposition, and declared they could not depend upon the army. He was, however, still desirous of securing the crown of France for his son, whom he had made king of Rome, and he offered to abdicate on this condition; but neither the allies nor the provisional government would accede to it.

Accordingly, on the 6th of April, the senate acknowledged Louis XVIII. as king of France, and invited him to ascend the throne, while to Napoleon was offered the possession of the island of Elba, on the coast of Italy. Against all expectation he calmly signed the abdication of all his imperial power and sovereignty, and departed, on the 20th of April, for his new dominion, where he arrived and fixed his residence. Louis XVIII. made his entry in the capital on the 3d of May, and mounted the throne of his ancestors twenty-one years after his brother's execution.

On the 30th of May the first peace of Paris was concluded between France and Europe. France retained the same limits as she had possessed under her kings, and consequently held possession of Alsace and Lorraine, which in former times belonged to Germany; while she also had secured to her an extent of territory conquered during the wars of the republic. She had likewise, in addition to this, no share to pay of the expenses of the war; the city of Paris was not obliged to restore the valuable productions of art and science, collected from all parts of the world, and all the thousands of French prisoners in Germany, Russia, and England, were forthwith set at liberty.

---

We have now traced the history of Germany from the earliest time down to the moment when it was fervently hoped, that the peace of that severely-dealt-with country, together with that of Europe generally, was finally and permanently established. The restless ambition, however, of Napoleon produced a renewal of hostilities, and once more, but for the last time, all the sovereigns and princes of Germany, as well as the whole of Europe, armed and advanced against him, and Providence crowned their wishes with success. On the memorable plains of Ligny and Waterloo, the pride and ambition of that dangerous man were forever crushed, his troops completely beaten and almost annihilated, and he himself forced eventually to yield himself a prisoner, and end his days on the rock of St. Helena.

It is not necessary here to describe the well-known details of a victory unparalleled in history, the beneficial results of which have been, and still continue to be so distinctly felt and gratefully acknowledged. The great and glorious achievements of the arms of combined Europe under Wellington and Blücher, can never be forgotten or too highly appreciated.

According to the arrangements made in the general and—happily as it has proved—lasting peace, concluded by all the powers of Europe at the congress of Vienna, in 1815, Germany received back all the provinces she possessed anteriorly to the Revolution, but of which she had been deprived during that and the subsequent period. They were now so divided among the members of the newly-formed Confederation of Germany, that the majority received either the same territories they previously owned, those granted to them by the peace of Lunéville, or such as they held at the period of the Rhenish league.

The members of the Confederation constituted at first a body of thirty-eight, viz.: Austria, Prussia, Bavaria, Saxony, Hanover, Würtemberg, Baden, Hesse-Cassel, Hesse-Darmstadt, Holstein, Luxemburg, Brunswick, Mecklenburg-Schwerin, Mecklenburg-Strelitz, Nassau, Saxe-Weimar, Saxe-Gotha, Saxe-Coburg, Saxe-Meiningen, Saxe-Hilburghausen, Oltenburg, Anhalt-Dessau, Anhalt-Bernburg, Anhalt-Coethen, Schwarzburg-Sondershausen, Schwarzburg-Rudolstadt, Hohenzollern-Hechingen, Hohenzollern-Sigmaringen, Lichtenstein, Waldeck, Reuss, (senior branch,) Reuss, (junior branch,) Schaumburg-Lippe, together with the free cities of Lübeck, Frankfort-on-the-Maine, Bremen, and Hamburg. Subsequently was added Hesse-Homburg; but, on the other hand, the house of Saxe-Gotha becoming extinct, in 1825, it was incorporated with that of Coburg, so that the number of members still remained thirty-eight. The ducal houses of Saxony are divided thus: Saxe-Coburg

Gotha ; Saxe-Meiningen-Hilburghausen ; and Saxe-Altenburg.

Austria has received back her faithful Tyrol, together with Salzburg and the country around; Bavaria rules over her own hereditary lands as well as Franconia; while, as an indemnification for the losses she sustained, she has been accorded the palatinate of the Rhine; her entire population thus forming more than 4,000,000 of subjects. Würtemberg holds dominion in Swabia over more than 1,500,000 subjects, and is separated by the Black Forest from Baden, whose possessions extend along the Rhine to Basle, and beyond Manheim, through a beautiful and fertile country. Hesse-Darmstadt has likewise enlarged her former line of territory very considerably, and holds in her possession the city of Mentz, the most important stronghold of the Confederation. Above all the rest, however, the king of Prussia has under his sovereignty the greatest number of subjects speaking the mother tongue, amounting to more than 14,000,000. So that Prussia is at the present moment one entire, and all but exclusively, German state.

As regards the government of Germany, it has been converted by the so-called Holy Alliance into a confederation of free and independent states, according to the following decrees :—

"The object of the alliance is the maintenance of the internal and external security of Germany, together with the independence and inviolability of the confederated states.

"All the members of the alliance have, as such, equal and uniform rights.

"The general interests of the body shall be discussed and arranged at a Diet, the seat of which it is appointed shall be fixed at Frankfort-on-the-Maine, and at which Austria shall hold the presidency; this diet is perpetual, and the period for the adjournment of the session, when the state of business allows, must not extend beyond four months at the most.

"The assembly must devote its attention especially to the subject of the fundamental laws of the Confederation and its organic regulations, in connection with its internal, external, and military relations.

"All the members of the Confederation promise to unite together against any and every attack, and when a war takes place they pledge themselves not to enter upon any secret compact, nor conclude any partial armistice or peace with the enemy. Meantime they reserve to themselves the right of forming alliances of every kind, but they bind themselves down not to conclude any one such alliance which may injuriously affect the welfare and security of the country, or be opposed to the interests of any one individual member. At the same time the members shall not be allowed, under any pretext whatever, to carry on a war against each other, but shall lay all matters of dispute before the Diet, which shall either mediate or adjudge accordingly, and to the decision of which the parties must submit.

"In all the states of the Confederation there shall be a constitutional government, (Landständische Verfassung.)

"The difference of Christian sects cannot affect the enjoyment of civil and political rights in any of the states of the Confederation; but as amelioration is necessary in the civil condition of those professing the Jewish faith, the Diet of the Confederation shall advise and determine upon the matter.

"The subjects of the German princes shall have the right to pass from one state into the other, and to accept of either civil or military service therein, if no military engagement already binds them to their native place.

"The Diet shall occupy itself with the formation of laws for the liberty of the press and against piracy, as well as for the commercial and trading intercourse between the states of the Confederation.

"Further, the Diet has decreed the exact numerical force of the army of the Confederation to be maintained in peace and war; of what arms it shall consist; a fixed contingent to be supplied by each member; to whom and by whom the chief command shall be given; and, finally, how many and what fortifications shall be garrisoned and maintained by the Confederation."

The army of the confederation consists of 300,000 men: to which Austria contributes 94,000; Prussia, 79,000; Bavaria, 35,000; Würtemberg, 13,600; Hanover, 13,000; Saxony, (the kingdom,) 12,000; Baden, 10,000; Hesse-Darmstadt, 6000; Hesse-Cassel, 5400; and thus in proportion the other members. The whole army is placed under the command of one general-in-chief, who is appointed by the Diet, to whom he renders the oath of duty and ser-

60

vice, and from whom he receives authority and orders, and to which body, likewise, he is bound to send in his reports. The Diet also appoints a lieutenant-general as his representative or successor in command. The army is divided into ten distinct corps, the leaders of which receive their orders only from the general-in-chief. Of these ten corps Austria contributes three; Prussia, three; Bavaria, one; and the remaining three are formed out of the other contingents. The fortified places garrisoned and maintained by the Confederation are Mentz, Luxemburg, and Landau.

THE END.

# INDEX.

THE END.

www.ingramcontent.com/pod-product-compliance
Lightning Source LLC
LaVergne TN
LVHW020919110826
845150LV00004B/719

* 9 7 8 1 4 2 5 5 5 4 4 2 2 *